Twentieth-Century Literary Criticism

Twentieth-Century Literary Criticism

**Excerpts from Criticism of the
Works of Novelists, Poets, Playwrights,
Short Story Writers, and Other Creative Writers
Who Lived between 1900 and 1960,
from the First Published Critical
Appraisals to Current Evaluations**

**Sharon K. Hall
Editor**

**Gale Research Company
Book Tower
Detroit, Michigan 48226**

STAFF

Sharon K. Hall, *Editor*

Dennis Poupard, *Associate Editor*

Thomas Ligotti, Marsha R. Mackenzie, James E. Person, Jr.,
Lizbeth A. Purdy, Anna C. Wallbillich, *Assistant Editors*

Phyllis Carmel Mendelson, *Contributing Editor*

Carolyn Voldrich, *Production Editor*

Robert J. Elster, *Research Coordinator*
Jane C. Thacker, Carol Angela Thomas, *Research Assistants*

Linda M. Pugliese, *Manuscript Coordinator*
Marie Lazzari, *Manuscript Assistant*

Earlene M. Alber, Ann Kathleen Crowley, Francine M. Melotti-Bacon, Denise Michlewicz,
Ada Morgan, R. Bruce Young, Robyn V. Young, *Editorial Assistants*

L. Elizabeth Hardin, *Permissions Coordinator*
Filomena Sgambati, *Assistant Permissions Coordinator*
Janice M. Mach, Mary P. McGrane, Patricia A. Seefelt, *Permissions Assistants*

Copyright © 1981 by Gale Research Company

Library of Congress Catalog Card Number 76-46132

ISBN 0-8103-0178-4

CONTENTS

PREFACE

It is impossible to overvalue the importance of literature in the intellectual, emotional, and spiritual evolution of humanity. Literature is that which both lifts us out of everyday life and helps us to better understand it. Through the fictive life of an Emma Bovary, a Lambert Strether, a Leopold Bloom, our perceptions of the human condition are enlarged, and we are enriched.

Literary criticism is a collective term for several kinds of critical writing: criticism may be normative, descriptive, textual, interpretive, appreciative, generic. It takes many forms: the traditional essay, the aphorism, the book or play review, even the parodic poem. Perhaps the single unifying feature of literary criticism lies in its purpose: to help us to better understand what we read.

The Scope of the Book

The usefulness of Gale's *Contemporary Literary Criticism (CLC),* which excerpts criticism of current creative writing, suggests an equivalent need among literature students and teachers interested in authors of the period 1900 to 1960. The great poets, novelists, short story writers, and playwrights of this period are by far the most popular writers for study in high school and college literature courses. Moreover, since contemporary critics continue to analyze the work of this period—both in its own right and in relation to today's tastes and standards—a vast amount of relevant critical material confronts the student.

Thus, *Twentieth-Century Literary Criticism (TCLC)* presents significant passages from published criticism on authors who died between 1900 and 1960. Because of the difference in time span under consideration *(CLC* considers authors living from 1960 to the present), there is no duplication between *CLC* and *TCLC.*

Each volume of *TCLC* is carefully designed to present a list of authors who represent a variety of genres and nationalities. The length of an author's section is intended to be representative of the amount of critical attention he or she has received in the English language. Articles and books that have not been translated into English are excluded. An attempt has been made to identify and include excerpts from the seminal essays on each author's work. Additionally, as space permits, especially insightful essays of a more limited scope are included. Thus *TCLC* is designed to serve as an introduction for the student of twentieth-century literature to the authors of that period and to the most significant commentators on these authors.

Each *TCLC* author section represents the scope of critical response to that author's work: some early criticism is presented to indicate initial reactions, later criticism is selected to represent any rise or fall in an author's reputation, and current retrospective analyses provide students with a modern view. Since a *TCLC* author section is intended to be a definitive overview, the editors include between 30 and 40 authors in each 600-page volume (compared to approximately 140 authors in a *CLC* volume of similar size) in order to devote more attention to each author.

The Organization of the Book

An author section consists of the following elements: author heading, bio-critical introduction, principal works, excerpts of criticism (each followed by a citation), and, beginning with Volume 3, an annotated bibliography of additional reading.

- The *author heading* consists of the author's full name, followed by birth and death dates. The unbracketed portion of the name denotes the form under which the author most commonly wrote. If an author wrote consistently under a pseudonym, the pseudonym will be listed in the author heading and the real name given in parentheses on the first line of the bio-critical introduction. Also located at the beginning of the bio-critical introduction are any name variations under which an author wrote, including transliterated forms for authors whose languages use non-roman alphabets. Uncertainty as to a birth or death date is indicated by a question mark.

- The *bio-critical introduction* contains biographical and other background information about an author that will elucidate his or her creative output.

- The *list of principal works* is chronological by date of first publication and indentifies genres. In those instances where the first publication was other than English language, the title and date of the first English-language edition are given in brackets. Unless otherwise indicated, dramas are dated by first performance, not first publication.

- *Criticism* is arranged chronologically in each author section to provide a perspective on any changes in critical evaluation over the years. For purposes of easier indentification, the critic's name and the publication date of the essay are given at the beginning of each piece of criticism.

- A complete *biliographical citation* designed to facilitate location of the original essay or book by the interested reader accompanies each piece of criticism. An asterisk (*) at the end of a citation indicates the essay is on more than one author.

- The *annotated bibliography* appearing at the end of each author section suggests further reading on the author. In some cases it includes essays for which the editors could not obtain reprint rights. An asterisk (*) at the end of a citation indicates the essay is on more than one author.

Each volume of *TCLC* includes a cumulative index to critics. Under each critic's name is listed the author(s) on which the critic has written and the volume and page where the criticism may be found. *TCLC* also includes a cumulative index to authors with the volume number in which the author appears in boldface after his or her name.

Beginning with Volume 2, *TCLC* added an appendix which lists the sources from which material in the volume is reprinted. It does not, however, list every book or periodical consulted for the volume. Beginning with Volume 4, *TCLC* is adding another new feature—portraits of the author.

Acknowledgments

No work of this scope can be accomplished without the cooperation of many people. The editors especially wish to thank the copyright holders of the excerpts included in this volume, the permission managers of many book and magazine publishing companies for assisting us in locating copyright holders, and the staffs of the Detroit Public Library, University of Michigan Library, and Wayne State University Library for making their resources available to us. We are also grafteful to Fred S. Stein for his assistance with copyright research.

Suggestions Are Welcome

If readers with to suggest authors they would like to have covered in future volumes, or if they have other suggestions, they are cordially invited to write the editor.

AUTHORS TO APPEAR
IN FUTURE VOLUMES

Ady, Endre 1877-1919
Agate, James 1877-1947
Agustini, Delmira 1886-1914
Alain-Fournier (Henri Alban
    Fournier) 1886-1914
Aldrich, Thomas Bailey 1836-1907
Annensy, Innokenty Fyodorovich
    1856-1909
Anstey, Frederick 1856-1934
Arlen, Michael 1895-1956
Barbusse, Henri 1873-1935
Barea, Arturo 1897-1957
Baring, Maurice 1874-1945
Baroja, Pio 1872-1956
Barry, Philip 1896-1949
Bass, Eduard 1888-1946
Belloc, Hilaire 1870-1953
Benét, Stephen Vincent
    1898-1943
Benét, William Rose 1886-1950
Bennett, (Enoch) Arnold
    1867-1931
Benson, E(dward) F(rederic)
    1867-1940
Benson, Stella 1892-1933
Beresford, J(ohn) D(avys)
    1873-1947
Bethell, Mary Ursula 1874-1945
Betti, Ugo 1892-1953
Biely, Andrei 1880-1934
Binyon, Laurence 1869-1943
Bjørnson, Bjørnstjerne 1832-1910
Blackmore, R(ichard) D(oddridge)
    1825-1900
Blackwood, Algernon 1869-1951
Blasco Ibáñez, Vicente
    1867-1928
Blok, Alexandr 1880-1921
Bojer, Johan 1872-1959
Bosman, Herman Charles
    1905-1951
Bottomley, Gordon 1874-1948
Bourne, George 1863-1927
Broch, Herman 1886-1951
Bromfield, Louis 1896-1956
Buchan, John 1870-1953
Bunin, Ivan 1870-1953
Byrne, Donn (Brian Oswald
    Donn-Byre) 1889-1928
Cabell, James Branch 1879-1958
Caine, Hall 1853-1931
Campana, Dina 1885-1932

Campbell, (Ignatius) Roy
    1901-1957
Cannan, Gilbert 1884-1955
Capek, Karl 1890-1938
Chesnutt, Charles Waddell
    1858-1932
Chopin, Kate 1851-1904
Churchill, Winston 1871-1947
Corelli, Marie 1855-1924
Corvo, Baron (Frederick
    William Rolfe) 1860-1913
Crane, Stephen 1871-1900
Crawford, F. Marion 1854-1909
Croce, Benedetto 1866-1952
D'Annunzio, Gabriele 1863-1938
Davidson, John 1857-1909
Davies, W(illiam) H(enry)
    1871-1940
Davis, Rebecca Harding 1831-1910
Day, Clarence 1874-1935
Delafield, E.M. (Edme
    Elizabeth Monica de la
    Pasture) 1890-1943
DeMorgan, William 1839-1917
Doblin, Alfred 1878-1957
Douglas, Lloyd C(assel) 1877-1951
Douglas, (George) Norman
    1868-1952
Doyle, Sir Arthur Conan
    1859-1930
Dreiser, Theodore 1871-1945
Drinkwater, John 1882-1937
Duun, Olav 1876-1939
Eluard, Paul 1895-1952
Fadeyev, Alexandr 1901-1956
Feydeau, Georges 1862-1921
Field, Michael (Katharine
    Harris Bradley 1846-1914
    and Edith Emma Cooper
    1862-1913)
Field, Rachel 1894-1942
Flecker, James Elroy 1884-1915
France, Anatole (Anatole
    Thibault) 1844-1924
Freeman, John 1880-1929
Gide, Andre 1869-1951
Glyn, Elinor 1864-1943
Gogarty, Oliver St. John
    1878-1957
Golding, Louis 1895-1958
Gorky, Maxim 1868-1936
Gosse, Edmund 1849-1928

Gould, Gerald 1885-1936
Grahame, Kenneth 1859-1932
Gray, John 1866-1934
Grey, Zane 1875-1939
Güiraldes, Ricardo 1886-1927
Gumilyov, Nikolay 1886-1921
Gwynne, Stephen Lucius
    1864-1950
Haggard, H(enry) Rider
    1856-1925
Hale, Edward Everett 1822-1909
Hall, (Marguerite) Radclyffe
    1806-1943
Harris, Frank 1856-1931
Hearn, Lafcadio 1850-1904
Heidenstam, Verner von
    1859-1940
Hergesheimer, Joseph 1880-1954
Hernandez, Miguel 1910-1942
Herrick, Robert 1868-1938
Hewlett, Maurice 1861-1923
Heyward, DuBose 1885-1940
Hichens, Robert 1864-1950
Hilton, James 1900-1954
Holtby, Winifred 1898-1935
Hope, Anthony 1863-1933
Housman, Laurence 1865-1959
Howard, Sidney 1891-1939
Howells, William Dean
    1837-1920
Hudson, Stephen 1868-1944
Hudson, W(illiam) H(enry)
    1841-1922
Ivanov, Vyacheslav Ivanovich
    1866-1949
Jacob, Max 1876-1944
Jacobs, W(illiam) W(ymark)
    1863-1943
James, Will 1892-1942
Jerome, Jerome K(lapka)
    1859-1927
Jones, Henry Arthur 1851-1929
Kipling, Rudyard 1865-1936
Kraus, Karl 1874-1936
Kuzmin, Mikhail Alekseyevich
    1875-1936
Lang, Andrew 1844-1912
Lawson, Henry 1867-1922
Lee, Vernon (Violet Paget)
    1856-1935
Leverson, Ada 1862-1933
Lewisohn, Ludwig 1883-1955
Lindsay, (Nicholas) Vachel
    1879-1931

London, Jack 1876-1916
Lonsdale, Frederick 1881-1954
Louys, Pierre 1870-1925
Lowndes, Marie Belloc
    1868-1947
Lowry, Malcolm 1909-1957
Lucas, E(dward) V(errall)
    1868-1938
Lynd, Robert 1879-1949
MacArthur, Charles 1895-1956
Macaulay, Rose 1881-1958
Manning, Frederic 1887-1935
Marinetti, Filippo Tommaso
    1876-1944
Marriott, Charles 1869-1957
Martin du Gard, Roger
    1881-1958
Martínez Sierra, Gregorio
    1881-1947
Mencken, H(enry) L(ouis)
    1880-1956
Meredith, George 1828-1909
Meynell, Alice 1847-1922
Milne, A(lan) A(lexander)
    1882-1956
Miro, Gabriel 1879-1936
Mistral, Frédéric 1830-1914
Mitchell, Margaret 1900-1949
Monro, Harold 1879-1932
Moore, George 1852-1933
Moore, Thomas Sturge
    1870-1944
Morgan, Charles 1894-1958
Morley, Christopher 1890-1957
Murray, (George) Gilbert
    1866-1957
Nervo, Amado 1870-1919
Nietzsche, Friedrich 1844-1900
Norris, Frank 1870-1902
Noyes, Alfred 1880-1958
O'Grady, Standish 1846-1928
Olbracht, Ivan (Kemil Zeman)
    1882-1952
Orczy, Baroness (Emmuska)
    1865-1947
Owen, Wilfred 1893-1918
Palamas, Kostis 1859-1943
Pinero, Arthur Wing 1855-1934
Pontoppidan, Henrik 1857-1943
Porter, Eleanor H(odgman)
    1868-1920
Porter, Gene(va) Stratton
    1886-1924

Authors to Appear in Future Volumes

Powys, T(heodore) F(rancis) 1875-1953
Proust, Marcel 1871-1922
Quiller-Couch, Arthur 1863-1944
Rappoport, Solomon 1863-1944
Reid, Forrest 1876-1947
Reymont, Ladislas (Wladyslaw Stanislaw Reymont) 1867-1925
Riley, James Whitcomb 1849-1916
Rinehart, Mary Roberts 1876-1958
Roberts, Elizabeth Madox 1886-1941
Robinson, Edward Arlington 1869-1935
Rölvaag, O(le) E(dvart) 1876-1931
Rolland, Romain 1866-1944
Rostand, Edmond 1868-1918
Roussel, Raymond 1877-1933
Runyon, (Alfred) Damon 1884-1946

Sabatini, Rafael 1875-1950
Santayana, George 1863-1952
Scott, Duncan Campbell 1862-1947
Seeger, Alan 1888-1916
Service, Robert 1874-1958
Seton, Ernest Thompson 1860-1946
Slater, Francis Carey 1875-1958
Sologub, Fyodor 1863-1927
Squire, J(ohn) C(ollings) 1884-1958
Stockton, Frank R. 1834-1902
Storni, Alfonsina 1892-1938
Supervielle, Jules 1884-1960
Sutro, Alfred 1863-1933
Swinburne, Algernon Charles 1837-1909
Symons, Arthur 1865-1945

Synge, John Millington 1871-1909
Tabb, John Bannister 1845-1909
Tarkington, Booth 1869-1946
Tey, Josephine (Elizabeth Mackintosh) 1897-1952
Toson, Shimazaki 1872-1943
Trakl, George 1887-1914
Turner, W(alter) J(ames) R(edfern) 1889-1946
Twain, Mark (Samuel Langhorne Clemens) 1835-1910
Vachell, Horace Annesley 1861-1955
Valle-Inclan, Ramon del 1869-1955
Van Dine, S.S. (Willard H. Wright) 1888-1939
Van Doren, Carl 1885-1950
Vazov, Ivan 1850-1921

Verne, Jules 1828-1905
Wallace, Edgar 1875-1932
Wallace, Lewis 1827-1905
Walpole, Hugh 1884-1941
Wassermann, Jakob 1873-1934
Webb, Mary 1881-1927
Webster, Jean 1876-1916
Welch, Denton 1917-1948
Wells, Carolyn 1869-1942
Werfel, Franz 1890-1945
Wister, Owen 1860-1938
Woollcott, Alexander 1887-1943
Wren, P(ercival) C(hristopher) 1885-1941
Wylie, Francis Brett 1844-1954
Zamyatin, Yevgeniy Ivanovich 1884-1937
Zangwill, Israel 1864-1926

Readers are cordially invited to suggest additional authors to the editors.

Henry (Brooks) Adams

1838-1918

(Also wrote under pseudonyms of Frances Compton Snow and Tauraatua i Amo) American autobiographer, historian, essayist, and novelist.

Adams's work is less pertinent to the history of literature than it is to the history of ideas. In the latter context Adams embodies for many a particularly modern viewpoint, one which sees the world becoming less stable and coherent than it once was and which predicts this trend will continue, never to be arrested. Adams developed this doctrine most thoroughly in his best known work, *The Education of Henry Adams*.

Adams was born into a prominent American family. His grandfather was John Quincy Adams and his great-grandfather John Adams. For a time Adams expected to take a politically active part in his family's heritage of power and influence, but he ultimately chose a literary life, which he thought better suited his temperament. He attended Harvard and later traveled to England, where he served as private secretary to his father, then Minister to Great Britain. Returning to the United States, Adams moved to Washington and published a number of articles on politics. He was offered a teaching position at Harvard and the editorship of the *North American Review*, both of which he accepted. Not dependent on a career to support himself, Adams eventually resigned these positions and devoted himself exclusively to writing.

Throughout his life Adams was recognized chiefly as a historian and biographer. With his first book, *The Life of Albert Gallatin*, Adams began research into the era that would result in his magnum opus, *History of the United States of America during the Administrations of Thomas Jefferson and James Madison*. This nine-volume work continues to be valued as an insightful analysis of the period and is ranked with the histories of Edward Gibbon and Thomas Macaulay.

During the years Adams worked on the *History* he anonymously published two novels. The first, *Democracy*, was popular in its time as a satire in which contemporary political figures were disguised as characters in a fictional Washington, D.C. Just as *Democracy* followed its main character's disillusionment with the world of politics, the second novel, *Esther*, did the same with that of religion. Each novel significantly features a woman as its protagonist, and later Adams turned his conception of the feminine principle into a philosophical emblem associated with the Virgin. Both novels have been critically regarded as competent works, though largely devoted to unfolding predetermined judgments and lacking a sufficient degree of narrative vitality.

More than his biographies, history, and novels, the works essential to Adams's literary reputation are *Mont Saint Michel and Chartres* and *The Education of Henry Adams*. He subtitled the first book "A Study in Thirteenth-Century Unity" and the second "A Study in Twentieth-Century Multi-

plicity." Critics often consider the two works in conjunction, each representing a polar extreme. The clash between these opposing concepts is at the heart of Adams's thought, which in *Mont Saint Michel* poses the Virgin as the symbol of the social and spiritual harmony that once existed in the Middle Ages and in the *Education* presents the dynamo as a symbol of the modern world's fall from a state of unity to one of conflict-ridden multiplicity.

Adams wanted to establish a scientific method for examining history, and in *The Degradation of the Democratic Dogma* he predicts the progressive disorganization and ultimate collapse of all life-energy, a conclusion substantially premised in *Mont Saint Michel* and the *Education*. Critics sometimes disparage this historical view as promoting an unwarranted degree of pessimistic determinism, arrived at by diligent but possibly flawed reasoning. In general, a critic is more likely to find intellectual value in Adams's questions and his conscientious approach to answering them than in the conclusions he reached. Adams's importance, then, is primarily that of a privileged man of broad learning and cultural experience who employed his considerable attainments to the fullest in dealing with both perennial and modern issues in history, literature, and philosophy.

PRINCIPAL WORKS

The Life of Albert Gallatin   (biography)   1879
Democracy   (novel)   1880
John Randolph   (biography)   1882
Esther   (novel)   1884
History of the United States of America during the
*   Administrations of Thomas Jefferson and James*
*   Madison.* 9 vols.   (history)   1889-91
Memoirs of Arii Taimai e Marama of Eimeo, Teriirere of
*   Tooarai, Teriinui of Tahiti*   (history)   1901
Mont Saint Michel and Chartres   (essay)   1904
The Education of Henry Adams   (autobiography)   1907
A Letter to American Teachers of History   (essay)   1910
The Degradation of the Democratic Dogma   (essays)
    1919

THE NATION   (essay date 1879)

In its superficial make-up [*The Life of Albert Gallatin*] falls little short of being an outrage both on Albert Gallatin and on every one who wishes to know anything about him. . . . Mr. Adams has sinned knowingly, and is accordingly entitled to no mercy. He seems, very wrongly, to have made up his mind when he took his task in hand that Gallatin's was not a picturesque character or an interesting life, and could not be made the one or the other; and, accordingly, he set to work in a spirit of defiance, and made every detail of publication as repelling to the general reader as he knew how. (p. 128)

He certainly did not lack material, and that he has the faculty of using his material artistically is from time to time apparent in this volume, in spite of himself. It would almost seem as if he had argued himself into the German professorial belief that vivacity is trickery, and that there is some positive merit in dulness. Accordingly, what is in fact one of the most valuable contributions of the day to an almost unknown period of American history is likely to find its way unread to the shelves of the library.

Having said thus much of the unfortunate get-up, and detail of this work, it is proper to add that, in spite of its appearance, it is in fact neither long nor dull, except in parts. . . . But in putting his material together Mr. Adams has not only succeeded in imparting to it an appearance of ponderosity, but he has also kept himself altogether too far in the background—sunk the author too much in the editor. Gallatin was undoubtedly a brilliant talker, but he was far from being a lively letter-writer. Now, it is very proper that a biographer should allow his subject to tell his own story, provided he tells it tolerably well. If, however, he tells very little and writes a great deal, letters, familiar or otherwise, become as dry a form of light literature as can find its way into print. This was the case with Mr. Gallatin. Putting him forward to tell his own story wherever he can, Mr. Adams, to Gallatin's great loss, does not tell it himself; and Mr. Adams's work is a great deal better than Gallatin's. It is, in fact, extremely good, and those portions of the volume in which Mr. Adams cuts loose from his hero and comes to the front in a fresh, clear, connected narrative of events which he thoroughly understands, are not only good but very interesting. (pp. 128-29)

"Albert Gallatin," in The Nation *(copyright 1879 The Nation magazine, The Nation Associates, Inc.), No. 738, August 21, 1879, pp. 128-29.*

THE ATLANTIC MONTHLY   (essay date 1880)

[With] all due respect to the clever author, [*Democracy*] seems to us not to have caught the best or the fairest view of what its title intends. (p. 421)

[The] judgment to be passed upon the book itself is that the author makes a mistake if it is intended that we shall take this story for a real exposition of American life at its core. Mrs. Lee, with all her equipment, was scarcely qualified to discover the secret of democracy. She had not the esoteric initiation. Again, it may be doubted if Washington presents, after all, the true point of view. The book itself very clearly displays the essential masquerading character of life there, and strongly prejudices us against accepting a judgment founded exclusively upon observation formed within one circle of political life. If we could divest ourselves of sensitiveness we should find it easier to praise this book. As it is, we confess its skill and adroitness. In one point especially it shows ability. It sketches public characters without unerringly pointing to men actually occupying public positions. One thinks he is on the scent of some particular person, and is presently thrown off in the most skillful manner. Able as the book is, it lacks the essential quality of the higher truthfulness. The writer has left out of account forces which, if wisely considered, would crowd back the life here presented into narrower bounds. (p. 422)

"Recent American Fiction: 'Democracy'," in The Atlantic Monthly *(copyright © 1880, by The Atlantic Monthly Company, Boston, Mass.), Vol. XLVI, No. CCLXXV, September, 1880, pp. 421-22.*

THE ATLANTIC MONTHLY   (essay date 1890)

Mr. Adams has given us a history [*History of the United States of America, during the First Administration of Thomas Jefferson*] which, if the subsequent volumes maintain an equality of merit with the first two, will be almost great. That he should have added much to the store of facts previously known concerning the period was impossible; but he has shed upon the old facts many new lights, has established for them fresh relationships and hitherto unappreciated proportions, and has illustrated them by comments and reflections of very great value.

The opening chapters contain a sketch of the moral, political, intellectual, social, and industrial condition of the country about the year 1800. Infinite rereading and research have gone to the making of this sketch, and probably in its accuracy not a flaw can be detected. Yet in dealing with the New England and Middle Atlantic States, Mr. Adams's point of view is very unfortunate; he is too obviously possessed by a carping, critical spirit, which enables him to discern no good whatsoever in a community which can hardly have been altogether devoid of abilities and of serviceable qualities. (pp. 274-75)

In describing the Southern States he lapses into gentler paragraphs; and at last, in taking leave of this part of his book, he frees himself for a brief while from his contradictory habit; even his style, which thus far has been dry, labored, and uneasy, suddenly improves; the reader, who has felt himself jolting uncomfortably over a cobblestone road, through scenery very distasteful to him, rolls out on a smoother way and is cheered by a fairer prospect. Perhaps it is a cloudland that now seems ravishing; for Mr. Adams, laying aside the rôle of historian for that of seer and orator, engages in sketching, by dim rhetorical innuendo, the destiny and the mission of the new country, and he does it with a swelling enthusiasm which pleasantly offsets his earlier denying disposition. One only wonders a little where, in the society which he has been sketching, he finds a basis for this cloudy palace of his imagination. (p. 275)

Mr. Adams admires Jeffersonianism, and so depicts it that his readers will admire it likewise, at least as an abstraction. But the observant ones among them will separate Jeffersonianism from Jefferson. The doctrine Mr. Adams sets forth attractively, but his position as towards the man is curious. He constantly interrupts his narrative to attribute some fine quality to his hero, yet it is impossible not to remark how widely the Jefferson of his fancy differs from the Jefferson of his facts; for no sooner does he ascribe a trait than he seems to adduce evidence to disprove it. He utters repeatedly the undeniable assertion that Jefferson was a great man, but he wholly fails to set forth how or wherein he was great.... Many students of Jefferson's career think that as chief administrator and head executive of the country his greatness was less apparent than it had previously been. But Mr. Adams does not hint at all this, contenting himself with alleging the greatness at frequent intervals throughout a history in which he shows his hero abandoning every principle he has ever avowed, creating no new policy in place of that which he throws away, yielding to others, failing to carry his own points, drifting along the current of circumstances. Even if Mr. Adams were Jefferson's detractor instead of his admirer, this would be unfair; and as it is, the reader feels a little irritation at a display falling so far short of the advertisement, and is justly provoked that the showman will not make his monkey perform his boasted tricks.

In other ways more trifling Mr. Adams pursues the same course, impelled apparently by that strange vein of contradictoriness which too often sets him obliquely and very uncomfortably across the stream of received belief and universal opinion. (pp. 275-76)

Our author reaches the extreme of audacity in his strenuous reiterations of Jefferson's honesty, even his guilelessness and simplicity. Now Jefferson's honesty has been much more seriously impugned than ever were his greatness and his purity; and his best friends have preferred to describe him as astute rather than as artless. In this, as in all the rest of his description, Mr. Adams alleges one thing and proves another. (p. 276)

[It is certain] that no writer, Federalist or Jeffersonian, has ever yet set forth Jefferson's desertion of his published faith with such painstaking elaboration, such conclusive elucidation, as Mr. Adams has brought to the task. The result is that the reader finds himself hopelessly bewildered between that which he is bidden to believe and that which the facts, as narrated and explained, compel him to believe. Mr. Adams's condition of mind as towards Jefferson becomes almost a psychological study, though such an element of perplexity is not altogether agreeably introduced when the reader would like to be clearly guided to sound conclusions.

In praising Jefferson Mr. Adams buries very deep the ancestral hatchet. But he cannot do the same for Hamilton. During the last hundred years four generations of Adamses have clung to the faith that Hamilton was nothing greater than an ingenious treasury clerk, and no more fit to meddle with statesmanship than Jefferson would have been to conduct a campaign against Napoleon. (pp. 276-77)

Mr. Adams is not especially happy in depicting persons; he leaves Madison no more lifelike than a mummy, and even his favorite Gallatin performs acts after the fashion of a marionette rather than a man. But with Randolph Mr. Adams achieves greater success, and we have many lively glimpses of that erratic creature. Chief Justice Marshall also seems to bring some little inspiration. Yet on the whole the portraiture of these volumes is disappointing.

In narration our author is happier, telling a story with clearness and force. The most interesting and novel portion of his work relates to the acquisition of Louisiana, and the history of this transaction has never been so exhaustively given. (p. 277)

It may be thought that we have spoken of these volumes in a somewhat critical temper; it is therefore only fair to say that it is the very importance of the work and the high ability shown in it which tempt, and in some degree necessitate, the mention of its peculiarities, and of those of its views which seem questionable. It is those writings which have such merits as to insure them a far-reaching influence that stimulate discussion, criticism, and in some particulars inevitably also dissent. The historian is a guide to his less instructed reader through the domain of history as the compass is to the mariner, and the personal bent of the writer must be discovered and allowed for no less than the deviation of the compass. It is certainly true that by this sample of his whole work Mr. Adams appears to have written a history which will not be soon or easily displaced from the important function of largely shaping the views of Americans concerning the interesting changes and developments carried on during the Jeffersonian era. It is evident that he has exhausted all accessible knowledge, has turned it to and fro and churned it, so to speak, in his mind, until accumulation, analysis, and comparison can no further go. The period may be discussed with different predilections; it will never be discussed more keenly or more profoundly. In a word, the book is one of marked ability and very great value. It is also to be said that Mr. Adams's idea of the way in which history should be written leaves nothing to be desired. He has an excellent sense of the proportion to be preserved between the narration of facts, the presentation of political arguments, and the explanation and comments properly to be furnished by the historian. His own elucidations and reflections, strung thickly, but not too much so, along the thread of his story, are always an important aid, always a stimulus to independent reflection. He has many of the best qualifications for historical writing: not only is his industry untiring, his research unlimited, but he is thoroughly trained in the difficult art of thinking historically; he is also, perhaps, as impartial as a man who has ideas and strong convictions ever can be. His style is a trifle uneven in its quality; possibly it is because his pages are so full of condensed thought that they often cannot be read without a sense of exertion. Yet, on the other hand, he is usually clear; often he glides onward with a pleasant current, but anon he shows inflexibility and hardness. If he is seldom brilliant, he is nearly always correct and scholarly. In a work which manifests so much care and painstaking, more observant proofreading ought to have eliminated some grotesque disfigurements in such little details as the division of words; but on the whole the accuracy in all matters of literary finish is highly commendable. (pp. 277-78)

"Recent Books on American History: 'History of the United States during the First Administration of Thomas Jefferson'," in The Atlantic Monthly (copyright © 1890, by The Atlantic Monthly Company, Boston, Mass.), Vol. 65, No. CCCLXXXVIII, February, 1890, pp. 274-78.

HENRY W. THURSTON   (essay date 1891)

Mr. Adams is always clear and interesting, but clearness and interest are perhaps sometimes gained at the expense of perfect truth [in *History of the United States of America during the Administration of James Madison*]. To illustrate: When Joel Barlow went, in September, 1811, as American minister to Paris, he was instructed to act upon the assumption that France had changed her system of commercial restriction. Says Mr. Adams:

> Of all the caprices of politics, this was the most improbable,—that at the moment when the Czar of Russia and the King of Sweden were about to risk their thrones and to face certain death and ruin of vast numbers of their people in order to protect American ships from the Berlin and Milan Decrees, the new minister of the United States appeared in Paris authorized to declare that the President considered those decrees to be revoked and their system no longer in force.

Probably the author himself does not intend to claim that Russia and Sweden went to war with France simply as champions of the United States, but the statement above given is nowhere sufficiently qualified.

As an example of the author's vivid style, and his power to group events far apart in space but close together in time and in significance, the following will serve:

> The Orders in Council were abandoned at Westminster June 17; within twenty-four hours at Washington war was declared; and forty-eight hours later Napoleon, about to enter Russia, issued the first bulletin of his Grand Army.

No author could well be more diligent than Mr. Adams in the examination of material, nor more successful than he in the arrangement of what he had chosen in order to present a series of dramatic pictures of the period under consideration; but one may well question whether or not another, having had access to the same sources, would have found so little of which to approve.

These five volumes close Mr. Adams's "History." Taken as a whole, the work covers the period of Jefferson's and Madison's administrations as no previous history has covered it and as no future history need cover it. Mr. Adams is not a Hero-worshipper and he detects the faults and failures of public men unerringly, but he has taken a broad view of the whole field and has shown the relation between cause and effect in every quarter.

Owing to the "undertone of detraction" that runs through many of his chapters and his dramatic style of writing, which sometimes expresses what his own best judgment does not sanction, Mr. Adams can hardly fail to be severely criticised by those who lean toward optimism and by those who demand judicial accuracy in expression. But when all allowances have been made, the fact remains that Mr. Adams has carried out a worthy plan in a worthy manner. (pp. 308-09)

Henry W. Thurston, *"Madison and Commercial Restriction,"* in The Dial (copyright, 1891, by The Dial Publishing Company, Inc.), Vol. XI, No. 130, February, 1891, pp. 307-09.

THE SPECTATOR   (essay date 1893)

The manner in which Mr. Adams has carried out his scheme [in *History of the United States of America during the Second Administration of James Madison*] is, on the whole, excellent. Though his style is not picturesque enough to make his book read like one of Macaulay's essays, it is one which the serious students of history will admire. Quiet, polished, scholarly, and always perfectly clear and intelligible, it will be the envy and admiration of all who know how difficult it is to reduce a confused mass of historical facts to an even narrative. But Mr. Adams's style has more than the negative virtues of good-taste and perspicuity. There runs through it a silver thread of irony, which, while never forced and never falling into mere caricature, keeps it from degenerating on the one hand into rhetoric, or on the other into flatness. One effect of Mr. Adams's Olympian gift of irony is to prevent his book being filled with either angels or devils. There are no heroic figures and no villains. Some men, of course, come out better than others; but there is neither a shouting either of paeans over the Americans, or a calling down of curses on the English. Mr. Adams has far too keen a sense of humour to be unfair.

"History of the United States," in The Spectator (© 1893 by The Spectator), Vol. 71, No. 3407, October 14, 1893, p. 490.

SIDNEY FISKE KIMBALL   (essay date 1914)

The fundamental unity of [*Mont-Saint-Michel and Chartres*] is not in its method or in its title, but in its real subject —the Middle Ages as a whole. Its implicit idea is that the different manifestations of the Middle Ages, more perhaps than of any other period, are each intelligible only in the light thrown by the others. Architecture must be elucidated by poetry and religion, religion by chivalry and art and philosophy. If here and there fragments are thrown pell-mell into the crucible, it does not prevent their fusion, and the sympathetic reader will not be disturbed. . . . [The] book is not written for scholars, and most readers will perhaps welcome a method which introduces them to so many interesting worthies they might not otherwise meet, and which places them together at their ease. (p. 246)

Mr. Adams is concerned not so much with description as with vitalization. He interprets the entire life of the Middle Ages as an assertion, in defiance of evidences of relativity and dissonance, that the world is an obvious and sacred harmony. (pp. 246-47)

Sidney Fiske Kimball, "The Life and Art of the Middle Ages," in The Dial *(copyright, 1914, by The Dial Publishing Company, Inc.), Vol. LVI, No. 666, March 16, 1914, pp. 246-47.*

FREDERICK BLISS LUQUIENS (essay date 1914)

The title [of "Mont-Saint-Michel and Chartres"] tells us nothing of the book's real character. It is the history of the spirit which informed the architecture of mediaeval France. There are many books, in many languages, which explain the development of the Gothic out of the Romanesque from the merely structural point of view; but "Mont-Saint-Michel and Chartres" explains, for the first time in any language, the development of the spirit which was born, lived, and died in those mediaeval stones. . . . Its author has realized that an exposition of the spirit of mediaeval architecture must be documented, so to speak, by evidences of the same spirit in contemporaneous forms of art and, indeed, in contemporaneous forms of life. His book, therefore, is much more than a treatise on architecture. Its name is rather a text than a title. The many pages devoted to mediaeval literature, history, and theology, in order to reveal through the writings and thoughts and deeds of the men and women of those days how they were used to feel, make it the complement of Mr. Taylor's "Mediæval Mind." It might well be called "The Mediæval Soul." This explains its great value. . . . (pp. 826-27)

Mr. Adams's scholarship is of the truest kind, for it achieves a definite advance in knowledge. It is to be regretted, however, that it is not proof against lapses in matters of detail. His treatment of mediaeval French literature is typical in this regard. The quotations from originals, and the charming translations which accompany them, are not without errors. He himself waives all claim to exact scholarship. . . . His occasional mistakes are probably to be defended simply and solely by conceding that it is impossible for any man to be a specialist in all the fields of mediaevalism at once. Mr. Adams has come as near to it as possible, for his errors are few and insignificant. (p. 829)

By some the book will doubtless be severely criticised as too imaginative. There is no denying that Mr. Adams is a mystic, and his book will therefore find little favor with matter-of-fact readers, whether scientists whose science must be pure and undefiled, or tourists pressed for time. To such Mr. Adams might say, changing slightly a sentence of his book: "You may, if you really have no imagination whatever, reject my ideas of the Archangel and the Virgin; the feebleness of our fancy is now congenital, organic, beyond stimulant or strychnine, and we shrink like sensitive-plants from the touch of a vision or spirit; but at least you can accept my essential conclusions." (p. 830)

Frederick Bliss Luquiens, "Book Reviews: 'Mont-Saint-Michel and Chartres'," in The Yale Review *(© 1914 by Yale University; reprinted by permission of the editors), Vol. III, No. 4, July, 1914, pp. 826-30.*

T. S. ELIOT (essay date 1919)

It is doubtful whether [*The Education of Henry Adams*] ought to be called an autobiography, for there is too little of the author in it; or whether it may be called Memoirs—for there is too much of the author in it; or a treatise on historical method, which in parts it is. . . .

Adams is perpetually busy with himself. Many of the best autobiographies have been by men who considered themselves more interesting than anybody else, even exclusively interesting; and their effrontery interests you in them. But Adams is superlatively modest, diffident. Conscience told him that one must be a learner all one's life, and as he had the financial means to gratify his conscience, he did so. (p. 361)

[A] great many things interested [Henry Adams]; but he could believe in nothing: neither in the sagacity of British statesmanship, nor in the perfection of the American form of government, nor in the New World, nor in the Old; not in Darwinism, or in Karl Pearson, or Ernst Mach, or in the wickedness of large issues of paper currency. . . . Wherever this man stepped, the ground did not simply give way, it flew into particles; towards the end of his life he came across the speculations of Poincaré, and science disappeared, entirely. He was seeking for education, with the wings of a beautiful but ineffectual conscience beating vainly in a vacuum jar. He found, at best, two or three friends, notably the great John Hay, who had been engaged in settling the problems of China and Cuba and Manchuria. Adams yearned for unity, and found it, after a fashion, by writing a book on the thirteenth century.

The Erinnyes which drove him madly through seventy years of search for education—the search for what, upon a lower plane, is called culture—left him much as he was born: well-bred, intelligent, and uneducated. He had attended to everything, respectfully, had accumulated masses of information and known nearly everybody; but he was unaware that education—the education of an individual—is a by-product of being interested, passionately absorbed. He had been too respectful of whatever was important, he laughed at nothing. It is not at all that he was an *amateur;* he would have liked to have been professional in everything; he abandoned lecturing at Harvard because of his doubts of the value of lecturing and the capacity of his pupils; but he had gone at the task in a thoroughly professional way. His extreme sensitiveness to all the suggestions which dampen enthusiasm or dispel conviction may be responsible for what one feels in him as immaturity, indeed as a lack of personality; an instability. The immaturity is marked: we are acutely, painfully aware of an elderly man approaching a new subject of study with "This will be good for me!" *That* is the type of egotism of Henry Adams; it is not a kind which we should expect to provide an agreeable autobiography; but Adams's is a remarkable confession of that peculiar mind.

For the immaturity there may be another reason. It is probable that men ripen best through experiences which are at once sensuous and intellectual; certainly many men will admit that their keenest ideas have come to them with the quality of a sense-perception; and that their keenest sensuous experience has been "as if the body thought." There is nothing to indicate that Adams's senses either flowered or fruited: he remains little Paul Dombey asking questions. (pp. 361-62)

T. S. Eliot, "A Sceptical Patrician" (copyright Mrs. Valerie Eliot; reprinted by permission of Mrs. Valerie Eliot and Faber and Faber Ltd), in The Athenaeum, *No. 4647, May 23, 1919, pp. 361-62.*

HENRY COMMAGER (essay date 1927)

[The] tragedy of Henry Adams was that he was born out of his time. He was an eighteenth century soul with a twentieth century intellect. It is this curious dualism, this paradox of the dynamo and the Virgin, of the Puritan and the physicist, of the New Englander and the cosmopolitan, that permeates much of the philosophy and of the writing of Henry Adams. It was an occasional outcropping in the family, and it spelt destruction. . . .

The mind of any Adams is an alluring study, but the mind of Henry Adams is positively fascinating. Either by inheritance or by environment and training, it should have been the best mind of its generation, and it probably was. (p. 253)

[In the *History of the United States During the Administrations of Jefferson and Madison*] Mr. Adams' approach is intellectual; his point of view is philosophical. Yet the result is a history of the old type,—a political and diplomatic history. With all the appreciation of a McMaster, a Green, a Lamprecht, for social, cultural, even for economic forces, he gives us only political history. The *History* is the apex of conventional historiography, the climax of the nineteenth century, and it is with this superlatively fine work that the new school must compete.

This conventionality is at once its virtue and its defect. The defect is that it fails fully to appreciate some of the economic and social phenomena of the period. The virtue is that, within its scope, the *History* is definitive. Especially in the handling of diplomatic history, Adams comes as near perfection as any historian can; to such an extent has he exhausted his subject that no one has yet had the hardihood to do it over again. In this Adams resembles Parkman. Built almost entirely on sources, very largely on unprinted archive material, it meets the technical demands of the most exacting historical critics. It is, further, a very real contribution to European and Napoleonic studies. (pp. 257-58)

Probably *Mont-Saint-Michel and Chartres* is the most perfect thing Henry Adams ever wrote. Into it he poured all the finer elements of his soul, and the composite is infinitely lovely. There is a radiance and a splendour and a mellow beauty about this volume, and with it all a gracious humor and a penetrating understanding. It was Adams' profession of faith. . . .

The Education of Henry Adams is a study in Twentieth Century multiplicity, with Henry as exhibit A. Introspection was his vice and his glory. (p. 263)

Intellectually Adams outgrew his New England heritage, but psychologically he never did. Intellectually he represents that steady Europeanization, that internationalization, of the American character, but he never reconciled himself to the inevitable. And so he sums up the tragedy of his country, which had outgrown provincialism and yet stubbornly refused to abandon her splendid isolation, which had developed an economic and social and cultural order essentially like the European, yet clung with a sort of pathetic obstinacy to her shibboleths and her culture of the eighteenth century. Henry Adams became as far removed from John Adams as Andrew Mellon from Albert Gallatin, but neither the individual nor the nation succeeded in effecting a recognition of the reality. Both Adams and America were married to the present—to multiplicity, but their real love was the past—unity. . . . (pp. 263-64)

Henry Adams had chronicled the evolution—or devolution —from unity to multiplicity, had formulated the problem, had attempted to solve it with the application of science. He saw the world and his country hastening to their doom, and he tried to warn them, but his was a voice crying out in the wilderness. The tragedy had assumed universal significance. (pp. 264-65)

> Henry Commager, "Henry Adams," in South Atlantic Quarterly *(reprinted by permission of the Publisher; copyright 1927 by Duke University Press, Durham, North Carolina), Vol. XXVI, No. 3, July, 1927, pp. 252-65.*

GRANVILLE HICKS (essay date 1935)

[The] *Education* gives one an excellent idea of the development of American thought from about 1800 to 1925. The first ideas that [Henry Adams] imbibed were not those of his generation, not those current in the forties and fifties in Concord and the more intellectual portions of Boston; they were, as he stated, eighteenth century ideas, the ideas of his great-grandfather. Very rapidly he caught up. In England he became acquainted with the writings of Lyell and Darwin, Comte and Marx. On his return to America he began his study of capitalism, and, because he remained outside the struggle for wealth and power, he went a long way towards understanding America in the decades after the war. Finally, with the breakdown of personal ambition, he arrived at an attitude that has only become common in the last fifteen years. It is amazing to note at how many points Adams anticipated the writers of the twenties, and it almost seems as if his work had been written, as theirs was, at a time when capitalism was rapidly decaying. He worshipped force, boasted of his ennui, complained of the sexlessness of Americans; he preached the general futility of action and the particular hopelessness of political effort; he made elaborate generalizations, not in order to influence the age in which he lived but merely to amuse himself; he pointed out the value of Catholicism as a refuge from struggle and a bulwark against change. It is little exaggeration to say that *The Education of Henry Adams* carries us from the adolescence of American industrial capitalism to its senility. (pp. 138-39)

> Granville Hicks, "Struggle and Flight: Henry Adams," in his The Great Tradition: An Interpretation of American Literature since the Civil War *(copyright © 1933, 1935 by Macmillan Publishing Co., Inc.; originally published in 1933 by The Macmillan Company, New York; new material in the revised edition copyright © 1969 by Granville Hicks; reprinted by permission of Russell & Volkening, Inc., as agent for the author), revised edition, Macmillan, 1935, Quadrangle Books, 1969, pp. 131-39.*

LOUIS KRONENBERGER (essay date 1939)

[The "Education"] remains an important document of American intellectual and moral inquiry, if only because not a dozen Americans of any period were intellectually and morally of a stature to produce it. It is predicated of very nearly a first-rate mind and something like a first-rate experience. If the mind fails us, it is chiefly from not being purposeful enough; if the experience, it is from being largely of one kind. Adams came to know everything within the reach of the cultivated man of the world, everything to be had of drawing-rooms and libraries, colleges and clubs, churches and ruins, senates and courts; but, though such contact was capable of a thousand variations, its bounds were immovably fixed. (p. 46)

If the "Education" were no more than a worldling's reminiscences and a student's recapitulations, all tied together with philosophical ribbons, we might praise its prose and wit and acknowledge its intellectual expressiveness of an era; but we should put it among the memorials, and not the textbooks, of American experience. But the "Education" is a grand-scale study of maladjustment, of the failure of an exceptional personality to mesh with a prodigious civilization: posing, with one gesture, the problem of the man and his times. (p. 48)

Like most serious autobiographies, the "Education" is an attempt, not to record a man's life, but to explain it. It is the work, at bottom, of one who set out both to judge and to justify himself. This dual intention is significant, even though what Adams attempted to justify was failure. We may take the liberty of supposing that this dual intention was embodied very simply: Adams judged himself by asking a question, and justified himself by returning an answer. Why—he asks in effect—should someone who started off with every opportunity, and with faith and eagerness, have ended up with so little achieved, dissentient and in utter flight? Because, he answers, the world he had set out to serve had been seized by forces he would not accept for master; and nothing better remained than to try to understand those forces and inveigh against them.

The "Education" is, then, a perfectly *conscious* study of frustration and deflected purpose; of the failure of a superior man to find the right place, or any tolerable place, in a civilization growing ever more corrupt, rapacious and vulgar. No one ever wrote a more deliberate apologia of his life than Henry Adams. (pp. 48-9)

[The] great documentary merit of the "Education" is its demonstration of what nineteenth-century America had become, and by what process, and on what terms.

The philosophical merit, which once seemed a merit so much greater, is by no means so great. For the intellectuals of the twenties, the "Education" was an epic after their own hearts. *Epic* is no idly used word; the scale and severity of the book are important. In one sense, the most misleading thing about it is its impressiveness. Written with much of the formality that Gibbon used in his "Memoirs," it comes at the reader with so magisterial an air that halfway through it he grants it the confidence reserved for an attested masterpiece. The Adams manner confers on the Adams apologia a definite extrinsic weight. There is the sense of a large mind and an imposing personality; there is the sense—unimpaired by the irony of the book—of deep purpose and high seriousness. Henry Adams, who lived his life in a minor key, took every precaution to write about it in a major one. The "Education" is a completely full-dress performance. (pp. 50-1)

[Impressive] as the "Education" is, and definitive as is its mood, it somehow is not profound. It befits very few of us to condescend to Adams on the score of his cultural background, his political knowledge, his cerebral weight; but the fact remains that it is not for his "discoveries," or his clarifications of the human struggle, that we can seek him out.

Those celebrated later chapters of the "Education"—The Dynamo and the Virgin, A Dynamic Theory of History—are superb intellectual exercises, but it is hard to believe that they offer a synthesis which is more than personally brilliant and picturesque. When Adams looked to the past, for example, it was originally in search of perspective. He set about contrasting twelfth-century "unity" with twentieth-century "multiplicity," and the contrast is striking. But to what end? He conceived the earlier age as the better one, but must have known that it was impossible to return to it. The structure of twelfth-century life has no application in ours; the old wheels went round from a social force that had become inoperative and spent. Yet, more and more in the manner of an escapist, Adams tried to go back; there came to be more than an esthete's interest in his medieval studies, in the long twilit mystic spell of Chartres. Coldly judged, does not one pamper one's maladjustment by pining for what one cannot have?

There was nothing shallow about Adams's inquiry into human culture, either in its feeling or its facts; but it failed to produce any profound philosophy of life, even a profound skepticism. Adams knew too much, he knew (or thought he knew) too well whither things were drifting, he had—too arrogantly—a disbelief that any good could come of it, ultimately to profit from his career of "education." The philosophy he did evolve is understandable enough, and one must grant that there was a basis in experience for it. But it comes to no more than the pessimism of one who sees the world being ruined, and the cynicism of one who gives up trying to reclaim it. And in Adams there was also an uglier cynicism, of sitting back and watching the world, with a not unmalign satisfaction, go to Hell. The motif of effort and education which carefully governs Adams's autobiography tends to obscure this uglier cynicism; but from a reading of the "Letters" one knows that it was there, and one sees how, after a time, the moralist in Adams gave up being in any sense a crusader and became a merely captious and querulous censor. (pp. 52-4)

[The "Education"] compels respect for a sense of weight behind, not in, it. It suggests tragedy; but it is not—at least on the terms it set out to be—tragic, because the author chose the less costly form of defeat, and the less noble. Impotence, to Adams, was preferable to mutilation. Psychologically—by which I mean that were Henry Adams the problem of a novelist—his life followed a convincing pattern. But in real life, an ultimate failure of character is not to be excused by being explained; nor does a lifetime of self-analysis compensate for a failure to see things through morally. If a crude capitalist era "crushed" Adams, it was as much from being enervated by the fruits of it as from being poisoned by its roots. Was Adams willing—was he ever willing—to lose just part of the world to gain his own soul? It is just possible to say Yes; but if so, Adams's reason was purely pride.

However great the merits of the "Education," its "method" can already be seen to have failed. Culture and education are of the highest importance—according to some philosophies, the very end of living. But for Henry Adams they were clearly intended to be a means, carrying him forward to a better understanding and fulfillment of his obligations. Instead, they produced in him the indecision of a Hamlet; they became a kind of luxury, a kind of solace, and a kind of escape. It may be that Adams has taught us more in autobiography than he could have in action. It is at least certain that he has warned us more unforgettably. (p. 56)

Louis Kronenberger, "'The Education of Henry Adams'," in The New Republic *(© 1939 The New Republic), Vol. LXXXXVIIII, No. 1267, March 15, 1939 (and reprinted in* Books That Changed Our Minds, *edited by Malcolm Cowley, Doubleday Doran & Company, Inc., 1939, pp. 45-57).*

YVOR WINTERS (essay date 1943)

Henry Adams saw modern history as a progress from unified understanding, or the illusion of such, in the century following the year 1150, toward the dispersion of understanding and force in the twentieth century; and he saw himself as the product of an earlier New England. In regard to himself he was correct; and as for modern history, his view of it, though scarcely defensible, provides a clue to certain historical processes of which the history of New England is perhaps the most dramatic single illustration. (p. 374)

Adams' theory of history is really a philosophy and a theory of human nature; it is wholly indefensible and perverse, and we should be hard pressed to understand how a man of genius could conceive it if we had not some understanding of the history which is largely responsible for his state of mind. Briefly, he possessed the acute moral sense of New England . . . and the New Englander's need to read the significance of every event which he saw. (pp. 390-91)

He had no faith, however, and hence he could not believe that there was anything back of the event: the event was merely isolated and impenetrable. Yet he possessed the kind of mind which drove him to read every event with a kind of allegorical precision; and since every event was isolated and impenetrable, he read in each new event the meaning that the universe is meaningless. (p. 391)

[Adams] was as passionate an allegorist as [Cotton] Mather had been; instead of seeing God's meaning in every event, he saw the meaninglessness of a godless universe, but with a Calvinistic intensity of vision. He had, as he confessed in writing of Henry James the "obsession of idée fixe." And not only had he the passion to see his allegorical vision, but he had the true Calvinist's passion to provide his vision with his own theology. He wrote:

> Chaos was the law of nature; Order was the
> dream of man.   (p. 405)

[Adams'] Emersonian disguise of his own disintegration . . . was something that he could not consistently maintain: his disintegration was not a voyage, governed by absolute standards, on a supernatural current in the direction of Unity; it was merely disintegration. And the only way to find Order in it, was to discover the reason for the disintegration and chart its rate.

He was too good a determinist and too devoutly sorry for himself to seek any part of the reason in himself, and partly because of these facts, and partly because he was committed to an obscurantistic view of history, he failed to seek it in any segment of history definite and limited enough to imply that the difficulty was due to human error that might in some measure be corrected. Like a true Calvinist and a true determinist, he turned at once, for his answer, to the Nature of the Universe, and sought to show that the whole

universe, as a single mechanism, was running down. The cosmological scope of the doctrine appears most fully in the volume of essays posthumously published as *The Degradation of the Democratic Dogma;* but in *Mont Saint-Michel and Chartres* and in the *Education* he seeks to illustrate the tendency by defining the difference between two extremes of civilization. . . . (pp. 405-06)

[Adams] is bent on proving the existence of a unified mind in the 13th century, because he is bent on proving that man has disintegrated since, and his discussion of Aquinas centers wholly in the theological difficulties, for he assumes that the philosophy derives from the theological solutions, whereas in reality the philosophy and the philosophical method derive very largely from Aristotle, who was a scientific observer and analyst and neither a Christian nor a theologian. And since the theological difficulties were real, and since the answers of Aquinas are less satisfactory to Adams than they must have been to Aquinas, Adams asserts that the entire structure, philosophy as well as theology, depends from faith, and "if Faith fails, Heaven is lost." . . . [And] when Adams says that Heaven is lost, he means that everything is lost. (p. 408)

The Cosmology which expands Adams' view of history to its ultimate generality is to be found in [the essays of] *The Degradation of the Democratic Dogma.* (p. 412)

The most important of these essays is *A Letter to American Teachers of History.* It begins with the unquestioning acceptance of two theological principles, both the product of the age which he is endeavoring to prove to be one of ultimate confusion: the Law of the Dissipation of Energy, and the assumption that man is governed by physical laws. Whether we regard Adams as the contemner of his own age, or as the apostle of scepticism, this acceptance is sufficiently startling. It can be understood only if we remember that he was the heir of the Puritans and that sooner or later his heritage was certain to overtake him completely. In order to prove the impossibility of absolute truth, he had to start from absolute truth and create what he could believe for the moment to be a comprehensive system.

The Revelation discloses that Energy is being dissipated steadily in a godless universe. . . . The principle explains why heat ends in cold, life in death, motion in station. And the principle once established, it follows that each succeeding manifestation of energy is inferior to the last. Man is thus inferior to the early animals, and civilization is a process of decay. The emergence of human reason during this process does not trouble Adams in the least: Reason, as we have seen, leads only to confusion and inaction and is of no help in the attainment of truth; this in spite of the fact that Adams probably believed that he was using his own reason in arriving at the truths which he elucidates. Reason is a degraded form of will. . . . (pp. 412-13)

[Man's deterioration] becomes a matter of cosmology, of Revealed Truth, and there is no help for the matter. The best thing man can do is trust his instincts, for they are worth more than his reason, and they will guide him infallibly along the current of his time to progressively more complex degeneracy. Art is a human function, and will be governed by the general law. Art also is deteriorating, but it must deteriorate to express honestly the general deterioration of man. . . . (p. 414)

If the chaos of the subconscious is the only reality, and if the subject-matter of art determines the form of the work, then we have arrived at *Finnegans Wake* and the poetry of Pound and Eliot as the finest expression of civilization, that is to say, of degeneracy, although in some way which almost eludes me, we have left that other product of degeneracy, the Reason, a little way behind us in arriving at our goal.

I have dealt very harshly with the later work of Adams; I have stated my opinion that this work represents the radical disintegration of a mind. The mind, however, had been a great one, though its true greatness is suspected only by professional historians at the present time and is little more than suspected by most of them. Of the early work, the novels and the life of Randolph are trivial; but the life of Gallatin is still regarded by historians as one of the great works in American biography, and although it is long and heavily documented, and is very different from the birds-eye views of biography which have been so popular during the past ten or fifteen years, it is a massive and distinguished work of literature. (pp. 414-15)

All things considered, I suspect that [*History of the United States During the Administrations of Thomas Jefferson and James Madison*] is the greatest historical work in English, with the probable exception of *The Decline and Fall of the Roman Empire,* although any such judgment by one who is not an expert scholar in a number of historical fields, as well as something of a critic of literature, must be very tentative. (p. 415)

[Adams] gives the impression of adhering very closely to his documents, and of judging them carefully and with a watchful attention to the possibility of his being prejudiced. If there is a constant prejudice in his history, in any wise comparable to the political bias of Hume or of Macaulay, it is a distrust of democratic procedure, a distrust which was to reach a state of violent exasperation in his later years. His fascination with confusion is already apparent, although in the history it is restrained; on the other hand, the confusion in the American government during the period which he treats was assuredly real, and it would be hard to convict him of over-emphasis or of drawing unwarranted conclusions. (p. 417)

Adams introduces a new style and an entirely new conception of historiography. The Adams who wrote the history was in the full possession of his intellectual powers, but he was the same Adams who was to deteriorate in the particular manner which we have seen. He was not heroic, and he did not see men as heroic, or at least he did not see those as heroic who were close to him in time and civilization. But he had a curiosity about psychological motives and action comparable to that of Henry James; his gift was for high comedy. (p. 422)

To the reader who habitually assumes that the great historians are necessarily in the heroic tradition, and that the only other historical type is that of the schoolroom text or the professional monograph, Adams' history may at first glance appear disappointing: it employs the method of the learned monograph, in a sense, but it raises the method to a form of art. This is what one should not overlook. The style is expert and flexible; it is never too exalted for its subject, as is sometimes the style of Gibbon; it never carries too much conviction to be convincing, as does sometimes the style of Macaulay or that of Motley. It is a style that can

offer a sequence of dates or the summary of a document, without loss either of accuracy or of distinction. It is in the passages dealing with the play of character that the book is most brilliant, but if one reads and rereads it carefully, one discovers that the play of character is comprehensible as a result of the author's careful preparations, and that the style is adequate with respect to everything it touches.

The history is penetrated with precise intelligence in all its parts: it is in this quality, I think, that it surpasses any other historical masterpiece with which I am acquainted. There is greater magnificence in portions of Gibbon, Macaulay, and Motley, but there is seldom the skill of penetration, and there is not the uniformity of success in any of them. And the wit of Adams is invariably the result of understanding instead of the result of its absence. (pp. 428-29)

> *Yvor Winters, "Henry Adams, or the Creation of Confusion" (originally published in his* The Anatomy of Nonsense, *New Directions Publishing Corporation,* © *1947 by Yvor Winters; reprinted by permission of Ohio University Press, Athens), in his* In Defense of Reason, *Swallow Press, 1947, pp. 374-430.*

R. P. BLACKMUR (essay date 1943)

Adams' two novels, *Democracy* and *Esther,* unlike those of a professional novelist, do not show their full significance except in connection with his life. In the case of *Democracy,* the first of the pair, the connection will be obvious when once set up, for it had to do with that part of his life which had been absorbed in the effort to make a career of politics. That is to say, it focused, and judged, an objective ambition. With *Esther,* it is a very different matter, which it will not be easy to make clear, and upon which different opinions are possible; for in *Esther* Adams made his first attempt to express what was to most of his contemporaries an outer lack as an inner and inaccessible need. Where *Democracy* dealt with man in his relation to society in terms of existing institutions which, whether they controlled or failed to control political power, at least represented it, *Esther* reached out to seize, to bring to rebirth, the spiritual power which the existing church, as Adams saw it in 1883, represented only by a kind of betrayal in terms of Pilate's question. Adams was no Pilate, as who would wish to be, but he could not help asking his question in the form peculiar to his generation just as he could not help repeating it later, in his two great books, in forms which seem in their vitality to have transcended those of his generation.

Adams was a lover of Matthew Arnold's poetry, not as he loved Swinburne for intoxication and lyric escape, but because Arnold expressed for him, as the two novels show, his own dilemma. . . . Adams was above all one of those for whom Arnold spoke in his famous lines, as

> Wandering between two worlds, one dead
> The other powerless to be born.

That the dead world had a singular tenacity and assiduity as a haunt and that the coming world had an overwhelming, if uncertain, necessity as a conception, made the distress of such an image the more severe. If a man cannot act upon his dilemma, or escape it in blind action, he will sometimes attempt to make symbols or fables of what would otherwise drive him to action; and it is as such symbols, such fables, that Adams' two novels best clarify themselves. (pp. 201-02)

[Adams] borrowed what he wished from the outsides of the popular novels of his day, and not from the best popular novels either or the newest, but from Lytton and Disraeli, from a romancer and a fabulist. His practical conception of what a novelist could do with difficult or interesting or obsessive material (and his material *did* obsess him) was not keen; and he lacked the native gift of the storyteller and the native necessity of the imagination that is able to create character. Thus he mixed in random proportions a love story, social comedy, social satire, and, for *Democracy*, the drama of politics or, for *Esther*, the drama of faith; and among these elements he set his chosen puppets to play and be played upon through arbitrary actions and dialogue either rootlessly brilliant or desperately conventional. Only when the author's intellect takes hold do the scenes come alive in the sense that the reader participates in them, and what the author's intellect takes hold of was what he knew when he began to write and not what the process of writing —of dramatizing—discovered for him. In short, if the novels were not by Henry Adams they would hardly be read today except to satisfy an omnivorous taste in the detritus of the third quarter of nineteenth-century American fiction.

But they were by Adams; and that fact provides us with enough good will so that we can take them, not as the third-rate novels they seem, but with the maximum significance that can be extracted from them in terms of Adams' life and work. . . . The idea or attitude in *Democracy* became in *The Education of Henry Adams* the idea or attitude by which Adams envisaged intelligence as playing the supreme role in American political life, but in the novel *Democracy* that same intelligence is shown as defeated by the very inertia which Adams later showed as its source. In *Democracy* American politics is shown as failing by the accident of corruption, as it were by the inattentiveness of human intelligence. In the *Education*, political life is shown, not as failing but as in abeyance; and the question is put: whether human intelligence is, or is not, adequate to controlling the vast forces which had shaped its forms. The difference is between the mere corruption of public life and the question whether public life will, or will not, cohere. (pp. 203-04)

As, in a way, Adams showed us in *Democracy* a state where the only responsible power was the police power and other powers were held irresponsibly, so, in *Esther*, he shows us a religion where the only effective power wielded by the church was also a kind of police power, and the great problems of faith were either received in indifference or were left to those outside the congregation. He shows us the figure of Hawthorne's Esther Dudley, with a difference. She does not hold the faith in an alien world, but she waits in an indifferent world for someone to bring the faith to her. Her struggle, then, is not to reject the false comer, but to see if she can accept him when he comes. (pp. 219-20)

Neither of Adams' novels reached conclusions; they were rather fables of the inconclusive; complementary to each other, they represented the gropings of a maturing mind after its final theme. Taken together they make the turning-point of a mind which had constructed itself primarily for a life of political action into a new life which should be predominantly imaginative and prophetic. But the turning had not finally been made. Adams lived still between two worlds. (pp. 224-25)

R. P. Blackmur, "The Novels of Henry Adams" (1943), in his A Primer of Ignorance, *edited by Joseph Frank (copyright © 1967 by the Estate of R. P. Blackmur; reprinted by permission of Harcourt Brace Jovanovich, Inc.),* Harcourt, 1967, pp. 201-25

ROBERT A. HUME (essay date 1945)

A knowledge of Adams's family background and of his literary tastes . . . confirms what is an easy enough hypothesis for even the most casual reader of his books: that here is, beyond any possibility of mistake, a scholarly American; and, more specifically, a scholarly New Englander. It is a scholarly New Englander whose thought and emotion give the paragraphs of the *Education* their particular dignity and formality. . . . Seldom if ever is there a lapse into colloquialism or a loss of cultivated poise; the vocabulary is learned and delicately weighed; the grammar is correct; the punctuation painstaking; the syntax disciplined. To be sure, sometimes the freedom from technical defect is a kind of defect in itself. Many a reader may feel that a construction like the following might be more readable if less correct: "One does what one can with one's means, and casting up one's balance sheet, one expects only a reasonable return on one's capital." It is impossible to escape that impersonal pronoun—re-repeated to the bitter end, as no doubt Boston pedagogy required. So marked an instance of pedantic stiffness, however, does not often occur. All in all, the prose of the *Education* is strong and "elegant" in an eighteenth-century sense, seeming to carry, even to readers not deeply sympathetic with its author, a highly civilized quality. (pp. 301-02)

One of [the more prominent stylistic features of the *Education*], of course, is the consistent avoidance of the first person singular pronoun. . . . [Presumably] the avoidance of "I" in the book is Adams's way of effacing the ego, or at least of diverting attention from the "manikin" whose "garment," or education, is his subject. Whether this result is attained may be doubted. Did Adams think to depress the ego by the same means which Julius Caesar in his *Commentaries* used to exalt it? Just as the reader may not forget that it was Caesar in Gaul, so he may not forget that it was Adams in America: the surname stands forth in mock-modesty on every page. True, the use of the third person may to some extent separate narrator from narrative. Though one is incessantly reminded that it is Adams whose story is being told, one is not often reminded that Adams is doing the telling; and it may have been this apparent detachment, instead of a true effacement of the ego, that Adams desired. Particularly in the concluding chapters, devoted mainly to an exposition of his dynamic theory of history, Adams wished to treat himself impersonally—merely as a "point" in the twentieth century to which he might draw a line of historical sequence emanating from the thirteenth. He was thus devoting these pages not to autobiography so much as to an elaborate social and historial hypothesis, and using himself only as a convenient working item.

What Adams sacrificed stylistically by avoiding the first person pronoun is the converse of what he gained. Most of all he sacrificed that naturalness which, as a critic, he prized. Almost all readers, consciously or not, must experience a slight psychological jar at encountering "he" where they would normally expect "I." (pp. 304-05)

A result accompanying this unnaturalness of style in the *Education* is that the reader seldom feels a sense of intimacy, or warmth, or chattiness, such as may be found often in Adams's correspondence. (p. 306)

It must be noted, too, that one reading the *Education* finds in every chapter, paragraph, and sentence a quality of self-possession which goes beyond the mere self-command of a writer of disciplined prose. It is a quality so personal, as well as stylistic, that on encountering it one is impelled to invoke at once the classic dictum of Buffon, "Le style est de l'homme même," and name it, again, a New England quality, deriving from one who was the inheritor of Puritan restraint, if not actually of Puritan belief. (p. 307)

[Irony is] a quality which Adams's style in the *Education* possesses to a marked degree. As applied to that style, however, the term seems often to require special defining. Much of the time one must use it to refer to a slightly different quality from that one discernible in Defoe or Swift or Fielding, which leads the reader to infer at once the direct opposite of the literal purport of the words. Paradoxically, perhaps, the writer who employs irony in this traditional sense is one who possesses clear-cut convictions. Concerning many important matters, certainly, Henry Adams lacked such convictions. (p. 309)

Recently Yvor Winters has pointed out with considerable trenchancy that from his earliest years Adams was prone to create difficulties where few or none existed, and that thus he brought himself at last to the point of not understanding or believing in anything [see excerpt above].

Hence it is not surprising to discern that for Adams irony frequently was valuable not in conveying to the reader the exact opposite of the asserted meaning, but in achieving a confused and ambivalent compromise between the two extremes. It was a method, for which he must have been grateful, of saying something and at the same time not saying it. (pp. 310-11)

When he deals specifically with his own career, many if not most of his comments are, obviously, couched in this tone of ironic evasion. His chapter "Twenty Years After" contains observations that the cognizant reader can neither accept nor reject, as, for example: "Perhaps Henry Adams was not worth educating. . . ." Even with the "perhaps" this is inescapably a titbit of mock-modesty. . . . (pp. 311-12)

Perhaps the Janus-faced element in his style may be defended, after a fashion, because it so strikingly reflects the state of confusion in Adams's mind and soul; and, of course, it helps to make the *Education* a challenging and a baffling problem in scholarly reading, the kind that a sly teacher may safely hand over to a brilliant undergraduate as antidote to the latter's intolerable pride in his own critical faculties. Nevertheless, many intelligent readers must lay down unfinished a book which so persistently avoids both of the comprehensible extremes of cutting irony and lucid direct statement.

One can turn with a certain relief to considering Adams's stylistic faculty for conciseness. Not only do the pages of the *Education* show, in general, noteworthy economy and efficiency; they are studded with terse observations, characterizations, and witticisms. Ordinarily these do not quite reach the quality of epigram: they lack the ultimate nicety

of balance, or, perhaps, depend too much on the context to stand brilliantly alone. (p. 312)

In Adams's sentences and paragraphs, few if any "devices" are noticeable. He does not overemploy alliteration, inversion, or repetition, nor suffer the intrusion of verse rhythms. There is little about his writing, in short, to suggest T. E. Hulme's conception of prose: a museum where all the old weapons of poetry are kept. Without conspicuous strain, he usually achieves the union between matter and manner; the result is an individual style that yet does not thrust itself on the reader. By consistently varying the length of phrases and sentences, he avoids the monotony against which he warned young Lodge, but still customarily retains a natural movement and organization. Now and then he exhibits a fondness for parenthesis, though he never carries it to the point of inescapable mannerism, as his friend Henry James finally did.

The most difficult reading in the *Education* is in the final chapters. Any obscurity derives, however, not from any basic change in his method, but from the introduction at this point of a different and more complex subject matter. An exposition of the dynamic theory of history cannot be easily perused, since the theory is filled with scientific technicalities and logical confusions. It may have been the virtual unintelligibility of this concluding section of the book which prompted the author of the Editor's Preface to remark: "The point on which the author failed to please himself . . . was the usual one of literary form." (p. 314)

Robert A. Hume, "The Style and Literary Background of Henry Adams," in American Literature *(reprinted by permission of the Publisher; copyright 1945 by Duke University Press, Durham, North Carolina), Vol. 16, No. 4, January, 1945, pp. 296-315.*

ROBERT E. SPILLER (essay date 1946)

Tahiti is not one of the major works of Henry Adams, but it is interesting because it is the product of a lull in his writing and it marks the transition between the two phases of his career, as historian and as man of letters. . . .

Here for the first time in Henry Adams' writings a tiny segment of man's history became the symbol of the history of man. The method of his later work, the *Education* and the *Chartres,* is suggested, even though it is wholly undeveloped. From a mass of geographical, genealogical, and historical facts, interspersed with characterization and lore, there emerges a portrait of a people representative of all people. Potentially *Tahiti* is a work of art of the kind its author later learned to write; actually it does not quite succeed in filling out the meaning of its massed data, largely because there was no central symbol like the Virgin or the Dynamo about which to group fact and idea. (p. v)

Robert E. Spiller, "Introduction" (1946), in Tahiti *by Henry Adams (copyright 1947 Scholars' Facsimiles and Reprints), Scholars' Facsimiles and Reprints, 1947, pp. iii-vii.*

RICHARD F. MILLER (essay date 1947)

All [Henry Adams's] works, except his historical writings, are, in varying degrees, studies of women. Such, certainly, are his two novels: *Democracy—An American Novel . . .* and *Esther. . . .* Even the *Education,* despite its exasperating omissions of much personal data, contains numerous discussions of women and candidly admits that Adams's life had been influenced by them. (p. 291)

[How] did Woman attract Henry Adams? There are, I believe, four ways. The clue to the first can be found in the *Education.* There, as elsewhere—in his letters, for example —he regrets men's inability to understand the true significance of Woman. Woman and sex had to be understood, the latter for its force, if one hoped ever to understand history. . . . (p. 292)

Woman was force or energy; that is one reason she attracted Adams. She was, in other words, one more study for which Adams could find some equation or formula. Her appeal in this sense is mainly intellectual.

The second reason is that he found in woman the generic symbol of the great comforter, in a sense the great mother of all gods. This much can be said dogmatically—so far as anything can ever be said dogmatically about Henry Adams: his irony was always absent when he dealt with, or discussed, women. (pp. 293-94)

The third quality that beguiled Adams was the importance of faith in Woman as a means to truth and as a guide in all her actions. Woman had to be convinced by faith; and gradually Adams himself came to believe that reason by itself was inadequate. (p. 295)

Although [in *Esther*] Esther's reason tells her that she loves Stephen Hazard, her intuition tells her that he will never be her husband. Hazard's reasoning and that of Strong merely make Esther panicky. Ultimately, both *Democracy* and *Esther* end in question marks; nothing is resolved, for neither heroine can be convinced by reason even though reason has able champions. Both are as puzzled about life as Adams.

At first glance *Democracy* is merely a picture of forces and energies in a corrupt capital, but it ends by becoming a study of a woman's mind. Madeleine Lee is essentially intuitive, and "Her final judgment of her own case is in terms of her intuitive understanding of moral forces. . . ."

Esther is a profounder examination of a woman's faith as a test of truth than is *Democracy,* but one has to turn again to *Mont-Saint-Michel and Chartres* to find this aspect analyzed most completely. I believe Professor [Robert E.] Spiller had this in mind when he said: "The trail from Esther to the Virgin of Chartres is a long and intricate one, but it is straight." Reason, fond as he was of it and unhappy as he would have been had he had to abandon it, was for Adams the means by which men arrived only at antinomies.

Women represented one other thing to Henry Adams. She embodied regeneration. Although man had but a secondary, uneasy role in the universe, woman felt at home. She knew intuitively the universe was a *uni-verse* ". . . because she had made it after the image of her own fecundity. . . ." (p. 296)

Even though we do not know all the facts, Adams appears to have been a victim of a poignant irony; he, probably more than any other man in his age, sought to understand Woman; yet his own wife committed suicide. (p. 298)

Richard F. Miller, "Henry Adams and the Influ- ence of Woman," in American Literature (*reprinted by permission of the Publisher; copyright 1947 by Duke University Press, Durham, North Carolina*), Vol. 18, No. 4, January, 1947, pp. 291-98.

NEWTON ARVIN (essay date 1951)

One gets the strongest impression in reading [his] letters that, when Adams sat down to write them, the discomfort that so often afflicted him elsewhere quite fell away and he became simply a man with a pen—a man for whom, moreover, the pen was a predestined implement. Now he was wholly at one with himself and with his perfect audience of a single person, and all his powers as a writer—powers of sharp attention to people and things, of responsiveness to impressions, of insight and judgment, and above all of expression in language—found themselves in free and unembarrassed play. (p. xiv)

It is the letters he wrote in the sixties that chiefly show how capable [Adams] was of competing with Horace Walpole on his own terrain. He is at one disadvantage here: he was never present at any event that offered itself to the chronicler quite so gratefully or so enviably as the trial of the rebel Scotch lords or the coronation of George III. And in any case Adams's writing rarely has just the qualities of briskness, amenity, and careless precision—as of eighteenth-century music—that one comes to expect of Walpole. It is usually a little lower in pitch and more astringent in savor than his predecessor's. If it has less sprightliness and charm, however, it of course has greater density: Adams's mind, only too obviously, was a far more complex one than Walpole's, and yet his eye was no less quick and keen. It need hardly be said now that his interest in the events that passed before him was a philosophical, not a gossipy, one—but along with this he had some of the gifts of the novelist too. And what gives his letters of the sixties their special character is the union one finds in them of the general and the particular, of the broadly historical and the sharply personal, of the sense of large affairs sweeping on their way and the eye for the human actors, not always heroic actors, who are carried along with them. (pp. xv-xvi)

No reader of the *Education* needs to be told what a genius Adams had for the personal sketch, for the quick penciled drawing of the individual subject that, isolating a detail or two and giving them their full salience, has an effect of serious and truth-telling caricature. . . . This gift of portraiture exhibits itself in the letters too—intermittently, to be sure; with more intermissions than one could wish; one misses any serious attempt to evoke Disraeli in the House of Commons or Grant at the White House—but at times it is in full play. . . . The great display-piece of Adams's achievements in this vein . . . is certainly the wonderful series of sketches of Stevenson, whom Adams encountered several times when he was in Samoa in the early nineties. (p. xviii)

The picture [of Stevenson] may be a one-sided picture, a brilliant caricature rather than a sober portrait, but of its brilliance, at all events, there can be no question. Quite by itself it would make the fortune of the letters in which it appears, yet as it happens these letters from Samoa are so rich, so spirited, even so genial, that, if the remarks about Stevenson were entirely deleted from them, they would still remain among the purest triumphs of Adams's career as a writer. In general, he was never more consistently good—never more uninterruptedly animated and vivid, or less liable to his special vices of mind and style—than in the great body of letters he wrote on his very considerable travels about the globe. (p. xix)

[The] letters enable one to follow the *development* of [Adams's] mind from phase to phase as, of course, none of his books or even all his books taken together quite do. The intellectual story they tell is, quite naturally, much less artfully shaped and organized than that in the *Education*, but it is a more complex, shifting, indecisive, and credible story.

What one gets in the letters, and fails to get in the *Education,* is the whole process by which Henry Adams moved from the great Unitarian synthesis of his fathers—from its pure, cold, arid, eighteenth-century rationality and optimism—to the mechanistic catastrophism with which he ended. This latter was, of course, his final testament to posterity, but only the reader of the letters has a full sense of the delicacy with which Adams's mind was for many years balanced between the poles of hopefulness and despair, affirmation and denial, belief and skepticism. (pp. xxiv-xxv)

But the strictly personal dimension cannot be left out, and the letters would tell one, if nothing else did, that the final tipping of the balance of his mind to the side of darkness was as much the consequence of personal tragedy as it was of historical decay. What his wife's suicide did to Adams was to destroy for good all the capacity he had ever had for reading the auguries cheerfully. (p. xxvii)

[Only] a reader of the letters will quite realize how great was the variety of ideas to which at one time or another Adams turned his mind, or with what agility and boldness his mind played over most of them. Now it is the shallow careerism of Alexander Hamilton, now the particular place of sex in Japanese life, now the vulgar mercantile quality of the architecture of the Valois and Touraine. He glances at Anglo-Saxon poetry, and his quick, offhand remarks might have come from a literary critic of genius; he animadverts on the evolution of finance capital, and seems to have given most of his life to the problem; he finds himself reflecting on the unself-consciousness of his father and that whole generation of New Englanders, and suggests in half a dozen sentences a sustained and searching essay in psychological history. Meanwhile he has been willful, petulant, illiberal, and superficial at a hundred points; he has ridden a few hobbies—and even a few phrases (his "gold bugs," for example)—to the brink of prostration and over; he has obstinately shut his eyes to every manifestation of new life that he does not wish to consider, and allowed his prophetic catastrophism to waste and weaken itself in senile hysteria. It has all mattered relatively little to the responsive reader: the foibles of a first-rate mind are always a small price to pay for its real fruits, and among the fruits of Adams's mind his letters come very close, at the least, to holding first place. (pp. xxix-xxx)

Newton Arvin, in his introduction to The Selected Letters of Henry Adams, *edited by Newton Arvin (reprinted by permission of Farrar, Straus and Giroux, Inc.; copyright 1951 by Newton Arvin),* Farrar, Straus & Giroux, 1951, pp. ix-xxx.

WILLIAM H. JORDY (essay date 1952)

Failure is the paradoxical unity in Adams' thought. Imagine

his thought without the unifying theme. Loose ends would appear everywhere. How easy to count up the loose ends and conclude that Adams did indeed fail. But by admitting his failure—more precisely by his *method* of admitting it—Adams forestalled this easy conclusion. He failed in his logic; but the logic was mere illustration for a larger pattern. His pattern was faulty; but the pattern allegorized his society. His social views were exceedingly narrow; but his picture of the contemporary world provided a background for self-portraiture. To complete the circle, his autobiography was actually that of modern man whose traditions in knowledge and society had both lost significance. His failure defied precise measurement. It was as though Adams were at one end of an elastic yardstick, stretching or bending the stick whenever measurement threatened. Make any number of measurements; others always remained, each qualifying all. It was in this process of stretching and bending that the unity occurred. Indeed, the lack of fixed points for measurement intensified the sense of multiplicity which was the real measure of failure.

If, however, Adams manipulated the pliable measure of failure in terms of himself, he was always just outside the area measured, while in eluding measurement he asserted his sense of superiority over his measurer. He was the oracle speaking in enigmas; and lest his reader take as fact what he intended as enigma, Adams reinforced the riddle by interlarding his personal account of decline and fall with reminders of his accomplishments. Although he failed as a teacher, the erstwhile professor did not forget to add that President Eliot had commended him; while (in the event that his reader had not come across the volume) John Fiske "went so far in his notice of the family in 'Appleton's Cyclopedia,' as to say that Henry had left a great reputation at Harvard College . . ." As for the *History* which he pretended to disparage, "The 'Life' of Lincoln [by Nicolay and Hay] had been . . . published hand in hand with the 'History' of Jefferson and Madison, so that between them they had written nearly all the American history there was to write. The intermediate period needed intermediate treatment . . ." By implication, less distinguished scholars could chronicle the intermediate period scorned by Adams and his friends. If he were ignorant, he considered himself only as ignorant as the "best-informed statesman." If he were a failure, Adams managed to imply that no one had enjoyed more success. By thus condemning as failure what to most would have seemed success, he chided his society for its standards, while crediting himself not only for his achievement but also for his perception in seeing its limitations. Moreover, the limitations to his success were those of his society rather than himself. So his failure served not only to give form to whatever was formless in his thought, his artistry, his world, and his life; it also served as the device to redeem his wounded vanity. In short, he made his failure heroic. (pp. 256-57)

William H. Jordy, "The Failure," in his Henry Adams: Scientific Historian *(copyright 1952 by Yale University Press), Yale University Press, 1952, pp. 256-88.*

EDMUND WILSON (essay date 1955)

[*The Education of Henry Adams*] is perhaps the most uncanny example of Adams' equivocal attitude in relation to the social world of Boston and to the official world of Washington out of which he had come and to which he had inevitably reverted, but with which he never ceased to express his extreme dissatisfaction. He assumes that Lodge, as a Lodge and the son of a friend of Adams, is worth taking seriously and writing about, but he turns the poor young man into a shadow, and withers up his verse with a wintry pinch [in *The Life of George Cabot Lodge*]. (p. 744)

[Lodge] was kept under glass, and he dried up from "lack of air to breathe"; and Adams himself was a part of the stifling. He composes for his young friend an epitaph which buries his aspirations with him. The stealthy and elusive malice which lies in *The Education* here colors what is meant as a tribute with an irony so ready and pervasive that it is hardly aware of itself. J. P. Marquand could not do so well . . . the irony of the final picture—how far is it deliberate on Adams' part?—of poor Lodge arriving back in Boston, weighted down with family, nurses and baggage and in a panic for fear he has lost his manuscripts in the confusion of the North Station; and Henry Adams' own gingerly justification of the element of violence in Greek tragedy: "The better informed and the more accomplished the critic may be, who reads the *Herakles* for the first time, knowing nothing of the author, the more disconcerted he is likely to be in reading it a second time. His first doubts of the poet's knowledge or merits will be followed by doubts of his own."

This double-edged doubt, so characteristic of Adams—the doubt that peeled the gilt off the Gilded Age yet despaired of Adams' strength to stand up to it, the doubt which, in envying the faith that had erected the cathedral at Chartres yet found in the weakness of the church's foundations a symbol for its own painful fears—this doubt is all through the life of Lodge, the last of Adams' published books. One feels that he dislikes Lodge's poetry. He would like to see something in it; but he shrinks—from what?—from finding in the younger man the reflection of his own sterility or from the disquieting possibility that Lodge may have really been a poet and hence have lived in some richer way than Adams had ever known? He wants to think that Lodge was a nonconformist as he imagines himself to have been; yet he meets in him all the old round of the life-cycle of people from Boston, of people like oneself; and he cannot repress a shiver. We people all come to nothing—not, of course, that we aren't better than the others.

With all this, there is even here that candor in dubiety and impotence which has the accents of a kind of strength and the rare sensitive-cynical Adams who is himself a kind of poet, as it were, signs the little memoir with the passage at the end of the seventh chapter in which he tells of the solitary writer weaving secret enchantments at night like a drug-merchant or a magician. (pp. 745-46)

Edmund Wilson, in his introduction to "The Life of George Cabot Lodge," in The Shock of Recognition: The Development of Literature in the United States Recorded by the Men Who Made It, *edited by Edmund Wilson (reprinted by permission of Farrar, Straus & Giroux, Inc.; copyright 1943 by Doubleday Doran and Company, Inc.; copyright © 1955 by Edmund Wilson), Farrar, Straus and Cudahy, 1955, pp. 742-46.*

EDWARD N. SAVETH (essay date 1956)

Before it was popular to think and say so, Henry Adams

evolved a theory of feminine superiority. Compared to the American woman, Adams once said, the American man was a "chump" who wanted to be ruled by her; "a peaceful, domestic animal, fond of baby-talk" and who yearned for "love and doughnuts." (p. 231)

Woman's sheltering strength allegedly afforded "solace and comfort" to Adams—a refuge from the harsh man's world of politics and business for which he had no liking. Adams himself said so, and so has practically everyone who has written about him. However, after a study of Adams' heroines—fictional ones like Madeline Lee, Esther and the Virgin; as well as the women who shared his life—his sister Louisa, his wife Marian, and his nieces; it is difficult to discover how Adams or anyone else could have found "solace and comfort" in them.

Adams' heroines are in many ways alike as though modelled upon a prototype. They are strong women and unyielding, dominating the men who surround them and posing a contemptuous challenge to masculine institutions. These women wanted no male interference with what Chaucer, centuries earlier, called their "soveraintee." They preferred weak men who were willing to be reduced to the level of manageable children and to accept mother's dominion unquestioningly. They occupied a world of their own, surrounded by an impenetrable world of feminine "feeling," as inaccessible to masculine "thought" as the planet Venus. For a man to attempt to possess an Adams heroine was to woo disaster or the promise of disaster. Adams, who liked nothing better than to turn over the reins of his life to certain of his heroines, must have felt at least some misgivings in doing so.

Adams' first fictional heroine, if not his first heroine, was Madeline Lee, central figure of the novel *Democracy*. . . . (pp. 231-32)

Mr. Robert Spiller has interpreted *Democracy* in terms of Madeline's bout with political corruption and Adams' second novel, *Esther*, as the heroine's conflict with established religion. This understanding is valid of the intellectual content of the novel. But Adams, particularly in so personal a book as *Esther*, avowedly written in his "heart's blood," seems to be saying something very basic about the emotional relationships of the characters. (p. 233)

Like all of Adams' heroines, Esther is endowed with "more strength than men" as well as an "instinct for power." At the same time, Adams made her less of an ironsides than Madeline Lee and with a brittleness inherent in her strength. She gave the impression "of a lightly-sparred yacht in mid-ocean; unexpected you ask yourself what the devil she is doing there." (p. 234)

Adams' greatest heroine was, of course, the Virgin, whom Adams made into a not very different woman from Madeline Lee or Esther Dudley. Like them, she is independent and defiant of men and institutions. Her power differed in degree, not in kind, from that exercised by Madeline and Esther; the Virgin dominated heaven and earth in the thirteenth century, even as Madeline and Esther ruled over their narrower milieux. As with Adams' other heroines, intellect was not Mary's strongpoint. The Virgin, Adams writes, had "very rudimentary knowledge, indeed, of the principles of political economy as we understand them" and her failure to comprehend the philosophy of St. Thomas Aquinas was matched by her scorn of it.

At the same time, Adams makes plain, it was the Virgin and not St. Thomas who ruled the thirteenth-century roost. In the heavenly hierarchy, Adams wrote, "not only was the Son absorbed in the Mother, or represented under her guardianship, but the Father fared no better and the Holy Ghost followed." If encapsulation in Mary was the fate of the Holy Trinity, so powerful a Mother could be approached by mere man, not through the logic of Aquinas but by complete surrender of will, not unlike the kind Madeline Lee and Esther Dudley demanded of their suitors and that was implied in Adams' willingness to have the woman in his life lead him where she willed. (pp. 237-38)

Mary, as Adams presents her, is undeniably a woman of charm as well as power. Yet, she who was above the law; who was capable of turning hell into an ornament; who trampled arbitrarily upon man-made institutions and distinctions—is also a little frightening. Her nature being "pity, not justice," no man could appeal to Mother on the merits of his case, since the approach to Mary, unlike that to other members of the thirteenth-century heavenly hierarchy, is through faith, not reason. Reason, unlike faith, involves a certain amount of give and take between mother and child, on the basis of which the child develops independence and maturity. But Mary in Heaven, Queen Eleanor and Queen Blanche on earth, and the rest of the thirteenth-century mothers and wives, in exchanging absolute protection for absolute faith, sanctioned no such developmental process. (pp. 239-40)

In his imaginative rendering of history, Adams parallels a decline in the world's energy and its eventual eclipse with a weakening of mother's power. Mother, like all else in Adams' world, loses strength and energy; and even as Adams in fantasy exalted mother—he degraded her too.

Students of Adams have taken for granted his wish to destroy father's world because of the frustrations he encountered in it. But were his frustrations any less real in mother's realm? Adams' heroines, alas, had a habit of disappointing him by failing to provide enough "love" and enough "doughnuts." Adams' ideal heroine was supposed to be fecund—Louisa and Marian were childless; Esther was unmarried, destined apparently to remain so, and Madeline Lee's child was dead. After he had placed the direction of his life in the hands of Louisa and Marian—they died inopportunely. Adams' ideal heroine has her proper milieu in the world of artistic creativity, but Marian had the temerity to commit suicide by swallowing chemicals she used in her photographic work. Adams sought peace and contentment in the arms of a woman powerful enough to bring them to him—but his earthly heroines, real and fictional, were cold comfort to a man.

And so, having condemned the world of mother and father to death, Adams in "The Prayer to the Virgin" hoped that he might live forever in another world in the arms of his supreme heroine. Here the man-child would find sufficient "love" and sufficient "doughnuts"; but knowing Adams we cannot be sure. (p. 242)

> *Edward N. Saveth, "The Heroines of Henry Adams," in* American Quarterly *(copyright, Fall, 1956 Trustees of the University of Pennsylvania), Vol. VIII, No. 3, Fall, 1956, pp. 231-42.*

ERNEST SAMUELS   (essay date 1961)

The *Mont-Saint-Michel and Chartres* of Henry Adams is a book as paradoxical as it was unexpected. It came into being unheralded by any forerunner in American literature. Its kinship was rather with John Ruskin's *The Stones of Venice* and the poetry of Dante Gabriel Rossetti than with the literary modes of the turn of the century. . . .

The . . . book marked a radical departure from [Adams'] earlier writing, not only in subject but in style. The severe precision of statement with which he had tried to fix American history at the point of his pen was replaced by an almost lyrical freedom of expression. In going back nearly seven hundred years for his subject, his imagination found full release at last. (p. v)

In two anonymous novels of the early eighties, *Democracy* and *Esther,* novels whose authorship remained a secret known only to a few intimates, Adams had begun his exploration of [the eternal question of man's nature and his relation to an indifferent or hostile universe], for a new urgency attached to [it] as a result of the impact of Darwin's *Origin of Species.* Besides, the industrial and financial revolution after the Civil War left no human relation undisturbed. Like Matthew Arnold, Adams felt himself hovering between two worlds, "one dead, the other powerless to be born." All the tensions of society seemed to come to a focus in the Woman Question. The emancipation of women was the most momentous social fact of the nineteenth century. The future of the family and of human society depended upon woman's remaining true to her natural role—maternity. Both of her heroines suffered the tragedy of divided natures. The atomizing tendency of the modern world was also stifling a whole side of man's nature: his capacity for feeling and art, for love and poetry.

After the Panic of 1893 and the triumph of money values, Adams found himself thoroughly at odds with the drift of the centers of American power. He demanded a nobler aim than a banker's materialist paradise. Like Ruskin and the Pre-Raphaelites, he rebelled against the vulgarity and ugliness that had come to be associated with middle-class life, and like them he was thrown back upon the idealized values of the Middle Ages. To the poet the Middle Ages offered a kind of refuge; to the historian they provided an anchor for a philosophy of history. Adams' quest for a form and a myth through which he might voice his criticism of contemporary values culminated in the *Chartres,* a criticism all the more profound for the ironic perspective of his parable. (pp. vi-vii)

The radiance of the stained-glass windows [of Chartres Cathedral] seemed to revive buried senses of color and form. The Norman churches, especially the Abbey of Mont-Saint-Michel, touched him on another side. In his imagination he identified himself with the archaic wholeness of his Norman ancestors. In this awakening there arose the polarities of the new book: the Abbey as the highest expression of the masculine nature, the Cathedral of Our Lady of Chartres as the triumph of the womanly nature. Beneath the art and theology of the twelfth-century renaissance Adams sensed a lost reality, the reality of sex and maternity. (p. vii)

Adams was one of the first in literature to recognize that the Religion of Beauty rested upon the laws of biology. In his daring imagery the Virgin Mary symbolized the popular rebellion against the artificial male-centered theology of the early Church. In the twelfth century she emerged as the last and greatest of the Mother Goddesses, the goddesses of fertility known to all early religions. Her portrayal as the Virgin of Majesty in the sculpture and iconography of Chartres reflected the harmony, for an all-too-short span of time, of appearance and reality, of the form and substance of men's beliefs, of the graceful submission of man to woman.

At one level the book is, of course, a brilliant guide to the treasures of the two great edifices. No other writer has assimilated with such grace and wit the physical details of these structures. Read in the iridescent twilight of the great nave of Chartres, the description of the rose windows, freighted with history and legend, is evocative beyond the reach even of Rodin's rapturous prose. There is still before one, however, the superb architecture of the book itself, buttressed upon the themes that make it a tract for the times. (pp. vii-viii)

> Ernest Samuels, "Introduction" (copyright ©
> 1961 by The New American Library, Inc.; re-
> printed by arrangement with The New American
> Library, Inc., New York, New York), in Mont-
> Saint-Michel and Chartres by Henry Adams, The
> New American Library, 1961, pp. v-ix.

GEORGE HOCHFIELD (essay date 1962)

Every student of Henry Adams comes sooner or later to feel that the *Education*, the book with which Adams makes his strongest claim to prominence in American literary history, is the greatest obstacle to a proper understanding of the man and his work. The *Education*, in some respects, is a fascinating deception; it seems to offer unreserved self-disclosure, but it is so stylized and so qualified by irony that it ends by creating a myth. The myth is indispensable in its own way, for it is a product of Adams' imagination, but it is not the whole, or even the essential, truth about Henry Adams.

In order to correct the impression left by the *Education*, it is necessary to place that book in a perspective which includes the rest of Adams' literary career. He was a prolific and exceptionally varied writer, and everything he did is touched with his genius. And, as with all writers, there is a continuity and development of thought in his intellectual history which relate his books to one another in a coherent order. (p. v)

Three basic facts of vital significance to the understanding of Henry Adams' mind are revealed by the *Life of Albert Gallatin*. The first is that he conceived of Republicanism as a system designed to realize an ideal of human perfection. Given such a conception, the lives of all those involved in the Republican movement were necessarily seen by him in a certain way, namely as deriving their meaning from the effort to achieve the ideal. The second basic fact is that the writing of biography meant to Adams primarily a study of the pursuit of ideal ends. Gallatin's life, insofar as it discloses a form to the biographer, is nothing else than just such a pursuit. The third fact we learn from this book is that Republicanism did not succeed in establishing its ideal society; Gallatin's life was a pursuit that terminated in failure. The failure of Gallatin portends quite definitely the failure Henry Adams attributed to himself in his autobiography, and the context of Gallatin's failure—the context of

democratic idealism—helps suggest a way of interpreting Adams' failure. (p. 23)

[*Democracy*, subtitled *An American Novel*] is steeped in the same current of thought that flows through the historical works and has much to reveal about Adams' state of mind during the period of their composition. Indeed, it seems that by the act of putting aside history and creating a set of symbolic personalities and events, Adams was liberated to discover, or at least to express, some of his most deeply felt convictions. (p. 24)

Beyond its importance within the framework of Adams' literary development, *Democracy*'s claim to consideration is supported by its own literary merit, its independent quality as a novel. Although it is partially true that, as R. P. Blackmur has said, Adams "lacked the native gift of the story-teller" [see excerpt above], still the subject of *Democracy* is a difficult one, its interest in human beings is serious, and its structural craft, though occasionally mechanical or still, is adequate to its intention. Instead of exhaustiveness it aims for verbal dexterity, a dry, witty economy that compresses its material and communicates insight in the form of epithet. Its mode of complexity, as therefore might be expected, is paradox or, more generally, an irony that plays over much of its surface, lighting up unexpressed motive, thought, or desire. A measure of Adams' success, in fact, is the extent to which his wit enlivens and deepens the book without diminishing its seriousness or reducing the stature of its heroes and their moral plight. (p. 25)

[The] action and moral judgment of *Democracy* are dependent upon one principle which is more important to Henry Adams' mind than any other that can be elicited from his books. For him, value or meaning is only conceivable as originating in final, impersonal ends. He cannot think of life as having meaning apart from a goal that is outside of and larger than the individual. This is the most fundamental and omnipresent manifestation of his Puritanism; it is a mental habit shaped by the obsessive need of his conscience to relate every event, every moral act, and every individual self to some ultimate and all-embracing unity. (p. 32)

All of Henry Adams' early works, except [*History of the United States of America during the Administrations of Thomas Jefferson and James Madison*], have been largely ignored by readers and critics alike, but *John Randolph* has more nearly fallen into oblivion than any of the others. If this indicates that a low opinion of the book is commonly held, even among close readers of Adams, then a great injustice has been done to a minor masterpiece of critical biography. (p. 34)

To be sure, *Randolph* is not, like the *Gallatin*, a full-scale biography; it is not even exhaustive with respect to politics; nor is it thickly sown with the documents of "scientific" historiography. But in page after page it is luminous with a prose equal to the best of the *History*, which is very good indeed. Its style is for the most part swift, supple, and epigrammatic, perfectly suited for the trenchant condensation and irony required by Adams' intention. It is a beautifully controlled style, capable of summarizing the major issues of political debate without damage to nuances of meaning, capable too of sharply drawn portraiture that nevertheless retains the flavor of complex life (pp. 34-5)

The chief difference between the *Life of Gallatin* and *John*

Randolph is that in the former, democratic idealism fails because it cannot control all the circumstances of life and cannot bend to them without breaking, while in the latter it is "perverted by the possession of power." Adams does not go quite so far as to say that idealism necessarily leads to such perversion, but power does, and idealism, therefore, must fail once it acquires power. The idealistic impulse, in short, is a hopeless one. But this does not excuse corrupted idealists from moral responsibility. Adams holds the Republicans to strict account for the loss, not of perfection, but of their integrity. The whole force of his ironic method is concentrated on this point: they professed idealism; they acted weakly or selfishly; they must be judged ignominious failures. Moral condemnation is perhaps the most lasting impression the book makes. Adams simply could not digest with equanimity the fact of Republican self-betrayal; he returns to it again and again with a kind of fascinated horror. (pp. 42-3)

Esther, as might be expected, bears certain striking resemblances to *Democracy.* Most important of these is in its plot, which again consists in the effort of an intelligent and sensitive woman to ascertain a meaning for her life. As in *Democracy,* the woman is confronted by a male embodiment of meaning whose motives of love and domination are so intertwined as to be inseparable. The novel, therefore, like its predecessor, culminates in a choice between acceptance and rejection of the male, a choice on which the issues of personal integrity and spiritual security depend. Esther's decision to reject her suitor, like that of Mrs. Lee, saves her freedom and integrity, but at the expense of cutting her off from an almost achieved purposefulness.

Despite these important similarities, however, it is a mistake to regard *Democracy* and *Esther* as thematically identical, differing only in subject matter, artistry, and degree of the author's involvement. The later book goes far beyond the earlier in its exploration of moral values and its effort to give these values a philosophical justification. (p. 45)

[The essential difference between *Democracy* and *Esther* is that] Mrs. Lee starts out in conscious search of a purpose in life; after finding out the truth about democracy—which is the point of the book—she is back precisely where she started. But Esther moves from ignorance to achieved realization of her life's purpose, forced by the logic of events and her own responses to them to a new state of awareness —which is the point of the book. This concentration upon the development of the heroine explains the greater psychological depth of *Esther,* and is the key to its divergence from *Democracy.* (pp. 45-6)

Esther fits coherently into the logic of Adams' development. The effect of his previous work was to undermine democracy as an end, to remove democratic politics from consideration as a field of action because it was no longer a struggle to realize ideals. Yet the compulsion to see life's meaning in absolute terms did not leave him; rather it inspired a lifelong effort to reconstruct a purposive scheme, if not for himself then for history of which he was a part. (p. 54)

Henry Adams' *History of the United States of America during the Administrations of Thomas Jefferson and James Madison* is the last fruit of his absorption in the era of American Republicanism. By virtue of its breadth and fullness of detail, its insight and superb narrative art, it ranks among the greatest of historical works in English. In every way it brings to completion the various themes of Adams' earlier writing, and adds a cool, objective detachment that gives the *History* the solidity of a monument. Whereas in the *Life of Gallatin* Adams had been drawn into what was for him a warm partisanship by the tragic heroism of Gallatin's defeat, and in *John Randolph* had been repelled by the spectacle of corrupted idealism, in the *History* he regards the current of men and events from an elevated distance, his sympathies under careful restraint and his eye probing always for the threads that hold the story together and make it meaningful as "a necessary sequence of human movement."

Nevertheless, despite such detachment and restraint, Adams succeeds in evoking an emotional response to the *History* more enduring than that aroused by any or all of his previous books. The reason is that in the *History* he broadens the drama of democratic idealism to make it inclusive of the whole American people. For the first time in Adams' work the horizon extends beyond the limited field of party theory and practice. Republicanism is now interpreted as a national ethos rather than a more or less accidental and localized phenomenon; the Republicans themselves become symbolic of the national character and the forces latent in national society. To be sure, the *History* is still chiefly occupied with political events, but these events are significant not merely to a handful of political leaders but to the people who have brought themselves to expression in these leaders. (p. 55)

["The Tendency of History"] is a landmark in Adams' intellectual development. In it, for the first time, he publicly announced his view that the study of history must become a science basing itself on the methods and laws of the more highly developed physical sciences. What he wanted as a result was something simple and grand, a law capable of making clear, for example, "the purely mechanical development of the human mind in society." The outcome of this desire, in "The Tendency of History" and all his subsequent works on the subject, was a complete merging of history with the natural sciences, a uniquely daring attempt to treat the record of the human past as a problem in physics.

"The Tendency of History" is significant as a first statement of certain basic general propositions that Adams was to explore more fully and in concrete detail in the concluding chapters of the *Education,* and in *The Rule of Phase Applied to History,* and *A Letter to American Teachers of History.* But "The Tendency" contains the seeds of all later developments. It asserts, in the first place, that historians are committed to the treatment of man as an object of scientific investigation. . . . Furthermore, Adams assumes that the primary object of a science of man's history is the discovery of "a great generalization that would reduce all history under a law as clear as the laws which govern the material world." He has in mind such a law as Darwin's under which all animal life may be subsumed. . . . Now Adams' anticipation that such a law must necessarily provide the groundwork for a science of history is extremely important because of the assumptions it reveals. Back of his confidence that a single, comprehensive law will be sufficient to explain the operations of historical reality is the supposition that reality is some sort of material or meta-empirical unity. Only a unit can be adequately dealt with by one "great generalization." The method of scientific analysis was for Adams a means of uncovering the essential unity of reality, a unity *assumed* to characterize reality; and the drift of his work prior to "The Tendency" suggests very strongly that he was drawn to science *because* of his assumption about reality, because he could only conceive of reality as meaningful, as having an end, in terms of unity, and such meaningfulness, whether in his own life, in history, or in the universe, was for him the ultimate value and the generating motive. (pp. 94-6)

[*Tahiti*] is the least interesting and least important of Adams' works composed during the 1890's. (p. 96)

Tahiti manifests in its devious way Adams' identification with "the objects of [his] horror or compassion." Its essential story is that of the degradation of a healthy and stable culture as a result of its contact with European civilization. The Tahitians were the victims of the same society by which Adams felt himself to have been defeated; that is the core of his interest in them. (pp. 97-8)

Mont-Saint-Michel and Chartres is an essay in scientific history, an effort to apprehend imaginatively the interior "faith" created in men by "the greatest force the Western world ever felt" and presumably to assign that faith some mathematical value in the "sequence of force" which is all of history. (p. 103)

The proclaimed scientific intention of *Mont-Saint-Michel and Chartres*—to fix a point from which the subsequent history of the West might be calculated mathematically in a "sequence of force"—falls to pieces upon examination of the book. Indeed, such an intention, although it provides a useful insight into the working of Adams' mind, is, in the light of what he actually wrote, blatantly irrelevant. How could he have hoped to give mathematical value to the Archangel Michael and the Virgin Mary? How could the rays of energy of the twelfth and thirteenth centuries, translated into faith by his own mind, be retranslated into numerical symbols possessing scientific validity? The task was an impossible one, and there are no signs in *Mont-Saint-Michel* that Adams made any effort to accomplish it. . . . (p. 114)

[In] the writing of *Mont-Saint-Michel* Adams discovered the theme toward which his mind had long been tending, "unity" vs. "multiplicity." With this apparently simple formula Adams achieved the self-understanding and the historical perspective that made the very idea of such a book as the *Education* possible. (p. 115)

For Adams education functions somewhat like Darwin's natural selection; it preserves the individual best adjusted to his environment, helping him triumph in the race for survival. It tries to penetrate to the steady undercurrent of force that drives life on its way in order to destroy illusion, wishful thinking, mental inertia, whatever stands in the way of smooth, efficient action. Education, in brief, is the means to power. (p. 118)

Power as a goal is in the back of Adams' mind throughout the *Education*. Often he thinks of it in a narrowly political sense because his own ambitions tended that way, but more generally it figures in his thoughts simply as the antithesis of his many failures. One distinguishing feature of the *Education* is the author's reiterated judgment of himself as a failure; the essence of this judgment is Adams' notion of success as the control of power. Had he succeeded, with

President Grant's permission, in aiding the cause of governmental reform through the press, he would have exercised power over the course of national life. Had he succeeded in finding a way of teaching history intelligibly, he would have "help[ed] the boys to a career," exerted power, in other words, over the "vigor and economy" of their future lives. He failed, he said, because his own education was at fault; he could never succeed in practically adjusting himself to the lines of force that attracted his world. His "failure" was essentially a failure to gain power, and at its root was "multiplicity," both internal and external, making failure a predestined necessity. (pp. 118-19)

[The] Adams of the *Education* might be described as a defeated idealist almost from the start, who is compelled to penetrate the causes of his defeat in order to rediscover an impersonal basis of value. . . . The structure of the *Education*, therefore, is analogous to that of *Democracy* and *Esther*. It is a quest for an impersonal goal, or at least for knowledge of the goal that belongs to history, a search for what transcends the individual life and gives it final significance. (pp. 120-21)

The pattern of failure that dominates the form and tone of the first three-fifths of the *Education* culminates Adams' use of a theme which was present in his work from the very beginning. In the *Life of Albert Gallatin* Adams had treated Gallatin, somewhat tentatively, as a failure in his endeavor to realize an ideal political system. . . . In his novels Adams engaged both of his principal characters in a quest for meaning; both ended in failure and the abandonment of false ideals. The pattern of failure, or of quest ending in failure, is, in short, the basic pattern of all of Adams' books except *Mont-Saint-Michel and Chartres*. It embodies the quintessential drama of his mind. (pp. 129-30)

But there is another side to the *Education*, its heroic side. In the brilliance and intellectual daring of the quest itself, Adams converts failure into heroism. What else gives the *Education* its right to claim a place among the masterpieces of American literature? The *Education* is one of those books in which a man charts unexplored territory, in which he risks seeming a perfect fool to his most sympathetic contemporaries and a madman to posterity. What Adams did was to subject his age, and in particular the historical formulas of his age, to a new and searching kind of criticism. It was a criticism that originated in the Puritan mode of perception—the inverted allegorical mode of the disbelieving Calvinist—and its daring consists in the opening up of innumerable perspectives of ambiguity, or "multiplicity," behind the generalizations and assumptions that passed for truth in the world at large. (p. 130)

Insofar as the theme of "multiplicity" is a challenge to the easy, the satisfying, and the false; insofar as it compels the mind of the reader to entertain a difficult and unresolvable view of reality; insofar as it creates a permanent disturbance in, and requires a permanent readjustment of, American self-consciousness, *The Education of Henry Adams* is much more than a cosmic blind alley, but an enduring and invigorating work of art. . . .

The "Dynamic Theory of History," [*The Rule of Phase Applied to History*], and [*A Letter to American Teachers of History*] comprise a solution to the quest for meaning which is the main object of the *Education*. They represent the attainment of unity in a manner foreshadowed by "The Tendency of History'' written more than ten years before the *Education* was begun. Having failed to establish unity within the limits of his own experience or within the range of his practical ideas, Adams turned to science as a way of fixing a meaning for all of history and hence, by indirection, for his own apparently pointless life. (p. 131)

In his final writings Adams carried his thought to one of the limits inherently possible to it from the start.

In doing so, in reaching the end of his quest, he arrived at a colossal irony. For what Adams discovered was that life had no meaning; the quest ended in a sheer, blank void from which there was no way of escape. Always pressing for certainty, for nothing less than absolute certainty, he found it in universal death, an event no less meaningless than certain. The unity which he had insisted on as a necessary condition of thought turned, in the very moment of its achievement, into an impenetrable chaos; in death, unity and chaos are one. The end which was to give life its form robbed all purpose of significance; the reality which was to give nature its order and history its truth turned nature and history into the merest dream from which humanity would one day wake only to be drowned. The bitter paradox of Adams' career is that the motives which impelled him to brilliant acts of creation were insatiable in their demand for perfection. His last works evidence the craving of a religious mystic for universal dissolution, for an end to the torment of finite intelligence through union with the ''ultimate ocean of atoms.'' (p. 139)

[In] his last book [*Life of George Cabot Lodge*] Henry Adams presents himself once again as a failure, this time in a light both more pathetic and more rebellious than before. He was a sensitive and timid nature, born for art in a time when art was a dying instinct, and living the life of a thwarted alien among his uncomprehending fellows. Indeed, the *Life of Lodge* terminates the theme of failure in Adams' works. Lodge's quest was that of the artist seeking in achieved poetic expression the reason for his being. In his failure Adams witnesses and objectifies the ultimate hopelessness of his own life. For after all, and despite his unwillingness to admit it to himself, Adams' career had been that of an artist. All the best of himself—his Puritan integrity, his love of clear, rational form, his power to conceive of life as a disciplined effort to realize impersonal goals—all these, which he had never stopped thinking of as somehow intended for a life of power, had gone into his books as the stuff of art. The *Life of Lodge,* however, is Adams' dismissal of his work as inadequate to redeem the disappointments it had cost him, and it is his curse upon the world that had blighted even this last possibility of success. (p. 144)

> *George Hochfield, in his* Henry Adams: An Introduction and Interpretation *(copyright © Barnes & Noble, Inc. 1962; by permission of Barnes & Noble Books, a Division of Littlefield, Adams & Co., Inc.), Barnes & Noble, 1962, 150 p.*

AUSTIN WARREN (essay date 1966)

[Adams'] legacy in the form of philosophy of history seems to me neither final nor impressive. The last two, the famous two, books are *Mont-Saint-Michel and Chartres: a Study of Thirteenth-Century Unity;* and *The Education: a Study of Twentieth-Century Multiplicity;* and both periods, he

thought, might be studied at once in philosophy and mechanics. But the mind is incapable of satisfaction in chaos, and Adams—at least in old age—couldn't master enough physical science (mathematics and physics in particular) to discover the unity which lay beyond twentieth-century multiplicity.

Nor is his famous antithesis of the Virgin, the Force which created thirteenth-century civilization, and the Dynamo, corresponding force of the twentieth century, an antithesis which can well be borne down upon. The two symbols, so to say, are not parallel. Men did once worship the Virgin, as a theological person who answered prayer, gave favors; men do not worship the dynamo in any corresponding sense. They value and desire the gadgets and effects of steam, gas, and electricity. The Virgin is a 'First Cause'; the products of the dynamo are 'material causes.' (p. 178)

What is the 'lesson' of Henry Adams? The lesson of an 'intellectual' never satisfied with his intellectual achievements or what he knew, one whose education was never completed and never could be completed. His was not primarily a *personal moral* conscience. Even in *The Education,* I find little self-analysis and that of an elementary sort. Much analysis there is, and that of an acute variety—at its best in Chapters VII through XI, given to the English statesmen's attitudes and actions during the American Civil War. . . . (p. 179)

I see the intellectual conscience of Adams as beginning, where it should begin, with one's private history—with the Adams family and Quincy and Boston and New England, then moving on and outward to the ever-larger questions—which are, indeed, really involved even when one deals with the seemingly nearest and most particular concerns. The dialectic relation between the smallest 'fact' and the most grandiose generalization can never be overcome.

Adams never quite says this: I can offer no ready 'proof-text.' But it is implicit in his work. Nor does he ever say—or quite see—the two almost universally disjunct characters of the researcher (the antiquarian, the fact-finder) and the interpreter and philosopher of history—this doubtless because, like his favorite historian, Gibbon, he had the leisure and the talent for both. Each of these two characters (poles, really) requires conscientiousness of intellect: the scholar must be sure that his 'facts' are 'facts'; the interpreter must be sure that there are no relevant facts with which he has not dealt, and sure that his generalizations are not merely rhetorical and that the evidence on which he bases them is clearly indicated.

Adams died with his education still incomplete. Complete it could never be, if only because it was a New England conscience which was to be educated. But, in the declining years of that conscience, he is a figure of honor. Though he reached no solutions which permanently satisfied him—or us, he went on asking questions, and those questions were central ones, for they concerned Sex, Politics; the State, the Individual; Art, Science; Power, Integrity. (pp. 180-81)

> *Austin Warren, ''Henry Adams,'' in his* The New England Conscience *(copyright © by The University of Michigan 1966), University of Michigan Press, 1966, pp. 170-81.*

MELVIN LYON (essay date 1970)

The sensibility expressed in the writings of Henry Adams

has eight or nine primary aspects: intellectualism; moralism; didacticism; a concern with contemporary and future relevance, and especially with relevance for the individual in relationship to society; historicism; scientism; and two elements—imagination and intuition (or feeling or instinct) —which are best discussed together and for that purpose may be called, collectively, subjectivism. Of these the most basic aspect is intellectualism: throughout his work Adams' sensibility operates ultimately in terms of concepts. He changes his mind about how the most adequate concepts are derived from reality; he even loses most of his faith in the ability of concepts to affect and express reality; yet he is never satisfied with facts or intuitions (or images or feelings) until they are translated into abstract terms. The particular abstractions he is concerned with are largely determined by his insistence that ideas be relevant to the good life in his own time and the future, and his persistent attempt to persuade other men to achieve that life. Hence, he tends to embody his ideas in some more or less specific program for improving society. The lifelong focus of this tendency is national politics, although in later years its primary focus becomes university education.

Intellectualism, moralism, didacticism, and a concern for contemporary relevance function most independently of the other aspects of Adams' sensibility in his early essays. The subjects of these essays are contemporary rather than historical, but here, as always in his work, when the subject is not specifically historical it is at least set in a historical context. The importance of the past for Adams lies in its relevance to the present and future, for these, he believes, can be understood and directed—insofar as they can be directed —only by viewing them in relationship to the past. The past has such value because, in his view, the validity and value of ideas can be tested only by experience. History as the totality of past human experience, is the repository of such tests and thus a means of gaining perspective upon the present. Throughout his career Adams also tries to improve the ability of history, as an *account* of human experience, to demonstrate the relative value and validity of ideas by making it more scientific. At first, he emphasizes the rigorous use of the scientific method both in research and in presenting its results; later, he tries to develop laws of history analogous to those of natural science and based upon them. In these efforts he acts essentially not as a scientist but as a historian trying to adapt to his discipline the methods of reaching truth accepted as most valid by his age. This historicism reaches its most autonomous expression in *The Life of Albert Gallatin* and especially *The History of the United States During the Administrations of Thomas Jefferson and James Madison*.

Subjectivism becomes a primary aspect of Adams' sensibility later than the other seven aspects, although, like them, it is present in his work from the beginning. The a priori moralism of his early essays anticipates the importance of intuition (or instinct) as a means of knowing in his later work. Even more clearly related to the later work is Adams' recognition in these rationalistic essays that man has an affective and imaginative as well as rational side to his nature and that the most effective writing appeals to the whole man by making use of images as well as abstractions and by appealing to feeling as well as reason. Hence imagination and feeling as important aspects of expression appear in such early essays as "The New York Gold Conspir-

acy" and, in the middle period, in *The History*, whose greatness is due in part to its being a literary as well as a scientific work. Subjectivism is most autonomous in Adams' work in the novels. . . . In *Democracy* the larger role of subjectivism appears in the greater importance of symbols in the work and in the appearance of a character who attaches as much importance to feeling as to thinking and makes her ultimate decisions on the basis of intuited moral principles. Yet subjectivism still remains largely under the control of intellectualism and didactic moralism, and a historical context is used to give greater veracity and conviction to the contemporary testing of ideas. In *Esther* there is a character who acts even more in terms of feeling than her counterpart in *Democracy*. Otherwise, the aspects of sensibility which appear have much the same relationship as in the earlier novel—until the last one-fourth of the work, where intuition and imagination become freer from intellectualism than anywhere else in Adams' work. The character who relies on feeling gains ideas intuitively from a natural object functioning as a symbol whose meaning is never fully intellectualized. Here in a far more profound way than in the earlier works subjectivism becomes an aspect of perception as well as expression. This basic change continues in *Mont-Saint-Michel and Chartres* and *The Education of Henry Adams,* where subjectivism, though less free than in the novels, is more complex, more pervasive, and more important than in any of Adams' works except the last part of *Esther*. Now Adams himself has come to let intuition or feeling rather than reason lead him to subjects for contemplation. As always, contemplation leads to conceptualization, but now the participation of subjectivism in perception produces a balance between intellectualism and subjectivism—or a fusion of the two—in works which are the expression of a sensibility not on a holiday but functioning in its totality. Of all Adams' works, *The Education* most fully fuses the eight or nine principal aspects of his sensibility and thus represents its fullest fruition. (pp. 1-3)

Most of [Adams'] ideas are related to the most pervasive theme in his work—the problems of distinguishing in human experience between illusion and reality and of ascertaining the value of each for human life. He examines these problems in a context of human experience, more especially in a historical context (though this is sometimes in the background rather than the immediate foreground), where he finds certain versions of recurrent human ideas and attitudes brought to the test of different sets of circumstances and thus proved false or true, valuable or not. Up to 1892 American history is the context in which Adams tests the validity and the value of democracy as an ideal and a form of government. The specific questions this test involves are whether men are naturally good; to what extent their wills are free; whether men and their wills, or circumstances, are more important in bringing about historical change; and to what extent the aims of American democracy have been in harmony with historical circumstances in the eighteenth and nineteenth centuries. After 1892 world history becomes the context in which Adams is testing what he believes is the innate human belief in unity. He is concerned again with the extent to which man's will is free and efficacious, but now he also asks whether man can know absolute truth, to what extent man's belief in unity and desire for it are in harmony with reality, and whether religion or science approaches closer to truth.

In all of the major works in which these tests and their results appear (except *The Life of Albert Gallatin*), symbolism is a pervasive and often major literary technique. (pp. 3-4)

The flag is an important symbol in *The History*. "Flag" is a word referring to an object which is a sign and a symbol—and a symbolic gesture—in the world which Adams is recording and interpreting. But the same object also has a related literary meaning in the book: the tendency of any country—though particularly the United States—toward unity and political centralization, toward an effective national sovereignty. On a higher level of abstraction, the flag seems to represent unity in general. Adams' use of the symbol to mean a unifying tendency is specific and explicit; his use of it to mean unity is also specific though only implied. A different and better known symbol is the Virgin in *Chartres* and *The Education*. In the medieval world, she was considered not a symbol but a fact. In Adams' work, she is a symbol for the sexual force of woman and its expression in the emotion of love. As such, she is also explicitly a symbol for unity in the form human beings find most desirable when their sense of unity is strongest and their desire for it most intense. In this case, even more clearly than in that of the flag, the symbolic object is significant on two levels of abstraction, but in this case the significance on both levels is specific and explicit. In *The Education*, the death of Adams' sister is also a symbol in two worlds, the world of Adams' life and that of the book—though in this case (as the event is presented in the book) there is not the disparity between the meaning of the symbol in the two worlds that there is in the case of the flag and the Virgin. Adams intermixes description of the event with a full statement of its significance for him. It is his first full realization that reality is chaos. As such, it is also the climactic example of the experience which he repeatedly undergoes throughout *The Education* and eventually decides is the essential process in man's relationship with reality: the disintegration of human unity into nature's chaos. This event both epitomizes and symbolizes the multiple variety of such experiences in the book. Moreover, since the Henry Adams who is the subject of *The Education* is also Everyman and his story is that of mankind, the death of this particular woman becomes a universal symbol for all men's relationship with nature. (pp. 4-5)

The symbols in the novels have a more poetic function than do the earlier symbols [in *The Life of Albert Gallatin* and *The History*]. As in all of Adams' work, however, they are tightly controlled—with one possible exception—by a body of clearly defined concepts explicitly stated in the work. In *Esther* three of the four major structural divisions determined primarily by the action also involve in a crucial way the three major symbols of the work. One symbol in each novel also functions as a means of cognition for the chief character in the novel. In both cases, most of what the protagonist learns is stated or suggested earlier in the book. In *Esther*, however, the main character's discovery of her own idea of reality through personal confrontation with a symbol adds a great deal both to what she and the reader know of her. Also in this novel, for the first time in Adams' work (and the last, with the possible exception of *The Education*), the conceptual basis for a symbol is not made clear in the book. Of all Adams' major symbols, Niagara Falls, Esther's symbol for reality, has the most ambiguity and multiplicity of reference. Yet it too is set in a rational context

which at least points toward an explication of its meaning in abstract terms.

Chartres and *The Education* are the culmination of Adams' use of symbolism. In them the symbolism is more pervasive, more complex, more important, and more poetic than in any other of his works. In them, too, the symbols are valued more equally with their conceptual meanings than in Adams' other works (with the exception of the falls in *Esther*). In part, this is the climax of Adams' steady movement away from a purely rational sense of reality to an increasing belief that irrational elements are essential to any adequate version of such a sense. (p. 8)

[Discussion] of individual symbols does not exhaust Adams' use of symbolic entities. Some of his symbols are related to systems of thought, and thus move in the direction of "myth." (p. 10)

I am using [the term "myth"] in the modern and literary way it is used when W. B. Yeats's system in *A Vision* is called a "myth" or a "mythology" (a system of myths). In this usage a myth is simply "the iconography of a world view," as Henry Murray has said. . . . [Adams is] less a mythical (or imaginative) writer and always more of an intellectualist than Yeats. Nonetheless, his system does share many of the qualities of myth in the modern literary usage of that term. (pp. 11-12)

[Adams' primary role was that] of a profound and witty man of the world, mediating between the two realms of thought and action. It is in this role that his principal value seems to lie. Disinclined to action by temperament, provoked to action by background, led to thought by temperament and background, dissuaded from too much reliance upon thought by both temperament and background, Adams ultimately combined these tendencies into works which provide a bridge between action and thought, between experience and its meaning, a bridge difficult to achieve in any age, but particularly so in our own complex and chaotic era. This bridge is largely provided by the "imaginative symbolism" which . . . pervades Adams' work. Such symbolism is a fusion of experience and significance which stimulates the emotions as well as the intellect and thereby becomes capable of influencing conduct. In Adams' work it is not mere rhetorical ornament but a primary means whereby he realizes his dual purpose of explicating experience and of making that explication an active influence upon the lives of others. (p. 230)

> *Melvin Lyon, in his* Symbol and Idea in Henry Adams *(reprinted by permission of University of Nebraska Press;* © *1970 by the University of Nebraska Press), University of Nebraska Press, 1970, 326 p.*

ADDITIONAL BIBLIOGRAPHY

Adams, Brooks. Introduction to *The Degradation of the Democratic Dogma*, by Henry Adams, pp. v-xiii. New York: Peter Smith, 1949.
>   Comments that the ideas developed in Adams's essays are indicative of an intellectual trend present in the Adams family from the time of John Quincy Adams.

Auchincloss, Louis. *Henry Adams*. Minneapolis: University of Minnesota Press, 1971, 48 p.

Introductory essay to Adams's life, work, and the major critical issues involved in the study of this author.

Barber, David S. "Henry Adams' 'Esther': The Nature of Individuality and Immortality." *New England Review* XLV, No. 2 (June 1972): 227-40.

Discusses Adams's ideas on the place and destiny of the individual with respect to society, nature, and death, commenting that his protagonists in *Democracy, Esther,* and the *Education* "seek harmonious, often self-effacing relationships with their social and natural environments."

Baym, Max I. "Henry Adams and the Critics." *The American Scholar* 15, No. 1 (Winter 1945-46): 79-89.

Discusses various critical views of Adams's admissions of "failure" in *The Education of Henry Adams,* linking this sense of failure with romantic pessimism.

Beach, Joseph Warren. "The Education of Henry Adams." In his *The Outlook for American Prose,* pp. 202-14. Port Washington, NY: Kennikat Press, 1968.

Considers Adams as a "distinctly American" author.

Bishop, Ferman. *Henry Adams.* Boston: Twayne Publishers, 1979, 157 p.

Introductory study of Adams's life, work, and the history of his reputation as a historian, literary figure, and modern thinker.

Blackmur, R. P. "The Revival: Henry Adams' *Mont-Saint-Michel and Chartres.*" *The Kenyon Review* n.s. II, No. 2 (Spring 1980): 126-49.

Analysis of the themes and symbols of *Mont-Saint-Michel and Chartres.*

Conder, John J. *A Formula of His Own: Henry Adams's Literary Experiment.* Chicago: The University of Chicago Press, 1970, 202 p.

Follows Adams's ideological and literary development which culminated in *Mont-Saint-Michel and Chartres* and *The Education of Henry Adams,* and analyzes the stylistic structures in these works.

Hume, Robert A. *Runaway Star: An Appreciation of Henry Adams.* Ithaca: Cornell University Press, 1951, 270 p.

Critical study designed for the nonspecialist reader.

Mane, Robert. *Henry Adams on the Road to Chartres.* Cambridge: The Belknap Press of Harvard University Press, 1971, 288 p.

Traces the origins of Adams's medievalism and examines his scholarship as a historian of thirteenth-century France.

Maud, Ralph. "Henry Adams: Irony and Impasse." *Essays in Criticism* VIII, No. 4 (October 1958): 381-92.

Examines Adams's use of scientific concepts in his later works, pointing to flaws in his facts and reasoning.

More, Paul Elmer. *Commemorative Tribute to Henry Adams.* New York: The De Vinne Press, 1922, 7 p.

Retrospective sketch of Adams's intellectual career, stating that "the variety of his intellectual achievement is more remarkable than their magnitude."

Mumford, Lewis. "The Pillage of the Past." In his *The Golden Day,* pp. 199-232. New York: Boni & Liveright, 1926.

Critique of Adams's pessimistic view of history.

Samuels, Ernest. *The Young Henry Adams.* Cambridge: Harvard University Press, 1948, 378 p.

First volume of the most comprehensive biography of Adams.

Samuels, Ernest. *Henry Adams: The Middle Years.* Cambridge: The Belknap Press of Harvard University Press, 1958, 514 p.

Second volume of the Samuels biography.

Samuels, Ernest. *Henry Adams: The Major Phase.* Cambridge: The Belknap Press of Harvard University Press, 1964, 687 p.

Third volume of the Samuels biography.

Tanner, Tony. "Henry James and Henry Adams." *TriQuarterly,* No. 11 (Winter 1968): 91-108.*

Contrasts James's optimistic views in his letters and autobiographical writings to the more pessimistic positions of Adams.

Taylor, Henry Osborne. *"The Education of Henry Adams."* *The Atlantic Monthly* Vol. CXII (October 1918): 484-91.

Appreciation of the *Education.*

Whipple, T. K. "Henry Adams." In his *Spokesmen: Modern Writers and American Life,* pp. 23-44. New York and London: D. Appleton and Co., 1928.

Discusses Adams's pessimistic philosophy in *The Education of Henry Adams.*

Zukofsky, Louis. "Henry Adams: A Criticism in Autobiography: I, II, and III." *The Hound and Horn* III, Nos. 3, 4 (April-June 1930, July-September 1930): 333-57, 518-30; IV, No. 1 (October-December 1930): 46-72.

Three-part biographical essay.

George Washington Cable

1844-1925

(Also wrote under pseudonyms of Drop Shot and Felix Lazarus) American short story writer, novelist, essayist, historian, and journalist.

Cable achieved his most enduring success with his early works of local color fiction about Louisiana Creole life. Though his work often suffered from the incorporation of melodramatic plots popular at the time, he is nevertheless acknowledged to be one of the first novelists to accurately portray post-Civil War southern society.

The best of Cable's work presents a unique and richly detailed vision of southern life. In *Old Creole Days*, *The Grandissimes*, and *Madame Delphine*, Cable captured the mood and tone of New Orleans society. Many critics consider these works to be pioneering efforts in the use of dialect. *The Grandissimes* has also been praised as the first important work of fiction by a southerner to deal honestly with complex southern racial issues. In addition to his fictional portrayal of Creole life, Cable also wrote several historical studies of Louisiana. These early works were widely praised, though Cable's objective portrayal of the cruelty as well as the charm of Creole life, and his espousal of civil rights for disenfranchised slaves, angered many southerners.

Cable's concern with civil rights led him into pamphleteering and works of social criticism. Of these, *The Silent South* and *The Negro Question* are still valued as historical documents. Cable's fiction of this period reflects his social and political interests, an example being *Dr. Sevier*, which presents a strong case for prison reform. Unfortunately, many critics feel that Cable's melodramatic plot devices and sentimental stories are unsuited to novels concerned with pressing social problems.

Throughout his writing career Cable also used the lectern to present his views to a wider public. He gave frequent readings and lectures (including a famous tour with Mark Twain) and was involved in educational programs such as the Home Culture Clubs.

About the turn of the century, Cable lost his zeal for social reform, and altered his conception of fiction accordingly.

Beginning with *The Cavalier*, Cable espoused a theory that the function of literature was to entertain, not teach. For the most part his later works are substandard romances that are all but forgotten today.

Even though he is a minor figure, critics stress the importance of Cable's early work in the development of the modern southern novel. Edmund Wilson, for example, has stated that *Old Creole Days* and *The Grandissimes* ought to be read by every student of American literature.

PRINCIPAL WORKS

Old Creole Days   (short stories)   1879
The Grandissimes   (novel)   1880
Madame Delphine   (novel)   1881

The Creoles of Louisiana   (historical essays)   1884
Dr. Sevier   (novel)   1884
The Silent South, together with the Freedman's Case in Equity and The Convict Lease System   (essays)   1885
Bonaventure   (novel)   1888
Strange True Stories of Louisiana   (short stories)   1889
The Negro Question   (essays)   1890
John March, Southerner   (novel)   1894
Strong Hearts   (short stories)   1899
The Cavalier   (novel)   1901
Bylow Hill   (novel)   1902
Kincaid's Battery   (novel)   1908
Gideon's Band   (novel)   1914
The Flower of the Chapdelaines   (novel)   1918
Lovers of Louisiana   (novel)   1918

HJALMAR H. BOYESEN   (essay date 1877)

The magnificence of the material for your novel quite dazzled me. . . . You have such a superb grip on reality—that is what I have always admired in your sketches & still you are so far removed from being a mere dry, materialistic photographer of actual events. . . .

Yours is going to be the kind of novel which the Germans call a "Kulturroman," a novel in which the struggling forces of opposing civilizations crystalize & in which they find their enduring monument. (p. 346)

> *Hjalmar H. Boyesen, in his letter to George W. Cable on March 17, 1877, in "A Novelist Discovers a Novelist: The Correspondence of H. H. Boyesen and George W. Cable" by Arlin Turner, in* Western Humanities Review, *Vol. V, No. 4, Autumn, 1951, pp. 343-72.*

HENRY C. VEDDER   (essay date 1894)

["Old Creole Days"] had not only the good fortune . . . of freshness of substance, but the additional advantage of novelty of form. Mr. Cable was one of the pioneers in the dialect tale, and dialect was not reckoned in those days as something to be forgiven an author, but as one of his titles to distinction, provided it were skilfully managed. (p. 266)

A natural aptitude for literature . . . gave him command of a style almost perfect for his purposes. It is a style of limpid clearness, of easy grace, not much given to ornamentation, and pleasingly destitute of mannerisms; a style of pure English, instinct with life and passion, sometimes reaching the borderland of poetry, but still oftener delighting by its delicate humor. In these stories laughter and tears lie near together, their pathos and even tragedy being as true and moving as their humor. It is seldom given to any author to sweep the whole gamut of human emotions with a touch so sure, yet so light and easeful, as that of Mr. Cable. (pp. 267-68)

Mr. Cable is remarkable among American novelists for a rare combination of aesthetic and religious endowments. In no other American fiction, unless it be in Hawthorne's, do we find the highest artistic instinct and the profoundest moral purpose so wedded. In truth, even the exception of Hawthorne cannot be allowed, for he is psychologic rather than moral, an observer, and analyzer of moral problems, and coldly critical, not sympathetic, in his treatment of them. But in Mr. Cable the moral purpose is almost stronger than the aesthetic instinct; rather they exist in his work in a balance so perfect that neither can be said to overtop the other. (p. 270)

> *Henry C. Vedder, "George Washington Cable," in his* American Writers of To-day *(copyright, 1894, by Silver, Burdett and Company), Silver, Burdett, 1894, pp. 261-74.*

WILLIAM MALONE BASKERVILL   (essay date 1897)

[The stories of "Old Creole Days"] showed that the author was a born storyteller.

In this first volume there are no suggestions of the amateur, nothing crude, unfinished. The pictures of life are as exquisitely clear as they are delicately tender or tragically sorrowful. Arch humor and playful fancy throw a bright ray into scenes of pure pathos, or give a joyous note to the tender tones of happy loves, which would otherwise grow monotonous. . . . (p. 314)

[Cable's first novel, "The Grandissimes," was] a genuine romance of Louisiana at the beginning of this century. Over the differences of race, the bitterness of caste prejudice,

restiveness under imposed rule, jealousy of the alien ruler, and suspicion of the newcomer, which largely constituted the situation at that time, was cast the warm coloring of a poetic imagination. But a note struck only here and there in the short stories now becomes the theme of all Mr. Cable's writings. It did not occur to him, it would seem, that an artist out of his domain is not infrequently the least clear-sighted of mortals; that the poet, if he is to be our only truth-teller, must let politics alone. . . . Indeed, [Cable] belongs to the class of thoroughgoing men, actuated by thoroughgoing logic, lovers of abstract truth and perfect ideals, and it was his lot to be born among a people who by the necessities of their situation were controlled by practical expediency. They were compelled to adopt an illogical but practical compromise between two extremes which were logical but not practical. This conflict between theory and actuality, of abstract truth with practical expedience, has so affected the sensitive nature of an extremely artistic temperament as to make this writer give a prejudiced, incorrect, unjust picture of Southern life, character, and situation. This domination of one idea has vitiated the most exquisite literary and artistic gifts that any American writer of fiction . . . has been endowed with since Hawthorne, though in respect to intellectuality, to imagination, to profound insight into life, to a full, rich, large, and true humanity, one would be overbold to institute comparison between him and America's greatest writer.

Both the time and Mr. Cable's methods, now that of the ardent controversialist espousing the extremest measures of partisan politics, and again that of the consummate artist holding up a people to the scorn and detestation of the world, were unsuited either to a philanthrophic and benevolent, or to a true artistic handling of this theme. (pp. 317-19)

[In "The Grandissimes"] Mr. Cable has forsaken the beaten track of character study with its brilliant, indefinite conversations and subtle moral and intellectual problems, and returned to the old romance. Yet he is modern, and has taken with him into the older field an artist's nice eye for color and the picturesque, an artist's fine sense of workmanship, and an artist's aim of producing effect in a natural way and by dramatic skill. (pp. 320-21)

Over the entire romance, over action and incident and scene and character, hangs the pall of slavery, with just enough light and color introduced to deepen the shadows. The effect upon the individual and society is brought out admirably, now by skilful word-painting and again by still more skilful dramatic action. But too frequently the author throws his puppets aside and appears in person upon the scene. The man with a mission throttles the artist. At such times he makes sententious comments or utters commonplaces now universally accepted, and still more frequently he indulges in sharp thrusts and biting sarcasms—all from the point of view of art not only blemishes, but "palpable intrusions." (pp. 324-25)

[In "Madame Delphine"] we see the most perfect specimen of the author's literary art and constructive ability. The story is so quickly told and so skilfully handled as almost to leave us unaware of the utter improbability of the plot. . . . While the compass does not admit of the exhibition of strength shown in "The Grandissimes," it also prevents the digressions and extravagances which mar that romance. (pp. 328-29)

["Dr. Sevier"], a beautiful story told with the same exquisite literary art and with even an added grace of simplicity, presents the author with eyes toward the setting sun; for his lack of ability to construct a plot, and of power to grasp the situation, is all too evident. His canvas is so crowded with a multiplicity of details that it is impossible to obtain the right perspective, to give a true artistic grouping. . . . In addition to the impossibility of handling so many details, the author's skill in narration at times deserts him. . . . But the chief defect of the book is the author's treatment of the hero. His trials and his difficulties are real, true to life, though an insufficient reason is assigned for them. . . . John Richling is at the mercy of the caprice of the author. It is easy to see that the poor fellow has no chance, that the author intends first to make him a failure, and then to kill him. Why these useless efforts, this hopeless suffering? (pp. 332-35)

As Richling seems to be one part of Mr. Cable, Dr. Sevier is another, now hard and repellant in his theories and then tenderly beautiful and poetic and loving in his life. If Richling had been developed into Dr. Sevier, a purpose would have been given to his life and a unity to the novel which would have insured to both the highest success. (p. 337)

Mr. Cable's historical writings . . . are marked by the same clear, picturesque style and exquisite finish observable in his romances. The facts have been collected with the most diligent research and painstaking labor. . . . When, however, the author essays to give "the derivation and final effect of influences," we become aware of the same spirit, too, which characterizes his imaginative productions. In truth this volume should be studied rather as the framework of the author's romances than as history; for it is to a large extent beautiful, picturesque, poetic-fiction. (pp. 343-44)

> *William Malone Baskervill, "George W. Cable,"
> in his* Southern Writers: Biographical and Critical
> Studies, Vol. I, *Publishing House of M. E.
> Church, 1897 (and reprinted by Gordian Press,
> 1970, pp. 299-356).*

W. D. HOWELLS (essay date 1901)

["The Grandissimes"] seems to me one of the few American fictions which one can think of without feeling the need of forbearance; or without wishing, in the interest of common honesty, strongly to qualify one's praises of it. Ample, yet shapely, picturesque in time and place, but essentially faithful to the facts of both, romantic in character but realistic in characterization, it abounds in varieties and contrasts of life mellowed but not blurred in the past to which they are attributed. . . . [The] political situation is subordinated to the social and personal interests, and the dark presence of slavery itself is perceptible not in any studied attitude, but in the casual effects of character among the Creole masters and the Creole slaves. (p. 235)

Mr. Cable's studies of Creole character in his New Orleans of the early nineteenth century seem affectionately, almost fondly, appreciative, and they convince of their justice by that internal evidence which it is as hard to corrobate as to overthrow. No dearer or delightfuller figures have been presented by the observer of an alien race and religion than Mr. Cable has offered in Aurora and Clotilde Nancanou, and in none does the artist seem to have penetrated more

sympathetically the civilization, so unlike his own, which animated them with a witchery so diverse yet so equal. (p. 236)

[In] reading Mr. Cable's novel one is afraid that nothing short of entreating the reader to go to it and do it justice himself will suffice. . . . [One] may remind him of the opalescent shimmer in which the story is wrapped, and from which keenly sparkle its facts and traits of comedy and tragedy. For a certain blend of romance and reality, which does no wrong to either component property, I do not know its like in American fiction, and I feel that this is saying far too little; I might say in all fiction, and not accuse myself of extravagance. Short of this I may safely declare it the author's masterpiece, on which he has lavished his happiest if not his most conscious art; and Aurora Nancanou is its supreme grace. (p. 240)

> *W. D. Howells, "Mr. G. W. Cable's Aurora and
> Clotilde Nancanou," in his* Heroines of Fiction,
> Vol. II *(copyright © 1901 by Harper & Brothers),
> Harper, 1901, pp. 234-44.*

RANDOLPH BOURNE (essay date 1918)

Mr. Cable has always blended his romance and sociology. . . . From the very first he seems to have seen the South as an impartially criticizable society as well as the beloved Dixie of romance. . . . To my Northern mind he seems the fairest of critics, with a justice that is sincerely tempered by love. His defense of the freedman, those pamphlets he wrote in the eighties about the "silent South" and the post-slavery problems, are restrained in tone and earnest with a high-minded persuasiveness. Only a South that would stand for nothing but a servile adulation of its ways could resist such a prophet. . . .

Those Southerners who do not complain about Mr. Cable's strictures on the South put their complaints against him on the ground that he is too much the sociologist at all times and too little the artist. I do not know whether he wrote *John March, Southerner* . . . to prove his impartiality. But it happens that this story . . . is one of his best novels. Mr. Cable was artist enough to draw vivid portraits which were the reverse of special pleading for the sociological idealisms he had been expressing. Into that book he got pretty nearly the entire life of a turbulent and proud Southern community in its welter of personal and political feuds and aspirations to develop its suddenly discovered resources. No mere apologia could have been so convincing.

But in *Lovers of Louisiana* the reader who missed the artist in Mr. Cable would have a better case. [Philip Castleton, the hero,] rarely becomes more than an abstraction. . . . Philip is always less a lover, less even a reformer, than he is a walking idea of what Mr. Cable would like the effective modern Louisianan young man to be. . . .

[Cable] spares us much of the enormity of dialect, and is thus able to save [his characters] from that belittling and patronage which seems the inevitable effect of dialect on the modern taste. In this book Mr. Cable's phonetic atrocities are so much milder than usual and his conversations so much briefer as to bring his story completely within the range of what, I take it, is our demand today. Nothing cuts off his school from us quite so much as that lavish cultivation of dialect. Our eye simply balks at untangling the paragraphs of a character like Narcisse in *Dr. Sevier,* so that that youth, who is so obviously intended to be a most amusing and winning figure, falls as flat as a Petrouchka who has lost his sawdust. (p. 364)

[*Lovers of Louisiana*] helps us to understand, I think, the limitations of that "national" school of fiction. For our interest today is vaguely in "life" itself rather than in the distinctive trappings of life, picturesque as they may be. We like to understand characters from their cradles to their graves. . . . It is not even "American" life we are after. We are on a restless search for "human life," almost as the thing in itself. We feel a craving to look beyond and through the particular type or the odd individual to some calm, immemorial current of personal truth. Any deliberately sectional portrayal comes to seem dangerously near an exploitation. The novelist is exploiting his material, digging out his marketable ore instead of making his human landscape reveal some significant veracity. This is the difference between books like *John March, Southerner* and *The Grandissimes.* In the latter one feels the exploiting touch. But fundamentally, to Mr. Cable's honor, it must be said that he does not deserve that stigma. He has felt deeply enough about his land to be its sound and bravely passionate counselor. And he has been artist enough not to let either this idealism nor his own very strict personal moralism impede his portrayal of all the sweetness and gayety of that life which his youth loved. (p. 365)

Randolph Bourne, "From an Older Time," in The Dial *(copyright, 1918, by The Dial Publishing Company, Inc.), Vol. LXV, No. 776, November 2, 1918, pp. 363-65.*

ROBERT UNDERWOOD JOHNSON   (essay date 1926)

[With] the possible exception of Hawthorne and Poe, Cable is the greatest figure in American fiction. Hawthorne and Irving had more continuous suavity of literary method; Poe a more arresting fancy; Mark Twain subtended a larger arc; Henry James vibrated a more purely intellectual gamut; Bret Harte was more uniformly, though often artificially, picturesque: but Cable seems to me to share all these qualities in a combination not found in any one of the others. (pp. 1-2)

Style, of course, is the essence of the writer, and, in Cable, this quality is composed of many qualities: grace, force, range, suggestiveness, imagination, large and unconventional vocabulary, shimmering humor, easy movement, contrast, tenderness, surprise and dramatic progression to an adequate climax. Thus his style has intense personality. I cannot find for it any provenance: it seems to derive from no master of literature.

When we turn to the substance of Cable's writing it is not less notable. Here was a man of Puritan instincts who could interpret the Cavalier as no other author has ever done. He portrayed women as understandingly and as sympathetically as Tolstoy. . . . Marcel Proust has said that "the writer who does not naturally think in images is far better without them." Here lies part of Cable's strength: instinctively he thinks in images, apposite and precise, and, therefore, is free from artificiality.

When I said that Cable is the greatest writer in American fiction, I forgot part of my climax. I believe the final verdict

of criticism will be that "The Grandissimes" is not only the greatest American novel to date but that it stands in the front rank of the fiction of the world. It is amazing in the bigness of its plot, its grasp of human nature, the charm of its execution, the suffusion of atmosphere, its firm dramatic construction and the sculpturesque roundness of its figures. (pp. 2-5)

Robert Underwood Johnson, "George Washington Cable" (1926), in Commemorative Tributes to Cable, Sargent, Pennell *by Robert Underwood Johnson, Edwin Howland Blashfield, and John Charles Van Dyke (copyright 1927 by The American Academy of Arts and Letters), American Academy of Arts and Letters, 1927, pp. 1-8.*

GRANVILLE HICKS   (essay date 1935)

[New Orleans was] America's most picturesque city, rich in traditions, blessed with a long-established culture, populated with as colorful a mixture of races as could be found on the continent. . . . But the fertility of the literary soil was, especially for so untrained a writer as George W. Cable, a danger. Like Bret Harte in California, he was tempted on every hand by bizarre incidents, extraordinary characters, strange manners of speech, and he had only to reproduce this kaleidoscope to win popularity among a people eager for new sensations and in love with the eccentric. It would have been easy for him to become a dealer in picturesque trifles.

That he did yield to temptation the title of his first collection of stories betrays: *Old Creole Days*—New Orleans' romantic past. . . . But even in these stories there is a sober recognition of the bases of human conduct and a critical spirit that does not abandon itself to the grandiose absurdity of the theme. That spirit asserted itself even when Cable planned for his novel a picture on the grand scale of romantic Creole life. *The Grandissimes* is not merely a record of feuds and balls, of black revenge and lily-white love; it is, as H. H. Boyesen called it [see excerpt above], a *Kultur Roman,* a substantial and detailed re-creation of New Orleans life at the beginning of the century, revealing, not at all in a complacent spirit, the effects of slavery and the caste system on the civilization of the times. The romantic element dominates the book, it is true, but not to such an extent that evil is ignored or suffering unrepresented. When . . . in writing his second novel, *Dr. Sevier,* the author chose to represent the period of the Civil War, he permitted his critical faculties to control its construction, based the story upon the abuses of vaunted southern virtues, and directly attacked the corruption and inefficiency of his native city. He could not resist the impulse to exhibit in tedious detail his facility in the variety of dialects to be heard in New Orleans, nor was he above the introduction of secondary plots that made room for whimsy, sentiment, picturesqueness, and piety. But the chief impression that remains is of the honesty and inclusiveness of his picture of New Orleans life and the basic austerity of his characterization of Dr. Sevier and the Richlings. (pp. 52-3)

During the next decade he was occupied with his writings on southern problems. . . . [After] these ten years he gathered himself for another major effort, and. . . produced *John March, Southerner.* Cable had been changing. Early in the eighties, speaking at the University of Mississippi, he had pointed out the necessity of regarding southern literature as part of the national culture. . . . Now, in this new novel, he proposed to turn upon southern life in the critical period of reconstruction the light of a thoughtful regard for the nation as a whole. With surprising clarity he saw the principal task of regional fiction and attacked it.

Unfortunately there were difficulties that he could not foresee. His great problem was to discover some vantage point, some intellectual eminence, from which the whole pattern of national life, with his chosen section in its proper position, could be discerned. . . . What he had to do was to understand the relations of the virtues and vices of both sections. In terms of the novel, he had to show that John March was right in opposing the old-fashioned southern gentry and allying himself with northern capitalists, and at the same time to show that the hero retained the highest southern virtues and acquired none of the northern vices. The problem was too difficult: the dice had to be loaded in favor of John and his victory granted him by an act of Providence. Even the characterization fails at the same point, for, though we are told that John March kept all the chivalrous qualities of his tradition the while he became a successful man of affairs, we are never allowed to see this combination of attributes in practice.

For most of the books that he wrote during the thirty years of life that remained to him, Cable returned to the New Orleans of his youth. More and more his critical acumen weakened, and he contented himself with either picturesque sketches or tales of adventure. He had tried and failed. . . . [He] could temper his account of past glories with realistic details of the lives of the oppressed. But he could not escape from the provincialism of his upbringing, from the effects of narrow orthodoxy and the long exposure to southern values. He could not penetrate below the superficial manifestations of the change that was taking place. Nevertheless he tried, and that attempt entitles him to respect. (pp. 53-5)

> *Granville Hicks, "A Banjo on My Knee," in his* The Great Tradition: An Interpretation of American Literature since the Civil War *(copyright © 1933, 1935 by Macmillan Publishing Co., Inc.; originally published in 1933 by The Macmillan Company, New York; new material in the revised edition copyright © 1969 by Granville Hicks; reprinted by permission of Russell & Volkening, Inc., as agent for the author), revised edition, Macmillan, 1935, Quadrangle Books, 1969, pp. 21-67.**

KJELL EKSTRÖM (essay date 1950)

With *Dr. Sevier*, Cable had, by the age of forty, finished all the literary work on which his reputation as an author was primarily to rest. To the plane of excellence of the short stories of *Old Creole Days*, the novelette *Madame Delphine*, and the two novels *The Grandissimes* and *Dr. Sevier* he never reached in his later fiction. . . . Soon he was engrossed by a violent campaign for the civil rights of Negroes, and he did not find much time for creative writing. The artist, it is usually said, was destroyed by the reformer.

This may be true of *John March, Southerner* but it is hardly true of later novels such as *The Cavalier, Bylow Hill, Kincaid's Battery,* and *Gideon's Band.* The fact is that in those books Cable consciously refrained from being a reformer, the reason being either a desire not to antagonize the South

in the way he had done in the 1880's or in a complete revision of his attitude towards literature. Such a revision is, in fact, in evidence in his articles and letters. While at the time he wrote his early masterpieces he held the view that literature should present and defend truth, assert rights, and rectify thoughts, morals, manners, and society, . . . he came to believe, in the 1890's, that the main purpose of fiction was to entertain. In this changed attitude of his lies, no doubt, part of the explanation of his deterioration as a novelist; being no longer fired with a reformatory zeal, he was unable to create really moving literature. (pp. 183-84)

> *Kjell Ekström, in his* George Washington Cable: A Study of His Early Life and Work *(originally a dissertation delivered at the University of Upsala on December 14, 1950; excerpted by permission),* Cambridge, Mass.: Harvard University Press, 1950, 197 p.

RICHARD CHASE (essay date 1956)

[In *The Grandissimes*] Cable transcended his usual limitations and wrote a minor masterpiece. (p. 373)

As a novel of political analysis that sees society both in ideological terms and as having "an atmosphere of hints, allusions, faint unspoken admissions, ill-concealed antipathies, unfinished speeches, mistaken identities, and whisperings of hidden strife," *The Grandissimes* makes [William Dean] Howells' most ambitious social novel, *A Hazard of New Fortunes,* seem like child's play. Cable's powers of intellectual analysis as well as his power of presenting manners and morals dramatically and symbolically are not matched at all in Mark Twain.

Strictly as such, they are not matched in Faulkner either, yet parts of *The Grandissimes* are closer to Faulkner than to anyone else. If one can imagine Faulkner suddenly turned into a witty, intellectual, teetotalling, genteel Presbyterian but retaining a large share of the genius that produced *Light in August,* one will have a fair image of Cable.

The episode of *The Grandissimes* which directly anticipates Faulkner is the story of Bras Coupé, a heroic negro prince brought from Africa in the slave ship *Egalité.* He refuses to work and there follow scenes of violence, of flight and pursuit, and of torture which are presented with tremendous effect. The story is made to serve as a kind of archetypal image which gives meaning and resonance to the book. It is referred to at various points and is told in the middle of the novel by three different persons on the same day.

As a novel of ideas which describes an intricate society full of both demarcations and ambiguities of class, caste, and race, *The Grandissimes* is something of a rarity in American fiction. . . . [Cable] had also the classic situation of the novel of manners—the dissolution of one class (the Creole aristocracy) and its replacement by another (the bourgeois "Américains").

Old Creole Days and *Mme. Delphine,* among the early writings, are well worth reading. Despite their realism, however, Cable put into them a rather gratuitous mystification about who is who and who is doing what, and it was only in *The Grandissimes* that he made mystification into mystery, that he dealt, in other words, with some of the inscrutable facts at the foundations of modern society and did his best to articulate these facts dramatically and ideologically. Only one other 19th Century American novel does this as well—James's *Princess Casamassima,* and if Cable has the less piercing intuition and the more parochial subject he in part makes up for it by being more at home among general political ideas than James. (pp. 373-75)

In the person of Frowenfeld, Cable finds a way to make capital out of the Jamesian theme of the innocent Yankee whose views are enlarged and humanized by contact with an old, rich, corrupt social order.

The rather preachy Frowenfeld and the contemplative Honoré Grandissime learn a good deal from each other because of their differences. But they have something in common too—namely, they are both in quest of reality. Frowenfeld is "as fond of the abstract" as the Creoles are "ignorant of the concrete." And much of the moral action of the novel is concerned with the successful attempt of the two friends to come, in their different ways, into contact with social reality as well as with their own deeper emotional natures. (pp. 375-76)

There is a good deal of highly effective symbolism in Cable's novel, mostly having to do with light and dark and the ambiguity not only of racial strains but of reality itself. This symbolism (used with equal effectiveness in American literature perhaps only in *Light in August* and in Melville's *Benito Cereno*) stems from the dread and guilt which remain unconscious in most of the characters but is articulated by Honoré when to Frowenfeld he professes himself amazed at "the shadow of the Ethiopian—the length, the blackness of that shadow." We sit, he says, "in a horrible darkness."

Nevertheless the novel should not be regarded as "symbolistic," despite the recent tendency to re-read the older American fiction as dramas of meaning. We do not have in *The Grandissimes* an epistemological symbolism. The book does not ask the intelligence to concern itself with meaning but rather to grasp and cleave to the concrete conditions of life. We have, as in so many American fictions, a realistic novel tending away from strict realism toward the "romance" by way of melodrama.

The symbols are involved in the intricacies of experience but (as in Cable's ancestral Calvinism) they move, not toward ambiguity and multiple meaning, as in symbolistic art, but toward ideology and dialectic. The structure of the book is melodramatic. That is, it conceives of life as a hazardous action between very marked, perhaps irreconcilable extremes which, appropriate to the subject, are racial, social, and political extremes. Alternative fates are offered to the actors—they can transcend the contradictions of their experience by an act of horror, violence, or suicide, or they can mollify or accommodate the contradictions by a reasoned and loving connection with the ordinary realities of nature and the humanities of men. (pp. 377-78)

In trying to suggest the quality of *The Grandissimes* I have inevitably made it sound more compact, intense, and rapid than it actually is. Despite the political intelligence, social passion, and symbolic poetry which Cable marshaled in this novel, a good deal of it is written in the rather loose manner of the Howells age. There is some facetiousness, some sentimentality, and too much genteel maundering. (p. 380)

> *Richard Chase, "Cable and His 'Grandissimes',"
> in* The Kenyon Review *(copyright 1956 by Kenyon
> College), Vol. XVIII, No. 3, Summer, 1956, pp.
> 373-83.*

ARLIN TURNER   (essay date 1956)

[The] method of "'Sieur George" is reminiscent of Hawthorne in the location of the action in a hazily defined past, real in atmosphere rather than circumstantial details, and in the reliance on hints and speculation instead of direct assertion. . . . Though Cable's attention was not mainly on plot, he was yet uncertain what methods were most suitable to his purposes and what liberties he might take in constructing a story. In consequence "'Sieur George" employs artificial concealment and contrivance of plot that suggest an author attempting to stay within a narrative method unsuited to his materials. . . .

"'Sieur George" is in a style which in every sentence, especially in the abundant figurative language, reflects the author's fondness for whimsical turns of thought and expression. If this trait seems at first strained, after a page or two its delicate, ironic turns become integral to the place and the action of the characters. . . . The flavor of the dialect is unobtrusive but unmistakable in its effect. (p. 57)

He was the first . . . to give his characters real speech, finely reported in its details of intonation and syntax as well as in pronunciation and grammar. Few if any realized the extent to which his had been the pioneer's task in determining an acceptable use of dialects in fiction and in working out a satisfactory orthography. (p. 87)

[*Bonaventure* was planned as] three separate stories that could stand together as a novel [but] something was lost to the whole book and also to each part. The three parts are not drawn together by the action, for the three plots are distinct, or by the characters, for the focus shifts from one story to another. Rather the unifying thread is the region and the people. (p. 236)

The book has a simplicity in its action not found in either of Cable's earlier novels, a simplicity the reader feels is appropriate to the directness and outward naivete of the Acadians which conceal the intensity and the depth of their characters. The author's purpose is to hold close to the line dividing reality from absurdity; if he avoids falling into absurdity . . . he is saved because his characters are of such directness and simplicity that the action of melodrama is natural to them. The three stories all bear out one theme—selfless devotion to others as the key to happiness. (pp. 236-37)

Bonaventure has the charm of the Acadian villages. Elemental in their natures and devoid of intricacy or subtlety, the characters live a story similarly direct and uncomplex. The book has no characters and no scenes to stick in the reader's mind as do those of Cable's earlier books, but the total picture is impressive, the picture of a gentle people, delightful in their simplicity and heroic in their minor way. (p. 237)

[*The Cavalier*] is a war romance. As the author looked back thirty-five years to his cavalry experiences, a softening glamour obscured the dirt and blood, the fatigue and pain of war. The cavalrymen saddle their horses at the end of a pleasant walk or an evening of dancing to gallop away for a skirmish with the blue-coats, and ride back afterwards to the arms and tears of the ladies. Wounds and death are blurred in the heroic view, except for occasional touches such as the odor of the narrator's healing wound and the tatters of the Louisiana infantry. The characters are faced with the Elizabethan conflict between love and duty and reach a satisfying reconciliation by subordinating their private wars to the public one. (p. 316)

The Cavalier lacks the realism that sinews Cable's first two novels; it was not inspired by the kind of urgent human problems that inspired those books. The issues back of the war are not mentioned; there is no more direct social criticism than the condemnation of bigoted religiousness. . . . It is the kind of book the author intended to write, and it is a good one. He caught the spirit of the cavalry forays he had known himself. (pp. 316-17)

[A similar treatment of war is found in *Kincaid's Battery;* there] is never a glimpse in the novel of the issues of the war or of the suffering. It is glamourized war in which the bravery, the intrigue, and the pain are beautiful, or perhaps better, pretty and pleasant. There has been bravery on both sides, as one would remark of an athletic match, and when all is over, members of the battery return home to resume their lives, proud of their heroism, and with no particular regrets at their defeat. All controversy and unpleasantness is expunged from the war of the story. . . .

Even so, the military incidents are the best in the book, for in them the reader is caught up in the rush and excitement the author habitually put into such scenes. The other scenes, mainly in boudoirs and parlors, employ hinting and allusiveness, but the reader may not find enough weight in them to justify the attention required to follow the development. The only issues in these scenes are the love entanglements. Cable had remarked to his wife ten years earlier that his fiction had suffered because he had withdrawn from the problems of the world around him. *Kincaid's Battery* calls this remark to mind. It seems appropriately the work of a man with half a dozen daughters who touches the world chiefly through the Home Culture Clubs and the Garden Clubs—not a man fighting the battles of right and justice against both his neighbors and the institutions of his time, as Cable had done during the first twenty years of his literary work. (p. 338)

In his last book, *Lovers of Louisiana,* Cable returned to the matter of his early books: the Creoles and the race problem. . . . [In the plot resolution found in the marriage between a Creole and an American it is shown that the] best of the old in both civilizations will be cherished, but it will be modified to profit from improvements that can be learned locally and from the outside. In the persons of Rosalie and Philip the old and the new of the two cultures are married. The sentiment is no less genuine and no less valid in its reflection of the intangibles involved for the fact that it respects good social theory and good sense. (pp. 352-53)

[The plot of *Lovers of Louisiana*] is one of the simplest he employed. The story is worked out mainly in dialogue rather than action, as had been true of the four other novels he had published since 1900, but in this one the topics discussed are of moment enough to give weight which is lacking in *The Cavalier* [and] *Kincaid's Battery*. . . . Cable had returned to the social criticism which had been such an important element in his first books. (p. 353)

> *Arlin Turner, in his* George W. Cable: A Biography *(reprinted by permission of the Publisher; copyright 1956 by Duke University Press, Durham, North Carolina), Duke University Press, 1956, 391 p.*

PHILIP BUTCHER   (essay date 1959)

[The] important consideration in an appraisal of Cable's record as a man and an author is his achievement. When his powers were at their height he risked his material security and devoted his intellectual and physical energies to the service of the oppressed and exploited and thus, in a democratic society, to the service of all. His controversial essays, "restrained in tone and earnest with a high-minded persuasiveness," are brilliant arguments for extending democracy to America's second-class citizens, white and black. They were so far ahead of their time that it is only within the past decade that the nation has officially adopted his definition of the nature of civil rights and has begun to take steps to guarantee these rights to all Americans.

Cable was not a professional social scientist, and it was in literature, primarily, that he sought his livelihood and his fame. Fortunately he contrived in his finest writing to combine his chief interests. . . . He did this effectively in *Old Creole Days, The Grandissimes,* and, for the most part, *Dr. Sevier;* critics and anthologists damn Cable to an unmerited obscurity when they praise these works as local color and ignore Cable's significance as a social critic. As he grew older he kept the same ingredients, sentiment and sociology, but altered their proportions, and the resulting blend, neither a bitter medicinal stimulant nor a soothing opiate, was less successful. In the early books Cable is an incisive critic of a bygone regime, but his real attack is on the injustices of his own time rather than on those of the past; the Creole is a romantic symbol for the white South. In the later novels Cable seems hardly more than a dispassionate observer, the historian of the dated culture he depicts. When he obscured his beliefs, or said only what was expedient, or, as in *The Cavalier,* wrote to fit a vogue, he added little to his stature, but when his pen was driven by his convictions he produced works of lasting value. (pp. 258-59)

> *Philip Butcher, in his* George W. Cable: The Northampton Years *(copyright © 1956, 1959 Columbia University Press; reprinted by permission of the publisher), Columbia University Press, 1959, 286 p.*

EDMUND WILSON   (essay date 1962)

[George Cable's] work during the seventies and eighties—influenced though it partly was by the more banal conventions of Victorian fiction—is astonishing, in a stuffy period and coming from the demoralized South, for its intelligence, its boldness and its brilliance. George Cable emerges in New Orleans as a phenomenon which could not have been predicted and of which, as a matter of fact, neither Northerners nor Southerners knew what to make. Not merely did the author of *Old Creole Days* possess a remarkable literary gift; he had a kind of all-around intellectual competence that was very unusual at that period in men of letters in the United States. . . . It has been said of George Cable that he possessed at that time a more detailed and comprehensive knowledge of the state of Louisiana than anybody else alive. (pp. 557-58)

But with all Cable's intimate knowledge of his region, there is something quite alien to New Orleans in the temper of mind he brought to it: in his striving for accuracy of observation, his naturalist's interest in varied types, in the eventual objectivity of his judgments. With his feeling for the languorous landscapes and the vivid social contrasts of Louisiana, he combines an intellectual rigor and an instinct for nonpartisan morality that was by that time excessively rare in the South on the part of those Southerners who wrote about it. It was no doubt the New England blood which was mingled in him with that of Virginia. (p. 559)

What is unique in the work of this Southerner is the exercise of a Protestant conscience in a meridional and partly Catholic community, in which it is, however, completely at home. The violence and the scandal he writes about are the conditions of the world he lives in, but presented from a point of view that is quite distinct from the point of view of those who commit them or suffer them. (p. 562)

In George Cable's first novel, *The Grandissimes* . . . , this able and gifted man gets the best out of the elements of his unique experience. *The Grandissimes* is made to take place in 1803-04, and it aims at historical accuracy; but Cable was quite explicit in declaring that its moral applied to the present: "I meant to make *The Grandissimes* as truly a political novel as it has ever been called." The resentment felt by the French and the Spanish, just after the Louisiana Purchase, against "American" domination—that is, against the descent on them of the English and Scottish—suggests an analogy with the Southerners in the period of Reconstruction, humiliated by the presence of the Northerners. But another problem figures in *The Grandissimes*. Though the slaves had been freed at the end of the war, the situation between Negroes and whites was in other ways not very different from what it had been eighty years before. . . . The mixture of white and black blood had already been treated by Cable in some of the stories of *Old Creole Days*, but he now attacked the subject on a larger scale and with unprecedented audacity and candor. This subject of miscegenation, so determinedly kept out of sight in the South, had hitherto been written about little and then mainly by outsiders. . . . George Cable was the first Southern writer to try to deal in a serious work of fiction with the peculiar relationships created by the mixture of white and Negro blood; and it was not to be till fifty years later, when William Faulkner wrote *Go Down, Moses, Absalom, Absalom!* and *Intruder in the Dust*, that a Southerner who had lived with these situations would have the courage to treat them in fiction again. . . . [It] is interesting to note that their methods are in certain respects rather similar. . . . In Cable and Faulkner both, the truth about family imbroglios in which a mixture of blood is involved is likely at first to be concealed from the reader, then presently in an unobtrusive way implied—allowed to leak out in some confidence of a character or made suddenly to emerge like the cat from the bag. It is treated, in other words, in the way that the Southerners treat it, and in Faulkner and Cable the suspense for the reader is likely to be created by the presence of a secret, and the climax will be a surprise.

There is in Cable's case a certain machinery of the conventional Victorian plot, but the effectiveness of his early fiction depends on the startling relationships, the unexpected courses of action that result from the queer situation of two races living side by side, entangled with one another but habitually ignoring this fact, proceeding more or less at cross-purposes but recurrently brought up short by love, sympathy or consanguinity. Hence the violence, the scandal, the constant frustration—to which is added that other

frustration of intervention by an alien power: in the early days the "Americans," in the years after the war the Yankees. The pretense that the past has not happened, that ancient history is not still with us here, makes the terror of this Southern world, the tragic irony of Cable's fiction. . . . *The Grandissimes* is Cable's best book, and the other strong things in his work are likely to repeat this theme. (pp. 563-65)

One is surprised when one picks it up and finds it—partly tedious, partly brilliant—so observant, so sharp, so humane in its handling of the maimings and distortions, the comic and tragic involvements of its complicated embarrassing subject. (p. 566)

[When Cable] persisted—through public statements as well as through his subsequent fiction—in his searching inquiry into Southern affairs, he eventually roused up against him virtually the whole white South. . . . [A] whole series of studies of conditions in the states of the late Confederacy . . . [were] collected in two small books, *The Silent South* and *The Negro Question*. These are among his most valuable writings, and they ought to have been recognized as classics in their field, but they appeared at a time when it happened, for reasons to be noticed later, that neither the North nor the South desired to be harassed further by these problems for which the proposed solutions could never be made to come out right. (pp. 566-67)

The influence of the Northern editors was to prove in the long run as lethal [as the South's hostility to his views on race]. The slow strangulation of Cable as an artist and a serious writer is surely one of the most gruesome episodes in American literary history. . . . [Editors] really wanted nothing from Cable but little love stories of queer old New Orleans—the romance and charm of the French Quarter, those Creoles with their droll way of talking—and they did not care in the least that Cable had no natural bent for the conventional kind of romance, that his interests and his capabilities all lay in the direction of imaginative history and realistic social observation. (pp. 579-80)

It is impossible to know what Cable's second novel, *Dr. Sevier* . . . , would have been like if he had been allowed to publish it as he wrote it. The dreadful conditions in the local prisons were apparently to have played a more important role than they do in the final version. . . . The unsatisfactoriness of *Dr. Sevier* may be due partly to the soft-pedalling of editors and partly to the author's desire to show lovable and worthy characters who would appeal to the Victorian appetite for reading about respectable virtue and humble people with hearts of gold. Here Cable was evidently aiming to supply his readers, also, with a liberal allowance of another product of his which was popular. One of the features of his early fiction had been his scrupulously accurate rendering of the dialects. . . . His skill at this kind of mimicry was one of the things that made his readings successful, and he seems to have set out in this novel to provide a certain number of scenes which would keep his mainly well-schooled audiences in gales of good-natured laughter. You have in *Dr. Sevier* not merely Negro and Creole, but also the imperfect English of Irish, German and Italian Americans, all set down with phonetic precision and stuck full of so many apostrophes that their dialogue becomes an obstacle. This conscientious book suffers, too, from a kind of miscalculation that sometimes occurs with novelists when a curious or striking true story, transposed into a work of fiction, turns out to give an impression of implausibility and, in the case of *Dr. Sevier,* to seem rather pointless as well, and hence uncharacteristic of Cable. *Bonaventure,* which followed . . . when Cable had been warned off the subjects that aroused his unwelcome emotions, turned out, in spite of careful descriptions of the "Cajuns" and their rather wild country—the author calls the book a "prose pastoral" and is trying for the poignant-idyllic—to have been rendered completely nonmemorable by a kind of wholesome insipidity and a sentimentality that fails to function. (pp. 581-82)

[Similiarly, Cable's editor] was quite right in declaring that there is no literature in *John March* and that its salutary purpose is irritating. For one thing, the novelist had by this time been away from the South too long to be steeped, as he had once been, in the local life, and, furthermore, the locale of the novel is entirely a notebook product, the result of a visit to a small town in Georgia, a state that Cable did not know well. He has tried to invent a community that will serve to show typical situations, but neither characters nor situations can be accepted by the reader as real. Between the Northern characters and the Southern ones and between the blacks and the whites, Cable shrewdly holds the balance as usual: there are good people and bad people on both sides. (p. 583)

In all this, the novelist has become far too conscious of his social responsibility. Every character, almost every scene, is intended to illustrate some point, and the moral of the whole thing is that the South can be born again only if the decent elements can succeed in disentangling themselves from the corrupt and reactionary ones. The novel is completely synthetic, and it was most unfortunate that Cable, in attempting so serious a book, should have played into the hands of his critics by producing so thorough a bore. . . . A book that follows *John March, Strong Hearts* . . . , is made up of three stories, two of which show Cable at his sickliest, but the third of which has at least the merit of containing one of the few bright spots of writing to be found in the later Cable. The experiences of a drunkard who reforms himself by escaping to an island in the Gulf of Mexico, destroying his adored sailboat and living alone on the sand, where he barely survives a hurricane, has something of Stephen Crane and something of Ernest Hemingway. It is the old American theme of the isolated man at grips with nature and entirely dependent on his own resources. The Sunday-school Cable is here, but there is also the shrewd psychologist. The drunkard, disappointed in love, can get himself under control only by accepting and intensifying his solitude. (p. 584)

The real canon of Cable's books, the five of them that ought to be read by every student of American literature—*Old Creole Days, The Grandissimes, Strange True Stories of Louisiana, The Silent South* and *The Negro Question*—were all written by 1890. Though somewhat hampered in the novels that immediately follow by the demands of the popular taste, the author of *The Grandissimes* is still trying to maintain his standing on the higher level of literature; but these books show Cable at a serious loss—witness *Bylow Hill*—as to what to do with his talents. And in the interval between *Strong Hearts* and *Bylow Hill,* he had, for the first time in his life, deliberately mustered his powers for a full-scale exploitation of the popular taste. (pp. 584-85)

[In *The Cavalier*] he was for the first time letting himself go

on his youthful adventures in the Civil War. "The author," he exultantly declares, "did not have to read up to write this story." He *had* had to do a great deal of reading-up in order to give his other writings the historical solidity at which he always aimed; he had labored and strained at his responsible thinking; and he had perhaps bored himself with *John March* as much as he bored others. But he was right from one point of view in believing that *The Cavalier* was "far better" than *John March:* it is at least a good deal more readable.

The truth is, however, that this popular novel is almost wholly meretricious. The fundamental thing about it is that Cable has made the decision to give up being a serious writer. He avows this when he says of his later books that he is frankly writing "romances," stories that might "make you feel today that you are entertained, and find tomorrow that you are profited." . . . Poor Cable cannot know how pathetic he is when he compares the execution of *The Grandissimes* unfavorably with that of *The Cavalier.* He has actually—in dropping the discipline of his rigorous moral code—become suddenly debauched in an alarming way. It is as if he has gone on a spree. (p. 594)

The result is erotic fantasy that seems not characteristic of Cable, and a deliberate contrivance—not far from Hollywood—of situations that create suspense. But *The Cavalier* does generate excitement. The "love interest" is hot and gasping. The medium of the writing—never employed save in this one book by Cable—is that heightened first-person narrative, a counterfeit of breathless and wondering youth and a conductor of pseudo-emotion, which had made the fortune of *Lorna Doone* and which probably derived more remotely from *David Copperfield* and *Henry Esmond.* . . . The admirer of Cable may be somewhat shocked to note with what conscious competence he has mastered the formulas of the period, how wholeheartedly he is here attempting to satisfy the feminine public that was dictating American taste. One of the primary requirements of the fiction of that time was that events should be presented from a woman's point of view, or, if not through a woman's eyes, in such a way as to appeal to a woman, and the results are often embarrassing. (p. 595)

Poor Cable is not quite up to this, but he makes a terrific effort, and it is distressing to find this fighter for justice going to pieces over the virility of his heroes. (p. 596)

The Cavalier was a kind of fluke. George Cable was never afterwards to repeat his success in this genre. It may be that his return to the memories of youth had made it easy for him to set off a gusher of adolescent romancing. But its successors [*Kincaid's Battery, The Flower of The Chapdelaines,* and *Gideon's Band*] are as synthetic as *John March, Southerner* and have nothing of *The Cavalier*'s liveliness. . . . Cable's intellectual conscience and the complexity of his point of view still forced him to construct, in these potboilers, most elaborate close-fitted machines. *Kincaid's Battery* was as carefully worked out in advance, carried through as systematically, as *Ulysses. Gideon's Band* . . . took Cable as long—six years—as *Madame Bovary* had taken Flaubert. But the expenditure of first-rate powers on situations which are artificial must become, to the admirer of Cable, most depressing and even repellent. (pp. 598-99)

Edmund Wilson, "Novelists of the Post-War South: Albion W. Tourgée, George W. Cable, Kate Chopin, Thomas Nelson Page," in his Patriotic Gore: Studies in the Literature of the American Civil War *(reprinted by permission of Farrar, Straus & Giroux, Inc.; copyright © 1962 by Edmund Wilson), Oxford University Press, New York, 1962, pp. 529-616.**

LOUIS D. RUBIN, JR. (essay date 1969)

The quality of the stories that make up *Old Creole Days* arises in large part out of the dynamic tension between their author's strong fascination with so much of Creole life and his disapproval, as a progressive-minded Protestant of Calvinistic descent, of their tribal ways. (p. 58)

What appeals to him as artist, and so distinguishes his New Orleans stories, is the physical texture of Creole life. For all his religious belief, as a writer he is secular in a way that almost no other American novelist of his century is.

The stories of *Old Creole Days* present a densely packed social panorama of class and caste. Cable's art is very much of the everyday, the ordinary; it is not the sometimes highly romanticized plots . . . that constitute the chief appeal. Rather it is the social scene, the rich variety of social life, with the coming and going of people, the confrontation of Creole and Anglo-American attitudes and customs, the impact of racial admixture. The art of the stories in *Old Creole Days* is founded upon realistic social observation.

When one views these stories in terms of Cable's later work, one sees both similarities and dissimilarities. That fine texture of experience that marks the best of *The Grandissimes* and his other work is already very much in evidence. In embryo, most of Cable's themes are present: the clash of Creole and Anglo-American ways, problems of race and caste, the delight in dialect . . . , the decadence of the Creole establishment, the city falling into neglect and disrepair, above all the sensuous, carnal quality of human experience in a Southern city of mixed races and languorous ways. Present, too, is Cable's taste for plots based all too strongly on romantic sentimentality: in "Belles Demoiselles Plantation" he sacrifices plausibility to melodrama, and in "'Tite Poulette" and "Café des Exilés" (but not "Madame Déliceuse") his lovers, insofar as they are lovers, behave woodenly in the conventionally sentimental tradition of the genteel romance. Significantly, the best of the stories, "'Sieur George" and "Posson Jone'," are those in which the plot is least complex.

What is largely missing from these stories, however, is any important attempt at social *criticism.* . . . [There] is relatively little evidence of the author's desire to protest social inequities. The attack on racism that is so prominent even in his next book, *The Grandissimes,* is hardly evident here at all. Only in occasional remarks . . . does Cable touch on racism, except in "'Tite Poulette." To be sure, there is considerable *implied* criticism. . . . But the point is precisely that most of this is suggested obliquely; it grows out of the fiction, and is in most instances a part of the characterization and the story line. The stories generally succeed on their own merit as fiction. (pp. 58-60)

In an important sense, *The Grandissimes* may be said to be the first "modern" Southern novel. For if the modern Southern novel has been characterized by its uncompromising attempt to deal honestly with the complexity of Southern racial experience, then *The Grandissimes* was the first important work of fiction written by a Southerner in which that intention is manifested. (p. 78)

What is most striking about *The Grandissimes* is its rich social texture. Though the story had its romantic elements, in particular the conventional love story plot of the day, more than almost any other Southern novel of its time it was, to use the distinction set forth by Hawthorne in his Preface to *The House of the Seven Gables,* a Novel, as opposed to a Romance, in that it presumed to deal with the "probable and ordinary course of man's experience" rather than the fanciful, the "Marvellous." . . . The dynamics of the story arise from the problems of caste and class, and human beings are portrayed to a remarkable degree as they exist in everyday life. Cable's chief concern is with social problems, and the weaving of a dense social fabric, in which what transpires among the characters is presented as part of a complex community existence, is absolutely necessary to the meaning of the novel. (p. 79)

[In] making the problem of race and caste the central theme of his novel of the Louisiana of 1803, Cable was dealing with the single most controversial and inflammatory issue of post-Civil War Louisiana life. . . .

[The] episode of Bras-Coupé is made into the principal thematic motif. The violation of the Negro's humanity involved in his enslavement is dramatically symbolized by the depiction of the tall, handsome African prince standing regally among the Creoles, and the curse he pronounces upon his owner's plantation when he is mistreated signifies the blight that the South brought upon itself and its lands by the moral crime of human slavery. (p. 84)

The wrong done to Bras-Coupé is emblematic of the basic corruption that runs through Creole New Orleans. . . . In his terrible pride, his furious insistence upon purity of race at the expense of justice and of blood ties, his invincible belligerence, and his championing of Creole rights and Creole virtue, Agricola Fusilier typifies the unreasoning atavism of the Creoles, and by inference, of the white South.

Yet such are Cable's insight and artistry that the basic characterization of the fiery old Creole is by no means totally unsympathetic. For Cable recognizes the pathos and dignity of the proud old man, the heroic quality of his misguided loyalty to Creole tradition and his zeal in a miserable cause, and the warmth of his friendship as well as of his hatred. . . . Here, as indeed throughout the novel, the literary artistry of Cable takes precedence over the politics and is responsible for much of the success of *The Grandissimes.* For it is impossible, more so perhaps than Cable had consciously intended, not to admire the old man's conviction and his resolution. If, as is likely, Cable intended Agricola Fusilier to represent not simply a passionate old man, nor merely the embodiment of Creole virtues and vices, but those of the South itself, then his very name, signifying the planter and the soldier, is quite appropriate. (pp. 85-6)

In any event, it is what Cable was able to do with Agricola Fusilier that makes his novel so compelling an examination of his society. For it enabled him to portray Creole society with considerable fondness and sympathy even while he was engaged in searching out its essential defects, and to save his story from becoming a didactic censuring of Creole deficiencies alone. (pp. 86-7)

It should be noted that Cable's dislike and disapproval of the Creoles does not extend to their women. Though occasionally he enters a sarcastic remark . . . , Cable generally portrays Creole ladies as soft, tender, and financially impractical. . . . As women, they feel rather than think; their emotions are their chief concern, and they live for love. (pp. 89-90)

[Cable's female Creoles] are indicative of the kind of attraction that the sensuous and the voluptuous held for Cable; that he conceived of Creole women as so very feminine, and so sensuously appealing in their helplessness and impracticality, is an index to his ambivalent attitude toward them. . . . Cable's own conscious disapproval of so much that the Creoles stand for is accompanied by a considerable delight in their sensuous, languorous ways; as an artist he is drawn to their impracticality, their hedonism, their love of ease, and their addiction to creature comfort. (pp. 90-1)

But if an eye for sensuous beauty is very much a part of Cable's art, it is emphatically not made into an aspect of Joseph Frowenfeld's character. That young man is almost unbelievably high-minded and out of touch with the baser realities of the world around him. . . . Frowenfeld's moral rectitude pointedly differentiates him from almost all the Creole males. (p. 92)

[Cable fails completely to] study Frowenfeld in terms of the remarkable social mobility that he displays. His *Kulturroman* describes in great depth the impact of Anglo-American culture upon the Creoles, but almost nothing of the reverse of the process. . . . In place of what might have been a fascinating delineation of the way in which an outsider responds to the attractions of a richly complex, formidable, but ultimately vulnerable society, we are given only the high-minded but wooden and lifeless characterization of Joseph Frowenfeld.

It is this, I think, that prevents *The Grandissimes,* for all its undoubted excellence of social texture and its unflinching realistic dramatization of the evils of caste and of racism, from being a novel of the first rank. In the best of Twain, Hawthorne, Melville, one finds no such area of experience within the novel so completely neglected. Because of this neglect, the love plot of *The Grandissimes* remains a romantic stereotype; and the author's strictures on Creole society, since they are not examined in terms of motive, tend toward didacticism. (p. 94)

The Richlings are subjected to one disaster after the other, and yet there is no buildup, no progressive enlargement or depth resulting from the experience, that would have given the novel a development, either of theme or of characterization. What development there is is entirely one of narrative chronology. . . . (p. 138)

It is not until almost the very end of the novel that we find a real clue to the explanation for what it is that sets Richling apart from his society, and then only by inference. . . . When he met Mary, and proposed to marry her, his family disinherited him, for no reason except "simple sectional prejudice." (pp. 139-40)

[We have] to ask ourselves what lies behind that past that might conceivably account for such a schism. The answer is, though as a theme it plays no part in the novel at all, *Negro slavery.* In other words, not only does Richling espouse a Northern girl; at one point we are told that when the war came, he wanted the North to win. The issue that separated North and South was Negro slavery. The *only* issue that could really account for Richling's suffering what he does, and being so cut off from his society, is the Negro issue. *But the novel says nothing whatever about the Negro issue.*

What I am getting at is that what Cable did was, through imaginative extension, to give his protagonist the net results of *his own* incipient estrangement from Southern society, without at the same time going into the causes of that estrangement. It was the Negro issue, and nothing else, that was steadily isolating Cable from Southern society, and that in his own life constituted a very clear, credible reason for and explanation of that isolation. Cable put John Richling in something of the same position as his own *vis-à-vis* New Orleans, but said nothing whatever about the Negro. Instead, he attempted to make it into a matter involving a general other-worldliness, a lack of aptitude for practicality and success, and the result is unconvincing. (p. 140)

Why could he not have portrayed Richling as being in much the same circumstance that Cable himself had been during recent years, and indeed was in at the time of writing, by showing him holding racial attitudes at strong variance with those of the New Orleans community, yet forced to suppress them? (p. 143)

For Cable to have developed his characterization of Richling in this fashion, it would have been necessary for him to have examined and understood his own personality in a way that there is no evidence he was ever capable of doing. He would have had to perceive the logic, the motives, the conflicting drives and attitudes of a man in such a situation of enforced repression—a situation very much like his own during the years when he was writing his novel. But the necessary introspective self-examination that would have been involved in the working out of such a characterization was beyond his capacities. He did not view himself in such a light; he did not recognize the contradictions within his own personality—the desire for social approval in New Orleans as contrasted with the desire to protest the injustice being done to the Negro; the desire for approval by the Genteel Tradition in literature as contrasted with the desire to deal with the often raw and unpleasant realities of the life around him; the Calvinist disapproval of Creole sensuality and indolence as contrasted with the sensuous and voluptuous attraction that such attitudes held for him. Much of Cable's finest writing had come out of just the two-way pull of those polarities and the resulting dramatic tension it had produced in his fiction. The polarity, the ambivalence, are abundantly present in his best fiction; but to judge from his letters and his other writings, apparently it was only *as fiction,* in the concrete particularity of characters and situations, that he was ever to express them. (pp. 143-44)

Because Cable could not do this he was able, as a novelist, to create characters of only limited depth and complexity. The result was that the variety and the profundity of meaning that Cable could give to his fiction was limited: he could develop the characterization, which is to say the form, of his fiction only so far, and no further. In dealing with the picturesque folk of *Old Creole Days* and *The Grandissimes,* that limitation had not been so apparent. With *Dr. Sevier* it began to reveal itself. (p. 145)

There is in Cable, as there is not in Whitman, James, or Twain, a point at which as an artist he stops, draws back, and refuses to go beyond. It involves a failure of self-scrutiny. . . . It accounts for Joseph Frowenfeld, John Richling, and all the romantic sentimentality of plot and characterization that to greater or lesser degree bedevils almost all Cable's fiction save some of the stories in *Old Creole Days*. (p. 149)

[*John March, Southerner*] is not Cable's best novel; *The Grandissimes* is probably that. But in terms of its author's life and career, it is his most interesting work, and certainly his most ambitious. (p. 212)

[Almost] all the major characters in the novel [are very realistically drawn], with the exception of Barbara Garnet and, in his role as romantic lover, John March himself. What is most remarkable in Cable's novel is the roundness and thoroughness of his characterizations. Where we might, in the typical Southern fiction of the period, expect local color stereotypes, Cable gives us characters such as rarely appear in Southern novels before William Faulkner. (p. 226)

It is chiefly with John March . . . that the fortunes of Cable's novel about the New South rise or fall. John is a character of mixed success and failure—and what is right and wrong about him is in effect what is successful and unsuccessful about the novel. . . . [Insofar] as John is the male romantic lead, he is a figure of conventional magazine romance and, to modern tastes at any rate, neither very interesting nor very believable. Unfortunately, Cable gives us a great deal of John in this role. . . . (p. 231)

I would nevertheless insist that the essential characterization of John March is not a failure, and that John's role as romantic hero may flaw, but does not spoil, Cable's novel. For when not occupied with Barbara Garnet, John March is not a stock figure, and is neither unconvincing or oversimplified. Instead, in his pride, his innocence, and his capacity for painful learning, he successfully embodies the meaning of Cable's novel. He is indeed John March, *Southerner*. . . . John March must learn to think and act for himself, and to do so he must understand what is going on in the society around him. Tradition, prejudice, loyalty, piety, all conspire to make it exceedingly difficult for him to attain that understanding; and the long, painful struggle whereby he comes to such knowledge is very much the structural development of the novel.

It is to Cable's credit that he does not make the achievement too easy, and does not invest John with any sort of easy moral superiority over his less high-minded fellow Southerners. (pp. 231-32)

[John March stands] for George W. Cable—a less articulate, less logical Cable, a ''man of action'' rather than of contemplation. . . . Cable himself had learned a bit more readily than John, but he too underwent a long apprenticeship before he was able to recognize what he considered the true condition of Southern society in his time. And unlike Cable's previous ''autobiographical'' protagonists, such as Frowenfeld or John Richling, there is sufficient distance between author and spokesman so that believable characterization is possible; Cable was able to show March slowly and painfully learning to recognize the errors of his way of thinking. Perhaps it is fortunate in this respect that Cable chose to set his novel far away from New Orleans; it enabled him to dissociate the people and the situation from his immediate personal experience.

Edmund Wilson [see excerpt above] has repeated the general verdict on the novel when he says that it is polemical, didactic, a ''notebook product'' without believable people. Here I can only say that, in this instance at least, Wilson is simply mistaken. The novel is not argued polemically, and it does not preach self-consciously. . . . (pp. 236-37)

It is a flawed but notable novel, representing the attempt of a writer of insight and skill to describe and define a situation of considerable human importance. The authenticity of the situation, growing as it does out of Cable's foremost concerns, provides an embodiment for the problems presented that results in convincing and moving fiction. . . . It is an impressive, sometimes even stunning examination of a region filled with torment and passion, stung by defeat, emboldened by opportunity, grappling with the problems of commerce, race, class, and belief, facing the challenge and hope of change. Before Faulkner, before Ellen Glasgow, before any other important Southern writer, Cable was working in this novel with the specific problems of human definition that have enabled the best Southern writers to produce literature of stirring dimensions. (p. 237)

With the publication of *John March, Southerner* in 1895, the literary career of George W. Cable, so far as its principal achievement goes, all but comes to an end. He was fifty years old, and was to live for three decades longer. During that time he was to publish nine more books, including five novels. Yet with the exception of several short stories also written in the 1890's, little that he produced after *John March* is of any literary significance or adds to his artistic reputation. He became a writer of romances devoid of social importance, designed to entertain and, vaguely, to provide some sort of moral uplift, in that the characters were supposedly ennobling and worthy of emulation. (p. 239)

> *Louis D. Rubin, Jr., in his* George W. Cable: The Life and Times of a Southern Heretic *(© 1969 by The Bobbs-Merrill Co., Inc.; reprinted by permission of the publisher, The Bobbs-Merrill Company, Inc.), Bobbs-Merrill—Pegasus, 1969, 304 p.*

ELMO HOWELL   (essay date 1972-73)

One of the most delightful scenes in [*The Grandissimes*], which at the same time betrays [Cable's] weakness as an artist, is the visit of Joseph Frowenfeld . . . with Madame Aurora Nancanou and her daughter Clotilde. It is a social occasion, a time for small talk, but Frowenfeld with Puritan self-righteousness turns it into a Chautauqua lecture on the shortcomings of Creole character. (p. 46)

Louis D. Rubin, Jr. [see excerpt above], finds an inconsistency in Frowenfeld's stark ethics and his attraction to the Creole ladies and suggests that he is trying to raise himself socially when he marries the younger one. . . . But Frowenfeld is no ''social climber,'' as Rubin suggests, but an iconoclast, whose aim is to supplant the Creole way of life with what he considers the superior Anglo-Saxon Protestant ethos. (p. 47)

[The] ladies Nancanou are unusual among his Creole characters. For the most part, he dislikes and distrusts them, particularly the men, and cannot let them alone to act and think for themselves. . . . Some of them spring to life, like old Fusilier the Creole apologist, for example, only to be buried again in the necessities of the argument. . . . All of his characters, however multifarious and rich in suggestion, are circumscribed by his thesis and strictly speaking have no life of their own.

His Creole antipathy is conveyed with most art in the use of dialect, to which his local audience objected from the beginning. . . . What probably offended . . . Creoles was not so much the kinship to Negro speech as the patronizing air that Cable's phonetics suggest. . . . Cable has a comic flair with dialect which he can turn to malicious purpose. (pp. 48-9)

Cable made no secret of his views in *The Grandissimes*. . . . Louisiana, says Frowenfeld, will become more and more an illiterate country, "as it persists in the system of social and civil distinctions." The Creoles are "amateurish" in their art, they are provincial in their hostility to the outsider, and any people who contemn physical labor and relegate it to a servile class are degenerate. (pp. 49-50)

But the Creoles will overcome their faults, or some of them, "under the gentler influence of a higher civilization," by which he means Protestant and Anglo-Saxon. It was the burning passion of Cable's life that the same should happen to the white South in the period of Reconstruction. He looked forward to the time when everything "Southern" should be forgotten, annihilated. . . . His novel *John March, Southerner* is a dramatization of his radical views, which were offensive even to the North, willing at last to let the South settle its own problems. He became a sort of postbellum Abolitionist. (p. 51)

[This indicates that] the fundamental weakness in Cable as an artist is not in his political or social views. Other Southerners, from Mark Twain to Faulkner, have taken views at variance with those of their region, because, as Faulkner once said, they have both loved and hated it. Cable seems only to have hated it. (p. 52)

Cable lacked the broad tolerance essential to the novelist who deals with a wide spectrum of human affairs. There was little reverence in his nature. He felt nothing of the Southerner's traditional loyalty to person and place—only the humanitarian's zeal. . . . In spite of their differences in temperament, Cable and Mark Twain had the parallel experience of a self-imposed exile, from which both were articulate concerning the faults of the South. But there the parallel ends. Mark Twain loved the life he knew as a boy in Hannibal, Missouri, and on his uncle's farm in Madison County, and his best work is a nostalgic recreation of "those old simple days."

Cable stands outside and aloof, coldly observant of the rich panorama of his native Louisiana. He feels none of the pathos of the Creole's situation in the early nineteenth century, nor of the white Southerner's after 1865. . . . His deficiency is a deficiency of the heart. (pp. 52-3)

> Elmo Howell, "George Washington Cable's Creoles: Art and Reform in 'The Grandissimes'," in The Mississippi Quarterly (copyright 1973 Mississippi State University), Vol. XXVI, No. 1, Winter, 1972-73, pp. 43-53.

DONALD A. RINGE (essay date 1973)

[In *The Grandissimes*] the central problem is not, as many

critics suppose, the conflict of two societies, but the strong influence that Joseph Frowenfeld and Honoré Grandissime exert on each other. . . . [To overemphasize the social] aspect of the novel is to slight the developing relationship between the German-American immigrant and his Creole friend, whose growing mutual respect is built, not upon their differences, but upon the important qualities they share. Each begins, of course, at a different stage of moral development. Frowenfeld plays a role that Cable more than once assigns to an *Américain* character: he assumes a high moral position that cannot in itself be argued with, but which takes little cognizance of the social and personal realities that surround him. (p. 54)

Frowenfeld's moral position is, of course, a sound one. The strong proponent of social justice, he attacks the caste society he finds in Louisiana as destructive of human rights, and he espouses the cause of the black man—both free and enslaved. Yet Frowenfeld has to learn that being right is not enough, if he wants to do more in society than merely argue. . . . Thus, although Cable presents the apothecary as a sincere advocate for truth and justice, he makes it abundantly clear that he can accomplish little or nothing in the practical world. Certain traits of character stand in his way. (p. 55)

[In] his "ardent zeal for truth," . . . [Frowenfeld] does not pay sufficient attention to the social reality in which he finds himself. . . . Frowenfeld must learn to be practical if he hopes to see his ideals become realities. The problem, of course, is to accomplish this end without so compromising his principles that he becomes false to his ideals.

This is the danger faced by Honoré Grandissime, the accomplished young Creole who seeks out Joseph Frowenfeld and becomes his friend. Honoré shares many of Frowenfeld's views. . . . We learn, indeed, that he even espoused the cause of Bras-Coupé, an enormous slave who had struck his master and run away. . . . That he failed in his pleas, Honoré attributes to his own temerity. "One can . . . condemn too rashly," he tells the American at their first meeting. . . . In the practical world, it can lead to a result precisely the opposite of what one might wish to obtain. (pp. 55-6)

This course of action, however, brings its own difficulties. If one can condemn too rashly, he can also "condemn—too cautiously—by a kind of—elevated cowardice." . . . Honoré confesses that this has been his failing, and the events of the story bear him out. . . .

Each of the heroes, then, faces a similar problem: to adjust theory to practice in such a way that social change can be furthered without the surrender of principle. (p. 56)

But if the double heroes of *The Grandissimes* arrive at the same moral and social position by the end of the novel, it is a point neither could have reached without the other. . . . Because these characters are so intimately involved with each other, therefore, the meaning of the book cannot be said to reside in either alone. Cable's theme is much more complex than such a theory might suggest and can only be seen as arising from the interrelation of the two main characters, around whom the story itself turns "as on a double center." (pp. 57-8)

[Like *The Grandissimes*], *Dr. Sevier* turns on a "double center," shifting its focus between the two main characters, both of whom are essential to the development of the theme. Dr. Sevier and John Richling learn related lessons, for both are taught the need for charity and humility in their relations with others. Both are afflicted with pride when the story opens: Dr. Sevier in the critical attitude he maintains toward the rest of the world, and John in his belief that he can preserve his independence from the rest of society. If John learns from the doctor the need to involve himself with society on its own terms and render it service, the older man learns from his friend's experience the need for Christian charity in his dealings with the poor and erring. (p. 60)

To seek a spokesman for Cable in *Dr. Sevier,* therefore, is as serious a critical error as to look for one in *The Grandissimes,* for the author has written both novels in such a way that the theme can emerge only through the interaction of his two main characters. The consequences of this practice are important. It would seem to indicate that, in Cable's view, the social problems that concerned him were extremely complex and not to be solved without taking into account both the moral principles involved and the social realities in which those principles are to be applied.... [Cable seems] to have understood that the abstract principles of a Joseph Frowenfeld and the cold austerity of a Dr. Sevier must be tempered by human understanding and Christian charity if desirable social change is to occur....

The device of the "double center," then, enabled ... Cable to urge his social reforms in fiction without doing violence to the moral and social realities of the world as he found it. To have made any character his spokesman would have entailed, inevitably, an oversimplification of the social context and the melodramatic division of his characters into heroes and villains. There are, of course, hateful and callous acts in both these books and men whose moral blindness is extreme, but most of the characters have both their virtues and vices. None of them are depicted as unqualified heroes, not even Joseph Frowenfeld. All share in the common fallibility of men, and though each of the major ones may express a part of the truth, none speak all of it.... Through this device ... Cable avoided the pitfalls of propagandistic fiction and created a pair of books that can still be admired today not only for their moral and social themes, but also for the artistic integrity of their expression. (p. 61)

> *Donald A. Ringe, "The 'Double Center': Character and Meaning in Cable's Early Novels," in* Studies in the Novel *(copyright 1973 by North Texas State University), Vol. V, No. 1, Spring, 1973, pp. 52-62.*

JOHN CLEMAN (essay date 1975)

[Cable's use of] local color in *The Grandissimes* is special, at the very least by virtue of the region he was delineating. That is, New Orleans and its environs were inescapably exotic to some degree and Cable developed his locale with full attention to its color, that is, to atmosphere. However, it has not often been recognized how thoroughly and artfully functional that atmosphere is in the work. In particular Cable creates a sense of mystery or ambiguity that is integrated but dramatically and significantly deepened in the use of the natural environment, and a close examination of these aspects of *The Grandissimes* argues not only that

Cable was highly artistic in his use of local color, but that the novel is great, not despite its local color elements, but through them.

We may begin to understand this artistry in Cable's local color by recognizing that he creates atmosphere in the novel, the sense of an early, cosmopolitan, semitropical city, by more than street and place names, patois dialect, and historical events.... [This] is the result of the right amount of indirection in narrative technique and a suggestiveness of style that goes so far as to reflect the action of a given scene in the rhythm and cadence of the sentences.... Such techniques contribute to the intimacy, quaintness, and languor that Cable felt was part of the life he was describing, but even more, the indirectness, particularly in introducing characters and at the novel's outset, creates a sense of mystery that is, more than Gothic overlay, a profound part of the civilization depicted. Cable, in fact, takes some pains to create a number of confusions of identity ... which owe something to eighteenth and nineteenth-century novel conventions, but which in *The Grandissimes* contribute to a feeling of ambiguity intricately linked to the social fabric on which the whole novel is based. (pp. 396-97)

Cable seems determined to register the quality of a culture he sees characterized by "hints, allusions, faint unspoken admissions, ill-concealed antipathies, unfinished speeches, mistaken identities and whisperings of hidden strife" ... ; it is a culture not open and simple, but covert and tangled. The lines of conflict between family and family, the history of political, social, and economic complexity, have been absorbed and partially hidden in the present culture, but they have shaped and are, therefore, represented in its mysterious, confusing, vaguely foreboding features.

The opening scenes of *The Grandissimes,* thus, are dense and confusing for a particular reason. Quite obviously there is too much in those scenes for a first-time reader to grasp, but this is precisely the situation facing Frowenfeld.... In a way that strikingly foreshadows Faulkner, the progress of the book in its early stages is a gradual journey into the heart of a civilization, a careful unraveling process by which Frowenfeld and the reader come to know not only the core but also how the ball was wound. One of the key aspects of the way Cable does this is that he is able to unravel the central features of Creole civilization without wholly dispelling the sense of profound mystery that is its characterizing trait. The mystification is too thoroughly worked out. It is an atmosphere permeating so much of the work, from the fictional manner, the techniques of style and narration, the modes of characterization, down to the nature of the material itself, that it is simply a part of our experience of the Creoles in this book, however much else we learn about them.

The art in Cable's treatment of locale, however, is even more profoundly felt in his use of the natural environment.... [Like] *The Scarlet Letter* and *The Pioneers, The Grandissimes* depicts a civilization in its early stages of formation, not exactly at its birth, but when the conflict between man and the natural environment is still a vital issue. It is not surprising, then, that nature figures in *The Grandissimes* beyond the mere descriptions of it, rather in ideas, values, and characters associated with the landscape. (pp. 398-400)

[There] is much of the idyllic and Edenic in Cable's some-times florid descriptions of the natural beauty, but at the outset the sense of prelapsarian innocence and delight in the cypress swamp is mostly in the elder Frowenfeld's head. (p. 400)

What the Frowenfelds seem to anticipate and what Cable seems to have expected his readers to anticipate in their image of a tropical paradise is some kind of spiritual restor-ative or lift—grand mountains, refreshing shady bowers, a land of milk and honey. What they find instead is "a land hung in mourning, darkened by gigantic cypresses, sub-merged; a land of reptiles, silence, shadow, decay." ... (pp. 400-01)

The atmosphere of the landscape in these early scenes ex-pands on what he describes in his history of the region, *The Creoles of Louisiana* ... , as "incessant and curious para-doxes," and it is, therefore, appropriate to the initial im-pressions of Creole society as "a thick mist of strange names, places and events," colored with the atmosphere of mystery. In this way, the setting maintains an atmosphere with particular social and cultural implications. ... Just as Cable is able to integrate style, narrative pace, theme, and characterization in treating some of the more purely social aspects of Creole life ... , he begins here also to blend those effects in the treatment of landscape. The continuity of atmosphere and technique thereby aids the impression of the Creoles' special connection to the landscape, an impres-sion that becomes more pronounced as the novel proceeds. In this light Cable's local color from the very outset is seen to be more than sentimental patina. It has its connection to reality, to the concrete, but much of its major importance is in the impressions, the atmospheric qualities. Quite simply, what Cable does is generate in the reader's imagination an image of the natural environment with multiple layers of meaning, wholly insinuated with the impressions and the themes of Creole culture he develops in the main plot. (p. 401)

[Beyond pleasantness and beauty] Cable saw the close presence and special quality of the natural environment to shape Creole culture as well. The general sense of this is indicated when ... Frowenfeld points out that "the climate has its influence, the soil has its influence—dwellers in swamps cannot be mountaineers." ... The "main defect," of course, is caste, but Frowenfeld's reference to natural influence is an idea Cable expressed and worked out more explicitly in *The Creoles of Louisiana,* where he asserts that "a soil of unlimited fertility became, through slavery, not an incentive to industry, but a promise of unearned plenty," and "a luxurious and enervating climate joined its influence with this condition to debase even the Gallic love of pleasure to an untrained sensuality." ... [This argues] that the paralleling of atmospheres in the treatment of na-ture and culture tends to interfuse one with the other in the reader's imagination, to suggest both specific and general connections between them. In particular, while the land has a unique beauty and charm, much of what imparts that ap-peal also weakens the Creoles. ... [It] seems altogether safe to see the Creoles' languorous charm—their manner of speaking as well as the casual way they conduct their business—and their sometimes weak morality as part of the prevailing atmosphere in which light and dark areas easily shade off into each other. Further, at the heart of *The Gran-dissimes* is the clash between the Creole and the rising

Anglo-American cultures, in which openness and industry (or business) are among the prime virtues of the latter in contrast to the Creoles' secretiveness and indolence, values which are suggestively echoed in the natural setting. (pp. 402-03)

The wilderness surrounding and influencing Creole culture comes to represent the base line of primitive existence for the Creoles as well as the Blacks, the level that the whole history of New Orleans points away from but never entirely escapes, not, in theory at least, until it can rid itself of the brutality of slavery, caste, ignorance, superstition, and pro-vinciality. (p. 408)

This is not to argue that social themes and concerns—the issues of slavery and caste—do not exist in the novel, but that they are inextricably linked to the natural issues, which are in turn intertwined with the overall atmosphere of the novel. ... If we recognize the role of nature we must also recognize that that role is shared and developed in several phases of the novel—character, setting, narrative pace, tone—each informing or adding dimension to the other. (p. 409)

To read *The Grandissimes,* therefore, as an example of early realism in which most of the novel is ignored or only tolerated, is to miss a good deal of its artistry and perhaps much of its central concern. And, if we are to describe the novel as local color we should not do so ... , with a sneer or an implied "only." Within that "color" ... are some of the same psychological tensions that give power to the dark romances by some of America's greatest nineteenth-cen-tury writers, and that local color, moreover, is no simple effect. Certainly, there is tough realism in the book and some sentimental twaddle, but most of the latter is in the love plot, and the realism is not really the significant part of the novel's special character. ... Cable wrote a number of other novels about the South, novels such as *John March* and *Dr. Sevier* ... , which in many ways are far more dev-astating in their realism, but which lack the power of *The Grandissimes* because they are thin in their sense of culture and more particularly in their sense of place. They lack the feel of cultural density, of complex family relationships, of a mysterious past, of intricate involvement with the land, but mostly they lack the sense of wholeness, the continuity of atmosphere, style, setting, and character, that together are Cable's rendering of local color and his greatest achievement in *The Grandissimes.* (p. 410)

> *John Cleman, "The Art of Local Color in George W. Cable's 'The Grandissimes',"* in American Literature *(reprinted by permission of the Pub-lisher; copyright 1975 by Duke University Press, Durham, North Carolina), Vol. 47, No. 3, Novem-ber, 1975, pp. 396-410.*

ADDITIONAL BIBLIOGRAPHY

Bikle, Lucy Leffingwell Cable. *George W. Cable: His Life and Letters.* New York: Charles Scribner's Sons, 1928, 306 p.
    A biography by Cable's daughter concerned exclusively with the facts of his home life and career. Though the work con-tains no critical comment, it is valuable in that it reprints many of Cable's letters to friends and family.

Cable, George W. "After-Thoughts of a Story-Teller." *The North American Review* 158, No. 1 (January 1894): 16-23.

A discussion by Cable of his methods of composition and his ideals of fiction.

Campbell, Michael L. "The Negro in Cable's *The Grandissimes*." *The Mississippi Quarterly* XXVII, No. 2 (Spring 1974): 165-78.

An examination of the role of the four main Negro characters in the novel and their relation to Cable's social themes. Campbell explores Cable's ambivalence toward the Negro: Cable's pity as well as his fear and fascination denote the complexity of race relations in the South.

Clark, William Bedford. "Cable and the Theme of Miscegenation in *Old Creole Days* and *The Grandissimes*." *The Mississippi Quarterly* XXX, No. 4 (Fall 1977): 597-609.

A summary of Cable's use of the quadroon and half-caste in his early fiction. The author finds that Cable often sidesteps interracial conflicts in his short stories but confronts the problem squarely in *The Grandissimes*.

Eaton, Richard Bozman. "George W. Cable and the Historical Romance." *The Southern Literary Journal* VIII, No. 1 (Fall 1975): 82-94.

A study of the elements of realism and of historical romance in *The Grandissimes*.

Fulweiler, Howard W. "Of Time and the River: 'Ancestral Nonsense' vs. Inherited Guilt in Cable's 'Belles Demoiselles Plantation'." *Mid-Continent American Studies Journal* 7, No. 2 (Fall 1966): 53-9.

A reading of the short story "Belles Demoiselles Plantation" which demonstrates Cable's intricate balance of romantic theme and realistic point of view.

Pugh, Griffith T. "George W. Cable's Theory and Use of Folk Speech." *Southern Folklore Quarterly* 24, No. 4 (December 1960): 287-93.

A brief examination of Cable's use of dialect which contends that Cable used dialect sparingly to give a sense of character, and was not concerned with a literal representation of Southern speech.

Tinker, Edward Larocque. "Cable and the Creoles." *American Literature* 5, No. 4 (January 1934): 313-26.

A biographical study which depicts the South's vilification of Cable for his racial position and portrayal of Creole life. Although Tinker feels that much of Cable's work will not survive, he still considers Cable important as the first novelist to examine truthfully Southern social conditions.

Countee Cullen

1903-1946

(Born Countee Leroy Porter) American poet, novelist, journalist, and dramatist.

Cullen was one of the outstanding poets of the Harlem Renaissance, and one of the first black poets after Paul Laurence Dunbar to achieve national recognition. Influenced by John Keats, his poetry is based on traditional forms of meter and rhyme, often treating his subjects in a mannered, romantic vein.

Of an obscure early background, Cullen was adopted by the Reverend and Mrs. Frederick Cullen of New York in 1918. He was raised in the fairly comfortable surroundings of his family's Methodist parsonage, a background conducive to reflection on spiritual matters, a common preoccupation in his work. Immersing himself in the genteel literature that surrounded him at home, Cullen proved to be an excellent student. His poetry was widely published and quoted during his high school and college years, bringing him many awards. One of his first major successes was "The Ballad of the Brown Girl," his reworking along racial lines of that English ballad. He also was the first American to publish a poem in rhyme royal, according to one of his Harvard professors, Robert Hillyer. Cullen's first book of poetry, *Color,* drew great critical praise, but the promise of that book was not fulfilled in his subsequent works. The volumes of poetry that followed *Color* contain what critics consider weak reworkings of the themes of the first book. It could be, as Jean Wagner suggests, that Cullen's source of inspiration, a sharing of the beliefs and hopes of common black people, was stifled after long years of sheltered living and close association with white culture.

Cullen worked for the National Urban League periodical, *Opportunity,* from 1925 to 1928, writing "The Dark Tower," a column of thought and literary criticism. He lived in France on a Guggenheim Fellowship during his brief marriage to Yolande Du Bois, daughter of prominent educator W.E.B. Du Bois, and it was there that he wrote the bitter poems of lost love collected in *The Black Christ.* For the last dozen years of his life Cullen taught junior high school in New York and wrote a play and two children's books.

Cullen's works published after *Color* exhibited occasional brilliance, but he received criticism for his traditional poetic style, sentimentality, and the mildness of his attacks on racial injustice—characteristics untypical of the work of other Harlem Renaissance artists. Yet it is for his racial poems that he is best known: for his pride in being black, his bitterness over the black experience in America, and his wonder at being born of an oppressed people but gifted with the ability to write well.

(See also *Dictionary of Literary Biography,* Vol. 4)

PRINCIPAL WORKS

Color (poetry) 1925

The Ballad of the Brown Girl (poetry) 1927
Caroling Dust [editor] (poetry) 1927
Copper Sun (poetry) 1927
The Black Christ and Other Poems (poetry) 1929
One Way to Heaven (novel) 1932
The Medea and Some Poems (poetry and drama) 1935
The Lost Zoo (A Rhyme for the Young, but Not Too Young) (poetry) 1940
My Lives and How I Lost Them (juvenile fiction) 1942
On These I Stand (poetry) 1947

CARL VAN VECHTEN (essay date 1925)

One of the best of the Negro writers, Countée Cullen, is the youngest of them all. He was barely twenty-one when *The Shroud of Color . . .* created a sensation analogous to that created by the appearance of Edna St. Vincent Millay's *Renascence* in 1912, lifting its author at once to a position in the front rank of contemporary American poets, white or black. *The Shroud of Color* was emotional in its passionate eloquence, but Countée Cullen sometimes . . . strikes the strings of his inspirational lyre more lightly, although a satiric or bitter aftertaste is likely to linger in his most ostensibly flippant verse. All his poetry is characterized by a suave, unpretentious, brittle, intellectual elegance; some of it—*To John Keats, Poet, at Spring Time* is an excellent example—by a haunting, lyric loveliness. It is to be noted that, like any distinguished artist of any race, he is able to write stanzas which have no bearing on the problems of his own race. In this respect his only Negro forebear, so far as I can recall at the moment, is the poet Pushkin, whose verses dwelt on Russian history and folklore, although he was the great-grandson of a slave.

Carl Van Vechten, "Countée Cullen," in Vanity Fair *(courtesy The Condé Nast Publications, Inc.; copyright © 1925, renewed 1953, by The Condé Nast Publications, Inc.), Vol. 24, No. 4, June, 1925, p. 62.*

BABETTE DEUTSCH   (essay date 1925)

[The lyrics in *Color*] by the youngest of the Negro poets—Countee Cullen is just past his majority—are likely to be considered less as the work of a gifted individual than as the utterance of a gifted, and enslaved, people. And indeed Mr. Cullen's poems are intensely race-conscious. He writes out of the pain of inflamed memories, and with a wistful harking back to the primitive heritage of his own folk. The peculiar flavor which the book gets from the fact that it was written by a colored man is to be had most sharply in the first section, from which the volume takes its title. This tang is the essence of such pieces as "Atlantic City Waiter," "Fruit of the Flower," and "Heritage," with their insistence on the savage past; it is the essence, too, of the lovely "Song of Praise," and of that shrewd lyric "To My Fairer Brethren." . . . (p. 763)

Again and again Mr. Cullen strikes the harsh note which carries the scorn of the oppressed, the arrogance of the insulted and injured. He is engaged by the somber power and terrible brilliance of Africa as a Jew might be engaged by the purple days of Solomon's glory, or as the Gael is moved by the bright bloody history of his island. The poem by which Mr. Cullen is perhaps best known, "The Shroud of Color," could have been written only by a Negro. It is a piece which, in spite of its sad lack of concision and its many cliches, yet abounds in true spiritual vigor.

But though one may recognize that certain of Mr. Cullen's verses owe their being to the fact that he shares the tragedy of his people, it must be owned that the real virtue of his work lies in his personal response to an experience which, however conditioned by his race, is not so much racial as profoundly human. The color of his mind is more important than the color of his skin. The faint acridness that gives an edge to many of these lyrics is a quality which one finds in Housman, or even in the minor strains of Herrick and of Horace. There is, for example, the song "To a Brown Girl"; and the same pungency is felt in the companion piece, "To a Brown Boy," or in "Wisdom Cometh with the Years." The twenty-eight rhymed "Epitaphs" have, almost without exception, a pure Gallic salt, as witness the one "For a Lovely Lady":

> A creature slender as a reed,
>   And sad-eyed as a doe
> Lies here (but take my word for it,
>   And do not pry below).

And even in what might be called his African poems it is Mr. Cullen's endowment of music and imagery and emotional awareness that matters, over and above the presence of jungle shapes and shadows.

These excellences—fantasy, lyricism, and fine sensitiveness—the book undoubtedly has. It has also faults, the faults of youth. The poet does not shrink from such rubber-stamp phrases as "costly fee," "crimson vintage," "ensanguined mead," "coral lips." He clutches at stars and clings to dreams like any neophyte, and lives in the pleasant reassurance that after death he will return to talk to his love "in liquid words of rain." But there seems little doubt that he will shed these puerilities before his youth is over, that he will discipline and develop his unquestionable gift. (pp. 763-64)

Babette Deutsch, "Let It Be Allowed," in Nation and Athenaeum, *Vol. CXXI, No. 3156, December 30, 1925, pp. 763-64.*

JESSIE FAUSET   (essay date 1926)

Color is the name of Mr. Cullen's book and color is, rightly, in every sense its prevailing characteristic. For not only does every bright glancing line abound in color but it is also in another sense the yard-stick by which all the work in this volume is to be measured. Thus his poems fall into three categories: Those, and these are very few, in which no mention is made of color; those in which the adjectives "black" or "brown" or "ebony" are deliberately introduced to show that the type which the author had in mind was not white; and thirdly the poems which arise out of the consciousness of being a "Negro in a day like this" in America.

These last are not only the most beautifully done but they are by far the most significant group in the book. I refer especially to poems of the type of "Yet do I Marvel", "The Shroud of Color", "Heritage" and "Pagan Prayer". It is in such work as this that the peculiar and valuable contribution of the American colored man is to be made to American literature. For any genuine poet black or white might have written "Oh for a Little While be Kind" or the lines to "John Keats"; the idea contained in a "Song of Praise" was used long ago by an old English poet and has since been set to music by Roger Quilter. But to pour forth poignantly and sincerely the feelings which make plain to the world the innerness of the life which black men live calls for special understanding. (p. 238)

Here I am convinced is Mr. Cullen's forte; he has the feeling and the gift to express colored-ness in a world of whiteness. I hope he will not be deflected from continuing to do that of which he has made such a brave and beautiful beginning. I hope that no one crying down "special treatment" will turn him from his native and valuable genre. There *is* no "universal treatment"; it is all specialized. . . . In a time when it is the vogue to make much of the Negro's aptitude for clownishness or to depict him objectively as a serio-comic figure, it is a fine and praiseworthy act for Mr. Cullen to show through the interpretation of his own subjectivity the inner workings of the Negro soul and mind. (pp. 238-39)

Jessie Fauset, "Our Book Shelf: 'Color'," in The Crisis *(copyright 1926 by The Crisis Publishing Company, Inc.), Vol. 31, No. 5, March, 1926, pp. 238-39.*

WALLACE THURMAN (essay date 1928)

There is hardly anyone writing poetry in America today who can make the banal sound as beautiful as does Mr. Cullen. He has an extraordinary ear for music, a most extensive and dexterous knowledge of words and their values, and an enviable understanding of conventional poetic forms. Technically, he is almost precocious, and never, it may be added, far from the academic; but he is also too steeped in tradition, too influenced mentally by certain conventions and taboos. . . . [In his poem "Heritage" and] in other far too few instances he reaches heights no other Negro poet has ever reached, placing himself high among his contemporaries, both black or white. But he has not gone far enough. His second volume [*Copper Sun*] is not as lush with promise or as spontaneously moving as his first. There has been a marking time or side-stepping rather than a marching forward. If it seems we expect too much from this poet, we can only defend ourselves by saying that we expect no more than the poet's earlier work promises.

Mr. Cullen's love poems are too much made to order. His race poems, when he attempts to paint a moral, are inclined to be sentimental and stereotyped. It is when he gives vent to the pagan spirit and lets it inspire and dominate a poem's form and context that he does his most impressive work. His cleverly turned rebellious poems are also above the ordinary. But there are not enough of these in comparison to those poems which are banal, though beautiful. (pp. 559-60)

> *Wallace Thurman, "Negro Poets and Their Poetry," in* The Bookman *(copyright, 1928, by George H. Doran Company), Vol. LXVII, No. 5, July, 1928, pp. 555-61.**

JAMES WELDON JOHNSON (essay date 1931)

One of Cullen's earliest poems, "I Have a Rendezvous with Life," reveals him as an adventurer in spirit. Even as a boy he had a lively and penetrating curiosity about life, and this quality in him is the mainspring of nearly all his poetry. It is the chief reason that the body of his poetry, young as he is, constitutes a "criticism of life." It does this more completely than the work of any other of the major Negro poets.

Cullen is a fine and sensitive lyric poet, belonging to the classic line. The modern innovators have had no influence on him. His models are Keats and Shelley, and he might be called a younger brother of Housman. He never bids for popular favor through the use of bizarre effects either in manner or subject matter. He would disdain anything approaching sensationalism. All of his work is laid within the lines of the long-approved English patterns. And by that very gauge a measure of his gifts and powers as a poet may be taken. These old forms come from his hands filled with fresh beauty. A high test for a poet in this blasé age.

Some critics have ventured to state that Cullen is not an authentic Negro poet. This statement, of necessity, involves a definition of "a Negro poet" and of "Negro poetry." There might be several definitions framed, but the question raised is a pure irrelevance. Also there is in it a faint flare-up of the old taboo which would object to the use of "white" material by the Negro artist, or at least, regard it with indulgent condescension. Cullen himself has declared that, in the sense of wishing for consideration or allowances on account of race or of recognizing for himself any limitation to "racial" themes and forms, he has no desire or intention of being a Negro poet. In this he is not only within his right; he is right.

Yet, strangely, it is because Cullen revolts against these "racial" limitations—technical and spiritual—that the best of his poetry is motivated by race. He is always seeking to free himself and his art from these bonds. He never entirely escapes, but from the very fret and chafe he brings forth poetry that contains the quintessence of race-consciousness. It is through his power to deepen and heighten these inner experiences that he achieves his finest work. It is pardonable for me to repeat here that the two most poignant lines in American literature, lines that surged up from the vortex of these experiences, are in the sonnet of his in which he expresses the faith that God can explain all the puzzling paradoxes of life; then, gathering up an infinity of irony, pathos and tragedy in the final couplet, says:

> Yet do I marvel at this curious thing
> To make a poet black and bid him sing.

Cullen's poetry demonstrates high lyric quality, sure artistry, rich imagination, and intellectual content. He has, too, the gift for witty and the power for epigrammatic expression. Pessimism is, perhaps, the pervading note in his poetry —it is in this note that he often sings of the ephemeral quality of love—but rarely does he fail to give it a sudden ironic turn that raises it above pathos or peevishness. (pp. 219-21)

> *James Weldon Johnson, "Countee Cullen," in* The Book of American Negro Poetry, *edited by James Weldon Johnson (copyright 1922, 1931 by Harcourt Brace Jovanovich, Inc.; copyright 1950 by Grace Johnson; copyright 1959 by Mrs. Grace Nail Johnson; reprinted by permission of the publisher), revised edition, Harcourt, 1931, pp. 219-31.*

BENJAMIN BRAWLEY (essay date 1937)

No account of Negro poets of the present day can fail to include Countee Cullen. If we may judge by the volumes issued and the prizes received, he has been the most successful of all. . . . [His sympathies, unlike those of Claude McKay and Langston Hughes,] are with tradition and convention. In some lines he has proclaimed that he is a Negro poet, but again he has said that he wishes his work to be judged on its merit, "with no racial consideration to bolster it up''; and when he wrote a long poem on lynching, he dated it from Paris. Something of this cleavage runs through all that he has written and gives to it an artificiality, a thinness of substance, of which one is not conscious with his two compeers. Yet, in spite of its obvious faults and sometimes its lapses in taste, his work shows much delicate perception and a keen instinct for beauty. (pp. 224-25)

Color, that appeared when the author was but twenty-three years of age, was a work of promise. The details of color conflict suggest a struggle that is more than racial and common to all mankind. Such poems as "Yet Do I Marvel," "The Shroud of Color," and "Heritage" challenged the attention of any reader. *Copper Sun* hardly indicated the advance that was expected. The book was thinner than its predecessor in both form and content; and when all due credit was given to the lyric impulse of the author, one could hardly fail to note the awkward lines and the faulty rhythms that were all too frequently in evidence. The fact is that there is a sophomoric note in the work of Mr. Cullen that he finds it hard to outgrow.

Benjamin Brawley, "Protest and Vindication," in his The Negro Genius: A New Appraisal of the Achievement of the American Negro in Literature and the Fine Arts *(copyright © 1937 by Dodd, Mead & Company, Inc.), Dodd, Mead, 1937, pp. 190-230.**

J. SAUNDERS REDDING   (essay date 1939)

[Countee Cullen] for himself (as well as others for him), has written numerous disclaimers of an attitude narrowed by racial influence. He may be right. Certainly *Caroling Dusk,* his anthology of "verse by Negro poets," represents a careful culling of the less distinctive, that is to say, the less Negroid poetry of his most defiantly Negro contemporaries. Nevertheless it remains that when writing on race material Mr. Cullen is at his best. His is an unfortunate attitude, for it has been deliberately acquired and in that sense is artificial, tending to create a kind of effete and bloodless poetry in the manner of Mr. [William Stanley] Braithwaite. The essential quality of good poetry is utmost sincerity and earnestness of purpose. A poet untouched by his times, by his conditions, by his environment is only half a poet, for earnestness and sincerity grow in direct proportion as one feels intelligently the pressure of immediate life. One may not like the pressure and the necessities under which it forces one to labor, but one does not deny it. . . . Now undoubtedly the biggest, single unalterable circumstance in the life of Mr. Cullen is his color. Most of the life he has lived has been influenced by it. And when he writes by it, he *writes:* but when this does not guide him, his pen trails faded ink across his pages. (pp. 108-09)

Mr. Cullen's first volume, *Color,* . . . is far and away his best. Here his poetry (nearly all of it on racial subjects, or definitely and frankly conditioned by race) helps to balance the savage poetic outbursts of Claude McKay. Countee Cullen is decidedly a gentle poet, a schoolroom poet whose vision of life is interestingly distorted by too much of the vicarious. This lends rather than detracts. It is as if he saw life through the eyes of a woman who is at once shrinking and bold, sweet and bitter. His province is the nuance, the finer shades of feeling, subtility and finesse of emotion and expression. Often however, with feline slyness, he bares the pointed talons of a coolly ironic and deliberate humor which is his way of expressing his resentment at the racial necessities. (p. 110)

When he leaves work of this kind for the heavier moods and materials so popular with Hughes, McKay, . . . and *The Crisis* and *Opportunity* poets, Mr. Cullen bogs down. He is the Ariel of Negro poets. He cannot beat the tom-tom above a faint whisper nor know the primitive delights of black rain and scarlet sun. After the fashion of the years 1925-1928, he makes a return to his African heritage, but not as a "son returned in bare time." He was not among the Negroes who were made Africa conscious and Africa proud by the striding Colossus, Marcus Garvey, by Vandercook's *Tom-Tom,* and O'Neill's *The Emperor Jones.* Cullen's gifts are delicate, better suited to bons mots, epi-

grams, and the delightfully personal love lyrics for which a large circle admire him.

The title poem of his third volume, *The Black Christ,* illustrates at once the scope and the limit of his abilities. Bitter and ironic in its mood, revealing but slight narrative and dramatic powers, the poem is feeble with the childish mysticism of a bad dream, penetrating the realm of emotional reality no more than does a child's relation of a nightmare. Here in this poem Mr. Cullen's lyricism is smothered, his metrical faults exaggerated, and his fear of stern reality italicized. (pp. 111-12)

J. Saunders Redding, "Emergence of the New Negro," in his To Make a Poet Black *(copyright © 1939 by the University of North Carolina Press), University of North Carolina Press, 1939 (and reprinted by McGrath Publishing Company, 1968), pp. 93-125.**

BERTRAM L. WOODRUFF   (essay date 1940)

Contemporary criticism seems hardly to have perceived that Cullen has a theory of poetry and life and it has overlooked almost entirely the question of the validity of his poetic intuition. (p. 213)

Upon the first casual reading, Cullen's attitude toward life seems to be a pessimistic one. In moods ranging from witty irony to cynical realism, he writes of the transience of life. Nevertheless, we may have in this life, where all things must change, a short hour for happiness. But to be happy, even for a time, a man must snatch his happiness when and where he may find it. (p. 214)

[Life] must be lived. Therefore, in the Schopenhaurean manner, self-will and the determination not to be frustrated by the world in realizing his desired ideals are Cullen's motives for living.

The ideals which Cullen proposes to realize as his human birthright in a grudging world are by no means unheard of conceptions. To assuage the anguish of living he presents five anodynes, namely, Love, Beauty, Faith in Man, Belief in Christ, and Poetry. To the theme of Love, as might be expected of a poet, Cullen devotes much consideration. . . . It may range from the lust of hedonistic passion to the noblest way the human heart can beat. . . . His experience tells him

> that nothing lovely shall prevail
> To win from Time and Death a moment's grace.

Yet in spite of himself, he cannot think that his faith in a whole-hearted love

> shall ever taste of death,
> Or perish from the false, forgetting earth.

Love, therefore, in this poetic philosophy, is a beautiful ideal in life, inasmuch as that which Cullen's logic tells him of the ephemeral nature of love, his whole experience discredits. And herein lies the clue to the unresolved dichotomy of Mr. Cullen's poetic experience. In his cynical realism, love is a variable; in his subjective idealism, love is an absolute.

A similarly unreconciled inner division characterizes Cullen's treatment of the theme of Beauty. In the cosmic mutability of life Cullen affirms, "Though beauty wax, yet shall it wane.'' Beauty seems also to him to be a variable. Indeed, the beauty of earth may be a snare to self-deception, concerning the perpetuity of this life. . . . (pp. 214-16)

To Countee Cullen some definite images of Beauty in Nature are those of the silver snakes of Africa, of scattered dogwood petals in springtime, of a red and white star over a windy hill, and of the blue color of the Mediterranean Sea.

With regard to external images of the human form, Cullen indicates that the bodies of Negroes are not less beautiful than those of white people. Both types are beautiful and serve as complements to one another. . . . Nor will he grant that the beauty of a fair woman is lovelier. . . . Beauty is indeed more than skin deep, for its concrete manifestation in dark women is associated with deep race pride and esoteric aesthetic standards.

By far the greatest number of Countee Cullen's poems have to do with the acting and suffering of human beings. To him the anguish of living is best realized in the reflection that, enveloped in cosmic vastness, men are like animals caged in a zoo. Surveying ironically the patterns of human life, Cullen writes philosophic epigrams for a Cynic, a Singer, a Virgin, a Lovely Lady, an Atheist, an Evolutionist and His Opponent, an Anarchist, a Magician, a Pessimist, a Mouthy Woman, a Philosopher, an Unsuccessful Sinner, a Fool, One Who Gayly Sowed His Oats, a Skeptic, a Fatalist, Daughters of Magdalen, a Preacher, and One Who Died Singing of Death. Most of the beautiful actions of the soul portrayed are those of Negroes. . . . For his race Cullen has much pride and interest, but sometimes he expresses the revolt of Negroes against discrimination and injustice. . . . His defiance of the scorn and indifference of the white race is flung with the boast that though as a Negro he has had to work three times as hard to score, yet he has, nevertheless, scored. . . . Cullen's discussions of race problems are emotional, but his emotions are given point and justification by his intellectual restraint.

Although the injustice of racial proscription enrages him, yet there runs ''Through all a harmony of faith in man.'' But here again he is torn between his materialistic and theistic concepts of life. (pp. 216-18)

The sacrificial glory of Christ is to Cullen a source of poetic inspiration and consolation. Cullen does not think of Christ as the Last Judge of orthodox Christians but as the kind Savior of Judas Iscariot and Mary Magdalene. The poems ''Heritage'' and ''The Black Christ'' affirm the belief that the redemption of Negroes was also included in Christ's sacrificial death upon the cross. Indeed, of all men, Negroes love Christ most for his promised mercy. The ''Litany of the Dark People'' is remarkably explicit in its union of the confident trust of the spirituals with a sophisticated knowledge of pagan freedom. . . . From the pagan, mad doubt of Christ in ''Pagan Prayer'' to the full-hearted acceptance of Him in ''The Black Christ,'' Countee Cullen sounds all the notes of warfare in modern civilization between primitive passions and spiritual light.

It is as a lover of poetry, however, that Cullen is most uplifted from the grievances of existence. Of all the arts, poetry, he believes, is the most powerful. . . . (pp. 218-19)

Countee Cullen believes that poetry is able to perform an ethical function. By objectifying suffering and the miseries of life in the beautiful forms of poetry, the poet is able to make a beautiful thing of the wretchedness of existence. Poetry, therefore, is a safety valve for the emotion of the poet, since he may contemplate his creation and from it derive pleasure. . . . The poet, therefore, by using his creative power to change sadness into gladness, is able to offer consolation to men. With the healing force of its high ideals of Love, Beauty, Faith in Man, and Christian Belief, poetry is a balm for the evils and frustrations of life. (pp. 221-22)

All in all, Cullen's philosophy is a tentative ordering of what is inchoate in his experience. If his poetic intuition fails to bring order out of chaos, it is not because he is a victim of self-deception. His poetry reveals his sincere attempt to discern whatever spiritual adjustment there may be for suffering, passionate, and weak souls in a hostile world. In the treatment of his poetic themes he sifts minutely the wheat from the chaff of human ideals, leaving as hoped-for verities his faith in Love, Beauty, Mankind, the Sacrifice of Christ, and Poetry. In his moments of weakness and doubt, he feels too keenly the everlasting strife and frustration in the world and the awesome mystery of Death. (p. 223)

> *Bertram L. Woodruff, ''The Poetic Philosophy of Countee Cullen,'' in PHYLON: The Atlanta University Review of Race and Culture, 1 (copyright, 1940, by Atlanta University; reprinted by permission of PHYLON), Vol. I, No. 3, Third Quarter (September, 1940), pp. 213-23.*

HARVEY CURTIS WEBSTER   (essay date 1947)

Reading and rereading the selections [in *On These I Stand* that] Cullen himself made from his six volumes of verse, one re-experiences the varied reactions his career provoked. *Color* . . . promised more than any other first volume that had been written by an American Negro. Although most of the poems were about social-racial ironies, the range of substance was very broad compared, say, to the range of Dunbar and Johnson. . . . Altogether, it seemed that Cullen was an unusually gifted craftsman who might, if he developed an original reading of life and a style peculiarly his own, become a poet of great distinction.

The too quickly following *Copper Sun* . . . was almost totally mediocre. Except for the unusually complex dexterity of the close of *To Endymion* and the amusing irony, *More Than a Fool's Song*, all of this volume consists of banal race poems or exercises in the imitation of Millay or Housman. *Ballad of the Brown Girl* . . . was better, an expert retelling of one of the oldest ballads of race prejudice. *The Black Christ* . . . Cullen's most ambitious volume to date, included a variety of metrical experiments (a tetrameter sonnet, a poem in dimeter), a number of poems in which an integrating figure controls the whole, . . . and a long narrative about a lynched Negro, who, like Christ, rises from the dead. Unfortunately, the lynch narrative seems strained—altogether inferior to Richard Wright's prose story, *Big Boy Leaves Home*, for example—and the experiments are uniformly failures. The poems that do succeed continue to be occasional in substance, conventional in technique: *That Bright Chimeric Beast; At a Parting; Ghosts.*

But *The Medea and Other Poems* . . . promised again and more maturely. In the short poems . . . he developed a more complex and daring use of imagery than he had ever employed before. Such poems as *Only the Polished Skeleton* and *What I Am Saying Now Was Said Before* suggest that he had been reading older and modern metaphysical poets with great profit. But nobody noticed the development and this was the last volume of serious verse Cullen published during the eleven remaining years of his life. (pp. 222-24)

Probably no-one can tell just how or why Cullen's promise faded into mediocre fulfillment, but it is possible to suggest some of the reasons. Cullen neither accepted nor developed a comprehensive world-view. As a consequence, his poems seem to result from occasional impulses rather than from direction by an integrated individual. Unlike Hardy, Yeats, Eliot, and Frost—and like hundreds of modern poets—he reacted to parts of the world—love, dancing girls, Scottsboro, Christmas, The-Snake-That-Walked-Upon-His-Tail—as if they had no relationship to each other or to any pattern in the universe. He was, in other words, an able and perplexed intelligence and a sensitive and confused heart.

Cullen was singularly unaware of what was going on in the world of poetry. In the age of Pound and Eliot, he tortured syntax and used such words as "aught" and "albeit." He nowhere shows any evidence of studying the styles of any modern poets other than Millay, Wylie, and Housman, although, according to Robert Hillyer, he wrote imitations of most of the older poets in the days at Harvard that preceded the publication of *Color*. Perhaps because of his failure to absorb the technical discoveries of his contemporaries, he was singularly unselfcritical and could allow such monstrosities as *Dear Friends and Gentle Hearts* to be printed. Certainly his failure to study carefully what other poets did is in part responsible for his never developing a style peculiarly his own. Even the good poems in *On These I Stand* could have been written by any other talented craftsman, they bear no stylistic signature. (pp. 224-25)

One of Cullen's great misfortunes must have been that he was usually commended by both Negroes and whites for extra-poetic reasons. He was praised by Negroes because he was a Negro of distinction, by whites because they feared dispraise might be called prejudice. Consequently, Cullen's poetry was never severely and sympathetically criticized while he was alive to benefit by it. (p. 225)

> *Harvey Curtis Webster, "A Difficult Career," in* Poetry (© *1947 by The Modern Poetry Association; reprinted by permission of the Editor of* Poetry), *Vol. LXX, No. IV, July, 1947, pp. 222-25.*

WILLIAM STANLEY BRAITHWAITE (essay date 1947)

[What] did Countee Cullen stand for as a poet, and as a poet who was also a Negro? He has given a partial answer to this question in that famous and often quoted couplet closing the sonnet "Yet Do I Marvel."

> Yet do I marvel at this curious thing:
> To make a poet black, and bid him sing.

Now some critics have demanded that because a poet is *black* he must sing always with a social and ethnical implication, and that his importance lies in the degree to which his propaganda is vital and colorful rather than in the quality of his work as an artist. A recent review of [*On These I Stand*] in an important publication, though not by a particularly discerning reviewer, made this demand, and

not being satisfied that Countee Cullen was painfully social or histrionically ethnical denied him the full accomplishment as a poet to which he is entitled. Such a mind, and others like it, miss wholly both the ideas and evocative emotions of poems like "Heritage" and "The Black Christ," to name but two poems where the triumphant nature and power of the poet transcends racial limitations while at the same time, in treating a racial theme, bestows upon it a universal significance.

Countee Cullen as a poet was a traditionalist in line with the great English poets, and an apostle of beauty with the fountainhead of his inspiration in the poetic philosophy of John Keats. If his imagination was scorched by the injustice and oppression of a people with whom his lot was thrown, like Keats whose sensitive nature was also wounded, he soared, not by way of escape, but by precept and counsel, into the abstract realm of the spirit. . . .

No poet we have as yet produced was so complete and spontaneous a master of the poetic technique as Countee Cullen. His octosyllabic line has not been more skilfully handled by any modern poet. He has used the sonnet for many moods and themes and carved its fourteen lines of varied temper and structure with a lyrical unity that earns him a place in the company of Wordsworth, Rossetti and Bridges. He possessed an epigrammatic gift and turn of wit that gave uncommon delight as witnessed in the series of "Epitaphs" among which the one "For a Mouthy Woman" is a masterpiece. His translations from Baudelaire, especially the sinuous felinity of cats, rank with those of Swinburne, Arthur Symons and George Dillon, in the rendering of that feverish and fantastic French poet into English. The fantasy of the "Wakeupworld" from the mythical narrative of "The Lost Zoo," established his poetic kinship in imaginative humor to the delightful foolery of Richard H. Barham's "Ingoldsby Legends."

No one will deny that Countee Cullen escaped the aches that come to a sensitive spirit aware of racial prejudice and insult, but he did not allow them to distort or distemper the ideals and visions which endowed him as an artist and poet. He had as deep a sensibility for the human denials and aches, which absorbed the lesser racial ones, and strove through the exquisite creation of imagery and music to evoke and communicate the spirit of Beauty as a solacing and restorative power. Time will, I think, accept him on the spiritual terms he set for himself in the poem "To John Keats, the Poet at Spring Time," and know that though he could sing a "Ballad for a Brown Girl" and make a "Litany of the Dark People" the blood and soul of mankind were alike in its passions and aspirations.

> *William Stanley Braithwaite, "New Books: 'On These I Stand',"* in Opportunity (*copyright 1947 by National Urban League, Inc.*), *Vol. XXV, No. 3, July-September, 1947, p. 170.*

ARTHUR P. DAVIS (essay date 1953)

In poem after poem, Cullen states or implies that the Negro in America is a perpetual alien, an exile from a beautiful sun-drenched Africa, his lost home land. As an alien, he suffers all of the insult, injustice and humiliation which unassimilated foreigners endure; and, as a consequence, he naturally possesses the mistreated alien's deep resentment against and distrust of his adopted country. For Cullen, the

Negro is both a geographical and a spiritual exile. He has not only an idyllic homeland; but equally as important, he has also lost understanding pagan gods who would be far more sympathetic to his peculiar needs than the pale Christian deities. This latter loss was extremely important to Cullen, as we shall see later; but both aspects of the alien-and-exile theme are significant and are basic to a full understanding of his racial poems. (p. 390)

Africa in his poems is not a place but a symbol; it is an idealized land in which the Negro had once been happy, kingly, a background for the heroic characters in his early poems, so Cullen postulated for the Negro a beautiful past existence in this mythical Africa. The point of many of these racial poems is an implied tragic contrast between the Negro's present state as an oppressed alien and that happy existence long, long ago in his native land. This, in brief, is the alien-and-exile theme as found in Cullen's works.

With this overall pattern in mind let us turn now to the various aspect of the theme, the first of which is: the alien's sad remembrance of a lost paradise. For example, in "Brown Boy to Brown Girl," the young man assures his loved one that "these alien skies do not our whole life measure and confine," but that "once in a land of scarlet suns" we found a quiet place to love. Our love, he is saying, cannot be wholly satisfactory here because we are despised exiles, but let us take comfort in remembering a happier day for our people. (pp. 390-91)

All of the superior qualities in the alien are to be traced to the mother country. For Cullen, the swift-footed "Atlantic City Waiter" is not just another efficient servant; his feet have been shaped through "ten thousand years on jungle clues," and though he smiles and is deceptively gracious, he remembers his old freedom, and behind his "acquiescent mask" the jungle flames through.

The Negro's former royal qualities are played up in many of these poems, for there were fabulous African kings and queens in the days before the exile. Jim the handsome hero of "Black Christ" is described as being of "imperial breed"; the dark heroine in *The Ballad of the Brown Girl* "comes of kings" and her dagger had once been used by a "dusky queen" in a faraway "dusky dream-lit land." After reading Vandercook's *Black Majesty,* a "chronicle of sable glory" dealing with the Haitian rulers, Cullen used the title of the work for one of his better sonnets. In this sonnet he points out to the "dark guttersnipe, black sprawler-in-the-mud" modern Negro that Christophe and Dessalines though black had once been kings, and "a thing men did a man may do again." The exile must ever keep his former greatness before him as solace and as inspiration.

The two longest poems in *Color* are the most revealing examples of Cullen's use of the Africa theme. The first of these, "The Shroud of Color," though far too wordy and abstract to be a good poem, is highly interesting because it is so typical of the poet's racial attitude at the time. . . . [The poem] gives one important aspect of the alien-and-exile theme—the constant "pull" of the jungle on the civilized Negro. . . . (pp. 391-92)

This pull of the home land, this appeal of Africa to the alien's "echoing breast," giving him freedom from the agony of exile living, is much more brilliantly stated in the second poem, "Heritage," one of Mr. Cullen's finest works. . . . What the poem [says] is simply this: the Amer-

ican Negro, hopelessly frustrated by the horrible ugliness of Jim Crow living, as one means of escape, must create in his own mind a beautiful world—a dream world, if you will, of past loveliness—to which he can turn for consolation and relief. In short, it is the typical romantic search for a better world in the distant past and in a "far countree." This, it seems to me, is the message of all of these glorification-of-Africa poems in the works of Cullen.

Let us turn now to another aspect of the alien-and-exile theme: the practical, everyday means taken by the Negro to obtain relief from the crushing burden of race. One obvious way of escape is through superiority, that is, excelling the oppressor. . . . (pp. 392-93)

There is also another and a deeper kind of superiority that the black man may possess. It is the kind that comes from suffering. . . . The compensatory wisdom that comes from oppression lifts the black soul above the oppressor's power to insult and hurt.

Another way out for the alien is to glorify his differences, to make attractive those racial characteristics which the other world ridicules. . . . (pp. 393-94)

Suicide is always a means of release when the alien's cup becomes too full to bear, and we are not surprised to note how many of Cullen's poems are concerned with this theme. "The Wise," "Suicide Chant," "The Shroud of Color," "Harsh World That Lashest Me," and "Mood" all deal with suicide. . . . Death, too, is a way of escape, bringing not only rest for the weary alien but also an explanation of his suffering. (pp. 395-96)

One of Cullen's best sonnets, "From the Dark Tower," deals with this theme, expressing in moving terms the black man's belief that he will some day take his rightful place in the sun. . . .

These then are some ways of escape for the Negro in an alien world, and we note here an interesting fact: Except in the lines of *The Black Christ* (and they are subsequently repudiated), Cullen nowhere makes a frontal attack on American injustice. Nevertheless, he has built up by suggestion and implication a most devastating picture of the Negro's plight in America—a picture showing a helpless, black and degraded minority, cut off from the beauty and fullness of majority living, desperately and futilely grasping at straws of consolation and escape.

As this is Cullen's pattern of protest one may well ask at this point, how effective is it as a type? Is it too subtle and vague and indirect? Is it too intellectual for the average reader? Does it suffer by comparison with the bluntness and directness of the protest methods of [Langston] Hughes and [Claude] McKay? I believe the answers to most of these questions must be in the affirmative. Cullen, it seems to me, was handicapped as a protest poet by his central theme. The average reader, failing to understand that Cullen relied on the basic alien-and-exile theme to give meaning to many of his racial poems, oftentimes overlooked the full significance of these works. Moreover, the theme itself has been a difficult one for the Negro to accept. In spite of its appropriateness and essential truth, the idea that we are cultural aliens and exiles has never been seriously entertained by any considerable number of American Negroes. No matter how much he has been thrust "outside" by prejudice and segregation, the Negro still considers himself an American; he, therefore, is incapable of becoming enthusiastic about a hypothetical home land in Africa. So deeply ingrained is this core of Americanism, he cannot even "poetically" conceive of himself as an alien and exile. It is this rejection . . . of Cullen's basic theme which destroys some of his effectiveness as a protest poet. (p. 396)

As stated above, for Cullen the Negro was a spiritual as well as a geographical exile, having lost along with his home land the sympathetic pagan gods of Africa. In Christianity with its doctrine of restraint and the other cheek, the exile cannot find an answer to the questions of his dark and rebellious heart. . . . In "Gods," the poet states that heaven's "alabaster turrets" are too high for him; there are "other" gods that "revel" in his pagan heart, and unless the Almighty allows him to bring his gods in, salvation is out of the question. The strongest expression of this pagan attitude is found in the latter part of "Heritage." After confessing sympathy for "quaint, outlandish heathen gods, black men fashion out of rods," the poet pleads guilty to rank hypocrisy on his own part. . . . He wishes God were dark so that he could have some "precedent of pain" to give Him understanding of the black man's oppressed and sorrow-laden soul.

Although here as elsewhere we must not take the poet's statements literally, Countee Cullen at the time . . . really felt very strongly on the pagan-Christian question. . . . As he grew older he seemed more and more inclined to repudiate his early pagan beliefs. Let us trace briefly the progress of this change of heart.

In *Color* . . . , as we have seen, the prevailing attitude is boldly and frankly pagan, and at least one poem is pantheistic in nature. In *Copper Sun* . . . the mood begins to change, and we find a tendency on the part of Cullen to return to the Christian fold. Even though there is a hint of scepticism in "Epilogue," the poem "In Spite of Death" seems to imply faith in an after-life; and "The Litany of the Dark People" reads like a direct denial of the stand taken in "Heritage" and "Pagan Prayer." . . . This attitude of repudiation comes to full cycle in *The Black Christ*. . . . In "Counter Mood" we have what is tantamount to a confession of Christian faith. . . . The title-poem in *The Black Christ* volume is a racial saint's legend of deep and moving faith, and as such represents an even more emphatic denial of the poet's youthful paganism. Cullen has made the heroic mother of the poem a symbol of the power of orthodox faith; and to show his complete change of heart, he parades all of his old antagonism against Christianity in order to repudiate it through the miracle which climaxes the narrative. The poem is really a *debat* between the pagan, younger Cullen and the reclaimed Cullen of 1929, which the latter wins. And what is equally significant, the poet seems through the mother to be repudiating the alien-and-exile attitude toward America which his earlier volumes expressed. . . . The mother certainly does not consider herself an alien or an outsider. This is her land, her home in spite of oppression and hate. If we take the mother's stand as Cullen's message in this poem, he seems to imply that a deep religious faith will overcome all racial difficulties; all we have to do is "love, trust, and wait."

With *The Black Christ* volume, Cullen took leave of that narrow concern with racial matters which had characterized his poetry up to and including that work. . . . From now on,

he [says in "To Certain Critics"], "no racial option" will circumscribe my subject matter; I shall write as a free man. And he stuck to this resolve. He wrote no more poems on the alien-and-exile theme and precious few of any kind touching on race. (pp. 396-99)

Why did Countee Cullen drop racial poetry so suddenly and completely? What happened after the publication of *The Black Christ* to dry up the springs of racial verse? It has been argued that Cullen turned from racial themes because he came to feel too keenly the inner conflict which his status as poet and Negro imposed upon him. . . . Undeniably, Cullen the poet was disturbed by the added burden of race, but I am inclined to believe that he turned from racial themes for a much more realistic and down-to-earth cause; namely, a consciousness of waning powers in this particular area of poetry. He had worked the racial lode to depletion, and he realized it. . . . Cullen's heart had had its say on the matter of race, and he preferred a "stony silence" to futile sound. We can easily understand his position. After all, there are only so many things that one can say on the race problem. The alien-and-exile theme with its glorification of Africa had become discredited even while Cullen was using it. Protest, like religion, is a very narrow subject for poetry. (pp. 399-400)

Arthur P. Davis, "The Alien-and-Exile Theme in Countee Cullen's Racial Poems," in PHYLON: The Atlanta University Review of Race and Culture, 14 *(copyright, 1953, by Atlanta University; reprinted by permission of* PHYLON*), Vol. XIV, No. 4, Fourth Quarter (December, 1953), pp. 390-400.*

JEAN WAGNER (essay date 1962)

Together with Claude McKay, Countee Cullen was the black poet gifted with the most intense inner life, but he was also a most tormented personality. The particular circumstances surrounding his youthful years, an intellectual preparation acquired almost entirely outside his racial milieu, and, furthermore, particularly haunting personal problems—these were some of the influences that help to explain the strange note sounded by his lyric poetry. Its tone constituted a seemingly impassable barrier between the poet and the people of his own race.

Cullen, for them, soon became a great, misunderstood figure, and he found their lack of comprehension a burden hard to bear. But his direct experience of suffering was, for his inner life, a source of extraordinary enrichment.

His lyric gift was incontestable and, indeed, exceptional. But his poetry has none of McKay's fiery virility, and the treasures it encloses are, rather, those of a soul that at times indulged in an excess of sensibility and preferred to express itself in the half-tones and nuances of a high scrupulousness. (p. 283)

[The] real substance of his lyric gift came from his individual experience at least as much as, if not more than, from the experience of the racial group to which he belonged and against whose encroachments he never ceased to defend himself with vigor. Even at those moments when the poetic élan is most directly inspired by his color, his individual voice always dominates that of the group.

Thus it is hardly possible to treat him fairly unless one

takes good care to allot its proper share to each of these two elements. (pp. 292-93)

[What] an excessive burden the shame of his origins was for him: the shame of his birth, which diminished him in his own eyes; the shame of the sin which, as he envisaged it, surrounded the circumstances of his adoption, and which exposed him to God's judgment; and especially the shame he felt at his color, whch debased him in the eyes of other men and bent him beneath a weight he longed to shake off in death. (p. 293)

Nor can there by any doubt that his feeling of inferiority is also derived, by a more direct route, from his partial or total inability to lead a normal sexual life. Where he sees a sin committed before God, in the physical reality there is also a humiliating defeat before the love of woman. His marriage demonstrates this, and the poet is not oblivious of the fact. (p. 295)

The sense of inferiority that overwhelmed him did not have a purely racial cause, and one must take fully into account the other emotional perturbations we have noted if one wishes to understand why Cullen, unlike the other poets of the Negro Renaissance, did not regard his race primarily as an object of pride. (pp. 295-96)

An examination of the tendencies manifested in the evolution of his poetic themes enables one to distinguish, in Cullen's work, two different periods marked off by the moment of reassessment represented in his life by the year 1927.

In his inner development, the primacy of race is scarcely noticeable after an early extroverted phase, during which his behavior tended to seek an adjustment to the surrounding environment. This reaction to racial tensions is an instinctive phenomenon, on a par with the attitude of most of his racial brothers. There is no point in looking elsewhere for any deeper reason that would explain the success of *Color* . . . from the moment of its publication. When he sang of the burden of color and of its nobility. . . . and above all when he nostalgically evoked the memory of the African homeland, black America had no difficulty in recognizing its own states of soul in those of the poet. (p. 302)

Despite surface appearances, his racial experience was indeed but one factor in what might be called his problem, and the basic urge behind his poetry must be sought in his scruples of conscience. . . .

Even while Cullen was exploring the dimensions of his color, there occurred an imperceptible shift in its value. Its significance, which had been a collective one, now shrank until it corresponded to the limits of the poet's individual consciousness. As the demands of the spirit grew more insistent, color itself became spiritualized and amounted, in the end, to no more than an array of symbols that swirled around Cullen's reflection on his destiny.

This tenuous thread of symbolism, whose purely inner relevancy was not at first appreciated, enabled the racial community to maintain for some time longer the illusion that, through a shared loyalty to color, it was in communication with the poet. But they were no longer speaking a common language. The poet's eyes, raised above the contingency of race, were already turned toward the Creator who bore the ultimate responsibility and to whom he, the black poet-prophet, sought to lead his whole people. Unfortunately, his own followed him not on the rugged paths of the spirit.

Little by little, a gulf widened between them and him, so that the poet found himself a stranger in the midst of his own people. His lonely itinerary to the heights then became an actual Calvary on whose summit he, like another Christ, was crucified between the exigencies of his color and his loyalty to his individual ideal. . . . Thus the first period is followed by one characterized by introversion, during which Cullen retreats ever further within himself. He has not severed all contacts with the external world, but this world is ever more often experienced as a cause of suffering for which he seeks a balm in his mystic dialogue with Christ.

It need scarcely be said that there is no absolute rupture between these two phases of his inner development. The last echoes of the African theme still resound faintly in [*The Black Christ*], and the colloquy with Christ had been inaugurated in *Color*. From one end of his work to the other, and more markedly than in the case of any other black poet, color and spirituality are inextricably intertwined. But as the former loses importance, his spiritual preoccupations take on ever clearer shape and soon outrank all else.

It is a change of course that happens rather early in the poet's career, and by the time *Copper Sun* was published . . . it may be considered an established fact. The critics were quite taken aback by that volume. Meeting with hardly any of the racial hyperboles they had noted in *Color,* they reached the conclusion, as we have seen, that the writer "has borrowed the temperament of his poems," and that his verse no longer had its source in his own inner experience. In a word, the blunt indictment was that his lines lacked sincerity.

Cullen is already a much more characteristic product of the black bourgeoisie, having been exposed to all its pressures as he grew up in the Harlem home of a Methodist minister. The whole course of his education took place in schools and universities with a majority of whites, and theirs were the standards and prejudices he unconsciously absorbed. He had scarcely any close associations with the people of his own race, and he had no sense of communion with them. The people, as a result, make no genuine contribution to his work in verse, and popular Negro themes and forms are entirely absent from it.

It would even seem that Cullen always sensed the existence of some incompatibility between restrictions of any kind that might be imposed on the poet because of his color, and the universality that is the distinguishing mark of poetry. . . . In any event, up to the very end Cullen will maintain his determination to be independent of his racial group, even at the risk of being called a traitor by his own. . . . (pp. 307-08)

Among the religious themes of which Cullen's poetry has an unusual abundance, exceptional importance is given to Christ's figure, which haunted the poet throughout his life. Every volume of his poetry, except perhaps *The Medea,* turns to the theme which, in his mind, was to have found its culmination in his longest poem, "The Black Christ," published three years after his visit to Jerusalem. (p. 329)

Even at those moments when Christ appeared to him most hostile, Cullen thirsts for the Christian ideal of perfection and self-transcendence, and no one could have suffered more than he did from the sense of guilt that awareness of his sinfulness aroused in him. But since he found himself on hostile terms with Christ on the spiritual plane because of his sin, and on the racial plane also because Christ seemed to have abandoned the black race, it was tempting to unite the two terms on either side of the barrier—to promote the urges of the flesh to the rank of a positive value, indeed, of a black value that had been consecrated by the African gods who thus came to challenge the place held in his soul by the white Christ. . . . (p. 332)

In the Negro folk tradition that predated Cullen, blacks had become accustomed to recognizing themselves in the Hebrew people, the chosen of God, whereas white people, especially southern whites, were equated with the Egyptians and their Pharaoh, who held captive the people of Israel. The choice of the crucified Christ to symbolize the lynched Negro was a new idea, and it appears that its originator was indeed Cullen. (p. 335)

The poet, after making Christ black, shows his dexterity by treating his color as worse than a crime. . . .

But not only in the person of the lynched Negro is Christ's sacrifice undergone once more. His Calvary prefigures also that of the whole black people, crowned with thorns and crucified on a cross of the same color as the oppressors, for this people, after having foresworn the ancestors' African gods, had entrusted itself completely to Christ, for better and for worse. . . . (p. 336)

His mystic intimacy with Christ finds its culmination in "The Black Christ." This great poem is also his spiritual testament, where all the fundamental themes of his poetic achievement are taken up once more and placed in their ultimate perspective. (p. 341)

[The scope of "The Black Christ"] would be lost if one paid attention only to the narrative aspect, for with Cullen this is also, ultimately, a way of activating symbols so that they may confront one another. In this perspective, "The Black Christ" is a masterly reconstruction of the poet's inner drama. It retraces the long debate, already launched in "Heritage," whose protagonists are incredulity and faith, each of these parties to the confrontation being endowed with its entire accompaniment of racial and personal overtones, which in this poem are orchestrated into an imposing *da capo*.

In this internal confrontation, in which the poet functions not only as the narrator but also as the moderator whose role it is to synthesize the opposing elements, the mother stands for the people's unshakable Christian faith. She is one of the humble who believe without having seen and to whom, for this reason, the Lord has revealed mighty things he keeps hidden from the proud and the argumentative.

The voice of the mother, as she speaks to her son in the humble setting of a southern cabin, at the same time is clearly that of faith speaking to the poet within his own heart. But the mother represents more than faith. She also symbolizes the people and, beyond them, the doubly ungrateful southern soil from which they draw their deep roots.

Thus Countee Cullen discovers . . . the perennial strength of the trinity made up of earth, folk, and faith, all irrational values against which the young intellectual had revelled in fiery protest in the days when he was winning his first triumphs as a poet.

Standing over against the values represented by the mother is the figure of Jim, who in many respects might well be looked on as the incarnation of the "New Negro." His whole being breathes pride of race and intolerance of any yoke. He also symbolizes the religious skepticism that sprang up in the heart of a whole race that had to witness unpunished injustice. (pp. 343-44)

One is reminded of Keats in reading the celebration of spring that is placed at the beginning of Jim's speech, as he is about to tell how the white man came upon him unawares. From the narrative point of view, this forms too lengthy a parenthesis, but because of its symbolic value it rounds out the portrait of Jim. It cannot be doubted that in it Cullen sought to depict everything within himself that represented an obstacle on the path that ultimately led him to God.

The arguments advanced by the mother and by Jim do battle, throughout the poem, in the poet's own heart, and doubt appears to be on the point of winning when, after the lynching has been carried out and the mother and her surviving son abandon themselves to their grief inside their cabin, Jim suddenly manifests himself in the glory of his resurrection. Before this revelation of divine power and mercy, doubt finally is routed forever and the poet, another Doubting Thomas, falls to his knees. He is overcome with remorse at the thought of all the blasphemies he had hurled at God, and which have been answered by the Divine mercy.

It is easy to understand why this long poem of 963 lines finally lost Cullen the sympathies of the black public. For the poem, with its mystical character, and despite the title and the theme of the narrative, is not essentially Negro in any way. Its very mysticism was condemned as childish, and one critic actually reproached the author for having dated the poem from Paris. (pp. 345-46)

"The Black Christ" must be read as a poem of thanksgiving for the bestowal of the light of faith, as well as the translation into words of a contemplative experience. The religious exaltation that dictates the poem's entire structure bears the marks of the neophyte's sense of wonderment and his whole touching naïveté. With such characteristics, however, "The Black Christ" was inevitably inaccessible to all but a handful of readers.

It must be confessed that the poem has all the defects that correspond to its virtues. A mystical experience always retains a certain incommunicability, and in the present case the reader has to make a considerable effort of self-adaptation to remain attuned to the poet who, in his exaltation, sometimes leaves all trammels so far behind that he falls into incoherence and neglects the external form. The tetrameter, which he had always favored and which he uses throughout the poem, may be appropriate for the narrative passages, but the prolonged meditations, which occupy an important place, might have moved more freely in a less constricting meter. The presence of rhyme, too, disposed with impenetrable arbitrariness, awakens a vague malaise and does injury to the sobriety of the whole. (pp. 346-47)

These reservations made, it must be avowed that this most sustained effort of Cullen's poetic inspiration finds, to the very end, accents of a deeply moving sincerity, and the undeniable beauty of a number of scenes within this great poetic fresco bespeaks the writer's quality of soul no less than his genius. . . .

[While] he appears to have discovered the permanent value embodied by the people, it is less likely that his sympathy went beyond the strictly spiritual. He had grown up apart from the people, and to the very end the people seem to have remained an abstraction for him.

All in all, and in spite of its extraordinary density, his poetic achievement will stand less as a mirroring of the black soul than as a living testimony to the great spiritual adventure of a poet named Countee Cullen. (p. 347)

> *Jean Wagner, "Countee Cullen," in his* Black Poets of the United States: From Paul Laurence Dunbar to Langston Hughes, *translated by Kenneth Douglas (copyright 1973 by the Board of Trustees of the University of Illinois; reprinted by permission of the author; originally published as* Les poètes nègres des Etats-Unis, *Librairie Istra, Paris, 1962), University of Illinois Press, 1973, pp. 351-77.*

ROBERT BONE (essay date 1965)

Among the poets of the Negro Renaissance there was none more talented than Countee Cullen.... [He] was more sophisticated in technique and choice of subject than most Negro poets of the period. A Keatsian idiom, a biblical emphasis on moral paradox, and a somewhat self-conscious espousal of African primitivism are the distinguishing characteristics of his verse....

Countee Cullen has often been described as one of the more "respectable" Renaissance novelists, with the implication that he avoided the "sordid" subject matter of the Harlem School. Nothing could be farther from the truth. Cullen neither exploited low-life material for its own sake nor avoided it when it served his artistic ends. Though distinctly not of a Bohemian temperament, neither did he value respectability above art. His mischievous sense of humor and his penchant for satire differentiated him from those Renaissance novelists who were forever defending the race before the bar of white opinion. Countee Cullen had a lighter and truer touch, which speaks for itself in *One Way to Heaven*.

Sam Lucas, the protagonist of the novel, is as typical a Harlem-School creation as Banjo or Jimboy. With the help of a missing arm, he makes his living as a professional convert. (p. 78)

The narrative interest of *One Way to Heaven* centers upon Sam's relationship with Mattie Johnson, an attractive, hard-working dark girl. (pp. 78-9)

The aesthetic design of the novel consists of variations on a theme. The moral ambiguity of Sam's life and death is echoed in the lives of the other characters. Both the evangelist and the Reverend Drummond are sincere men of God, but neither is above a little showmanship for the Lord's sake.... The author's point is clear: he that is without sin among you, let him cast the first stone at Sam Lucas.

Sam's cards and razor provide an appropriate symbol for Cullen's theme. Like people, the cards and razor contain potentialities for either good or evil. In Sam's hands, they are the tools of deceit, yet they are no less the instruments of Mattie's salvation.... In Cullen's view the moral universe is infinitely complex. Form is unimportant; there is more than one way to heaven.

Attached to the main body of the novel by the thinnest of threads is a subplot which deals satirically with Harlem's intelligentsia. By the simple expedient of hiring Mattie out to Harlem's most popular hostess, Cullen creates a vantage point from which to launch his barbs. Constancia Brandon's *soirées* are attended by Harlem socialites, New Negro poets, inquisitive white intellectuals, Garveyites, and even a Southern Bourbon. Cullen deflates them all indiscriminately, exposing their foibles while respecting their essential humanity. Yet it is difficult to see how these satirical episodes are related to the rest of the novel. Clever but shallow sketches, they do not approach the depth of moral insight which Cullen achieves through Sam and Mattie.

In spite of its faults, *One Way to Heaven* overshadows the average Renaissance novel. Countee Cullen has a poet's way with words, for which much can be overlooked. He also has a sure instinct for drama, which at times invests the novel with surprising power. He manages symbols skillfully, and for the most part achieves convincing characterization. Yet in making a final appraisal, it is difficult to disagree with Blyden Jackson, one of the younger Negro critics, who speaks of Countee Cullen's *two* novels: the one "with the charm of a fairy tale," the other "too stilted and self-conscious for good satire." (pp. 79-80)

> *Robert Bone, "The Harlem School," in his* The Negro Novel in America *(copyright © 1965 by Yale University), revised edition, Yale University Press, 1965, pp. 65-94.**

DARWIN T. TURNER (essay date 1971)

From the beginning in *Color* ... to the end of his poetic career in *Medea* ... Cullen was a lyricist, best when writing subjectively and most effective when his feelings derived from subjects sufficiently universal to encourage a reader's interest and, possibly, identification. (pp. 63-4)

[In the 1924 poem "The Shroud of Color,"] Cullen prophesied his future psychological agonies. At twenty he refused to base his reason for living on either God or white men. In all of nature only the black man could inspire him. But what if he lost this one faith? Then nothing would remain for him except the desire to die.

In 1925 Harper and Brothers published *Color,* which is heavily weighted with poems oriented to racial consciousness. Twenty-three poems, approximately one-third of the book, focus on Afro-Americans. Included are some of his best-known poems: "Yet Do I Marvel," "A Brown Girl Dead," "Incident," "Saturday's Child," "The Shroud of Color," and "Heritage."

The despair of "The Shroud of Color" is underscored in the couplet which ends his sonnet, "Yet Do I Marvel." ... Although he accepts even the seemingly paradoxical blindness, death, tortures, and frustrations of life, he, nevertheless, is amazed that God would expect unrestrained artistic expression from one restricted and oppressed because of the color of his skin.

In the other poems, however, Cullen did not despair. Instead he praised the courage and the beauty of Afro-Americans, exulted in their glory, exuded sympathy for them, and chanted his faith in his heritage. In "To My Fairer Brethren," for example, he boasted of achievements by blacks, who must defeat their white brothers three times before the victory is considered anything other than an accident.

In *Color,* Cullen perpetuated the unprovable idea that African heritage endows a black man with passion and rhythm superior to a white man's. In "A Song of Praise" he did not merely commend the beauty of the dark-skinned girl; he even demeaned the blond, whose blood is "thin and colder." In "Atlantic City Waiter" he described the graceful movements of a black waiter: "Ten thousand years on jungle clues / Alone shaped feet like these."

A popular stereotype of the Afro-American in twentieth century American literature is that of a child of nature, whose uninhibited behavior is directed by unrestrainable passion, innate rhythm, and an inherent talent for music. . . . Whereas some blacks have exploited the myth consciously, others, like Cullen, have succumbed to it. (pp. 66-7)

Cullen's atavistic urge is most apparent in "Heritage," the lyric cry of a civilized mind which cannot silence the memories of Africa that thrill the blood, of a heart which responds to rain and which, prostrate before the Christian altar, yearns for a black god who might comprehend suffering as no white god can. Despite the atavism, "Heritage," which surpasses "The Shroud of Color" in imagery and diction, is the most successful lyric poem Cullen ever wrote.

Only one-third of *Color* is concerned with Afro-Americans. The other two-thirds include a section of epitaphs, a section of love poems, and a section of poems on miscellaneous subjects. Skillfully chiseled cameos, the epitaphs reveal Cullen's ability to compress thought and image. . . . Anarchists, evolutionists, atheists, pessimists, philosophers, unsuccessful sinners, fools, skeptics, fatalists, wantons, heroes, and saints: all earn appropriate four-line summations. But he emphathizes most with wantons and fools, and he praises most highly the people who wisely have seized every treasurable pleasure from life's brief course.

In many of the miscellaneous poems, Cullen revealed significant elements of his thought. There is an abundance of love poems on the "carpe-diem" theme. A reminder of Cullen's habitual sympathy for outcasts echoes from his speculation that Jesus commanded Judas to betray Him so that His mission would be fulfilled. In four poems, Cullen repeated the death wish of "The Shroud of Color." Although the yearning for death is not unexpected in poetry written by sensitive youths, the juxtaposition of this theme and the "carpe-diem" theme of other poems suggests that his occasional challenge to life was merely a mood which could evanesce into despair. His brash boast to battle the world in "Harsh World That Lashest Me" ends with a reminder that he can leave whenever he wishes. (pp. 68-9)

Although they were his first, the poems of *Color* are representative of the talent which he maintained throughout his writing. His poetry differs from that of Paul Laurence Dunbar or Jean Toomer. More specific and more thoughtful than Dunbar in imagery but less impressionistic than Toomer, he concentrated upon conventional rhythms, pretty images, and provocative thought.

Cullen did not experiment with rhyme and meter; his needs were satisfied by iambics in four- or five-foot lines, ballad meter, rhymed couplets, and blank verse. Generally, he handled metrics competently; however, he sometimes faltered. (p. 69)

He pictured more precisely than Dunbar did, but he lacked the sensuousness of John Keats or even Toomer. In carefully chosen phrases, he communicated emotions through the mind and the eye rather than through the senses or the blood. He succeeded in such lines as, "for a fitful space let my head lie / Happily on your passion's frigid breast;" and his description of life in Africa—"a land of scarlet suns / And brooding winds, before the hurricane / Bore down upon us;"—or such an effective phrase as, "My heart is pagan mad." . . . Perhaps the major weakness is that a reader becomes too conscious of the craftsman manipulating deceptively simple phrases, of the artist who occasionally delighted in irony and deliberate ambiguity. (pp. 69-70)

Despite occasional flashes of brilliance which remind a reader of his potential for greatness, Cullen failed to distinguish himself in *Copper Sun.* He reexamined racial themes which he had explored previously in *Color.* Too frequently, he wrote phrases and images which echo artistically superior passages from Percy Shelley, John Donne, Edna St. Vincent Millay, and A. E. Housman. He included several love poems which are so personal or so petty that they cannot evoke empathy from sensitive readers. He wasted paradoxes, conceits, and sparkling images on trivial subjects and themes.

Nevertheless, despite Cullen's limitations, *Copper Sun* is not a poor book. Some poems are quite good. "From the Dark Tower" is one of his most respected poems despite its ambiguous ending. "Lovers of the Earth: Fair Warning" and "More than a Fool's Song" present provocative thought about the values of life and about social outcasts. If *Copper Sun* had appeared before *Color,* it would have persuaded readers to anticipate masterful lyrics by the author in his more mature years. Published after *Color,* however, it disappointed readers because it evidenced no significant improvement in metrics, imagery, or thought. In fact, Cullen seemed to be weakening rather than improving. (pp. 73-4)

[His next volume, *The Black Christ,*] is an unpleasant book. The imagery and the language evoke admiration. But the subject matter produces embarrassment comparable to that experienced when, visiting during a domestic quarrel, one is compelled to listen to the self-pitying despair of someone who cannot, who will not, be consoled.

Amid the self-pitying cries and childishly petulant defiances are some well-conceived poems and vivid images. (p. 74)

The best poem in the book is the title poem, "The Black Christ," the story of a miracle which converted the black narrator from atheism to a belief that Christ will save the world. (p. 75)

"The Black Christ" is an impressive failure. Cullen proved his ability to sustain lyric intensity throughout a long poem. He created images as effective as any others in his poetry, and he created persuasive, although somewhat stereotyped characters. Above all, he skillfully developed a somber mood through subtle contrasts: nature's springtime beauty is scarred by man's ugliness; the innocence of [black] Jim's friendship with the [white] girl is soiled by the lascivious inferences of the white man who sees them; skeptical, rebellious Jim contrasts with his mother, who suffers in the South but who refuses to leave her home.

Despite these achievements, Cullen failed both in conception and in execution. First, he carelessly contradicted his theme. Ostensibly, the theme is that each day Christ is killed by man's injustice and violence.... Yet He sacrifices Himself to save a murderer. Although he was attacked physically as well as verbally, Jim did not allege that he killed in self-defense; instead, he said that he killed the white man because the man was destroying springtime's beauty. By sacrificing Himself, Christ, therefore, sanctions murder, which, He has said, destroys Him each time it is committed. (pp. 75-6)

Cullen also revealed weaknesses in poetic techniques. By writing iambic tetrameter, he forced a sprightlier rhythm than seems appropriate for solemn incidents, and he frequently failed to sustain the metrical pattern. Furthermore, the movement is impeded by the end rhyme, and inverted or artificial phrasings evidence Cullen's willingness to sacrifice artistic expression to the demands of the rhyme scheme. (p. 77)

In 1935 Cullen published *The Medea and Some Poems*. The subtitle to "The Medea," "A New Version," suggests more changes than are apparent. When Cullen's version is compared with [Gilbert] Murray's prose translation of Euripides' play, there seem to be few significant differences in structure and characterization. Cullen departed from Euripides, however, in some interesting and revealing ways. In addition to limiting the number and the length of the choral odes—a concession to the tastes of a modern audience, he eliminated Euripides' pronouncements against divorce and his pleas for greater freedom for women. Cullen added imagery reflecting lust and greed for money, and he emphasized the alienation of Medea, an African woman who has betrayed her family for the love of an ambitious white opportunist.

The language vacillates between eloquence and colloquial stammering. Written in the idiom of twentieth-century America, the dialogue reads more smoothly than do most translations from the Greek. Yet Cullen too often sank into bathos in hackneyed colloquialisms and folk proverbs.

It is startling and distressing that King Creon, at a moment of tension, should exclaim, "Forewarned is forearmed," or "I'm not one for beating about the bush," or "Charity begins at home," or "I'm one who 'says his say'." At first, a reader presumes that Cullen consciously intended to deride the commonplace mentality of Creon, but Jason and Medea also speak tritely.... Confusing banality with naturalness in diction, Cullen failed to write either a great poetic drama or dramatic poem, for either must be measured by the excellence of its language.

Cullen's emphasis upon Medea's African ancestry, however, is significant. Even though he continued to insist upon his right to select his own subjects and ridiculed the idea that Afro-Americans should return to Africa, Cullen re-created the situation of [one of his earliest works] *The Ballad of the Brown Girl:* once again, an African woman is betrayed by a white man who has exploited her. As Medea proclaims herself a foreigner and castigates Jason for his willingness to abandon her while he seeks to ingratiate himself with the ruler of the land, a black reader suddenly perceives a new dimension in an old "Greek" story. Since it is doubtful that Cullen could have been unaware of this emphasis, which seems consciously developed, one must sur-

mise that, no matter how much he insisted upon his right to be judged without reference to his race, Cullen could not erase from his mind the conviction that whites exploit and betray blacks.

In the twenty-four original poems included in the volume with "The Medea," Cullen showed his characteristic strengths and weaknesses. Not straining for complicated measures, he contented himself with short forms which he could compose quickly. Fifteen of the poems are Shakespearean sonnets, written chiefly on the theme of lost love. He maintained greater artistic detachment than he had in *The Black Christ;* but, regardless of the subject or the theme, the mood of the shorter poems is melancholy.... He generally developed clear, appealing images, but he continued to publish carelessly finished poems. (pp. 82-4)

Two books of poetry—*Color* and *On These I Stand*—one novel—*One Way to Heaven*—and a children's story—*My Lives and How I Lost Them:* these represent the contribution to American literature by Countee Cullen, poet laureate of the Harlem Renaissance, a prodigy who failed to fulfill the promise of his first book and who ended his productivity in a world of cats and children where, free from social and literary demands, he could evoke sentiment in a smoothly narrated tale. Ariel, in mask, finally found a base on which to rest. (p. 88)

Darwin T. Turner, "Countee Cullen: The Lost Ariel," in his In a Minor Chord: Three Afro-American Writers and Their Search for Identity *(copyright © 1971 by Southern Illinois University Press; reprinted by permission of Southern Illinois University Press), Southern Illinois University Press, 1971, pp. 60-88.*

BLYDEN JACKSON and LOUIS D. RUBIN, JR.
(essay date 1974)

[Cullen] saw no incompatibility between following in the footsteps of Keats and being, at the same time, a Negro poet and a New Negro.... The lesson of his poetry seems to be, indeed, that regardless of what might have happened in his poetry had all gone exactly right, in what *did* happen, many things—the most important things—went wrong. Cullen failed to make his interest in Keats and, by extension, his affiliation with the cultural tradition of which Keats was a part, assimilate with his espousal of the interests of the New Negro. In "Heritage" Cullen is at great pains to claim kinship with Africa, just as at times elsewhere he has been at pains to claim kinship with Keats. He specifies, moreover, in "Heritage," the intensity of his ties to Africa. Africa is a continent, he contends, which is absolutely indivisible from the bone and marrow of his deepest self. It walks with "cruel padded feet" through his "body's street." It recalles itself to him in dreams. Its "quaint, outlandish heathen gods" elevate themselves in him and fight against the pale Jesus Christ upon whom the white religion of his white upbringing has sought to make him exclusively dependent.

Cullen's point is, obviously, that Africa is really his alpha and omega, that he is black not white, and that the quaint, outlandish gods, the world of the Negro African past, its beat within his blood, its ultimate sovereignty over his humanity—these are, after all, indestructible atavisms which he cannot banish from his mind or art. Moreover, in its final stanza, "Heritage" resolves itself, even though by innuendo rather than by outright statement, into a criticism of white culture, a criticism that can hardly be called less than a repudiation. Nevertheless, at the beginning of this poem, Cullen directs his gaze to Africa, seeing there its sun and sea, its jungle, and its men and women, *his* ancestors; he speaks of these ancestors as the foreparents *from whose loins he sprang,* but he speaks also of springing from those loins "when the birds of Eden sang." Yet there can be no birds of Eden in a truly African Africa. Eden comes from the very culture which Cullen is trying to demonstrate as being not a part of his fundamental self. For both Eden as a word and Eden as a concept are white. And it is Eden the concept, as well as Eden the word—and not concepts or words associated with Africa—which emanates from Cullen when he speaks off his guard and when the conditioned reflexes deeply rooted in his involuntary nervous system do express themselves without direction from his conscious intent.

Most Anglo-American poetry tends to employ an iambic beat. In "Heritage" Cullen resorts to the use of a trochaic measure. It seems valid to assume that his choice of the descending line was no accident. Under such an assumption, it also seems highly possible that in the rhythms of "Heritage" Cullen hoped to suggest the throb of African drums, for certainly the percussive movement of a trochaic line may fall upon the ear like the big and small booms of tom-toms in the African bush. Moreover, if the trochees of "Heritage" are tom-toms, and especially if they are consciously so, they might be further proof of how un-African Cullen really was. They might tell us again that Cullen's Africa existed only when Cullen was able to put his mind on what he was doing, as he could put his mind on the *selection* of a beat. So it may be that his Africa was contrived and synthetic, not integral within him as it must have been to justify the claims he makes in "Heritage" of the presence of his forefathers' continent in his "blood." How significant, then, might be Cullen's allusion in "Heritage" to rain: "I can never rest at all when the rain begins to fall." The rain brings back, that is, so Cullen is implying, the drums and Africa. And very probably it did, at the literary level. . . . (pp. 47-9)

Cullen's integrity is not at stake in his evaluation of his own credentials as a representative of his race. Neither, for that matter, is [Claude] McKay's. Both men must have sincerely believed that they were New Negroes. (pp. 49-50)

But Cullen and McKay, in spite of all the sincerity and rectitude of their professions, were in practice deficient as New Negroes. They broke, undoubtedly, with the tradition of the school of Negro dialect. They repudiated the plantation school. Consciously, they satirized the "dicty." What they could not, or certainly did not, do was to break with their own conditioned reflexes, reflexes dependent upon their experience of life and the bookishness of their training. The locutions, rhythms, imagery, and inflections native to black agrarians in the South and their transplanted cousins in the North, McKay and Cullen had not taken into part of themselves from which their poetry emanated. Hence their poetry was only New in that they were more educated, more sophisticated, and less conciliatory in their assertion of the good qualities of blackness than some of their predecessors. It was, not insignificantly, good lyric poetry. As a record of Negro life in America or in the Af-

rica from which American Negroes came, it was based too much on doctrine and not enough on anthropological and historical fact. (pp. 50-1)

> *Blyden Jackson and Louis D. Rubin, Jr., "From One 'New Negro' to Another, 1923-1972," in their* Black Poetry in America: Two Essays in Historical Interpretation *(reprinted by permission of Louisiana State University Press; copyright © 1974), Louisiana State University Press, 1974, pp. 37-98.**

HOUSTON A. BAKER, JR.   (essay date 1974)

Countee Cullen never achieved the "Vision Splendid." He can be classified as a minor poet whose life and poetry raise major problems. If we condemn him for his lack of independence and his rise to fame through the agency of noted American critics and periodicals, we are forced to do the same for a host of others. If he is judged and sentenced to exile on the basis of his aesthetic, a number of excellent statements on the Black artist's tasks and difficulties are lost. If he is upbraided for his lack of directness and his reliance on a longstanding tradition, our evaluation of the entire corpus of Black American poetry must be modified. It is possible that we are now whirling about fiercely in the maelstrom of a Black poetic revolution, but a careful view of Countee Cullen brings doubt. There is much continuity between the career of the Harlem Renaissance poet and the generations that have followed. As one glances from Cullen to present works and back, it is sometimes hard to tell the difference. In short, Cullen offers a paradigm in the Black American creative experience, and summary appraisals of his work lead to obfuscation rather than the clarity we so sorely need. He wrote a number of outstanding romantic lyrics and contributed racial poems that will endure because they grant insight into the Black American dilemma. (p. 52)

> *Houston A. Baker, Jr., in his* A Many-Colored Coat of Dreams: The Poetry of Countee Cullen *(copyright © 1974 by Houston A. Baker, Jr.), Broadside Press, 1974, 60 p.*

RONALD PRIMEAU   (essay date 1976)

Almost without exception, commentators on Cullen cite Keats as his chief "poetic model." While the similarities in structure, imagery, and theme are unmistakable, critics have stressed overt links evidenced in direct allusions and have, at the same time, neglected even more crucial (though more subtle) thematic connections. Cullen's attempts at once to grow through identification with Keats and to free himself from such influences in the very process of assimilating them exemplify many of the tensions in his career.

Cullen was attracted to (indeed, almost obsessed by) Keats's repeated and even ritualized insistence that pleasure and pain are always bound up in each other in the sensuous complexity of felt existence. While the suffering of the artist has become almost a cliché in literary history, the creative dimensions of pain and uncertainty—what Keats called the "Vale of Soul-Making"—above all else drew Cullen to the distant poet with whom he had little else in common. (p. 74)

The emphasis that Cullen gives to the creativity inherent in bittersweet experiences is paralleled throughout the Afro-American literary tradition. . . . From his own experiences, Cullen fuses joys and difficulties to create what Keats called "the sweetness of the pain."

Ironically, poems in which Cullen refers directly to Keats display far less of the intensity he achieves in his other more subtle treatments of the same material. In "For John Keats" he accomplishes little more than an echo of the epitaph on Keats's grave in Rome's Protestant Cemetery. . . . Although the imagery reflects elemental human quests, the patterns he achieves are neither original nor particularly striking. Similarly, "To Endymion" expresses "the bright immortal lie / Time gives to those detractors of your name" . . . in a series of Keatsian allusions that are for the most part too explicit. "Your star is steadfast now" suggests "Bright star. . .," and "long shall she stammer forth a broken note" echoes Keats's wish in his *Endymion* that he might "stammer where old Chaucer us'd to sing." Other examples, though this one suffices, reinforce the critical opinion that Cullen was more hurt than helped by this encounter with Keats. (pp. 75-6)

Most often in direct allusions, invocations bordering on idolatry, and blatant parallels, Cullen fails to overcome an influence that truly became a burden. But Cullen also read Keats creatively, and in poems where he is able to establish a distance between his precursor and his own experiences, the influence is stronger even where it is least perceptible. (p. 77)

Beyond such observable parallels, what has usually been overlooked in discussions of Cullen's indebtedness to Keats is his own distinctive reworking of themes and techniques. In his more subtle modifications of Keats, Cullen selected, rearranged, and reshaped poetic materials by impressing his own experiences on his responses to what he read. The poems most successfully forged from his reading communicate a sense of authentic existence. Ironically, then, his reading of Keats is most influential not in what is sometimes called his "non-racial" verse but rather in poetry he created out of his most intensely personal experiences as a black man and black poet. (pp. 77-8)

Everything that attracted Cullen to Keats (or to anyone else) depended in large part on his ability to come to grips with his own experience. In short, Cullen's personal experiences as a black man and poet within a given historical reference helped to shape his responses to Keats in distinctive ways and prompted him at the same time to transform what he found in his reading into the creation of his own poems. In what is usually considered his "racial" poetry, Cullen's absorption of Keats is more pervasive and liberating than in the obviously allusive and formal elegies.

In "The Shroud of Color" the speaker describes "being dark" in terms similar to the intensity of contraries central to Keats's odes. . . . Grappling with tensions and contradictions, the speaker embodies both the intensity of Keats's "burst joy's grape" in "Ode on Melancholy" . . . and the hopelessness characteristic of Keats's poems and letters to Fanny Brawne. . . . Cullen's poem may be likened to a long Keatsian dream-vision in which the speaker explores elemental feelings and attempts to place all the world's sufferings and joys together in epic panorama. . . . (pp. 78-9)

Structurally and thematically Cullen creates striking parallels with what he found regularly in Keats. But his subject is clearly the experience which is both personal and collective as it is embodied in the Afro-American oral tradition which Cullen knew well. His conclusion is therefore experientially authentic and shaped into poetic conflicts very like what he found in Keats's odes. . . . Cullen often repeats this basic pattern of Keats's odes: a speaker in pursuit of a seemingly unrealizable goal modifies his quest to accept, and in the process to reaffirm and to remake what is difficult but realizable in day to day human experience. His affirmation brings pleasure and pain as the speaker trades escape for a difficult, inevitable, yet imaginative involvement in human existence in time. (pp. 79-80)

"Heritage," Cullen's most famous poem, needs no commentary here. In the long soliloquy the speaker captures the contraries and poised energy typical of the concentrated expression and expansive paradox in Keats's odes. . . . [Within the poem] parallels to Keats's themes (distress and joy allied), imagery ("dammed within"), and fusion of theme and structure ("burst the fine channels") are both overt and sufficiently blended into Cullen's own experience as he transforms his influences into his own statements. The result is a more subtle and effective influence that often is ignored. (p. 85)

His obsessive drive to create at least a workable balance between the intellectual and the sensuous, the mythological and the deeply personal further attracted him to Keats. Cullen's subject was always—in a variety of forms and in repeated reworkings—again in his own words, "the heights and depths of emotion which I feel as a Negro." (p. 86)

Ronald Primeau, "Countee Cullen and Keats's Vale of Soul-Making," in Papers on Language and Literature *(copyright © 1976 by the Board of Trustees, Southern Illinois University at Edwardsville), Vol. 12, No. 1, Winter, 1976, pp. 73-86.**

ADDITIONAL BIBLIOGRAPHY

Bontemps, Arna. "The Harlem Renaissance." *The Saturday Review of Literature* XXX, No. 12 (22 March 1947): 12-13, 44.*
> Biographical sketches of Cullen and Langston Hughes, stressing their importance in the Harlem Renaissance.

Bronz, Stephen H. "Countee Cullen." In his *Roots of Negro Racial Consciousness: The 1920's: Three Harlem Renaissance Authors,* pp. 47-65. New York: Libra Publishers, 1964.
> Critical study of the individual works of Cullen's canon.

Brown, Lloyd W. "The Expatriate Consciousness in Black American Literature." *Studies in Black Literature* 3, No. 2 (Summer 1972): 9-12.*
> Examination of "Heritage," which is seen as an expression of a black artist in search of cultural roots.

Canaday, Nicholas, Jr. "Major Themes in the Poetry of Countee Cullen." In *The Harlem Renaissance Remembered,* edited by Arna Bontemps, pp. 103-25. New York: Dodd, Mead & Co., 1972.
> An examination of Cullen's treatment of the themes of religion, love, death, and racial conflict in his poems.

Emanuel, James A. "Renaissance Sonneteers: Their Contributions to the Seventies." *Black World* XXIV, No. 10 (August 1975): 32-45, 92-7.*
> Critical examination of three Cullen sonnets, explaining the racial thought expressed in them.

Ferguson, Blanche E. *Countee Cullen and the Negro Renaissance.* New York: Dodd, Mead & Co., 1966, 213 p.

Simply written biography of Cullen. Prominent black writers and educators of Cullen's era are profiled as well.

Huggins, Nathan Irvin. "Art: The Ethnic Province." In his *Harlem Renaissance*, pp. 190-243. New York: Oxford University Press, 1971. *
    Examination of Cullen's poetic style, in which the critic sees Cullen firmly grounded in the genteel tradition.

Larson, Charles R. "Three Harlem Novels of the Jazz Age." *Critique: Studies in Modern Fiction* XI, No. 3 (1969): 66-78.*
    Presents, largely by plot synopsis, Cullen's *One Way to Heaven*, Claude McKay's *Home to Harlem*, and Carl Van Vechten's *Nigger Heaven*, with a brief comparison of the three novels.

Perry, Margaret. *A Bio-Bibliography of Countée P. Cullen: 1903-1946*. Westport, CT: Greenwood Publishing Corp., 1971, 134 p.
    Valuable index to writings by and about Cullen, and a short biography.

Rubén Darío
1867-1916

(Pseudonym of Félix Rubén García Sarmiento) Nicaraguan poet, short story writer, journalist, critic, essayist, autobiographer, and novelist.

Darío is recognized as the leading figure of the *modernista* movement in Spanish-American literature. In thematic scope and artistic invention he surpassed his contemporaries and achieved the role of a prominent world author. Darío is credited with initiating a revival in Spanish literature following an artistically dormant period which extended back to the seventeenth century. Classical mythology, Christianity, American and English literature, and particularly the Symbolist movement in French literature were utilized by Darío to form a unique and coherent literary identity.

Darío's life was that of a world-traveling journalist, and he acquired a cosmopolitan perspective at an early age. He began his journalistic career working for newspapers in Central America and by 1886 was writing for a number of publications in Chile, where he found a more diverse literary and social scene than in his native Nicaragua. At different times he served in a diplomatic capacity as consul to Paris and Minister Plenipotentiary to Madrid.

Foremost among Darío's works is *Azul . . .*, critically considered the first important work of the *modernista* movement. The short stories and poetry in this collection reveal the author's efforts to revitalize the Spanish language, and critics have commented on Darío's striving for stylistic novelty as well as his original blending of various movements in contemporary literature. Reviewing *Azul . . .*, the Spanish novelist and critic Juan Valera wrote of Darío: "You are neither Romanticist, nor Realist, nor Naturalist, nor Decadent, nor Parnassian, nor Symbolist. You have taken the very quintessence of all that literature and made it your own."

In his next important collection of poetry, *Prosas profanas*, Darío pursued the Symbolists' ideal of poetry that aspires to the formal purity of music. His experimentation with unconventional metrical forms was revolutionary, and critics frequently cite this as one of his most significant contributions to Spanish literature. This collection is also the high point of a period of pure aesthetics and decadent exoticism in Darío's work.

In contrast, his later collections were less concerned with aesthetics and more concerned with themes of humanism and social conscience. *Cantos de vida y esperanza* is comprised of a wide range of poems, from examinations of mortality to expressions of South American solidarity before the burgeoning power of the United States. In *El canto errante*, however, Darío's concern for the human spirit transcends nationalism, achieving universality in its discussion of the fundamental dilemmas of human existence.

Though not widely known in the English-speaking world, Darío's work transformed Spanish poetry by introducing to it the technical achievements of contemporary world literature. In the eyes of many critics he is one of the most important figures in South American literature.

PRINCIPAL WORKS

Primeras notas   (letters and poems)   1885
Abrojos   (poetry)   1887
Emelina [with Eduardo Poirier]   (novel)   1887
Azul . . .   (short stories and poetry)   1888
Los raros   (essays)   1893
Prosas profanas, y otros poemas   (poetry)   1896
   [*Prosas Profanas and Other Poems*, 1922]
Peregrinaciones   (travel essays)   1901
Cantos de vida y esperanza   (poetry)   1905
Opiniones   (criticism)   1906
El canto errante   (poetry)   1907
Autobiografía   (autobiography)   1912
Canto a la Argentina, y otros poemas   (poetry)   1914
Eleven Poems of Rubén Darío   (poetry)   1916
Selected Poems   (poetry)   1965

SALOMÓN de la SELVA   (essay date 1916)

Rubén Darío's work has a threefold significance: aesthetical, historical and social. As an aesthete, in the purest meaning of this term, Rubén Darío is the Spanish Keats: he taught that "beauty is truth, truth beauty," and that sincerity is the highest virtue. This message is delivered to his people, the family of Spanish-speaking countries, with such power that through his influence and that of the other poets and writers who, with him for a leader, formed the revolutionary modernist school, Spanish poetry during the last generation was changed from the rhetorical, conventional sort of thing into which it degenerated after it had flourished gloriously in the time of Góngora to vibrant, real, sincere song. (p. 200)

[Seeking] orientation for his genius in that pilgrimage of discriminate assimilation that all great poets must make before they find themselves, Darío worshiped at many a shrine. Nor did our poet lose his own personality, but rather enriched it. . . . To critics who would tag him as belonging to this, that or the other school, he would cry: "I am myself!". . . . Sincerity of expression only can bring forth real poetry, and this he knew could not be attained through mere imitation. But he was eager to learn, and the Pre-Raphaelites of England, the Parnassians and Symbolists of France, Carducci among the Italians, and Poe and Whitman of the Americans, as well, of course, as the classics of all languages, had much to teach him. And the wealth of knowledge that he made his own, brought to bear upon his work, gave it that cosmopolitan bigness that made him a truly universal poet. His work, like America, as he would often say, is for all humanity.

With this ideal always before him, it is not surprising that he should be, as the phrase goes, a coiner of words, and an enemy of steel-ribbed grammars. His work, always impeccable and rich in form, is of supreme importance in the history of Spanish literature not only because of the spiritual renaissance of which it was the dawn—the awakening of Latin America to a realization of its literary individuality—but chiefly because of the changes that he wrought in the language, giving it a treasure of new expressions, new turns of phrase, *nuances,* in prose as well as in verse.

To appreciate this achievement justly, it must be remembered that for centuries the Spanish language had hardly been free to follow new paths of development such as English and French and German had taken. The dykes of linguistical traditions raised by the conservative and tyrannical Royal Academy of Spain had all but stagnated literary style. Up to Darío's time Spanish prosody was perhaps the poorest in Europe; it is true that sundry measures new to the language, such as the Graeco-Latin hexameter, the French alexandrine, and verses based on a four-syllable foot, had been essayed now and then; but there had not been a poet of sufficient power to use them as medium for great poetry and so to give them permanence.

The enneasyllabic verse, for instance, in which Rubén Darío wrote some of his best poems, had for a long time been used by comic opera libbretists in Spain, but the makers of serious poetry had always shown utter disregard for it, never realizing its musical virtues and possibilities. And so with less than a score of other metres which Darío invented or introduced and gave permanence to, or dignified, or revived. He was an indefatigable prosodist; and his poetry, magnificently sonorous at times, always elfin-touched, reveals the master craftsman no less than the born

poet. His verse possesses the very magic of pure music. Rubén Darío was a virtuoso of words fully as great as Swinburne or D'Annunzio, with more ideas than either. (pp. 200-02)

Darío, by his singing, united all the Latin-American countries, intellectually and morally, arousing them to a sense of their true grandeur. (p. 203)

Salomón de la Selva, "Rubén Darío," in Poetry *(© 1916 by The Modern Poetry Association; reprinted by permission of the Editor of* Poetry*), Vol. VIII, No. IV, July, 1916, pp. 200-04.*

PEDRO HENRÍQUEZ UREÑA (essay date 1916)

[Darío's] most important achievement was the book of *Cantos de vida y esperanza.* There he attained (especially in the autobiographical *Pórtico*) a depth of human feeling and a sonorous splender of utterance which placed him among the modern poets of first rank in any language. His later work did not always rise to that magnificence. but it often took a bold, rough-hewn, sort of *Rodinesque* form, which has found many admirers.

As a prosodist, Rubén Darío is unique in Spanish. He is the poet who has mastered the greatest variety of verse forms. . . . Darío, and the *modernist* groups which sprang into action mainly through his stimulus, gave vogue, and finally permanence, to a large number of metrical forms: either verses rarely used, like the enneasyllabic and the dodecasyllabic (of which there are three types), or verses, like the alexandrine, to which Darío gave greater musical virtue by freeing the accent and the cæsura. Even the hendecasyllable acquired new flexibility when Darío brought back two new forms of accentuation that had been used by Spanish poets during three centuries but had been forgotten since about 1800. He also attacked the problem of the classic hexameter, which has tempted many great modern poets, from Goethe to Swinburne and Carducci, and, before these, a few of the Spanish in the XVIIth century, chiefly Villegas. He introduced, finally, the modern *vers libre,* the type in which the number of feet, but not the foot, changes (as in the *Marcha triunfal*), as well as the type in which both the number of syllables and the foot vary frequently.

In style, Rubén Darío represents another renewal. He not only fled from the hackneyed, from expressions which, like coins, were worn out by use: it is the natural outcome of every new artistic or literary tendency to do away with the useless remains of former styles. He did much more; together with a few others, like Manuel Gutiérrez Nájera of Mexico, Darío brought back into Spanish the art of nuance, of delicate shading, in poetical style. This art, all but absent from Spanish poetry during two centuries, had been substituted by the forceful drawing and vivid coloring which foreigners expect to find in all things Spanish.

In the spirit of poetry, Rubén Darío succeeded in giving "des frissons nouveaux." If not the first, he was one of the first . . . to bring into Spanish the notes of subtle emotion of which Verlaine was arch master; the gracefulness and the brilliancy which emerge from the world of Versaillesque courts and feigned Arcadies; the decorative sense of a merely external Hellenism, which is delightful in its frank artificiality; the suggestions of exotic worlds, opulent storehouses of imaginative treasures.

But, while he did all this, he never lost his native force: he was, and he knew how to be, American,—Spanish-American, rather. He sang of his race, of his people,—the whole Spanish-speaking family of nations,—with constant love, with a tenderness which at times was almost childlike. If he did not always think that life in the New World was poetical, he did think that the ideals of Spanish America were worthy of his poetry. And, as he upheld the ideals of Spanish America, and the traditions of the whole Spanish race, . . . both Spain and Spanish America saw in him their representative poet. (pp. vi-ix)

> *Pedro Henríquez Ureña, in his introduction to* Eleven Poems of Rubén Darío, *translated by Thomas Walsh and Salomón de la Selva (copyright, 1916, by The Hispanic Society of America), G. P. Putnam's Sons, 1916, pp. v-ix.*

S. GRISWOLD MORLEY (essay date 1917)

Modernism is a term used in Spain to denote a movement in its world of letters which began there not long before the disaster of 1898, and still continues to develop. It is not easy to define, since nebulosity is one of its aims. But Darío, who was engagingly frank in his self-criticism, discloses without reserve his own literary ancestry, and with it that of the school. (p. 509)

Darío and his followers say, with justice, that they have renewed Spanish poetry, freed it from age-old shackles. It is invariably the formal, metrical side of their achievement that they stress. . . . [Darío] was, indeed, an indefatigable experimenter with rhymes and rhythms, but one must not forget that he never discarded a system till he had become proficient in it, and that this daring innovations sprang consciously from supreme technical skill, from a minute understanding of the intricacies of metrics, ancient and modern. He was not trying, like a cubist painter or some poets of the day, to escape the bonds of rules that he had not patience to master. It is noteworthy that, in spite of the liberty he preached, he was not a *vers librist,* except in occasional unimportant poems. His anarchy developed within the limits of rhyme and syllable-count. It is not likely that his more extreme licenses, such as *enjambement* with a pendant definite article, will remain in the language.

As might be expected in view of its origins, Darío's art is more French than Spanish. Not that he was unpatriotic or neglectful of the glories of his race. He was intensely loyal to his native tropics always and did not share the antipathy for Spain that many Spanish-Americans harbor. He came to love her national history and ancient honors. But the spirit of his art was quite unlike what we are accustomed to consider Castilian. To be sure, it may be all the more universal art for that. The savor of Spanish soil is so strong that, undiluted, it appears not to be much relished away from home.

Darío was un-Spanish, first, in the meticulous polish of his verse. "Slap-dash methods and indifference to form," says Fitzmaurice-Kelly, "are characteristic of the greatest Spaniards." The impeccable choice of words, the sapient harmony of line, the alliteration, the silvery combinations of vocables, the inspired placing of the cæsura,—all these qualities, dropping at times into mannerism and preciosity, are something new in Spanish poetry. One must go back to Luis de León and Góngora to find anything resembling it, and then remotely.

He is un-Spanish in the lack of that sonorous, mouth-filling rhetoric which impresses any reader of Castilian lyrics. Darío worked for lightness, freedom, and delicacy, and to that end substituted short words for long as much as possible. He is un-Spanish, too, in his lack of realism. Like many another poet who worked hard for a living, he put into his verse as little as possible of the sordid side of his life. To him his art meant an opportunity to retire into an ideal world, "within an ivory tower," as he put it, to regale himself with the joy of creation in a realm of dreams and illusions. Even in his erotic poetry, much of it a veritable hymn to Pan, the divinity of sex, the fundamental idea is clad in such a magical veil of imagery and mythology that it is incapable of offending. The great excesses of his own life found only an idealized echo in his verse. He was a robust, full-blooded product of the tropics, . . . but such was the aristocracy of his intellect that he would no more have soiled a blank sheet with slops than he would have cheapened it with rhyme-tags. I am speaking, naturally, of Darío in his prime, the Darío of "Azul," "Prosas Profanas," and "Cantos de Vida y Esperanza."

Lastly, Darío is un-Spanish in his vacillating religious faith. Every critic recognizes the duality of his nature, the "cosmic sensualism" of his pantheistic mythology, paralleled or contradicted by yearnings toward revealed religion. Darío himself affirmed that he was "a Christian if not a Catholic," and some of his admirers have tried to claim him for the Church, but it is indubitable that paganism was the essence of his soul, while his faith was hesitating and frail. Repeatedly, in both prose and verse, he describes the horror of death, a purely physical fear of annihilation, that beset him from his earliest years: "in my desolation," he says, "I have rushed to God as a refuge, I have seized prayer as a parachute." . . . Nor did Darío possess the equally Spanish courage of consistent materialism. He was bold toward the world, but timid toward himself. His lyrics are the quintessence of pantheism, and yet he could snatch at prayer as a parachute.

A like fluctuation is apparent in his poetry. His protean nature is the hardest in the world to pin a label to. Usually he is dubbed an apostle of imprecision, a translator of delicate nuances of mood into lines shaded with equal delicacy. He is, very often, that kind of Verlainian. . . . No sooner have you decided that Darío stands for nothing else than this, when, at some turn of a leaf, you come upon a sonnet of robust contour, firmly imagined and strongly chiselled, an ode of frosty brilliance, a martial and aggressive polemic. He is often assumed to be a pure æsthete, but he gives proof of clear reasoning and exactness, when he wishes. Now a pagan lover of fleshly beauty, at times he dallies with a wholly sensuous Christian mysticism; again, he is overcome by a sense of the futility of life. His one constant trait is the worship of art for art's sake, of the rare and delicate in every manifestation.

Somewhere in his work there is meat for every taste. Is this the dilettantism of a roving assimilator? Is it rather the full many-sidedness of genius? I incline to the latter hypothesis. It is early to declare with the novelist Valle-Inclán, in a *boutade* meant perhaps only to startle the bourgeois, that "all Spanish poetry may be reduced to two names, Jorge Manrique and Darío." It is early even to boast, with a French critic, that "Darío had a hand in the funeral of Nuñez de Arce and all that his art represents." The world of letters is probably not ready to discard forever, in favor of modernism, the poetry of definite ideas. What cannot be denied is that Darío, single-handed, initiated a movement in Spain that affects to-day nearly every branch of literary art; that he renovated the technique of both poetry and prose; that he made his own many diverse styles; and that his verse is often so inevitable as to touch the finality of art. (pp. 510-11)

S. Griswold Morley, "A Cosmopolitan Poet," in The Dial (copyright, 1917, by The Dial Publishing Company, Inc.), Vol. LXII, No. 744, June 14, 1917, pp. 509-11.

GEORGE W. UMPHREY (essay date 1919)

[We] find little to detain us in [Darío's] first volume of precocious verse, *Epístolas y Poemas*, of importance only in the study of the gradual evolution of a clever imitator of the French and Spanish poets of the preceding generation into the strongly individualistic leader of the *Modernistas*. The poems of his next volume, *Los Abrojos*, indicate a transference of his allegiance from Victor Hugo and Zorrilla to Bécquer and Campoamor. The influence of his models is still apparent, although the introduction of a more personal note into some of the poems shows that he is on the way toward independence. . . . [Many] of these short poems are filled with the bitterness and cynicism of a young man upon whom disillusionment has come with the first close contact with the real world. . . . Fortunately, this mood of skepticism, moral agitation and despondency did not outlive his twentieth year; a different mood is that of the following year when he published the collection of poems, *Azul. . . .* (p. 66)

It is in the prose selections of *Azul . . .* that we find unmistakable signs of a literary revolution, literary qualities that place the author among the great masters of contemporary Spanish prose, Valle Inclán, Benavente, José Enrique Rodó. In the content of these prose selections, fantastic, idealistic impressions, rather than stories in the ordinary sense, it is still the poet that creates. (pp. 66-7)

The innovations in the prose in which these stories were written were due mainly to Darío's careful study of French writers. . . . In the exquisite prose of *Azul . . .* we find flexibility, delicacy, fine shading, clarity and precision of expression; rhythmical flow of language; absence of provincialism and of all local color, characteristic of the prose *Modernistas*. (p. 67)

The collection of poems published . . . with the curious title, *Prosas Profanas*, established for all time Darío's leadership in the literary movement known as *El Modernismo* in Spanish America and in Spain; he it was who first completely assimilated the poetic principles of the French symbolists and made of them an integral part of modern Spanish poetics. He had indeed his precursors in Spanish America to whom due credit should be given, the three poets [Gutiérrez Nájera, José Asunción Silva, and Julián del Casal], any one of whom might have disputed with Darío the title of leadership had he been permitted to live a few years longer. In the writings of these poets may be found almost all the innovations of the *Modernistas*, but in none of them so completely and definitely as in the writings of the Nicaraguan poet. (p. 69)

[Darío's] breaking away from conventional forms of verse was due, in part, to another characteristic of symbolism, the close association of poetry and music. Just as Parnassianism was closely allied to painting and sculpture, was the poetry of color and form, symbolism had its closest affiliation with music, was the poetry of sound and rhythm. Unable to produce the desired musical effects by means of the conventional meters, the symbolists cast aside many of its bonds and delighted in new combinations. In *Prosas Profanas* are many masterpieces of melodious verse (*Sonatina, Era un aire suave, Sinfonía en gris mayor*), in which to the lyric melody of other great Spanish poets was added the suggestiveness of Wagnerian music.

This musical suggestiveness is closely associated with the chief characteristic of symbolism as regards content, the suggestion of ideas, sensations, moods, by means of symbols; by allusion merely not by direction mention or description. Darío's fine literary taste and capacity for self-criticism kept him from going to the absurd extreme of some of the *Symbolistes* and *Modernistas*, who attempted to work out a definite scheme of sense associations, color in music, music in color, color and perfume in vocal sounds. Quite apparent, however, in his *Prosas Profanas* is this tendency of the symbolists, the result of the strong reaction from the precision and objectivism of the Parnassians. (pp. 70-1)

Associated with [the] expression of purely personal sensations and the suggestiveness of symbols and sounds are other qualities in *Prosas Profanas* that are readily excused in the exquisite poetry of Rubén Darío, but that brought his influence into disrepute in the abuses of his servile imitators. With him the disassociation of art and morality did not result in licentiousness of thought, because of his innate refinement and his belief in the identity of truth and beauty, the object of his life-long cult. The refined sensualism that made physical love the motive for many beautiful poems was held in check by this love of the beautiful, by his instinctive shrinking from all that is vulgar or ugly in the moral as in the material world. His aristocratic exclusiveness . . . to which he retired for poetic inspiration, broke, for the time being, all vital contact with the world of reality, a contact that was to be re-established fortunately at a later period. The cosmopolitanism that permitted his spirit to wander at will through all ages and all countries in search of the beautiful and the rare resulted in his temporary "anti-americanism," the studied avoidance of local color and racial traditions that became mere affectation in his imitators. . . . The elegant artificiality of the court-life of Versailles in the 18th century made its irresistible appeal during this period and inspired some of his most beautiful verses. . . . (p. 71)

The exoticism of the poet of *Prosas Profanas* found expression also in many lines and poems of Hellenic inspiration,— a Hellenism, it should be noticed, not of ancient Greece, but that of Italy of the Renaissance (*Friso, Palimpsesto*, etc.), or that of France in the early years of the 18th century and in the late years of the 19th. . . .

The strange title that Darío gave to this collection of poems was as a red flag in the eyes of conservative critics, who either lacked understanding of its significance or were out of sympathy with the author's poetic ideals. On the other hand, it cannot but seem strangely appropriate to one who appreciates the literary qualities of the poems contained in the volume and the etymological history of the two words *prosa* and *profana*. In his study of the Old Spanish poets Darío became familiar with their use of *prosa* in the sense of "poem in the vernacular." He knew, too, the sequences of *proses,* Latin hymns that resulted from the setting of words to the music following the Alleluia in the Roman Catholic liturgy, a practice that became popular in the early 10th century. That the title was suggested by these sacred *proses* of the liturgy is clearly indicated by the second element, *profanas,* that is, "not sacred." This conjectural explanation of the title and the literary qualities already noted in the poetry indicate its appropriateness. Just as the liturgical hymns, the "sacred proses," broke away from the quantitative meters of Latin verse and came to depend for their rhythms upon accent, so the "profane proses" of Darío broke away from conventionality in form and content. (p. 72)

The volume of poetry . . . with the significant title, *Cantos de Vida y Esperanza* gives [Dario] an important place among the most vigorous poets of contemporary literature.

These poems composed during the six years from 1899 to 1905 show no absolute break with the poetic theories that underlie the poems composed during the preceding ten years and published as *Prosas Profanas* in 1896 and in 1900; there is, however, in many of them a new note that clearly differentiates the third stage of his literary evolution from the two preceding. With the avowed purpose of breaking the bonds of conventionality and tradition in both the form and content of poetry, he had consciously avoided local color and racial feeling; he had even sought remoteness from the actualities of life, taking refuge in his high tower of ivory, his *alcázar interior,* to which pure art alone could find an entrance. The result was the production of many poems of exquisite beauty in form, of rare refinement in thought and sentiment, of great metrical variety. The result was, too, the suppression of that part of his nature that was ready to respond to the call of race and of humanity when permitted to do so. That pure art alone could not satisfy him he tells us in the preface to his *Cantos de Vida y Esperanza.* . . . (p. 76)

If the charge of effeminacy was not without foundation when applied to the poet of *Prosas Profanas,* it could surely no longer be made against the poet who had written *Marcha triufal,* with its strong free verse and bold rhythmic swing in the Whitmanesque manner. Equally vigorous in form and content is the ode, *A Roosevelt,* in which the poet voices the widespread suspicion of Spanish Americans in the first years of the century toward the imperialistic tendencies of the strong Anglo-Saxon Republic. (p. 77)

The volume of poems entitled *Cantos de Vida y Esperanza* represents most fully Darío's third and last phase. Other poems, singly and in collections, have appeared at longer or shorter intervals since, representative of all three phases; the great majority of them, however, belong to the third stage of his literary evolution, in which he is still one of the greatest poets, although no longer the undisputed leader. In this [latest] literary movement young and vigorous poets, called the "New Poets" for lack of a better name, having gained freedom from the bonds of traditional rhetoric and prosody, have sought freedom from foreign influence in the content of their poetry; they have turned to national or racial themes for inspiration and are striving to bring about the complete *Americanization* of Spanish-American litera-

ture. Darío was in sympathy with the new tendency, in which strength is the quality desired above all others, but was not willing to go so far as his younger contemporaries in the new direction; he was too much of the cosmopolitan to limit thus his sources of inspiration, too ardent a lover of beauty in all its forms to restrict his manner of expression, too complex of character and variable of mood to attempt to be consistent in all his literary productions. (p. 79)

George W. Umphrey, "Spanish-American Poets of Today and Yesterday," in Hispania *(© 1919 The American Association of Teachers of Spanish and Portuguese, Inc.), Vol. II, No. 2, March, 1919, pp. 64-81.*

ISAAC GOLDBERG   (essay date 1920)

[Rubén Darío] has written works of dazzling technical perfection and of penetrating vision; he is the outstanding representative of modernism in poetry; he is a chiseler of luminous, glittering prose rich alike in imagery, melody and substance. He is not merely a Spanish-American poet, nor a Castilian poet; he is of the consecrated few who belong to no nation because they belong to all.

I believe that many Spaniards, on both sides of the Atlantic, have stressed Darío's technical perfection and innovating significance at the expense of his essential humanity. I believe that despite his aristocratic search after flawless form, despite his hatred of the crowd, despite his intellectual sybaritism, he was as human in a great part of his poetry as in his life. This wanderer sought to distil beauty from joy and sorrow, and at the bottom of this beauty the joy, the sorrow, the vain questioning, the doubt, the vacillations of the age are vibrant. (pp. 101-02)

The poetic career of Rubén Darío is another striking proof that the great artist may not be hooped in by critical symbols. The progress of his labors exemplifies what I may call a creative eclecticism. . . . From the study of Darío's poetry we may discover the spiritual counterpart of his wandering existence, ranging from the earliest romantic efforts, through a renovation of prose technique, poetic technique, the acquisition of a more human outlook, and the final emergence of these combined powers in masterpieces that belong to world poesy.

Darío's earliest efforts are contained in the collections *Epistolas y Poemas* . . . and *Abrojos.* . . . In the first his great god is Hugo; in the second his affections have shifted to Bécquer, Campoamor, Nuñez de Arce and Zorrilla, particularly the last. As may be expected, there is little in these lines from the pen of a youth between his eighteenth and twentieth years to reveal the dominant personality of the future. He is as yet diffident as to his powers and asks the Muses (*El Poeta á Las Musas*) whether his humble plectrum is better suited to martial hymns, or to harmonious eclogues. . . . He feels the influence of the past, yet is tempted by the modern. . . . (pp. 122-23)

Thus early do we find indications of a certain "Americanism," as in the poem *El Porvenir;* it is of interest as a germ that lies many years undeveloped. Thus early, too, do we discover the poet's Horatian hatred for the crowd, which is to him a mere beast to be discouraged every time it tries to raise its head. "The people is dull, filthy, evil; clap on the yoke; it complains of the taskmaster, then give it drubbings and more of them." . . . To this little sociologist . . . , the common toiler was born for the yoke, must remain content with it and eat his bread and onions in silence.

Equally enlightening are the poet's early views on women. Of course there is nothing cryptic in this misogyny. We know Darío now better than he knew himself then; it is easy to see that his woman-hatred was symptomatic of his excessive love of them, as is most misogyny. That is why, when we read some of his early lines with the music and passion of his later ones ringing in our ears, we smile at such platitudinous condemnations as the verses in which he refers woman's beauty to alien aids, and tells them that though he covets their kisses, they are nothing but flesh and bone. "Carne y huesos!" The very words which he was later to deify as the best incarnation of the Muses!

Abrojos, as its name—Thistles—indicates, represents the varied reactions of the melancholy, love-sick adolescent to the bitterness, grief and desires of his youthful career. It is now cynical, now humorous. . . . It is aware of man's envious nature and his cruelty to his own species. (pp. 125-26)

[There are] in *Abrojos,* touches of beauty as well as of youthful cynicism and disillusionment. Some of these touches have been coupled with the names of de Musset and Heine. On the whole, however, the collection is what its name implies; the verses, of uneven worth and of easily recognized parentage, are based upon the young poet's daily experiences. They indicate the storing up of an immense hoard of emotions in the bosom of an ideally-minded, little communicative, intense youth. Only gradually does Darío fully disburden himself of his inner life; his early Parnassianism, indeed, may have been an artistic symptom of his characteristic aloofness. (p. 127)

In the prose tales of *Azul* . . . may be discerned the intense idealism of their youthful author. Whether the scene be the fabled land of *The Bourgeois King,* the realms of *The Deaf Satyr,* or the garret of the starved artists over which floats the *Veil of Queen Mab,* the real background is the land of the ideal,—a land where art reigns in the telling, even though it be defeated by the tale. And how much self-revelation there is in these seemingly impersonal, delicate, airy traceries of language! (p. 130)

It is not part of my purpose to summarize the various productions [of *Azul*] under consideration; what is important, however, is to seek the spirit that informs them. This, I believe, is a glowing idealism, attended by the passing pessimism that all idealism must inspire. There is a mingling of styles,—Hellenism, realism even,—but at bottom it is the idealistic note that rings out loudly, whether the particular bell, so to speak, be such a hymn to Mother Earth as occurs in *El Rubí* or such a neo-Greek evocation as *La Ninfa.* (p. 133)

From the revolutionary standpoint, it is the prose part of *Azul* . . . that is more important; the language had become swollen, limited in resources, artificial and stagnant in expression; in these tales of Darío (which, if one must tell the truth, are of delicate fibre and contain little to set the literary world afire for either depth or intrinsic significance) the language flows with remarkable clarity. Not so much for what they say as for how they say it are the tales of *Azul* . . . worthy of notice. They represent an innovation in style, not in thought. The coming master is preparing his tools for the sculpturing of the new statue. . . . (p. 134)

There is in *Prosas Profanas* a variety, a melody, a suppleness, that was not evident in the poetry of *Azul. . . . Prosas Profanas,* indeed, has been recognized as having accomplished for poetry that same innovatory purpose worked by the prose of *Azul. . . .* (p. 141)

It is in the *Coloquio de los Centauros* that the book reaches its highest point. For the *Colloquy of the Centaurs* is the essence of the poet's personality as it was developed up to that date; it embodies and harmonizes the varied elements of the collection. It is classic in background, yet modern in feeling; it betrays an impeccably refined taste, yet throbs with something deeper than formal perfection; it is rich in imagery as in meaning; it blends the old and the new in the eternal. What is the meaning of the poem? That is for every reader to decide for himself. It has many meanings, because [the] centaurs gather to discuss our whole existence. They voice the poet's own queries before the enigma, and suggest his own inadequate reply which is but another question. (p. 144)

Among the technical innovations of *Prosas Profanas* have been noted the following: a new musicality of verse,—new strophic forms, such as the single-rhymed tercet,—the metrical interruption of the grammatical connection,—free movement of the cæsura, considered independently of the pauses in meaning. (pp. 145-46)

As a matter of record I indicate the innovations, but let us not deceive ourselves; they belong to history, not to literature, and the poet himself later protested that his poems were born whole, not first the skeleton of form and then the flesh of thought. There is, of course, a natural explanation of Spanish preoccupation with Darío's technical aspect; he brought freedom, amplitude, and blazed new paths. But within that freedom he spoke of his age; over those paths he drew new vehicles of beauty. And after all, mankind feeds upon feelings and thoughts, not hexameters and heptasyllables. I would not be understood as underestimating the technical aspect of art. The temple of technique is an imposing edifice, but a god must dwell within. By all means let the temple be beautiful, but do not leave it empty. . . . (pp. 147-48)

Quite futilely Darío, in his *Prosas Profanas,* had expressed dissatisfaction with the age into which he was born. He would have been a poet in any age; he was rich in response to the most varied stimuli. This book, in which there is more of life than hope, in which the intensity of the melancholy is more impressive than the exultant optimism, should prove, even without the collection which followed [*Cantos de Vida y Esperanza*], that Darío was not merely the poet of grace, delicacy and subtle charm, but a modern personality with more than one chord to his lyre. There is a surprising continuity of growth in the man, as is shown by a reading of his works in chronological order. We have already noted his remarkable faculty of assimilation; add to this that the assimilation was complete; wherever the impulse came from, it had been transformed into Darío's own before it issued from his pen.

In *Cantos de Vida y Esperanza,* then, we are to expect a poet of the multiform early twentieth century, afloat upon the turbulent waters of a very real and agitated life. It is just possible, too, that Darío was affected by [José Enrique] Rodó's criticism of *Prosas Profanas,* particularly in its statement (made without reproach) of Darío's non-Americanism. . . . At any rate the poet himself is deeply conscious of the inner change, which, with greater concision and beauty than any critic could state it, he confesses in the affecting opening poem of the collection. . . . The very first lines announce a change; the poet of yesterday's blue and yesterday's profane proses prepares us for a new orientation in his verse; there are lines of sincere self-revelation and certain overtones of repentance or apology for previous divagations. There is, too, I believe, a protest against the narrow conception of his previous work which looks upon it as beautiful Parnassianism without any essentially human implications.

The poet realizes the various epochs of his progress as keenly as any biographer; this is but another indication of the self-consciousness with which the man proceeded in his labors,—perhaps not only self-consciousness but that morbid introspection so characteristic of neurotic natures. He knows that he has been dwelling in a dream garden . . . ; that he has been very much of the eighteenth century and very modern; audacious, cosmopolitan; "with Hugo strong and ambiguous with Verlaine, and thirst of infinite illusions." (pp. 149-52)

[In *Cantos de Vida y Esperanza* Darío] seems to have abandoned his ivory tower and to have emerged into the hurly burly of life. He has now become undoubtedly American . . . and signalizes not only his Americanism, but a certain type of Hispanism, in poems that are as remarkable for their metrical innovations as for the indication of a new orientation of the poet's thought.

Chief among these is the *Salutación del Optimista,* with its sonorous hexameters that sounded so new to Spanish ears, and much less acceptable than Longfellow's similar experiment in *Evangeline* to his English audience. (pp. 155-56)

The poem is a ringing call to all of Spanish blood; away with sloth, diffidence and apathy; there is a renaissance of the ancient virtues that distinguished Hispania; it breathes in the two continents wherein repose the glorious bones of the great dead. The poet seems to have foreseen the cataclysm of 1914; he speaks clearly, and without the haze of prophecy, of muffled roars heard in the entrails of the world, and the imminence of fatal days; amid this universal upheaval it is no time for the Spanish race to remain dormant; let the blood of Spain unite and yield glory as of yore. (pp. 156-57)

Is it too great a fondness for the Darío of personal revelation and of the inner struggle that makes us see, in such poems as the *Salutación* and *A Roosevelt,* more of the indignant recipient of outward suggestion than the pure poet? I do not mean to question the genuineness of the writer's views, nor to deny the moments of intense poetry that he achieves in the expression of them. They are poetic, however, only at moments; they are, if I may so express it, the poeticization of views rather than poetry itself. They are more important as revealing the man's reaction to the times than for that intrinsic merit which all art should retain after the circumstances of its origin have disappeared. It may be said that . . . despite some brilliant poems like the *Canto á la Argentina,* Darío is not the poet of America, and that America,—Darío's own America—gains by it. On the other hand a good case may be made out for Darío not only as the poet of America, but as a poet who, in a few notable poetic works, voices a Pan-Americanism that is less ambiguous

than [José Santos] Chocano's. The more one reads the later Darío, the more one feels that this is the true man in all his expansion,—that he is in a very true sense universal, not merely in the statement of that universality . . . , but in the evidences of it as presented by poems of intensity and depth that are . . . "beyond art." (pp. 159-60)

As a collection, the *Cantos de Vida y Esperanza* is the keystone of Darío's poetical arch. It most exemplifies the man that wrote it; it most reveals his dual nature, his inner sincerity, his complete psychology; it is the artist at maturity. There is a wider sweep, a subtler music, a closer approach to universal amplitude of expression and linguistic sonority. In the *Prosas Profanas,* says Gonzáles-Blanco, the poet's æsthetic was at its highest; in the *Cantos de Vida y Esperanza* it is his technique that triumphs. Yet how much more than technique it contains in its pages! (p. 167)

The poet of *El Canto Errante* continues the varied manner of the preceding volume. He is outspokenly opposed to any narrowing conception of art, which he considers "not a combination of rules, but a harmony of caprices." He has no use for such terminology as old and new. . . . *El Canto Errante* secures Darío's reputation as a universal poet and emphasizes, perhaps, the pantheistic element in that universality. How far we are from the ivory tower of the *Prosas Profanas!* As the poet says in his Ballad to Martínez Sierra, the exquisite stylist and translator of Maeterlinck, the best muse is of flesh and blood. Darío has now become a wandering Jew of poesy. He is the singer who journeys over all the world, "reaping smiles and thoughts, amid white peace and red war." . . . Here we may see why Darío is not the poet of America; his mission, like that which he discerns in the soul of Mitre, is to reach humanity; he feels himself, it is true, American in spirit and in origin, but his patriotism does not blind him to the larger importance of the human unit. (pp. 170-71)

Apply this universality of humanity to the sphere of nature and a modern pantheism is the result. Measured by the totality of his work, which forms a rarely ordered rising curve, Darío is nothing less than cosmogonic; he identifies himself with all times, all moods, all animate nature, all peoples. (pp. 171-72)

Nor was this mood a new one to Darío, in whom from the very first, as a collation of his poems with his autobiography may show, existed the germs of all his later moods and manners. It seems that his frequent questioning of self led to a deeper knowledge of humanity. It has been said that all genius is neurotic. Without pressing that point, it is quite safe to assert that certain types of neuroticism enlarge appreciably the sufferer's view of himself as well as of mankind. (p. 172)

The *Canto á la Argentina* . . . is an inspiring, polyphonic, vast hymn,—the longest of Darío's poems, in forty-five stanzas of a length varying from eight lines to seventy-six, with lines of from six to twelve syllables,—sung as much to liberty as to Argentina. The longer Darío lived the closer he drew to that crowd which he thought he despised, and the more Pan-American, as well as universal, he became. He acquired, too, a certain noble magniloquence that one might scarcely have suspected in the poet of an *Azul* . . . or of *Prosas Profanas.* As a celebration of the centenary of Argentina's independence, the *Canto* is fully matched to its lofty theme. There is an epic sweep to the sonorous stanzas, which scatter upon the air a proclamation of freedom; there is a biblical fervor that welcomes the exiles of all nations to this new Promised Land. (p. 176)

The poem is in more than one way remarkable. First, for its sustained flight and the genuine inspiration. It produces upon the reader the effect of having been written (even declaimed) in a single outburst. Then there is a human outlook which contrasts markedly with the early aristocracy of the singer. To me, at least, the international sentiments ring more genuinely from these lines than from earlier ones. The Darío who began as a Romantic, then ranging through Parnassianism and Symbolism, here seems to revel in the pure, untrammeled, uncatalogued joy of creation. *El Canto á la Argentina* is a logical development of the two collections that preceded it.

Later poems, as well as the various posthumous collections issued, add little the poet's fame. The master was capable of writing some most pedestrian verse, such as the poem to *La Gran Metropolis,* in which New York's contrast of wealth and misery is sung in limping verses of lustreless facture; . . . he can become most unpoetic in his political utterances, as witness the verses of farewell written to the actress María Guerrero shortly after the publication of *Prosas Profanas.* On the other hand, in his marvellous *Poema del Otoño* he intones a hymn to love that pulses with the passion of eventide; for beneath its bacchanalian rhythm is the slackening gait of resignation. (pp. 178-79)

With the exception of the prose section of *Azul . . .* Darío's prose labors were the outgrowth of his journalistic career. (p. 179)

There is little necessity here for an extended consideration of the poet's prose works. Everywhere may be discerned the mind of the poet which never quite lost its aristocratic cast, however much it recognized the value of the crowd as a background of art. If I mention *Los Raros* as my favorite, it is because in that book Darío the poet and Darío the extremely sensitive human being are most evident in Darío the writer of prose. It is questionable whether such a prose would prove acceptable to the majority of English readers; the non-Spanish element in it, of course, would not bother them. What might, however, seem not fully acceptable, is the quasipoetic glow that shines from every page. (p. 181)

Can Darío really be pinned down in the critic's sample case like the entomologist's butterfly? Perhaps, by some refinement of the critic's art an appearance of inner unity may be imparted to the man, his life and his labors. To me, however, he is most human in his questionings, his fears, his vacillations, his wavering, his unresolved doubt. From the very first he reveals these dominant characteristics. He is of the past, of the present, of the future. From the very nature of poetry and its incapability of being transferred into another tongue it is inevitable that he will never be to other peoples what he will remain to Spaniards; that is one of the disadvantages under which the poet, more than any other creative artist, labors.

He crystallized an epoch; he transformed a language; he infused new life into the Castilian muse; he retained his own personality while absorbing all the currents that appeared during his career; he became . . . a legendary figure even during his own life. He belongs not only with the greatest poets that have written in the Spanish tongue, but with the masters of universal poesy. For above the early

Parnassianism, the later Symbolism and the final complex humanism, is the eternally human of a poet who was peculiarly of his day and, by that same token, of all ages. (pp. 182-83)

Isaac Goldberg, "Rubén Darío," in his Studies in Spanish-American Literature *(copyright 1920 by Brentano's), Brentano's, 1920 (and reprinted by Kennikat Press, 1968, pp. 101-83).*

F. M. KERCHEVILLE   **(essay date 1933)**

Rubén Darío, although the leader of the Modernist movement, should not be considered as the head of any certain school. He seemed to combine and take the best from all the literatures of the past—Spanish, French, American, and even Latin and Greek. He was able to assimilate the best from every influence, transform it, and make it his very own. Indeed, this is one of his most outstanding characteristics. He saw the need for new forms, new words, new subjects—in other words, new life; and, at the same time, he saw the beauty of the Spanish and Greek classics and did not fail to use this knowledge in his choice of subjects and in his treatment. He took the best of the French without actually becoming French. . . . (p. 9)

Darío has an unlimited range of subjects. He sang of everything worthy of being placed in song. Abstract love, love of women, love of nature, and above all, the love of the beautiful, wherever it is found, are his favorite themes. Yet he writes of battles, of doubts, of death, of politics, of religion, and of the sea. There have been very few poets with a wider range of themes. (p. 14)

[Darío] seems to have a special preference for themes of a classical nature, yet into the subject he puts his own personality, his own peculiar interpretation, and therein lies his strength. He may treat a theme of Eighteenth Century France, yet he makes the scenes live again, makes them universal. He has taken his subject matter from all three sources: classical, medieval, and modern. (p. 15)

In his choice of words, the poet has equally as wide a range as in his choice of themes. Very old words, words taken almost directly from Latin, words taken from the French, and even English words are found in his poetry. Rubén Darío has a marvelous talent for choosing his diction, and rarely, if ever, does he make a mistake. It must be said, however, that, although Darío searched for new words in foreign languages, he always preferred to use the Spanish. In his search for new expressions he seemed to be guided by his own personal taste and by the needs of the Spanish. (pp. 15-16)

It is especially interesting to note Rubén Darío's treatment of his subjects or his themes. He is essentially a lyric poet, and, therefore, largely subjective in his treatment. (p. 18)

Whatever interpretations the reader may wish to give Darío's poetry, the fact that he was truly in love still remains: in love with life, in love with beauty, and, above all, in love with beautiful musical verse. Perhaps this last was his real love, and women were rather symbols of that beauty to him.

By far the most outstanding characteristic of Darío's poetry is the musical quality of his verse. Few poets in the entire history of poetry knew better this wonderful secret of producing haunting music in verse by the selection and arrangement of words. . . . The poet studied his diction carefully, after reading the musical verse of certain of the French poets. With the beautiful and supple Spanish language he wrought wonders. At times Darío uses regular rhyme, at times a rather exotic rhyme, while at times he uses no rhyme at all. Yet that rhythm, that inward cadence, that eternal music is there in all of his best poetry—there to such an extent as to fascinate and to haunt him who reads the verse. (pp. 21-2)

In conclusion, we can say of Rubén Darío that he is a truly great poet; one who has taken the best he could find in other literatures, and in his own native Spanish made it his own and given it to the world as beautiful, musical verse. We must not, however, in seeking for influences forget the man's own genius, his own powers, his own individuality. He was no servile imitator. He possessed a rare genius of his own. (p. 27)

> F. M. Kercheville, *"Modern and Contemporary Spanish Poetry,"* in The University of New Mexico Bulletin *(reprinted by permission of the University of New Mexico), Vol. 4, No. 2, December 15, 1933, pp. 1-64.**

FEDERICO GARCÍA LORCA and PABLO NERUDA (essay date 1933)

García Lorca: [Rubén Darío] gave us the murmur of the forest in an adjective, and being a master of language, like Fray Luis de Granada, he made zodiacal signs out of the lemon tree, the hoof of a stag, and mollusks full of terror and infinity. He launched us on the sea with frigates and shadows in our eyes, and built an enormous promenade of gin over the grayest afternoon the sky has ever known, and greeted the southwest wind as a friend, all heart like a Romantic poet, and put his hand on the Corinthian capital of all epochs with a sad, ironic doubt.

Neruda: His red name deserves to be remembered, along with his essential tendencies, his terrible heartaches, his incandescent uncertainties, his descent to the hospitals of hell, his ascent to the castles of fame, his attributes as a great poet, now and forever undeniable.

García Lorca: As a Spanish poet he taught the old and the young in Spain with a generosity and a sense of universality that are lacking in the poets of today. He taught Valle-Inclán and Juan Ramón Jiménez and the Machado brothers, and his voice was water and niter in the furrows of our venerable language. From Rodrigo Caro to the Argensolas or Don Juan Arguijo, Spanish had not seen such plays on words, such clashes of consonants, such lights and forms, as in Rubén Darío. From the landscape of Velázquez and Goya's bonfire and Quevedo's melancholy to the elegant apple color of the Mallorcan peasant girls, Darío walked the Spanish earth as in his own land.

Neruda: He brought a tide to Chile, the hot northern sea, and he left that sea there, abandoned on the hard, rock-toothed coast, and the ocean battered it with spume and bells, and the black winds of Valparaíso filled it with sonorous salt. Tonight let us carve his statue out of air, crisscrossed with smoke and voices, with circumstances, with life, like his own magnificent poetry, crisscrossed with sounds and dreams.

García Lorca: But I want this statue of air to show his blood, like a branch of coral shaken by the tide; his nerves, like a photograph of sheet-lightning; his minotaur's head, where the Gongoresque snow is painted by flight of hummingbirds; his vague, absent eyes, the eyes of a millionaire whose millions are tears; and also his defects: the weeds and the empty flute notes in his book-shelves, and the cognac bottles of his dramatic drunkenness, and the impudent padding that fills the multitude of his lines with humanity. The fertile substance of his great poetry stands solidly outside of norms, forms, and schools.

Neruda: Federico García Lorca, a Spaniard, and I, a Chilean, dedicate the honors bestowed on us today to that great shadow who sang more loftily than ourselves, and who saluted, in a new voice, the Argentinian soil that we now tread.

García Lorca: Pablo Neruda, a Chilean, and I, a Spaniard, are one in our language and one in our reverence for that great Nicaraguan, Argentinian, Chilean, and Spanish poet Rubén Darío. (pp. 140-41)

> Federico García Lorca and Pablo Neruda, *"Al Alimon"* (orginally a speech delivered to the Pen Club in 1933), in Selected Poems of Rubén Darío, *translated by Lysander Kemp (copyright © 1965 University of Texas Press), University of Texas Press, 1965, pp. 139-41.*

G. DUNDAS CRAIG (essay date 1934)

In [*Blasán* from *Prosas profanas*], Darío brings together all the pleasing myths that in his mind were associated with the swan; first, the myth of Leda and the Swan, and, by association, Leonardo da Vinci, who painted a great picture on this subject. . . .

The reference to the Danube has puzzled the commentators; it is separated from the Lohengrin story by the reference to Leonardo, and seems to have nothing to do with the operatic legend. It may point to the widespread fame of the swan, because the Danube in ancient times was the limit of civilization; but perhaps a simpler explanation is nearer the truth. It is probably connected with the Lohengrin legend, for, although the incidents of that story are supposed to have occurred on the lower Rhine, any other German river would have done as well, and "Danubio" happened to offer a novel and interesting rhyme for the later epithet, "rubio." (p. 260)

The swan is the aristocrat among birds, as Darío felt himself to be an aristocrat of the spirit in the midst of a sordid democracy. . . . Hence, his mind turns naturally to courtly scenes. In imagination he sees the blue expanse of the lake crossed by the glittering white swans, and this reminds him of the fleurs-de-lis, the emblem of the kings of France. This again carries him back to the court of Louis XV, to the lake at Versailles, and to the king's favorite, Madame de Pompadour, lavishing her favors on the swans. (p. 261)

Darío's interest in classical mythology and his method of adapting it to his own purposes find illustration in *Friso* [from *Prosas profanas*]. This may be regarded as another effort on the part of the poet to escape from the dullness and materialism of his immediate surroundings and to find in the myths of ancient Greece the beauty that forever eluded him. There is evidence that he was not a profound classical scholar; but no more was Keats. Like Keats, however, he had so steeped himself in the ancient myths that their spirit lived again in him; their world became more intensely real than the actual world about him. Like Keats, too, he had the power to put life into the dry bones of the Dictionary of Classical Mythology. (pp. 262-63)

In *Friso* he essays a picture of Greek life in the Golden Age. He has seen, or imagined, the frieze of some Grecian temple; the figures take life before him, and the whole procession passes the lover and his beloved. Almost inevitably this poem suggests a comparison with Keats's *Ode on a Grecian Urn*. Both are Greek; but the latter preserves the restraint and severity of tone that we associate with the art of Athens, while the former is warm, pulsing with life, luxuriously sensuous—Corinthian, in fact, as is suggested by the reference to the Corinth vine under which the action develops. It is a picture of life looked at with the eyes of the Italian Renaissance, or of France under the *ancien régime*.... There is a difference, also, in the point of view: Keats looks on from the outside, detached from the emotions animating the figures before him; Darío identifies himself with the speaker, puts himself into the heart of the scene, and is the central figure presented in the frieze, fixed by the sculptor at the supreme moment in the life of the lover. (pp. 263-64)

Darío, it is evident, has definitely aimed at producing the effect of a sculptured frieze, that is to say, of a thin line of figures in movement, the action never being allowed to cease entirely, each group leading on the group that follows, and eventually bringing the reader back to the point from which he started.... (p. 264)

> *G. Dundas Craig, "Commentary: Rubén Darío," in his* The Modernist Trend in Spanish-American Poetry: A Collection of Representative Poems of the Modernist Movement and the Reaction *(copyright © 1934 by The Regents of the University of California; reprinted by permission of the University of California Press), University of California Press, 1934, pp. 255-75.*

E. ALLISON PEERS   (essay date 1949)

Vitality, in the fullest sense of that word, was Rubén Darío's great gift to literature and to Spain. Surging through both the content and the form of his work, it is perhaps the more obvious in the latter—in, for example, the extraordinary flexibility of his alexandrines and the sensitiveness and skill with which he adapted them to every kind of mood; in his demonstrations that the Classical hexameter, which had been but timidly essayed by Spaniards, could be used by them as confidently as by the natives of any other country; in the boldness with which he re-introduced *enjambements* of a type hardly known since Calderón. And to such specific indications, which space curtails, must be added more general ones: the discovery of a new world of colour and music, the revivification of well-worn themes, the creation of new atmospheres and the energizing of the verse-form with the poetic spirit.

With the name of Darío is generally connected the literary manifestation known as Modernism—a "direction" or a "mode", rather than a "movement" or a "school".... This association of Modernism with the greatest of its exponents is justified. For, although the ideals which it sought to

implant had arisen, independently of him, both in Spain and in Spanish America, it was he who carried them with the greatest distinction into practice and to whom poets in both continents looked as to their chief exponent. (pp. 581-82)

[*Cantos de Vida y Esperanza* is a] semi-autobiographical poem, prefacing the collection of the same title, with no very notable features in vocabulary or metre—giving the impression, in fact, of being rather carelessly written. The sidelights thrown by the poet, in familiar phrases, upon his character and literary tastes will give the reader food for thought and discussion. More elusive is the curious naïveté of tone, sometimes breaking into a half-defiant candour.... This is a poem of capital importance for an understanding of its author. (p. 586)

[Taken] from the *Cantos de vida y esperanza*, [*A Roosevelt*] is noteworthy almost wholly for its subject. It was addressed to Theodore Roosevelt, at a time when his "Big Stick" policy was antagonizing the Latin-American peoples, whose cause the poet takes up against the potential invader with a savage but dignified irony and a finely-controlled passion. Here and there the rhetoric verges dangerously on rant and some of the effects employed are facile, even childish. But these flaws are insignificant beside the positive achievements of the poem—notably the handling of the emotional tension as it first rises and then falls, before rising again, in the final section, to its tremendous climax. Unlike most of his other work though this may be, Darío would be remembered by the people of two continents had he written nothing beside. (pp. 591-92)

> *E. Allison Peers, "Rubén Darío," in his* A Critical Anthology of Spanish Verse *(reprinted by permission of the University of California Press), University of California Press, 1949 (and reprinted by Greenwood Press, 1968), pp. 580-98.*

OCTAVIO PAZ   (essay date 1965)

Rubén Darío was the bridge between the precursors and the second generation of Modernism. His constant travels and his generous activity in behalf of others made him the point of connection for the many scattered poets and groups on two continents. He not only inspired and captained the battle; he was also its observer and critic. The evolution of his poetry, from *Blue* to *Poem of Autumn*, corresponds with that of the movement, which began with him and ended with him. But his work did not end with Modernism: he went beyond it, beyond the language of that school and, in fact, of every school. Darío was not only the richest and most ample of the Modernist poets: he was one of the great modern poets. At times, he reminds us of Poe; at other times, of Whitman. Of the first, in that portion of his work in which he scorns the world of the Americas to seek an otherworldly music; of the second, in that portion in which he expresses his vitalist affirmations, his pantheism, and his belief that he was, in his own right, the bard of Latin America as Whitman was of Anglo-America.

Darío loved and imitated Verlaine's poetry above all other, but his best poems have little resemblance to those of his model. He has superabundant health and energy; his sun is stronger, his wine more generous. Verlaine was a Parisian provincial, Darío was a Central American globetrotter. His poetry is virile: backbone, heart, sex. It is clear and rotund even when it is sorrowful. It is the work of a Romantic who was also a Parnassian and a Symbolist. The work of a hybrid, not only because of the variety of his spiritual and technical influences but also because of the very blood that flowed in his veins: Indian, Spanish, with a few drops of African. A phenomenon. A pre-Columbian idol. A hippogriff. (pp. 11-12)

There was a certain incompatibility between the aesthetics of *Profane Hymns* and Darío's temperament. He was sensual, many-sided, gregarious, never a hermit. He was lost in the worlds of the world but he never withdrew into contemplation of his own self. What gives unity to the book is not its ideas but its feelings. It is a unity of accent and tone, very different from the spiritual unity which makes *The Flowers of Evil* or *Leaves of Grass* self-sufficient worlds. Darío's book is a vast repertory of rhythms, forms, colors, and sensations. It is not the history of a conscience but the metamorphosis of a sensibility. Its central theme is pleasure. But pleasure is a game, and for that very reason it is also a ritual which includes sacrifice and pain. Darío was not the first to know that the religion of pleasure is a rigorous one.

In my opinion, the last poem in *Profane Hymns* is the greatest poem in the book. It is both a résumé of his aesthetics and a prophecy about the future course of poetry. Its first line is a definition of his verse: "I seek a form that my style cannot discover." He seeks a beauty that is beyond beauty, that words can evoke but can never state. All of Romanticism—the desire to grasp the infinite—and all of Symbolism—an ideal, indefinable beauty that can only be suggested—are contained in that line. In the sestet there is an abrupt change of tone. After hope and confidence, doubt: "And I only find the word that runs away." The feeling of sterility and impotence appears as constantly in Darío's poetry as it does in that of the other great poets of the epoch, from Baudelaire to Mallarmé. At times it resolves into irony; at other times, into silence. In the concluding line, the poet sees the world as an immense question mark. It is not man who questions existence; it is existence that questions man. The line is worth the whole poem, and the poem is worth the whole book: "And the neck of the great white swan, that questions me."

In 1898 Darío became a correspondent for the Buenos Aires newspaper *La Nación*. . . . During this epoch he published many books in prose and his great volumes of poetry: *Songs of Life and Hope, The Swans and Other Poems, The Wandering Song, Poem of Autumn and Other Poems,* and *Song to the Argentine and Other Poems*. A good many of the poems are in his previous manner; in fact, some of them were written during the time of *Profane Hymns* or even earlier. But the larger and more valuable portion reveals a new Darío, graver and more lucid, stronger and more virile. This does not imply a major break between *Profane Hymns* and *Songs of Life and Hope*. New themes appear, and the verse is more masterly and more profound, but there is no diminishing of his love for brilliant words. There is also no lack of rhythmic innovations: on the contrary, the rhythms are even more daring, and at the same time more secure. *Songs of Life and Hope* is not a negation of his earlier style but rather a natural development of it. (pp. 13-15)

Although Darío found rationalist atheism repugnant—his temperament was religious, even superstitious—it cannot be said that he was a Christian poet. Fear of death, the horror of being, self-disgust, expressions which appear now

and then after *Songs of Life and Hope,* are ideas and feelings with Christian roots; but the other half, Christian eschatology, is absent. Darío was born in a Christian world, but he lost his faith and was left, like so many of us, with the inheritance of a guilt that no longer has reference to a supernatural sphere. The sense of original sin impregnates many of his best poems: ignorance of our origins and our end, fear of the inner abyss, the horror of living in the dark. . . . In the poems of this nature, written in a temperate and reticent language, varying between monologue and confession, I am especially moved by all three of the nocturnes. The first and third conclude with a presentiment of death. He does not describe death and only names it with a pronoun: She. In contrast, he sees life as a bad dream, a motley collection of grotesque or terrible moments, futile actions, unrealized projects, flawed emotions. It is the anguish of a city night, its silence broken by "the rumble of distant wheels" or the humming of the blood: a prayer that becomes a blasphemy, the endless reckoning of a solitary as he faces the blank wall that closes off the future. But all would resolve into a serene happiness if She would appear. Darío's eroticism never ceased, and he even made a marriage of dying.

In "Poem of Autumn," one of his last and greatest works, the two streams that feed his poetry are united: meditation on death and pantheistic eroticism. The poem is a set of variations on the old, worn-out themes of the brevity of life, the necessity of seizing the moment, and the like, but at the close the tone becomes graver and more defiant: in the face of death the poet does not affirm his own life but that of the universe. Earth and the sun vibrate in his skull as if it were a seashell; the salt of the sea is mingled in his blood as it is in that of the tritons and nereids; to die is to live a vaster, mightier life. Did he really believe this? It is true that he feared death; it is also true that he loved and desired it. Death was his Medusa and his siren. Dual death, dual like everything he touched, saw, and sang: his unity is always dual. That is why, as Juan Ramón Jiménez said, his emblem is the whorled seashell, both silent and filled with murmurs, an infinity that fits in one's hand. A musical instrument, speaking in an "unknown voice." A talisman, because "Europa touched it with her sacred hands." An erotic amulet, a ritual object. Its hoarse voice announces the dawn and the twilight, the hours when light and darkness meet. It is a symbol of universal correspondency, and also of reminiscence: when he presses it to his ear he hears the surge of past lives. He walks along the beach, where "the crabs are marking the sand with the illegible scrawl of their claws," and finds a seashell: then "a star like that of Venus" glows in his soul. The seashell is his body and his poetry, the rhythmic fluctuations, the spiral of those images that reveal and hide the world, that speak it and fall silent. (pp. 16-17)

"The seashell I found is in the shape of a heart." It was both his living breast and his dead skull. (p. 18)

Octavio Paz, in his introduction to Selected Poems of Rubén Darío, *translated by Lysander Kemp (copyright © 1965 University of Texas Press), University of Texas Press, 1965, pp. 7-18.*

SOLOMON H. TILLES (essay date 1966)

[*Emelina*] is Darío's only novel. Chronologically, it predates *Azul . . .* and all the other prose fiction for which

Darío achieved fame. In terms of the value of his total production the work must be written off as a youthful and unfortunate caprice. It is a rather poor effort which suffers from most of the excesses of its type (the late Romantic *folletín*) and so is completely unworthy of the great esthetic sensitivity which marked his subsequent efforts. Yet it has historic interest precisely because of its shortcomings. . . . In *Emelina*, though all the shopworn Romantic artifices are still present, the narrator no longer takes them seriously. Darío in this novel was following a literary convention in which he no longer believed.

That the work is a *novela de folletín* is perfectly obvious from its plot. (pp. 218-19)

The traditional nature of the work is further evidenced by many of its facets. Its structure, for instance, is highly episodic and mystery and suspense are employed very heavily as conscious techniques. Characters are introduced as cloaked figures in the night and not identified until later in work. Sudden changes of action are introduced that remain unrelated to the main current until several chapters later. The role of the narrator is also traditional in this type of novel. He is an omniscient puppeteer who, in spite of his prior knowledge, is constantly being goaded into outbursts of virtue by the machinations of the villain. The mysterious nocturnal assignations, the salons, the rustic paradise in the final scene are all very typical *folletín* settings of both American and European Romantic novels.

Especially Romantic are the ethical qualities of the work. Good and Evil represent an absolute dichotomy and the nature of the characters, the development of the action, the direct intervention of the narrator, the very tone of the language (a highly formal, courtly Castilian), all contribute to this basic vision. The major characters fit perfectly into this stereotyped construction. Thus the hero is a man of unblemished virtue, noble, tall, handsome, elegant, who, though poor, has proudly made his own way in the world while supporting his widowed mother. The heroine is blond, beautiful, of noble carriage, serene sweetness and melancholy expression. The chief villain is smooth, polished, a gambler, drinker and ladies' man who possesses all the social graces. Underneath however he is absolutely heartless, immoral, diabolical. The heroine's father is a truly noble patriarch, controlling his estate with strength and largesse.

Yet there are some deviations from these standard characterizations. One such departure is the extreme caricature, done with a light, humorous stroke, of the unscrupulous Boston Jew, Josué Humbug, who succeeds in embezzling a large sum of money from the arch villains themselves. His genius for accumulating other people's money is admirable in its scope.

A fine piece of levity is found in the description of Paris in Part II, Chapter IX. This amusing recreation of Paris has God crumbling Mohammed's paradise and Dante's hell into a huge flask. To this brew he adds Pandora's box, a mob of cupids followed by "gentílicos coros de placeres" and behind them, woes and bitternesses. God then thoroughly shakes this brew and pours it out on the face of the earth, exclaiming: let there be Paris, and Paris was. This image of Paris as a kind of delightful but turbulent witches' brew cast out upon the earth as one of God's greatest acts of creation, and indeed God himself, in the role of a mad scientist blending wondrous concoctions in his test tubes, are highly imaginative strokes, almost worthy of the later Darío. (pp. 219-20)

The departure from the traditional content of the *folletín* novel is evident in a number of other ways as well. Darío's great emphasis on aristocracy is present here. Much is made of the qualities of natural grace, elegance and polished, exquisite bearing. The palatial settings are described in great detail in all their wealth of jewels, silks and garlands of flowers. (p. 220)

The aesthetic elegance reaches its peak at the reception for the nephew of the Shah of Persia, where the aristocratic setting is lavishly drawn with its luxuriant garb and plentiful jewelry. The highlight of the affair is the piano recital given by Sara, the inseparable friend of Emelina, and in the description of her performance we can easily see the poetic vision that was soon to follow in *Azul*. (p. 221)

It is [the] few moments of artistic insight in what is otherwise a completely undistinguished novel that forecast the narrative form that jelled soon after and appeared full blown in the short stories of *Azul*. . . . (p. 222)

> *Solomon H. Tilles, "Rubén Darío's 'Emelina',"*
> *in* Hispania *(© 1966 The American Association of*
> *Teachers of Spanish and Portuguese, Inc.), Vol.*
> *XLIX, No. 2, May, 1966, pp. 218-22.*

BRENDA SEGALL (essay date 1966)

Many critics having detected the undeniable influence of such literary movements as Parnassianism and Symbolism on Rubén Darío *Azul*, have criticized what they considered to be Darío's lack of originality. I believe that their censure has come largely from not taking sufficiently into account some distinctive characteristics that play a decisive role in the meaning of these stories. (p. 223)

Darío himself would not have denied the strong influence of the French Parnassians—especially that of Catulle Mendès —on the innovations to be found in the *cuentos* of *Azul*. . . . However, Darío was far too skilful a writer merely to reproduce the tendencies of his French sources. In *Azul* he added a new dimension to the plastic and evocative expression of the Parnassians and other who had constructed a serious world of beauty. The distasteful excesses which critics . . . found in Darío's work may well be due to these critics' failure to consider the language of his poetry and *cuentos* within the structural context of each individual poem or *cuento*. They tended, for the most part, to view language usage superficially in terms of sources rather than in terms of its function in the context of the work in which it is employed. (pp. 223-24)

In the "Estudio Preliminar" to his edition of the *Cuentos completos de Rubén Darío* Raimundo Lida recognizes the presence of irony in Darío's *cuentos*, and points out isolated examples of its usage. . . . However, Lida does not show how the irony in the *cuento* is sustained throughout "El Rey Burgués" as a constant stylistic device. A detailed analysis of the structure of the *cuento* will help to clarify this statement.

"El Rey Burgués" bears, as we know, the subtitle "Canto alegre". . . . The reader therefore expects a happy story which will conform with the promise of the story-teller. The so-called "Canto alegre" contrasts strikingly with the sad, melancholy "día triste" . . . which forms the external atmosphere of the *cuento*. Darío plunges directly into his story, and describes the rich material possessions of the Rey Burgués. It is apparent from the initial description of the king and his possessions that Darío is satirizing him, and treating him in an ironic manner, for the *cuento* is filled with hyperbolic clichés . . . .

Everything in the world of the Rey Burgués is shown in a state of over-perfection. . . . [Darío describes] the idyllic and luxurious atmosphere in which his protagonist lives by accumulating fantastic details of the physical setting. . . . Such objects as white-necked swans, and caged birds which sing harmoniously are stock images in the poetic world of the French Parnassians; but Darío, by deliberate exaggeration, makes fun of them as he accumulates phrase after phrase of description of the possessions of the Rey Burgués, who is preoccupied with beautiful form. (p. 224)

The favourite elements of the Parnassians are present in new and surprising ways: their love for the exotic orient, their predilection for plastic beauty, interest in eighteenth-century France, and the world of classical mythology. (p. 225)

The debt which Darío owes in inspiration to contemporary literary movements cannot be denied. . . . There is undoubtedly much that is French in the *cuentos* of *Azul;* but there is a great deal more which is undeniably Darío. . . .

By using the plastic and evocative expression of the Parnassians and others ironically, Darío infused a new and special life into his *cuentos*. There are hardly more grounds for complaint about the lack of originality of Darío's imagery in these stories than there would be, for example, about Cervantes's use of the elements of the *libros de caballerías* in *Don Quixote*. Like Cervantes, Darío breathed new life into previously used forms transforming them into a vital ironic universe of his own. (p. 226)

> Brenda Segall, "*The Function of Irony in 'El Rey Burgués',*" in Hispania (© 1966 The American Association of Teachers of Spanish and Portuguese, Inc.), Vol. XLIX, No. 2, May, 1966, pp. 223-27.

HOWARD M. FRASER (essay date 1973)

[In the fantastic stories in *Azul*] Darío emerges as a writer with a deep social commitment and not as some critics . . . have appraised him, merely exotic, artificial or escapist. In Darío's fantastic stories precious objects and exotic scenes are impregnated with a metaphysical quality within settings of classical antiquity and the luxuriant glitter of Versailles. Against these magical backdrops appear real dramas of human existence, illuminated by the persistent device of irony, the tension between what is said and what is meant. (p. 37)

The irony in Darío most often underscores a tragic sense of life which is the product of the delicate relationship between the fantasy this author depicts and the realities of our own world. . . . Darío offers us fables and mirrors our era in his ironic brand of fantasy. A realism pervades several of his first stories and fantastic aspects are seen in clearly definable contexts as in "La Ninfa" ["The Nymph"]. Here, an actress masquerades as a nymph and in so doing mocks

an "obese scholar" who believes in the existence of such creatures in antiquity. Darío also creates a mythological universe, whose inhabitants are not unlike those of our own world. Some of his most successful stories combine real and dream-like elements in a mixture that erases the limits between reality and fantasy. The story "El Palacio del sol" ["The Palace of the Sun"] examines the spiritual as an element inseparable from the physical. Here, Darío's concept of reality is baroque, a *chiaroscuro* in which Man is ruled by occult forces which are beyond his human understanding or control.

The stories of Darío have a varied, polychromatic effect. They are a mixture of the everyday world of human experience and the idea world of dreams and possibilities, all of which are combined in differing proportions. Moreover, in all Darío's fantastic tales, irony is the element he uses to draw our attention to this mixture. His irony first commands the reader's attention and focus upon the essential duality of his world. The consistent ironic tone also creates a resonance that unifies the disparate subjects of his tales.

"El Rey Burgués" ["The Bourgeois King"] is a story of a clash between two realities, clearly definable and oppositely charged. The *Rey Burgués* himself is a caricature of the rich bourgeoisie. He has a "vientre feliz y la corona en la cabeza, como un rey de naipe" [content belly and a crown on his head like a king in a deck of cards]. . . .

One day an intruder is brought before him, a poet who is soon viewed as a new kind of possession by the *Rey Burgués*. (p. 38)

In "El Rey Burgués" the reality of the impoverished poet is contrasted with the fantastic parnassian imagery of the *Rey Burgués* himself. The glitter of the palace is clearly a grand artificiality but one the king is incapable of appreciating. Thus, the poet becomes just another "object" beyond the taste of the king. The exaggeration of the king's court is suddenly placed in sharp relief by the poet's invective. The poet awakens us to the existence of another reality ironically opposed to the material aggrandizement of the king. The king's opulence lacks the spiritual qualities of the poet's poverty. (p. 39)

The "Cuento griego—el sátiro sordo" ["Greek Tale—The Deaf Satyr"] is an example of Darío's mythological fantasy which strongly employs the effects of irony. Briefly, the story deals with the king of the forest, a satyr who has been deafened by the gods for his ascending to Olympus. As a monarch he has advisers, a lark and an ass. The latter is looked upon, erroneously, as a beast of intellectual possibilities—he seems to be thoughtful as he forages.

One day, the poet Orpheus arrives in the forest, looking for a hospitable place to live. He is disillusioned with the wretchedness of Man and, as in the version of mythology, retires to the forest and enchants its creatures. The birds, trees, and even the rocks respond to his harmonious song. Then, after giving his audition, he approaches the deaf satyr and asks him if he can stay. The king defers judgment to his advisers. The lark incants lyrical praise upon the poet but the deaf king cannot understand him. The ass is unable to speak but, the king thinks, eloquently communicates a negative answer as he grazes. Orpheus is banished.

This version of mythology is subject to several levels of interpretation. The obvious irony is the impassiveness of the deaf satyr confronted with the inhuman and fantastic beauty, first of Orpheus' song and later of the lark's praise. On another level of interpretation, we find a fine parody of court life. Here, the king is compared to an ignorant monarch who lacks the mental equipment necessary to make a judgment within the capability of any reasonable man. The king's court is replete with caricatures. The lark and the ass as advisers are of no profit to the king.

But above these views of the "Sátiro sordo" rests a greater irony, that of the world of men transposed into a mythology. Orpheus is that individual who cannot perceive the results of his own actions. The reaction of the forest is overwhelming to the reader, and Orpheus is blind to it. There is nothing mythological about blindness and deafness or the effect of man's imperfections on his fellow man. Orpheus has fled the world of wretched men only to escape to an environment which is for him equally upsetting. This is the real world dressed in mythological trappings.

The satyr and Orpheus both suffer defeat because each has encroached upon another's sphere of influence. The punishment they receive is due to the intolerance directed against them by those they intrude upon. The process of intrusion and rejection becomes interminable in human affairs as seen in Darío's exotic mythology when Orpheus must leave the forest and, ironically, marry Euridice.

It is in Darío's metaphysical stories where we see fantasy operating within everyday reality. In these tales, the author makes no attempt to separate reality from fantasy but steps back and allows the strange forces of the occult universe, those later to be explained by the theosophists as supernatural revelation, to control his characters' existence. (pp. 39-40)

The supernatural . . . invades the real world in "La Muerte de la Emperatriz de China" ["The Death of the Empress of China"]. In this metaphysical tale, a parnassian statue is the cause of the unhappiness of a sculptor's wife because the sculptor, like Pygmalion, finds his affections drawn to a work of art. Marital bliss is restored only after the piece of porcelain is smashed. Darío affirms the humanly carnal aspects of interpersonal relationships and underscores social commitment alongside the "ivory tower."

As an examination of the stories of *Azul* shows, Darío was interested in many areas of human experience. In fact, in them may be found evidence to support a rebuttal to the view that Modernism is escapist in character. He uses irony to point out the relationship of a fantasy bound to reality and, as we can see, goes far beyond the mere writing of pretty tales for the amusement of young ladies. (p. 41)

> *Howard M. Fraser, "Irony in the Fantastic Stories of 'Azul'," in* Latin American Literary Review *(reprinted by permission), Vol. 1, No. 2, Spring, 1973, pp. 37-41.*

GORDON BROTHERSTON (essay date 1975)

[Commentators have noted] Darío's cultural catholicity, his exoticism, the literariness of his references, and so on. Much more important are the inflexions of his conversational tone, the ease with which he not only moves through space and time but effectively denies a normal understanding of them, and the rhetorical persuasion which leads to the ecstatic close. An American writing in Spanish, he

shakes off the weight and claims of history while recognizing it and wanting its glamour, his own position being assured by nothing but errant energy. (p. 66)

In conjuring prior and established cultures [Darío] made a virtue of the absence of origin, term and identity. His huge limitation is of course that operatic sense of culture which marks this 'first stage' of Modernism, the total absence of a recognizably real world. But effectively converting his solitary palaces into the scenario of a Weltstadt, he was creating a potential, a margin of movement, even if . . . he did not specify it to become 'the poet of America'. (pp. 68-9)

> *Gordon Brotherston, "Modernism and Rubén Darío," in his* Latin American Poetry: Origins and Presence *(© Cambridge University Press 1975), Cambridge University Press, 1975, pp. 56-76.*

ADDITIONAL BIBLIOGRAPHY

Cardwell, Richard A. "Darío and *El Arte Puro*: The Enigma of Life and the Beguilement of Art." *Bulletin of Hispanic Studies* XLVII, No. 1 (January 1970): 37-51.
    Examines philosophical attitudes in Darío's work.

Davis, Harold E. "Leaders of Thought: Rubén Darío." In his *Latin American Leaders*, pp. 134-40. New York: H. W. Wilson Co., 1949.
    Biographical sketch.

Ellis, Keith. *Critical Approaches to Rubén Darío*. Toronto: University of Toronto Press, 1974, 170 p.
    Study organizing critical works on Darío into categories such as biographical criticism, structural analysis, and general assessments. There is also an appendix on "Rubén Darío as a Literary Critic."

Ellison, Fred P. "Rubén Darío and Brazil." *Hispania* XLVII, No. 1 (March 1964): 24-35.
    Examines the role of Brazil and Brazilian literature in Darío's life and work.

Englekirk, John Eugene. "Poe's Influence in Spanish America: Rubén Darío." In his *Edgar Allan Poe in Hispanic Literature*, pp. 165-209. New York: Instituto de las Españas, 1934.
    Examines Darío's acquaintance with Poe's works both in English and in translation, observing the strong influence of the American author on him.

Fiber, L. A. "Rubén Darío's Debt to Paul Verlaine in 'El Reino Interior'." *Romance Notes* XIV, No. 1 (Autumn 1972): 92-5.
    Contends that Darío's poem is not derivative with regard to Verlaine's "Crimen amoris" as previous critics have maintained.

Fiore, Dolores Ackel. *Rubén Darío in Search of Inspiration: Greco-Roman Mythology in His Stories and Poetry*. New York: Las Americas Publishing Co., 1963, 178 p.
    Scholarly investigation of Darío's knowledge of the myths and languages of Greece and Rome, concluding that his contact with these cultures was primarily through French and Spanish readings.

Fitzmaurice-Kelly, James. "Some Later Poets." In his *Some Masters of Spanish Verse*, pp. 153-84. London: Oxford University Press, Humphrey Milford, 1924.*
    Believes that Darío's chief accomplishment was extending the possibilities of metre in Spanish poetry.

Fraser, Howard M. "Magic and Alchemy in Darío's 'El rubí'." *Chasqui* III, No. 2 (February 1974): 17-22.
    "Examines an antecedent of the institution of magic [in con-

temporary Spanish-American fiction] as it appears in one of the short stories of Rubén Darío.''

Predmore, Michael P. ''A Stylistic Analysis of 'Lo fatal'.'' *Hispanic Review* 39, No. 4 (October 1971): 433-38.
    Analyzes symbols and linguistic structure of this poem.

Skyrme, Raymond. *Rubén Darío and the Pythagorean Tradition.* Gainesville: The University Presses of Florida, 1975, 107 p.
    Relates themes and allusions in Darío's work to philosophical currents in the nineteenth century having their source in Pythagoras.

Stewart, Watt, and Peterson, Harold. ''Rubén Darío: Poet of the Americas.'' In their *Builders of Latin America*, pp. 258-68. New York, London: Harper and Brothers Publishers, 1942.
    Biographical sketch.

Trueblood, Alan S. ''Rubén Darío: The Sea and the Jungle.'' *Comparative Literature Studies* 4, No. 4 (1967): 425-52.
    Detailed analysis of these motifs in Darío's work, stating, ''Sea and jungle appear . . . as significant links in a vast chain of being.''

Umphrey, George W., and Prada, Carlos García. Introduction to *Selections from the Prose and Poetry of Rubén Darío*, edited by George W. Umphrey and Carlos García Prada, pp. 3-32. New York: The Macmillan Co., 1928.
    Biographical sketch, with a descriptive examination of *Azul . . .*, *Prosas profanas*, and *Cantos de vida y esperanza*, supplying literary background of these collections.

Watland, Charles D. *Poet-Errant: A Biography of Rubén Darío.* New York: Philosophical Library, 1965, 266 p.
    Contains descriptive examinations of Darío's work, tracing his many influences and giving much information on both his literary career and his personal life. This biography is designed for the general reader.

Walter (John) de la Mare

1873-1956

(Also wrote under pseudonym of Walter Ramal) English poet, novelist, short story writer, critic, essayist, anthologist, and dramatist.

De la Mare is considered one of modern literature's chief exemplars of the romantic imagination. His complete works form a sustained treatment of romantic themes: dreams, death, rare states of mind and emotion, fantasy worlds of childhood, and the pursuit of the transcendent.

De la Mare's life was outwardly uneventful. As a youth he attended St. Paul's Cathedral School, and his formal education did not extend beyond this point. Upon graduation he went to work for the Anglo-American Oil Company, remaining with the firm for eighteen years. During this time he also pursued a literary career. In 1908 de la Mare received a government pension which made possible a life devoted exclusively to writing.

The appearance of his first book, *Songs of Childhood*, introduced de la Mare as an exceptionally talented author of children's literature, a genre in which he produced collections of fiction and verse, and several highly praised anthologies. The world of childhood, however, is only a facet of de la Mare's work, though critics have remarked that a childlike richness of imagination informs everything he wrote.

As a poet de la Mare is often compared with Thomas Hardy and William Blake for their respective themes of mortality and visionary illumination. His greatest concern was the creation of a dreamlike tone implying a tangible but nonspecific transcendent reality. This characteristic of the poems has drawn many admirers, though also eliciting criticism that the poet indulged in an undefined sense of mystery without systematic acceptance of any specific doctrine. Some commentators also criticize the poetry for having an archness of tone more suitable for children's verse, while others value this playful quality. It is generally agreed, however, that de la Mare was a skillful manipulator of poetic structure, a skill which is particularly evident in the earlier collections. With *The Burning Glass and Other Poems* critics perceived a falling off from the author's past artistic virtuosity, which afterward was only periodically regained. Closely linked with his poetry in theme and mood are de la Mare's short stories. Collections like *The Riddle* are imbued with the same indefiniteness and aura of fantasy as his poetry.

The novels of de la Mare rival his poetry in importance. De la Mare's early novels, such as *Henry Brocken,* are works of fantasy written in a genre traditionally reaserved for realistic subjects. In his tale of supernatural possession, *The Return,* de la Mare deals with a primarily naturalistic world while maintaining a fantastic element as the thematic core. Even though it contains no fantasy in a strict sense, *Memoirs of a Midget* includes a strong ingredient of the unusual and is considered by many critics to be a masterpiece. The definitive de la Mare novel, *Memoirs* is a study of the social and spiritual outsider, a concern central to the author's work.

For his extravagance of invention de la Mare is sometimes labelled an escapist who retreats from accepted definitions of reality and the relationships of conventional existence. His approach to reality, however, is not escapist; rather, it profoundly explores the world he considered most significant—that of the imagination.

PRINCIPAL WORKS

Songs of Childhood [as Walter Ramal] (poetry) 1902
Henry Brocken (novel) 1904
Poems (poetry) 1906
The Return (novel) 1910
The Listeners and Other Poems (poetry) 1912
Peacock Pie (poetry) 1913
Motley and Other Poems (poetry) 1918
Crossing (drama) 1921
Memoirs of a Midget (novel) 1921
The Veil and Other Poems (poetry) 1921
The Riddle and Other Stories (short stories) 1923
The Connoisseur and Other Stories (short stories) 1926
At First Sight (novel) 1928
On the Edge (short stories) 1930
Pleasures and Speculations (essays) 1940

The Burning Glass and Other Poems (poetry) 1945;
    published in the United States as *The Burning Glass
    and Other Poems, including The Traveler,* 1945
Winged Chariot (poetry) 1951
Private View (essays) 1953
A Beginning and Other Stories (short stories) 1955
Complete Poems (poetry) 1969

THE SPECTATOR   (essay date 1910)

Mr. de la Mare's somewhat rare excursions into the field of
fiction are welcome for their twofold distinction,—of style
as well as of thought. In his earlier ventures there was a
tendency to a deliberate preference for recondite and
bookish phrases; but this has largely disappeared [in *The
Return*] and his avoidance of the commonplace has in great
measure ceased to suggest affectation or mannerism, and
appears as the natural and unstudied method of a subtle and
fastidious mind. The majority of contemporary novelists are
painfully anxious to exhibit their familiarity with the equipment of modern life, and seek to produce an illusion of actuality by copious references to existing institutions, places
of entertainment, newspapers, even public characters or
notorious nonentities of the day.... People who adopt
these methods may achieve an immediate success, but they
neglect the obvious consideration that the more a book is
immersed in "actuality," the more faithfully it represents
the spirit of the moment, the more ephemeral is its popularity.... Of all this paraphernalia of modernity, this cult
of the "up-to-date" in dress, upholstery, and equipment,
Mr. de la Mare has a sovereign disregard. He writes a story
of to-day, but leaves us in the dark as to where the scene is
laid, what is the profession of the central figure, where he
went to school.... Mr. de la Mare would probably make a
bad witness if he were cross-examined about his characters,
and could not tell us how many chimney-pots there were on
Arthur Lawford's house. But that does not prevent him
from having written a very curious and unusual story which
has precisely that emancipating effect which novels of actuality can never attain. He has the gift of the magic carpet,
though the journeys on which he takes us are through
psychic regions rather than from Fleet Street to Samarcand.

An additional and powerful reason for this detachment from
realism is to be found in the occult character of the plot of
The Return. The central figure is a man in early middle age,
the victim of an extraordinary visitation while recovering
from illness. Fatigued by the exertion of a walk, he falls
asleep in a country churchyard near the tomb of a French
exile who committed suicide a hundred years back, and
returns home to find that he has undergone a facial and
physical change so complete as to disguise his identity....
Such a situation might seem to open the door for farce, but
Mr. de la Mare never oversteps the borders of a discreet
and ironical comedy. The situation, as it affects the transformed hero, is almost tragic. As Arthur Lawford he had
been a thoroughly commonplace, phlegmatic, "stodgy"
Englishman; now that his body has been raided by this *revenant,* he is a vastly more interesting, intelligent, and attractive personality. At the same time, the more that he
learns about the antecedents of the Frenchman, the less he
likes him, and the dread of being wholly submerged by the
alien personality fills him with horror and dismay.... The

problems, ethical and otherwise, that arise out of this
strange case of possession, dual personality, or whatever
else one may call it, are handled with great subtlety, and
what is more remarkable, with singular good feeling and
delicacy. Though, as we have seen, Mr de la Mare discards
the minutely circumstantial method, he succeeds in diffusing an atmosphere in which one is prepared to believe
that such a change is possible. (pp. 698-99)

> *"Novels: 'The Return',"* in The Spectator *(©
> 1910 by* The Spectator; *reprinted by permission of*
> The Spectator*), Vol. 105, No. 4296, October 29,
> 1910, pp. 698-99.*

CONRAD AIKEN   (essay date 1919)

Mr. de la Mare's "Peacock Pie" consists of lyrics ostensibly for children; in reality it contains some of the most
delightful work he has done. It is doubtful whether any
other living American or English poet can weave simple
melody as deftly as Mr. de la Mare, melody both as regards
words and ideas. If after a century has passed one may recall Leigh Hunt's categories of imagination and fancy as the
two springs of the poetic, it would be no violence to say
that Mr. de la Mare's power over us is rather in fancy than
in imagination. It is delicate, elusive, impalpable; over the
simplest lyrics hangs an overtone of magic. And now and
again, as in the "Song of the Mad Prince," this magic
reaches a grave intensity which strikes well to the marrow
of things. Mr. de la Mare is not an innovator, and his scope
is not great; but within his scope he has no superior. (pp.
213-14)

> *Conrad Aiken, "American Richness and English
> Distinction: Ralph Hodgson, Harold Monro,
> Walter de la Mare," in his* Scepticisms: Notes on
> Contemporary Poetry *(copyright © 1919 by
> Conrad Aiken; reprinted by permission of Brandt
> & Brandt Literary Agents, Inc.),* Knopf, 1919 *(and
> reprinted by Books for Libraries Press, 1967; dis-
> tributed by Arno Press, Inc.), pp. 206-15.*

STORM JAMESON   (essay date 1922)

[Mr. de la Mare's] eyes catch the grotesque aspect of
mortal loveliness, and his ears are attuned to the half-
human note that underlies the human voice of the created
world. Some part of him is often aloof and unresponsive to
the human call, as if the listening spirit were half withdrawn. Throughout his work an elfin mockery peers
through the words, with a sidewise glance for the mocker.
It is not unkind; Mr. de la Mare is incapable of a sneer; it is
the protective irony of a mind compelled to live awry in the
procrustean bed of circumstance.

Viewed thus, from an angle only half human, the world of
men and women shows faintly ridiculous, even while it
keeps its aspects of courage and loving-kindness. Mr. de la
Mare never insists upon the ridiculous aspect of humanity
and rarely forgets it, looking at life with a smiling irony
which is sometimes uncertain and always self-regarding.
The Miss M. of [*Memoirs of a Midget*] shows often less like
the elf she was than like an ordinary human adrift in a
world of monstrous appearances, visited at times by a spirit
far greater than her puny body, from which anon it departs,
leaving her cowering, afraid, and wretched. She is mean
and generous, capable of purest devotion and cruel egoism.

Suffering teaches her, and joy escapes her, after the fashion of life. She worships beauty and sees it spoiled and self-defiled, craves kind love and loses that in the instant of achievement. It is as if her creator said: ''This Midget is your mirror, discovering to you the whimsicalities of your bearing, which are my very own. Yet is it not a brave puppet?''

Gentle self-mockery pervades even Mr. de la Mare's mystical faith. A mystic he is, for whom the world of appearances exists as the transparent covering of things eternal. His imagination . . . , like Blake's, is rather a power of spiritual apprehension. . . . For him, as for Blake, ''a Spirit and a Vision are not, as modern philosophy supposes, a cloudy vapour or a nothing''; they are passionate realities in a world of unreal show. (pp. 424-25)

There is a deep-rooted and seemingly involuntary melancholy in his art. It is apparent behind his swift smile and behind his passionate adoration of beauty. He would be bitter were he a worse artist and a more worldly thinker. He is sad because he loves beauty with a sharp, intimate love, and can be hurt to the heart by loveliness. His sadness goes deeper than to the gentle Greek melancholy. He grieves little for the passing of beauty; that may be gracious, and at last is dignified by austere death. He grieves because most often beauty is betrayed by the heart that cherished it. It is slain by its own lovers, since human love grows weary and unkind. . . .

But if Mr. de la Mare is without illusion . . . he is indeed not without hope, having a sure refuge in humanity, which although mean and puny and cruel, is able to measure the paths of the stars, to suffer all things, to outface pain, to be kind, and to lay aside life for a dream or a word. Mr. de la Mare cannot always take mortal men seriously, but he does not forget that they are to be respected as well as to be pitied. . . . [He] sees through courage and meanness alike to the resolute secret dreamer which is man. (p. 426)

Memoirs of a Midget is the most notable achievement in prose fiction of our generation. A man writing of a woman with intent to penetrate through the shadow show of her adventures to the secret of her attitude to them, is hindered less by any inherent impossibility in the task than by the barriers which his own mind raises against his attempt. He will sometimes achieve complete understanding—when his mind has slipped into that world where all thought is one—and he will sometimes be baffled, imprisoned in his obstinate and inessential maleness. It may be that the diminutive size of Miss M., by allowing her creator to see her always as a little different from other women, removed one barrier. We do not and cannot know; but we do know that Mr. de la Mare has penetrated to the heart of this woman—never more woman that when her bodily insignificance is exaggerated by Fanny's triumphant charm—with an amazing and delicate audacity. He has divined, and conveyed with precision and a charming patience, the most subtle, emotional changes in one woman's adoring affection for another. (p. 427)

In an age of scamped and hurried work Mr. de la Mare has written a book of such exquisite and finished art that its words have the importance of threads in some tapestry of fabled beauty. (p. 430)

Storm Jameson, "Mr. de la Mare and the Grotesque" (reprinted by permission of A D Peter &

Co Ltd), in The English Review, *Vol. XXIV, May, 1922, pp. 424-30.*

J. C. SQUIRE (essay date 1922)

[''Memoirs of a Midget''] is a poet's book. I can think of no prose book by an English poet which is a more substantial achievement, but of many in which poets have escaped to a greater extent from the manner and matter of their poetry. Mr. de la Mare is one and indivisible. The world of his poetry, that strange assembly of pictures and sentiments drawn in from the daily world, from childhood's memories, and from art, contains elements familiar separately but nowhere else found in such combination. He can write of familiar decorative things . . . as though nobody had ever seen them before: he makes everything he touches his, and he touches nothing to which he does not sincerely respond. The world of his poetry is a quiet world of moonlight in still places, of evening waters, of gardens, woods, and wild roses, of quiet parlours sleeping in sunlight, of midnight silences broken by small sounds. Yet it is a world never made for decoration; it is haunted by the most secret whispers of the heart, and in every corner of it we encounter a gentle, bewildered, suffering human spirit. (pp. 137-38)

The book is a close tissue of lovely images and perfect phrases. Every page is crowded, so crowded that it can be read only slowly if the mind's eye will see everything that is presented to it and the heart receive every quiet message. But in all this elaboration and complication of picture and language, thought, and fancy, there is never anything false or faked, not a word that is dishonest, or that strikes one as having been put in for effect. The major elements in our landscape are shown with surpassing freshness: the Midget helps here, for she was secluded until grown up, and the author, looking through her unaccustomed eyes, has realised many common things—the stars over a wood, the sensation of being alone in the fields at night, the sea, trains, tea-parties, streets—as though they had all just broken on him for the first time. (p. 138)

[I cannot] deceive myself into thinking that [''Memoirs of a Midget''] will be understood, or even read, by a large public. A few people will read it; but those who read it at all will read it many times. It is a book for poets and their kindred, and unlike any other book that ever was written. The symbol may be queer. But are we not all Midgets, making terms with a foreign world, and tiny under the heavens? (p. 143)

J. C. Squire, "Mr. de la Mare's Romance," in his Books Reviewed: Critical Essays on Books and Authors, *George H. Doran Company, 1922 (and reprinted by Kennikat Press Corp., 1968), pp. 136-43.*

J. B. PRIESTLEY (essay date 1924)

[Mr. de la Mare] is one of those writers who have a few obvious characteristics known to everybody, characteristics that are complacently indicated by the reviewer whenever such writers publish a book; but if we wish to press forward and examine him more closely, he becomes curiously elusive, almost playing Ariel to our Caliban. There is no difficulty if we are simply prepared to enjoy and not to analyse, for we can always recognise his hand; the work is all of a piece. . . . Superficially, his work may appear somewhat fragmentary and casual, the spasmodic creation of a gifted dilettante—a few bundles of short lyrics, some short tales, and a fantasy or two, so many lovely and quaint odds and ends; but nothing could be further from the truth, for actually his work is one of the most individual productions this century has given us, every scrap of it being stamped with its author's personality and taking its place in the de la Mare canon. . . . Nevertheless, he remains to criticism an elusive figure, whose outline and gestures are not easily fixed in the memory—a shadowy Pied Piper.

One fairly common misconception must be brushed aside before we can begin to examine Mr. de la Mare, and that is the notion that he is primarily a creator of pretty fancies for the children. . . . Regarded as a general view this popular misconception is so preposterous that if we go to the other extreme, if we argue that Mr. de la Mare is a writer that no child should be suffered to approach, we shall not be further from the truth. We could point out that his work is really unbalanced, decadent, unhealthy, poisonous fruit for any child's eating. Consider his subjects. *The Return* is the story of a man who is partly possessed by an evil restless ghost, who comes back from a meditation among the tombstones in the local churchyard, wearing the face of a long-dead adventurer—a nightmare. The poetry is filled with madness and despair, wonders, and witchcraft, lit with a sinister moonlight; some crazed Elizabethan fool sitting in a charnel-house might have lilted some of these songs. The *Memoirs of a Midget* is the history of a freak who moves elvishly in the shadow of some monstrous spirit of evil; it is a long dream that never turns to the waking world, but only changes, when it does change, to nightmare. The tales in *The Riddle* are worse; they are the chronicles of crazed or evil spirits, Miss Duveen, Seaton's Aunt, and the rest; their world is one of abnormalities, strange cruelties and terrors, monstrous trees and birds and dead men on the prowl; their very sunlight is corrupt, maggot-breeding. And is this, we might ask, the writer of pretty fancies for the children; as well might we introduce [John] Webster, Poe, and Baudelaire into the nursery and schoolroom. Such an account of Mr. de la Mare as an unwholesome decadent is manifestly absurd, but on the whole it is probably less absurd than the more popular opinion of him as a pretty-pretty children's poet. (pp. 33-4)

The world he prefers to move in is one that has been pieced together by the imagination of childhood, made up of his childish memories of life and books, nursery rhymes, fairy tales, ballads, and quaint memorable passages from strange old volumes. Behind this, using it as so many symbols, is a subtle personality, a spirit capable of unusual exaltation and despair. There is nothing conscious and deliberate, I fancy, in all this; his mind instinctively seeks these forms in which to express itself; his imagination, when it is fully creative, instinctively avoids the world of common experience and runs back to this other world it created long ago.

The world we discover in Mr. de la Mare's poetry has some superficial resemblance to that in Mr. Yeats', but Mr. de la Mare could not casually wave away (as Mr. Yeats has done) his fairies and witches and ghosts and Arabias and Melmillos and Princess Seraphitas, not because they are really anything more than exquisite images and symbols, but because they are part of a world to which his imagination instinctively turns, in which it probably actually lives,

not so much a beautifully embroidered coat that his Muse wears for a season, but her actual form and presence. One of the most beautiful and significant of Mr. de la Mare's earlier poems, *Keep Innocency,* puts before us the paradox of innocent childhood's love of what seems to its elders terrible and cruel, such as warfare. . . . And we may say that there is a central core in Mr. de la Mare's imagination that has "kept innocency," though his spirit should walk the awful borderlands and proclaim its despair; a man has *felt* the world he shows us, but a child's eyes have *seen* it, lit with strange stars or bright with unknown birds. (p. 36)

[It] is worth remarking that the later work is better and more personal, more characteristic than the earlier, both in poetry and prose. Thus, both the *Memoirs of a Midget* and the collection of short tales called *The Riddle* are better, on any count, than—to go no further back—*The Return*. This last is, of course, a fantasy, but it differs from the later work not so much in its theme as in its treatment, which brings it nearer to the ordinary realistic fiction of the time than the later stories are. The style is not so mannered, not so subtly cadenced and bright with imagery, as the style of the other two volumes, and it does not lure us on to forget this world of offices and the witness-box as the later one does, but really has the contrary aim of making the one fantastic stroke credible. Mr. de la Mare has not boldly entered his own world, and the result, for all the art he has plainly lavished on the story, is unfortunate; the story itself is one, or at least is of the kind, that we are more accustomed to seeing treated comically . . . than treated tragically as it is here, and though this would not have mattered in the least had the author lured us away into his own world, it matters a great deal when he is making terms with this one. . . . Mrs. Lawford, a commonplace, conventionally-minded wife, is the kind of character the ordinary realistic novelist sketches in between a few puffs of his (or her) cigarette; but just where such inferior chroniclers are happily in their depth, Mr. de la Mare is well out of his, and Mrs. Lawford is appalling, a crude monster from a first novel by a third-rate writer. Her friend and their conversations are on the same level of crudity. In short, the conventional element, which would not be present at all in the later stories since the whole pack of characters, with their houses and furniture, would be subtly translated, is so badly done that it almost wrecks the fantasy, which is presented with some characteristic strokes of genius. Here, then, the normal, with its commonplace tangle of adult relations and interests, has baffled our author's imagination.

Then in his next story he boldly obliterated all the common relations and affairs of life by choosing a theme that was bristling with difficulties, that probably every other storyteller we have would have rejected at a glance, but that required just such an imagination as his and no other for its successful treatment. The *Memoirs of a Midget* overshadows *The Return* not so much because it is later and the author has improved his craft, but because he has now boldly entered his own world and has left off trying to come to terms with that of most novelists. Many people have wondered why Mr. de la Mare should choose such a queer subject, the history, in autobiographical form, of a year or so in the life of a freak, for what is easily his most ambitious single performance, a novel on the old heroic scale. But if our account of him has any truth in it at all, he could hardly have done better; the choice of subject itself, let alone his treatment of it, was a stroke of genius. (pp. 38-9)

At first sight it may appear that our theory of Mr. de la Mare's imagination will break down when we pass from the *Midget,* which triumphantly proclaims its truth, to the collection of short stories in *The Riddle.* In these tales the author creeps along the borderlands of the human spirit, and in a style that is even more artful, mannered and highly coloured than that of the *Midget,* he describes the corroding evils and moonstruck fantasies that visit those on whom the world's common burden of affairs presses most lightly, the very young and the very old, and those whose reason has been fretted away and whose ordinary faculties have fallen into desuetude; it is a book of "atmospheres," of adventures on the edge of things, crumbling away the homely and comforting reality, and confronting us with the heaving and crawling darkness. But not all the stories are set in this queer spiritual twilight; some of them seem little more than exquisite memories, clustered about some slight theme, and have something of the bright loveliness, the happy magic, of those clear dreams that only too rarely visit our sleep; their brightness and their suggestion of old ways and scenes point to their author's having made a poetical kind of camera obscura out of his memory. Many of them are related as the experiences of childhood, notably two of the most exquisite, *The Almond Tree* and *The Bowl,* both of which have the air of being fragments from some greater context (though perhaps existing only in the writer's mind); and none of these things could have been created by a man who had not kept alive his childhood and never lost sight if its world. Some of the tales have the appearance of bright nursery pictures that have suffered some curious change and become symbolical representations of a spiritual life that no nursery ever knew. And even the stories that seem furthest away from anything we can connect with childhood reveal, after some scrutiny, their indebtedness to the kind of imagination that has already been described. . . . There is a curious suggestion throughout these stories . . . that this world of Mr. de la Mare's is, as it were, the other half of the Dickens' world, the poetical, mysterious, aristocratic half that Dickens, with his eyes fixed on the democratic, humorous, melodramatic elements, never gave us. This suggestion was something more than an odd fancy, for both these lovable geniuses (Mr. de la Mare is certainly a genius), different as they are in almost every essential, have at least one thing in common, their method of building up their worlds, the process of the creative imagination. (pp. 40-1)

[Mr. de la Mare] remains one of that most lovable order of artists who never lose sight of their childhood, but re-live it continually in their work and contrive to find expression for their maturity in it, memories and impressions, its romantic vision of the world; the artists whose limitations and weaknesses are plain for any passing fool to see, but whose genius, and they are never without it, never mere men of talent, delights both philosophers and children; the artists who remember Eden. (p. 43)

*J. B. Priestley, "Mr. de la Mare's Imagination,"
in* The London Mercury, *Vol. X, No. 55, May,
1924, pp. 33-43.*

EDWARD DAVISON   (essay date 1928)

Most readers appear to regard Mr. de la Mare primarily as a poet who writes for children. Others would enlarge his appeal to include . . . "the young of all ages." (p. 117)

Songs of Childhood, with the exception of one or two pieces like "Haunted" and "The Pilgrim" which quietly anticipate the more complex character of his later work, cannot be mistaken for anything but a collection of nursery rhymes and poems, ingenious and delicious verses. . . . But even so early as 1901 Mr. de la Mare had invented that glamorous, magical atmosphere which culminates in his volume *The Veil.* "Tartary" is not unlike a thin version of his famous "Arabia." . . . Here, however, there is nothing symbolic, no suggestion of a secondary significance as in the later poems. The book is crowded with miniatures of his more serious work, faint foreshadowings of the poet's full-grown imagination. . . . [In *Poems*] he leaves the nursery almost entirely only to return at odd moments through the rest of his poetic journey, and even then (as in some of the poems in *Peacock Pie*) seldom with quite the same innocent music on his lips. . . . Other writers of children's verse cease at the point where the essential Mr. de la Mare begins. Those who have coupled his name with the names of Mr. A. A. Milne and Robert Louis Stevenson completely mistake this poet.

This common misunderstanding is not only due to the fact that the poems which first won Mr. de la Mare his current popularity were the admitted nursery rhymes and children's poems of his earliest books. Even his later work contains certain elements which are usually associated with fairy-tales and many of his most deeply significant poems have the superficial appearance of his earlier pieces. He has always been attracted by the more grotesque, fantastic, and curious appearances of people and things. . . . [There] is usually some faint strangeness about the people who inhabit his verse. They are like people remembered in a dream. . . . For the full glamour of the dream-like quality in which his poetry is saturated we must look less to the particular figures it contains (many of them are mere symbols for abstractions) than to the atmosphere of a world they inhabit. It is the atmosphere of a world hushed in mysterious, but slightly sinister calm, . . . thronged with invisible presences, unheard whispers. . . . Moreover, in this atmosphere there is frequently a vague sense of supernatural forces lurking invisibly. To Mr. de la Mare the gulf between reality and unreality is so small that he can doubt whether our waking life is more real than our dream life. The shapes and shadows of both lives enter into the world of his poetry. (pp. 118-124)

[The epitome of his] most pregnant spirit, that characteristic melancholy which permeates all his finest work, is stated continually throughout [*Poems*] which is conceived on infinitely more serious lines than the bulk of his work in *Peacock Pie* and *The Listeners.* (p. 126)

[The] bulk of his really thoughtful work appears in *Poems, Motley,* and again particularly in *The Veil* where the melancholy mood turns grim. These books include very few of his children's poems. He is increasingly concerned with those "dark and livelong hints of death". . . . Transience, age, decay, mortality, always the trouble and despair of the philosophic poet observing mankind and nature, are the chief preoccupations of his subsequent work. But this deepening of his mood does not immediately disturb the glamorous surface of his poetry. In *Peacock Pie* his famous double-edged "Song of the Mad Prince" is still superficially a nursery rhyme, the neighbour of innocent little lyrics like "The Bandog" and "Miss T." . . . To a child this poem may be nothing more than a delightful nursery rhyme. But the older and more sophisticated reader cannot escape hearing through the quietly chiming verse the haunting *cri du coeur* that is repeated in many a poignant variation of baffled thought and intense feeling ever and again throughout the poet's work. Even a stupid or insensitive person, deaf to this sound and asking no more of verse than its apparent surface charms of rhythm and rhyme, may still, like the child, find everything here to surprise and delight him. But, little by little, this concern for "life's troubled bubble" increases as the poet's work develops. The true de la Mare is gradually revealed as a brooding, melancholy spirit, puzzled and bewildered by the quarreling claims of reality and unreality, and attempting to reconcile things imagined or dreamed or desired with things accepted or known. . . . His metaphysical speculations are so unsatisfactory as to throw him back upon the most beautiful aspects of reality in his effort to interpret the signigicance of the shadow of even the loveliest thing on earth. He tries to comfort himself with the realization of beauty. (pp. 128-130)

[In] prose and verse alike (his poetry belongs to both) Mr. de la Mare's melancholy, stripped of its many disguises, is a match for anything in Thomas Hardy or Mr. A. E. Housman in their most pessimistic moods. Not all the cloud cap't towers and gorgeous palaces of his imagination can quite obscure the dark horizons of his view in the two later volumes, *Motley* and *The Veil*. . . . The note of futility sounds deeper and stronger. Even those poems wherein he most seeks to escape from the apparent conclusion of his philosophy are touched by some sense of hopelessness. (pp. 132-33)

> *Edward Davison, "Walter de la Mare," in his* Some Modern Poets and Other Critical Essays *(copyright 1928 by Harper & Row, Publishers, Inc.; reprinted by permission of Harper & Row, Publishers, Inc.), Harper, 1928, pp. 113-40.*

G. K. CHESTERTON (essay date 1932)

The fairy-tales of de la Mare are not those of the Sceptic but of the Mystic. Take the primary idea with which all the best work for imaginative infancy, as supplied by Stevenson and Barrie, really began. It began with an idea which is called, "make-believe". That is, strictly speaking, it is written by men who do not believe; and even written for children who do not believe; children who quite logically and legitimately make believe. But de la Mare's world is not merely a world of illusion; it is in quite another sense a world of imagination. It is a real world of which the reality can only be represented to us by images. De la Mare does not, in the material sense, believe that there is an ogre who crawls round houses and is turned back by the influence of the Holy Child; any more than Barrie believes that there is an immortal little boy who plays physically in Kensington Gardens. But de la Mare does believe that there is a devouring evil that is always warring with innocence and happiness; and Barrie does not believe that innocence and happiness go on having an uninterrupted legal occupation of Kensington Gardens. (pp. 48-9)

It is the first paradox about [Walter de la Mare] that we can find the evidence of his faith in his consciousness of evil. It is the second paradox that we can find the spiritual springs of much of his poetry in his prose. If we turn, for instance,

to that very powerful and even terrible short story called *Seaton's Aunt,* we find we are dealing directly with the diabolic. It does so in a sense quite impossible in all the merely romantic or merely ironic masters of that nonsense that is admittedly illusion. There was no nonsense about Seaton's Aunt. There was no illusion about her concentrated and paralysing malignity; but it was a malignity that had an extension beyond this world. . . . [There] are rhymes, even nursery rhymes, of Walter de la Mare in which the shiver is a real shiver, not only of the spine but of the spirit. They have an atmosphere which is not merely thrilling, but also chilling. They lay a finger that is not of the flesh on a nerve that is not of the body; in their special way of suggesting the chill of change or antiquity. To do this was against the whole purpose and origin of the fairyland of the later Victorians. (pp. 50-1)

> *G. K. Chesterton, "Walter de la Mare," in* The Fortnightly Review *(reprinted by permission of Contemporary Review Company Limited), Vol. 138, July, 1932, pp. 47-53.*

JOHN ATKINS (essay date 1947)

[De la Mare's] obsession with the tomb and with life on the other side is apparent to even the most casual reader. His best novel, *The Return,* begins in a churchyard and is haunted by the churchyard throughout, as Shakespeare's *Julius Caesar* is haunted by the spirit of Caesar. The tendency came to a head when he devoted a whole book, *Ding Dong Bell,* to thoughts and emotions resulting from visits to cemeteries.

Put as baldly as this it might appear that de la Mare is an unnaturally morbid and unbalanced person. Nothing, of course, could be less true. His delightful books on Childhood, Dreams and Desert Islands refute any such accusation. Despite his admiration for the writings of Poe, he is no Poe himself. (p. 8)

De la Mare's tomb points towards Egypt because the Ancient Egyptians preceded him in his absorption in the phenomenon of death. Their social lives were ruled by the never-forgotten fact that life was not eternal (in this world, at least) and that when life is important, so is death. . . . De la Mare is Egyptian in this respect, for he also can never forget it, although the conventions of our time force him to be less candid and more subtle. But any enclosed space reminds him of a tomb. Anything with walls is a grave-symbol. His walls are never on the defensive against the mind's expanding, roving spirit. Rather are they being battered from the outside by the unknown menace. (pp. 8-9)

The tomb is never far from de la Mare's active mind. It should be understood that the word "tomb" in this context stands for a great many more things than a sarcophagus. It is a symbol of all that belongs to the dividing line between life and death. No-one knows how fine this line is. The physiologist may be able to state that it is a matter of breath or heart-beats, but de la Mare, like his primitive ancestors, is suspicious of this simple explanation. He cannot forget, for instance, that the boundary between waking and sleeping is not a fine one. It is wide enough to contain daydreams; he himself refers to it as the territory between Dream and Wake. He is rather impatient with people who believe that physical definitions are sufficient to cover anything. (pp. 11-12)

[What] is the relation between [Poe and de la Mare]? On the outermost layer it is obviously one of teacher and taught, admired and admirer. But behind this is a subtle shift of ground. De la Mare is not content merely to copy Poe's method. What he has done is to analyse Poe's work into its constituents of subject and atmosphere. But instead of re-tracing ground and adapting atmosphere and sensation to his own time, he has made them the subjects of his work. Thus most of his stories are really concerned, not with human beings in a particular psychic state, but with the psychic state itself. Naturally, he has to employ human beings, otherwise his stories would be essays and would not reach the public he wishes to reach—those readers who keep clear of psychological treatises. The atmosphere is the hero and, as is to be expected, the human characters are often no more than cyphers, unreal and not very human. Poe's first consideration was the individual, though always the individual under stress. De la Mare has used Poe as a stepping stone in his advance into the unknown land which lies somewhere between life, death, sleep, dream, wake and revery. That is all we know of its topography.

And now we come to that aspect of these two writers which is most obvious, and which has already been referred to. Few others have managed so efficiently the horror theme. It is this, more than anything else, that brings the two together. But it is only the subject that is common, for in its treatment and presentation they are in constant divergence. Poe's horror is visual and extremely objective; de la Mare's can only be sensed by some hidden instrument of the mind and is intensely subjective. This does not mean that he writes impersonally of horror, or tries to analyse states of mind of the horrible or horrified; he is never so explicit as this, never presents horror as does a film magnate, but allows a sensation of alarm and apprehension to creep across the reader's mind. Poe's situations are horrible to the least and most sophisticated minds; his devices, the living in the tomb, the pit and the pendulum, are frightening even to the most insensitive. But de la Mare, with his mastery of nuance and suggestion, palms his menace off on to the reader like an expert salesman. His harmless Victorian furniture and harmlessly eccentric old ladies (Seaton's aunt, for example) are objects and people we know and meet almost daily without the smallest shudder, yet he transforms them into dark threats and menacing witches.

What he has done, in effect, is to establish the existence of a subterranean link between horror and beauty. This Poe never did. In his world of maniacs we would be foolish to expect anything but the unnatural. . . . But there is nothing like this in the stories of de la Mare. Gradually one becomes conscious of an eeriness which it is impossible to attribute to any one trick, but which must derive somehow from an expert use of words. And that is about all that can be said. (pp. 14-17)

Two forms of beauty are to be found in de la Mare: the physical beauty of nature and the psychological beauty of character. As has been said, his horror is subjective and psychological. Although he makes effective use of objects and their properties, they never provide the horror sensations in themselves. They are always provided by the impact of these objects on impressionable minds *in the story*. The reader is led to sense the result of this impact, of this psychic relationship. None of the ingredients are evil, but the effect of their collusion is. In fact, de la Mare does not

appear to recognise the existence of fundamental evil. He knows the stupid and the stubborn, but not the malevolent. But one of the disquieting facts of life is that the chance association of two goods often results in the production of an evil. This is the philosophic basis of his work. He goes further: evil is more likely to be produced by entities furthest removed in character from evil than by others which stand in closer proximity. Hence, the marriage of beauty and beauty can produce ugliness, and that of good and good can produce evil. This is an easily verifiable thesis. Intellectual marriages are sometimes spoiled by moronic offspring; the play of children is often marred by unfortunate accidents.

This is the explanation of de la Mare's apparently magic formula for the evocation of horror. It is based on a premiss that is so universal as to be universally ignored. It explains why a girl of ten, when placed in a certain environment, may appear repulsive. It is not the girl, and it is not the environment, but the association of the two. Association is both physical and psychic. Processes are set to work between the two poles, and they, the unseen epiphenomena of normal and everyday existence, provide the horror. They are the ghosts of de la Mare, they are the sinister influences, they are the pregnancy of his atmosphere. (pp. 17-18)

It is impossible to go any further with a portrait of de la Mare without entering more fully into the question of social criticism. Although many essays and biographies have been written of him, none that I know of is much concerned with this important aspect. It is not very difficult to see that his interest in subjects that are unpopular with and untouched by the majority of his contemporaries on the highest artistic and intellectual level is in itself a protest against the prevailing philosophy of our times. It is obvious that he must be extremely sceptical of the nineteenth century giants, the Darwins and Marxes. (''Marx is merely the boiled-up sentiment of a civilisation gone wrong''.) It is a revolt against a philosophy rather than a system. De la Mare would probably say that the idea comes before the act, and that the hideous living of our times is an accurate reflection of shabby minds. To argue thus one is covertly comparing one's own times with other times—in other words, one is drawing on an implicit reservoir of history. In this de la Mare is distinguished from his younger contemporaries. He has a sense of history, of the march of civilisation, that impregnates all his work. It is a dark backcloth to his scenes—one can make out very little detail but one is always conscious of its presence. The reader is aware vaguely of a distant Golden Age; any concrete features of this Age are difficult to define. There was an "otherness" about it. An extra sense was in use, perhaps, and language was heartily alive and not the almost valueless old invalid it is becoming to-day. (pp. 20-1)

The position we have reached in this examination of the mind and beliefs of Walter de la Mare is roughly this: The human race once possessed to an extraordinary degree a faculty known as Imagination. In the course of its history, however, the use of this faculty largely lapsed and was replaced by another one called Reason. Reason is a poor substitute. It has meant the closer investigation of a part of our world with a corresponding loss of knowledge of another. Reason utilises the five senses, and by skilful manipulation and co-ordination has elicited many truths from dark corners. But there are certain other truths that cannot be elicited without the aid of a sixth sense. It is a familiar controversy. Imagination is the poet's weapon; its links with religious experience and the old Mysteries are more than fine; it is Pascal's platform. Reason belongs to the scientist; it first flowered among the Greek oligarchs; it is Descartes's platform. (pp. 31-2)

A lot of de la Mare's poetry is for and about the mystery of childhood. Implicit in his theme is, if you like, an alternative to the historical Descent of Man. Confining his philosophy to a single lifetime one is aware of a circle, beginning with childhood and ending with old age, but where the end and the beginning are the same point. It is the Platonic theory of historical cycles applied to the life-span. The age of childhood is one of dimly remembered mystery; at about the age of eighteen, when the world forces itself upon the individual in its crudest form, mystery is dissipated and replaced by reality; reality holds sway until the world looks upon the individual increasingly as a liability; there is a gradual return to mystery, which one feels is akin to the first stage in more respects than a common opposition to reality. The process represents the author's dislike of and impatience with utility as a measure of value. The process, seen from his viewpoint, is Appearance—Disappearance—Reappearance. Reappearance is a recurring form of Appearance, the two are one. This is expressed in his stories by the close links that exist between children and old people, while the middle-aged are either unaware that such links exist or cannot understand them when they are aware. (p. 39)

With his strong sense of isolation and individuality, de la Mare is never at ease with the profanity of love. Each person is an island fortress in a rough sea strewn with privateers. It is perhaps possible for a person to know himself, but to know others is out of the question. We make fumbling attempts to explore the minds of our friends, just as I am making a fumbling attempt to explore the mind of Walter de la Mare, but we never penetrate deeply and only then at random points. The ghosts within, the filibusters of the mind, elude us always. How can two people, a man and a woman, dovetail into each other like the fingers of locked hands, and be no longer two, but one?

The novels and stories of de la Mare are still readable, after the lapse of many years, for a number of reasons. One is simply literary, his ease in the language. Another is his psychological accuracy, his nuances which ring so true and say so much. Throughout his writings are to be found chance phrases, often enigmatical or seemingly unimportant, which yet are like little daggers pointing at the hidden heart of a problem. From the core of his work fly streamers of many colours, which, if followed through the maze, lead invariably to something which one instantaneously recognises as truth or authority or perception. These are the documents of his own mental experience. And yet, with all this equipment, he never succeeds in creating a living character. In all his gallery—the Lawfords, Herberts, Bowaters, midgets and the thronging population of the stories—there is never a completely successful creation.

Here we have the greatness and shortcoming of de la Mare. Aesthetically he has no superior today; his mystic sense is of far greater value than most contemporary cerebration; his psychological perception is of a high order; but this perception extends only to parts, perhaps all the parts, yet never to the whole. The whole human being is as elusive to him as his ghosts are to us. (pp. 42-3)

John Atkins, in his Walter de la Mare: An Exploration *(reprinted by permission of the author), C. & J. Temple, Ltd., 1947, 45 p.*

EDWARD WAGENKNECHT   (essay date 1948)

[Of de la Mare's four novels], the first, *Henry Brocken,* is both the palest and the most "poetic." It opens with the picture of a little boy who has been left in charge of an elderly relative (a favorite situation of de la Mare's) starting out . . . to encounter the "wild and faithful" and "strange and lovely" people he has loved in books. De la Mare did not succeed in capturing the manner of the various authors whose characters are encountered, and the patterned beauty of his writing was less suited to fiction than was the rich, cerebrated prose he developed later. Yet, with all its immaturity, *Henry Brocken* is a book which only young genius could have written. The Criseyde episode, though a little vague, is very beautiful; even at thirty, de la Mare's comments on the subtlest creation of "the shrewdest and tenderest of [his] countrymen" went as deep as anything the Chaucerians have done. The passionate Puritanism of the Bunyan episode is pure de la Mare; and when the Yahoo loses his life to save Brocken in the stampede, Swift's bitterest creation is turned to the uses of faith and hope.

The passive quality of *Henry Brocken* disappears altogether in that glorious adventure story, *The Three Mulla-Mulgars.* Ostensibly written for the amusement of the de la Mare children, it is really an epic of courage, a song of loyalty and love. . . . (pp. 535-36)

In *The Return* we give our attention to the darker side of occult lore. It is interesting to remember that it was designed as a potboiler. . . . Of this book Forrest Reid has remarked that "it is the story of a spiritual upheaval such as might be produced by any violent emotional crisis, religious or otherwise." And it is true that a materialistically inclined writer might very well have taken his point of departure from some medically recognized maladjustment, while de la Mare preferred instead to have the convalescent Arthur Lawford possessed by the spirit of a long-dead French roué, Nicholas Sabathier, beside whose grave he had slumbered for a moment in a neglected cemetery. Once the element of "given" has been accepted, however, the situation is developed with psychological exactitude. Like a magic talisman, Lawford's strange experience tests his life in its every aspect. (pp. 536-37)

Few novels of our time have awakened such enthusiasm as *Memoirs of a Midget.* . . . It is much the longest and most closely wrought of Mr. de la Mare's novels, and while it is not obscure, it was written, and it should be read, imaginatively and intensely. But it is not a puzzle-book or a case-history. It is a picture of human life. The reader immerses himself in Miss M.'s experience with the same complete absorption encouraged by the great Victorian novels which the setting of the book suggests. And with such a protagonist, this is a great deal to say.

The fundamental idea is clearly the conflict between society and the individual; to accentuate the problem by making the heroine a midget was a very daring thing. . . . Though the first part of the narrative is studded with passages in which Miss M. is shown in relation to hairbrushes, watches, cats, books, etc., figures are never given. It is the mental and spiritual differences which result from her diminutive stature that really interest de la Mare; what might have been a mere trick is here filled full of creative significance, and we enter upon a tract of human experience hitherto unexplored. The data the midget accumulates are rather different from ours. (pp. 537-39)

[But having] separated her from humanity, [de la Mare] must at once unite her with it again; otherwise she is a freak and his book merely a tour de force. It must not be supposed that she is always right and society always wrong. For all his love of another world, de la Mare has never sacrificed this one to it; he loves solitude but he knows its dangers, its limitations; he knows, too, the social values. (p. 539)

There is no supernaturalism in *Memoirs of a Midget,* but Miss M. would not be a de la Mare heroine if she never looked over the edge; and it was more than a love of mystification which impelled her creator to remove her from the book—and our ken—with the laconic message, "I have been called away." So she typifies universal experience in the end, and so we get the marvelous suggestion that she goes on and on. . . .

Many readers of the *Midget* have wondered why de la Mare should not have seen fit to follow it with other novels in later years. Some ask still another question. Why should a man whose creative gifts have the quality of magic in them choose to devote so much of his time to non-creative work? . . .

At the outset one feels that such questions must come from those who have never read the books named. *Told Again* and *Stories from the Bible* are creative work; in *Come Hither!* . . .—incomparably the finest selection of poems for children that has ever been published—and in *Behold, This Dreamer!* . . . , whose field is "Reverie, Night, Sleep, Dream, Love-Dreams, Nightmare, Death, the Unconscious, the Imagination, Divination, the Artist and Kindred Subjects," anthology-making itself becomes a work of genius. As for *Early One Morning,* it seems to me worth all the scientific treatises on child-rearing ever written if for no other reason than because its pages are studded with the secrets which reveal themselves to love alone. (p. 540)

I think it significant . . . that in spite of all his love for children de la Mare is never sentimental about them. The small hero of "An Ideal Craftsman" (*On the Edge*) is positively sinister, and no "realist" could have given a less sentimental description than de la Mare has written of the "reactions" of Nicholas in "The Almond Tree" (*The Riddle*) when he finds his father a suicide in the snow. (p. 541)

[De la Mare's] shorter pieces classify themselves conveniently in several groups. First of all, there are stories of "real" life, like "The Almond Tree," "Miss Duveen" (*The Riddle*), "The Lost Track"—the only American story—(*The Connoisseur*), "Willows" (*On the Edge*), and "'A Froward Child'" (*The Wind Blows Over*). There is no supernatural element in these stories, but they are all brooded over by a sense of the mystery of human life and destiny; it is impossible to read them without feeling that they come from a mind with strong mystical tendencies.

Sometimes de la Mare's stories of this type are sinister, horrible, like "The Three Friends" (*The Riddle*), "Missing" (*The Connoisseur*), or "An Ideal Craftsman" (*On the Edge*). But the method is still indirect. . . . In some stories, though this world is our principal concern, we find ourselves subject to incursions from another. Such are "Miss Jemima," "Broomsticks," "Lucy," and "Alice's Godmother" (all in *Broomsticks*).

A special subdivision under this group might contain stories of ghosts and haunting, like "Out of the Deep" (*The Riddle*), "The Green Room" (*The Connoisseur*), "A Revenant" (*The Wind Blows Over*)—which is, however, a piece of literary and biographical criticism cast into narrative form rather than a ghost story per se. . . . Finally, there are a number of parables and apologues, all of which definitely seem to "mean" something, one is not always sure what: "The Riddle," "The Tree," "The Creatures," "The Vats" (all in *The Riddle*). (pp. 542-43)

Some of [de la Mare's] admirers see him suffering in later years from a spiritual nostalgia; the gates of the Kingdom of Dream are gradually closing themselves against him. (p. 543)

Probably every romanticist living in this day and age must, to a certain extent, find his fantasy trammeled; however uncompromising he may be in his romanticism, he can hardly avoid being a little self-conscious about it. It is true that de la Mare has some of the frank subjectivism of Stevenson; it is also true that he does not attempt to give us more than a glimpse of the Ultimate Vision. As he sees it, the "poet's faith" should express itself implicitly throughout his work. We have no right to ask of him that he "shall answer each of our riddles in turn; 'tidy things up.' He shares our doubts and problems; exults in them, and at the same time proves that life in spite of all its duplicity and deceits and horrors, is full of strangenesses, wonder, mystery, grace and power: is 'good.'" I find no nihilism in de la Mare, though I find much of the discouragement which touches all sensitive men in these troubled times. (p. 544)

Edward Wagenknecht, "News of Tishnar: Walter de la Mare," in his Cavalcade of the English Novel: From Elizabeth to George VI *(copyright © 1943 by Henry Holt and Company, Inc.; copyright renewed, 1971, by Edward Wagenknecht; reprinted by permission of the author), Holt, Rinehart and Winston, 1948, pp. 533-46.*

HENRY CHARLES DUFFIN (essay date 1949)

[In his poetry de la Mare] exhibits, generally, a perfection of art as flawless as Tennyson's. It is interesting to observe how this was achieved. The first volume, *Songs of Childhood* . . . shows none of this perfection of craftsmanship, but is rich in those delights that presently came to be recognized as characteristic de la Mare, though the final magic of rhythm is there only as an undertone. *Poems 1906* marks a great advance in art, and yet is deeply disappointing when read immediately after the [first] volume, because it contains so little of that entirely new thing—the spirit of Walter de la Mare—that made *Songs of Childhood* so precious. It seems that the poet was consciously disciplining himself to an exquisite artistry, but achieving this at a cost, giving us a greater number of excellent poems than were in the earlier volume, but very few to be remembered with equal pleasure. Yet the cost was well worth while. For in the first place, out of this conscious artistry was perfected the ultimate music of rhythmic form, embodied here in just one or two examples—*Age,* and *The Phantom.* . . . Moreover, the discipline of this volume was so effective that perfection of art became a habit, and in the next three volumes, far from being an obstacle to those special things this poet was born to create, it became the necessary medium and final voice of their utterance. (pp. 32-3)

De la Mare's ability to express in marvellous verse all the marvellous things he has to say is excelled by few even of the greatest poets. Moreover, it is progressive, and in *Motley* it is absolute. In this volume, as in *Hamlet,* content and form are perfectly balanced, and not to be distinguished. Here we find profound imaginative vision given utterance in poem after poem of flawless art. . . . (p. 35)

[The] poetry of Walter de la Mare is not essentially either a criticism of life or (as some think it) an escape from life. It will fulfill both these functions for those who require them, but the primary end of de la Mare's poetry is to heighten life. Life is much too good that any but the very unfortunate or the very dull should want to escape from it, but there are times when the pressure, perhaps the preponderance, of its lower constituents creates a sense of insignificance in life itself. At such times a draught, a breath, of de la Mare, even a fleeting memory of one of his poems, effects a miraculous restoration, so that life again is full of meaning and beauty. If the lower levels are your choice, if your interests are "business" and "sport", exalting your ego or overreaching your neighbour, you will have no use for de la Mare; but all the major themes of life he ennobles by making them eternal, part of the world of spirit. It is not altogether a matter of his special insistence on the necessity of magic, but of course it is partly this. He makes us feel in our hearts the strangeness of a phantom world, its stillness answering our cry. Dark hints and intriguing voices come out of the sounds that break the silence of nature, and the silence of a wood or a still house is burdened with meaning. The vaguely, deliciously disturbing atmosphere of quiet places is interpreted for us. Enchantment is ever at hand. . . . (pp. 196-97)

The themes which excite the intensity of de la Mare's passion, and which in consequence he makes more passionately intense for us, are all spiritual. Of love he speaks as of something special and strange, so that those to whom he has spoken can never let love sink into commonplace, but must always see it as godlike, breathing a speechless grace; an inexpressible union of the spirits of man and woman, a "selfless solitude in one another's arms". (pp. 197-98)

Life itself, the all that we have, the grand sum of our being and knowing from birth to death, is marvellously transmuted, transfigured, heightened in value and beauty by the poetry of Walter de la Mare, as he listens in his heart for what is beyond the range of human speech. He, more than most poets, keeps alive an endless wonder in the visible world suspended between God and man. (pp. 198-99)

Of happiness, life's profoundest truth, de la Mare has little explicitly to say, and that little comes late, but when it comes, it comes with an emphasis born of knowledge, a finality that gives it special force. It has always been there, silent, in the poetry, for all creation, whether of God or of genius, is in essence happy. But his ultimate word is that

love, beauty and happiness are the sacred triunity of life. Life so conceived, so lived, is hard to abandon, and to the poet with his intense life doubly so. Loving the light, he is impatient of the advancing dark—for to him it is Good night, not "in some other clime" Good morning. . . . (pp. 199-200)

> *Henry Charles Duffin in his* Walter de la Mare: A Study of his Poetry, *Sidgwick and Jackson Limited, 1949, 209 p.*

RANDALL JARRELL (essay date 1953)

[When a reader finishes Walter de la Mare's] *The Burning Glass,* he is amused by how complicated his feelings about it are. To enjoy much of it much, you have to make great concessions, great allowances; yet you feel that you would be a fool not to, that the allowances are ordinary good sense, common politeness. De la Mare is a hopeless romantic? Yes; but whose Law is it that a hopeless romantic cannot write good poetry? Reading de la Mare, one often has a sense of delicate and individual boredom, and wishes him a better writer than he is; but the man who would wish him a *different* writer would wish the Great Snowy Owl at the zoo a goose, so as to eat it for Christmas.

There are two or three beautiful poems in *The Burning Glass;* it is a book which will interest and occasionally delight a reader of generosity or imagination. It will not satisfy his ideas of what poetry should be, unless his ideas are deplorable ones; but how many poems will? (pp. 149-50)

De la Mare comes so late in the development of romanticism that, though he still believes in the romantic's world, he believes in it helplessly and hopelessly, as a long and necessarily (though perhaps not "really") lost cause. For its sweet ghost—a spectre that is haunting the industrial and scientific world that has destroyed it—he feels a nostalgic, rapt despair. Restrained by considerations neither of expediency nor of possibility, his romantic doctrines have become extraordinarily characteristic and extravagant: the forlorn hope is always the purest hope. Yet he grieves not so much over what has happened to everybody as over what must necessarily happen to anybody: over Man and the Present and what Is, these terrible crippling actualizations of the Child and the Past and what Might Have Been. This world of potentiality that he loves and needs is the world of the child *as it seems to the grown-up.* What we are is made bearable for him only by his knowledge that we once were potentially—hence, are—everything that we are not; and dreams and myths and tales, everything else that would be except for the fact that it isn't, are a similar consolation. To him the ordinary rational or practical life resembles the mechanical and rationalized routine, the hysterical anesthesia, of the hypnotized subject: what is real lies above (God, Beauty) or beneath (dreams, animals, children) or around (ghosts, all the beings of myth or *Märchen*). It is children and animals and the Heart . . . that participate in Reality: the blinkers of reason confine our conscious, systematic knowledge to what is irrelevant. Yet de la Mare's Heart not only has its reasons but does a surprising amount of reasoning with them, and its sentences are grammatical and full of semi-colons. He does not share the characteristic superstition of much modern opinion: that generalization or "statement" has no place in poetry. (pp. 151-52)

It is easy to complain that de la Mare writes about unreality; but how *can* anybody write about unreality? From his children and ghosts one learns little about children and nothing about ghosts, but one learns a great deal of the reality of which both his ghosts and his children are projections, of the wishes and lacks and love that have produced their "unreality." (We read religious poems not to learn about God but to learn about men.) At the very least de la Mare is a perspective of reality, a way of sight, that satisfies the limitations he and his readers share, and that exposes to his readers the limitations that are peculiar to de la Mare—or to themselves. He has made himself a fool for the sake of Faerie, for the sake of everything that is irrational, impractical, and at the same time essential; and because he has persisted in his folly his best poems—limited and extravagant as they are—are full of the personal distinction, the involuntary individuality that are marks of a real poet. But his poetry represents our world only as the flickering shade-pattern of leaves upon an arm can represent the arm; the hard hot flesh in the sunlight has nothing to stand for it but vacancy. (pp. 153-54)

> *Randall Jarrell, "A Verse Chronicle: Walter de la Mare," in his* Poetry and the Age *(copyright © 1953 by Randall Jarrell; reprinted by permission of the Literary Estate of Randall Jarrell), Alfred A. Knopf, Inc., 1953, pp. 149-53.*

DAVID CECIL   (essay date 1957)

[De la Mare's] prose tales are of an unusually "poetic" type. A great many of them deal with fantastic material, more often thought suitable subject matter for verse. And even when this is not so, even when, as in "Crewe" or "Mr. Kempe," he writes about contemporary human beings at a railway station or a London teashop, the impression he makes is unprosaic. Incident and character alike are fanciful and mysterious, the emotional tone heightened and lyrical. Every aspect of the world to which he introduces us is steeped in "the light that never was on sea or land, the consecration and the poet's dream." (pp. 219-20)

De la Mare's world is composed of diverse and incongruous elements. Its cast and settings are homely; he writes mainly about children, old maids and bachelors, old-fashioned servants, the keepers of lodging houses and small shops, living in country towns, or placid seaside resorts, or parsonages and cottages lost in the depths of a tranquil countryside. But—here we come to the second distinguishing feature of de la Mare's world—there is always something odd about them. And it is this oddness that he emphasizes. The houses are secret and irregular, full of dark nooks and twisting staircases and dusty accumulated junk: quaint ornaments, obscure books, dim portraits with histories attached to them. The children are queer children, with their demure manners and solemn eyes and heads buzzing with fancies; the bachelors and old maids are solitary, eccentric, often a trifle crazy; the landladies and shopkeepers are "character parts," as full of grotesque idiosyncrasy as the personages of Dickens. (p. 220)

De la Mare is, in the truest sense of a misused, overworked word, a symbolist. The outer world he shows us is the expression of an inner world, the external drama the incarnation of an internal drama. And that internal drama is concerned with some of the profoundest and most critical issues that confront the human soul. Indeed, de la Mare is occupied with nothing less than the ultimate significance of experience. What does life mean? he asks. What is the nature of the world we see around us? Not, at any rate, he seems to reply, what it might appear to a superficial glance. He is filled with a sense of the fleetingness, the insubstantiality of what looks so solid and permanent. Has the world indeed any objective existence, he wonders; is it not merely a reflection of our own minds, altering according to the mood and character of the observer? To de la Mare, as to Blake, what appears to one man to be a thistle, to another may be a grey-headed old man. Who can say with certainty which is right? "It seemed to him," so he says of the child hero of "Visitors," ". . . almost as if the world was only in his mind, almost as if it was the panorama of a dream." (pp. 222-23)

To convey so unusual a vision of life, de la Mare has evolved an unusual mode of expression. The style is a complex, highly orchestrated affair, rich with imagery, freaked with archaic words and poetical turns of speech, and moving in slow, winding, incantatory rhythms. And even when, as in "The Almond Tree," the style is relatively simple, the method of narration is not. Here Henry James's influence shows itself, and de la Mare's method is at least as devious as his master's. There is very little straightforward exposition or direct statement in these tales: their events are conveyed to us mainly by hint and suggestion and implication, made still more elusive by the crepuscular opalescent haze in which de la Mare veils his scene, in order to induce in the reader the spellbound mood in which he can respond rightly to this kind of story.

It must be admitted that he does not always so respond. Only a minority of de la Mare's stories are complete successes. Sometimes he tells them so subtly and tentatively as to become unintelligible. Even the simpler stories must be read very carefully if we are not to miss their full significance; for they are presented in a continuous series of delicate, minute, unemphasized touches, all of them important, but any one of which may easily escape attention. For this reason de la Mare is better at short flights. Every page of *The Memoirs of a Midget* is marked by a beauty and originality, but as a whole it does not make the impression it should, simply because it is too long for the scale of its presentation. Reading it is like looking at a large mural drawn with the myriad light miniature strokes of a mezzotint engraver. (pp. 226-27)

As for de la Mare's open and avowed excursions into the world of dream and ghost, the world of "Seaton's Aunt" and "All Hallows" and "Bird of Travel," it is unsurpassed in literature. He has a Coleridge-like faculty for giving a local habitation and a name to those basic nameless terrors and ecstasies and bewilderments which lurk far below the level of consciousness. It does not matter if we do not accept his interpretation of these phenomena. The rationalist may admire these beautiful, enigmatic, disquieting stories simply for the true picture they give of the movements of the subconscious mind. Understood as de la Mare intends us to understand them, they reveal a penetration into the spiritual regions of man's experience deeper than is to be found in the work of any other English author of this century. (pp. 229-30)

> *David Cecil, "The Prose Tales of Walter de la Mare," in his* The Fine Art of Reading and Other

Literary Studies (*reprinted by permission of Harold Ober Associates Inc.; copyright © 1957 by David Cecil*), The Bobbs-Merrill Company, Inc., 1957, pp. 219-30.

KENNETH HOPKINS (essay date 1957)

To say de la Mare writes 'a poet's prose' might do him a disservice, for the phrase sometimes suggests the whimsical, even the effeminate. But although in de la Mare there is a good deal of fanciful, elaborate, or even mannered writing, he is capable of prose as direct and simple as that of Dryden. This may be sufficiently demonstrated by reference to his essays.

The essays take several forms, and are all more or less 'occasional'. They occur as introductions to books—his own, or those of other writers—as contributions to symposia, as lectures reprinted, as long critical reviews. Of essays written simply as such, and so published, there are few. The long 'Desert Islands' is the most important of these. Most of the rest come into the categories first mentioned—but they are none the worse for that. And they afford an impressive body of critical prose quite separate from the prose of the tales.

In *Pleasures and Speculations* . . . the author gathered a dozen of these essays and *Private View* . . . contains a further gathering almost wholly of reviews. These, if the reader adds the long introductions to *Love,* and *Behold This Dreamer,* with *Desert Islands* and *Early One Morning* make a readily accessible collection as necessary to the understanding of de la Mare's work as the other prose.

To say 'introductions' in speaking of the prose commentaries in *Love* and *Behold This Dreamer* is misleading. These anthologies are full examinations of their subjects (I don't say 'final') and in both cases the introduction is well over a hundred pages long; the anthology is as much a commentary on the introduction as the introduction is on the anthology. These two works are more nearly conventional anthologies, in that the chosen pieces are grouped separately from the commentary, than the third, *Early One Morning.* In this the quotations and citations are blended with the commentary; are sometimes paraphrased; sometimes, indeed, are 'digested' into the writer's own; so that at first sight the whole long book appears to be 'de la Mare on children and childhood'. A glance at the index disproves this impression: it seems, indeed, that he has gathered thoughts, memories, glimpses of childhood from every writer of standing in the past twenty centuries. De la Mare looks for his material in the life of Al Capone, or the writings of the learned Sir William Jones. Indeed, as these three anthologies, and the other, *Come Hither,* amply demonstrate, the range of de la Mare's reading is prodigious. He seems to have read everything. In *Come Hither,* a 'collection of rhymes and poems for the young of all ages', there are nearly five hundred poems from three hundred writers; and he finds 'rhymes for the young' in Wolcot, Lydgate, and Alexander Scott. In *Love* he quotes nearly three hundred writers, including writers on this subject as apparently unrewarding as Erasmus Darwin.

His range as a critic can well be indicated by a few titles: 'The Early Novels of Wilkie Collins', 'Rupert Brooke and the Intellectual Imagination', 'Poetry in Prose', 'Flowers and Poetry', 'Lewis Carroll', 'Tennyson'. His Warton Lecture, *Poetry in Prose,* . . . delivered before the British Academy, is an interesting contribution to the study of English prosody, for it discusses how far 'poetry' can enter into 'prose'. (pp. 19-22)

Kenneth Hopkins in his Walter de la Mare *(© Kenneth Hopkins 1957 Longman Group Ltd., for the British Council), revised edition, British Council, 1957, 44 p.*

W. H. AUDEN (essay date 1963)

[De la Mare's] most obvious virtues, those which no reader can fail to see immediately, are verbal and formal, the delicacy of his metrical fingering and the graceful architecture of his stanzas. Neither in his technique nor his sensibility, does he show any trace of influences other than English, either continental, like Eliot and Pound, or Classical, like Bridges. The poets from whom he seems to have learned most are the Elizabethan songwriters, Christina Rossetti and, I would rashly guess, Thomas Hardy. Like Christina Rossetti, he is a master of trisyllabic substitution and foot inversion; the reader's ear is continually excited by rhythmical variations without ever losing a sense of the underlying pattern. . . . Like Hardy, he is a great inventor of stanzas and in command of every effect which can be obtained from contrasts between lines of different lengths, lines with masculine endings and lines with feminine endings, rhymed and unrhymed lines. (pp. 385-86)

Many poets have some idiosyncrasy or tic of style which can madden the reader if he finds their work basically unsympathetic, but which, if he likes it, becomes endearing like the foibles of an old friend. Hardy's fondness for compound and Latinate words is one example, de la Mare's habit of subject-verb inversion another. . . .

In his later work such inversions become much rarer. One can observe also a change in his diction. Though this continues to come from what one might call the "beautiful" end of the verbal spectrum—he never, like Yeats and Eliot uses a coarse or brutal word, and seldom a slang colloquialism—a chronological study of his poems shows a steady, patient and successful endeavor to eliminate the overly arty diction which was a vice of his Pre-Raphaelite forebears, and to develop a style which, without ceasing to be lyrical, has the directness of ordinary speech. (p. 387)

His late long poem, *Winged Chariot,* is a surprising performance. He still writes as a lyric poet, not as an epic or dramatic, and it is better read, perhaps, like *In Memoriam,* as a series of lyrics with a meter and theme in common, but readers who are only familiar with his early poetry will find something they would never have predicted, a talent for metaphysical wit. . . .

De la Mare wrote many poems with an audience of children specifically in mind. . . . [But] it must never be forgotten that, while there are some good poems which are only for adults, because they presuppose adult experience in their readers, there are no good poems which are only for children. (p. 388)

As a revelation of the wonders of the English Language, de la Mare's poems for children are unrivaled. (The only ones which do not seem to me quite to come off are those in which he tries to be humorous. A gift, like Hilaire Belloc's for the comic-satiric is not his; he lacks, perhaps, both the worldliness and the cruelty which the genre calls for.) They include what, for the adult, are among his greatest "pure" lyrics, e.g., *Old Shellover* and *The Song of the Mad Prince*, and their rhythms are as subtle as they are varied. Like all good poems, of course, they do more than train the ear. They also teach sensory attention and courage. Unlike a lot of second-rate verse for children, de la Mare's descriptions of birds, beasts, and natural phenomena are always sharp and accurate, and he never prettifies experience or attempts to conceal from the young that terror and nightmare are as essential characteristics of human existence as love and sweet dreams. (p. 389)

[De la Mare's] poems are neither satirical nor occasional; indeed, I cannot recall coming across in his work a single Proper Name, whether of a person or a place, which one could identify as a real historical name. Nor, though he is a lyric, not a dramatic, poet, are his poems "personal" in the sense of being self-confessions; the *I* in them is never identical with the Mr. de la Mare one might have met at dinner, and none are of the kind which excite the curiosity of a biographer. Nevertheless, implicit in all his poetry are certain notions of what constitutes the Good Life. Goodness, they seem to say, is rooted in wonder, awe, and reverence for the beauty and strangeness of creation. Wonder itself is not goodness—de la Mare is not an aesthete—but it is the only, or the most favorable, soil in which goodness can grow. (p. 393)

> *W. H. Auden, "Walter de la Mare" (originally published as an introduction to* A Choice of de la Mare's Verse, *Faber and Faber, 1963), in his* Forewords and Afterwords, *edited by Edward Mendelson (copyright © 1973 by W. H. Auden; reprinted by permission of Random House, Inc.), Random House, 1973, pp. 384-94.*

MICHAEL SCHMIDT (essay date 1979)

The uniqueness of [de la Mare's] poems is entirely thematic. A thematic personality emerges more powerfully than if he had written confessional verse. The unreality with which the poems deal—or the reality beyond language —*is* his reality. In expressing his world, he perfects a genre where cruelty, nonsense, mystery, fantasy and love exist together as constituting and complementary aspects of his world. But his limitations are clear. His and our realities hardly coincide, and where they do he is exploring only a limited range of our common experience. Yet within that range he is powerful, he gives us a poetry of wisdom before knowledge. He is the conscious poet of the unconscious— though in no facile psychological sense. To him 'unconscious' means inarticulate, the limbo in which language, to have power, can be used only connotatively. (p. 66)

When there is humour in the poems it is gentle and does not disrupt the stillness. D. H. Lawrence praised his 'perfect appreciation of life at still moments', and Edmund Blunden in his elegy, 'A Poet's Death', calls him 'A light of other days.' This unfairly restricts his achievement for, despite his romantic idiom and his lack of technical originality, thematic-ally de la Mare is timeless. It would be difficult for any poet to fuse the two worlds de la Mare did in 'The Song

of Shadows' with anything like his accuracy and unerring rhythms. From the Campion-like world of music and mystery, the poem focuses on a physical image whose mystery —the mystery of the actual, the known—exceeds the mystery of the unknown. . . . (pp. 67-8)

> *Michael Schmidt, "Walter de la Mare," in his* A Reader's Guide to Fifty Modern British Poets *(copyright © Michael Schmidt 1979; by permission of Barnes & Noble Books, a division of Littlefield, Adams & Co., Inc.), Barnes & Noble, 1979, pp. 64-8.*

ADDITIONAL BIBLIOGRAPHY

Barfield, Owen. "Poetry in Walter de la Mare." *The Denver Quarterly* 8, No. 3 (Autumn 1973): 69-81.
    Analyzes structure and rhetorical devices in de la Mare's poetry.

Gosse, Edmund. "The Fairy in the Garden." In his *Books on the Table*, pp. 311-17. New York: Charles Scribner's Sons, 1921.
    Discussion of de la Mare's early poems.

Gregory, Horace. "The Nocturnal Traveller: Walter de la Mare." *Poetry* LXXX, No. IV (July 1952): 213-32.
    Appreciation of de la Mare as poet, short story writer, and anthologist of children's verse.

Larkin, Philip. "Big Victims: Emily Dickinson and Walter de la Mare." *The New Statesman* 79, No. 2035 (13 March 1970): 368-69.*
    Characterizes de la Mare's poetry as attaining "a highly artificial 'childlike vision'."

Lucas, F. L. "The Poetry of Walter de la Mare." *The New Statesman* XX, No. 506 (23 December 1922): 356-57.
    Appreciation of de la Mare, seeing the combination of classical simplicity and a fascination with the strange as distinguishing features of his poetry.

McCrosson, Doris Ross. *Walter de la Mare*. New York: Twayne Publishers, 1966, 170 p.
    Critical study focusing on the novels.

Mégroz, R. L. "Walter de la Mare." In his *Five Novelist Poets of To-Day*, pp. 19-58. London: Joiner & Steele, 1933.
    Descriptive survey of the novels, short stories, and poetry.

Noyes, Alfred. "The Poetry of Walter de la Mare." *Contemporary Review* Vol. CXC, No. 1088 (August 1956): 70-3.
    Presents de la Mare as an example of the spirit of poetry in an era of "anti-poets."

Richards, I. A. "Reconsideraton: Walter de la Mare." *The New Republic* 174, No. 5 (31 January 1976): 31-3.
    Tribute to de la Mare's work.

Shanks, Edward. "The Poetry of Mr. Walter de la Mare." In his *First Essays on Literature*, pp. 68-85. London: W. Collins Sons & Co., 1923.
    General examination of the poetry, comparing de la Mare to Coleridge, Poe, and Christina Rosetti, and calling the author "the poet of lost paradises."

Williams, Charles. "Walter de la Mare." In his *Poetry at Present*, pp. 82-95. Oxford: The Clarendon Press, 1930.
    General appraisal of the poetry, comparing de la Mare with Yeats and criticizing the former for his undefined sense of mysticism.

Ernest (Christopher) Dowson

1867-1900

British poet, novelist, short story writer, and dramatist.

Ernest Dowson is generally considered the prototypical poet of the English *fin de siècle* (or decadent) period, a period which saw the emergence of a group of poets that W. B. Yeats characterized as "The Tragic Generation."

Dowson was primarily a lyric poet. His short, technically expert poetry is most often concerned with the transience of love, the corruption of innocence, and the inevitability of death. Like other *fin de siècle* poets, Dowson was an aesthete concerned with the creation of lyric beauty unburdened by messages or morals. Thus his poetry does not have characteristic themes so much as a characteristic mood of wistful melancholy and world-weariness. Dowson's style is melodically rich, and he was a master of several unusual forms of lyric construction. His influence is most often traced in the poems of Rupert Brooke and the early work of W. B. Yeats.

In addition to poetry, Dowson also collaborated on two novels with Arthur Moore, both of which are undistinguished. His two volumes of short stories, however, are highly regarded. More appropriately termed sketches than stories, they are generally most successful when most like his poetry: short, neatly constructed studies of mood, not of character development or action. His drama, *The Pierrot of the Minute*, is also reminiscent of his poetry: it is a brief, one-act fantasy in finely crafted heroic couplets, an elegy to the loss of a perfect love.

The unhappiness of Dowson's life, which receives almost as much attention from critics as his poetry, accounts for his concern with impermanence and mutability. His father's death left him financially insolvent and was a factor in his mother's suicide. Impoverished, he struggled to earn a living translating French novels.

There was one bright spot in Dowson's life during this period of family tragedy: he fell in love with Adelaide Foltinowicz, the twelve year old daughter of a restaurant owner. It was a platonic, worshipful love that appears to be the major emotional experience of his life. Dowson's love for Adelaide is characteristic of the nineties, a time when students at Oxford made a cult of the innocence and purity of young girls. Behind the phenomenon was a wistful regret for lost youth and innocence that reflected a fear of adulthood, rather than a desire to exploit children. When Adelaide was fifteen, Dowson proposed to her and was rejected. Many critics consider this love and its loss the inspiration for most of Dowson's poems of love and disappointment.

Dowson was an active member of The Rhymers' Club. Much of his early poetry was published in *The Yellow Book* and *The Savoy*, magazines which were the unofficial voice of the *fin de siècle* nineties. Although he was a minor poet, his work is a perfect exemplum of the aesthetic temper and melancholy mood of that period.

PRINCIPAL WORKS

A Comedy of Masks [with Arthur Moore]   (novel)   1893
Dilemmas   (short stories)   1895
Verses   (poetry)   1896
The Pierrot of the Minute   (drama)   1897
Adrian Rome [with Arthur Moore]   (novel)   1899
Decorations   (poetry and short stories)   1899
The Poems of Ernest Dowson   (poetry)   1905
The Stories of Ernest Dowson   (short stories)   1947
The Letters of Ernest Dowson   (letters)   1967

THE SPECTATOR   (essay date 1893)

Mr. Ernest Dowson and Mr. Arthur Moore are not merely a new pair of collaborators,—they are both new literary hands; but when they become old hands, and have learned what only experience can teach, they will have no valid reason for feeling ashamed of their maiden effort [*A Comedy of Masks*]. We cannot say that we discern any special justification for the title of their first venture, and indeed it was probably chosen as a good title *per se,* for persons as well as things are not what they seem, and any story which fairly represents life as it is will be, more or less, either a comedy or a tragedy of masks. Here the mask is worn habitually and with injuriously delusive effect only by one of the characters, who represents a type which, since the time when George Eliot drew Tito Melema, has made increasingly frequent appearances in fiction. A type, however, is common property; it cannot be monopolised, any more than a mechanical principle can be patented; and Dick Lightmark, the clever, popular young painter, stands so well upon his feet that he has a substantial claim to personal identity, even though he is not a creation, as he might have been forty years ago. He is the able, agreeable, good-natured self-seeker; and it is simply his self-seeking—so common and so apparently trivial a weakness—which transforms him from the pleasant, light-hearted fellow whom no one can charge with anything worse than lack of purpose, into the vile traitor who proves false to the two friends who trusted and to the two women who loved him. Lightmark is a really successful portrait, with just that kind of lifelikeness which will make many readers feel that they have known the original—much more successful, we think, than his immeasurably nobler friend, Philip Rainham. Rainham's heart, like Lightmark's heartlessness, is covered with a mask; but in his case the disguise seems somewhat purposeless, and when, in the central situation of the comedy, he masks his true self more effectually than ever before by taking upon himself the odium of Lightmark's villainy in order to preserve the happiness of the woman whom he loves, we feel that the truth of things is sacrificed to a dramatic effect which, though strong in its way, is showy and essentially meretricious. It is the kind of thing which brings down the house, but it is not art; and it is a blot on a novel which has genuine artistic merit, both in detail and in general exposition. From what has been said, it will be seen that we regard *A Comedy of Masks* with considerable favour; but we believe that the authors have it in them to do work that, if not stronger, shall be less faulty. (pp. 914-15)

"Novels by Old Hands and New," in The Spectator (© 1893 by The Spectator), Vol. 71, No. 3417, December 23, 1893, pp. 914-15.*

THE ATHENAEUM   (essay date 1895)

There is one exceedingly good story in [*Dilemmas*], 'A Case of Conscience.' At first sight it might appear unfinished, as one of the problems presented is left unsolved; but one soon feels that anything more would have spoilt the art with which the double tragedy of the two men's lives is flashed before the reader in a few pages. There are just two conversations, a few words of narrative, and yet the whole thing is complete, without a superfluous idea or incident. The episode is just the right one to choose for a short story, for it is one of those irremediable incidents which seem to explain all the past and future lives of the actors; and the sharpness and distinctness of outline with which the situation is presented show in the author a remarkable perception of literary values. Another story which has merit is the first one, but it is not so compact and direct in its effect. The last story is good in its description of Michael Garth's gradual descent to insanity, but it tails off feebly. The remaining pair of stories are of no account. (pp. 158-59)

"Short Stories: 'Dilemmas'," in The Athenaeum, No. 3536, August 2, 1895, pp. 158-59.

THE BOOKMAN   (essay date 1896)

A little fresh strength of nerves, a warmer coursing of the blood in his veins, and an ear more sensitively on guard against harsh sounds—these well-wishers might crave for Mr. Dowson. Perhaps the first two are unattainable; but it should not be difficult for him to train his sense of melody enough to make the use of "Sufficient for the day are the day's evil things" impossible as a refrain. His poetry is not inspiriting; why should it be? We freely admit the legitimacy of depressing verses, and the greyness of tone we mention uncomplainingly, and merely as a fact. But though a fine ear is a rare gift, better technical workmanship might be reasonably demanded from a writer of Mr. Dowson's ability and culture. It can be acquired to at least a greater extent than we find in ["Verses"]. Yet his book will be liked, and very rightly. There is a melancholy charm about it. It has a distinction of refinement, if not of poetic power. And five or six of the pieces so greatly surpass the others in wisdom, or melody, or sweetness, that we pause to reconsider our judgment of the whole, and think perhaps that Mr. Dowson is maybe only painfully reaching the true expression of himself.

"The Bookman's Table: 'Verses'," in The Bookman, Vol. 10, No. 58, July, 1896, p. 123.

THE ATHENAEUM   (essay date 1900)

['Decorations: in Verse and Prose'] is not indeed so good as ['Verses']. . . . But it contains enough charming and delicate work to prove that Mr. Dowson was a genuine poet, and here and there passages almost as good as anything he ever wrote.

Mr. Dowson was a lyric poet, and nothing but a lyric poet, and in attempting some years ago a dramatic scene in ten-syllable rhymed couplets, 'The Pierrot of the Minute,' he failed almost completely. He had neither sustained thought nor sustained passion, but he could set an exquisite moment to music. The music was faint, and did not seize upon the ear by an experimental boldness in its cadences. Owing much to French influences—to that modern French verse which has captured some of the haunting quality of the best English verse—Mr. Dowson's poetry was always quite simple, unaffected, really English. . . . Mr. Dowson's poetry is classical rather than romantic; seeming almost to dispense with imagination as it dispenses with all that exteriorizes vision in imagination, it is really suffused by imagination as by a gentle and constant light. Emotion, caught up into poetry before it has had time to grow too egoistically energetic, speaks as directly as if rhythm were its natural speech. And the rhythm itself has the same quality of subtle naturalness, avoiding, at its best, that too martial beat which verse-writers as a rule find it so difficult to avoid, or are irresistibly tempted to seek. Mr. Dowson was an exquisite artist in cadences, whether in long floating lines . . . or in short, sighing lines. . . . His poetry, more than that of any writer of the day, is "overheard," when it is heard at all; it has the essence of poetry, if scarcely more than that essence; and there will always be a few genuine *amateurs* to treasure it, as the genuine *amateur* treasures the rare, easily lost, little perfect things of the world.

"Literature: 'Decorations: In Verse and Prose'," in The Athenaeum, No. 3782, April 21, 1900, p. 490.

FERRIS GREENSLET   (essay date 1905)

In *The Poems of Ernest Dowson*, we find [an] endeavor to escape from the predicament of a prosaic and conventional society into paths of artistic freedom. In Dowson's case, however, there was a grievous disease of the temperament and of the will that led him into ways that were sordid and evil; and Mr. Symons in his introduction has been at no pains to conceal it [see excerpt below]. . . . The perusal of the memoir brings the reader to Dowson's poems, for all the delicacy of Mr. Symons's touch, with a certain preconceived repugnance. Yet as one reads the poems themselves the repugnance gives way to a pitiful and admiring interest. This poet of the docks and stews and cabmen's shelters, who led habitually a life such as Poe led occasionally, was a scholar and an aritst, who wrote in verse with sad sincerity, in exquisite lingering rhythms and a diction poignant in its reserved perfection. How almost classic is the acent of [the] stanzas from his "Nuns of the Perpetual Adoration." . . . (pp. 416-17)

The pathos of poetry such as Ernest Dowson's—a type more pathetically common in this unregardful world than any but readers of poetry in manuscript know—lies precisely in [a] conflict of the old vision with a volition diseased of a malady more insidious than that violent complaint of the romantic period whence the Byronic poets drew a large melancholy for their song. The note of Ernest Dowson's poetry more nearly resembles that of Leopardi's in its suggestion of a fine poetic faculty, a clear, undeluded mind, struggling for expression against a mortal weariness of flesh and spirit. Dowson's inspiration was never of the volume of Leopardi's, his idealism was more faltering and ineffective, but there is more than a passing likeness to such poems as *Il Sogno, Alla sua Donna*, and *Aspasia* in the mood and in the deeper meaning of the lyric entitled *"Non sum qualis eram bonae sub regno Cynarae."* . . .

There is in this, surely, something of the open-eyed supineness of what it is the fashion to call, perhaps too loosely, decadence, but there is in it, too, the old, piteous, significant cry of the soul. (p. 417)

> Ferris Greenslet, "Significant Poetry," in The Atlantic Monthly (copyright © 1905, by The Atlantic Monthly Company, Boston Mass.), Vol. 96, No. 3, September, 1905, pp. 414-23.*

ARTHUR SYMONS   (essay date 1905)

The death of Ernest Dowson will mean very little to the world at large, but it will mean a great deal to the few people who care passionately for poetry. . . . [He] was undoubtedly a man of genius, not a great poet, but a poet, one of the very few writers of our generation to whom that name can be applied in its most intimate sense. People will complain, probably, in his verses, of what will seem to them the factitious melancholy, the factitious idealism, and (peeping through at a few rare moments) the factitious suggestions of riot. They will see only a literary affectation, where in truth there is as genuine a note of personal sincerity as in the more explicit and arranged confessions of less admirable poets. Yes, in these few evasive, immaterial snatches of song, I find, implied for the most part, hidden away like a secret, all the fever and turmoil and the unattained dreams of a life which had itself so much of the swift, disastrous, and suicidal impetus of genius. (pp. v-vi)

We get out of life, all of us, what we bring to it; that, and that only, is what it can teach us. There are men whom Dowson's experiences would have made great men, or great writers; for him they did very little. Love and regret, with here and there the suggestion of an uncomforting pleasure snatched by the way, are all that he has to sing of; and he could have sung of them at much less "expense of spirit," and, one fancies, without the "waste of shame" at all. Think what Villon got directly out of his own life, what Verlaine, what Musset, what Byron, got directly out of their own lives! It requires a strong man to "sin strongly" and profit by it. To Dowson the tragedy of his own life could only have resulted in an elegy. "I have flung roses, roses, riotously with the throng," he confesses, in his most beautiful poem; but it was as one who flings roses in a dream, as he passes with shut eyes through an unsubstantial throng. The depths into which he plunged were always water of oblivion, and he returned forgetting them. He is always a very ghostly lover, wandering in a land of perpetual twilight, as he holds a whispered *colloque sentimental* with the ghost of an old love. . . . It was, indeed, almost a literal unconsciousness, as of one who leads two lives, severed from one another as completely as sleep is from waking. Thus we get in his work very little of the personal appeal of those to whom riotous living, misery, a cross destiny, have been of so real a value. (pp. xix-xxi)

Dowson was the only poet I ever knew who cared more for his prose than his verse; but he was wrong, and it is not by his prose that he will live exquisite as that prose was at its best. . . . The short stories [in "Dilemmas"] were indeed rather "studies in sentiment" than stories; studies of singular delicacy, but with only a faint hold on life, so that perhaps the best of them was not unnaturally a study in the approaches of death: "The Dying of Francis Donne." For the most part they dealt with the same motives as the poems, hopeless and reverent love, the ethics of renunciation, the disappointment of those who are too weak or too unlucky to take what they desire. They have a sad and quiet beauty of their own, the beauty of second thoughts and subdued emotions, of choice and scholarly English, moving in the more fluid and reticent harmonies of prose almost as daintily as if it were moving to the measure of verse. . . . He was Latin by all his affinities, and that very quality of slightness, of parsimony almost in his dealings with life and the substance of art, connects him with the artists of Latin races, who have always been so fastidious in their rejection of mere nature, when it comes too nakedly or too clamorously into sight and hearing, and so gratefully content with a few choice things faultlessly done.

And Dowson, in his verse . . ., was the same scrupulous artist as in his prose, and more feliciitously at home there. He was quite Latin in his feeling for youth, and death, and "the old age of roses," and the pathos of our little hour in which to live and love; Latin in his elegance, reticence, and simple grace in the treatment of these motives; Latin, finally, in his sense of their sufficiency for the whole of one's mental attitude. He used the commonplaces of poetry frankly, making them his own by his belief in them: the Horatian Cynara or Neobule was still the natural symbol for him when he wished to be most personal. I remember his saying to me that his ideal of a line of verse was the line of Poe:

> The viol, the violet, and the vine

and the gracious, not remote or unreal beauty, which clings about such words and such images as these, was always to him the true poetical beauty. There never was a poet to whom verse came more naturally, for the song's sake; his theories were all aesthetic, almost technical ones, such as a theory, indicated by his preference for the line of Poe, that the letter ''v'' was the most beautiful of the letters, and could never be brought into verse too often. For any more abstract theories he had neither tolerance nor need. Poetry as a philosophy did not exist for him; it existed solely as the loveliest of the arts. . . . He had the pure lyric gift, unweighted or unballasted by any other quality of mind or emotion; and a song, for him, was music first, and then whatever you please afterwards, so long as it suggested, never told, some delicate sentiment, a sigh or a caress; finding words, at times, as perfect as the words of a poem headed, ''O Mors! quam amara est memoria tua homini pacem habenti in substantiis suis.''

There, surely, the music of silence speaks, if it has ever spoken. The words seem to tremble back into the silence which their whisper has interrupted, but not before they have created for us a mood such a mood as the Venetian Pastoral of Giorgione renders in painting. (pp. xxii-xxvi)

He knew his limits only too well; he knew that the deeper and graver things of life were for the most part outside the circle of his magic; he passed them by, leaving much of himself unexpressed, because he would permit himself to express nothing imperfectly, or according to anything but his own conception of the dignity of poetry. In the lyric in which he has epitomised himself and his whole life, a lyric which is certainly one of the greatest lyrical poems of our time, ''Non sum qualis eram bonæ sub regno Cynaræ,'' he has for once said everything, and he has said it to an intoxicating and perhaps immortal music.

Here, perpetuated by some unique energy of a temperament rarely so much the master of itself, is the song of passion and the passions, at their eternal war in the soul which they quicken or deaden, and in the body which they break down between them. . . . Dowson could never have developed; he had already said, in his first book of verse, all that he had to say. Had he lived, had he gone on writing, he could only have echoed himself; and probably it would have been the less essential part of himself; his obligation to Swinburne, always evident, increasing as his own inspiration failed him. He was always without ambition, writing to please his own fastidious taste, with a kind of proud humility in his attitude towards the public, not expecting or requiring recognition. He died obscure, having ceased to care even for the delightful labour of writing. He died young, worn out by what was never really life to him, leaving a little verse which has the pathos of things too young and too frail ever to grow old. (pp. xxvii-xxix)

> *Arthur Symons, in his introduction to* The Poems of Ernest Dowson, *edited by Arthur Symons (reprinted in Canada by permission of The Bodley Head), John Lane, 1905 (and reprinted by Dodd, Mead and Company, 1929, pp. v-xxix).*

ALDOUS HUXLEY (essay date 1918)

Conquered by life, [Dowson] was yet in a sense its conqueror, for out of his life's ugliness and pain he created beauty. The cry that his agony extorted from him was an articulate music, always melancholy and pathetic, and possessing sometimes a plaintive loveliness all its own.

His poetry is always essentially lyrical and personal. He generalized no world-philosophy out of his experiences. Because life wearied him he did not, like Byron or Leopardi, postualte a universal ennui, did not rise in titanic curses against the Creator of a world where life was only supportable by illusions. Dowson did not see in his own misfortunes the Promethean symbol of persecuted but indomitable humanity. His poetry is the poetry of resignation, not of rebellion. He suffers, and records the fact. That is enough; he draws no universal conclusions, he does not rail on fate; he is content to suffer and be sad.

Weariness and resignation—these are his themes; weariness of life and a great desire for the ''quiet consummation'' of death, the annihilator; resignation, helpless and hopeless, to the fate that persecutes him. This constitutes his stock of poetical material. He sings the same song over and over, a thin, lamenting melody.

With no great desire to achieve originality, he made unashamed use of all the time-honoured poetical paraphernalia —lute and viol, poppy and rose and lily, with all those rare, remote precious things which the poets throughout the ages have appropriated to their peculiar use. He did not trouble himself to seek out a new diction, to invent new moulds of expression in which to cast his thought. The old conventional language of poetry, a language consciously archaic and aloof from the living speech of men, satisfied him completely. In his language he never passes the traditional bounds of nineteenth-century Elizabethanism.

What is it, then, which makes Dowson a poet? We have seen how limited was his stock of ideas, how familiar his images and diction. What is the quality in his work which raises it above flat mediocrity and makes it readable? Wherein does his magic consist? The answer to these questions is surely to be found in that quality of musical beauty which is characteristic of all his work.

Each poet has his musical beauty, each period is distinguished by its own harmony. To wed the musical form with the content of meaning so that the music expresses the thought in the purely sensuous symbols of its harmony— that is the achievement of the true poet. A great poet can tune his music to every mode.

Dowson, with his very limited poetical genius, knew of only one kind of music, the music of sadness. The rhythm of his lines is always slow and passionless. No harshness of abrupt energy breaks their melancholy sweetness, no eagerness quickens the weariness of their march. To heighten the effect of his music he makes frequent use of the refrain. Every reader of poetry knows how absurd or how deeply impressive this serial return to the same point may be. Dowson's use of the device is for the most part happy: ''I have been faithful to you, Cynara! in my fashion.'' ''Sufficient for the day are the day's evil things'' are haunting lines, whose return, stanza by stanza, produces a cumulative effect upon the mind, like the insistent moan of Dunbar's ''Timor Mortis conturbat me.'' Musical arrangements more elaborate than the simple periodical refrain are often used in Dowson's works. He has written several villanelles. . . . Well handled, the form is capable of being of great beauty. ''A little, passionately, not at all!''—he evokes here a drooping, evanescent music, a ''dying fall'' of poetry. Indeed, all Dowson's poetry possesses the quality of a music wearily drooping towards its close, trembling on the verge of silence. He reproduces the negative emotions of spent passion, the feelings of quiet sadness evoked by a song that draws to an end—a great period of human activity that closes. It is not for us to complain that he did not achieve more, as much as the great poets. Rather, we must be thankful for the contribution of beauty which he has brought to the general treasury—however small that contribution may be. (pp. 601-03)

> *Aldous Huxley, "Ernest Dowson (1867-1900)," in* The English Poets: Browning to Rupert Brooke, *Vol. V, edited by Thomas Humphry Ward (reprinted by permission of Mrs. Laura Huxley;* © *1918 by Macmillan Publishing Co., Inc.), Macmillan, London, 1918 (and reprinted by Macmillan, New York, 1923), pp. 601-03.*

W. B. YEATS (essay date 1922)

Dowson's poetry is sad, as he himself seemed, and pictures his life of temptation and defeat. . . . (p. 311)

I think Dowson's best verse immortal, bound, that is, to outlive famous novels and plays and learned histories and other discursive things, but he was too vague and gentle for my affections. I understood him too well, for I had been like him but for the appetite that made me search out strong condiments. Though I cannot explain what brought others of my generation to such misfortune, I think that (falling backward upon my parable of the moon) I can explain some part of Dowson's . . . dissipation:—

> What portion in the world can the artist have
> Who has awakened from the common dream
> But dissipation and despair?
>
> (p. 312)

> *W. B. Yeats, "The Trembling of the Veil: The Tragic Generation" (1922), in his* Autobiographies *(reprinted with permission of Macmillan Publishing Co., Inc.; in Canada by M. B. Yeats, Anne Yeats; copyright 1916, 1935 by Macmillan Publishing Co., Inc., renewed 1944, 1963 by Bertha Georgie Yeats), Macmillan & Co. Ltd., 1955, pp. 277-350.**

A. R. ORAGE (essay date 1922)

It is symptomatic of Dowson's state of mind, though Mr. Symons misses the subtlety of it [see excerpt above], that he was always repeating Poe's line: "the viol, the violet, and the vine." A special affection for labials and liquids is conclusive evidence of minority, not to say infantilism; and stylists with any ambition to excel, and to develop both themselves and their style, will be wise to watch their "v's" and "m's" and "l's," in fact, their labials and liquids generally. Dowson wallowed in liquids and labials to the end of his short life; his vocabulary never grew up, and I have no doubt that, had he been asked to quote his own best lines, he would have pointed, not to the notorious "Cynara," which is sufficiently pretty-pretty, but to these lines, in which he came as near to Poe as originality permits:—

> Violets and leaves of wine
> For Love that lives a day.

"One is essentially of the autumn," he wrote of himself. But that is not true, for Dowson was not ripe, but (I say it of course with respect) rotten. He remained in the cradle sucking sensations long after he should have been out in the world creating sensations. Life never got beyond his lips. (pp. 143-44)

> *A. R. Orage, "Ernest Dowson," in his* Readers and Writers *(copyright 1922 by Alfred A. Knopf, Inc.; reprinted by permission of Alfred A. Knopf, Inc.; in Canada by George Allen & Unwin (Publishers) Ltd.), Knopf, 1922, pp. 142-44.*

KATHERINE BRÉGY (essay date 1925)

[Ernest Dowson] has been scarcely remembered. He was not, as Beardsley was to so amazing a degree, vivid in his exoticism. Child he was, and singer also, of the twilight dusk. (p. 84)

He has left nothing more finished nor more arresting than [his youthful creation, the *Cynara* lament]; the posthumous poems are only less fresh, scarcely ever more mature, in their artistry. His was a genius which knew little development; like many another highly concentrated personality, it would seem to have sprung to birth fully armed and caparisoned. All his decisions were reached early—not one of his sentiments was outgrown. Indeed, there was a curious integrity in that simple yet sophisticated nature. One cannot conceive of him as a really innocent child nor as a really experienced man, but always as the youth—stung by exquisite dreams, hand-tied in the grip of sordid and insistent realities. (pp. 86-7)

[The seal of his] early, unfulfilled love was upon his life and upon his verse sacramentally, for better, for worse. *Mademoiselle* . . . was set up like a Virgin above his altar forevermore. Very gently, very reverently, he wrote of her [in several poems]. . . . (p. 89)

[But later,] in *Impenitentia Ultima*, there flamed a different mood of love—since love, surely, has many moods, and may be fierce or fine or tender with equal truth. Here we have Dowson's challenge to fate and time and death and change, his ultimatum to Almighty God Himself—all the more arresting because the poet dealt so little in ultimates or challenges. (p. 90)

The publication of *De Amore* [another love poem] did not come until after Dowson's death, but all that was best, highest, most steadfast in his soul soared into it. It would not be true (although it would be easy!) to picture Ernest Dowson as a poet of one single emotion; that is never quite true of any poet. But one would not go far amiss in remembering him as the poet of a single vitalizing passion. . . . [It] is notable that in only one poem has he accepted loss high-heartedly, and acknowledged the ministry of pain. And for this reason, *De Amore* registers the high-water mark of his passionate inspiration. It is a praise of love unfulfilled, unreturned, uncrowned by all "the certain peace which happier lovers know." It sings, almost as a Middle Age troubadour might have sung, the pride of the servitor who asks no guerdon in the Court of Love. . . . (pp. 91-2)

[In] the eternal justice of things, Dowson must go down to history as a literary decadent. Never as a literary degenerate—that would be a cruel and false arraignment! . . . In Ernest Dowson's work the memorable moods, the moods most perfectly and poignantly expressed, are *delicacy* and *disenchantment*. They are not the robust or heroic virtues of literature; none the less one takes them for such as they are. There was an almost infinite delicacy in Dowson's viewpoint and in his simple yet subtle craftsmanship; a sympathetic delight in all delicate things.... Often he chose quaint French forms for the expression of these aloof beauties; a villanelle of sunset, a rondeau to Manon, a refrain of love or sorrow or farewell. Not one of his contemporaries ... knew better how to use the airy and archaic beauty of these delicate verse forms. But ... Dowson made them serve a haunting and persistent melancholy. It is the saving grace of the poet's sometimes morbid outlook, of his often excessive sense of tragedy, that he never tore a passion to tatters. (pp. 94-5)

As for the poems of disenchantment, their name is legion. Here also delicacy prevails, but it is the ominous autumnal delicacy of fair things nearing death. Scarcely half a score of times do the verses reach the sinister power of *Bedlam;* only once or twice does their hopelessness quite darken the sun. For the most part they are the songs of a heartsick boy.... He is tired of love and of life, since he has rubbed the freshness from both of these; tired of beauty and of work; tired of body and of spirit, and of all the brave things he has abused. There was never anything more insidiously weary than these plaints of Ernest Dowson. They weigh us down with their suffocating sense of dissolution. The pages teem with requiems, vesperals, farewells, and salutations to "death, the host of all our golden dreams." Edgar Poe, also, had this preoccupation which may fairly be described as one hallmark of the decadent genius. There is, indeed, something in Dowson's poetry and more in his prose to suggest the work of Poe: but the young Englishman's touch —perhaps because of his intimacy with the French Symbolists—is more refined because more restrained.... [His stories] are slight things, meticulously observed, deeply meditated, sometimes witty and always fastidious in their expression. Often, as in *Eyes of Pride* or *Countess Marie of the Angels,* they tell a little sophisticated love story—always ending unhappily. Or else, as in that extraordinary prose-poem, *The Visit,* and the better known *Dying of Francis Donne,* they are, like many of the poems, studies in death. There is no denying their haunting quality; they smell of the grave; but—terrible as they are—they stop short of the horror of Poe's post-mortem colloquies. (pp. 96-8)

But after all, there is no defiance, very little *diablerie* in all this disenchantment. It was less a conviction than a sentiment with Ernest Dowson: the sentiment of a tired boy, a rejected lover, a runner who had lost the race. Perhaps its chief evil is that it vitiates the rest of his work. Critics ... insist upon asking whether the devotional strain, also, were less a conviction than a sentiment? Doubtless, it was both —nothing in human nature being quite so simple as the checkerboard philosophers would pretend. There is, in truth, the best of all reasons for believing in the sincerity of Dowson's religious poems. They express exactly the sort of religious emotion most native to what we (none too kindly) call inefficient people. *Lord, I believe—help Thou mine unbelief!* That is the one prayer open to no charge of hypocrisy; and it is the cry which trembles upon our poet's lips when he kneels for Benediction before the altar "dressed like a bride, illustrious with light," or sings the praises of Carmel, or kisses (as Villon might have kissed!) the habit of

the austere Carthusian. To each poet his own sacrament! ... [To] Dowson, meetly enough, the sacrament of death and the dying, Extreme Unction. His song of it should be better remembered by Catholic anthologists: there is scarcely another page of his work more simply dramatic in its appeal. Yet even higher is the strain throughout *Nuns of the Perpetual Adoration*—a thing of almost sculptural beauty, which, if it had not come to us from the hand of Ernest Dowson, we should perhaps have attributed to the convert-poet whose life ran so strangely parallel, that rare scholar and fine dreamer, Lionel Johnson.... (pp. 100-01)

We have spoken of him as the poet of a single passion—the passion of his hopeless love. But having the grace to be a poet, he transmuted this love into a symbol of all remote and inaccessible loveliness: of the Ideal which changes not (albeit *we* change!), of the spirit which *is* "when all things seem." And then, with that blending of vehement self-revelation and baffling aloofness common to the artist of every age, he wrapped his symbol in the classic robe of *Cynara.* And at the feet of Cynara, thinking not at all of men's judgment, the young poet who was never to grow old laid that one surpassing lyric gift for which men have thanked and consented to remember him. (pp. 102-03)

If that tragic thing had not come from Ernest Dowson's hand, one feels instinctively that neither Johnson nor any other could have given it to the world. What if there should be gathered into those brief stanzas the faith, the wistfulness, the insufficiency of a whole life? (p. 104)

> *Katherine Brégy, "Ernest Dowson: An Interpretation," in her* Poets and Pilgrims *(copyright, 1925, by Benziger Brothers), Benziger Brothers, 1925, pp. 82-104.*

GEOFFREY TILLOTSON (essay date 1935)

Like all good poets [Dowson] epitomizes significant developments in the poetical history of perhaps a hundred years. He clearly derives part of his quality from Swinburne and so also allies himself with Pater, Wilde, and the early Yeats in the belief that the value of a work of art is in proportion to the nearness with which it approaches 'the condition of music'. Arthur Symons recorded that Dowson's favourite line in English poetry was Poe's

> The viol, the violet and the vine.

But it would be a mistake to over-emphasize the importance of verbal music in Dowson's scheme. When he copies the effect of that line in such a line as

> Vine leaves, kisses and bay

he is not only trying to assemble beautiful words but is saying something exact. The line contains a symbol each for wine, women and song. Dowson derives from Swinburne, but he does not snatch at the first things that come to a poet's eyes for the sake of saying them divinely, does not transform a modicum of complex but limited impressions into a thousand lines of lyric. He may be dreadfully intent on writing poetry that shall be flawless as verbal music, and that music may be of an exacting and subtle kind, but all this is only half his activity. Dowson does give minute attention to working over and over his lines, to punctuation, to placing capital letters as a refinement for indicating accent; and yet, beside all this, he is putting in an equal amount of work on improving his meaning. He succeeds in the use of forms like the villanelle because he can write lines which are substantial enough to bear repetition, or to make minute variation worth while. (pp. 153-54)

More important for the way poetry has developed since, are Dowson's experiments and achievements in rhythm. In this he stands beside Mr Yeats. In the 'Trembling of the Veil' Mr Yeats calls 'Innisfree' the first poem he had written 'with anything in its rhythm of my own music. . . . I had begun to loosen rhythm as an escape from rhetoric'. This loosening of rhythm has been found important by later poets, Mr Eliot using late Elizabethan blank verse as a further solvent. Dowson's loosening was mainly carried out in the alexandrine, which in previous English verse had been either the hexameter or the six-iambic-footed line, the alexandrine, which Pope compared to a wounded snake. Dowson gave the English alexandrine the flexibility of the French alexandrine. . . . He even began to loosen syntax, but not sufficiently to make him more than a first straw in the rising wind. (p. 155)

> *Geoffrey Tillotson, "Ernest Dowson," in* The Times Literary Supplement (© *Times Newspapers Ltd. (London) 1935; reproduced from* The Times Literary Supplement *by permission), No. 1718, January 3, 1935 (and reprinted in his* Essays in Criticism and Research, *Archon Books, 1967, pp. 153-56).*

THE NEW YORK TIMES BOOK REVIEW (essay date 1947)

[Dowson's stories occupy] a classification of their own, one best summed up in Dowson's subtitle for the "Dilemmas" volume: studies in sentiment. The focus is in sensation, but sensation attenuated, remotely perceived—never, by the time it has emerged upon the printed page, sensational. Like the narrator in his "Souvenirs of an Egoist," Dowson is an epicure of old emotion, shy of garishness, consciously washing down his tones until the colors are almost too pale to see. It is emotion recollected, not so much in tranquillity as in desuetude. Yet one must further qualify it as an outwardly stylistic rather than an inwardly formal distinctiveness, a skill in verbal music (especially in the dying fall), rather than a true raconteur's planned mastery of timing or a true craftsman's attention to mass and pattern. Even the deliberate constraint of the style seems more closely allied to a fatigue of the imagination than to a desire to hold burgeoning power in check.

His favorite situation is that of the middle-aged man returned to brood and reminisce, rarely to act decisively, among the associations of his youth. . . . The texture is consciously stylized, as in this passage from "A Case of Conscience," the choicest story in ["The Stories of Ernest Dowson"]:

> It was in Brittany, and the apples were already acquiring a ruddier, autumnal tint, amid their greens and yellows, though autumn was not yet and the country lay very still and fair in the sunset which had befallen, softly and suddenly as is the fashion there.

Here are masks of Dowson's consuming interest in euphony and cadence, the choice of the word "befallen" as somehow more special and right than "fallen," the trick of

alliteration in "softly and suddenly," the studied simplicity of "very still and fair," the labored preciosity of "autumn was not yet." Here also is a hint of a characteristic of Dowson, the trembling before felicity rather than the full-blown and joyous embracement of it, so that one is not surprised to see that most of the stories turn upon some sort of unrequited love affair.

Reading stories like "The Eyes of Pride" or "The Statute of Limitations," one sometimes thinks momentarily of Henry James. But the master would have pressed these situations gaspingly dry of all they hold where Dowson merely agitates them gently with a polished spoon. Whatever he knew of terror he could not, or did not, transmit. (pp. 20, 22)

[Dowson's stories] are period pieces, pleasant enough to read in for a while, like the antique ladderback which hits one in most of the wrong places, but somewhat uncomfortable to live with on any permanent basis. There is little or nothing in this collection of what Keats called "the shadow of a magnitude." Only shadow. (p. 22)

> *C. B., "Epicure of Emotion," in* The New York Times Book Review (© *1947 by The New York Times Company; reprinted by permission), October 12, 1947, pp. 20, 22.*

MARK LONGAKER (essay date 1947)

Dowson's poetry stands out by reason of its classic simplicity and clarity. In his prose, however, there is not only a legibility which supports the conclusion that he was capable of sustained thought, but also a corroboration and amplification of much of the thought and sentiment which appears in the poetry. The narratives do much to supplement the poems, and as a result they are valuable in that they shed additional light on the mind and art of the author. (p. 1)

[There] is little in *A Comedy of Masks* and *Adrian Rome* to commend them to the interest of present-day readers. In plot they are plainly mediocre, for evidently neither Dowson nor Moore had the kind of creative imagination which could construct a story of compelling force. Their powers were not dramatic; suspense and climax were ineffectually handled; and the motivation was both conventional and thin. Nor were the characterizations vivid and completely convincing. . . . *Adrian Rome* is a better performance than *A Comedy of Masks* because the theme is more substantial, and the characters and plot are more skilfully integrated. (pp. 3-4)

Were it not for the frequently recurring passages of excellent prose, the novels would have little to distinguish them from the mass of fiction which has a deservedly ephemeral existence. There are descriptive passages, however, notably the description of Rainham's Dock and Brodonowski's in *A Comedy of Masks* which are both authentic and vivid; and the picture of the Thames at night is of rare beauty. . . . Although Dowson enjoyed epigram, and it is likely that Moore was appreciative of the glitter of phrase, they had none of the talent of Meredith and Wilde. Certainly Dowson, at least, cannot be called clever. A sincerity of purpose, characteristic of virtually everything he undertook, kept him from any temptation which might have presented itself to be humorous or smart. The best passages in the novels are those in which the authors tried to make articulate through their characters their own sentiments concerning art and life. The novels then become a sort of self-deliverance in which the manner is concise, spirited, and sincere. (p. 5)

[Dowson's stories] are not short stories in the usual sense of the term. Stories they can hardly be called: they illustrate a form which is virtually a *genre* unto itself. "Studies in Sentiment," the subtitle which Dowson gave to the collection *Dilemmas*, is perhaps as expressive a label for his short prose pieces as any that can be produced. They show little integration of character, setting, and plot in order to attain a unity of effect. In fact, they are devoid of real plot, of dramatic development, and stirring action. Furthermore, the characters are generally vague. His men and women are figures rather than characters, and as such they bear a faint resemblance to Hawthorne's. They are rarely exhibited in the full career of action. The action is either in the past or implied for the future; the present rarely comes into bold relief. Most of the space is taken up by a flashback into the past, leaving the present without action save the results of events in the past. All the tales are subdued in color, like paintings in *grisaille*, even when springtime in Brittany provides the setting. They are chaste, restrained records of suffering, of devotion to an ideal, and unselfishness, with nothing of the yarn-spinner's gusto, and with little on which the reader can take a firm grasp. They linger in the memory only vaguely, for there is nothing in their development which stands out concretely and boldly. (p. 8)

> *Mark Longaker, in his introduction to* The Stories of Ernest Dowson, *edited by Mark Longaker (copyright 1947, University of Pennsylvania Press), University of Pennsylvania Press, 1947, pp. 1-10.*

FRANCIS THOMPSON   (essay date 1948)

Dowson was a melancholy example of the decadent and (commercially) unsuccessful young poet,—an example more French than English. He has more affinity with the Quartier Latin than with Grub Street, with Verlaine than with Keats or even Savage, that eighteenth century decadent. (p. 559)

He wrote prose, which does not here concern us; and verse, with which alone we have to do. Swinburne influenced him, and Verlaine clearly yet more, with the later modern French poets at large. But if, in substance and spirit, Verlaine be writ large on his work, it is not Verlaine's manner that he seems to us to have attained. . . . The dainty sense of form, the diction delicately cut and graven, rather than (like Verlaine's and our own supreme lyrists') condensing from the emotion inevitably and freshly as dew; these features suggest Gautier or Gallic lyrism in general, not the spontaneous fluidity which Verlaine shares with so utterly different a lyrist as Hugo. It is the contrast between Greek artistry, reliant on the sculpturesque or architectural elements of form and structure, and Gothic or Celtic poetry, rooted in a peculiar spiritual intimacy, which we Goths distinctively recognise as poetry, and of which there are but the rarest examples in the classic poets (by "classic" meaning Greek and Latin). The French, as a nation, are classic and artistic rather than purely poetic. But Verlaine, with all his nation's instinct for external symmetry, had at his best the spiritual intimacy, both in substance

and style, which is un-Greek and un-Gallic. Dowson, enamoured of Verlaine as an ideal, and evidently suggesting him in substance, is too natively Gallic to recall him in style. Paradox though it seem, with his devout endeavour he might have come nearer Verlaine had he been more English.

As it is, we have an admirable symmetry, a chosen and conscious diction, with a too conscious defect of absolute inspirational power. Not that Dowson was insincere, despite a morbidity which courted the suspicion of resolved imitativeness. So many modern poets have professed a Parisian morbidity at second hand that the thing is suspect. But here it was the too sincere outcome of a life influenced by what to him was a compatriot-atmosphere. Derivative he was in his morbidity; but as a Parisian poet might be. Nevertheless, this derivativeness condemns him, as it would a French writer, to the minor ranks. The major poet moulds more than he is moulded by his environment. (pp. 560-61)

> *Francis Thompson, "'Poems of Ernest Dowson'," in his* Literary Criticisms, *edited by Rev. Terence L. Connolly, S.J. (copyright 1948 by E. P. Dutton & Co., Inc.; reprinted by permission of the publisher, E. P. Dutton), Dutton, 1948, pp. 559-62.*

FRANK KERMODE   (essay date 1963)

Dowson's positive virtues as a poet are a rhythmic subtlety which is well exemplified in the anthology-piece 'Non sum qualis eram' . . . . What in the end tires us is the repeated use of period epithets ('dim', 'enchanted', 'dreamlike' etc.) and the traces of Dowson's disastrous theory that you can't use the letter *v* too often: 'viols', 'violets', 'vines'. The new flexibility of rhythm was the important thing, but these trimmings often take over and make the poetry look like feeble attitudinising. . . .

Yet Dowson passes into modern poetry not only as a myth, but as poetry. Pound admired him, and his rhythms, and his Propertius, whom he modernised. It may not be too fanciful to find traces of him in the poetry of those 'who walked between the violet and the violet . . . In ignorance and in knowledge of eternal dolour.' Stevens, in such poems as 'Cy est pourtraicte, Madame Ste Ursule, et les Unze Mille Vierges', adapts the decadent title and ironises the decadent language. For such reasons it is worth undergoing the somewhat lowering experience of reading through Dowson's poems. (p. 866)

> *Frank Kermode, "Amateur of Grief," in* New Statesman *(© 1963 The Statesman & Nation Publishing Co. Ltd.), Vol. LXI, No. 1682, June 7, 1963, pp. 865-68.*

THOMAS BURNETT SWANN   (essay date 1964)

Ernest Dowson was predominantly and incomparably a love poet. He wrote about nature, he wrote about religion and death; but love was his favorite subject, a compulsion as well as a release. More than half of his poems in *Verses* and *Decorations* celebrate or deprecate love. . . . (p. 32)

Dowson's love poems are wistful even in their lightest moments and funereal in their darkest. Because he worships an ideal of inhuman perfection in a world of imperfections, he is faced with a painful and irresolvable conflict. A warm and sensitive man, he humanly yearns for his sweetheart's submission. But if she is flawless, as he believes, how can she lower herself to love him, a human and erring lover? Her yielding would be a confession of weakness, an abasement of her divinity. In spite of his yearning, then, he never allows her a total submission. (p. 35)

Readers have sometimes protested the gloom and frustration of Dowson's love poems. Why does he prefer funeral wreaths to bridal bouquets, they ask. Why does he doom his lovers as soon as they begin to love and make them shiver with winter in the flush of spring? At times, such a protest is justified. In his *carpe diem songs* . . . , the languor and darkness seem out of place. Much more often, however, the tension of his unresolved conflict—the war between his longing to possess and his fearing that possession means debasement of his ideal—becomes the stuff of fine poetry; it flickers behind his poems like firelight through leaf-thin ivory. Except in "Cynara," he is not a poet of passion, a Byron or an Edna St. Vincent Millay; but rarely have regret and yearning been sung with such haunting persuasiveness. (p. 36)

[Much] of Dowson's imagery is drawn from nature. Birds trill in his poems, boughs twine, roses and lilies flourish or fade. Where did he get them? Like most of the Decadents, Wilde in particular, he got them from books. (p. 57)

It does not follow, however, that because he borrowed from books he wrote about nature badly. Whether he planted violets in his garden and observed their color and configuration is less important than the use he made of them in his poems. One use is purely decorative. He liked some words for their sound. . . .

Much of his frequent nature imagery is drawn from the seasons. Often he names a month or a season either in his title ("Autumnal") or in the poem itself ("The air is soft with the sweet May showers"), and then he develops his images accordingly: "young, green grass" for spring; "gold and green" for summer; "pale amber sunlight" for autumn; "frozen hills" for winter. Almost always his use of seasons is symbolic: his poems symbolize the seasons in each man's life and heart, and they seem to say that youth and love, like spring, are brief and irrecoverable. (p. 58)

Dowson and the other Decadents, coming as they did in a highly civilized and increasingly mechanized era, were in no sense lovers of nature. They were dreamers, not doers; readers and talkers, not walkers; they mused, meditated, and brooded; they would rather meet in a pub than cultivate roses or ramble through blackberry thickets. Brandy and absinthe scented the air they breathed, not dogwood. Still, they were poets, and poets need symbols to show their moods and conditions: symbols more varied and permanent than those of the city and the tavern. As Dowson recognized, cities change and the poetry which reflects them dates; but roses and lilies are older than civilization and probably more enduring. Wishing his poems to endure beyond the limits of his own life, he resorted to a nature which he found in books and he borrowed her images to mirror his melancholy. His frequent success is the triumph of first-rate art over secondhand knowledge. (pp. 60-1)

The Pierrot of the Minute, Dowson's only play, is a one-act fantasy in heroic couplets. . . . In keeping with the trend of the times, Dowson has purposely limited his acts to one, his

characters to two, his scene to a park, and his time to a single night. But he has wrought as carefully as a craftsman of Tanagra modeling a terra cotta figurine. If he has not, like that craftsman, lavished many hues on his creation, he has painted so well in silver that few will lament the lack of flesh colors. (p. 73)

[The] action of the play is both brief and slight. The time allowed [Pierrot and the Moon Maiden] to love, though literally a whole night, is figuratively a single minute, in other words a moment in the stream of life; and the deeds allowed them are reduced to proportionate size. . . . In place of lusty Olympians and the heroic mortals who loved and sometimes battled them, in place of the less formidable but nevertheless robust goddess and mortal of Keats, Dowson has given us a pair of exquisite sylphs engaged in a pantomime.

It does not follow, however, that Dowson has therefore failed as a poet or as a playwright. There are other virtues besides power and magnitude. There are figurines as well as monumental sculptures. He has sought and achieved the intimate rather than the cosmic. He does not attempt to engulf his reader; only to charm him. (pp. 75-6)

To express and reveal his lovers, at once mannered and innocent, he has fashioned heroic couplets which glide like Poe's Nicaean bark, "gently o'er a perfumed sea." . . . Such lines, because of their ease, look easy to write, but their smoothness conceals art. It is no small achievement to sustain them through twenty-three pages. . . . The alliteration, frequent but not as in Swinburne excessive; the endstopped lines; and the usually perfect rhymes—all contribute to a seemingly effortless flow. To avoid monotony, the couplets are varied by the insertion of lyrics in contrasting meters, as nimble and airy as the lovers who sing them. . . . (p. 77)

If the lines please the ear with their flow, they also please the eye with their softly glittering images. Searchers after sensation, the Decadent poets reveled in images and cataloged flowers and insects, precious stones and even furniture, with the loving pride of a numismatist collecting rare coins. One gem was not enough; there must be a treasure trove. One color seemed to them colorless; there must be kaleidoscopes. Wilde, for example, enumerates gems in *Salomé* until they sing like an incantation. . . . Dowson also catalogs, with equal skill but less flamboyance. . . . (p. 78)

Dowson was above everything a lyric poet; but his stories and sketches and even, at times, his translations, show some of the grace and delicacy which characterize his poems. Unfortunately, the demands of prose are different from those of poetry, and the lyric impulse in Dowson's prose is not always sufficient to transcend his limitations as a storyteller. His prose succeeds in reverse proportion to its length: the longer the piece, the harder it was for the poet to show his hand. . . . Dowson once said of Poe that he was "a master of both prose and verse . . . his prose better than his verse, as mine is." Such a categorical statement, while true of Poe, must be amended for Dowson. On the contrary, his verse is better than his prose, which succeeds only when it approaches verse. (p. 80)

[Dowson's stories] suffer from pallid characterization and monotony of plot; but their flashes of poetry somewhat redeem them. The sketches on the other hand, most of them a page or less in length, do not pretend to tell a story or to present three-dimensional characters; hence, they arouse no large expectations. Promising less than the stories, they give much more. (pp. 80-1)

The power of the sketches, which resemble without echoing the prose poems of Baudelaire, is that of the best poetry—compression, rhythmical language, and provocative images. Had Dowson lived a little later, he might have written free verse instead of prose poems. ''Absinthia Taetra,'' especially, if broken into irregular lines, would make an excellent Imagist poem. . . . In short, the sketches have the virtues of Dowson's stories: their elegiac poetry, without their liabilities. In all of his work, only his best poems surpass them. . . .

[Dowson's short stories all] have a common theme: the loss of love. With one exception (''The Diary of a Successful Man'') love is lost not through fate or ironic coincidence as in Hardy, but through the deliberate choice of the characters. (p. 83)

The loss of love, which confronts us daily, is a rich and durable theme for short stories; but when eight stories, however different in setting, all concern characters who lose love, and when most of these characters invite the loss rather than having it thrust upon them, then the bias of the writer is evident. Even in the story in which the loss is an accident, ''The Diary of a Successful Man,'' the confusion of notes seems deliberately contrived: it is as if Dowson is saying that people are doomed to bring loss on themselves, if not consciously then accidentally. . . . The plain fact is that most of the characters are afraid to participate in life. They would rather withdraw from love, regardless of the consequences, than embrace it and risk being hurt or disillusioned. (pp. 85-6)

[The] same theme pervades his poems, his play, and his stories: life at best is joyless, pleasures are brief, death ends everything. . . . His heroes are himself; they mirror in prose the indecisiveness of his own life. They would rather renounce than participate. Behind them, however, one perceives not a shallow man, but one too sensitive for his own good. He feels so much and so deeply that even on the printed page he must limit experience until it becomes endurable.

The limitations of Dowson's method are severe. His pattern of love and loss is bound to grow monotonous, when every conflict is resolved by withdrawal. Nor does he compensate for weak plotting by the range and power of his characters. Most of his men, as we have seen, are Dowson himself; most of his women are the type of the innocent girl. . . . The heroines who depart from this type—the haughty Madame Romanoff in ''An Orchestral Violin'' and the proud Rosalind in ''The Eyes of Pride''—are welcome for the sake of variety but they are much less convincing. In painting scene, he is more successful though hardly exceptional. . . . If he did not choose to visualize his scenes through realistic details, he might have borrowed the method of Poe and substituted a cloudy but alluring exoticism; or borrowed from his own poems the bizarre Latin names, the mist, and the shadows. But strangeness too is lacking.

What remains is a single excellence which compensates for many limitations. The stories in their best moments approach poetry. The sentences are chiseled and balanced without being heavily formal; their length is varied to suit

the substance and also to please the ear. An almost funereal music beats behind the words. While the scenes as a whole are bare, isolated images throb and burn with color. . . . At times even the dialogue sings, though written in the candences of conversation. . . . Elegies written in prose, the stories make life musical if not meaningful. Dowson's heroes love and lose and grow no wiser, and his heroines climb to the compromise which is womanhood and decline to the ruin which is age. He offers them to us neither as examples to follow nor to avoid; he simply records their sighs. But the sighs are exquisite. (pp. 86-7)

The theme [of *A Comedy of Masks* which the] characters illustrate with their involvements and confusions is the old, familiar one that all the world is a stage where men and women conceal their tragic feelings behind their comic masks. (p. 92)

In illustrating their theme, the authors resemble at times their model, James. They people their pages with sharp-tongued dowagers and pliant, marriageable daughters, dedicated artists and smooth-tongued poseurs; and they conduct them through English drawing rooms and Continental watering places. But they lack James' mastery of language. Their writing is competent, no more. (pp. 92-3)

Furthermore, they lack James' ironic insights into the weaknesses of society. They have tried very hard to show a brilliant yet hollow circle, ''cultivated, very subtile, very cynical. Their talk, which flashed quickest around Lady Garnett, who was the readiest of them all, could not possibly have been better; it was like the rapid passes of exquisite fencers with foils.'' . . . Such a statement, however, should be followed by illustration: the talk should be *shown* to flash like the passes of fencers. Lady Garnett and her friends should scintillate and yet at the same time reveal themselves in their hollowness and cynicism. In actual fact, they talk with no more brilliance and no more self-revelation than a table of bridge players who mix bidding and gossip in equal portions. (p. 93)

Adrian Rome confirms what *A Comedy of Masks* suggests: Dowson is laboring in the wrong field. There is no sign of maturing abilities. The style is neither better nor worse; it remains merely adequate. The characters, for the most part, are as shallowly conceived . . . and the conflict in which they engage is no more gripping than a game of shuffleboard. . . . All in all, *Adrian Rome* represents a slight reversal rather than an improvement. (p. 97)

[The] novel has a theme: the conflict of an artist with society. Shall he do what others expect of him or lead his own life and thereby fulfill his gifts? (p. 98)

The theme could hardly be stated more plainly [than it is throughout the novel]. But it is not enough for a novelist to state or to make his characters state a theme. . . . (p. 99)

But the great, the unforgivable weakness is that, through most of the book, Adrian is a bore and a boor; and the truth he is meant to express, though always evident, is no more compelling than the man. . . . In a word, the theme of the novel fails to find adequate expression through the misadventures of a dullard. (pp. 99-100)

The author of a study devoted to a minor poet is obligated to justify his choice. Is Dowson after all worth extended attention? . . . Dowson was a traditionalist, and the twentieth century is an age which encourages experiment. He was clear, not ambiguous; emotional and often sentimental, not cerebral. (p. 101)

Never an experimentalist, Dowson perfected old forms rather than initiating new, and he has not been a major influence on later poets. The general reader more than the practicing poet has preserved his name.

What are the qualities which endear Dowson to that reader? An artful brevity is the first hallmark of his writing. Except for his two disastrous forays into the novel and his undistinguished translations, he wisely avoided the long and the massive. He lacked the power to sustain creation successfully in the larger forms, but he worked in miniature with unfaltering hands. (p. 103)

Littleness may extend to his content as well as his form. . . . Even when the subject is not normally small, even when it is adult love or death, he often reduces it to manageable dimensions by limiting the time and the scene along with the form: the time to a moment; the scene to a garden or a graveyard, a convent or a room in a madhouse. (pp. 103-04)

If brevity is the first hallmark of Dowson's writing, innocence is the second. . . . Most of the Decadents were more concerned with sin than virtue. With Swinburne they sang both the "rapture and roses of vice" and the "lilies and languor of virtue," but they much preferred the roses. Dowson reversed the balance in his poems. . . . (p. 104)

Dowson's brevity and innocence are irreproachable. His melancholy, however, is perhaps more open to criticism. There is no doubt that he is morbid, that he often wished to die and darkened his poems with the threat or presence of death. He can take a normally cheerful subject and infect it with his own black spirits. He can ask his sweetheart to help him seize the day and then make the day sound too dismal to be worth seizing. To read all of his poems at one sitting is to risk a surfeit of gloom. But taken in moderation they are highly pleasurable; their grief is remote enough not to be shattering, close enough to summon vicarious tears. Catharsis is perhaps too strong a word for the process they work in us; Dowson was not writing Greek tragedy. As he intended, his people are pensive rather than passionate and tragic. . . . There is still, however, a kind of cleansing. Because his subjects are smaller than life instead of larger, one feels protective toward them, proprietary, invited to share in their sadness without being overwhelmed. (p. 105)

With appropriateness, if not with originality, good minor poets are often said to represent the footpaths of literature. Dowson's path, it may be added, wanders through an antique garden where lilies nod languorously and rose petals redden the grass; where ivory-cheeked maidens weep beside quiet streams and wise children stare with the eyes of adults. The buoyant sun is a stranger to the place. Queen of the garden is the melancholy moon, and her beams are tears which silver the fallen petals. And yet her subjects do not resent her reign. For the zealous readers who ply them, the highways of Shakespeare and Milton are vital but a little terrifying in their crowded length and their hardness. With Dowson it is possible to meander at will through pleasant shadows with enough company for fellowship but not crowding. Literature has need of footpaths as well as highways. (pp. 107-08)

Thomas Burnett Swann, in his Ernest Dowson *(copyright © 1964, by Twayne Publishers, Inc., reprinted with the permission of Twayne Publishers, a Division of G. K. Hall & Co., Boston), Twayne, 1964, 122 p.*

KEITH CUSHMAN   (essay date 1974)

For the most part [Dowson's] stories and sketches are interesting period pieces, pale, delicate variations on [his] characteristic themes of lost love and the tragic gap between the flux of life and the perfection of art. (p. 45)

Only in "The Dying of Francis Donne" did Dowson break through to significant work in short fiction. . . . "The Dying of Francis Donne" is both artistically austere and rich in felt experience. More than any other Dowson story, it is capable of leaving a more than historical impact on a reader. . . . "The Dying of Francis Donne" is a masterly delineation of the psychology of dying; the pattern of Donne's death agony is scientifically verifiable. The story is also excellent in its own right, and deserves to endure as a fascinating expression of—and comment on—*fin-de-siecle* aestheticism.

Francis Donne is a successful physician who has risen to public eminence because of his writing and lectures. This dual profession is important, for Donne is an artist as well as a doctor; he is "great not only in the scientific world, but also in the world of letters." . . . (pp. 45-6)

But Donne is primarily a physician, not an artist, and in this profession he is even more a child of the end of the century. "The Dying of Francis Donne" is a very brief story, but it confronts no less a theme than the tragedy of being trapped in our mortality. Francis Donne's entire life has been devoted to coming to terms with his dilemma. His strategy is unmistakably that of the aesthete, and his "tired spirit" . . . and "morbid self-consciousness" . . . also place him in the 90's. Donne is above all detached: one of the technical accomplishments of the story is the brilliant manner in which the near-solipsism is rendered. The point, however, is that Donne's detachment is a defense. The only way he can confront the problem of decay and death is to remove himself from life itself. He copes with the "absurdity" . . . of the human situation by trying to keep that situation at a distance.

Donne is essentially a sort of decadent version of Roger Chillingsworth. He has lived exclusively with his mind, because the mind can order and control. . . . Death is kept at arm's length and studied for its own sake, as if it has no bearing on Donne's life.

Of course this distancing is illusory, and the story begins with the protagonist's moment of truth: Donne knows he is to die. He tries to deny this knowledge, but faced with reality, reason must yield to "casuistry." The detached observer is forcibly jerked back into life and started on the relentless process toward decay and dissolution. The image of mind as exquisite mechanism gives way to the image of "a hunted animal at bay." . . . Donne had known he was living in an illusion—one of his lectures is entitled "Limitations of Medicine"—but the fact remains that once the illusion is shattered, his entire world caves in. (pp. 46-7)

In its modest way the story is as much a depiction of the aesthete's yearning to get beyond flux and sensation as [Walter] Pater's *Marius the Epicurean*. (p. 47)

"The Dying of Francis Donne" is a success partly because for once Dowson has found a form that allows him to distance his own self-pity and world-weariness. The story is intensely personal of course, but it is also a self-contained artistic construct that needs no autobiographical interpretation. At the same time Dowson's characteristic nostalgia and ennui are unmistakably present, especially in the third section, which describes Donne's life in the fishing village "on the bleak and wave-tormented coast of Finisterre." . . . (p. 48)

Even more interesting, however, is the way Dowson describes the death. The "immense and ineffable tiredness" becomes "this utter luxury of physical exhaustion, this calm, this release." . . . Donne's life had been devoted to escaping from life, but his long dying had wrenched him back to the everyday world of change and decay. Much to his delight, he discovers that the transition into death is a release back into a sort of formal perfection, into a kind of changeless nirvana. The lifetime dedicated to living outside time had ended rudely and abruptly when the dying set in, but at the moment of death Donne is transported back to a world of timelessness, into the bliss of blankness and nirvana.

Donne is even granted a moment of ecstasy as he expires, an epiphanic point in time of complete clarity and perception. . . . This extended moment of clarity and insight is of course a surrogate for religious experience. Dowson can find no way to construct an order out of the chaos, and so he must settle for the heightened *moment* of order. Because the yearning for order is so intense, Dowson has a particularly high emotional stake in the moment when it comes. Thus there is an unmistakable ecstasy in the "singular mental lucidity" with which Donne passes from life. This moment of insight allows him to understand, order, and aesthetically arrange his entire life just as he leaves time for the timelessness he has always yearned for. The generation of the 90's were descendants of Arnold the poet, wandering between two worlds, one lost, and the other powerless to be born. This type of ecstasy is a commonplace in the poetry and fiction they wrote. (pp. 49-50)

"The Dying of Francis Donne" is richly cadenced and harmonious, and its sharp sense of experience is all the more effective because of its understatedness. The story is something of a miniature, but its economy and compression are such that it is able to confront the largest questions of all. At the same time "The Dying of Francis Donne" contains an important commentary on Dowson's own life and on *fin-de-siecle* aestheticism in general. It is a mistake to interpret aestheticism exclusively in terms of developments in the arts. The phenomenon is more directly a response to breakdown in the culture at large. Writers retreated to the formal perfection of art and to the doctrine of art for art's sake as a defense against chaos: "These fragments I have shored against my ruins." This link between the aesthetic stance of these writers and man's metaphysical dilemma is made clear by the life and dying of Francis Donne.

Dowson seems to be saying that the harmonies of art offer no real escape from the despair of living. Donne is able to escape the tyranny of time only by intellectual detachment and by death. These two forms of escape are directly related, and surely the effect is to question the detachment implicit in aestheticism, in attempting to convert one's life into a work of art. (p. 50)

[For] Donne is suffering above all from heartlessness. Instead of coming to terms with man's fate, he has tried to escape it, and as a result his life has been a living death, cold and sterile, without community, without love, without even emotion.

Donne learns that he cannot escape his mortality: no one can. But his decision to seek detachment is also a decision to deny life itself. The deepest and most profound meaning of this story is that the life of aesthetic detachment is nothing more than a long dying. "Dust thou art and to dust thou will return," Dowson's epigraph tells us; this is the main fact the story presents. Nevertheless, another message resonates through the carefully measured prose: the aesthete's headling flight from life is a horrible mistake. (p. 51)

> *Keith Cushman, "The Quintessence of Dowsonism: 'The Dying of Francis Donne',"* in Studies in Short Fiction *(copyright 1974 by Newberry College), Vol. 11, No. 1, Winter, 1974, pp. 45-51.*

ADDITIONAL BIBLIOGRAPHY

Ali, Raza. "The 'Decadent' View of Life and Dowson's Poetry." *Thoth* 13, No. 1 (Winter 1972-73): 19-32.
> Discussion of the ways in which Dowson's poetry reflects, and differs from, the attitudes and aesthetics common to the English decadent period. Ali concludes that, unlike most of the decadents, Dowson's integrity as a poet forced him to confront the emptiness of his life and the vanity of the aesthetic creed of *fin de siècle* decadence.

Baker, Houston A. "A Decadent's Nature: The Poetry of Ernest Dowson." *Victorian Poetry* VI (December 1978): 21-8.
> Discussion of Dowson's use of nature imagery in the presentation of his constant concern with the mutability of life.

Fowler, Rowena. "Ernest Dowson and the Classics." In *The Yearbook of English Studies, Vol. 3,* edited by T.J.B. Spencer, pp. 243-52. London: Modern Humanities Research Association, 1973.
> Discusses Dowson's use of classical epigraphs and concludes that he was influenced more by modern interpretations of Latin works than by actual reading of the classics.

Gawsworth, John, F.R.S.L. "The Dowson Legend." In *Essays by Divers Hands: Being the Transactions of the Royal Society of Literature of the United Kingdom, n.s., Vol. XVII,* edited by E.H.W. Meyerstein, pp. 93-123. London: Oxford University Press, 1938.
> An essay that should be read by the student concerned with Dowson's life. Gawsworth seeks to correct the impression of Dowson as a dissolute that was fostered by Arthur Symons's obituary.

Goldfarb, Russell M. "The Dowson Legend Today." *Studies in English Literature: 1500-1900* 4 (1964): 653-62.
> Survey of biographical material on Dowson. Goldfarb also attacks the inaccuracy of the Dowson legend.

Longaker, Mark. *Ernest Dowson.* Philadelphia: University of Pennsylvania Press, 1945, 282 p.
> The standard biography.

Plarr, Victor. *Ernest Dowson, 1888-1897: Reminiscences, Unpublished Letters and Marginalia.* New York: Lawrence J. Gomme, 1914, 147 p.
> An impressionistic reminiscence of Dowson by a fellow member of the Rhymers' Club.

Reed, John R. "Bedlamite and Pierrot: Ernest Dowson's Esthetic of Futility.'' *Journal of English Literary History* 35, No. 1 (March 1968): 94-113.

A close reading of Dowson's poetry concerned with his attempts to order the experiences of life through his poetry. Reed skillfully portrays the concern of a generation of poets with the search for a meaning to life through love, religion, and exaltation of the past.

José (María Waldo) Echegaray (y Eizaguirre)
1832-1916

(Also wrote under pseudonym of Jorge Hayaseca y Eizaguirre) Spanish dramatist.

Echegaray was the most important Spanish playwright of the late nineteenth century. Many of his dramas have been attacked for their weak dialogue and characterization, and for their melodramatic treatment of such timeworn themes as high honor and tragic love. But despite these weaknesses Echegaray is acknowledged as a master technician of his craft and was widely popular during his prolific career.

One of Spain's foremost physicists and mathematicians, Echegaray served in several important government offices following the overthrow of Isabella II in 1868. With the return of the Bourbons he fled to Paris, where he began his writing career. His first drama, *El libro talonario*, was produced in Madrid after his return from exile in 1874. However, it was his second play, *La esposa del vengador*, that won him popular acclaim. For the next thirty years Echegaray virtually ruled the Spanish theater, writing over sixty plays in both verse and prose.

Echegaray wrote dramas in two basic styles: the critically derided romantic style, reminiscent of the work of Calderón de la Barca; and the naturalistic style, in which he introduced Spain to the modern thesis play. *El hijo de Don Juan* (*The Son of Don Juan*) and *Ó locura ó santidad* (*Folly or Saintliness*), inspired by Ibsen's *Gengangere* (*Ghosts*) and *Brand* respectively, are chief examples of the latter type. Also written in this style is *El gran galeoto* (*The Great Galeoto*), his best-known drama. Echegaray's stature as a pioneer of the modern Spanish theater is due to his serious social dramas, although most of his work was written in the melodramatic romantic vein.

Echegaray was voted into the Royal Spanish Academy in 1894, and became the first Spaniard to win the Nobel Prize in literature, sharing the 1904 award with Provençal poet Frédéric Mistral. His selection as winner of the Nobel Prize was met with scorn by some members of the socially-concerned Generation of 1898, who regarded his drama as a remnant of Spain's distant past. Echegaray's work stands, however, as a definite link between the old and new schools of Spanish drama.

PRINCIPAL WORKS

La esposa del vengador   (drama)   1874
El libro talonario [as Jorge Hayaseca y Eizaguirre]
   (drama)   1874
Ó locura ó santidad   (drama)   1877
   [*Folly or Saintliness* published in *The Great Galeoto;
      Folly or Saintliness: Two Plays*, 1895; also published as
      Madman or Saint in journal *Poet Lore*, 1912]
El gran galeoto   (drama)   1881
   [*The Great Galeoto* published in *The Great Galeoto;
      Folly or Saintliness: Two Plays*, 1895]
Piensa mal . . . ¿y acertarás?   (drama)   1884

Vida alegre y muerte triste   (drama)   1885
Siempre en ridículo   (drama)   1890
   [*Always Ridiculous* published in journal *Poet Lore*, 1916]
Un crítico incipiente   (drama)   1891
El hijo de Don Juan   (drama)   1892
   [*The Son of Don Juan*, 1895]
Mariana   (drama)   1892
   [*Mariana*, 1895]
El loco dios   (drama)   1902
   [*The Madman Divine (El loco dios)* published in journal
      Poet Lore, 1908]
El preferido y los cenicientos   (drama)   1908

BERNARD SHAW   (essay date 1895)

Echegaray is apparently of the school of Schiller, Victor Hugo, and Verdi—picturesque, tragic to the death, showing us the beautiful and the heroic struggling either with blind destiny or with an implacable idealism which makes vengeance and jealousy points of honor. "Mariana" is a lineal descendant of "Ruy Blas" or "Don Carlos." In "The Son of Don Juan," the modern scientific culture comes in, and replaces the "villain" of the older school, the Sallustio or Ruy Gomez, by destiny in the shape of hereditary disease. In spite of the line "Give me the sun, mother," for which Echegaray acknowledges his indebtedness to Ibsen, his treatment of the "Ghosts" theme is perfectly original: there is not in it a shadow of the peculiar moral attitude of Ibsen. Echegaray remorselessly fixes all the responsibility on Don Juan (Alving), who is as resolutely vicious as Shelley's Count Cenci. Ibsen, on the contrary, after representing Mrs. Alving as having for years imputed her late husband's vices to his own wilful dissoluteness, brings home to her the conviction that it was really she herself and her fellow Puritans who, by stamping men and women of Alving's temperament into the gutter, and imposing shame and disease on them as their natural heritage, had made the ruin into which Alving fell. . . . There is not the slightest trace of this inculpation of respectability and virtue in "The Son of Don Juan." Indeed, had Echegaray adapted Ibsen's moral to the conditions of domestic life and public opinion in Spain, the process would have destroyed all that superficial resemblance to "Ghosts" which has led some critics hastily to describe Echegaray's play as a wholesale plagiarism. The fact that the doctor who is only mentioned in "Ghosts" actually appears on the stage in the "The Son of Don Juan" is a point, not of resemblance, but of difference; whilst the fact that Mrs. Alving and Manders have no counterparts in the Spanish play, and that the dissipated father, who does not appear in "Ghosts" at all, is practically Echegaray's hero, will make it plain to any one who has really comprehended "Ghosts" that the story has been taken on to new ground nationally, and back to old ground morally. Echegaray has also created a new set of characters. . . . Echegaray makes his puppets dance ruthlessly. He writes like a strong man to whom these people are all "poor devils" whom he pities and even pets, but does not respect. This again contrasts strongly with the Norwegian feeling. Ibsen never presents his play to you as a romance for your entertainment: he says, in effect, "Here is yourself and myself, our society, our civilization. The evil and good, the horror and the hope of it, are woven out of your life and mine." There is no more of that sort of conscience about Echegaray's plays than there is about "Hernani," or, for the matter of that, "The Babes in the Wood." The woman who looks at Hedda Gabler or Mrs. Alving may be looking at herself in a mirror; but the woman who looks at Mariana is looking at another woman, a perfectly distinct and somewhat stagy personality. (pp. 85-6)

> *Bernard Shaw, "Spanish Tragedy and English Farce" (originally published in* The Saturday Review, *Vol. 79, No. 2061, April 27, 1895), in his* Dramatic Opinions and Essays, Vol. 1 *(copyright 1906 by Brentano's; reprinted by permission of The Society of Authors on behalf of the Bernard Shaw Estate), Brentano's, 1906, pp. 81-9.*

WENTWORTH WEBSTER   (essay date 1895)

[The plays translated as "The Great Galeoto" and "Folly or Saintliness"] are undoubtedly two of Echegary's best.

The theme of "El Gran Galeoto" is derived from the well-known story of Francesca and Paolo in the *Inferno* of Dante. The great Galeoto who first suggests and then hurries on to the indulgence of passion is the power of calumny in the world. In this play the affection of Ernest and Teo-

dora would have remained pure but for the hints of slanderous tongues. It is this which gives them first consciousness of the danger of their position, and then multiplies these difficulties, until at length they sink under them. Though not guilty in act, the world declares them to be so, and nearly all the consequences of guilt follow. (p. 358)

"Folly or Saintliness'—"Insanity or Holiness," as it might be termed—recalls the writings of Tolstoi, just as *The Son of Don Juan . . .* recalls those of Ibsen. The theme is, that the acting up to the strictest laws of honour, conscience, and of unswerving moral rectitude in every case, must almost necessarily lead to the charge of folly or of insanity from those who have no such vivid sense of honour and of duty. This motive is well worked out in the body of the play, but is wholly spoiled in the *dénoûment*. The struggle in the minds of the persons interested, whether they shall believe in the lofty integrity of Lorenzo, or condemn him as insane, and trust to the decision of medical experts against their own truer instincts, is well given. We look on doubtful which will conquer. But when the one whose lot is most of all interested in the decision, the daughter Inez, is beginning to sympathise with the nobility of her father's action, all is cut short by the destruction of the only document which could prove his assertions. And thus, instead of the solution of the moral problem being laid before us, we have only the more commonplace result, that the world's sentence, or the sentence of experts, on a man's sanity or insanity may depend on a mere accident. Excellent as the drama is in the former acts, this makes it almost a failure as a whole. (pp. 358-59)

We cannot place [Echegaray] in the very highest rank, in spite of undoubted genius. His plays, as it were, all smell of the lamp. They are the work of a student: moral theses excellently reasoned out by a poet-mathematician. But they do not mirror actual life, with its almost infinite variety and complexity, with its joys and triumphs as well as its sorrows and defeats, its laughter and its tears, its frivolity and its cares and toil. It is with the latter aspects only that Echegaray deals: he either does not see or cares not to reproduce the brighter side. His painting is too uniformly dark, unbroken by the lights that are always existent in reality. But his works are, nevertheless, well worth study. They are earnest attempts to state and to resolve some of the most difficult problems of life; they are not mere enigmas of the fancy, still less are they the maunderings of erotic sentimentality, or of a feeble, whining discontent; and they have this peculiarity, that they may be enjoyed almost as much in solitary perusal as in representation on the stage. (p. 359)

> *Wentworth Webster, "Literature: 'The Great Galeoto, Folly or Saintliness',"* in The Academy, *Vol. XLVIII, No. 1226, November 2, 1895, pp. 358-59.*

JOSÉ ECHEGARAY   (essay date 1895)

In trying to interpret the idea of my last drama, "The Son of Don Juan," the critics have said many things. That the idea was the same as that which inspired Ibsen in his celebrated work entitled "Gengangere." That the passions which it sets in movement are more natural to the countries of the North than to our sunnier climes: that it deals with the problem of hereditary lunacy. That it discusses the law of heredity. That it is sombre and lugubrious, with no other

object than that of arousing horror. That it is a purely pathological drama. That it contains nothing more than the
progress of a case of lunacy. That from the moment when it
is perceived that Lazarus will go mad, the interest of the
work ceases, and nothing remains but to follow step by step
the shipwreck of the poor creature—and so forth. I think
that all this is but a series of lamentable equivocations on
the part of the great and little judges of the dramatic art.
The idea of my drama was not one of those mentioned. Its
motive is very different, but I shall not explain it. Why
should I? In all the scenes of my work, in all its personages,
in nearly all its phrases it is explained. Moreover, to explain
it would be dangerous; it might be imagined that my proposal was to defend the poor Son of Don Juan under the
pretext of exposing the central idea from which he drew
birth. . . . I neither wish nor ought, if only from good taste,
to defend my new drama; but it contains one phrase which
is not mine, which *is Ibsen's;* and that phrase I must defend
energetically, for I consider it one of extraordinary beauty:
"Mother, give me the sun," says Lazarus. And this phrase,
simple, infantile, almost comic, enfolds a world of ideas, an
ocean of sentiments, a hell of sorrows, a cruel lesson, a
supreme warning to society and to the family circle. Thus I
look at it. A generation devoured by vice; which bears even
in its bones the virus engendered by impure love; with a
corrupted blood which in its course drags along organisms
of corruption mingled with its ruddy globules, this generation goes on falling and falling into the abysses of idiocy:
the cry of Lazarus is the last twilight of a reason which
founders in the eternal blackness of imbecility. And at the
same time nature awakes and the sun comes forth—another
twilight which will very soon be all light. And the two twilights meet and cross and salute each other with the salutation of everlasting farewell at the close of the drama. Reason, which is precipitated downward, impelled by the
corruption of pleasure. The sun, which springs upward with
immortal flames, impelled by the sublime forces of nature.
Below, human reason which has come to an end; above,
the sun which begins a new day. "Give me the sun," says
Lazarus to his mother. Don Juan likewise asked for it from
between the tresses of the woman of Tarifa. On this point
there is much to be said: it gives room for much thought.
For, in truth, if our society. . . . But what the devil are
these philosophical speculations that I am plunging into?
Let every man compose such for himself as best he may,
and let him clamor for the sun or beg for the horns of the
moon, or ask for what suits his appetite. (pp. 25-7)

> *José Echegaray, in his prologue to his* The Son of
> Don Juan: An Original Drama in Three Acts; In-
> spired by the Reading of Ibsen's Work Entitled
> 'Gengangere,' *translated by James Graham (copy-
> right © 1895 by Roberts Brothers), Roberts Broth-
> ers, 1895 (and reprinted by Little, Brown, and
> Company, 1918, pp. 25-7).*

MAX [BEERBOHM] (essay date 1901)

Except that it contains two parts which may be very effectively acted, "Mariana," in English, is not of the stuff that
one raves about. Indeed, if its author's name were, not
Echegaray, but Smith or Jones, I should loudly decry it. I
should say that it was tedious in the first two acts, and
melodramatic in the last two. . . . Towards Echegaray,
however, I must take up a more respectful attitude. I must
assume that, in the original version, the caterpillaresque

progression of the first two acts is atoned for by a superla-
tive grace of language which Mr. James Monteith Graham,
the adapter, has not (despite many excellent qualities that
his style shows) been able to transmit for our delight. I
must assume, also, that Echegaray, a Spaniard, knows
more about Spaniards than I do, and that in Spain they do
the things which he would have us believe them to do. If an
Englishman had created the characters in this play, I should
twit him with having played the old trick of saddling them
with exotic names merely in order to enable them to behave
impossibly without destroying the illusion of possibility. I
should suggest, for instance, that no woman in the wide
world would make it a point of honour that her lover should
stay at her side and leave his dying father unvisited. But,
since it is Echegaray who makes a woman do this, and
since all I know of Spain is what it looks like on the map, I
am quite ready to believe that in Spain sexual passion is so
much stronger than in more northerly latitudes that filial
devotion is treated as impertinent for daring to co-exist with
it. That proposition I accept readily. Having accepted it,
however, I find myself in immediate difficulties. For filial
devotion is the very fulcrum of the play. When Mariana
was a little girl, her mother was seduced by a man who
turns out to have been the father of Montoya, the man with
whom now Mariana is in love. This discovery having been
made, the heroine, still loving the man passionately, marries somebody else, in order that she may escape contamination. . . . Even in England, where sexual passion is evidently a less lurid affair than in southern countries, a
woman in love with a man would not be diverted by such a
discovery as that which is made by Echegaray's heroine. It
is only the English dramatists (the situation is common
enough in English melodrama) who try to persuade us that
she would be diverted. In lurid Spain how much less possible would such diversion be! Yet Echegaray asks us to
believe in it. How can we do so? Only by assuming that in
Spain, as in China, the filial passion is a more real and potent passion than any other. But Echegaray's Mariana has
already in the first act, shown us how lightly the Spaniards
esteem filial passion in proportion to sexual passion. Thus
we behold the sharp horns of a dilemma. Either Spain is not
like China (in which case the whole play is impossible and
must be treated as mere melodrama) or Spain is like China
(in which case Mariana, showing herself to be an unnatural
monster in the first act, behaves quite incredibly in the last
two, and thus reduces the play to mere melodrama). It matters not on which horn we impale ourselves. Either compels
us to regard as mere melodrama this work of a distinguished and much-lauded foreigner, whose very name we
are afraid to pronounce. (p. 702)

> *Max [Beerbohm], "Several Theatres" (reprinted
> by permission of Mrs. Eva Reichmann), in* The
> Saturday Review, *Vol. 91, No. 2379, June 1, 1901,
> pp. 702-03.*

NORA ARCHIBALD SMITH (essay date 1909)

The fact that [Echegaray's] dramas and dramatic studies
are written in a noble language, used, for the most part, as
nobly as it deserves, might serve perhaps to blind the eyes
to some of their imperfections, but if we pierce behind this
glowing color we shall find the forms upon which it is laid
well worthy our attention. There is a profound idealism
about the dramas, a lofty impatience of conventional moral

standards, an intense conviction of the inherent relations of sin and retribution, a stern and rugged grandeur which remind one of Victor Hugo, to whom Echegaray is, in fact, often likened by the Spanish critics. (pp. 218-19)

Echegaray entered upon the dramatic arena at a critical time, when the political disorder and disturbance which followed the revolution of 1868 were paralleled by similar disorder and disturbance upon the stage. The Spanish drama, in its golden age perhaps without a peer in Europe (and for generations afterwards the cynosure of other nations), had thrown off the fetters of French classicism at the beginning of the century, but, weakened by its long slavery, feebly groped for a leader. Echegaray appeared at the right moment, and again peopled the stage 'with noble and heroic figures in whom the chivalric spirit of the Middle Ages'— and this gives the fillip to the modern taste—'is strangely joined to the casuistries of the modern conscience.'

Echegaray's first great dramatic triumph was "The Wife of the Avenger" ["La esposa del Vengador"], which somewhat lurid title, over-suggestive of Calabria and the 'Black Hand,' gives no idea of the tragic beauty of the play. The pair of lovers, Carlos and Aurora, are as exquisitely young and as passionately enamored with a love that breathes of nightingales and roses and moonlit gardens as ever were Romeo and Juliet, and the resemblance is heightened by the feud which exists between their respective families. . . . (pp. 220-21)

The entire atmosphere of this play is one of romance. The author shows in this, his first success, as in all the subsequent plays, that whatever his achievements in the weighty branches of learning, he is at heart a lover and a Spaniard, for the two terms are synonymous. Never language so made for love-making in the softness of its fall, its thrilling change, which English has so long abandoned, from the formal you to the tender thou as passion deepens, its poetic terms of endearment, its lyric swing and chanted syllables. (p. 221)

Echegaray's plays seem to my vision immeasurably above the ordinary line of modern dramatic productions. . . .

That [the] plays of Echegaray's are not without defects, it goes without saying, chief among which, perhaps, may be counted the gloom in which many of them are wrapped, their consequent lack of humor and their tremendous weight of moral purpose. The secondary characters are not always carefully drawn, the plots are sometimes overweighted with incident, there are occasional interminable speeches, and in one or two of the plays there are frequent artificial phrase-inversions and too great symbolic use of certain words in the effort to produce the desired atmosphere.

Still these defects are but small compared to their unusual plots, their striking situations, their wonderful grasp of passion, their noble flow of language, their felicity of invention, their strongly marked characters full of life, action, and good red blood and the powerful surge of moral conviction which upholds and bears them all upon its bosom. (p. 228)

> *Nora Archibald Smith, "José Echegaray," in*
> Poet Lore *(copyright, 1909, by Poet Lore, Inc.),*
> *Vol. XX, No. III, May-June, 1909, pp. 218-28.*

ELIZABETH R. HUNT (essay date 1914)

It is easy to fancy that no one who was not fond of a struggle against odds would ever have attempted to write "The Great Galeoto," for the theme presents peculiar difficulties. It is easy to fancy, too, that only a mathematician would have framed the play so symmetrically, stating the problem in the Prologue, and then working it out so precisely to a catastrophic Q. E. D. Even the six characters are exactly balanced, three in one household, a corresponding three in the other. (p. ix)

[In *El gran galeoto*] it was Echegaray's high ambition to make neither a comedy of gossip, like *Le Misanthrope*, nor a tragedy of slander, like *Othello*, but a unique play, midway between—a tragedy of idle, non-malicious gossip, the only achievement of its kind in dramatic literature.

The villain of the play is "They," "Everybody," the entire social mass, a monster of a thousand heads, a being too vague and dispersed to be set down in the play bill or to make his way to the stage. But as he must for theatrical purposes be somehow objectified, he is represented by the three members of a meddlesome family. . . . However, in the matter of idle, aimless talk, it is difficult to make individuals fairly represent a community. The most significant line in the play is from one of Pepito's soliloquies, when he recalls the fact that Ernesto and Teodora, the innocent victims of many dispersed trivialities, hardly ever went out alone—that possibly they had never been seen alone more than once. But he adds, "That's enough. If a hundred persons saw them on that occasion, it is quite the same as if they had been seen in public a hundred times." (pp. ix-x)

This play, for all its greatness, is in a sense a failure. Now and then there is a colloquy which seems hardly better than a heavy-handed Spanish school for scandal. But such loss of distinction is only temporary. There are many scenes, notably in the first and third acts, where the difficulties are triumphantly overcome, and impressions almost unknown to the stage are subtly created.

The shading and grading of effects, which always taxes the finest dramatic art, is especially well conserved. The action begins with a situation of perfect balance and repose, in which Teodora, Julian, and Ernesto, described as an innocent woman and two honest men, are quite harmonious. Inside the narrow limits of three acts it culminates with the tragic wreck of the household, and then passes on to a catastrophe of marvelous power and pathos. As a whole, the work is a marked instance of the almost complete vanquishing of intangible and insurmountable difficulties.

Moreover, it is of a kind not common to the stage of to-day. One result, by no means desirable, of Ibsen's all-pervading influence, is that modern tragedy has become so sordid, so austerely and bleakly realistic, as to depress and devitalize. Here, for our relief, is tragedy in the grand style, thrilling, inspiring, commingling fate and moral responsibility so as to produce, as an ultimate effect, the true tragic reaction and stimulation. When the final curtain rings down, Aristotle's pity and fear seize all minds and hearts. The pity is for the sad end of Don Julian, mortally wounded in a duel fought to avenge himself and save his dearest friend, and for Teodora and Ernesto, the innocent victims who kneel at his feet in the last pathetic scene. The fear that spreads among the spectators is lest they, too, may some time be victims of "Everybody," the monster of a thousand heads;

and perhaps also lest they may at any moment, by careless word or glance, strengthen the baleful power of this vague and vast Galeoto over their neighbours and friends. (pp. xi-xii)

Elizabeth R. Hunt, in her introduction to The Great Galeoto: A Play in Three Acts *by José Echegaray, translated by Hannah Lynch (copyright 1914 by Doubleday, Page & Company; reprinted by permission of Doubleday & Company, Inc.), Doubleday, 1914, pp. v-xiii.*

STORM JAMESON (essay date 1920)

[Echegaray wrote] comedies after the fashion of Scribe and Dumas, some with a grace beyond their reach. There are also tragedies, in the tradition of Calderon—not the highest Spanish tradition. (p. 231)

To these comedies after Dumas and tragedies after Calderon, Echegaray, politician, scientist, mathematician, added a curious problem drama. He was influenced by the work of the French Naturalists.... He observed, dissected, attempting the dispassionate faithfulness of the Théâtre Libre. His study of social questions and psychological cases is a mixture of that theatre's adherence to the document, and of the mechanical analysis of Scribe and Dumas. Not content with thus destroying the purity of the problem drama, he further complicated it by clinging to his traditional desire for terrific scenes and moving passions. He made of *Ghosts* a horrid melodrama. Imagination, fancy, audacity, true and forced, jostle scientific observation and notebook accuracy. These dramatic medleys form the greater part of his plays, their characters too often the puppets of an imaginary psychology. He attempted too much: the creation of the complex characters of modernity in the spirit of the highest tradition is not for him; it requires a greater dramatist. His problems are badly filled out with passion and poetry: their effects are too often cheap, and the verse of such as are nearest traditional form is too often banal and crude. His worship of the document, struggling with his love of striking situation and exceptional character, has destroyed both. Scientific accuracy is lost: poetic and emotional effect weakened, and the power to create character sometimes entirely lacking. Tradition and emotion predominate in these plays. (pp. 232-33)

Of these three kinds in his drama, the light comedies are most successful. Their construction is delightfully smooth, their dialogue witty and natural. The influence of the French society drama is strong, but the tiresome aridity of Scribe is replaced by a keen sense of reality.

In the plays according to tradition this is lost in a sense of emotional effect, always approaching the melodramatic. *O Locura O Santidad (Folly or Saintliness)* may be taken as typical.... It is impossible to say which is our dominant emotion, uneasy boredom, or a sort of shame at the play's lack of restraint.

In most of these plays the construction is more ambitious and less successful than in the comedies. What life a gloomy romanticism leaves in them is murdered at the point of honour. Tricks after the fashion of the misdirected letter are everywhere, and the emotions of jealousy and honour are almost sole dramatic props. (pp. 233-34)

Echegaray is in the tradition: his plays, sometimes ill-con-structed, their emotion strained to absurdity, have at their best not a little truth to humanity. At their worst, they have neither restraint nor truth, the characters mere passion-tossed puppets. Every one of these dramas falls short of greatness: yet they have in them a sense of life that would prove the Spanish drama not decadent, but waiting the master-hand to gather up a glorious tradition and fill it with a wider modern life, a more complex faith. (pp. 235-36)

Passion, strained to the negation of passion; characters made shadowy by their psychological confusion, jerked on the wires of the problem: these are the worst things of Echegaray's drama.... Where his work is bad, it is viciously bad: futile violence and jealousy, frenzy and wearisome exaltations, savage clutchings at sensation, forced situations, due half to an exaggeration of Calderon's dangerous bequest, half to a meddlesome realism from the drama of the north. At his best, music of verse, a grace and beauty not unworthy the past, and the need, ever felt, for the ennobling of life. His failure is not the decadent betrayal of a glorious heritage, but the failure of a creative intellect, defeated by a task beyond its strength. He belongs to the confusion of yesterday: he has little value for modernity save to remind it of its swaddling clothes. (pp. 238-39)

Storm Jameson, "The Drama of Italy and Spain," in her Modern Drama in Europe *(copyright 1920; reprinted by permission of A D Peters & Co Ltd), W. Collins Sons & Co. Ltd., 1920, pp. 221-70.**

RUTH LEE KENNEDY (essay date 1926)

As might be expected, the direct influence of Henrik Ibsen on the drama of José Echegaray has in some regards been overestimated, partly because of the obvious indebtedness of the Spanish dramatist to the Norwegian in *El hijo de Don Juan* and *El loco dios*, partly because of certain sweeping statements that have been echoed and re-echoed. All that glitters Ibsen-esque in Echegaray's theatre is not, however, from Ibsen, as a comparison of dates will readily prove.

A case in point is *Piensa mal y ¿acertarás?* ..., which contains a symbolic story of a wounded bird that immediately recalls the use of the wild duck in Ibsen's drama of that name. (p. 402)

[Striking similarities exist between the two dramas, which] would certainly justify the critic in supposing a relationship, if dates did not preclude the possibility. Echegaray's play was staged on February 5, 1884, and must therefore have been written too early to have been influenced by *The Wild Duck,* whose first sketch was not completed until June, 1884, and was not available to German readers until 1887. (p. 403)

After reading the plays of Echegaray, I have found only four which, in my opinion, show the direct influence of Ibsen.... It will be readily admitted that there is an indirect influence of Ibsen pervading the dramas of Echegaray. It is much the same general influence, I believe, as has been felt on all modern drama.... Because of Ibsen's widespread influence, there has been a temptation to ascribe to him much that Echegaray may have done, yes must have done, under the trend of modern social and dramatic tendencies.

Though the drama of the Spaniard looks backward only too

frequently to the theatrical effects of romanticism and to the Calderonian themes of honor, it is evident in various ways that these modern tendencies have touched his theatre. First of all, it is worthy of note that both Ibsen and Echegaray began their literary careers with dramas in which their protagonists were men . . . and that this interest gradually shifted towards their women characters. The title of "feminist," which Mr. Moses applies to Ibsen at the time when he was writing [*A Doll's House, Ghosts, Rosmersholm,* and *Hedda Gabler*] . . . , is equally applicable to the Spanish dramatist when he was constructing such dramas as [*El poder de la impotencia, Mariana, La duda, Silencio de muerte,* and *La desequilibrada*]. . . . As with Ibsen, too, his later women are individualists, though never to the extent of being Hedda Gablers or Rebecca Wests. . . . Nothing, perhaps, shows the contrast between the two dramatists' methods better than the fact that one always puts [the "wayward woman"] in contrast to the "saintly hero," the other never. Helmer (*A Doll's House*), Tesman (*Hedda Gabler*), Rubek (*When We Dead Awaken*), Captain Alving (*Ghosts*)—not one has given his wife any reason to love him. [Pablo (*Como empieza y como acaba*), Bernardo (*Lo sublime en lo vulgar*), Eugenio (*Siempre en ridículo*)] . . . are, on the other hand, diamonds in the rough. (pp. 404-05)

This increased interest in his women characters may be directly traceable to a study of the genre of Ibsen, but more probably it is derived from the general influence of the modern realistic drama. Certainly the feminine characters of the Spaniard show few direct traces of the Northern dramatist's. For all their independence, [Mariana (*Mariana*), Valentina (*A la orilla del mar*), and Teresina (*La desguilibrada*)] . . . are so far removed from the individualistic heroines of Ibsen that it is hardly possible to think of the former group as related to the latter. Mariana is sister to Hedda Gabler or Rebecca West in one respect only: she enjoys the thought of having absolute power over one man. This independent spirit of Echegaray's women and their position in the home may just as well be due to the freer atmosphere that surrounded the woman of his time, both in drama and in life, as to any direct influence of Ibsen.

The same doubt occurs when one begins to study the use of light effects in the drama of the two men. Both have used light symbolically. It is a curious coincidence that *Catalina* (1850), Ibsen's first boyish attempt, and *El libro talonario* (1874), Echegaray's first drama to be staged, should close with a reconciliation scene symbolized by the dawn, though there could be no question of direct influence here since *Catalina* was not translated into the German until 1896. Also, *Un sol que nace y un sol que muere*, written as early as 1867, though not published until much later, is in the very title, symbolic of two sisters . . . , that go to form two corners of the eternal triangle. This use of light as a symbol was to remain an element in the drama of both men. (pp. 405-06)

The effect of reading Ibsen is seen more clearly in Echegaray's interest in the abnormal character. Don José had, as early as 1865 in *Morir por no despertar*, vaguely concerned himself with the close relation of a high strung nature to insanity, and in 1877 had flatly put the question as to whether a man who follows his ideal of "All or nothing" in matters ethical is a madman or a saint. . . . [Lorenzo (*O locura o santidad*), and Gabriel (*El loco dios*)] . . . can be traced to definite characters in Ibsen's drama.

Various ideas found repeatedly in Ibsen's dramas, as well as certain similarities in characterization, may be found here and there in those of Echegaray. The ennobling power of suffering, which is brought out clearly in *Brand* and *The Emperor and the Galilean,* may be seen in at least five of Echegaray's dramas: [*O locura o santidad, Un milagro en Egipto, El hijo de carne y el hijo de hierro,* and *El loco dios*]. . . . It is not a new idea, however, with either and is quite in harmony with the ideas of the century. On the other hand, Ibsen's ideas concerning the "compact majority" and its power to cripple genius as seen in *An Enemy of the People* . . . seem reflected in [*O locura o santidad,* in *El hijo de carne y el hijo de hierro,* and particularly in *El poder de la impotencia*]. . . . (pp. 406-07)

When Brand [title character of Ibsen's *Brand*] would follow his ideals regardless of the danger involved, [an] old peasant mutters to himself, "Nay, but his wits are gone astray!" The verse might be taken as the theme of Echegaray's drama, *O locura o santidad*. Lorenzo [the protagonist] would carry out the dictates of conscience regardless of the pain caused; the world thinks "his wits gone astray" and shuts him up in the mad-house. For the first time we see in Echegaray's theatre a hero struggling against society in his effort to carry out his high ideals. The conflicts within the hearts of Brand and Lorenzo are much the same: each must choose between abstract duty and the life of his child.

In spite of great differences in the conception of Brand and Lorenzo, they touch at innumerable points: both are as proud as Lucifer; both are immense egoists; both are men who "with sacrilegious ambition would be as perfect as the God of the Heavens." Their views of mankind show similarity; "people without conscience and free will are atoms which today are joined, tomorrow separated." To Lorenzo as to Brand, God is one who demands sacrifice and martyrdom. Like the Norwegian's protagonist, Echegaray's hero would fulfill divine laws without respect to human passions. There are still other characters who recall those of *Brand*. Don Tomás, although he is a far more integral part of the drama, bears a likeness to the practical doctor in *Brand*. The representatives of the law are about as stupid in the one play as in the other. Finally, old Joanna brings to our mind Brand's mother: both women are thoroughly selfish; both have committed their crime for money; both are dying when the action of the story begins; neither the one nor the other can understand her idealistic son. Such a concurrence of circumstances seems to warrant the opinion that Echegaray's drama has been directly influenced by *Brand*, though the evidence is not conclusive. Echegaray himself tells us that it was inspired by a visit to the insane asylum. (pp. 408-09)

El hijo de Don Juan, through its connection with Ibsen's *Ghosts,* has become one of the best-known of Echegaray's dramas, at least outside of Spain. (p. 409)

In its broad outlines . . . Echegaray's drama is identical with *Ghosts* in plot. While the cast of characters shows important changes, particularly in that the father of Lorenzo is still living and in that poor little consumptive Carmen supplies the love story which is never lacking in Echegaray's theatre, it is the attitude of the two writers toward their characters that draws the line of division between the two plays. Echegaray has not caught the spirit of the Norwegian original. As Bernard Shaw expresses it, "The story has been taken . . . back to old ground morally.'' Don José has laid the whole blame for the terrible tragedy squarely on the shoulders of Don Juan. It was immaterial to Ibsen whether such a character as Captain Alving paid for his sins or not. Echegaray saw to it that an avenging Nemesis overtook Don Juan in this world, even as Tirso de Molina had seen to it that his Don Juan paid the penalty for his irreverence. Echegaray saw in *Ghosts* ''a cruel lesson, a supreme warning to society and to the family circle.'' That to him was the significance of Oswald's final words. Ibsen had laid much of the blame on the narrow environment which society offered individuals of the type of Captain Alving. The absence of a Mrs. Alving and of a Pastor Manders in the Spanish play is as significant as the presence of the father. Dolores is only a very pale copy of Mrs. Alving, and her responsibility as mother is only dimly and indirectly suggested by her conversation with the doctor. Thus the incisive questions in *Ghosts* concerning a conventional morality are wanting. There is no satire on social hypocrisy in *El hijo de Don Juan;* there is no method suggested for social regeneration; there is no question of divorce. As a good Catholic, Echegaray may not have cared to discuss this last, perhaps, but he could have emphasized the crime of the father in allowing Dolores to marry such a libertine as Don Juan was, or even that of Dolores herself in giving consent to such a marriage. But Echegaray has concerned himself with the one idea only: the sins of the father descend unto the third and fourth generations. And to prevent future Don Juans, he shows just how terrible the results may be. Don José is first and last the moralist.

El loco dios . . . shows clearly that Echegaray had read *The Emperor and the Galilean.* . . . So far as the plot is concerned, however, there is no similarity of detail. Gabriel, like Julian, gradually persuades himself that he is the supreme God, but whereas one is a ''rod of chastisement'' for whose soul the world must answer, the other is nothing more nor less than a pathological study in insanity. (pp. 410-11)

[Although there are many places in *El loco dios*] where the dialogue brings to us echoes of that from Ibsen's drama, it is difficult nevertheless to find the exact sources in any instance.

This is usually true of Echegaray's work. He read broadly, but apparently without attempting to retain more than the general thought, as is shown by the rareness of direct quotations. Consequently, his reading fused into a mass and became so thoroughly his own that it is extremely difficult to say with any degree of assurance that Echegaray had read this or that, especially since he was primarily a teacher and moralist and for the most part selected only those ideas which would fit into this kindly, didactic outlook on life. Armed with his idea, Echegaray seems to have chosen with scientific precision the episodes and characters necessary to bring about an explosion which would serve as a Q.E.D. to the moral theorem he had chosen to prove.

The exact measure of success that should be meted out to such a *modus operandi* is as yet somewhat doubtful. (pp. 413-14)

[It] is only fair to point out the element of injustice that is inherent in any comparison of a dramatist such as Echegaray with Ibsen. The latter was during the last years of his life ''the dominating personality of the literature of both Europe and America,'' and today his theatre remains the best example of the drama of ideas. To get any evaluation of the works of the Spaniard, his drama should be compared with what was being written in England, France, Italy, and Germany from 1874 to 1884. . . . [By] 1881 Echegaray had written both *O locura o santidad* and *El gran galeoto,* dramas that certainly, from the standpoint of technique, bear comparison with anything written during that decade. And in my opinion the former (though not so well known to English readers as the second mentioned) is a little masterpiece of characterization which represents a real contribution to the European stage of the nineteenth century. At least, they both entitle Don José to the double honor of being the first tragic writer of Spain to seek to combine the play of ideas with that of intrigue and the first to put his protagonist in sharp conflict with a conventional society that would swallow up the individual. And this last, I doubt not, represents a real borrowing from the ''grand old man of the north.'' (pp. 414-15)

Ruth Lee Kennedy, "The Indebtedness of Echegaray to Ibsen," in The Sewanee Review *(reprinted by permission of the editor; © 1926 by The University of the South), Vol. XXXIV, No. 4, October-December, 1926, pp. 402-15.**

FRANK W. CHANDLER (essay date 1931)

Echegaray was old-fashioned in some respects, and new-fashioned in others. His stress upon situation, his focusing of interest upon crises in the life of a single character, his fondness for the concept of honor, remind us that he descends from Lope and Calderón. Yet, for him, as for most moderns, honor is subjective and not merely the matter of a code; fate, too, is no longer arbitrary, but rather the result of heredity and environment. He delights to portray high-strung characters, intense hysterical souls, driven by passion or idea. He shows the individual struggling with himself or against social institutions. He loves the moral, the heroic, the perfervid. He is a natural rhetorician, less poetic than theatric. At his worst, Echegaray sinks to the level of extravagant melodrama; at his best, he rises to the heights with such original creations as *Folly or Saintliness* and *The Great Galeoto.* The influence of Ibsen became apparent in his work during the 'nineties. (pp. 465-66)

Much that Echegaray has written is sensational and artificial, journeyman's work by a man brought up in the school of Calderón, but lacking his master's romantic finesse. Thus, *The Steps to a Throne* [*La escalinata de un trono*] is an historical melodrama which might have come from the pen of Sardou. (p. 466)

More purely theatrical is *The Man in Black* [*El hombre negro*], the study of a modern Tartuffe, the middle-aged guardian of a girl who loves an impetuous young sculptor. (p. 467)

The play is half melodrama, half mathematical demonstration of the truth of a formula. But it affords occasion for high-sounding speeches and some tense theatrical scenes. D'Annunzio would have adorned it with gorgeous poetry; Echegaray has decked it out in tinsel rhetoric. Here is the same intensity and overstrain in the characters shown more convincingly in *The Great Galeoto,* in *Folly or Saintliness,* and in *The Son of Don Juan.* The defect of Echegaray's psychology lies in the fact that the motives of his people so often fail to justify their deeds. (p. 469)

Among the poorer plays of Echegaray are *Mariana* and *The Madman Divine*. The latter, indeed, is strained and over-drawn in situation, impossible in psychology, and written in the flowery language of a penny-dreadful. It shows how low one of talent may stoop in striving for theatrical effect. A girl married at seventeen to a man of seventy and left a widow, is encompassed by scheming relatives who would capture her fortune. Incidentally, they would prevent her marriage to a crazy suitor [Gabriel]. (pp. 469-70)

One difficulty [in the play] among many lies in the fact that Gabriel is set forth as half crazy from the first. Accordingly, we must sympathize with the scheming relatives, who, for their own ends, would save Fuensanta from him. They may be avaricious, but surely they are right to protect the heiress from marrying such a husband. Had Gabriel been shown as maligned by the relatives, who were wrongly imputing to him an insanity to which they finally drove him, the play might have meant something.

The motives in *Mariana* may be warped and artificial, but the characters at least bear some semblance to human beings, although their actions are determined by an out-worn and external ideal of honor. The heroine [Mariana], on discovering that the man she loves is the son of one who had injured her mother, dismisses him and marries a gen-eral [Pablo] twice her age because she knows that with his rigorous military concept of honor he will slay her should she ever be tempted to yield to Daniel. This is precisely what happens. (pp. 470-71)

However dramatic the climax and the scene when Mariana first ascertains her lover's identity, the play is unduly drawn out by reason of its indirect exposition. An archeolo-gist and a youth enamored of the scholar's wife are intro-duced for comic relief, but the comedy passages are only faintly humorous and clog the main action.

Best among the plays of Echegaray are two in which honor is treated more subjectively. These are *Folly or Saintliness* and *The Great Galeoto*. In the former, a sense of honor so delicate that it runs counter to every worldly consideration determines the fate of Don Lorenzo. (p. 472)

In this harsh world, too nice a conscience will make a saint seem a lunatic. Folly or saintliness? Which is the trait of Lorenzo? How slight is the barrier between sanity and in-sanity! The passion of the honor-loving Lorenzo is admir-ably set forth. His dilemma, however quixotic, is poi-gnantly perplexing. Indeed, lest the audience fail to note the relationship of this modern idealist to the Knight of La Mancha, Echegaray has shown Lorenzo at the opening of the play reading from Cervantes' novel and extolling the nobility of that famous madman. (p. 473)

Best of all the plays of Echegaray and known the world around is *The Great Galeoto*, which suggests, as does Mae-terlinck's *Monna Vanna*, that doubt of one's honor may in due course make real the situation which it had merely con-jectured. (p. 474)

In his Prologue, Echegaray has shown Ernesto casting about for the theme of a new play, and catching his sugges-tion from reading in the *Inferno* the story of Paolo and Francesca, whose perusal of the medieval tale of Launcelot and Guinevere united by Sir Gallehaut—in Italian Galeotto, and in Spanish Galeoto—incited them to yield to love. The go-between, or Galeoto, in his own play shall be the

scandal-talking crowd. Admirable in idea, the drama is also theatrically effective. . . . The characterization is more con-sistent than usual with Echegaray, and Don Julian, although an intense emotionalist and the victim of a suspicion con-firmed by circumstantial evidence, has only a touch of the madness of Don Lorenzo or Don Gabriel. Here beneath the local trappings and the cape and sword dueling appears truth universal, the truth that busy tongues will tend to in-duce what they profess to condemn. (p. 475)

Frank W. Chandler, "The Peninsular Tradition," in his Modern Continental Playwrights *(copyright 1931 by Harper & Row, Publishers, Inc.; re-printed by permission of Harper & Row, Publish-ers, Inc.),* Harper, 1931, pp. 465-86.*

E. ALLISON PEERS (essay date 1940)

Both superficially and in a much deeper sense [Echegaray] may be considered the chief perpetuator of the tradition of the Romantic revolt, which died out only with the last of his followers. . . . Echegaray could no doubt have followed with distinction in the footsteps of [Manuel] Tamayo y Baus and written plays that would have commanded greater re-spect in the future though less success in the present. But against this policy there were two potent considerations. First, it was for financial reasons that Echegaray began to write and the history of the Spanish stage showed him that the public could always be attracted by melodrama. Sec-ondly, he was by temperament an impenitent and thorough-going Romantic—"revolution incarnate", a critic has called him. He loved the clap-trap of the past; and, when he started to write, he warmed to the grandiloquent language, the effective devices and the violent catastrophes the day of which most of his contemporaries believed to be over.

The last supposition, if we knew it from no external source, could be deduced from the fact that, when after some years Echegaray elected to swim for a time with the prevailing current and to write plays of a social character, which were being received just then with such success, he did so without in any way forsaking the Romantic tradition. In his late, as well as in his early dramas, we find the same char-acteristic affection for sensation and horror, his breathless melodramatic moments, his grandiose language, his sweeping rhetoric, his picturesqueness and colour, his hur-ricane stage effects, his frequent use of coincidence and his grotesque improbabilities. The conventional comes as easily to him as the sensational and he indulges freely in both. Not only in the trappings of his plays but in his very conceptions of them, he takes his spectators back to the eighteen-thirties. Themes which by nature lend themselves to realism he treats romantically. Social problems he dis-cusses in a contemporary environment, but, although in essence the problems are real enough, as he presents them they are intolerably artificial. His frequent use of the vengeance-*motif* and the *pundonor* has led critics to de-scribe him as continuing the tradition of Calderón. But Spain had made some social progress since the Golden Age and Calderonian vengeance in nineteenth-century Madrid is so anachronistic that it is surprising that even Spain could endure, much less applaud it.

Another of Echegaray's predilections was for Romantic paradox and antithesis, which are apt to invade even the ti-tles of his dramas. An undetermined motive which may proceed from either of two opposite causes; a character of unstable mental equilibrium rushing from the one extreme of action to the other; a conflict (often patently unreal) between society and the individual: such are the themes which he loved to handle and to adorn.

Echegaray underwent many influences, but, with the exception of that of Ibsen, they reinforced his existing inclinations rather than modified them. . . . All that has been said about him emphasizes his affinities with the Romantic revolt—indeed, in many of his crudenesses he goes back to the unliterary melodrama of the late eighteenth century. Perhaps above everything else he stands as an example of the force of imagination. (pp. 348-50)

> E. Allison Peers, "Romanticism in Drama After 1860," in his A History of the Romantic Movement in Spain, Vol. II, Cambridge University Press, 1940, pp. 345-54.*

WILMA NEWBERRY (essay date 1966)

Echegaray criticism to date is remarkably simple to summarize. The general opinion is that his contribution to the Spanish stage is not much to be admired, although it is recognized that the public, unimpressed by the other playwrights of the time, joyfully accepted Echegaray's more appealing variety of drama. He is usually classified as a neo-romantic, he is accused of being much too melodramatic, and, although his debt to Ibsen and his incorporation of the modern drama of ideas within the romantic framework is acknowledged, he is called anachronistic and is criticized for blocking the Spanish realist movement in the theater, which, of course, was well on its way by his time. The wisdom of the committee which awarded him the Nobel Prize in 1904 has even been questioned, and the adverse manifesto of certain members of the Generation of '98 is often cited.

It is true that some of Echegaray's techniques, the passionate emotions expressed by his heroes, the violent situations and general atmosphere of many of his plays remind one strongly of the most exaggerated romanticism of the eighteen-thirties. However, there is another current in his plays that goes beyond superficial romantic characteristics and puts forth several of the ideas with which Pirandello later would revolutionize twentieth-century theater. Some of these ideas were Echegaray's development of his legacy from Cervantes and Calderón (a legacy which goes beyond international borders, and which is shared by Pirandello); others were products of his time, and many were based on his own intellectual and artistic life. (p. 123)

Echegaray's true position in the procession of dramatists who have made important contributions to the history of ideas should be reevaluated. Although some aspects of his work may seem anachronistic at the end of the nineteenth century, in many essential ways he looks forward to the twentieth century, while often drawing inspiration from the great literature of the past.

Echegaray and Pirandello coincide, first of all, in the manner in which they present the theme of the position of honesty for its own sake in our modern corrupt society. The brutal devotion to honesty displayed by Echegaray in *Ó locura ó santidad* and by Pirandello in *Il piacere dell'onestà* shows the isolation of a man who will not compromise with his own standards in order to conform to what society expects of him.

A psychological theme to be found prominently in both authors is that of many variations on the subject of madness as a solution. Both Echegaray and Pirandello have portrayed characters who are sent to an asylum in order to avoid ruining their lives and those of all around them because of their attempt to be completely honest. Both playwrights have also studied characters who lucidly decide to be insane rather than face life as it is. Interestingly, in both dramatists the themes of honesty and madness often overlap, as they do in Cervantes' great novel.

Both dramatic authors question the nature of reality, have written theater-within-the-theater, use the problems connected with play production as conflict in drama, and have attempted to describe the creative process. Both Echegaray and Pirandello satirize romanticism, and they anticipate or answer the criticism they know they will receive or have received for the romantic characteristics of their own work.

Very similar and unusual duel situations are found in Echegaray's *El gran galeoto* and in Pirandello's *Il giuoco delle parti*. The similarity is especially interesting because it involves the problem of identity, so essential a part of Pirandello's theater. Another problem of identity is found in the two plays *Un crítico incipiente* by Echegaray and *Quando si è qualcuno* by Pirandello. Both treat the desire of a well-known writer to present a work to the public without eliciting the preconceived opinions which their authorship would cause, or without changing the image which their public already treasures. (pp. 123-24)

In both [*Ó locura ó santidad* and *Il piacere dell'onestà*] the reaction of the friends and relatives is the same as the one we find in *El Quijote*: this brutally honest man in search of justice cannot be real; therefore the only possible explanation is that he is a lunatic. . . .

Echegaray, under the influence of Ibsen, often treated hereditary insanity. Of course madness is a common topic and does not belong exclusively to any generation or to any playwright. However, the most significant aspect of this theme in which Echegaray and Pirandello coincide is not true madness, but a convenient retreat into madness to avoid the consequences of one's actions, or because reality is too difficult for a sane person to bear. This type of dementia depicted in both Pirandello and Echegaray is also calculated to suggest the small difference between sanity and lunacy and to question the difference between reality and appearances.

When Lorenzo is carried away at the end of *Ó locura ó santidad*, he has been driven to show all the characteristics of a madman and even calls himself mad. . . . He then sends his wife a kiss with a horrible shout of desperation and to all appearances attempts to strangle his daughter, although he is really just trying to keep her with him—convincing evidence for all observers that their action in sending him to an asylum is justified. (p. 125)

In Echegaray's *La realidad y el delirio* are . . . found his most frequent remarks reminiscent of one of Pirandello's typical obsessions: the problem of truth and illusion, being and seeming. . . . They compare theater with life and introduce the life-dream theme of Calderón. (p. 126)

[In Echegaray's *Un crítico incipiente*] Don Antonio has

written a play anonymously, he prizes it highly, and he is extremely concerned about its success. Most of the play takes place during the actual performance of don Antonio's play—in a rather amusing way the characters run in and out of the theater where don Antonio's play is being given and go to his home to present their reactions. Don Antonio himself had left the theater because of a fainting spell brought on by emotion, and thus is present to hear the other characters' reactions.

Although Echegaray has not equaled the extreme measures of Pirandello in his continuation of the theater-within-the-theater tradition, and although Echegaray's plays do not contain the improvisation element which is so important in this type of Pirandello's play, following the *Commedia dell'arte* tradition, it is apparent that Echegaray has carried the play-within-the-play beyond Calderón, Shakespeare, Moratín, and Tamayo y Baus toward Pirandello's theater, especially in the treatment of the role of the creative function of the author and in the attempt to describe the difficult struggle involved in the creative process.

Furthermore, they both show the difficulty, if not the impossibility, of recreating life situations on the stage. They use the word "fantasma" in referring to a character and think of him as an entity, independent of the author. . . .

Fully conscious of their position in the history of the theater and aware that they could be criticized for the romantic characteristics of their work, both Echegaray and Pirandello have deliberately satirized romanticism, although neither playwright is known for his satire. (p. 127)

[A] revealing example of the spiritual kinship between these two authors is found in Echegaray's *Un crítico incipiente* and Pirandello's *Quando si è Qualcuno.* Both are autobiographic and express the desire of an older man, well-known in the world of literature, to write sincerely, without the weight of the preconceived opinions which his name carries with it. Echegaray's Antonio writes a play anonymously, but includes passages in the style of another playwright to add to the deceit. (p. 128)

The motives of Antonio . . . for writing anonymously are at first not clear, since he needs the money, and his name, already well-known in the theater world, would seemingly help him toward this goal. Subsequently, however, it is obvious that Antonio's financial motive is secondary. This play means more to him than the work he has published under his own name. He loves and defends it passionately, just as [Pirandello's] XXX loves and defends his poems written under the name of Délago, and he too has obtained artistic freedom by the anonymous device.

Since it is generally supposed that Echegaray's own chief reason for writing for the theater was financial, it is reasonable to assume that in this autobiographical play he is communicating his own deeper motives. . . .

In both of these plays there are sub-themes, which again stress the similar thoughts of Echegaray and Pirandello. Perhaps the most important is the contrast between youth and age. In *Un crítico incipiente* the romanticism, enthusiasms, and optimism of young people are represented by Antonio's son and daughter, Luisa and Pepe, and Luisa's *novio,* Enrique. Three young people also represent these qualities in Pirandello's play. . . .

Both Pirandello and Echegaray acknowledge their debt to

the past in these plays. The settings call for busts of Lope, Calderón, and Shakespeare in Echegaray's play, and portraits of [Dante, Lodovico Ariosto, Ugo Foscolo, and Giacomo Leopardi] in Pirandello's, perhaps with the additional purposes of showing an understanding of literary figures in death which was not always awarded them during their lifetime and contrasting the fixed images of past poets with those of the present which are still being formed.

Thus, in shifting the emphasis away from the obvious characteristics of his theater, Echegaray emerges as a playwright who is not exclusively a late development of romanticism but also a forerunner of the twentieth century. . . .

Criticism is usually based on the five or six most popular plays of the sixty he wrote, half in prose rather than in typically romantic poetry. One of the plays listed among his preferred ones, *Un crítico incipiente,* is not easily obtained. In spite of its subtitle "capricho cómico" and its often-exaggerated emotions and situations, it more truly reveals that Echegaray did aspire to communicate a certain intellectual content in his plays, which would make his relationship to Pirandello and the twentieth century more obvious. (p. 129)

> *Wilma Newberry, "Echegaray and Pirandello," in* PMLA, *81 (copyright © 1966 by the Modern Language Association of America; reprinted by permission of the Modern Language Association of America), Vol. LXXXI, No. 1, March, 1966, pp. 123-29.**

DONALD L. SHAW (essay date 1972)

Although Echegaray began with the little *comedia de salón* [*El libro talonario*], in which a young wife ingeniously turns the tables on her unfaithful husband, he made his name in the 1890s with a series of historical verse-melodramas which have led to his being frequently referred to as a 'Romantic' or 'neo-Romantic'. But it is necessary to make a distinction here. What saves the small group of major Romantic dramas from the oblivion into which Echegaray's other plays have deservedly fallen is their theme: the struggle of man, supported by love, against the hostility of life and fate. Deficient as their expression of it sometimes is, that theme gives them grandeur and literary significance. Echegaray's theatre, whether historical or modern in setting, lacks such thematic importance. It has only situations. With one or two exceptions—not among his best-known plays—everything in Echegaray is subordinated to situations. His essential quality as a dramatist was his astonishing ability to invent and exploit to the uttermost, with characteristic humourlessness, the most grotesquely improbable theatrical situations. Psychological verisimilitude and significant commentary on human life and behaviour are thus, for the most part, automatically ruled out. Suspense, and suspense alone, reigns supreme. We marvel that a middle-class theatre audience could applaud such a production as *En el puño de la espada.* . . . In a small number of plays (*El gran galeoto, Dos fanatismos, El hijo de Don Juan*) Echegaray attempted to break away from melodrama and write social drama of ideas. The first of these three plays, Echegaray's greatest success, widely translated and played outside Spain, illustrates the tragic effects of malevolent gossip, in an exaggerated thesis drama which makes an interesting comparison with a similar type of play by Tamayo, such as *Lances de honor. El hijo de Don Juan* reveals the influence of Ibsen's *Ghosts* and demonstrates

Echegaray's genuine desire to extend the range of his work. But he remains for us the maximum representative of Spain's theatrical decadence in the late nineteenth century. The award to him of the Nobel Prize in 1904 was the occasion of a spirited protest by several members of the Generation of 1898. How futile that protest was is shown by comparing the extremely successful *La muralla* of Calvo Sotelo in our own time with *O locura o santidad.* Despite the passage of more than seventy years we perceive an unmistakable similarity of manner. (pp. 88-90)

> *Donald L. Shaw, "Drama from Romanticism to the End of the Century: Echegaray," in his* The Nineteenth Century *(copyright © Donald L. Shaw 1972; by permission of Barnes & Noble Books, a Division of Littlefield, Adams & Co., Inc.), Barnes & Noble, 1972, pp. 87-90.*

ADDITIONAL BIBLIOGRAPHY

Gardiner, Fanny Hale. "Echegaray: Spanish Statesman, Dramatist, Poet." *Poet Lore* IV, No. 3 (July, August, September 1900): 406-16.
A life of Echegaray, with brief comments on some of his plays and a long synopsis of *La muerte en los labios.*

Graham, James. "José Echegaray: A Sketch." In *The Son of Don Juan: An Original Drama in Three Acts; Inspired by the Reading of Ibsen's Work Entitled 'Gengangere',* by José Echegaray, translated by James Graham, pp. 5-23. Boston: Little, Brown, and Co., 1918.
A biography of Echegaray, review of his canon, and appraisal of his talent.

Graham, Katharine A. "Some Aspects of Echegaray." *Poet Lore* XXI, No. III (May-June 1910): 234-39.
An essay on four of Echegaray's dramas. The critic applauds that dramatist for upholding the values of honor and virtue in defiance of the cynical artists of his day.

Lynch, Hannah. "José Echegaray." *The Contemporary Review* LXIV (October 1893): 576-95.
A lengthy plot analysis of *El hijo de Don Juan* and *El gran galeoto.*

Marble, Annie Russell. "Two Spanish Dramatists—Echegaray (1904), Benavente (1922)." In her *The Nobel Prize Winners in Literature,* pp. 239-52. New York: D. Appleton and Co., 1927.*
A chronological tracing of Echegaray's dramatic canon, supplying criticism of his major plays.

Shaw, Bernard. "The Echegaray Matinées." In his *Dramatic Opinions and Essays with an Apology, Vol. 2,* pp. 186-94. London: Constable and Co., 1910.
A reprint of one of Shaw's *Saturday Review* essays, offering his playfully mocking opinions of the plot, characters, and execution of an 1897 performance of *Mariana.*

Wallace, Elizabeth. "The Spanish Drama of Today." *The Atlantic Monthly* 102, No. 3 (September 1908): 357-66.*
A discussion of *El hijo de Don Juan, El gran galeoto,* and *El loco dios.*

Sergei (Aleksandrovich) Esenin

1895-1925

(Also transliterated as Sergei, Sergey, Sergéy, Sergej, or Sergyey; also Alexandrovich; also Esénin, Essenin, Yesenin, or Yessenin) Russian poet and essayist.

Esenin commands prominence in Russian literature as one of the most powerful poetic voices during an era of revolution. Born to peasant parents, he made their heritage central to his poetry, his poetic themes deriving from the traditional peasant values of religion and an intimate sense of the natural world. Esenin feared that this old agricultural order was rapidly becoming obsolete in the new political order of his country, and a side of his poetry expresses feelings of alienation as a consequence of disappointed hopes for the future of post-revolutionary Russia.

As a young man Esenin trained to become a teacher. Abandoning the pursuit of this career, he left his village for the cultural centers of Moscow and Petrograd. In Moscow Esenin studied Russian literature at the Shanyavsky Popular University, and in Petrograd he met the poets Alexander Blok and Nikolay Klyuev. Klyuev in particular guided and encouraged the young poet, and at this time *Radunitsa*, his first collection of poetry, appeared. Shortly afterward Esenin was drafted into the military, from which he became a fugitive when the February revolution broke out.

After the revolution Esenin published several more collections of poetry and was becoming noted in the literary world. With a group of Moscow poets he helped establish the Russian imaginist movement, a trend in poetry which considered imagery the primary vehicle for literary expression, similar to the imagist theories of Ezra Pound and T. E. Hulme. Due to aesthetic differences and his ambition for personal renown Esenin finally broke away from the imaginists. Works from this time include his narrative poem *Pugacev* and *Ispoved' khuligana* (*Confessions of a Hooligan*).

From the imaginist period to the end of his life Esenin became known for leading a self-destructively disordered existence, autobiographically chronicled in collections such as *Moskva kabatskaia*. During his marriage to the American classical dancer Isadora Duncan, Esenin continued his hectic style of living, traveling through Europe and the United States and eventually entering a sanatorium in Paris. After the poet's suicide his name became synonymous with mental and moral dissolution, the term "Eseninitis" designating this syndrome.

The most popular national poet during his lifetime, Esenin was derogated and officially neglected in the Soviet Union after his death. Not until the 1950s did Esenin's poetry begin to reclaim recognition, and since then his work has regained much of its former status. For his sheer artistic force, Esenin is now widely appreciated as one of the significant lyric poets of the twentieth century.

PRINCIPAL WORKS

Radunitsa   (poetry)   1916
Goluben'   (poetry)   1918

Inoniya   (poetry)   1918
Isus-mladenets   (poetry)   1918
Sel'skii chasoslov   (poetry)   1918
Preobrazhenie   (poetry)   1919
Ispoved' khuligana   (poetry)   1920
  [*Confessions of a Hooligan*, 1973]
Treriadnitsa   (poetry)   1920
Tripitkh   (poetry)   1920
Pugacev   (poetry)   1922
Stikhi skandalista   (poetry)   1923
Moskva kabatskaia   (poetry)   1924
Persidskie motivy   (poetry)   1925
Rus' sovetskaia   (poetry)   1925
Poems by Esenin   (poetry)   1970

MAXIM GORKY   (essay date 1919)

I first met [Sergei Yesenin] in 1914 in the company of [Nikolay] Klyuev. I got the impression of a lad of between

15 and 17, curly-haired, in a blue blouse, peasant-style top-coat and high-boots, highly reminiscent of . . . sugary post-cards of young boyars. . . . Yesenin produced a vague impression of a diffident and somewhat perplexed lad who felt quite out of his element in the huge city of St. Petersburg. (p. 349)

Later, when I read his vivid, sweeping and heartfelt verse, I found it hard to believe that it had come from the selfsame picturesquely attired lad. . . .

Some six or seven years later I saw Yesenin in Berlin, at A. N. Tolstoi's apartment. Only the clear gaze remained of the curly-haired comely boy I had met, and even that seemed to have lost much of its lustre. It flicked nervously from face to face, now defiantly or scornfully, now with uncertainty, embarrassment or distrust. It seemed to me that on the whole he felt unfriendly towards people, and everything went to show that he drank. His eyelids were swollen, his eyes red, and his skin pallid and lifeless, as is usual with such who breathe little fresh air and get little sleep. His hands were on the move all the time, and he looked harassed and *distrait,* like a man who has forgotten something important and has but a hazy recollection of precisely what he has forgotten. (p. 350)

I asked him to recite his poem of a dog whose seven whelps have been taken away to be drowned.

"If you aren't tired. . . ."

"Verse never tires me," he replied, then asked shyly, "Do you like that story about the dog?"

I told him that in my opinion he was the first in Russian literature to have written about animals with such skill and sincere love.

"Yes, I'm terribly fond of all sorts of animals," he said thoughtfully, and when I asked him whether he knew Claudel's *Animal's Paradise* he made no reply, touched his head with both hands and commenced his *Song of a Dog.* As he uttered the concluding lines:

> And the poor, sad tears of the mongrel
> Fell like golden stars on the snow.

his eyes also filled with tears.

After hearing these verses I could not help thinking that Sergei Yesenin was not so much a human being as a sensitive organ created by Nature exclusively for poetry, for the expression of the boundless "sadness of the fields," to quote S. Sergeyev-Tsensky, of love for everything living in this world and of that compassion that Man has deserved more than anything else. (p. 354)

> Maxim Gorky, "Sergei Yesenin" (1919), in his On
> Literature, *University of Washington Press, 1973,*
> *pp. 349-56.*

CLARENCE AUGUSTUS MANNING   (essay date 1929)

No modern poet has suffered more in reputation than has Sergyey Aleksandrovich Esenin. His mad fits of intoxication, his marriage with Isadora Duncan, his visit to America, all attracted the public fancy, and under the mass of scandalous tales that drifted around concerning him his real merits and his real position in Russian literature escaped attention. Despite all the incidents in which he figured, de-spite all the nonsense and the scandal of his life, Esenin was one of the most prominent figures in the literature of his generation, and had his life been cast in happier times, he would have won for himself a place respected and prom-inent in the field of literature. As it is, when the stories that cloud his career die away and his works are seen in a real perspective and as a whole, the attitude of the world to him will change and he will be recognised for qualities which have been unnoticed in the storm and stress of the last decade.

Culture is a deadly poison. The civilised world does not recognise this, for an established and settled society learns to control its ravages and builds up a strong internal resis-tance against its extremes. We may pride ourselves to-day on our democracy, but the unhappiness of the self-made man when he finds himself in society is often painfully evi-dent. It is the exceptional person that can pass from one class to another and be at home in all.

In this fact lies the tragedy of Esenin. He was never able in his short life to master the new environment into which he was thrown by fate. He was always the peasant boy with the ideals and the aspirations of the peasant. He could never free himself from his childish faith and his childish superstitions. He might try to show himself sophisticated; he might try to fly in the face of respectability and bour-geois principles; but in all his strivings there was something naïve, something strained, which showed how far he was from accomplishing his purpose. He was never at home in the world of revolution, in the world of art, and in his saner and calmer moments he must have felt what an unhealthy and unnatural rôle he was playing. (p. 676)

Esenin, when he came up to Petersburg, was forced in his own person to face that same clash of culture which had shaken Russian society two centuries earlier. He was thrown abruptly from the village of the past into the varied life of the capital, and he had barely arrived when the World War broke out. The turmoil was beginning. The young man still unused to the rich culture of the capital was forced to witness the disintegration of that culture before the rude assault of war and revolution. It was natural, and only natural, that he should take the side of the October Revolution. Culture meant little or nothing to him and the promises of the Bolshevik leaders attracted him. Yet, as he said himself, he accepted the Revolution with a peasant tinge. He saw in it the removal of those evils which he had noticed in his village life. He saw in it possibilities of change as they affected the life which he really knew. (p. 678)

Esenin had broken with the village. When he came to the city, and tasted its magic broth, he realised that the doom of the village had been sounded. He could not go back. He could not once again find refuge and peace in the simple life of the peasant. The cabaret and the night-life had entered his head and he was lost. That sense of loss becomes more apparent in his later poems. There is a pathos about them that makes them strangely appealing. (p. 679)

Soviet critics, carrying their theories and their doctrines into the world of literature as well as politics, see in him a failure to accept the world of facts. They feel that he should have spoken more fully and more satisfactorily in the lan-guage of the new day. They see in him a mystic who greeted the revolution in the belief that a miracle would happen and that a new and better day would come without a struggle and a contest. . . . They sorrow that so gifted a poet had written poems that could not speak to the class-conscious proletariat and peasantry. (pp. 679-80)

Reared as Esenin was to a hard and rugged life, with the simplest and most natural pleasures, we should not expect him to join the class-conscious peasantry. We should not expect him to narrate the wrongs of the poor, the hardships of the village hut, the injustice of the seasons. All those are for him the basis of existence, the very essentials of the life which he must lead.

Once this is understood, we can see at once the virtues of his poetry. He sings of the village and the country. He does not need to seek high themes, but he finds them near at hand. The village, the seasons, the beauty of the landscape, the colours of the sunset and the sunrise, the plains, the grain-fields, all are subjects for his pen. Few of his predecessors have been so able to express this simplicity and the naturalness of this rural life which surged around him. Nearly all of his earliest and best work deals only with the country. There is little or nothing of love, and love at no time seems to have driven Esenin into song. It is Russia and its Faith that inspires him. . . . (p. 680)

It is such themes which occupy Esenin until the beginning of the World War and which mark the clearest and most harmonious product of his genius. (p. 681)

The years of the World War are marked by relative silence on the part of Esenin and he only resumed vigorous production on the outbreak of the Revolution. Here he was wholeheartedly and vigorously expressing in naïve and unassimilated jargon the new elements that had come into being, but he was still thinking in terms of the old peasant life. (p. 682)

[His] love of description and of nature led Esenin to join the group of the Imagists, the group which was established to lead poetry away from the wilds of symbolism into the clearness and brightness of the visible and the tangible world. Through the dark days of the Revolution Esenin went his way singing as he would. He acquired the unbelief of the day and in "Inonia" he throws to the winds the old mystical conception of Kitezh, the hidden city of piety and holiness. He indulges in rude and naïve blasphemy as he seeks to develop the new ideal of "Inonia." The poem he dedicates to the Prophet Jeremiah and he begins with a curious mixture of conceit and less pleasing qualities. . . . (pp. 682-83)

With this preface he [describes] the new world which is coming into being, where mankind will rest solely on its own efforts and be judged by its own accomplishments. That was the net product of the Revolution for the peasant boy from Ryazan. He had licked in fight all the neighbours' children. Now he was merely taking God and the universe on, in the hope that thereby he would become stronger.

The notes of hooliganism begin to sound more and more clear in his works. He describes the revels and the scandals that made him notorious and a terror even to his friends. He revels in cynicism, and at the same time we have the curious and interesting "Confession of a Hooligan," written in 1920. He glorifies his wildness and his unbridled character, and at the same time he bemoans what he has lost. . . .

The two themes sound together as the peasant boy from Ryazan in patent-leather boots and a high hat tries to persuade himself that he is, after all, a cynical leader of a progressive society as well as the foremost poet of Russia.

Such a conflict could not long continue, and, as might have been expected, the solution was disadvantageous for Esenin. His hope was to master himself, to leave the city which he detested and feared and to go home to the country to live. The poison of culture had eaten into him too deeply and he returned to the village only to say farewell. He became all too conscious that the doom of the old world had been sounded. (p. 683)

The city, the all-devouring city, had caught him in its meshes, and once that was decided, he was forced to bid farewell to the land which he loved and to throw in his lot entirely with the new environment.

To do this required strength. To struggle and to hold one's own against the backward peasantry and the wild life around him was impossible. That is the theme of *Pugachov*, a lyric drama describing the career of that strange genius in the eighteenth century. Esenin pointed out the hardships, the injustice of the peasant life, the troubles of the Kalmyks and the Tatars, all of them unable to unite and demand relief until Pugachov comes and unifies them with a lie, the lie that he really is the Tsar. Success attends their efforts, but at the first sign of defeat and setback, the old feuds and superstitions reassert themselves, and the very men who were loudest in glorifying him are the ones who plan to hand him over to the authorities in return for their own safety. Pugachov can hardly believe that human nature is so petty. The whole poem, the largest continuous work of Esenin, is a remarkable production. In its lyric beauty, and in its keen analysis of the different characters, it shows what was latent in the poet, if only he could have mastered himself and found himself in a proper environment.

After all, he had left the country for the city, but the new urban culture of the Soviets had no message for him. "The Land of Rascals" he left unfinished, but it could hardly be anything but an exposition of the corruption of the Soviet bureaucracy and of the new evils which were growing in the Russia which was to have been cleansed and purified. What use was it all, the destruction of the old, if crooked and stealing communists were to take the place of corrupt and stealing servants of the Tsar? (pp. 684-85)

Esenin's life was a real tragedy. For him the country was health, the city disease, but his organism was not strong enough to throw down the challenge, to break with either one side or the other and to have done without remorse or without recall. He fluttered like a moth to the fire of the life of the city, and in it he saw only the dissipation, the wildness, the night-life, all those sides which were most hectic and unnatural. Into this he plunged with all of his vital energy, and in the struggle he perished. Yet it is his rural poetry that will live the longest, and the world of letters will more and more come to see that that is the real man, the real poet who deserves a place in Russian literature, and who is one of the foremost poets of country life in the twentieth century in any literature. (p. 686)

Clarence Augustus Manning, "The Tragedy of Esenin," in The Slavonic Review *(reprinted by permission of the University of London), Vol. VII, No. 21, March, 1929, pp. 676-86.*

ALEXANDER KAUN (essay date 1943)

[Yesenin's] allegiance to the imagists should be taken less seriously than . . . that of [Vladimir] Mayakovsky to the futurists. For Mayakovsky did introduce and practice a number of poetic innovations in form and substance that might be labeled futuristic. As for Sergey Yesenin's poetry, it defies all -isms; when good, it is just good poetry, in regular and occasionally varying metric verse, in rhymed lyrics or in long blank-verse poems like *Pugachov*. Only occasionally does he make one aware of imagist trickery, and then his lines are overladen with similes and charged with labored coarseness. Otherwise his wealth of images merits the label of ''imagism'' no more than does that of Homer or the Russian heroic ballads, the *byliny*. Yesenin is nearer to the symbolists, except for their aristocraticism and cosmopolitan urbanity, than he is to any other modern school. Yesenin is an autochthonous Russian peasant; this fact accounts for the fundamental characteristics of his poetry. The pungent aroma of rural Russia permeates his verse, its imagery as much as its ideology. . . . (pp. 72-3)

> Alexander Kaun, ''Postsymbolists,'' in his *Soviet Poets and Poetry (copyright © 1943 by The Regents of the University of California; reprinted by permission of the University of California Press), University of California Press, 1943, pp. 35-97.**

JANKO LAVRIN (essay date 1948)

[Sergey Esenin] on the one hand, and [Vladimir] Mayakovsky on the other, are the two dominant figures among the crop of the poets who came into their own during the first decade of the Soviet regime. Yet what a contrast between these two gifted youths. . . . While Mayakovsky became the poetic voice of the rising proletarians, Esenin preferred to turn his enormous gift into a lament for the old peasant Russia, and he could hardly have made any other choice. Born and brought up in the depths of rural Russia (the district of Ryazan), Esenin was so much steeped in the soil and the peasant lore that he was never able to detach himself from them, not even when he did his best to fit into the life of the capital, or into the spirit of the revolution. It would be a mistake, though, to regard his rural poetry from the angle of mere village folk-lore or local colour. It goes deeper. In a way it could be defined as poetic self-assertion of the ''eternal peasant'' against the encroaching machine and the mentality of the industrial town. The village in its primeval quintessence, sifted through his individual temperament, found in Esenin's verse one of the most poignant expressions in the whole of modern poetry. It was and remained the basic and perhaps the only source of his inspiration. (p. 263)

Esenin's pastoral motifs, far from being a repetition of . . . hackneyed old melodies, vibrate with such freshness and sincerity that, in spite of his calculated experiments in poetic technique (new rhythms and forms), they sound as if extemporised. He often achieved surprisingly original texture and inflection by the manner in which he used peasant imagery and peasant idioms as one of his expedients. Religion, poetic superstition, naive animism and pantheism seem to vie with each other to make him produce that intimate yet strangely remote atmosphere which permeates the poems of his early period. But this was only one facet of Esenin's work. Its second and for a while hidden aspect was that potentially anarchic spirit of the steppes which,

lurking in their unconscious, was perhaps more typical of the pre-revolutionary Russian peasants than were their seeming quietism and submissiveness. Whereas in the West the word freedom is associated with society, in Russia it used to be inseparable from the idea of the boundless spaces where everything seems to be on a bigger and more lavish scale than in Europe. This spirit in particular was responsible for their inner restlessness, as well as their frequent excess in everything: in piety and sacrilege, in meekness and cruelty, in active idealism and anarchic destruction. Esenin—an ''essential'' peasant from those spaces, stretching into the heart of Asia—actually confessed in one of his lyrics: ''I cherish my secret purity of heart; but still I may murder someone to the whistle of the autumn wind. . . .'' It may be that the same unruly spirit rather than any convictions made him hail the revolution even while he, too, expected from the latter a renewal of life. The sentimental-idyllic and the turbulent elements were intertwined in him as in a fugue, out of which emerged some of his most remarkable melodies. (pp. 265-66)

Unhampered by education or excessive reading, Esenin relied, like Nekrasov before him, on the sureness of his poetic instinct which made him glean the right kind of words, metaphors and images in the depths of the folk-genius itself. Most of his symbols, especially in his early poems, were connected with the archaic life of the village, and he enlarged them now and then—in a mythological sense—to cosmic dimensions. God and the saints are treated by him as something inseparable from the fields, the seasons, and the cattle. (p. 267)

The ''essential'' peasant was so strong in Esenin that he could not shed him even after he had turned to other themes and interests. While piling up laurels and disillusionments in the two Russian capitals, he still regarded the hut and the cornfields of his childhood as his only home. And when the revolution came, Esenin welcomed it in a spirit which was entirely different from that of [Alexander] Blok or Mayakovsky. He hailed it neither as a dissatisfied intellectual who thought he had found an outlet in the new Apocalypse; nor as a proletarian, dancing on the ruins of the old world, but exclusively as a peasant and a villager. It was the turbulent yet Utopian villager in Esenin that made him write . . . the revolutionary paean *Inonia*—a peasant counterpart to Blok's *The Twelve*. (p. 268)

Inonia is, together with Blok's famous poem, Klyuyev's *Lenin*, and Andrey Bely's *Christ is Risen*, among the most outspoken Messianic affirmations of the Russian Revolution on the part of the still lingering symbolists on the one hand, and the village poets on the other. Louder and more exuberant than *The Twelve*, Esenin's *Inonia* expresses the vision of a millennium ruled, not by the proletarians and their machines, but by the peasants inhabiting a free and universal Arcadia: quite in the style of those ''populists'' who once dreamed of a Russia untainted by the horrors of industrialism. Revolutionary in its tone and language, the poem thus seems to be anti-proletarian in its very subject.

If *The Twelve* can be likened to a disciplined and almost fettered ecstasy, *Inonia* is delirium passing into emotional and rhetorical debauch. As though intoxicated with his own words and visions, Esenin here lets loose not only his Utopian moods, but also his latent turbulence, verging on spiritual hooliganism. The result is a strange torrent of poetry and of verbal hysteria. ''I will shear the blue firmament like a mangy sheep of its wool," he shouts almost with foam on his lips. "I will bite through the Milky Way. I will raise my arms as high as the Moon and will crack her like a nut. . . ." And so on—one "colossal" simile hurled upon another. Forgetting the meek peasant Saviour of his former days, Esenin now yells in a raucous voice: "The body, the body of *Christ* I will spit out of my mouth." But what he offers instead is his vague Arcadian idyll "where the Deity of the living resides;" where there is faith in power, and Truth is to be found only in man himself. The worn old phrases, repeated in a new fortissimo.

This poem is a landmark between Esenin's early lyrics and his "imaginist" experiments, the limitations of which he recognised soon enough. . . . But for the fact that Esenin happened to be one of its temporary members, [the imaginist movement] might have passed unnoticed, and even he cleared out of it before long. (pp. 269-70)

Associated with a few other turbulent though less talented poets, Esenin must have felt strangely out of place in the turmoil of the Soviet capital. Yet he forced himself to fit into it and to satisfy at least the unruly element in him. He did all he could to beat the bohemians on their own ground, in which he seems to have succeeded. (p. 271)

But there was despair in his excesses. His buffoonery was that of a sentimental-romantic peasant boy who came too soon into the bedlam of a big city and was crushed by its grip. . . . [His] instincts and the very roots of his being had remained in another and totally different pattern of existence. . . . And when the trend of events took the direction of industrialism on a gigantic scale, Esenin—with his ideal of rural Arcadia—felt more dismayed than ever. Crushed by the depth of his own frustration, he arrived, in his tavern poems, at the conclusion that, together with him, everything else was doomed also. (pp. 272-73)

In moods such as this Esenin called himself the "last of village poets" and predicted that rapid mechanisation of the land which, according to him, was to destroy all the romance of patriarchal life he had known and loved in his boyhood. . . . (p. 274)

Provocative in his manners and in his verses, Esenin paraded, at times, words and expressions which are banished from civilised intercourse. As he could no longer invariably rely upon his inspiration, he often piled up images some of which were tiresomely laboured. Yet his tavern poems have a genuine tragic ring and produce, now and then, the effect of lived hallucinations. (p. 275)

It was during those years of riot and scandal that nostalgia for his lost and therefore poetically embellished Arcadia became particularly painful. One can feel it in his *Confessions of a Hooligan* . . . , and somewhat differently in his *Return Home* . . . , where the encroachment of the new Soviet village left little or no room for his old dreams. . . . For, with all his puzzling ways, Esenin was much too simple for the age and the conditions he was compelled to live in. Having tasted of glory and adulation; of riot and scandal; of travels . . . in America, Germany and France, he yet remained inwardly tied to the village—inert and "patriarchal" because of its very inertia. But while refusing to outgrow it, he suddenly saw himself outgrown and left behind by the new sovietised village which he did not want to accept. Hence his aimlessness and bewilderment. And as for his premature fame, it only unbalanced him like strong adulterated wine indulged in by a child.

Too sensitive and much too weak to face the unpleasant realities, he remained hanging in the air—a stranger to the world in which there was no room for his archaic dreams and ideals. . . . [A last visit] to the haunts of his early years only made things worse. Instead of recovering his paradise lost, he felt that he was a walking anachronism—out of joint with everybody and everything, his native village included. All he could do was to translate his sorrow into lyrics, or else stifle it in riotous night life.

With regard to form he now underwent another change. Having abandoned the "imaginist" eccentricities, he chose for his model the lucid genius of Pushkin. Once more he sang in simple intimate strains. In his *Persian Themes* he even caught something of Pushkin's serene insouciance which lasted, however, only during his wanderings in the East. On his return home he was plunged into the former welter, but this time the gap between fancy and reality was steadily widening. . . . At the age of thirty he was like an old man who had nothing to hope for, nothing to work for, nothing to look forward to. A victim of hypochondria, disgust and self-disgust, he saw only one way of escape and he took it. A juvenile melodramatic touch was lent to his death by the fact that he wrote his last poem in his own blood.

Such was the literary career of the poet whose personal fate was in a way symbolic of the transition period between the two Russias—the old and the new; between the agricultural pattern of existence on the one hand, and the birth-pangs of the industrialised socialist society on the other. The inner conflict involved by this change found in Esenin a pathetic voice which, in its turn, appealed to thousands of readers and was responsible for his vogue during and immediately after the revolution. It was his pastoral nostalgia that found a ready response in all those contemporaries who regretted the passing away of the old rural Russia, and they consisted by no means of mere *kulaks*. (pp. 275-78)

> *Janko Lavrin, "Sergey Esenin," in his* From Pushkin to Mayakovsky: A Study in the Evolution of a Literature, *Sylvan Press, 1948, pp. 262-78.*

D. S. MIRSKY (essay date 1955)

[Sergéy Esénin] is a product of south Great Russia (Ryazán), which has not the ancient and archaic civilization of the north, and where the peasant had always a tendency to be semi-nomadic with no firm roots in the soil. . . . [Esénin] had no interest in religious symbolism and ritual; his mysticism was skin-deep, and the quasi-blasphemous poems he wrote in 1917-18 were nothing more than his contribution to a fashion that raged among the belated symbolists of the day. These poems are in point of fact the sheerest and most shamefaced nonsense. Fortunately for Esénin his reputation does not stand and fall with these poems. He is a genuine poet and has a rare gift of song. He is genuinely akin to the spirit of the Russian folk song, though he does not adopt its meters. This blend of wistful melancholy and insolent daredeviltry is characteristic of the central Russian; it is present in the Russian folk song, and in Esénin it manifests itself both in the pensive sweetness of his elegies and in the aggressive coarseness of his *Confession of a Hooligan*. There is no genuine mystical or religious background in Esénin but a certain gay and careless nihilism that any moment may turn into a sentimental wistfulness under the influence of love, drink, or recollection. There is no vigor in

Esénin; . . . [he] is a sort of peasant Turgénev who sees the disappearance of all the beauty that is dear to him, laments it, but submits to the inevitable. His short lyrics are often very beautiful, though in the long run monotonous. All their charm lies in the sweetness of their melody, and his "tragedy" *Pugachëv* . . . is not a tragedy at all but merely a succession of (often exquisite) lyrics put into the mouths of a famous rebel and of his companions and enemies. (pp. 493-94)

> D. S. Mirsky, "Poetry after 1910," in his A History of Russian Literature, *edited by Francis J. Whitefield (copyright 1958 by Alfred A. Knopf, Inc.; reprinted by permission of Alfred A. Knopf, Inc.), revised edition, Knopf, 1955, pp. 485-503.**

RENATO POGGIOLI (essay date 1960)

Unlike [Vladimir] Majakovskij, whose destiny it was to become the poet of history and of "October," Sergej Esenin remained forever the poet of nature and of the decaying season. . . . (p. 269)

There is at least a minor vein in the poetry of Esenin which is not too different from certain aspects of Majakovskij's work. This is the apocalyptic vein which appears in *Transfiguration* and *Inonija* (the latter is a word coined by the poet, meaning "Other-Land"). In both pieces the poet condemns the dying old world, while exalting the Revolution as a kind of cosmic rebirth. Here Esenin's verse, like Majakovskij's, overflows with "hyperbolic" and "iconoclastic" images, which in this case, however, derive from a morbid and perverted mysticism, often turning into heresy and blasphemy, into a parody of Christian hopes, myths, and beliefs. In these two poems Esenin became the secular apostle of a new Gospel, the announcer of a new earthly kingdom, the seer of the Revolution as the earthly paradise of the peasant and the shepherd. These two pieces greatly differ from the long poems of the later years, predominantly autobiographical in character and expressing the disappointment of the poet with the Revolution, as well as the complaint of a peasant's son uprooted from the countryside, and living as an outcast in the alien world of the city.

Both the early revolutionary pieces, which are the weakest part of his work, and the later autobiographical poems may all too often seem to a foreign reader the most important fruits of this poet's talent. Certainly nobody can deny their significance as human and social documents. Yet the most genuine of Esenin's masterpieces are to be found among his shortest, least ambitious lyrics, written in the pure and simple modes of the elegy and the idyll, devoid of any rhetorical and anecdotal structure, and lightly woven as a cobweb of transparent words around the cluster of a few bright and striking images. Each one of these songs may be reduced to a landscape and to the mood it evokes within the soul of the poet. Although the narrative element is lacking, or hardly present, such poems partake of the magic aura of the legend and the fairy tale. They recreate a private and intimate universe, domestic and rustic, where all things are humanized by a naïve animism, by a pathetic anthropomorphism. The ingenuousness of Esenin's vision is evident in the central image of each one of these lyrics, defining its object by a kind of childish puzzle, which follows or accompanies its name.

It is from the same simplicity of outlook that Esenin derives his gusto for the colorful, the vivid, the picturesque. His favorite color is the color of the sky, in all its shades; and he loves it so much as to attribute it to his native land, to his "blue Russia." But his poems are equally full of white and yellow patches, so enameled as to give the effect of gold and silver, and to remind us of icons and miniature painting, of Byzantine mosaics and popular prints or cuts. This chromatism is not merely a decorative, but also a compositional, element and intensifies the stylization of the poet's vision, so evident in the stillness of the landscapes, with their motionless figures and timeless moods. But almost always this stillness is broken by a sudden burst of song, by a hidden stream of music, changing the stasis into ecstasis, and flooding the entire scene with a melodic grief which makes a vibrant chord of every fiber.

This feeling of cosmic pain is suggested through a constant parallelism, a continuous identification between men, beasts, plants, and stars. For Esenin there is no difference between our tears and the tears of all other creatures, and even of things. Since only the humble may be exalted, the poet celebrates even the heavenly creature he loves most, the moon, through a series of animal metamorphoses: by converting it, metaphorically, now into a bear, now into a frog. In the same spirit, when wishing to express his own sorrow at the passing of time, he changes himself into an old maple; or when wishing to declare his love for a girl, he addresses instead a young birch.

It is the beasts that play a central role in the poet's belief that there exists a universal, brotherly and mystical bond, joining together the human and the nonhuman, the animal and vegetable kingdoms, the organic and inorganic worlds. Animals are for Esenin the most human and humane of all the creatures of God. Thus, in one of the most beautiful and moving poems of his later years, he projects the horror of the Revolution through the vision of animal, rather than human, slaughter: through the ordeal of starvation and famine, when human beings are forced to kill their domestic animals, and to eat of their flesh. This poem is "Mare Ships," in which the tragedy of Revolution is reduced to the tragedy of hunger, symbolized by a fleshless carrion abandoned in a city street.

As the poet of wooden Russia, Esenin also protested against the invasion of the Russian countryside by the technological monsters of modern civilization: the telegraph poles and the electric cables, the steam engines and steel derricks demanded by the Soviet drive for industrialization. This theme is fully developed in "Requiem," especially in its final scene, describing a foolish colt that vainly challenges to a race the train crossing the Russian plains as a ghostly and awful "iron guest." The two themes of the sacrifice of the animals and of the countryside's martyrdom dominate the poetry of the late Esenin, in which they merge with a more individual note, with the poet's lament about his plight as a man and an artist. Such a lament and the poet's foreboding of his own ruin reflect in personal terms the cruel destiny of any uprooted villager, living as an exile in the foreign and harsh world of the city. . . . Esenin conveyed this feeling of alienation and corruption in "Soviet Russia," a poem describing a visit to his native village, and vented his indignation against a way of life he could neither reject nor accept by acting, in both imagination and reality, as a bohemian and a hooligan, as an eccentric and an outcast. (pp. 272-75)

The lesson we may learn from his fate, as from the fate of Majakovskij, is that in no country do poets find it harder to live or survive than in that Red Russia which they once saluted as a promised land. (p. 275)

Renato Poggioli, "The Poets of the Advance Guard," in his The Poets of Russia: 1890-1930 *(copyright © 1960 by the President and Fellows of Harvard College; excerpted by permission), Cambridge, Mass.: Harvard University Press, 1960, pp. 238-75.**

VERA ALEXANDROVA (essay date 1963)

Yesenin is a peasant poet through and through. This is expressed in the entire vocabulary of his poetry. The horse, the most important factor in the simple peasant economy, is Yesenin's favorite image. Even in ears of wheat this great artist found a resemblance to horses' manes. (p. 69)

In the spontaneity of his lyrical talent Yesenin is reminiscent of one of the greatest poets of fifteenth-century France —François Villon, who spent the greater part of his life wandering the land, whose friends were vagrants and thieves, but who left behind imperishable poems ("Petit Testament" and "Grand Testament"). The resemblance to Villon becomes even more pronounced in the poems Yesenin wrote during the last two years of his life, when he plunged into wild extremes of drinking and brawling. (p. 73)

Yesenin's poetry of nature is full of melancholy loveliness. In a single image he evokes a complete picture in the reader's mind. . . .

But Yesenin's muse is by no means devoted only to love of his native land and landscape. Very early, before the revolution, Yesenin also wrote poems dedicated to animals: "The Cow"—"Senile, toothless . . ."; and "Song about a Dog." . . . (p. 74)

Yesenin's poetry is marked by deep tenderness for every beast—a village dog, cats, sheep. He calls them all his "younger brothers." But love of animals is only a part of the poet's spiritual equipment. Still more characteristic is his sympathy with humbled man; he has a quick sense of kinship with the thief, the bandit, and the homeless waif. One of Yesenin's best poems, "Homeless Russia" . . . , is devoted to the *besprizorny*—the homeless children of the early years of the revolution. . . . (p. 75)

The poet's keenly emotional social awareness was vividly expressed in *The Song about the Great Campaign*. . . . The image of Peter the Great . . . is as monumental as it is in Alexey Tolstoy's novel *Peter I*, but Yesenin's attitude toward him is diametrically opposed to Tolstoy's. The nameless workmen of Peter's day, brought to life under Yesenin's pen, warn the Czar that he must be ready to die with dignity, should he fall into their hands. Neither these workmen nor the poet can forgive Peter for "favoring the nobles and ministers," and building a capital for them "upon the blood" of the homeless poor. (p. 76)

Vera Alexandrova, "Sergey Yesenin," in her A History of Soviet Literature, *translated by Mirra Ginsburg (copyright © 1963 by Vera Alexandrova-Schwarz; reprinted by permission of Doubleday & Company, Inc.), Doubleday, 1963, pp. 69-83.*

NIKOLAY TIKHONOV (essay date 1965)

Sergey Yesenin is a remarkable Soviet Russian poet. In his work he conveyed magnificently that great lyrical force, that song-like quality and extreme sincerity which is so close to popular (*narodny*) feelings, popular lyrical creations.

Not for nothing has he entered so deeply the consciousness of various generations of Soviet people. (pp. 508-09)

When you have before you such a complete, whole, beautiful phenomenon as Yesenin's verse, you can say a lot about it, but it is very hard to rebuke the poet for writing as he did, and not, say, as [Vladimir] Mayakovsky or anyone else.

A different, purely individual, approach to his verse is possible. I, for instance, do not think that the early period of the young Yesenin's verse is powerful. The poet is just beginning to build up his strength. I don't much like all his poems with a marked religious content. They are very pink, from [Nikolai] Klyuyev and Church pictures. And his attempt later to combine the new revolutionary theme with something divine in Imaginistic images was not successful.

In his last period, his verse, technically weak, ordinary, basically classical, would have been pale and inexpressive if he had not imbued it with his biography, and then this verse began to sound tragically and convincingly, because there already predominated in it that ultimate sincerity which made up for all the beauties of figurative language. In it the poet's fate spoke for itself. These poems are like milestones on the way to a hopeless dead-end. (p. 512)

Nikolay Tikhonov, in his letter to G. McVay on January 19, 1965, in "Soviet Poets Discuss Sergey Yesenin," edited by G. McVay, in The Slavonic and East European Review *(© University of London (School of Slavonic and East European Studies) 1970; reprinted by permission), Vol. XLVIII, No. 113, October, 1970, pp. 506-19.*

VSEVOLOD ROZHDESTVENSKY (essay date 1967)

Yesenin's pure lyric voice, so beloved by our people and, moreover, by men of different intellectual levels, stands out very sharply against a background of what one might call "literary" poetry, by means of its remarkable immediacy and vividly expressed melodiousness. One feels like singing his poems, and indeed they often do become songs. He himself used to sing them slightly when performing them.

This predominance of . . . a song-like structure could not, of course, fail to influence the creative manner of a number of poets, both contemporaries and those of following generations. Yesenin's musicality was mainly reflected in the work of those poets who themselves stemmed from the people and were close to song-like and folkloric motifs: I mean the early and subsequent works of [Mikhail Vasilyevich Isakovsky and Alexandr Trifonovich] Tvardovsky. But if one takes a broader look at this question, then the agitated tone of Yesenin's lyric verse has exerted a great influence on very many poets who have sought directly to express deeply personal experiences.

There can be no doubt also that his fresh bold *imagery*, which is rich in content (and nearly always linked with Nature and least of all with urban motifs) has been perceived and grasped by poets whose character differs greatly from the methods and themes of Yesenin himself. . . .

Finally, one may say that Yesenin's wide popularity—both among readers and writers—is caused by the fact that his poems are simple and clear in form, are always filled with profound inner agitation, and express with maximum sincerity the truth of his heart. And the tragic circumstances of his life, about which he himself speaks with exceptional sincerity, make his works especially memorable, because they are the confession of a man for whom life and art merge into one organic whole. . . . (pp. 517-18)

> *Vsevolod Rozhdestvensky, in his letter to G. McVay on June 12, 1967, in "Soviet Poets Discuss Sergey Yesenin," edited by G. McVay, in* The Slavonic and East European Review *(© University of London (School of Slavonic and East European Studies) 1970; reprinted by permission), Vol. XLVIII, No. 113, October, 1970, pp. 506-19.*

GEOFFREY THURLEY (essay date 1973)

The facts of Esenin's life can be derived from the poems, which form . . . a continuous and frank autobiography of the sensibility. By this I mean that the state of mind experienced and the stages of awareness reached by the poet do not have to be inferred or translated out of mandarin symbolism, but are hawked and proffered by a man who never —thank God!—outgrew a certain peasant crudeness and emotionalism. . . . [Although] Esenin lacked the intellectual sophistication to probe very subtly into himself—we cannot help admiring the courage and fundamental honesty of Esenin's response to what his life had become [after the Russian Revolution, his alcoholism, the Isadora Duncan farce, and the rowdy trips abroad]. If we turn from him to any Western poet who might offer parallel with him—say Hart Crane or Dylan Thomas—we cannot, I think, refrain from granting to the Russian poet a superior openness and frankness. In fact, Esenin's very absence of introspection aids him in this. Dylan Thomas's verse, for instance, offers practically no evidence of the shoddy disorder of so much of his later life; Hart Crane acknowledged the falling apart of body and soul under the stress of violent debauch with a fullness that at times attains sublimity: there is nothing in Esenin, I think, to equal the majestic transmutation of material we see in Crane's 'Island Quarry' or 'North Labrador'. But Crane's very sublimity contains an element of fraud: the conception of poetry implicit in Esenin's much more human ordinariness is surely saner and sounder than Crane's consistent concentration on what the imagination spans 'beyond despair'. (pp. 8-9)

[Esenin's work] begins with a simplicity that shames the premature nobility of the early [Alexandr] Blok. Lyrics like 'Night' . . . and 'Already Evening' . . . owe something perhaps to the indirect influence of Goethe, but Esenin's pristine clarity is his own. Like other writers of working-class stock—one thinks of D. H. Lawrence and Maxim Gorky— Esenin was a child in his childhood, unlike Proust, for instance, or Yeats or Rilke, bourgeois poets who seem to have been born middle-aged. [Vladimir] Markov and [M.] Sparks' dismissal of the very early work as 'extremely unoriginal and inept' must certainly be rejected. (p. 9)

Still, there is no denying the greater interest of the poems Esenin began to produce under the shadow of the Revolu-

tion. Esenin's greatest gift perhaps is a certain peasant fullness of gaze which was never quite allowed to cloud over. The peasant is far from the Arcadian stereotype, of course: he is crafty and hard as well as simple, and his very naïveté is cunning, compact of hidden knowledge and the residue of ancient cults. He is also incurably superstitious: scratch any Russian, indeed, and you get not a Tartar (that is a White Russian romanticism) but a hopeless, medieval Believer. It is a combination of all these qualities that gives Esenin's pre-Revolutionary lyrics their special beauty. Blok was the last poet of the sublime in Russia, and we shall look in vain through Esenin's work for the exalted majesty of a poem like 'Spring' ('At the crossroads Where distance begins'); moreover, Blok subsumes traditional Christian orthodoxy under a Goethean calm, if never quite a Wordsworthian depth. . . . Precisely the greater spiritual breadth and cultural awareness of Blok's work deny it the devastating, simple sophistication of Esenin's Christian symbolism. (pp. 9-10)

The clear, emphatic Christian symbols and personifications of the poems of these years provide some of the richest effects in Esenin's work. The man in the 'smock of sunshine', the sparrow reading from his Psaltery in the forest, the red calf of the sunset, the red prayer-book of dawn, St. Andrew piping among the willows, Isaiah tending the golden herds —these symbols and personifications leap from the page with the freshness of great, primal poetry: Esenin interprets the facts of Nature through the symbolic filters of Christian and pagan myth, yet with no loss of directness and naïveté. . . .

This pristine early phase of Esenin's career culminates in the series of brilliant poems and sequences in which he acclaimed the Revolution. The Revolution cauterized Blok into *The Twelve,* then left him for dead, a worn-out shell. Esenin was a generation younger . . . and of peasant, not high bourgeois stock. He greeted the Revolution with 'Otherwhere', 'The Dove of Jordan' . . . and 'Requiem', among others—poems which translate the political events into ecstatically mystical terms. (p. 11)

It would be a simple matter to demonstrate that Esenin's lyrics are put together solidly and simply, on a basis of sustained situational points of view. In other words, they follow the principle of Romantic verse in 'taking place'—in a field, on a highroad, in a hotel room. The structure is guaranteed both by the integrity of the situation and locale and by the poet's tone of voice: Esenin uses the analogical techniques of Symbolism, but the tone of his verse is insistently personal and inflected, like that of Byron and Lermontov. . . . Far from there being any break in his development, the movement of his early verse converges upon the Revolution, funnels through it, so that the bright, simple, yet age-old Christian beliefs are simply lifted to a new socio-philosophical level of application.

But between these poems of 1918, acclaiming the Revolution, and those even of the following year, there is a terrible gulf. In 1919, in quatrains markedly close in style to those of 'The Dove of Jordan', Esenin wrote 'Mare Ships'. The intensity of this poem—an intensity bordering upon derangement—betrays the sheer strain that had underlain the exultations of the 'Dove': in place of its apocalyptic fervour, with its brimming religious light and its transfigured fields, 'Mare Ships' is compact of bitter disgust, the disgust of physical filth, decay, hunger, wretchedness. . . . (p. 13)

Soviet critics have stressed Esenin's ignorance of the real aims of the Revolution. He was, like Blok, happy to acclaim the millenium and to rejoice in the transfiguration of souls; but when the mystic transfiguration failed to take place, and the new state had to get on with the business of administration, he lost interest and felt betrayed, in true bourgeois fashion. But on their own level, the poets understood very well what had happened—too well for Soviet critics. Blok's *The Twelve* and Esenin's 'Mare Ships' don't tell us much about the economics of Revolution, but they tell us a lot about the human mind's more basic needs. (p. 14)

The next phase of Esenin's creative life begins with the first of the 'Hooligan' poems. . . . Many of the most moving poems of this period turn on the mechanization of the countryside he loved so much. In poems like 'I am the last poet of the village' . . . , Esenin deplores the horrible depredations of technology. The new roads strangle the villages, and the animal servants of the old life attempt vainly to compete with the 'iron guest' of the new order. (pp. 14-15)

Esenin's great quality is often held to be his lyricism, his gift of 'song', which challenges comparison, so we are told, with that of Pushkin. Yet although this view can't be dismissed out of hand, it certainly represents a distorting simplification of the truth. For one thing, the memory of Pushkin is often a curse to Esenin. One tires of the easy trick of the metre, the plangent though often casual rhymes, the almost invariable quatrains, the couplets brought back again with a crashingly 'moving' impact, the battery of the effects Russian poets still find it so hard to resist for long—flying cranes, nightingales, snowstorms, troikas, sleigh-bells etc. Often it is hard for a Western reader to believe that this verse was being written at the same time that Pound was writing the *Cantos,* Eliot *The Waste Land,* Lawrence *Birds, Beasts and Flowers,* Apollinaire his *Calligrammes.* The metres are often metronomically tied to their text-book models, and everything is sacrificed to the emotive impact of the rhyme. . . . So Esenin was something of a dinosaur—a peasant, with the small-town hick's ambitions to be a new Pushkin. Thus, he restored, or rather tried to maintain in currency, the emotion-soaked balladry Pushkin had purveyed so incomparably. (pp. 16-17)

The poems Esenin wrote in the 'twenties fall into two main groups: first, heightened, tautened versions of the lyric quatrain; second, almost-free-verse conversational narratives, anecdotal, confessional and even ideological. It is presumably this latter group of which [Boris] Pasternak so stringently disapproved, and presumably it is the sometimes orthodox Communist content as well as the apparently slovenly versification which made Pasternak shudder. Yet although there are certainly signs of fatigue hereabouts, signs that Esenin could no longer sustain the weight of the formal lyric as easily as he had earlier, the success of longer poems such as 'Soviet Russia' . . . and 'My Path' . . . , and the various verse letters he wrote to his relations, proves that Esenin knew what he was up to. The lyric quatrain is useful for expressing crystallized situations and symbols; for narrative, it is practically useless. Thus when, later in life, he cast his mind back over his career, he used a freer, more dilatory rhythm, only loosely bound together with rhyme, which allowed him to reflect, to discuss, to describe and to narrate without awkward transition. It is an impressive achievement, and the finest of these poems—'Soviet Russia' and 'The Black Man' . . . are among his best work. The other group, the quatrain lyrics, have a different purpose. It is in these poems—['The Rowan Tree Fire', 'I will not weep', 'This present sadness is not eased', 'Now little by little we depart'] . . .—that Esenin distils himself most clearly: these poems achieve at times a classical purity of movement that fully justifies the Pushkin-like manner. They are an important part of the small body of great twentieth century poetry: the classical structure and tone are not superadded, but derive from a full assimilation of refractory experience never rejected, even when most regretted. Esenin's repeated assurance that he regrets nothing must, I think, be accepted in all good faith. It is neither Stoic attitudinizing nor stubbornness; on the contrary, no one ever acknowledged his mistakes more wisely ('Little of what has passed is dear, And many the errors made'). It is rather a refusal to disown himself or to disclaim responsibility for what he has done and become. (pp. 17-18)

Esenin's is a lonely poetry. It rarely admits others into its world. . . . [The] essential situation in Esenin, as in Hart Crane, is one of solitude, the solitude of the poet in the 'golden grove' in what is perhaps his greatest lyric ('The Rowan Tree Fire'); or the much more horrible solitude of the alcoholic, in 'The Black Man', and the various poems written in sanitoriums and jails. Esenin paid the usual price for hoarding a great gift and making it the price of his acceptance by other men—sterile isolation and despair. As he hardened in his despair, as the release of alcohol became more and more enclosing, so his isolation became the more unbreachable. But perhaps only a very isolated man is forced into a genuinely political relation with other men: it was precisely Esenin's refusal to stop analysing and dramatizing his own 'greatness' that opened up for him the nature of society itself. For this sort of reason, I think 'Soviet Russia' has claims to being his greatest single poem. It preserves the classical sweep of his finest lyrics . . . along with the reflective, flexible discursiveness that allows him to register the complex facts of the social revolution he is witnessing. The poem is *about* a Sovietized Russia, but it *is* Esenin's rather pitiable situation within it. . . . Esenin's political views, like his alcoholism and his kinship with the whores and thugs of the Moscow taverns, only emphasized his aloneness. This aloneness seems more convincing than the good-hearted but ultimately abject attempts, described in 'Stanzas' . . . and 'Return to my Homeland', . . . to get to grips with Marx and Engels. There is something sad about a great spirit grubbing among the worms.

No poem dramatizes this aloneness more devastatingly than 'The Black Man', which takes the form of an address to a character who turns out in the end to be Esenin himself, reflected in the mirror. Esenin had been horribly lucid about his condition in many of his earlier lyrics: he had seen himself as a 'yellow skeleton', and a heap of 'damp and yellow dust'. In a truly terrifying image, he saw himself as being devoured by his own eyes, 'as a maggot chews a blue petal'. As always, Esenin finds his imagery in the commonplace objects of his own life and memory. In 'The Black Man', he extends the image of the plain of snow, which many Russian writers—one thinks of Pushkin and Gogol—had used with powerful symbolic effect, forcing it to yield a new dimension of meaning: the whole plain, he observes, is 'covered In a soft quick-lime'. Thus, a bare month before he wrote his last words in his own blood, he saw deep into his own dissolution. (pp. 18-19)

Geoffrey Thurley, in his introduction to Confessions of a Hooligan: Fifty Poems by Sergei Esenin, *translated from the Russian by Geoffrey Thurley (copyright © Geoffrey Thurley 1973; reprinted by permission), Carcanet Press, 1973, pp. 7-21.*

CONSTANTIN V. PONOMAREFF   (essay date 1978)

[The period of Esenin's early poetry], though it did produce a number of personally representative poems, was on the whole imitative. In form and content his work at this time was largely inspired by the oral and literary modes of Russian folk poetry. (p. 20)

Esenin's poetry is rich in impressions of nature and village life. The proximity of man as poet to nature, and especially his mysterious association with her—that anthropomorphic relation between the natural and human worlds—ultimately casts its own poetic spell over everything.

But in the very beginning, there are—apart from a rustic's awareness of nature—no clearly discernible lines of perceptive development. Spring's shared exuberance yields to stylized love songs, that may then give way to a budding cosmic sense of wonder, as in "The Stars." Poems such as ["Vospominanie" ("Remembrance")] and "Pesnia starika razboinika" ("The Song of the Old Robber")] . . . are undoubtedly poetic reminiscences of Aleksey Koltsov's poetry. Such sentimentalized self-reflections as those found in "Moia zhizn'" ("My Life" . . .) on the other hand, recall both Ivan Nikitin's and Spiridon Drozhzhin's peasant poems. That this latter poem provides one of the few examples of anapest meter only underlines its imitative quality. The elegiac note in most of these poems, so typical of the Russian folk song, is amplified by such motifs as the passage of time, the fading of love and youth, and the onslaught of old age and death.

But Esenin was already beginning to be aware of his peasant roots. In a poem called "Poet" ("The Poet . . .), he spoke of himself as the bard of the Russian soil. . . . Esenin's preoccupation with the well-being of the Russian peasant again emerged in the image of peasant victory over outside enemies as developed in his poem "Egoriy" (the popular form of St. Gregory . . .). . . . [Vital] to Esenin's poetic perspective were the protective, regenerative aspects of this agrarian nature saint; his popular image as a symbol of fertility, earth power, and the coming of spring; and his function as the patron of livestock and the animal world. The figure of Egoriy reemphasized Esenin's peasant orientation and pointed directly to his vision of a Russian terrestrial peasant paradise as developed in "Inoniia." (pp. 22-3)

[In *Mourning for the Dead*] Esenin sought to express the essence of his early poetic vision.

The early poems of this collection were stylized love songs, and read like a "Russian" counterpart to his "Persian" poems of 1924. Still, the important emotional events of man's life in these poems occur in nature. But nature's linkage to human events was increasingly touched and colored by a religious, otherworldly poetic perception. Nature images were suddenly transformed into religious symbols: russet haystacks in the field under the moon's light turned into churches, and the wood grouse became a bell calling the faithful to an all-night service. . . . It was, however,

characteristic of Esenin that it was not man as human intermediary, but rather nature which here sanctified human existence. (p. 26)

Esenin's early poetry shows him in search of a poetic self. His peasant orientation is reflected not only formally, in his utilization of folk poetics and imagery, but also thematically, in his poetically sustained vision of a future Russian peasant utopia on earth. The imagery of his early poetry is sufficiently consistent to illustrate the gradual development of his dream. . . . (pp. 32-3)

The clearly discernible vision of a future peasant paradise was welded together out of four basic motifs: God, nature, peasant life, and utopia. If Esenin's vision was ultimately this-worldly, its spiritual motivation originated in God and, passing through nature, centered his particular blend of poetic intuition. In this sense, Esenin was, apart from his peasant Imagist poetics, essentially a Romantic. In this sense too, Esenin was poetically quite correct in his autobiographical statement of October 1925, when he observed that it was impossible for him to reject his prerevolutionary *religious* motivation without doing violence to the organic development of his poetic imagination. . . . (p. 33)

For Esenin, art was no branch of culture, no summation of knowledge and craftsmanship with an expanded autobiography. The theme of his poetry was himself—lost, doomed, perishing as a poet—a theme that was as difficult for him to bear as was wearing felt boots in summer. He wrote no poems, but only developed his theme in the form of poems. His inability to distinguish between skill and theme was possibly the blunder of a peasant who had always lived with an eye to festive occasions only. (p. 124)

Esenin's strength did not lie in novelty, his leftist orientation, or his independence. Even less convincing was his kinship with the Imaginists, who were neither novel nor independent. His strength lay instead in the emotional tone of his lyrical poetry. His basic poetic inspiration derived from a naive, primordial . . . , unusual, and vital . . . poetic emotion. His entire poetic creativity amounted to a continuous attempt to embellish naked emotion. Thus his church slavonicisms, his traditional peasant Christ, and his abusive language taken from the Imaginists promoted only this single aim of ornamentation. An art based on primordial emotion was always closely connected with individuality, and Esenin's personality came through, in "Pugachev," for instance, allowing the reader to glimpse the man in Esenin. But his poetic personality had become so enlarged as to border on the illusive. The reader treated his poems like documents or letters received through the mail. This was, of course, good, and made for poetic power; but it was also dangerous, because poetic personality might come to live a life of its own, quite apart from the poetry, and the poetry then would turn out to be poor.

Esenin's literary personality, on the other hand, left much to be desired. Profoundly shaped by literary influences, it almost seemed borrowed, an unusually schematized [Alexander] Blok made worse, or a parody of Pushkin. (pp. 124-25)

In his last poems—(after *Tavern Moscow*)—the hooligan did penance . . . and repented of his scandals, thereby weakening the dramatic tension of his poetry. It developed that, once the poetic personality no longer acted as a screen for his poetry, the latter was exposed in all its "literariness.'' The reader suddenly realized that the literariness of Esenin's poems had all along been concealed by his primitive emotionalism, and the almost tiresome, intrusive spontaneity of his poetic personality. Esenin now at times resembled an ''anthology'' of poets from Pushkin to the present. . . .

Esenin's poetry had become a disappointing utilization of exhausted traditions, a collection of commonplaces that could in no way take the place of poems. Banality became so epic and so thorough as to surpass even previous banalities. Poetic intonation became a lie, and the poem, addressed to no one, expressed only a general poetic intonation, which had become inert. Poetry of this caliber pointed toward the flatness of the simplified poetry written at the end of the nineteenth century. (p. 125)

[Esenin's] poetic vision was generated by two innate and opposing forces: one dynamic and visionary, constructive and liberating, essentially socially oriented, idealistically directed toward the future and therefore personally centrifugal; the other—which in the end proved to be the more powerful of the two—static and oppressive, a self-destructive and centripetal force, tending toward final dissolution.

These two dialectical streams of poetic consciousness in Esenin, genetically and psychically determined, were undoubtedly shaped by his experiences in the countryside and by his folk and Symbolist sources of inspiration. In fact it was probably Symbolism—with its emphasis upon poetry as a free spiritual force bringing transcendental knowledge, and the poet as a unique carrier of such poetic impulse—that enabled Esenin to shape his poetic imagery in terms of a utopian and equally Romantic vision of a Russian peasant paradise on earth. It was, however, these streams of consciousness taken together that engendered the poetic tension of Esenin's lyrical energy. He said as much metaphorically when, in a poem of 1925, he asked his sweetheart to light a fire in the stove and make the bed for the night: without her, the snowstorm within him would rage on without stopping. . . . Without her, in other words, without his beloved, without the warming energy of a utopian ''life'' vision, he would succumb to the cold force of ''death'' within. (p. 162)

Esenin's poetic vision as the integral of his life and art, the unity between the lyrical motifs of his work and the important personal ''poetic'' events of his life, bring to mind the scattered remarks—intuitively correct, but too general to be of any critical use—to the effect that Esenin's life and poetry were indeed inextricably linked. Esenin's attempt to come to terms with Marxism . . . was but an act of expediency, a desperate try to sustain himself poetically in an unfavorable environment. (p. 166)

Esenin, that ''Don Quixote of the village,'' as [Vadim] Shershenevich called him, whose Muse encountered a stirring emotional response among the reading public of his day and later, could not simultaneously fend off his inner spiritual and an outer historical upheaval, was unable to survive the two-pronged offensive mounted against him by the inner events of his poetic being and the sociopolitical realities of the outside world. But the bitter experience he encountered on the road between his vision and its interpretation was incorporated in a poetry that has found its readers across all political barriers. In this, Esenin belongs to that distinguished fellowship of poets whose work testifies to the indomitable creative spirit of man. (pp. 166-67)

Constantin V. Ponomareff, in his Sergey Esenin *(copyright © 1978 by Twayne Publishers, Inc.; reprinted with the permission of Twayne Publishers, a Division of G. K. Hall & Co., Boston), Twayne, 1978, 194 p.*

GORDON McVAY (essay date 1980)

Esenin welcomed both the February and the October Revolutions of 1917 enthusiastically, even if he did not perceive their real purposes and implications. Together with other peasant poets, he misguidedly viewed these Revolutions as heralding the approach of a peasant paradise. At this time Esenin was linked with the left-wing Socialist Revolutionaries and a group of writers known as the ''Scythians.'' He wrote a number of long poems picturing the Revolutions of 1917 in Biblical imagery, as a ''new Nazareth,'' Advent, Transfiguration, or Crucifixion. Not surprisingly, Marxist and proletarian critics soon condemned him for ''mysticism'' and otherworldliness, and his attempt to be a peasant ''prophet'' quickly foundered. (pp. 14-15)

From early 1919, for the next three years and more, his name was to be closely linked with that of a group of poets who called themselves the ''Imaginists.'' Although Soviet critics today are almost unanimous in condemning Imaginism as ''bourgeois'' and harmful to Esenin's talent, his alliance with the group was by no means fortuitous. Throughout 1918 he had sought new poetic allies, and his own poetic voice, and the path to national fame. He found, or so it seemed to him for a long time, all three in ''Imaginism,'' with its emphasis on the primacy of the ''image'' in poetry. (pp. 15-16)

During his Imaginist years the poet plunged into the whirlpool of urban bohemia and neglected the village. He might write nostalgically about his peasant childhood, and lament the decline of rural Russia, but he himself was gripped by the spell of city life.

Some people claim that this period was the ''healthiest'' in his life, for he worked hard and his fame continued to grow. . . . His life, although few can have suspected it then, was increasingly to be a fight against boredom and a deepening melancholy. (pp. 16-17)

The tone of his verse became funereal. In a poem of 1920, ''I'm the Last Poet of the Village'' . . . , he lamented the imminent encroachment of the ''iron guest'' (the railway, symbol of the town and the Revolution) upon his beloved countryside. His aesthetic sympathies undoubtedly lay in the pre-industrial past—and yet he seems to have espoused the cause of old Russia, at least in part, as a means of expressing his own more private sorrow. Moreover, the mourning of lost illusions was in tune with one aspect of his personality—a tendency towards nostalgia, bordering at times on sentimentality and even self-pity. . . . (pp. 17-18)

He wrote few poems in 1919-20, but his new themes, of the tender hooligan and the doomed village, brought him a wider fame than ever before. . . .

In November 1920 his poem ''The Hooligan'' . . . was published, in which he called himself a hooligan, robber and boor, but also the only bard of rural Russia. In that same month he wrote ''The Hooligan's Confession'' . . . , where the lyrical hero was shown as desperate and kind; full of flagrant vulgarity, and yet also ''gently sick with childhood recollections.'' The poem was bound to provoke scandal and indignation—and also compassion and admiration. For the first time in his verse Esenin described himself as the ''very best poet in Russia.'' (p. 18)

[Esenin] had to be the picture-book peasant, the prophet, the dandy, and then the last village poet, the best poet, and the husband of famous women. This was not merely child-ishness and ambition: it was an ingrained aversion to any-thing prosaic. It was in a way a despairing and doomed struggle against death, which repelled and attracted him always. (p. 19)

Gordon McVay, in his Isadora & Esenin *(copy-right © 1980 by Ardis), Ardis, 1980, 335 p.* *

ADDITIONAL BIBLIOGRAPHY

de Graaf, Frances. *Sergej Esenin: A Biographical Sketch.* The Hague: Mouton & Co., 1966, 178 p.
    Biography that includes a more descriptive than critical exami-nation of Esenin's poetry and prose.

Fisher, Lynn V. ''Esenin's Literary Reworking of the Riddle.'' *Slavic and East European Journal* 18, No. 1 (Spring 1974): 20-30.
    Scholarly study of Esenin's use of folklore elements in his po-etry.

Koshechkin, Sergei. ''Sergei Esenin (1895-1925).'' *Soviet Litera-ture* 9, No. 330 (1975): 139-47.
    General appreciation of Esenin's poetry, commenting on the poet's affection for Russia.

Mayakovsky, Vladimir. ''Sergei Esenin.'' In his *Poems,* translated by Dorian Rottenberg, pp. 64-8. Moscow: Progress Publishers, 1972.
    A poem written in reaction to Esenin's suicide and the critique of post revolutionary Russia that this act implied.

McVay, Gordon. ''Yesenin's Posthumous Fame, and the Fate of His Friends.'' *The Modern Language Review* 67, No. 3 (July 1972): 590-602.
    Examines Esenin's critical reputation in the Soviet Union, from the condemnation of ''Yeseninitis'' just after his death to his reinstatement as an important Russian poet.

McVay, Gordon. *Esenin: A Life.* Ann Arbor: Ardis, 1976, 352 p.
    Definitive biography in English.

Slonim, Marc. ''Sergey Essenin: The Confused Peasant.'' In his *Soviet Russian Literature: Writers and Problems: 1917-1967,* pp. 11-18. New York: Oxford University Press, 1967.
    Discusses Esenin's literary career, his involvement with the imagist movement, and his life under the Soviet regime.

Struve, Gleb. ''The Poets: Mayakovsky and Esenin.'' In his *Soviet Russian Literature,* pp. 165-69. London: George Routledge & Sons, 1935.*
    Brief sketch of Esenin's life and work.

Lewis Grassic Gibbon

1901-1935

(Pseudonym of James Leslie Mitchell) Anglo-Scottish novelist, short story writer, science fiction writer, essayist, biographer, and journalist.

Gibbon was a major figure in the Scottish Literary Renaissance and the foremost literary proponent of the Diffusionist theory of civilization. In the trilogy *A Scots Quair*, a chronicle of the vanishing agricultural way of life in northeast Scotland, Gibbon successfully reproduced the cadence and vocabulary of the Scots idiom, giving a new impetus to the development of a vernacular prose literature in Scotland. Gibbon's "English" novels and short stories, published under his own name, James Leslie Mitchell, have provoked little critical comment and it is agreed that his best work is found in his "Scottish" fiction—notably *Sunset Song, Cloud Howe,* and *Grey Granite,* later published in one volume as *A Scots Quair*. In his Scottish fiction Gibbon rejects the sentimentalism of the Kailyard school, represented by J. M. Barrie, and the brutal realism of George Douglas Brown, to recreate a mode of expression closer to the style the Scottish novelist John Galt used a hundred years earlier.

The son of a crofter, Gibbon grew up in Kincardineshire in northeast Scotland, the Mearns country depicted in his Scottish stories. While still in his early teens, he decided to be a writer, and after an unhappy year, academically and personally, at the Mackie Academy at Stonehaven, he abandoned formal education to pursue a career in journalism. After working on a paper in Aberdeen, he accepted a post with the *Scottish Farmer* and moved to Glasgow. Appalled by the grinding poverty of the city's slums, Gibbon became active in the dissemination of Communist propaganda. He lost his job in a dispute over his expense account and, subsequently, spent the next eight years of his life in various branches of the armed services.

While stationed in the Middle East, Gibbon renewed a boyhood interest in anthropology and archaeology. He studied George Elliot Smith's Diffusionist theory, which purports that civilization was an isolated accident "diffusing" from the banks of the Nile, and that primitive men and women lived in a kind of Rousseauesque Golden Age until the onslaught of civilization corrupted their essential goodness. Gibbon embraced this theory, which seemed to explain scientifically the genesis of social inequality, poverty, and war, not only in his scholarly archaeological essays, but in his fiction as well. In both his Scottish and English fiction, Gibbon is most concerned with portraying his characters' efforts to achieve a primitive state of peace and innocence in a modern, industrial society.

H. G. Wells, to whom Gibbon sent his first short stories for criticism, encouraged the young writer's efforts, and introduced him to agents and editors. Thereafter, Gibbon produced a steady stream of romantic adventure stories, science fiction, and archaeological and historical essays, but with limited success. Not until publication of *Sunset Song* did Gibbon achieve a work of originality and lasting worth. In this novel, and in the sequels *Cloud Howe* and *Grey Granite,* Gibbon traces, in rhythmic Scots prose, the life of Chris Guthrie and

her family as they move from farm life to city life. To many critics *A Scots Quair* is a multifaceted work in which the upheavals in one woman's life symbolize the flux of a nation, and fundamentally of civilization itself. The return to the Scots dialect of his youth unleashed in Gibbon a power and beauty of expression absent from his English fiction, but his early death prevented the full flowering of his talent.

Critics have noted that Gibbon's adherence to the Diffusionist dogma sometimes obtrudes in his fiction. He is also criticized for writing too hastily and carelessly, for dwelling on gory descriptions of torture and maiming, and for the generally uneven quality of his work. Yet, in his time, Gibbon was hailed as the great hope of Scottish literature, and his masterpiece, *A Scots Quair,* was called by James Barke "the greatest Scots novel in Scottish literature."

PRINCIPAL WORKS

Hanno; or, The Future of Exploration [as James Leslie
    Mitchell] (essays) 1928
Cairo Dawns [as James Leslie Mitchell] (short stories)
    1931; published in England as *The Calends of Cairo,*
    1931

Sunset Song [as Lewis Grassic Gibbon] (novel) 1932
Cloud Howe [as Lewis Grassic Gibbon] (novel) 1933
Spartacus [as James Leslie Mitchell] (novel) 1933
Grey Granite [as Lewis Grassic Gibbon] (novel) 1934
Nine against the Unknown [as James Leslie Mitchell and
    Lewis Grassic Gibbon] (essays) 1934
Scottish Scene [as Lewis Grassic Gibbon with Hugh
    MacDiarmid] (essays and short stories) 1934

*These novels were collected as *A Scots Quair* in 1946.

L.A.G. STRONG (essay date 1932)

Sunset Song is the biggest book I know which has come out
of modern Scotland. Mr. Lewis Grassic Gibbon . . . has the
real thing. His story has its faults, and its occasional absurdities. . . . Some of its writing is magnificent; some of it
is bad. . . . [But he] is a first-class writer; of that there can
be no doubt. *Sunset Song* makes no concession to the
reader, avoids the usual devices of punctuation, and goes
its own way with the power of a river in spate. It is the
work of real strength, able, as all real strength is, to express
the extremes of tenderness and delicacy. The love story of
Ewan and Chris, with the grim background of which its
own apparent defeat is a symbol, winds through a landscape which is as deeply realized, materially and spiritually,
as the background in any modern book which is known to
me. It is absurd, on the strength of one reading, to say how
good a book Mr. Gibbon has written. I can only say that I
think he has written something permanent, which his countrymen will treasure proudly as a testimony to the things
they love. I had better add that the book is exceedingly outspoken, and that those whose idea of a good Scottish book
is of the idyllic, kailyard type may get a few shocks if they
read it.

> *L.A.G. Strong, "Fiction: 'Sunset Song'," in* The
> Spectator *(© 1932 by The Spectator; reprinted by
> permission of* The Spectator*), Vol. 149, No. 5439,
> September 24, 1932, p. 380.*

BASIL DAVENPORT (essay date 1933)

["*Sunset Song*"] is intended to be a picture of the Scottish
crofters, the independent peasantry who came to an end
with the war. The author is not concerned with either the
sociological or the dramatic possibilities of the actual downfall of the class; his principal couple are not concerned in it
at all, since they have both ceased to be crofters before the
end of the book; he wishes solely to portray a little society
as it was in 1911 and thereafter, and as it is no more.

In his portrayal he is evidently torn between the desire to
leave an authentic, realistic testimony to the future, and the
desire to give an idealized picture, an impression of how
this little state looked to a lover of it. At least, this seems to
be the only way to account for the bewildering changes of
tone, and the lack of organization in the narrative. The
second and third quarters of the book are taken up with a
really lovely, but singularly static idyll; Eean and Chris,
two young people, fall in love with each other, and encounter no difficulties, and walk together in beautiful landscapes, and are married; that is all. But the first quarter of
the book makes a very different impression; it is a realistic

depiction, almost against the author's will, it seems, of a
peasantry who are indeed independent, and rather humorous, but who are represented as brutal in every way; they
are cruel, they delight in malicious gossip, they are so gross
that almost it seems as if every character in the book, from
the minister down, was found lying coupled in the hay.
Again at the end, the love-story suddenly and quite unexpectedly turns to tragedy; and the mood is not left unbroken even here, for there is an unconvincing patched-up
happy ending for the heroine. In consequence of this constant change of key, the narrative is extremely jerky; it will
stand still at an incident for thirty pages, and then advance
to the next one with a violent jolt.

The parts of the book are far better than the whole. The
gnarled villagers are vital, convincing, and strongly individual; one likes to hear them talk, to gather up their good,
stout prejudices and their vivid country expressions; and if
the author has not quite the supreme gift of communicating
to us the affection with which he evidently regards them in
spite of their faults, still he has the great talent of introducing us to an actual and human society. The language of
the book is on the whole excellent; it is full of Scottish
words and expressions, introduced so skilfully that they
usually explain themselves, and warm the heart as such
earthy talk always does. Even here, however, the author
has a curious trick of printing the speeches of his characters
in italics instead of using quotation marks, which seems to
be an affectation, and is at first distracting.

There are many admirable pages in the book, and some delightful ones; but it is impossible not to feel that here was
the material for two or three books, each of which would
have been better than the present volume.

> *Basil Davenport, "A Scottish Pastoral," in* The
> Saturday Review of Literature *(copyright © 1933
> by Saturday Review; all rights reserved; reprinted
> by permission), Vol. IX, No. 35, March 18, 1933,
> p. 489.*

WILLIAM PLOMER (essay date 1933)

Cloud Howe, in spite of the lack of euphony in its title, is a
powerful and beautiful novel. . . . *Sunset Song* dealt with
the Scotch countryside; *Cloud Howe* describes life in a
Scotch village, and the scene of the third part, *Grey Granite*, which is to appear next year, will be set in a Scotch
town. The present volume tells of post-War years in the
Lowland village of Segget, to which Chris Guthrie comes as
the wife of the new minister Colquohoun. . . . The life Mr.
Gibbon has set himself to describe may be largely characterized by meanness, squalor, and even horror, but his descriptions of it are either moving or entertaining. He does
not condemn the people he is writing about, because they
are his own people, whom he knows and loves. He sees
them as victims. . . . Mr. Gibbon sees the local in terms of
the universal; he writes in a remarkable style of his own,
which exactly suits his theme; he has a robust and racy
sense of comedy, with the healthy coarseness inseparable
from true vigour; and he is full of poetry and imagination. It
would not be in the least surprising if he came to be regarded as the chief living novelist of his country.

> *William Plomer, "Fiction: 'Cloud Howe'," in* The
> Spectator *(© 1933 by The Spectator; reprinted by
> permission of* The Spectator*), Vol. 151, No. 5484,
> August 4, 1933, p. 168.*

BASIL DAVENPORT (essay date 1934)

"Cloud Howe" takes us into one of the little manufacturing towns which are emptying the countryside, and pictures for us the turbulence in which the war has left it. In the cloth-making town of Segget, the young people have left the Kirk and grown cynical about the King; many of the spinners are on the dole and discontented, and, still worse, many of them are on the dole and content; there are strikes and labour troubles; and yet there is left some of the worst of the feudal spirit, servility surviving loyalty.... Into this harsh town come Chris, the girl whose first love was killed in the war, her son by him, Ewan, and her second husband, Robert Colquhoun, the minister who is trying to show the people the vision of brotherhood which has possessed him by flashes ever since he was shell-shocked.

To tell their story, and that of the town, Mr. Gibbon uses a Scots idiom, harsh and warm and good as tweed. It goes much deeper than the use of dialect words; there is no glossary, and none needed; but the whole style is subdued to an un-English mode of thought. And the whole story, like a gossiping carline, never introduces a new character without a few or a many words about him....

In "Sunset Song" one felt that Mr. Gibbon, from a natural sentiment toward a passing society, was inclined to claim more admiration for the crofters than by his own showing they deserved; but in "Cloud Howe" he manages the difficult feat of presenting his town with all its faults and filling us with a warm kindness for it; so that we sympathize both with the magnitude of Colquhoun's task in regenerating his people, and with the ardor of his desire to save them. In the two volumes already written, of countryside and small town, this trilogy is an enduring memorial of a land.

On the other hand, it must be said that if the method employed is excellent for sketching in the whole background, it is much less excellent for depicting the principal characters, Chris and Colquhoun, who are always in danger of being lost in the crowd of supernumeraries. Their situation, that of two romantics united in a marriage which has affection, integrity, everything except romance, is one which would repay a searching analysis; but instead of this it really seems as if they were made to go round and round in a mechanical cycle of exaltation, quarrel, tenderness, and then, after a good deal about the minor figures, exaltation again. Nevertheless, this is a fine book, and there is a promise that the next volume will be concerned with Chris's son Ewan, who is growing into so sturdy and straightforward a boy that the author's chosen manner will not be so great a disadvantage in portraying him. In any case, one anticipates with great interest the fulfilment of this work.

Basil Davenport, "A Novel of the Scottish Lowlands," in The Saturday Review of Literature *(copyright © 1934 by* Saturday Review; *all rights reserved; reprinted by permission), Vol. X, No. 31, February 17, 1934, p. 489.*

PETER MONRO JACK (essay date 1935)

"Grey Granite" completes [Lewis Grassic Gibbon's] trilogy on Scottish life in the country, town and city, begun in "Sunset Song" and continued in "Cloud Howe"; together making up "Scots Quhair" (or book).... In general it is the movement in time and space from agricultural to industrial conditions, and though the former are not idealized nor the latter unfairly drawn, it is seen as a movement from a quiet self-contained culture to a dissentious and precarious civilization, heading for civil war. (p. 6)

The scheme of the book is Ewan's, divided in four parts: the background; the wedge of industrial life; its full emotional impact; and the granite hardening, the front of steel that must be put on unless one is to become utterly soft and useless. But around and below this is a warm and living picture of city life in boarding house or tenement, humorous, realistic, charged with pity or indignation, or merely contemptuous....

It is Gibbon's most swiftly moving book and his most adventurous in ideas—and most deeply dyed in his love of Scotland and passion for humanity, neither of which prevents a clear-eyed anger and scorn at injustice. Ewan is Scotland's Pelle, done in small and done, I think, more rightly. (p. 20)

Peter Monro Jack, "Lewis Grassic Gibbon's Story of Scotland," in The New York Times Book Review *(© 1935 by The New York Times Company; reprinted by permission), April 7, 1935, pp. 6, 20.*

JOHN LEHMANN (essay date 1940)

[Lewis Grassic Gibbon] might have made a profound mark on our literature if he had not died so early in his career.... His chief title to fame rests on his trilogy of novels, *A Scots Quair*, written in a vernacular Scots which is nevertheless sufficiently diluted not to present too appalling an obstacle to the mere Englishman; his language is simple, full of colour, and keeps very close to everyday talk without mannerisms. He can create warmly living characters, he can make a crowd scene as vivid as in a film, and his narrative has underlying currents of lyrical feeling and irony which give it a strong individual flavour. It is a fault, perhaps, that the mood is rather continuously emotional—it has a curiously feminine quality which suggests the influence of Katherine Mansfield—but his sincerity and his imaginative power cannot fail to carry you along. He is one of the very few among his contemporaries not strictly *of* the working-classes who have managed to write convincingly *about* the working-classes. His setting is a Scottish manufacturing town, and he succeeds in describing the life of the working population from almost every angle; but his aim is not merely to give a panorama of that life, it is above all to show the revolutionary ferment developing. (pp. 130-31)

Gibbon can clothe the skeleton of his ideas—unlike some other writers of the 'thirties who have been more ardent for their political faith than gifted for creative art—with the flesh and blood of his imagination. And he can also present every side of a question; he has no sentimental illusions about "the workers" and refuses to picture them as oppressed heroes any more than their leaders as infallible prophets; he scoffs at the idea that the apocalypse of the Revolution is round the corner. His breadth of vision would, I think, have increased if he had lived to write more novels, for he had an extremely independent and lively mind. (p. 131)

John Lehmann, "Allies and Independents," in his New Writing in Europe *(reprinted by permission of the author), Penguin Books Ltd, 1940, pp. 130-40.*

IVOR BROWN   (essay date 1946)

[James Leslie Mitchell] was the voice of Scotland's past, almost of all antiquity in his great sense of pre-history and his addiction to primitive (the very opposite of barbaric and savage) men and things. He was a voice of humanity in his anger and compassion; his wrath flamed against oppression. . . .

Even more than any other of his qualities did I admire his superb mastery of words and rhythms, his spate of images, his prose of the earth which continually dissolved into air to become the poetry of sky and cloud. Has anybody ever written better about the mist of Scotland and the 'far-off mountains turnéd into clouds,' the steam of the land in summer, the sharp savours of the root-fields after rain, the aroma of fir-trees on the hillside, and the glitter of dew as it melts into the morning's canopy of jewelled Grampian air? (p. 5)

[*A Scots Quair* is] the story of a small farm among the peesie-haunted 'parks' of the Mearns, a story linked with the early age of Scotland, a story returning continually to the standing stones of the ancient colonists who came, metal-hunting and exploring, from the Mediterranean to these far hills.

Two points of explanation must be made. Leslie Mitchell's philosophy of life was a belief in original innocence. The early, unpropertied men, who are usually regarded as warring savages, he believed to have been care-free and peaceable. (All the evidence about the real primitives, simple food gathering folk, is on his side.) Then came, with the discovery of agriculture in Egypt and the misuse of the civilisation which settled farming created, the flow of follies and corruptions, the worship of tyrannous gods and tyrannous kings, the cults of property and power, war, and all the miseries of modern man. To him the savage and the barbarian were the primitive in decay and his creed was a passionate assertion of the initial, the pre-savage, the primitive goodness which man must somehow recover.

This is no place to expound his whole doctrine of the archaic civilisation, its diffusion, and its decay. . . . I mention it here because the reader of this trilogy may be puzzled by the constant return to the standing-stones above Blawearie, the standing-stones which in his view linked Scottish earth to all enduring and universal things, symbol of the early men who were happy until they missed the way.

A second point needing explanation is the idiom and the rhythm of these books. Leslie Mitchell was born a peasant and his mind was divided about the peasant and his lot. At one moment he would hate the drudgery of the land; at another he was conscious of a powerful pride that the land was so closely and intimately his. . . . These divisions of opinion, love of the earthy savours and the tang of the wind, resentment of the servitude under the 'on-ding' of the rain, hatred of the sweat and the shivering and the poverty, are constantly occurring in *Sunset Song* and *Cloud Howe.* There the Scottish peasants appear in all their roughness and coarseness as well as in their humours and their honour, just as the land itself appears in all its grudging and grinding dominion over labouring flesh as well as in the shimmering beauty of the Mearns upon a summer's day and in the foison of earth well dunged and well cropped by Scottish skill and endurance.

To utter this voice of the land and the landsman Mitchell chose a mannered, lilting style. When I first met this, it struck me as an affectation. But suddenly I realised what he was attempting and indeed achieving, which was 'to mould the English language into the rhythms and cadences of Scots spoken speech.' He used dialogue scantily, but in a sense he used it all the time. For his descriptions of men and places were the voice of one talking, say, the voice of Scotland itself. The vocabulary was a little antique, a trifle old-fashioned when it was first made. (So, they say, was that of Robert Burns.) That boy meets girl so often as 'childe meets quean' may irritate some. I am not here to defend all the means employed to achieve a certain result. That result was to make Scottish earth vocal, and I would claim that in the lilting, anapaestic prose of Lewis Grassic Gibbon you can indeed feel the swing of the horses at the plough, the rhythm of the wind upon the woods, the surge of the tumbling land where the mountains run down to the sea, and 'the speak' of the men who toiled and loved and quarrelled, the men of the little farms upon whose passing there is so noble a valediction at the close of *Sunset Song.* (pp. 7-8)

Ivor Brown, "Lewis Grassic Gibbon," in A Scots Quair *by Lewis Grassic Gibbon, Jarrolds Publishers London Limited, 1946 (and reprinted by Schocken Books, 1977), pp. 5-9.*

HUGH MacDIARMID   (essay date 1947)

[It] is still far from sufficiently understood in Scotland that in Lewis Grassic Gibbon we lost a great writer, the greatest novelist we have had since George Douglas Brown, author of the *House with the Green Shutters,* and one who seemed likely to prove able to resume the entire independent Scottish tradition, literary and political, at its farthest remove from English literature and politics, and bring it fully abreast of our own times. . . . (p. 309)

Gibbon had to go back to Scots, and did his best work in it (his English work is extremely "thin" in comparison), . . . just as every Scottish writer, either in prose or in poetry, who has used both media, has done. (pp. 313-14)

[Despite] his Socialism he is mainly concerned—at any rate in *Sunset Song,* the first, and by far the finest, of the trilogy —with rural Scotland. When he comes to deal with city life he doesn't know it half so well despite all his surface sophistication. . . . [We] have had no writer yet big enough to carry over the independent Scots literary tradition from the bucolic and nonindustrialized milieu in which it flourished into the contemporary scene. . . . It is a very difficult undertaking and calls for a major artist. Only Gibbon has seemed to have been potentially big enough to essay it. And I have little doubt but that he would have faced up to it and achieved it if he had been spared. He was certainly tending in that direction and he had already achieved enough, alike in his novels and in his short stories, to give ample earnest of the likelihood of his success. Certainly all the other contemporary Scottish novelists are childish in their content in comparison with Gibbon, lack the autochthonous authenticity which was one of his great qualities, utterly fail to share his ability to use the demotic speech, and, above all, have none of that "breadth of vision"—that ability to "present every side of a question"—which was one of Gibbon's outstanding characteristics. He completely out-tops, alike in the veracity and the magnitude of his work, other recent Scottish writers who have been concerned with rural material such as he uses in *Sunset Song* . . . : he is on a different plane altogether, of course, from that of the Kailyard novelists, and no less that of the regional novelists. . . . [Gibbon] had a magnificent narrative power and a mastery of all the resources of expression in prose. His use of Scots did not clog his story or his prose style—on the contrary, it gave passage and power to both in a way English could never have done. (pp. 314-16)

His best book, apart from his Scottish novels, is probably *Spartacus,* a splendid reconstruction in fictional form of the slave revolt in Ancient Rome, but vitiated to a large extent, too, by [sadism]. . . . He describes tortures and scenes of unbridled lust and ruthless cruelty with a telltale gusto, and the same thing keeps cropping up in his Scottish novels too, with the constant use by his rural characters of the term "brutes" as a half-critical, half-endearing epithet they incessantly apply to each other . . . , and the minister with his playful little habit of bottom-slapping.

But all these criticisms do not detract in any way from recognition of the fact that he was a splendid writer with great narrative powers, an abounding vitality of expression, a wide range of interests, and was, in T. S. Eliot's phrase "alive in his own time." His achievement, despite his early death, was massive and the best of it will live. Scottish literary historians of the future will undoubtedly rank him as the greatest writer in our native Scottish tradition since Galt. (pp. 318-19)

> *Hugh MacDiarmid, "Lewis Grassic Gibbon," in* Modern British Writing, *edited by Denys Val Baker (copyright © 1947 by The Vanguard Press, Inc.; reprinted by permission of the publisher, Vanguard Press, Inc.), Vanguard, 1947, pp. 309-19.*

GEOFFREY WAGNER (essay date 1952)

Chris Guthrie [the central character in *Sunset Song*] represents Scotland in many ways; . . . and from the first, she is split schizophrenically. . . . (p. 299)

Two Chrises, Highland and Lowland Scot, contemplative and active man, go to the college at Duncairn each morning. . . . There is even another level of this split suggested when we read of 'the English Chris', the Chris, who, like her author, wins the bursary, conjugates Latin verbs and pleases the Dominie. There is no doubt which of these two Chrises wins out; it is the active Chris, the Chris of the soil, and the Scots Chris. . . . (pp. 299-300)

The antiphonal split in Chris as character is reflected in the whole technical presentation of the work which is for the most part a mental monologue on Chris's part, with narrative and dialogue only differentiated on the page by italics. This, in its turn, is another reflection of that split between Scots speaking and Scots reading, between lower and upper-class culture, which Gibbon was trying to unify in his choice of medium. . . . (p. 300)

This is not a happy story, but life at that time for the crofter was not a happy one. Consequently, the few moments of solace from their lot, as in Chris's marriage, stand out in more moving relief. Indeed, despite the prejudices and smallnesses of the Kinraddie folk, despite the souses, lech-

ers, unprincipled ministers and the veritable Greek chorus of malicious gossips kept up on all sides, what emerges from *Sunset Song* is a positive feeling of corporate society. . . . A feeling of nobility and health pervades the work. Birth, marriage, death—ploughing, seed-time and harvest—all move in tune and the cosmic relationships are mirrored in the human relationships, for man is here at his closest with the elemental movement of the universe. . . . (pp. 301-02)

[In *Cloud Howe* the drama of Robert Colquohoun's] life, which characterizes one aspect of the social spirit of the times, is played against a carefully contrived background. Segget, the scene also of Gibbon's Scots short stories, is exactly divided, in population figures, between the farm folk and the spinners at the jute mills. The external social struggle is worked out also within the minister's own breast, for Robert comes to the parish, full of enthusiasm and hatred of war, apparently on the side of the spinners . . . in ideology. (p. 303)

Robert Colquohoun is that characteristic socialist of the Scots twenties, the sympathetic visionary with hopelessly inadequate practical tools: thus, when the spinners organize and take their first social action of the book, a moment of decision comes for Robert which is partially prepared for. (p. 304)

[The spinners'] strike fails and the baby of Robert and Chris dies, a moment after birth, at the same time. . . . More than the strike and the hope of socialism die in this child therefore, for Chris (Scotland), allied with the kirk (Robert), cannot produce a third force. (p. 305)

In *Cloud Howe,* as in *Sunset Song,* there is the same interrelationship between macrocosm and microcosm that is typical of Gibbon's work. Social change is knit in with the movement of nature; to give one instance, at the end of 'Cumulus', Chris sees a star in the night sky, beside the sickle moon, which she had never noticed before though she was familiar, as a country person is, with the face of the heavens. As she walks with Robert, he also notices something different in the air—'*Funny, there really is something about.*' The march of the spinners is coming, the new star in the social universe of Scotland. Then, as the strike is about to begin, and Chris's baby to be born, nature also responds, it is 'a waiting world of Spring'. Meanwhile the young Ewan was finding his first neolithic flints, the broken blade of a spear and the first sliver of that grey granite of which Scotland is partly made. (p. 306)

[In *Grey Granite* Ewan is characterized] in terms of the city, Duncairn, where he and his mother go after Robert's death, just as Chris is described in terms of the land. He has grey granite eyes and a grey granite smile. . . . [We] are well prepared from the start of this work for the later depiction of Ewan as the vehicle for a creed rather than a human being, and our chief sympathy is always left with Chris. Ewan is, after all, well equipped for life in a harsh Scots city like Duncairn, as his reactions prove; Chris is not. She is never at peace with the industrial class. . . . (p. 307)

For Chris there is only one reality, one constant, 'nothing in the world she believed in but change', and she is tied to it, body and soul. . . .

There are three books in *A Scots Quair* and three marriages for its principal character. None of these marriages, as

Chris herself points out, is lucky for the men concerned. Scotland must live by itself, as it does at last, when Chris returns, completed and unconquered, to Blawearie at the end. Each marriage has meant a hardening of the central problem for Chris as Scot; first, with Ewan, she knew love killed by capitalism; second, with Robert, we see the unsatisfactory nature of the union of utopian idealism with a stern and uncompromising country; third, Ake Ogilvie leaves her when life with her becomes too hard even for him. . . . As such, as a political allegory, *A Scots Quair* gives a message of independence. Of all the various political factions represented—an aspect of the work which is reflected in the increase in characters who take up the soliloquy—Chris alone stands out with no political viewpoint expressed; her politics are contained in her natural humanity.

Thus the cycle of Gibbon's masterpiece is complete and its many meaningful analogies may be taken one stage further, to what is perhaps the very core of all—the five ages of man. We know, from Gibbon's 'Michell' fiction, what he believed to be the age of gold, the age, as he called it, of 'golden hunters'. Ewan's flints are, however, only 'late Bronze Age.' . . . (p. 309)

But the fifth age of man, of which we are, according to most early cosmic chronologists, approaching the end, were divided between iron and clay. Is this, then, the central division in Scotland? We must not forget that Gibbon wrote, at the end of 1933, a story entitled 'Clay' and was constantly, throughout his writings, stressing the clayey nature of the soil of the Mearns, as much as he was the iron, or granite, aspect of Scots towns. Possibly the younger Ewan and Chris were intended to represent this division in modern civilization. (p. 310)

> *Geoffrey Wagner, "The Greatest Since Galt," in* Essays in Criticism, *Vol. II, No. 3, July, 1952, pp. 295-310.*

KURT WITTIG (essay date 1958)

In his trilogy *A Scots Quair*, J. Leslie Mitchell . . . produced the most ambitious single effort in Scottish fiction. The story moves on three distinct levels: personal, social, and mythical. On the purely personal level, it is the life story of Chris Guthrie, a crofter's daughter, who is pulled hither and thither between love and hate of the land, and of English and Scottish culture, but ultimately decides in favour of Scotland and the land. On the social level, the first of the three novels of Mitchell's *Scots Quair* deals with the breakdown of the crofting system after the artificial boom of the war; the second with the disintegration of small-town society, which it represents as a consequence of lack of understanding and co-operation between the crofters and the working classes; and the third (which is sometimes doctrinaire, and artistically inferior to the other two) with the fermentation in the city and the resultant upsurge of socialism and communism.

The trilogy only achieves its meaning on the third level. The personal and the social history are part of a larger, mythological cycle. All is change, nothing endures but the land, while the forms of social organisation are blown away like chaff. . . . What remains is the age-old link with the past, our dim ancestors. Not only with those who created the present form of social organisation in the Middle Ages, but more potently with our deepest roots in the time before history began. The standing stones on the hill in the Mearns, the flints of the primeval hunters before kings and culture and classes perverted the natural disposition of man. We must regain these essential, innate, unspoilt roots of life before we are able to find a way out. (pp. 330-31)

If Mitchell's *Scots Quair* succeeds on this mythological plane (and many will probably agree with me that it does), that is largely because the whole story is told subjectively. Unlike most other novelists, Mitchell does not present an "objective" picture of outer reality; instead, we are given the picture of reality as created in the mind of his characters. . . . One consequence of this dramatisation of the ego and its mind is the peculiar fact . . . that a person can view himself as "you"; another is the intense animism or demonism that colours the resultant subjective vision of reality. Different images are flashed together, "dead" things are animated ("snow stroked the window with quiet soft fingers"), and the whole landscape, the whole environs become a living impersonation, an active force. There is always the moor round the standing stones; "it was Time himself she had seen, haunting their tracks with unstaying feet"; after a bout of religious melancholy, Robert comes "seeking her, sad and sorry for the queer, black beast that rode his mind in those haunted hours". . . . All this clearly is what we have called animism, made to serve the trilogy's essentially mythological purpose.

As we are always listening to one speaker or another, the story is told throughout in Scots—but, according to the character who is imagined to be speaking, with a varying degree of modification by the English (or pseudo-English) that has long been taught in Scottish schools. Mitchell's narrative style has consequently a transitional character. . . . Yet it has the same music, the same cadences, the same dramatic intensity, the same way of presenting abstract thought in terms of a concrete picture, the same grotesque distortion as a first step towards creating one's own reality, as the spoken Scots of earlier periods. . . . As the story flows on through the minds of the speakers, we gradually begin to recognise it for what it is—namely Scotland's modern folk speech transformed into a literary language which perhaps lacks polish, but has all the vitality of folk imagination. Mitchell's *Scots Quair* was perhaps the first major Scottish work of fiction in which any kind of Scots was used throughout for narrative as well as dialogue—that is to say, as a first-order language. And with all its crudities, his Scots is by far the most promising attempt that has yet been made towards the creation of a modern Scots prose. (pp. 331-33)

> *Kurt Wittig, "Breakers: The Scottish Renaissance," in his* The Scottish Tradition in Literature *(copyright © 1958 by Kurt Wittig; reprinted by permission of James Thin Ltd), Oliver and Boyd Ltd., 1958, pp. 280-340.**

DAVID MACAREE (essay date 1964)

[Gibbon's trilogy, *A Scots Quair*,] showed no signs of lack of premeditation; in fact, considered at the personal level as a novel of the soil dealing with the life of Christine Guthrie, daughter of a small farmer, in the years between 1911 and 1934, it has been criticised for its excessive neatness of construction with its tripartite division corresponding to youth, young adulthood, and middle age; each with its appropriate husband, farmer, minister, and poet-craftsman; in three settings: countryside, small town, and industrial city. What is more, the parallels extend even to the structure of the individual books, each of which consists of four sections with titles suggestive of the progression of the narrative. In *Sunset Song* there is the cycle of the farming year: Ploughing, Drilling, Seed-time, and Harvest; in *Cloud Howe,* the cloud formations in order of increasing gloom: Cirrus, Cumulus, Stratus, and Nimbus; in *Grey Granite,* minerals ranked by hardness and purity: Epidote, Sphene, Apatite, and Zircon. Such tidy schematization annoyed some of the novel's first critics for it suggested a preoccupation with issues wider than those they considered strictly relevant to what they saw as regional fiction dealing with lower class life on the Scottish countryside. (pp. 45-6)

The carefully balanced structure indeed hints strongly that Gibbon was aiming not at naturalism solely, or even at a social documentation, but a myth arrived at through allegory. Besides its structure, there are elements in the story, too, that lend themselves best to such a reading. To give but one instance, Robert Colquhoun, Chris's second husband, greets the news of her pregnancy with, "Oh Chris Caledonia, I've married a nation"; . . . words that are meaningful only if we see Chris as Scotland herself, which was presumably Gibbon's intention. (p. 46)

In examining the individual books of the trilogy, we find that Gibbon has supplied us with clues to the larger time scheme that operates in addition to the one which records the passage of twenty-odd years in the life of the central character. Thus, both *Sunset Song* and *Cloud Howe* open with preliminary chapters sketching the political and social history from the Middle Ages of Kinraddie and Segget respectively. (p. 47)

[Besides] the personal story of Chris as a member of a social organization which, after eight centuries of existence, has collapsed through its own debility in the face of changes in the world outside,—besides this, there is yet another time scheme in operation, for the Guthries who come to settle in the Howe of the Mearns in the year 1911 are, in a special sense, representative of all those who, over the ages, have battled natural difficulties to make their homes in Scotland and become part of the land they have created. So their journey across the hills in the blast of a Scottish winter, described in epic terms, becomes a migration of peoples moving with their possessions through darkness to an unknown destiny. . . . (p. 48)

Chris the girl, then, whom we meet first by the Stones on a summer's day dreaming over the countryside from her vantage point, carries it all within herself. (p. 49)

Tavendale [her first husband] is Highlander as she is Lowlander, or rather he is Celt as she is Teuton, and it is this marriage that should produce the complete Scot from the fusion of the cultures that they represent. Under these circumstances, it is fitting that they plight troth among the ruins of Dunottar Castle with its mementoes of past battles between the two races. The marriage itself is consummated on a night of winter storm, appropriate symbol of the political and religious storms that have swept Scotland, and from that consummation is born young Ewan whose birth coincides almost exactly with the outbreak of a war that will engulf all that is best of the manhood of Kinraddie before it is done. (pp. 49-50)

Once again, though he never forces the matter on the reader's attention, Gibbon has created characters who function as individuals and as typological representatives. (p. 50)

With [Tavendale] and the others dead *Sunset Song* ends in a kind of *Vale* to the agricultural way of life. . . . Chris's departure from Kinraddie, then, becomes more than an event in the life of an individual, it serves to turn the page on one aspect of Scottish life and the characters it fostered. Now it is the turn of the small town to receive attention. (pp. 50-1)

Read simply as an account of life in a small Scottish mill- and market town in the grim years of the twenties, *Cloud Howe* is fully satisfying. The personal tensions between Robert Colquhoun and Chris are mirrored in social tensions for which there seems to be no alleviation in any of the religious and political faiths that Gibbon, through various characters, explores. Colquhoun's own Christian socialism is dismissed as an unsubstantial dream; socialism as a faith for workers, independent of religion, fails also because its leaders are too easily seduced by a taste of power and because its rank and file relax as soon as they themselves are comfortable. (p. 52)

But just as in *Sunset Song* Chris as Scotland serves to show us the men of Kinraddie as representative Scotsmen, so in *Cloud Howe* Chris as Scotland is seen in relation to the Presbyterian Church whose close links with the nation sustained it in the troubled centuries that followed the Calvinist Reformation until the advance of science in the last hundred years or so caused a retreat into hair-splitting disputes on points of dogma on the one hand and increasing indifference on the other. In the novel the beginning of the rupture is signalled by the death, stillborn, of Chris's child by Robert Colquhoun, an event that we might take as recognition that the union of Kirk and Nation is incapable of bearing lasting fruit. (p. 53)

Chris plays a less active part in *Grey Granite* which is largely Ewan's story as he seeks a faith to live by. . . .

The difficulty that Gibbon faced in the last volume of his novel was the necessity of removing attention from Chris so that he might focus on Ewan. Her actions, therefore, are pushed aside by the main current of the narrative: her third marriage to Ake Ogilvie, for instance, is treated in an offhand manner and he is shuffled out of the way as soon as possible. At the last, however, with Ewan gone the full spotlight turns again on Chris; we have a division of interest therefore, that has not been present in the first two members of the trilogy. In fact *Grey Granite* falls below these, partly for the reason just outlined, but more basically because it deals with the future and the referents which have been present hitherto are now lacking and there is no body of myth or history to which the allegory may point. Granted that Gibbon was presenting Communism as the stark, sure creed that Robert Colquhoun preached in his last sermon as a replacement for an outworn Christianity—and this appears to have been his intention—he denies in advance its efficacy by having Chris reject it as just another of the idle delusive dreams of men. (p. 54)

The suggestion that *Grey Granite* suffers by comparison with its predecessors in its lack of suitable correlatives for allegory shows wherein lay their power. In them the narrative flows smoothly at the personal, social, and mythological level with the one bound to the other by extended metaphor so that the surface realism achieved by a prose style that catches the varied accents of the speaking voice or the passing of ideas through the mind easily leads on to deeper levels of meaning, and the cadences of individual utterance become representative voices of movements or types of men. And for much of the novel the effect that Gibbon achieves by this narrative method is a richness of texture that sets it far above the common run of fiction and gives it a strong claim to be the exemplar of a genre, mythic realism, which other Scottish novelists have favoured but few have employed so well. (p. 55)

> *David Macaree, ''Myth and Allegory in Lewis Grassic Gibbon's 'A Scots Quair','' in* Studies in Scottish Literature *(copyright © University of South Carolina 1964), Vol. II, No. 1, July, 1964, pp. 45-55.*

IAN S. MUNRO   (essay date 1967)

[The greater part of James Leslie Mitchell's] achievement was the work written under the pseudonym of Lewis Grassic Gibbon, and in particular the three novels *Sunset Song, Cloud Howe,* and *Grey Granite,* which make up the great trilogy of the Mearns *A Scots Quair,* probably the most ambitious single effort in Scottish fiction. (p. viii)

Although *A Scots Quair* is undoubtedly the major achievement other Grassic Gibbon writings have a similar quality; the short stories and essays in particular are not only outstanding examples of difficult arts but are an integral part of the writer's treasury. It would be difficult to find the equivalent of *Clay* as a short story or the equal of *The Land* as an essay.

Certainly the five short stories of the Mearns are among the best of the century. In locale and idiom they are of the same genre as *Sunset Song* and in their own medium match the effect and accomplishment of the famous novel. The best of the essays are also vital to a full appreciation and understanding of the writer. For instance a study of *The Land* in relation to *Sunset Song* suggests a key as well as a parallel to the major work. (pp. viii-ix)

Like most great writers Mitchell was uneven in his work. Hasty composition, over-pressure of work, excesses in style and matter all have contributed to lapses in taste and standard. Nevertheless the greater part of this subsidiary material can stand by itself, while the remainder is important as background, source, and development material. Comparison between the English and Scottish material is inevitable, and while the former suffers in comparison to the latter, each has its relevance in the moulding and development of the finished writer. . . .

Despite the bitter loss of a writer of this stature at the height of his creative power, the work remaining is impressive by any standard. It is common now to measure this writer's work against the best in any modern literature, and to talk of the Mearns of Grassic Gibbon in the same sense as one speaks of the Wessex of Thomas Hardy or the Dublin of James Joyce. *A Scots Quair* must remain as the peak of the achievement but the smaller pieces . . . can be said to mark significant and at times spectacular stages in the progress towards the heights. (p. ix)

> *Ian S. Munro, ''Introduction'' (© Hutchinson & Co. (Publishers) Ltd. 1967), in* A Scots Hairst *by*

> *Lewis Grassic Gibbon, edited by Ian S. Munro, Hutchinson of London, 1967, pp. vii-ix.*

DOUGLAS F. YOUNG   (essay date 1973)

As a Scot [Mitchell] was always aware of a lack of assurance in Standard English and believed that no Scottish writer could handle that medium satisfactorily. His own efforts in Standard English were rarely wholly successful. . . . His English is very mannered and one often gets the impression of a journalist indulging in 'fine writing', full of overblown ornateness and poetic cliché. . . .

It has blatant flaws, which often come of the desire to preach a particular doctrine or to appeal to the popular taste, yet one is nearly always aware of a genuine literary craftsman exploring, with a varied degree of success, the potential of his medium. (p. 32)

The novel [*Spartacus*] uses history as the basis for the dramatization of certain contemporary social themes. The main interest of [the novel] is political rather than historical and the book might be better described as a political fable.

Spartacus can be interpreted as a Marxist novel, dealing with the revolutionary process, but it is given a wider meaning by the underlying Diffusionist philosophy. . . . The attempt of the slaves to overthrow the power of Rome is representative of the class struggle, but also of the more universal struggle of natural man to reassert himself. The state to which the slaves aspire is at once the Marxist's state of perfect communism and the Diffusionist's new golden age.

The first thing that is given emphasis is the corrupt and corrupting nature of Roman civilization, and Mitchell indulges in some of those scenes of horror in which he takes delight. All the evils which the Diffusionist associates with civilization are to be found here: superstitious devotion to cruel gods, sexual perversions, a general moral laxity, inhumanity and a widespread atmosphere of unhappiness and malaise. (p. 64)

In *Spartacus* Mitchell seems to be in charge of his medium. His irritating mannerisms and excesses of style, evident in all [his] earlier English fiction, are not now so obtrusive; the writing in *Spartacus* displays terseness and precision, economy and restraint. The complicated and bewildering convolutions of syntax are less apparent, and the vocabulary is handled with a much surer touch. . . . (p. 66)

The notion of the golden age recurs throughout the book. . . .

The golden age may be a dream, an impossible ideal, yet this vision must be behind our plans for the future. This is Mitchell's political conclusion; he is not a simple primitivist seeking to reverse the flow of history, but he does insist that a recognition of primitive values must be the basis for present and future action. (p. 71)

The ending of the book is weak. . . . The slaves are crucified, but we are left with the pious hope that there will arise other great leaders and somehow someday one of them will succeed.

Despite this flabby conclusion, *Spartacus* is the best work of fiction written under the name of J. Leslie Mitchell. At the simplest level it is a good, stirring adventure story, told in such a way as to make the most of the tension and excitement, and not allowing the propagandist's message to come between us and the adventure itself. The descriptions of the settings and the incidents are vivid, the battle scenes being particularly well realized. (p. 72)

[It] was the discovery of his unique Scottish prose style which was the making of Mitchell as a writer. That vision of man and of human destiny which had for so long been finding inadequate expression in English prose was now to be more fully realized than ever before. . . . *A Scots Quair* should not be seen as standing wholly apart from his other work, but as the fulfilment of the same endeavour. (pp. 84-5)

In *Sunset Song* [Mitchell's] boyhood experience in the Mearns combines with his mature Diffusionist philosophy to produce a novel which is at once a vivid evocation of a particular people in a particular place at a particular time, and also a universal commentary on human progress or the lack of it. Like all great novelists Mitchell discovers the universal in the particular, so that when he casts his eye over the Howe of the Mearns he sees mankind's past, present and future. It is not just the story of Chris Guthrie and of Kinraddie but a total critique of human civilization. (p. 86)

This brings us to the great technical achievement of *Sunset Song*. . . . [The] prose is Scottish not because of the extensive use of dialect but because it is infused with the rhythms of Scottish speech. It is a dramatic prose and we must always think of it as being *spoken* by someone. The important thing is *who* is speaking, the question of point of view. In *Sunset Song* the point of view is continually shifting: sometimes it is definitely placed, sometimes it is not defined. Mitchell achieves an incomparable flexibility and ambiguity of point of view so that the voice behind the prose may be that of one of the characters, or of an anonymous folk narrator, of the community itself, or any amalgam of any of these.

It is this subtle manipulation of point of view, by which Kinraddie is given a voice of its own to reveal its own character . . . that gives *Sunset Song* its unique ability to express the whole nature and quality of life in a peasant community. . . . *Sunset Song* is permeated by the Diffusionist myth and unless we analyse it in these terms we will miss much of its significance. (pp. 90-1)

At its most significant level *Sunset Song* is the story of the last few years of the genuine Pictish folk of the Mearns and their final defeat by the forces of civilization.

As we have seen with his earlier novels, Mitchell was in the habit of choosing his titles with care, and the title of *Sunset Song* is intended to convey this essential meaning of the book. . . . [Mitchell] uses the sun as a symbol of the golden age, so that the disappearance of the golden age and the advance of civilization become equivalent to the setting of the sun. This is the sunset of which we are singing, and the point is made throughout the novel by repeated use of the sun image. (pp. 91-2)

[A] point over which there has been some confusion [is] the significance of the Blawearie Standing Stones. It has been loosely assumed that they have something to do with primitive man but their full significance has not been made clear. The Standing Stones are not to be thought of as a remnant of the primitive golden age. As a good anthropologist Mitchell knew that they had a religious function, and as a good Diffusionist he knew that religion had no place in the golden age and came only with the coming of civilization. As the minister makes clear, it was the bringers of civilization who raised up the Standing Stones on the primitive, wild moorland around Blawearie loch, and the stones are reminders of that great and tragic step in Scottish history. They are memorials to the golden age only as reminders of the first bringers of civilization who destroyed it. . . .

Only Chris is aware of the importance of the Standing Stones. The others think of them as evil; only she sees that their existence provides a source of comfort and understanding. Symbolizing as they do the confrontation of primitive values and civilized values, they enable her to interpret her experience, to see meaning behind the unhappinesses that befall her. (p. 93)

It is an essential point in Mitchell's theory of human nature that no matter how great an influence civilization may have, the essential primitive still lives in us, deep down but unspoiled. Our moments of greatest happiness are those when we are most natural, when we recapture our essential selves. At such moments of supreme personal happiness and fulfilment the golden age can live again, but only for a time, until the encroachment of the civilized world destroys it and brings another sunset. (pp. 94-5)

[The] story of Chris Guthrie is also the story of human history; the pattern of her experience is the pattern which has shaped the destiny of man. Her early state of innocence and happiness is destroyed by the encroachment of civilization. But, as with man in general, civilization can never conquer completely; the essential Chris is never destroyed. It is the way that she retains her primitive naturalness, despite all external opposition and influence, and goes her own way, that makes her so attractive a personality, and makes her capable of moving beyond the sunset.

This preservation, despite all, of the natural, primitive self is symbolized by Chris's attachment to the land itself. (pp. 95-6)

To the Diffusionist civilization means in the first place the coming of agriculture, and a large theme of *Sunset Song* is concerned with the ways in which the agricultural life destroys the natural goodness of man. Here Chris's father is the outstanding example. We have a picture of him in his youth, at the ploughing match at Pittodrie, where he first met his wife, and he is handsome, competent, and kind, a young man in his prime. But by the time that Chris is a teenage girl he has changed into a dour, cruel, and bad-tempered man. The agricultural life has destroyed his spirit. (pp. 96-7)

Although religion may not be inherent in their nature, it yet has had a sad effect upon the people of Scotland. Calvinism, we are asked to believe, has been an oppressive force of great magnitude. Chris's father is not really a religious man in any spiritual sense, yet the teachings of the Kirk are the cause of much of his inhumanity. Christianity is so distorted that, far from being the religion of love, it becomes a major divisive force between Guthrie and his family. (p. 97)

[The] result of Mitchell's adherence to this view of Scottish religious history is that the characterization of John Guthrie sometimes seems rather exaggerated and doctrinaire. . . .

The evil influence of religion is perhaps most damaging in the attitudes which it has created towards sex. The general attitude of the parish can be seen from the gossip which is so much a part of the book. There is an essential unhealthiness where people take such a delight in dirty, sniggering gossip. (p. 98)

Chris's mother is altogether a more natural and instinctive person than her father, less influenced by the distortions of civilization. She is associated with the land and the sun, with the gold of her hair, and the conflict within Chris can be seen as the conflict between the Murdoch in her and the Guthrie in her. Mother is destroyed by the forces of civilization, first the gold disappears from her hair and then she is driven to suicide, but the destruction is not complete for she passes on her instinctive nature to Chris. (p. 99)

The First World War provides the climax to the book, for with that war comes the final disappearance of the old, primitive quality in the lives of the peasants. That we are meant to see the war as simply as the end of a long, continuous process, beginning with the first coming of civilization, is made clear in Chae Strachan's vision of the ancient, helmeted warrior when he comes back from the front on leave, up on the moor by the Standing Stones. (p. 102)

With the end of the war comes the sunset of a people and of a whole way of life. Civilization seems to have triumphed completely in Kinraddie. . . .

But the important thing about a sunset is that, though it may bring temporary darkness, the sun will rise again. Though these men are dead and their way of life gone, the land itself endures; the essential goodness of human nature, despite the distortions of civilization, remains. Thus there is reason for hope; we can look beyond the sunset for the Morning Star. (p. 103)

Sunset Song is certainly Mitchell's greatest achievement and it is one of the great works of modern literature. It presents us with a group of magnificent characters, thoroughly realized and extremely memorable, and involves them in situations which reflect the depths and complexities of real life. I can think of no other book in which the world of the Scottish peasant is presented so vividly and authentically. And to project his characters and their world, Mitchell evolved a highly original and effective technique which carries the reader along with the speech rhythms of his prose and gives a dramatic sense of hearing the voice of the Mearns itself. But most important, the book has a significance beyond that of personal and social history, a universality which derives from the underlying Diffusionist myth, and which asks us to examine our fundamental values in life, to look at the pattern of human development and to work for a more sane and natural world. (p. 104)

At every level of meaning [in *Cloud Howe*] there is a marked falling off. The writer is not engaged with his material to the same degree of imaginative intensity as he was earlier, and this becomes apparent in the realization of the characters, in the authenticity of the action and setting, and perhaps most strikingly in the quality of the prose. The uniquely evocative style of *Sunset Song*, with its magnificent subtleties of rhythm and mood, now becomes strained, mechanical and self-consciously mannered. (pp. 104-05)

In the first book, Mitchell's ideas on the nature and history of man are important but they have been related to his own experience of life to produce a world that is both real and significant. *Cloud Howe* comes from a different level of his being, and the Diffusionist theory is now not so much the basis for a fully-imagined myth about man's battle with civilization, as merely the means of an intellectual analysis of a particular political situation at a particular time. The result is that *Cloud Howe* lacks both the universality and the imaginative reality, the felt life, of *Sunset Song*. . . .

To my mind, *Grey Granite*, with all its faults, is a better book than *Cloud Howe*. (p. 120)

Until this third part, there was always some concrete symbol of the presence of the past in the here-and-now—the Standing Stones of Blawearie and the Kaimes of Segget—but in Duncairn there is no equivalent, nothing to remind us of the golden age that was. All links with the past appear to have been broken and civilization dominates completely. . . .

We have progressed from the clouds of *Cloud Howe* to the fogs of *Grey Granite*, shutting out the sunshine, shrouding the city in almost complete darkness. Throughout the book the imagery of cloud and smoke serves the same purpose, emphasizing that Duncairn is the City of Dreadful Night, cut off from all natural light. (p. 121)

In *Grey Granite*, unlike *Sunset Song*, Mitchell's theory of history leads to a lack of individuality in his workers, for he believed that, whilst the peasants retained something of their true selves, the urban proletariat had suffered under civilization to such an extent that their essential humanity had been destroyed, and they had reached a state of uniform wretchedness. With a sweeping judgment they are all lumped together as the sad victims of civilization. Like the foreigner who thinks all Chinese look alike, Mitchell the peasant cannot see any difference between one member of the proletariat and another. They are never seen as distinctive individuals but simply as 'keelies', all one type. (pp. 122-23)

[Ewan] is the key figure in the novel and his gradual acceptance of Communism provides the main movement of the theme. Mitchell means to portray him as the type of leader that is required if the downtrodden masses, useless on their own, are ever to contribute to any effective political action. He is a character very like Spartacus. . . . (p. 127)

The key point in the 'humanizing' of Ewan comes, according to a pattern with which we are now familiar, when he returns to the land. . . . [We] come to the crucial issue of the whole book, the question of the compatibility of socialism and Diffusionism, the suggestion that what true socialists are trying to do is recreate the quality of primitive life, without gods and without classes. The meaning of the trilogy as a whole is contained in the idea that we must reintroduce essential primitive values into life and that the best way to do this, indeed the only way, is through Communism. This, however, is never argued out convincingly, and one wonders whether Mitchell himself was really convinced that the methods of socialist revolution would bring about the kind of new golden age that he was seeking. (p. 128)

Chris herself still plays an important part in the book, and at the personal level of the drama of her life *Grey Granite* is very much better than *Cloud Howe*. In *Cloud Howe* the personality of Chris had dimmed somewhat, she had become rather a vague figure. Now she is treated with something of the sympathetic insight which we saw in *Sunset Song*. . . . We see in her a sensitive study of a woman approaching middle-age, regretting the passing of the years, afraid of the future, but finally reconciling herself to her new role in life. (pp. 130-31)

It is Chris's insistence on the maintenance of . . . essential primitive values in life which is symbolized by her return to Echt at the end of the book. We are not, I am sure, meant to see this as an advocacy of a return to peasant life but simply as an insistence that each of us, as individuals, must rediscover the essential primitive naturalness within us, must re-establish our roots in the land.

What Mitchell meant us to see in the relationship between Ewan and Chris at the end of the novel is not conveyed in a satisfactory way. . . . We are meant to see Chris and Ewan not in conflict but approaching the same goal by different routes, effecting the reconciliation of Mitchell's Communism and his Diffusionism. (pp. 133-34)

I think that in the drama of Chris and Ewan at the end of *Grey Granite* Mitchell projects his own political dreams and uncertainties. Partly he put his faith in the Communist movement, desperately hoping that it could produce the world he wanted, but essentially he felt that all political action was futile because it did nothing to change the character of the individual man or woman. Change must begin at the individual level, and the world will return to sanity only when man rediscovers the essential, primitive self within him. This is the real Mitchell, the Mitchell that we find in Chris. The other is a theoretical posture in which he himself does not really believe, and this is why the character of Ewan is so markedly less real and convincing than that of Chris.

It is significant that the book ends not with Ewan and his march towards the Communist revolution, but with Chris and her return to the land, with her discovery of her personal salvation in renewed contact with primitive reality. (p. 135)

> *Douglas F. Young, in his* Beyond the Sunset: A Study of James Leslie Mitchell (Lewis Grassic Gibbon) *(© Douglas F. Young 1973; reprinted by permission of the author), Impulse Books, 1973, 162 p.*

IAN CAMPBELL (essay date 1974)

[During] his literary apprenticeship [James Leslie Mitchell] showed a strong interest in utopian and science fiction. . . . The two titles which most concern us are [*Three Go Back* and *Gay Hunter*]. (p. 53)

[It] may at the outset be worthwhile investigating the "spirit" with which Mitchell approached his fantasy writing. It was the spirit of a propagandist for what he himself called the "diffusionist heresy." Very briefly, Mitchell believed that civilization had been spread—"diffused"—over the world as a result of the chance discovery in the Nile valley that settled agriculture was possible, rather than the shifting nomadic life which had gone before it. . . . The very violence of the arrival of civilization led to crudities and barbarisms which haunted Mitchell's imagination, and which haunted his Scottish novels in the shape of the Standing Stones of *Sunset Song*. Cruelty, injustice, and persecution obsessed Mitchell. Some would criticize him for dwelling

too long on the miseries of the slums in *Grey Granite* or the fate of the industrial proletariat in Glasgow. . . . [The] sufferings of the poor in every country depicted in Mitchell's work, are attributable to the decay of civilization, a blight which spreads through the world and degrades an originally wonderful being . . . man.

Three Go Back does not invite instant admiration. . . . [The] book opens on an airship flying across the Atlantic, introducing a thrill which was definitely new and exciting. (p. 54)

With skill and subtlety, Mitchell slowly breaks the news to his audience, as he does to the characters in his plot: they have been precipitated by the force of the undersea explosion through from one time-zone to another. . . .

They are lost, they have gone back to an island in a time unknown and unguessed, an island whose history is unknown because buried under Atlantic waters. It is a bold and ingenious setting, with the virtue of being neutral. . . .

In this setting the interaction of character is, admittedly, prosaic and predictable. The militant pacifist and the successful arms manufacturer run through the predictable arguments of a generation uneasily preparing for World War II, and Clair, in watching them, analyzes the process for the audience. (p. 55)

The plot ceases to be the observations of three who "go back." They become involved in a fight for survival which leaves them no time for mere observation. The golden hunters [natives of the island] are under double threat: first, from the fourth ice age (about to happen) and secondly, from Neanderthal man, their natural enemy. (pp. 56-7)

It is easy to see the characterization as an insuperable barrier to any claim to merit for this novel. But that would be too easy to do. Whatever the development of individual character, Mitchell's grasp of a moment's cultural history on a doomed island—a doomed sub-race of people threatened by ice-age and by natural enemies fleeing the destruction of Atlantis and probably fleeing to death in the glaciers of the North—is grippingly achieved. (p. 57)

If *Three Go Back* explores a beautiful past, *Gay Hunter* projects itself into a disquieting future. (p. 58)

What distinguished these novels of Mitchell's is not their scientific vision nor their handling of quasi-scientific themes . . . : rather it is Mitchell's passionate involvement with the fate of Mankind. (pp. 58-9)

Both *Three Go Back* and *Gay Hunter* have their indebtedness to the tradition of Rider Haggard and those novels which sought a primitivism in place of the new industrialization. Neither is considerable *science fiction* in the normal sense espoused by some. The scientific content is demonstrably thin; yet like so many of his predecessors, Mitchell used it to create a framework for his statement regarding his own times. Actually his attitude toward science itself is ambivalent. . . . Man has the capabilities in science, and Mitchell has confidence that there are men who have the powers of character and intellect to justify this cosmic effort. These qualities are reflected in numerous heroic figures of Mitchell's fiction who have flashes of intuition across space and time. (p. 59)

Mitchell's anger both at the systems which blunt men's feelings toward each other and at the degradation which "civilization" had brought on the unemployed of the 1930's, thwarted his writing ability often; his novels (none more so than his science fiction) preach and, as novels, stand still until the author has made sure his point has come across. (p. 60)

Mitchell's Diffusionism gave him a cause to fight against this civilization, but it would be wrong to think that his interest in science fiction allowed him an escape from an unlovely present. Beneath the too-easy plots and woolly scientific theorizing, the concern with the enduring qualities of kindliness and genuine human feeling, which civilization can never entirely eradicate, carries Mitchell thousands of years back and forwards from his own, particularly unloved, present. His strength of feeling was genuine, and it is that strength which makes *Three Go Back* and *Gay Hunter* remarkable works of science fiction. . . . (p. 62)

> *Ian Campbell, "The Science Fiction of John Leslie Mitchell," in* Extrapolation *(copyright 1974 by Thomas D. and Alice S. Clareson), Vol. 16, No. 1, December, 1974, pp. 53-63.*

IAN CAMPBELL   (essay date 1974)

Mitchell was in the familiar Scottish dilemma of a love/hate relationship with the environment from which he drew his very considerable artistic strength and originality. *A Scots Quair* eloquently shows the conflicting emotions and loyalties of its creator, yet (because it is a novel) *fails*. I suggest, as a wholly satisfactory artistic presentation of these conflicts, and in the failure may lie the root of the unease many feel (quite apart from the very evident blunders of artistic tact) in *Grey Granite* as the end of the trilogy.

In real life, Chris and Ewan were one. Mitchell, their creator, shaped the relevant parts of their characters, widely divergent, from the conflicting parts of his own experience and sympathy. Chris carries the weight of his love for the land and for Arbuthnott (along with a skilfully-applied coating of distaste for its unpleasantness), Ewan the less emotional political creed which grew to dominate his thinking. Chris is a real person, she embodies feelings he had known all his life and knew to be shared by his readers, his family, the originals behind his fictional characters. Ewan is an invention, a man embodying ideas which were developed, did not grow naturally like love for the smell of the land, or the sound of a peewit's cry. Ewan, in short, is intellectualised while Chris is a more emotional creation, natural, known longer, easier for the artist to portray than a more contemporary figure, less familiar to traditionally minded readers.

In the splitting of Mitchell into Chris and Ewan, the Scottish dilemma is brilliantly given shape, and can be seen in conflict over a prolonged period. So far, this is an artistic innovation of great merit. Nor are the characters oversimplified, for we have seen Chris's distaste for her environment, and Ewan's occasional flash of sentiment. Yet the inequality of conception (one is familiar, unconscious, the other consciously created, more recent) must tell, and Ewan is a far less 'sympathetic' character than Chris, as well as one far less fully developed. The interest of *Grey Granite* lies far more in action, and in the description of city life divorced from Ewan's experience (and even Chris's); in *Sunset Song* the interest of the plot revolves to a far greater extent round Chris's own experience, and round the reac-

tions to this of her immediate environment. Mitchell's method, then, while offering an opportunity to analyse a Scottish dilemma, imposes a strain on the book which grows more obvious as the trilogy nears its end.

The method imposes another weakness, perhaps even more serious. Chris and Ewan, it has been argued, embody different sides of the character of their creator. In Chris he embodies his yearning for the old life of the land which (as the end of *Sunset Song* makes abundantly clear) is forever gone. She knows this, yet at the end of the novel, in a conclusion unsatisfactory in its enigmatic character, she returns to her native Barmekin. Ewan, on the other hand, with a clear-eyed perception of the realities of life, marches off to London. The two sides of the author's personality, then, are not reunited at the end of the book, but quite the opposite. They are completely sundered, without apparent hope of reconciliation. And this, I would suggest, imposes a great strain on the credibility of the reader who accepts the symbolic structure the novelist has built round his character. The non-realistic and atypical compartmentalising of character into Chris and Ewan *for the purposes of argument* was quite acceptable, but this argument has no real close, or rather it has two. The reader, left perplexed, cannot accept that the quasi-mythical treatment of Chris and Ewan has been wholly successful, as it leads to nothing final, except perhaps the irreconcilability of the problems in contemporary Scottish life which they represent. Yet if this is their conclusion, it is one achieved at the expense of a satisfactory end of the trilogy.

This argument does not deny the extraordinary depth and richness of the examination of the Scottish scene, or the virtuosity of style, writing, or handling of language. It suggests, however, the proposition that the search for the distinctive excellence of *A Scots Quair* must lie in these directions rather than in a satisfactory solution of the problems which faced its creator. (pp. 55-6)

> *Ian Campbell, "Chris Caledonia: The Search for an Identity," in* Scottish Literary Journal *(reprinted by permission of* Scottish Literary Journal*), Vol. 1, No. 2, December, 1974, pp. 45-57.*

ADDITIONAL BIBLIOGRAPHY

Johnson, Roy. "Lewis Grassic Gibbon and *A Scots Quair*: Politics in the Novel." *Renaissance and Modern Studies* XX (1976): 39-53.
> Contends that *A Scots Quair* expresses a militant working class point of view.

MacDiarmid, Hugh. "Lewis Grassic Gibbon, William Soutar, Sydney Goodsir Smith, Norman McCaig and Others." In his *The Company I've Kept*, pp. 216-36. London: Hutchinson & Co., 1966.*
> Evaluates Gibbon's contribution to the Scottish Renaissance Movement.

Macdonald, Alastair A. "Lewis Grassic Gibbon and the Regional Whole." *The Dalhousie Review* 39, No. 4 (Winter 1960): 503-10.
> Discussion of the qualities of *A Scots Quair*, such as its transcendence of strictly parochial concerns, which in the critic's view make it a classic.

Munro, Ian S. *Leslie Mitchell: Lewis Grassic Gibbon.* Edinburgh and London: Oliver & Boyd, 1966, 224 p.
> Biography, with a foreword by Hugh MacDiarmid.

Whittington, Graeme. "The Regionalism of Lewis Grassic Gibbon." *Scottish Geographical Magazine* 90, No. 2 (September 1974): 75-84.

Analysis of the topography, customs, and attitudes of the rural and urban communities depicted in *A Scots Quair*.

Frederick Philip Grove

1879-1948

(Pseudonym of Felix Paul Berthold Friedrich Greve; also wrote under pseudonyms of Konrad Thorer, Elsa Greve, Friedrich Carl Gerden, Felix Grafe, and Edouard Thorne) German-born Canadian novelist, essayist, editor, short story writer, poet, translator, autobiographer, and dramatist.

Grove is best known as a naturalistic writer of life on the Canadian farmlands, prairies, and marshlands. His novels concern the plight of the individual struggling with fate and in search of identity; the struggles between the generations; and the effects of agricultural and industrial society. Throughout his life Grove felt compelled to conceal his name and background, cementing his ruse with an award-winning "autobiography," *In Search of Myself.*

Felix Paul Greve was born in Prussia and raised in Hamburg, the son of a city transit official. After a brief stint at Bonn University, he lived a decadent, debt-ridden life, earning money by translating the works of other European writers, including those of his acquaintances Stefan George and André Gide. Greve married, served a jail term for financial fraud, and published several novels and volumes of translations, a drama, and a book of poetry. He fled his creditors in 1909, leaving with his wife letters predicting his suicide aboard ship to Sweden.

Little is known of his whereabouts until 1912, when he applied for a teaching position in Winnipeg, Manitoba, using the name Fred Grove. For the next dozen years he taught school in several Manitoba towns, where he gained a reputation as a raconteur with bizarre, naturalistic beliefs.

Grove published his first book in English, *Over Prairie Trails,* in 1922. He wrote and rewrote a dozen books during the rest of his life, but only one, *A Search for America,* was a commercial success. His *Settlers of the Marsh* was banned from some Canadian libraries for its alleged obscenity. Grove's stubborn refusal to take even the least editorial advice, as well as the grim nature of his books, often made it difficult for him to publish.

Grove served as an editor with *The Canadian Nation* magazine and the short-lived Graphic Publishers from 1929 until 1931. He was elected to the Royal Society of Canada in 1941 for his pioneering contributions to Canadian literature, and he spent the last years of his life dabbling in politics and writing.

Grove's European past was discovered by Douglas O. Spettigue a full generation after his death, in the early 1970s. As a result of Spettigue's work, Grove's own story appears as interesting as that of any character he created.

PRINCIPAL WORKS

Wanderungen [as Felix Paul Greve] (poetry) 1902
Fanny Essler [as Felix Paul Greve] (novel) 1905
Maurermeister Ihles haus [as Felix Paul Greve] (novel) 1906
 [*The Master Mason's House,* 1976]

Over Prairie Trails (sketches) 1922
The Turn of the Year (sketches) 1923
Settlers of the Marsh (novel) 1925
A Search for America (novel) 1927
Our Daily Bread (novel) 1928
The Yoke of Life (novel) 1930
Fruits of the Earth (novel) 1933
Two Generations (novel) 1939
The Master of the Mill (novel) 1944
In Search of Myself (autobiography) 1946
Consider Her Ways (novel) 1947
Tales from the Margin (short stories) 1971

ARTHUR L. PHELPS (essay date 1926)

If during the last twenty-five years to grasp a convenient handful of time, a second novel suggesting genius has come out of Canada, this "Settlers of the Marsh" is that novel. Its faults lie on the surface, its merits are fundamental.

There are two tremendous scenes in the book and a multitude of intensely vivid little pictures of all sorts, there is detailed, subtle characterization and the presentation of many folk who appear physically alive to us and whom we might wish to know; there is presentation of a prairie settlement rising out of the gumbo and becoming articulated into Canadian life. Under all, upholding all, is the prairie landscape, over all, as a presence, is the prairie sky at night and by day. This vivid, compelling intensity of the book is blurred and offset from time to time by what appear to be tricks of style—the spendthrift use of dots suggesting that anything but the prolific linotype would have run out of periods by the end of the first chapter; a nervous haste destroying the reader's desire for leisure as he reads; the apparent lack of verisimilitude in the speech of certain characters; in one or two places an inartistic amount of detail in handling the sex elements of the book, and a rather hurried ending. . . .

The note of Grove's book is tragic. . . . The struggle within Niels [Lindsteadt], the struggles of the two women, Ellen and Mrs. Vogel, the battle of the whole community with the land—all of it involves the old pitiable disaster against which the heart and mind of man forever unavailingly rebel, the disaster of waste. But the book ends quietly and serenely. . . . In the end the book becomes one more localization of the warfare of the human spirit. Thus it fuses with the universal and out of Manitoba landscape creates spiritual territory of the soul.

Mr. Grove's knowledge is so thorough, his style so economical and effective, that his literary product becomes one of those inescapable things carrying with it an undeniable challenge to our attention. One is tempted to the statement that no pen at work in Canada suggests the capacity, not primarily to tell a story, but to interpret the actuality of Western prairie life in the making, as does the pen of Frederick Philip Grove; no one is creating as Grove is creating it the kind of literature to which one goes in order to get the sense of life, of men and women alive body and soul, of landscape under foot and eye. With this book, "Settlers of the Marsh," Canada makes contribution to contemporary world fiction.

Arthur L. Phelps, "Books of Special Interest," in The Saturday Review of Literature *(copyright © 1926 by* Saturday Review; *all rights reserved; reprinted by permission), Vol. 2, No. 27, January 30, 1926, p. 529.*

ISABEL SKELTON (essay date 1939)

Frederick Philip Grove's first published books, *Over Prairie Trails* . . . and *The Turn of the Year* . . . , are a fitting overture to all his writings. In them are heard his dominating themes and sentiments. The subject-matter of the first is found in seven intimate drives the author with us, his readers, takes "in the southern fringe of the great northern timber expanse"—a district which later affords a setting for various parts of his novels. We shall not have accompanied Mr. Grove very far before we discover we are on no expedition to get acquainted with our fellow-men, or to take any cognisance of them. We shall have no genial give and take, passing the time of day with residents or fellow-travellers, no humorous stories or sad tales connected with this one or that one we meet. On the contrary, we find ourselves taken up, as it were, into a travelling hermitage and enjoying a holiday away from our kind. (pp. 147-48)

[This] very exclusion of human interest is the characteristic of Mr. Grove's most personal books. (p. 148)

Again, we shall not have accompanied Mr. Grove very far until we discover how intensely absorbed he is in the transient natural phenomena taking place in the world about him. He seldom takes a sweeping view out towards the horizon. It is upon what is close behind him, what may be scrutinised with the greatest care and detail, that he likes to exercise his thought. He then searches to discover the truest word in which to pass his experience on to us. His description of hoar-frost-laden woods is an illustration, but too long to quote here. . . . There are many accurate, delicate details recorded [in the lengthy passage]: "It looked heavy, and yet it was nearly without weight. Not a twig was bent down under its load." And yet it is impossible to read such a length of lines without feeling the tendency to overdo which is latent in it. . . . It is the kind of picture which needs only one apt line or word of poetic insight to kindle the imagination of the reader to recreate it for himself. In *The Yoke of Life,* Mr. Grove himself has this sentence:

> As the picture which he had seen decomposed itself into its elements, Len felt sorry with that sadness which overcomes us when we see or hear a beautiful marvel rationally explained.

Mr. Grove holds us wholly intent on a very narrow world, for it is only a limited field could come into such a scrutinising ken. Still, all the time we feel there is at the back of his interest a deep realisation of the vast universe which envelops us. (pp. 149-50)

Considering the trend of passages like these, the mysterious sense they disseminate that we are wrapped round by immeasurable and impenetrable elements of creation, and then remembering the determined interest in conditions immediately beside us in both time and space to which Mr. Grove holds us, it would seem as if we distinctly heard him command: "Occupy yourself with this, poor, helpless, puny human atom that you are, because it is all that is given you to know." (p. 150)

[If the lines of his poem *Science*] speak Mr. Grove true, he looks upon life as something man must be "deluded into living on." Conrad has a phrase which from this point of view describes the armored protection against life Mr. Grove reveals in his work: "The detached curiosity of a subtle mind, and the high tranquillity of a steeled heart."

But this is not the right note to leave sounding as these books of beautiful word pictures are closed. The rich, musical, polished prose tempts one to make many and long quotations. The whole series of evening, sunset, and twilight scenes called *The Harvest* might be quoted to show how we are allowed to see through a very artistic and cultured eye the full gorgeousness of hue and shade in earth and air and cloud. Then, as the climax on this sloping field, passing into the shadows of evening while yet the heavens are full of light, there come two black horses drawing a wagon with a hayrack and a single man. This man, his wagon, his team, etched against that golden west, make a picture Millet himself might have wrought. And Mr. Grove's method of depicting the man has not a little in common with that master's method. He shows him to us doing his work, lifting his sheaves with his fork and building his load with such a rightness of the worker's movements—of a practised good worker's movements—that all weight, all motion in the picture and the posture are most satisfyingly right. (p. 151)

Settlers of the Marsh, a novel, was Mr. Grove's next book. . . . The opening up of this novel leaves nothing to be desired. There is a rightness about the descriptions and a harmony between them and the undertone of mood and feeling. Mr. Grove introduces his hero, Niels Lindstedt, a strong, well-built, quiet chap, and his guide and friend Lars Nelson, in a natural way. They are pushing along from the end of rail to the farm on the edge of the bush, thirty miles distant, where they are to dig a well. The hard work and its deadening effect, which are to be emphasized in the life before them, are foreshadowed by this long tramp. And there is also foreshadowed that almost passive "stick-to-it-iveness" which will characterise their acceptance of New World conditions and summarise, in their limited view, the complete fulfilling of their own duty in the life of the community around them. . . .

The same naturalness marks an interesting account of their early days. Their thrifty progress, their schemes and dreams are convincingly set forth. (p. 152)

So far this circumscribed study is thoroughly well done, and written in a style exactly suited to it, quiet, simple, precise, and with besides an undertone of understanding sympathy running through it. But the author at length finds he must broaden out his hero's life, if his book is to be anything beyond a commentary on working conditions in a rather poor section of country. This is not easy because Niels, while attractive-looking, energetic, and intelligent, is devoid of that interest which a copious outpouring of the gifts of the spirit or the intellect would give to him. To carry on his life successfully in the same vein, the author would require to be very familiar, one might almost say intuitively and lovingly familiar from childhood, with such prosaic surroundings and passive prosaic lives.

But this familiarity with the lives and thoughts of humdrum, ordinary, "low-brow" folk is what Mr. Grove's birth and training did not give him, and the interests and moods of the grown man could not cultivate. (p. 153)

[Grove] has carried [Niels] along his prosaic way as far as he has knowledge of that type—he has depicted his working life. Now to broaden out his study he marries Niels, forges off on another trail, completely changes the tone of his book, alters with it the style of his writing, and the result is that the account of Niels's life ceases to ring true. It becomes incredible. (p. 154)

There is another serious and fundamental weakness in the romantic side of Mr. Grove's novels. It is this. Mr. Grove himself has, at heart, no interest in it. He tells us in his article *The Novel*:

> I abominate the common love story—the story of prenuptial love, almost as violently as I abhor the gramophone, the telephone, or the radio. In life both young men and young maids are peculiarly uninteresting at the time when they see each other as they are not. (p. 155)

With this feeling on the subject, he produced in *Settlers of the Marsh* the unreal, sensational scenes between Niels and Mrs. Vogel, and the likewise unconvincing, wooden ones between Niels and Ellen. . . . Thus the artist "delimits his work by his own personality." (p. 156)

But it is pleasant to turn from Mr. Grove's treatment of "pre-nuptial love" to his delineation of the old man's character in *Our Daily Bread*. It is a sharp turn. A turn from a theme abhorred to one doted upon, and the reader's interest mounts in accordance.

It is not that the old man's character is a pleasant one to follow. It is the very reverse. But it is that Mr. Grove has herein a problem he finds worth while, and therefore spreads it out before us with detailed, ambitious thoroughness and seriousness which make it not only impressive but often very human. Occasionally when taking his readers into his confidence, Mr. Grove tells them that he has a scent for tragedy, by which he frequently means for failure. And certainly anyone with a scent for failure would have a topic very much to his liking in *Our Daily Bread*. The protagonist, John Elliot, in the last score years of his life, reaps a sorry harvest after living what he conceived to be a life of serving God through all the previous years.

Mr. Grove's problem, then, is so to work out John Elliot's character that his destiny will be seen to have been bound up in it. He does this largely by showing the interplay of character between John Elliot and his ten children. In this study he is more happy in less ambitious, casual lines than in his larger dialogues and set scenes. Whenever lengthy conversation is indulged in, Mr. Grove's limits in the knowledge of human kind make it painfully unreal. In such pages we forget the characters and live with the author. Mrs. Elliot's talks with John and with Isabel before their approaching marriages illustrate this. But John Elliot's brief utterances and meditations, snapped out here and there, have a human, living ring. (p. 157)

[As it is the reader,] like his children, has lost interest in him before his end. He is not great enough, he has too meagre an endowment of heart and spirit and intellect for his fate to move one as tragic. A tragedy demands a noble man defeated by ignoble circumstances, whereas John Elliot was a selfish man betrayed by his own selfishness.

It is not necessary to treat at length the third novel, *The Yoke of Life*. It is largely working over the same ground and garnering a poorer crop. (p. 158)

Unlike *Our Daily Bread*, a large part of this third novel is concerned with the story of "pre-nuptial love", and again the author's violent abhorrence of his topic brings it to grief. . . . So far removed from credible character drawing are Len and Lydia that a reader thinks of them only as some kind of a footnote exercise to illustrate the opinions on proper endings for novels or on realism in literature expressed by Mr. Grove in *It Needs to be Said*. The foundation for their existence has been evolved out of theories, and in no scene does it hold the reader as a page of life and truth. (p. 159)

Mr. Grove's next study, *Fruits of the Earth*, seemingly attempts, as did *Our Daily Bread*, to carry on the pedestrian everyday life of a prairie farmer throughout his maturity—the very material, therefore, he shied away from in *Settlers of the March*. (p. 160)

However, it is not as fiction or a novel Mr. Grove himself intended this book. He considers it as a sort of fictionised economic history of the district. In that light, it would not be very valuable for a research student of the future, who would require a great many more facts and figures to base his own conclusions upon. It thus unfortunately falls between two stools. It is not a novel and it is not history. And moreover it is written in the most pedestrian, unimaginative narrative style of all his books. To use his own adjectives applied to the settlers, his whole chronicle might be called ''slow, deliberate, earthbound.'' . . .

But the book which has been kept for the last, *A Search for America,* is one that has a dramatic, lifelike variety which does not pall. It is a unique *Pilgrim's Progress,* partly autobiographical, partly allegoric, showing how the author's outlook upon life became changed by the encounters he had with all sorts and conditions of men in the United States and Canada. . . .

[There] is gained for Frederick Philip Grove a priceless tuition in the ties linking a man to his fellows. Henceforth his demands from life for himself were supplemented by feelings of necessity for sympathy and responsibility towards his fellowmen. And dutifully did he try not to slur over this lesson. (p. 161)

The result was that there were from now on two Mr. Groves, and they are never wholly reconciled to each other. There is first the self-disciplined Mr. Grove, the teacher, the champion, the counsellor, and the guide of his less able fellow-immigrants. So earnest has he been about this that for some thirty years it has been one of the chief factors determining his habitation and avocation.

And secondly there is the European-trained Mr. Grove—the cultured, widely-read student, the sensitive artist, sufficient unto himself, yet eager in himself to create in literature what he confidently feels he can do and what, when done, will be of value to his fellowmen. He is an accurate and delicate observer within the limits of his academic interests, and a pondering philosopher, who, however, often contents himself, in this field, with inexplicit words which he would cast aside impatiently as most inadequate were he in his rôle of observer trying to catch some transient phase of a fog or mist or other natural phenomenon. This man wishes to be solitary and laborious. . . .

In the patient, thorough finish of his workmanship, in the fastidious rightness and accuracy of his words, phrases, and descriptions, in the sensitive recording and discriminating of the delicately shaded moods of a solitary man, Mr. Grove has given us an example and set a standard of superiority which even to himself—his own best critic and his own best guide—must give great artistic satisfaction. (p. 162)

Isabel Skelton, ''Frederick Philip Grove,'' in The Dalhousie Review, *Vol. 19, No. 2, July, 1939, pp. 147-63.*

B. K. SANDWELL   (essay date 1947)

It may sometimes occur to even the most ardent admirers of *A Search for America* to wonder whether Frederick Philip Grove the man—that granite figure upon whch the storms of implacable fate have beaten in vain for forty years—may not outlive Frederick Philip Grove the novelist. Posterity can hardly fail to be interested in a life so continuously and profoundly at odds with the predominant forces of its era, especially if it turns out that the struggle was due to that life being prophetic of new forces to come. But posterity might conceivably cease to be interested in more than

a few of the creations of Grove's imagination, not because they are not greatly imagined, but because they are not bodied forth in a great literary style.

Almost the whole of Grove's writing produces, to a singular degree, the impression of being a good translation of a much better original in some other language. . . . In a sense he has no mother tongue. His style has the clarity of a man writing with great care in a slightly foreign language, but not the beauty or the grandeur of a man writing in his own language which he passionately loves. The overmastering drive of literary creation as he describes it, and he describes it in [*In Search of Myself*] very fully, seems to relate entirely to the visualizing of the characters and situations, not to the getting of them down in words, which in Grove's mind seems to be a journeyman's job not clearly distinguishable from the labour of typing the script. (p. 202)

Whether Grove is a Canadian author is a matter of definition. He certainly elected of his own choice to do his writing in Canada. But he is not an author in the current Canadian tradition. At a time when Canadian literature is reacting from colonialism to an exaggerated nationalism he is a cosmopolitan and an ardent anti-nationalist. At a time when Canadian writers are still held down by the inhibitions of Victorianism (a Puritanism run to seed and decaying on the stalk) he practices the honest frankness of a continental Europe which never knew Puritanism—a very different thing from the exhibitionist frankness of the current American output. At a time when Canadian authors are called upon to depict the Canadian scene to the patriotic end that Canadians may learn to understand it and to love it better, he depicts only that part of it which imposes on mankind the bitterest hardships in the struggle for survival. By this means he has influenced Canadian literature, and much for its good, by diverting it slightly from its too facile optimism. (pp. 205-06)

B. K. Sandwell, ''Grove's Autobiography,'' in University of Toronto Quarterly *(reprinted by permission of University of Toronto Press), Vol. 15, No. 2, January, 1947, pp. 202-06.*

NORTHROP FRYE   (essay date 1948)

Frederick Philip Grove was certainly the most serious of Canadian prose writers, and may well have been the most important one also. . . . Many of his books are out of print, and it is easy to pick up a hearsay impression that he wrote nothing but gloomy epics on the ''no fun on the farm'' theme. Those who read him, however, will find that he not only reads very well, but is full of surprising insights and an unflagging sincerity and power.

Like many Canadian writers, he has a significance for Canadians that it is difficult to share with other countries. Perhaps it is only to the Canadian reader that his faults seem to be, not only inseparable from his virtues, but curiously instructive in themselves. . . . He is perhaps our only example of an artist who made his whole life a drama of the artist's fight for survival in an indifferent society. Yet one cannot help wondering how far his integrity merged with a self-conscious pose of integrity, how much of his frustration sprang out of an obscure but profound will to be frustrated. . . . [The] question would seem impudent if even the novels did not show a conflict between integrity and something else. A fine flash of ribald comedy may be smothered by a distrust of humor far deeper than prudery, or the logical development of a scene may be suddenly twisted into moralizing. There is something profoundly Canadian about this fear of letting oneself go, and Grove speaks for a whole era of Canadian literature when he says . . . "We (the artists) aim at creating that which will live beyond Christianity and in spite of whatever sublimation may take its place. We shall most certainly fail in that; for . . . this is not a time for the production of great art; but we are content to be the forerunners of such a time; and, to say it once more, we are not much concerned about our ultimate failure or success. Failure may be tragic; but we do not shrink from tragedy." As Christianity would say, the time is at hand. (pp. 121-22)

Northrop Frye, "Canadian Dreiser," in The Canadian Forum, *Vol. XXVIII, No. 332, September, 1948, pp. 121-22.*

LORNE PIERCE   (essay date 1949)

Although Grove wrote two long books which had for their main theme his search for himself, he failed to understand his own world and his own times, much less understand himself. (p. 113)

Grove has said that all life is meeting, that meeting was the very essence of the matter. Certainly Grove had been fortunate above most of those who wrote in Canada because of the interesting places and people he had known [in Europe]. . . . Whether his contacts with the myriad new scenes and with the crowding new faces were too brief or too casual to leave any distinct impression, it is true that in none of his books has he left a commentary upon an eminent man or important town that reveals any flashing insight, any fresh probing of a man or his milieu that we desire to remember.

Perhaps it was because the chief object of his search was after all himself, the only thing that mattered to him, just as in all his novels the principal male character is a reflection of some aspect of his own character. It may be that as we fail to comprehend men and the currents of the times about us, we also fail to understand what goes on within us. There is no overwhelming belief in anything outside himself, no overmastering love, no ineffable name, and no sanctuary. He plods patiently from detail to detail, slaving at his accumulation of data, indomitable in writing and rewriting, but somehow failing to seize the core of the matter.

His tragic view of life did not so much derive from the Greeks, as from the lack of an overmastering passion that drove him out beyond himself, a sublime faith. This was the reason for the sense of futility that came in time to weigh him down and overwhelm him in bitterness. All life is conflict: man against hostile Fate, against unfriendly Nature, against the menacing advance of Time; parent against child, man against woman; the deathless dream of greatness, with no armour but courage, and the end failure and despair. Why? Grove had no answer. Grove held that the artist with his insights and experiences must meet his audience before his art is complete. That he regarded as the final irony of his own life. He and his audience had failed to meet; his books hardly sold at all, many of his MSS could not find a publisher. (pp. 114, 117)

Over Prairie Trails is the ripe fruit of the long drives Grove

made to and from his school, his reading of Thoreau and Burroughs, and his almost mystical contemplation of the prairies at all hours and under all weathers. Grove once described art as "essentially the activity of the human soul," feeling that it derives its immortality from that. Everything of value in art or life was bound up with humanity. The foundation of all life was human nature. So it is that in this book of nature essays, and its companion *The Turn of the Year* . . . , Grove not only achieves some of his most memorable descriptions but, at the same time, presents one of the most revealing disclosures of his own mind and heart. His sincerity and sanity, his integrity both as artist and man, the hard clean core of his fine intelligence, are here revealed for all to see.

Settlers of the Marsh . . . announced the appearance of a Canadian novelist who would thereafter have to be reckoned with. It dealt with the problem of personal suffering, a problem often to appear in Grove's work, and one that he hoped to deal with comprehensively and adequately in his last great book "The Seasons"—never to see the light of day. . . . With the publication of *In Search of America* . . . , an autobiographical novel, Grove's position as a leading Canadian author was secure. Then at the height of his popularity *Our Daily Bread* . . . appeared, regarded by many as his best novel. A lecture tour resulted in a collection of addresses entitled *It Needs to be Said* . . . , in which Grove discourses upon the plight of Canadian fiction, on democracy, education and kindred matters. He appeared as a crusader, something of a prophet and reformer, and essayed to be a spokesman for his race in a limited way. His cosmopolitanism prevented him from becoming sentimental and naïve. As always he is serious, revealing little humour but a good deal of irony. Irony was his most trusted weapon. (pp. 117-18)

With *Fruits of the Earth* . . . , one of his three best books, Grove took leave of the Canadian West and placed his characters over against a rural Ontario background. *Two Generations* . . . , with this setting, brought nothing particularly new to the Canadian novel, while its understanding of Ontario and its people was not impressive. Grove often sounds like an outsider. Even where he is most at home, in his Western novels, not infrequently he seems at times to be translating into English, and to be observing the scene before him from a great distance. This is even more obvious in his Ontario novels. He treats his characters always with respect but not always with understanding, and while there is no flippancy or coyness there is often little subtlety or swift insight. Especially is this true of his women characters, who are rarely portrayed with success. However, only *The Master of the Mill* can be said to be a failure. It is melodramatic and unreal. His determination to tell all results in his saying little. Where he has usually avoided sentimentality he gave way entirely, losing not only the humour that had once saved him, but even his irony. His last book, *Consider Her Ways* . . . sums up what he had been thinking about the ant, an interesting work partly scientific, partly allegorical—something of a homily on man and fate. (pp. 118-19)

Lorne Pierce, "Frederick Philip Grove," in Proceedings and Transactions of The Royal Society of Canada: Third Series *(reprinted by permission of The Royal Society of Canada), Vol. XLIII, June, 1949, pp. 113-19.*

WILFRID EGGLESTON (essay date 1957)

[Grove] in his lifetime tried many literary forms: the novel, the short story, the essay, the lyric, autobiography, literary criticism, allegory—even the detective story and the juvenile. One of the pleasant surprises to any student of Grove is his excellence in some of the minor fields. Popular attention has been focused generally on Grove's longer fiction. His most perfect work, however, is almost certainly to be found in his nature essays, his short stories, his literary criticism and his lyrics. His most perennially interesting work is to be found in his two books of autobiography. However, it is as a Canadian novelist that Grove is generally presented today. . . . (pp. 117-18)

Grove passionately wanted to write a great novel or group of great novels; I think there is no doubt about that. He greatly admired the masters in this field: Turgenev, Conrad, Meredith, Hardy, Tolstoi. He envied Hamsun, Rolvaag, Thomas Mann and Galsworthy their contemporary successes. (p. 118)

Possibly he guaranteed his own failure in advance by setting his sights impossibly high. . . . If Grove really wanted to be the Joseph Conrad or Thomas Hardy of Canada—and there is some evidence that he so aspired—it can be contended that defeat was ensured in advance.

He possessed, certainly, some of the qualities of a great literary artist. He had a thorough intellectual grasp of the nature of tragedy, as can be seen from his essays in *It Needs to be Said*. He possessed an unusually intimate acquaintance with the outstanding literary works of Europe. He was an acute student of nature. He was versed in anthropology and archaeology. His writing style was adequate. He confessed that when he was writing *Over Prairie Trails* he realized that he had at bottom no language peculiarly his own. Instead, he had half a dozen of them. But this, he was shrewd enough to see, was a disadvantage and even a misfortune. . . . But such a limitation was not in my opinion the critical one in his ambition to write great novels. For that he needed one gift above all, the divine gift of being able to give his creations abundant life. Had he possessed that gift in high degree, any stiffness in his style would have been readily forgotten.

As it is, the occasional clumsiness of his expression is not a serious defect. He mastered the essentials of English grammar, and his essay style rose at times to grandeur. His vocabulary could be painfully precise, and did not often become elegant or notably felicitous. For a novelist perhaps his most serious lack was mastery of the vernacular. He had a very limited ear for the colloquial rhythms of common speech. Indeed, it may be that his hardness of hearing and the effect it had in making him something of a recluse robbed him of the opportunities of registering often and deeply the raw stuff out of which a fine novelist creates his conversations. Grove's dialogue, especially the speech attributed to the younger generation, is one of the weaker elements of his fictional technique. Above all, he lacked humour.

He was handicapped, too, I think, in failing to find in time friendly critics and editors who might have helped him greatly to attain virtuosity in literary style. . . . [Any] conscientious editor, reading Grove's published work, itches at times to make minor textual changes here and there, to remove irritating flaws in diction or sentence construction.

To be completely fair, some of these were due to excessive haste in preparing manuscripts for the printers.

A more serious handicap for the novelist has been suggested by both Edward McCourt and Isabel Skelton. Was Grove passionately interested in the fate and welfare of mankind? He said himself that he loved nature more than man. Did he really love people well enough to understand them? His portrayal of certain types of humanity was superb, particularly old men, masterful and ruthless, and men in their senile decay. But when he tried to portray adolescents or young lovers he usually faltered. (pp. 118-19)

"What then is tragic?" Frederick Philip Grove asked in one of his essays. "To have greatly tried and to have failed; to have greatly wished and to be denied." But like Prometheus, even in our failure we exult, because we have fought with courage against the odds of life. In his later years, it is true, Grove sometimes yielded to despair and even declared his life to be an abject failure. . . . I do not think that the pessimism of his last years was warranted. . . .

Grove was the first serious exponent of realism in our fiction. He left behind him a few exquisite essays, a few penetrating pages of criticism, some powerful short stories, two fascinating books of autobiography and a group of moving lyrics. There was, perhaps, no flawless masterpiece among his seven novels, but in some of the fragmentary and truncated efforts there is more sheer power and vitality than in any of the polished minor successes of Canadian fiction. (p. 127)

> *Wilfrid Eggleston, "Frederick Philip Grove," in* Our Living Tradition: Seven Canadians, *edited by Claude T. Bissell (copyright © Canada, 1957, by University of Toronto Press), University of Toronto Press, 1957, pp. 105-37.*

THOMAS SAUNDERS (essay date 1963)

Not many people are aware of Grove as a poet, and the manuscript now housed in the University of Manitoba collection would not encourage rhapsodies over his achievements in verse. Yet it is interesting to note his apparently life-long respect for poetry and his attempts to write it. For, while most of what is contained in the University of Manitoba collection was written after 1927, and was apparently motivated by the death of his daughter, there are indications that he dabbled in poetry during most of his writing life. . . .

Grove's interest in writing poetry, however, does not seem to have given him any great mastery of the craft. (Perhaps it would be more accurate to say that he reveals mastery of the craft but little beyond that—technical proficiency within imitative limits but not the true poet's ability to give words implications and ramifications beyond themselves.) (p. 236)

Written almost exclusively in unvarying iambic pentameters, Grove's verse, . . . while technically correct, is pedestrian and dull. It seldom gets off the ground. It is obviously imitative and much of it could as well have been written in prose. (pp. 236-37)

At times he is positively banal. . . . [Aside] from their merit as verse, the poems are not without value in assessing the man. They give us something of his basic philosophy, throw light on the content and form of the novels; and in the long poem, *The Dirge*, written after the death of his daughter, we have as searching an account as we are likely to have of his emotion and thought during what was undoubtedly one of the most tragic and critical periods in his life. This poem, though philosophically more pessimistic than anything that could have come from Tennyson, is reminiscent in its form —though not in its rhyme-scheme—of *In Memoriam*. This may make its sincerity suspect by some readers. Long poems in the form of dirges over someone we profess to love can have an aspect of falseness about them. But from those who knew Grove at the time of his daughter's death, and from all we know of the rapport that seems to have existed between father and daughter, plus the natural affection that can be assumed, this does not seem to have been the case here. (p. 237)

[Something] in him clings to the thought that death cannot have the last word. Beauty changes but never dies. (p. 239)

In all his poems, [*The Dirge*] is as positive a statement on the great issues of life and death as Grove ever allowed himself. There is no suggestion of a belief in personal immortality—only an assertion of the unextinguishable nature of beauty. It is still the tragic concept that prevails—a belief in the earthly immortality of the values he cherishes, values that may be buffeted by an improvident providence but can never be totally destroyed. (p. 240)

> Thomas Saunders, "A Novelist As Poet: Frederick Philip Grove," in The Dalhousie Review, Vol. 43, No. 2, Summer, 1963, pp. 235-41.

DOUGLAS O. SPETTIGUE (essay date 1969)

[Grove] denied angrily the charge that the heroes of his prairie novels were variations on himself, that their opinions were his own. The pioneer type is one, he explains, that he personally dislikes because of its necessary materialism, its bullying aggressiveness, its readiness to sacrifice others to its aims. . . . But these may also be characteristics of the artist, and Grove shares with his pioneers at least their solitariness, their rather stoic condescension to weakness and self-indulgence, their awareness of building not for themselves but for another generation and even their grimly acquired wisdom of the futility of building at all. The artist, as Grove presents him in the essays of *It Needs to Be Said* and in *In Search of Myself,* is the creator of order. The leader is the man who can communicate his vision to others such that they will work toward its practical achievement— but the romantic artist's concern is only with the vision; he stands alone and aloof from the application. (pp. 135-36)

Grove's Marsh and prairie heroes are concerned to realize a vision of order conceived in the only terms they know— large acreage, a large house, a large crop, a large family. John Elliot's is specifically the patriarchal dream of a large family that will continue in his image. Continuity of course is the essence of vision—the order one foresees is to be realized and to be fixed. Grove's pioneer farmers may realize their material vision just because it is material and within the limits of their strong grasp. They cannot impose their vision on even the nearest of their followers. Inevitably children, followers, the future itself, betray them. (p. 136)

Phil and Alice Patterson and Phil Branden are another breed of visionary, whose goal is not a material one, not something to be grasped but a process to experience, a

state to be entered into. Phil Patterson, Phil Branden, Felix Powell (for the initials F. P.), these are obviously relatable to their author by their names. Felix, like Len Sterner and Phil Patterson, is a seeker after education. But neither Len nor Felix has Phil's great advantage, his sexlessness or at least his ability to sublimate sexual urges into intellectual activity. The protagonists who come closest to the narrator of *In Search of Myself* are seekers after fulfilment; their achievement would be not a structure of order but the order of repose, a state of rest.

When Grove entered or re-entered Canada in 1912 he hoped, according to the autobiography, to realize two aims: to establish "a domestic island in the wilderness" and to write. The domestic island, the house, the wilderness and the writing are equally part of the quest though the house image is highly ambiguous. . . . [A house,] pretentious and half-empty, inspires *Fruits of the Earth,* and *Our Daily Bread* ends with a terrible pilgrimage back to the ruin of a house. For Grove's young builders and questers the house connotes achievement, security, fixity; for the older and wiser it suggests futility and decay. *In Search of Myself* begins with a "castle"; it ends with regretful longing for a hut in the wilderness.

Grove's account of his childhood in "The House of Stene," in "The Boat" and in *In Search of Myself,* emphasizes the big, turreted house. Clark House of *The Master of the Mill* seems in many ways to be the same building; some of the same incidents occur in it. The Sam Clark who spies on Maud playing to Dr. Fry in the music room of Clark House, for instance, is a variation on the account of the boy Grove watching his mother play to the rapt old nobleman in *In Search of Myself.* And Clark House is only a small child of the master-building, the mill itself, culmination of Grove's edifice imagery. To Niels Lindstedt the house combines achievement and domestic security, to Abe it is the sign of his victory over the land; the Clark's mill, we are told, means many things to many people, from the abode of goblins to the ultimate human creation. The image of a building —and the shape of the pyramid here is appropriate—does suggest on the one hand the realizing of man's vision of order, his accomplishment seen in his terms, his own celestial city bathed in light of his own making. But then the irony that the Clarks and the workers alike are slaves of what they have built—the mill is the monument of human work imperfectly conceived. (pp. 136-37)

We do not often think of Grove as a satirist, though many readers have noticed the transition in *The Master of the Mill* from the novelist's material at the beginning toward the satirist's more abstract material at the end, and the irony of its two-part structure. But *Consider Her Ways* is a fully realized satire in which the solitary visionary struggles on against the physical assaults of nature, the destructive machines of man and the treasons of her own kind. The house image was central to the chronicles and the tragic novels; it is not the least of the ironies of *Consider Her Ways* that the visionary structure should be an ant-hill. Nor is it inappropriate that the last of Grove's publications should emphasize the single questing spirit and should associate the ideal with the agricultural way of life according to the American agrarian dream. (pp. 137-38)

The solitary self in the formicary, the lone self betrayed and abandoned and yet valiant, and surviving to complete the quest and offer to the world the wisdom gleaned in both triumphant leadership and despairing adversity, this was not only Wawa-quee but the aged author of *In Search of Myself.*

In *A Search for America* Phil Branden touched the realities behind the facade of American civilization and concluded that the frontier myth had been abandoned. Phil had been Grove's first questing visionary.... America had abandoned the dream; the quester of *In Search of Myself* must soon have learned that Canada had abandoned it too—if a nation at work can be said to abandon a vision of human order of which very few of its people could ever have been aware....

The later Grove quester knows where he is going; his teachings are not often simple, but all are related to the crusade against materialism and toward a more ethical orientation of society.... Grove did stand head and shoulders, intellectually, above his peers; though his learning is not always deep, he acknowledges that he managed to make a little go a long way. Perhaps he says too many things in his fictions; he is always teaching because there is so much the New World needs to understand about itself, so much that could not wait for slower, more palatable lessons. Grove was both by inclination and profession a teacher. If that is a fault, it is the fault we find in his writings.

It is insufficiently recognized that only Grove among our between-war novelists has commanding stature as a critic. Only Grove has organized his criticism into a coherent, a total, view not only of the specific work and author he may be examining but also of the forms of literature themselves and the necessary relation of any literary structure to the great tradition of literature. (pp. 139-40)

The addresses in *It Needs to Be Said,* and the unpublished essays and addresses, have for their subjects the nature and aims of art, the function of criticism, the characteristics of realism and the novel, the definition of tragedy, the goals of nationhood, and all to the end of making Canadians simultaneously aware of the threat they face from American materialism and the legacy that can be theirs from the high civilization of Europe. The universal response to life is tragic; the true critic is steeped in the great tradition of European literature; the greatest artist is he who can respond, and articulate his reaction, to the most varied conditions of life. In these addresses Grove returns to the image of himself and to his motives for teaching in Canada and on the frontier. Characteristically, he identifies himself as an autodidact, as one who has never had a formal education, but as one who, like the true critic, has roamed through the wide field of European literature. He condemns with surprising virulence all that America represents and applauds Canada for her two achievements: her recognition of individual nationalities within her mosaic structure, and her success to date in retaining her own individuality in the face of the almost overwhelming flood of American standardized mediocrity. He approves the pioneer districts of the Canadian West because there he still can find the uneducated but independent mind laboriously culling the riches of the Bible.... In all he says and writes he is hopefully preparing, as a precursor, a Canadian public for a Canadian literature. (pp. 144-45)

The self Grove was searching for was a complex one; so no doubt was the self that was searching.... We can say only that his supposedly autobiographical writing is largely fic-

tion. The fictional Grove, however, we do know as the Canadian representative of that old, old archetype of literature, the exile. Sometimes the exile, like the Viking crossing the Atlantic and penetrating into western America —why else does Grove make himself Swedish?—is seeking a new land in which to settle. Sometimes too he is a persecuted minority seeking a place to enshrine his values in his own way. Sometimes he is the political or social rebel planning a better society in the New World. And sometimes he is the artist as exile expressing the ultimate loneliness of all mankind in his own, seeking as his goal the place where he can create, whatever sacrifices the search and the writing may entail, but seeking also an end to his loneliness. (p. 147)

A rational man, Grove was also a romantic. His abhorrence of what he calls romanticism in fiction seems to have two bases. The first is emotional, a simple reaction against the romantic tendency he sees in himself that is linked with the determination to face life without compromise. The second is its intellectual equivalent, insofar as these can be distinguished, and might aptly be called his atheism, if that word could be freed from its taboos. He sees himself often in the role of Prometheus and yet he is not really a rebel; the call for a return to plain living and high thinking is a conservative one which only seems radical because it is so much at odds with the times. (pp. 150-51)

In romantic imagery Prometheus is the god within, struggling to break free, and in this sense romanticism is radical. The romantic supposes that his potential, an undeveloped power, is the "real" self inside him or inside oppressed society.... Grove's lesson is that no external agency, no "God," exists apart from this principle of growth which is our share in nature and which our function as evolving human beings requires us to develop as far as our potential allows. His objection to literary romanticism as he detects it in Hamsun is thus not really directed against romanticism at all but against the comic ending.... The comic ending depends on taking the short-range view, whereby the action ends with the getting of the money, the winning of the girl, the marriage, with the achieving of whatever the author has caused the audience to consider desirable. But Grove says, *a propos* of sex in literature, that marriage does not solve the problems of the relation between the sexes, it begins them ..., and he shows in the sequel to *Settlers of the Marsh* how the past continues into the future to blight the apparent promise of that novel's comic ending. Much of the flatness, the abstraction, the remoteness complained of in Grove's fiction is due to his insistence on taking the long view, whereas the novel characteristically gains its effects from concentrating on the short-range and enlarging the trivia of the twenty-four-hour day. In the very long view life is an increasingly meaningless cycle, the round of evolution-devolution with which *The Master of the Mill* ends, or all but ends except for that last statement of faith in Promethean man's potential. (pp. 153-54)

It is Grove's romanticism which insists there can be nothing outside himself to build on and which gives the bleakness to his books. Yet he is stronger in his bleak loneliness than when, as in the poems, he tries to create a Hardy-like god to defy in the role of Prometheus. But it also is true that the bleak view was intolerable without the immediate comfort to be secured through the "domestic island." And therefore the somewhat paradoxical combination of Grove's domestic details with his role as rootless wanderer. . . . [Grove] thought he could be for Canadian literature the Emerson and the Thoreau, the pioneer, the prototype, the model and the master of literature in an unformed society, the saint and martyr of spiritual values in a primitive materialistic setting, the last survivor of the great tradition perpetuating its record for posterity, the tragic example of the good life whose story would purge, through pity and fear, the consciousness of a nation.

His reach exceeded his grasp, by far. There are areas of sensibility of which he seems totally unaware. His symbolism, often powerful, lacks subtlety. Compared with the European authors he claims to have known, his artistic experience, the sense of an "esthetic," in his confessional writings seems lamentably absent. He opens whole new areas for the Canadian novel, but we never become intimately involved with his characters even when we acknowledge their reality. Grove was not ultimately a novelist but a confessional writer and essayist. In the novel many Canadians would attempt in part what he attempted and with greater success in their narrower fields, particularly in their ability to take us inside their characters. But when we consider all his fiction, Grove's single hero-with-variations is seen to complete and absorb his predecessors and even in his failures to point the way for many of his successors. He therefore plays now, twenty years after his death, something of the exalted and tragic role he set out to play in Canada between the wars. He chose the road less travelled, when there were few to choose it with him, and that, in the story of Canadian fiction, has made all the difference. (pp. 154-57)

> *Douglas O. Spettigue, in his* Frederick Philip Grove *(reprinted by permission of Douglas & McIntyre Ltd.), Copp Clark, 1969, 175 p.*

RONALD SUTHERLAND (essay date 1969)

The title [of *Consider Her Ways*], of course, is from Proverbs 6:6, King James Version of the Bible: "Go to the ant, thou sluggard; consider her ways, and be wise." Grove had begun the book more than twenty-five years before it appeared in print, and it is a unique accomplishment in many respects. It is partly in the tradition of the beast fable, being the story of a "scientific" expedition by a group of ants from Venezuela to examine conditions in North America. On the other hand, it has something in common with the best science fiction, for it incorporates, dramatizes and extends a mass of fascinating information on the actual nature and behaviour of ants. (p. 33)

Consider Her Ways, however, is by no means a mere popularization of ant lore. The story, purportedly communicated to the human recorder by means of mental telepathy, is told from the point of view of an old ant called Wawa-quee, commander-in-chief and, eventually, sole survivor of the expedition. Grove succeeds in giving each of the leading ants a distinct personality; and with respect to suspension of disbelief, *Consider Her Ways* is a tour de force equal to if not better than *Gulliver's Travels*. The reader is quickly involved in a developing drama, which features not only a series of physical challenges but a conflict of personality and motivation between Wawa-quee and Assa-ree, commander of the army of 10,000 warrior ants acting as an escort for the expedition. In the course of the story, Grove

manages to illustrate with novel perspicacity the age-old yet very current dichotomy between the aims of pure science and those of the military, a dichotomy which can disappear if the scientist is willing to ignore methods and ulterior objectives and to concentrate rather on immediate goals. (pp. 33-4)

Like Jonathan Swift, Grove achieves the suspension of disbelief by careful attention to detail and point of view. Once the reader has granted telepathic communication between the aged Wawa-quee and the entomologist-recorder, then the book progresses without strain to the imagination. (p. 34)

[*Consider Her Ways*] abounds with fascinating incidents skillfully presented. For sustained narrative interest it is probably Grove's best book.

There is, of course, a great deal of irony in the book, arising especially from the ants' observations of man and his habits. Ant scholars, for instance, have difficulty understanding how the same man can appear at different times in different coverings, and they come to the studied conclusion that man can "molt at will." . . .

Where *Consider Her Ways* falls far short of *Gulliver's Travels* is in the poignancy of the satire. It seems likely that Grove intended the book indirectly to attack man's self-centered arrogance and such shortcomings as materialism, philistinism, and wastefulness. The book does indeed attack these things, and if an argument against slavery were needed, then the section dealing with the slave-holding Polyergus ants would serve admirably. But Grove defeats his own satirical purposes by focusing the reader's attention too exclusively on the adventures of the ant characters he has created. Implications and observations pertaining to the human race appear irrelevant, sometimes forced. As social satire, *Consider Her Ways* is ineffectual; as an intriguing, highly informative, and singular narrative, the book is a success. (p. 35)

> *Ronald Sutherland, in his* Frederick Philip Grove *(© 1969 by McClelland and Stewart Limited; reprinted by permission of The Canadian Publishers, McClelland and Stewart Limited, Toronto), McClelland, 1969, 64 p.*

DESMOND PACEY (essay date 1971)

The general image of Grove is of a powerful but rather awkward and gloomy novelist whose portrayal of pioneer life in the Canadian West has documentary value but is somewhat deficient in literary subtlety and sophistication. This is not altogether fair to Grove the prairie novelist, since there is considerable stress in the four prairie novels [*Settlers of the Marsh, Our Daily Bread, The Yoke of Life,* and *Fruits of the Earth*] . . . on man's capacity to endure, and more literary skill than critics have yet perceived. It is less fair to Grove the novelist, since the other four of his novels [*A Search for America, Two Generations, The Master of the Mill,* and *Consider Her Ways*] . . . are not set on the prairies, are not especially gloomy, and are quite experimental and varied in technique. It is still less fair to Grove the writer, since his three books of essays [*Over Prairie Trails, The Turn of the Year,* and *It Needs to be Said*] . . . show him to have been a man of great literary and social sophistication, alert to the most delicate nuances of natural beauty, erudite in the literature and philosophy of the ancient and modern world, knowledgeable about political history and theory, and intelligently concerned about contemporary social issues. Most important for our present purpose, the short stories of Grove simply do not fit the stereotype of him and his work.

One's dominant impression on reading the twenty-five short stories in [*Tales from the Margin*] is of their variety. They vary in setting. . . . They vary also in their characters—most of the characters are prairie farmers and their wives, but there are also storekeepers, travelling salesmen, horse drovers, school-teachers, auctioneers, doctors, French aristocrats, unemployed wanderers, and a mountainous midwife. As they vary in their occupations, the characters vary in age and personality. . . . Above all, as a corrective to those who think of Grove as the master of a single mood of tragic bitterness, they vary enormously in mood and tone. There is the grim resolution shading to eager hopefulness of ''Lazybones,'' the boyish excitement and adventurousness of ''Drovers,'' the farcical comedy of ''A Poor Defenceless Widow.'' . . . (pp. 5-6)

The second most powerful impression that one gets from reading these stories is of Grove's basically affirmative vision. On the whole, the stories are much more affirmative, much more optimistic, than the novels. From the novels one tends to carry away an impression of man's puny vulnerability in the face of Nature's hostile power and Time's less spectacular but no less fatal attrition; in the stories, on the other hand, one is impressed more with the ingenuity, variety and resourcefulness of human nature, and the destructive forces of storm and decay are given less emphasis. (pp. 6-7)

It is interesting, in view of the snobbery and austerity often attributed to Grove's outlook, that even the failures or villains of these stories elicit his compassion rather than his contempt, his tolerant sympathy rather than his arrogant scorn. . . . They are not Grove's types, obviously—but he is rather pleased that such people exist, to add to the variety of the human parade. A warmer, if half-reluctant, sympathy is obvious in Grove's portraits of ne'er-do-wells such as the lazy husband in ''Lazybones,'' the young brother who cannot be persuaded to be prudent in ''The Spendthrift,'' the bewildered hired man in ''The Extra Man,'' and the gullible husband in ''The Dead-Beat.'' We feel ourselves drawn to these characters in spite of their manifest inadequacies—and it is clearly Grove who does the drawing.

A concomitant surprise for those who hold to the stereotype image of Grove is the gift of comedy that these stories reveal. It has become one of the clichés of Canadian criticism to say that Grove is humourless. . . . [But these stories] prove that he had a sense of humour, and that his humour could vary from farce through irony to satire. ''A Poor Defenceless Widow'' is a good, though by no means a distinguished, farce; ''The Agent,'' a much better story, mingles irony and pathos in a very poignant and memorable fashion. . . . (pp. 7-8)

The final rather surprising feature of these stories is the frequent excellence of their dialogue. It is often said that Grove did not have a good ear for colloquial language, and that therefore his dialogue is at best overly formal, at worst awkward and stiff. There are occasional awkwardnesses of

style in these stories—we shall look at some of them later—but they are seldom found in the dialogue. . . . Part of Grove's claim to documentary accuracy may certainly be based on his adroitness in catching the exact words, rhythms and tones of the speech of his time and place.

But if the stories contain some surprises, and decisively modify the conventional view of Grove's work, they also confirm some of his recognized strengths.

There is first of all Grove's descriptive power, especially the power to describe the prairie landscape which he so brilliantly displayed in *Over Prairie Trails* and *The Turn of the Year* and in the prairie novels. No other writer—and there have been some very good prairie writers, such as Robert Stead, Martha Ostenso, Sinclair Ross and Margaret Laurence—no other writer has so clearly brought out the variety of landscape to be found in that huge area which we lump under the simple name of the prairie. (pp. 8-9)

Setting is obviously very important in Grove's stories. He is always at pains to tell us quite exactly where the action of the story takes place: he never allows his characters to lack a local habitation. His descriptions are often so sensitive as to enrich the story: he sees beauty and mystery in landscapes which a lesser writer would pass over as commonplace. . . . The symbolic use of landscape is often found in Grove's work alongside his precise, almost scientifically accurate notations of natural phenomena. In such cases, the setting ceases to be a mere background for the characters and events and becomes an organic part of the story. Grove's skill with this kind of writing is almost clearly apparent in ''Saturday Night at the Crossroads.'' (pp. 10-11)

This combination of accurate observation with symbolic suggestiveness is found not only in Grove's descriptions of landscape and wild creatures, but also in his descriptions of people and domestic animals. (p. 12)

Another facet of Grove's descriptive power is his sensitive awareness of and detailed attentiveness to weather, climate, and the seasons. Almost always we are told the time of day, the season of the year and the state of the weather. In ''Lazybones'' the action runs from dawn to dusk, and we are made aware of all the gradations in the turn of the day by references to the light, the temperature, the preparation of meals, the freshness of tiredness of the characters; the season is early summer, as we know from the fact that the haying is just finished and summer-fallowing is about to begin; the weather is sunny but a strong wind is blowing (''the grass was bending before the wind of the day''). This story is almost as intricately and carefully constructed as any ode by Milton or Keats. Not all of the stories are constructed so perfectly, but the best of them are. . . . (p. 14)

Grove's eye for significant and symbolic detail is almost equally apparent in his descriptions of the exteriors and interiors of houses, barns, stores and other man-made structures. Kalad's store, in ''Saturday Night at the Crossroads,'' becomes a multifaceted symbol. The fact that it has a huge store room in front, and tiny cubbyholes for living in at the rear, symbolizes Kalad's materialism: he cares more for trade than for living. The rickety nature of the structure —black tar paper held in place by laths nailed to ''the thinnest of box lumber''—suggests both Kalad's thriftiness and the fragility of human structures in the face of a powerful wilderness. . . .

A more unusual feature of Grove's descriptive capacity is his detailed and almost delighted observation of daily work: one has to go to Hardy, Zola or Dreiser to find other writers who find such congenial material in what are usually dismissed as humdrum tasks. (p. 15)

This faithful attention to the exterior world suggests that Grove is a very objective writer. The same objectivity is noticeable in his creation of character: Grove appears as a very minor character—the schoolteacher—in "Saturday Night at the Crossroads," and it might be argued that there is something of himself in Dave Chisholm, since the latter reads Tolstoi, Swift, Thoreau and Hamsun, but for the most part his characters are quite unlike himself, and there is little or no autobiography in the stories apart from "The Boat." His characters are mainly uneducated manual workers of undereducated salesmen, and yet Grove manages to enter into their consciousness, to share their feelings. Indeed his psychological acumen almost matches his sensitivity to landscape and climate.... There is no patronage or condescension in Grove's accounts of the dreams of these people, nor in any of his attitudes towards them.

The prevailing attitude of the author in these stories, in fact, is that of compassion. Whatever may be true of Grove's novels—and the conclusions to be drawn from these stories make another look at the novels imperative—the short stories reveal him as a humanist and a meliorist rather than a naturalist and pessimist. (pp. 16-17)

As one reads and re-reads the stories—and since they are subtle they demand and deserve re-reading—one accumulates a gathering sense of a single imaginative world as surely as one does from reading the fiction of Thomas Hardy. The fact that characters recur from story to story—characters such as Abe Standish, Dave Chisholm, Kalad, Cundy, Bill Orting—helps to create this impression, but is not decisive. The decisive fact is that the stories all give us a sense of a real, physical world in which credible human beings struggle to realize their dreams and to maintain their identities in face of an environment which is only occasionally beneficent and which frequently challenges them with hostility.

Technically, the stories have certain flaws. Sometimes the language is too formal, as when Elizabeth Hurst reflects that Walt "had enabled her to remain within her own tradition" or Grove uses slightly archaic words such as "afoot," "alighted," or "espying." Sometimes there are unnecessary words, as when in "Marsh Fire" he speaks of "retreating before the heat that made itself felt," and sometimes his sentences are so long and cumbersome as to be virtually unintelligible.... (p. 18)

Apart from such minor flaws, Grove's stories occasionally have deficiencies in structure. The best of them, as we have seen, are cunningly constructed, but some of them tend to be diffuse and rambling. "Herefords in the Wilderness," for example, moves slowly and circuitously, and only justifies its inclusion in this collection by its descriptive power and its powerful atmospheric effects.... One wonders whether some of these less cunningly constructed stories were originally part of novels rather than stories in their own right, as "The First Day of an Immigrant" seems to be a discarded first chapter of *Settlers of the Marsh* and one or two of the other stories read like left-over chapters from *Our Daily Bread*.

These technical deficiencies, however, are not frequent enough to impair seriously the value of this collection. As a whole, the stories impress us by their power to create a most varied group of characters set in an environment which is described both accurately and suggestively, and to evoke in realistic and yet compassionate terms a moving sense of man's struggle to endure and slowly to prevail. (p. 19)

> *Desmond Pacey, in his introduction to* Tales from the Margin: The Selected Short Stories of Frederick Philip Grove, *edited by Desmond Pacey (copyright © McGraw-Hill Ryerson Limited, 1971; reprinted by permission), Ryerson Press, 1971, pp. 1-19.*

ANTHONY W. RILEY (essay date 1973)

The title of this paper is a deliberate misnomer: it *should,* of course, read "The Novels of Felix Paul Greve." ... No one, I think, would maintain that they are great novels, and yet for the Canadian Literature specialist they are well worth reading, if only because they represent the first attempts of the young Grove to express himself artistically through the medium of the novel. (p. 55)

[The] influence of Naturalism is manifest in his novels, just as George's influence is to be felt in his poems. ...

Both *Fanny Essler* and *Maurermeister Ihles Haus* are mainly concerned with women from the lower-middle or middle classes. (p. 56)

[Grove] was not an innovator as far as form was concerned, nor, may I add, in style or language. Both novels are narrated omnisciently in the third person, the action of the novels is seen mainly from the point of view of the protagonists (from Fanny's on the one hand, and in the case of *Maurermeister Ihles Haus* from that of the three main characters [Ihle, his wife and their daughter Suse], though Suse is in fact the person who provides the focus of attention of the novel as a whole). (p. 59)

What is fascinating about both novels is in my view the extraordinary empathy Greve is able to create in his readers for the heroines: Fanny is not a "likeable" person—intelligent, but poorly educated, though with aspirations to higher things, vain, selfish, cruel—both to her family and relatives and to her various lovers—with sensual appetites bordering at times on the nymphomaniacal, and yet ... by some strange means we feel with her, sympathize with her plight, understand her dreams and longings for the fairy-tale prince who would take her out of the confines of the life or lives she leads. When she dies at the end of the novel at the age of thirty, one cannot help but feel the waste of her life, which perhaps in different circumstances might have been productive. Fanny is certainly not a "schematic figure lacking credibility," as some critics have said of Grove's characters. My major criticism of *Fanny Essler* is its prolixity: Greve dwells too long on Fanny's psychology and tends to lack any sense of artistic economy. (p. 62)

Greve's skill—and daring—in conjuring up the emotional life of a woman of the 1890's is great. But the sexual theme is balanced by another just as important and all-pervading topic: money.... The power of money—and the things it can buy—in Wilhelminian Germany is felt on every page of the novel. The material things of life: the furniture, clothing, the food, the apartments of both the rich and the lower classes are all depicted in great detail. Money is, in a way, Fanny's downfall, and at the same time Greve creates sympathy for her in the reader by showing that she is the victim of the system rather than a manipulator of it. Time and again, Fanny stubbornly refuses to ask her lovers for money, thinking that they should give it to her simply because they love her. But as he says in the motto of his novel, Greve never passes judgement: he depicts, like his Naturalist forbears, leaving the reader to draw his own conclusions.

In *Maurermeister Ihles Haus* money plays an equally important role. Ihle is no miser, but he has no comprehension of what money could buy if he were open-minded and more cultured. The pathetic scene . . . where Frau Ihle cuts out pictures from illustrated magazines and has them expensively framed while her husband is away is particularly telling. True, Frau Ihle is on the verge of madness, but the tragedy of a woman, brutally dominated by a husband, kept short of money, and yet who aspires to higher things, is moving. Indeed, the theme of women's aspirations blocked off by circumstances, education, and above all by domineering husbands and lovers, who keep their women in their place, i.e. in the kitchen and in bed, is one of the most interesting in both novels. Fanny Essler manages to become emancipated, yet she is no Hedda Gabler—she is not calculating or cold enough, even though she once wanted to play the part in a theatrical performance. . . .

It is the psyche of Fanny and Suse (and I would draw your attention to Greve's skill at depicting a child's and adolescent's mind in the case of Suse, especially her relationship with school friends, her teachers, and parents—this I find to be one of the best parts of the novel)—it is the female psyche into which Greve probes. Fanny's sexual problems, for example, are revealed in an almost clinical description worthy of Freud. . . . Fanny's dreams are also recorded carefully by Greve, and her fantasies—culminating in the delirium before her death—as well as the development of Frau Ihle from a frightened woman to paranoiac—might well have been taken from Freud's case book. The power of eros—Suse's and above all Fanny's slow sexual awakening—dominates pages of the novels just as the power of money does. The men, on the other hand, do tend to be rather schematically portrayed in *Fanny Essler*; the swashbuckling, moustache-twirling Prussian officers, the men-about-town, the artists and writers, are not portrayed with anyting like the vividness and depth [of] the women. The lower classes, both petite-bourgeoisie and workers, men and women alike, remain a sort of backdrop, albeit an important one, to the stage dominated by the heroine. Nevertheless, Greve's portrayal of, for example, the working-class family from whom Fanny rents a room in Berlin, whose hard struggle to earn a living does not embitter them but rather highlights their kindness and humanity to Fanny, is of remarkable sensitivity. . . . I may add that the evocative depiction of a sunset in the lowlands of Pomerania, as observed by Suse, reminds one of Grove's later descriptions of prairie landscapes.

True to Naturalistic precepts, Greve reproduces local dialect and speech-patterns (including Pomeranian, Berlin, and Cologne dialects) in dialogues involving members of the working-classes. He does this sparingly and effectively, but where his Naturalism does tend to irritate is his habit of

describing each new character, even those who appear only very briefly and who have no influence on the development of the plot, in great detail. For example, each of Suse's school teachers is described in this way: peculiarities of their eyes, nose, hair, lips, figure, clothing, etc. are dwelt upon with loving care, and the result is that after the reader has realized that this person has no further role in the novel, he asks himself why Greve took all the trouble. A comparison, say, with the narrative techniques used by Thomas Mann in his early works (e.g. in novellas like *Tonio Kröger* or *Tristan*) reveals how fumbling Greve's art is in this respect. . . . Nor does Greve use his numerous descriptions of the physical characteristics of a host of minor characters to bind together, musically, as it were, different parts of his novel as Mann does in his virtuoso technique employing the same sort of characterizing *leitmotif*. It is perhaps unfair to compare Mann and Greve, but it does give a measure of their relative rank. . . . To my mind, [Greve's] novels are still too firmly anchored in Naturalism—and in this sense he is an epigone—to allow him to break new ground. . . . It is in a sense an irony of fate that Greve probably left Germany in 1909, the year before the publication of Rilke's extraordinary novel *The Notebooks of Ilte Laurids Brigge*, a psychological novel (and much more besides) of European significance; and 1910 was also the year from which literary historians date the beginnings of literary Expressionism in Germany, the movement that was destined radically to change the face of German literature. Just as in his poetry, Greve had leaned heavily on the liturgical incantations and the cult of the beautiful typical of the George-Kreis (Greve's only published volume of poems, *Wanderungen* . . . might be taken as a parody of George!), so in his novels he remained a follower rather than an innovator. Had Greve stayed in Germany he might (with his undoubted talents) have produced more innovative work of better quality in German. By emigrating to North America he deliberately cut all ties to his native culture and language, but retained in my view the cast of mind which had produced his early German novels. (pp. 62-5)

> *Anthony W. Riley, "The German Novels of Frederick Philip Grove" (originally a speech delivered at The Grove Symposium at the University of Ottawa in May, 1973), in The Grove Symposium, edited by John Nause (copyright © Canada, 1974, by the Hopkins Club), University of Ottawa Press, 1974, pp. 55-66.*

DOUGLAS O. SPETTIGUE (essay date 1973)

[Felix Paul Greve's] early poems were rather unsuccessful attempts to imitate his model [Stefan George]. The difficulty was that he was too subservient; he could reproduce the settings and tones of George's lyrics but he could not make them his own. He chose George as his model not only to win the master's patronizing favour but because he saw or thought he saw one large general movement in nineteenth-century arts which linked them all together and led them toward Aestheticism and Decadence—and thence, perhaps, to himself. At first he may have thought of himself, like George, as the culmination of the movement, the poet to whom all the others had tended and in whom they now would find their perfection. If so, the illusion did not long survive publication.

Ironically, or prophetically in view of his later career, the poems were entitled *Wanderungen,* the Wanderings of Felix Paul Greve.... (pp. 63-4)

The book's rubric, "Vernimm! Ich bin aus Tantalos' Geschlecht" is from Goethe's *Iphigenie auf Tauris* . . ., which may suggest a young man who feels he has lost the favour of the gods but is still aspiring. The poems lack immediacy; they are dreamy, romantic, and they tend to show a youth prematurely beaten down, a loser in love, an aspirant to the heights who so often finds himself back down on the flats, just going on. He is a divided person, half the time imagining himself great, even divinely inspired, the other half doubting his mission. The first poem, "Question," has a participant in a religious festival draw suddenly apart to ask himself "Am I chosen, or only called?"

There are 23 poems in the booklet, but anyone who has wondered at the monotony of form in the typescript of Grove's unpublished Canadian poems—those endless rhyming quatrains—will find their original here. "Question" is a sonnet; all the rest but one are pentameter quatrains, most of them rhyming alternately. They are arranged, like George's lyrics, in titled sections.... (p. 64)

The "Caesar's Time" verses are directly modelled on Stefan George's historical poems. George, who considered himself the chosen leader, seems to have felt an affinity with the Rome of the first centuries of the Christian era, particularly that of Heliogabalus the priest-emperor.... The affinity is not evident in Greve, but only the similar subject. The poems of "Caesar's Time" picture, with a minimum of detail—purple tapestries, silken throne—a man of almost godlike power over whom broods nonetheless the shadow of fate. The great man disdains the crowd at his feet, but he has no illusions: all life is mummery. The "Wanderings" poems are romantically melancholy. The first of them has the speaker—it sounds like the poet himself—regretting his misplaced youthful scorn for his homeland and his idealizing of Mediterranean landscapes, which he now renounces.... The "Times of Day" poems are similar in setting: three impressionistic responses at dawn, midday and evening. In the last of them the poet looks back on the poems once inspired in him by Italy as flaccid vessels of sorrow bound together by the sound of parting bells. "Vagrant" records an allegorical solitary journey among mountains. The poet blunders into the realm of spirits who threaten him. But his high ambition and his jaded worldly wisdom are proof against fear: "I do not value my life. If ye can take it, then take it!" Characteristically, he means to ascend to the peaks and look down on the world of men below him. For the modern reader, all these poems seem to be written from some such remoteness —there is nothing in them to suggest any commitment to mankind or to actual life.

The long "Legend" or "Saga" is the most interesting of the poems. It is the tale of an allegorical eagle which, wounded, is caught by peasant children and subjected to cruel indignities until rescued by a herbalist, the local healer, who binds its broken wing and cares for it. But legend reports that a tame eagle brings good luck to the village. The peasants therefore storm the healer's hut, kill him when he resists, and steal the eagle, which they then keep in a cage. But one day as they walk to church the healer appears before them and as they flee in terror passes through the village to set the eagle free. The eagle soars again but now in a spirit of revenge returns frequently to the area to raid—like Nietzsche's eagle—the peasants' flocks.

Here again one detects in the poet something of the disappointed or socially withdrawn youth who feel himself superior to his fellows, one who may have been encouraged, "saved" for learning or art by a mentor—such figures are frequent in Grove—and who, his promise still not acknowledged by the crowd, seeks for himself a vicarious revenge: some day he will get back at them and they will have to acknowledge him. One notes, too, that for all the poet's romanticism, this poem has no illusions about peasants or children: their cruelty is indifferent, amoral, perfectly natural. (pp. 65-6)

Of the 23 *Wanderungen* poems, sixteen locate the subject or the viewer on a mountain or hilltop, an upper window or stair, or set him apart in a socially exalted position; and even those that are not so set are detached in unapproachable melancholy or alone on "the mountain of individual being." This suggests to us a young man steeped in the Byronic manner, a pose reinforced by Stefan George's belief that the poet was a person apart, divinely inspired, virtually divine himself, and above the petty interests of the bourgeois, the workman and the peasant. At the same time the degree to which this role is emphasized in *Wanderungen* implies the young poet's actual isolation and the absence of any sustaining social commitment or purpose that might have given direction and meaning to his early life and work. (p. 68)

Douglas O. Spettigue, in his F.P.G.: The European Years *(copyright © 1973 by Douglas O. Spettigue; reprinted by permission of Oberon Press), Oberon Press, 1973, 254 p.*

A. W. RILEY and DOUGLAS O. SPETTIGUE (essay date 1976)

Both *Fanny Essler* and *The Master Mason's House* deal broadly with the emancipation of women or at least with their struggle against male tyranny as manifest in late 19th-century Germany. Perhaps it is not too much to say that Greve's setting, like Grove's, is darkest domestica no matter where its location. His care for the feel of place makes him a regionalist in a sense, whether of German Pomerania or the Canadian prairies, but his broader subject is the human condition—man wound in the web of mortality, trapped in the cycle of time. And the setting in which he dramatizes the age-old predicament, whatever the geography, is the domestic arena in which the sexes and the generations battle without quarter and without reconciliation. Richard Ihle is only the first of FPG's defeated strong men; his successors are Niels Lindstedt, John Elliot, Abe Spalding, Ralph Paterson. Bertha Ihle is the precursor of Bertha Rutherford, Martha Elliot and Ruth Spalding. Susie Ihle has her successors in Ellen Amundsen, Jane Atkinson and Maud Clark, as Fanny Essler has in Clara Vogel, but Susie is on her way to being a Fanny Essler—or another Elsa—herself. (pp. 7-8)

The charge made against Greve's novels (and against Grove's) that they lack a focus and a controlling thought, may therefore be countered by the recognition that this is their thought: that there is no peace in this life because there is never equality and hence no lasting truce between the contending forces on the domestic battleground.

It is possible, then, to read *The Master Mason's House* with some appreciation of the apparently superfluous detail. Some episodes seem to have no purpose—the schoolroom scenes for instance, . . . but in retrospect they are seen to have unity. Young sexuality, Freudian complexes, fear, successful deceit or vain flight, these are their common thread. Even the children's excursion to the "Sold" and their being lost in the marsh and rescued only accidentally by one literally deaf to all cries, has its point in this novel in which fate is merely the human condition.

And so with the fine detail: every character must appear full-face and with every item of his or her dress complete, every room with all its furnishings must be visually present. As the reader of Grove would expect, Ihle's house is bigger than others, and all its appointings individualize it for us and tell us that individuality is in its particularity—while it lasts. But like the Clarks of Grove's *The Master of the Mill*, Ihle is its master only while his children are young enough to believe he is. (p. 8)

> *A. W. Riley and Douglas O. Spettigue, in their introduction to* The Master Mason's House *by Frederick Philip Grove (copyright © 1976 by Oberon Press; reprinted by permission of Oberon Press), Oberon Press, 1976, pp. 5-10.*

ADDITIONAL BIBLIOGRAPHY

Birbalsingh, Frank. "Grove and Existentialism." *Canadian Literature*, No. 43 (Winter 1970): 67-76.
> Examination of Grove's literary treatment of his conceptions of free will and humanism, and a comparison of his beliefs with those of Sartre, Camus, and other writers.

Holliday, W. B. "Frederick Philip Grove: An Impression." *Canadian Literature*, No. 3 (Winter 1960): 17-22.
> Sketch of Grove's character and beliefs by a man who at one time served as custodian of the author's farmhouse.

Keith, W. J. "F. P. Grove's 'Difficult' Novel: *The Master of the Mill*." *Ariel* 4, No. 2 (April 1973): 34-48.
> Study of *The Master of the Mill*, examining its thematic divergences and similarities with Grove's other novels, and assessing Grove's difficult style as a function of his purpose.

MacDonald, R. D. "The Power of F. P. Grove's *The Master of the Mill*." *Mosaic* VII, No. 2 (Winter 1974): 89-100.
> Essay on the theme of the absurd quest as found in *The Master of the Mill*.

McCourt, Edward. "Spokesman of a Race?" In his *The Canadian West in Fiction*, pp. 56-69. Toronto: The Ryerson Press, 1970.
> A discussion of several of Grove's prairie novels. The critic hails Grove's talent, but underscores the author's inability to create convincing characters.

McMullin, Stanley E. "Grove and the Promised Land." *Canadian Literature*, No. 49 (Summer 1971): 10-19.
> An examination of the various elements of the Mosaic Promised Land motif present in Grove's novels.

Mitchell, Beverly. "The 'Message' and the 'Inevitable Form' in *The Master of the Mill*." *Journal of Canadian Fiction* III, No. 3 (1974): 74-9.
> An examination of three levels of meaning to be found in *The Master of the Mill*.

Nause, John, ed. *The Grove Symposium*. Ottawa: University of Ottawa Press, 1974, 110 p.
> A collection of papers delivered at the University of Ottawa's Grove Symposium in 1973. Aspects of Grove's published and unpublished work, German and Canadian, are examined by such scholars as Lorraine McMullen, Anthony W. Riley, and Wilfrid Eggleston.

Pacey, Desmond. "Frederick Philip Grove: A Group of Letters." *Canadian Literature*, No. 11 (Winter 1962): 28-38.
> Correspondence between the critic and Grove, illuminating some of Grove's beliefs and intents in his writings.

Spettigue, Douglas O. "The Grove Enigma Resolved." *Queen's Quarterly* 79, No. 1 (Spring 1972): 1-2.
> Article in which Grove's real name and details of his well-hidden past were revealed for the first time.

Stobie, Margaret R. *Frederick Philip Grove*. New York: Twayne Publishers, 1973, 206 p.
> Excellent biographical and critical book on Grove and his works.

Thompson, J. Lee. "In Search of Order: The Structure of Grove's *Settlers of the Marsh*." *Journal of Canadian Fiction* III, No. 3 (1974): 65-73.
> Examination of *Settlers of the Marsh*, centering on four themes found throughout the novel.

Woodcock, George. "Possessing the Land: Notes on Canadian Fiction." In *The Canadian Imagination: Dimensions of a Literary Culture*, edited by David Staines, pp. 69-96. Cambridge: Harvard University Press, 1977.*
> Notes Grove's European literary heritage of symbolism and naturalism. The critic sees *The Master of the Mill* as Grove's greatest work.

Thomas Hardy

1840-1928

English novelist, poet, dramatist, short story writer, and essayist.

Hardy is considered one of the greatest novelist in English literature. His work resembles that of earlier Victorian novelists in technique, while in subject matter it daringly violated literary traditions of the age. In contrast to the Victorian ideal of progress, Hardy depicted human existence as a tragedy determined by powers beyond the individual's command, in particular the external pressures of society and the internal compulsions of character. His desire to reveal underlying forces directing the lives of his characters led him to realistically examine love and sexuality in his fiction, a practice that often offended his readers and endangered his literary reputation.

Hardy was born and raised in the region of Dorset, which he used as the basis for the Wessex countryside of his novels, short stories, and poems. Hardy initially sought recognition as a poet but turned to novel writing as a more realistic way to literary success. His unpublished first novel, *The Poor Man and the Lady,* was rejected for being overly satirical. George Meredith, then a reader for Chapman & Hall Publishing Company, advised the young author to incorporate the plot devices of popular novels into his work.

Taking this advice Hardy wrote *Desperate Remedies,* a novel that embodies many of the characteristics associated with the author's style. Hardy considered strict realism an insufficient method for creating interesting fiction; consequently his novels display artificially elaborate plots, highly unrealistic use of coincidence, and sometimes Gothic melodrama. The first major novel to display the definitive strengths of Hardy's narrative art was *Far from the Madding Crowd.* The psychological portrait of Bathsheba Everdene foreshadows Hardy's genius for sympathetic portrayal of a feminine protagonist, which would reach its height in *Tess of the d'Urbervilles.* Some critics have remarked that Hardy's strongest analysis of a male character is to be found in Michael Henchard, the protagonist of *The Mayor of Casterbridge.* This novel introduces the concept that "character is fate," and develops this theme into a tragedy of psychological determinism. The heroine of *Tess of the d'Urbervilles* is sometimes considered to be the single figure in Hardy to escape this determinism, her tragedy deriving largely from conflict with a restrictive social order. In addition to profound character studies, Hardy is esteemed for the vivid sense of natural forces in his novels, an intangible mood most dramatically symbolized by Egdon Heath in *The Return of the Native.*

Hardy achieved enormous success as a novelist, but his work was often compromised by the demands of popular taste. He consistently veiled the morally volatile situations in his novels with ambiguous description. Always subject to criticism, Hardy incurred especially harsh attacks for his unidealized portrayal of human relationships in *Jude the Obscure.* His reaction to this criticism was to cease writing novels and devote himself to poetry, which he had written intermittently throughout his career.

Hardy's poems express the same pessimism that serves as the foundation of his novels. Critics have noted, however, that Hardy's emphasis on abstract ideas in the poems interferes with their literary value, much of his poetry constituting a sermon on pessimistic themes. Though faulted for their sometimes clumsy structure, these poems are often praised for a lyric power unique in its particular blend of traditional and experimental forms. Critical opinion for the most part agrees that only a fraction of Hardy's poetry warrants serious consideration, though conceding this sufficient to rank him as a major poet. In addition to novels and poetry, Hardy also wrote several volumes of short stories. Like his poems, the stories are frequently concerned with grotesque situations in the lives of rural characters, and are often bitterly ironic. "The Three Strangers" and "The Withered Arm" exemplify Hardy's best work in this genre.

Hardy called his last major work, *The Dynasts,* an "epic drama" and designed it as a summation of his views on existence. Juxtaposing the historical drama of the Napoleonic wars with a Greek chorus made up of "Phantom Intelligences" such as the Spirits Ironic and Sinister, this work is the author's ultimate statement concerning the forces that influence life. Thematically central to the epic-drama is the concept of the Immanent Will, the all-pervasive force in which Hardy perceived faint signs of progress toward improvement in the human condition. Many critics consider *The Dynasts* more successful as an examination of Hardy's philosophy than as a drama, finding it vital to a complete understanding of Hardy's ideas.

Criticism of Hardy has accommodated a diversity of interpretations. Early views see the author as a consummate realist, while later evaluations of such critics as Albert J. Guerard suggest that Hardy may be recognized as a predecessor of anti-realist trends in twentieth-century fiction. Hardy's reputation has survived disparging as well as excessively adulatory opinion. For the integrity of his moral and philosophical views, and for the imaginative achievement in creating the world of Wessex, he continues to receive undiminished acclaim from critics, scholars, and the reading public.

PRINCIPAL WORKS

Desperate Remedies (novel) 1871
Under the Greenwood Tree (novel) 1872
A Pair of Blue Eyes (novel) 1873
Far from the Madding Crowd (novel) 1874
The Hand of Ethelberta (novel) 1876
The Return of the Native (novel) 1878
The Trumpet-Major (novel) 1880
A Laodicean (novel) 1881
Two on a Tower (novel) 1882
The Mayor of Casterbridge (novel) 1886
The Woodlanders (novel) 1887
Wessex Tales (short stories) 1888
A Group of Noble Dames (short stories) 1891
Tess of the d'Urbervilles (novel) 1891
Life's Little Ironies (short stories) 1894
Jude the Obscure (novel) 1895
The Well-Beloved (novel) 1897
Wessex Poems, and Other Verses (poetry) 1898
Poems of the Past and the Present (poetry) 1901
*The Dynasts (drama) 1904-08
Time's Laughingstocks, and Other Verses (poetry) 1909
A Changed Man, and Other Tales (short stories and novel) 1913
Satires of Circumstance, Lyrics and Reveries (poetry) 1914
Winter Words (poetry) 1928
**An Indiscretion in the Life of an Heiress (novel) 1934

*This work appeared in three installments and was collected in a single volume in 1910.
**This work is a later adaptation of Hardy's unpublished first novel, *The Poor Man and the Lady.*

THE ATHENAEUM (essay date 1871)

Desperate Remedies, though in some respects an unpleasant story, is undoubtedly a very powerful one. We cannot decide, satisfactorily to our own mind, on the sex of the author; for while certain evidence, such as the close acquaintance which he or she appears (and, as far as we can judge, with reason) to possess with the mysteries of the female toilette, would appear to point to its being the work of one of that sex, on the other hand there are certain expressions to be met with in the book so remarkably coarse as to render it almost impossible that it should have come from the pen of an English lady. . . .

As to the story itself, it is, as we have said, disagreeable, inasmuch as it is full of crimes, in the discovery of which lies the main interest of the tale. We will not particularize them . . . ; but we may say that they are never purposeless, and that their revelation comes upon us step by step, and is worked out with considerable artistic power. (p. 1)

The characters are often exceedingly good. The parish clerk, 'a sort of Bowdlerized rake', who refers to the time 'before he took orders', is really almost worthy of George Eliot, and so is the whole cider-making scene at the end of the first volume. The west-country dialect is also very well managed, without being a caricature. . . .

There are a few faults of style and grammar, but very few. . . . On the whole, the chief blemish of the book will be found in the occasional coarseness to which we have alluded, and which we can hardly further particularize, but which, startling as it once or twice is, is confined wholly to expressions, and does not affect the main character of the story. If the author will purge himself of this, though even this is better than the prurient sentimentality with which we are so often nauseated, we see no reason why he should not write novels only a little, if at all, inferior to the best of the present generation. (p. 2)

"'Desperate Remedies'" (originally published in The Athenaeum, *April 1, 1871), in* Thomas Hardy: The Critical Heritage, *edited by* R. G. Cox, Barnes & Noble, 1970, pp. 1-2

HAVELOCK ELLIS (essay date 1883)

[It] is difficult to find anywhere fit comrades for the quaint and worthy fellowship, so racy of the earth, who greet us from the pages of *Far from the Madding Crowd,* and *The Return of the Native.* They seem to be born of the earth in a more special sense than her other children. The forms which pass in procession along the ridge in the twilight at the beginning of *Under the Greenwood Tree,* who look, as they are silhouetted on the sky, like the processions on the walls of Egyptian chambers, have grown to have something of the contours of the things among which they live; their 'nature is subdued to what it works in, like the dyer's hand'. And Mr. Hardy reveals the same lines in the contours of their mental and emotional nature. Perhaps the most marked general characteristic of them is their limited range. They never soar very high, or, indeed, at all; but, on the other hand, they never sink very low. Timorous they often are without a cause. Mr. Hardy represents them as, on the whole, a rather feeble folk, but they are never besotted, never coarse; the only effect of an immoderate pull at the cider-can is to render the receiver's humour rather more *spirituel* than usual. And that humour, how delightful! It is the grand characteristic of these men, a delicate and involved humour, which carries itself solemnly, with a tone of gentle banter in it, which is instinctively tolerant without always seeing a reason for tolerance. There are many distinct individualities, but in this respect they are all alike—this humour is common to them all.

And then, secondly, we have to note Mr. Hardy's heroines, those instinct-led women, who form a series which, for subtle simplicity, for a certain fascinating and incalculable vivacity which is half ethereal and half homely, can hardly be matched. . . . [It is] easy to be content with the type of womanhood which Mr. Hardy gives us in all its delicate variations. So great, however, is the general resemblance among the fresh and piquant figures in this gallery of fair women, that there is scarcely a dominant quality in one of them which is not shared by the whole group. . . . There is, in truth, something elemental, something *demonic* about them. We see at once that they have no souls. And that is why the critic, who called them 'Undines of the earth', was striking the keynote of every one of them. In their ever-varying and delicate moods and caprices, which are never untouched by the elemental purity of nature, in their tenderness, in their unconscious selfishness, Fancy, Elfride, Eustacia, Lizzie, Anne, they are all Undines. And few, probably, will care to say that they are, for that, less women. (pp. 105-07)

These Undines are not too good. Woman, in Mr. Hardy's world, is far from being 'the conscience of man'; it is with the men always that the moral strength lies. It is only necessary to think of Bathsheba Everdene and Gabriel Oak, of Eustacia Vye and Clym Yeobright, of Anne Garland and John Loveday. The women may be clever, practical, full of tact; they are always irresistibly fascinating; but veracity, simplicity, rectitude are with the men. . . .

In [*A Pair of Blue Eyes*] the delicate power and fine insight of Mr. Hardy's work were first fully revealed. Elfride's character, in a last analysis, would probably be indistinguishable from Fancy Day's [of *Under the Greenwood Tree*], but the elements are here united in a more complex, a more unstable, manner. There are finer possibilities about her; she is more refined, she is braver, she is more candid. She has, too, a sweet and clinging tenderness which is not hidden by the *grata protervitas* which characterizes all Mr. Hardy's heroines. In *Under the Greenwood Tree* we breathe throughout an atmosphere of pure comedy; Elfride is shrouded from us at last in a tragic gloom. And this tragedy is wrought with an art so like artlessness, so overwhelming in its simple and passionate pathos, as Mr. Hardy has never quite attained since. *A Pair of Blue Eyes* contains the first serious study of Mr. Hardy's favourite hero, who belongs to the class that enters modern literature as *Wilhelm Meister*, and finds its most prominent recent representative in *Daniel Deronda*. It is true that in Goethe's novel, and in George Eliot's, larger issues are involved than anywhere in Mr. Hardy's. . . . Nevertheless, he succeeds in escaping weakness; perhaps because, as George Eliot says, receptiveness itself, like fortitude, is a rare and massive power; perhaps because of a certain moral strength which we have seen in Dick Dewy and which is elsewhere brought out still more distinctly. (p. 112)

With all its great and fascinating qualities, *A Pair of Blue Eyes* is by no means free from faults. Mr. Hardy was breaking new ground, reaching after higher things than those he had so perfectly expressed in *Under the Greenwood Tree*. This may be noticed especially in regard to a characteristic which appears first in *A Pair of Blue Eyes*, and to which the pathos of it is so largely owing, which constitutes, indeed, a new point of departure in Mr. Hardy's art. This is a quality which at its best should be called

a kind of tragic irony, but which too often appears as a series of impossible coincidences and situations, connected sometimes with a pointless cynicism. These are the more irritating to the reader, as that by which Mr. Hardy's work is so fascinating, far from consisting in any tricks of cleverness, lies, rather, in the fresh and direct qualities of genius. (p. 113)

Far from the Madding Crowd is, on the whole, perhaps the finest, as it is certainly the most popular, among Mr. Hardy's novels. Not because it is faultless, but because it is more than any other distinguished by power. It is not deficient—Mr. Hardy's work never is—in subtlety; but here the subtlety is subordinate to the production of effects which are broad and strong rather than subtle. There is a certain sure and easy sense of mastery about it, which dominates the growing tendency towards extreme elaboration. From the first page, with its minutely realized portrait of Gabriel Oak, to the last, where Gabriel and Bathsheba are united, and the familiar group of rustics join in their chorus of delightful comment, there is nothing so distinct about *Far from the Madding Crowd* as this adequacy of power. It is here also that Mr. Hardy has lavished most freely his intimate knowledge of rural life. The description of the storm, with its elaborate details of Nature's hints of the coming catastrophe, given by the toad, the spider, the dog, the sheep, could not be surpassed for vivid intensity. (pp. 114-15)

Like most of Mr. Hardy's [novels, *The Hand of Ethelberta*] represents a new point of departure and a new development; for he is a writer who moves within a limited range, but is yet capable of producing many variations within that range, variations in the defects as well as in the merits of his work. If *Under the Greenwood Tree* is a comedy, and *A Pair of Blue Eyes* a tragedy, if it is possible to find traces of melodrama in *Far from the Madding Crowd*, there is something of farce in *The Hand of Ethelberta*. Mr. Hardy begins by accepting what may be called an impossible situation, and then works it out *ad libitum*. It is necessary to recognize this before the story can be appreciated at all. There is much of the irony of *A Pair of Blue Eyes*, much of the dramatic power of the work which immediately preceded it, and the whole is worked out with a facile—a too facile—brilliance, which, since then, Mr. Hardy has wisely restrained. In method and style it may be said to occupy the same place among the author's works as *Maud* among Mr. Tennyson's. (p. 116)

In *The Return of the Native*, Mr. Hardy has found more adequate expression than elsewhere for the instincts of love and art which bind him to the familiar heath-land of Wessex. The book is full of passages which show with what fine appreciation he has entered into the meaning of that country whose general aspect is one of weird and silent gloom. To Mr. Hardy it is rich with all the complex possibilities of an organic life; he has discerned its varying moods of day and gloaming and night; he has heard and understood its mysterious voices, from the almost inaudible recitative of the dead heath-bells in autumn to the wind's chorale at midnight. All the harmonies that air makes with earth Mr. Hardy has learnt to discriminate and to love; and he writes of them with at once the accuracy of a specialist and the enthusiasm of an artist. (p. 120)

In *The Trumpet Major*, forsaking for a while the carefully elaborated method of *The Return of the Native*, Mr. Hardy adopted a style which recalled *Far from the Madding Crowd*. It is slighter and less powerful, possesses less unity of effect, but the same fresh Dorset air blows through it, the same wanton fancy plays pleasant or mischievous tricks; it is marked by the same touch of melodrama. (p. 122)

[The] hand that drew Anne Garland and the Trumpet Major has gained a new mastery of art since *Under the Greenwood Tree* was written, exquisite as was the early effort. There is here a precision, a delicacy, an easy adaptation of means to end, which can only come late. *The Trumpet Major* is full of passages etched in, as it were, with slight workmanship, where the touches are few, but where every line tells. It cannot be claimed for *The Trumpet Major* that it equals several of its predecessors in colour and intensity; it is inferior also in architectonics, though it is impossible to pass over without mention the beautifully wrought frame in which the story is set. . . . It is not, however, by any impression of power and unity in the whole that *The Trumpet Major* is chiefly remarkable; but rather by its *verve*, its fresh and careless vivacity, the proof it offers that Mr. Hardy's genius is yet far from being exhausted.

A Laodicean has scarcely a single point of resemblance to *The Trumpet Major*. All the characteristic features which go to make up the charm of the latter are here absent. Mr. Hardy had set himself to write a story which is perhaps more faultless, and certainly less mannered, than anything that he had yet produced. The fancy which ran wild in *The Trumpet Major* is here chastened to one or two delicate touches. The eager and animated narrative has given place to a single thread of love-story, and, for the rest, relies on the charm of exquisite workmanship. (pp. 123-24)

In *Two on a Tower*, Mr. Hardy has to a great extent proceeded on the lines laid down in the previous novel. It is less delightful, but even more finished. . . . One characteristic which comes out here may be noted. Mr. Hardy has given to each of his later novels a distinct and dominating background. In *The Return of the Native* the Dorset heathland formed a landscape in the manner of Old Crome which was visible throughout. The bustle of military preparation is used with admirable skill and reticence in *The Trumpet Major*. *A Laodicean* is an architectural novel, and *Two on a Tower* is astronomical. This method adds to the charm of freshness and variety which distinguishes Mr. Hardy's work; but on the whole is progressively unsatisfactory. The astronomical enthusiasm is wanting in spontaneity. . . . If, however, *Two on a Tower* may be said to lack inspiration, it is still the work of a writer who has a finer sense of his art than any living English novelist; and, notwithstanding the light and delicate touch that Mr. Hardy has attained, there is no sacrifice of breadth. (p. 125)

The time has not yet come for forming a final estimate of Mr. Hardy's work. We may hope that it is far distant. It may be safely said, however, that he will scarcely write another novel of the peculiar power, and, it might be added, the peculiar weakness, of *Far from the Madding Crowd*. It seems more probable that he will pursue the vein of comedy which began in *The Hand of Ethelberta*, and is, perhaps, the most characteristic outcome of his genius— that subtle and unimpassioned tracing of aspects of life at once delicate and simple, which are best touched by the fine observation, the tender irony, that we have found to be the most constant elements in Mr. Hardy's work. What fresh variations are possible within these limits it would not

be well to predict, but it is probable that, of stories in this manner, *A Laodicean* and *Two on a Tower* will not be the last. (pp. 131-32)

> *Havelock Ellis, "Thomas Hardy's Novels" (originally published in* The Westminster Review, *Vol. CXIX, No. LXIII, April, 1883), in* Thomas Hardy: The Critical Heritage, *edited by R. G. Cox, Barnes & Noble, 1970, pp. 103-32.*

EDMUND GOSSE   (essay date 1890)

[Mr. Hardy's] two masterpieces are, without question, *Far from the Madding Crowd* . . . and *The Return of the Native* . . . ; in these he has filled large canvases with complete success. A second class consists of novels sketched on the same broad and generous plan, but, for one reason or another, executed with less *bravura*, and more unequal in their evolution; these are [*A Laodicean, The Woodlanders*, and perhaps *A Pair of Blue Eyes*]. . . . Yet another class contains books of smaller compass, but, more obviously than the last mentioned, masterpieces of their kind: *The Trumpet Major* . . . ; *Under the Greenwood Tree* . . . ; and, less perfect in its proportions than either of these, *The Mayor of Casterbridge*. . . . Finally come two books which, although full of cleverness, and cleverness characteristic of Mr. Hardy, are yet partial failures, *The Hand of Ethelberta* . . . and *Two on a Tower*. . . . If this classification be conceded, it will be seen that there has been no definite rise or fall, but a fluctuation due to temperament or choice of subject. In point of fact, the quality of Mr. Hardy's books is singularly steady, and the worst chapter in *The Hand of Ethelberta* is recognizable, in a moment, as written by the author of the best chapter in *The Return of the Native*. No novelist of the day, moreover, has produced a body of work so coherent and so little confused by extraneous matter. Mr. Hardy is almost unique in being a novelist or nothing. He is neither a poet nor a theologian, a journalist nor a politician; his reputation lives or dies on the strength of his romances alone. (p. 168)

It has been eminently fortunate for Mr. Hardy that he has identified himself with an interesting and wholly unexhausted population. If all that is not directly or indirectly inspired by the people and scenery of the county of Dorset were expunged from his books, they would lose little in bulk and less in value. He is the laureate alike of the open wastes of *The Return of the Native*, of the undulating, pastoral country of *Far from the Madding Crowd*, of the market-towns, as in *The Mayor of Casterbridge*, and of those apple-growing parishes of *The Woodlanders*. . . . (pp. 168-69)

The unpopularity of Mr. Hardy's novels among women is a curious phenomenon. (p. 169)

[There] is something in his conception of feminine character which is not well received. The modern English novelist has created, and has faithfully repeated, a demure, ingenuous, and practically inhuman type of heroine, which has flattered womankind, and which female readers now imperatively demand as an encouragement. . . . But Mr. Hardy's women are moulded of the same flesh as his men; they are liable to flutterings and tremblings; they are not always constant even when they are 'quite nice'; and some of them are actually 'of a coming-on disposition'.

This feminine realism, which, whether the ladies are pleased or no, is one of the author's charms, would probably have been excused, however, if Mr. Hardy had not shown a proclivity towards placing a more unique and singular species of womanhood as the central figure of each of his books. She is dignified and capable, like Bathsheba; she is a belated pythoness, like Eustacia; she is an innocent adventuress, like Mrs. Charmond; or she is a delicate razor cutting hones, like Lucetta. But these variations are external, and all these ladies belong to the same family. All are women lifted by circumstances a little distance out of their sphere—educated too highly for it, rendered too fine for it, yet excluded from a superior status, which they are too simple to succeed in reaching. Very often they are contrasted, in their tragic failure, with their humbler and less intelligent sisters, and the novelist loves to show that their beautiful and dignified heads, lifted into solitude above their fellows, offer a special aim to the shafts of ill-fortune. (pp. 169-70)

Besides his ten great oil-pictures, Mr. Hardy has occasionally hung up in his gallery a water-colour sketch of extraordinary charm and quality. . . . But Mr. Hardy has written one short story so complete, so admirable in execution, so novel and brilliant in conception, that it raises him for a moment to the level of Tourgéneff himself. If all his works but one were doomed to perish, he might safely depend for immortality on *The Three Strangers* . . . , with its unrivalled picture of the sheep-stealer jammed into the shepherd's chimney-corner, hob-nobbing there with his own intended hangman. From the first word to the last, this amazing little composition never flags for a moment. It is not a small thing that it contains the best of the group of Mr. Hardy's peculiarly happy pictures of country parties. But its highest merit consists, of course, in the tension of its wild emotion, raising common scenes and common speakers, in the midst of their ludicrous humours, to the heights of tragedy. (pp. 170-71)

[Mr. Hardy] is one of the very few living English writers who can be measured with the great masters without sinking into insignificance; and if his strongly defined, consistent, charming gift is not to be designated genius, we may as well resign that word as obsolete and not suited to our degenerate age. (p. 171)

> *Edmund Gosse, "Thomas Hardy" (originally published in* The Speaker, *No. II, September 13, 1890), in* Thomas Hardy: The Critical Heritage, *edited by R. G. Cox, Barnes & Noble, 1970, pp. 167-71.*

W. D. HOWELLS   (essay date 1895)

[In *Jude the Obscure* Mr. Hardy] has given me the same pity and despair in view of the blind struggles of his modern English lower-middle-class people that I experience from the destinies of the august figures of Greek fable. I do not know how instinctively or how voluntarily he has appealed to our inherent superstition of Fate, which used to be a religion; but I am sure that in the world where his hapless people have their being, there is not only no Providence, but there is Fate alone; and the environment is such that character itself cannot avail against it. We have back the old conception of an absolutely subject humanity, unguided

and unfriended. The gods, careless of mankind, are again over all; only, now, they call themselves conditions.

The story is a tragedy, and tragedy almost unrelieved by the humorous touch which the poet is master of. The grotesque is there abundantly, but not the comic; and at times this ugliness heightens the pathos to almost intolerable effect. But I must say that the figure of Jude himself is, in spite of all his weakness and debasement, one of inviolable dignity. He is the sport of fate, but he is never otherwise than sublime; he suffers more for others than for himself. The wretched Sue who spoils his life and her own, helplessly, inevitably, is the kind of fool who finds the fool in the poet and prophet so often, and brings him to naught. She is not less a fool than Arabella herself; though of such exaltation in her folly that we cannot refuse her a throe of compassion, even when she is most perverse. All the characters, indeed, have the appealing quality of human creatures really doing what they must while seeming to do what they will. It is not a question of blaming them or praising them; they are in the necessity of what they do and what they suffer. One may indeed blame the author for presenting such a conception of life; one may say that it is demoralizing if not immoral; but as to his dealing with his creations in the circumstance which he has imagined, one can only praise him for his truth. (pp. 151-52)

I find myself defending the book on the ethical side when I meant chiefly to praise it for what seems to me its artistic excellence. It has not only the solemn and lofty effect of a great tragedy; a work far faultier might impart this; but it has unity very uncommon in the novel, and especially the English novel. . . . This tragedy of fate suggests the classic singleness of means as well as the classic singleness of motive. (p. 153)

> *W. D. Howells, "Pleasure from Tragedy" (originally published in* Harper's Weekly, *December 7, 1895), in his* Criticism and Fiction and Other Essays, *edited by Clara Marbury Kirk and Rudolph Kirk (reprinted by permission of New York University Press; copyright © 1959 by New York University), New York University Press, 1959, pp. 150-53.*

MARGARET OLIPHANT   (essay date 1896)

The present writer does not pretend to a knowledge of the works of Zola, which perhaps she ought to have before presuming to say that nothing so coarsely indecent as the whole history of Jude in his relations with his wife Arabella has ever been put in English print—that is to say, from the hands of a Master. There may be books more disgusting, more impious as regards human nature, more foul in detail, in those dark corners where the amateurs of filth find garbage to their taste; but not, we repeat, from any Master's hand. It is vain to tell us that there are scenes in Shakespeare himself which, if they were picked out for special attention, would be offensive to modesty. There is no need for picking out in the work now referred to. Its faults do not lie in mere suggestion, or any *double entendre*, though these are bad enough. In the history of Jude, the half-educated and by no means uninteresting hero in whose early self-training there is much that is admirable—Mr. Hardy has given us a chapter in what used to be called the conflict between vice and virtue. . . . He is virtuous by temperament, meaning no evil; bent upon doing more than well, and elevating himself to the level which appears to him the highest in life. But he falls into the hands of a woman so completely animal that it is at once too little and too much to call her vicious. She is a human pig. . . . After the man has been subjugated, a process through which the reader is required to follow him closely (and Jude's own views on this subject are remarkable), he is made for the rest of his life into a puppet flung about between them by two women —the fleshly animal Arabella and the fantastic Susan. . . . In this curious dilemma the unfortunate Jude, who is always the puppet, always acted upon by the others, never altogether loses our esteem. He is a very poor creature, but he would have liked much better to do well if they would have let him, and dies a virtuous victim of the eternal feminine, scarcely ever blameable, though always bearing both the misery and the shame.

We can with difficulty guess what is Mr. Hardy's motive in portraying such a struggle. It can scarcely be said to be one of those attacks upon the institution of Marriage. . . . It is marriage indeed which in the beginning works Jude's woe; and it is by marriage, or rather the marrying of himself and others, that his end is brought about. We rather think the author's object must be, having glorified women by the creation of Tess, to show after all what destructive and ruinous creatures they are, in general circumstances and in every development, whether brutal or refined. Arabella, the first —the pig-dealer's daughter, whose native qualities have been ripened by the experiences of a barmaid—is the Flesh, unmitigated by any touch of human feeling except that of merciless calculation as to what will be profitable for herself. She is the native product of the fields, the rustic woman, exuberant and overflowing with health, vanity and appetite. The colloquy between her and her fellows in their disgusting work, after her first almost equally disgusting interview with Jude, is one of the most unutterable foulness —a shame to the language in which it is recorded and suggested; and the picture altogether of the country lasses at their outdoor work is more brutal in depravity than anything which the darkest slums could bring forth, as are the scenes in which their good advice is carried out. (pp. 381-83)

The other woman—who makes virtue vicious by keeping the physical facts of one relationship in life in constant prominence by denying, as Arabella does by satisfying them, and even more skilfully and insistently than Arabella —the fantastic *raisonneuse,* Susan, completes the circle of the unclean. She marries to save herself from trouble; then quits her husband, to live a life of perpetual temptation and resistance with her lover; then marries, or professes to marry him, when her husband amiably divorces her without the reason he supposes himself to have; and then, when a selfish conscience is tardily awakened, returns to the husband, and ends in ostentatious acceptance of the conditions of matrimony at the moment when the unfortunate Jude, who has also been recaptured by the widowed Arabella, dies of his cruel misery. This woman we are required to accept as the type of high-toned purity. It is the women who are the active agents in all this unsavoury imbroglio: the story is carried on, and life is represented as carried on, entirely by their means. The men are passive, suffering, rather good than otherwise, victims of these and of fate. Not only do they never dominate, but they are quite incapable of holding their own against these remorseless ministers of destiny, these determined operators, managing all

the machinery of life so as to secure their own way. (pp. 383-84)

I have said that it is not clear what Mr. Hardy's motive is in the history of Jude: but, on reconsideration, it becomes more clear that it is intended as an assault on the stronghold of marriage, which is now beleaguered on every side. The motto is, 'The letter killeth'; and I presume this must refer to the fact of Jude's early and unwilling union to Arabella, and that the lesson the novelist would have us learn is, that if marriage were not exacted, and people were free to form connections as the spirit moves them, none of these complications would have occurred, and all would have been well. 'There seemed to him, vaguely and dimly, something wrong in a social ritual which made necessary the cancelling of well-formed schemes involving years of thought and labour, of foregoing a man's one opportunity of showing himself superior to the lower animals, and of contributing his units of work to the general progress of his generation, because of a momentary surprise by a new and transitory instinct which had nothing in it of the nature of vice, and could be only at the most called weakness.' This is the hero's own view of the circumstances which, in obedience to the code of honour prevalent in the countryside, compelled his marriage. Suppose, however, that instead of upsetting the whole framework of society, Jude had shown himself superior to the lower animals by not yielding to that new and transitory influence, the same result could have been easily attained: and he might then have met and married Susan and lived happy ever after, without demanding a total overthrow of all existing laws and customs to prevent him from being unhappy. (pp. 384-85)

Margaret Oliphant, "Contemporary Reception: From 'Blackwood's Magazine' (January 1896)" (originally published under a different title in Blackwood's Magazine, *January, 1896), in "Jude the Obscure" by Thomas Hardy: An Authoritative Text, Backgrounds and Sources Criticism, edited by Norman Page (copyright © 1978 by W. W. Norton & Company, Inc.), Norton, 1978, pp. 381-85.*

THE SATURDAY REVIEW   (essay date 1899)

Mr. Hardy enjoys a great reputation for his very clear, and sometimes powerful, presentation of the limited life of the country folk who live in a backwater out of the main stream of the world. Even more, his work has for some years been one of the important influences determining the estimate of life of many thoughtful, if imperfectly educated, people. We come, therefore, to anything he chooses to publish predisposed to respect. But as we read this curious and wearisome volume [*Wessex Poems*], these many slovenly, slipshod, uncouth verses, stilted in sentiment, poorly conceived and worse wrought, our respect lessens to vanishing-point, and we lay it down with the feeling strong upon us that Mr. Hardy has, by his own deliberate act, discredited that judgement and presentation of life on which his reputation rested. It is impossible to understand why the bulk of this volume was published at all—why he did not himself burn the verse, lest it should fall into the hands of the indiscreet literary executor, and mar his fame when he was dead.

The pieces of verse at the beginning of the volume are expressions of the feelings natural to every thoughtful young man coming to his first grips with life, and finding that his imaginings surpass its possibilities. . . . The feelings do not ring quite sincere; they are not strongly felt; they are, in truth, the outpourings in verse common to all the weak, undeveloped natures of intelligent young men, and it is the custom to lock them away, or burn them. Only two of them, 'The Heiress and the Architect', and 'Neutral Tones', show any forecast of Mr. Hardy's mature strength. (pp. 319-20)

Of four of the other ballads it can only be said that they are some of the most amazing balderdash that ever found its way into a book of verse. In 'San Sebastian' a sergeant, harrowed by remorse, tells the story of the siege of that city, and how Heaven has punished him for ravishing a young girl during the sack of it, by giving his daughter her eyes. In 'Leipzig' a Casterbridge workman tells the story of Napoleon's defeat, as it was told him by his German mother. . . . In 'The Peasant's Confession' an improbable peasant tells how he led astray and killed an officer, who told him the gist of the orders he was carrying from Napoleon to Grouchy. The stories of the siege and of the battles are alike bald, mechanical and lacking in spirit; while that essential quality of the ballad, a lilting easy flow, is entirely wanting. . . . Even worse than these three is 'The Alarm'. (pp. 320-21)

Mr. Hardy is hardly more fortunate with the poems which purport to be dramatic, than with his ballads of the wars of Napoleon. The situations in 'The Burghers', when the husband surprises the flying lovers, and when he gives them gold and jewels for their livelihood, afford admirable opportunities for the display of dramatic power; but such is the poorness, the clumsiness rather, of the treatment that they lose all their inherent dramatic force, and are entirely unreal, lifeless and flat. (p. 321)

Mr. Hardy reaches a higher level in the verse which he calls 'personative' in conception. Such verses as 'Friends Beyond', 'Thoughts of Ph—a', 'In a Eweleaze near Weatherbury', are instinct with the intimate, penetrating charm of real feeling, completely, strongly felt; they have the value of originality of sentiment and idea; and were the form equal to the matter, they would be poetry. Last of all comes a veritable poem, 'I look into my glass'. It is an original thought realized and felt completely; and the expression is so clear and simple, that it will surely live when the rest of the book has been forgotten. (pp. 321-22)

"'Wessex Poems'" (originally published in The Saturday Review, *No. LXXXVII, January 7, 1899), in* Thomas Hardy: The Critical Heritage, *edited by R. G. Cox, Barnes & Noble, 1970, pp. 319-22.*

THE ATHENAEUM (essay date 1899)

It is not often that a writer at an advanced, if not quite the eleventh, hour essays two new arts at a blow. Nevertheless, this is the case with Mr. Hardy. . . .

[Many of the poems] that Mr. Hardy has amused himself by collecting [in *Wessex Poems, and Other Verses* are] quite trifling, conceived in the crude ferments of youth, and expressed with woodenness of rhythm and a needlessly inflated diction. On the other hand, there are certain things

which stand out unmistakably, not from their fellows merely, but from the ruck of modern verse as a whole. Two or three of these, which take more or less of a ballad form, are vigorous studies of types of Wessex character, and are marked by the observation and saturnine humour which one would naturally expect from the writer of Mr. Hardy's novels. Such are 'The Fire at Tranter Sweattey's' . . . and 'Valenciennes'. . . .

The majority, however, of Mr. Hardy's small cluster of really remarkable poems, even though they may be dramatic in their setting, are not so in their intention. They are personal utterances, voicing a matured and deliberate judgment on life, which has, indeed, found expression more than once in his novels. More than anything it was this that gave offence to the narrower minds in 'Tess of the D'Urbervilles.' "The President of the Immortals had finished his sport with Tess": this is the note upon which the tragedy ends. And this is the note, too, more or less, of all the poems in which Mr. Hardy really speaks, is really convincing. The tragedy of life as the outcome of the sport of freakish destinies: this is briefly the conception which dominates his inmost thought. And the mood of melancholy, or perhaps rather melancholic irritation, to which such a conception gives rise, is the one from which his verse must well, if it is to attain anything beyond a mediocre inspiration. From this spring the sombre irony and mournful music of what is perhaps his finest single effort, 'My Cicely.' . . .

Equally uncompromising in its pessimism is 'Friends Beyond,' with its dream—as all these things are but dreams—of the cessation of life, the deadening of desire, in the grave. (p. 41)

We do not conceal our opinion that Mr. Hardy's success in poetry is of a very narrow range. He is entirely dependent for his inspiration upon this curiously intense and somewhat dismal vision of life, which is upon him almost as an obsession. Where he is not carried along by this, his movement is faltering, and his touch prosaic. But within such close limits his achievement seems to us to be considerable, and to be of a kind with which modern poetry can ill afford to dispense. There is no finish or artifice about it: the note struck is strenuous, austere, forcible; it is writing that should help to give backbone to a literature which certainly errs on the side of flabbiness. (pp. 41-2)

"Literature: 'Wessex Poems, and Other Verses'," in The Athenaeum, *No. 3716, January 14, 1899, pp. 41-2.*

THOMAS HARDY (essay date 1911)

One word on what has been called the present writer's philosophy of life, as exhibited more particularly in [the] metrical section of his compositions. Positive views on the Whence and the Wherefore of things have never been advanced by this pen as a consistent philosophy. Nor is it likely, indeed, that imaginative writings extending over more than forty years would exhibit a coherent scientific theory of the universe even if it had been attempted—of that universe concerning which Spencer owns to the 'paralyzing thought' that possibly there exists no comprehension of it anywhere. But such objectless consistency never has been attempted, and the sentiments in [the novels and poems] have been stated truly to be mere impressions of the moment, and not convictions or arguments.

That these impressions have been condemned as 'pessimistic' —as if that were a very nice wicked adjective—shows a curous muddle-mindedness. It must be obvious that there is a higher characteristic of philosophy than pessimism, or than meliorism, or even than the optimism of these critics—which is truth. Existence is either ordered in a certain way, or it is not so ordered, and conjectures which harmonize best with experience are removed above all comparison with other conjectures which do not so harmonize. So that to say one view is worse than other views without proving it erroneous implies the possibility of a false view being better or more expedient than a true view; and no pragmatic proppings can make that *idolum specus* stand on its feet, for it postulates a prescience denied to humanity.

And there is another consideration. Differing natures find their tongue in the presence of differing spectacles. Some natures become vocal at tragedy, some are made vocal by comedy, and it seems to me that to whichever of these aspects of life a writer's instinct for expressions the more readily responds, to that he should allow it to respond. That before a contrasting side of things he remains undemonstrative need not be assumed to mean that he remains unperceiving. (pp. 497-98)

> *Thomas Hardy, "General Preface to the Wessex Edition of 1912" (1911), in his* Jude the Obscure, *edited by C. H. Sisson, Penguin Books, 1978, pp. 493-98.*

LASCELLES ABERCROMBIE   (essay date 1912)

[Of Hardy's six great novels], the two which were latest in publication show a marked difference from the others in their form. Roughly, but conveniently, the earlier books may be called dramatic, the two later epic, in form. The difference is chiefly in degree of complexity; but it is enough to put *Tess of the D'Urbervilles* and *Jude the Obscure* distinctly apart from the others. In the four earlier novels [*Far from the Madding Crowd, The Return of the Native, The Major of Casterbridge,* and *The Woodlanders*], the action is a woven intricacy of many curving and recurving lines, carrying the threaded lives of several persons through a single complicated pattern of destiny; for as the interest of the story concerns not one character, but several—a group, as a rule, of four contrasted personalities—its process is not a simple forward motion, but a system of vital currents ramified to and fro, the whole elaborate event obeying one general trend. They are polyphony, these four novels; whereas the two later books are great pieces of plain-song, each concerned with one human theme, which goes forward in unswerving continuity, not part of a broad stream of counterpoint, but accompanied by tones that follow it in unison. The difference between the two sets of novels is the difference between a history of an individual, and a history of the relationship in a group of individuals; and from this thematic difference, formal difference naturally follows. But *The Mayor of Casterbridge*, while clearly belonging, as regards its form, to the dramatic set, is in theme a partial anticipation of the epic set; since the history of the relationship which subsists in the principal group of characters is all focussed in the individual history of a single figure, Michael Henchard. (pp. 103-04)

The processes of nature, which are so carefully and vividly, and with such obvious symbolic purport, mingled into the substance of the three other dramatic novels, are scarcely present in *The Mayor of Casterbridge*. But they are not needed; Henchard himself takes their place. He is, probably, the greatest instance of masculine characterization in Hardy's fiction; Jude's history may be the more significant, but Jude is conceived in a narrower mould than Henchard. He himself altogether provides the two main elements which combine to produce tragedy. In the rest of Hardy's fiction, these tragic elements are, on the whole, separately provided, by personality, and by the circumstances which have hold of personality. But the elemental antinomy, which is the basis of Hardy's tragedy, is entirely Henchard's own. . . . [In] Henchard, human nature's dualism of personal and impersonal force is so intensified that his whole circumstance, as far as it is injurious to him, seems but the objectification of his own self-injuring nature. The significance of *The Mayor of Casterbridge* is, therefore, in every way a notable variation on the general theme of Hardy's dramatic fiction. (pp. 125-26)

The aesthetic manner of those four great [earlier] novels . . . admirably enabled [Hardy] to express his intellectual conception of life, from its outer show of events to the inmost primal discord of its nature, and even to the necessary tragic resolution of the discord. But it withheld him from adding to his formation of life the gloss of his own opinion of the tragedy. That tragedy is not an accidental accompaniment of life, but essential to its nature, this manner of art can be brought, without any violence, to assert; but it is very difficult for it to assert either that the tragedy is a fine, heartening business or, on the contrary, pitiable and unjust. Already, in *The Mayor of Casterbridge*, Hardy appears somewhat restive under the restriction; the book seems several times on the verge of indignantly protesting against the injustice of Henchard's fate—a fate which gave his personality a wealth of striving, aspiring vigour, and then punished him for possessing the gift. One has the feeling that the art is here constantly hoping to be able to do something which the artist's conscience will not tolerate. So a change of aesthetic habit becomes necessary, and *Tess of the D'Urbervilles* and *Jude the Obscure* are written in a form which the artist's conscience easily allows to contain an emotional as well as an intellectual judgment of life. (pp. 130-31)

Instead of being constructed round a progressive harmony of several individual themes, the form of these two novels [termed "epic" as a convenient label] develops a single theme, the life-history of one person, and sends this uninterruptedly forward. This is obviously the case in *Tess of the D'Urbervilles;* not quite so obviously in *Jude the Obscure,* for Sue Bridehead is a character drawn with as exact and penetrating a care as Jude himself. Yet she is only the subject of the book in so far as she affects Jude; with him the story begins and ends, and the whole form of the book is moulded to his single history. . . . With only the history of a single life to carry, there needs but continuity of events from end to end. . . . In the dramatic novels, [on the other hand], with their intricate linkages of events both lengthways and crossways, formal control finds a pretty full employment in keeping the mere matter of the story in order, and has about as much as it can do to relate the matter intellectually with the artistic metaphysic of the whole, leaving the emotional relation for inference. But in the matter of the epic novels, formal control is freed from a good deal of this employment . . . ; more of the intangible stuff can be woven in, and closely complicated with it. . . . So, in the epic novels, a great tune is played on a single human life; and because there is only one instrument, we are able to hear, instead of the harmony of human living, the whole quality of the one instrument's tone, all its intellectual and emotional overtones. (pp. 132-35)

The objective life in these two novels is shown as a phenomenon much more closely and intensely "complicated with the life beyond" . . . than in the others. . . . Indeed, we can hardly read these two disturbing books without feeling that their accusing passion is in them not merely on behalf of the lives they imagine; they surely confess, under the covert fiction of their histories, their author's personal sense of life, of its tragic compound of individual desire and the overriding force of general existence. . . . (pp. 135, 138)

> *Lascelles Abercrombie, in his* Thomas Hardy: A Critical Study *(reprinted by permission of the Estate of Lascelles Abercrombie), M. Secker, 1912 (and reprinted by Russell & Russell, 1964), 224 p.*

LYTTON STRACHEY (essay date 1914)

The originality of [Hardy's] poetry lies in the fact that it bears everywhere upon it the impress of a master of prose fiction. Just as the great seventeenth-century writers of prose . . . managed to fill their sentences with the splendour and passion of poetry, while still preserving the texture of an essentially prose style, so Mr. Hardy, by a contrary process, has brought the realism and sobriety of prose into the service of his poetry. The result is a product of a kind very difficult to parallel in our literature. . . . [What] gives Mr. Hardy's poems their unique flavour is precisely their utter lack of romanticism, their common, undecorated presentments of things. They are, in fact, modern as no other poems are. The author of *Jude the Obscure* speaks in them, but with the concentration, the intensity, the subtle disturbing force of poetry. And he speaks; he does not sing. Or rather, he talks—in the quiet voice of a modern man or woman, who finds it difficult, as modern men and women do, to put into words exactly what is in the mind. He is incorrect; but then how unreal and artificial a thing is correctness! He fumbles; but it is that very fumbling that brings him so near to ourselves. In that 'me one whom consequence influenced much,' does not one seem to catch the very accent of hesitating and half-ironical affection? And in the drab rhythm of that 'daytime talk of the Roman investigations,' does not all the dreariness of long hours of boredom lie compressed? And who does not feel the perplexity, the discomfort, and the dim agitation in that clumsy collection of vocables—'And adumbrates too therewith our unexpected troublous case'? What a relief such uncertainties and inexpressivenesses are after the delicate exactitudes of our more polished poets! . . . [The] flat, undistinguished poetry of Mr. Hardy has found out the secret of touching our marrow-bones.

It is not only in its style and feeling that this poetry reveals the novelist; it is also in its subject-matter. Many of the poems . . . consist of compressed dramatic narratives, of central episodes of passion and circumstance, depicted with extraordinary vividness. A flashlight is turned for a moment upon some scene or upon some character, and in that moment the tragedies of whole lives and the long fatalities of human relationships seem to stand revealed. . . . (pp. 221-23)

> *Lytton Strachey, "Mr. Hardy's New Poems," in* New Statesman (© *1914 The Statesman & Nation Publishing Co. Ltd.), December 19, 1914 (and reprinted in his* Literary Essays, *Chatto and Windus, 1948, pp. 220-25).*

ARTHUR SYMONS (essay date 1920)

In *Poems of the Past and Present* almost every poem has something to say, and says it in a slow, twisted, and sometimes enigmatic manner, without obvious charm, but with some arresting quality, not easy to define or to estimate. . . .

In [Hardy's] verse there is something brooding, obscure, half-inarticulate, as he meditates on men and destiny. In one of his poems, an ironical song of science, Nature laments that her best amusement, man, has become discontented with her in his self-discontent. Dumb and blind forces speak, conjecture, half awakening out of sleep, turning back lazily to sleep again. Here is a poet who is sorry for nature, who feels the earth and its roots, as if he had sap in his veins instead of blood, and could get closer than any other man to the things of the earth. There is an atmosphere not easily to be found outside this book, a mysterious, almost terrifying atmosphere which one finds again in the phantom love-poems, the phantom war-poems, and in certain reflective verses. Abstract thought takes form in some given symbol, as in "The Church-Builder," with its architectural imagery, its deliberate building up of spiritual horror. Nearly the whole book shivers with winter. (p. 67)

[Hardy] has studied the technique of verse more carefully than most of his critics seem to be aware of, and he has a command of very difficult metres which, if it were unvarying, would be really remarkable. But his command of his materials is uncertain. He crowds syllables together inharmoniously. He is always experimenting in metrical effects, and he has made some perfectly successful experiments of a very unusual kind; but he is too fond of long lines, in which the cadence gets lost by the way. He sometimes writes gaily and trippingly, as in the delightfully naughty jingle of "The Ruined Maid," which Congreve could not have done better.

Neither in verse nor in prose is Hardy a master of style. Both in prose and in verse he has interesting things to say, and he can say them in an intensely personal way. He can force words to say exactly what he wants them to. But their subjection is never even willing, they seem to have spite against him because he is stronger than they. That is why they have never given him all their souls along with their services. Some of their magic remains over: his verse does not sing. But so far as it is possible to be a poet without having a singing voice, Hardy is a poet, and a profoundly interesting one. (p. 68)

> *Arthur Symons, "Thomas Hardy," in* The Dial *(copyright, 1920, by The Dial Publishing Company, Inc.), Vol. LXVIII, No. 1, January, 1920 (and reprinted by Kraus Reprint Corporation, 1966), pp. 66-70.*

JOSEPH WARREN BEACH (essay date 1922)

[With] *The Return of the Native*, Hardy has taken up a theme which involves a clear-cut issue in the minds of the leading characters, and especially in the mind of Eustacia, which is the main stage of the drama. It is her stifled longing for spiritual expansion which leads her to play with the love of Wildeve, which causes her later to throw him over for the greater promise of Clym, which leads her back again to Wildeve, and at last—with the loss of all hope—to suicide. In every case it requires but the smallest outlay of incident to provoke the most lively play of feeling; and the play of feeling—the opposition of desires—is embodied here, in true dramatic fashion, in talk rather than in acts. It takes nothing more than the return of Thomasin from town unwed to set going the whole series of dialogues which make up the substance of the first book, dialogues in which Wildeve and Mrs. Yeobright, Venn and Eustacia, Eustacia and Wildeve do nothing more than fence with one another, each maneuvering for position in a breathless game of well-matched antagonists. These are scenes in the true dramatic sense, not in the popular sense that calls for violence and surprising action.

In the third book the main thing that happens is a quarrel between Clym and his mother over Eustacia. The wedding itself is not presented, having no dramatic value. The dramatic value of the book is indicated in its caption, "The Fascination," the drama lying in the resistless attraction to one another of two persons so far apart in mind. (pp. 90-1)

Never before in Hardy had the machinery of action been so masked and subordinated. Never again perhaps was it to occupy a place of so little prominence in his work. It is only once or twice in Meredith, and more generally in the later novels of James, that we find so great a volume of emotional energy released by events of so little objective importance. Only in them is found a greater economy of incident; and many more readers will testify to the dramatic intensity of *The Native* than to that of *The Egoist* or *The Golden Bowl*.

The whole course of the story was conceived by the author in terms suggestive of physics and dynamics. Each step in the plot represents the balance and reaction of forces expressible almost in algebraic formulas. Many readers have been impressed with the strong scientific coloring of Hardy's mind: with his tendency to view both external nature and the human heart with the sharpness and hard precision of a naturalist, and to record the phenomena observed with some of the abstractness of the summarizing philosopher. (pp. 93-4)

The division of a novel into parts is always a significant indication of an author's interest in the logical massing of his material, in the larger architectonics of his work. It is very little used by novelists like Dickens; very much used by novelists like George Eliot, Victor Hugo, Henry James, and . . . Mr. Walpole. It generally implies a bias for the "dramatic," in so far as it involves the grouping of the subject-matter around certain characters or great moments in the action, as that of a play is grouped in the several acts. In *The Native* this is especially notable. (pp. 96-7)

These five books are like the five acts of a classic play. And in each book the scenes are largely grouped around certain points in time so as to suggest the classic continuity within the several acts. (p. 97)

What we are concerned with here is the unity of tone—the steadiness with which the heath makes us feel its dark and overshadowing presence, so that men and women are but slight figures in a giant landscape, the insect-fauna of its somber flora. Mr. Hardy was bold enough to begin this grave history with an entire chapter devoted to a description of the heath at twilight; and his choice of a title for the second chapter but serves to signalize the littleness and frailty of man upon the great stage of inhospitable nature: "Humanity appears upon the scene, hand in hand with trouble." It is very quietly and without word or gesture that humanity makes its appearance, like a slow-moving shadow. (p. 101)

It is thus that Egdon takes its place as the dominating force of the tragedy, as well as its appropriate and impressive setting. So that the unity of place, in itself an artistic value, is but the counterpart of a unity of action rooted and bedded in a precious oneness of theme. Instead of being, as in *Far from the Madding Crowd,* brought together arbitrarily to make out the prescribed materials of a novel, plot and setting here are one, growing equally and simultaneously out of the dramatic idea expressed in the title. For the first—and almost for the last—time in the work of Hardy, the discriminating reader is delighted with the complete absence of mechanical contrivance. Contrivance there is as never before in his work, the loving contrivance of an artist bent on making everything right in an orderly composition; the long-range contrivance of an architect concerned to have every part in place in an edifice that shall stand well based and well proportioned, with meaning in every line. (p. 105)

The determinist may be equally impressed with the helplessness of man in the grip of strange forces, physical and psychical. But he is distinguished from the fatalist by his concern with the causes that are the links in the chain of necessity. Determinism is the scientific counterpart of fatalism, and throws more light on destiny by virtue of its diligence in the searching out of natural law. Mr. Hardy is rather a determinist than a fatalist. When he speaks most directly and unmistakably for himself, it is to insist on the universal working of the laws of cause and effect. (p. 228)

The point in which determinism and fatalism agree is the helplessness of the individual will against the will in things. Only the determinist conceives the will in things as the sum of the natural forces with which we have to cope, whereas the fatalist tends to a more religious interpretation of that will as truly and literally a *will,* an arbitrary power, a personal force like our own. Sometimes Mr. Hardy allows his characters the bitter comfort of that personal interpretation. . . .

What gives rise to such notions is the ironic discrepancy between what we seek and what we secure, between what we do and what follows from it. We have control of so very few of the factors that go to determine our fortunes that we can hardly help imagining behind the scene a capricious and malignant contriver of contretemps. (p. 229)

> *Joseph Warren Beach, in his* The Technique of Thomas Hardy *(copyright, 1922, 1949 by Joseph Warren Beach), University of Chicago Press, 1922 (and reprinted by Russell & Russell, 1962), 255 p.*

CONRAD AIKEN (essay date 1924)

Mr. Hardy was determined—by what motives we can leave a chartered psychoanalyst to ascertain—to take a tragic view. Leaving aside, then, both the personal and the philosophic aspects of this, and restricting ourselves to the aesthetic, we find in Mr. Hardy the extraordinarily interesting case of an artist with a powerful appetite for a tragic view, who, beginning with melodrama, has gradually and laboriously sought the "rationale" which would not only permit, but actually invite, the maximum of disaster, and carry him thus from melodrama to tragedy. In *A Pair of Blue Eyes,* and in all those novels in which chance, or mere coincidence, dominates—that is, a purely external and unpredictable force—we have melodrama; but by degrees Mr. Hardy substituted a gloomy determinism for chance, and thus greatly extended the dimensions of his tragic view, partly by increasing his plausibility (since the downfall of a protagonist could be derived from the defects of his own nature), but also by increasing the unity and aesthetic value of his "scene," which was now conceived not as chaos but as order. In this, the "philosophy" was perhaps simply derived from the appetite for disaster and pity.... Mr. Hardy's appetite for the disastrous and pitiful often outruns his inventive power, as his inventive power (especially in his prose) almost invariably outruns his sense of effect. The "idea" thus too often and too bleakly emerges in his prose, crippling or hypnotizing his characters, or reducing them to lifelessness. It is in poetry that the "idea" takes its place most naturally and effectively; and it is therefore not surprising that Mr. Hardy should have shown in poetry, most unmistakably and unintermittently, his tremendous power and individuality. (pp. 221-22)

Conrad Aiken, "Hardy, Thomas" (originally published under a different title in Nation & Athenaeum, May 24, 1924), in his Collected Criticism (copyright © 1958 by Conrad Aiken; reprinted by permission of Oxford University Press, Inc.), Oxford University Press, New York, 1968, pp. 219-22.

HENRY JAMES   (essay date 1924)

[Mr. Hardy] has evidently read to good purpose the low-life chapters in George Eliot's novels; he has caught very happily her trick of seeming to humor benignantly her queer people and look down at them from the heights of analytic omniscience. But [there is a] ... difference between original and imitative talent—the disparity, which it is almost unpardonable not to perceive, between first-rate talent and those inferior grades which range from second-rate downward, and as to which confusion is a more venial offense. Mr. Hardy puts his figures through a variety of comical movements; he fills their mouths with quaint turns of speech; he baptizes them with odd names ("Joseph Poorgrass" for a bashful, easily-snubbed Dissenter is excellent); he pulls the wires, in short, and produces a vast deal of sound and commotion; and [*Far from The Madding Crowd*], at a cursory glance, has a rather promising air of life and warmth. But by critics who prefer a grain of substance to a pound of shadow it will, we think, be pronounced a decidedly delusive performance; it has a fatal lack of magic.... Mr. Hardy's novel is very long, but his subject is very short and simple, and the work has been distended to its rather formidable dimensions by the infusion of a large amount of conversational and descriptive padding and the use of an ingeniously verbose and redundant style. It is inordinately diffuse, and, as a piece of narrative, singularly inartistic. The author has little sense of proportion, and almost none of composition.... Mr. Hardy's inex-

haustible faculty for spinning smart dialogue makes him forget that dialogue in a story is after all but episode, and that a novelist is after all but a historian, thoroughly possessed of certain facts, and bound in some way or other to impart them. To tell a story almost exclusively by reporting people's talks is the most difficult art in the world, and really leads, logically, to a severe economy in the use of rejoinder and repartee, and not to a lavish expenditure of them. *Far from the Madding Crowd* gives us an uncomfortable sense of being a simple "tale," pulled and stretched to make the conventional three volumes; and the author, in his long-sustained appeal to one's attention, reminds us of a person fishing with an enormous net, of which the meshes should be thrice too wide. (pp. 293-94)

The three unities, in Aristotle's day, were inexorably imposed on Greek tragedy: why shouldn't we have something of the same sort for English fiction in the day of Mr. Hardy? Almost all novels are greatly too long, and the being too long becomes with each elapsing year a more serious offence. Mr. Hardy begins with a detailed description of his hero's smile, and proceeds thence to give a voluminous account of his large silver watch. Gabriel Oak's smile and his watch were doubtless respectable and important phenomena; but everything is relative, and daily becoming more so; and we confess that, as a hint of the pace at which the author proposed to proceed, his treatment of these facts produced upon us a deterring and depressing effect. (pp. 294-95)

The chief purpose of the book is, we suppose, to represent Gabriel's dumb, devoted passion, his biding his time, his rendering unsuspected services to the woman who has scorned him, his integrity and simplicity and sturdy patience. In all this the tale is very fairly successful, and Gabriel has a certain vividness of expression. But we cannot say that we either understand or like Bathsheba. She is a young lady of the inconsequential, wilful, mettlesome type which has lately become so much the fashion for heroines.... But Mr. Hardy's embodiment of her seems to us to lack reality; ... she remains alternately vague and coarse, and seems always artificial. This is Mr. Hardy's trouble; he rarely gets beyond ambitious artifice—the mechanical simulation of heat and depth and wisdom that are absent. Farmer Boldwood is a shadow, and Sergeant Troy an elaborate stage-figure. Everything human in the book strikes us as factitious and insubstantial; the only things we believe in are the sheep and the dogs. But, as we say, Mr. Hardy has gone astray very cleverly, and his superficial novel is a really curious imitation of something better. (pp. 296-97)

Henry James, "Hardy's 'Far from the Madding Crowd'," in The Nation (copyright 1924 by the Nation Associates, Inc.), Vol. CXIX, No. 3103, December 24, 1924 (and reprinted in his Literary Reviews and Essays, edited by Albert Mordell, Twayne Publishers, 1957, pp. 291-97).

E. M. FORSTER   (essay date 1927)

Hardy seems to me essentially a poet, who conceives of his novels from an enormous height. They are to be tragedies or tragi-comedies, they are to give out the sound of hammer-strokes as they proceed; in other words Hardy arranges events with emphasis on causality, the ground plan is a plot, and the characters are ordered to acquiesce in its requirements. Except in the person of Tess (who conveys the feeling that she is greater than destiny) this aspect of his work is unsatisfactory. His characters are involved in various snares, they are finally bound hand and foot, there is ceaseless emphasis on fate, and yet, for all the sacrifices made to it, we never see the action as a living thing as we see it in *Antigone* or *Berenice* or *The Cherry Orchard*. The fate above us, not the fate working through us—that is what is eminent and memorable in the Wessex novels. Hardy's success in *The Dynasts* . . . is complete, there the hammer-strokes are heard, cause and effect enchain the characters despite their struggles, complete contact between the actors and the plot is established. But in the novels, though the same superb and terrible machine works, it never catches humanity in its teeth; there is some vital problem that has not been answered, or even posed, in the misfortunes of Jude the Obscure. In other words the characters have been required to contribute too much to the plot, except in their rustic humours, their vitality has been impoverished, they have gone dry and thin. This, as far as I can make out, is the flaw running through Hardy's novels: he has emphasized causality more strongly than his medium permits. (pp. 93-4)

> *E. M. Forster, "The Plot," in his* Aspects of the Novel *(copyright 1927 by Harcourt Brace Jovanovich, Inc.; copyright 1955 by E. M. Forster; reprinted by permission of the publisher; in Canada by Edward Arnold Ltd. in connection with Kings College, Cambridge and The Society of Authors as the literary representatives of E. M. Forster's Estate), Harcourt, 1927, pp. 83-104.**

HARRIET MONROE   (essay date 1928)

Rereading Hardy's four or five books of poetry, one must be struck by the narrowness of his range, by the relentless enthusiasm, the fierceness, with which he pursues and shows up his world's poor little man-made gods. The opening dialogue of *The Dynasts* strikes the keynote of his philosophy—a sombre theme of which his shorter poems are phrases or variations. (pp. 327-28)

In *The Dynasts* the furies are let loose over the troubled face of Europe—we have war with all its horrors and without its pomp and pageantry. Reading this vast poem skippingly, I wondered how many of the poet's most ardent admirers had read its 520 40-line pages word for word, including those terribly prosy and unconvincing debates in the House of Commons. A great book, a great poem, in spite of its excessive length and the heavy impedimenta of detail it carries, because it presents in harshly swinging rhythms the enormous confusions out of which battles are won and lost, nations made and unmade; rumbling ominously, as a basic motive, the thunders of its central theme, its haughty challenge of the Immanent Will. Always expending his most sinister ironies upon the exceptional man—evidently incredulous of "genius"—the poet leads us magnificently to the tremendous climax, the rush and clash of mighty masses of men driven murderously back and forth by dread command in the battle of Waterloo. (pp. 328-29)

Hardy's hero is humanity—that *masse-mensch* which certain German dramatists have tried of late to put on the actual stage. Hardy's hero, like the Oedipus of Sophocles, is the noble and ignorant sport of remorseless powers.

Whipped back and forth, blind and helpless, by ruthless beings jealous of their omnipotence and intent on their own designs, he is worthy of a happier destiny. No more than Sophocles, does Hardy promise to the harassed soul compensatory bliss after death; for injustice there is no atonement here or hereafter.

Thus in *The Dynasts* Hardy's motive was as proletarian as Lenin's own, though he had no illusions about the people even while he pitied them as pawns in a game. He pitied them, but gave no advice; nowhere, in *The Dynasts* or elsewhere, does he hint at revolution or offer hope of a change. He accepts things as they are, but with a bitter cry of protest that they are not happier, more just, with a shaking of his fist at the stone wall which conceals supernal intrigue or indifference. (p. 329)

> *Harriet Monroe, "Comment: Thomas Hardy," in* Poetry *(© 1928 by The Modern Poetry Association), Vol. XXXI, No. 6, March, 1928, pp. 326-32.*

SAMUEL C. CHEW   (essay date 1928)

The writer of one monograph upon Hardy puts *Desperate Remedies* aside as a sort of *Titus Andronicus* among the Wessex novels, unworthy of any consideration. This is quite uncritical. It is an immature and in some respects disagreeable book, a tale of mystery, crime, startling coincidence, and melodramatic incident, which in its use of entanglement, suspense and moral obliquity reveals the strong influence of Wilkie Collins. (pp. 21-2)

But though obviously the work of an imitator, the book offers, both in structure and in character-drawing, certain adumbrations of some of the most typical traits of the later novels. Hardy gradually abandoned the employment of mystery and suspense in favor of the equally effective and perhaps more philosophical method of tragic anticipation; but these cruder means of sustaining interest did not disappear immediately after *Desperate Remedies*. Already he exhibits his ability to weave a highly complicated plot while keeping a sure grasp upon every strand of the tangle of purposes and interests. . . . [There] is no sweetness in the book, and subtlety only in those passages which are obviously mere transcriptions of early poems. Such paraphrases often take the form of disconnected aphorisms of a philosophic sort and in sombre vein, generally stiffly and awkwardly expressed. But there is no large philosophic implication that raises the interest above the level attained by a merely ingenious plot. Beneath the conscientiously documented external "realism" of Budmouth and Knapwater House there is a thoroughgoing romanticism of treatment; and even the realism of setting is of a sort that [Charles] Reade could produce any day from his scrapbooks and pigeon-holes. In this respect Hardy had a long way to go before he became master of the art that is visible in the living presentation of Dorchester in *The Mayor of Casterbridge*. An exception must be made, however, of the modest but convincing beginning of his transcripts of country life. . . . The occasional rustic scenes—the innkeeper and his friends, the postman, and the bellringers—are not only promising but excellent in themselves. (pp. 22-4)

The West Country characters were singled out as the best part of the book by judicious reviewers, one of whom declared them to be "almost worthy of George Eliot."

This remark is the first appearance in print of an idea that has haunted critics of Thomas Hardy.... But as a matter of fact the dissimilarities [between George Eliot and Hardy] are far more marked than the resemblances. Each writer uses the novel as a medium for the communication of ideas, and in each the tendency to philosophize becomes more outspoken in later books. But the views of life that they set forth are poles asunder. The tragic conflict in George Eliot's conception is between desire and conscience; it is an internal war. Conscience plays a small part in Hardy's books. He envisages life as a struggle between will and destiny. Man is master of his fate in George Eliot; the problem is a moral one. Fate, according to Hardy, is beyond human control. The one preaches action and resistance; the other submission, quietism. In both writers hereditary taints and the contaminations of environment play a part; but in George Eliot their influence is preponderating, in Hardy they do not determine the outcome. Both introduce the rustics of their native counties into some of their novels.... But the older novelist's carefully realistic studies of country life lack the lightness, relief, and flavour afforded by the undertone of quiet amusement which while it lessens the realism enhances the charm of Hardy's country scenes. There is little in common between Hardy's peasantry and George Eliot's small townspeople, though her success in delineating provincial types may have suggested to Hardy to turn to artistic account the customs and traditions of the Southron folk among whom he had grown up and whom he best knew. (pp. 24-6)

At all events it was this vein of his genius, and quite evidently following the lead of George Eliot, that he worked exclusively in ... *Under the Greenwood Tree*.... This is unpretentious in scale and theme and far removed from the complexities of *Desperate Remedies*. It is an intimate, detailed, humorous and delicately ironical story of a rural courtship.... [It] would have been a shrewd critic who could have detected at the time the undertone of bitterness in the portrayal of the indecision and deceptiveness of the winsome heroine, Fancy Day. It is, indeed, possible to exaggerate the significance of this undertone, for as a whole the tale is blithe enough. The simple love-story is set against a background of village life.... Never, save in *Far from the Madding Crowd* and in some of the Wessex scenes of *The Dynasts*, has Hardy surpassed the quaint humour of the rustic talk. (pp. 26-7)

The first book to bear Hardy's name upon its title-page was *A Pair of Blue Eyes*.... The obvious immaturity of this story has been admitted by its author. In the contrasting scenes of comedy and pathos there is evidence of the influence of Dickens, though the alternations are accomplished with more dexterity and refinement than the master was generally capable of. And too much of the influence of Wilkie Collins still remains. Sensational events and coincidences are too frequently resorted to in order to sustain the interest.... Chance is certainly overworked, and the artist, several times barely escaping the farcical, has not sufficient mastery to render acceptable so formidable a conglomeration of its freaks. But one must bear in mind the part that ''Hap'' plays in Hardy's scheme of things and perhaps regard these strangely juxtaposed events as extreme illustrations of the whimsicality of chance in disposing of human affairs. ''Hap'' does not change character; it alters the course of events.... And we shall see later that it is in part responsible for the ruined lives of Tess and Jude. But in *A

Pair of Blue Eyes these shortcomings of character account only in part for the resulting tragedy. (pp. 27-9)

A Pair of Blue Eyes marks a distinct advance upon the two former novels. There was no telling that the author of *Desperate Remedies* would ever accomplish anything of genuine worth; and *Under the Greenwood Tree*, for all its charm, promises only such things as *The Trumpet-Major*, some of the short stories, and the rustic scenes in other books. The philosophic implications of the present story, on the other hand, are harbingers of many of Hardy's most mature ideas. Human action is seen to be fettered by Cause on the one side and by Effect on the other. The human will, thinking itself free, is nevertheless bound fast by the ''purblind Doomsters'' that unthinkingly ordain what is to be. (pp. 29-30)

What [*A Pair of Blue Eyes*] lacks is just that quality that Hardy was later to possess to a degree equalled by no other English novelist: the ability to read into a series of happenings to a group of unimportant people in a remote district a universal application, a suggestion of the inescapable oneness that enfolds all human affairs. The style, when it seeks to be urbane, is still often awkward and ungracious; sentiments intended to be of tragic import are generally merely harsh and bitter; the ''strong'' scenes sometimes overreach themselves and verge upon the ludicrous. But there is a sure command of his medium in the landscape drawing and in the dealings with the peasantry. On the whole there is a relapse from the flexible and confident grasp of *Under the Greenwood Tree*; but it is a relapse that comes from essaying a more difficult feat of the novelist's art. (pp. 32-3)

In *Far from the Madding Crowd* many sides of Hardy's genius are shown fully developed. There are still the flashily sensational incidents of which he never wholly rid himself.... The structural mastery is by no means flawless.... But the many excellences of the novel ensured not only its immediate success (which carried with it the inconvenience of attaching to its author's name the reputation of being a first-rate story-teller, thereby obscuring for a generation his significance as a thinker) but its permanent place among the classics of the English novel. These merits were especially the variety and vivacity of the moods and interests; the power of devising a series of convincingly connected yet surprising situations; the insight into character, especially the character of a certain type—for Hardy always the preeminent type—of woman; the minutely detailed and sympathetic nature-description in which the interrelationship of man and the natural world is brought out with a forcefulness that revealed to some contemporary readers the significance of this connection in the author's view of life; and the passages of intensely vivid narrative such as the burning of the rick, the bringing home of Fanny's body, and the doings of the gargoyle during the rainstorm. (pp. 34-5)

The novel which in the opinion of many critics is Hardy's most nearly perfect work of art as well as his most profound and least biassed study of human nature is *The Return of the Native*.... The situation presented is that of *Far from the Madding Crowd* with certain variations: a love-entanglement between three men and two women. Two of these persons—Eustacia and Wildeve—are highly complex natures, impulsive, passionate, selfish, but not without some qualities that in other circumstances might have been turned to good; two others—Thomasin and Venn

—are steady, simple, and courageous. The first two are at odds with life and in violent war with the conditions among which they are placed; the second pair are steeped in, and in harmony with, their environment. One may well question the grim note which Hardy, in the definitive edition of the book, appended to it, to the effect that only the exigencies of periodical publication caused him to arrange an ending with the marriage of the two children of the heath and requesting readers of "an austere artistic code" to imagine that Thomasin remained a widow and that Venn disappeared from the country-side. A protest against the conventional "happy ending" was needed at the time and would have been wholesome. But to have ended this particular story in such a manner would have eliminated the *catharsis,* the cleansing of the passions, which is part of the function of tragedy. As the book stands, the implied lesson is effectively brought home by the destruction of the two rebels against circumstance in contrast to the serene content awarded those who submitted themselves to circumstance. There is a greater emphasis than heretofore upon the power of environment over the fortunes of humanity. The novelist develops with full and confident strength the line of thought somewhat crudely adumbrated in *A Pair of Blue Eyes,* for the tale is a tragedy of the human will, believing itself free yet ceaselessly entangled and thwarted by external forces. Egdon is the type of that Power that moves the world, a Power which is not inimical (for hostility implies intention, and intention consciousness) but indifferent to man. In some later novels and in many poems Hardy tends to differentiate more completely between Nature—that is, the natural world—and the Will of Force which governs it as well as man. All phenomena come to be looked upon as fellow-sufferers with man under a conscienceless and implacable despotism. (pp. 39-41)

After the concentration required in the creation of this great romance refreshment was found in writing several books of slighter build. The first of these is *The Trumpet-Major.* . . . *The Trumpet-Major* is a remarkable resurrection of the life of a bygone time of crisis; the atmosphere of the village and of the old mill, the tranquil setting against the background of war are accomplished with a pleasing, quiet art. Hardy here gives freer rein than usual to imagery, to description for its own sake, to racy dialogue that has little bearing upon the action. As a whole his books lack the quality of gusto; that quality is certainly present here. The story is too protracted, but it leaves a pleasant taste in the mouth, and in tone it is the sweetest and serenest of all the novels.

The feminine flux of fancy portrayed in this book becomes the chief motive of *A Laodicean* . . . , by all odds the weakest of Hardy's books. . . . The involved love-story is not worth untangling. (pp. 42-4)

A third slight and in some respects rather tiresome story, *Two on a Tower* . . . , is notable for the manner in which the human emotions are projected against a background of infinite space, for the young hero is an astronomer; and a "stellar gauge" is thus afforded whereby may be measured the infinitesimal insignificance of the actions and emotions of such apparent importance to the actors themselves. (p. 44)

Then came *The Mayor of Casterbridge* . . . , an astonishing rebirth of power in thought and art.

Interest in this book is not divided over a group of four or five people all portrayed with about the same amount of detail, but is concentrated in a manner that anticipates the technique of *Tess* and *Jude* upon a single man who represents, as Jude was later to represent still more harshly, the conflict of reason and impulse. The tragedy of Henchard's life does not lie in combinations of external circumstances, though they play their part. . . . He carries his fate with him. . . . Character is Fate. Henchard's shrewd, proud, illiterate, forceful, generous, passionate nature dashes itself to pieces against its own qualities. . . . Fortune does not favour him; but the directing Force of the universe uses his own pride and high temper and stubbornness to work his ruin, notwithstanding his many splendid qualities of heart and head. This conception reaches to the very heart of tragedy, and the belated humility of his last visit to his foster-daughter renders the tragedy more poignant still. The other characters are less strongly imagined, and intentionally so in order to throw the picture of Henchard into high relief. (pp. 46-8)

In its employment of the marvellous and the fantastic *Wessex Tales* harks back to Hardy's earlier years and is in striking contrast to *Life's Little Ironies.* Three stories are particularly memorable in this first set. These are "The Three Strangers," "The Withered Arm," and "The Distracted Preacher." The first two of these, and several others in the book, are studies in the freaks of coincidence. [The well-known tale of "The Three Strangers"] . . . may well be taken as a model of what the short story should be. (p. 51)

"The Withered Arm" tells of the chance simultaneous occurrence of a dreadful dream or hallucination of an incubus and of the beginning of a terrible disease. The coincidence is so tremendous that, though it can be accounted for rationally, it almost forces the acceptance of a supernatural explanation. It shows the degree to which the power to suggest mystery and dread may take the place, in a rationalistic age, of the downright supernaturalism of an age of romance. (pp. 51-2)

Of one of his former books a critic of the time had remarked that Hardy "like a true artist, never attempts by any indication of his own preferences to bias his reader's judgment." In [*Tess of the D'Urbervilles*] Hardy abandons his "objectivity." He forsakes his impassivity; he has a thesis to propound, and he does so in a recriminating fashion. This is not to say that to employ the novel as a means of promulgating a writer's views is necessarily and inherently wrong. But in so doing Hardy left behind him one of the characteristics of the earlier Wessex novels that was most impressive. . . . This change may well have been prompted by the reception of former romances by a public that greeted him as a capital story-teller while refusing to recognize the substratum of philosophic implication. (pp. 59-60)

It is possible, by setting certain passages in *Tess* over against certain others, to involve Hardy in a maze of self-contradictions. Nature is depicted at times as cruel and without sympathy; yet there are repeated suggestions of advocacy of the free play of natural impulses. The very measures that have been taken for the protection of society against the mercilessness of Nature are harshly attacked. And this attack is in itself an admission (which Hardy has elsewhere indicated as the centre of his practical philosophy) that man can ameliorate the conditions in which he lives. Yet man is not a free agent. It is possible so to follow Tess's career . . . as to make her out very largely the victim of her own stupidity and needless timidity. But these very qualities are part of her nature and beyond her control. (pp. 60-1)

And yet, when all is said, the impression that *Tess* leaves upon almost every candid and clearsighted reader is one of power and insight and sympathy and beauty—and hopefulness. The conclusion we are asked to draw is that passivity, quietism, is the only remedy for the ills of human life. But we do nothing of the sort. We deny that the book presents any general indictment of life. For these evils are not inherent in the nature of things. They are open to cure. (p. 61)

[The] judgement of posterity upon [*Jude the Obscure*] will be partly determined in accordance with whether the novelist's function is held to be the impartial and impassive reflection of life or whether he may take as his mission the promulgation of new and important ideas. By the old test, the test of ''objectivity,'' *Jude* fails to a degree greater even than does *Tess,* for though there are no such philosophic digressions as occur in *Tess,* the novelist is here even farther removed from austere self-control. By the other test it may be regarded as a milestone of advance, for it opens up new avenues of thought, it poses deliberately and courageously questions that all the world now faces. (pp. 67-8)

There is far more matter in *Jude* than can possibly be condensed into a paragraph or two, more perhaps, as Hardy confesses, than the novelist consciously put there. But it is possible to indicate very briefly some of the lines of thought. The central theme is ''the tragedy of unrealized aims.'' . . . Here we are presented with a man who is well-meaning and who holds a high ideal before him. But he comes of tainted stock, he is of low birth and narrow circumstances, and he is constantly being dragged down by his temperament. In the very hour of his visions of Christminster, the ''City of Light,'' seen now in his dreams, now in reality far off at sunset, there rushes upon him an irresistible inclination towards women and presently he is entrapped into a sordid marriage. Jude experiences to the full ''the fret and fever, derision and disaster, that may press in the wake of the strongest passion known to humanity''; and behind the temptation of sexual passion lurks another: the desire for strong liquor. Some hostile reviewers charged Hardy with putting to the credit of this man every aspiration, every fine yearning, and to the blame of circumstance each backsliding, each error, each yielding to desire. The charge misses the point of the whole tragedy: the book is not a denial of the existence of those happy souls who rise above temptations to the realizations of their ideals. It is the story of a man who . . . is a ''poor, damned, incautious, duped, unfortunate fool, the sport, the miserable victim of . . . hypochondriac imaginations, agonizing sensibility, and bedlam passions.'' (pp. 69-70)

In moments of cool analysis one may be tempted to ask whether it is not the author himself who has doomed his puppets to disaster, for there is little individuality in the several characters who are differentiated one from another by little save differences in opinion. But the unquestionably powerful impression made is an answer to that criticism. Almost the opening words describe Jude as ''the sort of man who was born to ache a good deal before the fall of the curtain upon his unnecessary life should signify that all was well with him again.'' Here we have the final example in

Hardy of the substitution of the instrument of tragic anticipation for the instrument of tragic suspense. The theme is announced immediately; and the heart-aches, the needlessness, the falling curtain, and the return to ''dateless oblivion and divine repose'' succeed each other like movements in a sombre symphony. (p. 74)

Samuel C. Chew, in his Thomas Hardy: Poet and Novelist *(copyright © 1928 by Alfred A. Knopf, Inc.), Knopf, 1928 (and reprinted by Russell & Russell Inc., 1964, 196 p.).*

VIRGINIA WOOLF   (essay date 1932)

[As we read Hardy's early books, *Desperate Remedies* and *Under the Greenwood Tree,*] there is a sense of waste. There is a feeling that Hardy's genius was obstinate and perverse; first one gift would have its way with him and then another. They would not consent to run together easily in harness. Such indeed was likely to be the fate of a writer who was at once poet and realist, a faithful son of field and down, yet tormented by the doubts and despondencies bred of book-learning; a lover of old ways and plain countrymen, yet doomed to see the faith and flesh of his forefathers turn to thin and spectral transparencies before his eyes.

To this contradiction Nature had added another element likely to disorder a symmetrical development. Some writers are born conscious of everything; others are unconscious of many things. Some, like Henry James and Flaubert, are able not merely to make the best use of the spoil their gifts bring in, but control their genius in the act of creation; they are aware of all the possibilities of every situation, and are never taken by surprise. The unconscious writers, on the other hand, like Dickens and Scott, seem suddenly and without their own consent to be lifted up and swept onwards. The wave sinks and they cannot say what has happened or why. Among them—it is the source of his strength and of his weakness—we must place Hardy. His own word, ''moments of vision'', exactly describes those passages of astonishing beauty and force which are to be found in every book that he wrote. With a sudden quickening of power which we cannot foretell, nor he, it seems, control, a single scene breaks off from the rest. . . . But the power goes as it comes. The moment of vision is succeeded by long stretches of plain daylight, nor can we believe that any craft or skill could have caught the wild power and turned it to a better use. The novels therefore are full of inequalities; they are lumpish and dull and inexpressive; but they are never arid; there is always about them a little blur of unconsciousness, that halo of freshness and margin of the unexpressed which often produce the most profound sense of satisfaction. It is as if Hardy himself were not quite aware of what he did, as if his consciousness held more than he could produce, and he left it for his readers to make out his full meaning and to supplement it from their own experience.

For these reasons Hardy's genius was uncertain in development, uneven in accomplishment, but, when the moment came, magnificent in achievement. The moment came, completely and fully, in *Far from the Madding Crowd.* The subject was right; the method was right; the poet and the countryman, the sensual man, the sombre reflective man, the man of learning, all enlisted to produce a book which, however fashions may chop and change, must hold its place among the great English novels. There is, in the first place, that sense of the physical world which Hardy more than any novelist can bring before us; the sense that the little prospect of man's existence is ringed by a landscape which, while it exists apart, yet confers a deep and solemn beauty upon his drama. (pp. 268-70)

[Nobody] can deny Hardy's power—the true novelist's power—to make us believe that his characters are fellow-beings driven by their own passions and idiosyncrasies, while they have—and this is the poet's gift—something symbolical about them which is common to us all.

And it is when we are considering Hardy's power of creating men and women that we become most conscious of the profound differences that distinguish him from his peers. We look back at a number of these characters and ask ourselves what it is that we remember them for. We recall their passions. We remember how deeply they have loved each other and often with what tragic results. . . . But we do not remember how they have loved. We do not remember how they talked and changed and got to know each other, finely, gradually, from step to step and from stage to stage. Their relationship is not composed of these intellectual apprehensions and subtleties of perception which seem so slight yet are so profound. In all the books love is one of the great facts that mould human life. But it is a catastrophe; it happens suddenly and overwhelmingly, and there is little to be said about it. The talk between the lovers when it is not passionate is practical or philosophic, as though the discharge of their daily duties left them with more desire to question life and its purpose than to investigate each other's sensibilities. Even if it were in their power to analyse their emotions, life is too stirring to give them time. They need all their strength to deal with the downright blows, the freakish ingenuity, the gradually increasing malignity of fate. They have none to spend upon the subtleties and delicacies of the human comedy. (pp. 273-74)

But the opposite is equally true. If we do not know his men and women in their relations to each other, we know them in their relations to time, death, and fate. If we do not see them in quick agitation against the lights and crowds of cities, we see them against the earth, the storm, and the seasons. We know their attitude towards some of the most tremendous problems that can confront mankind. They take on a more than mortal size in memory. We see them, not in detail but enlarged and dignified. . . . They have a force in them which cannot be defined, a force of love or of hate, a force which in the men is the cause of rebellion against life, and in the women implies an illimitable capacity for suffering, and it is this which dominates the character and makes it unnecessary that we should see the finer features that lie hid. This is the tragic power; and, if we are to place Hardy among his fellows, we must call him the greatest tragic writer among English novelists. (pp. 274-76)

> *Virginia Woolf, "The Novels of Thomas Hardy,"
> in her* The Second Common Reader *(copyright
> 1932 by Harcourt Brace Jovanovich, Inc.; copyright 1960 by Leonard Woolf; reprinted by permission of the publisher), Harcourt, 1932, pp. 266-80.*

T. S. ELIOT   (essay date 1933)

The work of Thomas Hardy represents an interesting example of a powerful personality uncurbed by any institutional attachment or by submission to any objective beliefs: unhampered by any ideas, or even by what sometimes acts as a partial restraint upon inferior writers, the desire to please a large public. He seems to me to have written as nearly for the sake of "self-expression" as a man well can; and the self which he had to express does not strike me as a particularly wholesome or edifying matter of communication. He was indifferent even to the prescripts of good writing: he wrote sometimes overpoweringly well, but always very carelessly; at times his style touches sublimity without ever having passed through the stage of being good. In consequence of his self-absorption, he makes a great deal of landscape; for landscape is a passive creature which lends itself to an author's mood. Landscape is fitted too for the purposes of an author who is interested not at all in men's minds, but only in their emotions; and perhaps only in men as vehicles for emotions. It is only, indeed, in their emotional paroxysms that most of Hardy's characters come alive. . . . But as the majority is capable neither of strong emotion nor of strong resistance, it always inclines to admire passion for its own sake, unless instructed to the contrary; and, if somewhat deficient in vitality, people imagine passion to be the surest evidence of vitality. This in itself may go towards accounting for Hardy's popularity. (pp. 94-5)

> *T. S. Eliot, "Thomas Hardy" (1933), in his* Points
> of View *(reprinted by permission of Faber and
> Faber Ltd.), Faber and Faber, 1941, pp. 94-5.*

H. E. BATES   (essay date 1936)

[*Tess of the D'Urbervilles* is] almost the only novel of Hardy's in which a single character is great enough to transcend the too-crushing mechanisms of plot. *Tess* has for its sub-title *A Pure Woman*. Why? Why this careful preliminary emphasis on purity? Why this laboured attempt on Hardy's part to establish Tess as an emblem of chastity before the book begins? Obviously it is, I think, because the dice is loaded before the book begins, and that Hardy knows only too well that it is loaded for the simple reason that he has loaded it himself. Tess was not only doomed in the book but—in Hardy's day at any rate—doomed outside it too. Poor Tess!—she was victimized both ways, by Hardy on the one side and by Victorian England on the other. With Tess the cry is not *'Tis Pity she's a Whore!* but *'Tis Pity she is Pure!* And Hardy knew that—he knew that whatever he might think, Victorian England would think the opposite. Tess for him might be the purest of the pure, but for the Victorians that very purity was the secret of the trouble. A wanton labelled wanton, yes—but not a wanton labelled pure.

But today Tess is neither pure nor wanton. Why indeed should she be? Her little misdeed, on which after all the whole book depends, arouses in the modern reader no feelings of moral outrage or disgust. Why is it? Tess herself has not changed, the printed word remains as Hardy left it. But clearly there is a change somewhere, and clearly it must be either in us or in contemporary standards of morality. And since we are asked to judge Tess by standards of purity the change is clearly in morality itself. Morality in fact has done some quick-change tricks since Hardy's day, so that what was moral for him and immoral for his readers may have, and in fact has, a totally different aspect and meaning for us.

Which brings us at once to the great defect in Hardy's make-up as a novelist. Living in the heart of an age where morality was the great watchword he may perhaps be excused for not having rumbled morality, for not seeing that morality, as a fixed entity, does not really exist, that it is really nothing but a fashion, which changes from one year to another, from one country to another, from one place to another, and more especially from one person to another, as surely as the fashion and taste in hats or furniture. . . . In championing Tess as pure, Hardy was committing, as a novelist, just as grave an error as those who condemned her as a wanton. For it is not the novelist's business to champion at all, any more than it is his business to judge. His job is to create and interpret. Shakespeare does not champion Desdemona, nor does he give *Othello* the title of *Desdemona: a Pure Woman*, though he might have felt every bit as justified as Hardy in doing so. He creates and interprets, and manages also to do something else for which there is no recipe: he touches us to tears of pity. But for Hardy mere creation and interpretation was not enough. He must come boldly out on the side of purity. He took up, in fact, a Moral Attitude. With the inevitable result that we wonder today what all the fuss was about. We are no longer scandalized or outraged by Tess's behavior, and it is only by some intangible and touching quality of greatness in Tess herself that we are moved to any emotions resembling pity at all. (pp. 236-38)

[The] constant elaborated building-up of plot and the subordination of everything to it . . . has made Hardy, in many ways, a second-class writer. . . . Technically, in spite of that genius for the creation of atmosphere, Hardy can at times be the biggest bungler with words in the whole history of the novel. The latinized, slow-moving prose reaches its worst depths in such phrases, common on every page, as the "spectral, half-compounded, aqueous light", "a domiciliary intimacy", "equinoctial darkness", "a pulsating flexuous domesticity". Thousands of grandiose wasted words lie along Hardy's path as a novelist. Living in an age that adored elaborations he wrote for it as though he were saying to himself, "I have profound works to write. The longer and more elaborate the words I use the more profound I shall seem to be."

Oddly enough, that overburdened prose now creates the entirely opposite effect, an effect of something pompous and meretricious. Hardy seems far more profound when using the far simpler idioms of poetry. His knotty little poems are in fact his choicest works—the sharp little nuts of his own autumn, tense and bitterly flavoured with the refined salt of his irony. As a novelist, however, he suffers much from having to carry the burden of precisely those characteristics by which he was once judged to be great. His plots and his prose have revenged themselves upon him completely. (p. 239)

> *H. E. Bates, "Joseph Conrad and Thomas Hardy" (reprinted by permission of Lawrence Pollinger Limited, as agents for The Estate of H. E. Bates), in* The English Novelists: A Survey of the Novel by Twenty Contemporary Novelists, *edited by Derek Verschoyle, Chatto & Windus, 1936, pp. 231-44.**

D. H. LAWRENCE (essay date 1936)

It is urged against Thomas Hardy's characters that they do unreasonable things—quite, quite unreasonable things. They are always going off unexpectedly and doing something that nobody would do. That is quite true, and the charge is amusing. These people of Wessex are always bursting suddenly out of bud and taking a wild flight into flower, always shooting suddenly out of a tight convention, a tight, hide-bound cabbage state into something quite madly personal. It would be amusing to count the number of special marriage licenses taken out in Hardy's books. Nowhere, except perhaps in Jude, is there the slightest development of personal action in the characters: it is all explosive. Jude, however, does see more or less what he is doing, and acts from choice. He is more consecutive. The rest explode out of the convention. They are people each with a real, vital, potential self, even the apparently wishy-washy heroines of the earlier books, and this self suddenly bursts the shell of manner and convention and commonplace opinion, and acts independently, absurdly, without mental knowledge or acquiescence.

And from such an outburst the tragedy usually develops. For there does exist, after all, the great self-preservation scheme, and in it we must all live. Now to live in it after bursting out of it was the problem these Wessex people found themselves faced with. And they never solved the problem, none of them except the comically, insufficiently treated Ethelberta. (pp. 410-11)

This is the theme of novel after novel: remain quite within the convention, and you are good, safe, and happy in the long run, though you never have the vivid pang of sympathy on your side: or, on the other hand, be passionate, individual, wilful, you will find the security of the convention a walled prison, you will escape, and you will die, either of your own lack of strength to bear the isolation and the exposure, or by direct revenge from the community, or from both. (p. 411)

[In Hardy's novels] there exists a great background, vital and vivid, which matters more than the people who move upon it. . . . Upon the vast, incomprehensible pattern of some primal morality greater than ever the human mind can grasp, is drawn the little, pathetic pattern of man's moral life and struggle, pathetic, almost ridiculous. The little fold of law and order, the little walled city within which man has to defend himself from the waste enormity of nature, becomes always too small, and the pioneers venturing out with the code of the walled city upon them, die in the bonds of that code, free and yet unfree, preaching the walled city and looking to the waste.

This is the wonder of Hardy's novels, and gives them their beauty. The vast, unexplored morality of life itself, what we call the immorality of nature, surrounds us in its eternal incomprehensibility, and in its midst goes on the little human morality play, with its queer frame of morality and its mechanized movement; seriously, portentously, till some one of the protagonists chances to look out of the charmed circle, weary of the stage, to look into the wilderness raging round. Then he is lost, his little drama falls to pieces, or becomes mere repetition, but the stupendous theatre outside goes on enacting its own incomprehensible drama, untouched. There is this quality in almost all Hardy's work, and this is the magnificent irony it all contains, the challenge, the contempt. Not the deliberate ironies, little tales of widows or widowers, contain the irony of human life as we live it in our self-aggrandized gravity, but the big novels, *The Return of the Native*, and the others.

And this is the quality Hardy shares with the great writers, Shakespeare or Sophocles or Tolstoi, this setting behind the small action of his protagonists the terrific action of unfathomed nature; setting a smaller system of morality, the one grasped and formulated by the human consciousness within the vast, uncomprehended and incomprehensible morality of nature or of life itself, surpassing human consciousness. The difference is, that whereas in Shakespeare or Sophocles the greater, uncomprehended morality, or fate, is actively transgressed and gives active punishment, in Hardy and Tolstoi the lesser, human morality, the mechanical system is actively transgressed, and holds, and punishes the protagonist, whilst the greater morality is only passively, negatively transgressed, it is represented merely as being present in background, in scenery, not taking any active part, having no direct connexion with the protagonist. (pp. 419-20)

Thomas Hardy's metaphysic is something like Tolstoi's. ''There is no reconciliation between Love and the Law,'' says Hardy. ''The spirit of Love must always succumb before the blind, stupid, but overwhelming power of the Law.''

Already as early as *The Return of the Native* he has come to this theory, in order to explain his own sense of failure. But before that time, from the very start, he has had an overweening theoretic antagonism to the Law. ''That which is physical, of the body, is weak, despicable, bad,'' he said at the very start. He represented his fleshy heroes as villains, but very weak and maundering villains. At its worst, the Law is a weak, craven sensuality: at its best, it is a passive inertia. It is the gap in the armour, it is the hole in the foundation.

Such a metaphysic is almost silly. If it were not that man is much stronger in feeling than in thought, the Wessex novels would be sheer rubbish, as they are already in parts. *The Well-Beloved* is sheer rubbish, fatuity, as is a good deal of *The Dynasts* conception.

But it is not as a metaphysician that one must consider Hardy. He makes a poor show there. For nothing in his work is so pitiable as his clumsy efforts to push events into line with his theory of being, and to make calamity fall on those who represent the principle of Love. He does it exceedingly badly, and owing to this effort his form is execrable in the extreme.

His feeling, his instinct, his sensuous understanding is, however, apart from his metaphysic, very great and deep, deeper than that, perhaps, of any other English novelist. Putting aside his metaphysic, which must always obtrude when he thinks of people, and turning to the earth, to landscape, then he is true to himself. (p. 480)

> *D. H. Lawrence, "A Study of Thomas Hardy," in* Phoenix: The Posthumous Papers of D. H. Lawrence, *edited by Edward D. McDonald (copyright 1936 by Frieda Lawrence; copyright renewed © 1964 by the estate of the late Frieda Lawrence Ravagli; reprinted by permission of the Viking Press Inc.), Viking Penguin, 1936, pp. 398-516.*

AMIYA CHAKRAVARTY (essay date 1938)

[In *The Dynasts*] Hardy's mythopoeic mind could enfold an entire panorama of human events, link it up with the primal forces of Nature, and dwell on purpose and circumstance, details of history and local traditions, without making the drama suffer from any effects of super-imposition or of deliberate allegorical intent. The fusion is complete; the Homeric sweep of the poem is finely saturated with modern psychological interpretation; the general design and the minutiae of colour and curve take in the historical perspective as naturally as they weave into a pattern the multiform strands of character, commentary, and local traditions. It moves with the momentum of a vast unfolding drive of the time-spirit; *The Dynasts* in many ways is the most lucid and cogent exposition of the mind of our Age because its illumination comes from its power of suggestion. It is not a didactic drama set upon a rationalized platform, tortured by its own purposiveness. (pp. 8-9)

Hardy's 'philosophy' . . . will be found in the implications, rather than in any closely elaborated doctrine. *The Dynasts*, the final fruit and major event of his creative life, should be studied as one studies the *Heimskringla*, the Arthurian, the Niamh, or the Nibelung legends; and yet, being a saga of the modern Age, a new critical sense informing its whole has to be reckoned with. Its philosophical drive is no less keen than that of Langland's *Piers Plowman*, but, as in that intuitional poem, the bare bones of logic are entirely covered over with living significances which defy philosophical labelling. In this *The Dynasts* differs from Milton's Epic which sets out deliberately to justify the ways of God to men, and, incidentally, succeeds in finally establishing Satan in literature. (p. 11)

By substituting the word 'Will' or 'the Unconscious' for 'God' we would come close to the character of *The Dynasts*. But it is important to stress the curious blend of imagination with a philosophical theme in *The Dynasts* which makes it a modern mythology. The sense of 'prior relationships' is constant throughout Hardy's drama; the human relationships by themselves cannot tell the whole story. The drama of creation must be shown by the poet with the actors appearing in what to him is a proper order of relationship, so that we may begin to understand the meaning. The primal Unconscious; the consciousness of animal and man; reason and compassion, emerge as manifestations of some yet unrevealed urge of existence.

Hardy's drama is allegorical, but in the modern sense. (p. 13)

It has been necessary to dwell on [the] mythopoeic character of *The Dynasts* because otherwise we may be led to examine it either as a philosophical system or as a narrative, whereas in *The Dynasts* both processes meet in a curious imaginative fusion. Such methods of analysis may tend 'to constrict and prevent that fluidity of meanings which . . . are everywhere in ambience', and as post-War poetry shares the character of Hardy's drama, perhaps a new approach to the latter will be necessary in order that the contemporary trend can be clearly recognized. (p. 14)

The drama of *The Dynasts* is the drama of human consciousness, in which disruptive forces are at work; a part or quality of this consciousness detests these forces and tries to check them, or at least hopes they may be checked, but it cannot control them. Napoleon's blind energy is challenged by the heroism of Nelson, who, even if his methods are those of war, and often unavailing, believes in a moral purpose, and stands for justice. We are shown a titanic storm of the prime forces of Nature, and the torment of self-consciousness, itself a product of the former. Evil is struggling with itself, it is no longer free from some incipient germs of self-criticism; the events, good and bad, involve the comments and reactions of reason, and of the emotions. All the wars on the European continent, the tussle between the individual wills of king and commoner, of nation and nation, are enveloped within a single drama of consciousness. (pp. 24-5)

The workings of the human mind, especially of that no-man's-land between the body and consciousness, are yielding fresh extensions to reason every day; the study of the layers of consciousness has given remarkable results. And yet at the very threshold of immense achievements mankind is threatened by a world-wide cataclysm of disruption.

Hardy's *The Dynasts* shows the whole spectacle; its message is in its realization of the nature of the problem of consciousness. Evils can be dealt with by palliative measures, but only a combination of them resulting from the assiduous application of the higher Will of Man in every sphere can be remedial. (pp. 80-1)

> *Amiya Chakravarty, in his "The Dynasts" and the Post-War Age in Poetry: A Study in Modern Ideas (© Oxford University Press 1938; reprinted by permission of Oxford University Press), Oxford University Press, London, 1938, 174 p.*

JOHN CROWE RANSOM   (essay dates 1940)

Hardy is not one of the poets who have been much studied, and argued over, and finally assigned some rather fixed place in the line of poets, by the professional "scholars"; by the persons who canonize poets and put them into circulation officially through textbooks and classrooms. . . .

His kind of poetry is so much his own, and so far from standard as that might be defined by nineteenth-century tradition, that it is difficult to find the place for him in a poetic "line." Either he was not influenced by the current styles of poetry that were admired in his lifetime, or else he was not adaptive and could not change from the style which he came into at the outset, as into a style that suited him. For the one reason or the other he continued in it, though he widened its range. (p. 13)

At any time in Hardy's life there must have been twenty poets whose easiness with the formal proprieties of theme and diction exceeded his own. And this is not an observation which it would be a pleasure to document. I should avoid it by recording in advance my consent to the charge that Hardy is an uneven poet, and capable of marring fine poems by awkward and tasteless passages; and even of writing whole poems that now are too harsh, and again are too merely pedestrian. For some reason, however, I must confess that these lapses have often seemed to endear the poet to me, and to other readers I know, and I can think but of one way to rationalize so odd a reception: by the consideration that "bad form," though generally a thing to be reprehended, is possibly under one circumstance to be approved: where we feel that the ignorance behind it is the condition of the innocence and spontaneity which we admire in the general personal context. (p. 14)

He was an amateur who did not have the professional equipment to see how provincial and honest his poetry was, nor how rare. He played boldly with syntax and lexicon, as Shakespeare had done, and he knew, if only from his acquaintance with Shakespeare, what the rights of poets were. But when he looked at his object the object was the actual one under his eye, not one out of Shakespeare, or out of literary conventions elsewhere. A superior metaphysical validity belongs to his lyrics and little narratives in that the particularity of their detail is sharp and local. I think highly of that kind of genuineness. (pp. 14-15)

> *John Crowe Ransom, "Honey and Gall" (copyright, 1940, by John Crowe Ransom), in* The Southern Review, *Vol. 6, No. 1, Summer, 1940, pp. 2-19.*

F. R. LEAVIS   (essay date 1940)

[Though] I shouldn't think of calling Hardy a great poet, I do believe that he wrote a certain amount of major poetry. (p. 87)

Lack of distinction in Hardy becomes a positive quality. If one says that he seems to have no sensitiveness for words, one recognizes at the same time that he has made a style out of stylelessness. There is something extremely personal about the gauche unshrinking mismarriages—group-mismarriages—of his diction, in which, with naïf aplomb, he takes as they come the romantic-poetical, the prosaic banal, the stilted literary, the colloquial, the archaistic, the erudite, the technical, the dialect word, the brand-new Hardy coinage. (p. 88)

[In Hardy's poetry] one might find, perhaps, twenty or thirty pages deserving to be handed down; poems that present in quintessential form what is most living in the novels. But they would not of themselves have won for Hardy the repute of major poet. He owes this largely, no doubt, to his preoccupation with life's ironies and to his talk about the Immanent Will—to all those elements in his work which might encourage a belief that it conveys an impressive underlying metaphysic. But any real claim he may have to major status rests upon half-a-dozen poems alone: "Neutral Tones," "A Broken Appointment," "The Self-Unseeing," "The Voice," "After a Journey," "During Wind and Rain." (pp. 91-2)

Hardy is notable for limitation rather than breadth. The effect is rather to be explained by the tenacious simplicity of character that enables him to say, "I am just the same." His preoccupation with time brings with it no sense of unreality. . . . Moreover, the singleminded integrity of his preoccupation with a real world and a real past, the intentness of his focus upon particular facts and situations, gives this poetry the solidest kind of emotional substance. There is no emotionality. The emotion seems to inhere in the reality recognized and grasped. The effect is of a kind we call major in contrast with the specifically minor-poetical of "Tears, idle tears" or "Break, break, break," where the emotion is an intoxication and the poignancy a luxury. I don't think there is much more that need be said about Hardy's major status. (pp. 94-5)

> *F. R. Leavis, "Hardy the Poet" (copyright, 1940, by F. R. Leavis), in* The Southern Review, *Vol. 6, No. 1, Summer, 1940, pp. 87-98.*

R. P. BLACKMUR (essay date 1940)

Hardy was a free man in everything that concerns the poet; which is to say, helpless, without tradition; and he therefore rushed for support into the slavery of ideas whenever his freedom failed him. The astonishing thing is—as with Shelley and Swinburne to a lesser degree—that he was able to bring so much poetry with him into a pile of work that shows, like a brush heap, all the disadvantages of the nineteenth-century mind as it affected poetry, and yet shows almost none of the difficulties—whether overcome, come short of, or characteristic—belonging to the production or appreciation of poetry itself. (pp. 37-8)

Almost the only objective influence consistently exerted upon his verse is the influence of meter; from which indeed his happiest and some of his most awkward effects come. There remain, of course, besides, neither objective nor otherwise, but pervasive, the fermenting, synergical influence of words thrown together, and the primary influence of the rhythm of his sensibility; that double influence in language used, which a skillful poet knows how to invoke, and which *is* invoked in just the degree that he has the sense of the actuality wanted already within him, when it shows as the very measure of his imagination and the object of his craft, but which, in the poet who, like Hardy, has violated his sensibility with ideas, comes only adventitiously and in flashes, and shows chiefly as the measure of imagination missed. (pp. 41-2)

Surely no serious writer ever heaped together so much *sordid* adultery, so much *haphazard* surrender of human value as Hardy did in these poems, and with never a pang or incentive but the pang of pattern and the incentive of inadequacy, and yet asked his readers to consider that haphazard sordor a full look at the worst—a tragic view of life —exacted with honesty and power. (pp. 42-3)

Hardy never rejected the tradition of English poetry; probably, indeed, if he thought about it at all, he thought he followed it and even improved it by his metrical experiments. What he did was more negative than rejection. He failed to recognize and failed to absorb those modes of representing felt reality persuasively and credibly and justly, which make up, far more than meters and rhymes and the general stock of versification, the creative habit of imagination, and which are the indefeasible substance of tradition. (p. 47)

Hardy really lacked . . . the craft of his profession—technique in the wide sense; that craft, which, as a constant, reliable possession, would have taught him the radical necessity as it furnished the means, of endowing every crucial statement with the virtual force of representation. . . . In Hardy's case, the interesting fact is that he sometimes possessed the tradition and sometimes did not; and the fertile possibility is that possession or lack may explain what otherwise seems the accident of success or failure. (pp. 48-9)

> *R. P. Blackmur, "The Shorter Poems of Thomas Hardy," in his* The Expense of Greatness *(copyright, 1940, by R. P. Blackmur; reprinted by permission of Betty Bredemeier Davison, as literary executrix to the Estate of R. P. Blackmur), Arrow Editions, 1940 (and reprinted by Peter Smith, 1958), pp. 37-73.*

V. S. PRITCHETT (essay date 1942)

How little a novelist's choice of story and character widens or changes between his first book and his last. In an obvious way there seems to be no kinship between Hardy's *Under the Greenwood Tree* and *Jude the Obscure,* but reading these books again we see their differences are on the surface. Only age separates the youthful pastoral from the middle-aged tract. One is the sapling, pretty in its April leafage, the other is the groaning winter oak, stark with argument; but the same bitter juice rises in both their stems. Sue Bridehead is one of the consequences of being Fancy Day, Jude is a Dick Dewy become conscious of his obscurity; the tantalised youth has become the frustrated man. . . . What has changed, of course, is the stretch of the scene. After the *Greenwood Tree,* we are always struck by the largeness of the panorama and by the narrowness of Hardy's single, crooked, well-trodden path across it. And if the path is narrow, so is the man. He stands like a small, gaitered farmer in his field, dry, set, isolated and phlegmatic, the most unlikely exponent of human passion, but somehow majestic because he is on the skyline. (p. 99)

In the pastoral realism of *Under the Greenwood Tree* there is a visual vividness, despite some old-fashioned phrasing, which is what we especially like today and the talk of the cottagers is taken, rich and crooked, as it comes from their mouths. . . . But long before *Jude,* the visual brightness had gone. There appeared instead that faculty of instant abstraction in Hardy's eye, whereby the people, the towns, the country, became something generalised in the mind as if Time had absorbed them. The light catches the vanes of Christminster and they glint the more brightly because they are seen against an abstract foreground "of secondary and tertiary hues". One is looking at things not seen by an eye but known by a mind, by tens of thousands of minds. If society in the mass could see, if a town or village could look, this is what they would see. Masses themselves, they would see beyond the surface to the mass beneath. The realism of Hardy is a realism of mass, you are aware all the time that hundreds of other people are passing and bumping into Jude and Sue Bridehead when they stand in the street or go to the train, carrying their passion with them. They are tired, not fired, by passion. (pp. 102-03)

The chief criticism of Hardy's technique as a novelist usually falls upon his use of coincidence, melodrama and fateful accidental meetings. (pp. 103-04)

Far indeed from suffering from coincidence Hardy is the master of coincidence. He is its master because he is the master of the movement of people. What are the scenes we most vividly remember? They are, I think, the journeys. The whole burden of the story weighs upon them. The tragic idea of people circling further and further from the crux of their fate and yet mile by mile coming inescapably nearer to it, is very familiar; Hardy fills in the provincial detail of this conception. Again, it is not tragic feeling which is his subject, but the burden of feeling. At a high moment like the murder of the children in *Jude,* Hardy completely fails to convince or move us, and this is not only because the whole episode is too much in itself; the failure owes something to the fact that in the preceding pages which describe how Jude and Sue are turned out of one lodging after another in Christminster, either because they are unmarried or because they have noisy children, Hardy has described something far more real, more fated and more significant. (pp. 104-05)

Hardy was at his worst in attacking convention, because his interests were so narrow. What are his tragedies? Love stories only, the enormous Victorian preoccupation with sex. He seems never to have outgrown the tantalisation, the frustration which the Sue Brideheads brought down upon their husbands, making them expert, as only the true Puritan can be, on the pathetic subject of female vanity. (pp. 105-06)

V. S. Pritchett, "The First and Last of Hardy," in his In My Good Books *(reprinted by permission of A D Peters & Co Ltd; in Canada by the author and Chatto and Windus Ltd.), Chatto & Windus, 1942, pp. 99-106.*

HARVEY CURTIS WEBSTER   (essay date 1947)

The Return of the Native is the most pessimistic of [Hardy's] early novels. From the first description of Egdon Heath until the close of the story, this dreary and unfertile waste seems to symbolize the indifference with which Nature views the pathetic fate of human beings. Occasionally the reader is likely to look upon the long-enduring barrenness and apparent purposelessness of the heath as a sign of its kinship to man, to feel that it is like man, slighted and enduring. More frequently, its somber beauty, which, Hardy tells us, is the only kind of beauty that thinking mankind can any longer appreciate, reminds us that man is of no more significance than an insect against its far-extending barrenness. It is the unsympathetic background for the human scene. What happens to man is not its concern. Like the forces of Nature, it has participated passively in man's slow and unhappy progress through disillusive centuries, unconcerned with the joys or sorrows of petty humankind.

What the dreary atmosphere of Egdon Heath makes us feel, the author's interpolations emphasize. The modern facial expression portrays a "view of life as a thing to be put up with." A long train of disillusive centuries have shown the defects of natural law and the quandary in which their operation has placed man. Life causes one to set aside the vision of what ought to be and induces a listless making the best of the world as it is.

More than in any other Hardy novel, we feel the power of the forces that control man's destiny. Heartless Circumstance, this time *not* viewed as an environment that can be contended against, has placed Eustacia Vye in a situation in which her gifts are a plague rather than a blessing. Natural law leads man from one mistake to another. Chance, in the shape of accident and coincidence, joins itself with these other unsympathetic powers to assure man's unhappiness. . . . Undoubtedly Hardy believes that there is nothing actively malign in Egdon Heath, in natural law, or in the play of Circumstance or accident; but the very indifference of these forces to the fate of human beings results in such unhappiness that we are likely to assume that sinister gods control the action.

Against the somber atmosphere of an indifferent and Chance-guided universe, the characters move in accordance with natural law. Eustacia's physical attractiveness compels the love of Charley, Clym, and Wildeve. By a similar force Eustacia is drawn to Wildeve and Clym. None of them is fitted for each other, but their imaginations cause them to believe that their ideas of each other are real. Disillusionment and pain result. (pp. 120-21)

Harvey Curtis Webster, in his On a Darkling Plain: The Art and Thought of Thomas Hardy *(reprinted by permission of the author; copyright 1947 by The University of Chicago), University of Chicago Press, 1947, 240 p.*

JAMES GRANVILLE SOUTHWORTH   (essay date 1947)

In order to understand Hardy we must realize . . . that he is both Victorian and Modern. Prosodically we might call him the last of the Victorians. His difficulty is that technically he came too late to perfect any of the traditional forms of poetry. He has made no real contribution to English prosody in spite of his experimentation, which to me is halfhearted experimentation. This does not mean that there are not times when the force of his thought is sufficiently great to give new and almost unexpected life to old forms. In his few best poems this happens. Taken as a whole, however, Hardy is too fragmentary. Individual poems may satisfy the canons of criticism, may fuse thought and form to create a forceful aesthetic reaction, but the effect of the poems taken as a whole is unsatisfactory. He is a modern in his ideas. . . . These ideas, ideas which I think the elder Browning was more prepared to accept, or at least was less shocked than was Hardy, are those of the scientists of the Victorian Age, the ideas of Mill, Huxley, Darwin, and others. The ideas that impregnate his poetry are still too inexpertly grasped to be fused into workable materials. He did not fully comprehend their manifold implications. This accounts both for the tentative and the nostalgic qualities in his work. His successors, building on his foundations, will be able to improve upon his experiments. This failure fully to grasp the significance of ideas deprives his poetry of the cohesiveness that results from conviction, and because of this the reader is left with no unified impression. He senses a struggle, at times an intense one, to evolve a faith, but the struggle never resolves into the exaltation of achievement. The reader never moves steadily forward with the poet sensing that he is being led upward as he is with Dante, Milton, Shakespeare, and Goethe, nor as he is with Donne, Wordsworth, Keats, Hopkins, or Yeats. Nor has he done as did Browning, whose problem, as Sir Leslie Stephen has justly remarked, was "always to show what are the really noble elements which are eternally valuable in spite of failure to achieve tangible results." Consequently the reader is left with a sense of frustration and indecision. He sees beauty, occasionally great and carefully wrought beauty, in the individual fragments, but they lie scattered on the ground and form no edifice in a realm where there are many mansions.

The critic's problem is a perplexing one. Can he examine minutely these fragments and give them the praise that only the finished work merits? When praising this or that fragment he runs the risk of being understood as praising the whole achievement, of being inconsistent in his point of view when a consistent one is impossible.

Hardy does not take his place among the great poets, although greatnesses are in him. If by greatness we mean "the construction of an inner world and the communication of this inner world to the physical world of humanity" I think we could say that he is great in a few of his shorter poems in which he struggles with his faith—his desire to believe and his slavery to reason. In these he is never conciliatory, he is not self-conscious, and his feelings reveal nobility of soul, although a frustrated one. These poems are soul-searching. Because of these qualities we find in them his best although not his most obvious music. (pp. 221-23)

His poetry is in one respect not intensely personal. In another, it is. He is not primarily concerned with the joys or sorrows that he himself had experienced. He is not, in other words, essentially a subjective poet in the usually accepted meaning of the term. . . . This does not mean that his work is not drawn from his own experience; but it does mean that it was only rarely drawn from his own deepest inner experience, an experience which defies analysis in workaday terms. (p. 225)

Although Hardy's sympathies were broad and his tolerance was all embracing, the final effect of his poetry is not warm and pulsating. His poetry is of the head rather than of the heart. His preoccupation with form rather than color reveals the dominance of the intellectual over the emotional. One never experiences a nostalgic sadness when reading him in spite of the nostalgic quality in the work itself. Although he wrote some poetry early in life, the vast corpus of his work was the result of middle and old age when our spirits, as he himself said, "are less subject to steep gradients than in youth." It is the importance of this that many persons are inclined to miss when they speak of him as a pessimist. . . . Certainly, Hardy has such a ruthless honesty and sincerity when presenting his observations on life in general, and the people of Wessex in particular, that the worst that can be said of him is that he is a realist with a realist's limitations. He does not distort facts nor gloss over truths. (p. 226)

The pitch of his verse is more measured than that of a poet in early youth, and this general tone is contemplative rather than passionate, nostalgic; one might even say elegiac. This does not mean that he lacked vitality. . . . At times, however, the lyric impulse of his verse becomes definitely more pronounced than in the major corpus of his work; such, for example, as in those poems after the death of his first wife. Occasionally, too, he captures a Shelleyan quality which, could it soar higher, would burst into song; but this is rare rather than frequent. He was artist enough to realize that were he to attempt to capture in his middle and late years the ecstatic exuberance of youth, his work would have the ring of insincerity, a quality he vigorously fought against. . . .

His general inability to realize the concealed power of words in themselves and not only the power resulting from a strict pattern is another cause for his failure to achieve a place among the greatest. He waited too long before devoting his best efforts to poetry. (p. 227)

Had Hardy worked unremittingly at poetry during the years when his creative energy was at its best he might well have forged an instrument that would have been worthy his maturest deliberations. He might have been able to fuse his images into his thought until they were indistinguishable from the thought—until they were a part of it and from this fusion greater strength would have sprung. He might have accomplished this, but he did not. Evocative as his images often are, they remain in all but his best work—a small corpus—things of ornament and void of inner passion. He might, too, have arrived at a sense of the inevitability of words in association. And this he only rarely achieved. (pp. 227-28)

All this is not to say that Hardy failed; because he did not. He only failed to find a resting place on Parnassus. He achieved, I believe, that of which he was capable, something far above the ability of the majority of men. He has been a beneficent influence on poetry. He brought freshness of observation, a freshness which continued until the very end. He widened the horizon of English poetry. He gave new ideas and new forms to his generation and to ours. He examined the world about him and presented the results of his observations with lucidity. That in itself is much. (p. 231)

James Granville Southworth, "An Evaluation," in his The Poetry of Thomas Hardy *(copyright © 1947, 1964, 1966 by Columbia University Press; reissued, 1966, by Russell & Russell; reprinted by permission of the publisher), Columbia University Press, 1947 (and reprinted by Russell & Russell, 1966), pp. 221-34.*

MARK VAN DOREN   (essay date 1955)

The reader [of Hardy's *Collected Poems*] is forever making new discoveries: either of Hardy or of himself. If of Hardy, they have to do with dimensions of his thought and feeling not previously observed. If of himself, they have to do with certain poems he seems to be reading for the first time; or reading with a sense of power in them that startles him, for there had been no sign of it before. No poet has so changeable a surface as Hardy, no poet maintains in his reader so changeable a mind. Which are his best poems, and which are his worst? The question never seems to get settled; no wonder that he becomes the anthologist's despair. (p. 53)

We want more from a poet than a theory of life; we want, if such a thing is possible, the look, feel, sound, taste, and even smell of life itself. And that is what Hardy eventually provides, and provides so richly that his name is sure to last. Meanwhile there are [his] philosophical poems which tell us that he finds no intelligibility in events, no form or order in the world. They are such poems as only he could write; they say what they have to say in his own idiom, for he meant very personally what he said in them, and they make a solemn, piercing music which alone would certify their sincerity. But they are not the heart of the book as he must have supposed they would be. They take their place among the thinner tissues, the ones with the least blood in them. The heart of the book, assuming it can be located at all, is older and tougher than these poems are. The book was not a single effort like *The Dynasts*, conceived and carried through with little or no interruption; it was the work or almost seventy years, and Hardy himself changed much in all that time. Or if he did not change, he submitted himself to many chances, and caught on the fly a bewildering number of perceptions which in the nature of things could not have been alike. An assiduous taker of notes upon himself, he rendered on a wide front his experience of the world, so that there is scarcely anything he has not understood and said before he is finished. This is not precisely to say that the rest of the book contradicts or denies the philosophical poems. Rather, it absorbs them; it finds a place for them and leaves them there. (p. 54)

Hardy hugged time to himself as he hugged pain and gloom; they were the three dimensions of his universe, in which he felt so much at home that he could be surprised when readers complained of its barrenness. It was thick and warm for him, like an old coat that exactly fitted him, even if it looked a little long, and indeed drooped to the ground. It was what he recognized as reality, the one thing to which he was entirely committed. The bitterness of the world did not forbid him to embrace it: a poor thing, but his own. At times, to be sure, he wondered whether he missed something that others saw; he peered hard, and had the reward of any pessimist—something was better than he expected. For that matter, many things were; even all things, if one did not mind their being just what they were. Now and then he would offer an apology for the low tones in which he spoke: he but sang his part, as others must sing theirs. (p. 67)

Mark Van Doren, "The Poems of Thomas Hardy" (originally published in Four Poets on Poetry, The John Hopkins Press, 1955), *in his* The Happy Critic and Other Essays *(reprinted by permission of Farrar, Straus & Giroux, Inc.; copyright © 1955, 1957, 1961 by Mark Van Doren), Farrar, Straus & Giroux, 1961, pp. 50-70.*

FRANK O'CONNOR   (essay date 1956)

[Hardy] is a fascinating example of historic schizophrenia, standing on the frontier of two cultures, watching traditions older than the Celts, whose barrows topped the neighboring hills, disappear as the extending railway line brings in the latest music-hall song, the latest melodrama, the latest scientific theory. When two cultures clash in this way, what happens at the time is not that the more sophisticated one triumphs, but that the less sophisticated takes refuge in the depths of the heart. This is what he means when he says that half his time he believes in "spectres, mysterious voices, intuitions, dreams, haunted places, etc., etc." At the same time he is slightly ashamed of his own weakness. What takes place in the conscious part of a mind like that is the spread not of sophistication, but of naïveté. Hardy as a thinker is naïve because he thinks with only half his mind. His feelings, on the other hand, are profound.

The problem for the critic is to distinguish between the two Hardys. If one considers him as a novelist in the way in which one considers Tolstoy or Trollope, it soon becomes plain that he is not a novelist at all. More than any other novelist who ever lived he is socially limited and naïve. Naturally, he is a genius, but his genius is akin to that of the *douanier* Rousseau or an American primitive. (p. 241)

All Hardy's faults are faults of simplemindedness. His invention is largely meaningless and frequently highly embarrassing. The plot of *Far from the Madding Crowd* is as stagy as anything in Dickens, but it is unsatisfying because, unlike Dickens and, indeed, unlike most Victorian novelists, Hardy is not in the least a stagy man. He writes in this way only because he has read and seen too many melodramas and is lacking in the critical insight that would enable him to see how far removed they are from those things which came natural to himself. (pp. 242-43)

In *Under the Greenwood Tree* he wrote the only novel of his which does not depend on meretricious coincidence and melodrama; which is absolutely authentic; and, enchanting as it is, it is clearly not a novel at all. It is an idyll that will be remembered as long as fiction is read, not for the sake of its characters or their emotions, but for its picture of life in rural England before it was swamped by railway culture.

This was the real inspiration of the second Hardy, Hardy the poet. Whenever he looked forward, he saw only chaos and gloom; whenever he looked back, his memory filled with enchantment. He was not only one of the great folklorists and historians; he was also the greatest master of local color that the nineteenth century had seen, greater even than Dickens.

Here, whether or not he knew it—and probably he did not —Hardy was affected by the naturalists, and we can trace in him the development of a purely pictorial kind of writing which must ultimately derive from Flaubert. Unlike Flaubert, he never allows it to settle into neat little miniatures. . . . (p. 245)

If Hardy is not a realist like Dickens, it is that he is "not solid enough to influence his environment," but neither is he a Flaubert or Joyce, "like God, paring his nails." He is a ghost; a ghost that finds the spectacle of passing life intolerable, and can contemplate it only as if it were already gone by, its sufferings ended. All his characters are treated as though they were already dead, and even among the shadows he evokes he will turn from any face too fair or venturesome to contemplate some Celtic fort or fifteenth-century cottage that has already outlasted generations of such eager souls. It is almost impossible for the artist to evade the spirit of an age, and even in the west of England, far from the bustle of James's society world, the novel was closing in on itself and the novelist being pushed to the extreme periphery of experience. Hardy was as incapable as James of placing himself again where Trollope and Tolstoy stood, in its burning center. (pp. 249-50)

Frank O'Connor, "Thomas Hardy," in his The Mirror in the Roadway: A Study of the Modern Novel *(copyright © 1956 by Frank O'Connor; reprinted by permission of Joan Daves, Literary Agents), Alfred A. Knopf, Inc., 1956, pp. 237-50.*

SAMUEL HYNES   (essay date 1961)

Unfavorable judgments of Hardy's poetry have generally been of two kinds: either philosophical or stylistic. The philosophy has been criticized either because it is wicked—the "village atheist" school of Chesterton—or because it gets in the way of the poetry (Hardy, says R. P. Blackmur, was a "sensibility violated by ideas"). The style has been criticized either because it is not poetic, or because it does not exist. (p. 56)

[This] began with the first reviewers of Hardy's verse, and . . . still continues. In those early reviews, certain points were made again and again: Hardy's rhythms were prosaic, "arbitrarily irregular," "clumsy"; his language was "needlessly inflated," "persistently clumsy," "unexciting and unpoetic"; his range was narrow and monotonous. (pp. 56-7)

Any reader of Hardy's poetry must recognize that some of these judgments, at least, are just. Hardy's poems do seem awkward, halting, and often ungrammatical. The language ranges from the dialectal to the technical, and is full of strange, tongue-twisting coinages. . . . These are the things we think of when we think of the typical Hardy style; and they are all there in the poems. But in justice to Hardy we must add two substantial qualifications to this idea of his style: that his poems are not *all* awkwardness, and that awkwardness, like the melodiousness which he does not have, may be functional in the poem. (pp. 57-8)

It is a simple fact that, quantitatively speaking, Hardy is syntactically and grammatically orthodox more often than not. Many of the best poems are almost conversational in style, and do little violence to prose syntax or to the rules of grammar. "A Broken Appointment" is a slight, but entirely successful example of this kind of poem. . . . One recognizes at once that this is a Hardy poem; but "clumsy," "awkward," and "prosaic" are not the right terms to describe its distinctive style. In form it is an answer to the "blunt pencil" view of Hardy's art. The stanza is a fairly involved one: Hardy uses it with grace, adjusting long sentences to the rhyme scheme easily and employing inversion to make the rhyme only once. Its ease is not quite the ease of prose speech—Hardy always insists on the essential formality of poetry, on what Patmore described as "the necessity of manifesting, as well as moving in, the bonds of verse"—but this is true of conventional poetry in general, and describes nothing peculiar to Hardy.

It might be easier to define Hardy's style negatively, in terms of what it is not. First of all, it is not melodious or "lyric" in any conventional sense—only the most tedious (and least typical) of Hardy's poems can be said to sing. His characteristic pace is erratic and abrupt, the pace of thoughtful speech or of spoken thought. In "A Broken Appointment" this pace is to a considerable extent a function of the syntax, which is slow and involved in the first stanza, and is broken by many stops in the second. The syntax is not particularly odd, and it is not, as it often is in Auden and Eliot and even Shakespeare, ambiguous—one can always establish in Hardy's verse what modifies what. (pp. 58-9)

[The] exact location of stresses may be puzzling in spots, especially where the compound words of which Hardy was so fond leave the stress hovering over two or three syllables. This oral roughness has led some critics to conclude that he had no ear; but rather, I think, he heard a different kind of music, and a kind which should not sound strange to the modern reader's ear—it is not so different, after all, from the dissonances of Meredith and Patmore and Hopkins, or, for that matter, of Pound and Eliot. (p. 60)

At this point we can say, then, of Hardy's style that it is assertively unmusical and often harsh, and that this harshness is a function of the manipulation of syntax, sound, and diction so as to defeat lyric fluidity and to restrict the movement of the verse to a slow, uneven, often uncertain pace. The question of the way in which this style can be regarded as functional in the poems remains. The answer lies, I think, in the quality which Hardy praised in Barnes: "closeness of phrase to his vision."

The vision in Hardy's case is . . . "his sense of the irreconcilable disparity between the way things ought to be and the way they are: the failure of the universe to answer man's need for order." That failure is a constant in Hardy's writing; and because of that failure the idea of poetic order is a very different thing for Hardy from what it was for his predecessors. Hardy says in "In Tenebris," "if way to the Better there be, it exacts a full look at the Worst." The "worst" is suffering, mortality, change, death—all meaningless in a meaningless, indifferent universe. Hardy did not try to reconcile man to his predicament, or to resolve the

evident disparities and contradictions of existence—he merely recorded them. . . . Like other modern poets (notably Pound in the *Cantos* and William Carlos Williams), Hardy restricted himself largely to his vision of the actual, a poetic world without abstract ideals or absolutes, and strove for "closeness of phrase" to that vision.

One result, and this is also true to some degree of the other poets mentioned, was an uncompromising fidelity to fact and detail ("Oh, but it really happened" was, for him, a valid defense of a poem). One cannot read far in Hardy's poems without noticing the precision of observation, the command of minute detail. Sometimes there is nothing more and the poem seems merely trivial, a description, or more often, since Hardy's method was primarily dramatic, an anecdote; but often detail and vision fuse and support each other, and the poem succeeds. "A January Night" succeeds in this way. . . . The poem does not explain anything, nor does it set this particular experience in the context of any system of belief; rather it dramatizes man's *inability* to explain, his ignorance and his horror.

Man's ignorance, and his inability to reduce the universe to significant order, are the principal factors in Hardy's vision, and in his poetry. One result, as we might expect, is a style built upon tensions and disparities. These tensions and disparities function in many ways: form against idea, prose syntax against metrical necessity, one level of diction against another, image against image, or image against abstraction. The poetic materials are likely to be heterogeneous, and their combinations apparently whimsical—one rarely feels in Hardy's verse the force of poetic decorum at work. This is odd if one considers the Victorian decorousness of the man, but not strange in the light of his thought. For Hardy's thought, while it had not achieved a system of belief, had freed him from traditional belief, and with this philosophical freedom went a poetical freedom as great, and as empty. Chance rules Hardy's universe, and often it seems to determine his style as well. And why, after all, in a lawless universe should there be laws governing poetry? Why *not* make poems out of clashing incongruities, since this is the way the world is?

This argument seems to lead us to the conclusion that Hardy's poems are good or bad by accident, that he did not really have control of his medium. This critical conclusion did persist throughout Hardy's poetic career, and he was understandably annoyed by it: "The reviewer," he complained, "so often supposes that where Art is not visible it is unknown to the poet under criticism. Why does he not think of the art of concealing art?" (pp. 60-3)

Hardy tried . . . to write monistic poetry—poetry, that is, in which the actual is the only reality, and in which there is no other, invisible world above and beyond the actual, to which the things in a poem refer and from which they derive significance and value. (p. 66)

But Hardy apparently found the style proper to his belief, like the belief itself, inadequate. If the unseen reality could not come in the front door as philosophy, it could come in the back door as superstition; if it could not clothe itself in symbol and metaphor, it could appear as omen and abstraction—"our old friend Dualism," says Hardy, is "a tough old chap." Hence the phantoms, ghosts, and dreads in the poems; hence also the presence among the meticulous particulars of abstract words—Crass Casualty, Time,

Change—and personifications of the sort that populate the Overworld of *The Dynasts*. These terms have one quality in common: they all refer to the dark, inexplicable side of existence. The superstitions in the poems are all frightening superstitions ("Signs and Tokens" catalogues some of these); the Overworld includes spirits of Pity, Irony and Rumour, but not of Happiness or Joy or Peace. (pp. 66-7)

Hardy's style was often an effective medium for the expression of his personal vision, it was severely limited in range. This limitation is essentially the limitation of his vision, for in Hardy style and belief were one. He could not write poems of song or celebration—in his experience he found nothing to sing about and nothing to celebrate. He could neither reason nor argue in verse, and the occasions on which he tried—his "philosophical" poems—were disastrous. Certain themes and certain aspects of experience were closed to him: religion was something other people believed in, love was only available to him as a theme when it was either betrayed or past, sex was cruelty but never ecstasy, and human happiness was a delusion or a memory made bitter by the unhappy present. Art, politics, urban life —all common themes among his successors—he ignored; his world was the dark side of Wessex, and it was there that he succeeded as a poet.

But Wessex is a private country, and its accent is private, too; if he achieved "closeness of phrase to his vision" there, it was *his* vision, and no one else's. (p. 73)

> *Samuel Hynes, in his* The Pattern of Hardy's Poetry *(copyright © 1956 by Samuel Hynes), The University of North Carolina Press, 1961, 193 p.*

IAN GREGOR   (essay date 1962)

To examine [*Tess of the d'Urbervilles*] in any detail is to be made more than usually aware of two things—the varying levels of imaginative intensity which it contains, and the way in which these levels disappear to leave the reader with a dominant impression of unity. There is the art of the ballad writer: the beautiful village maid, seduced in the green wood, who rallies to find her true lover, only to be rejected by him when he discovers her 'past' and brought to a tragic end. There is the art of the writer who feels that such a world is dying in the shadows of the new industrial society which is growing up round it. And finally there is the writer who reflects philosophically on these things. . . . Nevertheless, the total impression that Tess leaves on the reader is undeniably one of unity. And we must start by asking how *that* is done, before going on to isolate the various elements that make it up.

The first thing to be noted is the extraordinary vividness and imaginative density with which Tess herself is presented. . . . Tess is continually before the reader as a living presence. She is the heart of the novel, giving it all the life it has, and that life remains a personal life; it doesn't transform itself into symbolic terms so that she becomes 'the agricultural community in its moment of ruin'. If an enlargement of the character takes place, it is to increase the force of the character, not to point out its significance. Tess 'felt akin to the landscape'—this is Hardy's way of providing a dramatic notation for material which, in another novelist, would have been handled psychologically. At every stage of the tale interior states are visualized in terms of landscape. (p. 451)

The character of the heroine, the profound sense of landscape, the interlocking pattern of symbol and image—these all contribute to give the novel its eventual unity, but within that enclosing rim there are several stresses and strains.

They proceed from varying levels of imaginative realization. At the heart of the novel is the ballad world. When Tess returns from a day in the fields after her tragic encounter with Alec, 'her female companions sang songs . . . they could not refrain from mischievously throwing in a few verses of the ballad about the maid who went to the merry green wood and came back a changed state'. That is the world—the maid, the seducer and the true lover. It is primal in form and content. . . . This primal world of love and grief, of omen and song, forms the centre of the novel, its densest presentation of what James called 'felt life'. Tess belongs to it entirely, and like all ballad heroines she is fundamentally changeless.

When we consider Alec D'Urberville, we move into a world different from this one, but the shift still lies completely within Hardy's power of dramatic presentment. It has been frequently urged against Alec that he is simply a stock-in-trade figure from Victorian melodrama. He is certainly a stock figure, but only because he belongs to a stock world; he is the eternal tempter. He describes himself to Tess as 'the old Other One who can tempt you in the disguise of an inferior animal'. To a large degree he is simply the anonymous villain of the ballad. . . . Here Hardy is establishing an historical perspective. The rural ballad world now comes to be seen more specifically as an agricultural community beginning to disintegrate under the threats of industrialism, the Changeless giving way to the Changeful. (pp. 454-55)

Just as Alec is lightly connected to the ballad world of Tess, but really 'lives' (in so far as he lives at all) in the new capitalist world, so Angel is lightly connected with that world of Alec's . . . but his real element is that of the Free-Thinkers' Hall. In either case he is a world away from Tess, too far for differences to become conflicts, and effective communication peters out in the vacancy between. In a novel less fiercely conceived such a dramatic crack, reaching practically to the centre, would have been fatal.

In the thin air in which Angel lives there is only debate, and languid debate at that. We notice primarily the ambiguous presentation of 'Nature'. To say this is not to take Hardy to task for his defects as a philosopher, but to suggest that he juggles with the word 'nature' in a way damaging to his artistic purpose. At times the protest would appear to be against the human conditions as such; this is surely the force of Tess's most uncharacteristic reflection that the world is 'a blighted star'. . . . This then is how things would appear to be, and, setting aside questions as to the legitimacy of calling something 'blighted' or 'cruel' if it is its nature to be so, and the futility of complaint against things being what they are, we can turn to Hardy's other, and more frequent, use of the word 'nature'. This relies for its effect precisely on the possibility of change; as they are, things are healthy, the blight is social custom and attitude. It is on this axle that the abstractly formulated 'defence' of Tess turns: 'Walking among the sleeping birds in the hedges, watching the skipping rabbits on a moonlit warren, or standing under a pheasant-laden bough, she looked upon herself as a figure of Guilt intruding in the haunts of Innocence. But all the while she was making a distinction where there was no difference. Feeling herself in antagonism she was quite in accord. She had been made to break an accepted social law, but no law known to the environment in which she fancied herself such an anomaly.' Innocence . . . Guilt, such is the kind of juxtaposition between the natural and the social environment; if men looked into their hearts things could be very different. This somewhat Rousseauistic view of nature contrasts strangely with the determinist one, which Hardy runs alongside it. . . . In exploring and assessing Tess's situation, Hardy is continually using a double standard. His immediate defence [of Tess] is by way of beneficent Nature. . . . But then, when Hardy is taking a remoter view, the tragedy is inherent in Nature's 'cruel law'—in the way things are. To take the force of one point, we have to forget the other; there is contradiction here, not complexity. On the other hand, the small measure in which this confusion, which is central to the theme of the novel, really decreases its artistic compulsion, suggests how effectively the latter is protected against the raids of philosophic speculation.

This ambivalence is related to the weakness in presentation of Angel Clare in the tale. The thinness of this aspect of the novel is due to Hardy's failure to integrate his 'thought' into his art. (pp. 456-57)

If *Tess* has a centre capable of formulation in abstract terms, then such a statement is found in Clare's reflections on 'the old appraisements of morality. He thought they wanted adjusting. Who was the moral man? Still more pertinently, who was the moral woman? The beauty and ugliness of a character lay not only in its achievements, but in its aims and impulses; its true history lay not among things done, but things willed.' This is a forceful passage, making the point succinctly and without rhetorical flourish. Hardy is here feeling his way towards a criticism of 'behavior' as an adequate moral register—'not things done, but things willed'. In James this criticism is vastly extended and subtilized, and the way is prepared for the characteristic twentieth-century novel, which takes as axiomatic the moral supremacy of 'things willed'. The citadel defended by the Victorian novelist was 'innocence', and 'innocence' can be seen most clearly in behaviour; the citadel defended by the modern novelist has shifted to 'integrity' and here we are more naturally at home in the psychological world of motive and intention. Abstractly Hardy could see the shifting strategy, but in practice he occupied the old position. (pp. 458-59)

[In] the last analysis what does come through is the force of Hardy's sub-title—'a pure woman' seen and presented within a social framework. Hardy may talk of 'things willed' but here everything is externally 'done', the gauntlet is visibly thrown. The individual physically confronts her antagonist. But the way is beginning to be clear for 'things willed' to find their imaginative expression in art, for the contest between corruption and innocence to take place not in a field, but within the human heart itself. For this we have to leave Hardy and enter the world of Henry James. (p. 461)

Ian Gregor, "The Novel As Moral Protest: 'Tess of the d'Urbervilles'," in his The Moral and the Story *(reprinted by permission of Faber and Faber Ltd.), Faber and Faber, 1962 (and reprinted in "Tess of the d'Urbervilles" by Thomas Hardy: An Authoritative Text, Hardy and the*
Novel, Criticism, *edited by Scott Elledge, W. W. Norton & Company, Inc., 1965, pp. 450-61).*

ALBERT J. GUERARD (essay date 1964)

Many more books about Thomas Hardy have already appeared than their subject found time to write himself, and to read them is a long and harrowing task. One rises from this task with the impression that Hardy was a gloomy philosopher (fatalist? mechanistic determinist? meliorist?) who wrote depressing but profound and technically admirable realistic novels. Perhaps the chief motive for still another revaluation is the grossly misleading simplicity of this portrait and, even, its irrelevance. . . . [We] must cling to a first untutored impression that Hardy's novels, read in sequence, are by no means uniformly gloomy. Academic schematizing . . . has done its worst by Hardy. It has fastened on certain obvious structural and didactic aspects of the major Wessex novels to the neglect of much else which remains readable and which can even be useful to a novelist writing today. Whenever a writer shows a certain surface obviousness and a discernible skeleton of intention, commentators may be relied on to gather in great numbers. And this has certainly been true with Hardy, whose art was not that which conceals either art or didactic intention. (pp. 1-2)

Between the two wars the most vital literary movements, following widely separated paths through reality, arrived at the same conclusions concerning it: that a cosmic absurdity pervades all appearance, that evil has an aggressively real existence, that experience is more often macabre than not. . . . And what both surrealism and naturalism discovered was a more than Gothic horror. This *littérature noire* may give a false picture of our world, but it does help us to suspend disbelief in Hardy's most startling excursions. (p. 4)

[We] are now willing to go back to Hardy for the qualities which in 1920 seemed so old-fashioned: the absurd coincidences, the grotesque heightenings of reality, the sense of mystery inhabiting hostile circumstance and nature itself. We go back too for the tales themselves—as stark and tragic and traditional as any ballads. We are no longer willing to dismiss some of Hardy's finest inventions . . . merely because they are "sensational" and "too remote from ordinary experience." (pp. 5-6)

It is certainly true that Hardy had a vision of the cosmic absurd—of man's longing for order and justice outraged by the eternal indifferent drift of things—and his attitude toward this conception of the human dilemma is one of the shaping forces of his work. But it is much less rewarding to dwell on his iteration of some of the intellectual conclusions of his time: whether those of John Stuart Mill or Comte or von Hartmann or Bergson. As a thinker Hardy is commonplace in juxtaposition to Bergson; he is commonplace even in juxtaposition to Comte. A poet's ideas on society or on the cosmos are no subtler nor more rewarding because they happen to be a poet's. Yet academic critics often applaud poetic speculation whose crudity they would never tolerate from a colleague.

The Dynasts has of course suffered most of all from these didactic interpretations; it has been treated, in spite of Hardy's forewarnings and protests, as a philosophical essay, rather than as a historical and dramatic poem. . . . The untutored reader must surely find *The Dynasts* an uneven but absorbing chronicle of historical events and persons: Napoleon and Pitt and Alexander are alive and interesting in spite of Hardy's theoretical determinism, just as Zola's characters are alive and interesting in spite of his theoretical determinism. And surely the Spirits, once they have helped us to a daring point of view, are little more than embodied attitudes. A familiar chain of reasoning can prove, however, that determined characters are not, properly speaking, characters at all, and it is this implacable logic which leads W. R. Rutland to conclude that the Spirits "are the only real characters in the *Dynasts*"! Flawless reasoning, as it appears, has led an intelligent reader as far away as possible from an unprejudiced reading of the poem, from the impression the poem actually makes, from what it really says. Nearly all discussions of Hardy's thought fail to distinguish between formulated belief and dramatically useful symbol or myth. (pp. 7-8)

Hardy was first of all a storyteller, and his attitude toward many problems was aesthetic. His pessimism was genuine enough, of course, but it was to a degree cultivated as artistically useful. He knew that if some natures become vocal in comedy, his own became vocal in tragedy. (p. 16)

We are thus confronted by a writer who, however sincere his convictions, thought first of all of his stories. Even the historian of Wessex knew that Wessex was dramatically useful, thanks to the presence of elementary passions in a circumscribed world, thanks to "the concentrated passions and closely knit interdependence of the lives therein." But should we accept the novels as a historical record of changes in Dorset from 1800 to 1889? One of Hardy's great "subjects" was, of course, the sad passing of the stable rural life, the decay of old customs and of local traditions, the death of ghost stories and the death of village choirs. (p. 17)

[The] decay of old customs was more significant to Hardy the novelist than the amelioration of the laborer's lot; the aesthetic changes were the ones which concerned him. The dialogue of his rustics was no more realistic than that of Shakespeare's rustics; their daily security and moral innocence were, perhaps, very nearly as idealized. Hardy was not the historian of Dorset but the novelist and poet of Wessex. He was a realist within a world he had reshaped to his vision and whose joys and sorrows he had quite deliberately heightened. (pp. 18-19)

With *Tess of the D'Urbervilles* and especially *Jude the Obscure,* Hardy left his idealized Wessex for the harsh realities and moral confusion of the modern world. (p. 31)

Jude the Obscure remains . . . the extreme point at which we must take Hardy's measure as a "thinker." And it becomes quite clear that we must base his importance as a novelist on entirely different grounds. Hardy was nowhere wrong, as I see it, unless in his bio-philosophical determinism, but he thought neither subtly nor originally on any of these problems. Just as the Wessex novels leave an idealized impression of an ancient and stable world rather than an accurate almanac of Dorset, so *Jude the Obscure* leaves a dominant and in a sense truthful impression of the world in which we live. This impression of unrest and isolation and collapse, rather than the diverse problems discussed, makes the book still seem true. Like all self-conscious spiritual history, *Jude* has many pages which date it: Sue's discussion, for instance, of the chapter headings to the Song of

Solomon. It is even conceivable that the picture of our world as rudderless and lost will some day date. But the novel will survive even this doubtful eventuality, I suspect, thanks to the rectilinear starkness and truth of Jude's personal history; the history is the truer, even, for its omission of Jude's rare happy hours. For there will always be men willing to whisper with him: "Let the day perish wherein I was born, and the night in which it was said, There is a man child conceived." (pp. 33-4)

Anti-realist is an embarrassingly comprehensive term, which may serve Huysmanns and Péladan as well as Melville; the term *symbolist* is scarcely more satisfactory and has the added disadvantage of referring also to particular literary groups. The anti-realists had this much in common: they found that the prevailing positivist complacency and bondage to hard fact threatened art or ethics or both. (p. 83)

Hardy's anti-realism was more popular and less metaphysical than that of his greatest contemporaries; he is one of the few anti-realists to whom the term *romantic* may at times be applied in other than a pejorative sense. Obviously he wanted to avoid the sterility of mere observation and Gradgrind common sense: he was an anti-realist on aesthetic grounds. But also he was a pure romantic, like Scott, appealing to the surprised child who lingers in us all; he was a popular teller of tales. The appearance of the Devil in the poetry and fiction of the last hundred years often signifies a skeptic's search for God. But Hardy, though he used the preternatural now and then, was very rarely concerned with damnation, with crime and guilt and remorse. His rare preternatural beings are there to puzzle and excite us, and because they have a time-honored place in the traditional ballad and tale. Significantly Conrad departs farthest from realism, in *The Secret Sharer,* to create a ghostly image of the divided and damning ego. Hardy departs farthest from realism, in *The Romantic Adventures of a Milkmaid,* to tell us a fairy story. Nearly all the anti-realists were intensely subjective writers and were often markedly neurotic; Hardy as a novelist was neither. He was less serious than many of them, but also in some sense purer. (pp. 84-5)

His anti-realism was more often the natural expression of a particular temperament (the "idiosyncrasy") and a great dramatic gift. A grotesque chapter may thus exhibit simultaneously the pessimist's disgust with the absurdity of things and the dramatist's delight in presenting that absurdity. A ferocious sense of fun may accompany a wholly genuine horror, in Hardy as in Dostoevsky or Kafka or Faulkner. The difference is that Hardy, unlike the others, seldom went "underground." He was startled rather than obsessed. (p. 85)

It is common enough for readers to express a mild and casual preference of [Hardy's] poetry over the novels; or, at least, to cite Hardy's own distinct preference. (p. 160)

The major question remains, nevertheless, as it did for the novelist. Why does this "simple" poetry, with its transparency of statement and shameless reiteration, have such a considerable appeal for readers bred on ambiguity and paradox? (p. 161)

Much attention has been given to Hardy's temperamental gloom, some to his diction, but little to his formal and metrical experiments. There are . . . two impulses in Hardy's poetry. The first is anti-poetic and conversational. It strives for a colloquial, realistic, unhurried, even prosy voice, a voice of many dissonances and cacophonies. This is a style of broken rhythms and often harsh phrasing consciously opposed to the lulling liquid euphonies of Shelley, Tennyson, Swinburne. Some of Hardy's critics . . . have assumed this roughness was undeliberate. But a considerable number of obviously graceful poems shows this to be untrue.

The second major impulse is formalistic, and reflects both an architect's interest in patterns and a musician's interest in new meters and odd rhythms. This is the Hardy of the verse skeletons and nonsense verses, the Hardy who tried out such a large number of verse forms, the Hardy who (in "The Respectable Burgher") wrote a thirty-six-line poem on a single rhyme.

There are . . . important relationships between the two impulses in Hardy's poetry. On the one hand, some of the metrical experiments are designed to bring out colloquial rhythms and dissonances, especially the experiments with long lines. On the other hand, there sometimes exists an ironic counterpoint between gravity of feeling and a playful intricacy of stanza and meter. Here we find, once again, the ironic use of form that is one of Hardy's important strangenesses.

The obvious medium for expressing the speaking voice realistically is the unpretentious but carefully modulated blank verse of "Panthera"—the familiar blank verse of a quiet "Conversation Poem." Here many lovely variations are possible, and, especially, great varieties in degree of accent, within a perfectly recognizable norm. But Hardy also tried for colloquial naturalness in a number of unusual meters, some of which refuse to recognize any norm. "Honeymoon Time at an Inn," to take an extreme example, is almost ruthlessly experimental. This is one of a number of Hardy poems, of deceptively familiar appearance on the printed page, which prove on close examination to be metrically very strange.

The look of this poem is wholly reassuring. We have eight stanzas, with the first, third, fourth, and fifth lines of each stanza fairly long, and the second and sixth lines short. There is every reason to expect an accentual-syllabic poem of considerable regularity. But the poem, so long as we preserve these expectations, simply cannot be read; the ear is perpetually baffled. If we scan the poem, looking for the sources of bafflement, we find that the "long" lines vary from ten to fifteen syllables and the "short" ones from six to eight. If we now look instead for a purely accentual norm based on true speech stresses, we find that the long lines run from four accents to seven and the short lines from three to four. These variations, though marked, are less extreme than in a number of poems that present less difficulty. If we look at our scansion again, our verse-skeleton, and note also the quantitatively strong unaccented syllables (one of the most important variations in English verse), and note of course the inversions of accent, we find something truly astonishing. The fifth line of the first stanza repeats the first line. This occurs again, with a slight change in wording, in the seventh stanza. This leaves us with a theoretical possibility, for a forty-eight-line poem, of forty-six different types of metrical line. *And this is precisely what we have!* Except for the lines noted above, no two are rhythmically alike. Granted the principle of monotony implicit in perpetual variety, such extreme variation is no mean tour de force. It is interesting to note that Hardy

made this extreme experiment in a serious and ambitious poem. (pp. 181-83)

Hardy, though he repeated himself a good deal, is a richer and more versatile poet than is commonly assumed. Yet behind the diverse subjects and multiplicity of experimented forms one nearly always hears the recognizable personal voice, the grave, sad, and unhurried voice with its accent of unmistakable sincerity—the mature expression, decade after decade, of an exceptionally pure and authentic temperament. (p. 188)

> *Albert J. Guerard, in his* Thomas Hardy *(copyright 1949 by The President and Fellows of Harvard College; copyright © 1964, 1977 by Albert J. Guerard; excerpted by permission), revised edition, New Directions, 1964, 207 p.*

EDWIN MUIR   (essay date 1965)

[Hardy] takes a short cut to tragedy by reducing life to a formula. He gets rid beforehand of the main obstacle to tragedy, which is man's natural inclination to avoid it. His characters are passive, or at the best endlessly patient. He does not believe that character is fate; so that for him tragedy does not proceed from action, but resides with the power which determines all action. (p. 111)

In Hardy's universe man's presence is ultimately inexplicable; so that while he sees nature as indifferent, he cannot help personifying it in some diabolical form. This is a measure of the intensity of his feelings towards it, and of the contradiction of his thought. To him man's position can be explained only by a universe which perpetually defeats him, unintentionally yet intentionally. The universe, seen in this way, is simply another term for evil. (p. 115)

Hardy was partial to man; to be partial is to be involuntarily unjust; and in taking evil from man's shoulders he robbed him of one of his indispensable possessions. For in relieving man of evil he did not improve his situation, but made it worse, since he concentrated all evil against him. His characters, therefore, are curiously neutral; they gain colour only when passion of misfortune touches them, and are quite convincing only in their helplessness and instability. He draws women better than men. He sees woman and her response to love almost with a woman's eyes. He is on woman's side against man, just as he is on man's side against nature, and for the same reason; for woman is the final victim. . . . In describing endurance Hardy is best, for by enduring man seems to rise above the malice of fate by a pure act of magnanimity comprehensible only to himself. The peasants who form a chorus to the novels are the final expression of this endurance, which has become so native to them that it has been transformed into a kind of humour. They are too low to fear a fall. They are in the position where the universe wants to have them; therefore beyond the reach of tragedy: the speakers of the epilogue to every action. (p. 119)

> *Edwin Muir, "The Novels of Thomas Hardy," in his* Essays on Literature and Society *(copyright © 1965 by the President and Fellows of Harvard College; excerpted by permission), revised edition, Cambridge, Mass.: Harvard University Press, 1965, pp. 111-19.*

EZRA POUND (essay date 1970)

A conscientious critic might be hard put to it to find just praise for Hardy's poems. When a writer's matter is stated with such entirety and with such clarity there is no place left for the explaining critic. When the matter is of so stark a nature and so clamped to reality, the eulogist looks an ass. At any rate he looks an ass the moment he essays the customary phrasings of enthusiasm. It is not life grim. It is not life *plus* ANY adjective the would-be eulogist can (at least in the present case) find. . . .

Expression coterminous with the matter. Nothing for disciples' exploitation. When we, if we live long enough, come to estimate the "poetry of the period", against Hardy's 600 pages we will put what? (p. 285)

No man can read Hardy's poems collected but that his own life, and forgotten moments of it, will come back to him, a flash here and an hour there. Have you a better test of true poetry?

When I say that the *work* is more criticism than any talk around and about a work, that also flashes in reading Hardy. In the clean wording. No thoughtful writer can read this book of Hardy's without throwing his own work (in imagination) into the test-tube and hunting it for fustian, for the foolish-word, for the word upholstered. (pp. 286-87)

> *Ezra Pound, "Happy Days," in his* Guide to Kulchur *(copyright © 1970 by Ezra Pound; all rights reserved; reprinted by permission of New Directions Publishing Corporation), New Directions, 1970, pp. 284-90.*

J. HILLIS MILLER (essay date 1970)

Two themes are woven throughout the totality of Hardy's work and may be followed from one edge of it to the other as outlining threads: distance and desire—distance as the source of desire and desire as the energy behind attempts to turn distance into closeness.

One version of these motifs in their relation is that distance of one person from another which creates love in Hardy's protagonists. Love is the urgent theme of his fiction and of his poetry. The experience of an "emotional void" within, a distance of oneself from oneself, drives his characters to seek possession of another person. To possess the beloved would be to replace separation by presence, emptiness by a substantial self.

The opposition between presence and absence also determines the temporal structures of Hardy's work. The horizons of time establish one important kind of distance—distance of one time from another time which makes up the temporal form of all those poems in which someone looks back at an earlier time in his own life; distance in the fiction between the narrator's retrospective view and the time of the characters as they live from moment to moment moving toward the future. The openings within time itself, as Hardy experiences them, are constitutive of these narrative and poetic structures. His writing attempts to close these fissures, to bring the perspective of narrator and character together, to reconcile then and now in the poetic persona's life, or to possess all time in a single moment, as do the choruses of spirits in *The Dynasts*.

The temporal distance of Hardy's narrators from the story they tell is also a spatial distance. His narrators and many of his protagonists are objective spectators of life. The relation of his writings to the personal and historical realities from which they spring or which they "mirror" involves a similar distancing. The narrators of his novels, like the speakers of his poems, are roles Hardy plays. The poems, he often insisted, are imaginary monologues, "dramatic or impersonative even where not explicitly so." The narrators of the novels exist on the other side of the mirror of fiction. They are witnesses within an imaginary or linguistic world who speak as if the characters and events of their story had had an historical existence. Hardy's writing is an indirect way of exploring the real world. It goes away from reality to try to return to it by a long detour, or to try to reveal the otherwise invisible nature of the real by means of the fictive. It attempts to reach reality by way of the imaginary, to close the gap between words and what words name or create.

To do this would also be to reveal that secret energy which moves both nature and history in their courses through time. Hardy calls this force the Immanent Will. The tracings of the Will in history or in nature are themselves a kind of writing, the patterned "mesh" or "contemplated charactery" which is the inscription on matter of the Will. His writing is also covertly motivated by the Will, for the Will is the hidden force behind each person. The Will is the ground of desire. It uses Hardy as it uses all men and women to add one more form of writing to the others. The author seated at his desk composing *Tess of the d'Urbervilles* is as much a victim or instrument of the Immanent Will as Tess herself. (pp. xii-xiv)

> *J. Hillis Miller, in his* Thomas Hardy: Distance and Desire *(copyright © 1970 by The President and Fellows of Harvard College; excerpted by permission), Cambridge, Mass.: Harvard University Press, 1970, 282 p.*

PENELOPE VIGAR (essay date 1974)

The Mayor of Casterbridge is unique among Hardy's novels in that it makes extensive use of an urban community setting to show the relationship of an 'exceptional' individual both to his immediate social environment and to the fixed and undeviating principles set down by the mass of humanity. In the earlier 'Novels of Character and Environment' the common people, usually rustics, almost invariably serve in the comparatively passive rôle of a chorus, a solid and credulous background to the action, or to provide comic relief. It was not until *The Return of the Native* that Hardy showed, in the character of Susan Nunsuch with her primitive fear and hatred of Eustacia, the directly opposing view of an inflexible section of humanity, suspicious of and hostile to a way of life which it does not comprehend. In *The Mayor of Casterbridge*, the active representatives of the 'commonplace majority', Joshua Jopp and the furmity-woman, bring into prominence the whole body of vociferous and down-to-earth citizens of Casterbridge as a foil for the depiction of individual lives. One has only to note how freely and frequently the narrative is carried on by the gossip of the local residents and how consistently the town or the townsfolk help directly to shape the action of the story, to realize that the survival of the main protagonists depends to a very large extent on their 'acceptance' by this limited and circumscribed social environment. . . . Henchard's history is acted out always against the existence of an uncompromising established human order. Always he must be seen both subjectively, as an individual, and objectively, as a mere fractional part of the great undifferentiated mass of humanity. Our conception of Henchard is essentially a combination of these views, and the contrasts inherent in Hardy's artistic presentation of his titular character also provide the bases for the working out of his underlying theme. (pp. 147-48)

The striking unity of *The Mayor of Casterbridge* is less the result of its carefully symmetrical structure than it is of Hardy's consistent and imaginative balancing of opposites in his seemingly unwieldy mass of material. Despite the complexity of the story and the regular points of suspense and climax which betray its serial origin, the novel succeeds primarily because the events in it are firmly embedded in and related to a background which is itself an intricate material reconstruction of the story's theme. Hardy's technique here is basically identical to that he used in *The Return of the Native,* but it functions on a rather different level. Whereas Egdon, though humanized itself, ultimately dwarfs the transient human lives which reflect its mystery, Casterbridge is the specific embodiment of its inhabitants, reflecting in its ancient brick and stone all the ambiguities of man's condition. This essential contradictoriness is subtly reflected in Hardy's depiction of a town which is in appearance 'as compact as a box of dominoes' but in character as diverse and unpredictable as the lives of the people existing within its boundaries. (p. 149)

The themes of deception and concealment contained in the main story-line are reiterated in countless smaller ramifications of plot; in such things as secret marriages, mistaken identities, shady propositions and false promises, clandestine meetings and unexpected encounters. The pattern of deliberate secrecy and evasion which shrouds the actions of one character from another at varying stages of the tale is subtly reinforced throughout the novel by Hardy's use of a consistent imagery of mistiness and obscurity, a pervasive dankness leading to decay. (p. 151)

The clash between Henchard and Farfrae which is the central action of the story is shown essentially as a conflict of their natures, a clash of the moody and unpredictable with the rational and consistent. Farfrae is clear-headed, resourceful and transparent, with the glow of poetry and romance about him; one whom even the plain townspeople view admiringly 'through a golden haze which the tone of his mind seemed to raise around him.' . . . Henchard is by comparison blundering and primitive, passionate and well-meaning, but lost in his own obscurity. . . . The relationship of the two men is so twisted and thwarted by false pride and misunderstanding that finally each can see only evil and treachery in the other, so much so that when Lucetta's life is in danger, Farfrae coldly and distrustfully chooses to ignore Henchard's earnest entreaties to go to her, because he has been so often wronged by him.

It is therefore with specific irony that Hardy uses the prevailing images of blurring and misting to underline metaphorically the lack of perception and the ultimate bafflement which exist between the rival men, and to point the defeat of the one by the other. (pp. 153-54)

With Hardy's concentration on one particular character in this novel, his use of specifically 'visual' techniques is

rather more subjective than it is in *The Return of the Native* or *Far from the Madding Crowd*. More than Clym or Eustacia—who are presented essentially as being the halves of a perfect aesthetic whole—Henchard's character, as well as his thematic rôle, is determined by how he appears and what he does. His portrait is nowhere definitive, even though all the conflicting elements in his densely wrought personality are carefully built up from a series of images which work together to create the 'meaning' of his character within the framework of the novel. Henchard's life as a wealthy mayor of Casterbridge is continuously contrasted with the lingering image of his past; the way we see him is constantly shown to be at variance with what he really is. (p. 155)

All through the novel Hardy has interwoven the details of Henchard's past with those of his present life, in preparation for the moment when they finally come together and betray him. For this reason he maintains, at all levels of his protagonist's life, a neatly ambivalent pictorial imagery by which external appearance is shown as having, on the one hand, the simple and obvious connotation of social status and importance, and, on the other, as demonstrating a contrary moral or actual truth. . . .

The sharpness of detail with which Hardy depicts Henchard's outward appearance at all stages of his life is countered by a consistent use of natural metaphorical equivalents which point to the characteristics always discernible beneath the palpable surface. Through this continually altering perspective, we view him both as he is seen by his contemporaries and as he really is. (p. 158)

The contrast between natural life and the false order of the artificial values imposed on it by society is shown not only in the dual presentation of Henchard himself, but also in Hardy's method of depicting all the main characters in this novel. Weaving his story around the motifs of truth and concealment, he shows, through a fluctuating pattern of deception and intrigue, all the differing ways in which these characters are blinded to actuality whilst at the same time they contrive to maintain for themselves an ideal of integrity in the eyes of their fellow-men. (p. 160)

Two days after he had finished *The Mayor of Casterbridge,* Hardy noted in his diary that 'The business of the poet and novelist is to show the sorriness underlying the grandest things, and the grandeur underlying the sorriest things.' . . . This, in brief, is the philosophy underlying the story of Michael Henchard. It does not necessarily imply a tragic point of view, but is merely a simple statement of what (to Hardy) is a universal truth. Nothing is consistent. . . . [Everything] is dependent, finally, on the manner in which it is viewed and understood. (p. 166)

Artistically, the story of Michael Henchard comes full circle, with what might be termed the 'spherical completeness of perfect art' which Hardy so admired in the parable stories of the Bible. . . . When the ex-mayor, dressed in the serviceable clothes of a workman, returns resolutely to his former occupation as a hay-trusser, we are urged to take note of the significance of this fact by a naively intrusive authorial aside couched in terms of Elizabeth-Jane's unconscious observation: 'Though she did not know it Henchard formed at this moment much the same picture as he had presented when entering Casterbridge for the first time nearly a quarter of a century before. . . .' . . . Partly because of the obviousness of this sort of artistic contrivance, there is undoubtedly a danger of seeing Henchard purely as an allegorical figure. . . . Yet, by his inclusion of the novel's subtitle, *A Man of Character*, Hardy emphasizes that it is Henchard himself who is uniquely the subject of the story. Ultimately, Hardy's elaborate methods of staging his characters and arranging his scenes must be seen to relate purely to the attempt to present this one man, and his relationship with his environment, by means of various contrasting perspectives. The contrived synonymity of his entrance into the world of Casterbridge and his exit from it points to the comparative unreality of his existence there. Those past events which vitally affected his life are shown virtually as fantasy or are left completely in obscurity; and yet these hidden episodes are the abiding reality by which all else is judged. (pp. 167-68)

> *Penelope Vigar, in her* The Novels of Thomas Hardy: Illusion and Reality *(© Penelope Vigar 1974), Athlone Press, London, 1974, 226 p.*

ROY FULLER   (essay date 1976)

[*The Poor Man and the Lady* is] a compelling narrative (if, here and there, a clumsy one) which in view of its origins is not obtrusively abrupt or deformed. Though the balance of the story and the rationale of the lovers' destiny would perhaps have gained from the missing social satire, no doubt we would have agreed with Alexander Macmillan's excellent and sympathetic letter of rejection that the bias in that department was too great for verisimilitude. In other words there has probably been a positive gain in the simple retention of a set of events showing the protagonists in the grip of those Hardyesque Powers which make for unhappiness.

The heroine, Geraldine, is the first in the long line of Hardy heroines whose sexual attractiveness is so masterfully depicted. . . . The hero is a very young provincial who goes to London and becomes a talked-of writer, Hardy avoiding most of the implausibilities and embarrassments in such a schema. One could not say that every rift of the writing was loaded with ore, but Hardy is sometimes observationally extremely alert and finds the poetically exact word. . . . Now and then there is a descriptive set-piece of mature power, like the opening scene in church where the pulpit candles and the girl's face shine increasingly in the deepening dusk.

A few of the incidents have the familiar and amusing Hardyan ambiguity: are they awful or rather good? . . . What is unambiguously excellent is Hardy's insight into feminine feelings—only a handful of touches, but all on target.

> *Roy Fuller, "Hardly," in* The Spectator *(© 1976 by The Spectator; reprinted by permission of* The Spectator*), Vol. 236, No. 7719, June 5, 1976, p. 23.*

ANNE Z. MICKELSON   (essay date 1976)

[Hardy] anticipates much of the thinking in the 1970s on men and women, especially women.

The vitality of Hardy's fiction and the note of modernism which surrounds it come not only from the individual's quest for identity—man seeking in woman a counterbalance for the loss of community and religious faith, woman searching for her place in a man-made world—but from the conviction that the coming of machines affects the emotional life of men and women. When his comments about men and women are gathered together, they dovetail into a coherent argument that outer and inner nature have been defeated. By this I mean that the outer world of nature, the natural world, is disappearing before the inroads of industrialization, and that part of human nature which is instinctual and intuitive is being smothered by the social self imposed on it. In Hardy's last book, *Jude the Obscure*, society's triumph over nature is complete. (pp. 1-2)

Tess of the d'Urbervilles is a penetrating study of a woman who battles to be recognized as a person in her own right, but who never gets the chance to realize her womanhood. Considered inferior as a woman and as a peasant, her self-esteem is constantly eroded by a society which brands her as socially, economically, and morally unacceptable. The hunted of predatory men like Alec and others, the scorn of the morally-righteous like Angel, the victim of family loyalty, it is no wonder that toward the end she looks like a woman out of whose body all the blood has run. The black flag which goes up on the prison roof as signal that her execution for murder is over becomes a symbol of a blighted life. The most poignant thing about Tess, though, is not her death but her loneliness in life—the special loneliness which comes from not being known by others. (p. 122)

The novel is a high point of maturity in Hardy's fiction. He deals with poverty and the woman, the double standard of morality, the role of passivity forced upon woman, and how woman's chances for happiness are eventually blighted. . . . [In] his last novel, *Jude the Obscure*, Hardy develops the psychological insights glimpsed in *Tess* through his portraits of Sue Bridehead and Jude Fawley. The interactions of the two, their isolation from society, their deep personal problems, and the psychic shelters they seek emphasize more starkly than previous works Hardy's concern with a society which refuses to change. (p. 123)

Most of the ideas concerning human relationships with which Hardy works, and which Lawrence is to develop later and give his special imprint of personality and interpretations, are in *Jude the Obscure*. Here are: the decline of family; the loss of community; nostalgia for the past; the suspension of accredited values; the deracination of men and women caught between two worlds and lost before town, machine, sex, religion. Here are also the struggles of a woman to find her place in a man-made world: the growing mechanization of life; the need for work which would yield some measure of fulfillment; the urge to regain a pagan love of living; the insistence that living is loving; the eternal conflict between the individual's outer and inner worlds; and the urge to build a private world of one's own. Jude and Sue . . . desperately want to stake out some private corner of their own in the world and come to private terms with the world. Hardy insists that the world will not let them. (pp. 146-47)

Hardy defies the tests ordinarily applied to fiction. He leans heavily on the old-fashioned devices of coincidence, chance, eavesdropping, and, as has been too often said, his plots sometimes creak. Yet our final impression of his novels is of a great imagination linked to an equally great compassion which strives to express the torments of men and women attempting self-fulfillment in an age which forces increasing conflict between the individual and society. Their true tragedy becomes revealed to us not so much in the societal conflict, but in the self-conflict. In this respect, Hardy's books are truly oriented to the future and point to problems in our own time. (p. 161)

Anne Z. Mickelson, in her Thomas Hardy's Women and Men: The Defeat of Nature *(copyright © 1976 by Anne Z. Mickelson), The Scarecrow Press, Inc., 1976, 172 p.*

R. M. REHDER (essay date 1977)

Hardy rejected the idea that the novel should be merely a representation of sensation or the world. He shared with Henry James the belief that the art of the novel depends on selection and treatment. . . . The lost letters, missed trains and unexpected encounters in his novels are part of his effort to keep the story going. They are also ways of holding the story together as tightly as possible. Hardy prefers the definite. Like Shakespeare, like all great poets, he has a metaphor-making mind. He is less discursive than George Eliot and more specific than Henry James. Their tendency is to expand, his instinct is to concentrate. The terse, twisted quality of his prose shows the marks of this pressure. As the descriptions focus on details and each becomes a nexus of metaphors, the plots of the novels seem to crystallise around a sequence of small, individual, closed scenes. *Far from the Madding Crowd* can almost be described as a series of images. Hardy does not seek to create space in his novels, but rather to fill it. He has a need to make things happen, while Eliot and James have the ability to contemplate a mood by itself and often prolong their delays.

Hardy emphasises the importance of strict, rigorous form. (p. 15)

He stresses symmetry and tightness. He deplores the spasmodic, the heterogeneous and the conglomerate. . . . [He believes] that each story has its own form and that a novel should be all of a piece. He intimates that the protagonists make their own plot, that each character is a plot. The one critic who looms up in all this is Aristotle. This is certainly because of Hardy's preoccupation with tragedy.

Most of Hardy's novels have markedly unhappy endings. This is a significant characteristic of their form. He is the first major English author to write a number of novels that end unhappily, although the conclusions of his best novels can only be called tragic. He does not simply negate happiness, he insists on sorrow. His achievement, in terms of form, is to have combined the tragedy and the novel.

Hardy is a writer of great subtlety. He makes full use of 'the force of reserve, and the emphasis of understatement', but he can be obvious, heavy-handed and unrelenting as well. He seems sometimes to resemble the man with the tin pot of red paint in *Tess of the d'Urbervilles* who paints Biblical texts in fiery letters around the countryside, but he, nevertheless, continues to surprise us by the fineness of his observations, as when he describes how the strangers drinking outside Rolliver's inn 'threw the dregs on the dusty ground to the pattern of Polynesia', or Clym tying Eustacia's bonnet strings after their quarrel. He uses the most delicate touch and the hammerblow. His harshness and his ruthlessness can obscure for us the fact that these qualities exist together. (pp. 16-17)

Hardy needs the tragic because of the overwhelming power of his feelings. It may be said that the novel as he found it was too slack and diffuse for his purposes. Tragedy may be considered the most rigorous of narrative forms, the novel is perhaps the most commodious. Hardy's combination of the two enables him to express sorrow as no other English novelist can. His work is remarkable for the varieties and nuances of sadness. Among English writers, perhaps only Shakespeare surpasses him in this capacity.

Hardy worked consciously and deliberately as an artist in the tradition of the greatest European art. His idea of tragedy represents a combination of Greek, Shakespearian and Biblical tragedy. He had Jesus and Paul in mind when he created Clym Yeobright. He found much of the form of *The Mayor of Casterbridge* in the histories of Saul and King Lear, and *Jude the Obscure* is reminiscent of Job. The customers in Warren's Malthouse, the old men in the Three Mariners and the people at Rolliver's perform some of the functions of a Greek chorus, as do many of the groups of folk in Hardy's novels. They are used to balance the novels. The way in which they are separated from, and contrasted with, the other characters is Shakespearian and derives from the ancient division between high and low styles. (p. 23)

Fifty years after Hardy's death it is clear that he is one of the greatest English novelists, with Jane Austen and George Eliot, Henry James and Joseph Conrad. (p. 26)

R. M. Rehder, "The Form of Hardy's Novels" (© R. M. Rehder 1977), in Thomas Hardy after Fifty Years, *edited by Lance St. John Butler, Rowman and Littlefield, 1977, pp. 13-27.*

JOHN BAYLEY (essay date 1978)

[We] may still respond today to the real pleasures of [Hardy's] text in ways quite different to those in which we are usually taken on by a novelist. For one thing his words may make us feel that the words of other novelists are much more settled in place, have the air of being dealt out for good. Hardy's words and sentences give the impression of continuing instability: while reading we are waiting for something unexpected, good or bad, to happen to them, and this kind of expectation is a characteristic part of the pleasure. (p. 2)

Instability grows less marked as the list of Hardy's novels grew longer. In the last three, from *Tess of the D'Urbervilles* onward, it is hardly in evidence at all. What suggests itself instead is a greater rigidity, a methodical build-up instead of deflations and relaxations. There is an air of concentration at the outset of *Tess,* a bent to get everything possible out of the scenic atmosphere of the rural drama; and there is a deliberation which seems to stabilise a method throughout both *Jude the Obscure* and *The Well-Beloved.* Hardy has become much more concerned with the completed achievement in a more ambitious sense. (p. 11)

Hardy secures our attention on his narrative mood by the absent-minded expression of the prose contrasting with the attention of its gaze. (p. 30)

This quality in the writing of both attention and inattention, shifting between the language itself and what it describes, is an aspect of what could be called Hardy conscious and unconscious; and our feeling is for the alternation of the two. The Hardy who is on duty does not seem aware of the one who unknowingly observes: this perceiver pays no regard to the artificer and craftsman. The text is like a landscape of which the constituent parts—cows, birds, trees, grass—pay no attention to one another, although they appear as a total composition to the beholder, the reader.

The metaphor does not quite do, but it may convey something of the complex pleasure in attending to Hardy. The conscious Hardy may not seem aware of the unconscious one, but is extremely sensitive to everything else, including the main chance of the story and what response his readers may show. The conscious Hardy is laborious in the pursuit of literature and the exploitation of verbal effect and allusions, erudite or worldly, meditative or melodramatic. This conscientiousness can give us the feeling of disappoinment, of let-down, but also the knowledge that the conscious Hardy augments the unconscious. The two are mutually dependent, perhaps on account of their seeming ignorance of each other. (p. 31)

> *John Bayley, in his* An Essay on Hardy *(copyright © 1978 by the Cambridge University Press), Cambridge University Press, 1978, 237 p.*

ADDITIONAL BIBLIOGRAPHY

Bailey, J. O. *The Poetry of Thomas Hardy: A Handbook and Commentary.* Chapel Hill: The University of North Carolina Press, 1970, 712 p.
> Supplies literary and personal background and other factual annotations to Hardy's complete poems. Bailey maintains that knowledge of Hardy's life is the key to a full understanding of his poetry.

Blunden, Edmund. *Thomas Hardy.* London: Macmillan and Co., 1942, 286 p.
> Critical study of the novels, poetry, and *The Dynasts.*

Brennecke, Ernest, Jr. *Thomas Hardy's Universe: A Study of a Poet's Mind.* New York: Haskell House, 1966, 153 p.
> Derives a "Hardy-system" of philosophy from the author's works, comparing his world view with that of Schopenhauer.

Brown, Douglas. *Thomas Hardy.* London: Longmans, 1961, 194 p.
> Focuses on Hardy as the literary voice of English agricultural society, examining how the author's "unserviceable, even shoddy" prose style effectively expresses this way of life.

Cecil, David. *Hardy the Novelist: An Essay in Criticism.* London: Constable and Co., 1956, 157 p.
> Delivered as a series of lectures, this thematic study includes chapters on Hardy's "Power," "Art," "Weakness," and "Style."

Cox, R. G., ed. *Thomas Hardy: The Critical Heritage.* New York: Barnes & Noble, 1970, 473 p.
> Useful compendium of early magazine reviews of Hardy's novels and poetry. Several of these reviews are excerpted in criticism above.

Drabble, Margaret, ed. *The Genius of Thomas Hardy.* New York: Alfred A. Knopf, 1976, 191 p.
> Essays divided into sections on Hardy's life and works, with special studies devoted to specific aspects of the author's writing such as architecture and history. Critics in this collection include J.I.M. Stewart, Elizabeth Hardwick, Sir John Betjeman, and Lord David Cecil, among others.

Draper, R. P., ed. *Hardy: The Tragic Novels: "The Return of the Native," "The Mayor of Casterbridge," "Tess of the d'Urber-*
villes," "Jude the Obscure." London: The Macmillan Press, 1975, 256 p.
> In three sections presents (1) Hardy's comments on his own work gathered from various sources (2) a chronological sampling of criticism, including essays by Lionel Johnson and D. H. Lawrence (3) modern thematic perspectives on the major novels.

Duffin, H. C. *Thomas Hardy: A Study of the Wessex Novels, the Poems, and "The Dynasts."* Manchester: Manchester University Press, 1937, 356 p.
> Primarily devoted to thematic and technical analysis of the novels, with a chapter on "Hardy's Use of the Marvelous."

Grimsditch, Herbert B. *Character and Environment in the Novels of Thomas Hardy.* New York: Russell & Russell, 1962, 189 p.
> Analyzes Hardy's characterizations with regard to environmental influences contributing to a given character's psychology and development, inferring from this the author's philosophical views of humanity and existence.

Guerard, Albert, ed. *Hardy: A Collection of Critical Essays.* Englewood Cliffs, NJ: Prentice-Hall, 1963, 180 p.
> Includes essays by Guerard, D. H. Lawrence, A. Alvarez, W. H. Auden, Samuel Hynes, and Delmore Schwartz, among others.

Hardy, Evelyn. *Thomas Hardy: A Critical Biography.* London: The Hogarth Press, 1954, 342 p.
> Considers the influence on Hardy of literary and philosophical trends in the nineteenth century, focusing on the interdependence of his life and work.

Hardy, Florence Emily. *The Life of Thomas Hardy, 1840-1928.* London: Macmillan & Co., 1962, 470 p.
> A biography mostly dictated by Hardy to his second wife.

Hawkins, Desmond. *Thomas Hardy.* London: Arthur Barker, 1950, 112 p.
> Survey of the novels.

Lee, Vernon. "The Handling of Words: Hardy." In her *The Handling of Words and Other Studies in Literary Psychology,* pp. 222-41. London: John Lane, The Bodley Head, 1923.
> Analysis of Hardy's stylistic flaws in a passage selected from *Tess,* concluding that these flaws are an expression of the author's particular genius.

Marsden, Kenneth. *The Poems of Thomas Hardy: A Critical Introduction.* New York: Oxford University Press, 1969, 247 p.
> Analyzes the structure, genesis, vocabulary, and fundamental ideology of Hardy's poems. Marsden takes issue with the prevalent critical attitude that only a fraction of Hardy's poetry is of enduring significance.

Orel, Harold. *Thomas Hardy's Epic-Drama: A Study of "The Dynasts."* Lawrence: University of Kansas Publications, 1963, 122 p.
> Contains chapters on the writing of *The Dynasts,* its philosophical foundations, its relationship to Milton's *Paradise Lost,* and "Hardy's Attitude toward War."

Pinion, F. B. *A Hardy Companion: A Guide to the Works of Thomas Hardy and Their Background.* London: Macmillan, 1968, 555 p.
> Survey of Hardy's work and its major influences, with biographical background. This study contains an insightful chapter entitled "Aspects of the Unusual and Irrational."

Roberts, Marguerite. *Hardy's Poetic Drama and the Theatre: "The Dynasts" and "The Famous Tragedy of the Queen of Cornwall."* New York: Pageant Press, 1965, 110 p.
> Examines Hardy's interest in the theater and considers the purely dramatic aspects of these two works.

Rutland, William R. *Thomas Hardy: A Study of His Writings and Their Background.* Oxford: Basil Blackwell, 1938, 365 p.
> Examines influences on Hardy's writings and philosophical

outlook; gives biographical and literary background to his works.

Sankey, Benjamin. *The Major Novels of Thomas Hardy*. Denver: Alan Swallow, 1965, 59 p.
Examination of major themes, characterization, and some aspects of style in Hardy's novels.

Southerington, F. R. *Hardy's Vision of Man*. New York: Barnes & Noble, 1971, 289 p.
Critical study of the novels and *The Dynasts,* noting in part autobiographical elements in Hardy's work and deriving a coherent view of his personal ideology.

Weber, Carl J. *Hardy of Wessex: His Life and Literary Career*. New York: Columbia University Press, 1965, 324 p.
Biography drawing in large part on Hardy's letters, which this prominent Hardy scholar edited for publication.

Wright, Walter. *The Shaping of "The Dynasts": A Study in Thomas Hardy*. Lincoln: University of Nebraska Press, 1967, 334 p.
Traces the creative evolution of *The Dynasts*, with a textual examination of the various drafts and revisions of the manuscript.

Jaroslav (Matej Frantisek) Hăsek

1883-1923

(Also wrote under pseudonyms of M. Ruffian, Benjamin Franklin, and Vojtěch Kapristián z Hellenhofferů, among others) Czechoslovakian novelist, short story writer, essayist, and poet.

Hašek's reputation rests entirely upon his four-volume series, *Osudy dobrého vojáka Svejka za svetoné války* (*The Good Soldier Schweik*). This unfinished work, which details the exploits of the apparently simple-minded Schweik, has been subject to various interpretations. While some view *The Good Soldier Schweik* as a slander against the Czech national character, others feel that it epitomizes the Czech attitude of resistance toward Austria during World War I.

Hašek was born in Prague and, despite his obvious lack of interest in business, attended the Prague Commercial Academy. While studying at the Academy, Hašek attended the literary club Syrinx, which included many future leading Czech writers and dramatists. He came to reject his literary peers' romantic conception of the artist as a being detached from society, however, and was most comfortable in working-class pubs. Hašek lived a life marked by dissipation and minor arrests, and became well known in Prague bohemian circles for his practical jokes, anarchism, and the founding of his satiric Party of Moderate Progress within the Limits of the Law.

When World War I broke out, Hašek shared the contempt most Czechs felt for their obligatory participation under Austrian authority. He served in the Austrian Army, was captured by the Russians, and endured a subsequent period of imprisonment. He eventually joined the Czech legions in Russia and then became a communist. When Hašek finally returned to Prague and began writing *The Good Soldier Schweik*, he drew heavily upon his wartime experience. Critics cite numerous parallels between this period of Hašek's life and the chronicle of his antihero Schweik.

Hašek had already spent a considerable amount of time developing the character Schweik before actually beginning *The Good Soldier Schweik*. A rough version of Schweik first appeared in a short story of 1911, and again in Hašek's novel *Dobrý voják Švejk v zajetí* of 1917. Written in Russia, this novel relates the adventures of Schweik while in Russian captivity, and reflects Hašek's own imprisonment in the Russian camps.

The Good Soldier Schweik both delighted and enraged its readers at home and abroad. Schweik is the Czech "little man" whose naiveté, whether real or assumed, carries him unscathed through the disintegration of the Austro-Hungarian Empire. Critics often compare *The Good Soldier Schweik* to the works of Rabelais and Cervantes. Like the works of these predecessors, Hašek's novel is bawdy, disrespectful, and unrelentingly ironic. In fact, some critics have called *Schweik* the most thorough attack upon bourgeois values ever written. But, even though Schweik has been analyzed on anarchist, nationalist, and socialist grounds, his in-

dividual and ambivalent nature defies absolute categorization.

Hašek also wrote approximately 1,200 short stories and comic sketches under more than eighty pseudonyms, as well as some poetry early in his literary career. Although *The Good Soldier Schweik* has been widely translated, filmed, and dramatized several times, including a dramatization by Bertolt Brecht, little of his other work has been translated or recognized. Hašek died with only three of the projected six volumes of his masterpiece completed. Despite the occasional repetition and inconsistency of its prose, *The Good Soldier Schweik* is regarded as one of the world's most thorough condemnations of war.

PRINCIPAL WORKS

Dobrý voják Švejk v zajetí (novel) 1917
Osudy dobrého vojáka Švejka za světoné války (four-novel series; volume four completed by Karel Vanek) 1920-23
  [*The Good Soldier Schweik* (abridged version), 1930; also published as *The Good Soldier Švejk and His Fortunes in the World War* (unabridged version), 1973]
Velitelem města Bugul'my (short stories) 1976

C. A. CHAPMAN (essay date 1930)

Schweik's adventures [in Hašek's *The Good Soldier: Schweik*] are good. If you like wholehearted burlesque with the material picked up pellmell in generous buckets . . . this is your book. The function of the allegedly feeble-minded orderly, Schweik, is to make fun of war in general and war as waged by the former Austro-Hungarian empire in particular; but he is not aware of this function. He is never out of trouble, yet his motives are never at fault. His fund of stories with which to point any moral, no matter how incredible, is inexhaustible. Of course he never gets to the front, but to have created him and given him such a pack of associates, to have made them vivid and real, is an achievement. . . . This is a long book and its greatest virtue is its fundamental humanity, its good-nature. It casts a spell. You can bury yourself in it.

> C. A. Chapman, "Behind the Lines," in The New
> Republic (© 1930 The New Republic, Inc.), Vol.
> 63, No. 807, May 21, 1930, p. 26.

ROBERT VLACH (essay date 1962)

Two noteworthy definitions of *poshlost'* were proposed by two prominent Russian *hommes de lettres*, Prince D. S. Mirskij and Vladimir Nabokov. Mirskij, in his *History of Russian Literature*, presents the following one: *Poshlost'* is "a self-satisfied inferiority, moral and spiritual." For Nabokov, in his *Nicolai Gogol*, the expression means "not only the obviously trashy, but also the falsely beautiful, falsely important, falsely clever, falsely attractive." Neither Gogol, nor Hašek had ever named it by its name, but they embodied it, in its acme, in their masterpieces. In [Gogol's] *Dead Souls* (as well as in the *Inspector General* or the *Overcoat*) and in [Hašek's] the *Good Soldier Schweik* we find the same magnificent, universal, exasperating trashiness. . . .

There are no positive characters in either [*Dead Souls* or the *Good Soldier Schweik*]. They simply do not live: *poshlost'* emptied them of all human content. They are caricatures, grotesques, but these traits only mask an immense, limitless, pure tragedy.

Poshlost' seems to have imposed upon both authors many identical artistic means, but there can be no doubt that Gogol was a much greater artist than Hašek. . . . *Poshlost'* does not favor plots. It permits one to see men only as caricatures. It makes laughter turn to tears of despair. It does not tolerate any system: its currents are those of hazard. People (or rather shadows) appear, perform something meaningless, promise something never fulfilled, then disappear. There is, significantly enough, no place for women. . . .

[In foreign countries,] Schweik is accepted as a kind of Sancho Panza. His name is often mentioned in relation to such characters as Hamlet, Don Juan, Faust and Oblomov, according to the critic's preferences. (p. 240)

Schweik unveiled all the formidable *poshlost'* of the Austrian military machinery and by this of the whole monarchy. But for this latter he would be gaily pardoned by the Czechs. The novel also brought to light the no less formidable *poshlost'* of a newformed, small-bourgeois State, with its not-yet-learned democracy, its self-glorification not only in the remote, but also in the very recent past and its heroic

revolutionary legends in particular. You are not Hussites but "Schweiks" was the challenge Hašek threw in the face of his countrymen, and he knew what he was saying, being one of them, being himself a "Schweik". . . .

Who is Schweik? According to American critics, he is either, as William E. Harkins proposes, "an apparently naive person whose simplicity protects him and helps him escape the hardships and responsibilities of life in the Austrian army during the First World War" or a "fat dogcatcher from the Prague area," "a coward and shirk who assumes the innocence and stupidity of an idiot to disarm railing officers, a happy-go-lucky skeptic as to war and military glory, and endless talker and coarse jester"—as René Wellek patriotically sees him.

For the Czech Communists, because he was accepted in the Soviet Union, Schweik became a positive hero, illustrating [as Jaroslav Kune expressed it] "the rascality, barbarity and nonsense of the imperialist war," a man "of common, realistic sense and opinions based upon his experience of daily life."

F. X. Šalda, the greatest Czech critic, found Hašek's novel "sorrowful to death: for here, an individual struggles with an enormous power, which has no superior—with the war . . . He struggles with the mean, insidious weapons which were imposed on him: he struggles as slaves always do." . . . Šalda, of course, put his finger on the Czech national wound: the Czechs were reduced then, as during World War Two, and as at the present time, to the weapons of slaves. But more than that: they have got used to these weapons and have since fallen back upon them even when they had free choice. They will be ashamed of Schweik as long as they manage to redeem themselves in their own conscience.

It is another story, that Hašek did not make this cruel diagnosis in order to heal them. His own despair, similar to Gogol's, limited him to diagnosing the condition. The process was not without delight for him. (p. 241)

Poshlost', which both Gogol and Hašek reflected so brilliantly and fully, seems to take possession of the hero as well as, through him, of the author. They were masters of *poshlost'* in their works, but in life they became its victims. . . . [Because] of *poshlost'*, which they were able to discern more sharply than anyone else, they detested men. (p. 242)

> Robert Vlach, "Gogol and Hašek—Two Masters
> of Poshlost," in Slavic and East-European Stud-
> ies, Vol. VII, Parts 3-4, Autumn-Winter, 1962, pp.
> 239-42.*

LESLIE A. FIEDLER (essay date 1962)

For a thousand years or so, roughly from the time of Charlemagne to 1914, the wars of Christendom, whether fought against external enemies or strictly within the family, had been felt and celebrated in terms of a single continuous tradition. And those who lived within that tradition assumed without question that some battles at least were not only justifiable but holy, just as they assumed that to die in such battles was not merely a tolerable fate but the most glorious of events. . . .

[Full of internal contradictions], nonetheless the Christian heroic tradition proved viable for ten centuries, as viable in the high verse of Dante and Shakespeare and Chaucer as in folk ballads and the sermons of country priests. Yet all the while it lived, of course, it was dying, too, dying with the civilization that had nurtured it, already mourned for by the time of Sir Walter Scott. So slowly did it die, however, that only under the impact of total war were those who fought shocked into admitting that perhaps they no longer believed in what they fought for. (p. 34)

[The] antiheroic revolt has itself become in two or three generations a new convention, the source of a new set of fashionably ridiculous clichés. Shameless politicians are as likely to use the slogans of between-the-wars pacifism to launch new wars as they are to refurbish more ancient platitudes. The wild freedom with which the authors of *The Enormous Room* and *Le Feu, The Good Soldier: Schweik* and *A Farewell to Arms,* challenged millennial orthodoxies has been sadly tamed; its fate is symbolized by Picasso's domesticated dove hovering obediently over the rattling spears of the Soviet war camp. Nevertheless, such books still tell us certain truths about the world in which we live, reveal to us certain ways in which men's consciousness of themselves in peace and war was radically altered some four decades ago.

The antiwar novel did not end war, but it memorializes the end of something almost as deeply rooted in the culture of the West: the concept of Honor. It comes into existence at the moment when in the West men, still nominally Christian, come to believe *that the worst thing of all is to die—* more exactly, perhaps, the moment when for the first time in a thousand years it is possible to *admit* that no cause is worth dying for. (p. 36)

There are in the traditional literatures of Europe, to be sure, characters who have believed that death was the worst event and honor a figment; but such characters have always belonged to "low comedy" i.e., they have been comic butts set against representatives of quite other ideals, Sancho Panzas who serve Don Quixotes, Falstaffs who tremble before Prince Hals, Leporellos who cower as the Don Giovannis tempt fate. They have been permitted to blaspheme against the courtly codes precisely because those codes have been so secure. . . . They represented not a satirical challenge but precisely a "comic relief" from the strain of upholding—against the promptings of our animal nature, the demands of indolence, and greed, and fear— those high values that were once thought to make men fully human. . . .

What happens, however, when the Leporellos, the Falstaffs, and the Sancho Panzas begin to inherit the earth? When the remaining masters are in fact more egregious Falstaffs and Leporellos and Sancho Panzas, and all that Don Quixote and Prince Hal and Don Giovanni once stood for is discredited or dead? What happens in a time of democracy, mass culture, and mechanization, a time when war itself is transformed by the industrial revolution? *The Good Soldier: Schweik* addresses itself to answering, precisely and hilariously, this question. And the answer is: what happens is what has been happening to us all ever since 1914, what happens is *us.*

We inhabit for the first time a world in which men begin wars knowing their avowed ends will not be accomplished, a world in which it is more and more difficult to believe that the conflicts we cannot avert are in any sense justified. And in such a world, the draft dodger, the malingerer, the gold brick, the crap-out, all who make what Hemingway was the first to call "a separate peace" all who somehow *survive* the bombardment of shells and cant, become a new kind of antiheroic hero. Of such men, Schweik is the real ancestor. (p. 37)

Not all of Hašek's book, unfortunately, is devoted to portraying a Falstaff in a world without Hotspurs or Prince Hals. Much of it is spent in editorializing rather obviously about the horrors of war and the ironies of being a chaplain, the shortcomings of the Emperor Franz Joseph and the limitations of the military mind; and toward the end it becomes rather too literary in a heavy-handed way, especially after the introduction of Volunteer Officer Marek, a figure obviously intended to speak directly for the author. From time to time, we feel it as dated, say, as *What Price Glory* or *All Quiet on the Western Front,* for we have grown by now as weary of the phrasemongering and self-pity of conventional pacifism as of the attitudinizing and pharisaism of conventional patriotism.

It is not Hašek's anticlericalism or anti-Semitism, not his distrust of Magyars or of the long-defunct Austrian Empire, not his Czech nationalism or his defense of the Czech tongue against German linguistic imperialism that moves us today. The dream of expropriation, too ("After this war, they say, there ain't going to be any more emperors and they'll help themselves to the big royal estates"), rings hollow for us now. . . . (p. 38)

It is only when Hašek turns Schweik loose among scoundrels quite like himself, the police spy Bretschneider or the atheist Jewish chaplain, Otto Katz, and permits him to speak his own language—only, that is to say, when the anarchist intellectual permits himself to be possessed by his *lumpen* antihero—that the book becomes at once wonderfully funny and wonderfully true. Schweik is fortunately one of those mythical creations who escape the prejudices of their creators even as they elude our definitions; and he refuses to speak with the voice of the 1920 revolutionary, even as he refuses to speak with the voice of councilors and kings.

He will not be exploited by his author any more than he will by the con men and bullies who inhabit his fictional universe; moving through a society of victimizers, he refuses to become a victim. Though Hašek would persuade us that he is surrounded by Pilates ("The glorious history of the Roman domination of Jerusalem was being enacted all over again"), Schweik certainly does not consider himself a Christ. He is neither innocent nor a claimant to innocence. (pp. 38-9)

To Schweik malice is simply one of the facts of life, the inexhaustible evil of man a datum from which all speculation about survival must begin. He neither looks back to a Golden Age nor forward to redemption, secular or heavenly, but knows that if he is to survive it must be in a world quite like the one he has always known. A communicant of no church and a member of no party, he considers that neither intelligence nor charity is likely to ameliorate man's condition. "Anybody can make a mistake," he says at one point, "and the more he thinks about a thing, the more mistakes he's bound to make." And at another, he remarks with a straight-faced nihilism before which we can seek refuge only in laughter, "If all people wanted to do all the others a good turn, they'd be walloping each other in a brace of shakes."

Return evil for evil is Schweik's anti-Golden Rule, though often he assumes the guise of nonresistance, along with the semblance of idiocy, to do it. He is, however, neither a pharisee nor a hypocrite, only a simple conniver—in civil life, a peddler of dogs with forged pedigrees; in war, a soldier who will not fight. His resistance to war is based on no higher principles than his business; both are rooted in the conviction that a man must somehow *live* and, if possible, thrive on the very disasters which surround him. In the end, he is a kind of success, as success goes in a society intent on committing suicide; he eats well, drinks well, sleeps with the mistress of one of his masters, and pummels another mercilessly. But above all, he does not die. What more can a man ask? (pp. 39-40)

No matter how hard history nudges him, no matter what his orders read, nothing will force him into battle. He marches resolutely backward or in circles, but never forward into the sound of shooting; and by the novel's end, he has managed blessedly to be taken prisoner by his own side. Refusing to recognize the reality of disaster, he turns each apparent defeat into a victory, proving himself in the end no more a *schlemiel* than a Victim, or one of those Little Men so beloved in sentimental protest literature. Yet he seems sometimes all three, for it pleases his native slyness to assume such roles, fooling us as readers, even as he fools his superiors in the fiction they share, and as we suspect he fools the author himself. Indeed, he is fond of speaking of himself as "unlucky," but when he explains what this epithet means, it turns out he is unlucky only to others, especially those unwise enough to entrust him with important commissions.

Schweik's affiliation runs back through all the liars of literature to the father of lies himself, back through Falstaff to the sly parasites of Roman comedy and the Vices, those demidevils of medieval literature. He is, in fact, the spirit that denies, as well as the spirit that deceives: but he plays his part without melodrama, among the clowns, his little finger on the seam of his trousers, and his chin tucked in. So plumb, affable, snub-nosed, and idiotically eager to please does he seem, that we are more inclined to pat his head than to cry, "Get thee behind me!"

Yet on his lips the noblest slogans become mockeries. Let him merely cry, "God save the Emperor" and all who listen are betrayed to laughter; for he speaks in the name of the dark margin of ambivalence in us all—that five or ten per cent of distrust and ridicule that lurks in our hearts in regard even to the cause to which we are most passionately committed. And in the world in which Hašek imagines him, there is none to gainsay him, since the spokesmen for the ninety or ninety-five per cent of ordinary affirmation are corrupted or drunken or dumb.

We cannot help knowing, moreover, that not only the slogans of a distant war and a fallen empire, but those most dear to us now—the battle cries of democracy or socialism—would become in that same mouth equally hilarious; our pledges of allegiance intolerable jokes even to us who affirm them. Surely Schweik is not yet dead, but survives in concentration camps and army barracks, in prison cells and before investigating committees, assuring his interrogators

of his feeble-mindedness and his good will as their pretenses to virtue and prudence crumble before his garrulous irrelevancies. (pp. 40-1)

It seems appropriate that Jaroslav Hašek and Franz Kafka lived at the same moment in the same city; for, though their politics differed as did the very language in which they chose to write, . . . their visions of the world's absurdity were much the same. Perhaps there was no better place from which to watch the decay of Europe and the values which had nurtured it than Prague; no better place to see how *comic* that catastrophe was. . . .

"Terribly funny," we say putting down [*The Good Soldier Schweik*] and not taking the adverb seriously enough. (p. 41)

> *Leslie A. Fiedler, "The Antiwar Novel and the Good Soldier Schweik" (1962), in his* Unfinished Business *(copyright © 1971 by Leslie A. Fiedler; reprinted with permission of Stein and Day Publishers), Stein and Day, 1972, pp. 32-42.*

EMANUEL FRYNTA   (essay date 1965)

The text of artistic prose is usually composed in two layers: one is provided by the voice of the narrator, the other by the vocal expressions of the individual characters of the work. In *The Adventures of Good Soldier Schweik* . . . a no less fundamental role is provided by a third layer, namely, the stream of quotations. They even have quite an important position statistically; there is an unusually large number of them in the book and their function, of course, is even more important. . . . (p. 79)

The narrator's voice in "Schweik", in other words the author's text in a narrow sense, is conspicuously sober and simple in comparison with the perfection of the descriptions and the evocative strength of classical prose; one might call it almost primitive. . . . It is really more the voice of a reporter than of a narrator, the author's words are free of the ambition "to make things come alive", they merely introduce them or present them in the simplest manner possible. And where the connections between the demonstrated facts are formulated on more general ideological parallels, we do not feel them to be persuasive efforts aimed to convince, but just simple conclusions, arising objectively out of certain mentioned facts. And not only that—Hašek's author's text is in many instances ostentatiously not "novel style", it violates the traditional enclosedness of a novel's setting, as for instance by pointing to the postwar fates of some of the characters. . . . *Hašek never ceases for a moment emphasizing the priority of existence of the proffered facts over his literary efforts. The apparent primitiveness or negligence of the author's voice in this case is an intentional stylistic medium: its aim is to keep the author in the background, to degrade him in a sense as a writer, so that the facts represented should carry greater weight. . . .* [Hašek] makes himself out to be an unskilful writer. He puts on the mask of naive simple-mindedness, which we know so well —from the figure of Schweik. That this stylistic device was successful is proved best by the contemptuous judgements of those who proclaimed that Hašek was only marginally a writer, and "Schweik" a careless bit of prose with no claim to the honourable title of novel. Hašek was of course not interested in contending with dense critics, his self-styled polish is simply an important component in the construction of the work. . . . [The] quotations by their very number and frequency led certain readers and critics to doubt whether Hašek was really a good and conscientious writer. Did he not simplify things for himself by the fact that he incorporated all sorts of foreign texts into the work in place of sentences of his own? . . . [The] most conspicuous are the rhyming quotations, all the national, popular, soldier and religious songs, the poems, the contemporary song hits, the pop songs, the official rhyming propaganda extolling Austro-Hungarian patriotism, the simple soldiers' rhymes or the rhyming couplets for advertisements. The quotations from official documents, such as the supreme army orders, instructions for police stations, circulars, protocols, telegrams, proclamations, commercial declarations and so on, are all well differentiated. Another important group is provided by the propagandist tales about model soldiers and the immense variety of comments on postcards, posters, parcel wrappings and presents for soldiers. (pp. 80-1)

True, we should take the words of the quotations in these inserted texts with a grain of salt, aware that they are not always alien texts. Not by any means all of them are documentarily authentic loans, many a one has been invented by the author *ad usum,* which also of course goes for the letters, all of which are fictitious. What is important, however, is that Hašek is able to invent perfect fictitious quotations in the spirit of the requisite real documents and, secondly, that he employs them as quotations incorporated aesthetically into the work as a whole.

What is the reason for this overabundance of quotations in the compositional framework of the novel "Schweik"? *First, it gives the reader the feeling of a reportage-novel, creating on the materialistic plane a historically truthful setting. Second, it facilitates the mutual mirroring of the various layers of language and the social and moral strata represented by them.* (pp. 81-2)

Hašek's aim, obviously, is to play around with and confront all possible planes of language, all their functional levels and their social shadings. (p. 84)

[The] period round about the time of the First World War introduced the *collage* as a suitable aesthetic means for expressing the conflicting social reality, for demonstrating the absurdity of the war, which had raided the optimistic world of modern civilisation with all its incomprehensible barbarism. Collage, as a grotesque and drastic means of confronting facts which we accept automatically as "normal", so long as they exist independently of one another, is a principle employed in Hašek's novel that is as obvious as it is legitimate. . . .

The entire Good Soldier Schweik *in its basic structure is a complex and cunning collage, the peculiar feature about this collage however is that all these clashes of such varying sections of reality are motivated, indeed are justified, as being necessary and not incidental to the course of the story and the natures of its chief characters. Secondly, it is constantly a question of demonstrating a very specific absurdity—namely that which is the expression of the absurdities of the social order. . . .*

Conflicting material descriptions, used in the same collage-like inlay style are somewhat of the same nature as the quotations in Hašek's novel. They concern such objects as the blatant demonstration of the conflict between the official, the authoritative and the popular point of view. (p. 87)

[The] monstrous "collage situation" was primarily the war itself. For Hašek, however, it seems to have been something more than just a subject. "Schweik" is not just a war novel. The chaos of war and the alienation of the soldier in the army, fighting for a cause that was unacceptable to him, probably seemed to Hašek to be, above all, a most suitable graphic form for depicting and expressing the utter discordance of social reality itself, even the most peaceful. To him war was not a crisis phenomenon against the background of an orderly peaceful life, but merely the extreme expression of universal moral poverty. We can conclude this also from the way that everything in civilian and peacetime life, again by means of collage confrontation, is shown to be wrong, unjust, prejudiced and false too. Hašek chose places and situations with the maximum collage potentialities: the police comissariat, the lunatic asylum, the prison cell, the garrison prison chapel, the field chaplain's home life, the constant and repeated babbling of drunkards, talking in sleep and after concussion, and so on and so forth. He never missed an opportunity to confront very antithetical facts taken from the full canvas of the given world.

His humour in bringing about these damning encounters seems inexhaustible. But then the natural, seemingly self-evident, motivation behind these repeated *montages* is also that they should be effective: if they are to convince they must not bear the slightest trace of the author's purpose. It must look as though even the grossest and most striking short circuits happen of their own accord, as if by mere coincidence. (pp. 89-90)

[In *The Good Soldier Schweik* Hašek uses] a special kind of associative principle, in which the juxtaposition of two facts brings about a kind of innocent secondary implication. Masked by this assumed innocence, Schweik makes it look as though he has no idea, in his simple-mindedness, that by his statements he is producing grotesque parodies, ironical confrontations, these strange comparisons. . . .

[It] is clear that *Schweik is in fact also operating with verbal collages. Their peculiarity is that they are masked by apparent innocent motivation, but, nevertheless, they have an intentional sharp edge. . . .*

We are justified in seeking one of the roots of this [collage method] of Hašek's in the traditional practices of the Czech press, which was forced to speak to its readers across the barriers of the Austrian censorship. We should not forget Hašek's journalistic experience and the fact that, in addition, he was a witty master of the finesses of indirect expression, irony and parody, ridicule and satire. There are countless examples of this in his prewar short stories and articles. . . . He likewise found the second basic element of his novel ready to hand, namely the pub story. And this was possibly his greatest discovery and contribution altogether, herein probably lies the corner-stone of his masterpiece. The reader of "Schweik" has no need to seek for the meaning of the term pub story—from the lips of Schweik alone he knows a whole multitude of them. He knows very well what it is all about and also what a variety of forms the pub story allows for. (p. 94)

In a pub story there is no mental barrier between the storyteller and his listeners. [The] stories are an integral part of the conversation, the teller is alternately this man or that, as occasion demands. . . . Just as in other traditional folklore genres, here also each speaker has his own limited and frequently repeated repertoire. Here, too, the individual stories are well or not so well "prepared". (p. 98)

[One of the main features of the pub story is] its grotesque, comedian-like stylization. Absurd moments are brought out in the tale, which climax in an unexpected punch line.

In contrast to the traditional folk tale or anecdote, the contents of which, in their own way, are "everlasting"and only brought up-to-date, the realm of the pub story is the present. (p. 99)

The pub story was not only an entertaining form of literary expression, but above all a perfectly tailored functional form nationalistically, socially, politically, and morally. It was the coded speech of . . . popular anarchism, the language of natural resistance to everything official. . . . (p. 102)

The reader is to believe that he is reading an unpretentious narration by a witness, out of whose mouth the whole multitude of experiences just comes tumbling. Joseph Schweik's characteristic method is in essence the same method as that used by Jaroslav Hašek, the author. Inevitably, the hero of the book draws all attention to himself. He seems to have been perfectly observed from reality, he seems at the same time to be natural and familiar and yet exceptionally original. The author of the novel, the modern European writer Jaroslav Hašek, is overshadowed by him. . . . [Hašek had] rediscovered the traditional figure of the wise fool in the modern world. (p. 103)

From the very first moment Hašek had in mind a man who was "good", "law-abiding", "honest", in other words one who conformed with the surrounding world right to its logical end, right to the proof of the idiocy of that world. (p. 106)

[Schweik is a] paradoxical type—the wise fool, who apparently never and at no point was a mere individual figure in the sense of story and narrowly conceived realism. His name had more the function of being the silken epic thread onto which more and more anecdotes were woven. Too much individualization would hinder the spontaneous additional telling of stories and, apart from this, would prevent the constant topicalization of their points. In this sense Schweik is also truly traditional; even in his blatant uncompletedness he resembles his countless predecessors in popular tales. (p. 114)

Characters of this kind—at one and the same time monumentally individual and completely impersonal in their generality—naturally invite interpretation, they just seem to be asking for it. On a different level let us merely recall Don Juan, Don Quixote, or Faust: the character appears to be unfinished, evokes the impression that the author somehow did not know what to do with him, as though the two had got out of step, and that he did not quite understand him. . . .

In Hašek's novel, Schweik holds a central position to the extent that the entire work seems to be Schweik's story and portrait and it seems to have been created entirely for him. From the very first page the Good Soldier draws attention to himself, and thus the significance of the message of the novel is frequently sought purely in an interpretation of him as a character. This is incorrect. Schweik is primarily a component part of the novel, one of its elements, albeit a

primary one. He is not independent, isolated. In fact the explanation of his character is only possible in relation to the novel, within its construction and the setting of its ideas. In other words: he is not created merely for himself. He can only reveal himself as the wise fool in the respective context, only under certain conditions. . . . The existential *prius* is the deformed, petrified, false, alienated world. Schweik's reactions are the gestures of a simple living being defending itself against it. (p. 115)

[To] Hašek the wise fool as a type was not the real aim of the picture, but simply the most suitable guide to the world depicted. To him, as the author, it is a perfect mirror-like apparatus for truthful examination and condemnation of the world in crisis. *Hašek's originality as an author lies in the fact that . . . he created a colourful language which enabled him to reinstate the wise fool type of hero, giving it back its proper function in modern literature.*

Josef Schweik, like all his typical predecessors and contemporaries, is by no means an exemplary hero, and Hašek quite definitely did not mean him to be. He is none other than a poor outcast, day by day, hour by hour, defending his very life. He is a tragic hero in his powerlessness to live according to natural human needs. He is not capable of it in a world which has no place for him, in which he could quietly cease to be. He is a man of exile, on the run, homeless, if home means not only a roof over one's head and family ties, but also the possibility of life as something creative. He is not expected to produce works of art, just simply this: he should fulfil the function allotted to him. The function allotted to him by the alienated, lifeless, artificial world of authority. (pp. 115-16)

In *The Adventures of Good Soldier Schweik* . . . there are all the basic dialects of the reality that is depicted. The novel is based on the confrontation of those language forms into which the various linguistic levels at a given moment crystallized most poignantly. The artificial, lifeless, false world of authority is represented by official phrases in all kinds of characteristic groupings; at the most remote, opposite end we have instinctive life, the vital, colourful language of the pub story.

Schweik's and Hašek's "dadaism" is unforced, natural, entirely functional. The verbal collage condemns the phrases for their emptiness and lack of life, unmasking them as a weave designed to ensnare people. (p. 116)

Kafka's Prague and Hašek's Prague, at first sight, seem to be two completely different cities. With the best will in the world, Kafka never lost the doubly isolated point of view of the German-speaking Jew, Hašek looked on Prague always and at all times through the eyes of the Czech man-in-the-street. (p. 125)

Owing to this polarized distinction between them, . . . it seems impossible to think of anything that would in the very slightest resemble a kindred relationship. And yet, maybe, the very oppositeness of their sociological positions and inner characters prompts something suggestive, namely the possibility of placing the literary works of Kafka and Hašek side by side as complementary phenomena. They both experienced the curious milieu contemporaneously, but from its opposite sides. They both created works in it and obviously based on it, which were penetratingly unconventional. They both, each in his own way but mutually unlike one another, set the language of prose moving at the threshold of this century.

First of all let us take the leading characters of Kafka's and Hašek's novels.

Josef K. in *The Trial* and surveyor K. in *The Castle* appear on the scene, as we all know, isolatedly and torn from all context, without mention of any preceding life, above all, however, without any relationship to it and with no natural connection with it. Their great solitude in the world surrounding them is brought about by the incomprehensibility of the laws which govern this world. (pp. 125-26)

Hašek's Schweik seems to be the very opposite of Kafka's great "alienated and solitary ones". He is clearly a typical "native" in every way, he is intimately acquainted with the whole of life and with all the snares of the environment. . . . Above all, in whatever situation he finds himself in, he always feels completely "at home" at once. Yes, it's exactly like that. Except that it is just in this that Josef Schweik conspicuously resembles those eternally surprised and eternally alien heroes of Kafka's. Schweik is at home everywhere—just because he is *homeless*. What a tragically coerced ability! What a paradox! . . . [As] the story of the novel progresses Hašek's solitary hero finds himself in a position of extreme alienation, he is involved in the incomprehensible machinery of war, functioning in the colossal dimensions of deadly absurdity. It is true, Schweik doesn't grumble, he smiles broadly and accepts things as they are. He knows what the conditions are for his self-preservation. (p. 126)

Prague at the turn of the century was a collage-city. Phenomena torn from different, mutually antagonistic, contexts met there and clashed, stage sets were grotesquely displayed there, set in motion on the one hand by the natural demands of the advancing *modern age,* on the other by the inert or artificially preserved *myths.* We can clearly consider this fact to have been exceptionally worthy of attention both as regards the works of Franz Kafka and the works of Hašek. The myths and pseudomyths quite undoubtedly influenced these two Prague authors, myths that substituted in so many ways for objective law and order, out-of-date, incomprehensible and unacceptable myths, ones that were still effective in institutions and in customs, in decrees and in prejudices. . . .

In the collage-like construction of his novel Hašek succeeded in systematically compromising the false myths by their simple confrontation with the live multiformity of elemental reality. . . .

Similarly, in Kafka's works, albeit from the opposite pole, there is also the manifest uneasy awareness of the multidimensionality of reality. (p. 127)

The specific "Prague" theme was posed to Hašek and Kafka from two opposite and literally complementary ends, not only sociologically but also linguistically. Hašek as a Prague Czech had at his disposal the whole gamut of colloquial and popular speech, the language of the indigenous strata that felt completely at home there, the live, alertly reacting language that was anchored in the ordinary activities of everyday life. . . . Kafka's German, to be more precise the Prague German of that time, was the very opposite of a people's language. It had the marks of an isolated and defective tongue, one that was torn from the lower strata of the social structure and from the natural nourishment of the ground. (p. 128)

[The] main weight in the works of both Kafka and Hašek is laid on improvisation, in other words on a special process of direct dealing with language. Empirical experience, obedient to causality and effect, is weakened in favour of free play with the possibilities of epic elements. It is by no means accidental that both withdrew from written literature and found fresh sources of inspiration in oral literature. Hašek in the pub story, Kafka in the Chassidic tales, to take only one genre in each case. The knowledge that the literary artist's task consists of work with words and that only in them and through them can the work of art grow into an idea, is the basis of their apparently arbitrary use of language. Here lies the root of their modernity, if we can call it such, for we could equally well speak of the rediscovery of original spontaneity. (p. 129)

In recent years we find the terms such as non-literature, anti-lyric, anti-drama, anti-theatre and so on, used over and over again. . . . [If] we are to understand these contemporary antis- and nons- we must go back to the start of the cycle of which they are an expression, to their original initiators and users, to the discerning founders of the artistic and literary present. And if Franz Kafka obviously and demonstrably is one of these writers, to whom a whole series of our contemporaries rightly refers, then Jaroslav Hašek, though less well known and conspicuous, is surely also an undoubted member of that generation of initiators. His non-literariness, his anti- and non- are of a special kind. (p. 137)

[Hašek] was one of that generation which first fully fought with the problems of the modern world, he was one of the artists at the start of the century who so splendidly cast light on the question of a live, valid, meaningful art worthy of the time. He was a curious, not easily understood person, too mobile and opaque for portrayal. As a creator apparently careless, natural, spontaneous, [he was] in reality sharply discerning and refined in his specific type of non-literariness, one who was working far-sightedly in the field of language and style, with something that was to become the shape of speech of the century. (p. 145)

Emanuel Frynta, in his Hašek: The Creator of Schweik, *translated by Jean Layton and George Theiner (© 1965 by E. Frynta; reprinted by permission of the author's agent, Dilia Theatrical and Literary Agency), Artia, 1965, 145 p.*

J. P. STERN (essay date 1968)

[Hašek's *The Good Soldier Schweik* is] a novel constructed on the pattern of "one damn' thing after another." It begins with the assassination of the Archduke Franz Ferdinand and the declaration of war in the summer of 1914. . . . That war and the bureaucratic and military machinery set up to keep it going are presented as corrupt and unjust, senseless and doomed to defeat, yet quite inescapable. . . . The Great War dominates each man's life—at least, its outward circumstances and events—and the movements of war give what shape there is to the novel as a whole.

The world that fills out this mosaic is constructed on a peculiar principle of verbal and factual associations and the language represents a very rich and original retracing of the Czech vernacular. (pp. 193-94)

The political intention behind the satire is obvious enough

throughout: it is anti-Austrian and anti-Hungarian, propatriotic Czech, and antimilitarist. (p. 195)

The several groups of men who are linked by Schweik's pilgrimage are all more or less at the mercy of a war machine to whose aims they are more or less indifferent or hostile. Various cogs in this machine . . . are drawn into the satire. . . . (p. 196)

The satirical vein is patent throughout, and occasionally it degenerates into unfunny abuse. . . . The satire is derived from absurd situations, not from corrupt language, and it is not absolute satire. By this I mean that it is essential to Hašek's scheme that Schweik, the medium through whom the corruption is satirized, should remain in constant contact with the world around him. Throughout, Schweik's patter finds ready listeners high and low; and the fact that he is not immediately interrupted by his superiors and brutally disposed of—this fact is, within Hašek's scheme of things, still credible (as it would not have been in Hitler's war). Hašek of course operates with an immense poetic license. Yet the license gains its foothold in our credence because the satire is not all black, because the condemnation it implies is not absolute: Schweik belongs to the world that encompasses him, and occasionally he can even change a bit of that world for the better. (pp. 196-97)

Similarly, Hašek's social concern is undogmatic and unemphatic: "ordinary people"—mainly the private soldiers—are right; the lower-middle and upper classes—Germanizing officers, Austrians, and Jews—are usually in the wrong, and one can easily tell in whose company one is. . . . Hašek upholds a private integrity in the face of bureaucratic intrusion, and implicitly recommends a behavior which, from the point of view of the organization against which Schweik defends himself, can only be described as asocial and anarchic.

The most intriguing question the novel raises concerns the "simplicity," "honesty," "wide-eyed naivety," and "goodness of heart" of its hero, which are asserted in countless passages. . . . Occasional remarks by the author suggest . . . that the character of "congenital idiot," "malingerer of feeble mind," and "certified moron" is consciously assumed. Yet these few disclosures of what Schweik "really" is appear to be inadvertent, they remain isolated from the rest of the text, and nothing is made of the knowledge they convey to the reader. There is thus a secret at the core of Schweik's character, but that secret is shared by no one, not even by Officer Cadet Marek, the nearest thing we get to a self-portrait of the author. Considering that all the figures in the book are seen in relation to the hero and hardly at all independently, Hasek's lack of psychological disclosures and depth appears at first surprising. Each man's relation to Schweik determines his place on Hašek's implied moral scale, which stretches from "decent-patriotic" to "corrupt pro-Austrian," yet none shares the secret of Schweik's integrity. . . . [Schweik's is] a mind whose complexity is not disclosed.

In other words, Hašek does not portray a man who knows one thing and does another, like Cervantes in Sancho Panza. *Don Quixote* is one of the few books actually mentioned by the author . . . , but the connection between the two novels, taken for granted by many critics, is far from simple. To establish it, one would have to endow Schweik with a combination of Sancho's practical astuteness (which

derives from a cunning Schweik does not display), and of the Don's naïveté and candor (which leads to disasters Schweik does not encounter). Nor does Hašek probe into the recesses of Schweik's consciousness in the manner of Dostoevsky's *The Idiot*. The kind of psychological unmasking that Dostoevsky achieves—one thinks of the revealing scene between Prince Myshkin and Madame Yepanchin on the subject of humility—has no parallel in Hašek's novel. What he stresses is Schweik's candor. The comic muse operates, as always, with a license. But here it is the license not to explore, to stop short of disclosure, to leave the hero's mind, and the huge joke of which the mind is a part, unanalyzed. . . . Author and hero alike seem to share a naive, or at least an unexplored consciousness. The result is a comic inspiration unique in twentieth-century literature, and comparable only with that of Mr. P. G. Wodehouse. (pp. 197-99)

The main narrative device Hašek uses to give substance to this enigma is association. . . . Hašek's novel opens with a conversation concerning the assassination of the heir presumptive to the Hapsburg throne, which leads to the declaration of war in August 1914:

> "So they've killed our Ferdinand," said the charwoman to Mr. Schweik . . .
> "Which Ferdinand, Mrs. Müller?" asked Schweik, continuing to massage his knees, "I know two Ferdinands . . ."

What happens here and throughout the book (to put the matter briefly and obscurely) is an exploration of the possible as opposed to the relevant data of a situation. . . . Hašek through Schweik disrupts and makes positive nonsense of the actual. . . . [It] is the outside world that becomes nonsensical, and it is the unexplored integrity of the hero that grows in assurance and strength. Thus, in that fabulous discussion about His Highness the Archduke Franz Ferdinand, Schweik makes nonsense of the actual—here it is the public sphere—by exploring it in terms of his own purely personal range of experience. . . . To be precise, his patter is meaningless; to be more precise still, this patter is the most meaningful protection of his person and integrity available to him against the meaninglessness of history. Schweik is thus the very opposite of the "existential" and "alienated" hero: he renders the hostile world harmless by domesticating it and making it familiar. (pp. 201-03)

Both [*The Good Soldier Schweik* and Joseph Heller's *Catch-22*] proceed from firmly realistic bases to the heights of humorous and satirical exaggeration—their humor is never disconnected from their realism. And both do this by way of a peculiar logic which is at once a joke *and* an illumination of the logic of "ordinary" life. (pp. 203-04)

Both novels are based on the premise that war is meaningless, or, to be exact, they portray war to the extent that it is meaningless. They avoid all questions relating to the consequences of victory or defeat, that is, any political questions. . . . Schweik was drafted against his will, Yossarian volunteered for flying duties. But at the point at which we first encounter them they are both concerned with one thing and one thing only: the protection of the threatened self against the accidents of war, against violent death. . . . They regard violent death not as glorious but unnatural, as the opposite of a normal, rational order of things. It follows from this premise that the social organizations which aim at the prosecution of war and thus at the efficient inflicting of violent death have, *qua* social organizations, the *appearance* of rationality; but they are, on that same premise, the opposite of normal and rational. (p. 207)

[I think we can] narrow down the principle of self-protection at work in both novels. The Italian island of Pianosa where Mr. Heller's novel is set encompasses the whole world at war in the same way as does the Bohemian, Hungarian, and Polish countryside of Hašek's; and the domination of each life by the war is equally powerful. Yet each hero retains the charm and the enigma of an essentially private person—Schweik unconsciously and passively, Yossarian aggressively and by means of conscious strategems. (p. 212)

The private person remains inviolate.... [Yet what the two novels] intimate is something more than survival at all costs.... What they intimate is human freedom. A freedom which is hedged in on all sides, heavily qualified, but to us as readers all the more valuable because it is so heavily, so realistically qualified. The condition of this freedom is not barren detachment or alienation, but the sentience *and* essential integrity of the self in the onslaught of history. (pp. 214-15)

> *J. P. Stern, "War and the Comic Muse: 'The Good Soldier Schweik' and 'Catch-22',"* in Comparative Literature (© copyright 1968 by University of Oregon), Vol. XX, No. 3, Summer, 1968, pp. 193-216.

THE TIMES LITERARY SUPPLEMENT   (essay date 1973)

[In early reactions to *The Good Soldier Švejk*] most people failed to see any greatness in what seemed to be a crude and vulgar story of an amiable half-wit, lacking entirely the note of heroic patriotism which prevailed in the war fiction of the newborn republic [of Czechoslovakia]. . . .

Though *Švejk* in the end achieved considerable popular success, serious critics ignored the book, with the exception of some left-wing writers like Ivan Olbracht, who was the first to describe both Švejk and the author as an "idiot of genius". (Hašek's reaction was typical: "I'm just an ordinary idiot.") Another favourable response came from Kafka's friend Max Brod, who compared the author with Cervantes and Rabelais. But the book was still seen as a danger to public morals. . . .

It was the first German edition, published in 1926, that started the discussion which has been going on ever since, centring on the question, Who is Švejk? Those anxious to build up an attractive image of the Czech nation abroad were horrified by the idea that it should be represented by Švejkian nihilism. . . . Karel Čapek admitted only much later that "Hašek was a person who *saw the world*. Many others just write about it." The reasons for this negative attitude were perhaps best summed up by the great Czech critic F. X. Šalda, who wrote in 1934:

> Švejk fights for his life with all his might and Shaw would tell us that he has every right to do so.... There is no question of Švejk showing awareness or intention and consequently he is not such a poetically great and significant figure as his admirers would have

us think. He is a document of his day rather than a work of great literary merit. Without a polarity of ideas there can be no great work of literature, and Švejk is too lacking in awareness, too muddily shapeless, to make a hero, albeit a passive one.

Marxist critics, on the other hand, found in Švejk's clashes with the authorities the makings of a proletarian revolt. . . .

It was this kind of interpretation which prevailed in Czechoslovakia in the 1950s, when Švejk was turned into a fighter against imperialism and the book became obligatory reading for soldiers, the Army publishing house issuing it in huge editions. The soldiers may, however, have enjoyed the book for the wrong reasons; it is hard to believe that they really felt that its antimilitarist message applied only to conditions in the bourgeois and imperialist armies of the First World War. (p. 1083)

More recently the discussion has been raised to a more sophisticated plane. In 1963 the Czech philosopher Karel Kosík examined the relationship between Hašek and Kafka and argued that, in spite of all differences, both writers expose the grotesque absurdity of the modern world, while their heroes reveal their characters and become meaningful only when confronting the Great Mechanism. Two years later, the usual parallel between [Alfred Jarry's] Ubu and Švejk was denied by Václav Černý, who on the contrary saw in the latter a victim of Ubu-like violence, the personification of the little man, not exactly bright, but smart with experience, who has to defend himself against the master Ubu. Reverting to Šalda's criticism, Professor Černý emphasized, however, that Švejk was a hero of minute moral proportions and, though a great *literary* character, personified the struggle against Ubuism only on the smallest possible scale.

Attempts have also been made to assimilate Švejk to theories of alienation, as one who attacks the dehumanizing power of modern bureaucracy and provides the one-dimensional man "with a reliable antidote against oppression of all kinds" (in Gustav Janouch's phrase). Others saw Švejk as the archetype of the anti-hero and Hašek as the precursor of black humour. Indeed, could not a sentence like, "I had my leg dislocated for ten crowns and three glasses of beer" come straight out of Pinter?

Who is Švejk, then? The answer lies in the book, and approaching it one should bear in mind Kosík's warning that Hašek's work is in a certain sense as enigmatic and mysterious as Kafka's. It is generally accepted that Švejk's imbecility, his zealous execution of orders showing up the stupidity of those who issue them, his inept bungling of important matters, and his innocent explanations of the disasters which he has brought about are all parts of a mask. . . . A consistent, maddening and more often than not successful pretence is his method of warding off danger to survive in difficult circumstances. Surrounded by a world which he cannot influence but which claims its right to rule him, he finds liberation by escaping into a world of his own which others may find incomprehensible. The innumerable stories with which he reacts to every possible situation are parables of a kind, though his listeners may fail to understand them as such, as they move along strange lines of reasoning. He gains an immense inner freedom through this trick, but the price he has to pay is almost total loneliness. Despite all the joviality, Švejk . . . has no intimate friend. He talks incessantly to avoid real communication. Thus, while he remains inscrutable, as a character he encompasses a vast proportion of the infinite variety of human qualities and attitudes: he is both cruel and kind, clever and stupid, openhearted and irritatingly elusive. It is in this sense that the character is open—open also to very various interpretations.

At the same time, this may be a too refined approach to the puzzle of Švejk. Some of the ambiguities, which today serve as subjects of lengthy analysis in learned articles and at literary conferences, could perhaps be explained more simply by the author's clumsiness and carelessness. In fact it is a wonder that there is not more evidence of this, considering the circumstances in which the book was written: Hašek often dictated it in a pub while at the same time engaging in conversation with his permanent entourage.

Perhaps a more pragmatic approach is appropriate. . . . Treating the book with too much reverence and too little sense of humour, as has been recently often the case, can be self-defeating; the reader should be allowed to enjoy it and to arrive at his own interpretation if he feels one is necessary. (pp. 1083-84)

> *"The Art of Survival," in* The Times Literary Supplement *(© Times Newspapers Ltd. (London) 1973; reproduced from* The Times Literary Supplement *by permission), No. 3733, September 21, 1973, pp. 1083-84.*

CECIL PARROTT (essay date 1973)

[Švejk is] a 'Mr. Everyman', in the sense that he resembles any 'little man' who gets caught up in the wheels of a big bureaucratic machine.

A true appreciation of the book requires a full understanding of Švejk's character. It is a complex one. Although he was discharged from military service for patent idiocy, as he proudly tells everyone, he is far from being a fool. He is quite capable of making himself *appear* a fool to save a situation, and it was probably to this resourcefulness that he owed his discharge from the army. Švejk speaks most of the time in double-talk. He pretends to be in agreement with anyone he is dealing with, particularly if he happens to be a superior officer. But the irony underlying his remarks is always perceptible. Not only are his observations and explanations ironical, but so too are many of his actions. One example of this is his *apparent* efforts to get to the front by protesting his patriotism and devotion to the monarchy, when it is clear that his actions only impede the achievement of his proclaimed objective.

Švejk is no ignoramus. He is the brother of a schoolmaster and is clearly an educated man. Although he expresses himself in the Prague vernacular he has a rich literary vocabulary combined with an almost encyclopedic knowledge, no doubt derived from considerable reading of newspapers and journals. He is a close observer of human nature and some of his deductions are penetrating. In dealing with his superiors he masks his real views and, indeed, even when talking to people of his own class he rarely reveals his true thinking. (pp. xiv-xvi)

Moreover, unlike his creator, Švejk is no anarchist. He believes in law and order and means what he says when he

asserts that discipline must be preserved. At the same time he is full of human feeling and compassion. 'Mistakes must occur,' he says, and he is always ready to excuse or defend, when others attack or complain. . . . Some of the characteristics are common to many who are placed in the position in which Švejk finds himself. But the combination of all these traits makes Švejk unique.

One writer who recognized the greatness of Hašek's novel soon after it was written was Max Brod, the man who had diagnosed the genius of Kafka and Janáček. 'Hašek was a humorist of the highest calibre,' he wrote. 'A later age will perhaps put him on a level with Cervantes and Rabelais.' Max Brod saw that there was something of the Sancho Panza in Švejk. There is some truth in this. (p. xvi)

The parallel with Rabelais is more valid. In this book Hašek comes near to scraping the barrel in coarseness and nastiness. Here of course he is showing his true colours as the anarchist who wants to shake the bourgeoisie out of its comfortable complacency and hypocritical respectability, and he does not scruple to rake about in the dirt just for the sake of the stench. . . . This is exactly Hašek's method of treating the Catholic Church. Some of the episodes dealing with the army chaplain can hardly be said to embellish the work. Hašek was consumed with such a bitter hatred of the Church and religion that in this book and many of his other stories he shot wide of the mark and the reader soon becomes surfeited, if not nauseated. (p. xvii)

Nor should one blind oneself to Hašek's shortcomings as a writer. He is certainly a master of character-drawing and dialogue. Indeed, it is his dialogue which often provides the material for the characterization. And he displays considerable ingenuity, inventiveness and imagination too in devising the innumerable stories which Švejk and the characters tell in the course of the book. But his own comments and descriptions are less successful. He was good at recording what he had heard in life, especially over a drink at the pub—the stories, the conversations, the adventures. But he can be surprisingly lame in his descriptions and unconvincing in his narrative style. His greatest achievement is to maintain the momentum of the book and the raciness of the narrative in spite of introducing so many stories which hold back the action. He wrote carelessly and quickly. Sometimes it is apparent that he must have been drunk when he was writing, so confused do his thoughts and sentences become. But with all its imperfections *The Good Soldier Švejk* is a classic and I know of no novel which conveys so poignantly not only the ugliness of war but the utter futility of anything connected with it. (pp. xvii-xviii)

> *Cecil Parrott, in his introduction to* The Good Soldier Švejk *by Jaroslav Hašek, translated by Cecil Parrott (copyright © 1973 by Cecil Parrott; reprinted by permission of Harper & Row, Publishers, Inc.; in Canada by William Heinemann Ltd), Thomas Y. Crowell Co., Inc., 1973, pp. vii-xxii.*

P. Z. SCHUBERT (essay date 1978)

[*Velitelem města Bugul'my (The City Commander of Bugul'ma)*] is a cycle of short stories based on [Hašek's] personal experience of the events of the civil war in Bugul'ma (Soviet Union) between 15 October 1918 and December of the same year. Hašek creates an image of an epoch from small details. These trivialities, however, are of primary importance to the people, who are more concerned with what surrounds them individually than with the idea of a great epoch. Hašek is interested in the little man and he sees History through the latter's eyes, the perspective being minor events, localities and details. The writer uses the precise optics of a tragicomic humoresque. He presents a sequence of irresistible stories about the occupation of the city abandoned by the Whites, into which the Reds dare not enter for fear of a trap, and about the revolutionary activity of the commander Jerochymov and his quarrels with the city commander, which, although very comical, involve life and death. Hašek in the Bugul'ma stories breaks down History into comic details. The book also contains one story which does not belong to the Bugul'ma cycle. It is a story in which the main protagonist of the cycle is back in Prague, and thus it brings his "Russian adventure" to a definitive end.

A key to *The Good Soldier Schweik* is said to be found in these stories. The first pages of the famous novel date from about the same time as this book. It is an open question whether Schweik would have eventually become the city commander of Bugul'ma just as Hašek has, but it seems to be a natural continuation of his story.

The importance and quality of *Velitelem města Bugul'my* cannot be questioned.

> P. Z. Schubert, "Other Slavic Languages: 'Velitelem města Bugul'my'," in World Literature

Today *(copyright 1978 by the University of Oklahoma Press), Vol. 52, No. 1, Winter, 1978, p. 139.*

ADDITIONAL BIBLIOGRAPHY

Arden, Stuart. "The Good Soldier Schweik and His American Cartoon Counterparts." *Journal of Popular Culture* IX, No. 1 (Summer 1975): 26-30.
    Examines the similarities and divergences between Hašek's Schweik and American military cartoon characters.

Enright, D. J. "The Good Writer Hašek." *The Times Literary Supplement,* No. 3961 (24 February 1978): 225.
    Review of Cecil Parrott's biography of Hašek, *The Bad Bohemian.* This essay provides a brief overview of Hašek's life.

Parrott, Cecil. *The Bad Bohemian: The Life of Jaroslav Hašek, Creator of the Good Soldier Švejk.* London: The Bodley Head, 1978, 296 p.
    Detailed account of Hašek's life.

Pynsent, Robert. "The Last Days of Austria: Hašek and Kraus." In *The First World War in Fiction: A Collection of Critical Essays,* edited by Holger Klein, pp. 136-48. New York: Barnes & Noble, 1977.*
    Biographical study of Hašek's development as a satirist. Pynsent demonstrates how Švejk's personality grew in complexity as Hašek reached artistic maturity.

"The King of Bohemia." *The Times Literary Supplement,* No. 3158 (7 September 1962): 665-66.
    Concise summary of Hašek's life and literary career.

Gerhart (Johann Robert) Hauptmann

1862-1946

German dramatist, novelist, poet, short story writer, and autobiographer.

Hauptmann's naturalistic plays of the late nineteenth century established him as a major artist in modern drama. Though he produced a vast assortment of works in various genres throughout his long career, it is these early dramas on which his literary standing was founded and endures. Hauptmann is recognized primarily for initiating the naturalist movement in German theater with his first drama, *Vor Sonnenaufgang* (*Before Dawn*). Influenced by the work of Ibsen and Zola, Hauptmann became his country's most prominent exponent of dramatic techniques that sought to portray human existence with extreme faithfulness, particularly focusing on the social problems of the lower classes. He did not, however, limit himself to this single artistic approach, and his work ranges over a variety of styles from naturalism to romanticism to symbolic fantasy. In 1912 Hauptmann was awarded the Nobel Prize in literature.

Hauptmann was born in Silesia, and he later used the dialect of this region in his dramas, along with local folklore and legendry. After an unsuccessful academic career, during which he studied agriculture, sculpture, and history, he settled in Berlin. There he entered Berlin literary society and began producing his first works.

Before Dawn was an immediate success. Although recognized as a powerful vision of life, this and the later naturalistic plays have received criticism for depicting existence in an undramatic and fragmentary manner. Some critics also claim that Hauptmann's dramas convey no clear ideology; others contend that, like Shakespeare, Hauptmann reflects life in its true state of diversity and contradiction, not confining himself to a single world view.

In his most famous play, *Die Weber* (*The Weavers*), Hauptmann made use of a collective hero, a device that would be much exploited by collectivist writers. This work once again portrays the harsher aspects of human reality for which Hauptmann's naturalism is frequently noted. *Der Biberpelz* (*The Beaver Coat*) presents similar naturalistic themes in the genre of comedy, as does *Florian Geyer* in that of the historical drama. In *Hanneles Himmelfahrt* (*Hannele*) Hauptmann combines the methods of naturalism with those of symbolic fantasy. He follows a thoroughly symbolic style in the dream play *Die versunkene Glocke* (*The Sunken Bell*). In these later dramas Hauptmann focuses on characters as individuals rather than as representatives of a social body.

In 1907 Hauptmann visited Greece, afterwards recounting the experience in *Griechischer Frühling*. Hauptmann's encounter with the birthplace of Western classical mythology proved a rich source of inspiration for his later works. The influence of pagan myth is visible in such novels as *Der Narr in Christo Emanuel Quint* (*The Fool in Christ, Emanuel Quint*) and *Der Ketzer von Soana* (*The Heretic of Soana*), these works being informed by a conflict between Christian compassion

for humankind and pagan delight in physical gratification.

Between the wars Hauptmann produced what he regarded as his greatest work, *Till Eulenspiegel*, an epic poem that is a summation of the author's lifelong thought and learning set against the turmoil of Weimar Germany. During the Second World War Hauptmann did not follow the example of many German artists who left the country, and he consequently incurred much personal criticism for his wartime inactivity. The literary result of this period is *Die Atriden Tetralogie*, a reinterpretation of the myths surrounding the curse of Atreus, which was both an incrimination of Naziism and a lament for the increasingly barbaric behavior of the German people.

Though highly praised during his lifetime as an innovative force in German literature, Hauptmann is no longer widely read. Ultimately his reputation seems to have suffered because of his versatility. Some critics contend that his concern for experimentation and innovation in drama, poetry, and prose kept him from attaining mastery in any single genre. Though his diversity has frustrated critical attempts to define his most essential concerns, one quality is often cited as a unifying element in Hauptmann's works—his humanism. A sincere compassion for humankind is fundamental to his entire literary achievement.

PRINCIPAL WORKS

Promethidenlos (poetry) 1885

Vor Sonnenaufgang (drama) 1889
[*Before Dawn*, 1909]

Das Friedenfest (drama) 1890
[*The Coming of Peace*, 1900]

Einsame Menschen (drama) 1891
[*Lonely Lives*, 1898]

Der Biberpelz (drama) 1893
[*The Beaver Coat*, 1912]

Hanneles Himmelfahrt (drama) 1893
[*Hannele*, 1894]

Die Weber (drama) 1893
[*The Weavers*, 1899]

Florian Geyer (drama) 1896
[*Florian Geyer*, 1929]

Die versunkene Glocke (drama) 1896
[*The Sunken Bell*, 1899]

Führmann Henschel (drama) 1898
[*Führman Henschel*, 1909]

Michael Kramer (drama) 1900

Rose Bernd (drama) 1903
[*Rose Bernd*, 1913]

Griechischer Frühling (travel diary) 1908

Der Narr in Christo Emanuel Quint (novel) 1910
[*The Fool in Christ, Emanuel Quint*, 1911]

Atlantis (novel) 1912
[*Atlantis*, 1912]

Der Ketzer von Soana (novel) 1918
[*The Heretic of Soana*, 1923]

Till Eulenspiegel (poetry) 1928

*Iphigenie in Delphi (drama) 1941

Der grosse Traum (poetry) 1942

*Iphigenie in Aulis (drama) 1943

*Agamemnons Tod (drama) 1947

*Elektra (drama) 1947

*These four plays comprise *Die Atriden Tetralogie* published in 1949.

WILLIAM NORMAN GUTHRIE (essay date 1895)

Hauptmann ventures to create tragedies in which he relies on the inherent power of the drama alone. Verbal and stylistic beauties are abandoned. Verse-forms to charm the ear are not used. And surely thereby the illusion of the drama is increased. The language is such as under given circumstances given characters might be expected to use with no external pressure, such as that exercised by the consciousness of a critical audience. When a tragedy of Racine has been played, we feel it was written and acted for us, with us in view. Hauptmann has not allowed his characters to take our existence into consideration and consequently we believe them to be real men and women not the puppets of the god of Fiction. Hauptmann has also abandoned the thought that the chief characters must be in themselves good or noble. The drama is concerned with action not characters. Its beauty is to be primarily that of the action. Its nobility and dignity must emerge from that and from its consequences. Hence he does not feel obliged to introduce us to a cloister of saints, or to a drawing room of gentle people. Like Shakspere he goes forth into the world, but, unlike

Shakspere he furnishes the characters it gives him for heroes with no wedding garments of conventional respectability or social importance. For Hauptmann is wholly of an age in which science has made accuracy a virtue, anachronism distasteful, and every disguise and compromise of recognized truth ridiculous, not to say offensive. He relies for his success on the mutual action of character on character. He is unsparing in his contempt of the unideal, and the ideal is perhaps all the more vividly presented to our minds because he somehow forces our consciences to present it to themselves, transmuting by a vital necessity the despair of his catastrophe into ecstatic faith, tranced vision of what he has made us feel must be. (p. 281)

[From Ibsen] our dramatist differs very materially. In the Norwegian's dramas the chief characters are usually persons, not maybe *in*sane but surely *un*sane. There is in them all a certain strained extraordinariness which marks them out as exceptional people. They are morbid results of an age of transition—"between two worlds," as Matthew Arnold expressed it—the consequence of the deadly feud of science and old beliefs that have not yet reexpressed themselves in its terms, which, in the meanwhile, gives men and women over to erratic fancy, whim, and mania as practical guides through the maze of life.

The characters in the dramas of Hauptmann are commonplace, familiar beings, such as we have all met or can readily meet if we choose to do so. We need no introduction. We know them by recognition or intuition. Their fate, therefore, concerns us if possible more nearly than that of Ibsen's characters. (pp. 283-84)

"Vor Sonnen Aufgang" gives us a fearful picture of unearned wealth degrading men below the level of brutes. (p. 284)

A terrible subject, awfully handled. Already in this first play Hauptmann succeeds in giving us the background so cleverly by quite natural chance hints that we can hardly tell how we got to know all we do about the previous history of the family. There is no narrative, no relation irrelevant from the point of view of the characters on the stage, no mechanical devices for giving us a clue.

We can readily understand that this piece should have been made a battleground between old school and new school. It was for the new movement what Hernani was for the literary France of the first half of our century. His next drama is "Das Friedensfest." Here the thesis is that disparity of education and instruction, and the consequent diversity of interests, manners, and moral standard, make congenial felicity and home life impossible. (p. 285)

Never was a more ghastly picture drawn of a wrecked home. A mere unwillingness to give each other the benefit of the doubt, the unhesitating ascription of malignant motives to each other, have undermined a family, and ruined morally every member of it but one, who is saved, as it were, by fire through the instrumentally of an unselfish devotion to a noble art, and contact with two noble self-oblivious women, both of whom he loves, one as mother the other as betrothed.

"Einsame Menschen"—"Lonely Souls"—is a marvellous study of how we cannot lift ourselves, ethically, above our age; how we may think, but cannot with impunity attempt to feel and act, apart from it. What was meant as pure and disinterested is besmirched by suspicions natural to those on a lower ethical plane, and actually becomes, through the instrumentality of those suspicious, what it seemed to them to be. (p. 286)

["Die Weber" is not] a Socialistic drama, still less one whose authorship could be in cold blood—or rather let us say in cold printer's ink—ascribed to a certain cisatlantic anarchist! It simply presents a strike, makes it live before us, shows us the misery that occasions it, and the misery it occasions; leaves us profoundly convinced of the solidarity of society, and the need that our conscience should correspond to our consciousness of that fact.... What impresses one chiefly however is that in this piece we are not dealing with the individuals so vividly presented, as much as with masses of individuals. The interest inheres in the cause, not in particular cases.... The movement then is the hero; it has many and various representatives, and when we have heard and seen the play, the actual human world has been before us in process of evolution, an evolution in which individuals are sacrificed to the clearer manifestation of the type. (p. 287)

["Hannele"] is one of those masterpieces that defy criticism. It is too winning and affecting to permit of unbiased scrutiny. From beginning to end, excepting a few songs, it is one quick, nervous dialogue. It is quite as realistic as any other piece of Hauptmann in treatment. He has made us acquainted in it with a bit of the world in which we actually live. Nor has he chosen some favored spot in it, where the envied few delight to dwell. It is a patch of common soil, not beautiful in itself, but the sort of thing we have all about us. The illumination is such as to impart to everything preternatural glory. He takes one human lot, but we know that behind it are the terrible millions. To make us feel more keenly, the lot is that of a child, the motherless little stepdaughter of a brutalized drunkard. Nothing could be simpler or more original. A painstaking study in child-psychology was not unheard of before "Hannele," but was there ever such a study? Furthermore it is the psychology of its dream state, less fettered, more subtly self-revealing, which is boldly set forth as real to us, quite as though we had been entranced and made to feel the child's fever pulse throbbing in our own arteries. (p. 288)

Shall we venture to assert that Gerhardt Hauptmann's work answers to the great modern demand for a new drama that may be to us what Shakspere's was to Elizabethan England? ... Whatever may be said against "Before Sunrise" and "The Weavers," and there is much that can be said with much plausibility, the charge of "brutal realism" cannot be maintained against "Hannele." If anything could convince us that the drama of actual life, using its language abandoning all traditional elegance, rhetorical exaggeration, in a word all stage-strut and stage rant, can attain to higher glories than the classicist supposed possible, it would be this piece, the effect of which is that of the work of an idealist infinitely strengthened by the realistic method.... We want to be shown the loftily tragic in the actual. Thus will our daily burden-bearing seem less ignoble, and our drudgery may acquire a majesty of its own. We want to be told, as only the poet can tell us, that it is the human soul, not the circumstances of life that make our dignity; not intellectual achievements and polish, only possibly to the few, but moral worth that distinguishes the hero from the common man.... (pp. 288-89)

William Norman Guthrie, "Gerhardt Hauptmann," in The Sewanee Review *(© 1895 by The University of the South), Vol. III, No. 3, Spring, 1895, pp. 278-89.*

OTTO HELLER (essay date 1905)

It is evident to us at this distance that the extreme naturalism of Hauptmann's first play in 1889 represents merely a played-out episode in the consistent movement of the modern drama towards greater truthfulness. (p. 120)

In truth, the temperamental or subjective coloring can never be absent from a work of art. So far as it goes, it will set apart the work of one writer from the work of all others. For this reason we find that with his peculiarly lyric temperament it is no easy task for Hauptmann, even in the beginning of his career as a dramatist, to conform strictly to the tenets of the new art code, and that occasionally he breaks away altogether from allegiance to the school [of naturalism]. (pp. 122-23)

Hauptmann apparently has not yet evolved [a theory of life]. Whenever he departs from the visible model and follows either an imaginative or a speculative bent, it at once becomes apparent that his poetry is not moored to a definite, consistent philosophy. Hauptmann as a thinker, say in *Einsame Menschen* or *Die versunkene Glocke,* is handicapped by the same intense impressibility that enables him in *Die Weber* or *Der Biberpelz* to show among all his contemporaries the greatest skill in the art of accurate and minute *milieu* painting. The specific nature of his prodigious lyric gifts, notably the lilting melody of his verse, which so often asserts itself triumphantly over the doctrinal veto, springs from a decadent predisposition. The much-abused word decadent is to be taken not at all in a sinister meaning, but to denote a state of overrefinement manifesting itself in a subtle yet sterile receptivity, brooding pensiveness, and—perhaps the chief criterion—in a certain debility of the volitional energy, which leaves this poet in a condition of tormenting doubt on major questions of life, and which even in his pursuit of an art ideal makes him seem vacillating and visionary. Hauptmann, too, is apparently as incapable of the higher self-discipline as are his heroes. With his peculiar mental and temperamental equipment he might well have become the foremost lyrist of his generation. When he leaves free rein to his poetic fancy (as here and there already in *Hannele* and throughout *Die versunkene Glocke*) he gives being to poems of exquisite beauty.... (pp. 123-24)

More than that, there is a fine lyric quality in all of Hauptmann's plays, a *Stimmungszauber* unmatched by any other modern dramatist; even the most crassly naturalistic among them, *Vor Sonnenaufgang,* contains one such scene of great beauty. In this power of drawing the spectator at will into the mood of the play lies Hauptmann's real strength. It is not, however, for his lyric genius but as a dramatist pure and simple that Hauptmann is worshiped by his contemporaries.... [Through] a natural fallacy of public opinion he has been proclaimed Germany's greatest living dramatist. Yet it may be, severely questioned whether he should be considered for that place of honor. (pp. 124-25)

Judged by a just dramaturgic standard, Hauptmann is deficient in three essentials. In the first place, he is weak as regards his dynamics. The characters are stationary, incapable of any real development. In a certain way they are very true to life, thanks to their author's prodigious power of observation and his absorbing attention to detail. . . . Hauptmann renders such accurate account that when his men and women make their first appearance their verisimilitude elicits our highest admiration. After a while, however, the interest in them flags, owing to their persevering sameness. Neither literally nor figuratively do they ever change their clothes. They evolve no new ideas from within, they admit none from the outside, and they never relent in their stubborn adherence to what ideas they happen to possess. The original stock, moreover, with which the author has set them up is so limited as to constitute another weakness of Hauptmann's plays. For truth to tell, the characters are wanting in ideas chiefly because the author has not much of this commodity to spare. Now fixed ideas are a dangerous equipment in proportion as they are few in number, and one is tempted to think that the characters in Hauptmann's plays meet their defeat through their own unyielding devotion to the single fixed idea that forms the dramatic viaticum of each. To come to the third defect: Upon the glorious authority of the ancients and of Shakespeare, we feel justified in demanding of a dramatist that in manipulating a theme of his own deliberate choice he shall turn his subject-matter to full account and make the most of the dramatic data it presents. Of this reasonable demand Hauptmann falls short. He does not convert all his metal into coin. His art is imposing but fragmentary. His pieces are counterfeits of life, but for the greater part they are not dramas; each constitutes a series of living pictures succeeding each other without an inevitable causal connection, coming somehow to a stop but often lacking finality. (pp. 126-27)

As a matter of fact, the plots of Hauptmann are structurally weak and do not even present a firm and definite outline. This may be a virtue in the eyes of some naturalists, yet the suspicion is strong that it is a virtue made of necessity.

Hauptmann is not primarily cut out for a dramatist. But there is a species of drama which is not at all conterminous with life, and in which a first-rate poet may excel even without any superior dramatic power. Over the domain of the fairy-tale play Hauptmann might wield an absolute sovereignty, were it not for that deep-seated lack of a consistent theory of life which debars him from interpreting the nature and destiny of man through symbolism of the grander stamp.

Hauptmann has up to this time given us fifteen specimens of his dramatic art. Obviously they belong to two essentially different, nay contradictory and hostile, spheres. Between these, however, they are not cleanly divided; for in several of the plays the attempt is made at least to bridge the chasm that separates the worlds of fact and figment. The first six plays, closing with *Kollege Crampton*, are patterned throughout after the extreme naturalistic precept. In *Hannele* the poet swerves aside from this path of unalloyed naturalism or "verism," to return to it again transiently in *Der Biberpelz* ("The Beaver Coat"). In *Die versunkene Glocke* ("The Sunken Bell") he once more turns into another road and finds the way, so it would seem, to the true sanctum of his genius. But the half dozen plays that have followed "The Sunken Bell" are so evenly divided between the realistic and the idealistic spheres that it would be obviously unfair to regard Hauptmann either any longer as an obdurate disciple of naturalism or as an apostate from its principles. (pp. 128-29)

Perhaps now, in the retrospection, we can better understand the apparently saltatory progress of Hauptmann. That he had outgrown the obstructive ordinances of naturalism there can be no question. Yet he did not turn utter renegade, because he recognized the permanent gain accruing to the drama from the late reform; rather he sought to find a means by which, without sacrificing this gain, he might attain a less one-sided manifestation of his powers. In *Hannele* . . . the theme was chosen with singular felicity so as to permit the unmixed coexistence of the seamy and the dreamy worlds. In "The Sunken Bell" naturalism was pushed to the wall by the long-repressed *furor poeticus.* But Hauptmann is naturally unwilling to relinquish a method which furnishes the sole opportunity for one of the most potent elements in his genius, namely, his unexcelled power of observation and reproduction. . . . [*Fuhrmann Henschel*] retains all the external verisimilitude of "The Weavers," yet the interest is never, as there, focused on the environment, but on the *Auswicklung,* the unfolding of the central character. (pp. 195-96)

[The] tramp-comedy *Schluck und Jau* . . . does not lay claim to any special weight or relative value among the works of Hauptmann. (p. 199)

[Yet in] *Schluck und Jau* Hauptmann approaches real comedy more than in any other work. The play is indeed documentary evidence of a "happy, careless mood." Such moods, with Hauptmann, are excessively rare. But genuine humor we miss even in *Schluck und Jau.* For genuine humor is the medium of an optimistic view of life, a medium by which all things are gilded or sublimated. To this poet whom the gods have otherwise endowed so richly, that one divine gift seems to have been denied, because he is at bottom a pessimist through whose mind the world is refracted as a confused and wrangling mass. All his works—the comedies not excepted—betray this pessimistic world-view which in the last analysis appears to be concomitant with the lack of a higher intellectual potency.

If it is a fact that *Michael Kramer* . . . was written to give the lie to critics like Richard M. Meyer, who had said of Hauptmann that he lacked "the higher intellect, the mastery in the realm of ideas, the power to deal with the abstract, the quick flash that lights up the mystery of things," he has only furnished his critics with an additional proof of their allegation.

In *Michael Kramer* . . . the poet undertook a bold and thoroughly original task. In this play what is customarily regarded as the "action" is not worked out through the agency, nor even with the coöperation, of the real hero,—Michael Kramer is in no way the author of his son's tragic fate. . . . In fact the "action" is of a very indirect and subordinate importance; it serves merely as a psycho-dynamic means for drawing to the surface the inmost soul-life of the principal character, for carding out, as it were, his very heart and entrails. So far this is the most ambitious and possibly the most successful psychological study undertaken by Hauptmann. (pp. 202-03)

[Michael Kramer] belongs to a type that has necessarily the greatest fascination for a man like Hauptmann, who is in love with his art,—desperately in love, as we sometimes say, or better, as we should always say, sacredly in love with it. He typifies the incompleted, fractional, or merely potential artist—*der unganze Künstler,* I should say in

German. But this man's failure has lost its sting. A life long he has striven without winning the prize, yet his loyalty has been rewarded. That divine spark which alone can engender the truly great in art is missing from his breast; but for the lack he is compensated by the stirrings of a serious and sober idealism. He is an unswerving advocate of the Joy of Working, and that makes him a great teacher. (p. 205)

Architecturally *Michael Kramer* relapses from the greater structural consistency of *Fuhrmann Henschel*. The action is pushed forward jerkily over the insipid first act to the most telling part of the play; then after the appalling interview between father and son in which the second act ends, it sinks to the level of hopeless banality in the third act. With [the son] Arnold out of the way, a higher plane is reached in the fourth act, which is cast in a sort of disguised soliloquy. . . . The thoughts uttered by Michael have a powerful, human charm, without, however, being either very new or remarkably profound. Wealth of ideas is certainly not a strong point of Hauptmann's art. (p. 209)

[Hauptmann has not yet produced] the work of transcendent dramatic merit which his countless admirers have been expecting from him year after year, to be disappointed again and again. The excellences of Hauptmann's later plays do not wholly compensate for certain inherent defects which make it look as though he were debarred by his make-up from the achievement of unqualifiedly great works. He is not destined, apparently, to be the Messiah of the German stage. (p. 226)

> *Otto Heller, "Gerhart Hauptmann," in his* Studies in Modern German Literature *(copyright 1905 by Otto Heller), Ginn & Company, 1905, pp. 119-228.*

ASHLEY DUKES (essay date 1912)

Gerhart Hauptmann is a poet and an artist. . . . His claim to be considered a great dramatist is more doubtful. . . . [We see] in Hauptmann the extreme of untheatricality, the erratic method of a sensitive genius who is not consciously striving after a new vehicle of expression, but who hurls refinement of observation, minute impressions of detail, poetry and beauty of tone, piecemeal upon the stage.

It has often been said that Hauptmann has created new forms, and that he is the only living dramatist who has passed beyond Ibsen. There is some truth in this. His plays are written in new forms. "The Weavers," with its extraordinary number of characters, its loosely-grouped five acts and its subordination of everything—personality, construction, often drama—to the central idea of a workmen's strike, is certainly a play that Ibsen would not have written. "Rose Bernd," a later play in which all the events of the drama occur between the acts, and the acts themselves are no more than discussions of what has happened, is another innovation. But a new dramatic form can only have lasting value when it is created by a great craftsman. . . . The dramatist who attempts a revolution must first count the cost, and endeavour to make his new form effectual. Hauptmann's dramatic method shows no such consideration. It is altogether tentative and incoherent. To say that many of his plays stamp him as a novelist who has wandered into the theatre by mistake is not to belittle his power as an imaginative writer. That would be impossible. The

only question is one of judgment; and a real combination of genius and judgment is rare enough. . . . Hauptmann is one of the most gifted of living writers, but the style in his case is not adapted first and foremost to the service of drama. No one can witness the performance of a series of his plays without feeling that many of their subtleties are being strangled at birth; and a reading of them confirms the impression. Hauptmann's men and women are real. His method is sincere, but it often fails of its effect. (pp. 78-81)

Hauptmann is distinguished most clearly by his sensitiveness. Every great imaginative writer is sensitive to impression. The quality is not only twin-born with intelligence; it is a part of the author's stock-in-trade. But Hauptmann is almost hyper-sensitive. His creative work is a history of "influences," good and bad. Only in the rarest flashes does he escape from them. (p. 83)

Nothing illustrates Hauptmann's insecure hold upon the Theatre more clearly than his incessant wavering between one dramatic method and another. (p. 85)

[Hauptmann] was the prodigy of the hour, and he suffered from the grossest overestimation. Pan-Germanic critics, determined at any cost to prove the superiority of the native German drama to all others, praised him extravagantly, and endeavoured to thrust him into a position among the classics. (p. 89)

Hauptmann's reputation, however, was always artificially maintained. His first striking success had been in the theatre, with "Vor Sonnenaufgang." . . . "The Sunken Bell" brought him fame. But with the plays from "Fuhrmann Henschel" onwards he drifted steadily out of touch with the real theatre-going public, and became the apostle of a literary cult. His followers applauded the growing obscurity of his work. They succeeded in making apparent successes out of actual failures such as "Rose Bernd." And the final result of this continual harrying into the theatre of an undramatic artist is seen in "Griselda." . . . This play hardly rises to the commonplace. As a "modern" treatment of Boccaccio's Griselda legend it is flat and uninspired; as the work of a poet of Hauptmann's standing, not yet past middle life, it is a tragic disappointment. There is clearly something fatally wrong with a playwright who, at forty-seven years of age, can produce a drama bearing all the signs of senile decay.

But "Griselda" does not represent the real Hauptmann, any more than "Misalliance" represents the real Bernard Shaw. It is well to turn to the Silesian peasant dramas, for in them lies the Hauptmann atmosphere which is his most real service to the theatre. All the Silesian plays are written in dialect. . . . (pp. 90-1)

Whatever may be said of them as drama, the Hauptmann dialect plays have contributed much to the literature of Germany. They are individual and national, and in the theatre their great service has been to show the way back from the mere cosmopolitanism of the "society drama" to the tragic problems near at hand, among the common people. (pp. 91-2)

> *Ashley Dukes, "Gerhart Hauptmann," in his* Modern Dramatists, *Charles H. Sergel and Company, 1912, pp. 78-95.*

THE NATION (essay date 1913)

Gerhart Hauptmann's ["Atlantis: A Novel"], like almost all

of his other productions, is concerned with a hero who can suffer, but not do, act, construct. From ["Sonnenaufgang" to "Emanuel Quint," "Die Ratten," and "Gabriel Schillings Flucht"] . . . , Hauptmann's leading characters do not "lead." In his dramas this fault is even more serious. The lack of defensive or constructive will, and the pessimistic philosophy that goes with such a lack, are well expressed in Hauptmann's play "Das Friedensfest" . . . , one of whose characters says: "The will is a straw! . . . One may will and will a hundred times, and everything remains as it was!" . . .

Throughout ["Atlantis"] the reader gets the effect of tremendous forces in combat, but upon careful examination sees that this impression comes from the masterly literary treatment of gigantic physical forces in action rather than from any spiritual struggle. . . .

The underlying theme of "Atlantis" is neither great nor unusual. The book's strength lies in its external form, its wonderful descriptions, its equally marvellous characterization, its vivid imagery, its record of accurate observation of men and things, its striking figures, in short, in its brilliant style. It is quite remarkable how even as skilful an artist as Hauptmann could paint the picture of storm and shipwreck (both moral and physical) and the hair-breadth rescue (also both moral and physical) without having gone through some such dreadful experience himself. He sees everything, he hears everything—even the sense of smell is alert and its experience recorded.

> *"Current Fiction: 'Atlantis: A Novel',"* in The Nation *(copyright 1913 The Nation magazine, The Nation Associates, Inc.), Vol. 96, No. 2479, January 2, 1913, p. 11.*

KARL HOLL (essay date 1913)

"Vor Sonnenaufgang" was produced . . . amidst unprecedented stormy scenes both of approval and dissent, and at once put its young author in to the foremost rank of German playwrights. . . . The chief interest is in social-ethical problems. By the discovery of coal on their property a peasant family has come to immense wealth, and thereby to unaccustomed luxury. Instead of giving up their life to daily work as previous generations had done, they spend it in idleness, and in consequence are driven to all sorts of base vices. Immorality rules the house. . . . It was due to this portrait of the lowest immorality that Hauptmann was hailed as the hero of Naturalism. It remained unnoticed that he already had departed from naturalistic dogma by depicting the growing love between the young girl Helen and the idealist Loth, in the course of which Hauptmann gives us, in the fourth act, the most charming love-scene which has been written in modern German drama. His own soft nature in its overflowing wealth of feeling breaks through. The portrait of Helen is one of his finest creations, and ranks with the best to be found in German literature. Her partner, Loth, on the other side, is an absolute failure. He is a blubbering theorist, invented to put forth the sociological problems the author has at heart, which are clearly indicated by the milieu. (pp. 24-6)

Hauptmann has also treated social problems in purely comic technique, and in this way gave us what may well be called the best modern comedy in German literature—"Der

Biberpelz" (The Beaver Coat). The contrast of bare reality with the presumptuous honesty of the heroine of the play, the washerwoman, Mrs. Wolff, produces the most comic effect. Hauptmann realizes that the field of the comic is the intellect, and he contrives to raise the aspect of all actions to this level, in order to prevent any ethical and moral ill-feeling from damaging its humour. He therefore chooses an old literary device—a scene in court—to form the setting of a comedy. The contrast of the blind and pretentious judge with the clever washerwoman who is the moving spirit in everything and pretends to know nothing, is perfect comedy. (pp. 36-7)

All [of Hauptmann's] prose dramas show a characteristic which is one of their most distinguishing features in comparison with the works of preceding playwrights: the dialogue. Perhaps Ibsen's influence is nowhere more keenly felt than here. (p. 50)

Ibsen's influence on Hauptmann's diction is, indeed, so strongly effective that it might almost be said to reach into our author's verse dramas. For there is another side of Hauptmann's dramatic genius which is unfolded in what he calls his "Fairy Dramas." There the lyrical strain of his artistic nature appears at its best. (p. 51)

On the whole, Hauptmann seems to be denied the gift of purely lyrical expression. His poems, as far as we know them, fail to carry us away by an impression of spontaneity and impetuosity. They are too full of intellectual reflection. It is strange that he should lack the power of writing lyrics. For his Greek diary is supreme evidence of the naïve and impressionable nature of his mind. As to the form, his Fairy Dramas reveal his mastery of poetic diction. In fact, his drama "Der Arme Heinrich" contains passages of the best verse in modern German literature. And he certainly has the gift of creating a uniform and harmonious atmosphere which, after all, is perhaps the highest perfection of a lyrical poem. He is so strongly gifted in this direction that it sometimes even endangers the realistic development of his dramatic plot. One might almost be tempted to divide his plays into two sections—lyrical and non-lyrical. To the former we would reckon his Fairy Dramas, but also plays like "Die Jungfern vom Bischofsberg," or even "Das Friedensfest" and "Gabriel Schilling's Flucht," in virtue of their unique atmosphere. Scenes like the love-scene in "Vor Sonnenaufgang" are pearls of lyrical feeling. And yet Hauptmann will never rank with such true lyrical poets as Stephan George, or Rainer Maria Rilke. (pp. 51-3)

His feelings, especially in the years of inward conflict, strove for dramatic lyrical expression. The first play of this series is "Hannele's Himmelfahrt" (Hannele). . . . It is permeated by the sincerity of his social compassion. The simple story is of a motherless and cruelly treated child, who is driven to death, and in her last hours sees in visions the heavens open and the angels with the Saviour Himself descending to take her up to happier regions. The intermingling of the crude reality and the golden vision is so artistic that we feel transported to the heavenly spheres. . . . (p. 55)

Naturalism is the daughter of materialism and, together with Ibsen's influence, is the most important element in shaping Hauptmann's style. It seems to me idle to discuss whether his talent lies more in the realistic or in the romantic drama, more in prose dramas or those which are in verse. His mastery of diction, be it prose or verse, is perfect, and in this he is indebted to Naturalism and to Ibsen. Its concise pregnancy is unthinkable without them. His early dramas are the best proof of this. In their realistic style monologues and asides are tabooed. But just as we saw the naturalistic drama drift toward the stringent rules of French classical tragedy, so this realistic style drifts towards symbolism. Complete sequences of thought cannot be expressed by words. (pp. 78-9)

Gerhart Hauptmann is a truly artistic genius. His technical execution may sometimes be lacking, yet the inner vision is always perfect and definite, and it is irresistibly felt throughout his works. (p. 93)

> *Karl Holl, in his* Gerhart Hauptmann: His Life and His Work, 1862-1912, *Gay and Hancock, Limited, 1913 (and reprinted by Books for Libraries Press, 1972; distributed by Arno Press, Inc.), 112 p.*

LUDWIG LEWISOHN (essay date 1915)

[The reality which experience furnishes—] so sensitively observed and so greatly rendered—has always inspired Hauptmann with a boundless compassion. To him the world's life has been the world's woe; his very austerity and apparent harshness pay tribute to the sacredness of human sorrow. Such a temperament adopted the technique of the naturalistic drama not only as an artistic but as an ethical act. It sought the tragic beauty that is in truth and almost instinctively rejected all the traditional devices of dramaturgic technique. From such a point of view artifice is not only futile, it is wrong. There could be, in the drama of Hauptmann, no complication of plot, no culmination of the resultant struggle in merely effective scenes, no superior articulateness on the part of the characters. There could be no artistic beginning, for life comes shadowy from life; there could be no artistic ending, for the play of life ends only in eternity.

This view of the drama's relation to life leads, naturally, to the exclusion of many devices. Thus Hauptmann, unlike the playwrights of France, but like Ibsen and Galsworthy, avoids the division of acts into scenes. The coming and going of characters has the unobtrusiveness but seldom violated in life; the inevitable artifice of entrance and exit is held within rigid bounds. In some of his earlier dramas he also observed the unities of time and place, and throughout his work practises close economy in these respects. It goes without saying that he rejects the monologue, the unnatural reading of letters, the *raisoneur* or commenting and providential character, the lightly motivised confession—all the devices in brief, by which even Hervieu and Lemaître, Wilde and Pinero, blandly transport information across the footlights, or unravel the artificial knot which they have tied. (pp. 111-12)

[Beside the speech of Hauptmann's] characters all other dramatic speech seems conscious and merely literary. Nor is that marvellous veracity in the handling of his medium a mere control of dialect. Johannes Vockerat and Michael Kramer, Dr. Scholz and Professor Crampton, speak with a human raciness and native truth not surpassed by the weavers or peasants of Silesia. Hauptmann has heard the inflections of the human voice, the faltering and fugitive eloquence of the living word, not only with his ears but with his soul. (pp. 112-13)

In the structure of his drama Hauptmann . . . met and solved an even more difficult problem than in the character of his dialogue. He rejects the whole tradition of structural technique. And he is able to do so by reason of his intimate contact with the normal truth of things. In life, for instance, the conflict of will with will, the passionate crises of human existence, are but rarely concentrated into a brief space of time or culminate in a highly salient situation. Long and wearing attrition, and crises that are seen to have been such only in the retrospect of calmer years, are the rule. Hence instead of effective rearrangement Hauptmann contents himself with the austere simplicity of that succession of action which observation really affords. The intrusion of a new force into a given setting, as in *Lonely Lives,* is as violent an interference with the sober course of things as he admits. From his noblest successes, [*The Weavers, Drayman Henschel, Michael Kramer, Rose Bernd*] . . . , the artifice of complication is wholly absent.

It follows that his fables are simple and devoid of plot, that comedy and tragedy must inhere in character, and that conflict must grow from the clash of character with environment or of character with character in its totality. In other words: Since the unwonted and adventurous are rigidly excluded, dramatic complication can but rarely, with Hauptmann, proceed from action. For the life of man is woven of "little, nameless, unremembered acts" which possess no significance except as they illustrate character and thus, link by link, forge that fate which is identical with character. The constant and bitter conflict in the world does not arise from pointed and opposed notions of honour and duty held at some rare climacteric moment, but from the far more tragic grinding of a hostile environment upon man or of the imprisonment of alien souls in the cage of some social bondage.

These two motives, appearing sometimes singly, sometimes blended, are fundamental to Hauptmann's work. (pp. 114-15)

Such is the naturalistic drama of Hauptmann. By employing the real speech of man, by emphasising being rather than action, by creating the very atmosphere and gesture of life, it succeeds in presenting characters whose vital truth achieves the intellectual beauty and moral energy of great art. (p. 127)

> *Ludwig Lewisohn, "The Naturalistic Drama in Germany," in his* The Modern Drama *(copyright 1915 by B. W. Huebsch; copyright renewed 1942 by Ludwig Lewisohn; reprinted by permission of Viking Penguin Inc.), B. W. Huebsch, 1915, pp. 110-28.*

PAUL H. GRUMMANN (essay date 1916)

[The protagonist of 'Emanuel Quint, Fool in Christ,'] is a man who resembles Jesus in many particulars, and the book suggests what would happen if a man attempted to apply the principles of Jesus to modern society. . . . Hauptmann divested his figure of its divine setting. Quint is the illegitimate son of a woman who after his birth has married a carpenter. The tragedy of his advent, the agonies of the disgraced mother have left their marks upon the son, for he is distinctly abnormal. Deficient in vitality, and robbed of the normal child's environment, Emanuel soon becomes a victim of his dreams. He is inefficient in his foster-father's workshop, and is unable to meet the requirements of the world generally. His Silesian environment supplies the pietistic atmosphere which naturally suggests a life of idle contemplation to the boy, and his abnormal imagination seizes the main precepts of the teachings of Jesus in a thoroughly uncritical fashion.

Unable to analyze his own subconscious mental activity, he looks upon every discovery which he makes through his inner consciousness as a revelation or an inspiration. In this manner he comes to accept the main doctrines of primitive Christianity with the stubborn conviction of the fanatic. (pp. 431-32)

At first the book strikes the reader as distinctly strange. One almost feels that the author was too conscious of the fact that he was writing his first novel; that in an attempt to get away from the terse structure of the drama, he has given his novel too much epic breadth. But very soon the book has the same effect that the dramas of the author produce. The reader begins to ponder and the remoter intention begins to unravel. He begins to see that very many things have been accomplished by the author for which he will look in vain in other books on kindred subjects. It becomes clear that Quint has been revealed with all his idiosyncracies by a psychological expert who has the sympathy of a solicitous friend. No vagary of Quint is too foolish to engage the serious interest of the novelist, and nowhere does he scoff at this fool in Christ. Yet his sympathy is rationalized, for Quint is nowhere exalted into a hero nor is he made the representative of a really valid cause. By maintaining the judicial attitude the author has succeeded in characterizing the eccentricities of Quint and revealing the tragedy of this individual who has shut himself up in his meagre personality, while the great world lay beyond him with its complex human interests, its joys and sorrows, its possibilities of enjoyment and service, from which he was forever separated because he became the victim of the ideals of primitive Christianity,—ideals which Christianity herself has outgrown and to which she will never return. (p. 435)

> *Paul H. Grummann, "Hauptmann's 'Emanuel Quint'," in* Poet Lore *(copyright, 1916, by Poet Lore, Inc.), Vol. 27, No. 4, July-August, 1916, pp. 430-38.*

T. M. CAMPBELL (essay date 1924)

Several years before the outbreak of the great war Hauptmann made a trip to Greece, the immediate record of which he published in the form of notes or sketches, under the title of *Griechischer Frühling.* (p. 353)

When Tolstoy ran across the New Testament comparatively late in life, he discovered that he was a Christian. When Hauptmann went to Greece, comparatively late in life, he discovered that he was a pagan. . . . Hauptmann in his Grecian journey is a man pilgrimaging to the long-sought altars of his soul. (p. 354)

[In reading *Griechischer Frühling,* we observe that its author is] true to his rôle as realist. Literally with notebook in hand he records his impressions, and less than most men, does he juggle with them. His passivity is at times amazing. He sucks in the sounds and colors of the Ionian sea with a delicious contemplation. . . . There is nothing mechanical in the way these impressions are recorded. His personality is tirelessly and subtly engaged.

This personality has two poles which it is ever seeking to contract into one point, exerting a kind of centripetal force on all the poet's work. To name them briefly, they are Christianity and paganism. The unity that Hauptmann over and over endeavors to throw around these two hostile, yet seemingly irreducible, elements of his soul is mysticism. Essentially Christian in Hauptmann is his sympathy with all sorrow, his compassion for the poor and needy, his pity for every suffering heart. Essentially pagan in him is his extreme sensitiveness to all beauty, and particularly to the beauty of women. He will never escape this peculiarly modern dualism. For Hauptmann in his own personality is struggling with the great problem now facing humanity. Humanity, like Hauptmann, is profoundly pagan and profoundly Christian, seeking the magic word that will bring peace between these warring elements without destroying either.

In *Greek Spring* the pagan element is naturally in the ascendancy. For here the poet discovers that he is a pagan. We see a Silesian mystic, a thorough student of pietism, a man in whose soul industrial misery had found a voice never heard before, painstakingly and eagerly reconstructing in his imagination the pagan world, with its sacred rites, its worship of beauty, its pantheism. (pp. 354-55)

[In] spite of the partiality and intensity with which he plunges into this different life, [Hauptmann] cannot deny the fundamental appeal of his Christian civilization. That is the significance of his praise of Demeter, the goddess whose maternal sorrow and resignation, as he says, have brought her closer to humanity than any of the Olympians. Thus involuntarily he seeks Christian elements in an ancient myth. (p. 356)

For the two tireless and energetic nuclei are busily organizing the impressions about themselves as centers: the necessity of compassion and the sense of beauty, the moral compulsion and the esthetic compulsion: comprehension of suffering, from which escape into Christian mythology is so easy as to be almost unavoidable, and sensual affirmation, which finds its classical form in Greek mythology. Neither of these powerful centers will yield to the other. Each grips and nourishes itself upon whatever material the world of experience brings within its reach. We cannot conceive of this poet's work aside from an actively tender and sympathetic heart, while in the presence of beauty he is delivered up to emotions that have elemental power over him.

Hauptmann has written no work in which a successful, or at any rate, a complete synthesis of these two forces of his being is achieved. Rather has he occupied each extreme point of view and reached out from that in the direction of the other. In *Emanuel Quint* he expresses without reserve the whole range and intensity of his Christian compassion with human life; and here his mind scales its loftiest heights of Christian mysticism. In the *Heretic of Soana* he revels with equal abandon in a pagan joy of the senses, an unrestrained worship of the earthly goddess of love and beauty; but again he extends the significance of this worship far beyond its tangible forms, identifies it ecstatically with the creative force in all phenomena, and ends in a mysticism as complete as that of the *Fool in Christ.* Thus, like parallel lines, the two emotions meet in infinity. (pp. 356-57)

T. M. Campbell, "Gerhart Hauptmann—Christian or Pagan?" in The Modern Language Journal, *Vol. VIII, No. 6, March, 1924, pp. 353-61.*

HARVEY W. HEWETT-THAYER (essay date 1924)

The hero [of "Der Narr in Christo; Emanuel Quint"] doubtless bears a resemblance to Dostoievsky's "Idiot." Like him, Emanuel Quint lacks the human trait of self-seeking, but in a much more positive way, for he is possessed with a veritable passion of self-effacing love. We are confronted with the same baffling mystery, quite unsolved, if we seek sources for the negative and positive qualities which separate this selfless one from his fellowmen. Hauptmann causes his story to develop into a kind of Messiad. It is, in its essence, the simple and pathetic tale of a Silesian peasant who tries to walk in the footsteps of Christ, and then, through a combination of strange vicissitudes, loses his mental balance and confuses his own identity with that of his Master. (p. 181)

The external events which make up the "plot" of the story, Hauptmann has constructed with great skill; there is a logical precision in the sequence of events, there is a unity of impression, a relevancy to ultimate purpose in the selective accumulation from possible happenings, which betokens epic power of a high order. Hauptmann's training in dramatic writing has given him also a plastic skill in presenting character vividly and completely within narrow limits; he imparts a fine semblance of life and reality to the individual disciples, the country folk, the wretched weavers in their filthy warrens, the country society of clergy and squirearchy, or the Bohemian dregs of a large city. But the main theme of the story is a spiritual one; it lies within the mind of Emanuel Quint. (p. 185)

[The] growth of the Messianic consciousness in his hero is to Hauptmann a vexatious stumbling-block. . . . At the beginning Emanuel insists that he is not the Christ, that he is merely one of many sent to heal the broken-hearted, only a man, the son of man,—and then he is startled and terrified when he realizes that he has thus used his Master's designation of Himself. But on reflection he decides that this is not an unwarranted presumption, for he lives Christ, walks in His steps, and is inspired by a transcending love. So he consents somewhat reluctantly to a kind of homage; his disciples kiss his hands; the wretched, who seek his aid, bow down before him. His overmastering love shrinks from disillusioning them, from shattering the pitifulness of their faith. Naturally the effort to imitate Christ, to reproduce the life of Christ in himself, leads Emanuel to invite experiences which correspond to the gospel story.

During the night of his first imprisonment, Emanuel has a dream of Christ; the vision is more actual to him than many of the attested happenings of waking hours. From that moment on, the transfusion of identity gradually becomes to him an established verity. . . . From this insidious identification of himself with the historical Christ follows the later repudiation of prayer. Why should he pray to himself? The Bible is also discarded; it is the work of erring men; the errors of centuries involving the wretchedness of generations are built upon it. Among the blasphemies which the authorities lodged against Emanuel was his violent treatment of the sacred book. He throws it angrily and irreverently across the room, the very tattered little volume out of

which his youth had drawn its faith. In the last period of Emanuel's ministry his love for suffering and deluded humanity is touched with a strange exultant assurance and mingled with occasional outbursts of indignation against the rulers of the world, temporal and ecclesiastical; and in a kind of apocalyptic vision, he prophesies their passing from the earth.

The assumption of Messiahship is a familiar phenomenon of mental unbalance. Throughout the Christian era, eager apostles have wearied at the tarrying of their Lord, and on the borderland between conscious volition and hysteria, they have surrendered themselves to the fateful presumption. On a lowlier level stand the numberless "Christs" whose pitiful delusions sadden the annals of the asylums. Hauptmann is plainly at a loss where to classify his "fool." Emanuel's life brings him into association with many kinds of people; he is a puzzle to most of them,—and he remains a puzzle even to his own creator. (pp. 185-87)

Hauptmann closes his narrative with an interrogation point. He has ended the story in his own bewilderment; he has conjured up a fictitious tale which grips him; it embodies an idea which has held him from boyhood and will not let him go. . . . Is there a sentient power which enfolds us, giving now and then to chosen spirits,—who then seem abnormal in this duller world,—their visions of human perfectibility? This is the question which puzzles and baffles. Hauptmann tries to reason it out, perhaps to reason it away. But he can not get away from the problem which he can not solve.

In telling the story of Emanuel Quint, Hauptmann makes use of a familiar method of indirect narration; he pretends that he is simply presenting the record of a chronicler who, interested in the reported phenomena of the apostle's life, has taken upon himself to investigate, to accumulate material, and then set it in an orderly narrative. If Hauptmann intended to tell the story through the medium of another personality, adding to its interest through the creation of a narrator in whose mind it is reflected, his purpose has signally failed. The reader is in no way aware of the personality of the chronicler, is only at rare intervals even reminded of the device of an intermediary narrator; and, as a matter of fact, Hauptmann himself seems to recall it only now and then, generally narrating, with the conceded omniscience of the novelist, matters which no chronicler, however minute his investigations, could ever have found out. The fiction of the chronicler is after all a rather transparent device; Hauptmann uses it as a cloak for his own uncertainty, but contrariwise perhaps, it merely uncovers more plainly his attitude of perplexity in the presence of the mystery. (pp. 189-91)

Harvey W. Hewett-Thayer, "The Novel and the Eternal Question," in his The Modern German Novel: A Series of Studies and Appreciations *(copyright, 1924 Marshall Jones Company), Marshall Jones, 1924, pp. 162-94.***

L. B. KEEFER (essay date 1934)

[Even] a superficial glance at the writings of [Gerhart Hauptmann] brings to light the fact that it is precisely and almost exclusively the love for woman which causes and conditions the conflict in his dramatic productions. She it is around whom the problem revolves, and from whom it obtains solution; she, whose traits determine the conception as well as the entire direction of the play. It is in her, the prototype of endlessly varied images, that the man, more often than not her inferior in vitality, intellect, and will, seeks obstinately, untiringly the light of salvation, and if she: Ida, Michaline, Ottegebe, Griselda, Tehura, at times mercifully bestows upon him the purport and entirety of existence, it is likewise the woman: Hanna, Elga, Rautendelein, who hurls him into the abyss.

Nowhere else does the gradual and unceasing evolution of Hauptmann's dramatic genius speak more tellingly, perhaps, than in the long multicolored gallery of his feminine portraits. Decided naturalist, romanticist, social reformer, creator of comedies or fairy tales, symbolist—all these phases of artistic growth, all these acceptances of new philosophic doctrine and repudiations of credo are emphasized and illustrated through the varied delineations of womanhood. (p. 35)

[Hauptmann's richest productions] are reserved for the numerous interpretations of the woman in the rôle of the more or less successful redeemer of the male, entrusted to her charge. Here one is confronted with an almost inexhaustible wealth of expression: the realistic contours of the early images—Helene Krause, Ida Buchner, and Michaline Kramer—give way to the more complex countenance of Anna Mahr, the first of the lonely souls from the world abroad to wear the veil of symbol: a concept which gains incessantly in breadth, phantasy, and inner vision, until it reaches a climax in the pregnant characterizations of Hannele and Pippa, Elsalil and Tehura.

Most relevant for the artistic evolution of Hauptmann is the fact that in spite of a seemingly infinite multiformity of treatment and of individual features with which he endows his pictures, the chief motives and the situations presented remain essentially static. The most universal and powerful, the broadest, all-absorbing theme is the woman-mother. A sharper contrast than that between Griselda and Frau Krause, both chronologically and stylistically the poles of Hauptmann's dramatic activity, would be difficult to visualize, yet the portrait of the peasant maid, elevated to a throne and finding her true employ in motherhood, is but the final pause in the development of an idea, whose single phases, in the positive as well as the negative aspects, are accented in all the representatives of the eternally feminine.

Next in importance, a concept which even in the eyes of the author borrows its significance not from the eternally human, but from the currents of the particular era, is the calling, conferred on woman previously by Ibsen, namely, that of the emancipated messenger from more enlightened regions. By far more episodic than the mother task, this function is totally absent in the later writing. (pp. 35-7)

In the end Hauptmann envisages as the only, great, all important, everlasting mission of woman that of motherhood. To her . . . , the sibyl of humility and understanding, of pity and compassion, to her, the splendid, powerful figure, great in her trivial tasks, he sings his most inspired, most impassionate praise. (p. 53)

> L. B. Keefer, *"Woman's Mission in Hauptmann's Dramas,"* in The Germanic Review *(copyright 1934 by Helen Dwight Reed Foundation), Vol. IX, No. 1, January, 1934, pp. 35-53.*

F. B. WAHR (essay date 1946)

[In his poems] Hauptmann's lyrical gift is a modest one. He is in no way an innovator. His distinctly original contributions, as we know, lie in other fields, particularly in that of the realistic drama. His lyrics are by-products, "gleanings," as he calls them. But they are not for that reason artistically insignificant. They are in large measure traditional in form. In his shorter pieces he reminds us of Eichendorff and the Romanticists, at times with touches of Heine. (p. 216)

Though the two volumes of verse [*Das Bunte Buch* and *Ährenlese*] contrast with one another in content and form, they have much in common. Both contain short, direct, impressionistic lyrics as well as longer, more sustained poems, some narrative and objective in nature, others more personal. But the earlier volume, though touched at times with the melancholy of youth, is forward looking, hopeful with its dreams and plans, some imbued with an enthusiastic, Promethean-like challenge, whereas the later volume is largely the work of an old and mature master, who is contemplatively looking back in retrospect over much that has transpired, in a spirit of resignation and accommodation, accepting rather than contending. The warm sympathy for social enlightenment and reform which was so much a part of the young idealists of the late eighties is missing in the *Ährenlese*. A more elegiac mood has taken its place; there are unhappy memories of things undone or done poorly that seem to haunt the poet; there are moments of regret and disappointment. Life's experiences are to be endured and accepted, even its futilities, because after all they are so much worth while and, in memory, so beautiful. Hauptmann, like his own Till Eulenspiegel, is prone to escape from life's bitter realities into a dream world of classic myth and beauty and idyllic simplicity. In *Das Bunte Buch* a northern atmosphere, that of Erkner, Rügen, and Hohenhaus, hovers over the poetic spirit; in the *Ährenlese*, on the whole, the poet seeks the sunshine and clear outlines of the south, the blue Mediterranean skies, and his own "dream islands" of Leuke and Hohenhaus.

Though the lyrics of *Das Bunte Buch* had all the imperfections of an early effort, they did have, nevertheless, the virtues of genuineness and sincerity. Faltering as many of the verses were, they contained an expression of the conflicting, militant ideas and ambitions of the time as well as of its seeking subjectivity. . . . From this standpoint alone the early volume deserves to be remembered, even though Hauptmann's verses lack much of the strength and robustness of his contemporaries. They betray a sensitive spirit that has not yet found itself and is therefore not yet sure of itself. (pp. 217-18)

[Hauptmann's] later lyrics are distinguished by moods of acceptance and resignation. Such moods and certain symbols recur again and again. There are moments of indignation and revolt, but the prevailing tone is one of forbearance, longing for peace and quiet. . . . The poet has turned away from the problems of human society; he seeks calmer communion with nature and adjustment to her inexorable and immutable ways. He ponders upon more eternal and universal questions. It is less man's role in the social structure than his position in the natural universe that holds his interest. (p. 220)

Characteristics of Hauptmann's poetic style which had long been evident in his verse dramas and longer poems recur of course in his lyrics. His propensity for unusual word combinations, his delight in sense impressions, the inclination to run the thought over the line with frequent cases of enjambment, together with his repeated use of certain symbols, figures, motives, and verse-forms impress one, but not always favorably. However in a few of the shorter lyrics as in the longer poems with a Greek setting, such as "Der Heros" and "Der Knabe Herakles," he has written poetry of great beauty and finish. His lyrics, like those of many other German writers chiefly distinguished in other fields, help to complete our evaluation of him and cannot be ignored in any appraisal of his complete work. Like all his writings they are expressions of his fertile and tirelessly creative genius. (p. 229)

> *F. B. Wahr, "Gerhart Hauptmann's Shorter Poems," in* The Germanic Review *(copyright 1946 by Helen Dwight Reed Foundation), Vol. XXI, No. 3, October, 1946, pp. 215-29.*

OSKAR SEIDLIN (essay date 1947)

In his early years Hauptmann was blamed because of his characters. Critics, prompted by energetic idealism and patriotism, clamored for "heroes" on the stage and felt repelled by the weakness and oversensitiveness of Hauptmann's characters. They found in his works a glorification of neurasthenia, and, rough-and-ready as they were, they insisted on firmness of character, which could serve as a shining example to the adolescent. They did not notice that someone was speaking who was unwilling and unable to offer guiding models and direct appeals—one whose heart was tortured by a great woe, an ardent compassion for those who were defeated in life, defeated by life.

Gerhart Hauptmann has had only one basic theme: the failure of the poor and naked human creature faced with an inexorable superior power, a failure which it would be wrong to term a fight, because there is no fight: only suffering, suffering unto death. Endless is the procession of sufferers, some of them eloquent, most of them mute as animals, who desperately raise their arms against a fate which, in the proper sense of the word, pursues them, and who at every attempt to resist know beforehand that they will succumb. (pp. 360-61)

An endless gallery of sufferers, human beings wounded in body and soul, a procession under the cross of human existence from which only death can relieve us: this is the sum of Gerhart Hauptmann's work. The visions which Hauptmann has called into existence—and some of them will survive our times—are not the creations of an activist who believes in deeds and action. This is not the sound of a trumpet calling to revolution, but the sound of weeping over the sufferings of mankind. (p. 361)

Hauptmann's work is a symphony in gray, a dark panorama, lit neither by a light from below nor by one from above.

And still, there is a strong, beautiful light in his work; it flows from the sentiment which is the center of the man Gerhart Hauptmann and from which every one of his creations has sprung: compassion with his fellow-men. Compassion is the message of Hauptmann's work, and for the sake of this message we love him. Whatever blemishes may darken this work . . . , this is the great gospel which he was

sent to preach and which he never tired of preaching. . . . (p. 363)

> *Oskar Seidlin, "Taking Leave of Gerhart Hauptmann," in* South Atlantic Quarterly *(reprinted by permission of the Publisher; copyright 1947 by Duke University Press, Durham, North Carolina), Vol. 46, No. 3, July, 1947, pp. 359-64.*

MARGARET SINDEN (essay date 1949)

Hauptmann's career was as varied as it was long. Until shortly before the First Great War he devoted himself in the main to the prose drama, to a realistic portrayal of contemporary life in Germany. But from an early date he had begun also to write verse plays, and from about 1912 his attention was drawn increasingly from realistic prose to verse, to symbol and philosophy; from Germany to Greece, America, the South Sea Islands, or simply into the realm of vision and myth; and even from drama to novel, *Novelle,* and verse epic. In an attempt to order this variety, critics have generally adopted some version of the two-souls-in-one-breast theory, and have considered Hauptmann as a man in whom naturalism struggled with romanticism, or Germany with Greece, or the rationalist cynic with the religious mystic. Any of these solutions may have much to be said for it, but they are all inadequate in the last analysis, I think, for one reason, because they ride rough-shod over obvious inequalities in Hauptmann's work, and, taking attempt for achievement, give to bad works and good an equally positive value. Also any sharp and distinct cleavage is foreign to what we know of Hauptmann as a man, and foreign to the characters which he created.

We must rather, I suggest, proceed from the assumption that if one group of works, fairly uniform in style, surpasses in bulk, and, on the whole, in excellence, any other group, there we shall find the essential Hauptmann, if such there be. This group undoubtedly exists in the realistic prose dramas, predominantly tragedies, which he wrote between 1889 and 1911, together with the greatest tragedy of them all, the novel *Emanuel Quint.* (p. 17)

Hauptmann's longest and most profound study in sublimation . . . and the point at which he has come to his closest grips with the mysticism of his native Silesia, is the novel *The Fool in Christ (Der Narr in Christo, Emanuel Quint),* the story of the development of a red-headed carpenter's son who leaves his father's bench to preach the gospel of repentance and love. . . . "Love," he says, and "love" again. In the end comes the bitter recognition that men cannot accept the absolute, cannot comprehend that the kingdom has nothing to do with the flesh or the healing of the flesh, that it is useless to pour love into the furnace of the world's hatred; until with the weary, "Aber alles ist müssig"—But all is in vain—he vanishes from Silesia. In the spring a frozen body is found, high in the Gotthard. (pp. 23-4)

Hauptmann, who once said that the highest form of human life appeared to him to be serenity . . . and whose sense of the power and beauty of the creative forces which spring from the earth and draw men together and upward is so strong that he embodied it again and again in convincing human form, is at the same time and almost before all else intensely sensitive to suffering, and constantly aware of the perils from within and without which menace the peaceful development for which he longs. (pp. 24-5)

[Nevertheless], sensitive as Hauptmann is, he is not obsessed with the vision of a suffering world to the point of distortion, of narrowly subjective interpretation. Some of his characters are indeed pathological, but his treatment of them justifies his assertion that the sorting of the healthy and the ill is the business of the doctor and not of the artist, that the bounds of the so-called healthy and normal are in any case overstepped in moments of passion, and that he must take men as he finds them and not confine himself to dealing with a fragment of a man. Though he was shaken into tragedy, his vision remains broad and objective, his focus straight and just. He is quick again and again to catch the humour of a situation. . . . (p. 26)

Such is Hauptmann, the "realist." That this is basically and essentially the true Hauptmann is borne out by those other works, be it verse drama or verse or prose epic, in which realism, in the sense of a detailed reproduction of the physical world and social setting, is a less important factor. For here too he remains first and foremost a tragedian, and he is at his best when his way leads not from the abstract but through the concrete, not from the general, but through the psyche of specific human beings, when a landscape (Greece for example) or the people who live in history, legend, and poetry have taken the same strong hold on him as those whom he knew in his youth. Thus poetic drama, for example, does not necessarily, in itself, pose for Hauptmann a new or different problem from prose, though he may well have felt after 1914 that the framework of realism was no longer adequate to cope with the magnitude of events, with the war and the subsequent German breakdown. Also he may have needed the distance afforded him by legend or history in order to be able to deal with them at all. But the main difference is that here, and above all in verse epic, the direct contact which he needed was sometimes broken; he sometimes tried to run counter to his own genius, and did not succeed. He quite comprehensibly sought relief from the strain of tragedy; he sought to embody his ideal of serenity. He sought also to speak in his own voice, as a seer and an interpreter. The very scope and variety of his later work makes it clear, even without a long series of parallels (*Till Eulenspiegel* with *Faust, Anna* with *Hermann und Dorothea, Hamlet in Wittenberg* with *Wilhelm Meister,* and so on), that he had, in such attempts, at least one eye on Goethe, the man who had mastered life, who strove in his workshop with divine purpose and human hand to evoke and call forth man, "den Menschen." These works make it clear that Hauptmann was attempting to do the same for the men of his own generation, in his own way, and yet in a way which was not always fundamentally his own.

For when he sets out to attack the problems of the world by direct onslaught, to place idea or conception before individual or picture, to philosophize or use deliberate, intellectually conceived symbolism, or to leave the medium of the human behind for the realm of mythological visions, then we must, I think, admit that in the ensuing works not only does he have little to say, but that what he wishes to say he does not express well. His philosophy is apt to resolve itself into platitude, if it resolves itself at all. The symbolism is often merely perplexing, and the only way out of the difficulty is to fall back on his own truly enlightening explanation of the last act of *Und Pippa tanzt,* namely, "Ja, was schwebte mir nicht alles vor"—Well, I had all kinds of things in mind. The verse in such works (and Hauptmann could write verse powerfully and distinctively) has a ten-

dency to stumble or jingle or relax into jarring colloquialisms. By and large, also, the characters become thin, their outlines indistinct; they appear cowed by the magnitude of the task which is, too obviously, being thrust upon them. (pp. 27-9)

[If we compare Hauptmann with others] in respect of characterization, we shall find that one dramatist has perhaps as subtle a touch, but works within a narrower sphere; that another depends to a greater extent than Hauptmann on the force of argument or thesis, and shapes his characters, however powerfully and convincingly, toward the demonstration of that argument; that yet others use sensational plot or situation, abstraction or allegory, or consciously and deliberately invest age-old themes in modern regalia, or call the resources of music, or of the dance, or of machinery to the aid of the spoken word; but in no case can we match Hauptmann's protean ability to project himself into a wide range of characters and make them live before us in all their shaded and complex individuality and variability. (p. 33)

This same ability, it would seem to me, and the resultant richness and breadth of his work, together with the modernity of his interpretation of men which parallels in so many respects that of the modern sciences, makes of him . . . something very close to the central figure of the modern drama. (p. 34)

> *Margaret Sinden, "Gerhart Hauptmann," in* University of Toronto Quarterly *(reprinted by permission of University of Toronto Press), Vol. 19, No. 1, October, 1949, pp. 17-34.*

HERMANN J. WEIGAND (essay date 1952)

Unlike his other great contemporaries in German literature, [Hauptmann] had little, if anything, of the passion of art for art's sake in his make-up. He seemed always more concerned with the matter than with the manner of what he had to say. Except in the field of drama, he was an indifferent craftsman. One may be shaken to one's depths by the total pathos of a human situation projected by Hauptmann; one is rarely entranced in his work by a conscious experience of aesthetic perfection in the phrasing, in the rhythmic and melodic values of his linguistic material. He does not give to the trained ear the ecstasy of mutation achieved in the powers of language. He has none of the metallic density of Stefan George, none of the incorporeal incandescence of Rilke. His prose has none of the disciplined suppleness and brilliant phrasing that characterize Thomas Mann's mastery of narrative and essay. But what Hauptmann does in a comprehensive way is to penetrate to the heart of all that is human. Thus he encompasses the contemporary scene in accents which are compellingly authentic. But also in the grand manner of poets like Shakespeare he recreates outstanding figures of history and myth to revel in an orchestration of passions of incomparably richer scope than the very limited range of modern civilized man. (pp. 317-18)

When I said above that Hauptmann was by and large an indifferent craftsman, that statement requires qualification. It does not hold for the early, spectacular phase of his career. On the contrary, Hauptmann's concern with living drama involved a very conscious craftsmanship, schooled by the great example of Ibsen. Hauptmann set out to advance the authenticity of dramatic representation of life beyond the point achieved by the great Norwegian master. (p. 319)

Hauptmann the naturalist is intent upon refining on Ibsen's quality of realism in a variety of ways: To a much greater degree than with Ibsen, the local setting, including the background of landscape, season, and weather, is integrally tied in with the dramatic action.—The dramatic emphasis has shifted to the lower strata of society. Social stratification of great complexity is a background phenomenon of prime importance.—The social group as such may stand in the focus of interest rather than a representative individual. —Folk dialect, or rather folk dialects are employed, in meticulously authentic rendering, Silesian, Saxon, Berlin; and even the speech of characters of the bourgeois level takes on a variety of dialect shadings in response to the degree of nervous excitation evoked by the situation.—The dramatic hero, no longer necessarily the focus of our sympathies, is replaced by the mere protagonist who happens to unite in his person a maximum number of the threads that make up the tissue of the segment of life presented.—The concept of tragic guilt, so strong in Ibsen's heroes of often monumental individuality, is attenuated, dissipated, and replaced by the inescapable web of circumstance.—Lastly, personality in terms of stable, static character, is replaced by multiple dynamic reactivity. As one might say, the matter of character is transmuted into energy. (p. 320)

Before long Hauptmann introduces another far-reaching modification in his dramatic method: a basic change in perspective. Ibsen had given us only the dénouement—the untying of the dramatic knot. The long, intricate process of the tying of all the fateful strands, usually begun many years ago in the past, is glimpsed only in retrospect, often by the device of a startling confession. Ibsen presents the past in highly foreshortened form. Hauptmann shifts the emphasis. Deeply influenced by the scientific trend of the times, the naturalist is concerned with the sympathetic comprehension of a social process. A process is a development. With Hauptmann, the acts presented on the stage come to be but significant moments of the process of development, separated by considerable intervals of time, by weeks and months. These time intervals count heavily. The dramatic configuration of forces presented in each new act has undergone a substantial realignment between the acts. Thus, already in *Einsame Menschen* there is an interval of approximately one week separating each of acts II, III, and IV from the preceding, and in each act there is a substantial task of reorientation. We are presented with a succession of states, each showing tensions, latent in the preceding, as emergent in the succeeding. The dimension of time as duration is experienced. It gets into one's bones and may leave one with a sense of having lived through, in the space of hours, a development of months or years. (pp. 320-21)

> *Hermann J. Weigand, "Gerhart Hauptmann's Range as Dramatist," in* Monatshefte *(copyright © 1952 by the Regents of the University of Wisconsin), Vol. XLIV, No. 7, November, 1952, pp. 317-32.*

F. GARTEN (essay date 1954)

Among the major dramatists of the present century, Gerhart Hauptmann is probably the least known outside his own country. . . .

The first and most obvious reason is undoubtedly that a large number of Hauptmann's plays—and, for that matter,

his most successful and most characteristic—are written in dialect, and that their essential flavour is lost in translation. However, there is a deeper cause which must be sought in the intrinsically 'German' quality of Hauptmann's work in general.

It is no mere accident that it was a dramatist who, during the sixty years of his creative life, was acclaimed as 'the greatest German writer'. For it can be said that in Germany the drama generally ranks foremost among the literary forms. A predilection for tragedy, for the sharp clash of passions, is deeply engrained in the German character. . . .

From the outset, the theatre has been regarded not so much as a place of entertainment as, in Schiller's phrase, a 'moral institution'. It is the platform on which the main issues of the time, social, moral, and spiritual, are joined. The drama is endowed with the full dignity of *Dichtung;* the dramatist is the *Dichter* par excellence: it is his essential task to create a self-contained world of independent characters who, wholly detached from their creator, enter into a life of their own.

Gerhart Hauptmann conforms fully to that ideal. His outstanding faculty is this very power of creation, of bringing to life a host of characters, each with his destiny, his individual soul. There is no rationally definable theory, no philosophy, no *Weltanschauung* which can be distilled from his work as a whole. What he has produced is a reflexion of nature, as multiform and contradictory as herself—but animated by a live and sensitive heart. (p. 9)

[Hauptmann] is essentially a tragedian; even in his comedies, tragedy is always close at hand. His approach to human problems is emotional, and he is at his best when he creates intuitively and, as it were, unconsciously. He is never concerned with ideas, but always with human beings. What message he has to convey is not explicitly stated by his characters, but implicit in their actions and their sufferings. Moreover, he soon abandoned the realistic and social plane on which he won his first successes. His work grew into new dimensions. He delved into history, legend, and myth. His poetic strain which, as an undercurrent, had run through his most naturalistic works, broke forth and carried him to regions far removed from any temporal or local limitations.

Although Hauptmann, particularly in the latter part of his life, contributed to every *genre* of literature, he will always be known first and foremost as a dramatist. It was in drama that his greatest faculty, the creation of live characters, found its fullest scope. . . . Hence genuine drama is for Hauptmann in the first place a drama of the mind, of character, and not of action. 'The more complex the plot, the less there is of character. The simpler the plot, the richer the character . . . What you give to the plot you take away from the character.'

This basic conception of drama partly explains why Hauptmann's principal characters are throughout passive. They do not act; things happen to them. Their tragedy springs not so much from an excess of action, or of passion, as from an insufficiency, an incapacity to cope with the exigencies of life. Their keynote is suffering. However, Hauptmann's intrinsic philosophy is not one of fatalism. His central theme, shaped in countless variations, is redemption through suffering. In the end, when tragedy has taken its course, the victim, though felled by the force of circumstance, emerges as the true conqueror.

It was always to the weak and suffering that Hauptmann felt himself irresistibly drawn—to those who are trapped in the snares of fate, and succumb. But fate is not outside and above man: it is born in his heart, shaped by his character, and is for that reason the more inescapable. In the early naturalistic plays, the causes of man's suffering are partly in his social environment, that is, in material circumstance. As Hauptmann develops, they shift more and more to man's innermost self; in other words, to the timeless problems of human existence.

It is scarcely justifiable therefore to see in Hauptmann's abandonment of the naturalistic form, and his growing inclination towards poetic drama, an inconsistency or even, as has often been done, a yielding to changes of literary fashion. His entire life-work, though encompassing a great diversity of subject-matter and literary form, springs from a single basic concept of man and of life.

The mainspring of Hauptmann's work has often been stated to be *Mitleid*—compassion. But this compassion is devoid of any sentimentality or condescension; it is rather a profound sympathy with man's suffering wherever he encounters it, a genuine understanding of all human frailties. (pp. 12-13)

This intensely human appeal made Hauptmann throughout his life one of the most cherished and venerated writers of his country. His person no less than his works inspired affection: the almost magical spell his appearance exercised could be felt on many occasions, when it turned a near-failure into undisputed triumph. Moreover, his works have the peculiar quality of growing independently, as though endowed with a life of their own; many of his plays which, at their first appearance, found little response, turned into successes when revived. Although so huge an *oeuvre* as his contains many single works which are second-rate or not fully perfected, there is scarcely one which does not fall into place when viewed as a link in the author's development. (p. 14)

Any critical assessment of Hauptmann's work—at any rate, of his dramatic work—will have to dispense with one of its most vital aspects, its impact in the theatre. Indeed, the continued life of his plays on the German stage for over half a century is in itself a proof of their vitality. Among them, the earlier realistic plays clearly stand highest in popular favour. Despite Hauptmann's own partiality for his later work, despite the occasional revival of some of his late poetic dramas, it is the sequence of plays from *Die Weber* to *Die Ratten* that really lives to-day. What is the secret of their superiority? Hauptmann was unsurpassed in his own field, the delineation of realistic character. When he turned to poetic and symbolic drama, although he gained an incomparably greater range and depth of vision, he lost his greatest asset—the intuitive contact with the *Volk*, the simple people, where he had his roots. His verse, particularly in the later phases, often shows signs of carelessness, and is marred either by a cumbersome heaviness or by jarring colloquialisms. Hauptmann did not add a new voice to German poetry. Both in his lyric and epic poems he employed a rather undistinguished poetic diction; he seemed too hard pressed by the throng of characters and images to give sufficient attention to their embodiment in language. As for his prose, a similar defect can be seen in his later works. Many of them are marred by a certain awkwardness of diction, and tend towards the ponderous and sententious.

Of all his prose writings, perhaps only two are quite devoid of these flaws—*Der Narr in Christo Emanuel Quint* and *Der Ketzer von Soana,* the two complementary novels written at the height of his power; here vision and language are in complete harmony. (pp. 61-2)

In his entire work Hauptmann was never concerned with personifying ideas or problems: he was exclusively interested in human beings as such. Nor did he conceive his characters as representatives of any given form of society. This is the essential mark distinguishing his work from Ibsen's or Chekhov's. Both these dramatists move in a given social setting which determines their characters—with Ibsen, the middle-class society of his time, with Chekhov, the pre-revolutionary Russian gentry. There is no such common denominator in the works of Hauptmann. Whenever society, with its conventions and moral concepts, enters his plays, it does so as an inimical power, antagonizing and ultimately destroying the isolated human being.

As a matter of fact, most of Hauptmann's plays are not set within the middle-class but on its lower fringes, that is, among artisans and peasants—and among artists. These stand outside the accepted standards of a circumscribed society and are more closely linked to the elemental forces of human existence. The same applies to Hauptmann's women, who so often hold the centre of the drama.

The conflict between man's innermost being and outer reality, his inability to realize himself fully in a world determined by social factors or by the callousness of others, is the essence of all Hauptmann's dramas. It is interesting to note how many of his central characters, both men and women, commit suicide. This has been wrongly ascribed to their inherent 'weakness'. It would be better to say that they are of a more subtle and complex nature, of a greater emotional capacity, than their fellowmen. . . . They all strive to realize their inward vision in the face of an adverse reality, and are broken in the attempt. Their guilt—if guilt it can be called—is not of a social or moral kind, but existential; it is inherent in their very existence as isolated human beings. Even the crowds of the weavers or peasants consist of so many individuals, each driven by his own inarticulate longing. '*A jeder Mensch hat halt 'ne Sehnsucht*'—these words of a simple weaver strike the keynote of all Hauptmann's characters; it is the longing for something ineffable, something beyond their reach, a fulfilment never to be granted in this life. (pp. 63-4)

Hauptmann's dramas are tragedies of man's isolation. All his heroes suffer from one fundamental failing—an inability to communicate with others. 'Everything tends towards unity', Michael Kramer meditates, 'yet over us lies the curse of dispersion'. The evil characters, those who inflict suffering instead of enduring it, are beset by the same inability. There are, in fact, no villains in Hauptmann's world, only men thwarted in their natural growth. Even in the blackest soul there is an indefinite longing for the light, a divine spark. (p. 64)

Hauptmann's plays are full of [moments that reveal,] in a sudden flash, the very core of a character. But they lose their significance when torn from their context. It is these momentary revelations, insignificant in themselves but striking to the heart, that make for the inimitable quality of Hauptmann's art. It is a quality which can only be defined as a profound humanism—an intuitive understanding of the timeless human drama.

Despite the prevalence of tragedy, the ultimate impact of Hauptmann's work is not one of pessimism. His negative attitude towards man as a social being is merely the reverse side of a positive belief in the healing powers of nature; all human existence is rooted in nature and longs to return to it. Throughout his work, nature is always palpably present. The narrative works are rich in glowing descriptions of its beauties, and in the plays its changing moods and manifestations form an essential component of the action. But nature is not merely the background of the human drama, it is the redeeming power and the ultimate refuge for man's suffering. (p. 65)

This close communication with nature, at once sensuous and spiritual, forms the very basis of Hauptmann's poetic world. All his characters, even the most realistic, are rooted in it. Their various tragedies spring, in the last resort, from the clash between this elemental basis and the limitations of outer reality. Each one fails through his inability to realize his innermost self. This basic conception is the unifying principle, spanning the gulf between the realism of the beginning and the mysticism of the end; at first, the accurately observed reality is predominant, later, the inward vision of the soul. (p. 67)

> *F. Garten, in his* Gerhart Hauptmann *(reprinted by permission of Anne Garten), Yale University Press, 1954, 72 p.*

H. F. GARTEN   (essay date 1964)

There is little doubt that Hauptmann was first and foremost a dramatist. . . . However, from his very beginnings, he turned again and again to epic forms, either in prose or in verse. . . .

Along with his narrative prose works, Hauptmann showed a special predilection for the epic poem. While his lyric poetry is only of subordinate importance, epic poetry plays an essential part in his creative output. It is in this form that he revealed his inner world—a world of dream and vision from which even his realistic works have grown. (p. 95)

The term "epic poetry" should be understood here in a very loose sense. I am using it in the German sense of a "Versepos", that is, a long narrative poem which has not sprung from a single lyrical mood. If we accept this definition, we have three large epic poems in Hauptmann's work: one at the beginning—*Promethidenlos*—and two in his maturity—*Till Eulenspiegel* and *Der große Traum*. (p. 96)

Promethidenlos is written in ottava rima which, in one or two dramatic passages, breaks up into plain blank verse. The language is throughout traditional, in a pseudo-romantic vein, the imagery cliché-ridden and hazy. . . . The influence of Byron's *Childe Harold* is unmistakable. The hero, called Selin . . . , alternates between lofty dreams and bleak despair. He sees himself as a bard, plucking the lyre, scorning the philistinism of the common herd. The passionate indictment of the present age, its materialism and "Fadheit", runs as a main theme through the whole work. (p. 97)

However, Selin's belief in a social mission proves only a passing phase. Soon he reverts to his former, self-centred and self-pitying meditations. In the final stage, during his stay in Capri, he abandons himself completely to Byronic *Weltschmerz*. For him, the serene beauty of the island is overshadowed by the memory of the emperor Tiberius, whose demented ghost still haunts the place. The evocation of his weird presence is one of the most vivid passages in the poem. The emperor's lament at the world's betrayal confirms Selin in his misanthropy and casts him into ever deepening gloom. Finally, with a truly Byronic gesture, he smashes his lyre and seeks death in the sea. . . .

The hero of *Promethidenlos* is the first in a long line of Hauptmann's characters who commit suicide. In his case, this solution is rather unconvincing, prompted merely by the literary models the young author was following. . . .

Promethidenlos has all the marks of immaturity, both in form and thought-content. It summarises what may be called the prenaturalistic period in Hauptmann's development. But its technique of proceeding from image to image, alternating between exultation and despair, already foreshadows the structural form of his later epics—only that the images are not yet fully visualised, but rather dissolved in abstract thought and philosophical comment.

Hauptmann returned to epic poetry only thirty years later, after he had completed his fiftieth year. (p. 99)

Till Eulenspiegel and *Der große Traum* must be counted among the chief works of Hauptmann's ripe age. . . . [His] creative activities shifted, after his fiftieth year, more and more from dramatic to narrative writings, both in prose and verse. While he never quite lost sight of the drama, epic works now predominated. Both *Till Eulenspiegel* and *Der große Traum* grew from the deep emotional and intellectual crisis caused in Hauptmann's development by the First World War. . . . (p. 108)

Of all Hauptmann's works, *Till Eulenspiegel* comes closest to the traditional concept of an epic poem: it has a hero, whose adventures, physical and spiritual, are related in a succession of cantos. However, there is a close link between that hero and the poet: the spiritual development he undergoes is to a large extent Hauptmann's own. Growing out of the mental and political chaos of post-war Germany, the work served him as a vessel into which he poured the sum of his knowledge, his despair, his dreams, his comments on the contemporary world. It does not concentrate on any one problem or conflict, but attempts to encompass the whole of life. (pp. 108-09)

The work is divided into 18 "Abenteuer", each of which is headed by a brief, largely humorous, summary, in the style of the picaresque novel. Altogether, the poem has a distinctly baroque quality. . . . This baroque quality is also manifest in the sumptuous language, the profuse imagery, and the constant interplay of realism and transcendental vision. Hauptmann's hexameters have been criticized for not conforming to the classical rules. However, his arbitrary use of the verse form is no doubt deliberate: the general pattern is rather that of rhythmical prose than of a strict metre. Often, the metric accent is at variance with the natural accent. This deliberate licence in the handling of the verse is much more in keeping with a "modern" epic than any faithful imitation of classical models would have been. The variety of the language is infinite: it comprises every linguistic level, from harsh colloquialism to sublime lyricism. In sheer poetic power and range of expression, it has no equal in Hauptmann's entire work.

The relationship between Hauptmann's epic and the 16th

century Volksbuch of *Till Eulenspiegel* resembles that between Goethe's *Faust* and the original Faust legend. It uses the figure of the popular jester as a point of departure, endowing him with a range and significance far beyond his original function; moreover, it transplants him into the present.

The central character is a German airman of the First World War, who finds himself on the street after the Armistice. Under the name of the legendary rogue, he drives his ramshackle cart through the misery and anarchy of postwar Germany, setting up his booth at village fairs. As a symbol of this transformation, his pilot's helmet has grown bells, turning it into a jester's cap.... However, Till is much more than a clearly defined individual; he has a superpersonal, symbolic significance, like Goethe's Faust, with whom he is linked in many ways. He is, first and foremost, specifically German.... Till is as German as Don Quixote is Spanish. However, his "folly" is the reverse of Don Quixote's: while the latter is enwrapped in his madness, amidst a sane world, Till is the only sane man in a world gone mad; while the world laughs at Don Quixote, Till laughs at the world. But his humour has a bitter flavour; it is a defensive weapon to save himself from despair.... (pp. 109-10)

Till's existence moves on two planes: to the outside world, he poses as a jester; but his real self is revealed in the dreams and visions by which he is beset. Through these dreams and visions, he is in communication with characters, real and imaginary, of all ages. Moreover, he is endowed with magic powers, which enable him to call forth the dead at will. It is through these powers that he touches on the innermost secrets of life....

From beginning to end, Till contents himself with the role of a passive onlooker, endowed with an infinite capacity for suffering and compassion. (p. 110)

The further he progresses, the more he succumbs to a state of dejection and the more he yields to day dreams and hallucinations. His way, leading from reality to inward vision, is Hauptmann's own. (p. 111)

Throughout, Till is haunted by memories of the war and its victims; he feels himself to be one of them. During the war, he felt at one with his country. But the German defeat has opened his eyes and filled him with deep compassion for the hecatombs of dead, including the enemies he has killed in battle. He sees himself as Cain, doomed for ever to wander the earth to atone for his guilt.... This self-identification with Germany and the pity he feels for her present plight are essential aspects of Till's personality. (p. 112)

However, the political level is only one of the planes on which the work moves. Against the background of contemporary events, Till is beset by visions which carry him into distant times and regions. It is these visions which give the whole work a range and depth far beyond its topical significance. Sometimes, they are genuine hallucinations, day dreams and oppressive nightmares to which he falls a victim; sometimes, Till relates them as plain "Lügenmärchen", conjuring up scenes and images by the sheer power of his imagination. In every instance, these visions are so vivid as to make them indistinguishable from reality; the borderline between "real" and "imaginary" happenings remains fluid throughout. (p. 113)

Like *Till Eulenspiegel*, with which it is linked in many ways, *Der große Traum* is a product of the First World War and its aftermath. But in contrast to the former, it abandons the realistic plane and moves entirely in a world of dream and vision. Moreover, the dreamer is the poet himself, and the visions are his own.

Both in form and in substance, the poem takes its cue from Dante's *Divina Commedia*. It is written in terza rima, divided into 22 cantos ..., and tells of the poet's imaginary journey through the under and upper worlds, led by a guide (who at one point is Dante himself). (p. 121)

Hauptmann's poem differs from Dante's in a significant way: while Dante's path leads through the fixed universe of medieval Christian doctrine, Hell, Purgatory, and Paradise, the modern poet has no such pre-established pattern to follow. His way unrolls in an arbitrary succession of visions and images, succeeding one another with the inconsistency of a dream. Nor is there any perceptible direction or development. The only pattern that can be discerned is within the single cantos, which generally—but by no means always—lead from dark to light. However, the dark predominates throughout. There is no paradise to reward the righteous, only everlasting struggle. Yet the poem does not purport to reveal merely a private world of visions. Although personal reminiscences and associations are inextricably mingled with symbols of universal significance, the poet calls his work repeatedly a "Weltgedicht". His dreams are the dreams of humanity; the subconscious from which they spring is part of the collective unconscious. (p. 122)

The place of Virgil in Dante's poem is taken by Satanael, a figure Hauptmann derived from Gnostic thought. According to this, Satanael is one of the two sons of God, an elder brother of Christ. Cast out from Heaven for his pride, he created the world and man in defiance of God. However, he has not withdrawn from his creation, but continues to live in it as the "Demiurg", sharing man's sufferings and joys, and spurring him to ever higher exertions. He thus has many features of Lucifer, the Fallen Angel, but as it were on a higher level. His relationship to Christ is ambivalent: partly, he is hostile to Him, partly, he acknowledges Him and will one day be reconciled to Him.

What fascinated Hauptmann in these Gnostic concepts was evidently their attempt to explain the Evil in the world, or rather, to bridge the gulf between Good and Evil, giving theological foundation to the dual nature of man. (pp. 122-24)

Satanael, who acts as a guide through Hauptmann's dream world, is the key figure to the whole work. His ambivalent nature reflects the fundamental dualism on which *Der große Traum*, indeed Hauptmann's entire work, is based. This dualism lies at the very root of the poet's thought. It finds expression in his frequent use of antithetic images, such as Light and Dark, Heaven and Hell, Olympos and Hades, sun and moon, black and white, and so on. The everlasting struggle between these opposing powers, which dominate man's life, represents the "Urdrama"—a basic concept of Hauptmann's. Its scene is the mind of man. But these opposing powers are not only locked in perpetual war; they also meet in a *coincidentia oppositorum*. In other words, there is a realm in which the antithesis of light and dark, heaven and hell, life and death is as it were neutralised. (p. 124)

In *Der große Traum*, Hauptmann seems to have travelled a long way from his starting point. There is, at first sight, no link between its fleeting images and the precisely defined reality of his naturalistic plays. Nevertheless, the two are merely the beginning and end of a consistent creative evolution. This evolution led from the particular to the universal, from reality to symbol. But the link is even closer. The epic poems of Hauptmann's old age reveal as it were the subconscious region from which his whole work has sprung. Hauptmann has emphasised countless times the prevalence of dream over reality, and the fallacy of distinguishing between the two. . . .

It is hardly necessary to point to the frequent incidence of dreams and the constant interplay of dream and reality in many of his works, from *Hanneles Himmelfahrt* onwards. Man is encompassed by a world of dream, compared with which his waking state is no more than a small island in an ocean. As Hauptmann grew older, this dream world occupied an ever larger place in his writings. All the works of his old age are steeped in it. (p. 133)

This borderline vanishes completely in his epic poems. Far from being of secondary importance, they lay bare the very roots from which Hauptmann's work has grown. Some of them . . . are perhaps too closely linked to his personal life to stand as works of art in their own right. But *Der große Traum,* and, still more, *Till Eulenspiegel* transcend this personal sphere and aim at establishing symbols of universal significance. How far they succeed is a question of critical evaluation. It can be argued that the time of the epic poem as a valid art form has passed, and that its place has been taken by the novel. However, what Hauptmann set out to do, he could not possibly achieve in prose. In order to find a form congenial to his mythological visions, he needed the emotive pitch of poetic diction, which only the epic poem could provide. The question remains whether the symbols he has used are only subjectively relevant, or whether they have objective validity in our modern age. Whatever the final assessment, these two works represent perhaps the last desperate attempt to encompass the spiritual heritage of Western Man, and to see our present age ''sub specie aeterni''. (pp. 133-34)

H. F. Garten, "Hauptmann's Epic Poetry," in Hauptmann, *edited by K. G. Knight and F. Norman (© The Institute of Germanic Studies, London; adapted by permission), University of London Institute of Germanic Studies, 1964, pp. 95-136.*

ANN B. DOBIE (essay date 1969)

Gerhart Hauptmann holds the lonely distinction of being a playwright who is anthologized and taught with some frequency but who, with equal frequency, is criticized and dismissed as minor, dated, and inconsistent. Indeed, *The Weavers*, his most significant play, is often found in textbooks for courses in modern drama with a notable critic such as John Gassner calling it repetitious and criticizing Hauptmann for not fully developing the characters. Gassner even comments that the actions of the weavers contribute nothing to ''an intelligent treatment of modern realities.'' . . .

Upon reading much of the Hauptmann study of the past few years one is led to wonder what all the enthusiasm could ever have been about. But upon reading Hauptmann himself, the old excitement returns and one wonders what the sneering was all about.

In light of the revolutionary aspects of the present day, *The Weavers,* is a surprisingly current and socially relevant play. (p. 165)

Certainly a close reading of *The Weavers* reveals that a basic misunderstanding of the themes of the play has led to a general misreading of the work as a whole. Whereas most analysts have seen the play as a social protest against injustice, one which rehearses the inequities and abuses of the industrial revolution, *The Weavers* is far more. In fact, it is a play of definition, a drama in which the actions of its collective hero of some seventy people probe and analyze the nature of revolution itself. They show its causes, its purposes, its results. True, Hauptmann based his play on the 1844 uprising of poverty stricken German cottage weavers, a protest against poverty and exploitation of labor. But through art the uprising becomes not a pathetic, if idealistic, cry against wrong. It becomes a broadly developed study of an abstraction. (pp. 165-66)

One difficulty the modern American reader has in seeing *The Weavers* as a definition of revolution is its ending. Our history has accustomed us to accepting revolution as progress. The American Revolution, even the Civil War, a social revolution against an inhuman system, led to ends which are now considered right and good. . . . In contrast, the revolution of the weavers in Hauptmann's play ends in disaster and defeat for those who declared it. The revolutionists are dispersed with little difficulty by well armed troops ordered to quell the uprising. This, then, is not revolution as we have known it. Hence the play has been called a futile social protest. But *The Weavers* is not dark in tone. The rebels feel not futility but joy and exultation as they lash out against the system which has enslaved them. The despair which precedes the revolt has no place in the revolt itself. Revolution, according to Hauptmann's play, is not a cycle of grievance, uprising, and immediate justice. It is a cycle of abuses which lead to revolution which is countered by forces which may ultimately defeat the rebels as well as the establishment. Its nature is destructive and violent. Its perpetration may look less than noble. Progress, in the form of immediate happiness or prosperity, may not be visible. It may be present only in the ultimate inability of a system to function as before once human dignity and human rights have been asserted. (pp. 166-67)

The audience which leaves *The Weavers* with a sense of futility misses the powerful statement which grows out of the violent final act. Certainly the most apparent results of the rebellion are negative; physical destruction lies on all sides. But less visible, though far more significant is the deep sense of dignity, nobility, and understanding experienced by the survivors that the world is not and can never be as it was. Social protest, yes, it is. But Hauptmann gives the world of *The Weavers* not simply a shake of the fist but a philosophical questioning of the causes, the nature, the purposes, and results of revolution itself. (p. 172)

Ann B. Dobie, "Riot, Revolution, and 'The Weavers','' in Modern Drama *(copyright © 1969, University of Toronto, Graduate Centre for Study of Drama; with the permission of* Modern Drama*), Vol. 12, No. 3, September, 1969, pp. 165-72.*

RENATE USMIANI (essay date 1969)

A great deal of critical controversy surrounds Gerhart Hauptmann's last dramatic work, the imposing tetralogy *The House of Atreus*. . . . While some have interpreted the entire work as a clearly political pronouncement directed against the Nazi regime, others see in it the aging poet's refuge from the grim realities of contemporary life into the distant past of Greek mythology. (p. 286)

[The] three later plays, at least (*Iphigenia in Aulis* in particular), definitely represent an indictment, not only of warfare in general, but of Nazi warfare and Nazi policies in particular. . . . I think that it can be established beyond doubt that the barbaric sacrifice of Iphigenia as treated by Hauptmann carries heavy symbolic overtones of that other most barbaric human sacrifice which was taking place at the time in the poet's Vaterland: the slaughter of the Jewish people. In the year 1943, the year of *Iphigenia in Aulis,* Goebbels had triumphantly announced to the German people the success of the "final solution," and the Reich was officially declared "judenfrei" (free of Jews). Hauptmann himself was deeply disturbed over these developments, occasionally braving personal persecution in his defense of Jews. The plays clearly reflect his attitudes. (pp. 287-88)

The mythological story of the sacrifice of Iphigenia at the hand of her father [Agamemnon] in order to free the becalmed fleet for the destruction of Troy became more than an artistic challenge to the author: it became a personal obsession. (p. 289)

The character of Agamemnon had undoubtedly become for Hauptmann an embodiment of the German people, whose greatness he never ceased to admire, but whose delusion he deplored. He is drawn here as a truly epic hero, whose barbaric action is not a result of free choice, but rather is due to the wild machinations of his counsellors, above all, Kalchas, and to the inexorable demands of the war-god. Hauptmann's growing determinism is clearly apparent in the attitude of Agamemnon, as he defends himself before his wife and the mother of the intended victim: "I am . . . a powerless toy in the hands of horrible gods and men. . . ." . . . This hero, who is willing to make a human sacrifice out of his own daughter, bears all the traits of the German nation of the 40's: helpless to distinguish between right and wrong under the spell of clever propagandists and the pressures of a threatening war situation; possessed of a rigid feeling of duty towards his "historical mission," the destruction of the enemy; almost god-like in his heroic determination, and at the same time totally enmeshed in madness, and thus capable of the most barbaric behavior.

The situation surounding the sacrifice of Iphigenia finds its perfect parallel in the contemporary situation. It is summed up in the very opening speech of the play by Kritolaos: ". . . Oh god, what horrors now surround us! And it all began with shouts of joy." In *Iphigenia in Aulis* chaos and destruction reign; the action takes place among smoldering ruins, while the stench of corpses fills the air, and the black and red ship of Hekate beckons from afar. Total war is proclaimed: a situation which overthrows the morality and rationality of peace time. The Greeks' war policies reflect exactly the policies of total war proclaimed by the leaders of the Reich. (pp. 289-90)

Besides the psychology of demagoguery and its brilliant

rhetoric, Hauptmann has captured in *Iphigenia in Aulis* another phenomenon typical of the Nazi era: the mass demonstration with its resulting outbursts of mass hysteria and drunk enthusiasm. . . . Exactly the same madness surrounds the sacrifice of Iphigenia. As Agamemnon brings Iphigenia before the assembled populace, he is greeted with wild shouts of "Hail King Agamemnon! Hail! Hail! Hail!" Agamemnon has put himself entirely under the aegis of the war god. . . . (p. 292)

The effect on the masses is predictable as a wave of unchecked war enthusiasm breaks out among the people. . . . Even Iphigenia herself, the victim, is caught up in the general madness, as she screams in a "shrill and demonic voice": "Victory! Victory! Victory!" . . . The play ends on this note of intoxication, as the assembled populace repeats after Agamemnon, "To Troy! To Troy! Off to Troy!" just as the audience in the Sportpalast used to repeat the slogans of Goebbels.

That Hauptmann had the slaughter of the Jewish people in mind when he described the barbaric sacrifice of Iphigenia at the hands of her father becomes quite clear if we examine the way in which the author treats the sacrifice in the play, and try to establish his views about the Jewish question.

The sacrifice of Iphigenia is nowhere treated as a glorious or noble deed performed in the pursuit of a national ideal. Rather, it is presented throughout by the author as a most gruesome lapse, by a formerly civilized people, into barbaric and unjustifiable behavior. (pp. 292-93)

The two one-act plays, *The Death of Agamemnon* and *Elektra,* fill in still further the background of war madness and horror outlined in *Iphigenia in Aulis*. Both are dominated by the image of the blood-axe, symbol of the curse of violence and destruction which lies over the house of Atreus, instrument of the murder of Agamemnon and Klytemnaestra.

The *Death of Agamemnon* emphasizes the author's feeling of despair and religious pessimism. It reveals a great deal about Hauptmann's political views in its merciless representation of tyrannical rule. (pp. 294-95)

The physical horror of the central event of the play, the murder of Agamemnon at the hands of Klytemnaestra, is overshadowed by the moral horror of the reign of tyranny which raises its head in the wake of the crime itself. The wild excesses of the murderess and Aegisthus undoubtedly echo the reign of Nazi terror under which the play was written. Following the psychological pattern of Nazi Jew policies, Klytemnaestra first tries to hush up the crime, then switches to proud boastfulness and full self-justification. Dissenters are threatened with drastic measures.

Elektra, last in composition of the four plays of the cycle, reflects clearly the gloom that lay over Germany in 1944, and the feeling of futility and despair which filled the poet's heart. The setting is the same one as that of *The Death of Agamemnon,* but gruesomely different: the temple buildings lie in ruins, "horrible vapors" rise out of the holy spring, and human bones lie scattered over the ground. Immediately, we feel transported back into the desolation of the ruined German cities, laid low by the terror of daily air raids. (p. 296)

In this atmosphere of evil and destruction, the curse which

lies upon the house of Atreus takes its inevitable course. The unspeakable horror of the final stages of the total war finds its counterpart in the equally unspeakable horror of the crime of matricide committed by Orestes. . . .

Clearly, then, all the parallels point to the fact that Hauptmann's poetic representation of the tragedy and guilt of the curse-ridden Greek clan . . . reveals his very direct and personal involvement in the tragedy and guilt of that other "blond master race" to which he belonged. Nevertheless, the scope of the *Iphigenia* cycle takes it far beyond this first and most immediate interpretation. On a more universal scale, it deals with man's helplessness in the face of powers stronger than himself, and with the fearful consequences of war. In this sense, it fits into the general picture of Hauptmann's literary works: classical in scope, and deterministic in philosophy. (p. 297)

> Renate Usmiani, "Towards an Interpretation of Hauptmann's 'House of Atreus'," in Modern Drama *(copyright © 1969, University of Toronto, Graduate Centre for Study of Drama; with the permission of* Modern Drama*), Vol. 12, No. 4, December, 1969, pp. 286-97.*

PETER BAULAND   (essay date 1978)

Hauptmann's play [*Vor Sonnenaufgang*] contains all the patented thematic ingredients of German Naturalism: the struggle of people in the grip of forces beyond their control, the dramatic delineation of interacting social classes, the hard bite of economics, the concentration on workers and farmers as well as the gentry with whom they come into contact . . . , the overweaned emphasis on heredity and environment, the frequent paralleling of the behavior of people and the beasts of the field, the deromanticized awareness of the power of sexuality, the juxtaposition of squalor and wealth living side-by-side and springing from the same conditions, the graphic depiction of the sordid and the degrading. Hauptmann had both compassion for and understanding of ordinary people, and he pioneered the dramatic presentation of their lives in modern drama. He made their destinies seem important, if for no other reason than that they are human beings entitled to some dignity; for as Chekhov was to say a bit later, "Each man is the hero of his own life." *Vor Sonnenaufgang* was not the first play of its kind, but it was the first significant one—a landmark of a dramatic form developed in the late nineteenth century that has left its imprint on the stage. Much of what we see to this day started with Hauptmann, and Hauptmann started with *Vor Sonnenaufgang*.

Among the devices Hauptmann sired was the play with a collective protagonist, the hero-less play in which the community of people whose story is being told serves as the main "character." *Die Weber* is surely his best known achievement in this vein, but *Vor Sonnenaufgang* already presents a dramatic situation in which the audience does not really identify with any single main character. The one who is most often "right," if we do not look beyond his pious pronouncements, the one whose broad social ideas might even be equated with Hauptmann's on occasion, is gratingly unsympathetic. Indeed, Alfred Loth bears a more than passing resemblance of Ibsen's Gregers Werle of *The Wild Duck*. . . . Hauptmann always demonstrated an inherent fairness in characterization, and Loth surely has his positive side. It is impossible not to be moved by his aware-

ness and articulation of outrageous social injustices, and we can consider his long-range goals nothing short of admirable. An audience must share Hauptmann's own ambivalence toward his reformer, and it cannot discount what Loth says just because it may not like him personally. At the same time that we agree with and approve of Loth, we find it hard to forget that he is a narcissistic, pompous, self-righteous, humorless ass who is insensitive to the needs of others and incapable of listening to them. Ever intent on the welfare of "the people," he does not even realize when he is trampling on the feelings of the individual persons in his life. Loth is so devoted to his principles that he fails to notice that his devotion is destroying the woman he professes to love. (p. xv)

Though the miseries of the poor are ever in the background of *Vor Sonnenaufgang*, they are seldom developed or made specific, as they are in *Die Weber*. Hauptmann's earlier play concentrates more on the nature of the alleged reformer than on that which, admittedly, needs to be reformed. Loth, simultaneously altruistic and egoistic, is unaware of any contradiction in his nature. He espouses and proclaims a substantial chunk of the Naturalists' philosophy of social reform, which allows Hauptmann to dramatize a far more balanced view of the points at issue than can be found in the more doctrinaire plays of his confreres and to give the play an objective texture not universally found in sociopolitical Naturalism. Hauptmann's dramatic strength was always that he concentrated on the delineation of characters rather than causes, and this strength is apparent in *Vor Sonnenaufgang* even if Loth, in his total predictability, is not as psychologically complicated as he should be. . . . Loth compels us to question the validity of a revolution that does not improve the lot of those in whose name it is generated. Most German Naturalists tended to heap uncritical praise upon such monomaniacally serious would-be redeemers and saved their scorn for bohemian rebels. Hauptmann, through his multifaceted characterization of Alfred Loth, whose principles we praise and whose behavior we deplore, gave an extra dimension of analytical honesty to his Naturalism. (pp. xv-xvi)

Vor Sonnenaufgang is not an unflawed play. Though Hauptmann often expressed his desire to write plays without tidy conclusions because they were about problems that had no clear solutions, the tradition of the well-made play is still pronounced in this first work. *Vor Sonnenaufgang* has too many crude and overwrought scenes with dialogue that today sounds almost like parody. Its denouement is airtight, mechanical, and melodramatic, even if plausible. The play also abounds in retroactive exposition coming at just the opportune moment, and too often Hauptmann explains where he should reveal. (p. xviii)

A more serious dramatic problem results from the functions of the two levels of plot in *Vor Sonnenaufgang*: (1) the background social conflicts at issue; (2) the central situational instability to be resolved—will Loth find out about the alcoholism in the Krause family? The latter yields the melodrama and the action of the play; the former, which is the real substance of the drama, yields the disputation within the play, its discussion and its rhetoric. *Vor Sonnenaufgang* would be a stronger drama were its main theme developed in its main action, or had Hauptmann raised fewer issues in the play and treated those in greater depth. It is easy enough to quibble with any dramatic work.

Hauptmann's merits far outweigh his inadequacies in this seminal play of the modern theater. . . . (pp. xviii-xix)

> *Peter Bauland, in his introduction to* Before Daybreak *by Gerhart Hauptmann, translated by Peter Bauland (© University of North Carolina Studies in the Germanic Languages and Literatures 1978), University of North Carolina Press, 1978, pp. xi-xx.*

ADDITIONAL BIBLIOGRAPHY

Brown, Frank Chouteau. "Critical Analysis of *The Sunken Bell*." In *The Sunken Bell: A Fairy Play in Five Acts,* by Gerhart Hauptmann, translated by Charles Henry Meltzer, pp. 127-43. Garden City, NY: Doubleday, Doran & Co., 1930.
    Scene by scene descriptive analysis of this play.

Clark, Barrett H. "The German Drama: Gerhart Hauptmann." In his *A Study of the Modern Drama: A Handbook for the Study and Appreciation of Typical Plays, European, English, and American, of the Last Three-Quarters of a Century,* pp. 72-83. New York, London: D. Appleton-Century Co., 1938.
    Outlines structures and techniques in *The Weavers, Hannele,* and *The Sunken Bell.*

Frenz, Horst. Introduction to *The Weavers. Hannele. The Beaver Coat.,* by Gerhart Hauptmann, translated by Horst Frenz and Miles Waggoner, pp. v-xix. New York: Holt, Rinehart and Winston, 1951.
    Introduction to Hauptmann's life and work, with a discussion of these three plays as they represent his treatment of the separate dramatic forms of tragedy, symbolism, and comedy.

Gassner, John. "Gerhart Hauptmann (1862-1946)." In *A Treasury of the Theatre: From Henrik Ibsen to Arthur Miller,* edited by John Gassner, pp. 132-33. New York: Simon and Schuster, 1950.
    States of Hauptmann, "No particular importance can be attached to the plays written during the last twenty-five years of his life, and today even the bulk of his work before 1921 rings hollow outside, and apparently inside, Germany."

Grummann, Paul H. "Gerhart Hauptmann." *Poet Lore* XXII, No. II (Spring 1911): 117-27.
    Survey of the major dramas.

Hodge, James L. "The Dramaturgy of *Bahnwärter Thiel*." *Mosaic* IX, No. 3 (Spring 1976): 97-116.
    Examines the structure and symbolism of this story.

Klemm, Frederick A. "Genesis-Thanatos in Gerhart Hauptmann." *The Germanic Review* XVII, No. 4 (December 1942): 273-81.
    Traces the development of themes relating to creation and death throughout Hauptmann's work.

Knight, K. G. and Norman, F., eds. *Hauptmann Centenary Lectures.* London: University of London, 1964, 167 p.
    Essays on Hauptmann and naturalism, themes in the dramas, with two unpublished letters and a bibliography of Hauptmann in England. Critics whose work is included in this anthology are J. W. McFarlane, E. O. H. McInnes, and H. F. Garten, among others.

Lewisohn, Ludwig. "Germans: Gerhart Hauptmann." In his *Cities and Men,* pp. 121-32. New York, London: Harper & Brothers, 1927.
    Examines the artistic quality of language in Hauptmann's work.

McInnes, Edward. "The Domestic Dramas of Gerhart Hauptmann: Tragedy or Sentimental Pathos?" *German Life and Letters* n.s. XIX, No. 3 (April 1966): 190-96.
    Perceives tragedy, and not the mere character analysis seen by earlier critics, as the dominant feature of Hauptmann's domestic dramas, including *Einsame Menschen* and *Die Ratten.*

Mann, Thomas. In his *The Story of a Novel: The Genesis of "Doctor Faustus",* pp. 194-200. New York: Alfred A. Knopf, 1961.*
    Personal reminiscence of Hauptmann's later years.

Osborne, John. *The Naturalist Drama in Germany.* Manchester: Manchester University Press, 1971, 185 p.*
    Traces the evolution of naturalism and its artistic theories, including analyses of Hauptmann's major naturalistic dramas. Approximately half of this book is devoted to Hauptmann.

Salpeter, Harry. "Gerhart Hauptmann." *The Bookman* (New York) LXVII, No. 6 (August 1928): 662-66.
    Overview of Hauptmann's life and work, contending that his art is essentially autobiographical.

Shaw, Leroy R. "Hauptmann's Suspended Present." *Texas Studies in Literature and Language* II, No. 3 (Autumn 1960): 378-82.
    Distinguishes between Hauptmann's early period of naturalistic *drama* and his later works of naturalistic *tragedy,* examining the author's use of time in the plays of each era.

Sinden, Margaret. *Gerhart Hauptmann: The Prose Plays.* Toronto: University of Toronto Press, 1957, 238 p.
    Critical survey of the prose plays, which the critic considers are among those works where "Hauptmann's truest insight into the wonders of the universe is to be found."

Wahr, F. B. "Theory and Composition of the Hauptmann Drama." *The Germanic Review* XVII, No. 3 (October 1942): 163-73.
    Examines similarities of form in Hauptmann's works.

Weisert, John Jacob. *The Dream in Gerhart Hauptmann.* New York: King's Crown Press, 1949, 120 p.
    Traces "development of Hauptmann's interest in dream phenomena" in his life and in his work.

Juan Ramón Jiménez (Mantecón)

1881-1958

Spanish poet.

Jiménez is considered one of Spain's finest contemporary lyric poets and an important influence on Spanish letters. His earliest poems, published when he was seventeen, drew the attention of the noted poets Rubén Darío and Francis Villaespesa, who invited Jiménez to join them and other modernists in the reform of Spanish poetry. Jiménez eventually moved beyond Darío's influence, forging his own poetic style. His poetry provided a link between the modernists and younger Spanish poets, such as Garcia Lorca, Rafael Alberti and Jorge Guillén.

Jiménez, born of wealthy parents, was raised in the small town of Moguer in the rich Andalusian countryside. He was a small youth of delicate health, and suffered repeated illnesses. His spirit, however, was bright. It was the sudden death of his father, when Jiménez was eighteen, that marked a change in his personality. From that time forward he struggled with a deep melancholy and a recurring obsession with death, both of which are evident in his verse.

Stylistically, Jiménez's writings fit into three periods. His earliest period includes poetry written in an impressionistic vein, with a florid and overwrought style. Much of the luster found in these early works reflects the poet's love for his native Andalusia. *Almas de violeta* and *Ninfeas*, representative of this stage, also evidence the influence of Darío.

Jiménez's second period is more abstract and is marked by the poet's search for "la poesia desnuda" (naked poetry), or pure poetry. These works are characterized by an emergent pantheism, the use of free verse, and a simpler, refined form. *Diario de un poeta recién casado*, his most important collection of this time, was occasioned by his voyage to America where he was to be married. Using free verse for the first time, Jiménez portrays in this work, through the symbol of the ocean, his struggle to let go of the securities of his past and to open himself to love. The popular and often-translated *Platero y yo (Platero and I)*, regarded as a modern classic, is also representative of this period. It is the simple story of the poet as a boy traveling with his donkey over the familiar landscape of Andalusia. Throughout this period Jiménez, generally a man of silence and solitude, was active publicly. He founded or edited a number of short-lived poetry reviews, which were especially significant for publishing the early works of such noted poets as Pedro Salinas, Rafael Alberti, and Jorge Guillén.

Jiménez's third period is best described as metaphysical. With the onset of the Spanish civil war, Jiménez, like many of his contemporaries, went into self-imposed exile. The mood of this period was expressed in the intensity of his poetry. Though his range of poetry was limited, focusing particularly on nature, it was continually deepening. He consistently strove, for example, through constant revision, for precision and purification. Jiménez had been preoccupied with God all of his life. "Poetry," he said to Ricardo Gullón, "is an attempt to approximate the absolute by means of symbols."

This lifelong search through poetry, the writing of which he considered a religious task, culminated in his powerful spiritual testament, *Animal de fondo (Animal of Depth)*. A sea voyage from Buenos Aires provided the experience that proved to be a "moment" when he sensed a divine and universal consciousness. *Animal of Depth* is an exultation, a hymn in celebration, a synthesis of this "aesthetic mysticism."

Jiménez's reputation as one of Spain's greatest contemporary writers is based on his dedication to poetry, his continual innovations, and his introduction of modern symbolism to Spanish poetry. In recognition of his contribution, Jiménez was awarded the Nobel Prize in literature in 1956.

PRINCIPAL WORKS

Almas de violeta (poetry) 1900
Ninfeas (poetry) 1900
Arias tristes (poetry) 1903
Pastorales (poetry) 1905
Laberinto (poetry) 1913
Platero y yo (prose poem) 1914
   [*Platero and I*, 1956]
Estío (poetry) 1915

Diario de un poeta recién casado (prose and poetry)
   1917; also published as *Diario de poeta y mar,* 1948
Poesías escojidas (poetry) 1917
Sonetos espirituales (poetry) 1917
Piedra y cielo (poetry) 1919
Segunda antoljía poética (poetry) 1920
Belleza (en verso) (poetry) 1923
Poesía (en verso) (poetry) 1923
Poesía en prosa y verso (poetry) 1923
Españoles de tres mundos (poetry) 1942
La estación total (poetry) 1946
Animal de fondo (poetry) 1949
Fifty Spanish Poems (poetry) 1950
Selected Writings (poetry) 1957
Three Hundred Poems, 1903-1953 (poetry) 1962

AUBREY F. G. BELL   (essay date 1925)

The chief Modernist poet of Spain, Don Juan Ramón Jiménez, evidently has the gift of infuriating some critics and of fascinating others. But studying his work impartially nearly ten years after the death of Rubén Darío, when modernism is seen to have been a passing craze, the critic finds that there is something in Señor Jiménez' poetry that endures. (p. 208)

As a rule [Señor Jiménez' body of verse] maintains an astonishingly high level. The poems in which he has employed rhyme show that his poetry might gain rather than lose by its more frequent use; for this poet, who is so careless of rhyme, and sometimes of rhythm, and goes out of his way to cut a word or a phrase in twain and introduces far sought newfangled words into his verse, is very quiet and natural in the use of rhyme, when he does use it, while the rhyme helps to shape and concentrate what might tend to be the indefinite flow of his verse. He would appear to have a keener sense of sound and colour in all their shades and subtleties than of definite shape; he is the impressionist painter rather than the sculptor, and his poetry is in fact an ever-flowing though transparent stream; it is perhaps interesting to notice that his favourite flowers are the scented flowers formed not of bold petals but of a hundred tiny flowerets: heliotrope, lilac, verbena, jasmine, whin, honeysuckle. Yet, in this minute and constant flow, how delicate is his ear for the pattern and construction of the verse! (pp. 209-10)

His poetry is like a nocturne of Chopin played in the twilight, full of faint sounds and rustling silences and from time to time revealing some concrete lovely presence, the gleam of a star, the note of a bird, the mellow ringing of an Angelus bell. . . . There is more of the concrete and the substantial in his work than one might imagine. This may be seen in the delicious prose of his *Platero y Yo,* in which poetry and reality are mingled without the omission of common things and with a charm and precision of words which produce definite pictures. (p. 210)

His soul is vexed with immortal longings (*afanes imposibles; anhelos de cien cosas que no fueron*); he searches for the "hidden beauty" of things; and his *poemas mágicos y dolientes* are filled with elegiac regret, until his song becomes the echo of a song rather than the song itself—or, as it were, a shadow cast before. . . . Few poets have shown a

more exquisite sensibility towards the moods of Nature; but if the Nature described is a reflection of the poet's spirit, . . . it also dwells concretely in his mind and heart. Nature, such as he sees it, and his soul are one. . . . (pp. 212-14)

It is perhaps scarcely necessary to remark that this Nature in which the poet's soul merges itself and which merges itself in the poet's soul until they are completely identified, is not the whole of Nature but a limited if exquisite view of it. The poet may declare that the dawn is in his breast and the sunset in his back, but mountain ranges and rushing torrents and sounding forests are more discomfortable guests; the *desgarradura* would have to be even greater if they are to be harboured. These wilder aspects of Nature have no echo in his lyrics. (p. 214)

His Nature is confined chiefly to gardens and scenes such as Watteau painted. He himself describes the poems of *Laberinto* as "scenes and editions of a literary Watteau, a little more subjective and less optimistic than his pictures." (p. 215)

Señor Jiménez is not a poet to be imitated; one hopes that he will not found a school. He himself changes and develops and has now shed most of his modernist trappings. Mannerisms matter but little when there is a fundamental sincerity; Señor Jiménez is sincere and a true poet. His aim is to be simple and spontaneous, as he has recently informed us. His poetry holds a high place in the Spanish literature of the Twentieth Century and it will retain it. Señor Jiménez repeats himself, quotes himself, and imposes himself; the reader may at first be disconcerted and try to protest, but very soon he becomes fascinated, as a bird by a snake, and it is noticeable that the repetition of this poet's verse seems to increase its value, bringing out much that had escaped one on a first reading. (pp. 215-16)

> *Aubrey F. G. Bell, "The Modernist Invasion," in his* Contemporary Spanish Literature *(copyright © 1925 by Alfred A. Knopf, Inc.), Alfred A. Knopf, Inc., 1925, pp. 199-220.**

WALTER T. PATTISON   (essay date 1950)

Juan Ramón Jiménez has never written a long-deliberated poem with an analytical catalogue of his poetic ideas and attitudes. His failure to do so reveals much of his concept of the nature of poetry. It is an interplay between the poet's soul and reality, a flash of comprehension, a moment of ecstatic oneness with some natural beauty, a wave of emotion disclosing the essence of some thing. . . .

Since Juan Ramón Jiménez writes for "la inmensa minoría," he feels that his readers can make their way through his kingdom without a guide. Yet the fleeting, fragmentary nature of his individual works makes desirable some kind of a chart of his realm of gold. If each poem is a glimpse, what is the total vision? Only after many readings and much meditation and feeling do we get a mountain-top view over the whole area.

As we assemble the fragments, we find that Juan Ramón's attitude toward reality is fundamental to our understanding him. His reality is immensely rich in facets. Most of it—the real, or inner meanings of things—remains hidden to the eyes of the average mortal, but stands partly revealed to the eyes of the poet. . . . (p. 18)

Given the infinite variety in both reality and poetic reaction to it, it is obvious that the poet must limit himself to a part of the whole. In a general way the realities Juan Ramón Jiménez prefers are, in order of descending importance, nature, man-made things, humanity, and individuals. But each one of these categories must be limited further, for within the class the realities Juan Ramón Jiménez prefers frequently correspond to his favorite emotion—an elegaic, sweet sadness. Nature as seen through his eyes is one of gardens and parklands, usually lighted by the sunset, the moon, or the stars, where fountains and beds of flowers give a rather domestic effect, and where the strains of a Beethoven sonata come tearfully from a distant piano. Most prominent in the category of things are household objects. . . .

The love of humanity is the feeling of emotional unity with the nameless, shadowy inhabitants of the poet's world. . . .

Juan Ramón is naturally most interested in the more gifted, more poetic element of humanity. . . .

The vagueness which characterizes humanity is also typical of the few individuals appearing in Juan Ramón's poems. The bodiless spirit of the person and the poet's emotional reaction to it are the all-important things. A woman momentarily glimpsed, whose image and impression the memory cannot quite bring into sharp focus; another woman whose spirit captures the quintessence of springtime, such are the women in Juan Ramón's lyrics. Most of them are not only individuals but symbols of the highest beauty of nature. Men, except as decorative figures—the shepherd, the ox-driver—are practically never found. The one ever present individual is the poet himself.

Although these favorite elements of reality can never be thoroughly understood, the poet's love for them can lead to an ecstatic oneness with nature, a mystic exaltation in which comprehension or knowledge is superseded. . . . (p. 19)

Juan Ramón's attitude parallels that of Christian mystics point for point. The one great difference is that the poet substitutes an infinite, incomprehensible reality for an infinite, incomprehensible God. Not that Juan Ramón's reality is devoid of God, for the contemplation of nature's beauties is frequently fused with an awareness of the divine presence. . . . The difference lies rather in emphasis; for Juan Ramón's thoughts are oriented toward things of this world while the mystic usually disdains terrestial things to concentrate all his intensity on the Creator alone. . . .

Juan Ramón's first great contribution to the modern concept of poetry is precisely the idea of the poet as a mystic of nature. The idea was already implicit in Bécquer, but Juan Ramón gave it its complete development and modern emphasis. In this century most Spanish poets have followed his lead.

But Juan Ramón goes on to even more radical concepts and attitudes in which he leaves the mystics behind and joins hands with the exponents of the subconscious mind. . . .

Poetry, we have said (for Juan Ramón), is an interplay between the poet's soul and reality. The sense impression received from reality provokes an emotion, which emotion then goes forth from the poet to become part of the original object. A sunset seen with the eyes may arouse a vague, elegiac, sweet sadness, which mood, working outward,

becomes the "meaning" of the sunset. But sometimes the poet's subconscious reactions carry him above and beyond this normal process. The sense impression may stir all sorts of subconscious associations so that the emotion which goes forth from the poet toward the object is greater than the emotion inherent in it. The poet is a creator (through his wealth of subconscious "associations"), and his contribution to the poem (or poetic ecstasy, which results in the poem) is at times even greater than the contribution of reality. (p. 20)

Every poem of Juan Ramón Jiménez gives evidence of his skill at noting down the emotional-realistic aspect of things. . . .

The poet, utilizing his poetic gift and struggling with his poetic task, catches and transmits fleeting beauty to less artistic souls. . . . But since he can at least partially note down beauty—unique and fleeting though it may be—not only for his contemporaries but also for people in ages to come, the poet imparts immortality to that beauty. What he catches remains for posterity; what he fails to catch is lost forever. (pp. 21-2)

> *Walter T. Pattison, "Juan Ramón Jiménez, Mystic of Nature," in* Hispania *(© 1950 The American Association of Teachers of Spanish and Portuguese, Inc.), Vol. XXXIII, No. 1, February, 1950, pp. 18-22.*

GERALD BRENAN (essay date 1951)

Jiménez's first style in poetry can be seen in the three books of verse that he brought out between 1903 and 1905 —*Arias Tristes, Jardines Lejanos* and *Pastorales.* They consist of short poems in octosyllabic metre in which a state of mind is expressed through a landscape. Frequently this landscape is an Andalusian garden and more often than not the moon is shining. There is an air of autumnal vagueness and melancholy: we note the influence of Verlaine's early lyrics and occasionally of [Francis Jammes and Jules Laforgue] but these influences have been well assimilated through the choice of a classical Spanish metre. Jiménez did not borrow rhythms and cadences from the French Symbolist poets as Rubén Darío had done: rather he was writing the same sort of poetry, but with a smaller and more delicate gamut. (p. 436)

In his next volume but one, *Baladas de Primavera,* his manner is firmer and there is an invigorating influence that comes from the popular song-books of the sixteenth century and from children's ditties. . . . Then in his next two books, *Elegías* and *La Soledad sonora* . . . , Jiménez leaves the short measures for alexandrines. Here one sometimes feels the touch of Mallarmé. . . . After this the poetry gets richer, more ornate and coloured: the metaphors develop, but the influences are classical Spanish rather than French and there is little trace of Baroque. Among the best of these poems are the sonnets, which are in the condensed manner of the sixteenth century. But one begins, among all this poetical paraphernalia of birds and roses, to feel a certain weariness, in spite of the continual attention given by the poet to the discovery of new epithets and images and of the artistic perfection of the verse.

Then in 1916 his style changes. He speaks of this in a poem numbered 411 in his *Anthology.* His first verses, he says, had all the charm of innocence. Then he began to dress them, to load them with jewels as a queen and to find that he secretly detested them. A moment came when he could bear them no longer, and he began to undress them. Now they were completely naked. . . . What this means is that in 1916 Jiménez abandoned rhyme, assonance and fixed metres and began to write in *vers libre*. The aim he set himself was *depuración*, to take out of his verse everything except its pure poetic essence. This change in his method coincided with a great change in his life. He had fallen in love and his *amada* had sailed for New York; he had followed her, won her and brought her back as his wife. This is the story described in the book of verse that he published at this time, *Diario de un poeta reciencasado*.

Vers libre is a difficult form for a poet who relies upon his fine artistic sense rather than upon the strength of his poetic imagination, because it requires the abandonment of all artificial aids. Jiménez was entirely lacking in Whitman's force and rhythmic power. But he was at this time under the influence of strong feelings, and it is the new tone of seriousness that these feelings gave that raises some of these short poems to a higher level than anything he had written up to now. Particularly fine are the poems on the sea, which he was crossing in the stormy month of January. . . . (pp. 437-39)

What are we to make of this poet who seems so remote from the English scene? His early verse is all spun out of sensibility—a fine eye, a delicate ear and the passive attitude of the aesthete, savouring the poetic moments of life on his palate. Professor [J. B.] Trend has well compared these poems to the piano pieces of Debussy. His poetic philosophy at this time might be described as a sort of adolescent solipsism: the landscapes and gardens he writes about do not exist independently, but are extensions of his mind. Later this attitude is modified and he dreams of a disembodied life, fed by memory. . . . We see Juan Ramón Jiménez as a poet who lives very much on his own resources and, from the convent security of his study or sick-room, keeps at a distance that rude and disturbing thing called Life.

What distinguishes him from other poets of sensibility is the extreme self-consciousness of his artistic sense and the urge he felt not to rest on what he had done, but to advance and explore. He used his fine intelligence to organize and analyse what his sensibility gave him, and his delicate ear to fix it in flawless lines. From his first poems onwards we can watch the increasing subtlety and precision of his metaphors, just as we can with the Spanish Arab poets of the eleventh and twelfth centuries, of whom he often reminds us. In his second period we see his verse reduced largely to a texture of metaphorical expressions and allusive statements, yet, note well, metaphors which are not conceits, but which are intended to convey as simply as possible a recondite perception or experience.

In one of his later poems he asks his muse, whom typically he calls *Inteligencia*, to give him the 'exact names of things.' . . . Can we say that this request was granted? The power of naming and creating (as a younger poet, Gerardo Diego, was a few years later to assert) has hitherto been effected only through rhythm and melody. Jiménez's early poems are melodious, though their melody is often faint and has to be listened for. But the melody of his *vers libre* poems is, I would say, essentially speech melody. Their

total impression, too, is not so much of a thing caught or seen as of a state of mind in which the outside world mingles and takes part. There is a constant interchange of elements between the poet and the object. Nature appears saturated with thought. These poems seem to me therefore to represent not so much an attempt to create *things* as to seize an almost unseizable experience, and we may observe that there is a necessary correspondence between their thin, diaphanous texture—which demands an exceptionally receptive state of mind from the reader—and the abstruse, elusive character of what is conveyed. Jiménez is most decidedly one of those poets who set out to extend the limits of consciousness. In this respect we can compare much of his later work with T. S. Eliot's *Four Quartets*, although both his method and his cast of mind are entirely different. Jiménez looks out at nature to find himself: Eliot looks inward.

The last book of Jiménez's poetry that I have seen is *La Estación Total*. . . . In this he takes another step towards 'naked poetry'. In some of these poems he develops the *vers libre* themes of his 1916 volume. A very beautiful (and difficult) example of this is his poem on the Guadarrama, which he calls *Pacto primero*. Others seem to have taken shape round words, rhymes and scraps of old poetry, out of which he builds something new. The forms are more symmetrical and regular and the content very elliptical. A few of these poems are very lovely: I would single out *Cuatro* and two which copy the forms of the sixteenth-century *villancicos—Mi triste ansia* and *Viento de amor*. The latter has the *a-i* rhyming system of the Galician *cossantes*. So we see the most abstruse and recondite of modern Spanish poets returning—but how differently!—to the forms of the medieval dance poetry.

If Jiménez's position as a poet is difficult to assess, there can be no doubt about his great importance as an influence. The whole of contemporary poetry comes out of him. For some of these poets he is the continuer of the introspective and analytical verse of Bécquer: for others an experimenter in form and imagery. Again and again he has provided the themes which more forceful and exuberant poets have developed. Most indebted of all was García Lorca. One cannot read his *Romances Gitanos* without realizing that many things that one regards as characteristic of his style— rhythms, melodies, turns of phrase, uses of refrain—are derived from Jiménez's early poems. But greatly amplified. What in Jiménez is delicate and faint becomes a music of flutes and guitars in Lorca's rich, fully blooded, triumphant poetry. (pp. 441-43)

Gerald Brenan, "The Twentieth Century," in his The Literature of the Spanish People from Roman Times to the Present Day *(copyright Gerald Brenan, 1951; reprinted by permission of the author and his agents C & J Wolfers Ltd), Cambridge University Press, 1951, pp. 417-54.**

CLAUDIO GUILLEN   (essay date 1957)

No one questions the extraordinary historical importance of Jiménez. He is not only the dean of the Hispanic poets, but the pioneer and the source of all those who wrote in the Spanish tongue after him. Many readers believe his works to be unequaled in their precision and taste, models to be admired today without any reservation. Others, on the contrary, consider his supremely delicate, supremely limited poems to be—to borrow a term from the Surrealists—a *cadavre exquis*. Juan Ramon, to those readers, is simply the master who was not only surpassed by his disciples, but obliterated by them. . . .

From 1900 to 1919 he had published nearly a book of poems a year. From then on (he was only 38) his poetic efforts consisted mainly in correcting and editing his previous works. Thus he attempted to live not for, but from his poems: to exist to *be*, in a return to romanticism, by virtue of the vital power conferred upon him by his own words. . . .

In a nation where art is often associated with a kind of willful roughness, Jiménez will be remembered always for certain exceptionally "perfect" compositions. Most typical of this perfection is a form of necessarily short poem (song, lullaby, picture, emotional moment, fleeting sense-perception, etc.) where unity resides in the sensibility, the feeling or the symbol, not in the fully developed or connected succession of lyrical comments. (p. 17)

Jiménez reconciles . . . restraint and intensity: tirelessly sincere, but never given to prattling or gesticulation, he will express moments of plenitude or of rapture while preserving a muted tone, a singular poise and weightlessness. This is especially evident in his folkloric pieces, where colorful effects are shunned. Restraint is also compatible in Juan Ramon with the boldness of the experimenter. Here his role as an innovator must be recalled once more, for he never ceased to invent, to search for that straightest line between the emotion and the reader which would be the purest form. He has been, like Gide, always a young poet, for whom every book was a beginning. Hence his considerable variety and—to mention a final wedding of opposition—the fusion of it with a remarkable singleness of intent and style. Jiménez concentrates in each poem on almost a single device, plays but one of the many strings on his instrument at a time. If one virtue or one method may be considered characteristic of his poetry, it is that of concentration. Concentration on the indispensable effect, surrounded by silences, concentration above all on the single word, on the force and the magic of which language is capable. (pp. 17-18)

I have underlined the significance in Jiménez of the creation of a language, of a poetic instrument, because I believe this to be his principal contribution—not only to art in general, but to the poets who followed him. It is true that Juan Ramon's works, unlike those of the school of Rubén Dario, are not without spiritual content and intensity (his vision is basically a kind of exasperated romanticism). But his *originality* is chiefly formal or stylistic. He did not attain the depth of Antonio Machado, nor the coherence and the breadth of the poets of Lorca's generation. His quest and his richness are linguistic, and in this fact—that he put old wine in new bottles—one may find the explanation of his equivocal destiny. Without him the instrument would not have existed from which a Lorca, a Salinas, an Aleixandre wrested vast poetic worlds (such as Lorca's tragic one). Yet his better poems reached verbal heights which are permanently admirable for their elegance and their purity. (p. 18)

Claudio Guillen, "The Problem of Juan Ramón Jiménez," in The New Republic *(reprinted by permission of* The New Republic; © *1957 The New Republic, Inc.), Vol. 137, No. 26, December 16, 1957, pp. 17-18.*

GRACIELA P. NEMES (essay date 1961)

[Juan Ramón Jiménez] and his wife became collaborators in the translation of Tagore's works. (p. 319)

Tagore and Jiménez were one in sensitivity and one in lyrical expression.

In a comparative study of these two poets the easiest and most direct method is to notice the parallelism between Tagore's *The Crescent Moon* and Jiménez's *Platero and I.* Both works are spiritual biographies, both works contain a philosophy of life based on simplicity, both enhance the lesser people and the commonplace through an attitude toward nature and people, which speaks with the greatest tenderness that exists in the hearts of men. However their approach to the subject is different. Tagore enters the inner life, his life, by way of a child's soul, Jiménez by way of Moguer, his native town.

The coincidences are many. In Tagore's work there is a shaggy-headed banyan tree. . . . In Jiménez's work, he, the child, also had a tree, an acacia ("The Tree in the Yard"). It was the first source of his poetry, as Tagore's banyan tree had been to the Hindu child. (pp. 319-20)

Tagore's *The Crescent Moon* and Jiménez's *Platero and I* are poetic interpretations of reality, a reality which reappears later in life in other works of biographical character. . . . The Indian poet relishes the childhood memory of the view from the terrace, the Spanish poet the enchantment in childhood of the view from the roof. (p. 320)

Besides those works of Tagore and Jiménez reminiscent of their childhood and early youth, there are other works which merit comparison. They are of a more complex nature as they project the "Inner Self" of the poets in a mystical way which at times coincides in expression and thought. There is, in the literary production of Jiménez after 1916, a new poetic vision, a mystical attitude toward his artistic endowments, and a subsequent exalted satisfaction in his poetic creation much like that which prevails in Tagore's works. (p. 321)

Three important topics in [Tagore's] *Gitanjali* can be found in Jiménez's works after 1916: a depuration of the verse, an awareness of his other self, and a great concern with the time devoted to artistic creation. In a metaphor, Tagore speaks thus of his new poetry:

> My song has put off her adornments. She
> had no pride of dress and decoration. . . .

Jiménez puts forth his famous concept of "naked poetry" in *Eternidades,* in 1916, in a metaphor which refers also to having put off the adornments. . . . The concept of "naked poetry" became the best known feature of Jiménez's works. (pp. 321-22)

Artistic creation became in Jiménez as in Tagore, the prime source of delight. Like Tagore, Jiménez learned to trust his "Inner Self." He first had worshipped beauty as an outsider, and through beauty he had discovered the key to Being. . . .

Having attained mystical union with creation, they check their ledgers and report their findings with the same metaphor, "the fruit." (p. 322)

In one of his aphorisms Jiménez said: "An Easterner and a Westerner I am, Alas! For me there is no way out!" . . .

His pronouncement had to do with his poetic personality. Although greatly indebted to the West for certain disciplines of his art, Jiménez was, nevertheless, breaking away from Western orthodoxy. Of Tagore it can also be said that he was breaking away, but from Eastern orthodoxy. (pp. 322-23)

Jiménez defined poetry as "all essential feelings related to beauty," adding that "one who lives in poetry is living in God." To the end of his life he adhered to this belief. Like Tagore, Jiménez cultivated the emotions while cultivating the intellect and the will, thus developing his nobler desires through emotions of beauty which were voiced in his poetry. It is not strange, then, to find in the works of Tangore, a great poet of the East, and of Jiménez, a great poet of the West, so many coincidences in expression and thought. (p. 323)

> Graciela P. Nemes, "Of Tagore and Jiménez," in Books Abroad (copyright 1961 by the University of Oklahoma Press), Vol. 35, No. 4, Autumn, 1961, pp. 319-23.

HOWARD T. YOUNG   (essay date 1964)

[Jiménez'] world of refinement and sensitivity is ultimately a spiritual world that exists for its own sake. We are so used to demanding practicality that we forget the world of pure essence. But Jiménez was wedded to it. After an early affair with *modernismo* and the *albo lirio* (white lily) of sensualism, he devoted his entire energy and talent to exploring the essence of poetry. In the end, this led him to a consideration of the creative process itself, and much of his best final poetry is a metaphor of the creative human mind.

His preciosity, especially apparent in translation which cannot preserve the niceties of distinction, is something we must put up with, like Wordsworth's lapses of taste or Yeats's private cosmogony. For Jiménez at his best is a very great poet—one who expanded the limits of the Spanish language and created a new idiom. (p. 78)

The approach to this vast canon, however, can be facilitated by dividing it into three main periods: melancholy impressionism; the search for beauty and the struggle with time; the encounter with absolute beauty or eternity. In distinguishing these epochs, we must keep in mind, as he did, the ultimate goal of his labors: the need for an absolute experience, the desire that his total human nature should transcend the limits of time and space. (p. 80)

Water Lilies (Ninfeas) and *Violet Souls (Almas de violeta)* . . . are his first books. They are strongly marked by Rubén Darío's *modernismo,* as well as a general sense of *fin de siècle* malaise. He quickly freed himself of this influence, exhibited most disagreeably in a cloying morbidity, and began the characteristic effort to refine his perceptions, all the while experimenting with new techniques. In *Pastorales,* . . . he also broke with the forms of *modernismo* and used the traditional ballad meter. Despite uncertainty and a return to despondency under the influence of Baudelaire in *Laberinto* . . . , he reached the height of his first period with *Spiritual Sonnets (Sonetos espirituales* . . .) and *Summer (Estío* . . .). During these years, his reading consisted mainly of Bécquer, the *romances,* the French symbolists, and Heine.

The year 1916 is one of change, marking the beginning of Jiménez' intermediate period. He went to America and married there. His encounter with the sea produced a great restlessness which, in turn, resulted in one of the most remarkable books of Spanish poetry, first published . . . under the title of *Diary of a Newly Married Poet (Diario de un poeta recién casado)*, and republished . . . as *Diary of Poet and Sea (Diario de poeta y mar)*, a title which more aptly describes the contents. (pp. 80-1)

The third period embraces his residence in America, occasioned by the Spanish Civil War. His desire for perfection finally led him to a highly particular form of mysticism, his logical goal from the outset. The best Spanish poetry is fated to be mystical, with or without a god, he averred in 1941. During an ocean voyage to Buenos Aires . . . , he wrote *Animal of Depth (Animal de fondo)*, a triumphant celebration of his life's work. (p. 81)

[Juan Ramon's early volumes from his melancholy impressionist period] exaggerate his morbidity and rejection of society. Yet, although we react unfavorably to the excessive preoccupation with the demise of children and virgins, we can also see therein the kernel of a basic theme: the fate of beauty. And if his petulant espousal of sadness leaves us initially unmoved, we soon find it woven with genuine feeling into the remainder of his youthful works. Melancholy was a ruling emotion of his life and not a mere pose. He did not begin to transcend it until middle age and did not triumph over it until his final years. (p. 83)

Nature, in particular, gave him cause for sweet sadness, and his early contemplation of the natural world was the beginning of a long, complex, and loving relationship. He took from nature nearly all the metaphors and images which embellish his art. (p. 84)

The marked sensuality of Jiménez' early poetry was soon suppressed or, more accurately, channeled into his consuming desire to transcend. (p. 92)

Jiménez was partially guided in his search for the absolute by the conviction that there did exist a platonic archetype, an ideal norm which he could know by means of poetry. (pp. 94-5)

A favorite symbol for the "unique norm" is the rose. The poet himself must become, like the rose, "all essence" . . . , in order to apprehend perfection; his soul is a branch, constantly ready to sustain the perfect rose. Once he has prepared himself, his creation will be "the norm of roses." . . . A second common symbol of perfection is the star, variously presented as light or gold; it is the medium by which his soul is purified. Finally, woman symbolizes the incarnation of beauty. In *The Total Season (La estación total)* . . . he acclaimed his trinity: "woman, star, and rose, / the three most beautiful forms in the world." (p. 95)

The style of his early poetry was inspired by French symbolism and impressionism. To this effect, he employed elliptical phrases, made liberal use of questions, and was fond of interpolation. His general plan was to comply with the injunction of the symbolists: suggest rather than state. (p. 97)

Another technique inherited from symbolism is synaesthesia, the association of disparate senses. . . . The indiscriminate mixture of the senses is part of the effort to savor all possible angles of an experience; eyes that hear and feel, as well as see, would be the supreme endowment for a poet.

Among the early stylistic devices, the one with deepest implications is that of fluctuation (*vaivén*). It is also the device most constantly utilized throughout his entire work. In Jiménez' poems, everything comes and goes, nothing seems to be defined exactly in time or space (or, if it is, there is an immediate interpolation of a new aspect). Partly this is commensurate with the vague malaise, the amorphous sense of indisposition, characterizing his youth. Partly, also, it is his unwillingness to select any one experience as typical when his kaleidoscope shows him literally thousands of other brilliant patterns. Thus, things are always both near and far away, great and small, ethereal and concrete. But this apparent imprecision is in reality a mania for exactness and responds, as do all the impressionistic techniques, to his wish to describe all aspects of reality and thereby transcend it. (pp. 98-9)

In order to pin down this hovering presence, to capture the subtle (but perhaps mocking) laughter, style would have to become an overwhelming preoccupation. He was ready to succumb to the passion for the "exact word." (p. 99)

Two factors were responsible for transforming Jiménez' poetry [into the poetry of his middle period]. The first was his marriage. (p. 100)

The second factor that caused a change was the sea. . . . The record of [his ocean] voyage was first called the *Diary of a Newly Married Poet* (*Diario de un poeta recién casado*), but in 1948 was changed to *Diary of Poet and Sea*. Although love plays a significant part in the book, it is subordinate to the experience of the ocean, which is the leitmotif. (p. 101)

Travel is an unsettling experience for the sensitive and meditative soul. Having thought a great deal about time, space, and reality, the voyager suddenly discovers himself in the grip of what was heretofore only a concept. Thrust upon him in all its force, literally clamoring for clarification, is the puzzle of the true nature of the relationship between man and the world. Since he was constantly preoccupied with such relationships, Jiménez found the very depths of his nature bestirred by this ocean voyage.

The sea, therefore, became a riddle in creativity: how to incorporate it into his aesthetic outlook and thereby account for it in terms of his longing for spirituality. The immediate attraction was balanced by an aversion, for the sea was coldly and vastly independent, not sounding with the sweet chords of nature he had heard in his Spanish landscapes. In the end, he apprehended the image of his own mind in the ocean's rapidly changing, yet fixed, nature. Its fateful mutations would mould the rest of his work. (pp. 101-02)

Everything is in the sea, and yet the sea seems to be without itself, lacking identification. . . . The sensation of something so imposing, incomprehensible, and separate from himself creates one of his new preoccupations: nomenclature—the art of choosing the exact word. Neither the sea, nor the sky, as characterized by the sea, has a name. Until he can learn the proper designation he cannot make the sea his own. Baptism (or creation) is an act of identification. (p. 102)

Everything flows forth from the *Diary* like sunlight from its source, bathing the ensuing books in a brilliant new light. All the revelations of the ocean voyage are intensely pur-

sued. At this time also, the incessant correction, or re-creation, of past work begins. (p. 107)

In this middle period, that unreasonable desire to go forth from himself, which he had perceived one night at sea, became more and more dominant. . . . (p. 111)

At certain moments, he felt an urge to become part of the unquestionable existence of sky and leaves and earth, but his sense of his own identity was so sharp that one feels he lacked the true pantheist's willingness to surrender himself. . . . (p. 112)

With his environment exploding in violence [the Spanish Civil War] and the disquieting experience of travel forced upon him again, Jiménez turned to his final phase, or, as he baptized it, his "third road," notable for the successful conclusion of his siege of beauty and the achievement of the unity he so faithfully sought. . . .

The Total Season (*La estación total*), comprising verse written from 1923 to 1936, is another transitional book. . . . (p. 116)

The "total center" houses the chief themes of his work—love, poetry, woman, and death. Brought together they provide a new awareness of the world, and Jiménez is quick to use "awareness" (sometimes called "loving awareness") as a synonym for the "total center." All elements and ideas flow inward now into the receptacle of mind. The formula *poetry equals spirit* is about to be established. . . . (p. 118)

[Although] Jiménez forever sought [mystic] experiences, he very much wanted to keep one foot on earth; accordingly, he was not tempted to make the classical mystic denunciation of mundane matters. Instead, he tried to enrich the here and now of existence, to bring to his point in space and time an aroused and loving awareness. Only then, in accordance with his last definition of poetry, could he raise the personal to the universal. (p. 119)

The publication of *Animal of Depth (Animal de fondo)* . . . marks Jiménez' joyful acclamation of mysticism as the final end of poetry. The book, which appeared in a bilingual French and Spanish edition, is both a spiritual autobiography, recapitulating his career in terms of the need "to depart without reason" that he first perceived during the ocean voyage to meet his bride, and a fusion of his poetic ideals in a new sense of creative unity with the world. (p. 125)

Animal of Depth contains no abrupt break with the past. What is new is the shout of joy, the exultation that tugs at the reader. At the pinnacle of his years, Jiménez saw the labor of a lifetime finally resolved, and wrote his first book in which there is not a trace of despondency nor a touch of shadow. From the first word "transparency" to the last word "air," everything is bathed in light. . . . (p. 126)

In *Animal of Depth,* he coined a new word—*cuerpialma,* bodysoul—to describe the intimacy between matter and spirit, or, as he called it, the encounter of reality and its image. Precisely because he refused to discard the root element of the body, he can never be accepted as an orthodox religious mystic. The flesh sheltering his spirit is fully recognized. . . . (p. 130)

Jiménez, in his challenge to the soul to find a better house than the body—*his* body—is raising a unique cry, one that stamps his entire work.

The import of the title can now be appreciated—*Animal of Depth,* that is, a human being of earth and dust but containing also a deep well of light. . . . (p. 132)

> Howard T. Young, "Juan Ramón Jiménez: The Religion of Poetry," in his The Victorious Expression: A Study of Four Contemporary Spanish Poets (copyright © 1964 by the Regents of The University of Wisconsin), University of Wisconsin Press, 1964, pp. 75-135.

PAUL R. OLSON   (essay date 1967)

[There is important] evidence offered in the thought and work of a writer like Juan Ramón Jiménez that the pursuit of pure poetry—poetry in its authentic being—leads itself to a consideration of the questions of first philosophy. So far as intellectual disciplines are concerned, Jiménez's area of activity was almost exclusively literary, and unlike [Antonio] Machado, he never undertook any systematic study of philosophy. . . . (p. vii)

[There is] a particular value in the study of Jiménez's work for what it reveals about the essence of all poetry, the relation of poetic essence to essence generally, and of both of them to time. (p. viii)

A large part of Jiménez's contribution to twentieth century poetry is in what he has shown us about the very nature of the poetic phenomenon, so that we have received from him as readers a fuller understanding of the whole of poetic literature, while poets coming after him have been enabled to perceive more clearly the basic goals of their art. (p. 5)

One of the primary characteristics of the poetry of Juan Ramón is . . . its temporality, by which it expresses, with striking profundity of intuition, the perpetual mutability and elusiveness of all beloved objects. This quality is a constant in the whole of his work, but perhaps it is most immediately striking in his First Period, previous to the *Diario de un poeta recién casado.* . . . (p. 9)

Change, movement, and the lack of fixed forms—all are the measure of temporality, and in Jiménez's early poetry the qualities of mutability, errancy, and transience are suggested in countless details: scenes set in the transitional seasons of spring and fall or at the transitional hours of dawn and dusk; an abundance of delicate, 'transitional' colors—mauve, rose, *mate,* or unique shades like "a noncolor, almost green." Temporality is suggested too by the constant flow of water in fountains and arroyos, by the music which wanders through the night, and by the fact that objects are so frequently seen in the perspective of flight, so that their only visible facet is the obverse. In all of these details, and many more, the poetry of Jiménez displays the marked temporal accent which Machado regarded as definitive in distinguishing all true poetry from rhymed logic.

In addition, however, to the quality of temporality, and often concomitant with it, this poetry also contains with great frequency a note of quietude, of contemplative ecstasy expressive of the longing for the eternal which may be equated with Machado's 'imperative to essentiality.' (pp. 11-12)

As a profoundly contemplative and lyrical poet, Jiménez doubtless tends very strongly to evoke the mood of ecstasy, and the movement of narrative or discursive language is almost wholly absent from his poetry. Within his apparently static images, however, there can be felt the vital palpitation which is nothing other than the rhythmic flow of time itself.

Certainly the antivital implications of a pure stasis were evident to Juan Ramón, and he constantly sought to retain within the static moment the kinetic qualities of life itself. The ideal, as he expressed it in an aphorism of his *Etica estética,* was "An ecstasy which does not kill what is alive. Anxious longing and pursuit and even falling back in failure are aspects of human experience which can be preserved in their authentic reality only if their intrinsic temporality is preserved as well, and although in Jiménez's later years the moments when his poetry expresses the joy of possession become increasingly frequent, the long period which preceded these moments produced a poetry expressive chiefly of the pursuit of objects of beauty which are themselves in constant flight through time. The dynamics of desire within the poet and of elusiveness within its objects are, like the dynamics of life itself, essential to each of them, and Jiménez strives to preserve these dynamics in an eternal—but not purely static—perception of the essences which transcend and survive temporal existence. (pp. 13-14)

[For] Jiménez eternity and the essences within it are the permanent realities which survive the passing of every moment, every being, every *thing,* and which forever *are* because they once have been.

Man, of course, can perceive these realities only in memory, and for that very reason Jiménez could at one moment express his eagerness for the present moment to pass in order that its essence might become the possession of memory. (pp. 15-16)

Of principal interest to us [in *Piedra y cielo*] is the fact that the poem expresses the intuition that produced a complete reversal in the poet's attitude toward the past. Beginning with the assumption that the passing of the present and its experience into the past constitutes a transition from being into non-being, he suddenly sees that remembered experience is greater than present experience, for it is as memory that an experience triumphs over the passing of time and becomes eternal. Indeed, as Jiménez concludes in the final lines, it is only by 'dying' (that is, moving into the past), that the experience of the present moment and the self which is the subject of that experience really begin to 'be,' to 'have essence.' (p. 17)

The world of created names, which is the world of poetry, survives the passing of love and life and beauty because, in the first instance, the entities of which it is constituted have at least the possibility of preservation in their empirical existence beyond the lives of their creators. But, in a profounder sense, that world is eternal because behind the empirical form of every word, every 'name,' stands the phenomenon of meaning, which is the essence of the objects to which it refers and is timeless—in effect, eternal—because experience reveals that it can and does survive the passing of both its *signifiants* and its referends.

The idea that linguistic meaning, the psychic content of any verbal artifact, is eternal and independent of the fate of the artifact as an empirical entity is fully developed in the first poem in *Belleza.* . . . (p. 19)

When Jiménez writes that only names will remain, he clearly is looking beyond their empirical entities to those essences. This, indeed, was his constant tendency in all his efforts at *depuración* and the improvement of poems through revision (reliving, he called it) of form so as to make it as transparent as possible and ultimately to disappear. (p. 20)

For Jiménez, it is because objects and their names are regarded with love that they contain an infinite depth of meaning, and it is this infinity which gives them the quality of eternity. (p. 22)

To call a thing eternal-for-an-instant, however, is to speak in a paradox, and we thus have here an example of one type of paradox ... constituting a principal source of affective and logical tension within [Jiménez's] poetry. The only possible conceptual resolution of the paradox is to see the eternity of the instant as an infinity of depth, a dimension which intersects the linear successiveness of time at every moment. This depth is, then, the *qualitas* of the moment, that is, its essence, and therefore the paradox of the eternal instant is clearly a reflex of the primary paradox of temporality and essentiality.

Another frequent paradox in Jiménez is that of the synthesis of a concept of motion with one of quietude or rest. In the early Juan Ramón, whose verses are so markedly colored by the Verlainean tone, the principal image of this paradox is the fountain. . . . (pp. 22-3)

The diamond of water, combining a gemlike permanence with eternal motion, is, then, a perfect icon of the synthesis of contemplative stasis and vital kinesis, that is, of essentiality and temporality.

In his later years, Jiménez gave this phenomenon the name *éstasis dinámico,* and he used it on more than one occasion to express his concepts of art and poetry. (p. 24)

Concepts of dynamism and motion suggest, in the first instance, movement in space, but obviously temporal motion is always implicit in them. In the poetry of Juan Ramón, the latter concept is actually the primary one. If for Aristotle time is the 'number of movement,' for Jiménez motion is, above all, the measure of time, and therefore this second paradox is also a clear analogue of the basic one of essentiality and temporality. 'Dynamic ecstasy' is, then, simply Juan Ramón's way of saying both 'time within essence' and 'essence within time,' and in so far as it is a principle of poetic art, it is strikingly similar to Machado's definition of poetry as "the essential word in time."

A third type of paradox is that found in the deliberate juxtaposition of concepts of magnitude and brevity. . . . (p. 25)

Perhaps the clearest expression of the paradox of magnitude in brevity in the work of Jiménez is in the prose poem, *Espacio.* . . . (p. 27)

In most of the poetry of the first decade of his Second Period, Jiménez took this paradox as a creative principle, and constantly sought to express a maximum of poetic sentiment with a minimum of words. (p. 28)

The principle of 'the greatest in the least' may not, at first, seem directly analogous to the paradoxical synthesis of temporality and essentiality, and it is, indeed, at some remove from it; but clearly the immensity which is qualitative is of the realm of essence, and literal quantitative dimensions are of the empirical world of space and time. Thus our third paradox, too, may be seen as analogous to and ulti-

mately derived from that of the tension between time and essence.

A fourth type of paradox is one borrowed directly from St. John of the Cross in the phrase *la soledad sonora,* 'the sounding solitude.' It appears, in fact, as the title of a book by Jiménez published in 1911, but the phrase itself, or a variant of it, appears elsewhere with sufficient frequency to constitute an identifiable type. (p. 30)

[As an example of the paradox, in a brief poem from *Belleza,* music] is a perceived sound which is like a bright darkness or a brightness in the dark; and this in turn is like a sound not heard.

This paradox is probably at the farthest remove of all from that of time and essence, but the analogies are still clear: in so far as it is affective form, music is of the realm of quality —that is, of essence; in so far as it is mere physical sound, it is of the realm of empirical realities, it is temporal—intrinsically so; but if the physical sound is reduced to complete silence, the essential music becomes all the more clearly audible to the spirit of the poetic idealist.

In such a reduction of the empirical reality to silence, that is, to nothing, it is a natural step to the last of the types of paradox which can be discussed here. The 'sounding silence' is, indeed, simply a special case of the more general phenomenon which may be called the paradox of 'being in non-being,' although by their very nature the two terms at times suggest a compenetration which would make them freely reversible. The starting point is the simple expression of the poet's awareness of the possible disappearance of any or all things, as they pass from being to non-being, and in this form it is not actually a paradox. (pp. 31-2)

What keeps the concept from being a paradox is the fact that being and non-being are seen as successive rather than as simultaneous. In the later poetry, however, such simultaneity becomes very striking, as in [the] lines from *Poesía* on the death of the poet's mother. . . . (p. 32)

Here, then, there occurs the ultimate possible diminution of empirical and temporal existence, as the time of a human life ends in eternal nothingness. Human time itself is continued because another life, that of the poet, continues its own existence, but nowhere is the incommensurability of time and essence felt more profoundly than in such simultaneous moments of cognition: the empirical cognition of the undeniable non-existence of a beloved being and the intuitive one of an eternal reality in that essence of personality which traditionally is called 'soul.' ... Juan Ramón believed his poetic work itself would one day be "(borrada) esistencia inmensa," an immense existence, even when canceled; which is to say, a reality in essence, not an empirical reality. (p. 33)

[The] intuition of non-being—the fear of death—was a source of extreme anguish for Jiménez, and the determinant of some of the major themes within his work. The recurring periods of emotional depression which afflicted him during his entire life, from the time of his father's death in 1900 until shortly before his death in 1958, are a clear indication of his personal inability ever to subdue definitively an anguish so basic and metaphysical. But in his poetry itself there occurs a definitive change from the bitter-sweet melancholy or dark depression of the First Period ("... and everything which is / sinks in the nameless pit of nothingness . . .'') to the serene acceptance, in the Second Period, of death and non-being as realities which are themselves a form of 'existence,' and therefore not the same as total negation. (pp. 34-5)

[Jiménez] has come to see that the presence of death and the void which men experience in their souls, that is, in their essential natures, does not effect a negation of their empirical existences, for men may think of death, yet continue to live; and therefore it is possible to conceive of the empirical reality of death, which awaits every man, as equally ineffective in negating the personal essences which we call souls. To state this concept of being in non-being and of life in death in terms of the contrast between time and essence with which this study of paradoxes began, it might be said that just as it is possible to conceive of things timeless and essential from within the flow of time—to think, that is, "the essential word in time"—, so it may be possible to conceive of the reality of a vital time within the realm of essences, the realm in which time itself is an essence.

The five types of paradox examined here can all be seen, then, to be analogous to and expressive of the basic one of temporality and essentiality, which [Antonio] Machado calls the two imperatives of poetry. By deliberately linking opposites, asserting that a thing is both minute and immense, that there are sounds both heard and not heard, that things both move and do not move, and, in patent opposition to the first principle of logic, that a thing may at the same time both be and not be—in all these ways Juan Ramón makes clear the incommensurability of the two sets of terms. He thus can save as timeless essences those values which otherwise, in the inexorable flow of time, would be carried to sure destruction. Time is, to be sure, the very substance of life (Jiménez is no less aware of this truth than is Antonio Machado), but it is also the chief problem of life, which the poet seeks to solve through his art.

It is, clearly, as metaphors that the five specific types of paradox express the fundamental one. As such they reveal a number of important aspects of the nature of the poetic art of Juan Ramón Jiménez and of the particularity he has made manifest upon the ground of the universal poetic themes of time and essence. . . . [The] poetry of Juan Ramón can be understood in its beginnings only from the point of view of its ultimate development, and the values of the latter can be fully felt only through a constant awareness of what had come before. (pp. 37-8)

> *Paul R. Olson, in his* Circle of Paradox: Time and Essence in the Poetry of Juan Ramón Jiménez *(copyright © 1967 by the Johns Hopkins Press), The Johns Hopkins University Press, 1967, 236 p.*

LEO R. COLE   (essay date 1967)

The highly subjective nature of Juan Ramón's quest for a personal god, for some ultimate deity which gives life its fourth dimension, does not allow us to support the view that he subscribed to an orthodox religious dogma such as Christianity or to a specific religious philosophy such as Buddhism. Any attempt to pigeon-hole the poet's religious concepts and philosophical outlook into a traditional framework of a clearly defined character fails to do justice to the complexity of his thought. (p. 15)

Mystic-artist as he was, he could never allow any depersonalising or codifying of what he considered to be the personal experience of communion with some hidden power. (p. 17)

The religious instinct, as reflected in Juan Ramón's poetry, is best studied from a viewpoint not too closely allied to a specific accepted code of religion. It is when placed in the framework of mysticism that much of Juan Ramón's poetry becomes pregnant with meaning and acquires value and purpose. . . .

Juan Ramón attributed some magical potency to the word in spite of the outward manifestation of apparently rational philosophising. However, whether we treat the poet as a sceptic, a non-believer, or as a deluded egoist, it remains a fact that he was constantly preoccupied, and at times obsessed, with the idea of God. It is, moreover, true to say that the far-reaching and practical consequences of this preoccupation do not lead us to suppose that the poet's ideas discredit religion in the generally accepted use of the term. (p. 18)

Even when placed in the framework of mysticism, however, Juan Ramón's ideas on religious matters are still not easily understood. Mysticism alone does not give an account of that magical potency of the word, of that tendency of mind which considers the word as an instrument in reaching the godhead. Juan Ramón was in search of a personal God who would reveal Himself through the poet's creative activity which makes the word part of the living consciousness. For an understanding of the more fundamental ideas of his religious philosophy it is necessary to view the poetry of Juan Ramón within the context of the Symbolist poetic. . . .

Juan Ramón's work, therefore, besides reflecting a search for some kind of mystical experience, may be interpreted from the aesthetic point of view as a Symbolist poetry in that it attempts to convey a spiritual essence which lies in the word after it is abstracted from the material objects of the external world to which it refers. Words, in short, are used to allude to a kind of Platonic Idea on which the concrete objects of the physical world depend for their meaning. The spiritual essence lies within the poet's consciousness as that function in it which gives names to mental images or concepts.

In Juan Ramón's poems the tangible objects of the natural world are converted to concepts in the mind with the expressed intention of using them as symbolic references to a deeper spiritual reality which bathes them in a divine splendour. The actual words and images in a poem often seem to be used, manipulated, in such a way that they become pointers indicating something more mysterious and greater than the material objects to which they might normally refer. (p. 19)

Juan Ramón's poetry gives the impression that he was for ever striving to give form and substance to something which by its very nature is elusive and eternal. (p. 20)

Juan Ramón's quest is for some elemental power in man and Nature which reveals itself through the medium of the word. Reacting against the idea of a God who manifests Himself in the human form of Jesus Christ, Juan Ramón desired a God who would reveal Himself through Nature, and more precisely, through Nature's most highly valued product, consciousness, the consciousness of each individual human being. Towards the end of his life Juan Ramón came to formulate a philosophy which might be broadly termed pantheistic. (p. 21)

An examination of Juan Ramón's poetry shows that Juan Ramón himself made no distinction between the spiritual world on the one hand, and the external physical world on the other. The ordinary everyday world perceived by the senses seems in his poetry to be a dull reflection of its real self, which is spiritual in essence. . . . God is conceived as a finality which emerges from Nature, an end product of a search which begins with the contemplation of Nature's beauty. The reality of God's existence, however, is not inferred from the reality of beauty as inherent in the external object but rather from man's consciousness of beauty. . . .

Although it is with some difficulty that we are able to distinguish Juan Ramón's aesthetics from his metaphysical and religious thinking, a study of his poetry seems to indicate that his idea of God grows out of aesthetic ideals. Juan Ramón's pursuit of perfection in poetry and his ideal of 'poesía desnuda' gradually undergo a transformation of character. This transformation, evident in the poet's thought and diction during the period 1916-1949, may be described as a process of deification of the object of striving. (p. 22)

What becomes important in Juan Ramón's poetry is the fact that the poet makes the pursuit of the ideal, which in itself remains inexpressable, the very subject-matter of his poems. The emphasis is not on the eternal truths (which are only intuitively grasped), nor indeed on their expression (since they are ineffable), but rather on the desire, the fundamental impulse, to strive towards the unattainable. Juan Ramón became less concerned with external reality as reflected in his poems and more concerned with his own creative processes, making these the subject of his poetry. After about 1916 Juan Ramón's poetry might be defined as a self-conscious poetry in that it becomes a world in its own right, self-contained and hermetically-sealed against outside influences.

Juan Ramón's intention was to catch himself on the wing and contemplate his own flight. The Symbolist tradition does not raise its whole aesthetic on Idealism, as some might argue, but on the impulse of man to believe in a spiritual reality. (p. 23)

The rose is perhaps the most complex and mysterious of all the symbols in the poetry of Juan Ramón. (p. 24)

[We] can at least state, with some degree of exactitude, that the rose, in spite of the fluctuations of meaning, remains throughout the course of Juan Ramón's poetry a symbol of some hidden spiritual reality. As Juan Ramón progresses in his poetic evolution, however, the associations of the word 'rosa' become more complex and ambiguous. In a poem entitled '¡Amor!' (in 'Poesía' . . .) it has already attained to metaphysical import in that it is a kind of microcosm of the universe and a symbol for an all-embracing love which unifies the diverse elements of the external world. . . . (p. 28)

In the poetry of Juan Ramón ideas of death, eternal life, mystic ecstasy, and God are so woven together that the reader cannot help coming to the conclusion that the poet sustains himself not with positive answers but with the knowledge that the object of his desires is wrapped in mystery. (p. 31)

Although Juan Ramón can never be sure about the mysterious object of his search, he can at least convey to us the anxiety and uncertainty engendered by the search itself. The object can, in the actual poetry, take the form of a symbol, and this symbol can in turn be understood in terms of something within our experience: beauty, perfection, love, a longing for immortality, a woman. Finally, however, the term which is found to embrace all these things is the name of God. Each name given to the object of the poet's search seems to supersede the previous name, which it takes up within itself. The fact that one name does not replace another but rather includes it as a lesser term is exemplified by the final integration of love and the poet's god in 'Animal de fondo.' . . . (p. 37)

> Leo R. Cole, "The Nature of the Search," in his The Religious Instinct in the Poetry of Juan Ramón Jiménez *(a revision of a thesis given at University of London in 1965; © Leo R. Cole), The Dolphin Book Co. Ltd., 1967, pp. 15-38.*

MICHAEL P. PREDMORE   (essay date 1970)

As one of the most famous prose poems in twentieth-century Spanish literature, *Platero y Yo* stands as an early masterpiece in the long and distinguished career of Juan Ramón Jiménez. . . . It has always been popular, even and especially among its critics, who unite unanimously in praising the artistic qualities of the work. . . .

It will be remembered that *Platero y Yo* does not tell a conventional story; there is no strict narrative ordering of events, no causal relationship linking one lyric chapter to the next. There are sudden shifts of scene and changes in time. . . . One looks in vain for the inner thread which must weave these chapters together. Yet, if *Platero* is a prose poem, if it is indeed an artistic masterpiece, there must be some principle of organization, some basis for poetic unity and wholeness. . . .

[In general,] pain and suffering (and, in some cases, death) in *Platero* are not accidental or gratuitous, but are seen as the result of specific conditions. . . . (p. 56)

[Effort] to find exceptions to the general rule, to find incidents of accidental injury or bloodletting, are rewarded, though only up to a certain point in the book. . . . Finally, as if to confirm further the fact that there is something significant and mysterious about so much bloodletting during the early chapters of *Platero*, the image of blood even invades the metaphorical description of a sunset. . . . In the same chapter, Platero goes to a pool of water to drink, and the reflected light from the sunset makes it appear as though he is drinking waters of blood. . . . It is important to note, I think, that this description is unique in the entire work. There are no other instances in which the image of blood is associated with the countless descriptions of sunset in *Platero*.

That there is violence and misery and suffering in this "Andalusian Elegy" is well-known and has been noted on a number of occasions. What concerns us for the moment is the vein of gratuitous suffering and bloodletting in *Platero*. . . . (pp. 56-7)

At this point three sets of related observations can be introduced. Each one governs both the beginning and the ending of the book. The first observation is that Platero dies in the month of February. The second is that the book begins in March, passes through the cycle of a year, and ends in April. (*Platero* begins in late winter—early spring and ends in spring.) And the third observation, which reveals the significance of the first two, is that the book begins with the introduction of butterfly imagery, the "mariposas blancas" in Ch. ii, and ends with a cluster of butterfly imagery. . . . Clearly "mariposas blancas" must be read on a symbolic level. Platero is carrying spiritual goods; he does not participate in the material and economic life of the village. The significance of the butterflies, which is a recurring image throughout the work, is established in five final chapters . . . (dealing with the death of Platero) . . . [and] (the rebirth and metamorphosis of Platero). . . . Platero's body is part of the earth and soil that is giving birth to flowers. His death contributes to life processes and becomes part of creation. In this way, Platero like the butterfly has undergone metamorphosis. It is not essential to the argument, but highly interesting as an extrinsic factor, to learn that Jiménez had planned, in a future revised version of *Platero*, to make explicit precisely what seems to be the principal expressive value of the butterfly imagery. . . . [The] answer to the poet's question when he asks if Platero still remembers him is that Platero has never really died. He is still there alive in nature, a spiritual companion of the poet as always. His soul like a butterfly has undergone metamorphosis and is attending the spiritual condition of the irises just as his decomposed heart will nurture their physical being in the next chapter. Therefore, when Platero carries symbolically white butterflies in Ch. ii, he carries within him the principle of regeneration and transformation. Platero, like all plants and creatures of the natural world, participates in nature's vital processes. (pp. 57-8)

Platero is introduced to us in the month of March, he dies in the month of February, and is resurrected again in the season of spring—through his spiritual and physical metamorphosis into yellow irises. The underlying theme, then, of *Platero y Yo*, put in its most abstract formulation, is the theme of death and rebirth as a process of metamorphosis. And the principle of metamorphosis, linked to the seasonal cycle of nature, constitutes the key structural principle.

Now the special pattern of gratuitous violence and accidental bloodletting, identified earlier, assumes its full significance. All the incidents that belong to these categories occur during the season of spring. . . . This is the seasonal sacrifice and the letting of blood that ensures the renovation of spring and the well-being of society. These events can be interpreted as the symbolic enactments of the rites of spring. The treatment of blood, it seems to me, makes a convincing case for a symbolic reading of these events as ritual elements in a great seasonal drama, in which Platero himself is the protagonist. (p. 58)

[Disparate] images such as those of blood and butterflies help account for the expressive organization of material in *Platero*. The occurrences of gratuitous bloodletting become comprehensible as ritual elements in the rebirth of spring. The pattern of butterfly images serves to express the underlying theme of death and rebirth in nature's annual cycle. The significance of these patterns is sufficient, I think, to allow us to define the general structural framework within which *Platero y Yo* must be read and interpreted. Events must be read on a symbolic level as well as a literal level. The clue to the expressive value of a given lyric chapter

should be sought in the season (and at times even in the month) in which it occurs, whether spring, summer, autumn, or winter. What is being established in each case is the emotional climate, or the climate of feeling, of each season. Events are symbolic of meanings and feelings and rhythms that belong to the different seasons of nature and that have been preserved and maintained through ancient traditions of myth and ritual. Thus the rebirth of spring, the plenitude of summer, the decline of autumn, and the death of winter are enacted and relived through every page of *Platero*. (pp. 59-60)

What strikes the attention immediately about the section devoted to summer is its extreme brevity. It contains only twelve chapters as compared to approximately forty-eight chapters devoted to spring, forty-two devoted to autumn, and twenty-three to winter. . . . This provides a dramatic example of what seems to be true of many other early works of Jiménez's poetic world. There is almost always a marked preference for the transitional seasons of spring and autumn. In *Platero y Yo*, the relevance to the theme of death and rebirth as a process of metamorphosis accounts, I think, for the greater elaboration of spring and autumn as opposed to summer and winter. (p. 60)

While butterfly imagery is perhaps the key expressive pattern, dominating as it does both the beginning and the ending of the work, it is certainly not the only pattern of its kind. . . . [The] treatment of autumn gives rise to a variety of metaphorical language, equally expressive of the theme of death and rebirth. The treatment of winter offers a significant departure from the expression of seasonal moods and feelings. . . . There is a whole series of chapters dominated by a sense of happiness and even exhilaration. . . . [We] must take into account one final significant pattern, which has been a constant up to now, throughout all of *Platero*. We note that the pattern of violence both conditioned and gratuitous, seems mysteriously to disappear, precisely in the season where one might expect its greatest concentration. It will be remembered that incidents of human cruelty and human and animal misery are regularly distributed through the pages of *Platero*. They are juxtaposed repeatedly with moments of vitality and harmony in nature. It is as though the forces of violence and harmony are constant conditions that govern all life, to a greater or lesser degree, in all seasons. . . . As the season of winter progresses, the gradual reduction of violence and sordidness becomes notable (a reduction which begins almost imperceptibly in autumn). . . . [We] suddenly realize that the gradual reduction and, finally, the elimination of all instances of cruelty and violence is a deliberate attempt to purify the environment, the climate of feeling, in which Platero is to die. Just as Platero is instructed through the season of autumn in the mysterious ways of death and rebirth, so he is especially prepared in winter, even his environment is prepared, for the final event of his death. (pp. 62-3)

A cluster of butterfly imagery symbolizes the significance of his death as a process of rebirth. And finally, at the crucial moment, the sun is shining straight overhead at noon. (p. 63)

The companions of rebirth are the forces of darkness and winter. The companions of death are the forces of light and spring. The experience of birth is long and painful; the experience of death is quick and painless. With this symmetry in mind, we can now make more fully explicit the structure of *Platero y Yo.* Earlier it was established that the principle of metamorphosis, linked to the seasonal cycle, constitutes the key structural principle. Now this can be modified and refined in a way that accounts, I think, for nearly all the expressive material, seen as an organic and unified whole. The organization of *Platero* into an expressive form involves the following sets of interrelated principles: the symbolic treatment of the sense and feeling of life embodied in the seasons of nature; the expressive manipulation and elaboration of the seasonal pattern to fit the special needs of Platero's death; the juxtaposition and distribution of expressive material in terms of life and death, light and darkness, violence and harmony, with the gradual reduction of death and violence and the triumph of life and harmony, reborn through the mysterious process of metamorphosis. (p. 64)

> *Michael P. Predmore, "The Structure of 'Platero y Yo'," in* PMLA, 85 *(copyright © 1970 by the Modern Language Association of America; reprinted by permission of the Modern Language Association of America), Vol. 85, No. 1, January, 1970, pp. 56-64.*

ÁNGEL MANUEL AGUIRRE (essay date 1970-71)

Like Rimbaud and the other French Symbolists Jiménez makes use of the symbol with a complete awareness of its effects and limitations. (p. 212)

According to Ramón de Garciasol, *Rimas,* written in France in 1902, is Juan Ramón's response to [his] encounter with the poetry of Verlaine, Rimbaud and Mallarmé. However, the influence of the French Symbolist poets on Jiménez does not end with *Rimas,* as Garciasol implies. . . . (p. 213)

Jiménez, like Rimbaud, had linguistic gifts and engaged in the creation of neologisms. (p. 216)

A point of greater interest is that of the creation of the prose poem in modern French and Spanish literatures. Frérédic St. Aubyn states that the prose poems are Rimbaud's greatest invention. . . .

In 1914 Jiménez published *Platero y yo,* a book consisting of 107 short, lyrical prose poems whose mission was to renovate Spanish prose. This symbolic book has been called a lyrical autobiography and an elegy to a donkey (who actually existed) and to the poet's past youth. Platero and the poet are the symbols of the close association that exists between man and nature. For this prose-poem genre Jiménez is undoubtedly indebted to Baudelaire and more directly to Rimbaud.

Rimbaud was a poet of revolt (social, political, psychological, metaphysical) who sought the expression of his poetry through the disordering of all the senses. He was a poet of action both physical and spiritual. Jiménez's poetry, like Mallarmé's, was rather of an interior nature, in contrast to Rimbaud's. . . .

There are many points of contact between Mallarmé and Jiménez and the most obvious one is the search for the ideal, pure poetry. Jiménez was a fastidious poet who worked on a poem for years before publishing it, and destroyed those he judged to be mediocre. He used to burn copies of his first books of poetry and worked constantly to perfect the ones that had survived. Likewise, Mallarmé

reworked and polished the already refined vocabulary of his poems. (p. 217)

[Wallace Fowlie] remarks that in Mallarmé's theory of the poet's function, poetry becomes an activity of the human mind whose nature and purpose are spiritual. The poet in this sense is both priest and god. Jiménez seems to have had the same belief and he desired to become the god of poetry, the creator of a world through the word. . . .

Like Mallarmé, Jiménez realized that there is a point when poetry passes into the realm of the unexpressed or the ineffable. (p. 218)

Both Mallarmé and Jiménez wrote occasional poetry. Among Jiménez's most famous is the poem he write upon hearing of his friend Darío's death. They felt the same concern for "pure poetry," and in an article entitled "Poesía cerrada y poesía abierta" Jiménez wrote that the most representative classical poets were Villon, Baudelaire and Mallarmé. (p. 219)

Mallarmé and Jiménez shared also the same respect for music. . . . Up to the year 1915 Jiménez is concerned with rhyme and classical molds. After that time he writes in "vers libres," probably another contribution coming from Rimbaud, who had written the first "vers libres" in 1873. When Jiménez wrote *Pastorales* and especially *Jardines lejanos,* works inspired entirely by music, he confessed that music was filling a great deal of his life. (pp. 219-20)

Both Mallarmé and Jiménez had a delicate sensibility. They wanted to create beauty. For Mallarmé absolute beauty is venerable: "comme tout ce qui est absolument beau, la poésie force l'admiration." Jiménez's greatest ideal is perfection, a perfect beauty. . . .

Many of the poetic images used by Mallarmé in some of his poems (as well as by Verlaine in *Fêtes galantes*) are present in Jiménez's early books of poetry: "la lune, les sanglots, le jardin mélancolique, le parc, le couple qui se promène et dialogue, le jet d'eau, la lumière de la lampe, le crépuscule." Jiménez's works possess a certain sensuality, especially in the poems dealing with the important theme of woman. This sensuality could be the influence of Mallarmé. . . . (p. 220)

Of all the French Symbolists, Verlaine is the one with whom Jiménez has more obvious points of contact. We have pointed out the pre-eminent position of music is Jiménez's poetry, a factor that links it with Verlaine's *art poétique:* "de la musique avant toute chose." Verlaine, like Mallarmé and Jiménez, had the same love of beauty. . . . Unlike Mallarmé, Verlaine was not a theorist, and neither was Jiménez. Verlaine departed from traditional rhythms and created some of the most lyrical poems in all French literature. Jiménez did likewise for Spanish literature when he wrote his crucial *Diario de poeta y mar.* Verlaine was the leader in the search for freedom in verse. Jiménez and Verlaine identified with their art. (p. 221)

In the fashion of Verlaine, Jiménez dedicated several of the poems included in his early books to different friends and fellow writers. Many other poetic images and devices used by Verlaine [are present in Jiménez's poems]. (pp. 222-23)

In a manuscript page entitled "Fuentes de mi escritura" Jiménez enumerated all the writers who had influenced his books. Included in the list were the names of the major

French Symbolist poets and that of Maeterlinck, famous for his Symbolist plays. . . .

It is very difficult to state how much influence a writer has received from another and exactly where that influence begins and ends. But, contrary to Garciasol's opinion that *Rimas* is Jiménez's only response to the Symbolist movement, we can conclude that regardless of date the influence of the French Symbolists, especially Verlaine, is present in many of Jiménez's works. Later on, in his final creative period, Jiménez will continue to write symbolic poetry, but on a metaphysical level, and concerned more with his own religious and philosophical quest. (p. 223)

> *Ángel Manuel Aguirre, "Juan Ramón Jiménez and the French Symbolist Poets: Influences and Similarities," in* Revista Hispánica Moderna: Columbia University Hispanic Studies, *Vol. XXXVI, No. 4, 1970-71, pp. 212-23.*

DONALD F. FOGELQUIST (essay date 1971)

Among [the] pine-clad hills, some two or three kilometers from Moguer, lies Fuentepiña the country retreat of the Jiménez family. . . .

A solitary pine, with the spreading limbs and round crown peculiar to the common Spanish species, casts its shadow over a large area of the yard at one corner of the house. It is much older and larger than the rather spindly pines that grow in dense clusters on the surrounding hill tops. The big pine delighted Jiménez, and he mentions it often in his writings. . . . The Fuentepiña pine, and pine trees in general, became deeply ensconced in Jiménez' poetic consciousness. . . . The pine appears often in his poetry, not only in the compositions written in Moguer, but in those of a much later period, when virtually the only ties the poet still retained with his native town were his nostalgic memories. Somewhat analogous to the live oak (*encina*) in the poetry of Antonio Machado or the birch in that of Robert Frost, the pine became an affective, not simply a descriptive image, in the poetry of Juan Ramón Jiménez. (p. 452)

It was an extended visit to the Guadarrama mountains that inspired *Pastorales*. . . . Pine trees belong to this enchanted realm, and they appear for the first time in his poetry. Whether seen in the brightness of day, the waning light of evening, or under the stars, they are to Jiménez a wonder that never grows old. With rapid impressionistic touches he captures the beauty and the mystery of their varying form, movement, color, scent and sound in light or dark, wind or calm. The opening stanza of one of the poems of *Pastorales* gives [the] glimpse of a world in which sun, water and pines unite in a rhapsody of light, exaltation, and song. . . . (pp. 452-53)

Late in 1905, afflicted with nervous fatigue and nostalgia, Jiménez abandoned Madrid and returned to his home in Moguer, where he was to remain for an unbroken period of six years. Throughout the works of this period pine trees are often present in the poet's nature imagery, particularly in *Baladas de primavera*. . . . It is evident from the tone of these poems that the return to family, to the tranquility of provincial life, and particularly the renewed communion with nature, worked a beneficent change in the poet's health and outlook. (p. 453)

The appeal of the pine tree was something quite distinct from that of other trees which belonged to Jiménez' world of poetry. Unlike the acacia, the almond, or the magnolia it was never transformed by the miracle of blossoms; not did it have the grace, the shimmering beauty, the "música verde" of the poplars. However, its enduring greenness, its strong and rugged contours could, when touched by nature's magic, attain a splendor which none of the other trees could surpass: "la luna naciente / encendía de oro el verdor de los pinos." The wind could draw from the pine soothing or majestic music: "rumor idílico de pinos," "murmullo de pinos," to cite two auditory images used by Jiménez. . . .

[Jiménez felt the pine] was one of the few constants in a world where all beauty was ephemeral and in which man's life itself was but a "vapor." Other trees, with leaves ablaze, once each year, with autumn glory, were a poignant reminder of this inexorable erosion of beauty and life, and their presence in Jiménez' imagery often accentuates the decadent tone of the poetry of his so-called "first" period. . . . The pine trees with their perennial greenness and their powerful thrust toward the sky were, by contrast, a source of strength and affirmation. In none of his works is this sentiment more explicit and intense than in the chapter of *Platero y yo* entitled "El pino de la Corona." A giant pine tree on a hill near Moguer, has for centuries been a landmark to the inhabitants of the region, and a guide to the seafarers along its shores. Its grandeur has not diminished with the poet's transition from childhood to manhood. To him it is a living being; it offers him a haven of peace, a source of strength and exaltation, the visible evidence of eternity. . . .

In *La soledad sonora* there is a poem unmistakably inspired by the pine tree which stands near the house at Fuentepiña. . . . The point of departure in the creation of the poem was clearly reality, a tree the poet saw every day, a common pine. However, the moment he apprehends in the poem is one in which the pine tree is resplendent in the sun, its branches reach into the depths of a blue sky, the breeze gives it a rhythmic movement, and ripples of joyous song come from the birds in the dark, green crown. The reality of the tree persists, but it is at once a wonder which nature may never again perform in exactly the same way. The poet's reaction to it transcends his sensory awareness of the pine tree; he is transfigured, in tune with the infinite. . . . (p. 454)

[It] is significant that Jiménez expressed his wish that a pine —in preference to all other trees—shelter his grave and accompany him after death. . . .

Canción contains a poem entitled "Con el pino" in which Jiménez discovers his own identity in the pine, a tree he endows with the human attributes to which he himself aspired. . . .

In other poems of *Canción* the pines contribute to the nature imagery both in the visual and affective sense. (p. 455)

The long prose poem *Espacio,* written at Coral Gables [Florida], contains [a] nostalgic reminiscence of two pine trees of Moguer, which emerge in the poet's consciousness with a fondness and nostalgia one usually feels only for human friends. . . . By the time Jiménez established his residence in Coral Gables his poetry had evolved through romantic, elegiac, decadent and impressionistic stages toward one of more abstract imagery and metaphysical content. The poems of *Romances de Coral Gables,* which were, in fact, written during the poet's residence in the city that gave its name to the collection, reflect the change. The simplicity of these romances belies their intellectual and emotional complexity. The natural world to which the pines belong undergoes a transmutation which corresponds to that which the poet senses will be his own final destiny. . . . (p. 456)

It is significant that the pines which had been a part of the poet's world ever since his first awareness of it, and which had given him vital, esthetic, and emotional sustenance throughout his life, should in his late maturity acquire an ideal dimension transcending the physical, perishable world. . . .

To summarize and conclude: the pine has left both real and ideal images in Jiménez' work through all its stages of evolution, contributing to its beauty, profundity and universality. The rose, real and metaphoric, is associated much more often than the pine with Jiménez and his poetic world; the delicate form, the fragrance, and the fleeting beauty of the rose suggesting perhaps that only what was exquisite, ephemeral, and feminine . . . struck any response in his sensibility. However, his thirst for immortality was even more intense than the ecstasy with which he contemplated earthly beauty. The eternity for which he yearned so ardently is symbolized as effectively by the pine tree as by any other image in his poetry. (p. 457)

> *Donald F. Fogelquist, "Poet and Pine," in* His-pania *(© 1971 The American Association of Teachers of Spanish and Portuguese, Inc.), Vol. 54, No. 3, September, 1971, pp. 452-58.*

MICHAEL P. PREDMORE (essay date 1972)

It will be remembered that the *Diario* was written in 1916 between January and July on the occasion of the poet's trip from Spain to the United States to marry Zenobia Camprubí. The book is divided into six parts, and records, in the manner of a diary, the poet's day-to-day impressions. . . . An analysis of the structure of the work, treated not as a diary now, but as an expressive form, will reveal, I think, the complete form of a spiritual quest.

To penetrate into a work as symbolically dense and complicated as the *Diario* is a difficult task. It seems to me instructive at the outset to heed the words of the author himself, for Jiménez as a critic is often the best source of the most perceptive insights about his own work. . . . Jiménez's own testimony of the importance of the sea in the genesis of his work has understandably influenced the attention of many of the critics. . . . [Jiménez has also observed] that the book is in some sense metaphysical, that it deals with a discovery of sky, love, and sea which seems to involve a struggle between these three elements [and] that it initiates the beginning of modern symbolism in Spanish poetry. . . . (pp. 54-6)

Part I opens with a series of poems expressive of the poet's love of his bride-to-be. (p. 62)

The poet's deep attachment of his native Moguer is a well-known constant in nearly all of his work. . . . The poet does not want to leave his world of familiar landscapes and sunsets. . . . This, then, is the essential inner conflict of the *Diario de un Poeta Reciéncasado:* the constant struggle

between the child's attachment to the familiar boundaries of his early existence . . . and the pull toward love, emotional maturity, and independence. The opposite pull of these two forces results in the conflict that the poet himself has observed both within and outside of his poems. (pp. 64-6)

Against the background of the central theme (of an adult love struggling to realize itself), the significance of Part II becomes clear. The poet's experience of the sea intensifies and deepens his doubts concerning himself, for he is suddenly in a new and strange world, alienated from all the familiar surroundings with their deep emotional attachments. . . . [He] cannot reconcile himself to the sea, which is too fundamentally different from his nest in southern Spain. The constant impression of the sea in Part II is one of solitude. It is lifeless, companionless, monotonous; it produces overwhelming boredom, insufferable tedium. The most effective portrayal of the sea, from the standpoint of one in quest of a new springtime in life, is the cluster of images expressive of sterility and desolation, in "Monotonía" (["Monotony"], Poem 30). . . . The strong emotional attachment to his land as if it were "mother" reflects the child's longing for warmth and security. The metaphorical intercalation ("tomb of eternal life / with the same ornament renewed") suggests the static, timeless world of Moguer; the innermost depths of mother are like the innermost depths of land—both are sources of new life. But if the land, the "distant mother, land asleep," is a "tomb of eternal life," the sea is no such thing. The sea continues to offer a vision of desolation, ruin, and sterility. (pp. 67-9)

Part III of the *Diario,* "América del Este" ["America of the East"], consists of one hundred poems and is the longest and perhaps most difficult section of the work. Part of its difficulty lies in the fact that the underlying theme of the work is diluted by a series of ironic sketches and commentaries on the overwhelming and dehumanized phenomena of New York City. Another factor obscuring the meaning of the section is the symbolic character of certain elements, which continue to develop the central theme. . . . "La primavera" ("Spring") appears in at least one-third of all the poems of Part III. . . . [The] poet's concern is not only with the "discovery and interpretation of America's spring," it is also with the search and the struggle for his own springtime. (p. 72)

Enough has been seen already to show that the poet's search for the springtime of love and maturity is interfered with by his familiar childhood longings—the fascination for the crepuscular sky or the starry night or the attraction to cemeteries and children (which we will see later). That the poet is in a kind of limbo, caught between two kinds of springtime (the unconscious springtime of nature in which the child delights and the inner springtime of love and adulthood. . . . The conflict is not resolved at the end of Part III. The poet is still searching, united and yet not united with his loved one. (p. 74)

Part IV continues to develop the inner conflict, the struggle of opposing forces within the poet. It opens with the poem "Nostaljia" (["Nostalgia"], Poem 157), expressive of a momentary mood of peace and repose. The tranquil sea within the poet stands in striking contrast to other moods in which the soul is tormented by doubts and fears that rage within it. . . . (p. 75)

Though the forces of Moguer and childhood continue to

exercise their influence over the poet into Part IV, there is dramatic evidence to indicate that the poet's relation to the sea has undergone a profound change. There are two magnificent poems especially in which the sea is transformed into a wild, raging giant. The sea of "El Mar" (Poem 163) is an enormous, drunken creature that seems to resent this intruder and to taunt and frighten him deliberately.... Despite the rage and anger, the humanization of the sea for the poet is a positive sign. It reflects his own humanization, his own timid first attempts to establish contact ("If I touch a finger of his") with powerful, natural forces—instead of longing for the quiet of a natural landscape, or the security of mother, or gazing from afar at the stars of the night. The sea of Poem 168 seems to increase the fury of its assault upon the intruder.... Thus, as the sea of Part II serves as an oppressive force, through images of sterility, desolation, and monotony, to deny the poet his will for love and rebirth, the sea of Part IV, wild, irreverent, blasphemous, serves as a liberating force to shock the poet back into the real and human world. To recognize this difference is to understand the gradual process of spiritual transformation that leads to the soul's liberation in "Oro Mío" and "Nocturno" and to the final resolution of the inner conflict in "Todo." (pp. 78-81)

[The] vision of and feeling for the unity of land and sky, permeated as it is with the feeling and unity of mother and child, is precisely the world the poet must struggle to overcome and replace if he is to realize his own independence and his love of woman. And this is what he does do as announced in "Todo": "You, sea, and you, love, all mine / as the land and the sky were before!" (p. 84)

Though the childhood attachment to the past (and fear of the future) continues to manifest itself well into Part IV, this aspect of the poet's madness (the platonic conception of an ideal love situated amidst the celestial spheres) is treated very little now. That the poet is engaged in a search for truth and reality and the truth of reality (his personal reality) is becoming increasingly clearer. An important factor in this search is the awareness that he must rid his mind of these dreams and illusions of fantasy.... (p. 92)

[The] treatment of "dream" is an important expressive medium for the revelation of the poet's inner conflict. The dreams of the poet, daydreams and nightdreams, voluntary and involuntary, reveal perhaps more than any other expressive device the nature of the poet's madness and infantile obsessions. They reveal him to be a man oscillating between two conditions of the mind and soul, between the forces of "dream" and "not being born" and the force of "dawn" and "springtime." The former pull him toward the innocent world of mother, nest, and childhood where the soul strives to unite itself with the harmony of its familiar landscapes. The latter pull him toward a new world of experience, of love and adulthood, in which the soul must journey through a sea and storm of violence. One world is the tranquil world of childhood; the other, a great sea of new adventure. The agony and pain of the conflict of opposing forces arise from the mutually exclusive nature of the two worlds. The one threatens and denies the other.

The poet, in a painful moment of awareness, realizes that he fears his loved one. He knows that a full acceptance of her would spell the end of his childhood illusions and fantasies. He would have to live in a world of men and be denied his dream-world of moon and stars and sunsets. He is thus

confronted with two real possibilities in life—a possibility for growth and development and another which would arrest these natural impulses. He is from the very beginning of the work in doubt about the outcome of this inner struggle. He imagines that he will be shipwrecked on this sea of adventure. He fears that his springtime will never open and flower. Yet he continues his journey and is aided by the forces of love and sunlight, denied and then aided by the powerful colossus of the sea. Throughout his struggle he is possessed with visions and dreams and illusions and fantasies. Such a stimulation and agitation of the mind and the imagination bear on the essential nature of his quest, which is a search to resolve the conflict within him, to know himself fully and to find the world he must live in. This is what the author means, I think, when he says that the *Diario* "is a metaphysical book." It is an inquiry into the fundamental nature of truth and reality—one man's truth and one man's reality. What is to be his destiny? Which of the two worlds competing within him will eventually prevail?

An important resolution of the poet's quest for identity, his struggle to determine the true nature of his own reality, is neatly provided by the treatment of the theme of rebirth. In this context, the symbolic formulation of the inner conflict in terms of "sueño" and "amanecer" ("madrugada" and "aurora") ... now takes on added significance. Indeed, the theme of rebirth (rebirth of the day, and rebirth and awakening from the dreams, illusions, and fears of the child), couched in terms of "amanecer" and its synonyms, is one of the key structural principles of the *Diario*—it accounts, perhaps more than anything else, for the expressive organization of the poetic work. (pp. 95-6)

All of the expressive elements in [Part IV] operate to prepare, herald, and finally convey, in symbolic terms, the complete resolution of the poet's inner conflict.... [The] theme of rebirth, expressed in terms of "dawn" is one of the key symbolic developments of the *Diario*. It heralds the advent of a new order and leads immediately to the liberation of the soul in "Oro Mío" and "Nocturno." These, indeed, are the decisive events that lead to the dramatic redefinition of self in "Todo." "You, sea, and you, love, all mine, / as the land and the sky were before!" can now be clearly seen as an explicit rendering of this "new arrangement of the universe." The child's experience of the land and the sky (permeated with the values of Moguer) has been replaced by the new adult's experience of the sea and of love. (pp. 100-01)

Part V both opens and closes on the theme of rebirth and makes explicit the relation between the rising sun and the soul's condition. (p. 101)

The theme of rebirth, then, expressed through the frequent opposition of and final collaboration of "amanecer" ("dawn") and "sueño" ("dream"), is clearly the key organizing principle of the *Diario*. It opens and closes the work, dominates Parts I and V, occurs always and significantly toward the end of each major section, and plots the gradual resolution of the central, underlying theme—the inner conflict of opposing forces. And as the "Soñando" of Part I indicates the source of one of those forces (the child's fear of and resistance to the demands of "dawn" and rebirth), the "Soñando" of Part V indicates the origin of an opposing force—contact with the sea, with forces of nature that bring about the spiritual transformation and the final, eager acceptance of rebirth and adulthood ("Dawn at Sea").

It is . . . possible, I think, to make explicit the special features of the *Diario* as hermetic poetry and to explore its historical importance within the context of twentieth-century Spanish lyric poetry. It is clear that Jiménez's masterpiece is a highly complex structure of recurring clusters of images and recurring patterns of association. The patterns and configurations of images invest the work with a consistent symbolic density. Each recurring image acquires symbolic value and each poem is a symbolic poem, subordinate to and dependent upon the coherence of the system as a whole. . . . I would argue, then, that the two hundred and seventeen poems of the first five sections of the *Diario* must be read as a single poem. . . . Within [the] great tradition of "architectonic" composition, Jiménez must stand as one of its most distinguished practitioners. The *Diario de un Poeta Reciéncasado* is one of the most tightly-knit, highly organized works in modern poetry. Not one of its major parts can be rearranged or altered without severely damaging the meaning of the whole. In fact, to alter or modify even an individual poem within a given part would risk sending a disruptive tremor throughout the entire organism. The nature of the journey itself is the most powerful factor controlling the rigorous order assumed by the poems. (pp. 102-03)

[Jiménez] was the most powerful and influential force to introduce a new conception and a new practice of poetry into twentieth-century Spain. With the *Diario*, a new practice of poetry achieves its maturity. The individual poem loses its relative autonomy, become vitally dependent upon a greater whole, and acquires meaning only through the coherence of an entire system. The private symbolism and the resulting hermeticism require a new kind of reader, a reader who is willing to suspend his attachment to traditional and conventional meanings of literary language and who is willing to be reeducated to respond to the poetic experience of private semantic systems. . . . A new practice of poetry, a new kind of ordering and structuring of poems within a greater whole, within a symbolic system—this is the legacy of the *Diario* to the succeeding generation. (pp. 104-05)

> *Michael P. Predmore, "The Structure of the 'Diario de un poeta reciéncasado': A Study of Hermetic Poetry," in* Contemporary Literature (© *1972 by the Regents of the University of Wisconsin), Vol. 13, No. 1, Winter, 1972, pp. 53-105.*

ADDITIONAL BIBLIOGRAPHY

Allen, Rupert C. "Juan Ramón and the World Tree: A Symbological Analysis of Mysticism in the Poetry of Juan Ramón Jiménez." *Revista Hispánica Moderna: Columbia University Hispanic Studies* XXXV, No. 4 (October-December 1969): 306-22.
    An interesting study of the "World Tree" archetype in Juan Ramón's poetry. The critic suggests that the "World Tree" archetype serves as symbol of the transcendence of ego-consciousness in Jiménez's "secular" mysticism.

Cardwell, Richard A. *Juan R. Jiménez: The Modernist Apprenticeship 1895-1900.* Berlin: Colloquium Verlag, 1977, 323 p.
    An in-depth discussion of Jiménez and the "modernist" poets, authors, etc., their influences on literature, and their evolution from the original style of the generation of 1898. Critical references are interspersed throughout the book, but most of the critical terminology is in Spanish.

Duran, Manuel. "Juan Ramón Jiménez: The Poet as Philosopher." *Books Abroad* 42, No. 3 (Summer 1968): 391-93.
    A review of Paul R. Olson's book *Circle of Paradox: Time and Essence in the Poetry of Juan Ramón Jiménez* with some period and biographical background information.

Frank, Rachel. "Juan Ramón Jiménez: The Landscape of the Soul." *Poetry* LXXXII, No. 4 (July 1953): 224-39.
    Traces the theme of the "landscape of the soul"—qualities of sensuousness and spirituality—throughout his poetry.

Gullon, Ricardo. Introduction to *Juan Ramón Jiménez: Three Hundred Poems, 1903-1953*, by Juan Ramón Jiménez, translated by Eloise Roach, pp. xvii-xxxiv. Austin: University of Texas Press, 1962.
    General introduction to his poetry which gives a brief explanation of some of his poems along with biographical information.

Olson, Paul R. "Structure and Symbol in a Poem of Juan Ramón Jiménez." *Modern Language Notes* LXXVI, No. 7 (November 1961): 636-47.
    Good analysis of structure and symbolism in "Viene una música lánguida" from *Arias tristes*.

Olson, Paul R. "Time and Essence in a Symbol of Juan Ramón Jiménez." *MLN* 78, No. 1 (January 1963): 169-93.
    Analysis of Jiménez's poetry and the use of the rose as a symbol.

Trend, J. B. "Juan Ramón Jiménez." In *Fifty Spanish Poems*, by Juan Ramón Jiménez, translated by J. B. Trend, pp. 9-25. Oxford: Dolphin Book Co., 1950.
    Thorough introduction to various biographical and literary influences on Jiménez's career with comments on many of the poems.

Young, Howard T. "Two Poems on Death by Juan Ramón Jiménez." *Modern Language Notes* LXXV, No. 6 (June 1960): 502-07.
    Analysis of meaning and symbolism of Jiménez's poems, interspersed with a few critical comments.

Selma (Ottiliana Lovisa) Lagerlöf

1858-1940

Swedish novelist, short story writer, autobiographer, poet, biographer, and dramatist.

Lagerlöf is one of the major figures of the romantic revival in Swedish literature. Noted for their narrative grace and potent imaginative quality, her works are rooted in the legend, history, and peasantry of her native Värmland. Her many works illustrate an abiding faith in the supremacy of love and goodness, and a fascination with the supernatural.

Nearly ten years elapsed between the conception of Lagerlöf's first novel, *Gösta Berling's saga* (*The Story of Gösta Berling*), and its publication. Influenced by the current Swedish realism, Lagerlöf struggled to reconcile her interest in legends and Icelandic sagas with the extreme objectivity of her literary peers. After experimenting with several genres, she finally accepted her affinity with the romantics and proceeded with her own imaginative and richly descriptive prose.

The influence of Thomas Carlyle's romantic lyricism and fervent prose, which Lagerlöf discovered in his *Heroes and Hero Worship*, is obvious in Lagerlöf's first period, most notably in *The Story of Gösta Berling*. Lagerlöf gradually modified this early overwrought style, however, and by the time *Jerusalem* and *Antikrists mirakler* (*The Miracles of Antichrist*) appeared, Carlyle's influence was no longer evident. *Jerusalem*, a novel in which she explores the religious conviction of the Dalecarlian peasants, displays a more sober style characteristic of the middle period of her career. A grant from the Swedish government made possible Lagerlöf's travels which supplied the material for this period. Lagerlöf's return to her family home of Märbacka provided the impetus for her final period. The works of this period, which include the *Löwensköld* trilogy and her autobiographical writings, were inspired by childhood memories and Värmland folklore. Many feel that her best works emanate from Värmland, where she was most at home, and that her writings drawn from other sources are not nearly as convincing.

Because she defied every literary ideal of her day, Lagerlöf baffled her Swedish critics. They criticized her work for its naiveté, moralistic psychology, and weak characterization. Despite this uneasy critical reception, she achieved great popularity among the Swedish people and a loyal international following. She earned the distinction of being the first female recipient of the Nobel Prize in literature, as well as the first woman member of the Swedish Academy.

PRINCIPAL WORKS

Gösta Berling's saga (novel) 1891
  [*The Story of Gösta Berling*, 1898; published in England as *Gösta Berling's Saga*, 1898]
Antikrists mirakler (novel) 1898
  [*The Miracles of Antichrist*, 1899]
Jerusalem: I Dalarne (novel) 1901

P. Ruler

[*In Dalarne* published as Part 1 of *Jerusalem*, 1903]
Jerusalem: I det heliga landet (novel) 1902
  [*In the Holy Land* published as Part 2 of *Jerusalem*, 1903]
Herr Arnes penningar (novel) 1904
  [*Herr Arne's Hoard*, 1923; published in the United States as *The Treasure*, 1925]
Kristus legender (short stories) 1904
  [*Christ Legends*, 1908]
Nils Holgerssons underbara resa genom Sverige (juvenile fiction) 1906-7
  [Published in two volumes: *The Wonderful Adventures of Nils*, 1907; *Further Adventures of Nils*, 1911]
Troll och människor (short stories) 1915
Bandlyst (novel) 1918
  [*The Outcast*, 1920]
Mårbacka (autobiography) 1922
  [*Mårbacka*, 1924]
Charlotte Löwensköld (novel) 1925
  *[*Charlotte Löwensköld*, 1927]
Löwensköldska ringen (novel) 1925
  *[*The General's Ring*, 1928]
Anna Svärd (novel) 1928
  *[*Anna Svärd* published in *The Ring of the Löwenskölds*, 1931]
Ett barns memoarer (autobiography) 1930

[*Memories of My Childhood*, 1934]
Dagbok för Selma Lagerlöf (diary) 1932
[*The Diary of Selma Lagerlöf*, 1936]

*These novels were collected as *The Ring of the Löwenskölds*, 1931

WILLIAM ARCHER (essay date 1899)

Sometimes the situations in which [Selma Lagerlöf deals in *Gösta Berling's Saga*] belong to a high order of romantic melodrama; sometimes (in the case of Marienne Sinclaire, for instance) they pass into the sphere of spiritual tragedy. Nowhere do we find a point of clear and steady light in the murky atmosphere. Least of all does Gösta Berling himself provide such a luminous centre. He is the most unreal character in the book (a fact which strengthens the supposition that he is imposed on the writer's imagination from without, not created from within); and both in his strength and his weakness he is almost always maleficent. So far as its matter goes, then, it would be hard to conceive a sadder book than *Gösta Berling's Saga*. But its spirit, its "spirits," render it the reverse of depressing. The writer loves intensely, she revels and glories in the life she is describing. She is not blind to its barbarisms; her personal point of view is not inhuman; but her delight in the sheer vigour, the rough-hewn individuality of the characters of her myth-cycle, is everywhere keen and infectious. She projects them with an energy that carries all before it. She never wavers in her faith that life was eminently worth living in her (real or imaginary) Värmland of seventy years ago; and she leaves the reader, for the moment, at any rate, fascinated by the spectacle of all this primitive vitality. (pp. 394-95)

> *William Archer, "Pessimism and Tragedy," in* The Fortnightly Review, *n.s. Vol. 71, No. 65, March, 1899, pp. 390-400.**

WILLIAM MORTON PAYNE (essay date 1899)

[Lagerlöf's *Gosta Berling's Saga*] is certainly impressive, although we cannot say that it is altogether a work of art. It is too incoherent, too rhapsodical, to deserve that title. But it is an exceedingly interesting example of what young Scandinavia is now doing in literature, for its author, Miss Selma Lagerlöf, is one of the very newest of Swedish writers. Its success, moreover, in its present form, has been such as to warrant the speedy preparation of another of Miss Lagerlöf's romances for the English-speaking public, and to this second work we will now direct our attention.

"The Miracles of Antichrist" is a work that represents a maturer stage in the development of this talented writer, although it still has the incoherent and episodical character of the earlier book. In this case, Miss Lagerlöf has turned from the Swedish to the Sicilian peasantry for her subject, and her insight into the racial and temperamental characteristics of a people so remote from her own is really remarkable. . . . There is no continuous story of much interest, but there are many faithful and sincere studies of character, and many portions of the work glow with a strange poetical beauty. Miss Lagerlöf is assuredly a writer to be reckoned with in the new development of Scandinavian literature. (p. 310)

> *William Morton Payne, "Two Epochs of the Roman Empire," in* The Dial *(copyright, 1899, by The Dial Publishing Company, Inc.), Vol. XXVI, No. 309, May 1, 1899, pp. 306-11.**

EDWIN BJÖRKMAN (essay date 1913)

Selma Lagerlöf is one of the greatest of an increasing group of writers who represent a synthesis of two past literary epochs, and who, for this reason, must be held especially representative of the literary epoch that is now coming. She has revived not only the courage but the ability to feel and dream and aspire that belonged to the scorned romanticists of the early nineteenth century. But this recovery of something long held to be lost and outlived forever she has achieved for us without surrender of that intimate connection between poetry and real life which was established by the naturalists in the latter half of the same century. The romanticists spoke to our hearts alone. The naturalists spoke only to our heads. For the men and women of the new epoch we have not yet found an adequate name, but we know that they are speaking to head and heart alike. We know that Selma Lagerlöf's brightest fairy raiments are woven out of what to the ordinary mind would seem like the most commonplace patches of everyday life—and we know as well that when she tempts us into far-off, fantastic worlds of her own making, her ultimate object is to help us see the inner meanings of the too often over-emphasized superficial actualities of our own existence. (pp. 139-40)

> *Edwin Björkman, "The Story of Selma Lagerlöf," in his* Voices of To-morrow: Critical Studies of the New Spirit in Literature *(copyright © 1913 by Mitchell Kennerley), Mitchell Kennerley, 1913, pp. 139-153.*

THE NEW YORK TIMES BOOK REVIEW (essay date 1915)

Not only did ["Gösta Berling"] take Sweden by storm, but it was translated into most modern languages, and was everywhere pronounced a masterpiece.

It was an extraordinary and beautiful story, and it was written in a style of singular clarity, and revealed what seemed an inevitable comprehension of the hearts of men and women, the strange workings of human nature. . . .

[In her book Selma Lagerlöf] appeared to understand every one, to have done and seen everything, to be at home with the wildest and fiercest, the greatest lovers, the hopeless, the strong, to know youth and age, to be surprised at nothing, to sympathize with points of view as far apart as good and evil. In her book was life in its thousand aspects, good and bad, subtle and simple, passionate and cold, presented with an art so simple and direct that it is only occasionally the reader realizes its beauty and effectiveness. . . .

"Jerusalem" is the story of a revival. In telling it the writer presents a picture of universal human nature swaying between the poles of warm, comfortable, conventional, and time-honored bodily ease, sanctioned by tradition, and the chill, self-denying, fanatical, disturbing demand of the spirit, setting father against son, wife against husband. The story, to be sure, is intensely local. . . . It is all a close, true study of a small group, with its little comedies, its bitter tragedies, its love stories, its tension between members of families or neighbors held together or strained apart by early, casual occurrences long since become rigid rules and traditions. Here they are, these Ingmars and Halvors and Elofs and Hellgums, plucked living from their immemorial farms and huts, and set in the mesh of the story; so real, so individual, man, woman, and child, that they touch every one in the world. The Volapük of human emotion is spoken through them, and every human being understands and sympathizes. . . .

There are strange happenings in the course of the story, for the author sets down what strikes upon her characters in the way it appears to them. . . . In this power of completely identifying herself and her reader with her characters Miss Lagerlöf's genius reaches its heights; and it seems futile to employ another word in speaking of her.

The exquisite art of the book is only completely revealed when you have finished and are looking back upon it. The solid foundation of character and habit, the settled ways of these people, with their flashes of idealism, their courage of conviction—these are made familiar and understandable as they would be if you had grown up in Dalecarlia yourself. Then, working on that idealism, that courage, the gradual invasion of religious upheaval, the oversetting of ancient rules and beliefs, the dawning of new demands and needs, the rise of a spiritual enthusiasm powerful enough to sweep the home-loving, tradition-sworn creatures away from their green farms and ancient houses to the desperate hazards of a pilgrimage to Jerusalem, there to set up a colony that was to exemplify the teachings of Christ anew to a world that had drifted far—how clearly, how wonderfully it is all done, while all the while you seem simply to be following the village happenings and personal problems of a few rather slow-thinking, earnest, sincere folk, who believe in walking in the ways of God, but who are not averse from feathering the nest of life.

The description of the final exodus is rarely beautiful. Only an incident here, another there, a face, a figure, an isolated experience or two, are related. But when all are gathered together you realize that every emotion which must have moved the pilgrims, and also those left behind, has been illuminated. It is all there.

"The Woman Who Won the Nobel Prize," in The New York Times Book Review (© *1915 by The New York Times Company; reprinted by permission), October 31, 1915, p. 413.*

HENRY GODDARD LEACH   (essay date 1915)

What is the secret of the power that has made Miss Lagerlöf an author acknowledged not alone as a classic in the schools but also as the most popular and generally beloved writer in Scandinavia? She entered Swedish literature at a period when the cold gray star of realism was in the ascendant. . . . Wrapped in the mantle of a latter-day romanticism, her soul filled with idealism, on the one hand she transformed the crisp actualities of human experience by throwing about them the glamour of the unknown, and on the other hand gave to the unreal—to folk tale and fairy lore and local superstition—the effectiveness of convincing fact. . . . Furthermore, the Swedish authoress attracts her readers by a diction unique unto herself, as singular as the English sentences of Charles Lamb. Her style may be described as prose rhapsody held in restraint, at times passionately breaking its bonds. (pp. vii-viii)

[It] is by intuition that she *works* rather than by experience. Otherwise, she could not have depicted in her books such a multitude of characters from all parts of Europe. She sees character with woman's warm and delicate sympathy and with the clear vision of childhood. . . . Selma Lagerlöf takes her delight, not in developing the psychology of the unusual, but in analyzing the motives and emotions of the normal mind. This accounts for the comforting feeling of satisfaction and familiarity which comes over one reading the chronicles of events so exceptional as those which occur in "Jerusalem." (pp. viii-ix)

"Jerusalem" is founded upon the historic event of a religious pilgrimage from Dalecarlia in the last century. (p. x)

The novel is opened by that favourite device of Selma Lagerlöf, the monologue, through which she pries into the very soul of her characters, in this case Ingmar, son of Ingmar, of Ingmar Farm. Ingmar's monologue at the plow is a subtle portrayal of an heroic battle between the forces of conscience and desire. (p. xi)

The underlying spiritual action of "Jerusalem" is the conflict of idealism with that impulse which is deep rooted in the rural communities of the old world, the love of home and the home soil. . . . Among the peasant aristocracy of Dalecarlia attachment to the homestead is life itself. In "Jerusalem" this emotion is pitted on the one hand against religion, on the other against *love*. Hearts are broken in the struggle *which* permits Karin to sacrifice the Ingmar Farm to obey the inner voice that summons her on her religious pilgrimage, and *which* leads her brother, on the other hand, to abandon the girl of his heart and his life's personal happiness in order to win back the farm.

The tragic intensity of "Jerusalem" is happily relieved by the undercurrent of Miss Lagerlöf's sympathetic humour. When she has almost succeeded in transporting us into a state of religious fervour, we suddenly catch her smile through the lines and realize that no one more than she feels the futility of fanaticism. The stupid blunders of humankind do not escape her; neither do they arouse her contempt. She accepts human nature as it is with a warm fondness for all its types. (pp. xii-xiii)

Henry Goddard Leach, in his introduction to Jerusalem: A Novel *by Selma Lagerlöf, translated by Velma Swanston Howard (copyright 1915 by Doubleday, Page & Company; reprinted by permission of Doubleday & Company, Inc.), Doubleday, 1915, pp. vii-xiv.*

V. SACKVILLE-WEST   (essay date 1931)

Selma Lagerlöf, like a skilled juggler, has contrived over a respect-worthy number of years to spin her two plates, the plates of realism and of fantasy, without either of them coming disastrously to the ground, and continues to catch and reject each alternately, without a shattering of either. . . . [The] feat of equilibrium never degenerates into a trick. Her dexterity remains always as an integral form of the self-expression of her mind. The gesture of her hand (which may stand symbolical for her literary, realistic skill), works in perfect accord with the wilder, twirling throws of her imagination. (p. v)

[Selma Lagerlöf combines] two methods. Wild, romantic, and improbable happenings are confirmed by the thousand threads and strands attaching them firmly to a basis of sensible and homely observation. The warp and woof of 'Gösta Berling' alone is enough to illustrate this point. For the Swedish reader, all may be plain-sailing; perhaps 'pensioners' did, or do, behave in that extravagant way in Sweden; for English readers, the stormy and prodigal excess of Gösta Berling, his beauty, his adventures, his conflict with the Devil in the shape of Sintram, his many mistresses—whether they struggle for the salvation of his soul, perish in the snow, or suffer in sleighs from pursuit by wolves—are removed into a world of the true fairy-tale prodigality, justified as are all fairy-tales from Scheherazade to Hans Andersen by a foundation of observed and potential fact. (p. vi)

Of such a mixture is the art of Selma Lagerlöf made. The landscape of Sweden, and the escape of the fairy-tale.

But if I have a quarrel to pick with a great artist, it is that her realism remains slightly subordinate to her romanticism —'romanticism,' as she herself says, 'with a vengeance.' Subordinate, not inferior. Mark the difference. It is tantamount to saying, that her realism is deliberate, whereas her romanticism (with a vengeance) is instinctive. (p. vii)

Reading 'Gösta Berling,' admirable as is the juggling between romance and naturalism, one cannot help regretting that Selma Lagerlöf should have been born in the nineteenth instead of in the ninth century. Then, she would have been forced into no compromise. She could have indulged her romanticism to the full.

Indeed, one may observe that in spite of her close acquaintance with the spirit and the details of her country, she is at her happiest and most secure so long as she keeps to myth, saga, and story, whether of her own or another's inventing. Human events, human psychology, in the ordinary sense, are not her strong line. She moves easily upon two planes only: the plane of peasant life, with its perennial anxieties, small meannesses, and sudden generosities; and the plane of high emotions, with its poetry, apparent unreality, and essential truth. The middle distance is almost entirely left out, save for some queer lapses into a bourgeois snobbishness and a concession to second-rate values, difficult to explain away. . . . Selma Lagerlöf could deal with tragedies of the soul, not of the body. She could deal with symbols, not with events.

She is, I suppose, a poet writing in prose. (pp. vii-viii)

[Her] prose lifts itself, if not on the wings of an eagle, then on the wings of a gander, into the upper air of poetry. Let us add, too, that she writes always as a woman: not one of her books could have been written by a man. Her art is essentially feminine, not masculine, yet without the slightest consciousness of sex. (p. x)

> *V. Sackville-West, "Preface" (reprinted by permission of the Estate of V. Sackville-West),* Selma Lagerlöf: Her Life and Work *by Walter A. Berendsohn, translated by George F. Timpson, I. Nicholson & Watson Ltd., 1931 (and reprinted by Kennikat Press, 1968), pp. v-x.*

WALTER A. BERENDSOHN (essay date 1931)

The inner unity of [Selma Lagerlöf's 'The Story of Gösta Berling' ('Gösta Berling's Saga')] is greater than that of any other work of literature which has grown out of isolated

stories, such as the Folk-book of Dr Faust or de Coster's 'Till Eulenspiegel.' The constructive achievement is all the more remarkable because so many characters are built into the framework. (p. 40)

At first reading the wealth of incidents and characters may seem so great as to obscure the main issue. The individual adventures grip the imagination and hold it; in them the author's powers reach their highest achievement. On repeated reading one sees more and more clearly the artistry of the weaving, the delightful variation of passionate onrush and comforting pauses, of moving pathos and restrained humour. An inexhaustible wealth of experience has found expression within the wide, yet well defined, limits of the form. . . . 'Gösta Berling's Saga' has no exact parallel in English literature, but there burns in it the same passionate intensity which glows through the pages of 'Jane Eyre.' (p. 41)

[Her novel 'The Miracles of Antichrist' ('Antikrists mirakler')] is full of vivid pictures of the life and landscapes of Italy, pictures so interwoven with breathless action that they remain permanently in the memory. . . . The book contains the same wealth of incident as does 'Gösta Berling,' and falls naturally into short stories which can be read independently, although they are like pearls strung on the thread of the main subject. (pp. 44-5)

The ground-plan of the work is clear and definite, but it is not an entirely successful one. Socialism is an almost religious devotion to the well-being of future humanity on earth, and a false Christ-image is not a fortunate symbol for such a wholly secular philosophy. The contrast with Catholicism is thereby blurred. . . . Catholicism is not really depicted; Selma Lagerlöf seems to have identified it with her own sunny faith. Its main influence is seen in the superstitious reverence which makes all the characters worship the false image without perceiving that they are submitting to another faith. . . . Despite the charm of the individual scenes, the book seems to me a failure as a philosophical novel. It is as if Selma Lagerlöf had wandered mentally and actually too far from her native soil. (p. 47)

In contrast to 'The Miracles of Antichrist' Selma Lagerlöf has treated in 'Jerusalem' [('Jerusalem 1. I Dalarne,' 'Jerusalem 2. I det heliga landet')] a theme taken from her own country, the story of a religious revival which culminates in the emigration of half a Dalecarlian parish to the Holy Land. . . .

The people of Dalecarlia are wholly different from the light-hearted Värmlanders. A remarkable depth of character, with a capacity for dreaming dreams and seeing visions, makes them more akin to the Biblical Hebrews. The reader, therefore, is conscious of a complete change of atmosphere as he passes from 'Gösta Berling' to 'Jerusalem.' (p. 51)

[The] importance of Selma Lagerlöf's book lies in its emphasis on those qualities and forces which run counter to all mysticism. Though she has striven with all her might to understand the rise of this religious movement, and though she acknowledges its genuineness, she has nevertheless not been able to enter into the experiences of the believers. Every moving incident is carefully described, but every important event is associated with some counter-balancing character who has her innermost affection. (p. 53)

Selma Lagerlöf has herself stated that the ancient Sagas had been her model while composing 'Jerusalem 1.' . . . Selma Lagerlöf has succeeded in blending these traits from old-time sagas with events in the 1880's in such a way that the resultant characters become symbolic of the highest virtues of her race. . . . [They] stand for all its best traditions, above all for an unwavering righteousness, which shrinks from no self-sacrifice in the cause of justice. (pp. 53-4)

'Jerusalem,' like 'Gösta Berling,' transcends its Swedish setting and appeals to universal humanity. . . . 'Jerusalem' is a eulogy of family loyalty, faithful affection, practical goodness and sane morality guided by a profound trust in a good and just Providence. The author's mature faith finds full expression in this book, and shines the more clearly by contrast with a mysticism which is wholly foreign to it. (p. 56)

The two important works of [Lagerlöf's imaginative period] have had a world-wide response from children, and from all who retain a child's delight in pure fancy. (p. 57)

['The Christ Legends' ('Kristuslegender')] are written around the central Figure of the Gospels, but they are little concerned with the prophetic, moral and religious character of the Saviour in his maturity. . . . [Although] the author draws back in reverent awe from the public work and teaching of Christ Jesus, His essential message forms the theme of all her stories. (pp. 57-8)

The very subject of the Christ Legends assures them of readers beyond the bounds of Sweden, but they would not win a permanent place did not they embody the highest qualities of literary art. The author's distinctive gifts are here revealed in their full power. The miraculous element in popular lore is enhanced by a rich and varied setting, and is then employed to reveal the deepest feelings of the human heart and to portray a whole-hearted and glowing charity. (p. 61)

The most successful book of this imaginative period is undoubtedly ['The Wonderful Adventures of Nils' (Nils Holgerssons underbara resa genom Sverige')]. (p. 62)

[It is] something more than a children's story. 'Nils Holgersson' gives the reader such a vivid impression of the land and its people, that it is an excellent preparation for a visit to Sweden. . . . [The adventurous flight of the bewitched peasant lad] affords countless opportunities for describing both isolated scenes and broad landscapes in words which remain naturally in the memory. Happy comparisons and ingenious stories sharpen the impressions, and forestall any risk of didactic dullness. (p. 63)

[The] wealth of information would be wearisome, were it not a setting for the endless variety of adventures which befall Nils Holgersson on his journey, and if nature were not so frequently pictured in its most stirring moods. (p. 64)

Nils Holgersson is a Swedish Mowgli, for a substantial proportion of the book is taken up with his varied, and often dramatic experiences among the animals, yet it is in no way an imitation of [Rudyard Kipling's] 'The Jungle Book.' Nils is very definitely a Swedish boy with human standards of conduct, and a fair knowledge of the world; he comes among the animals as a grown lad and learns to hold his own among them, and he is not, like Mowgli, more animal than human in his feelings. In the intimate pictures of natural lore it unfolds, the Swedish book can fairly claim a place beside Rudyard Kipling's masterpiece. . . . But the

wealth of human figures woven into the story give it a different tone from that of 'The Jungle Book.' (pp. 64-5)

In many ways 'Nils Holgersson' is the most successful of Selma Lagerlöf's longer books. The long chain of adventures is most happily forged into organic unity. . . . A great love for childhood, for all the forms of nature, for every part of this far-flung Fatherland has found its full artistic expression in 'Nils Holgersson.' . . . (pp. 66-7)

Dr. Lagerlöf's work follows a definite line of development from the day when she attempted to make herself known as a poet. 'Gösta Berling' was like the bursting of a dam. Parts of the first book and some of her early stories reveal her mastery of narrative art, but before arriving at the full development of her powers in the 'Christ Legends' and 'Nils Holgersson,' she feels impelled to grapple with the currents of thought around her in a series of problem novels, which serve to clarify her own philosophy. The return to her old home re-opens the treasure-chest of childhood memories, and old legends of Värmland become the principal subject of her work. . . . (p. 80)

The development of her art throws rich light on the character of the author. The wide range and great variety of subjects she has handled show her to be a woman, not only of highly sensitive imagination, but of great strength and sturdiness. Her excitable fancy, her motherly affection, her profound sympathy and her enlightened philosophy are combined with a great depth of character. She is most profoundly attached to home and family and to the traditions of her nation and fatherland, so that no outside influence can detach her from the affections of her youth. . . . Her strongly marked individuality has left its mark on all her works, which are an embodiment of her own character and faith. (pp. 80-1)

[Selma Lagerlöf's] narrative method was decided by an intimate acquaintance with the traditional oral narratives of her home district. This oral narrative exists in a world of its own, wholly distinct in origin and nature from that of the written word. The distinctiveness of her contribution to the national literature was due to her absorption in this strange, confused, inconsequential, miraculous realm. . . . Collections of oral narrative of every type had already been made; but in the hands of Selma Lagerlöf these traditional stories, gathered for the most part by herself from the mouths of skilled narrators, became the rarest creations of a lofty genius. The art of telling stories to an intimate circle of listeners has had an immense influence on her work, greater than on that of any poet or novelist in literature; yet in her own outlook on life and in her creative endowment there are powerful characteristics not to be found in oral tradition. Her art is by no means naive; even its simplest creations are animated by an intelligence, a wealth of feeling and a spirituality not to be found in folk-lore. The real content of all her works is the inner spiritual development of her characters; her object is to reveal this, and to make it of value to universal humanity. (pp. 92-3)

The story-teller depends for his effect on the strong emotions he arouses in his hearers, and the art of Selma Lagerlöf has the same quality. . . . [The division of her] books into short chapters each with its own climax makes possible a perpetual stirring of the emotions to fear, horror, laughter, compassion, sorrow. Not even in Dante is there a more moving picture of the realm of the damned than in 'The Christ Legends.' . . . (pp. 96-7)

Though she draws freely on folk-lore, Selma Lagerlöf does not incline to the mere fairy story. . . . Her works resemble rather the didactic sagas, with their earnest presentation of actual existence, true to daily life, yet introducing supernatural elements to enforce a profound moral. Although Dr. Lagerlöf's stories contain supernatural elements, they never break away entirely from reality; when she incorporates such elements in her narrative she makes them intensely actual, and they play a decisive part in the unfolding of the plot. (p. 97)

Though we have dwelt at some length on Selma Lagerlöf's debt to folk-lore, this in no way implies that she owed to it her whole art. She is not a mere teller of old stories, but a profoundly original author, endowed with a range of abilities far beyond those of the popular narrator. Her real goal, the goal of all the best modern literature, is the disclosure of the human heart, whereas the folk-tale is very weak in the description of feeling. (pp. 98-9)

[Selma Lagerlöf's] faith is firm and simple. From the manifold and multi-coloured doctrines of Christendom she has singled out one central theme and made it her own—faith in an all-embracing, omnipresent spiritual Power. . . . Dr. Lagerlöf's philosophy is liberal and broadminded. Her faith, one perceives, is not besought of God in daily prayer as a special favour; rather is it the fundamental basis of her thought and action. Although the miraculous has an irresistible attraction for her, she is in no way a mystic. Nowhere does she describe mystical states of mind, nor seek unity with God through exalted feeling, nor sink into the depths of her own soul; like Goethe, she draws reverently back from this inscrutable realm. Her works do not deal with the everlasting realities, nor with the relation between God and the individual soul, nor with eternal bliss. . . . [Humanity] is made for work in the market place of this world, and only the last longings of the released soul may wing their way to heaven. (p. 101)

Frequently her works exhibit paganism and Christendom in strong contrast. . . . Without particular reference to paganism Dr. Lagerlöf constantly depicts the struggle between hard-heartedness and kindness. In a hundred forms the same story is retold; it is the fundamental subject of her work. It is therefore not surprising that her imagination always dwells with horror on war. For her war is sheer paganism, and the banishment of it is the inescapable task of Christianity. (p. 103)

[Throughout her work] she is striving to portray the warp and woof of Divine purpose in the lives and destinies of men, and never once does she waver in her certainty of the justice and kindness of Providence.

It is only fair to confess that Dr. Lagerlöf's conception of human life has definite limitations. The scene of her stories is mostly laid in small towns or in the country, among people still governed by a faith similar to her own. She generally avoids any detailed description of town life. . . . The grosser elements of town life she indicates . . . , but she would seem to make the reader feel that all poverty is self-induced and that normal charitableness of heart should dispel it.

Hardly anywhere in her work does she portray those scenes, too common in modern civilisation, calculated to shake one's faith in a good and just Deity. . . . (pp. 104-05)

Wherever Selma Lagerlöf traces the workings of God in the human heart, her philosophy is strong, indisputably genuine and comforting; but whenever she permits supernatural powers to interfere with the normal course of events, its limits are at once obvious. The logical pursuit of her fundamental thesis under every circumstance brings about such a simplification of human destiny, that a thoughtful and experienced reader cannot be fully satisfied, and begins to question where she ceases to do so. (pp. 105-06)

[Love] is the power animating all her work. The tense and thrilling action of her plots, the stately and flowing rhythm of her style are only the transparent glass through which shines a profound spiritual experience. To the superficial reader, Selma Lagerlöf may appear a recluse, unacquainted with the world; but whoever pierces below the surface finds there a mental realm which includes wide tracts of reality. However her mother-love came into being and ripened into such an all-embracing affection, it is the beginning and the end, the seed and the fruit, the innermost being of her art.

Im this great motherliness there is certainly an element of self-conquest, of freedom from the world and yearning for a more spiritual experience, but there is no self-repression, mysticism or asceticism. The fairy-like quality of her work is therefore blended with a strong attachment to the actual world. (p. 109)

Were it not for this actuality in her work, the reader might weary of its supernatural elements and of the simple philosophy it unfolds. The inexhaustible wealth of incident, the objective reality and the striking portrayal of unique characters prevent this. . . .

[Selma Lagerlöf's] poetic imagination constantly transcends the human circumstances. Yet she is no romanticist. Her soul is doubly bound to reality, for instead of sublimating the actual world, she compels the supernatural to act in and for it. . . . However rich her stories may be in poetic imagination, they never become fantastic, but remain true to reality. (p. 110)

Dr. Lagerlöf has her rich flow of poetic imagery under perfect control. When she is deeply interested in a plot or a character, her imagination always comes to her aid, and the loose-knit nature of her stories gives free play to her rich fancy. Yet the author does not give full rein to her feelings, but exercises a stern discipline over her imagination, which is always brought into the service of man's spiritual life.

Her poetic fancy is ceaselessly employed to give life and colour to description. . . . Her whole work is filled with this rich poetic power, which distinguishes it wholly from other forms of literary art. . . .

Selma Lagerlöf's favourite occupation is, as she has said, the study of character. . . .

Her attention has been fixed on the fundamental qualities of human character, and the more profound revolutions of human destiny. (p. 111)

It may be true that Selma Lagerlöf's characters lack something of every-day reality. Her outstanding personalities are always clothed with a certain magic power which lifts them above the common run of life. They have an inner kinship with the figures of folk-lore, which are personifications of elemental forces, and thus they are more than individuals. But they are by no means mere types representing ideas, virtues and vices, for their personality is rich and vivid, with unique and charming characteristics.

Dr. Lagerlöf's work is distinct from the naturalism, the impressionism and the expressionism of our age. She is less concerned with man in his relation to actual life than with his innermost being, his deepest longings, his purest purposes, his secret idealism—with all that he might be and so often cannot be. (p. 113)

The perfect balance of her powers gives to her work the stately calm of the true epic. She is not dramatic, because for her all passionate struggle is over; nor tragic, because her character contains no insoluble contradictions; her rich powers continue to produce a gentle harmony. (p. 114)

[The] great literary achievement of Dr. Lagerlöf [is] the inner fusion of rich objectivity and vivid description with profound moral and spiritual insight in a style so simple that it can be understood by all. (p. 117)

> *Walter A. Berendsohn, in his* Selma Lagerlöf: Her Life and Work, *translated by George F. Timpson, I. Nicholson & Watson Ltd., 1931 (and reprinted by Kennikat Press, 1968), 136 p.*

HANNA ASTRUP LARSEN (essay date 1936)

[Selma Lagerlöf's *The Story of Gösta Berling*] was the accumulated sum of her childhood's memories, her girlhood's dreams, and the affections of her whole lifetime. As it grew and took shape in her mind, it became not the story of a few individuals but the epic of a countryside, a world revolution in miniature. The form, a cycle of related stories, is artfully adapted to the purpose. We are introduced to myriads of people, who are flashed on our consciousness and then fade into the background again. We see them only in bold outline, often only in a single incident, but they all advance the momentum of the story.

Gösta Berling, who gives his name to the book, is an incarnation of its spirit. . . . The author has seen him as a certain Swedish type, the brilliant, volatile artist temperament. (pp. 32-3)

[Selma Lagerlöf's works are shot through with] very old legendary lore. How much does she want us to believe? She does not say. She tells the stories as they existed in the minds of those who believed them. The supernatural and the real are so closely interwoven that they could not be separated without tearing the fabric to pieces. Selma Lagerlöf does not attempt to extricate the one from the other. (p. 37)

The author was able to create her fairy-tale atmosphere by placing the action of the book in a period that even in her childhood lay far enough back to have become tradition, a time of gay cavaliers and lovely ladies, of wild sleigh rides and merry balls, of people who were impulsive, wholehearted, and unreflecting. Towards the end of the book, however, she shows the influence of her own time. There is an Ibsenesque casting up of moral accounts, and the gentle Countess Elisabeth turns on her husband (Gösta) with Nora-like denunciations, bidding him do his duty "quite simply and without heroics." (pp. 38-9)

When many people, especially in the neighborhood, have thought that *The Story of Gösta Berling* purported to be a narrative from real life or from local legends, it is in part

because the physical background is true to reality. The author's method has been first to create the characters and then invent the story, which she has staged in the environment she knew from childhood. (p. 42)

[*The Story of Gösta Berling*] did not at once win the approval of the critics. (p. 44)

[Georg Brandes, a Danish critic,] praised the author's firm grasp of her subject and her successful blending of the lyric and the epic, but he hoped that in her next book she would be less lavish of her material and remember that a single human being "has in him a whole Värmland, nay many Värmlands." . . . In an age when authors aimed to dissect every fiber of emotion within the narrow confines of one person or one incident, she squandered the creatures of her imagination as if her wealth were inexhaustible, as indeed it seemed. When objectiveness was the parole, she was intensely subjective, throbbing with personal emotion in every line. (pp. 45-6)

As a picture of Italy *The Miracles of Antichrist* is charming. Involuntarily one compares it with George Eliot's *Romola*, which also grew out of a visit to Italy. . . . Her touch is as light and graceful as George Eliot's is heavy. She seems to understand the people of the South by that subtle divination which is her peculiar gift. She turns on them the same loving gaze that she directs towards her Swedish neighbors, and the little quaint town of Diamante with its simple, kindly people comes to life under her hand. (pp. 54-5)

In style and method of approach *Jerusalem* is as different from *The Story of Gösta Berling* as Dalecarlian peasants are different from Värmland cavaliers. It is written with a sobriety and a restraint that fit the subject, and sometimes there is a suggestion of the folk tale. There is no longer the intense personal feeling; the author seems to stand more aloof and does not apostrophize her readers as in her first book. The influence from [Thomas] Carlyle is no longer evident.

The supernatural element is strong in *Jerusalem* and is closely intertwined with the religious emotions of the people. (p. 66)

To the Dalecarlian period belongs also Selma Lagerlöf's greatest non-fiction work, the two books about Nils Holgersson and his journey through Sweden. . . . (p. 69)

Artfully and without a single "thus we see," Selma Lagerlöf leads her young readers first to see what pleasure they can enjoy in the companionship of animals and then to understand the broader principle that no one can be happy without feeling affection for others. (p. 71)

[*Nils Holgerssons underbara resa genom Sverige*] has no doubt done more than any other book to acquaint both children and grown-ups with Sweden. (p. 72)

It is a striking fact that an author who never wrote an equivocal line, and whose own life has never been touched by a breath of gossip, let alone scandal, should have so little condemnation for what is generally called illicit love. Her severest censure is always reserved for selfishness, cruelty, and hardness. I cannot remember any occasion when she has shown that love itself can be selfish and cruel.

Perhaps one reason for her large charity is that she has never quite plumbed the depths of human passion. She knows that it exists, of course; there are few things in human nature that this seeress does not know, but she does not choose to dwell on the physical side of love. She thinks of the yearning between men and women chiefly as a longing of the soul and an emotion of the heart. Therefore she is able to draw it within the circle of that love which she conceives as the great regenerative force in the life of the individual. (p. 78)

If Selma Lagerlöf's fame did not rest so securely upon her great novels and her Nils Holgersson books, she would be known as one of the most distinguished short story writers of the Scandinavian North. The smaller format enables her to isolate an idea or an episode and present it with epic strength and simplicity. Her extraordinary fertility of imagination is almost more striking here than in the longer works. Every story is different from every other, each conceived with boldness and worked out with exquisite delicacy.

Her first volume of short stories, *Invisible Links,* which appeared after *The Story of Gösta Berling,* gave evidence of her versatility. Perhaps the most interesting story in the collection is "The Outlaws," dealing with primitive Sweden. . . . [The] story was written in a period when Selma Lagerlöf was deeply wrought up over the cruelties that were masked under religion or patriotism or progress. In the same volume are several stories protesting against the horrors of war.

In her later collections of short stories, more especially in those based on legends of saints, she almost always emphasizes love as the one regenerative force, cruelty as the one thing that shuts human beings out from God. (pp. 81-3)

[There] is certainly no lack of imagination in the Löwensköld Cycle [*The General's Ring, Charlotte Löwensköld,* and *Anna Svärd*] which was completed in her seventieth year. (p. 86)

The seeming perversion of justice in [*The General's Ring*] is something very unusual with Selma Lagerlöf, who nearly always uses the supernatural to vindicate right against wrong. As we cannot believe that she wrote it merely to entertain us with a goose-flesh thriller, we wonder whether she has lost her old faith in goodness and right. Has she seen evil prevail so long that she has begun to despair of justice? The only answer, it seems to me, must be that evil breeds evil and vengeance leads to more vengeance, and human beings are so bound up one with another that the innocent cannot escape suffering. (p. 88)

In *Charlotte Löwensköld* we are back in the manors and parsonages that we know from *The Story of Gösta Berling.* The time is about the same, the twenties and thirties of the nineteenth century, but the youthful glamour and golden haze of that first work of her genius are gone. The treatment is much more realistic, the outlines clearer and sharper, the language terser and quicker. We get closer to the people in their intimate daily life, and the humor is broader. In spite of the baleful influence of the fatal ring, this book and the following have less of the mystic and supernatural than almost any other work by the author. (p. 89)

With Anna Svärd and her friends [in *Anna Svärd*] Selma Lagerlöf takes us back to the scene of *Jerusalem,* but here again the treatment of peasant life is much more realistic

than in the older book. She makes, for instance, free use of the Dalecarlian dialect. Anna herself is a substantive character and has plenty of native wit and shrewdness, though she can neither read nor write. The difference between her and Karl Arthur is of course abysmal, but she loves him and is attractive enough to win a certain regard from him. The study of Anna's development is done with penetrating psychologic insight. It is clear that in the struggles of marital adjustment the author's sympathy is entirely on the side of the woman with her sound natural instincts and unreflecting warmth of heart. (pp. 90-1)

In some respects [Karl Arthur] resembles Gösta Berling in his beauty and charm, his power of inspiring affection, his visionary eloquence, and the emotionalism that swings between exaltation and despair. But Gösta Berling has the one thing that redeems all his faults, the power of unselfish affection. Karl Arthur lacks it, and therefore all his virtues are sterile. (p. 91)

In Karl Arthur the author castigates the self-righteous fanatic who thinks chiefly of achieving a special holiness for himself and recks little of how much he hurts others. It is evident that she finds more Christianity in . . . simple kindly people who take their religion as a matter of course without emotional spasms, who enjoy the pleasant things of the world without scruple, and do good to all who come within their circle. (p. 92)

[Karl Arthur] finally learns that one cannot love God without loving men.

It is significant that the Löwensköld Cycle . . . should end with the message which in one form or another runs like a red thread through all Selma Lagerlöf's varied production. (pp. 92-3)

That which impresses [Selma Lagerlöf's readers] first is the creative wealth of her imagination. Her mind teems with ideas and images that are bodied forth seemingly without any effort on her part. For pure inventiveness her stories have rarely been equaled, and her skillful use of the element of surprise has been noted by many critics.

Closely allied to her imagination is the almost psychic intuition that enables her to enter into the mood of distant ages and climes and to put herself in the place of people who are immeasurably removed from the even tenor of her own ways. Her fancy is equally at home in the natural and the supernatural. . . . True, there are domains of the human soul which she has never explored, but within her own field the richness of her mind seems inexhaustible.

In her interpretation of spiritual things she is a mystic; in her treatment of bygone days she is a romanticist, and yet she is a realist in her grasp of actualities. She possesses in full measure that sense of intimate homely details which is often the asset of the woman novelist, and by means of it she brings us so close to the scenes she describes that we seem to have been there and lived through them with her.

She is always sincere, and her style is so simple that it is accessible to the most unliterary. The sophisticated will enjoy its naïve charm, but at the same time they will perceive a delicate irony which plays over her sturdy honesty as a sunbeam plays among the foliage of an oak. Often the irony is turned on herself, as if she needed it to keep in check her too fervent enthusiasm. Her humor is seldom tangible enough to raise a laugh; it is present rather as a flavor that gives a subtle pungency to the whole dish.

But the strongest of the strands by which Selma Lagerlöf holds us is her faith in goodness.... [The] one theme, which she treats with infinite variations, is the struggle between light and darkness. She has faith that light will prevail, and she makes us believe it because we feel the goodness and purity of her own heart. It is possible that her very limitations, her refusal to look upon what is stark or hideous or gross, may have added to her popularity. Nevertheless, she could not have won and held the love of millions of readers if her goodness had been insipid. It is no mere negation, but an active, regenerative force, and it is the deepest source of her power over others. (pp. 94-6)

> Hanna Astrup Larsen, in her Selma Lagerlöf (copyright, 1935, 1936 by Hanna Astrup Larsen; reprinted by permission of Doubleday & Company, Inc.), Doubleday, Doran & Company, Inc., 1936, 117 p.

ALRIK GUSTAFSON (essay date 1940)

Gösta Berling's Saga disturbed most of the Swedish critics of the day because it was so *different*. As prose fiction it fell into no easily recognized type. Besides, it was too rich in emotional overtones, and entirely too naïve in its glorification of materials and themes which a decade of "sober reason" had come to look upon with disfavor and identify with a clearly outmoded Romanticism. It would seem, indeed, considering the literary tastes of the day, that a young schoolmistress was risking all opportunities for a literary future by making her début at this time with a novel that defied practically every ideal of literary composition which her generation held dear. In place of the photographic realism characteristic of the fiction of her time, Selma Lagerlöf indulged freely in what seemed to be a whimsical, utterly capricious selection of detail both in her highly lyric descriptive passages and in her loose development of plot. In place of a rigidly objective measuring of cause-and-effect relations in human life, Selma Lagerlöf occupied herself quite frankly with the unbelievable, the fantastic and miraculous, at times even with miracles. In place of the hopelessly decadent tone of much of the fiction of her day, Selma Lagerlöf created a world of romantic adventures, of heroic action, a world in which the sense of joy in life was permitted to be unobstructed, abandoned, complete. (pp. 185-86)

The central fact about Selma Lagerlöf as a novelist is that she is a born story teller. It can be said without exaggeration, I think, that not since Hans Christian Andersen delighted old and young alike with his fairy tales had a Scandinavian story teller so fascinated his public with pure *narrative* abilities as did Selma Lagerlöf in her tales of the Värmland Cavaliers.... In the handling of scene the author of *Gösta Berling's Saga* is equalled by many, and distanced by some; in variety and profundity of character analysis she must be said to rank rather low among Scandinavian novelists of first importance; but as a direct, spontaneous, vividly moving teller-of-tales she remains in her fictional achievements all but alone in the long line of Scandinavian novelists down to our day.

The chief secret of her story telling ability in *Gösta Berling's Saga,* as well as in a host of other Värmland tales more or less closely related to the Cavalier legends, lies in the frank and unabashed naïveté of her narrative point of view. Impatiently casting aside the elaborate machinery of fictional techniques that had become characteristic of the novel of her day, she resolved to write spontaneously, without reflection.... Selma Lagerlöf resolved to tell these tales as they had been told to her ... naïvely, with none of the reservations of a sophisticated maturity, and as if by word-of-mouth.... It was an artistic accomplishment of no mean order to do this, and do it well, in "the enlightened 1890's"; but she did it so well that even the cosmopolitan, worldly wise tastes of Georg Brandes, whose custom it was to make short shrift with the imaginative vagaries of "Romanticism," was forced to admit her narrative triumph. (pp. 189-90)

Gösta Berling's Saga is made up of a succession of more or less closely related tales, each of them an entity in itself, and the whole held together in a rather loose narrative pattern. This pattern centres, on the one hand, upon the adventures of Gösta Berling, the hero of the novel, and, on the other hand, upon the strange fate of the Major's Wife at Ekeby, whose strength of character and thoroughly masculine abilities had made her the most notable person in the whole province of Värmland. The unity of the novel, such as it is, cannot alone be maintained, however, by centring our attention upon the double story of Gösta Berling and the Major's Wife.... The more constant, immediate unifying elements of the novel are those of time and place—most of the action taking place within the limits of exactly a year and a day, and all of the stories converge intimately upon Lake Löfven.... More particularly it might be said that the action tends to converge upon Ekeby Manor, the then famous residence of the wealthy Major's Wife. (p. 191)

[Tale] follows upon tale in rapid succession, each of them more or less related to life at Ekeby, all of them in the high romantic tone of the opening episode—some filled with a pathos just short of the tragic ("Ebba Dohna's Story"), others adventurous in the grand manner ("The Ball at Ekeby" and "The Paths of Life"), some inspired by the half-dismal terrors of native superstition ("Ghost Stories"), and still others packed with a sparkling, rollicking humor ("The Old Carriages" and "Squire Julius").

The plot of the novel—in the sense that there is a discernible plot in this strange congeries of Värmland legends—develops around the conflict between the Major's Wife and the Cavaliers for the possession of Ekeby. (p. 192)

Selma Lagerlöf identifies herself with her characters with the same naïve intensity as do many of the writers of the older sagas.

It may have some significance also that, like the heroes of the Icelandic biographical sagas, Gösta Berling is not a successful man as his saga comes to a close. It must be pointed out in this connection, however, that the spirit of Christian resignation with which Gösta takes his exit in the final scene of the novel is hardly the note on which most of the old biographical sagas close. It is rather on a note of genuine tragedy—such as that of *Lear*—that the Icelandic saga usually is brought to an end. It seems, however, that neither the general spirit of the largely carefree Värmland Cavalier legends, nor the essentially sunny temperament of Selma Lagerlöf, could permit a more severe judgment upon Gösta than is implicit in the Christian spirit of resignation. (p. 193)

Gösta Berling's Saga differs in narrative technique from the old sagas, moreover, in the constant intrusion of its author upon the story in the form of those lyric outbursts which so frequently interrupt the smooth flow of the narrative movement—introducing episodes, commenting upon the action, and offering, not infrequently, the author's generalizations, often in a moralizing manner, upon the world in general and upon human fate in particular. This is the note of Carlyle rather than that of a typical saga narrator. At times these extra-narrative intrusions do not unduly disturb the reader's concentration upon the story; at other times they seem somewhat forced and unnecessary, definitely breaking the narrative spell that Selma Lagerlöf has previously cast upon us.

Scene, as we have observed, is one of the elements in the novel which give to it a rather closely knit unity not always apparent in the conduct of the medley of tales in themselves. Very early in her novel Selma Lagerlöf pauses long enough in the progress of her story to give us what might be called a full-length portrait of Lake Löfven. . . . To refer to her description of the valley of the Löfven as "a full-length portrait" is hardly exaggerated, for to her sensitively active imagination Lake Löfven *is a personality.* . . .

[Throughout her description] the same tendency to personify natural scene is dominant. All of nature, even its inanimate forms, take on a pulsing, personal life. (pp. 194-95)

Everywhere in *Gösta Berling's Saga* action is directly motivated by an ebulliently spontaneous impulse; never is an action the result of mature, deliberate reflection. (p. 199)

[Even] at the end of the novel, where impulse might conceivably be expected to submit to some "higher law of being," we find it still the determining power in the final action of Gösta; though at this point Gösta's impulse has undergone a kind of transformation—it is less violent than heretofore, and more socially constructive in its motivation, combining at the last, curiously enough, with a partly chastened spirit of Christian resignation. It is important to note, however, that Gösta has not *changed* essentially when he makes his final decision to live a simple life of humble service among the peasant-folk of his beloved Värmland. . . . [He] is still the same creature of impulse that we find in the opening scene of the *Saga.* . . . (pp. 199-200)

It is important to note, moreover, not only that the characters in *Gösta Berling's Saga* are essentially children of impulse, but also that their impulses, almost without exception, are fundamentally in intent *good.* These characters are scarcely ever motivated by mean or ignoble impulses, though they may often for a moment be weak and childish enough. (p. 200)

Little wonder is it, in the light of these facts, that the chief fault which Georg Brandes had to find with *Gösta Berling's Saga* was the over-simplified treatment of character which results inevitably from Selma Lagerlöf's optimistic view of human impulse. The Danish critic objected vigorously to the child-of-impulse psychology that lay at the base of character portrayal in the novel; and by implication he rejected Selma Lagerlöf's easy acceptance of that sentimental view of human nature which found impulse almost invariably good at base. Brandes is ready to applaud without reservations the fresh naïveté of manner which animates Selma Lagerlöf's strictly narrative technique; but he condemns heartily the carrying over of this naïveté into the author's

treatment of human character. . . . Of Gösta Berling himself, Brandes points out, we know only "the outlines of his person," though he is the hero of the *Saga;* and nowhere in the novel, with the single exception of Marienne Sinclaire, do we come upon a character which is even remotely conceived in the penetrating lights and shades of a thoroughly modern view of human psychology. (pp. 201-02)

The childlike naïveté in point of view, so eminently successful in the purely narrative technique of the novel, could hardly be maintained in the processes of character analysis without certain serious consequences. The modern reader —perhaps in some cases against his will—seems forced to conclude that the characters in *Gösta Berling's Saga* tend to be superficially rendered, over-idealized, reduced almost to the psychological level of the nursery tale. It should be recorded, however, that Selma Lagerlöf herself was at least partly conscious of the difficulty. In defense of her own procedures she suggests at one point in the novel that "One must treat old tales with care; they are like faded roses. They easily drop their petals if one comes too near to them." (p. 202)

It might very well be argued that any other method of character analysis—particularly a thoroughly modern one— would be quite inconsistent with her narrative material, a simple body of local folk legends. It seems, in short, that Selma Lagerlöf may have deliberately chosen to simplify her characters in the interests of artistic congruity. . . . [Marienne Sinclaire] is a character sketched in a thoroughly modern spirit. Deliberately introspective, a curiously sterile example of the split-personality, Marienne Sinclaire seems made to order for the sophisticated present-day reader of fiction. But Marienne Sinclaire, it is to be noted, is felt to be exceptional in the world of Värmland folk legends; and her story remains in consequence only a disturbing interlude in Selma Lagerlöf's novel—a fragment sketched only in the barest of outlines. (pp. 203-04)

[It] is clear that Selma Lagerlöf's best creative powers were active only when she busied herself with such characters as were dominated by impulse alone—Gösta, the Major's Wife, the Cavaliers, and in one way or another nearly all the other individuals who people the pages of her first novel. Each of these characters is interesting enough in himself; and yet each of them is perhaps even more interesting as an individual who personifies, each in his own way, the general folk-character of Värmland. It is a collective, almost racial conception of character which is after all Selma Lagerlöf's primary preoccupation in *Gösta Berling's Saga.*

For this novel is primarily the saga of a province—not a story whose chief concern is with individual characters. The real hero of *Gösta Berling's Saga* is not Gösta Berling but *the collective character of Värmland.* . . . Gösta is to be considered by the reader, not as an individual in the ordinary sense of the word, but rather as the most profound individual representation of the collective character of Värmland. A highly individualized character in keeping with modern psychological demands would seem in this instance to be curiously inappropriate.

It is customary among even sympathetic critics of *Gösta Berling's Saga* to decry the serious moralizing tone with which the novel is brought to a close. Gösta, they reason, should not be reduced at the end to a moral being, sober, reformed, and contrite. . . . The chief contention of these critics—that the moral has been gratuitously "dragged in" near the close—is a fundamentally false one; for in almost every chapter of Selma Lagerlöf's novel the moral emphasis is present, sometimes being given direct expository expression, at other times unmistakably implied in the conduct of narrative episode. (pp. 204-06)

It is true that we are permitted on occasion in *Gösta Berling's Saga* to revel as children in a fictional world of pure high adventure; but never for long in these pages are we allowed to remain forgetful of the sterner demands of an actual world governed by certain severe moral laws. . . .

[Selma Lagerlöf's] genius has revealed a thoroughgoing ethical bias. (p. 207)

In Selma Lagerlöf's general conception of the world the fundamental conflict in life does not lie between good and evil. To her essentially sunny, almost naïvely optimistic temperament evil does exist, to be sure—but only as a shadow that may cast itself temporarily over experience, not as a basic, constantly present determining condition of existence. The human soul is not to her primarily a Manichaean battle-ground between the power of evil and the power of good. She conceives of the world rather as a state of existence fundamentally good in all essential respects—disturbed, perhaps more than occasionally, by evil, but never for long dominated by it. It is therefore that she looks upon the central problem of life as a seeking, on the part of the individual soul, for a proper balance between joy and virtue, gaiety and goodness. It is to be noted that the Cavaliers, including Gösta, must at last depart from Ekeby because their gaiety, though innocent in intent, was often evil in its consequences. (p. 208)

Flesh and spirit are viewed by Selma Lagerlöf as possible of combination toward a common noble end. And as there is no basic conflict between the flesh and the spirit, so is there none between the spirit of joy and the spirit of goodness properly understood. Nor is impulse to be stultified—rather is it to be guided carefully into channels of goodness. Resignation, the will to endure, has its place in Selma Lagerlöf's view of life, and likewise penitence of a kind. . . . In the central ethical implication of *Gösta Berling's Saga*—that impulse is fundamentally good—Selma Lagerlöf joins hands with the primitivistic ethics of Rousseau, though she might hesitate to admit the kinship.

Her positive ethics in *Gösta Berling's Saga* reminds one, perhaps, even more definitely, however, of [Thomas] Carlyle, particularly in the late chapters of her novel, where she preaches with an ever increasing emphasis the constructive doctrine of work. . . . Swedish critics have occupied themselves more frequently with Selma Lagerlöf's stylistic indebtedness to Carlyle in *Gösta Berling's Saga* than with the possible influence of Carlyle's ethics on the novel; and this is perhaps the proper emphasis. (pp. 209-10)

I am convinced, indeed, that no merely literary source had the importance in shaping Selma Lagerlöf's general view of life as expressed in *Gösta Berling's Saga* that her parental home had. Any student of the sources of Selma Lagerlöf's characteristic attitude toward life must constantly return to Mårbacka; for here it is that her deepest and strongest roots have sunk. (p. 213)

One could play at Mårbacka, but one must also work; both activities were equally welcome, each had its natural and appointed place. . . .

Certainly it is fitting that Selma Lagerlöf should find her ethical roots in Mårbacka, even as she had found at Mårbacka her tales, her characters, and many of the details of her fictional method; though some modern readers will doubtless feel a certain limitation in the optimistic ethics of Mårbacka. . . . Selma Lagerlöf never outgrew the simple, optimistic ethics of Mårbacka. This explains why she deals so satisfactorily with legends and with peasant characters in semi-primitive environments; and this explains also why her art is so uncertain when it seeks to come at grips with other, more complicated materials. (p. 214)

The novel *Jerusalem,* though its action takes place in Dalarne and in the Holy City, might be said to be more closely related to *Gösta Berling's Saga* than any of the other volumes which came from Selma Lagerlöf's pen between her literary début . . . and the publication of *The Wonderful Adventures of Nils.* . . . The quietly dignified movement of the sober religious tale which is unrolled for us in *Jerusalem* seems to have none of the characteristics of high romance so typical of the earlier *Saga*—its venturesome action, its rapid, colorful movement, its stylistic vehemences, and its fanciful world of dream and ideal. . . . (p. 216)

[Yet] the two novels have much in common. *Jerusalem* is hardly less lyric in its basic tone than is *Gösta Berling's Saga.* Its lyricism is merely conceived in a different manner: less spontaneous, though no less intense; less ecstatic, yet no less elevating; less brilliant, and yet just therefore, perhaps, more substantial, more profound, more penetratingly sensitive in its seeing and in its feeling. In short, Selma Lagerlöf's lyricism in *Jerusalem* is a more mature lyricism. If *Gösta Berling's Saga* may be said to represent Wordsworth's definition of poetry as "the spontaneous overflow of powerful feelings," the novel *Jerusalem* may be held to typify the more characteristically Wordsworthian definition that "poetry is emotion recollected in tranquillity." (pp. 216-17)

[The strangely moving religious story of the picturesque parish of Nås in Dalarne] gripped her no less deeply than had her earlier Värmland materials, and the result, stylistically, was a prose of delicate, restrained, and yet strong lyric power. The very subject matter of *Jerusalem* called, of course, for a sober and restrained stylistic lyricism; and in addition it seems very probable that outward literary influences to an extent determined the prose style of this novel. The prose style of *Jerusalem* seems to reveal even more consistently the imprint of the ancient Scandinavian sagas than does *Gösta Berling's Saga.* (p. 217)

The chief charm of [Selma Lagerlöf's autobiographical reminiscences from her childhood, *Mårbacka* and *A Child's Memories*] lies in their utter self-forgetfulness. It is doubtful that autobiography has ever been written with a more complete exclusion of self. . . . [Neither] of the two volumes, curiously enough, can be said to deal immediately with *Selma Lagerlöf herself*—except insofar as her childhood character is revealed indirectly through these childhood memories.

This artistic reticence is one of the most ingratiating elements in Selma Lagerlöf's character. It is natural with her. She never takes the reader into her confidence in the manner that has become so popular with authors since the years when the vogue of Romantic egotism first swept the literary world with its confessional strain—a manner which soon came to harden into a confessional pose or degenerate into a confessional hysteria. Selma Lagerlöf's artistic reticence grows naturally out of her essential modesty of person. Always has she been ready to give to others the credit for her own success as a novelist. Never does she take credit to herself. (pp. 222-23)

> *Alrik Gustafson, "Saga and Legend of a Province," in his* Six Scandinavian Novelists *(© copyright 1940 by the American-Scandinavian Foundation), American-Scandinavian Foundation, 1940, pp. 177-225.*

N. ELIZABETH MONROE (essay date 1941)

Miss Lagerlöf is a Protestant whose serene, unquestioning faith has followed an unbroken course. She is the supreme example in modern literature of the charm of simple goodness. . . . She has no interest in dogma nor in the intellectual elements of Christianity, and her novels do not concern themselves directly with social problems. This does not mean that Miss Lagerlöf's religious perception is unintelligent, but it has its roots so deep in her life and environment that it needs no examination. She is content to show Christianity flowering in goodness and kindliness in the lives of very simple people or leading them to devote everything to God. (p. 88)

The peasants Miss Lagerlöf writes about are dour and self-willed and gauche, but at the roots of their consciousness is the persistent desire to do God's bidding. Their lives are made significant by two loves, the love of land and the love of God, and when the two come into conflict, as they do in *Jerusalem,* it is the love of God that triumphs. (pp. 88-9)

It is hard to see how her particular ability would have flowered in any other environment than the one she knew. She is not a realist; she establishes the motives of her characters but not the outlines of personality, and has little to do with passion and sin. Her exploration of religious themes does not get at the roots of conscience, but concerns itself with a sense of God's nearness and a persistent brooding over motives and with various forms of obsession and mystical experience. She does not write, to any extent, of ideas, but quietly recreates the life of Värmland. (p. 90)

Selma Lagerlöf's description of Värmland is warm and homely and clear. She simply invents stories to describe the home she has always known. (p. 93)

It is in the first part of *Jerusalem* that Miss Lagerlöf gives the most complete picture of her native culture. . . . It provides one of the most remarkable interpretations of peasant life in fiction. Hardy's peasants are as natural as life itself, but they are never allowed to emerge from the background and are alien to the temper of the novel and to the laws that govern it. Miss Lagerlöf's story is based on a deep and penetrating vision of the peasant soul. Although she observes artistic economy in this story, the incidents give the effect of having been set down in a seemingly artless manner. The peasants are not relegated to the background nor sacrificed to the exigencies of a rigid plot; they are unfolded naturally and completely. They are imbued with a deep spiritual life and a particularity of their own and are

never made into pegs to carry the author's philosophy. (pp. 94-5)

[*Jerusalem*] is a remarkable interpretation of religious psychology, given with sympathy and understanding and sometimes with a quiet smile at the excesses to which man is open when he begins to interpret God in his own way. At times [the peasants'] piety leads them into spiritual arrogance, as when their leader turns child against parent, brother against sister, in the interest of unity. Sometimes it leads them into cruelty. (p. 96)

Selma Lagerlöf's greatest achievement lies in her reconciliation of imagination with the homely uses of everyday. Her novels are unique in this regard. The modern novel has little traffic with imagination. It is an incalculable element, except when used to fathom the motives of men or to weld the parts of a story together. . . . [Selma Lagerlöf] touches off the reader's mind and gives it the imaginative freedom of childhood or of dreams.

The fusion between real and unreal is effected very often by making supernatural phenomena the counterpart of conscience. With her the unreal always has its roots in the real, preferably in the realities of everyday living or in moral motives. There is a subtle connection between the moral and artistic conscience. To make use of this connection is the first requirement of a good folk tale or fairy story. (p. 97)

Selma Lagerlöf leads with ease from a troubled conscience to strange signs and omens and disasters. With her the supernatural is never allowed to take the lead in the narrative but simply intensifies the action of conscience. . . . Miss Lagerlöf has been careful to combine the unreal with the real and to have the unreal spring from moral aberration. (pp. 98-9)

It is thus that Miss Lagerlöf naturalizes superstitious and imaginative phenomena by making them appear to be projections of the conscience or the artistic equivalents of well known psychological states. . . .

Miss Lagerlöf's gift of subduing the wildest imaginings to the sphere of the credible amounts to genius. It derives in part from the fact that everything in her stories, both the real and the visionary, has a basis in actuality. (p. 99)

Certain oddities of character appear again and again in Miss Lagerlöf's stories. The Swedish people she describes are introspective in the extreme; they examine motives with scrupulous care and are often prone to obsessions of one kind or another. (p. 100)

The Ring of the Löwenskölds illustrates how superstition and magic can be naturalized by being made to conform to reason and the moral law. The three books of *The Ring of the Löwenskölds* are remarkable for their use of causality and their closely-knit tragedy and for the deep sense of mystery that runs through their strange events. (p. 103)

Miss Lagerlöf's stories are told on three and sometimes four levels. There is first a narrative about human beings; this is accompanied by an apparatus of legend and superstition; then the meaning of each incident is given, somewhat after the manner of a fable, and finally the spiritual significance is implied. *Gösta Berling* illustrates how supernatural motives may deepen and enrich a story in this way. The main action of *Gösta Berling* tells the story of a wayward minister, who, thinking that God has mocked at him, throws himself into a life of mad dissipation. He meets the little people of the woods, has strange adventures with the Devil, and undertakes superhuman exploits. Each incident is followed by its moral meaning. When the Countess Marta is driven from her home by magpies we see that she has given all her life to frivolity, which in the end has turned into a self-destructive malice. In the spiritual realm the story as a whole is meant to shadow forth the mad doings of fools and wayfarers who wander over the land until they find rest in God. As the reader contemplates each successive level, the story takes on deeper significance and becomes a rich, imaginative experience.

On all levels of her narrative Selma Lagerlöf stresses causality. Her characters, almost without exception, try to read the riddle of the universe, and when they are unskilled in the ways of thought, gain a dim intuition into the meaning of the world through signs and portents. Even the wise and learned are not above signs and portents as a clue to the mystery of the world and as a guide to their lives. Both their moral sense and their lively imagination, which leans toward superstition, make them sensitive to the law of cause and effect. (pp. 105-06)

[*The Miracles of Antichrist*] is the only one of her novels that concerns itself with an ideological theme. . . . The deceptive appeal of socialism is described through a vivid and intricate story of modern Sicily. Although the story has had high praise, it does not hold together as a novel. The suspense is not maintained beyond the separate incidents; the story rises to a peak, then falls off, rises again and falls off. Its real merit lies in the skill with which the appeal of Antichrist is used to implement the confusing story. It is bodied forth in signs, and miracles, and fables, and revolutions, and in the every-day narrative of Sicilian life. (pp. 106-07)

In spite of their remarkable use of causality Miss Lagerlöf's novels do not always hold together. The parts of her vision are not fused but remain separate incidents, dramatic in themselves, but not moving the story on. As in *The Miracles of Antichrist*, the action in her novels rises and falls, rises again and falls, and might very easily be ended a half dozen times before the novel is closed. The incidents themselves are moved by the law of cause and effect and the story as a whole has design; the difficulty is that interest is not sustained from one incident to another. (p. 107)

Miss Lagerlöf is at her best in the short story or in a novel that resembles fable. The incidents of *Gösta Berling* are simply laid end to end, but the imaginative interest holds the reader and releases his own myth-making capacities. (p. 108)

In summary it is enough to say that Miss Lagerlöf has certain traits rarely found in the modern novel. First of all she has the gift of imagination. . . . [She uses] legendary material as a springboard for her own imagination. It also acts as a release to the reader's mind. It is evident, too, that Miss Lagerlöf is a born story teller. Her stories all have the sound of tales told round the fire at night. . . . Stories told in this way must engage the attention and hold it by a simple flow of narrative. The naïveté of the point of view needs no excuse, and the author is free to turn prose into the enraptured medium of romance or to carry it along in pedestrian fashion. These are the qualities of Miss Lagerlöf's art. It is to her credit that she was not afraid to be simple and childlike when the narrative was simple, and that she knew by instinct that simple forms were the best medium for imaginative material. Her characterizations lack depth, but they are never unreal, and the stories she invents or remembers have their springs in truth. She has the virtue of good folk or fairy art; the strangeness of the unreal is brushed off by its affinity with the humble little things of every day. (pp. 109-10)

> *N. Elizabeth Monroe, "Provincial Art in Selma Lagerlöf" (originally appeared in a different form in* The Scandinavian Review, *Summer, 1940), in her* The Novel and Society: A Critical Study of the Modern Novel *(copyright, 1941, by The University of North Carolina Press), University of North Carolina Press, 1941, pp. 88-110.*

ELSA PEHRSON (essay date 1945)

[For Selma Lagerlöf] there was a reality behind our reality, a subtler world behind our concrete one. When people attributed her descriptions of this other world to her vivid imagination, she did not contradict them. She let them think as they pleased about her, in this as in so many other matters. (p. 42)

It was Selma Lagerlöf's great passion in life to explore the hidden powers and possibilities of man. She has always said that human beings are and can do much more than they themselves are conscious of, and has loved to describe the moments when they suddenly become conscious of these powers. . . . Nothing happens without a meaning. She was a firm believer in the law of cause and effect. Therefore she could not accept the Christian doctrine of vicarious atonement. What we have sown we must reap. In book after book she has described how human beings are purified and transformed by making good what they have broken. Few writers have so relentlessly traced what one might call the genealogy of a wrong deed in all its ramifications, or described in such glowing terms the final happiness when full atonement is won. It would seem a harsh doctrine were it not for the power of love which to Selma Lagerlöf is the supreme force, the axis on which everything turns both in the life of individuals and in the universe. It is the instrument through which the most hardened offenders can be transformed. If they have only a spark of love glowing somewhere deep down in their being, Selma Lagerlöf is on their side, and in her books she does not rest till she has fanned the spark into a great fire. (p. 43)

It is hardly surprising to find that Selma Lagerlöf accepted Freud's theory of the subconscious. For her the subconscious was not only a theory. It played a too important part in her work. What Freud calls the subconscious corresponds to her "inner workshop." She speaks about her own power to receive inspiration from this hidden source. . . . Sometimes she reaches so deep down that she seems to touch those strata where the common memories of the human race are stored.

Everything is alive in Selma Lagerlöf's world. Even stones. Nothing is isolated, everything is related, and there is a constant though invisible interchange between all things, great and small. The whole creation is one big family, where all the members are dependent on each other. What happens to one affects all. Nothing we do is unimportant or wholly private. Therefore it is a great responsibility to be a human being. When men do wrong, the whole of nature suffers. . . . This intimate relationship of everything gave any situation she described in her books extraordinary depth and breadth.

To have genius meant in Selma Lagerlöf's opinion to be receptive to the rays of intelligence that enlighten the universe. She saw it as her mission in life to spread these rays to those who could not themselves receive them. (pp. 43-4)

> *Elsa Pehrson, "Glimpses from the Hidden Workshop of Selma Lagerlöf," in* The American Scandinavian Review *(copyright 1945 by The American-Scandinavian Foundation), Vol. XXXIII, No. 1, March, 1945, pp. 41-4.*

ERIC O. JOHANNESSON   (essay date 1960)

Selma Lagerlöf and Isak Dinesen have both written autobiographical works considered by many to be their finest literary products. The former's *Mårbacka* and the latter's *Out of Africa* have several significant features in common. They do seem to suggest, first of all, the sources of the motives underlying the literary works of their respective authors. The two books describe a lost paradise, a way of life that will never return. In both instances we find ourselves on a farm on the verge of civilization. . . . The two worlds are self-contained, and within these worlds the authors found happiness and fulfillment. In both instances these worlds were lost, and the loss was felt as a great tragedy. (pp. 18-19)

The worlds [*Mårbacka* and *Out of Africa*] project are very similar to the fictional worlds of their authors, which leads us to conclude that both Selma Lagerlöf and Isak Dinesen rely heavily on personal experience even in their stories and novels. (p. 19)

Both writers rely heavily on the oral tradition of storytelling. If they do write novels, as they have done, these novels tend to fall apart at the seams. *Gösta Berlings Saga* is a collection of tales loosely strung together, and *Jerusalem* shows how difficult it was for Selma Lagerlöf to restrain herself from adding a good story ("The Loss of L'Univers" episode). (p. 21)

[Selma Lagerlöf and Isak Dinesen] are both very affirmative in their outlook on life. Both have a fine sense of humor, a strong piety toward the past and its traditions, but, above all, they have a great faith in life and in the power of myth.

In *Gösta Berlings Saga* Selma Lagerlöf speaks critically of the beautiful Marianne, because she has within herself the persistent itch for self-analysis, the dissecting spirit, which the author felt to be the characteristic feature of her age. And she cries out for vitality, instinct, wholeness, and faith. Many of Dinesen's figures have this dissecting spirit within them, and they are, consequently, unable to act. . . . (pp. 22-3)

[*Seven Gothic Tales* by] Isak Dinesen, like *Gösta Berlings Saga* some forty years earlier, marked the return to myth and storytelling. Both works appeared at a time when Scandinavian literature was either sociological or psychological in emphasis. The element of storytelling had been lost sight of in favor of analysis. With Isak Dinesen and Selma Lagerlöf the story regained its position of supremacy. (p. 24)

[No] comparison between these two writers would be complete without an indication of some of the ways in which they differ. . . .

Dinesen's tales tend to represent epiphanies. The most common figure in them is the young man who is waiting for fate to lend him a helping hand, to provide him with a new vision. A story is told, a little comedy is staged: thus the epiphany is induced.

Selma Lagerlöf's stories tend to represent conversions. The figures in them are often radically changed, but not through a change of vision. They do not come to see life in a new way, but change morally, from vanity or meanness to goodness and humility. . . .

Selma Lagerlöf's universe is essentially a moral one, in which the conflict is between good and evil, and in which God guides all for the best. For this reason her stories tend to be didactic in tone.

Dinesen's figures, on the other hand, live in an esthetic universe, in which God is a great artist, indifferent to good or evil. (p. 25)

The didactic tone which mars many of Lagerlöf's works is probably responsible for their lack of appeal to modern readers. Furthermore, the tales of Isak Dinesen meet, I believe, with a greater response today, because they express an underlying sense of despair, a tragic vision, that is lacking in the tales and novels of Selma Lagerlöf. There is in Selma Lagerlöf's works . . . an affirmation and praise of life, which is difficult for us to accept, since it is without this underlying tragic vision. . . . (pp. 25-6)

Thus, while Isak Dinesen has shown the young generation of writers in Scandinavia the path to the rediscovery of myth and the story, Selma Lagerlöf has not had much influence on younger Scandinavian writers. (p. 26)

> *Eric O. Johannesson, "Isak Dinesen and Selma Lagerlöf," in* Scandinavian Studies, *Vol. 32, No. 1, February, 1960, pp. 18-26.**

ERLAND LAGERROTH   (essay date 1961)

Let us first look at the relationship between characters and setting in Selma Lagerlöf's fiction. Let us try to see how these two parts of the poetic machinery work together and see how Selma Lagerlöf has composed with them as with different tunes in a counterpoint piece of music. . . . [Throughout Selma Lagerlöf's] writing, we find everywhere characters who are related to their setting and are explained and interpreted by all that is told about it. . . . Selma Lagerlöf's setting never becomes an articulated symbol . . . , for then the device would have become boring and ineffective. She simply describes man and his setting together and then we who read the story can experience the similarity spontaneously, and in this way it becomes more effective. (pp. 10-11)

The impression of the characters in *Gösta Berling's Saga* is, for instance, to a large extent due to compositions . . . so elaborately worked out, that there cannot be any doubt that they are conscious devices of art. But they are found not only in *Gösta Berling's Saga*—they constitute an important part in Selma Lagerlöf's craft all through her production. (p. 12)

[Almost] every episode in *Gösta Berling's Saga* is inscribed in the course of the seasons. . . . [The] changes and variations of the seasons in the landscape of Värmland constitute the most excellent sound-board for what happens among the people.

In this way motives of character and nature, events and setting everywhere co-operate in Selma Lagerlöf's poetic machinery, and it is hard to overrate what this kind of composition means in bringing out the individuality of characters and events more clearly and sharply, to give them color and substance and force. Of not least importance is it that so much *description* in this way can be transformed into narration. Instead of *describing* the characters, Selma Lagerlöf tells us about their relationship with their settings. . . . Instead of motives of character and setting being described each by themselves, they become as it were parts of a machine, parts moving and working in relation to one another. Thus the poetic experience becomes richer and stronger.

This can be said the more inasmuch as it is not only the characters that are "narrated forth" in this way. It is also the setting itself, because the interplay between man and setting is double-acting. (pp. 12-13)

[In] her writings men everywhere are standing around nature: worrying about it, struggling with it, rejoicing at it, working with it. And the rendering of their impressions and reactions pictures nature much better than long descriptions —and the long descriptions are not found in Selma Lagerlöf either.

Indirect description by overradiation and reflex light from characters and events is the most important secret in Selma Lagerlöf's rendering of landscape and nature. She is a story teller also in her description of nature, she "narrates forth" her landscapes, narrates them into us, and that is the foremost explanation why they have such a power over people. . . . (p. 14)

Let us now direct our attention in another direction, which also displays Selma Lagerlöf's craftsmanship and gives us insight into the poetic machinery of her writing. Now it is a question of the device, by which she succeeded poetically in transforming the tension and contradiction in her view of life. . . . Ever since [Selma Lagerlöf] came into contact with modern thought and science . . . she was torn between faith and knowledge, mysticism and rationalism. She was caught between the belief in the supernatural of the people in the milieu where she was brought up and the belief in the rational idea of the universe of her contemporaries, and faced by this choice she could never finally make up her mind. . . .

[At] the end Selma Lagerlöf found a solution in her dilemma. It was not a philosophical solution, because Selma Lagerlöf could no more than anyone else finally disprove mysticism or rationalism or synthetize them. It was an aesthetic and in a way a personal solution. Instead of choosing and rejecting, *she involved herself along both lines at the same time.* . . . Selma Lagerlöf succeeded in creating a form of fiction that made such a double commitment possible. That was achieved by letting her different ideas be announced, partly by different characters or social groups in her books, partly by different kinds of narrators, telling the story in the first person singular. In this way she did not need to stand as guarantor for any of the two views of life.

She could give knowledge what belonged to knowledge and then freely involve herself in what she called her "attraction towards the mystical, towards old popular beliefs in ghosts and elemental powers." (p. 15)

[Usually she presents] two points of view side by side without any disturbance as two equivalent possibilities. In this way *Gösta Berling's Saga* is written on two levels at one and the same time: the mystical-popular level, where the events are given a supernatural or religious explanation and the psychological-rationalistic where the events are looked upon as produced by the qualities of the characters themselves, the circumstances of the time and so on. And principally it is done in the same way in her other books.

Sometimes Selma Lagerlöf herself felt inferior—or at least pretended to—because she had chosen the way of double involvement instead of clearly and firmly choosing sides. (pp. 16-17)

The fact that throughout her life Selma Lagerlöf was directed towards listening, receiving and rendering instead of choosing, deciding and denying was probably sometimes a weakness in her personal life. But in her authorship it was a strength, which became the foundation of her greatness as a writer. . . . [She] was forced to develop the form of narration that can be called the art of double involvement. And in her hands that form was carried to a kind of perfection of the craft of fiction, where faith and knowledge are put side by side as they are in reality, and where the interplay and the gliding from one to the other recreates the ambiguity and contradiction of life itself. And with this richness and exuberance of ideas the basic melody of Selma Lagerlöf's fiction is not missing either. It is there and its name is tolerance, empathy and human understanding. (p. 17)

> *Erland Lagerroth, "The Narrative Art of Selma Lagerlöf: Two Problems," in* Scandinavian Studies, *Vol. 33, No. 1, February, 1961, pp. 10-17.*

LARRY W. DANIELSON (essay date 1975)

[*Gösta Berlings saga*] is an excellent example of Lagerlöf's use of Swedish folk materials toward literary ends. (p. 187)

It is the use of traditional demonic lore in *Gösta Berlings saga* that is of substantial interest to students of folklore-literature relations. Lagerlöf incorporated folk belief and legend into the novel for reasons other than the mere establishment of setting and tone. She used Värmlandian and more general Swedish and European traditions to delineate a major character and to enrich the ambiguities that surround him. Supernatural traditions, specifically demonic beliefs and legends, provided the powerful psychological stuff out of which Sintram was shaped. (pp. 192-93)

Sintram is not the stereotyped villain of the romantic novel. An ambiguous character, he assumes various shapes of evil. Sometimes he seems to be a wicked human being in league with the Devil. At other times he appears as the Devil himself. In one of the last scenes in the book, . . . Sintram perceives himself as the essence of evil. . . . In the next paragraph, he is described as a madman who once played devilish tricks for his own pleasure, but now is compelled to believe that he is a demonic figure in truth. Throughout the novel Lagerlöf emphasizes that Sintram and his satanic activities are the subjects of often-told stories that he nurtures, sometimes dressing in Devil costume in order to spread them. In these related shapes he transcends the character of the dramatic villain. His ambiguity forces the reader to consider the meaning of this evil figure from various perspectives and the significance of his relationships with the other characters of the novel. In order to describe him and attribute to him his various guises Lagerlöf relies on demonic folk belief and legend.

Sintram is often described in terms of the popular European conception of the Devil. He first appears in the novel dressed as the Devil, with horns, a tail, cloven hoofs, and a hairy body. He materializes from the Ekeby forge furnace on Christmas Eve and joins the twelve cavaliers in their Yule drinking. (pp. 193-94)

It is not difficult to trace the traditional elements used by the author in this scene. Sintram's appearance has behind it a long and widespread association with the Devil, both among the cultivated and folk strata of Indo-European societies. The Devil's representation as a goat, for example, in Sintram's horns and cloven hoofs, has been found in many Indo-European cultures. His hairiness is traditional as well. In Swedish folklore he is described as fearfully ugly, hairy, horned on the head or knees, and sporting claws rather than fingers and often cloven hoofs rather than feet. . . . In his initial appearance in the novel, as in several other instances, Sintram is associated with the forge fireplace. Legends and folk beliefs collected in Sweden in the nineteenth and twentieth centuries corroborate this relation with the fireplace and chimney, one of the favorite entrances and exits of the Devil.

It is important, too, that the demonic Sintram first visits the cavaliers on Christmas Eve. In nineteenth-century Swedish folk belief this night, like every festival eve, was a dangerous one in which spirits traveled about. (p. 194)

Lagerlöf has drawn on traditional materials to describe Sintram as a demonic figure, perhaps a wicked human being in league with Satan, perhaps the Evil One himself, or a grotesque, somewhat demented trickster. By ascribing to him demonic characteristics she has symbolized his evil character, but has left it to the reader to puzzle out his exact relationship with dark powers.

As Sintram is developed in the novel, other satanic details are accumulated. These details are also traditional, have long been the subject of European folk belief and legend, and were probably first encountered by the author in the oral traditions of her childhood. For example, Sintram's diabolical pacts with the cavaliers, and supposedly with their mistress, correspond in detail to the pacts contracted with the Devil that one finds in Swedish folklore. (p. 195)

[Characteristics] associated specifically with the Devil in Swedish folk belief and legendry delineate Sintram as intrinsically evil and shape him in the form of the Devil himself. Concurrently Lagerlöf attributes to Sintram characteristics which make him out to be not Satan, but a human being who has sold his soul to the Devil for certain rewards and who aids the Devil's work among men. The ambiguous nature of Sintram's character is again structured by the author's use of satanic Swedish folklore.

Several animals are closely associated with Sintram, and all of them have traditional demonic significance: black bulls, wolves, and a fierce black dog. Sintram is said to leave his manor drawn by horses and to return drawn by monstrous black bulls whose hoofs strike sparks against the road gravel. . . . (p. 196)

Sintram's black dog is perhaps his most striking animal familiar, especially since the satanic dog is so important in Swedish oral tradition. . . . In these contexts Sintram appears to be a man in league with the Devil rather than the Devil himself in human form. . . . This alliance is portrayed in other scenes as well. (pp. 196-97)

Lagerlöf has worked out a third implication which presents itself in concurrent references with the suggestions of Sintram as Devil and Sintram as man in league with the Devil. In this characterization he is a misanthropic old man with a grotesque sense of humor who eventually believes himself to be the cause of the year's misfortunes. (p. 198)

This third role, rationalized and closer to our own world and its psychology, does not rely on Swedish folk tradition, but is used once again to amplify and complicate Sintram's ambiguity. Without the folkloric references to Sintram as actual demon and to his wicked pact with the Demon as depraved man, he is a lesser figure, too simply comprehended. Through the imaginative use of Swedish folk belief and legend Lagerlöf has created a multi-dimensional villain, now a sinister human being in league with the Devil, now the Devil himself, and, if we like, a pitiful psychotic. We may see him through the lens of nineteenth-century folk traditions concerning a sinister Fryken Valley foundry superintendent, we may observe at a distance the native fears about the man, and we may watch the psychological disintegration of a malcontent. The richness and depth of the demonic figure are due both to the author's talent and to the potency of the folk traditions upon which she drew. (p. 199)

> *Larry W. Danielson, "The Uses of Demonic Folk Tradition in Selma Lagerlöf's 'Gösta Berlings saga'," in* Western Folklore *(© 1975, by the California Folklore Society), Vol. XXXIV, No. 3, July, 1975, pp. 187-99.*

ADDITIONAL BIBLIOGRAPHY

Afzelius, Nils. "The Scandalous Selma Lagerlöf." *Scandinavica* 5, No. 2 (November 1966): 91-9.
   Chronicles the critical response of Lagerlöf's contemporaries to her work.

De Vrieze, F. S. *Fact and Fiction in the Autobiographical Works of Selma Lagerlöf.* Assen, Netherlands: Royal VanGorcum, 1958, 380 p.
   Documents autobiographical fact in Lagerlöf's work. This detailed study includes excerpts from speeches, articles, letters, and the author's diary.

Fleisher, Frederic. "Selma Lagerlöf: A Centennial Tribute." *The American-Scandinavian Review* XLVI, No. 3 (September 1958): 241-45.
   General commentary on Lagerlöf's style and her place in world literature.

Howard, Velma Swanston. "At Mårbacka." *The American-Scandinavian Review* XVI, No. 12 (December 1928): 743-47.
   Account by Howard, Lagerlöf's translator, of her three-week visit at Mårbacka Manor.

Lagerroth, Erland. "Selma Lagerlöf Research 1900-1964: A Survey and an Orientation." *Scandinavian Studies* 37, No. 1 (February 1965): 1-30.

Survey of the major critical works written on Lagerlöf during the years 1900-64.

Lagerroth, Ulla-Britta. "The Troll in Man—A Lagerlöf Motif." *Scandinavian Studies* 40, No. 1 (February 1968): 51-60.*
Critical analysis of the troll motif in Lagerlöf's collection of short stories titled *Troll och manniskor* (*Trolls and Men*), with particular emphasis on "The Changeling." The critic also draws some insightful parallels between Lagerlöf and Jonas Lie.

Larsen, Hanna Astrup. "Four Scandinavian Feminists." *The Yale Review* V, No. 2 (January 1916): 347-62.*
Examines the significance of Lagerlöf, Camilla Collett, Frederika Bremer, and Ellen Key in relation to the Scandinavian feminist movement.

Marble, Annie Russell. "Selma Lagerlöf—Swedish Realist and Idealist." In her *The Nobel Prize Winners in Literature*, pp. 104-23. New York: D. Appleton and Co., 1925.
Provides general biographical background as well as a brief critical overview of Lagerlöf's major novels.

(Harry) Sinclair Lewis

1885-1951

(Also wrote under pseudonym of Tom Graham) American novelist, short story writer, dramatist, journalist, and poet.

Lewis was one of the foremost American writers of the 1920s. Along with H. L. Mencken he was the scourge of provincialism, greed, smugness, and other negative elements of American society. Like Dickens, he was the creator of caricatured but disturbingly recognizable characters. In George Babbit Lewis created an American archetype equal in stature to Mark Twain's Huck Finn.

The son of a country doctor, Lewis was born in Sauk Centre, Minnesota, a town that may have served as the model for Gopher Prairie in *Main Street*. He worked for a time at Upton Sinclair's Helicon Hall, a socialist experiment, and then went on to graduate from Yale in 1908. Lewis married writer Grace Hegger, and drifted about the country from job to job. During this time he sold ideas for stories to Jack London.

Lewis wrote a handful of average novels, receiving little commercial or critical success until 1920. In that year he completed a novel he had long wanted to write—*Main Street* —in which he exposed provincial dullness and intolerance, attacking the myth of the panacean quality of small town life after the tradition of Anderson and Masters. During the prosperous twenties Lewis prodded the "booboisie" (Mencken's term) and its institutions in several satires which, along with *Main Street*, are deemed his master works: *Babbitt, Arrowsmith, Elmer Gantry,* and *Dodsworth*. These books added new stock characters to American literature. In 1926 Lewis won, but refused to accept, the Pulitzer Prize for *Arrowsmith*, claiming that the award was given only to champions of American wholesomeness. In 1930 he became the first American to win the Nobel Prize in literature.

Lewis mottled his career with many rather weak and mediocre novels. The publication of *Dodsworth* in 1929 marked the end of his tenure as a great satirist. For the rest of his writing career Lewis turned out relatively undistinguished novels, none possessing the quality of his earlier work.

Critics have noted a certain ambivalence in Lewis's novels: he displays a definite love/hate relationship with the George Babbits and Will Kennicotts of the world. Critics also point to the naiveté of some of his satirical attacks, for, although he was an excellent caricaturist and mimic, he lacked a consistent vision of humankind to inform his work. Nevertheless, his work performed the important function of documenting and criticizing life in provincial America. As his biographer, Mark Schorer, said, "In any strict literary sense, he was not a great writer, but without his writing one cannot imagine modern American literature."

PRINCIPAL WORKS

Hike and the Aeroplane [as Tom Graham]   (novel)   1912
Our Mr. Wrenn   (novel)   1914

P. Puller

The Trail of the Hawk   (novel)   1915
The Innocents   (novel)   1917
The Job   (novel)   1917
Free Air   (novel)   1919
Main Street   (novel)   1920
Babbitt   (novel)   1922
Arrowsmith   (novel)   1925
Mantrap   (novel)   1926
Elmer Gantry   (novel)   1927
The Man Who Knew Coolidge   (novel)   1928
Dodsworth   (novel)   1929
Ann Vickers   (novel)   1933
Work of Art   (novel)   1934
It Can't Happen Here   (novel)   1935
Jayhawker [with Lloyd Lewis]   (drama)   1935
Selected Short Stories of Sinclair Lewis   (short stories)   1935
The Prodigal Parents   (novel)   1938
Bethel Merriday   (novel)   1940
Gideon Planish   (novel)   1943
Cass Timberlane   (novel)   1945
Kingsblood Royal   (novel)   1947
The God-Seeker   (novel)   1949
World So Wide   (novel)   1951

THE NATION   (essay date 1914)

One puts down [*Our Mr. Wrenn*] in a pleasant frame of mind, with the feeling of having wandered awhile in an odd and delightful world of make-believe. Mr. Lewis's is better than the average first book, and best of all, holds promise of more telling work in the future. There is simplicity, a grateful lack of straining for effect, in this story of a little New York clerk's seeking for the world of adventure and romance conjured up in his fancy by the Fourteenth Street moving-picture palaces, and nurtured on the gaudy circulars of steamship companies and tourist agencies. The girl, Istra Nash, is a very real figure. . . . She is a stock character of modern fiction, of course, the unconventional, cigarette-smoking girl artist, but she is flesh and blood as Mr. Wrenn sees her. The narrative of Mr. Wrenn's voyage to England on a cattle-steamer and the scenes of boarding-house life in New York are well done. It is a story out of the ordinary, with an individuality that atones for a certain slowness in pace.

"Current Fiction: 'Our Mr. Wrenn'," in The Nation *(copyright 1914 The Nation magazine, The Nation Associates, Inc.), Vol. 98, No. 2541, March 12, 1914, p. 266.*

STANTON A. COBLENTZ   (essay date 1921)

"Main Street" is not primarily a novel of plot. There are few complications to the story; the tale itself might easily be condensed to five or six pages; the narrative interest is everywhere subservient to character and situation. Against the grey, monotonous background of Gopher Prairie the two principal characters stand out in sharp outline; while behind them, in various shades of distinctness, may be seen the incidental personnel, some of them vividly defined, some of them barely distinguishable from thousands of a common type. The story is concerned principally with Carol Milford, the throbbing, active city girl who comes to Gopher Prairie as the wife of Will Kennicott, the country physician. In Gopher Prairie not much happens to her—not much happens to anyone in Gopher Prairie—and it is the very drabness and monotony of life in the small town that makes the story. (p. 357)

Paradoxically, the solution of the problem of Carol Kennicott seems to be that no solution is to be found. Though life in Gopher Prairie is narrow, prosaic, and uninspiring, without breadth and devoid of outlook, yet they who go there are by degrees so innoculated with the "village virus" that they discover escape to be meaningless as imprisonment, and in the end resign themselves to Gopher Prairie and to "the humdrum inevitable tragedy of struggle against inertia".

In a sense, that tragedy is not confined to Gopher Prairie, nor to all the Gopher Prairies on earth. It is the universal tragedy of human life, a tragedy far more profound than that of the hero of the epic; it is the tragedy of the denizen of office and factory and apartment house; the tragedy of the decay of youth and of youthful aspirations; the tragedy of the all-consuming drabness of life; of the normal, the conventional, and the commonplace. And it seems to be Mr. Lewis's message that just as Carol felt herself confined when beyond Gopher Prairie, even as when within it, so many another person, through externally he reside in New York or Philadelphia, is living within a Gopher Prairie of his own, a Gopher Prairie of pettiness and triviality, of suppressed ambitions, and of inevitable greyness and monotony.

It must be said for Mr. Lewis that he has made his case convincing. Life in Gropher Prairie, small and changeless and perpetually narrow, is made photographically real; yet while the author writes with the most minute and unerring sense of detail, he peers beneath the surface with a keenness that is more than photographic, and interprets life in a way that should make his novel of interest and value even to those already exhaustively acquainted with the small town. . . . However insignificant the subject-matter, everything has some essential bearing on life in Gopher Prairie; and the total impression one derives is that neither Jane Austen nor George Eliot depicted the provincial England of the past with more vividness than that with which Mr. Lewis portrays the present-day American small town, its humor and its pathos, its meanness and its potential greatness, its innumerable petty comedies and its hidden, sordid tragedies. (pp. 357-58)

Stanton A. Coblentz, "A Shelf of Recent Books: 'Main Street'," in The Bookman *(copyright, 1921, by George H. Doran Company), Vol. LII, No. 5, January, 1921, pp. 357-58.*

H. L. MENCKEN   (essay date 1922)

Babbitt is at least twice as good a novel as *Main Street* was —. . . it avoids all the more obvious faults of that celebrated work, and shows a number of virtues that are quite new. It is better designed than *Main Street;* the action is more logical and coherent; there is more imagination in it and less bald journalism; above all, there is a better grip upon the characters. If Carol Kennicott, at one leap, became as real a figure to most literate Americans as Jane Addams or Nan Patterson; then George F. Babbitt should become as real as Jack Dempsey or Charlie Schwab. The fellow simply drips with human juices. Every one of his joints is movable in all directions. Real freckles are upon his neck and real sweat stands out upon his forehead. I have personally known him since my earliest days as a newspaper reporter, back in the last century. (p. 20)

To me his saga, as Sinclair Lewis has set it down, is fiction only by a sort of courtesy. All the usual fittings of the prose fable seem to be absent. There is no plot whatever, and very little of the hocus-pocus commonly called development of character. Babbitt simply grows two years older as the tale unfolds; otherwise he doesn't change at all—any more than you or I have changed since 1920. Every customary device of the novelist is absent. When Babbitt, revolting against the irksome happiness of his home, takes to a series of low affairs with manicure girls, grass-widows and ladies even more complaisant, nothing overt and melodramatic happens to him. He never meets his young son Teddy in a dubious cabaret; his wife never discovers incriminating correspondence in his pockets; no one tries to blackmail him; he is never present when a joint is raided. (pp. 20-1)

[Not all the story's merit is] in the central figure. It is not Babbitt that shines forth most gaudily, but the whole complex of Babbittry, Babbittism, Babbittismus. In brief, Babbitt is seen as no more than a single member of the society he lives in—a matter far more difficult to handle, obviously, than any mere character sketch. His every act is related to the phenomena of that society. It is not what he feels and aspires to that moves him primarily; it is what the folks about him will think of him. His politics is communal politics, mob politics, herd politics; his religion is a public rite wholly without subjective significance; his relations to his wife and his children are formalized and standardized; even his debaucheries are the orthodox debaucheries of a sound business man. The salient thing about him, in truth, is his complete lack of originality—and that is precisely the salient mark of every American of his class. What he feels and thinks is what it is currently proper to feel and think. . . .

Babbitt gives me great delight. It is shrewdly devised; it is adeptly managed; it is well written. The details, as in *Main Street*, are extraordinarily vivid. . . . I know of no American novel that more accurately presents the real America. It is a social document of a high order. (p. 22)

> H. L. Mencken, "Portrait of an American Citizen" (reprinted by permission of Mercantile-Safe Deposit and Trust Company, Baltimore, Trustee of the Estate of Henry L. Mencken), in Smart Set, October, 1922 (and reprinted in Sinclair Lewis: A Collection of Critical Essays, edited by Mark Schorer, Prentice-Hall, 1962, pp. 20-2).

VIRGINIA WOOLF (essay date 1925)

[It is] by its hardness, its efficiency, its compactness that Mr. Lewis's work excels. . . . [His] books, one is inclined to say, are all shell; the only doubt is whether he has left any room for the snail. At any rate *Babbitt* completely refutes the theory that an American writer, writing about America, must necessarily lack the finish, the technique, the power to model and control his material which one might suppose to be the bequest of an old civilisation to its artists. In all these respects, *Babbitt* is the equal of any novel written in English in the present century. . . . [But study] of Mr. Lewis more and more convinces us that the surface appearance of of downright decision is deceptive; the outer composure hardly holds together the warring elements within; the colours have run.

For though *Babbitt* would appear as solid and authentic a portrait of the American business man as can well be painted, certain doubts run across us and shake our conviction. But, we may ask, where all is so masterly, self-assured, and confident, what foothold can there be for doubt to lodge upon? To begin with we doubt Mr. Lewis himself: we doubt, that is to say, that he is nearly as sure of himself or of his subject as he would have us believe. For he . . . is writing with one eye on Europe, a division of attention which the reader is quick to feel and resent. He . . . has the American self-consciousness, though it is masterfully suppressed and allowed only to utter itself once or twice in a sharp cry of bitterness ("Babbit was as much amused by the antiquated provincialism as any proper Englishman by any American"). But the uneasiness is there. He has not identified himself with America; rather he has constituted himself the guide and interpreter between the Americans and the English, and, as he conducts his party of Europeans over the typical American city (of which he is a native) and shows them the typical American citizen (to whom he is related) he is equally divided between shame at what he has to show and anger at the Europeans for laughing at it. Ze-

nith is a despicable place, but the English are even more despicable for despising it. (pp. 118-19)

Mr. Lewis it would seem was meant by nature to take his place with Mr. [H. G.] Wells and Mr. [Arnold] Bennett, and had he been born in England would undoubtedly have proved himself the equal of these two famous men. Denied, however, the richness of an old civilisation—the swarm of ideas upon which the art of Mr. Wells has battened, the solidity of custom which has nourished the art of Mr. Bennett—he has been forced to criticise rather than to explore, and the object of his criticism—the civilisation of Zenith—was unfortunately too meagre to sustain him. (pp. 121-22)

> Virginia Woolf, "American Fiction," in The Saturday Review of Literature (copyright © 1925 by Saturday Review; reprinted by permission), Vol. II, No. 1, August 1, 1925 (and reprinted in her The Moment and Other Essays, Harcourt, Brace and Company, 1948, pp. 113-27).*

PERCY H. BOYNTON (essay date 1927)

Mr. Lewis is not primarily a story-teller; he is an expositor who uses the narrative form. To follow an individual through his experiences as one would follow and observe a force in nature, to see him always as an individual and yet to see in him the human elements which are timeless—this is neither his interest nor his gift. To Mr. Lewis . . . a story if it has any power must serve not merely as a story but also as a vehicle. Life for him is not inherent in John Smith or Babbitt. It is the force that surrounds the man. . . . It is small wonder in the circumstances, that with one exception he has not made a character strong enough to dominate the stories of which they are only incidental features. (p. 184)

Excellence in a thesis novel . . . requires excellence in the novel as well as in the thesis; and it requires incomparably good story-telling to carry the double pack. . . . *Main Street* pretty largely íakes its case, as a case, but leaves in the memory no imperative episode and no unforgettable person. (p. 188)

The creation of a character is, of course, what Mr. Lewis did achieve in *Babbitt*. The success of George F. as an artistic creation lies in the fact that he is not the caricature that he is often said to be. He is sufficiently complicated to belong to the race of little people, who are usually more multiplex than the great ones of the earth, whose greatness is in their relative simplicity. And his failure as an individual lies in the pathetic fact that he actually does struggle to save his own soul and to free himself from the web of circumstance which is too much for him, but to which he is never completely resigned. (pp. 188-89)

Martin Arrowsmith stands at the far intellectual pole from George F. Babbitt; yet he has the same history, and, granting the gifts with which he is endowed, he comes off very little better. . . . Arrowsmith is a genius but a scientist. He has a conception of science which makes it one with art and religion. . . . He is an intolerant, but he works for human welfare though he has little respect for most human beings. He does not expect intelligent sympathy; and he is ready to sacrifice. (pp. 190-91)

The story which is told of him is a story of the scientist in conflict with his avowed allies. (p. 191)

[Arrowsmith descends] on the metropolis armed with a

deadly thesis. [He is] prepared to demonstrate that inhospitable as the countryside is to the fine enthusiasms of the scientist, the great city is more dangerous. The country is stupid, but the city, with its show of friendliness, is subtly and insidiously dangerous. It offers the scientific investigator a laboratory and assistance and a living wage, but it begrudges him the time to follow his curiosity to its final goal, to be certain of his findings, to be deliberate and modest in his statement of results. According to this thesis the control of the great research foundation inevitably falls into the hands of men who are managers, exploiters, publicity-seekers. To yield to them is to compromise with the devil. (p. 192)

This is a striking proposition, and there is a good deal of reason for maintaining it. The man who knows of philistinism in the medical world has no quarrel with Mr. Lewis on the score of his truthfulness. . . . But the story falters in two respects. The lesser is the result of attempting to put unfamiliar and technical material into a story-fable. . . . The major weakness arises from his insistence on the thesis. He tells the truth but not the whole truth about the medical world. Pasteur, facing every obstacle, fought the French government to a finish—and won. If America is arraigned as being less corrigible, there can be cited American men in medical research who have not compounded with principle, who are free agents in full career with abounding honors and troops of friends. There is no hint of such a figure in the fable; yet Arrowsmith's retreat to the hills is recorded as inevitable not only to his nature but also to the nature of the situation. It was inevitable for him only because he was an unheroic figure. (pp. 193-94)

Elmer Gantry is Mr. Lewis' first attempt at a rake's progress, the point of which, as a narrative genre, is that the rake is not a unique character but a typical product of the social order. His progress is a series of intrigues, all but one of them shabby. . . . (pp. 194-95)

He is a timely figure, and in his timeliness he is likely to achieve a smashing *succès de scandal* for his author; greater than the success of *Arrowsmith,* for a hundred entertain a personal feeling for religion to every one who harbors any loyalty to abstract science. But Gantry's timeliness makes him and the book about him a contribution to journalism rather than to literature. He is, like Martin Arrowsmith, a proponent for a thesis, and like Arrowsmith again he is the proponent of a thesis with which the author has acquainted himself through deliberate gathering of the material more than through the intimate knowledge that arises from experience and unconscious observation. (pp. 195-96)

In the attack on his thesis Mr. Lewis attempts to write a story about an individual and to draw up an indictment of an institution. These two tasks could be one if the career of Elmer Gantry were actually an indictment of religion and the church. But this is not the fact. Gantry is not a product of the church; he is the product of a philistine and stupid social order which makes it possible for him to exploit the church without ever in any real sense belonging to it. (p. 196)

It is fair to say that *Main Street* is not the easiest of stories to understand; it is perfectly safe to say that *Babbitt* has been quite misunderstood by the vast majority oreaders. But in turning away from these two criticisms of life Mr.

Lewis turned to criticisms of institutions—from the soul of a whole community to single organizations and their besetting faults. In doing which he began to document and argue and harangue. It is an experience almost exactly the reverse of Mr. [Sherwood] Anderson's in the same years, and in this contrast the advantage is indubitably with Mr. Anderson in so far as art is to be taken into the reckoning.

As Mr. Lewis knows what art is, showing thi,s in both criticism and creation, some experience, either in life or in reading, may lead him back toward his ideal. (pp. 197-98)

Percy H. Boynton, "Sinclair Lewis," in his More Contemporary Americans *(reprinted by permission of The University of Chicago Press; copyright 1927 by The University of Chicago), University of Chicago Press, 1927, pp. 179-98.*

T. K. WHIPPLE   (essay date 1928)

As a novelist Lewis has several peculiarities and limitations all of which point to a poverty of invention or imagination. One of these [is] his fondness and aptitude for mimicry. . . . Closely allied to this trait is his extreme dependence on his own experience and on his power of observation. Another indication of the same weakness is the care with which he gets up his subjects, as he got up aviation for *The Trail of the Hawk,* or medicine and bacteriology for *Arrowsmith.* Furthermore, it is significant that his interest is in social types and classes rather than in individuals as human beings. With few exceptions, his treatment of his characters is external only; he confines himself largely to the socially representative surface, rarely exercising much insight or sympathy. He is above all a collector of specimens. May the explanation of this clinging to actuality and to externals not be that his imagination has failed to find adequate nutriment in his experience, especially in his social experience?

However that may be, of one thing there can be no doubt: that he has hated his environment, with a cordial and malignant hatred. That detestation has made him a satirist, and has barbed his satire and tipped it with venom. . . . His eye is always alert and keen for inconsistencies or weaknesses in his prey—and how quickly he pounces! . . . Such observation is but one sign of a defensive attitude. Undoubtedly, his hostility is only a reply to the hostility which he has had himself to encounter from his environment, such as every artist has to encounter in a practical society. But for the artist to adopt an answering unfriendliness is disastrous, because it prevents him from receiving and welcoming experience. From such a defensive shield, experience, which ought to be soaked up, rattles off like hail from a tin roof. I should judge that Lewis had been irritated rather than absorbed by his experience. His observation seems at the other extreme from realization; it seems vigilant and wary, whereas realization demands self-surrender and self-forgetfulness, and is possible only in friendly surroundings. If it be true that his imaginative power is somewhat lean and scanty, the fact would be in part accounted for by the enmity between him and his surroundings.

But to have evoked this enmity is not the only unfortunate effect which his environment has had on Lewis. Although he has changed not at all in essentials, some of his characteristics are disclosed more plainly in his early than in his later novels. *Our Mr. Wrenn, The Trail of the Hawk, The Job,* and *Free Air* assist materially toward an understanding of the author of *Main Street* and *Elmer Gantry*. In the former, for example, he betrays his defensive attitude in the extraordinary precautions he takes lest his readers misjudge him. He makes greater use of irony as a defensive weapon than any other writer I know of; he early made the discovery that if only he were ironical and showed that he knew better, he could be as romantic and sentimental and playful as he pleased. He writes as if always conscious of a hostile audience. He takes needless pains to make clear that he is more sophisticated than his characters, as if there were danger of our identifying him with them. He makes fun of their ingenuous enthusiasms, even when these enthusiasms have the best of causes. The result of it all is that he often seems unduly afraid of giving himself away.

In this respect he resembles his characters; nothing in them is more striking than their morbid self-consciousness. Only Will Kennicott and Leora are free from it. The others, especially those in the early books, are always wondering what people will think, always suspecting that they are the objects of observation and comment—and in Lewis's novels they are generally right. They are constantly posing and pretending. . . . [They] conceive the object of life to be to pass themselves off as something they are not. This idea the author himself seems to share; he seems to think that the solution of all problems and difficulties is to find the one right pose, the one correct attitude.

Just as his people have no inner standards of their own, because they are not integral personalities, because they have not, in fact, developed any real personality at all, so Lewis himself shifts his point of view so often that finally we come to wonder whether he has any. One of the great advantages of *Arrowsmith* over its forerunners and its successor [*Elmer Gantry*] is that in it there seemed to emerge an almost established point of view. Otherwise, one would be inclined to call Lewis a man of multiple personality—save that all these personalities have a look of being assumed for effect. All the Lewises are disdainful of one another. When he has been romantic, he throws in a jibe at sentiment lest we think him sentimental; when he has been cynical, he grows tender lest he be thought hard; when he has been severe with a member of the Babbittry, he emphasizes the virtues of the common people and the absurdities of highbrows and social leaders. All his manifold attitudes, however, may be resolved into four: most conspicuously, he is the satirist who has flayed American society; least obviously, he is the artist whom one feels sure nature intended him to be; in addition, and above all in the early novels, he is a romanticist, and he is a philistine—these two bitterly abusive of each other. That is, besides his other reactions, he has tried to escape from his environment, and he has tried, with more success, to conform to it. (pp. 218-22)

Wonder has often been expressed at Lewis's popularity—that attacks such as his on American life and the American gods should meet a reception so enthusiastic. Yet I think his vogue is easily understood. For one thing, no doubt all the Zeniths enjoyed *Main Street* and all the Gopher Prairies *Babbitt,* and all who live on farms or in big cities liked both books. Moreover, Lewis caters to all tastes because he shares all points of view. . . . [Whatever] one's likes and dislikes, whether boosters, malcontents, romantics, radicals, social leaders, villagers, bohemians, or conventional people, one can find aid and comfort in the work of Sinclair Lewis.

Furthermore, Lewis's style must have contributed enormously to his success. It is of just the sort to please the people of whom he writes. His technique of raillery he has learned from Sam Clark and Vergil Gunch; he merely turns their type of wit and humor back upon themselves. All his satire is a long *tu quoque*. His crusade against the shortcomings of the clergy is conducted in the same spirit as Elmer Gantry's crusade against vice. His irony and sarcasm are of the cheap and showy variety popular on Main Street and in the Zenith Athletic Club. . . . Lewis seems to aim at much the same stage of mental development as the movies, which is said to be the average age of fourteen. His manner is founded on the best uses of salesmanship, publicity, and advertising. It is heavily playful and vivacious, highly and crudely colored, brisk and snappy. He avails himself of all the stock tricks of a reporter to give a fillip to jaded attention. His people do not run, they "gallop"; instead of speaking, they "warble" or "gurgle" or "carol." . . . No wonder Lewis has sold satire to the nation—he has made it attractive with a coat of brilliant if inexpensive varnish. The excellence of his rare intervals of real writing is lost in the general glare. (pp. 224-26)

[But] there are such intervals, and they serve to remind us from time to time of Lewis the artist, by no means insensible to beauty or devoid of the tragic sense of life. . . . Will Kennicott, who is little analyzed or dissected, is the best evidence before *Arrowsmith* that Lewis has the ability to create people. *Arrowsmith* itself, however, is the final proof of his creative power. Leora, Martin's first wife, is by general consent Lewis's masterpiece in the creation of character. Not only is she likable, but she is indubitably real; though she is protrayed casually and without effort, few other characters in American fiction equal her in absolute final reality. And Martin suffers only in comparison with Leora; although far more difficult than either Carol or Babbitt, he is more understandingly and more successfully portrayed. Yet even Leora interests Lewis less than his national portrait gallery of typical frauds and fakirs. He prefers to stay safely on the surface of social appearances. He shows little of Sherwood Anderson's hunger to delve into the lives of men and women.

The very mention of Anderson brings into sharp relief Lewis's limitations—his superficiality, his meretricious writing, his lack of passion and of thoughtfulness. If it were objected that the comparison has no point, Lewis being a satirist, I should reply that it is possible for a satirist to manifest penetration, strong feeling, and intellectual power, seeing that other satirists have obviously possessed these qualities. Yet I feel sure that Lewis has many unrealized capabilities. Underneath all the masks he puts on to rebuff or to placate the world, there seems to lurk a boyish artist, immature and shy and eager, full of fancy and sentiment, who has never grown up and ripened—denied his proper development, probably, by the necessity of manufacturing those protective masks. . . . The world would have none of him; so he will have none of the world. His world was a poor one at best, but he has denied himself even what little it might have offered. That is why he is still a boy, with a boy's insecurity and self-doubt hidden behind a forced rudeness and boldness.

In *Arrowsmith* . . . Lewis showed signs of beginning to develop a point of view, an inner standard of measurement. But that it is too late now for him to abandon his assumed attitudes and adopt the position proper to the artist, with the self-reliance which can come only from a sense of there being a pivot or point of rest in himself, *Elmer Gantry* is sufficient evidence. To the present, at any rate, Lewis is significant mainly as a social rather than as a literary phenomenon. And though this fact heightens his immediate importance, it detracts ultimately even from his social importance. While many of his contemporaries, who have succeeded in maintaining their integrity unimpaired, impart to their readers an intenser realization of the world they live in, the net result of Lewis's work is not a truer apprehension or a deeper insight, but an increase in mutual dissatisfaction: he has made Americans more outspoken and more hostile critics of one another. But perhaps after all it is better so: Lewis's romanticism and philistinism and vulgarity of style make him powerful because they make him popular. The attack on American practicality needs its shock troops—could we afford to give up so effective a critic for a better writer? (pp. 226-28)

> *T. K. Whipple, "Sinclair Lewis," in his* Spokesmen: Modern Writers and American Life *(copyright © 1928 by Prentice-Hall, Inc.), D. Appleton & Co., 1928, pp. 208-29.*

ALFRED KAZIN (essay date 1942)

[There] is a certain irony in Lewis's career that is now impossible to miss, and one that illuminates it as a whole. Here was the bright modern satirist who wrote each of his early books as an assault on American smugness, provincialism, ignorance, and bigotry; and ended up by finding himself not an enemy, not a danger, but the folksiest and most comradely of American novelists. Here was the young rebel who had begun *Main Street* as his spiritual autobiography, who even wrote dashingly in his foreword that it preached "alien" doctrine and who painted that whole world of endless Main Streets where "dullness is made God"—and found that people merely chortled with delight over how well he had hit off the village butcher, the somnolent afternoons on Main Street, the hysterical Sunday-night suppers, and the genteel moneylender's wife, with her "bleached cheeks, bleached hair, bleached voice, and a bleached manner." Here was the crusading satirist who spared none of the hypocrisies by which Babbitt and his group lived, least of all their big and little cruelties, and gave Babbitt back to his people as a friendly, browbeaten, noisy good fellow. Here was the indignant critic of commercialism in science who portrayed the tragedy of Max Gottlieb in *Arrowsmith* and the struggles of Martin Arrowsmith against those who threatened his disinterested worship of truth, yet succeeded even more significantly in making out of Arrowsmith a gangling romantic American hero. Here was the topical novelist, with his genius for public opinion, who tried to describe the nightmare coming of Fascism to America in *It Can't Happen Here*, but really described his own American optimism in the affectionate portrait of Doremus Jessup, that good American small-town liberal.

In the first flush of his triumph in the twenties, when Lewis did seem to be the bad boy breaking out of school, the iconoclast who was Mencken's companion in breaking all the traditional American commandments, it was easy enough to enjoy his satiric bitterness and regard him as a purely irreverent figure. But today, when his characters have entered so completely into the national life and his iconoclasm has become so tedious and safe, it is impossible to look back at Lewis himself without seeing how much native fellowship he brought into the novel and how deeply he has always depended on the common life he satirized. The caricature will always be there, and the ugly terror that Babbitt felt when he tried to break away for a moment from the conventional life of his society. There is indeed more significant terror of a kind in Lewis's novels than in a writer like Faulkner or the hard-boiled novelists, for it is the terror immanent in the commonplace, the terror that arises out of the repressions, the meannesses, the hard jokes of the world Lewis had soaked into his pores. But in a larger sense his whole significance as a writer rests on just his absorption of all those commonplaces, for Lewis has seemed not merely to live on the surface of public reality, but for it. . . . Lewis has always led so mimetic an existence that his works have even come to seem an uncanny reproduction of surface reality. Not so much revelations of life as brilliant equivalents of it, his books have really given back to Americans a perfect symbolic myth, the central image of what they have believed themselves to be; and it is this which has always been the source of his raucous charm and his boisterous good-fellowship with the very people and ideas he has caricatured.

For what is it about Lewis that strikes one today but how deeply he has always enjoyed people in America? What is it but the proud gusto and pleasure behind his caricatures that have always made them so funny—and so comfortable? Only a novelist fundamentally uncritical of American life could have brought so much zest to its mechanics; only a novelist anxious not to surmount the visible scene, but to give it back brilliantly, could have presented so vivid an image of what Americans are or believe themselves to be. It was the satire that always gave Lewis's books their design, but the life that streamed out of them impressed people most by giving them a final *happy* recognition. Lewis caught the vulgarity and the perpetual salesmanship. . . . But he caught also, as almost no one did before him, the boyish helplessness of a Babbitt, the stammering romance of a Martin Arrowsmith on his first day at the McGurk Institute, the loneliness of a great Sam Dodsworth before all those Europeans in Paris. (pp. 219-21)

Yes, and for all their sharp thrusts and irritable mutterings, his books also confirmed in Americans the legend of their democratic humility, the suspicion that every stuffed shirt conceals a quaking heart. . . . Lewis's men are boys at heart, living in a world in which boys are perpetually stealing through their disguise as men, and glad to know that a certain boyishness in the native atmosphere will always sustain them. Businessmen, scientists, clergymen, newspapermen, they are forever surprised at their attainment of status and seek a happiness that will encourage them to believe that they are important. (pp. 221-22)

Lewis's characters have often been criticized as "types," and they are, partly because he memorialized some of them as such, gave people in George F. Babbitt what seemed the central portrait of a businessman. But what is really significant in his use of types is that his mind moved creatively in their channels. With his ability to approximate American opinion, his lightning adaptability to the prejudices, the fears, the very tonal mood, as it were, of the contemporary American moment, Lewis has always been able to invest his tintypes with a careless energy that other writers would not have been able to understand, much less share, since they did not work so close to the surface. Lewis restored life; he did not create it. Yet what that means is that for him the creative process lay in the brilliance of that restoration. . . . (p. 223)

Just as Lewis has always worked from type to type, embodying in them now the cruelty, now the sentimentality, now the high jinks, now the high-pressure salesmanship of one aspect of the national life after another, so he has always moved in his books from one topic to another, covering one sector of American life after another—the small town, Rotary, business, medicine, the smoking car, travel, religion, social work. More than any other American novelist since Frank Norris, he felt from the first the need to go from subject to subject that would lead him to cover the entire national scene. . . . Yet this could work only up to a certain point, as the steady decline of his novels after *Dodsworth,* reaching a really abysmal low in *The Prodigal Parents,* has proved. . . . In a sense Lewis depended on an America in equilibrium, a young postwar America anxious to know itself, careless and indulgent to his friendly jokes against it, ambitious even to improve its provincial manners in the light of his criticism; but when that America lost its easy comfortable self-consciousness, Lewis's nervous mimicry merely brushed off against it.

It followed also from Lewis's whole conception of the novel that his brisk mimetic energy would become a trick repeating itself long after he had lost his sense of design and purpose. In some of the early brilliant descriptions in *Ann Vickers,* he seemed to be blocking out perfect scene after perfect scene that led to nothing; there is a forlorn flashiness about them that reveals Lewis running over his old technique even when he had little to say. In Lewis's first works his verve had always been able to light up an inconsequential book like *Elmer Gantry* with dozens of hilarious scenes, or, as in *The Man Who Knew Coolidge,* even to make one long monologue out of it; but now, with nothing more substantial to write about than Barney Dolphin in *Ann Vickers,* Ora Weagle in *Work of Art,* or Fred Cornplow in *The Prodigal Parents,* he could keep on bringing in his "trick," his special gift and charm, while the books merely sagged. They were tired, evasively sentimental books, and full of a hard surface irritability and uncertainty. (pp. 223-25)

What these later works also signified, however, was not only Lewis's growing carelessness and fatigue, but an irritable formal recognition of his relation to American life. Far from even attempting iconoclastic satire, he wrote these books as moralities for a new time; and his new heroes—Ora Weagle, the poetic hotelkeeper; Doremus Jessup, the amiable and cautious liberal; Fred Cornplow, the good solid husband and father betrayed by his erring children—were the final symbols of everything Lewis had always loved best. He had lampooned Babbittry easily enough; but when the Babbitts themselves were threatened, he rushed forward to defend them. From his own point of view, indeed, there were no Babbitts now, or at least nothing to lampoon in them—Fred Cornplow was the mainstay of the times and Doremus Jessup a representative American hero.

Those who had missed Lewis's dependence from the first on the world Fred Cornplow represented, however, could only wonder at Lewis's sentimental tribute to him and his ugly caricature of those who mocked him. The thing didn't

jibe; Lewis wasn't supposed to like Cornplow-Babbitt; and how could Doremus Jessup ever seem enough for him? Yet what was it but Doremus, with his fishing tackle and his wise little small-town editorials, that Lewis had ever known and loved? What was it but the Cornplows he had run after for twenty years, trying to catch the warts, the buffoonery up at the lodge on Wednesday nights, the pleasure of the open road on Sunday? The village rebels had all failed, and that was tragic; . . . all [had] gone down before meanness and ignorance and terror. But if the Fred Cornplows remained, they were not so bad after all; and Carol Kennicott really had been just a little silly. The village atheist ended his tirade, and sighed, and went on playing a friendly game of poker with the local deacons. (pp. 225-26)

> *Alfred Kazin, "The New Realism: Sherwood Anderson and Sinclair Lewis," in his* On Native Grounds: An Interpretation of Modern American Prose Literature *(copyright 1942, 1970, by Alfred Kazin; reprinted by permission of Harcourt Brace Jovanovich, Inc.), Reynal & Hitchcock, 1942, pp. 205-26.**

LEO GURKO and MIRIAM GURKO   (essay date 1943)

An examination of [Lewis'] work, and more particularly the three principal divisions into which it falls, suggests that to the degree that Lewis practices the art of satire—and particularly satire against the Main Street which he made famous—to that degree his novels teem with an abundant life; conversely, his abandonment of satire drains his works of their élan and reduces them to pulpiness and routine. There are to be observed in him two distinct, fundamentally antithetical points of view with regard to his central theme. On the one hand, he satirizes the materialists of Zenith and Gopher Prairie for their ignorance, their standardized thinking, aggressive provincialism, and self-righteous tyranny over all those who do not rigidly subscribe to their ways. On the other, he finds in them much kindliness, honesty, a genuine idealism which on occasion assumes the guise of social reform, and even a certain poetic sensitivity. This antithesis, this alternation between attack and defense, permeates nearly all his novels and is to be found even in the great satirical classics of the 1920's.

Before the advent of these classics, however, Lewis wrote a number of little-known, small-scale novels, in which the roots of this antithesis are perhaps most clearly visible. He veers from whimsical apologias for the provincial, "folksy" people, later to be ridiculed in *Main Street,* to heated criticisms of them, their institutions, and their ways of life. If *Our Mr. Wrenn, The Innocents,* and *Free Air* represent the first attitude, then *The Trail of The Hawk* and *The Job* express the second. *The Job*—the most serious and perhaps the best of these early novels—straddles both sides. It begins with an exposure of what Lewis considers the uselessness and irrational mechanism of business life but concludes with roseate observations of this very life. The book —indeed, this whole early period—reveals the uncertainties within Lewis' mind. He has not succeeded, as, in a sense, he was destined never to succeed, wholly to resolve his central theme: whether to satirize or espouse Main Street. . . . This period of unfocused hesitation and doubt comes to an abrupt end with the spectacular appearance of *Main Street,* which opens the second large phase of Lewis' career—the phase of the great satires. . . . (pp. 288-89)

Main Street lays the groundwork of Lewis' campaign against a crassly materialist society wherever it appears.... As long as he maintains his satirical offensive, as long as Carol Kennicott rebels against the demoralizing philistinism of Gopher Prairie, the novel has enormous power. The point of the book is definitively clear, and the exposure of the soullessness of provincial life is deadly and all embracing. But Lewis is not content to let matters rest here. He blurs his focus by occasional confusing shifts in sympathy. At times he appears to side with Will Kennicott, who embodies and defends the solid qualities of Main Street; at such times it is Carol who appears ridiculous. More than once she and her cultured friends are accused of snobbishly pursuing a false and contentless spirituality. But perhaps the most formidable shift is Carol's inexplicable acceptance of Main Street at the end of the novel. She returns to Gopher Prairie, not resolved to make the best of a bad bargain, but suddenly and mystically enthusiastic.... (p. 289)

To describe Gopher Prairie as beautiful and filled with mystery and greatness is to negate everything that was said before. These shifts reveal Lewis' uncertainty, his alternate acceptance and rejection of Main Street. Though the first of his great satirical novels of the post-war period, *Main Street* contains, in an almost Hegelian fashion, the seeds of its own antithesis.

Lewis' affection for Will Kennicott introduces a whole series of curiously sympathetic portraits, which expose still further the duality of his feelings. The bellicose materialism of George F. Babbitt and the Rev. Elmer Gantry seems no more abhorrent to Lewis than does Kennicott's. For all their faults, Babbitt and Gantry are presented as pretty decent fellows at bottom. Gantry is a cheat, rogue, bluff, coward; but he is also good company, and Lewis obviously revels in his gusto. As for Babbitt, though Lewis pillories his ideas and associates, he displays a warm affection for the man himself....

The one towering exception to this duality, the one novel in which Lewis shakes himself free from the contradictions enmeshing him, is *Arrowsmith*. The satirical issues are at their clearest: his hostility to materialism is undiluted by affection for any of its representatives. Here, for the first time, Lewis is ranged entirely on the side of the rebels, who in the persons of Martin Arrowsmith, Terry Wickett, and Professor Gottlieb variously epitomize the spirit of Carol Kennicott....

If *Arrowsmith* marks the apex of the synthesis of Lewis' satirical convictions, *Dodsworth* as clearly foreshadows the dissolution of that synthesis and therefore marks the beginning of the third period of his work. For the first time Lewis draws a completely friendly portrait of a successful businessman; for the first time the rebel is projected unsympathetically. Lewis' focus has shifted from a broad attack upon Main Street to a broad defense of it. Underneath the probing into the lives of the Dodsworths, Lewis' change of heart becomes increasingly apparent. In this change Fran is the key figure. Here is a kind of Carol Kennicott in her forties, chafing under the dulness of life in Zenith, passing a great many devastating observations upon her husband's Main Street friends and upon the empty materialism of Zenith society.... [But] Fran is not the heroine of her story, as Carol is of hers and Arrowsmith of his. Quite the reverse. She emerges as a disagreeable snob, vainly seeking

to recapture her lost youth, utterly blind to the virtues of her faithful husband. The rebel here is more than a lost soul; she is an empty soul as well; and this emptiness signals what is to be Lewis' principal opinion of the rebel through much of his work in the 1930's.

In the struggle between Fran and Dodsworth, it is Dodsworth who comes out best. Like Babbitt, he is solid, dependable, dull, moved by a vague humanitarian desire to improve things, out of his depth in nearly all affairs outside the realm of business. But, whereas Lewis lampoons these qualities in Babbitt, he praises them in Dodsworth. In Dodsworth's triumph there lies foreshadowed, with an immutable finality, the new role of Lewis, no longer the satirist but the apostle of Main Street. (p. 290)

[Lewis] appears to lose all interest in satire, now that he devotes himself more or less completely to defending Main Street and upholding its ways of life. Paradoxically, he defends Main Street against his own attacks and now views the Carols and the Arrowsmiths of the 1930's through the eyes of Sam Clark, Vergil Gunch, and their Main Street cronies. By a circular and devious route, he returns to the "hominess" and the small civic virtues of his first published work, *Our Mr. Wrenn*.

The evidences of this *volte-face* abound in the novels of his third and most recent period. *Work of Art*, for example, glorifies that very Service which Lewis ridiculed in *Babbitt*. Lewis has changed his conception of materialist pursuits: they no longer constrict, but release, the creative energies of those engaged in them. (p. 291)

An inclusive examination of Lewis' novels from 1914 to 1940 makes a one-track view of his work impossible. It cannot be said that he hates or loves Main Street. He does both—and both simultaneously. This simultaneous coexistence of contradictory feelings is a source of much of the intellectual wavering present even in many of his great novels and is perhaps a major reason for his decline as a chronicler of the American scene. The hesitations and reversals of his first period, the satirical crystallization of the second, the apologetics of the third, are closely interwoven.... Lewis was at his best as a satirist in a challenging frame of mind and as a writer who helped siphon the satirical tradition of Flaubert, Butler, and Galsworthy into the contemporary American novel and helped clear its air of the prettifications of the William Dean Howells school. As a satirist he was able to exploit his considerable talent for mimicry and caricature. When he abandoned satire, vitality drained away from his work, to which the succession of undistinguished novels of the 1930's bears witness. (p. 292)

> *Leo Gurko and Miriam Gurko, "The Two Main Streets of Sinclair Lewis," in* College English *(copyright © 1943 by the National Council of Teachers of English; reprinted by permission of the publisher and the author), Vol. 4, No. 5, February, 1943, pp. 288-92.*

VINCENT SHEEAN (essay date 1947)

This century has been blessed with many great writers: one has only to think of Gorky, Valéry, Proust, Joyce and Kafka, more or less at random—and there are at least eight or ten more—to see that the period has been fecund. The work of Lewis is so violently American that it bears no resemblance whatever to that of such deliberate and lapidary European artists, preoccupied as they were with form. His appeal is to the largest public he can possibly reach, and to do so he uses the most widely established vernacular; he composes on a huge scale, with great, heavy lines, extreme foreshortenings and distortions of perspective; he is thus thought, as it says in the article on him in the Encyclopaedia Britannica, to exhibit a "lack of art"; in reality, it seems to me, he has an art which is altogether his own. Its vital power is shown in two phenomena characteristic of the giants: first, it is so personal that it bears his stamp in every part and thus defies imitation or rivalry; second, it transcends language itself and is felt with equal intensity in all parts of the world through the veils of translation.

This is not to say, by any means, that Lewis has all the qualities that belong to his greatness. The design was grandiose but it was not altogether filled in. His passion for justice and his comprehension of humanity may make us think of Goethe or Tolstoy, but the actual ectoplasm is not of their texture. In all its astonishing vigor and pungency, his prose is likely at times to weary the palate by its narrowness of range. It never sings; it cannot be made thicker or thinner, sweeter or harsher, at will; its pace or tempo, musically speaking, varies little. This is the principal limitation of a talent which otherwise towers above all others, I believe, in mature and serious novel-writing in the United States.

And yet for the themes that interest him and for the kind of composition in which he is a master, Lewis has the instruments he most needs. There is a kind of sardonic bitterness in his style, achieved mainly by incongruous juxtapositions . . . which reminds one of the most inspired inventions of Charlie Chaplin; there is a breathless speed in climaxes which makes me think of Toscanini; there are passages of dialogue . . . which cut with the sharp edge of horror. Technically speaking, none of these effects would be at all easy for another writer; they are part of the peculiar treasure which is his. (p. 191)

> *Vincent Sheean, "Sinclair Lewis," in* Commonweal *(copyright © 1947 Commonweal Publishing Co., Inc.; reprinted by permission of Commonweal Publishing Co., Inc.), Vol. XLVI, No. 8, June 6, 1947, pp. 191-92.*

MAXWELL GEISMAR (essay date 1947)

In the delicate and shifting marital relationship of Carol and Will Kennicott [in *Main Street*], Lewis has brought domestic drama almost to the point of classical tragedy; and in the beautifully controlled balance between Carol's view of Gopher Prairie and Gopher Prairie's view of Carol—an equilibrium of opposing human impulses in which nobody is to blame and everybody suffers—he seems for the first time to have the makings of a major realist. (p. 84)

[The] whole dramatic force of Lewis's novel depends upon the fact that the village society and the critic of that society are so evenly paired off. In another sense this is the story of Gopher Prairie's revolt against Carol Kennicott. But it is actually closer to a description of that familiar condition of our existence in which two equally imperfect forces are locked together in an irreconcilable conflict. (pp. 84-5)

Babbitt carries forward the chronology of *Main Street*, of course. Zenith, in turn, is Gopher Prairie come of age. The crossroads hamlet has become the replica of the eastern metropolis, if in miniature, and here the democratic revolution is embodied in what is practically an orgy of Tocqueville's 'virtuous materialism.' The opening pages of the novel are ripe with the promise of sleek, noiseless limousines, concrete bridges, dictaphones, gleaming railway tracks, immense new factories, and 'the song of labor in a city built—it seemed—for giants.' (p. 88)

[What] is remarkable about the novel's whole view of life is the 'muted tone,' as it were, to which everything in the novel must conform: there can be no full release, or the promise of release, for the characters' aspirations as well as their inhibitions. . . . No wonder—uneasy as Babbitt is in his own domain, restricted on the one hand by these rigid emotional taboos, surrounded on the other hand by these mysterious Economic Presences whose whims actually determine his every move: no wonder that the prevailing mood of this new Middle-Class Mogul should be one of increasing irritation.

—If not of actual fear, or dread. (p. 91)

[The] mangled specter of Dante is the true presiding genius of Zenith. . . . The central scenes of *Babbitt* can hardly be explained by the ordinary categories of 'satire'—and this almost classical example of photographic American 'realism' is realistic only in terms of its introductory setting—and there, also, only to a degree. In the central concept of the novel, in its final and dominant mood, and in the craft technics which first suggest and then fully project its true theme, *Babbitt* is, on the contrary, an imaginative work of a high order. It is, if anything, close to poetry. . . . [It] is almost a perfectly conceived poetic vision of a perfectly standardized money society; it is our native *Inferno* of the mechanized hinterland. Even the 'Great Strike' that grips Zenith toward the close of the novel is a middle-class nightmare of a workers' revolt in which the workers are as vague as they are ominous.

In this connection the familiar objection to the novel—the fact that even George F. Babbitt himself could never possibly be so *complete* a Babbitt—becomes, of course, the novel's main virtue; while the familiar criticism of the novelist's 'ear' must also be set aside, temporarily anyhow. The language of Lewis's people is certainly not the language of the small-town and city people who have hitherto existed in the United States, nor even that of our present-day Rotarians. . . . But it can serve very well—tricky, synthetic, and prefabricated as it is—as the medium for some future Utopia of Rotary. . . . [It] is the new global lingo of the machine and the cartel. (pp. 96-7)

[*Arrowsmith* returns] to the more realistic elements of Lewis's work. The opening sections of the novel . . . are more carefully and warmly done than has been the case in Lewis's previous descriptions of [the] older rural scene. . . . Like the young Carl Ericson of *The Trail of the Hawk*, Martin Arrowsmith himself is intended to be one of Lewis's few full-fledged heroes. . . . (p. 97)

[Lewis's main purpose is] to satirize the exploitation of medical research by the vested interests. Yet, in a curious shift of the novel's focus, his animus is directed not so much against medical or commercial institutions as against the chief victims of these institutions. Martin's bungling attempt to reform the public health system in Nautilus,

Winnemac—an attempt that is very similar to Carol Kennicott's Campaign for Culture in Gopher Prairie—leads, not, as one might suppose, to any sort of self-examination on the part of Lewis's hero, or to a further examination of the human elements in the situation, but to a sort of contempt for public service and the public welfare itself.... [It] is actually this tone of fashionable cynicism rather than of scientific skepticism that marks both the concluding sections of *Arrowsmith* and the last two novels of this period of Lewis's work [*Elmer Gantry* and *The Man Who Knew Coolidge*]. (pp. 100-01)

Just as *Arrowsmith* represents the upper range of human aspiration in the world of Lewis's fiction, and its positive pole, *Elmer Gantry* ... represents the lowest range, and the negative pole, of the Middle-Class Empire.... Moreover, if Martin Arrowsmith is meant to illustrate the purest type of Lewis's truth-seeker, so Elmer Gantry, in person, is the archetype of the opportunist and false prophet, the epitome of bourgeois villainy and vice—of sin in Winnemac.

And *Elmer Gantry* also marks a sort of increasing vitality in Lewis's realism as the 'Hell Cat' emerges ... in all the glory of a physical and sexual prowess— ... the bodies of the Lewis heroes have never been the secret of their charm —that is unhampered by a religious or even a moral sense. (pp. 101-02)

[If] Elmer Gantry himself is unmistakably a bounder, he is still a middle-class bounder: he is the Anti-Christ of *Zenith*.... And the fact that such a view of his leading figures stems quite as much from Lewis's own view of reality as from the satiric presentation of his material is clear from the whole intellectual framework of *Elmer Gantry*.

For there are sections of the novel which remind us of the best things in *Babbitt*. The later account of Elmer's rise to power as a religious 'crusader' and a pillar of organized morality does take on a kind of extra-realistic and extra-satirical quality. The descriptions of the New Thought in Zenith, of Elmer's famous Lively Sunday Evenings, his Committee on Public Morals, and his Salesmanship of Salvation ... make *Elmer Gantry* close to another excursion into the inferno: an inferno that is composed of the blind religious paroxysms of a society which has lost all sense of religion.

But this is also a vision of corruption in which the novelist's own view of life is separate from, but hardly superior to, the life he is describing, and in which even the novelist's craft has been affected by the taint in his subject matter. If the larger scene of *Elmer Gantry* presents a cross-section of religious activity in the United States, and if there are some witty descriptions of this activity, there is also remarkably little insight into the more fundamental aspects of religious motivation—either personal or cultural—or into that commercial exploitation of religion which is the ostensible theme of the novel. (pp. 103-04)

The Man Who Knew Coolidge probably deserves wider recognition than it has received. You may see very easily here what has been happening both to American life and to Lewis over this decade of Lewis's work.

For a whole range of earlier Lewis characters have been confused about the 'great world,' but Lowell Schmaltz is absolutely incoherent; political events are quite as esoteric

to him as artistic events were for Will Kennicott and George Babbitt. Yet, if Babbitt was naïve and complacent, Schmaltz is arrogant and assertive; his abysmal ignorance is matched only by his conviction of his own influence. Babbitt had his little moments of revolt against Rotary ... and even a certain confused generosity about life in general. Schmaltz is all narrowness and meanness; the epitome of complacency and conformity, of self-righteousness and moral virtue.... Babbitt, in short, was a second-class citizen; the hero of *The Man Who Knew Coolidge* is a second-class Babbitt. By comparison, Lewis's earlier figure is a rarely gifted and unique personage—a Leonardo of the Realtors—and one who marked the flowering of an individualistic society. (pp. 105-06)

Yet *The Man Who Knew Coolidge* is a blueprint, rather than a novel. Its hero, hardly so much an individual as the product of a standardized cultural mold of 'individualism'— of the mass-production temperament and the Woolworth personality—is presented simply *as* another standard brand on display. There is no longer an attempt on Lewis's part to face the socio-economic factors or the underlying cultural pattern of Lowell Schmaltz's cosmos; very much like his own businessmen, the writer is interested only in *results*, which are all taken for granted, which are even, in a way, enjoyed.... [The] artist himself, after illustrating the farthest vistas of the Middle-Class Empire, has withdrawn to the Olympian, or, say, the neo-Menckenian heights of exposé and mockery. (p. 107)

We have noticed the divided view of the contemporary scene in *Main Street*—a deeply ambivalent and sharply divided view—and also the almost completely destructive vision of the common American future in *Babbitt*. Yet nowhere after these novels has Lewis been able to come to grips with the real elements of his own literary projections, or, indeed, of the native scene itself. On the contrary, what has become increasingly clear in both the truth-seekers of *Arrowsmith* and the false prophets of *Elmer Gantry* is the curiously limited nature of Lewis's own view of reality. Just as there is really no sense of vice in Lewis's literary world, there is no true sense of virtue. Just as there is practically no sense of human love in the whole range of Lewis's psychological values, and no sense of real hatred— there is no genuine sense of human freedom. (p. 108)

It is easy to recognize all the ignoble aspects of human behavior that appear in Lewis's work: in a sense his virtue is that he continually reminds us of these, and only these. He hardly so much tries to destroy us in one stroke as to make us continuously uncomfortable. Similarly, in terms of Lewis's portraits of love itself, we may very well appreciate his recurrent scene: a scene in which the chief actors continually display all the ridiculous by-products of human desire, but never the desire itself—in which they are never really up to their rôle and never understand that they are not up to their rôle.

Yet, perpetually frustrated and distorted as the human passions are, they are nevertheless passions. They do exist in fact, whereas they never possibly can exist in Lewis's notion of the facts.... And this is not his main artistic intention but his chief artistic limitation.

For what is obvious is that the inner existence of Lewis's figures follows just as sharply defined a pattern as their outward behavior. But what seems curious in the end is that Lewis's own set of values should follow the same pattern as that of his people. It is almost as though the writer who has been describing over and over again one way of life . . . [and] always following the same circumscribed line of human behavior, had mistaken it for the perfect circle of human experience. . . . In the cultural area, also, if Lewis has followed up Carol Kennicott's directive that 'institutions, not individuals, are the enemies,' and that the only defense against them is 'unembittered laughter,' it is clear that his own laughter has become a substitute for, rather than an accompaniment of, a deeper insight or a bolder conviction. In both areas the surface of things, sharply and often brilliantly illuminated as it is in Lewis's work, has taken the place of the thing itself, and Lewis has turned from morals to manners, as they used to say. (pp. 109-11)

> *Maxwell Geismar, "Sinclair Lewis: The Cosmic Bourjoyce," in his* The Last of the Provincials: The American Novel, 1915-1925 *(copyright 1943, 1947, and 1949 by Maxwell Geismar; reprinted by permission of Houghton Mifflin Company), Houghton, 1947 (and reprinted by Hill and Wang, 1959), pp. 69-150.*

JOSEPH WOOD KRUTCH (essay date 1951)

Both [*Main Street* and *Babbitt*] are, each in its own way, tremendously well done in the sense that it is easy enough to understand why they produced the effect they were intended to produce. Yet, except perhaps in the case of George Babbitt himself, neither very often suggests the aims or the methods of that higher sort of fiction which either creates or reveals something that the mere description of observed fact cannot convey. Though Lewis had to a remarkable degree mastered his method, that method is a good deal like the one so successfully employed in the writing of many present-day best-sellers—the method, I mean, which produces books that are not so much naturalistic novels as "documentaries," pseudo-fiction in which everything is recognizable as true but with the fidelity of a waxwork and no suggestion of any sort of autonomous life. . . .

The literary gift that [Lewis] developed to an extraordinary degree was, of course, the gift for mimicry, which is as definitely something more than mere naturalistic reproduction as it is definitely something less than imaginative recreation. As he used to demonstrate in social gatherings—sometimes rather over-insistently—he could improvise at any length the conversation or the speech-making of a Babbitt on almost any topic, and his improvisations had, like what he wrote in the same style, an air of authenticity, heightened by touches of burlesque, which made them as astonishing in their way as anything of the sort ever achieved. Yet at the same time he rarely if ever escaped the limitations of mimicry as an artistic device. The typical fact or the typical gesture is one step above the merely authentic. But it is also one step below the symbolic. Lewis habitually achieved the one, habitually made one exclaim "How characteristic!" But rarely if ever did he rise to that point where a detail is so charged with meaning that it becomes a symbol whose significance all but defies analysis.

It is for this reason that his brilliant, parodistic mimicry must go on and on; so that Babbitt's speech at the Chamber of Commerce dinner continues for nine pages. Good as most of it is, no sentence or paragraph is good enough to make further elaboration unnecessary, and in the end one is reminded of that ultimate satire on the naturalistic method embodied in a stage direction for one of Ring Lardner's plays: "The curtain will descend for seven days to indicate the passage of a week." Lewis falls victim, therefore, to the mimic's nemesis, which condemns him to remain always insufficiently more entertaining than the victim of his mimicry. There is too much burlesque, not enough wit.

To realism in art there is a limitation which "Babbitt" all too frequently illustrates. A bore in literature should be different from a bore in real life in at least one respect: he should not be boring. If "Babbitt" is not really a classic, that is probably because in the midst of our laughter and admiration we are likely to remember Mr. Bennett's remark to his piano-playing daughter: "You have entertained us enough for one evening." (p. 180)

> *Joseph Wood Krutch, "Sinclair Lewis," in* The Nation *(copyright 1951 The Nation magazine, The Nation Associates, Inc.), Vol. 172, No. 8, February 24, 1951, pp. 179-80.*

J. B. PRIESTLEY (essay date 1960)

In the satirical-clown department, where social and literary criticism is represented by Mencken, Sinclair Lewis is in charge of the novel. Or it might be more accurate to say that the novel is in charge of him, compelling him to abandon realism for comic-cum-romantic fantasy. (We mean what we say here. Certainly for his earlier novels, Lewis, a good reporter, set to work like another Zola, filling notebooks with facts and observed details, and then shutting himself up with them, to write his novel. And it is when the method broke down, when the novel began writing itself, that he really created something.) He could not be a serious satirist because he did not possess any central fixed set of values and standards; he looks to Europe when he is in America, to America when he is in Europe, to Eastern America when he is in the West, to the West when he is in the East; as a man, and so as a writer, he was uncertain of the world and of himself, bewildered, confused, homeless and restless. (This is why, in *Work of Art*, he can take hotels so seriously.) He could not identify himself with any kind of life, was always the clever visiting journalist or the tourist. But only in his relation to the actual scene. His best work is raised high above journalism; sheer drive, applied to the mass of recorded detail, and a rare exuberance, bringing the unconscious into action, turn him into a genuine creator, not a conscious deliberate artist but a mythmaker. So his masterpiece, high above *Main Street*, is *Babbitt*, which is at once something less and something more than a novel, just as *Moby Dick* and *Huckleberry Finn* are. This is a truly American creative imagination at work, uncontrolled and outrageous by European standards, just as America itself seems uncontrolled and outrageous; rushing, in *Babbitt*, from heights of satirical buffoonery, often clowning for its own sake, to quick shuddering glimpses of depths where terror and despair are lurking. The real Sinclair Lewis, the enduring writer, should not be looked for in *Martin Arrowsmith, Dodsworth, Ann Vickers*, but, apart from *Babbitt*, in *Elmer Gantry, The Man who Knew Coolidge*, and some parts of *It Can't Happen Here*. He faded away, looking in his last years strangely empty, melancholy, spectral, because there was in him no creative and critical centre that could take over, once the necessary drive, energy, exuberance, were waning. But while they lasted, he was, as he remains, one of those creators who do not make works of art for the cultivated minority, but myths for the multitude. Even if criticism, quite mistakenly, should argue him out of literature, he will remain a figure in American history. (pp. 429-30)

J. B. Priestley, "Between the Wars," in his Literature and Western Man *(copyright © 1960 by J. B. Priestley; reprinted by permission of the author), Harper & Row, Publishers, Inc., 1960, pp. 376-440.**

IRVING HOWE (essay date 1961)

Lewis wrote the kind of novels—almost exasperating in their transparency—which lend themselves neither to extensive summary nor intensive analysis. They are primarily novels of performance, all spark and surface, bristling with a topicality that now makes them seem a trifle dated and, more important, blocks the deeper possibilities of fiction. They are still very pleasing for their vivacity, a kind of katzenjammer tumult of language. They are equally pleasing for Lewis' cleverness at satiric distortion—and his endless interest in the appearance of things, as a slight twist of perspective transforms staid objects into grotesque.

Lewis' novels do not sufficiently resist the temptation to reduce them to their motivating ideas; they contain few reserves of suggestion or mystery; they depend too much on the bludgeon of statement. That they yield pleasure is undeniable, but it is the kind of pleasure that pours out too quickly. After a time one tends to think of his places and his characters as if they were the common property of our culture, almost forgetting they were created for particular books by a specific artist. And that is both the triumph and the tragedy of Sinclair Lewis; for while his creatures do live, they seem steadily to be moving beyond the pages of his books. (p. 34)

Irving Howe, "The World He Mimicked Was His Own," in The New York Times Book Review *(© 1961 by The New York Times Company; reprinted by permission), October 1, 1961, pp. 1, 34.*

SHELDON NORMAN GREBSTEIN (essay date 1962)

[The early novels of Sinclair Lewis are] novels of and about education. The heroes and heroines are put through a learning process in which book learning has a strictly subordinate role. In this process they inevitably grow more sophisticated in their manners, improve their appearances and personal attractiveness, increase their practical or vocational skills, become keener observers of human nature and more adept at handling people, and develop a broader world-view. (p. 40)

While [Lewis's] style is not fully mature in *Our Mr. Wrenn*, it is already distinctive. Later, in the books appearing after 1920, he became a more adept and resourceful craftsman, his method more documentary, his tone more sober. However, his diction, dialogue, sentence types, narrative techniques (with the point of view usually third person-omniscient) remained essentially the same. The early books, as well as such later romances as [*Mantrap* and *Bethel Merriday*] . . . , are generally characterized by a playful, deliberately facetious approach, including an occasional now-dear-

reader passage. In Lewis's romances the reader is instantly made aware and kept aware that this is a *story* and that someone is telling it, which is typical of the psychology of popular fiction. Yet there is a leavening of realism, some harsh detail, a focus on the commonplace and ordinary. The cheerful voice, when Lewis describes his hero's tribulations or loneliness, sometimes begins to tremble; the sweet tones verge on the bittersweet.

Diction is the key to Lewis's style, early and late, especially the pivotal adjective or adverb, with the choice of verbs next in importance. Thus, Wrenn's mustache is "unsuccessful." (pp. 42-3)

Another basic technique is Lewis's employment of figurative language. He uses it a great deal, including a wide range of types and varieties: metaphor, personification, simile, metonymy and synecdoche, and others. (p. 43)

The result of Lewis's style is to produce an impression of speed and color rather than depth and intensity, especially when the tone is one of self-conscious cleverness. Furthermore, Lewis rarely gets into the character's head, either in *Our Mr. Wrenn* or thereafter; he habitually describes experience from the outside. We do not learn enough about the character as an individual from what he thinks and feels; instead we are given what he says and does. We have too little chance to interpret him or see him develop. All too frequently the development is accomplished by Lewis's loaded diction, so that the character's words and deeds only confirm the reader's ready-made judgment. Again, the technique is that of slick fiction and is ever-present in Lewis's romances. In his best books, of course, Lewis surmounted many of these limitations. He always had difficulty maintaining consistent tone, but the strength of his feeling usually carried him through, while the accuracy and amount of his realistic detail compensated for the superficiality of his approach. Moreover, such creations as Babbitt, Gottlieb, and Sam and Fran Dodsworth prove that at his peak Lewis was capable of bringing to life subtle and complex characters. Istra Nash of *Our Mr. Wrenn* gave promise of that ability. (p. 44)

Free Air, Lewis's last novel of the [early] period, . . . illustrates Lewis's weaknesses—at times his near-fatal weakness—for the romance of the commonplace. It is not quite so syrupy as [his earlier book] *The Innocents* . . . , nor so self-consciously cute, but with very little alteration it would still make a Grade B movie or *Post* serial. In fact, *Free Air* is a kind of summation of the popular fiction of Lewis's early period; for it has travel, adventure, romance, colorful characters, "problems," an upbeat philosophy, twists and turns of plot, and the necessary revisions of personality and attitude without hard struggle. The book's surface realism is provided by the narrative of driving across the country, when such a trip was still an adventure and the automobile still new enough to be fascinating. Without the bits of driving-lore and automobile mechanics, without the panorama of American terrain, the book would be totally shapeless and unconvincing. (p. 53)

The Job [is not typical of Lewis's early period in that he] specifically rejects what he has elsewhere asserted, that business is a modern form of high romance; he treats it instead as an enslaving force. Even the bosses, its priests, do not understand the religion they serve. . . . In passage after passage Lewis reminds the reader how business has driven beauty and passion out of life. There are dozens of pages which stress the dreariness of the heroine's job and daily routine, the ugliness and crush of the subway, the loneliness of the working girl's empty flat. Such descriptions manifest Lewis's special gifts: his solid grasp on materiality and his ability to suggest the spiritual poverty of modern life by conveying both the meretriciousness of its exterior and the inner pathos of its inhabitants. Nor does he hesitate to drop the mask of reportorial realist and speak out passionately against injustice. (p. 56)

[The] dominant tone and detail of *The Job* is realistic, so realistic that it was hailed in its time as one of the most candid and authentic American novels dealing with the life of the working girl. Even today, with a handicap of nearly fifty years, it reads surprisingly well. (p. 57)

Ann Vickers, [which came after the period of Lewis's great satires, is] an imperfect fusion of realistic-satirical novel and romance. (p. 125)

Despite the book's rather racy plot, the reader coming to it after Lewis's slashing books of the 1920's would immediately have detected a new and unsettling note in the novel's first paragraph, in which Lewis depicts children at play "blissfully unaware that compromise and weariness will come at forty-five." . . . There are other disturbing hints. Although the novel's heroine is described from the start as a free and proud girl, highly idealistic, Lewis's treatment of her village background is an interesting departure. For one thing, it is not stultifying. For another, we are told that it leaves a deep and favorable impression upon her, teaching her a basic and permanent sense of decency and values and also introducing her to a wide variety of human types. Furthermore, Ann shares with rural America the awakening awareness of national destiny and pride. In short, Lewis presents a portrait of the small-town environment which is not only autobiographical but also complimentary. (pp. 125-26)

[In *Ann Vickers* Lewis's] tone has changed. It is neither that of the raging satirist, filled with snap and snarl . . . nor is it the cheery and whimsical voice of the romancer. Now it is nostalgic; an older soldier *hors de combat* is questioning the need of the battles he once fought. It was to be the tone and attitude dominant in Lewis's work of the 1930's. He has become the historian, not the reformer; he is the scribe of what has been, rather than the maker of what should be. Further, he addresses an audience he assumes are friends he had met long ago, who are growing old with him and sharing his bemusement at the times. This self-admitted displacement, this bewilderment, this weariness are not what we had come to expect of Sinclair Lewis. . . . (p. 126)

Another unusual element in *Ann Vickers* is its sexuality. While it rarely becomes indecorous and while it completely avoids the erotic, sexuality is important to both the novel's story and message. Until *Elmer Gantry* Lewis had been proper, even puritanical about sex. Ann's affairs are the first in Lewis's books in which a hero or heroine engages in illicit relations without some feeling of shame. Will Kennicott and Babbitt had indulged in such relations, but in their cases Lewis had portrayed the situations as sordid. . . . In *Ann Vickers* he suspends judgment altogether. Moreover, he demonstrates quite emphatically that love and satisfying sexual experience may be had outside of marriage, that

women have as much right to sexual pleasure as men, and that, once awakened, they have need of it. He also justifies abortions under extenuating although not desperate circumstances. None of these concepts and suggestions were radical in the fiction or discussion of the 1930's, but for Lewis they were.

The novel's sexuality cannot be discussed as an isolated factor, however. It is woven into the heroine's destiny and it is part of the novel's larger moral statement. The biography of the heroine follows the pattern of Lewis's search-for-identity or growth tales: small-town environment, instruction by the village atheist, stimulating college years, career, travel, disillusionment, and deeper experience in love, all resulting in maturity and fulfillment. Although Ann Vickers, unlike Una Golden [of *The Job*], achieves prominence, like the earlier heroine, she finds that a career is not enough for a woman. She suffers loneliness; she even regrets her own talents and accomplishments because they frighten men away. Upon this base Lewis erects a Nietzschean theory of romance: that great women need great men to love them. Since both are rare, the superior will marry an inferior. Then, the inferior will strive to drag the other down, humble him, and thus remove the difference between them. (p. 127)

However, even as social commentary—Lewis's specialty—*Ann Vickers* is shaky. There are jibes at social work, communism, the too-clever talk at New York liberal-intellectual cocktail parties, but none are keen enough to cut. It advances a number of worthy causes, true, and it takes a firm stand on penology, but these episodes do not dominate the entire novel. On the whole, it conspicuously lacks the vision which had transfigured *Main Street, Babbitt,* and *Arrowsmith;* it is without *Elmer Gantry*'s sheer malice, nor does it possess *Dodsworth*'s deep seriousness. Lewis seems to have surveyed the panorama of American society in the first years of the thirties and found nothing worthy of his full and concentrated attention. (p. 128)

Of the thirteen stories in his *Selected Short Stories* . . . , all but a few range from the canned, slick, or unforgivably sentimental to the merely contrived. Such a collection forces conclusions hostile to Lewis. If we presume that these stories are Lewis's best or representative of his best short fiction, then his best was inferior. It is also impossible to trace any consistent values or standards in the stories; rather, they contain some direct contradictions. For example, "Things" . . . , attacks the materialism and values of a business society; "Go East, Young Man" defends those very values. The shift might be explained by saying that one is an early story and the other late; however, in another late story, "Land" . . . Lewis reverses his field again and denies profit, respectability, and urban life. Obviously, Lewis paid no attention to consistency or harmony of theme in issuing this volume. Although the better stories, "Things," "Young Man Axelbrod," and "Land," affirm individuality and integrity, the collection on the whole manifests the romantic, affirmative, and commercial Lewis. Perhaps most disturbing of all, these tales show no development or progress of any kind. The best of them, "Young Man Axelbrod" . . . , is the earliest; one of the worst, "Let's Play King" . . . , is the latest and a piece of pure claptrap.

Jayhawker . . . is less objectionable than the story collection, although it, too, stemmed from Lewis's commercial rather than artistic instincts. . . . [The] play abundantly reveals Lewis's hand in its characters and plot. . . . With its combination of romance, war, heroism, and political intrigue and with its Gantry-like central character, Ace Burdette, *Jayhawker* may have been diverting entertainment but, again, it was not a tribute to America's winner of the Nobel Prize. (pp. 131-32)

[Held] up against Lewis's best and against other notable political novels of its generation—*Man's Fate, Darkness at Noon, Bread and Wine, 1984,* to give only a partial list—we can see why *It Can't Happen Here* falls short as a work of art, or even as a permanently significant political document, where the others succeed. They are engendered not only by a set of conditions or a type of society but also by deeply held convictions about the nature of man. The events they describe are based not only upon a Depression, a period of political unrest, or even the characteristics of a single nation, but upon the writer's conclusions regarding the destiny of the human race. They are ultimately not about politics but about people. This is exactly where Lewis miscarried in his novel and where we may perceive one of his great failings. . . .

The only conclusion of which Lewis persuades the reader is that the ends of idealism and reform—the establishment of a utopian and edenic state—do not justify the means. However, because the aims of the Corpo regime were clearly ignoble from the start, *It Can't Happen Here* provides scant opportunity either to the hero or the reader for progress, change, or learning. The sole development which takes place in the novel is that in Doremus Jessup's concentration camp experiences he has beaten into his body the lessons about political tyranny that his head knew all along. The theme of the novel affirms that it *can* happen here if the decent folk, whom Doremus represents, merely stand by as well-behaved spectators of the legions of evil. We must all resist, Lewis says. But is this not a contradiction to the doctrine voiced by Doremus and so persistently by Lewis throughout the 1930's—that we would be better off without reformers and rebels and idealists? (p. 144)

What *It Can't Happen Here* most lacks, considering it thematically, is a code of political or economic or philosophical convictions which would serve as a frame of reference. The critics had always complained that Lewis diagnosed sicknesses without prescribing medication for them, and the same criticism might be applied even more appropriately to this novel, for in it Lewis is dealing with specific political and economic conditions as well as a particular state of mind. Yet the only remedy Lewis proposes is some sort of welfare state—a kind of benevolent democratic socialism—in which civic responsibility is rigidly enforced, and this proposal is given but a paragraph. The only solution Lewis advances for human betterment is the preservation of the free, inquiring, liberal mind. Well and good, but that's like being for Virtue. We are all in favor of it; how do we get it? I again admit that judged as a satirist and as a writer of fiction Lewis is not obligated to provide remedies. This is the work of statesmen, professors, and philosophers. But evaluating Lewis as a political scientist, and he leaves himself open to such an evaluation in *It Can't Happen Here,* we can call him to account here where we could not in his books of the great decade. (p. 145)

Quite apart from Lewis's hold on politics, the looseness of his grip as a novelist is apparent in *It Can't Happen Here* in the handling of characters, plot, and narrative structure. "Buzz" Windrip, for example, is the most incredible of all Lewis's creations. In Windrip and in such other characters as Adelaide Tarr Gimmitch, Hector Macgoblin, and General Emmanuel Coon—whose names in themselves testify to the state of Lewis's artistic sensibility—the distance between the concrete world and fantasy world of Lewis's imagination becomes too obvious. He conveys quite well the mood of the 1930's and a sense of the chaos in the decade's events, but the fantasy spills over into the reality and dilutes it, sometimes making a witch's brew of the whole thing. The book departs too often from a firm grounding in emotional and psychological truth for us consistently to project ourselves into it and shudder, as we do Orwell's *1984;* nor is *It Can't Happen Here* dignified by the total seriousness of Orwell's masterpiece. Because Lewis's material is itself so volatile, it should have been handled with more care and restraint. (p. 146)

The passage of time and a vital change in literary taste have . . . conspired to make Lewis seem worse than he is. He was never a very sophisticated novelist; yet we judge him, as we must judge the artist, by prevailing standards of criticism. As it happens, that criticism is itself highly sophisticated, more so than the work of Sinclair Lewis and more so than the work of many of the very novelists, poets, and playwrights to which it applies. Lewis's aims were simple: he told a story, he recorded a fact, he exposed an evil; or, most frequently, he did all three at once. He was too rarely a *novelist,* in the fullest sense. The novelist seeks to exhibit men and women and to search for a common emotion or basis of understanding. The satirist, on the other hand, pursues and scourges a common failing in men and women. His characters are most effective when they are "types of their failures." (pp. 161-62)

The characters who are types and not individuals are such because their society—as Lewis sees it—does not allow them development as individuals. America, the land of personal liberty and individual freedom, produces types: this is Lewis's recurrent thesis. His characters yearn to be individuals and some of them make progress toward it, but their environment and fellows enslave them. In Lewis's books the reader gets a far stronger impression of the milieu in which things happen than he does, with a few exceptions, of the people to whom they happen. To put it plainly, the "Character" writer disregards environment, while Lewis, in his best books, is concerned precisely with environment; if not in *how* the character became the way he is, at least—as in *Babbitt*—in *what* keeps him that way. (pp. 162-63)

[In] the limitations of Lewis's view, with its focus on surface and its belief that the exterior communicates the interior, we can see the distance between Lewis and Tolstoy, or Lewis and Flaubert. He has grasped a portion of the truth and has taken it for the whole truth. They knew what he did not, and they had the artistic resources to say what he could not. (p. 164)

Sheldon Norman Grebstein, in his Sinclair Lewis *(copyright © 1962, by Twayne Publishers, Inc.; reprinted with the permission of Twayne Publishers, a Division of G. K. Hall & Co., Boston), Twayne, 1962, 192 p.*

MARK SCHORER (essay date 1963)

When *Main Street* appeared, plunging literary America into a rare and heated controversy, it seemed that nothing like it, with its shrill indictment of village life, the middle class, provincial America, had been published before. For many years popular American fiction had been picturing village life as sweet and good, the middle class as kindly when not noble, the provinces as aglow with an innocence in sharp contrast to the cruelty and corruption of the cities. In the fifty years before 1920 there had, to be sure, been exceptions—novels a good deal more critical of village life than was the rule; but the prevailing view was that of Friendship Village, and it was this view that *Main Street* abruptly and perhaps forever ended.

Main Street seemed to those readers who had known Lewis' earlier work to be a complete rupture with everything he had done before. A look at those earlier novels [*Our Mr. Wrenn, The Trail of the Hawk, The Job, The Innocents,* and *Free Air*] now shows this not to have been the situation at all. All five works had essentially the same pattern: the impulse to escape the conventions of class or routine; flight; a partial success and a necessary compromise with convention. Realistic in detail, these novels were optimistic in tone in a way that was not generally associated with what was then thought of as the school of realism, and it was the combination of the optimistic view of human character with the body of observed social detail that critics remarked and some readers enjoyed.

There had been satirical flashes in the earlier books if not the generally sustained and less good-tempered satire of *Main Street,* but satire nevertheless and satire directed against the same general objects. Furthermore, when those earlier novels were effective, they were so because of the body of closely observed physical detail, but it was detail more impressionistically, less massively presented than in *Main Street.* Certain character types that were to be made famous by *Main Street* had already appeared—the hypocritical bigot, the village atheist, the aspiring idealist, and so on. And the basic pattern of *Main Street* was exactly the same pattern that has already been described: a young creature is caught in a stultifying environment, clashes with that environment, flees from it, is forced to return, compromises.

Carol Kennicott, the heroine of *Main Street,* has no alternative to compromise. Her values, her yearning for a free and gracious life, had only the vaguest shape, and when she tried to put them into action in Gopher Prairie, Minnesota, she found only the most artificial and sentimental means. To some readers even then (when thousands of women were identifying themselves with her) she seemed like a rather foolish young woman, and so today she must seem to every reader. In the end, the true values are those of her husband, "Doc" Kennicott, who, for all his stolidity, is honest, hard-working, kindly, thrifty, motivated by commonsense.... It is Kennicott who has the last word. In the end, then, it is the middle class that triumphs and the Middle West, and the middle-brow. And so it would always be in fact in the novels of Sinclair Lewis.

It is more accurate to say that the triumph is given to the *best* qualities of the middle class and that it is its worst qualities that the novel castigates: smugness, hypocrisy, a gross materialism, moral cant. These are the qualities that

Lewis' satire, even when the focus begins to blur as it does with *Dodsworth,* would continue to assail. (pp. 9-11)

[The essential narrative pattern established in Lewis's early novel] had not changed in *Babbitt:* the individual trapped in an environment, catching glimmerings of something more desirable beyond it, struggling to grasp them, succeeding or failing. Babbitt fails—or nearly does—with the result that the comic-satiric element here is both heightened and broadened over that of the earlier novels. (p. 13)

The novel makes it easy enough for one to name the values that would save Zenith and Babbitt with it. They are love and friendship; kindness, tolerance, justice, and integrity; beauty; intellect. For the first two of these Babbitt has a throbbing desire if no very large capacity. Of the next four he has intimations. The seventh he can approach only in the distortions of his reveries, as in his morning dream of the "fairy child." To the last he is a total stranger. (p. 14)

[*Babbitt* was the first novel] of its kind in two striking ways. American literature had a full if brief tradition of the business novel.... Business was synonymous with ethical corruption; the world of business was savagely competitive, brutally aggressive, murderous. The motivation of the businessman was power, money, social prestige—in that order. But the businessman in almost all this fiction was the tycoon, the powerful manufacturer, the vast speculator, the fabulous financier, the monarch of enormous enterprises, the arch-individual responsible only to himself. And his concern was production.

After World War I, the tycoon may still have been the most colorful and dramatic figure in the business myth, but he was no longer the characteristic figure, and *Babbitt* discovers the difference. This is the world of the little businessman and, more particularly, of the middle man. If his morals are no better, his defections are anything but spectacular. Not in the least resembling the autocratic individualist, he is the compromising conformist. No producer himself, his success depends on public relations.... And with the supremacy of *public* relations, he abolishes human relations. All this Sinclair Lewis' novel was the first to give back to a culture that was just becoming aware that it could not tolerate what it had made of itself.

And it did it with a difference. The older novels, generally speaking, were solemn or grandly melodramatic denunciations of monstrous figures of aggressive evil. *Babbitt* was raucously satirical of a crowd of ninnies and buffoons who, if they were malicious and mean, were also ridiculous. And yet, along with all that, Babbitt himself was pathetic. (pp. 14-16)

[After the brutal satire of *Elmer Gantry, Dodsworth*] once more assured Lewis' readers that he was a generous man, for while it again had its share of satire, the satire was directed largely at the frenetic pretentiousness and snobbery of Dodsworth's first wife, and it presented Dodsworth himself, with all his solidly American middle-class virtues, in full sympathy. Here there was no occasion at all for controversy. And what Sinclair Lewis himself believed in, at the bottom of his blistered heart, was at last clear: a downright self-reliance, a straightforward honesty, a decent modesty, corn on the cob and apple pie. (p. 25)

[In *Dodsworth,* Lewis] turned back to a reassertion of those very middle-class, middle-brow, and middle-western values that the decade of the twenties seemed to have destroyed forever, and that it had most emphatically modified at least; and with those values he, who would henceforth seem to be the most old-fashioned of modern American novelists, would henceforth abide. (p. 27)

[*Work of Art*] was probably the first of Lewis' serious novels since *Main Street* to be completely without distinction. . . . This novel brings to a climax, certainly, his old, uneasy suspicion of intellect and art, and his deep respect for middle-class virtue, for effort. A novel about the hotel industry in America, it deals with two brothers, Myron and Ora Weagle. Myron is steady and reliable and, even as a boy, dreams of some day owning a perfect hotel. Ora is "literary" and spends his good-for-nothing days mooning in romantic fantasies and in writing verse. . . . Ora grows up to be a commercial success and a hack, always self-deluded and scornful of his downright brother. But Myron is the true artist, and Lewis makes nearly his every effort analogous to an act of artistic creation. Ultimately, Myron even keeps a notebook, "what must, in exactness, be called 'The Notebook of a Poet,'" in which he jots down ideas for improving hotel management and reflections upon his experience as a hotelkeeper. . . . If one wishes to learn about hotel management the novel is no doubt an admirable handbook, and no duller than a handbook; if one wishes to learn anything about art, and especially the art of the novel, there is nothing here at all. *Work of Art* is the fantasy of the perfect Rotarian. It is almost as if George F. Babbitt had suddenly produced a novel.

It was no longer the best of the middle-class character that Sinclair Lewis was praising, but the very middle of the middle. (pp. 32-3)

And so he staggered toward his end. In *Kingsblood Royal* . . . he made his last strenuous effort to re-enter American realities by addressing himself to the problem of the Negro minority in American life. The book aroused some excitement as a social document but none whatever as a literary performance, and even its social usefulness, it is now clear, is minimized by Lewis' mechanical oversimplification of what is, of course, one of the most complex, as well as one of the most pressing, issues in the national life of the United States. From this attempt to deal with the immediate present, Lewis retreated into the historical past of Minnesota. *The God-Seeker* . . . is apparently the first part of what was finally projected as a trilogy about labor in the United States. But it is a wooden, costumed performance about which even Lewis' faithful publishers despaired. And his last novel, *World So Wide*, . . . is a thin attempt to write another *Dodsworth*. It is the final self-parody. (p. 37)

[It] is quite true that even [Lewis'] most famous novels have crass defects. He was, in the first place, the kind of writer who found it temperamentally impossible to objectify his own anxieties, the tensions of his inner life, or even to draw upon them except in the most superficial way, in his own writing, and the writer, after all, is not different from the man who contains him. Shunning the subjective, he often fell into the sentimental. Yet there are other realities than those that pertain to the subjective life. His twenty-two novels, so uneven in quality, do share in one likeness: they are a long march all directed toward a single discovery, the "reality" of America. . . . For Sinclair Lewis, America was always promises, and that was why, in 1950, he could say that he loved America but did not like it, for it

was still only promises, and promises that nearly everyone else had long ago given up. Sinclair Lewis had nothing else to turn to. (p. 39)

Generalized, [Lewis' America] becomes an idealization of an older America, the America of the mid-nineteenth century, an America enormous and shapeless but overflowing, like a cornucopia, with the potentialities for and the constant expression of a wide, casually human freedom, the individual life lived in honest and perhaps eccentric effort . . . , the social life lived in a spirit that first of all tolerates variety and individual difference. It was the ideal America of Thoreau, of Whitman. . . . Like Thoreau, Whitman, Twain, Lewis too could see the difference between the idealization and the actuality. (pp. 39-40)

The American defection from the American potentiality for individual freedom is the large subject of Lewis' satire. When he excoriated Americans it was because they would not be free, and he attacked all the sources by means of which they betrayed themselves into slavery: the economic system, intellectual rigidity, theological dogma, legal repression, class convention, materialism, social timidity, hypocrisy, affectation, complacency, and pomposity. These two, the individual impulse to freedom and the social impulse to restrict it, provide the bases of his plots in novel after novel. (p. 41)

But he was himself sentimental and a Philistine, and often these led him to settle for the very stolidity in American life that he flayed. . . . If he was the village intellectual, the village atheist, the rebel, the nonconformist crank for whom the dialect, the cracker barrel, and the false whiskers served as counterpoise to the stuffed shirt in his defense of what Lloyd Morris called "the old, free, democratic, individualistic career of the middle class," he was at the same time the pontifical village banker, the successful manufacturer of automobiles, the conservative, the very middle of the middle. His trust in "culture" was equaled by his trust in "things." His respect for science was certainly greater than his respect for art. Brought up in an environment that condescended to art and reverenced success, he managed, in that America, to make a success of "art." Often and increasingly it was bad art, and the success was in many ways abrasive and self-destructive. In his novels, he loved what he lamented; in his life, he was most secure and content with the kind of people who might have been the prototypes for his own creatures. (pp. 41-2)

He had other impressive qualities, among them the ability to create a gallery of characters who have independent life outside the novels, with all their obvious limitations—characters that live now in the American historical tradition. A number of them have become gigantic, archetypal figures that embody the major traits of their class. . . .

He performed a function that has nearly gone out of American fiction, and American fiction is thinner for the loss. Many American novelists today tell us about our subjective lives, and on that subject Sinclair Lewis could hardly speak at all. Fitzgerald, Hemingway, Faulkner—they all had some sense of the tragic nature of human experience that was denied to Lewis. Lyric joy, sensuous ecstasy—to these, too, he was apparently a stranger. But he had a stridently comic gift of mimicry that many a more polished American writer does not have at all. And a vision of a hot and dusty hell: the American hinterland. He gave Americans their first shuddering glimpses into a frightening reality of which until he wrote they were unaware and of which he himself may also have been unaware. . . . [He] could document for an enormous audience the character of a people and a class, and, without repudiating either, criticize and laugh uproariously at both. In any strict literary sense, he was not a great writer, but without his writing one cannot imagine modern American literature. No more, without his writing, could Americans today imagine themselves. His epitaph should be: *He did us good.* (pp. 43-4)

Mark Schorer, in his Sinclair Lewis *(American Writers Pamphlet No. 27;* © *1963, University of Minnesota), University of Minnesota Press, Minneapolis, 1963, 47 p.*

DANIEL R. BROWN (essay date 1966)

[Lewis'] satire is at its best, its most exciting, when he is totally armed as an opponent, as he is in *It Can't Happen Here* and *Elmer Gantry.* In these novels, he is undoubtedly one-sided and unfair, but all satire is this way. When the attitude becomes inconsistent, it becomes watery and tepid. Even *Main Street* and *Babbitt* lack directness and cohesion because of the author's ambivalent emotions toward his protagonists. His ambivalence could have heightened and deepened his novels but too often the ambivalence is uncontrolled, arising from uncertainty rather than subtlety. In addition, the novels offer a norm within themselves against which to judge the action. Because he provides no adequate alternatives to their lives, the characters scurry around pursued by Lewis' scourge, but presented with no escape. . . . The net result of his uncertainty is that the reader, once he has stopped laughing, is left grasping for some standard of comparison with which to identify. Even when he does provide alternatives to the dreary lives and anesthetizing aestheticism of his characters, the merely exotic becomes the desirable, for no doubt Lewis was a sentimentalist. Usually all he offers as substitutes to a hum-drum existence are Persian market-places, idyllic camp-sites, fairy girls, and jeweled roads to Samarkand. . . . His satire suffers most when, because he cannot provide legitimate substitutes, he throws sugar on the wounds he inflicts instead of salt.

Like all satirists, Lewis' animosities are more tangible than his loves. Just what he wanted for his characters is obscure. Unquestionably he felt strongly that people should be told that too many of them possess only a cheapened and degraded appreciation of beauty. He knew that make-shift shacks of hick towns, newspaper verse, and dull conversations are not the height of man's accomplishment, and he makes these feelings very vocal. Moreover, throughout his career he consistently opposed such things as racial intolerance, rich men's insensitivity, rudeness to waiters and servants, un-Christian Christian charity, and mores mistaken for the voice of God. Beyond these he went only into vague notions of something better. In general, Lewis approved of behavior which can best be described only by the nebulous word "moderate." He admired persons who fall somewhere between the excesses of an Elmer Gantry and the mental sterility of the citizens of a Gopher Prairie. (pp. 64-5)

Obviousness is, in large measure, the quality that made Lewis' satire popular. Probably too often he bludgeons his

characters to death when he might have, as Dryden said, decapitated his victims so dexterously that they would not have known it until they tried to move. Perhaps if there were fewer mangled bodies lying around, he would be taken more seriously by literary critics. Very often the way in which his blunted sword displays itself is in a too-obvious juxtaposition of ironic happenings. (pp. 68-9)

Fortunately, there are places where Lewis controls his tendency toward leaving fingerprints on the reader's mind. Subtlety is not unknown to him. . . .

Satirists can be more indirect, more adroit, but it appears that Lewis was afraid that his readers would fail to realize he had killed his character unless he shook the corpse like a terrier. (p. 69)

But ordinarily Lewis preferred to use the opposite method and gain attention by impaling his victims in a frontal attack. If he is often crude in his technique, it should be remembered that he is so because he chose not to be crude in his basic material. . . .

When he is too obvious, it is almost always because he wanted to club his subject without waiting, brooding, honing his prose. Yet when he was able to restrain his indignation and achieve aesthetic distance, he could be caustic and witty, fashioning many a stiletto-tipped sentence, without succumbing to his worst fault as a satirist—elephantine clumsiness. (p. 70)

Daniel R. Brown, "Lewis's Satire—A Negative Emphasis," in Renascence *(*© *copyright, 1966, Marquette University Press), Vol. XVIII, No. 2, Winter, 1966, pp. 63-72.*

JAMES LUNDQUIST (essay date 1973)

Lewis's reputation has rested, and most likely will continue to rest, on his notoriety as a polemicist—and he was a good one, deserving comparison to H. L. Mencken and perhaps even to Thomas Paine. In dealing with the new realities of the American industrial state and the concurrent economy of abundance, he took a moral position that was instructive yet not so radical as to be unacceptable to the middle-class audience that bought his books. His appeal was wide, perhaps wider than that of any other American writer. He received serious critical attention from high-powered critics and scholars . . . , yet at the same time he was read devotedly by hundreds of thousands of people whose literary acumen was anything but highpowered. He was that most unusual phenomenon, an important writer whose appeal to the masses was genuine. . . . But as much as Lewis deserves credit as an author of books that have been seen as publishing events and as markers in the history of American consciousness, he is nonetheless a novelist, and his place in the history of that literary form is a definite one.

The novel is, of course, many things, and the Lewis novel is a distinct type, never matched or really imitated by any other writer, however many bad or weak novels Lewis wrote. Although Lewis's presence was most certainly felt by other writers, he did not, in the strictest sense at any rate, inspire a school of followers: one reason for this is that his most memorable books are all *tours de force,* making imitation difficult. But a more sweeping explanation is that there is a quality of inimitableness in Lewis; . . . he is virtually a movement unto himself. (pp. 126-27)

The problem of understanding Lewis has not simply been a matter of evaluating his social pronouncements or of debating whether or not he is sufficiently artistic; it has been predominately the problem of his uniqueness. There is a wildness, an unpredictableness that is at the center of Lewis the man and Lewis the writer; and this tendency at once serves as an explanation for the dynamism of his writing and the inertia that has crept into many of the attempts to evaluate it. One is led to conclude that the nervous energy that is so much a part of Lewis's style, tends to wear readers and critics down. . . . There is no point in explaining away this characteristic of the Lewis novel other than to state simply that Lewis is no writer to read in large doses; he is too singular, too angry, too irritating in both style and statement. This, of course, is a major source of his power, a way he still makes the presence of his abrasive personality felt.

If there is a single word that may be used to describe and categorize Lewis's books, it is none of the adjectives so far mentioned. The best term is perhaps "garish." His better novels are all showy, harsh, glaring, and alternately positive or negative to the point of extravagance. They embody a particular kind of contemporaneity that is effectively defined in the word "pop" and its implication of obsession with the bizarre forms and life patterns that are part of the everyday world in the economy-of-abundance democracies of this century. In many respects Lewis was the first of our pop novelists (later ones include Dos Passos, Gore Vidal, Terry Southern, and the Charles Portis of *Norwood*), his imagination seemingly most stirred by the ticky-tacky eternal presence of mass culture seen on the big screen at the Rosebud Theater, listened to on the radio, tasted through a soda-shop straw, touched with gloves purchased at the Bon Ton store, and smelled through a miasma of automobile exhaust and industrial smoke. It is a culture in which the ultimate disillusionment is that in the midst of seemingly infinite variety so many things are the same and carry the same price tag—loss of freedom. But Lewis reveled in it nonetheless, inexplicably loving that which he invited us to hate.

But the nature of the Lewis novel and the reasons for his popularity should first and last be understood in ways that do not demand footnotes in the history of aesthetics. Lewis came on the scene at just the moment when twentieth-century American garishness was becoming apparent—even to Americans. It was a time when the very garishness of the reality of surplus production was short-circuiting the pioneer brain. His novels are partly histories of the painful transition that began sometime around 1920 and partly remedies for the pain. His fictionalizing of what was happening in the small town and in the city to the housewife, the businessman, the scientist, the preacher, and the industrialist was a purgation of fears that were widely and deeply felt, fears that are, of course, still with us. Had Lewis's novels not been written the way they were, had they been more tightly structured, more carefully thought-out, more Jamesian (for it is Henry James that most critics seem to have in mind when castigating Lewis), they would not have had the peculiar and lasting effect that they have. This itself is a measure of Lewis's artistry and a defense of his achievement as a writer, of the notoriety of his enduring fame. (pp. 127-29)

James Lundquist, in his Sinclair Lewis *(copyright*

© *1973 by Frederick Ungar Publishing Co., Inc.),*
Ungar, 1973, 150 p.

ADDITIONAL BIBLIOGRAPHY

Benét, William Rose. "The Earlier Lewis." *The Saturday Review of Literature* X, No. 27 (20 January 1934): 421-22.
    A friend's reminiscences of Lewis, including interesting insights into Lewis's love for the very people he satirized.

Bucco, Martin. "The Serialized Novels of Sinclair Lewis." *Western American Literature* IV, No. 1 (Spring 1969): 29-37.
    An examination of the differences between the serialized versions of Lewis's novels and the final editions.

Conroy, Stephen S. "Sinclair Lewis's Sociological Imagination." *American Literature* 42, No. 3 (November 1970): 348-62.
    A look at Lewis's great novels of the 1920s from a sociological perspective.

Dooley, D. J. *The Art of Sinclair Lewis.* Lincoln: University of Nebraska Press, 1967, 286 p.
    Synopses and criticism of Lewis's works. The book is sprinkled with critical excerpts by other essayists as well.

Fyvel, T. R. "Martin Arrowsmith and His Habitat." *The New Republic* 133, No. 3 (18 July 1955): 16-18.
    An assessment of Lewis's skill as a satirist of the middle class.

Hoffman, Frederick J. "The Text: Sinclair Lewis's *Babbitt*." In his *The Twenties: American Writing in the Postwar Decade,* rev. ed., pp. 408-15. New York: The Free Press, 1949.
    An essay on *Babbitt,* and close examination of the book's central character.

Hollis, C. Carroll. "Sinclair Lewis: Reviver of Character." In *Fifty Years of the American Novel: A Christian Appraisal,* edited by Harold C. Gardner, S.J., pp. 89-106. New York: Charles Scribner's Sons, 1952.
    An essay in which Lewis's strength as a creator of Theophrastian Characters rather than as a writer of novels is examined.

Light, Martin. *The Quixotic Vision of Sinclair Lewis.* West Lafayette: Purdue University Press, 1975, 162 p.
    A study of the relationship between reality and delusion in Lewis's characters.

Maglin, Nan Bauer. "Women in Three Sinclair Lewis Novels." *The Massachusetts Review* XIV, No. 4 (Autumn 1973): 783-801.
    Examines the female principals in *The Job, Ann Vickers,* and *Main Street* as creations Lewis used to explore the choices and pressures on women in the early part of this century.

Millgate, Michael. "Sinclair Lewis and the Obscure Hero." *Studi Americani* 8 (1962): 111-27.
    An examination of the main characters in several Lewis novels.

Schorer, Mark. "Sinclair Lewis and His Critics." In his *The World We Imagine: Selected Essays,* pp. 183-94. New York: Farrar, Straus and Giroux, 1948.
    An interesting survey of Lewis's critical reception throughout his career.

Schorer, Mark. *Sinclair Lewis: An American Life.* New York: McGraw-Hill Book Co., 1961, 867 p.
    The definitive biography of Lewis.

Sherman, Stuart P. *The Significance of Sinclair Lewis.* Freeport, NY: Books for Libraries Press, 1971, 20 p.
    Discusses Lewis's first seven novels, responds to critics of Lewis's satirical method, and provides an interesting comparison of Lewis and Flaubert as chroniclers of provincial life. This study was originally published in 1922.

Thompson, Dorothy. ''The Boy and Man from Sauk Centre.'' *The Atlantic Monthly* 206, No. 5 (November 1960): 39-48.
    A short biography of Lewis containing interesting insights into the man, his descendents, and his forebears.

H(oward) P(hillips) Lovecraft

1890-1937

(Also wrote under pseudonyms of Ward Phillips, Humphrey Littlewit, Gent., Lewis Theobald, Jr., Augustus T. Swift, Albert Frederick Willie, Edgar Softly, and Richard Raleigh) American short story writer, novelist, poet, critic, and essayist.

Lovecraft is the twentieth century's most significant author in the genre of supernatural fantasy. Often compared to Edgar Allan Poe, Lovecraft extended the Gothic tradition of his predecessor and ultimately established an independent literary domain. As is evident from his critical survey, *Supernatural Horror in Literature*, Lovecraft was a theorist as well as a practitioner of the weird story. In that essay he establishes a sophisticated and highly personal aesthetic for a category of literature not often subjected to lengthy critical examination. Lovecraft's own fiction serves as a model of his criteria for the ideally formed fantastic tale—emphasizing the clashing confrontation between the known and the unknowable, slighting character psychology to focus upon cosmic phenomena.

Lovecraft's stories are commonly divided into three types: those early works influenced by the Irish writer Lord Dunsany, those tales sharing a similar background of cosmic legend usually referred to as the Cthulhu Mythos, and a number of horror narratives set for the most part in New England. The short stories and novels connected with the Cthulhu Mythos, a term never used by Lovecraft, are the focal point for his literary reputation. In these works he fused a number of disparate, sometimes radically conflicting elements. Scientific studies and occult lore, nihilism and mysticism, beauty and decay all mingle in Lovecraft's stories, creating that dynamic tension which critics so often observe.

Critics often differ severely in their appraisals of Lovecraft. Most critical objections call attention to the author's prose style, dismissing it as awkwardly ornate and archaic. Defenders find Lovecraft's techniques well suited to the genre of the fantastic, where extravagant subjects are sometimes best portrayed by an extravagance of style. Jorge Luis Borges uses the term "comic nightmares" to describe Lovecraft's stories, indicating a level of irony in what are widely considered straightforward tales of terror. Even if indifferent to Lovecraft as an artist, many commentators are fascinated with him as a psychological case, portraying him as a night-wandering recluse who wasted much literary talent in profitless misuse of his energy.

Most of Lovecraft's writing, in fact, was not done for commercial outlets. In addition to his voluminous correspondence, he also wrote lengthy travelogues of Quebec and Charleston, South Carolina, much poetry, and many essays for amateur journalism publications, all of which were decidedly unremunerative. Nearly all of Lovecraft's professional work, and his chief source of income, was in the form of revision and ghost-writing assignments of various sorts, from textbooks to fiction. Some of these "revisions" are entirely his own work, including the story "Imprisoned with the Pharaohs," ghost-written for the magician Houdini.

Lovecraft's fiction was first published in nonprofessional journals and in pulp magazines such as *Weird Tales*. To the end, he considered himself essentially an amateur who wrote primarily for his own amusement. His work, however, attracted followers and imitators among his contemporaries, many of whom—such as Fritz Leiber, Robert Bloch, and Frank Belknap Long—have in turn become influential writers of fantasy and science fiction. In the field of the Gothic and the macabre, Lovecraft continues to be a major literary presence.

PRINCIPAL WORKS

The Shunned House (short story) 1928
The Shadow over Innsmouth (short stories) 1936
The Outsider, and Others (short stories, novel, and criticism) 1939
Beyond the Wall of Sleep (short stories, essays, poetry, and novels) 1943
Marginalia (short stories, essays, and juvenilia) 1944
Supernatural Horror in Literature (criticism) 1945
Something about Cats, and Other Pieces (short stories, essays, and poetry) 1949

The Shuttered Room, and Other Pieces (short stories, essays, and juvenilia) 1959
Collected Poems (poetry) 1963
Selected Letters. 5 vols. (letters) 1965-76
The Dark Brotherhood, and Other Pieces (short stories, essays, and poetry) 1966
The Horror in the Museum, and Other Revisions (short stories) 1970
To Quebec and the Stars (essays and travel essays) 1976
A Winter Wish (poetry and essays) 1977

WILLIAM POSTER   (essay date 1944)

Howard Phillips Lovecraft died . . . at the age of 47, leaving behind an imposing mound of manuscript, either wholly unpublished or confined within the coarse covers of the pulp magazines. His tales of supernatural horror, black magic, prehistoric demons and spirits that inhabit the outer rim of the universe never achieved, within his lifetime, the dignity of a [commercially published] book. But before he died Lovecraft had succeeded in constructing a complete and detailed imaginary cosmos and mythology, the realm of "Cthulu," the sticky, green, winged water-god, "Nyarlath-otep," forever howling in the outer darkness, and hordes of greater and lesser demons and deities, complete with genealogy, habitat and spheres of influence.

Lovecraft was one of those rare individuals who seem to have been perfectly fitted by nature to do one thing surpassingly well. Poor health prevented him from participating fully in the normal life of children and at an early age he took refuge in his imagination. Most of his mature life he spent as a recluse in an old Georgian house in Providence, charting his private cosmos and populating it in successive narratives, with fantastically horrible survivals of untamed antiquity and projections of the more fearsome elements of the unknown present.

He was a voluminous writer. His stories grew longer with the years and made publication increasingly difficult. But Lovecraft, spurred on by internal compulsion rather than profit, never made the slightest effort to alter them for a market. Purveyors of the supernatural still lean heavily upon the Lovecraft pantheon. His fabulous bible of evil, the "Necronomicon of the mad Arab, Abul-Alhazred," is constantly referred to by his successors and still frequently requested from bewildered librarians.

> *William Poster, "Nightmare in Cthulu," in* The New York Times Book Review (© *1944 by The New York Times Company; reprinted by permission), January 16, 1944, p. 19.*

T. O. MABBOTT   (essay date 1944)

Lovecraft is one of the few authors of whom I can honestly say that I have enjoyed every word of his stories. . . . His study, "Supernatural Horror in Literature," makes one feel he could have been a remarkable interpreter of Literature. And while his poetry seems to me mostly written "with his left hand," it includes that marvellous bacchanalian song (in "The Tomb") with the magnificent line,

> Better under the table than under the ground

which makes one think he might under some circumstances have been a fine poet. But it was a writer of weird fiction that he chose to be primarily, and that choice seems to me justified by what he wrote.

His gifts were unusual. He was a scientist at heart, and that gave him a love of clarity. But he was also a dreamer, and could command the record of his own dreams, so as to make his readers yield "to shadows and delusions here." But mere style and clarity and careful planning cannot make a writer outstanding. There must be a narrative power for the writer of stories to excel, and that narrative power was the greatest of Lovecraft's gifts. It could outbalance his one greatest weakness—as recognised by himself, a tendency to melodrama, to kill off a dozen victims where one would have served better. It could have outbalanced a dozen weaknesses he did not have.

From time to time he is compared to Poe. There is little basis and no necessity for comparison. He was a great appreciator, admirer, and even interpreter of Poe (his recognition of the central theme of the "House of Usher" as the possession of but one soul by brother, sister, and the house itself seems to have been as novel as it is obviously correct) and he shared to a large extent Poe's views of the purpose of literature and the attitude the artist should have toward the weird. . . . The chief difference is hard to explain although it is easy to feel; Poe was more interested in method of thought, Lovecraft more in a record of ideas; yet Lovecraft tried to make his tales consistent with each other, while Poe could allow the devil to read human minds in one tale and not in another with insouciance. It is also notable that Poe, like most writers, was only occasionally interested in the weird, while Lovecraft confined himself to a single *genre.*

But Lovecraft is not to be thought of as an imitator of Poe. . . . Lovecraft can stand on his own feet, and does this without reference to his influence or the influences upon him. Few writers have ever won their way with less ballyhoo. . . . I think it too soon to say what place Lovecraft will have in American Literature, I have no doubt that it is an honourable place that should be accorded this truest amateur of letters. (pp. 43-5)

> *T. O. Mabbott, "H. P. Lovecraft: An Appreciation," in* Marginalia *by H. P. Lovecraft (copyright 1944 by August Derleth and Donald Wandrei; reprinted by permission of Arkham House Publishers, Inc.), Arkham House, 1944 (and reprinted in* H. P. Lovecraft: Four Decades of Criticism, *edited by S. T. Joshi, Ohio University Press, 1980, pp. 43-5).*

WINFIELD TOWNLEY SCOTT   (essay date 1945)

In Lovecraft's complete work his verse remains secondary; it has less distinction than his best stories and it is presumably less interesting than his letters. (p. 73)

The bulk of the poems fall into one or the other of two manners of verse brought to perfection in Lovecraft's beloved eighteenth-century England. One is the neat, or as Keats called it, "the rocking-horse" couplet. This is emulated by Lovecraft in "Old Christmas" and "New England Fallen," and possibly carried on to Sir Walter Scott's narrative manner in "Psychopompos." The other is the more dulcet, bucolic or elegiac tone, usually in quatrains, as mastered by Thomas Gray and James Thomson. "Providence," "On a Grecian Colonnade in a Park," "Sunset," and "On a New England Village Seen by Moonlight" are Lovecraft poems in this manner. . . . All these poems, indeed most of Lovecraft's, are "early poems." . . . They are quite dull, even at time unreadable. Their inspiration is literary and they never escape from or overcome the derivative tone. Their eighteenth-century mannerisms refuse transposition into the twentieth century. They are completely out of touch with Lovecraft's actual time as no vital poetry can ever be. And they are further damaged by the strong racial and social snobbery of Lovecraft's earlier years; what they say is frequently as restricted and eccentric as the manner in which it is said. In short, the quaintness and old-world-ness, which in his horror stories became an attractive other-worldliness, remain wholly inefficient in his poetry. (pp. 73-4)

Oddly enough, Lovecraft got away from this. . . . A poem called "A Year Off," dated 1925, hints the first flicker of freshness in his verse. It is light, humorous, deftly done, an extravaganza of far travel which concludes with J. K. Huysmans' touch that the thoroughgoing and imaginative anticipation is probably better than the actuality. But in its course it has verbal fun with its ideas: "To dally with the Dalai Lama" is a particularly fortunate moment.

Then, far more impressively, came the prolific spate of poetry between December 1929 and early January 1930. In three or four weeks Lovecraft wrote "Brick Row" and "The Messenger" and—these possibly within a week—the thirty-six sonnets, "Fungi from Yuggoth." In general their style is simple and direct, the earlier poetic derivations sloughed off. The horror of his best stories is at last used with effective understatement in verse. "They took me slumming" is, for instance, a phrase from one of the "Fungi" sonnets that would have dynamited the artificialities of his earlier poems; and almost everywhere the language is equally alive, and the horror is all the sharper for being quiet-spoken. (p. 75)

Had there been, in place of the eighteenth century and Poe, another and newer influence? I am inclined to think, with nothing to go on but internal evidence, that Lovecraft had been reading Edwin Arlington Robinson. [The] phrasing, the tone, the general approach of the "Fungi" sonnets are repeatedly Robinsonian. (p. 76)

[Lovecraft's best verse] remains restricted. Unlike Robinson's, it touched no depths of human significance. Its terror, unlike *The Ancient Mariner's*, has no meaning beyond mere nightmare. To scare is a slim purpose in poetry. But when Lovecraft at last brought his undoubted talent for horror themes into unaffected verse he made his poetry an interesting if minor portion of his total work. (p. 77)

> *Winfield Townley Scott, "A Parenthesis on Lovecraft As Poet" (originally published in* Rhode Island on Lovecraft, *edited by Donald M. Grant and Thomas P. Handley, Grant-Handley, Publishers, 1945), in his* Exiles and Fabrications *(copyright © 1961 by Winfield Townley Scott), Doubleday & Company, Inc., 1961, pp. 73-7.*

AUGUST DERLETH   (essay date 1945)

Lovecraft was not in any sense of the word a prolific writer. [True, he wrote] a depressing amount of poetry pat-

terned after the Eighteenth Century; but such of his work as has any lasting quality is not voluminous, apart from his letters. . . . Save for the fine *Supernatural Horror in Literature,* his essays are negligible; his derivative poetry of nothing but curiosity value. (p. 64)

His poetry of the weird, which followed his earlier period, is of considerably more interest; there is a sense of "adventurous expectancy" such as Lovecraft was himself aware of for most of his life, about most of the poems, though they are uneven; there is often a note of true terror, particularly in the *Fungi from Yuggoth,* which represent the best of his verse, and, added to such lesser poems as the appealing and sentimental *Brick Row,* and the narrative werewolf poem, *Psychopompos,* merit critical attention. Winfield Townley Scott has suggested that the influence at work in Lovecraft when he wrote the *Fungi from Yuggoth* was that of E. A. Robinson [see excerpt above]; but this must remain a speculation, for there is nothing at present to show that Lovecraft had read any of Robinson's work. The poems utilize place-names and beings of the Cthulhu Mythos, and also draw upon Lovecraft's earlier tales, written under the influence of Lord Dunsany's work; they are consistent with Lovecraft's direction in prose, and might well have been a natural extension of that direction.

It is in his prose fiction that Lovecraft promises to survive. In the Gothic tradition, and yet markedly original in its concepts, the short and long stories of H. P. Lovecraft command critical respect. (pp. 65-6)

The Lovecraft tales generally fall into two major classifications, and one combination; that is, the tales are either fantastic, somewhat after the Dunsany pattern; or they are weird and terrible tales of cosmic outsideness, after a pattern which, though a compound of Poe, Machen, Chambers, and Bierce, manifests the influence of Arthur Machen and Algernon Blackwood, and yet manages to remain individually Lovecraftian to such an extent that it has influenced many another writer in the genre. The combination, manifestly, is of these two developments, and has not been notably successful. The weird and terrible tales subdivide into "New England" tales and stories of the Cthulhu Mythos. The best of these early tales are stories of pure horror, such as the unforgettable *The Rats in the Walls,* the Poesque *The Outsider, The Picture in the House,* etc. Of the Dunsanian pieces, *Dagon, The Cats of Ulthar* and *The Strange High House in the Mist* are the best of the earlier stories, and *The Statement of Randolph Carter, The Silver Key,* and *Through the Gates of the Silver Key* the best of the later tales. The one surviving fantasy novel, *The Dream-Quest of Unknown Kadath,* has a kind of eerie charm, but seldom any genuine terror; it has a dream-like quality, almost an Alice in Wonderland kind of fantasy, and is quite unlike the other short novel, *The Case of Charles Dexter Ward,* which is one of Lovecraft's most carefully wrought fictions. (pp. 67-8)

The Dunsanian influence waned rather quickly, though Lovecraft occasionally returned to the manner, considerably modifying it each time; and he devoted more of his creative energies to the fashioning of memorable tales in the purest Gothic tradition. To this second period belong, apart from those titles already mentioned, such fine stories as *The Shunned House, The Music of Erich Zann, The Picture in the House,* and *Pickman's Model.* The last and most promising phase was that of the Cthulhu Mythos, which some commentators are prone to think came into being with the story, *The Call of Cthulhu,* which is not factual, since the Mythos was evolved piecemeal, and very slowly, and the most that can be said for *The Call of Cthulhu* is that it began to give shape to the mythos and the pattern Lovecraft was beginning to evolve. As a matter of record, there is everything to show that Lovecraft had no intention whatsoever of evolving his Cthulhu Mythos until that pattern made itself manifest in his work; this explanation alone would account for certain trivial inconsistencies. (pp. 68-9)

Lovecraft's concept of the Cthulhu Mythos . . . is basically similar to the Christian mythos, particularly in regard to the expulsion of Satan from Eden and the power of evil. "All my stories, unconnected as they may be, are based on the fundamental lore or legend that this world was inhabited at one time by another race who, in practising black magic, lost their foothold and were expelled, yet live on outside ever ready to take possession of this earth again," he wrote. Given this frame, given Lovecraft's free-ranging imagination and his ability to bring his imagination vividly into being on paper, . . . the myth-pattern began to assume a dramatic reality. (pp. 69-70)

As examples of something new and different in the Gothic tradition, [the Cthulhu Mythos] stories of H. P. Lovecraft place him at once in the forefront of writers of the macabre in American letters. Without any suggestion of imitation, he belongs in the tradition of Poe, and in the line of Poe and Ambrose Bierce, rather than in that of Hawthorne, Mary E. Wilkins-Freeman, and Edith Wharton. (p. 73)

Lovecraft's prose style in his major work is suggestive of his beloved eighteenth century. It is grave and stately; it is deliberate, rather than studied; and there is throughout his later prose work an air of leisurely compulsion, however paradoxical that may sound—a compulsion which affects the reader with a desire to carry on and stems from that careful leisureliness of manner so typical of Lovecraft at his best. This is the mature style, as against the earlier manner of Lovecraft; it is the style which Lovecraft himself questioned as "verbose". The need to set the stage meticulously is a necessary aspect of the supernatural story, and Lovecraft held to the tradition. In its prose style alone, however, Lovecraft's work is akin to the past; for his recurrent preoccupation with time and space, with the tantalizing enigmas of the never-ending quest for scientific knowledge and the attempt to comprehend the universe and man's place in it belong to our own time. (pp. 78-9)

[There] is no basis for comparison of Lovecraft's work to that of any other contemporary writer; among writers in the field of the macabre, apart from occasional work by men and women who were better known in other fields—like Edith Wharton, Wilbur Daniel Steele, Gertrude Atherton, Gouverneur Morris, Irvin S. Cobb, Dubose Heyward, Conrad Aiken, etc.—there were only Clark Ashton Smith and the late Reverend Henry S. Whitehead whose work was consistently good enough to command attention, and yet was not on the Lovecraft plane. Comparison has thus had to be made to the Gothic writers of the last century, and as a result there is too often a kind of careless suggestion that there are great similarities between the work of Lovecraft and that of Poe or Bierce. That is simply not so. Apart from the single tale, *The Outsider,* which is similar, there are none of the similarities to Poe, so carelessly imagined; and of Bierce's work, only *An Inhabitant of Carcosa*

and *The Death of Halpin Frayser* suggest any similarities. Nothing more. Lovecraft was an original in the Gothic tradition; he was a skilled writer of supernatural fiction, a master of the macabre who had no peer in the America of his time. . . . (pp. 87-8)

> *August Derleth, in his* H.P.L.: A Memoir *(copyright, 1945, by August Derleth; copyright renewed, 1973, by April Derleth and Walden Derleth; reprinted by permission of Arkham House Publishers, Inc., Sauk City, WI), Ben Abramson, 1945, 122 p.*

FRITZ LEIBER, JR. (essay date (1949)

Howard Phillips Lovecraft was the Copernicus of the horror story. He shifted the focus of supernatural dread from man and his little world and his gods, to the stars and the black and unplumbed gulfs of intergallactic space. To do this effectively, he created a new kind of horror story and new methods for telling it. (p. 290)

[The new universe of modern science is] a highly suitable object for man's supernatural fear. W. H. Hodgson, Poe, Fitz-James O'Brien, and Wells too had glimpses of that possibility and made use of it in a few of their tales. But the main and systematic achievement was Lovecraft's. When he completed the body of his writings, he had firmly attached the emotion of spectral dread to such concepts as outer space, the rim of the cosmos, alien beings, unsuspected dimensions, and the conceivable universes lying outside our own space-time continuum. (p. 291)

For a while Lovecraft tended to mix black magic and other traditional sources of dread with the horrors stemming purely from science's new universe. In *The Dunwich Horror* the other-dimensional creatures are thwarted by the proper incantations, while witchcraft and the new Einsteinian universe appear cheek-by-jowl in *The Dreams in the Witch-House.* But when we arrive at *The Whisperer in Darkness, At the Mountains of Madness,* and *The Shadow Out of Time,* we find that the extra-terrestrial entities are quite enough in themselves to awaken all our supernatural dread, without any medieval trappings whatsoever. White magic and the sign of the cross are powerless against them and only the accidents of space and time—in short, sheer chance—save humanity. (p. 292)

The universe of modern science engendered a profounder horror in Lovecraft's writings than that stemming solely from its tremendous distances and its highly probable alien and powerful non-human inhabitants. For the chief reason that man fears the universe revealed by materialistic science is that it is a purposeless, soulless place. To quote Lovecraft's *The Silver Key,* man can hardly bear the realization that "the blind cosmos grinds aimlessly on from nothing to something and from something back to nothing again, neither heeding nor knowing the wishes or existence of the minds that flicker for a second now and then in the darkness." (p. 293)

Lovecraft's matured method of telling a horror story was a natural consequence of the importance of the new universe of science in his writings, for it was the method of scientific realism, approaching in some of his last tales (*At the Mountains of Madness* and *The Shadow Out of Time*) the precision, objectivity, and attention to detail of a report in a scientific journal. Most of his stories are purported documents and necessarily written in the first person. This device is common in weird literature, as witness Poe's *Ms. Found in a Bottle*, Haggard's *She*, Stroker's *Dracula*, and many others, but few writers have taken it quite as seriously as did Lovecraft. (p. 296)

The scientifically realistic element in Lovecraft's style was a thing of slow growth in a writer early inclined to a sonorous and poetic prose with an almost Byzantine use of adjectives. The transition was never wholly completed, and like all advances, it was attended by losses and limitations. Disappointingly to some readers, who may also experience impatience at the growing length of the stories (inevitable in scientific reports), there is notably less witchery of words in, say, *The Shadow Out of Time* than in *The Dunwich Horror*, though the former story has greater unity and technical perfection. (pp. 296-97)

There were three important elements in Lovecraft's style which he was able to use effectively in both his earlier poetic period and later, more objective style.

The first is the device of *confirmation* rather than revelation. (I am indebted to Henry Kuttner for this neat phrase.) In other words, the story-ending does not come as a surprise but as a final, long-anticipated "convincer." The reader knows, and is supposed to know, what is coming, but this only prepares and adds to his shivers when the narrator supplies the last and incontrovertible piece of evidence. . . . This does not mean that Lovecraft never wrote the revelatory type of story, with its surprise ending. On the contrary, he used it in *The Lurking Fear* and handled it most effectively in *The Outsider*. But he did come more and more to favor the less startling but sometimes more impressive confirmatory type.

So closely related to his use of confirmation as to be only another aspect of it, is Lovecraft's employment of the terminal climax—that is, the story in which the high point and the final sentence coincide. . . . Use of the terminal climax made it necessary for Lovecraft to develop a special type of story-telling, in which the explanatory and return-to-equilibrium material is all deftly inserted before the finish and while the tension is still mounting. It also necessitated a very careful structure, with everything building from the first word to the last.

Lovecraft reinforced this structure with what may be called *orchestrated prose*—sentences that are repeated with a constant addition of more potent adjectives, adverbs, and phrases, just as in a symphony a melody introduced by a single woodwind is at last thundered by the whole orchestra. *The Statement of Randolph Carter* provides one of the simplest examples. In it, in order, the following phrases occur concerning the moon: ". . . waning crescent moon . . . wan, waning crescent moon . . . pallid, peering crescent moon . . . accursed waning moon. . . ." Subtler and more complex examples can be found in the longer stories. (pp. 297-98)

All these stylistic elements naturally worked to make Lovecraft's stories longer and longer, with a growing complexity in the sources of horror. In *The Dreams in the Witch-House* the sources of horror are multiple: ". . . Fever—wild dreams—somnambulism—illusions of sounds—a pull toward a point in the sky—and now a suspicion of insane sleepwalking. . . ." While in *At the Mountains of Madness* there is a transition whereby the feared entities become the

fearing; the author shows us horrors and then pulls back the curtain a little farther, letting us glimpse the horrors of which even the horrors are afraid! (p. 298)

[It] must be kept in mind that no matter how greatly Lovecraft increased the length, scope, complexity, and power of his tales, he never once lost control or gave way to the impulse to write wildly and pile one blood-curdling incident on another without the proper preparation and attention to mood. Rather, he tended to write with greater restraint, to perfect the internal coherence and logic of his stories, and often to provide alternate everyday explanations for the supernatural terrors he invoked, letting the reader infer the horror rather than see it face to face. . . . (p. 299)

> *Fritz Leiber, Jr., "A Literary Copernicus" (originally published in a different version in* The Acolyte, *Fall, 1944), in "Something about Cats" and Other Pieces, edited by August Derleth (copyright, 1949 by August Derleth; reprinted by permission of Arkham House Publishers, Inc.), Arkham House, 1949, pp. 290-303.*

EDMUND WILSON   (essay date 1950)

The principal feature of Lovecraft's work is an elaborate concocted myth which provides the supernatural element for his most admired stories. This myth assumes a race of outlandish gods and grotesque prehistoric peoples who are always playing tricks with time and space and breaking through into the contemporary world, usually somewhere in Massachusetts. One of these astonishing peoples, which flourished in the Triassic Age, a hundred and fifty million years ago, consisted of beings ten feet tall and shaped like giant cones. . . . They propagated, like mushrooms, by spores, which they developed in large shallow tanks. Their life span was four or five thousand years. Now, when the horror to the shuddering revelation of which a long and prolix story has been building up turns out to be something like this, you may laugh or you may be disgusted, but you are not likely to be terrified—though I confess, as a tribute to such power as H. P. Lovecraft possesses, that he at least, at this point in his series, in regard to the omniscient conical snails, induced me to suspend disbelief. It was the race from another planet which finally took their place, and which Lovecraft evidently relied on as creations of irresistible frightfulness, that I found myself unable to swallow: semi-invisible polypous monsters that uttered a shrill whistling sound and blasted their enemies with terrific winds. Such creatures would look very well on the covers of the pulp magazines, but they do not make good adult reading. And the truth is that these stories were hackwork contributed to such publications as *Weird Tales* and *Amazing Stories*, where, in my opinion, they ought to have been left.

The only real horror in most of these fictions is the horror of bad taste and bad art. Lovecraft was not a good writer. The fact that his verbose and undistinguished style has been compared to Poe's is only one of the many sad signs that almost nobody any more pays any real attention to writing. I have never yet found in Lovecraft a single sentence that Poe could have written, though there are some—not at all the same thing—that have evidently been influenced by Poe. . . . One of Lovecraft's worst faults is his incessant effort to work up the expectations of the reader by sprinkling his stories with such adjectives as "horrible," "terrible," "frightful," "awesome," "eerie," "weird," "forbidden," "unhallowed," "unholy," "blasphemous," "hellish" and "infernal." Surely one of the primary rules for writing an effective tale of horror is never to use any of these words—especially if you are going, at the end, to produce an invisible whistling octopus. (pp. 287-88)

[Lovecraft] wrote also a certain amount of poetry that echoes Edwin Arlington Robinson—like his fiction, quite second-rate; but his long essay on the literature of supernatural horror is a really able piece of work. He shows his lack of sound literary taste in his enthusiasm for Machen and Dunsany, whom he more or less acknowledged as models, but he had read comprehensively in this special field—he was strong on the Gothic novelists—and writes about it with much intelligence. (p. 289)

Lovecraft's stories do show at times some traces of his more serious emotions and interests. He has a scientific imagination rather similar, though much inferior, to that of the early Wells. The story called *The Color Out of Space* more or less predicts the effects of the atomic bomb, and *The Shadow Out of Time* deals not altogether ineffectively with the perspectives of geological aeons and the idea of controlling the time-sequence. The notion of escaping from time seems the motif most valid in his fiction, stimulated as it was by an impulse toward evasion which had pressed upon him all his life. . . . (p. 290)

> Edmund Wilson, "Tales of the Marvellous and the Ridiculous" (originally published in a different version in The New Yorker, Vol. XXI, No. 41, November 24, 1945), in his Classics and Commercials: A Literary Chronicle of the Forties (reprinted by permission of Farrar, Straus & Giroux, Inc.; copyright 1950 by Edmund Wilson; copyright renewed © 1978 by Elena Wilson), Farrar, Straus & Giroux, 1950, pp. 286-90.

PETER PENZOLDT (essay date 1952)

Lovecraft's greatest merit was also his greatest fault. He was too well read. In his critical study *The Supernatural Horror in Literature* he displays an encyclopædic knowledge of supernatural fiction, and since he read that enormous amount of weird fiction with obvious pleasure he has been subjected to a corresponding series of influences. In fact he was influenced by so many authors that one is often at a loss to decide what is really Lovecraft and what some half-conscious memory of the books he has read. (pp. 165-66)

If one reads carefully Lovecraft's critical study on supernatural horror in literature, one is struck by his frequent remarks, on how much more some authors could have made of themes they used. It seems possible that Lovecraft deliberately shaped some themes that were already known into the type of story that he considered fitted them best. . . .

The fact remains that when Lovecraft adopted a motif which his forerunners had already used, he frequently handled it far better. His 'Call of Cthulhu' and other stories on the ancient gods rank high above Machen's 'The Novel of the Black Seal', 'The Shining Pyramid' or 'The White People'. His 'Shadow out of Time', a novel about strange trips through time and space, and the forced exchange of human bodies with those of the mysterious pre-human 'Great Race' is at once reminiscent of Wells' 'The Time Machine' and of Machen's Tales. It also contains many Poesque

scenes. Yet, as a whole, the story is infinitely more poignant and convincing than either Wells' or Machen's works. The hero's final descent into the ruined capital of the 'Great Race', where he discovers his own manuscript written quadrillions of years ago, is one of the most perfect climaxes in the history of weird fiction.

It would be unjust to say that Lovecraft's inventive powers were limited to a better presentation of old themes. In 'The Call of Cthulhu' he created a whole mythology of his own which now and then appears in his other tales. (p. 167)

The way in which he was influenced by so many other writers makes it very difficult to decide which symbols found an echo in his own personality, which were used for subtly calculated effect, and which arose from a more or less distinct recollection of his reading.

As it is, the most dominant motif in Lovecraft's work is the nameless, ancestral horror lurking beneath the earth, or ready to invade us from the stars; the dethroned but still potent gods of old. The symbol is a very common one and is not bound to any particular complex. It therefore strikes and horrifies more readers than would any theme having a single subconscious origin. Probably C. G. Jung's theories on the collective subconscious give the only explanation of such symbols as 'great Cthulhu', 'the father Yog-Sothoth'. According to him they would symbolise very old hereditary fears. Edgar Dacqué, the famous German palæontologist and philosopher, whose theories are somewhat different from Dr. Jung's, would, strangely enough, point to a similar origin. While the latter believes in an exceedingly ancient but yet subconscious origin of certain collective fears and spiritual tendencies, Dacqué suggests an equally ancient but materially existent basis for these terrors in the distant past. Perhaps such tales as 'Pickman's Model' or 'The Call of Cthulhu' are, after all, more than the result of purely intellectual search for effect.

Even if there is a true symbolism in Lovecraft's tales it is his realistic descriptions of pure shameless horror that strike one as the dominant feature. If any writer was able to cram his tales with more loathsome physical abominations than Crawford and Machen it is Howard Phillips Lovecraft. He delights in detailed descriptions of rotting corpses in every imaginable state of decay, from initial corruption to what he has charmingly called a 'liquescent horror'. He has a particular predilection for fat, carnivorous, and, if possible, anthropophagus rats. His descriptions of hideous stenches and his onomatopœic reproductions of a madman's yowlings are something with which even 'Monk Lewis' did not disgrace fiction. (pp. 168-69)

Yet when the details are not too ridiculous one cannot but praise his precision. There are no traces of nineteenth-century reticence left in his work. Though he sometimes speaks of 'unnamable' horrors, he always does his best, and perhaps even too much, to describe them. Even if he sometimes overshoots the mark, one may say at least that no author combined so much stark realism of detail, and preternatural atmosphere, in one tale.

It is strange how Lovecraft uses material details even if he is describing purely supernatural entities. He is unable to evoke the glorious spectral and half-material shapes we find in [Algernon] Blackwood's tales. A presence felt, rather than perceived by the senses, is beyond his inventive powers. . . . Nor was he able to make use of Dr. [M. R.]

James' indirect method of describing an apparition, with metaphors chosen from reality, but devoid of words directly alluding to horror. He would never have begun a climax with 'It seems as if'. Lovecraft's monsters are usually ridiculous compounds of elephant feet and trunks, human faces, tentacles, gleaming eyes and bat wings, not to mention, of course, the indescribable fœtor that usually accompanies their presence. The reader is often amused rather than frightened by the author's extraordinary surgical talents. (pp. 170-71)

> *Peter Penzoldt, "The Pure Tale of Horror," in his* The Supernatural in Fiction *(copyright 1952 by Peter Penzoldt; reprinted by permission of The Hamlyn Publishing Group Limited), P. Nevill, 1952 (and reprinted by Humanities Press, 1965), pp. 146-90.***

JOSEPH PAYNE BRENNAN (essay date 1955)

[Lovecraft's stories of the Cthulhu Mythos] were not his best tales.

Many of the Cthulhu stories, such as "The Dunwich Horror" and "The Whisperer in Darkness", are actually tedious. They are too long; our interest is apt to flag; our "willing suspension of disbelief" may not hold to the final page. All too often we read on without compulsion, without belief, without very much actual enthusiasm.

Lovecraft often seems so intent on introducing and exploiting the "Mythos", he loses sight of some of the basic elements which are essential in a good short story: economy of wordage, verisimilitude, mounting suspense sweeping to a single climax followed quickly by a final denouement. (p. 2)

When it still possessed the freshness of novelty, the Cthulhu Mythology afforded a vast amount of entertainment. But with the passage of time the novelty has evaporated and the myth has become threadbare. Lovecraft used it in story after story and his disciples have exploited it since his death and it now seems wrung nearly dry of interesting effects.

It remains, of course, an integral part of the bulk of Lovecraft's work. To attempt to dismiss it as incidental or unimportant would be to close our eyes to the facts.

In my opinion however, Lovecraft's future reputation as a writer of fine horror stories will rest on a very few of his early tales in which the Cthulhu Mythos is either entirely absent or at most still in its formative stages in Lovecraft's own mind. (pp. 2-4)

These stories are: ["The Hound", "The Rats in the Walls", "The Music of Erich Zann", "The Outsider", and "Pickman's Model."] (p. 4)

Of these I think the best of all is "The Music of Erich Zann." This piece, which might have been written by Poe, has everything which many of the "Mythos" tales lack: compression, sustained and rising suspense culminating in a powerfully effective climax followed almost immediately by the end of the story. Stylistically and structurally, I think Lovecraft never surpassed it. . . . This story, like Poe's masterpiece, "The Cask of Amontillado", seems literally above criticism. There are no wasted words. The brief story unfolds with a remorseless inevitability. Nothing could be

omitted, nothing added, nothing changed which would improve its quality. In its particular genre it remains a pure masterpiece.

After "The Music of Erich Zann", I would cite "The Rats in the Walls." Actually, I very nearly voted it first place because it achieves a pitch of sheer grisly horror which exceeds the taut terror of "The Music of Erich Zann." On the other hand, it does not possess quite the same degree of purity and compression. But it is a masterpiece of its type, and again I can think of no Lovecraft story after "The Music of Erich Zann" which equals it. (pp. 4-5)

"The Rats in the Walls" begins in the somewhat leisurely manner which has come to be associated with rather old-fashioned gothic ghost stories, and for some little time nothing really hair-raising happens. But once the full horror comes to light, it simply overwhelms us. We see at once that the leisurely start was intended to lull us a little. Certainly it kept us interested enough to continue, and we did perhaps expect some pretty formidable horrors—but nothing like what we finally encounter! For sheer inhuman horror those twilit grottos under the evil foundations of Exham Priory have yet to be surpassed. (p. 5)

"The Outsider" is one of Lovecraft's finest stories. It possesses the merit of compression; with rising intensity it achieves its single shuddery effect—and ends. (pp. 5-6)

"Pickman's Model" is one of Lovecraft's strongest stories. It has unity of effect, suspense, a highly original plot idea, and a climax which neatly and forcefully ends the story. It is not quite as tightly knit as "The Music of Erich Zann" or "The Outsider", but it is still Lovecraft writing at his top-level best. . . .

I have mentioned Lovecraft's "The Hound" because it has remained in my mind after I first read it many years ago. Its structure is somewhat slight and it does not have the power of Lovecraft's very best tales, but it has splendid atmosphere and, again, brevity and unity of effect. It might have been written by the early Poe. (p. 6)

Lovecraft's final place in American literature has not yet been determined. . . . But it seems certain that the very best of his work will endure, that it will remain important in the particular field which he chose. If he did not reach the summits attained by Poe, or Bierce, at his best he scaled some dizzy heights. (pp. 7-8)

> *Joseph Payne Brennan, in his* H. P. Lovecraft: An Evaulation *(copyright © 1955 Joseph Payne Brennan), Macabre House, 1955, 8 p.*

COLIN WILSON (essay date 1962)

Lovecraft carried on a lifelong guerrilla warfare against civilization and materialism, albeit he was a somewhat hysterical and neurotic combatant. (p. 1)

What is so interesting about Lovecraft is the extraordinary consistency of his attempt to undermine materialism. His aim was "to make the flesh creep": more than that, to implant doubts and horrors in the minds of his readers. If he had been told that one of his readers had died of horror, or been driven to an insane asylum, there can be no doubt that he would have been delighted. . . . In a tale called "The Unnameable," the writer claims that one of his horror stories, published in 1922, had caused a magazine to be withdrawn from the bookstalls because it frightened the "milk-sops." Whether this is true or not, there can be no doubt that Lovecraft wished it to be true. . . . [He] wanted to horrify the world. . . . To increase the illusion, he never set his stories in the remote past; in fact, he took care to date them close to the time they were written. (p. 3)

Lovecraft's early tales follow the usual pattern of ghost stories: man enters haunted house, leaves with his hair white. But he is very far from being satisfied with ordinary ghosts of the Shakespeare type. . . . The horrors have to be tangible. And in some of the stories, the effect is one of absurdity and bathos. A typical example is a tale called "The Lurking Fear," leaning heavily on the style of Poe and Mrs. Radcliffe. . . . The story takes place in modern times, in a remote place in the Catskill Mountains, where Washington Irving set some of his weird tales. This is typical of Lovecraft; he is willing to make his setting modern, but it must be remote from civilization, a kind of admission of defeat. A week before the story opens, a whole village has been destroyed by strange forces that are conjured up by a storm. There follows a characteristic episode; the narrator goes into a wooden hut to shelter from a storm, taking with him a newspaper reporter. The reporter looks out of the window, and stands there throughout the storm. When the narrator touches him on the shoulder he is found to be dead, his head "chewed and gouged" by some monster.

Anyone who has seen a modern horror film will recognize the technique; there have to be a number of innocent "fall guys" whose role is to be killed by the "horror." At the end of this story, the horror is revealed to be a horde of gorilla-like demons (of semi-human origin) who live underneath the "deserted mansion."

If it were not so atrociously written, this story would be funny. Lovecraft hurls in the adjectives ("monstrous," "slithering," "ghoulish," "thunder-crazed") until he seems to be a kind of literary dervish who gibbers with hysteria as he spins.

But he must have realized that this kind of thing would terrify no one but a schoolboy, and soon he set out to build a complicated and erudite myth that would convince by its circumstantial detail and plausibility. Recognizing that modern city dwellers are not likely to be impressed by ghosts and other such arbitrary exceptions to the laws of nature, he relies on the sense of disgust, and on a pseudo-historic or scientific framework. An early story, "The Picture in the House" . . . , is a nearly convincing sketch of sadism. An old man who lives alone is so fascinated by a book about cannibals that he becomes a cannibal himself. The scene in which the old man drools over the picture of the cannibal butchers' shop, losing his caution as he gets carried away while speaking to the narrator, is an accurate piece of psychological observation, recalling the sketch of a different kind of pervert in Joyce's story "An Encounter." But Lovecraft's clumsiness comes out in the catastrophic end of the story—the house is struck by a thunderbolt as the narrator notices blood dripping through the ceiling. (pp. 4-5)

[It] must be admitted that Lovecraft is a very bad writer. When he is at his best, his style might be mistaken for Poe's. (A tale called "The Outsider," about a monstrous-looking man who does not realize that he is monstrous until he finally sees himself in a mirror, owes something to "Wil-

liam Wilson" and perhaps to Wilde's *Birthday of the Infanta;* it might easily pass for an unknown work by Poe.) But he makes few concessions to credibility, in spite of his desire to be convincing. His stories are full of horror-film conventions, the most irritating of which is the trustful stupidity of the hero, who ignores signs and portents until he is face to face with the actual horror. (pp. 7-8)

But although Lovecraft is such a bad writer, he has something of the same kind of importance as Kafka. If his work fails as literature, it still holds an interest as a psychological case history. Here was a man who made no attempt whatever to come to terms with life. He hated modern civilization, particularly its confident belief in progress and science. Greater artists have had the same feeling, from Dostoevsky to Kafka and Eliot. . . . Only Kafka's approach was as naïve as Lovecraft's. He also relied simply on presenting a picture of the world's mystery and the uncertainty of the life of man. (p. 8)

All the same, Lovecraft is not an isolated crank. He is working in a recognizable romantic tradition. If he is not a major writer, he is psychologically one of the most interesting men of his generation. (p. 10)

> *Colin Wilson, "The Assault on Rationality: H. P. Lovecraft," in his* The Strength to Dream: Literature and the Imagination *(copyright © 1962 by Colin Wilson; reprinted by permission of Houghton Mifflin Company; in Canada by Bolt & Watson, as agents for the author), Houghton, 1962, pp. 1-10.*

E. F. BLEILER (essay date 1973)

Supernatural Horror in Literature is a magnificent achievement from many points of view. Structurally it is an accomplished tour de force, since it transmuted what might have been a catalogue with opinions into an organic unity. It reveals a mind of power and subtlety, a fine critical sense, and a feeling for development and cultural milieu that any historian might envy. Very few of Lovecraft's judgments have been overturned, even in mainstream criticism, and Lovecraft's acumen has been praised by critics as diverse as Vincent Starrett and Edmund Wilson.

One ability Lovecraft demonstrates to a supreme degree in *Supernatural Horror in literature.* No other writer has ever been able to summarize a supernatural story in a more enticing manner, penetrating to the heart of the work and restating it accurately, yet with an appeal that may at times exceed that of the original work. In his letters Lovecraft comments on a related facet of his mind: his memory keeps reworking the books he has read, and he is forced to retrace his steps to avoid distorting ideas. Yet he was successful in avoiding such contamination. Many passages in his essay, too, refute the charge that Lovecraft always wrote in a leaden and pompous style. The reader who has covered the same literature can marvel that Lovecraft could always find something fresh to say about what might seem an exhausted subject. (pp. iv-v)

> *E. F. Bleiler, in his introduction to* Supernatural Horror in Literature *by Howard Phillips Lovecraft (copyright © 1973 by Dover Publications, Inc.), Dover, 1973, pp. iii-viii.*

DIRK MOSIG (essay date 1976)

H. P. Lovecraft was a "mechanistic materialist," in the philosophical sense of the words, totally devoid of any dualistic belief in religion or the supernatural. (p. 48)

Lovecraft's fiction, and in particular his pseudomythology (which I prefer to call the Yog-Sothoth Cycle of Myth, to differentiate it from the distorted version labelled "Cthulhu Mythos" by Derleth [see excerpt above]) was *not* a reaction *against* his austere and parsimonious materialistic philosophy, but instead formed the natural outgrowth of the same. (p. 49)

The Yog-Sothoth Cycle of Myth centers around a certain group of alien entities from the "Outside"—from beyond the sphere of conscious human experience.... These Old Ones *were, are,* and *will be.* They are *not* mere symbols of the power of evil, although they may appear to be inimical to man, in the same way the man would appear to be inimical to ants, should these get in his way. The Old Ones are above and beyond mankind—they transcend man, and care no more for him than he does ants. (pp. 50-1)

And what could be more terrifying for man than the realization of his own impotent insignificance face to face with the Unknown and the Unknowable?

From the above sketch it should be readily obvious that there is *no* real parallel between the Christian Mythos and Lovecraft's pseudo-mythology, despite Derleth's assertions to the contrary. The "Elder Gods" does appear in HPL's *The Dream-Quest of Unknown Kadath* and in "The Strange High House in the Mist," but only to denote the "weak gods of the earth." It also occurs in *At the Mountains of Madness,* but only as a label for one of the extra-terrestrial species which inhabited the earth eons before man. Nowhere did Lovecraft use the expression to refer to any powerful benign deities which might intercede for man—in Lovecraft's indifferent universe, man cannot expect outside help in his confrontations with the Unknown. (p. 51)

[Lovecraft's *oeuvre*] is a work of genius, a cosmic-minded *oeuvre* embodying a mechanistic materialist's brilliant conception of the imaginary realms and frightful reality "beyond the fields we know," a literary rhapsody of the cosmos and man's laughable position therein.... The Lovecraft *oeuvre* can be regarded as a significant contribution to world literature.... (p. 55)

> *Dirk Mosig, "Myth-Maker," in* Whispers *(copyright © 1976 by Stuart David Schiff), Vol. 3, No. 1, December, 1976, pp. 48-55.*

PHILIP A. SHREFFLER (essay date 1977)

Lovecraft's tales root themselves in a mythos of unseen and undimensioned monsters that existed before the advent of man on earth, or else involve fantasy lands that are at once strange and familiar.... Prehistory, Lovecraft's theory might state, equals the unknown, and the unknown yields fear.

In this way the scope of Lovecraft's horror stories becomes cosmic in nature; vast sweeps of space and time are the rule rather than the exception. And this is what gives Lovecraft such a peculiarly American character. From the days when English Anglicans hacked Jamestown out of the Virginia swamps and the Puritan Separatists braved the hostile environment of eastern Massachusetts on through to the present time, American writers have responded one way or another to the sheer immensity of their national landscape. (p. 4)

American artists from the Puritans, the Romantics, the naturalists, and through to the present century have dealt chiefly with the most massive and perplexing problems of philosophy: the nature of being, the validity of knowledge, questions of universal morality and aesthetics.

Lovecraft, too, addressed himself to some of these same issues. Ontology and epistemology both play a role in stories like "Celephais" and "Through the Gates of the Silver Key"; moral allegory is the primary function of "The Street" and "The White Ship"; and the aesthetic question becomes the focal point of "The Unnamable" and "The Hound."

But confronting these philosophical questions in the way that a Hawthorne or a Melville would was not Lovecraft's main intent. If he could touch on them along the way, that was clear profit. The major impetus behind Lovecraft's fiction, however, was purely to frighten, to excite and elevate the sensibilities of the reader in such a way that he could experience not merely shock but horror on a cosmic level. (pp. 4-5)

At the same time, it is untrue to say that Lovecraft's fiction is informed wholly by American literature. Indeed, in his long essay survey of horrific fiction, "Supernatural Horror in Literature," Lovecraft cites as many British works as American ones as having a central influence on the genre of the weird tale. And there can be no mistake, as students of Lovecraft's work discover, about its being touched with the technical characteristics of the British horror story. (p. 5)

In terms of his literary intentions, then, Lovecraft was taking the best from both sides of the Atlantic—the cosmicism of America, the cosmic inclinations of some British writers, the literary philosophy of Poe, and to some degree the heavy atmosphere of Victorian and Edwardian horror stories. (p. 10)

In [one] respect, Lovecraft is strikingly modern. The sense of being alone and afraid in a world one never made is common among many writers of the twentieth century. (p. 21)

[Lovecraft had] witnessed, as had so many others, the horrors of the Great War—a war so terrible that it was thought by some to be man's final war. The world of 1900 through 1920 was a world that seemed to be falling apart, a chaos that pointed the way toward Armageddon. In "Arthur Jermyn," a story of a human being who had not quite "let go the hot gorilla's paw" ..., Lovecraft was simply responding sensitively and cynically to the world that he saw. (p. 22)

The question may arise as to whether or not Lovecraft's strange half-breeds, the offspring of horrible liaisons between men and monsters, can be seen as a return to the nineteenth-century tension between dark and light principles existing simultaneously in a human being.... [But in] these characters, though mixtures of men and monsters, it is the evil of the monster and the evil of the human parent that survive. In those cases in which Lovecraft surrounds a decent and pure main character (many of his first-person narrators are modeled upon himself) with wicked ones, it is the sheer enormity of the world's evil pitted against the pitiful insignificance of the hero's good that drives the hero into madness or actually into removing himself from the world by violence. There is a clearly perceivable paranoia in this version of reality.

Finally, and this is perhaps the most insidious dimension of Lovecraft's work, we come to understand that if we are looking for a moral, we might just as well forget it. There is none. This was a view taken by the post-Civil War naturalists who wrote in the generation preceding Lovecraft's. Represented by literary artists such as Stephen Crane, Jack London, Frank Norris, and Ambrose Bierce, the naturalists saw the universe as a blind, dead, uncaring beast that occasionally blundered against men and, without any particular malice, exterminated them. This kind of thing happens often in Lovecraft, particularly in the earlier stories like "The Other Gods," in which it is the encounter with monsters, which are only innocently going about their business of being monsters, that destroys men.

In the later stories, however, the monsters do take on malevolent characterisitcs and become creatures whose design it is to wipe out mankind and inherit the earth. This notion is pure survival-of-the-fittest philosophy (which is to say in this case survival of the most powerful). . . . (pp. 22-3)

Lovecraft's weakest moments tend to be those in which he describes a monster visually; and his strongest ones, those in which he only hints dimly at what may be lurking nearby. Like the rampant imaginations of Hawthorne's guilt-ridden characters, the imaginations of Lovecraft's readers fill in what Lovecraft has deliberately left out, but they fill in vaguely, so that they themselves may not be quite aware of what is causing their uneasiness.

Unlike Hawthorne, however, Lovecraft was little interested in dealing with life on a moral level. . . . Usually, in Lovecraft's mature work, the main characters find themselves caught in a universe of cosmic conspiracy, in a world that is impossibly evil and bent only on the destruction of men. In this way Lovecraft's fiction becomes strangely nihilistic, akin to that of Bierce. (pp. 27-8)

Lovecraft has been much criticized for his apparent disinterest in strong, flashy elements of plot. Indeed, plot is sometimes so de-emphasized that one may read forty pages or so of one of the longer stories in the course of which nothing much happens. But Lovecraft well understood what he was about. These long passages often amount to virtually Henry James-like descriptions of the main character's psychological state or are given to physicial depictions of setting. And it is this, rather than plot, that contributes to the total effect in Lovecraft's fiction. By focusing analytically on a man whose psychological state is deteriorating, Lovecraft is echoing Poe's treatment of the mind of Roderick Usher, and this technique casts an eerie and ghastly shadow over the entire work. (pp. 29-30)

[Every] bit as important as . . . the psychological examination of characters is Lovecraft's rhetorical style. It was, perhaps, through his attempts to imitate the heavily ornate style of Poe, as well as his exposure to British literature, that Lovecraft found himself given to immensely complex sentence structure and an archaic vocabulary. It has been said that readers are simply unable to deal with this, a charge also leveled at Henry James. Actually, Lovecraft almost certainly had less control over his diction than either Poe or James did, and his adjectival explosions and archai-

cisms often make his fiction sound a bit silly by comparison. What must be kept in mind here is not the frequent awkwardness and heavy-handedness of a given passage or set of passages but, rather, the cumulative *effect* of Lovecraft's stories—their weirdness, which is precisely what he wanted them to be invested with.

Perhaps this quality simply defies analysis; perhaps we should not analyze it. It should, however, be sufficient to say that it is exactly Lovecraft's rhetorical excesses that make his style consistent with his characters who feel madness growing on them against the backdrop of macabre, otherworldly settings. And this is the reason that strangely, and often against our will, we begin to feel that Lovecraft is not writing fiction, but a hideous version of truth. (p. 31)

Lovecraft's most important contribution to the overall framework of American literature was not altogether derivative. In the early twentieth century, a time when the older modes of literary thought were crumbling and when a writer like Hemingway could successfully machine-gun his readers with staccato diction and syntax, Lovecraft stood firmly in the midst of a syntax that was meant to be woven magically around the reader. And although the fantastic strain in American literature will probably always exist in one form or another, the Romance form in America as it was understood and practiced by both Hawthorne and Poe all but vanished with Lovecraft's death. Lovecraft was the last American writer to guide us, in the nineteenth-century tradition, on a fearful torchlight tour of witch-haunted New England. (pp. 31-2)

Philip A. Shreffler, "Lovecraft's Literary Theory," in his The H. P. Lovecraft Companion *(copyright © 1977 by Philip A. Shreffler; reprinted by permission of Greenwood Press, a Division of Congressional Information Service, Inc., Westport, CT.), Greenwood Press, 1977, pp. 3-38.*

GLEN ST JOHN BARCLAY (essay date 1978)

Lovecraft's concern is entirely with manufactured horrors. An effective writer of science-fiction must have some acquaintance with basic scientific principles if he is not to spoil his best effects with technical absurdities; a maker of myths must have some sympathy for genuine human hopes and fears if his myths are to evoke any emotional response from his readers. Lovecraft was as deficient in technical expertise of any kind as he was in the understanding of the human predicament.

Three main themes emerge from his writings. There is first of all the theme of miscegenation—presumably reflecting Lovecraft's loathing for all manner of men except the Anglo-Saxon protestants of whom he was himself hardly a successful exemplar—in which typically New England seaports are overrun by the products of mismatings between Yankee sailormen and assorted beasts of the sea and water, including, oddly enough, frogs. Lovecraft may not have been sufficiently interested in reproductive processes to have been aware of the fact that there was just no way in which even the most desperate Yankee sailorman could have impregnated a fish, or vice versa. More likely, he simply did not care about such technicalities. Secondly, there is the theme of the ghoul, which again is singularly lacking in any kind of message for the human race: nobody is really interested in whether or not supernatural, bat-winged hounds dine off the bodies of the dead in cemeteries at night. They don't, of course, but it would really make very little difference to anybody if they did. Finally, there is what has come to be extravagantly known as the 'Cthulhu Mythos'.

There are several angles to the Cthulhu concept. There is a mad Arab, Abdul Azred, the author of a terrifying work called the *Necronomicon*, all about 'nameless aeons and inconceivable dimensions to worlds of elder outer entity'. . . . The subject of this poetical effort is indeed Cthulhu himself, gelatinous, enormous, equipped with claws, bats' wings and tentacles growing out of his head, who sleeps under the Pacific in his house in the cyclopean city of R'lyeh. From time to time he is incautiously awakened, and then there is indeed hell to pay. Cthulhu originally came from the stars, along with his relations Yuggoth, Tsathoggua, Yog-Sothoth *et al*, or alternatively they might have come from Pluto, in the name of which Lovecraft sees the most gratifying implications. Since Lovecraft's idea seems to be that these and other Great Old Ones actually flew with wings, like bats, from wherever they came from to here, the actual point of origin hardly matters: as one cannot fly with wings in space, they would never have made the trip anyway. (pp. 84-6)

The definitive stories of the Cthulhu Mythos are [*The Call of Cthulhu, At The Mountains of Madness* and *The Haunter of the Dark*]. . . . Together, it might be said, they tell one more about Cthulhu than most people would want to know. Cthulhu himself is introduced in *The Call of Cthulhu*, which is in fact a succinct and well-constructed story, told with far more restraint than Lovecraft normally exercised. (p. 86)

There is no denying that Lovecraft has considerable narrative skill when he exercises any kind of self-restraint, as he does only in the shorter stories like *The Call of Cthulhu*; a considerable vocabulary, weighted on the polysyllabic side; and considerable though severely limited imaginative vision. His faults encompass every imaginable literary sin. His admirers interestingly tend to regard these failings as almost a positive virtue: for example his biographer and fellow aficionado of the occult, Sprague de Camp asserts that 'the essential quality of a good storyteller is neither accurate observation, nor warm human sympathy, nor technical polish, nor ingenuity in plotting, helpful as all these may be. It is a certain vividness of imagination, enabling the writer to grip the reader's attention and sustain it to the end. This Lovecraft had.' Indeed, de Camp suggests that Lovecraft 'stands on a level with Poe or even a shade above. . . . He exerted wide influence among writers in his genre. He turned out spine-chilling tales that provide first-rate entertainment; and that, after all, is the prime test of any popular fiction.' This is an arguable point of view, but it is hardly adequate support for ranking Lovecraft above Poe in any hierarchy of literary merit. There is no doubt that the comparison can hardly be avoided, because Lovecraft himself was obsessed with the thought of Poe as inspirator and exemplar. (pp. 89-90)

The thought that Lovecraft could have regarded himself as [Poe's] spiritual and literary heir would have been enough to make Poe turn in his grave. . . . Lovecraft's only real contribution to literature might indeed be to serve as a contrast to Poe, illustrating the difference between discipline and indiscipline, between genius and obsession, between genuine myth-making and contrived exercises in unconvincing horror. (p. 91)

One would hesitate to rank Lovecraft even among the second-rate. At the same time, however, there is such a thing as the Lovecraft achievement, which it is perfectly simple to define. He succeeded in influencing a number of other authors, one or two of whom write far better than he could. It is an achievement which is essentially inartistic, in the sense that the man is vastly more significant than his work. Bram Stoker is almost invisible behind the towering figure of Dracula. . . . With Lovecraft, the reverse is the case. There is no Cthulhu Mythos. There is only a Lovecraft Mythos. . . . (pp. 95-6)

Glen St John Barclay, "The Myth That Never Was: Howard P. Lovecraft," in his Anatomy of Horror: The Masters of Occult Fiction *(copyright © 1978 by Glen St J. Barclay; reprinted by permission of St. Martin's Press, Inc.; in Canada by George Weidenfeld & Nicholson Ltd.),* Weidenfeld & Nicholson, 1978, St. Martin's Press, 1979, pp. 81-96.*

DARRELL SCHWEITZER   (essay date 1978)

At his best, HP [Lovecraft] was a superior literary technician. Certainly he never possessed the subtle insight of Walter de la Mare or Henry James, but he also lacked the sometimes painful stylistic awkwardness of the latter. At his worst, he was one of the more dreadful writers of this century who is still remembered. . . . Lovecraft never equalled Dunsany in eloquence or deft invention, and he never won any awards or made much money from his work. But his stories had an intensity the Irish master never approached, and HPL is still being read, while his contemporaries at *Weird Tales* have largely been forgotten.

Fritz Leiber perhaps summed it up best when he called HPL "a literary Copernicus" [see excerpt above]. In his fiction Lovecraft is aware of the whole cosmos and man's place in it, while virtually all mainstream writing and early fantasy could just as well be set in a pre-Copernican universe, Lovecraft's uncontrollable horrors from other dimensions or distant space can only be confronted with stoic fatalism, an apt metaphor for the 20th Century condition. This is the source of Lovecraft's power: he writes with conviction about things which on a subconscious level are more believable than ghosts and goblins. Modern man is a materialist, even if he outwardly professes religion. Few people seriously expect the supernatural to intervene in their lives. But the Night Fears are still with us, and until mankind's outlook profoundly changes, Lovecraft's fiction will mean something. He was uniquely able to link the inner substance of former spiritual beliefs with the most recent scientific discoveries. He used a rational, mechanistic context to get his readers to the edge of the abyss—and then dropped them over. The result was an irrational horror grimmer than anything a Puritan could conjure up. His bleak pessimism doesn't comfort, but it does convince. Despite his eighteenth century affectations, Lovecraft was a *modern* writer, well ahead of his era, and perhaps even ours. In his constant emphasis on the tyranny of time and change, he perceived what we now call "future shock." His viewpoint borders on contemporary philosophical despair, existential or otherwise, with one difference: HPL insisted that only by clinging to tradition could we make life worth living amidst the chaos of modern civilization.

From a purely literary viewpoint, Lovecraft is important for revitalizing the horror story, which prior to his time seemed completely worked out. He provided a wealth of new material. And when he died in the spring of 1937, there was no one to take his place. There have been a lot of superficial imitations, mostly in the vein of [August] Derleth's Cthulhu Mythos, but none of these works (or their authors) have amounted to much. Lovecraft was also a positive influence on the young science fiction genre. Just when it needed a kick in the direction of greater realism and a higher level of craftmanship. He refused to churn out copies of the pallid formula fiction of his day. Virtually every major science fiction writer of the next generation was aware of him, and acknowledges his influence. HPL demanded that the fantastic tale be treated as art, not just a frivolous parlor game or an easy way to make a buck. The most constructive sentiments uttered by the "New Wave" writers of the 1960s were first aired by Lovecraft forty years before. The tragedy of the man, as far as the rest of the field is concerned, is that he didn't live long enough, and lacked the ambition when he was still alive, to push these ideals further. (pp. 60-1)

> *Darrell Schweitzer, in his* The Dream Quest of H. P. Lovecraft *(copyright © 1978 by Darrell Schweitzer), The Borgo Press, 1978, 63 p.*

ADDITIONAL BIBLIOGRAPHY

Bailey, J. O. "Beyond the Mountains of the Moon." In his *Pilgrims through Space and Time: Trends and Patterns in Scientific and Utopian Fiction,* pp. 119-87. New York: Argus Books, 1947.*
  Primarily plot outlines of *At the Mountains of Madness* and "The Shadow out of Time." The critic calls Lovecraft "one of the most sensitive and powerful writers of our generation in the field of the quasi-scientific tale of terror."

Buhle, Paul. "Dystopia As Utopia: Howard Phillips Lovecraft and the Unknown Content of American Horror Literature." *The Minnesota Review,* No. 6 (Spring 1976): 118-31.
  Views Lovecraft as a dissenting voice to the idea of social and political progress in America.

Carter, Lin. *Lovecraft: A Look behind the "Cthulhu Mythos."* New York: Ballantine Books, 1972, 198 p.
  Offers a thorough background on the nature and evolution of the "Mythos" stories, with largely descriptive rather than interpretive commentary.

Conover, Willis, Jr. *Lovecraft at Last.* Arlington, VA: Carrollton-Clark, 1975, 272 p.
  Personal chronicle of Conover's correspondence with Lovecraft during the last months of the author's life. This work vividly conveys the character of its subject and contains several facsimile reproductions of Lovecraft's letters.

de Camp, L. Sprague. *Lovecraft: A Biography.* Garden City, NY: Doubleday & Co., 1975, 510 p.
  Controversial biography that is informative and opinionated, designed to offer little extended criticism on the work though much on the personal life of its subject.

Derleth, August. Introduction to *The Horror in the Museum and Other Revisions,* by H. P. Lovecraft, pp. vii-ix. Sauk City, WI: Arkham House, 1970.
  Gives background to Lovecraft's revision work.

Fresco: Howard Phillips Lovecraft Memorial Symposium 8, No. 3 (Spring 1958): 68 p.
  Reminiscences, essays, and a bibliography by writers from the Lovecraft circle and others, including Samuel Loveman, Thomas Olive Mabbott, David Keller, and Joseph Payne Brennan.

Joshi, S. T., ed. *H. P. Lovecraft: Four Decades of Criticism.* Athens, OH: Ohio University Press, 1980, 250 p.
  Collection of seminal essays on Lovecraft, including studies by Barton Levi St. Armand, J. Vernon Shea, and Dirk W. Mosig, with a survey of Lovecraft criticism by the editor.

Mosig, Dirk W. "The Four Faces of 'The Outsider'." *Nyctalops* II, No. 2 (July 1974): 3-10.
  Analyzes "The Outsider" in turn as fictional autobiography, as a Jungian allegory of the psyche, as a refutation of spiritual afterlife, and as a declaration of philosophical materialism.

Mosig, Dirk W. "Towards a Greater Appreciation of H. P. Lovecraft." In *First World Fantasy Awards: An Anthology of the Fantastic: Stories, Poems, Essays,* edited by Gahan Wilson, pp. 290-301. New York: Doubleday & Co., 1977.
  Jungian reading of some of Lovecraft's stories.

Schweitzer, Darrell, ed. *Essays Lovecraftian.* Baltimore: T-K Graphics, 1976, 114 p.
  Collection of essays, including excellent pieces by Arthur Jean Cox and Dirk Mosig.

St. Armand, Barton Levi. *The Roots of Horror in the Fiction of H. P. Lovecraft.* Elizabethtown, N.Y.: Dragon Press, 1977, 101 p.
  Elaborate philosophical and psychological reading of "The Rats in the Walls," drawing in part upon Jungian symbolism in the course of explication.

Wetzel, George. "Genesis of the Cthulhu Mythos." *Nyctalops* II, No. 3 (January/February 1975): 21-5.
  Sees Greek mythology as an important influence on Lovecraft's structuring of his fictional myth-cycle.

Arthur (Llewellyn Jones) Machen

1863-1947

(Born Arthur Llewellyn Jones; also wrote under pseudonym of Leolinus Siluriensis) Welsh short story writer, novelist, essayist, translator, and journalist.

Machen is best known for his tales of bizarre occurrences and supernatural horror. In his stories he explores the ways in which occult forces reveal the opposing elements of good and evil within human nature. A complex writer, Machen approaches his material from the dual perspectives of humanist and mystic.

The only child of a clergyman, Machen spent a lonely childhood exploring the somber grandeur of the countryside in Gwent. His youthful fascination with the beauty of the countryside is reflected in his critically admired descriptions of natural phenomena. Similarly, his strong religious background influenced his fictional quest for a spiritual energy which could exert a regenerative power over human life. This pursuit is often symbolized in his work by the quest for the Grail.

Machen's success as a writer was limited and never provided him with a livelihood. Instead, he supported himself as a translator, journalist, tutor, and actor. Ironically, he achieved his greatest literary success with *The Bowmen*, a relatively trivial piece of fiction concerned with divine aid received by English soldiers at the battle of Mons, during World War I. The story was widely believed to be true, and Machen was compelled to publish a disclaimer stressing that he had invented it.

Critics consider Machen's best work to be *The Hill of Dreams*. A psychologically powerful novel of alienation and escapism, it was the first of his "long picaresque novels of the soul." *Things Near and Far*, the second volume of his autobiographical novels, is perhaps the best example of his imaginative writing, and is considered by some to be a masterpiece of humanism. In his essay *Hieroglyphics* Machen formulated a theory of fiction which held that all true works of art are distinguished by their quality of ecstasy, a higher form of knowledge that removed the reader from the realm of common life. Critics acknowledge that Machen successfully infused his work with just this sense of wonder and mystery.

Although Machen achieved little success in his own day and eventually abandoned writing, he was influential with other writers of the horror and fantasy genres, notably H. P. Lovecraft, Ray Bradbury, and Daphne du Maurier. Though Machen remains a minor author, he has become something of a cult figure among followers of the occult and supernatural horror.

PRINCIPAL WORKS

The Anatomy of Tobacco [as Leolinus Siluriensis] (burlesque) 1884
The Chronicle of Clemendy (novel) 1888
The Great God Pan and the Inmost Light (short stories) 1894

The Three Impostors (short stories) 1895
Hieroglyphics (essay) 1902
The House of Souls (short stories) 1906
The Hill of Dreams (autobiographical novel) 1907
The Angels of Mons: The Bowmen and other Legends of the War (short stories) 1915
The Great Return (novella) 1915
The Terror (novel) 1917
Far Off Things (autobiography) 1922
The Secret Glory (novel) 1922
Things Near and Far (autobiography) 1923
Precious Balms (criticism) 1924
The Children of the Pool and Other Stories (short stories) 1936

ATHENAEUM (essay date 1896)

Mr. Machen is hardly ever diverted from his unwearied quest of the uncanny, the gruesome, and—in the classical sense—the obscene. 'The Three Impostors,' produces on the normal waking mind much the same effect as a hearty supper of pork chops on the dream fancies of a person of delicate digestion. . . . It is Mr. Machen's chief joy, in the words of one of his characters, to dabble "with the melting ruins of the earthly tabernacle"; to hint, rather than describe, the unholy joys and infamous orgies of those whose diet is framed in accordance with the recipes of the devil's cookery book, and whose esoteric acquaintance with the black art enables them to practise short cuts to the sundering of body and spirit. The result is never agreeable, occasionally disgusting, but seldom really bloodcurdling, since in the last resort Mr. Machen generally takes refuge in a copious use of such words as "unutterable," "hideous," "loathsome," "appalling," and so on. Still these chapters present undeniable evidence of a sombre imagination, considerable descriptive power, and a keen sense of the mystery and picturesqueness of London.

> *"New Novels: 'The Three Impostors,'"* in Athenaeum *No. 3562, February 1, 1896, p. 146.*

ATHENAEUM (essay date 1907)

In 'The Hill of Dreams,' which is, we are told, the author's first long novel, Mr. Machen exhibits much the same qualities as those which distinguish his shorter and earlier essays in fiction. Here we find, but in a higher degree, the same exquisite feeling for words and colours, the same fine, if somewhat laboured artistry of style, together with a more complete mastery of what, for want of a better phrase, may be called the art of atmosphere. The last is perhaps the most striking, as it is certainly the most admirable, feature of the book. In the emotional adventures of the hapless youth who is a victim of a species of nympholepsy and intellectual loneliness combined, we cannot, after the first hundred pages, feel any adequate interest. His agonies while engaged in the long-drawn-out struggle with his stubborn literary gifts are too protracted, too remote from any human sentiment, to hold the interest of the reader. . . . But the spirit of place which informs the book, whether it is the forlorn, illimitable dreariness of suburbia that the author chooses to show us, or the mysterious and melancholy beauty of that wild Wales he knows so well, could only have found expression at the hand of an adept. It is perhaps a pity that so clever a writer as Mr. Machen should bestow such infinite pains on astonishing the bourgeois, who in all likelihood will never have the privilege of reading his books. . . . [But] the main matter for regret is the utter formlessness and the arid inhumanity of his work. His Muse is a kind of Lilith—not a drop of her blood is human —and thus, except from the decorative point of view, he leaves us cold.

> *"New Novels: 'The Hill of Dreams,'"* in Athenaeum *No. 4142, March 16, 1907, p. 317.*

DOROTHY SCARBOROUGH (essay date 1917)

Arthur Machen deals with strange, sinister aspects of supernaturalism unlike the wholesome folklore that other writers reveal to us. He seems to take his material chiefly from the Pit, to let loose upon the world a slimy horde of unnamable spirits of ageless evil. One reads of the White People, who are most loathsome fairies under whose influence the rocks dance obscene dances in the Witches' Sabbath, and the great white moon seems an unclean thing. Images of clay made by human hands come to diabolic life, and at mystic incantations the nymph Alanna turns the pool

in the woodland to a pool of fire. In *The Great God Pan* the timeless menace comes to earth again, corrupting the souls of men and women, rendering them unbelievably vile. . . . One feels one should rinse his mind out after reading Arthur Machen's stories, particularly the collection called *The Three Impostors.* (p. 247)

> *Dorothy Scarborough, "The Supernatural in Folk-Tales," in her* The Supernatural in Modern English Fiction *(copyright 1917 by G. P. Putnam's Sons), G. P. Putnam's Sons, 1917 (and reprinted by Octagon Books, Inc., 1967, pp. 224-50).**

J. W. KRUTCH (essay date 1922)

[Mr. Machen's] own concern is exclusively with transcendental Sin and transcendental Virtue—not with particular sins or particular virtues which, as James realized, have a way of turning out to be disappointingly petty, but with Good and Evil themselves, considered as the only mystic realities. Not even the Unforgivable Sin of Hawthorne's lime-burner would satisfy Machen, I suspect, for that sin was pretty definitely an anti-social sin, and Machen has a mystic's contempt for any attempt to interpret evil in human or humanitarian terms; what he seeks is something like that dark blasphemy which for the medieval mind was embodied in the Black Mass. (p. 258)

The horror which he would present is the horror of that unseen world which, for the mystic, surrounds the little spot of seeming light and seeming reality in which we dwell; it is the dissolving of the solid wall of actuality and the direct presence of the ultimate mystery; something so profoundly unnatural that, as one of the characters says, its evil affects one as a mathematician would be affected if he were brought suddenly face to face with a two-sided triangle—there is nothing left do do but to go mad. All his villains are Fausts, taking supernal knowledge by storm; all his heroes Blakes, gazing mildly at the tree full of angels and harkening to the chant of the morning sun.

"The Terror," though interesting in theme, is very markedly inferior to the other books in manner, for they reveal the fact that Mr. Machen is gifted with a very remarkable style, rich and colorful but always simple and clear. Yet though he is unmistakably an artist he has never enjoyed anything like popularity. . . . [Actually there is no possibility that] the peculiar temperament which not merely underlies but is the very texture of his work [will] win any wide acceptance. He belongs to the always small company of genuine mystics, and though his creed is superficially similar to that of Chesterton and Belloc he uses his position not primarily as a vantage point from which to shoot paradoxes but as a world into which to retire. He has only one theme, the Mystic Vision, and only one plot, the Rending of the Veil. In "The Great God Pan," one of the stories of "The House of Souls," he does the Faust side of the theme so well that it renders the other stories of the volume unnecessary, and in "The Secret Glory" he does the other side even better; but beautifully as they are done they remain a thing of fairly limited appeal—stories by a mystic and for mystics. (pp. 258-59)

> *J. W. Krutch, "Tales of a Mystic," in* The Nation *(copyright 1922 The Nation magazine, The Nation Associates, Inc.), Vol. 115, No. 2984, September 13, 1922, pp. 258-59.*

HAMISH MILES   (essay date 1923)

Things Near And Far really contains the core of most of Machen's creative writing. This second volume of his auto-biography (if the term is not too strict for an agreeably mazy monologue) covers the years between 1884 and 1901, during which he accomplished most of that imaginative work. And I incline to think that this meditation and self-portraiture is in many ways an indispensable gloss on his novels and tales of the occult. Machen set out to depict certain recondite states of the soul which are probably impossible to define, certainly intensely difficult even to indicate: the symbols are wavering and uncertain, now too vague, now too esoteric. But manifestly his stories (the best of them) were born of his own experience of the Hidden Country. They had been written out of so long a travail, and with such painstaking valuation of words, that they were obviously not just the glorified "shockers" they were often mistaken for. Yet the fact remains that when Machen writes (as here) directly of himself, of the actual houses he has lived in, of the actual adventures of his own youth, of the actual horrors of his own solitude, he writes with far more ease, and he carries a correspondingly greater conviction, than when he transposed these experiences, whether in the seen or the unseeable worlds, into fiction.

Look, for instance, at a highly characteristic work, *The Hill of Dreams*. Here he set out to write, as he says himself, "a Robinson Crusoe of the mind . . . to represent loneliness not of the body on a desert island, but loneliness of the soul and mind and spirit in the midst of myriads and myriads of men." The story, in effect, is Machen's imaginative summing-up of the years which he now returns to describe more or less objectively in *Things Near And Far*. . . . But the Lucian Taylor of the novel is a tediously laboured manipulation of character in comparison with this mature, cooly reticent narrative of the same (or similar) happenings. Lucian never emerges altogether solid and three-dimensioned from the page: he has something of the remote and disembodied quality of a "case" in the Proceedings of the Society for Psychical Research. That adolescent misanthropy of his is irksome. The girding at stupid schoolboys, frumpish relatives, "impossible people" in general, grows tiresome. The satiric touch is often strangely amateurish. And all this weakens the tremendous force of Lucian's story. But take this volume and its predecessor, *Far Off Things*, and turn back to *The Hill of Dreams* with the living Machen in your mind to sharpen the outlines of Lucian. The whole story is somehow quickened with a new vitality that transcends the irritating flaws in the telling. The smouldering glow burns suddenly up. It is as if an actor of genius had taken over a part from a stiff and puzzled beginner. (pp. 628-29)

[The] measure of Machen's success in these self-explanatory books is in a way a measure of his failure in earlier ones. The pity is that it is only in these late works that he has found an expression so free and adequate. His first matrix was fashioned after a pattern of Rabelais, Marguerite of Navarre, Béroalde de Verville; later came a congenial fluency in a Stevensonian manner; from this he deliberately broke away after 1895 in search of an authentic style. But only now does he seem to have found his way into an easy, unshackled, uninhibited speech. It may be, perhaps, that only now has he come into a settled tranquillity of the soul. Such things come late: and this is the book of a man who knows it. (p. 630)

Hamish Miles, "Machen in Retrospect," in The Dial *(copyright, 1923, by The Dial Publishing Company, Inc.), Vol. LXXIV, No. 6, June, 1923 (and reprinted by Kraus Reprint Corporation, 1966), pp. 627-30.*

VINCENT STARRETT   (essay date 1923)

More than Hawthorne or Tolstoy, Machen is a novelist of the soul. He writes of a strange borderland, lying somewhere between Dreams and Death, peopled with shades, beings, spirits, ghosts, men, women, souls—what shall we call them?—the very notion of whom vaguely stops just short of thought. He writes of the life Satyr-ic. For him Pan is not dead; the great god's votaries still whirl through woodland windings to the mad pipe that was Syrinx, and carouse fiercely in enchanted forest grottoes (hidden somewhere, perhaps, in the fourth dimension!). His meddling with the crucibles of science is appalling in its daring, its magnificence, and its horror. Even the greater works of fictional psychology—"Dr. Jekyll and Mr. Hyde," if you like —shrink before his astounding inferences and suggestions.

It is his theory that the fearful and shocking rites of the Bacchic cultus survive in this disillusioned age; that Panic lechery and wickedness did not cease with the Agony, as Mrs. Browning and others would have us believe. (p. 3)

There are those who will call him a novelist of Sin, quibbling about a definition. With these I have no quarrel; the characterizations are synonymous. His books exhale all evil and all corruption; yet they are as pure as the fabled waters of that crystal spring De Leon sought. They are pervaded by an ever-present, intoxicating sense of sin, ravishingly beautiful, furiously Pagan, frantically lovely; but Machen is a finer and truer mystic than the two-penny occultists who guide modern spiritualistic thought. (pp. 4-5)

The sin with which Arthur Machen is concerned is an offense against the nature of things, it has to do with evil in the soul, and has little or nothing to do with the sins of the statute book. (p. 6)

[Sin is] simply, "an attempt to penetrate into another and higher sphere in a forbidden manner . . . Holiness requires almost as great an effort; but holiness works on lines that *were* natural once; it is an effort to recover the ecstasy that was before the Fall." . . . Obviously, this is not the sin of the legal code. (p. 7)

One of his most remarkable stories—certainly, I think, his most terrible story—is "The Great God Pan." . . . [It] is told with exquisite reticence and grace, and with a plausibility that is as extraordinary as it is immoral. (pp. 7-8)

["The Hill of Dreams"] perhaps is Machen's masterpiece, a circumstantial narrative of martyrdom, told by a master of style. The background of the book is as rich and complicated as the bewildered mind of him who reads it—varying with that mind in some odd way; an accurate account of the transfiguration of a highly imaginative boy before the world has dulled and corrupted him. The story loses a certain health in the telling, however. A fastidious nature is stronger, more coherent, more organized, than one that is unfastidious, because it is selective, and because it rejects rather than permits itself to be rejected. Machen permits Lucian Taylor to be rejected, and on this account the boy often appears to be without the energy of passion, and becomes what we call decadent, although by nature he is intensely human and normal; for it is human to feel that sunsets are more than sunsets, and that girls are more than girls. (p. 11)

"The Hill of Dreams" is a study in the morbid; not that it is morbid to be a flagellant, for in the world of the soul, as someone has said, there is neither health nor disease; the lad Lucian Taylor performs his rites from an aesthetic necessity. He makes his body bleed not to kill his desire for Woman, but rather to glorify her fittingly. He is not disclosed, of course, in a world too credulously to be regarded as truthful; it is too solitary.

One's single objection to the story is its dearth of wit and humor, a deficiency that leaves the air oppressive at times. This is too bad, for with a greater alertness in this department it might even have got home to the "owls and cuckoos, asses, apes and dogs."

In this novel, as in most of his writings, Machen is deeply-concerned with the hidden mysteries of nature. The *occult* in clouds, in trees, in water, in fields and valleys, is for Arthur Machen the background of all mystery. I think he *fears* Nature. (p. 12)

Quite as important as what Arthur Machen says is his manner of saying it. He possesses an English prose method which in its mystical suggestion and beauty is unlike any other I have encountered. There is ecstasy in his pages. (pp. 14-15)

The "ecstasy" one finds in Machen's work . . . is due in no small degree to his beautiful English "style"—an abominable word which it is difficult, however, to avoid. But Machen is no mere word-juggler. His vocabulary, while astonishing and extensive, is not affected. His sentences move to sonorous, half-submerged rhythms, swooning with pagan color and redolent of sacerdotal incense. The secret of this graceful English method is a noteworthy gift for selection and arrangement. (p. 15)

He defines his method and exhibits its results at the same time. (p. 16)

[Machen's style] is not prose at all, but poetry, and poetry of a high order. And it is from such exquisite manipulation of words, phrases and rhythms that Machen attains his most clairvoyant and arresting effects in the realms of horror and dread and terror and beauty; from the strange gesturings of trees, the glow of furnace-like clouds, the somber beauty of brooding fields and too-still valleys, the mystery of lovely women, and all the terror of life and nature seen with the understanding eye. (p. 17)

> *Vincent Starrett, "A Novelist of Ecstasy and Sin," in his* Buried Caesars: Essays in Literary Appreciation *(copyright 1923 Covici-McGee Co.), Covici-McGee, 1923, pp. 1-31.*

JOHN GUNTHER (essay date 1925)

[The books of Arthur Machen] like the work of so many artists of similar nature, are chapters, I think, in one long book. Perhaps Mr. Machen himself thinks this way about them. I don't know. But it seems fairly obvious that "The Hill of Dreams", his first major book, is but the primary section of a long romance which by its very nature must be continued in each successive book as long as the author

lives and writes. That is, as a very young man, one theme compelled his attention to the exclusion of other themes; and his work shows little but a series of variations on that theme. With Mr. Machen it has always been a search for the relation of the inner realities of man, to put it crudely, to the outer realities: a search for and a compromise between the life of the spirit and the life of the flesh. In his own phrase, he has attempted in all his books a picaresque romance of the soul. (p. 572)

It is an ironic chance that his war tales, "The Bowmen" and "The Angel of Mons," his only two slight fictions, are the only things he has ever written which have sold well. "The Angel of Mons," vividly and plausibly written, so convinced the British public of the existence of such angels that frequently, even now, soldiers and former soldiers claim to have seen them. But the tale was entirely Mr. Machen's invention.

"Anyone who says otherwise," he told me, "lies." (p. 574)

> *John Gunther, "The Truth About Arthur Machen," in* The Bookman *(copyright, 1925, by George H. Doran Company), Vol. LXI, No. 5, July, 1925, pp. 571-74.*

PHILIP VAN DOREN STERN (essay date 1948)

[Machen] did not write a single ghost story. He was never interested in the unhappy revenant that lingers around ancestral houses to plague a new generation for the sins of the old. He wrote of things more ancient even than ghosts, which at best seldom have more than a few centuries of existence, for Machen dealt with the elemental forces of evil, with spells that outlast time, and with the malign powers of folklore and fairy tale.

A taste for his work has to be acquired; the writing is polished and elaborate, the thinking is subtle, and the imagery is rich with the glowing color that is to be found in medieval church glass. His style does not belong to our period of stripped diction and fast-moving prose; it stems instead from the latter part of the nineteenth century, and preserves some of the formality of the theater itself that attracted him. (pp. iii-iv)

In ["The Great God Pan" and "The Immost Light"] can be seen the author's interest in the inheritance of evil left us from the ancient world. They deal with malign, elemental forces that destroy modern man when he comes in contact with them. These two tales show Machen's mastery of the technique of the supernatural story, for he seems to have known, even in his earliest work in the field, that the best way to summon up horror is to do so by suggestion, by half-veiled hints, and by building up atmospheric effects rather than by the blood-and-thunder methods so often used in such tales.

These two stories were followed a year later by *The Three Impostors*, which the author himself has described as "an imitation of Stevenson's *Dynamiter* and *New Arabian Nights*." But two stories that were woven into the fabric of this picaresque romance may very well outlive the parent work. One of them, "The Black Seal," is literally a fairy tale, for it is based on the supposition that the "Little People" are descendants of the undersized pre-Celtic inhabitants of the British Isles. They are not the beneficent creatures of children's stories, however, but malevolent dwarfs bent on harming the invaders of their ancient land. The other tale, "The White Powder," is perhaps the most powerful of Machen's stories that deal with evil as an elemental force, for it builds up to an unforgettable climax that is terrifying in its impact. (pp. v-vi)

"A Fragment of Life" is the first statement of a theme that was to become almost obsessive with Machen. . . . From earliest childhood he had been impressed with the mystical idea that the world is not what it seems to be, but that there lies behind everyday events and common objects some inner secret that is the key to the great enigma of man's existence. In "A Fragment of Life" a London bank clerk discovers "that man is made a mystery for mysteries and visions, for the realization in his consciousness of ineffable bliss, for a great joy that transmutes the whole world, for a joy that surpasses all joys and overcomes all sorrows."

Machen restated this theme in his autobiographical novel *The Hill of Dreams*, in *The Secret Glory*, and in his autobiography *Far Off Things*. It is the keynote to nearly all his work, the most important clue to the understanding of his art, which is firmly based on the belief that the mystical interpretation of life is the only one worth holding. Machen is the artist of wonder, the seeker for something beyond life and outside of time, the late-born disciple of early Christianity who sees the physical world as the outer covering of a glowing inner core that may someday be revealed. (p. vii)

The Hill of Dreams is a strange book that owes much of its distinction to the fact that its author poured into it the bitterly distilled essence of his own frustrated and unhappy life. He described it as "a 'Robinson Crusoe' of the soul; the story of a man who is not lonely because he is on a desert island, but lonely in the midst of millions, because of his own mental isolation, because there is a great gulf fixed spiritually between him and all whom he encounters." (pp. vii-viii)

[*The Great Return*] is a poetically conceived and imaginatively written account of the return of the Holy Grail to western Wales in modern times. The Grail was one of Machen's major interests; he wrote about it more than once, and it apparently had some kind of personal significance for him that far transcended its ordinary meaning as a religious symbol. It should not be forgotten, of course, that he was born in the town from which the Knights of the Round Table are supposed to have set out on their quests for the sacred vessel. (pp. viii-ix)

Machen will be remembered for his tales of the supernatural, a genre in which he had few superiors. . . . [He] was equipped for his work with the kind of imagination that can see the wonder and the glory that reside in things so common that they escape most people's attention. He was sensitive to physical surroundings, so sensitive that his atmospheric backgrounds sometimes dwarf the human figures in his stories. This hardly matters, for his characters are not real people but symbolic representations of creatures in an eternal chase—a chase wherein evil is in full pursuit of its madly fleeing quarry. The reader knows that the hunter must overtake the hunted and prevail, but the tension holds him spellbound until the race is run. Fear dominates Machen's plots; he is the conjurer whose dumb show must end in death or disaster, for Punch is his master of ceremonies, and the hapless puppets must act in their traditional ways. (pp. ix-x)

Machen was a pictorial writer whose works are filled with magnificently rendered landscapes, but in them there is always some sinister note that betrays their origin. (p. x)

These, of course, are the sort of scenes a painter of the romantic school would choose. But Machen was a belated romantic who lingered on beyond his day. He was born in the middle of the century when romanticism reached its height, and he never forgot his heritage. The people of the nineteenth century had on precious asset that we have lost. They believed in something. It hardly matters what—religion, the family, tradition, the idea of progress, or anything you wish. But they believed, and on the firm foundation of their belief they were able to construct great and enduring works of fiction. Good fiction requires a solid core of belief; it cannot be written from the heart unless the heart is permitted to deal with matters of consequence and speak out the truth. The naturalistic writer seeks his truth in what his eyes have seen, in what his ears have heard, but Machen was a romantic writer who knew that the senses can be deceived, so he was satisfied only with the truth that comes from within. Works of the imagination cannot be written out of notebooks; they spring from the dark depths of the unconscious, and they can be produced only by a mind that searches for the eternal verities. They are often expressed in symbols and images, for they are concerned not with superficialities, but with inner meanings that sometimes cannot be stated in words. And it may be, when the final balance is struck, that there is more essential truth to be found in the tales told by such weavers of fantasy as Arthur Machen than in all the charts and graphs and statistics of the world. (pp. x-xi)

> *Philip Van Doren Stern, in his introduction to* Tales of Horror and The Supernatural, Vol. 2 *by Arthur Machen (copyright 1948 by Alfred A. Knopf, Inc.; reprinted by permission of Alfred A. Knopf, Inc.), Knopf, 1948 (and reprinted by Pinnacle Books, Inc., 1976, pp. iii-xi).*

WILLIAM FRANCIS GEKLE (essay date 1949)

It has been implied that there is a sameness about Machen's work. But do not imagine that you will read the same story, told and retold. You will come to realize that there is in Machen a definite pattern. He has said that most men, as well as writers, are men of one idea. And most writers create tales that are variations on one theme, that a common pattern, like the pattern of an Eastern carpet, runs through them all. And Machen's pattern? You will see, when you read him, that literature 'began with charms, incantations, spells, songs of mystery, chants of religious ecstasy, the Bacchic chorus, the Rune, the Mass.' And Machen has taken as his symbol and pattern the devices and signs of ecstasy, of the removal from the common life. The dance—the maze—the spiral—the wheel—the vine, and wine, these are the outward signs of ecstasy, the patterns of Machen. (p. 11)

The magic of Machen depends as much upon his style as it does upon the magical things of which he writes. His finest stories appeal to an essential and basic desire for "escape" from the common life. (p. 129)

Machen's magic is very simply achieved. In each of his tales an improbable, but not implausible, theme is stated; usually one that is based upon something involving an instinctive belief, for example: the existence of ''little people,'' the continuance of some ancient power under certain circumstances, and in explaining certain occurrences or events for which no rational explanation exists. Folk tales, superstitions, local legends and mythology, most of these embody certain elements in which most of us have at least an instinctive belief. Then, too, a great deal of Mr. Machen's own particular magic is achieved through his ability to see things and to present things that are ''removed from the common life.''

Most of Machen's characters are not unusual people, they are not especially ''peculiar'' in any accepted sense except as they may be affected by certain occurrences in the earlier development of the story. . . . But for the most part his characters are, or were, very ordinary people; ordinary, that is, in the sense that Dyson and Phillips, and even Lucian Taylor, are quite ordinary people. Indeed the very ordinariness of some of these people becames the starting point of an entire sequence of extraordinary events. (p. 130)

To the development of ordinary character . . . must be added one very important magical element—the influence of landscape upon character.

For the peculiar potency of Machen's magic owes much, if not most of its force, to landscape and to the subtle influence of the weird topography of his stories. Many of Machen's most telling effects are achieved through the mere portrayal of a brooding landscape, the sombre background of mountains, the deep, rutted lanes that run along between head-high hedges, solitary hilltops shimmering in heat waves, old grey houses that sit somberly at the edge of the forest and rivers that coil in slow esses through forests and skirt the walls of mountains. There is no doubt that the wild Welsh countryside had this effect upon Machen himself. (p. 131)

Many years ago Vincent Starrett wrote. . . . that there were three Machens—Machen the Saint, Machen the Sorcerer and Machen the Critic. . . . [It] is the works of Machen the Sorcerer that have been most widely anthologized. These are the stories one finds classified under such headings as ''supernatural stories, tales of terror, horror stories'' and the like. (p. 134)

The magic of Machen is due no less to his wonderful style than to his wonderful material. (p. 137)

Arthur Machen has a distinctive style, the perfection of which, while it appeals to the pedantic and soothes the scholarly, must be apparent even to the readers of those horrendous anthologies which have reprinted Machen while the scholars were busily interring him in their fascinating masoleums. (pp. 137-38)

Machen's style is a blend of many things; of words with magic connotation, of sentences that create moods, of passages that suggest, subtly and almost unconsciously, the exact atmosphere for which they were intended. Mr. Machen is a master at evoking the willing suspension of disbelief, and he does it without employing any of the stock properties listed by Coleridge and other authorities as having the proper connotative value for the creation of a ''Gothic'' mood or atmosphere. (p. 139)

[Machen defines his primary theme] in several places quite briefly and simply. It is, he says, ''The sense of the eternal mysteries, the eternal beauty hidden beneath the crust of

common and commonplace things: hidden and yet burning and glowing continously if you care to look with purged eyes.'' (p. 146)

[In] excerpts from Machen's autobiographical sketches one encounters over and over again certain keywords: 'escape,' 'common life,' 'eternal mysteries,' 'removal' and so on. And these same key words are, of course, the underlying themes of every story he ever wrote. They constitute the criteria by which he judged the literature of past and present as well. (pp. 147-48)

There are, undoubtedly, those who prefer Machen the essayist to Machen the story teller. . . .

And yet, in the essays no less than in the stories, the pattern is there and is recognizable. One is forever running across a phrase or a notion one has encountered before—some where, some time, some place—and the place usually turns out to be another Machen essay. For the pattern of Machen's thinking is as obvious as the pattern in the rug; as obvious, and as simple, as the definitions supplied in *Hieroglyphics*. The pattern is, as we know, summed up in the phrase: ''removal from the common life.'' It may be simplified further in the one word: ''ecstasy.'' (p. 158)

And *this* ecstasy is of the mind—it is an exultation of the spirit of men. It is, to go back to the more descriptive phrase, the removal from the common life.

This pattern exists everywhere in Machen, sometimes it is developed by the characters and circumstances in his tales, or again it is carried out by argument or analysis in his essays, but always, upon closer examination, the grand design is apparent. (p. 159)

> *William Francis Gekle, in his* Arthur Machen: Weaver of Fantasy *(copyright 1949 by William Francis Gekle), Round Table Press, 1949, 219 p.*

ROBERT L. TYLER (essay date 1960)

Machen published several novels, the most ambitious being *The Hill of Dreams*. Upon this book his reputation will depend. Malcolm Cowley has placed it in the genre of the ''Art Novel'' and has allowed it the status of a ''minor masterpiece.'' Superficially the book is indistinguishable from many novels about hyper-sensitive young artists or connoisseurs who are defeated in bootless struggles with an obtuse, bourgeois society. It is in bare outline very like *Au Rebours, Martin Eden, Three Soldiers,* to name only several of the type. The principal and virtually only character in *The Hill of Dreams,* Lucian Taylor, resembles Machen himself, a resemblance between protagonist and author not at all uncommon to the whole category of novels. (p. 22)

Machen's claque picked this novel as his masterpiece. If the reader can quiet a certain impatience with the now threadbare plot, he can understand some of the wild praise that the novel elicited from a small circle of smitten readers. The novel is puzzlingly original. The reader may finish the book, saying to himself, ''This is either good or unbelievably bad.'' The writing is lush, at times almost a kind of religious incantation with mouth-filling sentences that pour on and on with brief pauses on the ''ands'' to catch the reader's breath. Despite this saturated style, the feeling of spiritual silence, of corrosive loneliness, of what today we would sagely call a ''schizoid state,'' is presented effectively. The settings, Wales and London, are painted with an extravagance that succeeds in emphasizing those particular qualities needed by the story. The book is full of woodland pools that shine like brass or look like gouts of blood, London streets as fabulous as Baghdad's, and skies that would shame Turner. But these wild romantic excesses never quite become the literary counterpart of a Parrish calendar painting. Their function is controlled to present something besides mere prettiness, and even at their prettiest they convey more awe and wonder than sentimentality.

With a little reflection, it becomes obvious that the novel is really not an "Art Novel" at all. It is not another story of a sensitive plant withering in a philistine desert. The real theme of the story is the imminence of the supernatural, of the ultimate mystery just beyond banal appearances. (pp. 22-3)

In *The Hill of Dreams* Machen aimed at a quality he termed "ecstasy," the mystical experience.... Machen argued this particular literary theory in a little book entitled *Hieroglyphics*.... He presented his argument through the conversation of an imaginary literary hermit, a talkative eccentric whose one consuming passion was literature. *Hieroglyphics* is an informal, meandering monologue in Coleridge's "circular mode of discourse," as the hermit calls it several times in the book. The setting is a cluttered apartment in London. The stage machinery creaks, as it does in most of Machen's books; the plot reminds one vaguely of a Sherlock Holmes-Doctor Watson conversation. But the book possesses a certain nostalgic charm, however outrageous, naive, or crotchety the argument may seem. (p. 23)

Machen never really isolates [the] essential ingredient of ecstasy [in *Hieroglyphics*]. The argument, as argument, seems crankish and what is worse, imprecise. The book is interesting because of a more articulated, reasoned argument that always seems on the verge of presentation, because of the hints, asides, and allusions that suggest an esthetic elaborated in some detail since Machen's day, an esthetic that agrees with Machen on the autonomy of art but seeks art's reference not in some reality beyond human experience but in the immediate complexities and individuality of human emotion. Machen's ecstasy, from this perspective, strikes the reader as a desperate and somewhat too facile attempt to remove esthetic judgement from the blunt instruments of discursive reason. (p. 24)

[Explicitly] in *Hieroglyphics* and implicity in his fiction, Machen was advancing a view of art as some different or "higher" kind of knowledge. He has champions today, more than he had in his own day. But most critics on his side would probably want to jettison his outright mysticism, his ecstasy, and replace it with some more manageable term such as "significant form" or "expressive form" or some other current usage. (p. 25)

What makes Machen a minor writer was his inability to transcend his own situation, either artistically or intellectually. This judgment can be sustained by examining his mysticism and by observing how it actually weakened his fiction. Ironically, Machen was as much of a "message" novelist as the non-ecstatic sort he excoriated in his essay on criticism. However hard he tried to weave his charged symbols and his "style" into an autonomous work of art, he never really

succeeded. The stories and *The Hill of Dreams* remain curious machines to lead the reader to Machen's metaphysical position. At best his works become covert, but nonetheless, discursive arguments. Moreover, when the argument becomes explicit, as in *Hieroglyphics*, it ends with a frank admission of failure, an admission all mystics in an argument must honestly make. After all, ineffable *means* inexpressible. Machen accepted more than he knew the "rationalist" or "materialist" culture he so railed against, accepted it in a deeper sense than was easily recognizable. He accepted, for example, the form of its semantic, its conviction that words and symbols were tools with simple referents. So, for Machen, Art with its difficult reference to the immediate and unique inner life of man had perforce to refer either to the road and the street or to some other form of reality.

What makes Machen an interesting and significant writer, even though minor, are his near misses. He did at least resist the "positivism" of his age.... In his stubbornness he produced several curious, individual books worth the sampling of the inveterate book lover. Machen is a poignant figure, a writer of great dedication who held his lantern up boldly in the dark, though in slightly the wrong place. (p. 25-6)

> Robert L. Tyler, "Arthur Machen: The Minor Writer and His Function," in Approach (copyright 1960 by Approach), No. 35, Spring, 1960, pp. 21-6.

WESLEY D. SWEETSER (essay date 1965)

Like Poe, Machen was limited in range and esoteric in his ideas; but Machen lacked the imaginative genius of Poe; and in those works where he allowed his imagination full rein, Machen could not refrain from displaying intellectual guilt at his childish fantasies. With a little less intellectuality, he might have been a major writer. As it is, his present following, like that of mystery story addicts, is avid but small. (p. 9)

Machen, whose life was self-admittedly blighted by a slight tinge of genius, "a juxtaposition of desire and impotence," and whose works clearly illustrated that he lacked the fertile imagination of a writer like Dickens, who could populate his novels with whole cities of people and who could create situations and conversations more real than reality—Machen, the arid dogmatist, could not create those marvellous fictions; but he took what he had—a mystical worship of nature, a knowledge of Celtic folklore, a familiarity with occult doctrines, and a respect for style and for the world's great literary masterpieces—tinged them through and through with the spirit of romance, and blended the whole into an affirmation of spiritual ascendancy. His works, en masse, reflect not so much the literary art as a philosophy of life. They reflect the insignificant individual successfully pitting his strength against ever-increasing social pressures and maintaining his individuality to the end. They reflect spiritual certitude and provide a lifeline for those caught in an undertow of eclecticism. Machen accepted the challenge of life and remained indomitable unto death. (pp. 9-10)

Artistically speaking, his total literary output can be placed into three main categories—romanticism, mysticism and symbolism, and the weird and occult—with each one often permeating the whole. As far as romanticism is concerned, even his satire was prompted by his desire to denounce those attitudes and beliefs and forms of art which impeded the growth of romanticism and were destructive to it. . . . [He] was attempting to convey a sense of the unknown, to achieve withdrawal from common life. He effects this escape in many ways: by the use of medieval subject matter, by producing the illusion of antiquity through archaic diction, by the creation of pure fantasy in the field of horror and the supernatural, and by calling forth the sense of wonder in order to lend enchantment to ordinary occurrences. Although only a few of his tales have a medieval setting, he makes frequent references to Gothic architecture and to the Graal legend. . . . His style, though variable, is often imitative of the seventeenth century writers so much revered by Lamb and Coleridge. Several of his works are written in an archaic diction which gives them a quaint quality reminiscent of bygone eras. In works of pure imagination, he can hardly be called a Gothic novelist in the sense of Walpole and Radcliffe. He was led into the field of the supernatural by his great admiration of Poe and Hawthorne, and he seldom uses the Gothic machinery or pattern except in the general sense of magnifying the grotesque and macabre. Infused throughout his work is the sense of wonder and enchantment which transforms the commonplace existence into a world of magic and wonder. In his use of the wild natural setting of Wales to enhance atmosphere and mood, his return to nature is not often the same as that of the Romantics in the Wordsworthian sense of revealing the influence of nature upon the soul of man or in the sense of the return to the "noble savage" state of existence, but is romantic, rather, in the sense of returning to the primal nature of man, to Good and Evil. (pp. 10-11)

The second strong element pervading his works is that of mysticism and symbolism. The mystic is a man alone, living in a world apart; yet as if impelled by a power beyond his control, he has the insatiable urge to communicate his incommunicable experience. In Machen's case, he propounded again and again, so that there could be no shadow of a doubt, his underlying premise concerning life, nature, and the universe, that all is a profound and ineffable mystery. The surface realities are but symbols which both reveal and conceal the true nature of that mystery. . . .

To sum up Machen's philosophical position with respect to weird and occult phenomena, Machen considered himself somewhat of an alchemist whose business was far more embracing than mere trasmutation of lead into gold. He felt consistently that his artistic purpose was to transform the world of everyday reality into a world of magic and wonder, to convey to the reader the naked transcendental forces behind human existence. (p. 11)

Machen, as an artist, had many deficiencies, not least of which was his psychological obsession to write on every possible occasion. . . . [But despite] his inability to master some forms of writing, two virtues stand forth clearly in most of his work, even in some of his routine reviews—an insuperable style and an ability to suggest, to lead the reader to the brink of revelation. Through cadenced prose, he hints of the evolution of man from primordial slime, on the one hand, and almost reveals a glorious and ineffable mystery on the other. Vincent Starrett was thus induced to call him a novelist of "ecstasy and sin" [see excerpt above]. Primarily, Machen was concerned with matters of the soul, with the essence of man, with the paradise lost and never regained, and with the great errantry. (p. 12)

Machen was not a novelist. He was essentially a writer struggling, never quite successfully, to create the Great Romance; and he carefully avoided, indeed abhorred, the contemporary realistic and naturalistic movements in literature. His main claim to fame, ironically enough, lies in the field of tales of the weird and supernatural, tales which he wrote as potboilers and which he believed worthless. Numerically greater than any other fictional types in his total literary output, Machen's tales of the weird and occult are also the only ones being currently reprinted on a large scale. . . . [Only] in his weird and occult tales was it possible for him to express all of his latent proclivities—his romanticism, his bent for fantasy, and his symbolic and mystical concepts of the nature of the universe. In this field, Machen's horrors are always remote and suggested, never physical; and it is precisely in this small area of psychological, transcendental occult that Machen has never been surpassed. His peculiar knowledge of demonology, witchcraft, folklore, particularly Celtic lore, and occult societies and religions combined with his unique talent for suggesting the indescribable through the creation of atmosphere to make him the spokesman without peer for sorcery and sanctity existing always behind the veil of the ineffable mystery. . . . The impact of his tales lies not in their novelty as a new sensation, but in their spiritual import, in their emphasis upon the concealed aspects of human existence. The infusion of the element of humanism into everything he wrote provides the distinction which sets his work off from mere sensation fiction and gives it universal applicability.

Machen dreamed in fire, but he worked in clay; and his desire far exceeded his grasp. His great weakness as an artist lay primarily in his over reliance on the raw idea. He was too much the scholar, the humanist, the man of letters. He lacked the gift of narrative which expresses an idea implicitly, rather than explicitly, through character creation, conversation, and action. Nevertheless, he wrote a few works in addition to his penny dreads which are interesting, challenging, and artistically conceived and executed. The first of these is *Hieroglyphics*. . . . The second of his memorable but neglected works is *The Hill of Dreams*. This strangely original, symbolistic work, despite the disparate elements of satire and mysticism, is a notable experimental "novel" foreshadowing the stream-of-consciousness school. A third unknown work displaying Machen's diverse talent is "The Rose Garden," a mystical prose poem which produces the feeling of ecstasy resulting from annihilation of the self and which conveys remarkably the loss of substance and the resulting spiritual rebirth, the rare rapport and harmony necessary to consummate mystical art. Finally, *Dog and Duck,* written in a slightly archaic style like *Hieroglyphics,* is representative of a large body of journalistic essays which, despite their seeming ingenuousness, are artfully conceived. (p. 13)

In terms of his own critical dicta, as set forth in *Hieroglyphics,* most of these works will stand up under criticism as far as idea or conception is concerned. As to style, most of them are outstanding. In plot or construction, on the other hand, Machen was extremely weak. However, as he says, the idea is the most important; and a work can live on that alone. Machen's trouble was that he had only a few ideas for all of his works, stated in slightly different terms, but highly resembling one another. At any rate, he never failed to fulfil his unique principle for romantic art—withdrawal from common life. . . .

[In the final analysis Machen] shows us that even in the most drab and commonplace existence lies a beckoning land of wonder and enchantment beyond.... Machen's works are imbued with the same romantic spirit of discovery found in Keats' sonnet "On First Looking into Chapman's Homer" applied to everyday life in such manner as to excite the sense of wonder in everything everywhere. In the second place, some of Machen's works impart gusto, joy in living, joy in simple pleasures, in eating and drinking, enjoyment of the beauties of nature, and love of humanity. In addition to this optimistic outlook, so refreshing after the hopelessness and despair of the naturalists, his works have the quality of certitude which gives us courage to live according to our convictions—a reverence for simple virtues and a mystic faith in the order and harmony beyond the seeming disorder and chaos. Next, much of his work conveys the sense of timelessness, the historical continuity which joins each generation with all ages past and links each man into the great chain of being. Finally, his major fictional works present a progressive study from utter evil to the highest good, from pure diabolism to the attainment of sanctity and the occurrence of miracles. Such are the works, such are the visions, such is the spirit of Arthur Machen. (p. 14)

> *Wesley D. Sweetser, in his introduction to* A Bibliography of Arthur Machen *by Adrian Goldstone and Wesley Sweetser (copyright © 1965 by Adrian Goldstone & Wesley D. Sweetser),* Humanities Research Center, University of Texas at Austin, *1965, pp. 9-14.*

BERTA NASH (essay date 1967)

[In Machen's tale "The Great Return" there] is no word of Arthur, his Round Table, or the quest for the Grail, although Machen utilizes in a large measure fairly well known material associated with King Arthur and his knights.... The Grail, with its guardians, the three fishermen, visits a little coastal village for a few days. Because of its intervention, a deaf woman hears, a girl at the point of death is healed, unrelenting enemies are reconciled, the wealthy and the poor, the fox and the hound play together, and all Christians, of many different sects, worship together in the Mass of the Sangraal....

This is unexpected. Machen, when known at all, is known as a Welshman, a romantic, a purveyor of stories of horror. (p. 110)

[But the] story may be more typical of Machen than it first seems, in that it brings together—though in uncharacteristic fashion—his characteristic themes. It is mystic, supernatural, as are many of Machen's better-known tales—for example, "The Novel of the Black Seal," "The White Powder," "The Shining Pyramid," "The Great God Pan," "The Terror." But these are tales of evil and horror, whereas "The Great Return" is a tale of joy. It is, however, a tale of joy which perhaps can be read as symbolizing, fairly late in Machen's career, a kind of solution, or resolution, of the sharp dichotomy between the material and the spiritual world which underlies the tales of horror. (p. 111)

[In the early horror stories "The Great God Pan" and "The Novel of the White Powder"] are manifested, perhaps consciously, the already conventional opposition between the

scientist and the spiritualist, the materialist and the seeker after the invisible, the imponderable, the immeasurable. At first glance it would seem that Machen is fighting on the side of the angels and is wholeheartedly opposed to the scientific materialist. Actually, however, Machen does not oppose the material per se, but seeks a reconciliation of natural and supernatural. (p. 112)

He does not try to say that the physical is wholly representative of evil while the spiritual element symbolizes the good. These elements are never to be considered as irreconcilable opposites, but as typifying that diversity in unity which is humanity at its most noble.

The tales of horror, of evil, are nearly all occult and supernatural; they are also nearly all stories in which an immaterial evil prevails over a balanced human being because of the use of some material agency. In tale after tale horror prevails because of some effort made which destroyed that delicate balance. Indeed it would appear that the greatest depth of evil to which man can descend is to effect a separation between the physical and the spiritual in the human creature. (p. 113)

Although Machen was, in an earlier period, well dosed with medieval manuscripts, he does not use demons, fallen angels, in this role even though he is occupied with a supernatural story. What he requires is a wholeheartedly wicked being, superficially human but without any divine admixture—soulless. Finding no such race of creatures in the universe, he does what any creative writer would do in such an emergency. He invents one.

Essentially his myth starts with the wholly logical supposition that the British Isles were home to a different race before the advent of the Celt. With the coming of the Celtic tribes these beings neither departed nor were assimilated by the invaders; they went underground. To this day these troglodytes live on in the caves and hills of Cornwall and Wales.... Thus Machen creates an evil element for his tales of horror which represents the material wholly purged of any spiritual admixture. These creatures are not only evil; they are soulless. They are inhuman, and are not even animals. Animals at least are capable of evolving into higher forms but these have no such promise.

Such are the tales of horror; stories in which individuals sometimes accidentally, sometimes deliberately, so overturn the natural balance of a human creature that there occurs an unnatural separation of the elements which form its composition.... In the tales which he wrote in his later years the apparently supernatural visions or visitations seemed to occur spontaneously, as in "The Happy Children" the supernatural benefits seem to fall upon the recipients by chance, certainly through no intervention of their own. The winds of the spirit, whether malevolent or benevolent, blow when and on whom they will, without the need of any material agency or the directions of any external power. (pp. 114-16)

[A] look at one of the "tales of joy" will help us to understand this opposition of horror and joy. In *The Great Return* the supernatural visitation comes unbidden but through the medium of a material utensil, the Grail.... (p. 116)

For Machen, then, the Grail is not only an interesting literary legend of respectable antiquity, it is also a symbol of the Christian teaching, a symbol which possesses the special power of becoming that which it represents. (p. 119)

Perhaps others have found different answers, but for me *The Great Return* has led to a kind of insight into the nature of Machen's writings. At first it seemed a pleasant tale, but as I read more of his work I became aware of the curious dichotomy of his moods. His tales are either unutterably horrible or completely joyous. He knows no middle way. Initially I accepted him as a typical product of his time, an age of conflict between the scientist and the humanist, the good mystic opposed to the evil materialist.

However, the Grail for him is not spiritual but material, and furthermore he appears to be at some pains to establish the reality of the old woman's deafness, the illness of the girl, the enmity of the men. Furthermore, it appears that in the tales of horror, although the evil is initiated by a physical agency, it invariably culminates in a complete corruption. Even though the spirit is eliminated the material remainder is also dissolved, for no single element in the human compound may exist unsupported by the others. These stories are stories of diminution, in which a person is destroyed in an attempt to separate out an element which is an essential part of him. The other part of the canon, the happier tales, are sums in addition. The actors remain very human and alive. They are recognizable but changed.

For many readers, then, the Grail becomes a symbol of mankind as mankind ought to be, an indissoluble compound of elements. . . . [The] whole is something very different from the collection of parts which compose it. Evidently, in Machen's view, the human being is such another compound: infinitely various, capable of additions and elaborations, but to be analysed, dissected, and diminished only at the gravest peril. (pp. 119-20)

> Berta Nash, "Arthur Machen among the Arthurians," in Minor British Novelists, *edited by Charles Alva Hoyt (copyright © 1967 by Southern Illinois University Press; reprinted by permission of Southern Illinois University Press), Southern Illinois University Press, 1967, pp. 109-20.*

D.P.M. MICHAEL (essay date 1971)

Machen was not one of the first but certainly he was one of the most successful of those writers who have exploited the theme of horror. . . .

The Great God Pan was published, together with *The Inmost Light,* . . . and they caused an immediate stir. (p. 11)

The Great God Pan was the result of a conscious search for a subject and a style of his own, but Machen's theme was not wholly original since he was writing for *fin-de-siècle* readers at a time *when yellow bookery was at its yellowest.* An audience, supposedly interested in sin and decadence, suggested, directed and controlled the flow of the narrative. The demand was allowed to play too great a part in the writer's supply. He strained after temporary and topical effects and found reason to regret as time went by the exaggerated notoriety the story brought him. Judged not for its intrinsic value but as a transitional experiment, the work becomes more important. The manner is more interesting than the matter. His growing experience in journalism was teaching him to remove from his style the exotic elements. The Great Romance was an illusion. (pp. 11-12)

The real achievement of *The Great God Pan* remains even when one has admitted that the plot strains coincidence and the characters are insufficiently differentiated. Machen conjured up an atmosphere of pure evil. It was always one of his objects to communicate to others the glimpses he had of a deeper reality behind the commonplace. The spiritual world was angelic; it was also demoniacal. (p. 14)

The White People is remarkable for the power of its writing. Much of the story is told through the lips of a child and this may have some influence upon the style, but no small girl could have written so simple and so eloquent a journal describing how she stumbles upon a secret and sinister world. (p. 15)

Far Off Things is a delightful but discursive autobiography. It contains the quintessence of Machen and is perhaps the best introduction to the author for a reader not easily attracted to the longer, leisurely fiction characteristic of this writer. Machen's mind goes back wistfully to those far-off days in Gwent when he was learning to write. There is a kind of *hiraeth* for Wales, there is a sort of Virgilian *desiderium*, a Theocritan nostalgia. He realises that he has long striven to express in a variety of works his impressions of the magic land of his youth,

> those vague impressions of wonder and awe and mystery.

And obviously the epithet *magic* is transferrable between the land and the youth. In his six chapters he moves from boyhood to books and to a London at first exciting and then menacing, and comes full circle to a return visit to Monmouthshire. A summary gives a totally inadequate idea of the gentle beauty of the book. There is art in the construction as the melodious narrative that has continuously meandered comes at last once more to its point of origin. There is euphony too in the language. . . . (pp. 50-1)

Like Far Off Things, Things Near and Far is not so much an autobiography as a reverie. (p. 51)

Machen always writes with an unusual excitement of any mystery, whether something ordinary is seen in an extraordinary light or from an odd angle, or whether the supernatural invades the natural, or whether events seem simply to fall into an unexpected pattern. He apprehends a secret world which is more real than the outward appearance of things. The story of human life is a palimpsest where the original writing, almost wholly erased for the modern reader, is the true and valuable work. (p. 53)

The style of Machen's early prose was too conscious but . . . when he forgets that he is a prose-artist, his writing is excellent. When Machen is moved by passion, his words beat with a pulsating rhythm, and we begin to hear the melodious words chiming in harmony. He knew one secret of the Welsh preachers.

Years of labour purified his style of its youthful faults. His language takes on a new cogency as it gains in vigour and vivacity. The antiquarian affectation observable in his early prose almost disappears. The forced wit and humour of the first books is now urbane and relaxed. The dialogue is no longer stilted and unreal. *Far Off Things* is Machen's finest and best sustained expression, but the severe beauty of his mature style may also be found in his later fiction. Every word is chosen with due regard for its meaning and overtones and there is greater variety in the word-order. The vocabulary is less abstract: the verb drives out the noun and there is a reduction in the adjectival load. Machen's prose achieves a new lucidity without any essential sacrifice of beauty. (pp. 65-6)

Machen is always concerned with the things of the spirit and perhaps that is why there are still those of us who feel that, with all his faults, Machen's work is of greater value than that of many better-known novelists and short-story writers. He himself was never complacent about his achievement. He was a Romantic. As he himself said, he worked in clay, he dreamed in fire. There are reflections in Machen's best work of that fiery dream. (pp. 66-7)

> *D.P.M. Michael, in his* Arthur Machen (© *The University of Wales Press and the Welsh Arts Council, 1971), University of Wales Press, 1971, 80 p.*

DAVID VESSEY   (essay date 1973)

Machen was able to write a prose which is pure poetry: lyrical, sensuous and rhythmic, linking sense and sound in a symbolic unity. This talent is demonstrated to the full in *The Hill of Dreams* when he describes the strange splendours of his native Monmouthshire and the contrasting horrors of suburban London.

The novel recounts the story of the short and unhappy life of Lucian Taylor, a hypersensitive youth who finds the world intolerably hostile to his ideals and aspirations. . . . Lucian is in part Machen, but only in part: he shares many of his creator's tastes and ambitions, but he lacks Machen's warmth and humour. He is a Machen cast in a tragic mould. . . . Lucian Taylor is a *figura:* he had a subjective origin and was rooted in an act of self-dramatisation, but he passed beyond this origin to become an objective statement illustrative of certain Romantic preconceptions about art. By inexorable stages, he becomes utterly alienated from his fellow man; he is enshrouded in a dark frenzy of useless creativity—escape from his predicament can be found only in fantasy (when he creates for himself the fictive delights of the garden of Avallaunius), or in a solitary, unlamented death through an overdose of drugs. (pp. 124-25)

The Hill of Dreams is a paradigm of the literary trends which we associate with the 'nineties. . . . Lucian spurns bourgeois values in art and society; he shudders at the savagery that springs from the vulgarian smugness and middle-class prejudices of the genteel folk of Carmaen. But his dislike of the bourgeoisie and their soulless *Lebensform* is not inspired by radicalism, but by an idealisation of the illusory past, whether it be Roman, Celtic or Medieval. (p. 125)

Machen provides what is more or less a satirical commentary on the literary war of the 'nineties. He wittily reveals the unbridgeable gulf that yawned between the elitist decadents and the purveyors of healthy books for healthy minds. (p. 126)

In *The Hill of Dreams*, Machen shows great psychological perception, particularly in his analysis of Lucian's sexuality. Before Freud, Machen realised that art may be interpreted as a sublimation of erotic desire. Lucian fails to come to terms with his own sexual urges and, repressed, they break out in his obsession with writing. The sexual theme runs through the book; Machen is never scabrous, but, like other 'decadent' writers, he does not attempt to avoid the issue. He realised that no account of a young

man's psychic development could be complete without considering the sexual aspect. (p. 127)

In *The Hill of Dreams*, Machen pioneered a technique of integrated psychological narrative. He gives us a devastating picture of madness and alienation, and we are able to recognise in Lucian Taylor the characteristic symptoms of schizophrenia. Everything in the book is seen solely in subjective relation to Lucian's mental state; he is a cosmos with its own fantastic scale of values; the world of nature and of man is interpreted entirely through him. He is the measure of all things; the universe itself is involved in the decline and final dissolution of Lucian Taylor. It is a frightening and savage universe, in which reality and illusion are scarcely differentiated. At one point, Lucian remarks: 'I had rather call the devils my brothers. . . . I would fare better in hell.' . . . In those words lie the essence of his madness; because of his inability to adjust to the harshness of life, he turns within himself, seeking in fantasy an escape from hell. Lucian is a sacrificial victim slaughtered in honour of a god that he has himself created. His failure and despair were Machen's triumph. (p. 128)

> *David Vessey, "Arthur Machen's 'The Hill of Dreams': A Novel of the 'Nineties," in* Contemporary Review *(© 1973 Contemporary Review Co. Ltd.), Vol. 223, No. 1292, September, 1973, pp. 124-28.*

ADDITIONAL BIBLIOGRAPHY

Ellis, Stewart M. "Arthur Machen." In his *Mainly Victorian*, pp. 269-75. London: Hutchinson & Co., 1925.
  Biographical and critical study that discusses Machen as a product of the Victorian era.

Hillyer, Robert. "Arthur Machen." *The Atlantic Monthly* 179, No. 5 (May 1947): 138-40.
  Reminiscences by a friend of Machen's which includes a brief summation of Machen's importance as a writer.

Lovecraft, Howard Phillips. "The Modern Masters." In his *Supernatural Horror in Literature*, pp. 87-108. New York: Dover Publications, 1973.*
  An essay which stresses Machen's importance in the field of horror literature. Lovecraft's plot summaries are more substantial than his critical remarks.

Mais, S.P.B. "Arthur Machen." In his *Some Modern Authors*, pp. 211-20. London: Grant Richards, 1923.
  A biographical sketch that includes plot summaries of Machen's works.

Penzoldt, Peter. "The Pure Tale of Horror." In his *The Supernatural in Fiction*, pp. 146-90. New York: Humanities Press, 1965.*
  Study which sees Calvinist beliefs expressed throughout Machen's works of horror.

Sweetser, Wesley D. *Arthur Machen*. New York: Twayne Publishers, 1964, 175 p.
  Critical study of Machen's work that includes biographical information.

Van Vechten, Carl. "Arthur Machen: Dreamer and Mystic." In his *Excavations: A Book of Advocacies*, pp. 162-69. New York: Alfred A. Knopf, 1926.
  Biographical information and plot description that includes some criticism of *Hill of Dreams, Far Off Things*, and *Things Near and Far.*

Vladimir (Vladimirovich) Mayakovsky

1893-1930

(Also transliterated as Maĭakovskiĭ, Mayakovski, and Majakovskij) Russian poet, dramatist, screenwriter, and autobiographer.

Mayakovsky is considered the leading poet of revolutionary Russia and the most important innovator of the futurist school of verse. The Russian futurists, whose precepts were defined by the 1912 Cubo-Futurist Manifesto, "A Slap in the Face of Public Taste," sought to create a verbal equivalent to the cubist movement in painting. Their avowed aim was nothing less than the destruction of all traditional art and literature. Hyperbolic metaphors, syntactical inversions, and an idiosyncratic vocabulary were mixed with gritty, lusty street language to revitalize the language. Mayakovsky's efforts influenced many young Russian writers and revolutionized the nation's poetry.

A rebellious, bright youth, Mayakovsky came to live in Moscow as a teen after spending his early years in a Georgian village. Rejecting the Czarist political system, he joined a Bolshevik cell, serving as an errand runner. After several jail terms for his political activities, Mayakovsky briefly attended the Moscow Institute, where he took up painting. It was there he met David Burlyuk, an artist with a bohemian spirit like his own. Burlyuk coaxed the first verses from Mayakovsky, then joined him on a bizarre futurist speaking tour of Russia. Mayakovsky possessed a booming voice, a commanding personality, and a natural talent for public speaking. Most of his subsequent poetry was written to be delivered aloud.

Mayakovsky's prerevolutionary poems are characterized by their flaunting of bourgeois conventions, both in subject and form. *Oblako v shtanakh* (*A Cloud in Trousers*) is his best known work from this period. In addition to his literary activities, Mayakovsky also starred in the tragedy *Vladimir Mayakovsky*, in which he vividly presented his lifelong role as the boastful champion of his "beloved self." And in 1915 he met Lily Brik, the wife of one of his publishers, with whom he maintained a long romantic obsession and who figured in many of his poems.

With the triumph of the Bolsheviks in 1917 Mayakovsky enthusiastically devoted his work to the Communist cause, writing propagandistic verses and designing news posters for the Russian Telegraphic Agency. During the first years of Lenin's rule he wrote *Misteria-Buff* (*Mystery-Bouffe*) a drama celebrating the hoped-for triumph of the world's working class. This poem was followed by *150.000.000*, a reaction to American intervention in the Russian Civil War. He contributed poems to the major Soviet newspaper *Izvestia*, and founded the journal *LEF* (*Left Front of Art*) in 1923. Although he praised the Revolution in his poems, Mayakovsky nonetheless received criticism from the Russian Association of Proletarian Writers (RAPP) for his individualism and utilization of futurism, a style deemed a remnant of prerevolutionary decadence by members of that organization. The Revolution's comfortable bureaucrats and traditionalists of

RAPP's ilk were satirized in Mayakovsky's dramas *Klop* (*The Bedbug*) and *Banya* (*The Bathhouse*), which were written and performed in the last two years of his life.

Mayakovsky's lifelong stance was that of an unloved, unappreciated genius, who desperately wanted to feel persecuted. He was torn between the flamboyant originality of his poetry and a desire to "stamp on the throat" of his talent in service to the Party. His struggle against the regime's increasingly narrow artistic standards ended with his suicide in 1930.

PRINCIPAL WORKS

Poshchochina obshestvennomu vkusa [with David Burlyuk, Velimir Khlebnikov, and Aleksey Kruchonykh] (manifesto and poetry) 1912
Vladimir Mayakovsky (drama) 1913
  [*Vladimir Mayakovsky* published in *The Complete Plays of Vladimir Mayakovsky*, 1968]
Ya (poetry) 1913
Oblako v shtanakh (poetry) 1915
  [*A Cloud in Trousers* published in *Mayakovsky*, 1965]
Chelovek (poetry) 1916
Fleita pozvonochnik (poetry) 1916
Rossii (poetry) 1916

Sebe, lyubimomu, avtor posvashchaet eti stroki (poetry)
1916
Voina i mir (poetry) 1916
Misteria-Buff (drama) 1918
[*Mystery-Bouffe* published in *The Complete Plays of Vladimir Mayakovsky*, 1968]
Vse sochinennoe Vladimirom Mayakovskim (poetry and drama) 1919
150.000.000 (poetry) 1920
Liren (poetry) 1921
Lyublyu (poetry) 1922
Nash byt (poetry) 1922
Ya sam (autobiography) 1922
[*I Myself* published in *Mayakovsky and His Poetry*, 1942]
Pro eto (poetry) 1923
Vladimir Ilyich Lenin (poetry) 1924
[*Vladimir Ilyich Lenin*, 1970]
Amerikanskiye stikhi (poetry) 1926
Kak delat' stikhi? (essay) 1926
[*How are Verses Made?*, 1970]
Khorosho! (poetry) 1927
Klop (drama) 1929
[*The Bedbug, and Selected Poetry*, 1961]
Banya (drama) 1930
[*The Bathhouse* published in *The Complete Plays of Vladimir Mayakovsky*, 1968]
Mayakovsky and his Poetry (autobiography and poetry) 1942
Polnoe sobranie sochinenii Mayakovskogo. 13 vols. (poetry) 1955-1961
The Complete Plays of Vladimir Mayakovsky (dramas) 1968

KORNEY CHUKOVSKY (essay date 1920)

It would be hard to imagine two [poets] less alike than [Anna] Akhmatova and Mayakovsky. Akhmatova is shrouded in silence, in whispered, almost inaudible words. Mayakovsky shouts like a thousand-throated public square. ''The heart is our drum,'' he himself declares, and any page of his work will convince you of it. He is not only incapable of silence, but of any sort of measured conversation. He is ever shouting and raging.

Akhmatova is as devout as a prayer book. Angels, the Virgin, God are present in her every word. Mayakovsky cannot pass by God without hurling himself on Him with a shoemaker's knife. . . . (p. 42)

Of course it would be easy to dismiss him as a blasphemer, a simple outrage. . . . [But let] us look at Mayakovsky closely and conscientiously, without prejudice. (pp. 43-4)

[He] is the poet of the colossal. In his world, the smallest speck of dust becomes Mount Ararat. His poetry operates on a gargantuan scale beyond the imagination of our previous poets. He appears always to be in front of a telescope, as when using stupendous augmentatives: portentous conversation, enormous Hell, colossal neck, huge step, great Babylon, massive tail. ''Give me, give me a seventy-mile-wide superlanguage,'' one of his theatrical characters demands; it would appear that Mayakovsky himself already possesses such a language. Everything is blown up to such a size that words like ''thousand,'' ''million,'' and ''billion'' are commonplace. (p. 44)

Each of his poems is a great collection of exaggerations, and he can't do without them. Another poet might say that a flame burns in his heart; Mayakovsky asserts that his house is a roaring conflagration not to be extinguished even by forty-gallon barrels of tears (that's how he puts it—''barrels of tears''). Firemen bound up to him and pour water on his heart, but it's too late: his face is already burned, his mouth is in flames, his heat-cracked skull is split all the way open; his charred rib cage has collapsed.

Love caused this conflagration; such is Mayakovsky's love! Let Akhmatova, treating love, describe slight hand-touching and imperceptible lip movements—Mayakovsky needs a hundred-eyed flame, a ten-square-mile forest fire. (pp. 44-5)

We find here along with hyperbole another device: the concretization of everything abstract. His metaphorically flaming heart becomes an actual fire requiring hoses and fire chiefs.

His figuratively gyrating nerves turn into real dancers. This device of his is extremely interesting, but for the present we are concerned with giantism. Where did this ravenous need to aggrandize originate? Why does he describe himself as a towering titan, dwarfing other two-legged creatures, as though he saw even himself through a telescope? (p. 45)

[Let] us try to understand what is going on. Revolutions and wars have so accustomed our generation to large figures that it would be odd for poets reflective of the age *not* to pick up and use the thousands, millions, and billions now so clearly operative in life. . . . Isn't it as the poet of this new, grandiose system of measurement that Mayakovsky deeply senses the great mass of humanity, senses her thousands of peoples swarming about on our planet, continually addresses himself to them, never for a minute forgetting their existence? . . . On them one finds the Alps, the Balkans, Chicago, the Arctic Circle, London, the Sahara, Rome, the Atlantic Ocean, the English Channel, California—in fact the geography of the whole world.

Living in Moscow, he nonetheless (like anyone alive today) considers himself a citizen of the universe. This is a new feeling, heretofore unknown. At one time very few people had this feeling, but now it is quite common. . . . Our thinking has broken out of its closed circle and is expanding and growing.

And so a heightened awareness of great expanses is only natural to Mayakovsky's outsized scale of things. When he describes war in his poem *War and the World*, he doesn't single out a particular sector of war, a specific battle, but covers the whole worldwide field of slaughter, the million wrinkles of trenches that furrowed the earth, the thunder and lightning of billion-man armies—here blacks and Arabs, there Munich, Constantinople, the Marne—''the whole of blazing Europe'' suspended in the skies like a chandelier. His telescope is such that, unresponsive to details and particulars, his vision takes in enormous distances. And to encompass these distances indeed requires a seventy-mile language. (pp. 45-6)

[What] is the essence of [Mayakovsky's] work?

He is a poet of catastrophe and convulsion. Every word is earthshaking. In order to create a poem, he must first go mad. Only feverish and demented images are permitted on his pages. His skull is ''inflamed,'' words are ''frenzied,'' his face is more frightening than "sacrileges, killings, and slaughter." He says so himself. He has only to go out into the street, and the street collapses like a syphilitic nose and a crazed cathedral careens down the street, an insane god jumps out of a church icon and whirls about in the slush of the road, six-storied concrete giants break into a frantic dance....

Mayakovsky is a poet of movement, of dynamics, whirlwinds. Since his first verses in 1910, his objects haven't stopped rushing and springing about. This bounding of massive objects is in fact Mayakovsky's favorite device. All his images are aimed at movement, action. It is positively impossible for him to describe something stationary, peaceful, quiet. (p. 47)

The war and the Revolution broke out, as it were, just for his sake alone.... It's just such subjects that require the hyperbolic style, that giantism and penchant for the massive that are organic to Mayakovsky. To deal with great events created by a mass of millions, a scale of millions is required.

In the second place, as we have seen, he is the poet of thunder and lightning, roars and screeches; he is incapable of maintaining any sort of quiet. Another obligatory trait: the Revolution can in no way be carried out in a whisper. For some time revolutionary cries had been heard in his poetry, and inhuman, inarticulate sounds—such as those that fill the streets of insurrection—characteristically burst from his pages.... (p. 48)

Thirdly, as we have just seen, he is a poet of perpetual motion, cataclysmic convulsions, concussions between objects. This is another sine qua non: how can a poet of this cataclysmic era operate without such movement?

He was, in a word, expressly equipped by nature to sing of war and revolution. And, amazingly enough, he presaged and raved about the Revolution before it even began. As early as 1915, at the height of the war, I read with astonishment:

> —1916 is drawing near in the thorny crown
> of revolutions / . . . . And I am its harbinger,
> scouting it for you / . . . like no other, I can
> see the future approaching, / over the mountains of time.

At that time no other poet had even *sensed* the revolution, but he even prophesied the year. True, in his impatience he erred slightly—the Revolution took place a year later—but his impatience was really very great. (pp. 48-9)

This street idiom first expressed itself in his rhythms. His verses, with few exceptions, are based not on those formal metric schemes which are so alien to contemporary ears, but on a living, conversational, street rhythm. He put together his own rhythms, those we hear in the marketplace, on trolley cars, at meetings, the rhythm of shouts, conversations, speeches, squabbles, agitators' exhortations, swearing. His only aim is to canonize his street rhythms in spite of all the laws of prosody. (p. 50)

It is as though all of Russia is divided today between Akhmatovas and Mayakovskys. Between the two there are millennia. And they hate one another.

Akhmatova and Mayakovsky are just as antipathetic to each other as are the epochs that gave them birth. Akhma-

tova is the heir of all the precious riches of prerevolutionary Russian poetry; and she values her inheritance.... But Mayakovsky in every word and every line is the product of the present revolutionary epoch. The faith, the cry, the ecstasy, and the failures of that epoch are in his work. (p. 52)

In a word, we observe here not just a difference between two poets—who may be good, bad, or indifferent—but rather a contrast between two different worlds. Akhmatova and Mayakovsky are two incarnations of great historic forces, and each one of us must decide which of these opposites he will identify with.... (p. 53)

> *Korney Chukovsky, "Akhmatova and Mayakovsky" (originally published in* Dom iskusstv, *No. 1, 1920), translated by John Pearson, in* Major Soviet Writers: Essays in Criticism, *edited by Edward J. Brown (copyright © 1973 by Oxford University Press, Inc.; reprinted by permission), Oxford University Press, New York, 1973, pp. 33-53.**

NIKOLAI LENIN   (essay date 1922)

I do not belong to the admirers of [Mayakovsky's] poetic talent, though I fully admit my incompetence in that field. But it is a long time since I have experienced such pleasure from the political and administrative points of view. In ["Outsitters"] Mayakovsky makes deadly fun of 'meetings,' and ridicules communists who sit and oversit in sessions. I do not know about the poetry, but I vouch that politically this is absolutely correct. We do find ourselves in the position (and one must say, a silly position it is) of men who are perpetually in session, composing plans, commissions—to infinity.

> *Nikolai Lenin, in a speech delivered on March 6, 1922, in* Soviet Poets and Poetry *by Alexander Kaun (copyright © 1943 by The Regents of the University of California; reprinted by permission of the University of California Press), University of California Press, 1943, p. 56.*

LEON TROTSKY   (essay date 1924)

Mayakovsky is a big, or, as Blok defines him, an enormous talent. He has the capacity of turning things which we have seen many times around in such a way that they seem new. He handles words and the dictionary like a bold master who works according to his own laws, regardless of whether his artisanship pleases or not. Many of his images and phrases and expressions have entered literature, and will remain in it for a long time, if not forever. He has his own construction, his own imaging, his own rhythm and his own rhyme.

Mayakovsky's artistic design is almost always significant, and sometimes grandiose. The poet gathers into his own circle war and revolution, heaven and hell. Mayakovsky is hostile to mysticism, to every kind of hypocrisy, to the exploitation of man by man; his sympathies are entirely on the side of the struggling proletariat. He does not claim to be the priest of art, at least, not a priest with principles; on the contrary, he is entirely ready to place his art at the service of the Revolution.

But even in this big talent, or, to be more correct, in the entire creative personality of Mayakovsky, there is no necessary correlation between its component parts; there is no equilibrium, not even a dynamic one. Mayakovsky shows the greatest weakness where a sense of proportion and a capacity for self-criticism are needed. (pp. 147-48)

His subconscious feeling for the city, for nature, for the whole world, is not that of a worker, but of a Bohemian. "The bald-headed street lamp which pulls the stocking off from the street"—this striking image alone, which is extremely characteristic of Mayakovsky, throws more light upon the Bohemian and city quality of the poet than all possible discussion. The impudent and cynical tone of many images, especially of those of the first half of his creative career, betrays the all-too-clear stamp of the artistic cabaret, of the café, and of all the rest of it. (p. 149)

He has frequently a very high degree of pathos in his works, but there is not always strength behind it. The poet is too much in evidence. He allows too little independence to events and facts, so that it is not the Revolution that is struggling with obstacles, but it is Mayakovsky who does athletic stunts in the arena of words. Sometimes he performs miracles indeed, but every now and then he makes an heroic effort and lifts a hollow weight.

At every step Mayakovsky speaks about himself, now in the first person, and now in the third, now individually, and now dissolving himself in mankind. When he wants to elevate man, he makes him Mayakovsky. He assumes a familiarity to the greatest events of history. This is the most intolerable, as well as the most dangerous thing in his works. One can't speak about stilts or buskins in his case; such props are too poor. Mayakovsky has one foot on Mont Blanc and the other on Elbrus. His voice drowns thunder; can one wonder that he treats history familiarly, and is on intimate terms with the Revolution? But this is most dangerous, for given such gigantic standards, everywhere and in everything, such thunderous shouts (the poet's favorite word) against the horizon of Elbrus and Mont Blanc—the proportions of our worldly affairs vanish, and it is impossible to establish the difference between a little thing and a big. That is why Mayakovsky speaks of the most intimate thing, such as love, as if he were speaking about the migration of nations. For the same reason he cannot find different words for the Revolution. He is always shooting at the edge, and, as every artilleryman knows, such gunning gives a minimum of hits and tells most heavily on the guns.

It is true that hyperbolism reflects to a certain degree the rage of our times. But this does not offer a wholesale justification of art. . . . Mayakovsky shouts too often, where he should merely speak; that is why his shouting, in those places where he ought to shout, seems insufficient. The poet's pathos is destroyed by shouting and hoarseness.

Mayakovsky's weighty images, though frequently splendid, quite often disintegrate the whole, and paralyze the action. The poet evidently feels this himself; that is why he is yearning for another extreme, for the language of "mathematical formulas", a language unnatural to poetry. . . . Each phrase, each expression, each image of Mayakovsky's works tries to be the climax. That is why the whole "piece" has no climax. The spectator has a feeling that he has to spend himself in parts, and the whole eludes him. To climb a mountain is difficult, but worth while, but a walk across plowed-up country is no less fatiguing and gives much less joy. Mayakovsky's works have no peak; they are not disciplined internally. The parts refuse to obey the

whole. Each part tries to be separate. It develops its own dynamics, without considering the welfare of the whole. That is why it is without entity or dynamics. (pp. 149-52)

"The 150 Million" was supposed to be the poem of the Revolution. But it is not. The whole of this work, which is big in its design, is devoured by the weakness and defects of Futurism. The author wanted to write an epic of mass suffering, of mass heroism, of an impersonal revolution of the one hundred and fifty million Ivans. . . . [But the] poem is profoundly personal and individualistic, and in the bad sense of the term. It contains too much purposeless arbitrariness of art. The poem has these images: "Wilson swimming in fat", "In Chicago every inhabitant has the title of a general, at least", "Wilson gobbles, grows fat, his bellies grow story on story",—and other such. Such images are very simple and very rude, but they are not at all popular; at any rate, they are not the images that belong to the present-day masses. The worker, at least the worker who will read Mayakovsky's poem, has seen Wilson's photograph. Wilson is thin, though we may readily believe that he swallows a sufficient quantity of proteins and fats. The worker has also read Upton Sinclair, and knows that Chicago has stock-yard workers besides "generals". In spite of their loud hyperbolism, one feels a certain lisp in these purposeless and primitive images, of the kind grownups use with children. The simplicity that looks at us from these images does not come from a gross and wholesale and popular imagination, but it comes from a Bohemian silliness. (pp. 152-53)

Hurriedly and in passing, that is, without purpose, the author divides the whole world into two classes: on the one hand, there is Wilson, floating in fat, and with him are ermines, beavers and large heavenly stars, and on the other hand, there is Ivan, and with him are blouses and the millions of the Milky Way. . . . But in general, though the poem has a richness of expression and quite a few strong apt lines and brilliant images, it has in truth no iron lines for the blouses. Is this for want of talent? No, for want of an image of the Revolution worked over by nerves and brain, an image to which the craftsmanship of words is subordinate. The author plays the strong man, catching and throwing about one image and then another. "We shall finish you, romanticist world!" Mayakovsky threatens. That is right. One has to put an end to the romanticism of Oblomov and of Tolstoi's Karataiev. But how? "He is old —kill him and make an ash-tray of his skull."

But this is the most real and most negative romanticism! Ash-trays made of skulls are inconvenient and unhygienic. And its savagery is after all . . . meaningless? By making such an unnatural use of the skull bones, the poet becomes caught in romanticism; at any rate, he has not worked out his images, nor has he unified them. (pp. 154-55)

The poem has striking lines, bold images, and very apt words. The final "triumphal requiem of peace" is perhaps the strongest part of it. But the whole has been struck fatally, because of a lack of inner movement. There is no condensing of contradictions in order to resolve them later. Here is a poem about the Revolution lacking in movement! The images live separately, they collide and they bounce off one another. The hostility of the images is not an outgrowth of the historic material, but is the result of an internal disharmony with the revolutionary philosophy of life. However, when not without difficulty one reads the poem to the very end, one says to oneself: a great work could have been composed out of these elements, had there been measure and self-criticism! Perhaps these fundamental defects are not to be explained by Mayakovsky's personal qualities, but by the fact that he works in an isolated little world; nothing is so adverse to self-criticism and measure as living in a small group.

Mayakovsky's satirical things also lack profound penetration into the essence of things and relationships. His satire is racy and superficial. . . . Mayakovsky's satire is approximate; his racy observations from the side miss the mark, sometimes by the width of a finger, and sometimes by the width of the whole palm. (pp. 155-56)

Mayakovsky has risen from the Bohemia which brought him forth, to extraordinarily significant creative achievements. But the rod on which he has raised himself is individualistic. The poet is in revolt against the condition of his life, against the material and moral dependence in which his life, and above all, his love, is placed; and suffering and indignant against the masters of life who have deprived him of his beloved one, he rises to an appeal for revolution and to a forecast that it will fall upon the society that does not allow free space to Mayakovsky's individuality. After all, his poem, "A Cloud in Trousers", a poem of unrequited love, is artistically his most significant and creatively his boldest and most promising work. It is even difficult to believe that a thing of such intense strength and independence of form was written by a youth of twenty-two or twenty-three years of age. His "War and Peace", "Mystery Bouffe", and "150 Million" are much weaker, for the reason that here Mayakovsky leaves his individualist orbit and tries to enter the orbit of the Revolution. One may hail the efforts of the poet, for in general no other road exists for him. "About This" is a return to the theme of personal love, but is several steps behind "A Cloud", and not ahead. Only his wider grasp, and a deeper artistic volume, help him to maintain his creative equilibrium on a much higher level. But one cannot help seeing that his conscious turning to a new and essentially social direction is a very difficult thing. Mayakovsky's technique in these years has undoubtedly become more skilled, but also more stereotyped. The "Mystery Bouffe" and the "150 Million" have splendid lines side by side with fatal failures filled with rhetoric and with verbal tight-rope walking. The organic quality, the sincerity, the cry from within which we heard in "A Cloud" are no longer there. "Mayakovsky is repeating himself", some say; "Mayakovsky has written himself out", others add; "Mayakovsky has become official", others say maliciously. But is that so? We are in no haste to make pessimistic prophecies. Mayakovsky is not a youth, but he is still young. (pp. 157-58)

> *Leon Trotsky, "Futurism" (1924), in his* Literature and Revolution, *translated by Rose Strunsky, Russell & Russell, 1925 (and reprinted by Russell & Russell, 1957), pp. 126-61.**

ROMAN JAKOBSON (essay date 1931)

The poetry of Mayakovskij from his first verses to his last lines is one and indivisible. It represents the dialectical development of a single theme. It is an extraordinarily unified symbolic system. A symbol once thrown out only as a kind of hint will later be developed and presented in a to-

tally new perspective. He himself underlines these links in his verse by alluding to earlier works. In the poem "About That" . . . , for instance, he recalls certain lines from the poem "Man" . . . , written several years earlier . . . , and in the latter poem he refers to lyrics of an even earlier period. An image at first offered humorously may later and in context lose its comic effect, or conversely, a motif developed solemnly may be repeated in a parodistic vein. Yet this does not mean that the beliefs of yesterday are necessarily held up to scorn; rather, we have here two levels, the tragic and the comic, of a single symbolic system, as in the medieval theater. A single clear purpose directs the system of symbols. "We shall thunder out a new myth upon the world." (p. 141)

His first collection of poems was entitled *I*. Vladimir Mayakovskij is not only the hero of his first play, but his name is the title of that tragedy, as well as of his last collection of poems. The author dedicates his verse "to his beloved self." When Mayakovskij was working on the poem "Man" he said, "I want to depict simply man, man in general, not an abstraction, à la Andreev, but a genuine 'Ivan' who waves his arms, eats cabbage soup and can be directly felt." But Mayakovskij could directly feel only himself. This is said very well in Trotsky's article on him (an intelligent article, the poet said): "In order to raise man he elevates him to the level of Mayakovskij" [see excerpt above]. . . . Even when the hero of Mayakovskij's poem appears as the 150,000,000-member collective, realized in one Ivan—a fantastic epic hero—the latter in turn assumes the familiar features of the poet's "ego." This "ego" asserts itself even more frankly in the rough drafts of the poem.

Empirical reality neither exhausts nor fully takes in the various shapes of the poet's ego. . . . Weariness with fixed and narrow confines, the urge to transcend static boundaries—such is Mayakovskij's infinitely varied theme. No lair in the world can contain the poet and the unruly horde of his desires. (pp. 141-42)

Opposed to this creative urge toward a transformed future is the stabilizing force of an immutable present, overlaid, as this present is, by a stagnating slime, which stifles life in its tight, hard mold. The Russian name for this element is *byt*. (pp. 142-43)

Against [the] unbearable might of *byt* an uprising as yet unheard of and nameless must be contrived. The terms used in speaking of the class struggle are only conventional figures, only approximate symbols, only one of the levels: the *part for the whole*. Mayakovskij, who has witnessed "the sudden reversals of fortune in battles not yet fought," must give new meaning to the habitual terminology. In the rough draft of the poem "150,000,000" we find the following definitions:

> to be a bourgeois does not mean to own capital or squander gold. It means to be the heel of a corpse on the throat of the young. It means a mouth stopped up with fat. To be a proletarian doesn't mean to have a dirty face and work in a factory; it means to be in love with the future that's going to explode the filth of the cellars. . . . Believe me.

The basic fusion of Mayakovsky's poetry with the theme of the Revolution has often been pointed out. But another indissoluble combination of motifs in the poet's work has not so far been noticed: revolution and the destruction of the poet. This idea is suggested even as early as the "Tragedy" . . . , and later the fact that the linkage of the two is not accidental becomes "clear to the point of hallucination." No mercy will be shown to the army of heroes, or to the doomed volunteers in the struggle. The poet himself is an expiatory offering in the name of that universal and real resurrection that is to come; that was the theme of the poem "War and the World". . . . (p. 145)

Mayakovskij always regarded ironically talk of the insignificance and early disappearance of poetry (really nonsense, he would say, but useful for the purpose of revolutionizing art). He planned to pose the question of the future of art in the "Fifth International" . . . , a poem that he worked on long and carefully but never finished. According to the outline of the work, the first stage of the Revolution, a worldwide social transformation, has been completed, but humanity is bored. *Byt* still survives. So a new revolutionary act of world-shaking proportions is required: "A revolution of the spirit in the name of a new organization of life, a new art and a new science." The published introduction to the poem is an order to abolish the beauties of verse and introduce into poetry the brevity and accuracy of mathematical formulas. He offers an example of a poetic structure built on the model of a logical problem. When I reacted skeptically to this poetic program—the exhortation in verse against verse—Mayakovskij smiled: "But didn't you notice that the solution of my logical problem is a trans-sense solution?"

The remarkable poem "Homeward!" . . . is devoted to the contradiction between the rational and the irrational. It is a dream about the fusion of the two elements, a kind of rationalization of the irrational. . . . (pp. 146-47)

The idea of the acceptance of the irrational appears in Mayakovskij's work in various guises, and each of the images he uses for this purpose tends to reappear in his poetry. (p. 147)

Mayakovskij's central irrational theme is the theme of love. It is a theme that cruelly punishes those who dare to forget it, whose storms toss us about violently and push everything else out of our ken. And like poetry itself this theme is inseparable from our present life; it is "closely mingled with our jobs, our incomes, and all the rest." And love is crushed by *byt*. . . .

Eliminate the irrational? Mayakovsky draws a bitterly satirical picture. On the one hand, the heavy boredom of certain rational revelations: the usefulness of the cooperatives, the danger of liquor, political education, and on the other hand, an unashamed hooligan of planetary dimensions (in the poem "A Type" . . .). Here we have a satirical sharpening of the dialectical contradiction. Mayakovsky says "yes" to the rationalization of production, technology, and the planned economy if as a result of all this "the partially opened eye of the future sparkles with real earthly love." But he rejects it all if it means only a selfish clutching at the present. If that's the case then grandiose technology becomes only a "highly perfected apparatus of parochialism and gossip on a worldwide scale" (from an essay "My Discovery of America"). Just such a planetary narrowness and

parochialism permeates life in the year 1970, as shown in Mayakovskij's play about the future, "The Bedbug" . . . , where we see a rational organization without emotion, with no superfluous expenditure of energy, without dreams. A worldwide social revolution has been achieved, but the revolution of the spirit is still in the future. The play is a quiet protest against the spiritual inheritors of those languid judges who, in his early satirical poem "without knowing just why or wherefore, attacked Peru." Some of the characters in *The Bedbug* have a close affinity with the world of [Yevgeniy] Zamyatin's *We* . . . , although Mayakovskij bitterly ridicules not only the rational utopian community but the rebellion against it in the name of alcohol, the irrational and unregulated individual happiness. (p. 148)

Mayakovskij has an unshakable faith that, beyond the mountain of suffering, beyond each rising plateau of revolutions, there does exist the "real heaven on earth," the only possible resolution of all contradictions. *Byt* is only a surrogate for the coming synthesis; it doesn't remove contradictions but only conceals them. The poet is unwilling to compromise with the dialectic; he rejects any mechanical softening of the contradictions. The objects of Mayakovskij's unsparing sarcasm are the "compromisers" (as in the play *Mystery-Bouffe*). (p. 149)

In Mayakovskij's earliest writings personal immortality is achieved in spite of science. . . . At that time he regarded science as an idle occupation involving only the extraction of square roots or a kind of inhuman collection of fossilized fragments of the summer before last. His satirical *Hymn to the Scholar* turned into a genuine and fervent hymn only when he thought he had found the miraculous instrument of human resurrection in Einstein's "futuristic brain" and in the physics and chemistry of the future. (pp. 152-53)

Whatever the means of achieving immortality, the vision of it in Mayakovskij's verse is unchangeable: there can be no resurrection of the spirit without the body, without the flesh itself. Immortality has nothing to do with any other world; it is indissolubly tied to this one. . . . Mayakovskij's dream is of an everlasting earth, and this earth is placed in sharp opposition to all superterrestrial, fleshless abstractions. In his poetry and in [Viktor] Khlebnikov's theme of earthly life is presented in a coarse, physical incarnation (they even talk about the "meat" rather than the body). (p. 153)

The vision of a future that resurrects people of the present is not simply a poetic device that motivates the whimsical interweaving of two separate narrative levels. On the contrary—that vision is Mayakovskij's most cherished poetic myth.

This constant infatuation with a wonderful future is linked in Mayakovskij with a pronounced dislike of children, a fact which would seem at first sight to be hardly consonant with his fanatical belief in tomorrow. But just as we find in Dostoevsky an obtrusive and neurotic "father hatred" linked with great veneration for ancestors and reverence for tradition, so in Mayakovskij's spiritual world an abstract faith in the coming transformation of the world is joined quite properly with hatred for the evil continuum of specific tomorrows that only prolong today ("the calendar is nothing but the calendar!") and with undying hostility to that "broody-hen" love that serves only to reproduce the present way of life. (pp. 153-54)

There's no doubt that in Mayakovskij the theme of child-murder and suicide are closely linked: these are simply two different ways of depriving the present of its immediate succession, of "tearing through decrepit time."

Mayakovskij's conception of the poet's role is clearly bound up with his belief in the possibility of conquering time and breaking its steady, slow step. He did not regard poetry as a mechanical superstructure added to the ready-made base of existence (it is no accident that he was so close to the formalist literary critics). A genuine poet is not one who feeds in the calm pastures of everyday life; his mug is not pointed at the ground. . . . Mayakovskij's recurrent image of the poet is of one who overtakes and passes time, and we may say that this is the actual likeness of Mayakovskij himself. Khlebnikov and Mayakovskij accurately forecast the Revolution (including the date); that is only a detail, but a rather important one. It would seem that never until our day has the writer's fate been laid bare with such pitiless candor in his own words. Impatient to know life, he recognizes it in his own story. The "Godseeker" Blok and the Marxist Mayakovskij both understood clearly that verses are dictated to the poet by some primordial, mysterious force. . . . The poet is the principal character, and subordinate parts are also included; but the performers for these latter roles are recruited as the action develops and to the extent that the plot requires them. The plot has been laid out ahead of time right down to the details of the denouement. (pp. 154-55)

A simple résumé of Mayakovskij's poetic autobiography would be the following: the poet nurtured in his heart the unparalleled anguish of the present generation. That is why his verse is charged with hatred for the strongholds of the established order, and in his own work he finds "the alphabet of coming ages." Mayakovskij's earliest and most characteristic image is one in which he "goes out through the city leaving his soul on the spears of houses, shred by shred." The hopelessness of his lonely struggle with the way things are became clearer to him at every turn. The brand of martyrdom is burned into him. There's no way to win an early victory. The poet is the doomed "outcast of the present." (p. 156)

> *Roman Jakobson, "On a Generation That Squandered Its Poets," translated by Edward J. Brown (originally published as "O pokolnii, rastrativshem svoikh poetov," in his* Smert poeta; *copyright © 1931 Petropolis-Verlag; Petropolis-Verlag, 1931), in* Twentieth-Century Russian Literary Criticism, *edited by Victor Erlich (copyright © 1975 by Yale University; reprinted by permission of Yale University Press and the author), Yale University Press, 1975, pp. 138-66.*

C. M. BOWRA (essay date 1949)

Before the Revolution of 1917 Mayakovsky's poetry followed a natural line of development. . . . His poetry is entirely personal and displays the paradoxes and contradictions which we might expect from a man of his ebullient personality and restricted circumstances. It was only natural that at times he should be stridently self-assertive and self-confident, and at other times relapse into self-mockery and self-abasement. His confidence in his own powers was tempered by his knowledge that the age was hostile to him and that his chances of making a mark were small. Just as his fellow Futurists drew attention to themselves by painting pictures on their faces, so Mayakovsky wore an enormous tie, and found that it made an effect. His poetry has something of the same spirit. One of his first poems . . . is called *I* and speaks with candour about himself. *Vladimir Mayakovsky . . .* was an attempt to portray him as a fanciful hero in conflict with typical figures of his time. In *Spine-Flute . . .* his personal feelings are again the chief subject, and in *Man . . .* he composed a drama about himself in the manner of the Gospel story. . . . The self-assertion in these poems was partly a tactical move but more urgently a spiritual need. Mayakovsky had to unburden his feelings, to release his conflicting emotions, to take the world into his confidence. He was a powerful elemental being who knew that extraordinary powers were at work in him and that he must let them speak.

In these poems Mayakovsky fused his warring elements into a single result. His self-assertion and his self-pity, his caustic satire and his strange lyrical quality, are inextricably entangled not only in the same poem but often in the same line. The combination and quality of his gifts can be seen from *A Cloud in Trousers*. . . . The poem is planned in four parts, which deal successively with love, art, society and religion. But of course the treatment of these subjects is very much Mayakovsky's own and has a highly personal touch. Beginning with an unhappy love-affair he delivers his attacks on most aspects of the world which concern him and creates a special kind of poetry, crowded with images, violent in its expression, and yet undeniably melodious and striking and at times even touching. It shows what Mayakovsky felt at an important crisis of his career. The outbreak of war and the failure of a love-affair brought many powers in him to work and produced the most characteristic and remarkable of his early poems. (pp. 101-02)

A Cloud in Trousers is in the first place remarkably candid and intimate. Mayakovsky has no false modesty, and sets out his emotions exactly as they are. To this candour his art makes a special contribution. Though he habitually uses violent metaphors and hyperboles, he is always in effect true to what he feels. His violence reflects his real self and is not a means of rhetoric, and once we recognise this, we see how acute an observer Mayakovsky is of himself. (p. 102)

This intimacy is presented through a remarkable variety of effects. At first sight some are so surprising that we may fail to see how true they actually are, how well they reflect an extremely agitated and troubled mind in which the fancy is set to work by uncontrollable emotions. For instance, the third part contains an account of a stormy sky in which the poet sees signs and portents of political brutality. He does not spare the details of the comparison between the sky and the forces of reaction:

> From behind stormclouds thunder emerged, ferociously,
> Blew its colossal nose with a reverberating bark,
> And the skyface for a second twitched rapaciously
> In the grim grimace of an iron Bismarck.

Now that is not really in the least strained. To the poet's haunted fancy, full of fears of persecution and injustice, it is only too natural that the sky should take on this character and behave in this way. Against this he sets his hopes of revolution, and for the moment knows that they are useless. . . . Mayakovsky drew his imagery from his actual experience, and, through his great powers of fancy and emotional drive, was able to make it highly relevant to his lovelorn state.

Perhaps the most striking quality of *A Cloud in Trousers* is the way in which Mayakovsky brings off the most reckless experiments. At times he unleashes his fancies, lets them chase a theme which seems to have little relevance to his immediate subject, and yet bring it home successfully. His way of showing how violent his feelings are is that no comparison is too strong for them and that his nature is so primitive and primaeval that it can only be measured correctly against violent natural forces. Thus he takes up the notion that his heart is aflame with love,—but this flame is a conflagration, and he makes the most of the parallel. His words rush forth from him, "like whores from a burning brothel". He tries to jump out for safety:

> Let me escape from my ribs for a start.
> I jump! I jump! I jump! I jump!
> I crashed back.
> You can't jump out of your heart!

This is of course a trope, but a trope conceived so genuinely that it performs a special function. It shows that Mayakovsky is on the edge of hysteria and that the image which forms in his brain affects him so powerfully that he almost believes in it and must think in terms of it. . . . In 1913 this was certainly a new kind of poetry, but it is, for all its strangeness, perfectly sincere and true. This is what Mayakovsky felt, and his art is perfectly adjusted to his feelings.

A Cloud in Trousers shows the anguish and hysteria of a powerful personality when he finds circumstances beyond his control and attacking him in all the activities which he thinks important. Through it there breathes an angry spirit of revolt. But anger was not Mayakovsky's only weapon. He was a master of controversy in more than one form. Most characteristic perhaps is an ironical exaggeration which makes his opponent's case look absurd. By seeming to treat it with politeness and reason Mayakovsky grossly misrepresents it. He rejected with passionate disgust the religious orthodoxy of his time, but he did not allow his indignation to get the better of him or to make him heavy-handed. His method can be seen from *Listen,* where he tilts against the theological argument from design and the belief that the starry skies are evidence for the existence of God. . . . (pp. 103-05)

In this poetry Mayakovsky is extremely self-centred. He could hardly be otherwise, since he is defending his precious gift of poetry and all that it means to him against an unfriendly world. Even when he falls in love, he speaks chiefly of his misery, and tenderness or affection seldom competes with his desire for conquest and possession. And this, too, is to be expected. Mayakovsky's poetry rises out of his conviction that he possesses special powers to create and transform, and for this reason he writes about himself. But this self-absorption is not matched by an equal self-confidence. At times he suggests that he is not his own master but the plaything of uncontrollable powers which will break him if he is not careful. He seems to have felt this specially about love. He knew all too well what it meant, and he was uneasy about a passion which so under-

mined his self-confidence and made him the prey of incalculable forces. He gave expression to this fear in a remarkable poem, *To myself the beloved are these lines dedicated by the author. . . .* The poem moves through a resplendent series of fanciful hyperboles, but they cloak a real emotion,—the poet's desire not to surrender himself because he feels that if he does, strange powers will be unleashed and shake the world. (p. 110)

The whole poem moves at a level of delightful absurdity, but it is built on a real fear, and this playfulness is Mayakovsky's escape from it.

This sense of great powers in himself, and of their conflict with the world, dictated most of Mayakovsky's early poetry. For him the creative principle lay in this central, primitive strength which he found in himself. His conviction that he must at all costs preserve it and exercise it forbade him to yield to anything which demanded the submission of his will or his intelligence. This created difficulties for him in his approach to his art. It made him a rebel in literature because only by being true to his own unusual poetical instinct could he be himself, and his gifts were not those of other men. (p. 111)

[The First World War] called out Mayakovsky's most human and most tender qualities. He showed that underneath his irony and his display he hid a love for his fellow men. Though he was appalled by the carnage and the cant, he did not surrender to despair. He characteristically looked for a solution and found it in the new comradeship which the victims of war had learned through their common agony, and he proclaimed that before long this would lead to revolution. He believed that great natural forces were all on his side, that the Rhine and the Danube, China and Persia, would help his cause. He discovered that his own creative qualities were somehow those of the common people in many lands, and he was eager that the whole world should join him in abandoning war and promoting human brotherhood. This wild hope finally broke down Mayakovsky's defences and turned him from a self-centred into a public-minded poet. Here was a cause which responded to his conviction that the artist should be a man of action and made him at last feel that he was not a misunderstood oddity but a man who felt as the mass of other men felt. The war not only confirmed and justified him in his revolutionary views, but gave him a new insight and sympathy. He believed that mankind was changing. . . . This conviction and this hope united his different gifts and showed him what to do. His central flame was now single and shed its light on a prospect of a world free and active as Mayakovsky had known himself to be in his creative hours. Just as Blok saw in the Revolution the transformation of ordinary men into a nation of artists, so Mayakovsky foresaw an unleashing of enormous powers and the creation of a new humanity.

In 1917 Mayakovsky's hopes were realised. . . . In *Liberty for All* [Viktor] Khlebnikov sings his song of the triumphant proletariat. . . . (pp. 114-16)

Mayakovsky shared [his] exultant confidence and gave his own version of it in *Our March.* . . . Mayakovsky's poem is not pantheistic like Khlebnikov's, but it has the same sense of great events afoot, of enormous powers liberated, and of vast prospects in the immediate future. His old contempt for the past has produced a fierce desire to transform the present into something swift and marvellous: his Futurist's love of speed has turned from machines to human beings: his irreligion has become a spur to drive mankind on to the conquest of the physical universe. *Our March* is a peak in Mayakovsky's career. In it all his lyrical spirit is at work in harmonious unison. It is his finest and almost his final word on the dynamic urgency which he felt in himself and in mankind, his purest expression of the creative force which made him both a poet and revolutionary. (pp. 116-18)

[*Mystery-Bouffe*] was rightly hailed as a new departure in Russian literature. It is in fact a kind of Aristophanic fantasy, though Mayakovsky might not have appreciated the comparison. It is Aristophanic in its mixture of boisterous, knock-about fun and lyrical delicacy, in its great assortment of characters who vary from typical workmen and contemporary figures, like Clemenceau and Lloyd George, to machines and things, in its clean-cut distinction between the good and the bad characters, who are the Unclean and the Clean, the workers and the capitalists. . . . It is a myth of the struggles and triumph of Communism and bears as little relation to reality as Aristophanes' *Birds*. But it is a wonderful feat of creative imagination. . . . (p. 118)

Mystery-Bouffe is by no means a mere fantasy of ideas. It has a peculiar dramatic quality. There are excellent passages of comic dialogue and intrigue as when Lloyd George at the North Pole is mistaken for a walrus, or the Negus is thrown overboard from the ark, or the inhabitants of Heaven are fussed by the arrival of a lot of unexpected guests, or the devils complain of the dullness of their life. The characters, though sketched in broad lines, have at least the vitality of farce. . . . Though there is a slight thread of allegory in the persistent theme of the hunger which dogs the Unclean, it is not at all troublesome but gives an extra point to the struggles which the Unclean endure to gain some sort of happiness and freedom. The final scene has great variety and vitality. There is a delightful moment when the workers refuse to believe that the earth is theirs to be enjoyed and cling to their old notion that they will have to pay for it until the Things apologise for the trouble they have caused, owing to unjust masters, in the past, and promise a new and better order. . . . [The] chief quality is the lyrical exaltation which shows Mayakovsky's finest qualities of work in his conviction that natural powers will now serve man and lay the universe at his feet. (p. 120)

[Mayakovsky] had always been a child of nature, and now he believed that he was nature's ally and agent in bringing her gifts to a liberated world. How much this belief meant to him can be seen from *An Extraordinary Adventure*. . . . He tells of a hot summer in the country when he finds the sun unendurable. He playfully summons it to visit him—and the sun comes. . . . The vivid myth has its moments of fanciful absurdity, as when the sun shines "overtime" and smacks the poet affectionately on the back. But there is truth behind it. Mayakovsky really felt that he was inspired by natural powers and to some degree resembled them. He felt so sure of his task and his place in the new society that he could compare himself to the sun and think the comparison not entirely absurd. He believed that his own gifts were an example of what belong to most men when the bondage of an effete system is broken, that what matters most is this new confidence which he had found and thought that others had found too. If he had a gospel, it was that for free men nothing is impossible.

Yet while he was thus indulging his newly found liberty, Mayakovsky, with a curious contradiction that lay deep in his nature, was not entirely convinced that a poet must follow his own fancies and not make himself immediately useful by advocating urgent social and political causes. . . . In *Command to the Army of Art* . . . he shows how he interprets his task. He vents his old contempt on established writers and summons his Futurists to action. . . . He argues that there is still a need for poets because they give life to other men. He is convinced that they have a social task and that their place is in the midst of new developments and their work among the common people. . . . He did not at first notice that this conception of poetry was at variance with his own lyrical spirit, that it demands a different technique and a different outlook from what had hitherto been his. Mayakovsky still believed that he could combine his old gifts with his new social outlook, and for a short period he succeeded in creating a compromise between them.

Mayakovsky soon felt pressure not only from his own sense of social responsibility but from external powers. (pp. 121-22)

[*150,000,000,*] written with great force and with much of Mayakovsky's old brilliance, falls into two parts, the first dealing with a general justification of the Soviets, the second with a myth which portrays their future victory over the forces of Capitalism. In the first part Mayakovsky has hardened and clarified his ideas and brought them into harmony with current thought. His old playful blasphemies are replaced by a conscious conformist atheism. . . . So Mayakovsky created the poetry which his time demanded. His contemporaries, released from their old religion and trusting innocently in the promises of science, believed that with a little effort they could realise the dreams of Jules Verne and H. G. Wells. Mayakovsky agreed with them and proclaimed that theirs was a force that nothing could withstand. . . . Despite its purely mythical and fantastic air *150,000,000* is based on a dogmatic belief that the Communist system is bound to conquer because it makes a proper use of human nature and natural resources. Mayakovsky indicates the power behind mechanisation with his poetry of an enormous people on the march, and his irresistible Ivan, who is like a volcano or a tidal wave. The poem takes full account of revolutionary doctrine and is in many ways a glorification of it. It has been transformed into poetry and engages Mayakovsky's most characteristic gifts.

150,000,000 is Mayakovsky's last attempt to combine Futurism with political poetry, the last poem in which he gave full rein to his ebullient fancy. After it he wrote a great deal, but not in this way. He became more and more a public figure, a tribune of the Revolution, who through his rhetorical verse did much to convince the proletariat that it lived in a wonderful world and must make every effort to preserve and improve it. To make his message more effective he trimmed and simplified his style and abandoned most of his earlier wildness. The change in his art reflected a change in his time. The first ecstatic years of revolutionary optimism were finished, and the time of organisation and discipline followed. Futurism of Mayakovsky's kind was no longer appreciated, and Mayakovsky himself decided to compose in a different way. But in these first years, between 1912 and 1922, he had done something sufficiently remarkable. He had created a special kind of poetry in which his words were not only poured out in a white heat of excitement but succeeded in reflecting important elements in the contemporary consciousness. More than anyone he broke down the hieratic dignity of Russian poetry and replaced it with a special version of living experience. His technique, which owed so little to anyone else, was highly modern in the exactness and truth which it allowed. . . . His was a peculiar creative gift, half lyrical and half satirical. It was well suited to these years of change, and though some may not like it, we cannot deny its originality and its power. (pp. 125-27)

> *C. M. Bowra, "The Futurism of Vladimir Mayakovsky," in his* The Creative Experiment *(copyright; reprinted by permission of Macmillan, London and Basingstoke), Macmillan, 1949, pp. 94-127.*

HELEN MUCHNIC (essay date 1958)

There is no more tragic poet than [Mayakovsky] in Russian literature, and it will not do to hold society, nor even individuals, responsible for his tragedy; it was not by his world, but by himself that he felt oppressed, and it is difficult to imagine any external circumstances that would have brought him happiness. (p. 264)

Of all Russian writers, Gogol was the favorite of his youth. He must have sensed in him his own variety of loneliness, the kind that turned what was not himself into the monstrous, the cruel, and the alien. Like Gogol, he was a humorist, but it can be as truthfully said of him as of Gogol that those who think him funny do not know how to read him. Gogol's laughter, as he himself explained, was the product of despair; he escaped from depression into an imaginary world of absurdity, but he never proclaimed his misery so openly as Mayakovsky, for he had accepted his alienation to this extent at least, that he had no desire to exhibit it. Mayakovsky, on the other hand, instead of fleeing to a never-never land, caricatured his own experience. He remained the central figure of his tragic work, instead of obliterating himself in fantastic tales as Gogol had done. For since he had never fully accepted the difference between the *I* and the *non-I,* he wanted to explain himself and to unite himself to the world of men and things. There is, of course, this all-important difference between them, that whereas at the heart of Gogol's unhappiness lay a sense of loss and inadequacy, Mayakovsky's self-pity was based on a feeling of power, of an insufficiently appreciated grandeur. His tragedy had in it an element of paradox; it was the inarticulateness of the outspoken, the tragedy of those who seek to relieve pain by trying to explain it, although they know that pain is incommunicable and that when it is past cure, no one can be of help. A cry of pain is without purpose; and much of Mayakovsky's best work is in essence such a cry, disguised though it is as rational protest. (pp. 265-66)

[He] was nothing if not honest. His denunciations of society, of art, of morals and ideas were rooted in a loathing of pretense. It was honesty that made him blunt: the world was crude and ugly, his own experience was bitter; he despised artists who insisted on sweetness, and hated all men who loved comfort of body and ease of mind. There was much in him of the nineteenth-century Russian nihilists, of Turgenev's Bazarov. But he was not so independent as they. He needed people not only for approval but for self-

realization, and belonged to the type of rebel whom Albert Camus has called the Dandy, the man who does not know that he exists unless others can serve him as mirrors. . . . (p. 266)

[Roman Jakobson] has called his poetry "a scenario according to which he acted out the film of his life." . . . [Both] scenario and life were built on a process of mystification, that "playing with reality" which Boris Eichenbaum has shown to be the essence of Gogol's work. When Mayakovsky pictured himself as Man or Poet, as the martyred savior of humanity, or as the sun's comrade, he was indulging in a kind of solemn, baffling joke on the order of his other grotesques: the gruesome images of the bleeding world in *War and the Universe,* the huge fantasy of warring objects and the duel of giants in *150,000,000,* the pictorial caricature of history and religion in *Mystery-Bouffe.* All are exaggerations intended to teach a lesson. As pictures they are unambiguous; all is black and white in them, there are no complexities here, there is no shading. But they are jokes. . . . Whatever the motive—pride, vanity, or despair—this necessity to conceal lay at the heart of his work, although it appeared in the semblance of self-exposure.

Negation was the principle of Mayakovsky's life; and parody, which is a form of negation, was something more with him than a favorite trick of art. It was an ingrained habit of thought. His image of himself as a tragic hero was really a parody of the traditional concept of tragedy. . . . In his tragic role Mayakovsky was defiant and self-sufficient. He passed judgment on himself, annihilated death, and talked to posterity. But he parodied even his own idea of tragedy when, attempting to achieve something like comic catharsis, he burlesqued his suffering and presented himself as a kind of *miles gloriosus,* simulating absurdly the attributes of gods or nature. He did not manage to obtain what he desired; his performance was gravely earnest, even at its most preposterous; if he "stepped on the throat of his own song" he could not stamp it out, and his ultimate parody of artistic revelation lies in the doubt with which he leaves us as to how much of his clowning he intended to be taken seriously.

Ridicule absolved him of cosmic terror, and his anthropomorphism took rise in the opposite feeling from that which is usually presumed to motivate it. Usually, it would seem, the darker, the less explicable, the more awful an aspect of nature, the more does man seek to humanize it, wishing to diminish his fear of the incomprehensible by seeing it as human. But Mayakovsky's anthropomorphism is either a kind of camaraderie in which man fraternizes with nature, animals, and things, or a ghoulish force that turns what is perfectly familiar into something ominous and sinister. In his use of the pathetic fallacy, it is not nature that responds to man's experience, but man who sympathizes with nature —since in his view of life man is all-encompassing and nature is part of him, not he of nature. When he wishes to present whatever seems to transcend men's limitations— greater powers, greater achievements than theirs—he neither elevates the human being to the rank of deity nor invests him with supernatural qualities but, in a way that parodies heroic myth, extends men's capacities within the realm of nature and confers earthly status on the superhuman. . . . (pp. 267-69)

He loathed assent and had an imperative need to assert himself through contradiction, but his negation was not absolute, not like Rimbaud's, for instance. It was provoked by a respect for justice, and was aimed not so much at a transvaluation of values as at a redefinition of men's attitudes. He plotted, denounced, and blasphemed in the name of right, truth, and independence. Like Rimbaud, he wished to turn habitual concepts upside down, to shock men out of complacency; the stance of opposition was in itself important to him, and he delighted in blasphemy. But the blasphemy of *Une Saison en Enfer* has a suave elegance that Mayakovsky's lacks, for it is the witty statement of a personal experience, of one man's conclusions about human history and human ideals, whereas the parody of Christ and the Beatitudes in *Mystery-Bouffe*, for example, or the conclusion of *The Cloud in Trousers*, or the sketch of heaven in *About What? About This* are didactic, and purposefully grotesque, for they are tools in an ideological battle, not private visions. Mayakovsky and Rimbaud were kindred spirits, but in their most intimate experience they were each other's opposites. Rimbaud thought himself endowed with superhuman qualities which, being man, he was doomed to lose; from his idealistic heights he must come down to earth.... Mayakovsky, on the other hand, who held that there was nothing greater than to be simply man, felt in himself angelic qualities and powers that transcended the earth.... Rimbaud's negation was absolute, because it came of an embittered sense of loss; Mayakovsky's was a tentative first step on his way to the grand affirmation of a universal Utopia. (pp. 269-70)

[Not only] did Mayakovsky write for the street, he wrote in the street; and his verse swings to the rhythm of his [long, uneven] stride and bears the accent of his heavy step and the casualness of informal meetings. Loud, determined, staccato, beating with the pulse of the day, there is no intimacy in it, nothing of that "inner life" that Mayakovsky seems to have denied himself for the sake of an audience of which he was always aware. Powerful and defiant, he believed himself free, but he never could or would have said, like Beethoven about his quartets, that he was writing for himself. If he dreamed, he paid no attention to his dreams. Even his surrealist effects were consciously contrived; nothing welled up unasked from the unconscious, and his visions of the future give the impression of having come not of insight, but of fantastic desire. When from painting the real he passed to the imaginary, he refused to note the transition or admit the irrationality of his visions. Just as he himself had become indistinguishable from the part he had undertaken to play, so hyperbole, which he had originally adopted as an artistic device, came to stand in his mind for reality. His will was stronger than his judgment. His thought was as rhetorical as his style; his poetry, his life, and his reasoning were passionate and narrow. An immoderate and violent man, he had no capacity for analysis or detachment; he did not criticize, he damned; he did not love, but worshiped; he could hate and despise, but not dislike.... He made his reason fight unhappiness and his public voice shout down the private one.... His work was a process of willful exclusion, and it is strong by reason of its passion, not its wisdom. Sometimes it seems the poetry of a nihilist Beethoven, without Beethoven's melody or lightness, but with his power to record the grandeur of rebellious suffering. And sometimes it reminds one of those primitive sculptures, massive and rough, that seem to express the anguish of a child helplessly possessed by an overwhelming emotion. His self-analyses indicate a struggle between a sense of his own greatness and his desire to be at one with the masses of men. But he has nothing of that large, generous ease, that undiscriminating joy in life which Whitman makes a virtue and the basis of his love of men. Mayakovsky is all tension, striving, willing. He is united with humanity not in feeling, but on principle. The principle is the magnet of his vigorous emotions, and it is therefore passionately argued. A megalomaniac image is made to express the nature of humanity. It was as if a Russian Rimbaud had tried to make himself the Whitman of the proletarian revolution.

It is an indication of Mayakovsky's complex and paradoxical nature that he should have combined the characteristics of two such opposite souls as Walt Whitman and Rimbaud.... [His] poetry often reminds one of Whitman's. Like his, it is made to be spoken and has a similar loose, oratorical structure, the long line, the marked, emphatic beat, the calculated crudeness, and there are passages in it which unmistakably echo Whitman. But Whitman's long rhythms are Biblical; Mayakovsky's re-create the cadence of his own steps. Whitman's praise of man, his exultation in the body, his love of humankind must certainly have appealed to Mayakovsky. Yet in *150,000,000* he pictures him derisively as "rocking a cradle in imperceptible rhythm" and bearing the highest title which Americans bestow on a poet, "honored smoother of ladies' wrinkles." He was too much of a rebel to tolerate Whitman's open-hearted geniality. Never could he have been a Good Gray Poet; and even if like Whitman he loved things and men in the abstract, his feeling for them was not exactly comradely; his pride in them and in himself was too involved in suffering to be joyous; the violence of his love resembled hatred. In his rebelliousness he was closer to Rimbaud.

But his was a primal, Promethean revolt that took place in the void and was itself a kind of parody. There was no Zeus for him to defy, and, unlike Rimbaud, he had never believed in the God whom he addressed. His blasphemy was, in effect, denunciation of men's folly and a cry of resentment for his own suffering. He addressed himself to a nothingness, a cosmic injustice that had once been given a name, and which men worshiped as good—and he pitied men for adoring this embodiment of tyranny, and, wanting to cure them of error and to lead them out of torment, courted them in the dual capacity of martyr and jester.... (pp. 271-73)

As artist, Mayakovsky was the opposite of the Shakespeare once described by Coleridge as one who "first studied patiently, meditated deeply, understood minutely, till knowledge, become habitual and intuitive, wedded itself to his habitual feelings." Mayakovsky had respect for neither meditation nor patience. Instead of study and minute understanding, he pounced on events and molded them in the roughly hewn formulas of reason-masked prejudice. Nevertheless, his loud rhetoric, inflated imagery, propagandist simplifications, his broken rhythms and brutal words achieve aesthetic wholeness, because they contain in themselves their reason for being. There is grandeur in them, and the strength of immediacy, the sense, that is, of something lived, not borrowed from talk about life. They express the upheaval, willfulness, and negation which are the mark of his day; and neither the bold, bright way he used the language of the street, nor the raw agony of his impassioned love, nor his crude but pointed wit are likely to be soon forgotten. (p. 274)

*Helen Muchnic, "Vladimir Mayakovsky" (origi-
nally published in* The Russian Review, *Vol. 17,
No. 2, April, 1958), in her* From Gorky to Pasternak: Six Writers in Soviet Russia *(copyright ©
1961 by Helen Muchnic; reprinted by permission
of Random House, Inc.), Random House, 1961,
pp. 185-275.*

BORIS PASTERNAK   (essay date 1959)

I liked Mayakovsky's early lyrical poetry very much.
Against the background of buffoonery that was so characteristic of those days, its seriousness—so heavy, so menacing, and so plaintive—was quite unusual. It was a poetry
beautifully modelled, majestic, demonic, and, at the same
time, infinitely doomed, perishing and almost calling for
help. (p. 93)

[He] says:

> Not for you to understand why, calm
> Amid the storm of gibes,
> My soul I carry on a plate
> For the feast of coming years. . . .

It is impossible not to think of parallels from the liturgy:
"Be silent, all flesh of man, and stand in fear and trembling
and think not of earthly things. For the King of Kings and
the Lord of Lords cometh to offer Himself as a sacrifice
and as food to the faithful."

In contradiction to the classics, to whom the sense of the
hymns and prayers was important, . . . the fragments of
Church canticles and lessons are dear to Blok, Mayakovsky, and Esenin in their literal sense, as fragments of everyday life, in the same way as the street, the house, and
any words of colloquial speech are dear to them.

These ancient literary deposits suggested to Mayakovsky
the parodical structure of his poems. One can find in him a
great many analogies with canonical ideas, hidden or underlined. They called for something vast and mighty, they
demanded strong hands and trained the poet's audacity.
(pp. 93-4)

Compared with Esenin, Mayakovsky's genius was coarser
and more ponderous but, to make up for it, perhaps vaster
and more profound. The place nature occupies in Esenin is
occupied in Mayakovsky's poetry by the labyrinth of a
modern big city, where the solitary soul of modern man has
lost its way and become morally entangled and whose passionate and inhuman situations he depicts. (p. 97)

[My own] intimacy with Mayakovsky has been exaggerated. Once, at [Nikolai] Aseyev's, where we had a discussion about our differences, which have become more acute
since then, he characterized our dissimilarity in these
words: "Well, what does it matter? We really are different.
You love lightning in the sky and I in an electric iron!"

I could not understand his propagandist zeal, the worming
of himself and his friends by force into the public's consciousness, his idea that a poem could be written by several
hands, by an association of craftsmen, and his complete
subordination to the demand for topical subjects. (pp. 97-8)

With the exception of the immortal document *At the Top of
the Voice,* written on the eve of his death, the later Mayakovsky, beginning with *Mystery Buffo,* is inaccessible to
me. I remain indifferent to those clumsily rhymed sermons,

that cultivated insipidity, those commonplaces and platitudes, set forth so artificially, so confusedly, and so devoid
of humor. This Mayakovsky is in my view worthless, that
is, nonexistent. (pp. 98-9)

*Boris Pasternak, "Before the First World War,"
in his* I Remember: Sketch for an Autobiography,
*translated by David Magarshack (copyright ©
1959 by Pantheon Books, Inc.; reprinted by permission of Pantheon Books, a Division of Random
House, Inc.; in Canada by William Collins Sons &
Co. Ltd.), Pantheon, 1959, pp. 71-101.*

PATRICIA BLAKE   (essay date 1960)

Of the thirteen volumes of [Mayakovsky's] complete
works, about one-third consists of fulminations on patriotic
and political themes. Another third is composed of serious
"revolutionary" poems which are quite original in their
genre and which still to-day can evoke some of the fervour
of the early years of the Bolshevik revolution. What remains are his satiric plays, and his lyrics on the themes
which were central to Mayakovsky's life: a man's longing
for love and his suffering at the hands of the loveless; his
passion for life and his desolation in a hostile and inhuman
world; his yearning for the absolutes of human experience
and his rage at his impotent self. (p. 53)

Mayakovsky represented an affront to the values and sensibilities of the liberal intelligentsia. For all those who cared
for the sweet and solemn diction of Russian verse, Mayakovsky sounded a monstrous clangour. His thumping
rhythms, his declamatory style, his use of puns, neologisms, and *outré* images shattered every standard of verbal
behaviour. And, for all those who cherished the Russian
intelligentsia's humanistic traditions, there was something
horrifying about Mayakovsky's self-absorption—his craving
for melodrama, his penchant for high tragedy, and his fascination with the drumbeat of revolution. (p. 55)

[His] harsh and violent idiom was far closer to the mood of
elemental Russia than the elegant language of the "gentlemen poets" who warbled (in Mayakovsky's phrase) of
"pages, palaces, love, and lilac blooms." Yet in his early
poetry he was almost entirely absorbed by his personal
torments. Then, it was Pasternak, of all the writers bound
to the humanistic tradition, who understood Mayakovsky
best. Pasternak was later to reject his political verse, but in
Mayakovsky's early lyrics he saw "poetry moulded by a
master; proud and daemonic and at the same time infinitely
doomed, at the point of death, almost an appeal for help"
[see excerpt above].

Indeed, from these lyrics rises a single cry of pain, at times
barely tolerable to the human ear. His poetic techniques
served above all to sharpen the impact of his feelings on the
senses of the reader—or rather, of the listener—for his
verses were written to be read aloud. Poetry was his confessional, his lectern, and his soap-box. Here he always
assumed the first person, the "I" with which he could directly assail his audience with every detail of his personal
affairs, and every nuance of his feelings.

In . . . *The Cloud in Trousers,* he begins with an attack on
the sentimental drawing-room poets who cannot turn themselves inside out; then he proceeds to do just that. Rejected
by his beloved, he eviscerates first himself, and, ultimately,
the universe. His screams claw his mouth apart, a nerve

leaps within him like a sick man from his bed. He will root up his soul, and, trampling it to a bloody rag, offer it to his beloved as a banner. *"Look!"* he cries, *"again they've beheaded the stars / and the sky is bloodied with carnage."* Here, in these images of terror and violence, is Mayakovsky at his best and worst. Most often he is the master of his material, but sometimes he loses control and staggers out of the bounds of art into the realm of psychopathology. Then the poet's anguish appears unnecessary, excessive, artificial. It is at such moments that Mayakovsky's great weakness is most apparent. This weakness lay not in the over-abundance of passion, but, all too often, in the absence of it. Clearly, he felt a deadness in himself which demanded quickening. Hence, he was constantly exacerbating his feelings; only when he had thus roused himself to an extremity of emotion did he feel wholly alive. All the extravagances of this astonishing man's life—his dramatic involvements with women, his intoxication with Bolshevism, and, paradoxically, even his obsession with suicide— must be understood in this sense. (pp. 55-6)

Vladimir's love for Lily, and others, ... resulted in some remarkable lyrics, among them: *I Love* ..., an anguished declaration of love for Lily; *About This* ..., his cry of despair at Lily's infidelity; *Letter from Paris to Comrade Kostrov on the Nature of Love* ..., a direct expression of the rival claims of love and Communism on the poet.

The struggle within Mayakovsky between the propagandist and the lyric poet sharpened in the mid-'twenties. For one thing, his position as the foremost revolutionary poet was being questioned. (p. 58)

[*Back Home!*] is at once the most outrageous and the most pathetic expression of Mayakovsky's attraction to dictatorship—outrageous, as he calls upon the Gosplan, a commissar, a factory committee, and Stalin himself to command his work—and pathetic as he explains, *"I / from poetry's skies / plunge into Communism, / because / without it / I feel no love."* The mood did not last long. ...

During the two years before his suicide he came closest to an awareness of the nature of the society he had once acclaimed. He saw the conflict between the ideals and the reality of Communism, between the individual and the collective, between the artist and the bureaucrat. And although this knowledge ultimately proved intolerable, it is to Mayakovsky's honour that, at the last, he chose to confront it in his art.

In 1928, he wrote one of the most devastating satires of Communist society in contemporary literature: *The Bedbug (Klop)*. In the first half of the play, he sees the Russia of 1928 in terms of the Soviet bourgeoisie: the profiteers, the Party fat cats, the proletarian philistines. His villain is Prisypkin, the bedbug-infested, guitar-strumming, vodka-soaked vulgarian who is the possessor of a Party card and a proletarian pedigree. In the second half, Mayakovsky foresees the Communist millennium. Now, in 1978, the excesses of a Prisypkin are unthinkable. Sex, vodka, tobacco, dancing, and romance are merely items in the lexicon of archaisms. The hero? None other than Prisypkin who has been resurrected as a zoological curiosity and who begins to look nearly human in this dehumanised world. He is lost, frightened, utterly deprived of love—in short, he is a caricature of his author. To sharpen the resemblance on stage, Mayakovsky took pains to teach the actor who played Prisypkin his own mannerisms.

Mayakovsky was making fun of his own youthful hopes in the second part of *The Bedbug*. (p. 59)

His last important poem, the unfinished *At the Top of My Voice*, was conceived as a monument to a doomed man— Vladimir Mayakovsky. The poem was clearly inspired by Pushkin. ...

Here, in *At the Top of My Voice*, he made a final defence of the purity of his ideals and the quality of his accomplishments in the name of socialism, *"above the heads / of a gang of self-seeking / poets and rogues."* Here, too, he indicated the cost of these accomplishments: *"Agitprop / sticks / in my teeth too / ... But I / subdued / myself, / setting my heel / on the throat / of my own song."* (p. 61)

> *Patricia Blake, "The Two Deaths of Vladimir Mayakovsky" (reprinted by permission of the author; originally published in a different form in* The Bedbug and Selected Poetry *by Vladimir Mayakovsky, translated by Max Hayward and George Reavey, edited by Patricia Blake, Meridian Books, 1960), in* Encounter, *Vol. XV, No. 2, August, 1960, pp. 52-63.*

RENATO POGGIOLI   (essay date 1960)

From the technical standpoint, Majakovskij's greatest contribution to Russian poetry consisted of making a working instrument of *vers libre*. (p. 265)

[Unlike other poets of that medium, Majakovskij] preferred to use conventional strophic schemes in his lyrics, especially those having the character of odes and hymns, and used free verse only for his longer poems, in which he never completely renounced the ornament of rhyme. As a matter of fact, Majakovskij treated rhyme with full freedom, from the viewpoint of its richness and frequence, as well as from the viewpoint of its position and quality. Hypermetric, compound, and equivocal rhymes abound in his poems, where they produce striking, and often grotesque, effects. Majakovskij stretched the traditional rhyming freedom of Russian verse to the point of changing the identical endings into distorted echoes, vague phonetic approximations, consonances and assonances. If by doing this he followed the example of the popular songs of his time, generally urban or proletarian in origin, in the matter of rhythm he based his metrical reform on his unerring instinct, rather than on theory and experiment; the method which his insight made him choose was merely the spontaneous imitation of the accentual versification of the ancient Russian folk song.

Despite his keen sense for all the values of language and meter, Majakovskij was temperamentally the least interested, among the leading Futurists, in questions of craft and technique. A born poet, he conceived of his art as a medium toward an end, rather than as an end in itself. From this viewpoint he played within the Futurist movement a role not dissimilar to the one Blok had played within the Symbolist school. ... Despite all appearances to the contrary, his muse, like Blok's, was a muse of disaster: and the poet acted like an echo reproducing and repeating the noise of the storm then raging over Russia and the world. Majakovskij, however, was not content to remain a passive echo, and joined his voice with that of the storm. And unlike Blok, who almost against his will turned even the discord of the elements into a harmony and melody of his own, Majakovskij based the rhythms of his poetry on what he called "the cacophony of wars and revolutions."

The wordless music of Blok's poetry is better felt by the inner ear, while Majakovskij's verse is written to be read aloud, in a resounding voice. As such, it is the perfect verbal instrument of an inspiration which may be defined, without derogatory intent, and without contradiction of what has just been said, as essentially declamatory in character. (pp. 266-67)

The poems of Majakovskij must always be shouted, rather than recited or chanted, "at the top of *one's* voice," to use the title of his last, splendid, and unfortunately unfinished composition. In later years Majakovskij was forced to recognize that when a poet uses a loudspeaker, he is bound to utter alien words, and to speak, rather than with his own, with "his master's voice." One could even say that this revelation led him finally to his ordeal, and to his very death; yet it remains undeniable that there existed, for a brief span of time, an authentic affinity, and a kind of kinship, between the climate of the Revolution and the inspiration of its greatest poet.

This does not mean that his muse was anonymous or collective. Majakovskij paid only lip service to the early slogans of both Futurism and proletarian poetry, always being unable to replace the Romantic or Decadent "I" with the "we" of the group, or of the masses. A stentorian voice is not necessarily a choral one: it may be the voice of a heroic ego, or of a virtuoso singing solo his own tunes. Thus Majakovskij's poetry was public merely in the sense that it was often performed publicly, and with great effect. He was not so much a proletarian poet as an urban one, loving the open, and yet walled, spaces, of the metropolis, with its squares and avenues, alleys and streets. In other terms, he was a city poet, rather than a civic one; not a popular, but a plebeian artist. (pp. 267-68)

Majakovskij's poetry is as highly individualistic as [Konstantin] Bal'mont's or [Igor] Severjanin's, especially at the beginning of his career. His lyricism, always obsessive, becomes often sentimental and even pathetic. Even his humorism, when directed toward the self of the poet, is like the humorism of a suffering clown, producing grotesque effects, such as those in his youthful poems devoted almost exclusively to the unhappy love affairs of their author. In them self-irony may lower itself to the level of an unconscious self-parody. In one of those early pieces, the poet sings of his own passion by accompanying himself on the "flute" of his own spinal chord; in another one, he mirrors his own mood of love and despair in the self-image of "a cloud in trousers." These two metaphors show that the states of mind dominating his inspiration are exasperation and paroxysm. The poet cultivates and expresses his own psychic urges by employing two typical media of advance-guard poetry, the "hyperbolic" and the "iconoclastic" image, which are both the symptoms and the symbols of his own poetic pathos. The first type of image is directly derived from the poet's megalomania; yet it is sometimes able to sublimate itself into a kind of cosmic vision. The second type derives equally directly from his nihilism and cynicism; yet, not infrequently, it transcends the very ugliness of the experience it intends to convey.

The poetic practice of Futurism influenced Majakovskij's imagery in both form and matter, as is proved by its fre-

quent reference to the world of machinery. Like [Viktor] Khlebnikov, Majakovskij looks at the machine as an instrument of war and death, rather than as a working tool; yet this view is not derogatory in character, as is shown by a famous passage in *At the Top of My Voice,* in which he compares the series of his lines to rows and weapons, to armed ranks. This mechanistic imagery is nihilistic in essence; and one could say that Majakovskij exalted the Revolution as an engine of destruction, rather than as a machine helping to construct a new world. Although ideologically a Marxist, psychologically he was an anarchist; and this may help to explain certain aspects of his art, the crisis of his life, and the tragedy of his death. (pp. 268-69)

> *Renato Poggioli, "The Poets of the Advance Guard," in his* The Poets of Russia: 1890-1930 *(copyright © 1960 by the President and Fellows of Harvard College; excerpted by permission), Cambridge, Mass.: Harvard University Press, 1960, pp. 238-75.**

DALE E. PETERSON (essay date 1969)

Unlike Mayakovsky, Whitman was able to incorporate his "hankering, gross, mystical, and nude" self into a personally viable organicist mythology of Nature. In purely pragmatic terms, Whitman's persona proved to be a "live option." It worked as a life-model and kept Whitman afloat, a "Me Imperturbe," amidst the churning seas of his inner experience. (p. 417)

By contrast, Mayakovsky's lyric persona is neither therapeutic nor inspirational; he is a scapegoat without a cosmological rationale. Recoiling from life's inherent frustrations, he plays Harlequin, a holy fool, who enacts the Christian vicarious atonement, but without God (or History) in the wings to redeem the gesture. Whereas Whitman's "self" loafs in the cycles of the years, confident that a slight upward spiral marks the close of each cycle, Mayakovsky's persona writhes in anticipation, searching for a misplaced eschatology.... Time is experienced not in generous cycles but in vicious circles. Hence, whereas Whitman's chants are attuned to the ebb and flow of eternally recurrent energies (sprouting grass, tides, copulation), Mayakovsky's lyrics, as Renato Poggioli noticed, toss fitfully between hyperbole and iconoclasm, alternately arousing and razing expectations [see excerpt above]. Typically, the Mayakovskian persona, after indulging in brilliant verbal calisthenics, reaches a pathetic impasse: "the one who aspires to the role of the 'hero' cannot find or create a significant myth." True, both poets are primarily singers of outsized selves. But Whitman celebrates an "infinite and omnigenous" capacity to assimilate experience, while Mayakovsky bellows forth an inflated intensity of experience. The one strikes a pose of general hospitality to the chances of life; the other, curiously fastidious by comparison, "seized life in a death-grip," to quote [Roman] Jakobson's epigram. Whitman sexualized society and the universe, then saluted the world with libidinal gusto. Mayakovsky found life impersonal, so he impersonated the ideal lover and flaunted his bruised heart at a frigid world.

This radical disparity in content is formally ensconced in the linguistic structure of each poet's variant of "free verse." Neither Whitman nor Mayakovsky yields easily to traditional systems of scansion. When read, their verse produces the effect of a highly structured mode of expression; yet, when scanned, it reveals no recognizable pattern of syllabic, tonic, or even accentual regularity. (pp. 417-18)

The fundamental structural principle in Mayakovsky's free verse in no way resembles Whitman's syntactic organization. Although no consensus of expert opinion exists in Mayakovsky's case, the two most plausible structural explanations will suffice to indicate the . . . implications of Mayakovsky's mode of free verse. Roman Jakobson sees at the core of Mayakovsky's declamatory verse a return to Russian folk narratives which predated the academic scansions and rested firmly on conversational, "reduced" pronunciations. In Mayakovsky's verse the accentual sequences follow the factual and oral, rather than the lexical and academic stress patterns. But the typographical layout often burlesques the "reduced" pronunciation until a true *reductio ad absurdum* results: "Subsidiary, weakly stressed words receive strong stresses, as if these words were being spoken for the first time." The end effect of this accentological "estrangement" is a poetry of isolated, self-sufficient words and word-phrases. In such an atomized linguistic structure, words are simultaneously made new and made grotesque by the exaggerated and fastidious attention paid to oral patterns of enunciation.

Finding no adequate linguistic structural principle in Jakobson's stress on dislocated metrics, the Soviet scholar M. P. Shtokmar has advocated another approach to Mayakovsky's *vers libre:* "Rhyme is the genuine motive force of Mayakovsky's verse." Much like the Russian folk *raeshniki* and Pushkin's *Skazka o pope i rabotnike ego Balde,* Mayakovsky's verse, in Shtokmar's opinion, struck an unprecedented emphasis on a strictly acoustical patterning of rhyme consonances. Hence the prolific frequency of compound, hypermetric, and imperfect rhymes amidst a sea of metrical and syllabic irregularities. (p. 419)

As in Whitman's case, there are profound semantic implications embedded in the peculiar organization of the given free verse form. The autonomous rhyme system which Shtokmar finds in Mayakovsky clearly accommodates a comic content. . . . This comic thrust in Mayakovsky's verse form is significantly deflected, however, by the implications of Jakobson's accentological "estrangement." The typographical oddities of the Mayakovskian line have an ambivalent effect. On the one hand, they befit a declamatory verse form by forcing the reader into a precise oratorical enunciation of isolated words and word-phrases. The Mayakovskian line lends majestic possibilities of dignity and self-sufficiency to ordinary words which are so easily slurred in full sentence contexts. On the other hand, the arbitrary violence done to syntax reinforces the grotesque impact of hyperbole, burlesque, and semantic incoherence. In short, the raw linguistic data behind Mayakovsky's free verse provide a vehicle for a highly oral poetry that is comic, but pointedly mock-epic in context. It is a peculiar verse form, one loose enough to indulge in a shocking sort of buffoonery. Whereas Whitman's Biblical cadences can occasionally accommodate an exuberant jocularity, Mayakovsky's gruff staccatos often foster the wry humor of irreverent repartee.

Like Whitman, Mayakovsky did lend his name and biography to a hyperbolic persona poetically projected. But the image of man presented through this artificial personality is in no way derivative from Whitman. The Mayakovskian

Man is not the anthropocentric and representative "self" about which Whitman "yawped" so barbarically. In the simple juxtaposition of *Leaves of Grass* with *A Cloud in Trousers* we see dramatized the comparatively unearthly and impatiently otherworldly inclination of Mayakovsky's lyric gift. Whitman's "self" is a "caresser of life wherever moving"; Mayakovsky's "Man" is a homeless angel, trumpeting apocalypse to a deaf universe. (pp. 420-21)

Whitman chose ideally to be an imperturbable reflector of the world's panoply of colors. Mayakovsky chose to concentrate life's radiant energies to the point of a scorching, life-destroying intensity. Mayakovskian Man has his heart fixed on life *in extremis;* consequently, his rigid insistence on ecstasy makes him apocalyptic and world-demolishing by instinct. Whitman's persona is a jubilant litanist, celebrating a "self escaping a series of identities which threaten to destroy its lively and various spontaneity." The two poets share in common the fact that each purveyed in verse an exaggerated image of man. In Mayakovsky that exaggeration is expressed in a form that entertains hyperbole, puns, rhyme, and all manner of linguistic grotesquerie. In content, it is a poetry at war with the world; witty, bitter, and ultimately masochistic, it rages against the limits within which humans must enact life, from sex to syntax. In Whitman, who condemned rhyme as suitable only for persiflage, exaggeration is formally embodied in omnivorous, enumerative sentences. In content, his poetry expresses the psalmist's loving assimilation to the wonders of a world without end. Whitman's self is a personified mosaic of life. . . . Mayakovsky's Man is a walking icon, equally an abstract transfiguration and equally vulnerable to iconoclasm. As for the "Whitmanesque" in Mayakovsky, it does not go very deep. It is, indeed, little more than a false scent that has waylaid too many fine critics for too long. (pp. 424-25)

> *Dale E. Peterson, "Mayakovsky and Whitman: The Icon and the Mosaic," in* Slavic Review *(copyright © 1969 by the American Association for the Advancement of Slavic Studies, Inc.), Vol. 28, No. 3, September, 1969, pp. 416-25.*

HAROLD B. SEGEL (essay date 1979)

[It was in a spirit] of theatrical innovation and renovation that *Vladimir Mayakovsky: A Tragedy* was written. The title is well chosen, for the play is wholly a projection of Mayakovsky himself. Not only did Mayakovsky stage it, play the lead role, and assign himself the declaration of both Prologue and Epilogue, but he made himself—his poetic uniqueness, genius, and destiny—the subject of the work. (p. 138)

The Prologue and Epilogue, devices later to be used more effectively in the two versions of *Misteriya-Buff* . . . , establish an unmistakable theatricalist presence. The radical departure from illusionistic drama is still more pronounced in the case of characters. Apart from Mayakovsky himself we find such items as The Enormous Woman who does not speak and is fifteen to twenty feet tall; an Old Man with Scrawny Black Cats, who is "several thousand years old"; . . . a Woman with a Tiny Tear, and others. Whimsy, obviously, and theatrically realizable only by virtue of a director's imagination. The imagery of the dialogue sustains the fantasy of the characters. Exuberant, novel, at times brilliant, often excruciatingly obscure, it impresses ultimately as dazzling and narcissistic verbal showmanship. (pp. 138-39)

Analyzing *Vladimir Mayakovsky* for sense is as speculative as trying to invest an abstract painting with a specific meaning. Reacting impressionistically, the viewer, or reader, grasps the exaltation of poetic self-celebration. Mayakovsky projects himself as the embodiment of the spirit of poetry, of creative energy, as the dawning of a new era of poetic expression. But the dawning of the new must be preceded by the destruction of the old, and so the appeal to destroy resounds loudly through the two short acts of which *Vladimir Mayakovsky* consists. In subtitling his play "a tragedy" perhaps the poet intended more than whimsy or the response of disbelieving laughter. Extended throughout the play is the insinuation of spiritual anguish masked by the outward gaiety of the creative artist as jester. Endowed with a transcending, immortalizing power the poet nonetheless cleaves to a solitary path. Perceiving beyond the finite capacity of ordinary mortals, he knows the true pain of existence. The sorrows of others represented by the tears offered him in Act II only repel him; he is weighted down by his own burden. But in the end the poet cannot turn away. Self-fulfillment must be more than withdrawn self-adulation and a public mask of joy. And so, reluctantly, the poet accepts the tears. . . . The acceptance of the anguish of mankind becomes the ultimate self-realization of the poet whose creative power alone holds the possibility of a reordering of existence. (pp. 139-40)

Apart from the use of prologue and epilogue and the appearance of such fantastic characters as the Enormous Woman and the Old Man with Scrawny Black Cats, Mayakovsky's first play is considerably less noteworthy as an exercise in theatricalism than *The Fairground Booth*. That Mayakovsky was thinking along theatricalist lines when he wrote his "tragedy" is evident from the film and theater essays written in the same year. But *Vladimir Mayakovsky* is an immature work as drama, a platform from which a beginning author convinced of the magnitude of his poetic genius could publicly proclaim his own advent as a poet. This he sought to do by astounding, shocking, and mystifying, but the posturing and self-glorifying of the playlet relate more to Mayakovsky's own artistic development at the time than to the expansion of a Russian theatricalist art. (p. 141)

The burden the poet declares his willingness to accept, finally, in *Vladimir Mayakovsky* is borne positively, even rapturously in Mayakovsky's first postrevolutionary dramatic work, *Mystery-Bouffe*. . . . *Mystery-Bouffe* is a political play hailing the ultimate triumph of the workers of the world. Structured like a medieval mystery with the biblical account of Noah's Ark as its point of departure, it presents the boarding of a new ark by seven pairs of Clean (capitalists, imperialists, rulers, and their henchmen) and seven pairs of Unclean (workers) after the Flood inundates the earth's surface. When the Clean attempt to impose their will on the Unclean during the voyage, they are unceremoniously tossed overboard. . . . [The Unclean ultimately] enter the promised land where worker and machine are now united not for the enslavement of man but for the betterment of man, where a new society—a true paradise on earth—will be created.

The obvious ideology of the play, reinforced especially in the later version by an epilogue consisting of the singing in chorus by the Unclean of an adaptation of the Communist *Internationale*, may suggest a tedious exercise in tendentious drama, but this is by no means the case. The posturing and Futurist-Surrealist mannerisms of *Vladimir Mayakovsky* behind him, Mayakovsky created in *Mystery-Bouffe* a true revolutionary drama but at the same time a more impressively theatricalist play striking for its farcical action and humor.

The choice of form was no literary accident. Structuring a revolutionary political drama along the lines of a medieval mystery with all its traditional religious associations is an irreverence rich in mocking irony. *Mystery-Bouffe* is a repudiation of Christianity, of Christian concepts of Heaven and Hell. That this repudiation assumes the form of a mystery play only sets the mockery in bolder relief.

Other factors besides the satiric may have influenced Mayakovsky in his choice of dramatic structure. One, certainly, was the theatrical. Mayakovsky had a good knowledge of European drama and theater and was well aware that medieval religious drama accommodated laugh-provoking scenes of sheer buffoonery. There is much of this in *Mystery-Bouffe*, particularly in the journey of the Unclean through Heaven and Hell.

Medieval drama and such early manifestations of European domestic secular comedy as the fourteenth- and fifteenth-century German Shrovetide comedies (*Fastnachtsspiele*) also made extensive use of prologues and epilogues. . . . The direct communication with the audience on the part of the author himself or through a character or characters which prologues and epilogues made possible appealed to Mayakovsky's sense of the theatrical and confirmed his interest in medieval drama. (pp. 141-42)

Mystery-Bouffe was not Mayakovsky's last theatricalist play. Elements of theatricalism reappear in his two later satirical comedies *Klop* . . . and *Banya*. . . . (p. 144)

The fantasy [*The Bedbug*] begins with the fifth scene; until then, in a little less than half the work, the play is a satirical comedy of manners spiced by elements of the absurd and grotesque.

As the play opens to the cacophonous cries of typical NEP peddlers hawking everything from herring to fur-lined bras, interest rapidly centers on the comic hero of *The Bedbug*, Ivan Prisypkin, whom the dramatis personae identify as a former worker and Party member but now a fiancé. Although he piously mouths Party platitudes and sneers at anything to do with the petty bourgeoisie, it is obvious that Prisypkin himself has picked up something of the hedonism of NEP and its new bourgeois tastes. . . . [His] wedding celebration dissolves into chaos; a stove is overturned, the house catches fire and collapses, burying all the celebrants.

With the fifth scene, Mayakovsky moves the comedy onto the level of science-fiction fantasy. The time is fifty years later and the Institute of Human Resurrection learns that a human being was found frozen in an ice-filled cellar on the site of the former city of Tambov. It is, of course, Prisypkin, the only survivor, of sorts, of the fire. The decision is taken to resurrect him and the experiment succeeds.

The "resurrection" of Prisypkin, apart from the intrinsic humor of the situation, directly relates to Mayakovsky's satirical intentions in the play. The society in which Prisypkin is brought back to life is remarkably advanced technologically. It is automated and dehumanized; the emotional responses of earlier days are nonexistent—no more than terms of historical significance. It is, in effect, Mayakovsky's projection of a future machine-dominated Soviet society bereft of any trace of human compassion. In the broader context, it is the anxiety-ridden vision of European expressionism which beholds a future in which man, wholly subordinate to the machine, is reduced to the level of an unfeeling automaton. The dread this vision inspires pervades the literature of expressionism and a play such as *The Bedbug* shares the apprehension. Even considering the absurd and grotesque satire typical of NEP comedy and the play's topical aspect—the dehumanization of society brought on not only by technological advance but also by the rapid growth of a monstrous and impersonal Soviet bureaucracy—Mayakovsky's comedy can be related to such representative Expressionist dramas as the Czech Karel Čapek's once very popular *R.U.R.* . . ., and the German Georg Kaiser's no less famous "Gas" trilogy. . . . (pp. 204-06)

The evolution of Mayakovsky's outlook is interesting to consider at this point. In his early poetry and in his first major dramatic work, *Mystery-Bouffe,* he shared the ideas as well as the stylistic techniques of European futurism. The Futurists welcomed the advances of technology. They measured human progress in technical terms and saw the machine, about which they rhapsodized, as man's liberator and savior. The celebration of the machine with which *Mystery-Bouffe* comes to a joyous conclusion is a typical Futurist response.

But the Mayakovsky of a decade later had different ideas and these found expression in both *The Bedbug* and *The Bathhouse.* So dehumanized does man become in consequence of the advance of the machine and the machinelike bureaucracy that by contrast even a coarse vulgarian like Prisypkin seems attractive. This is the point Mayakovsky makes with the strange events that follow Prisypkin's "resurrection." Prisypkin's zest for life becomes infectious and is regarded as a dangerous malady. Worse than anything, however, is the gradual reawakening of love, long thought totally eradicated in the new society. . . . (p. 206)

The bedbug motif from which the play derives its title operates in a twofold way. The ultrahygienic society of the future, of course, is insect-free, so when a bedbug appears "resurrected" along with Prisypkin it has to be kept in a special glass exhibition cage in a zoo. On one hand, it cannot be allowed to wander about freely lest it spread contagion, while on the other, as a curious natural relic of the past it is worth preserving for public exhibit. The director of the zoo seizes on the idea of advertising for a human being willing to be caged with the bedbug so that it can feed on him and remain alive. Since Prisypkin's presence in the new society is becoming less tolerable with every passing day, the director's hope is that he will come forward and agree to be caged with the bedbug. This is precisely what happens. Prisypkin is not at all unhappy about the situation because in the exhibition cage he is at least able to drink as he pleases and to sing and play the guitar to his heart's content. By remaining in the cage, even though the bedbug feeds on him and his movements are restricted, he has some awareness of himself as a human being. And perhaps even the bedbug crawling on him is not wholly unpleasant, for this too remains a link with a more human past.

By having Prisypkin *prefer* to live in the zoo with the bedbug rather than remain abroad in the new society, Mayakovsky carries his indictment of his projected anti-utopian world to its logical extreme. In terms of his "human-ness," Prisypkin's decision in favor of cohabitation with a bedbug in a cage in preference to the dehumanized conditions he finds all around him in the new world of tomorrow is natural. But as Mayakovsky extends the bedbug motif it becomes apparent that the automated society of the future is not the only target of his satire. However attractive Prisypkin becomes by contrast with the society of the future into which he is resurrected, he remains the same vulgarian, the same travesty of a NEP social climber he was before, and once the satire of the "new world" is unequivocally established Mayakovsky returns to the satire of everything formerly represented by Prisypkin. (pp. 207-08)

The mingling of satire, absurd and grotesque humor, and fantasy reappears in *The Bathhouse.* . . . But compared to *The Bedbug, The Bathhouse* is less ambivalent in its satire. The target here is the new Soviet bureaucracy. It is embodied, above all, in the figures of Comrade Pobedonosikov, the head of the government Bureau of Coordination, and his administrative secretary Comrade Optimistenko (Optimistic). (p. 209)

Future time, which Mayakovsky makes the springboard of fantasy in *The Bedbug,* recurs prominently in *The Bathhouse* as well; but not exactly in the same way. In *The Bedbug,* roughly the second half of the play is set in Mayakovsky's future society. In *The Bathhouse,* a visitor from the future (the Phosphorescent Woman) appears by means of [a] time machine. She states her intention of taking into the year 2030 some of the best specimens of the new Soviet society for which she has such high regard. (p. 212)

[But when] the machine finally begins its trip into the future with a great explosion, Pobedonosikov, Optimistenko, and [other would-be time travellers] are sent sprawling to the ground. The message is clear: in the millennial socialist society of the far distant future there is no place for the Pobedonosikovs, Optimistenkos, and their like. (p. 213)

Although cloaked in absurdity and grotesqueness, Mayakovsky's last plays reveal an unmistakable undercurrent of disillusionment with the course of Soviet society. (p. 223)

Mayakovsky's use of utopian and anti-utopian motifs in drama goes back to his first version of *Mystery-Bouffe* in 1918. Coming almost at the same time as the Bolshevik Revolution, that curious mixture of mystery play, buffonade, theatricalist manifesto, and futurism hailed the anticipated, imminent paradise on earth of the Soviet state. It envisioned a utopia in which man emerges from the night of capitalist exploitation and degradation and enters into a day of socialist egalitarianism and humanism. By the end of the NEP period, however, Mayakovsky's utopian vision had soured into anti-utopian disenchantment. And this despair was bluntly expressed in his plays of 1928 and 1929 and even more eloquently by his suicide in 1930. (pp. 223-24)

Harold B. Segel, in his Twentieth-Century Russian Drama: From Gorky to the Present *(copyright © 1979 Columbia University Press; reprinted by permission of the publisher), Columbia University Press, 1979, 502 p.**

ADDITIONAL BIBLIOGRAPHY

Alexandrova, Vera. "Vladimir Mayakovsky (1893-1930)." In her *A History of Soviet Literature*, pp. 53-68. Garden City, NY: Doubleday & Co., 1963.
    A biographical sketch of Mayakovsky and chronological discussion of his poems and dramas.

Bunin, Ivan. "Six Miniatures." In his *Memories and Portraits*, translated by Vera Traill and Robin Chancellor, pp. 193-206. Garden City, NY: Doubleday & Co., 1951.*
    A contemporary's first-hand sketch of Mayakovsky, bitterly portraying him as a boorish hypocrite.

Humesky, Assya. *Majakovskij and His Neologisms*. New York: Rausen Publishers, 1964, 269 p.
    A compilation of Mayakovsky's linguistic innovations, and discussion of their structure and their stylistic and semantic value.

Katayev, Valentin. *The Grass of Oblivion*. New York: McGraw-Hill Book Co., 1970, 222 p.
    The author's remembrances of his friendship and conversations with Mayakovsky, including an account of the poet's activities on the eve of his suicide.

Lavrin, Janko. "Vladimir Mayakovsky." In his *Russian Writers: Their Lives and Literature*, pp. 305-25. New York: D. Van Nostrand Co., 1954.
    Cogent criticism of the high points of Mayakovsky's canon.

Slonim, Marc. "Essenin, Mayakovsky, and Prolecult." In his *Modern Russian Literature: From Chekhov to the Present*, pp. 249-68. New York: Oxford University Press, 1953.*
    A life of Mayakovsky, chronicling his literary career, and discussing his writings in relation to the events of his life and the artistic and political spirit of the times. His technique is also explained.

Stahlberger, Lawrence Leo. *The Symbolic System of Majakovskij*. Slavistic Printings and Reprintings, edited by C. H. Van Schooneveld, vol. XIV. The Hague: Mouton & Co., 1964, 151 p.
    A study of some of the basic types and symbols of Mayakovsky's work, attempting to demonstrate his consistent view of humanity and the world.

Woroszylski, Wiktor. *The Life of Mayakovski*. New York: The Orion Press, 1970, 559 p.
    A biography of Mayakovsky, composed of extracts from his autobiography, fragments of police records, and the reminiscences of his mother, acquaintances, and associates.

Edna St. Vincent Millay

1892-1950

(Also wrote under pseudonym of Nancy Boyd) American poet, dramatist, essayist, librettist, and translator.

Millay was an exceptionally popular poet whose poems, like F. Scott Fitzgerald's fiction, caught the mood of the postwar revolt against convention. She is remembered primarily for her early books of poetry, which collectively form an extended personal testament. The poems of this period are elegiac, their attitude hedonistic. Millay is at her best when conveying intense emotional experience, and for that reason has often been called a modern Romantic.

Some critics have noted that Millay's readers often seem more interested in the poet than in the poetry, and her life was colorful enough to support that position. She was at the center of Greenwich Village artistic life in the twenties and her self-dramatizing way of life caused her to be labeled a female Byron. Because she was born and raised in a small Maine town, some saw her hedonism as the bravura of an innocent who had decided to master the evils of city life.

Millay's success came early; her first major poem, "Renascence," was published when she was nineteen, and her early books were both critically and popularly admired. *Fatal Interview* in particular is often praised as one of the most artistically successful of modern sonnet sequences. Millay's popularity was at its height when she received the Pulitzer Prize in 1923 for *The Ballad of the Harp-Weaver*. The poems of this period were primarily concerned with her own emotional life. However, her concern for Sacco and Vanzetti in the late twenties led her to reexamine her poetic priorities. As she became more interested in social and international problems, her work became increasingly didactic and journalistic. Her popularity waned with a series of wartime propaganda poems and she died in relative obscurity.

After an initial period of resounding praise, critical opinion divided. She is most often discussed by later critics as a minor lyric poet who failed to develop beyond her early successes. Her work has been termed verbose, pretentious, and artificial. The latter charges stem from Millay's use of archaic word forms, traditional structures, and a coy, girlish tone which made even her strongest feminist statements palatable to the general public. On the other hand, there are critics, such as Edmund Wilson, who consider her one of the few modern poets whose stature matches that of great literary figures. To support their contention these critics point to her pervasive wit, lyric skill, and her distinguished contribution to the sonnet form.

Besides poetry, Millay wrote several lyric dramas and an opera libretto, *The King's Henchman*, which is considered an important contribution to American opera. Her fame rests, however, with her poems of love and loss, the work that made her the unofficial feminine laureate of the twenties.

PRINCIPAL WORKS

Renascence, and Other Poems   (poetry)   1917
Aria da Capo   (drama)   1921
A Few Figs from Thistles   (poetry)   1921
The Lamp and the Bell   (drama)   1921
Second April   (poetry)   1921
Two Slatterns and a King   (drama)   1921
The Ballad of the Harp-Weaver   (poetry)   1922
The Harp-Weaver and Other Poems   (poetry)   1923
Distressing Dialogues [as Nancy Boyd]   (essays)   1924
The King's Henchman   (drama)   1927
The Buck in the Snow, and Other Poems   (poetry)   1928
Fatal Interview   (poetry)   1931
Wine from These Grapes   (poetry)   1934
Conversation at Midnight   (poetry)   1937
Make Bright the Arrows   (poetry)   1940
Collected Sonnets   (poetry)   1941
Collected Lyrics   (poetry)   1943
Collected Poems   (poetry)   1956

JESSIE B. RITTENHOUSE   (essay date 1918)

[*The Lyric Year*] presented one poem of remarkable

imagination—*Renascence,* by Edna St. Vincent Millay. . . . Now, however, after six years in which Miss Millay, who was a school girl when she wrote the poem, has been at college, studying and developing,—appears *Renascence and Other Poems.*

One almost fears to re-examine a poem which, six years ago, seemed not only individual but unique, lest the rapid changes in form and theme through which we have been passing should have rendered it out of date and robbed it of vitality. One is relieved to find that this is not the case. While the poem has naturally its immaturities, it remains a remarkable production not only for a girl of nineteen, but for anyone. *Interim,* though written later, shows more of youth and has less certainty of touch than *Renascence.* This is largely due to its form. It is written in the diffuse, conversational style so much affected of late, a style that permits instant transitions from the sublime to the ridiculous. Between pathos and bathos there is but a letter, a hair's-breadth, which it is almost impossible not to cross in a soliloquy of this sort. Yet, immediately following some passage of love or loss that William Archer would call "domestic," may come one of stark poignancy which shows how deeply, after all, this young poet can feel.

If we emphasise Miss Millay's youth, it is because it is so obviously the cause of whatever limitations her poems yet show. *Interim* was written, if I remember correctly, only two years after *Renascence.* In *Suicide* the touch is much more sure, though in individual passages *Interim* rises higher. All of these poems reveal a gift whose potentialities impress themselves constantly upon the reader. This is just as it should be. A first book should be rich in foretokens, it should hint of something beyond its fulfilment, and no one can read Miss Millay's volume without recognising the authentic poet.

Aside from *Renascence* itself, the most successful poems in the book are certain lyrics such as *When the Year Grows Old,* and the group of sonnets at the end of the book. Here Miss Millay has both simplicity and magic. She is quite herself: promise and performance are one. (p. 682)

> *Jessie B. Rittenhouse, "Contemporary Poetry," in* The Bookman *(copyright, 1918, by George H. Doran Company), Vol. XLVI, No. 6, February, 1918, pp. 678-83.**

MAXWELL ANDERSON   (essay date 1921)

Edna St. Vincent Millay's *Second April* is [not] above criticism. In common with all other poets of the period she often searches in vain for a subject and at last contents herself with a theme too slight or too fantastic to be worth handling. There is small excuse for *The Blue-Flag in the Bog* or *The Bean-stalk*—none in fact, save the artistry wasted on them. The theme of *Doubt No More That Oberon* is so hackneyed that one is left flatly wondering why it should have been printed. The *Ode to Silence,* the longest venture in the volume, is an artificial ecstasy; exquisite treatment cannot save it.

But *Inland, Wild Swans,* the *Elegy,* and the third of the twelve sonnets are powerful, humanly moving, perfectly touched, said as only a first-class artist could say them. There are other things of nearly equal excellence, and the whole book rises above the tin-pan procession of the usual

by virtue of an almost flawless sensitiveness to phrase. Miss Millay, also, is one of the most clear-headed poets who ever put pen to paper. She is akin to Burns in the definiteness of her object and the astonishing accuracy with which she finds the exact homely image to clinch her meaning. . . .

Second April resolves a doubt, too, a doubt that the brilliant child of *Renascence* would ever grow up. That she has taken on a woman's stature is best proved by the sonnets.

> *Maxwell Anderson, "In Review: 'Second April'," in* The Measure *(copyright, 1921, by the Editors), No. 7, September, 1921, p. 17.*

PADRAIC COLUM   (essay date 1921)

Miss Millay is a poet with good gifts—a gift of music, a gift of proportion in verse, a gift of witty expression. These gifts are shown on nearly every page in the booklet ["A Few Figs from Thistles"], and "The Penitent," "She is Overheard Singing," and "Daphne" have the spontaneity, the lilt that goes with the songs of one born a singer.

As I read "Second April" I note how many of these poems might be written by the precocious, learned and subtle child that I see in Miss Millay—"City Trees," "Journey," "Weeds," "Passer Mortuus Est," "Pastoral," "Assault," "Travel," "Low Tide," "Song of a Second April," "Rosemary." None of these, it seems to me, has mature passion or mature experience. "The Beanstalk" is a breathless dramatization of a child's climb and is something that is very well done. "The Blue Flag in the Bog" is a distinctive poem—a mental journey such as Miss Millay has made before; an irregular progress with glimpses and visions. Then I come to "The Poet and his Book," and after that I cease to think of Miss Millay as the child. . . . Here is music and here is the sense of actual things, and the two mix as in a seventeenth-century poem. About the wide expanse of external nature Miss Millay says nothing that is at all impressive, but she surely gets the actuality of the things of the household, the things of the garden. "Wraith" has all the sense of the four walls of a house, the closed windows and doors, and the haunting rain outside, and "Lament" has overpoweringly the sense of things that are handled. . . . Then "Exiled" has the actuality that the seashore has from the door of a house—the "bobbing barrels," "the black sticks that fence the weirs." But what an unequal writer Miss Millay is! The six little poems that are a Memorial to D. C. are classic in their pagan feeling for youth and for death. But the "Ode to Silence," with its classic figures and its classic imagery, is, to me, nothing more than a literary exercise.

Then we come to the twelve sonnets that end "Second April." There is maturity here and an emotion that is not dwarfed by the high framing of the sonnet. The third in the sequence, "Not with libations, but with shouts and laughter," will be praised, I am sure; but I do not feel a profound emotion in it, nothing as profound as the emotion that is in the fifth sonnet and the twelfth. (p. 189)

> *Padraic Colum, "Miss Millay's Poems," in* The Freeman *(copyright, 1921 by The Freeman Corporation), Vol. IV, No. 86, November 2, 1921, pp. 189-90.*

LOUIS UNTERMEYER (essay date 1923)

["Renascence"] was written when Miss Millay was nineteen years old; it remains possibly the most astonishing performance of this generation. But it is far more than a performance; it is a revelation. It begins like a child's aimless verse or a counting-out rhyme. . . . After this almost inconsequential opening, the couplets develop into what first seems to be a descriptive idyl and then, growing out of a straightforward lyricism, mount into a rapt hymn to being. In this child's passion for identification with all of life, burns a splendor that attains nothing less than magnificence. (pp. 214-15)

This spiritual intensity drives her to the very heart of existence. In a vision, she sees herself resting deep in the earth where consciousness becomes still keener. . . .

It is a cumulative rapture in which the climax comes like a burst of sudden trumpets; one is confronted by the revelation of forgotten magnificence. Mystery becomes articulate. It is as if a child had entered the room and, in the midst of ingenuousness, had uttered some lucid and blinding truth. There is a Blake-like poignance in the ever-ascending cadence, a leaping simplicity. . . . (p. 216)

This lyrical mastery is manifest on all except a few pages [of *Renascence and Other Poems*] (such as "Interim" and "Ashes of Life," which lisp as uncertainly as the hundreds of poems to which they are too closely related); it shines particularly in the unnamed sonnets, the light "Afternoon on a Hill," the whimsical "When the Year Grows Old" and the remarkable "God's World," in which Miss Millay has communicated rapture in a voice that no lyricist of her time has surpassed for beauty. In the fourteen lines of "God's World" this poet sounds the same hunger which intensified "Renascence." Here the spiritual passion is so exalted that the poet trembles with and voices the breathless awe of thousands caught at the heart by a birdnote or a sunset. But where the others are choked in the brief moment of worship, she has made ecstasy articulate and almost tangible. (p. 217)

It is something of a shock to turn from *Renascence*, possibly the most amazing first book of the period, to the succeeding *A Few Figs from Thistles*. . . . Here Miss Millay seems to have exchanged her birthright for a mess of cleverness; it is nothing more than a pretty talent that gives most of these light verses the quality of a facile cynicism, an ignoble adroitness. (pp. 217-18)

Only the dilettanti of emotion could relish, after the radiance of her first poems, the sophisticated smirk that accompanies "The Penitent," "Thursday," "She Is Overheard Singing," "The Merry Maid," and others of the same easy genre. . . .

One resents such lines not because one feels the poet may lose her quality by playing with fire, but because she is merely setting herself off in theatrical fireworks and so is in danger of losing her soul. The author of "God's World" is the last person who should deck passion with tinsel.

But there are deeper penetrations even in this volume. When Miss Millay is less consciously irresponsible, less archly narcissistic, *A Few Figs from Thistles* bear riper fruit. (p. 218)

[*Second April*] recaptures the earlier, concentrated ecstasy. There is little rhetoric here, no mere imitation of prettiness;

the too-easy charm to which Miss Millay occasionally descends is replaced by a dignity, almost an austerity of emotion. Hers is a triumph not only of expression but above her idiom; she is one of the few living poets who can employ inversions, who can use the antiquated *forsooth, alack! prithee,* and *la,* and not seem an absurd anachronism. Possibly it is because Miss Millay is at heart a belated Elizabethan that she can use locutions which in the work of any other American would be affected and false. (p. 219)

[It is] felicity of language that gives the poetry of Edna Millay the power of resonant speech; hers is a voice that is both intellectually thrilling and emotionally moving. (p. 221)

　　　　Louis Untermeyer, "The Lyricists—1," in his
　　　　American Poetry Since 1900 *(copyright 1923 by*
　　　　Holt, Rinehart & Winston; reprinted by permission of Holt, Rinehart & Winston, Publishers),
　　　　*Holt, 1923, pp. 205-33.**

HARRIET MONROE (essay date 1924)

Long ago . . . I used to think how fine it would be to be the greatest woman poet since Sappho. . . .

I am reminded by that old dream to wonder whether we may not raise a point worthy of discussion in claiming that a certain living lady may perhaps be the greatest woman poet since Sappho. (p. 260)

[The] woman-poets seem to have written almost exclusively in the English language. Emily Bronte, Elizabeth Barrett Browning, Christina Rossetti, Emily Dickinson—these four names bring us to 1900. (p. 261)

Emily Bronte—austere, heroic, solitary—is of course the greatest woman in literature. Not even Sappho's *Hymn to Aphrodite* . . . can surpass *Wuthering Heights* for sheer depth and power of beauty, or match it for the compassing of human experience in a single masterpiece. But *Wuthering Heights,* though poetic in motive and essence, classes as a novel rather than a poem. . . . As a poet, she has not the scope, the variety, of Edna St. Vincent Millay, whose claim to pre-eminence we are considering. (pp. 261-62)

Renascence remains the poem of largest sweep which Miss Millay has achieved as yet—the most comprehensive expression of her philosophy, so to speak, her sense of miracle in life and death—yet she has been lavish with details of experience, of emotion, and her agile and penetrating mind has leapt through spaces of thought rarely traversed by women, or by men either for that matter.

For in the lightest of her briefest lyrics there is always more than appears. In the *Figs,* for example, in *Thursday, The Penitent, The Not Impossible Him* and other witty ironies, and in more serious poems like *The Betrothal,* how neatly she upsets the carefully built walls of convention which men have set up around their Ideal Woman, even while they fought, bled and died for all the Helens and Cleopatras they happened to encounter! And in *Aria da Capo,* a masterpiece of irony sharp as Toledo steel, she stabs the war-god to the heart with a stroke as clean, as deft, as ever the most skilfully murderous swordsman bestowed upon his enemy. Harangues have been made, volumes have been written, for the outlawry of war, but who else has put its preposterous unreasonableness into a nutshell like this girl who brings to bear upon the problem the luminous creative insight of genius?

Thus on the most serious subjects there is always the keen swift touch. Beauty blows upon them and is gone before one can catch one's breath; and lo and behold, we have a poem too lovely to perish, a song out of the blue which will ring in the ears of time. Such are the "little elegies" which will make the poet's Vassar friend, *D. C.* of the wonderful voice, a legend of imperishable beauty even though "her singing days are done." Thousands of stay-at-home women speak wistfully in *Departure;* and *Lament*—where can one find deep grief and its futility expressed with such agonizing grace? Indeed, though love and death and the swift passing of beauty have haunted this poet as much as others, she is rarely specific and descriptive. Her thought is transformed into imagery, into symbol, and it flashes back at us as from the facets of a jewel.

And the thing is so simply done. One weeps, not over *D. C.*'s death, but over her narrow shoes and blue gowns empty in the closet. In *Renascence* the sky, the earth, the infinite, no longer abstractions, come close, as tangible as a tree. *The Harp-weaver,* presenting the protective power of enveloping love—power which enwraps the beloved even after death has robbed him, is a kind of fairy-tale ballad, sweetly told as for a child. Even more in *The Curse* emotion becomes sheer magic of imagery and sound, as clear and keen as frost in sunlight. Always one feels the poet's complete and unabashed sincerity. She says neither the expected thing nor the "daring" thing, but she says the incisive true thing as she has discovered it and feels it.

Miss Millay's most confessional lyrics are in sonnet form, and among them are a number which can hardly be forgotten so long as English literature endures, and one or two which will rank among the best of a language extremely rich in beautiful sonnets. (pp. 263-65)

Beyond these, outside the love-sequence, the *Euclid* sonnet stands in a place apart, of a beauty hardly to be matched for sculpturesque austerity, for detachment from the body and the physical universe. Other minds, searching the higher mathematics, have divined the central structural beauty on which all other beauty is founded, but if any other poet has expressed it I have yet to see the proof. That a young woman should have put this fundamental law into a sonnet is one of the inexplicable divinations of genius. . . . If Miss Millay had done nothing else, she could hardly be forgotten.

But she has done much else. Wilful, moody, whimsical, loving and forgetting, a creature of quick and keen emotions, she has followed her own way and sung her own songs. Taken as a whole, her poems present an utterly feminine personality of singular charm and power; and the best of them, a group of lyrics ineffably lovely, will probably be cherished as the richest, most precious gift of song which any woman since the immortal Lesbian has offered to the world. (pp. 265-66)

> *Harriet Monroe, "Edna St. Vincent Millay," in* Poetry *(© 1924 by The Modern Poetry Association), Vol. XXIV, No. 5, August, 1924, pp. 260-67.*

CARL VAN DOREN (essay date 1924)

No one so well as Miss Millay has spoken with the accents credited to [Greenwich Village].

> My candle burns at both ends;
> It will not last the night;
> But ah, my foes, and oh, my friends—
> It gives a lovely light!

Thus she commences in *A Few Figs from Thistles.* And she continues with impish songs and rakish ballads and sonnets which laugh at the love which throbs through them. (p. 111)

[The] tincture of diablerie appears again and again in Miss Millay's verse, perhaps most of all in the candor with which she talks of love. She has put by the mask under which other poets who were women, apparently afraid for the reputation of their sex, have spoken as if they were men. She has put by the posture of fidelity which women in poetry have been expected to assume. She speaks with the voice of women who, like men, are thrilled by the beauty of their lovers and are stung by desire; who know, however, that love does not always vibrate at its first high pitch, and so, too faithful to love to insist upon clinging to what has become half-love merely, let go without desperation. A woman may be fickle for fun, Miss Millay suggests in various poems wherein this or that girl teases her lover with the threat to leave him or the claim that she has forgotten him; but so may a woman show wisdom by admitting the variability and transcience of love. . . . (pp. 113-14)

What sets Miss Millay's love-poems apart from almost all those written in English by women is the full pulse which, in spite of their gay impudence, beats through them. (p. 115)

Miss Millay has given body and vesture to a sense of equality in love; to the demand by women that they be allowed to enter the world of adventure and experiment in love which men have long inhabited. But Miss Millay does not, like any feminist, argue for that equality. She takes it for granted, exhibits it in action, and turns it into beauty.

Beauty, not argument, is, after all, Miss Millay's concern and goal. . . . For the most part, however, she stands with those who love life and persons too wholly to spend much passion upon anything abstract. . . . The shining clarity of her style does not permit her to work the things she finds beautiful into tapestried verse; she will not ask a song to carry more than it can carry on the easiest wings; but in all her graver songs and sonnets she serves beauty in one way or another. Now she affirms her absolute loyalty to beauty; now she hunts it out in unexpected places; most frequently of all she buries it with some of the most exquisite dirges of her time.

These returning dirges and elegies and epitaphs are as much the natural speech of Miss Millay as is her insolence of joy in the visible and tangible world. Like all those who most love life and beauty, she understands that both are brief and mortal. . . . Having a high heart and a proud creed, Miss Millay leaves unwept some graves which other poets and most people water abundantly, but she is stabbed by the essential tragedy and pity of death. Thus she expresses the tragic powerlessness of those who live to hold those who die. . . . (pp. 116-18)

Are these only the accents of a minor poet, crying over withered roses and melted snows? Very rarely do minor poets strike such moving chords upon such universal strings. Still more rarely do merely minor poets have so much power over tragedy and pity, and yet in other hours have equal power over fire and laughter. (p. 119)

Carl Van Doren, "Youth and Wings: Edna St. Vincent Millay," in his Many Minds *(copyright © 1924 by Alfred A. Knopf, Inc.; copyright renewed 1951 by The Estate of Carl Van Doren; reprinted by permission of The Estate of Carl Van Doren), Knopf, 1924, pp. 105-19.*

JOSEPH COLLINS (essay date 1924)

It is easy to enumerate Miss Millay's virtues, to define her charm, to explain her appeal, to make clear to any one our appreciation of her. But like many others of the endowed and the elect she has a besetting sin: she is careless. She is like a beautiful woman who has a varied, attractive wardrobe and if one may judge from some of her appearances she knows how to wear her clothes; but she does not always take the trouble to select discriminatingly or put them on properly, or at least as effectively as she might easily do. She gives the impression that she does not think it worth while. Unfortunately her last book, "The Harp-Weaver and Other Poems," discloses the fact that her sin is finding her out and it seems to me much more chivalric and gallant to say so than to throw bouquets. (pp. 118-19)

Miss Millay reveals her carelessness in some of her sonnets. There is more form and technique in a sonnet than fourteen lines. The form she violates continually. The stress does not fall naturally on the important syllable. She gives no heed to this and the result is that one has a jumpy feeling while reading them. And it is not only in the form but in the thought that she does not do herself full justice. The thought of a sonnet should be of a high motive or endeavour. She makes it commonplace, such as "Not risen," "Not writing letters." Many of the last series of sonnets are unfortunately commonplace. "I don't know exactly what you do when a person dies" is conversation but certainly not poetic expression and quite unsuitable for sonnet form.

Such criticism should not be construed to mean that her last volume is without merit. It has great merit. Some of the poems reveal her keen zest for beauty and for life, and her ability to express it in vibrant, compelling verse. She has a good eye and a good ear; she is an admirable pagan and she has genuine passion. She finds beauty not alone in the bizarre or exotic, but in the moulding forces of man's experience. (pp. 119-20)

However, one cannot but realise the nostalgia that has replaced some of the joy of life that ebbs from her earlier poems. (p. 120)

Joseph Collins, "Gallantry and Our Women Writers," in his Taking the Literary Pulse: Psychological Studies of Life and Letters *(copyright, 1924, by George H. Doran Company), Doran, 1924, pp. 118-29.**

SISTER M. MADELEVA (essay date 1925)

Edna St. Vincent Millay has been, for a decade past, one of our most diverting poets. One wonders, as he watches her maturing work, whether she will not become something more. The popularity of her poetry has rested unduly on its "Panlike quality," its "impudent philosophy," perishable trappings, proper to youth and bound to pass with it. But under these are an instinct for beauty, the technic to capture it, an equilibrium of mind and emotion that go to make

enduring song. One wonders where the bright trinity will lead. (p. 143)

[*Renascence*] celebrated a mystical rebirth, an awakening to nature, and a supersaturation with beauty. Then came *A Few Figs from Thistles*, witty, arrogant, and outspoken, which gave the girl poet a reputation for flippancy beyond her desire, one would think. For presently there followed *Second April*, singing her renewed allegiance to nature and to beauty. Then quite suddenly, to the public at least, a sequence of sonnets appeared that were consequential enough for a novel and so deeply rooted in New England soil that they might have been done by Robert Frost. All of our Q.E.D. conclusions about Edna St. Vincent Millay having been for a third time upset, we ask her in dead earnest, "Where are you going, my pretty maid?"

Whatever singing road this blithe girl may choose, she has been led by beauty until now—"waylaid by beauty," as she says; the beauty of the world that she cannot withstand, that lures her on resistlessly.... (pp. 143-44)

With almost precocious alertness to the dangers of excess, she has accustomed herself to the ultimate intensities of beauty.... (p. 145)

Against the danger of such excess she chooses the artifice of simple technic and the strength of mental poise. One feels that her poetry should be judged by its lyric qualities. But as indicative of her power and possible future achievement, it must be rated by these sterner tests. It is precisely her ability to restrain rather than to free, to balance rather than to heap up emotions that will set her yet plastic loveliness into the mold of strength and great beauty. A quality of asceticism is needed, a power to forego, to relinquish. (p. 146)

[The] three qualities of Miss Millay's poetry, the three strong tools with which she has to work for permanence [are:] exceeding sensitiveness to beauty, simplicity of technic which is the technic of simplicity, and a fine balance between thought and feeling.

Times she is not restrained, or simple, or level headed; notably in the dizzy, daring "Bean-Stalk," wildest, most typical of her poems, the bold biography of her headlong imagination in its gay climb up the sky. The poem is a swaying, reeling one, blown about by the winds of free verse but held taut by perfect rimes at every point.... By every token of its apparent lawlessness it points the primrose path to the poet's possible destruction, abandonment of an ecstatic imagination to less wholesomely alluring ventures of the day. But always an instinctive, beautiful poise forestalls a misstep. (pp. 148-49)

Another pitfall there is in the way of her flying feet, the trap of her own versatility. Already she has stumbled into it. She imitates with dangerous facility. She began in the manner of Anna Hempstead Branch; just now Robert Frost appears to be her model; a half dozen sonneteers and lyricists have come between. Imitation is the privilege of the young, a method commendable and well authorized. But when the imitations turn out to be prettier than the originals, as is so often true of Miss Millay's lyrics, there is the danger not only of forgetting that they are imitations, but of being satisfied with such. Her susceptibility extends to the form, no less than the spirit in which she writes; she has followed conservatively in blank verse, epigrammatic lyrics, and excellent sonnets the more erratic course of contemporary American poetry along practically the same broad path. (pp. 149-50)

A Few Figs from Thistles is a serious, albeit a very witty book. ''To the Not Impossible He'' and ''The Unexplorer'' sting with their satire the restlessness and the smugness with which life is beset; . . . ''Thursday'' combats fickleness with its own weapons. Altogether, Miss Millay has gathered dexterously among the brambles of social life, a field where stronger hands are needed for reaping. It has been a venture for her and has not gone beyond the limits of a mood. One almost hopes it will not do so; satire with such art as hers will yield more power as a force than as a form.

To judge the poetry of Miss Millay by her sonnets may seem like measuring a bird's songs by a metronome. She has become so much a synonym for lyric caprice, quick-witted poetic repartee that readers have been distracted by her tricks from her performances. Many of her sonnets are distinctly literary performances; all of them are sober indications of what she may be at her future best. They speak the familiar sonnet language of love and beauty with fluency and force. They leave no doubt at all as to the poet's accuracy of speech but they do leave doubt as to the conviction behind that speech. They give the impression that ability to express, more than the power to feel, has gone into their making, which is an injustice to Miss Millay's real capacities. Too many moods and styles are reflected. That of Rossetti is conspicuous and yet, one feels, it is not the one to which she will yield finally. ''Sonnets of an Ungrafted Tree'' in *The Harp Weaver* makes one sure of this.

Here, in a sequence of seventeen sonnets, Miss Millay has struck out into a new field with a new model. Robert Frost is unquestionably her teacher, and whether or not one prefers the music and fancy of her lyrics, he knows that she has got beyond loveliness at last. (pp. 151-53)

Here is, indeed, a departure not only from Miss Millay's other sonnets but from her other poetry, her other self. Until now she has been her own leading lady; here she has stepped off the stage completely to record the drama in which another woman has the lead. Her elimination of self is sudden, complete, and successful. She has freed herself from the chief encumbrance to real work. For always, one feels, there has been between her ability and its best expression, the supple plasticity of Edna St. Vincent Millay herself. She seems to have lost that here, unless, indeed, her pliancy has merely lent itself to this mold of strength. (p. 155)

The sonnet form used in the sequence is the target at which most darts of criticism will be aimed. Seventeen sonnets with uniform couplet endings of seven feet is not a license that tape measurers of meter are going to tolerate without a protest. Neither the story nor the poetry suffers from the spurious feet, but the form—aye, there's the rub—and deliberately to adopt the sonnet as one's medium is tacitly to respect its form. Miss Millay has been a ravisher here. However, ''Sonnets of an Ungrafted Tree'' are the best good work, the nearest great work she has done.

One always runs the risk, in looking at a thing too closely, of seeing it too large. Today Miss Millay looks important poetically. It may be that we are too near to her. It may be

that she has done her best work. All of which suppositions err, probably, on the side of conservatism. These things can be said for her: she has kept her head amid all the turbulent and wayward winds of free and erratic verse, she has withstood unguessed temptations to be clever rather than true, and she has reached in a decade a poetic stature half a head above a goodly number of contemporary poets. Her weakness lies in her strength—she is versatile. She adapts herself too easily to the forms and moods of the day. She can be mystical, epigrammatic, flippant, serious, dramatic. She can be neat and sweet and beautiful, and she usually is. Facility is a more perilous gift than ability. Miss Millay has both. Beauty, technic, poise she has. Whether she will rub her golden mind into a mirror for the reflection of loveliness or round it into a crucible for life, one wonders. (pp. 156-58)

> *Sister M. Madeleva, '' 'Where Are You Going, My Pretty Maid?','' in her* Chaucer's Nuns and Other Essays *(copyright 1925 by D. Appleton and Company), D. Appleton, 1925 (and reprinted by Kennikat Press, 1965), pp. 143-58.*

EDD WINFIELD PARKS (essay date 1930)

According to our convention, a woman feels rather than thinks, and is governed by emotion rather than intellect. Until she reached the age of thirty-five, Edna St. Vincent Millay seemed an almost perfect example of this belief: her poetry was intimate rather than conventional, emotional rather than intellectual, realistic rather than philosophical, and inconstant to an extreme. In brief, feminine. True, she occasionally exhibited remarkable insight into the problems of life, the miracle of death, but even these strengthened the conception: they seemed lightning-clarifying flashes of that intuition so freely granted to women, but behind them no philosophy of life, nor even a sustained intellectual curiosity.

Until the appearance of *The Buck in the Snow*, then, Miss Millay was in line for comparison with the gifted women poets of the world, Sappho, Mrs. Browning, Christina Rossetti, Emily Dickinson, and the feminine poets of the present day—a comparison that, in itself, would limit her work to a definitely narrow range.

There is a close unity, a cohesion of matter and manner in her work from *Renascence* through *The King's Henchman*. (p. 42)

Though her poems hint at embryonic intellectual processes and a growing interest in mortality, her best work and brief, lyrical moods clothed in gossamer silk, pointed *vers de société*, such work as might be expected from one whose mother was a leprechaun and whose father was a friar. *The Blue Flag in a Bog*, the *Ode to Silence*—these and other poems that attempt the philosophical are her poorest work. They drag, repeat, wander: common faults when a poet has nothing to say. (pp. 43-4)

[In the later poems] she has experimented with many techniques. Too often this experimentation with new forms is a first sign of sterility, the autumn of the mind. His vein of poetry almost exhausted, the craftsman attempts concealment by the dexterity of his rhyme and diction. One cannot believe this to be the case with Miss Millay. *The Buck in the Snow* is a richer, *fuller* book than any of its predecessors, the emotions, though changed, glow with the same intense flame. A tragic note replaces the old joyous one; mortality and the terrible uncontrollable machine that man has builded, society, are her chief interests: society menacing all who may endanger its peace or its dollars. (pp. 47-8)

[These] are transitional poems, the end of one poet and the birth of a new, perhaps a greater, poet. Something more than greater skill in craftsmanship, a more flexible technique, is present, though almost for the first time Miss Millay has tried new rhyme-schemes, assonance, slant-rhymes, a longer line, even free verse; in addition to this there begins to appear a philosophy of life, tragic, Hardy-esque, but immature. (p. 48)

Certain it is that her mind can no longer be called feminine, in the derogatory sense. For these poems, though they lack greatness in themselves, have the inherent qualities of which great poetry is made: not only emotion, but a philosophy of life appears; the intimacy remains, but surging underneath one feels universality. (p. 49)

Edd Winfield Parks, "Edna St. Vincent Millay," in The Sewanee Review *(reprinted by permission of the editor;* © *1930 by The University of the South), Vol. XXXVIII, No. 1, January-March, 1930, pp. 42-9.*

BABETTE DEUTSCH   (essay date 1935)

Miss Millay's poetry, like [A. E.] Housman's, like the delicate lyrics of Sara Teasdale, has found favor with a wide public because it is, after all, behind the times. She uses a traditional technique to express traditional themes, while her clear-eyed irony and the individual character of her verse, partly a matter of musical phrasing, partly of vocabulary, give it a freshness which surprises without alarming. One has but to contrast her performance with that of such contemporaries as Pound, Eliot, Edith Sitwell, Hart Crane, to make no mention of younger and equally audacious poets, to appreciate how old-fashioned is her method of attack, and how far she is from the pressure of contemporary thought. Her modernity lies in her willingness to let the commonplaces of daily living and dying intrude upon her verse, and in her acknowledgment that the relation between the sexes is not what it was painted by the poets of romantic love. But even these aspects of her work are not essentially of our own time. Her commonplaces are not those of the worker or the thinker caught in the wheels of our mechanical civilization, but those of a rural housewife, an artist in an attic, or an exile from some village on the east coast. If her attitude toward sex differs from that of Tennyson and Arnold, even from that of Keats or of Shelley, it can readily be paralleled in the verse of the Cavalier poets.... Even her later and more sober love poems and the sonnet sequence entitled, after Donne, *Fatal Interview,* do not probe the emotions with the peculiar sensitiveness of her contemporaries, but might rather be set alongside sonnets written before they were born: George Meredith's *Modern Love.* The thwartings, the conflicts, which harrow D. H. Lawrence, T. S. Eliot, Conrad Aiken, Robinson Jeffers, and which they expose, with varying success but unrelenting candor, are not fully admitted in her verse, or are confessed in a manner so archaic that it robs them of half their sharpness. It is in the gay rebellious lyrics of her youth that she strikes a more modern note. But the chal-

lenge which she flung a stodgy generation rings somewhat falsely on ears which have heard the cries wrung by a tyranny she has scarcely questioned. One returns to Miss Millay's poems less because they give the quality of contemporary experience than because they utter so piercingly the perennial cry against death of the lover of the sensual world. (pp. 98-9)

Babette Deutsch, "Bearers of Tradition," in her This Modern Poetry *(reprinted by permission of W. W. Norton & Company, Inc.; copyright* © *1935 by W. W. Norton & Company, Inc.; renewed 1962 by Babette Deutsch), Norton, 1935, pp. 84-107.*

ELIZABETH ATKINS   (essay date 1936)

Millay's first poetic drama, *The Lamp and the Bell,* is not her best one. *The King's Henchman* . . . will stand up beside any play of the seventeenth century, excluding Shakespeare's. One never believes that until he reads it while he is absorbed in seventeenth-century drama. But read *The Duchess of Malfi* and *The White Devil* and then reread *The King's Henchman.* There it still stands, untarnished, bold and beautiful as ever. Her college play, *The Lamp and the Bell,* is much slighter, but it, too, can be read among seventeenth-century plays without ceasing to be beautiful. (pp. 36-7)

[All] the spirit of [*The Lamp and the Bell*], the atmosphere and the theme, came from her undergraduate days. The kingdom of Fiori is Poughkeepsie on the Hudson, and college students and faculty keep looking straight through their Italian veils, very much as Elizabethan Londoners keep lifting their masks in Shakespeare's Illyria and Verona and Messina.

The theme is that one of burning concern to students in any girls' school—the theme of friendship; and the play takes up their endless arguments as to whether an ardent feminine friendship is healthy and whether it will last. (p. 37)

The theme is surely Elizabethan. From Lyly to Beaumont and Fletcher, Elizabethan literature is filled with asseverations that friendship is a stronger thing than sexual love. . . . The only novelty is that this twentieth-century play deals with the friendship of women instead of men. . . . (p. 38)

But of course it is not the theme or the plot that matters. The excellencies of *The Lamp and the Bell* lie in its dramatic movement, its interwoven moods, its characterization, its fluid blank verse, its lyrics, its imagery.

In its dramatic components *The Lamp and the Bell* is as like late Elizabethan tragi-comedies as they are like one another. . . . [In] *The Lamp and the Bell,* as in the seventeenth-century plays . . . , there is a current of life flowing through the action that makes all the stock situations fresh and real.

Stage tactics are handled with the daring of a beginner. When a character appears on the stage without an excuse, she simply announces that she cannot think why she is there and goes away to remember. It is far more plausible than many of the ingenious excuses for their presence that some more experienced playwrights have given their characters. Whenever an action is especially meaningful and difficult to present, it takes place off stage. This arrangement would seem to be all wrong, but as a matter of fact it underscores the most effective qualities of the play: its suspense and its foreboding. The audience is kept in the dark as to what has already happened in a way that is almost without parallel. (pp. 38-9)

Possibly the most important lesson that Edna St. Vincent Millay learned from the Elizabethans was that passion and exaltation are not divorced from one's bodily condition, and that dramatic poetry is most convincing when it makes us share the physical states of the characters. Most characters in modern poetic dramas are like shadows on a cinema screen, mere shape and sound, but Millay's people, like the Elizabethans, impress us as being able to eat and to smell. It is curious how intense a feeling of reality is given by odors. No other sense actually confuses illusion and reality as the sense of smell can do, if the artist appeals to it subtly enough. . . . Millay's plays bring us stenches and fragrances. Even her imagery is sometimes based on odor. (pp. 44-5)

The blank verse of [*The Lamp and the Bell*] is suited to . . . [the] feminine characters. It is not the mighty line of Marlowe, by any means; it walks with a light, swift, girlish tread. (p. 47)

A very feminine play it is, in subject matter and in style. Indeed, it is almost a childlike play, scarcely more than a fairy tale. But it has subtle qualities of greatness. (p. 48)

What Proust has called "the intermittences of the heart" made it possible for Edna St. Vincent Millay to be a light-hearted girl, accepting a mad and merry world, during lyric intervals of the same year when she was writing the maturest of ironical dramas and was staring at the life of her century with eyes as disillusioned as Jonathan Swift's. Her *Aria da Capo* is a bitterly hopeless analysis of the logic of all wars and of the irreversible machinery of tragic human history. And yet on the surface it is farce.

Aria da Capo is a most original play, in style, in theme, and in mood. . . . For in this play Edna St. Vincent Millay inaugurated a type of poetry that is usually thought of as stemming from T. S. Eliot's *The Waste Land* (composed in the following year), a complex poetry which telescopes time by presenting several historical periods simultaneously, and which, in the second place, uses a new method of writing tragedy, presenting it with deliberate reticence, under a surface of bitter jest. And, in the third place, it makes use of symbolism.

Millay solved the problem of telescoped time, or relativity, with a lucidity which accounts, I suppose, for the public's scarcely noticing how difficult her task had been. She represented her two courses of time as separate plays, acted in the same theater. In other words, *Aria da Capo* is deliberately removed one degree from reality by being played as two plays within a framing play. A sophisticated farce of the twentieth century and a prehistoric pastoral tragedy are dovetailed to make a complex allegorical drama. (pp. 77-8)

One reason for the success of *Aria da Capo* is that Edna St. Vincent Millay is so steeped in the seventeenth-century imagery comparing life to a stage play that she can make stage puppets of her characters without losing a jot of their appeal to our human sympathies. (pp. 89-90)

The other reason for her success, as I see it, is her sensitiveness to musical effects. (p. 90)

[The] influence of music on *Aria da Capo* goes much farther than the title and the tripartite division that the title imposes upon the play, with the third part repeating the first. The resemblance to music comes out most strongly in the interweaving of themes, so that, in much the same way as in *The Lamp and the Bell*, one hears echoes of the past and anticipations of the future while a certain action is going on. In *Aria da Capo* this is managed by having the voices of Pierrot and Columbine, off stage, interrupt the shepherd's story. Thus, as the shepherds take their first step toward modern civilization by making their wall, we hear the inane voices of the harlequins quarreling, reminding us that their futility is a sample of the civilization toward which the happy and serious shepherds are moving. . . . The play is very like a string quintette of eighteenth-century music, and the harmony with which the parts answer one another lends a sense of heightened significance to the simple or flippant speeches, giving them in combination a meaning far beyond their surface meaning. This formal symmetry, like that of classical music, is indispensable to a play in which the subject matter is so lawlessly ugly, and in which the author's mood is so blackly pessimistic. It was necessary that this play, depicting the endless nightmare of history, be written in a form of beautiful symmetry; just as it was necessary, later, that Millay's *Epitaph for the Race of Man* be written in a strict form such as a sonnet sequence, rather than in free verse. For a chaotic report of chaos is nothing at all. (pp. 91-2)

Human life, Millay believes, has always been beset by tragic problems, and so she makes *The King's Henchman* [her next play] a tragedy. And yet, beneath the tragedy, she shows us something marvelously and magnificently solid, something on which one may rest as on the foundations of the world.

This solid foundation is not a code of morals. The code of *The King's Henchman* is not ours, could not be ours. (p. 161)

But underneath the code is something else—a willingness to accept the noblest code that one can conceive of and try to live up to it. . . . [Aethelwold, the king's henchman,] believes from the depths of his soul that his highest duty is to obey literally and implicitly his king and his blood brother. He believes that only blood revenge can blot out a dishonor. And believing these things while they do not hurt him, he must believe them also when his tragic desire has made him wish to believe otherwise. By killing himself rather than to compromise with his beliefs, he becomes in our eyes a man—a man who is something more than the cleverest of all the beasts. Watching Aethelwold die by his own hand, we know, with something deeper than reason, that the strongest compulsion upon human nature is to find a code of behavior that satisfies the most lively intelligence and then to live up to it, however much it hurts. (p. 162)

Before Millay can reach our almost forgotten faith in aspirations after nobility, she must convince us that her story is true, must win us to what Coleridge calls "a willing suspension of disbelief." (p. 163)

She has chosen her period wisely. She has refrained from going back so far into the mists of time that human figures appear shadowy and ill-defined to us. She gives us a time when, we know, life sounded and smelled and tasted and looked more or less recognizably like the world today. And she chooses a century when she has the completed literature of a period to guide her. And she has chosen a century in which the language was changing sufficiently so that she can suggest its vigor without abandoning a natural modern English speech, though she has, with strictest fidelity, used not a single word of which the root, at least, had not entered the language before the Norman Conquest.... Therefore Millay, without too much incongruity, can represent the forceful everyday speech of her characters by an irregular blank verse, heavily alliterated, and can show them singing rhymed ballads. But she convinces us from the beginning that these are old English times, indeed, by opening the play with a song by the gleeman which is in the four-stressed alliterative and unmetrical (though heavily rhythmical) Old English verse. (pp. 164-65)

Literally and figuratively, then, Millay has given a very strong illusion of showing us actual early England. Why was it worth doing? . . . Well, nothing else takes the place of reading old literatures at first hand, of course, but *The King's Henchman* is, obviously, not presented as a substitute for that. It is not a mere imitation of Old English poetry, but an interpretation of it in terms of twentieth-century needs. (p. 170)

[Thus] with the full light of twentieth-century psychology beating upon them, we judge the people of Old English times as they are interpreted in *The King's Henchman.* So long as tragedy can move us in this way, the racial memory of some strange impulsion to seek good and to abhor evil is not dead within us. (p. 174)

[Millay] has traveled a long way since she wrote some of the poems of her girlhood. Her first volume of lyrics revealed a violent contrast of moods. The childlike faith and serenity of *Renascence* were set against *Interim,* expressing utter abandon to human tragedy as in her total inexperience she imagined it must be. . . . In the next volume of lyrics [*A Few Figs from Thistles*] actual grief has reached her, and the tone is very different. But the volume is made up entirely of variations on the theme of despair. In the *Harp-Weaver* volume her mood has become more complex. Joy and pain have become subtly interfused in her life, and every poem in the volume reveals a tempered mood. In *The Buck in the Snow* and still more in *Wine from These Grapes* the intense egotism of her moods is becoming transcended. She is becoming, as she travels up the long and steep hillslope of poetry, not less herself, but more a human being, and from personal agony she is climbing to the bleak grandeur of our mortal infelicity. All her troubles and joys she sees as those of the strange earth-dweller, man. . . . (pp. 242-43)

Man is becoming a simple and a piteous being to her. He is the "breather" and the "dust." And pitying herself in him she has begun to achieve a poetry of communism—very different from the polemic communistic verse that is so prevalent just at present, but not the less communal or poetic for that. The common fate of man is coming to be her own deepest sorrow; and her own death is scarcely distinguishable for her from the extinction which she so deeply fears for the race. . . . [Mankind] has become to her an individual being, like a character in a Dostoevski novel, a being who loves and fears and hates everything, and is monstrous and pitiable in his tragedy. Her genius for simplification has made all mankind as real and as individual to her as such a character. This, in spirit, is truly communal poetry. (pp. 243-44)

Elizabeth Atkins, in her Edna St. Vincent Millay and Her Times *(reprinted by permission of The University of Chicago Press; copyright 1936 by the University of Chicago), University of Chicago Press, 1936, 265 p.*

HILDEGARDE FLANNER   (essay date 1937)

In reading Miss Millay's poetry one is always struck by the thought that she has been fortunate in her time of emergence—or that the time was fortunate in her. After the War and during the early twenties she expressed, particularly for women and for youth, a spirit that was symptomatic of the moment. (p. 161)

It is interesting to note that many of her more serious poems coming at a later period, especially the sonnet sequence "Fatal Interview," are in celebration of the opposite practice, that of romantic love or what is more crudely (or exactly) called transference. It is this state to which literature is indebted for some of the most treasured examples of the poetic art. . . . Since the sonnets of "Fatal Interview," however, she has come a noticeable distance from the private drama of the early and middle poems. One cannot prophesy, but it is unlikely that she will return to write of romantic passion and the crises of personal attachment. That something is thus lost from poetry is true. But any gain in objectivity is, after a few years, a gain for feeling and hence for the heart, when it again enjoys authority.

Miss Millay is not to be classed among the "makers" who have left language altered and disturbed by their experiments, and ready for new forms and sensibilities. . . . She is one of those who take the known forms that offer the readiest vehicle, technically and emotionally, and thus save themselves much loss of time, much doubt. Of her own day in modernism of intellect, she has yet been nearest another age technically. The sonnet was ideally suited to her wants and she surrendered herself to the iambic line and all the machinery of the form, certain to work and work so musically in her hands. Its good brevity, its psychological moments, its fine style of being a capsule of infinity, the effect of an idea ravished and made quotable, all this she was familiar with. That she was able with no hesitation to accept the continuity of a traditional form meant that she wrote in measures already possessing emotional associations for all readers. There was an exchange of gifts, for the sonnet received something from Miss Millay. She took the principle of surprise common to the final lines and developed it into a clever note of drama. . . . She gave to it, as to her other lyrics, homely and modern details and sometimes the grandeur of folk heroism. . . . She brought to the sonnet the interest and ferment of conversation. She made the form sophisticated, versatile and highly feminine.

It is not easy now to recapture in one's own words the sense of freshness and transparent revelation that her early lyrics conveyed. In these also it had been her fortune to take frequently a traditional form, the elegy, and make it immediate and tender. Her contribution to method has been chiefly in two directions: an infusion of personal energy and glow into the traditions of lyric poetry, and the deceptively artless ability to set down the naked fact unfortified. She has pleased the fastidious and did not scorn to please the simple, for even a limited poetic appreciation found in the identical performance something that gave pure pleasure. (pp. 162-64)

It is true, however, that an extravagance of feeling, an indulgence of legendary anguish that belongs to the ultra places and not to the heart of poetry, have thrived beyond wisdom in her lines. One deplores the overdramatic ring in a brilliant measure. Yet it is equally true that an egotism never weak, and one of the best talents for lyrical anger in all literature, have saved her from a problem that other women poets have been torn by. Miss Millay has never been apologetic about the right to love or to suffer. (pp. 164-65)

[Miss Millay] contemplates the end of civilization. Her mind, however, is on the elegy, not the revulsion. "Epitaph for the Race of Man" is eminent writing. But now that the content of her work is changing, these sonnets still run as smoothly as perfect engines. That is the fate of a traditional measure, no matter how strong may be our sense of continuity in using it. It begins to alarm with the bland ease of the mechanical. One does not ask Miss Millay to forgo the exceptional command of her medium. Yet there could be possible an eloquence neither disinherited nor upstart, an eloquence closer to its own necessity than these sonnets are, a kind of language less dependent on the perfection of the form. (p. 166)

> *Hildegarde Flanner, "Two Poets: Jeffers and Millay," in* The New Republic *(© 1937 The New Republic, Inc.), Vol. 89, No. 1156, January 27, 1937 (and reprinted in* After the Genteel Tradition: American Writers Since 1910, *edited by Malcolm Cowley, Peter Smith, 1959, pp. 155-67).**

JOHN CROWE RANSOM   (essay date 1937)

Miss Millay is an artist of considerable accomplishments. She is the best of the poets who are "popular" and loved by Circles, Leagues, Lyceums, and Round Tables; perhaps as good a combination as we can ever expect of the "literary" poet and the poet who is loyal to the "human interest" of the common reader. She can nearly always be cited for the virtues of clarity, firmness of outline, consistency of tone within the unit poem, and melodiousness. Her career has been one of dignity and poetic sincerity. She is an artist. (p. 783)

[The limitation of Miss Millay] is her lack of intellectual interest. It is that which the male reader misses in her poetry, even though he may acknowledge the authenticity of the interest which is there.... It is true that some male poets are about as deficient; not necessarily that they are undeveloped intellectually, but they conceive poetry as a sentimental or feminine exercise. Not deficient in it are some female poets, I suppose, like Miss Marianne Moore; and doubtless many women are personally developed in intellect without having any idea that poetry can master and use what the intellect is prepared to furnish. (pp. 797-98)

Such are Miss Millay's limits.... We come finally to her quite positive talent or, if anybody quarrels with that term, genius. But I still have to identify by restriction the field in which I find it displayed.

The formal, reflective, or "literary" poems fall for the most part outside this field. She is not a good conventional or formalist poet, and I think I have already suggested why:

because she allows the forms to bother her and to push her into absurdities. (p. 801)

Then, the young-girl poems fall outside it; and I am afraid I refer to more poems than were composed in the years of her minority. This charming lady found it unusually difficult, poetically speaking, to come of age. *Renascence* is genuine, in the sense that it is the right kind of religious poem for an actual young girl of New England, with much rapture, a naïve order of images, and a dash of hell-fire vindictiveness.... But the volume *A Few Figs from Thistles* is well known as a series of antireligious and Bohemian shockers, and that stage should have been far behind her when she published the work at the age of twenty-eight. The college plays were exactly right for their occasions, but *Aria da Capo* comes long afterward and still suggests the prize-winning skit on the Senior Girls' Stunt Night of an unusually good year. And then come the poems of *Second April*, whose author at twenty-nine is not consistently grown up.... [Gradually] the affectations of girlhood in Miss Millay disappear.

When they are absent, she has a vein of poetry which is spontaneous, straightforward in diction, and excitingly womanlike; a distinguished objective record of a natural woman's mind. The structures are transparently simple and the effects are immediate. There are few poems, I think, that do not fumble the least bit, unless they are very short, but she has the right to be measured as a workman by her excellent best. Her best subjects are death, which she declines like an absolute antiphilosopher to accept or gloze, a case of indomitable feminine principle; personal moods, which she indulges without apology, in the kind of integrity that is granted to the kind of mind that has no direction nor modulation except by its natural health; and natural objects which call up her love or pity. I have to except from this list the love of a woman for a man, because, in her maturity at least, she has reserved that subject for the sonnets, and they are rather unconventional in sentiment, but literary, and corrupted by verbal insincerities. (pp. 801-02)

The most ambitious single work of Miss Millay's would be her operatic play, *The King's Henchman;* ambitious, but suited to her powers, and entirely successful.... Operatic drama lends itself to Miss Millay's scope. Its action is a little brief and simple, and it permits the maximum number of lyrical moments and really suits Poe's idea of the long poem as a series of short poems rather than a single consecutive whole. The work does not prove Miss Millay to be a dramatist, but it shows what an incessant fountain of poetry is a woman's sensibility in the midst of simple human and natural situations. It should be remarked that, being tenth century, the properties have the advantage of being a little picturesque, and the tone of the language slightly foreign, like a Scottish or Irish idiom perhaps. But these are the arrangements of the artist, of whom it cannot so fairly be said that she is in luck as that she is a competent designer. (p. 804)

> *John Crowe Ransom, "The Poet As Woman" (copyright, 1937, by John Crowe Ransom), in* The Southern Review, *Vol. 2, No. 4, Spring, 1937, pp. 783-806.*

DELMORE SCHWARTZ   (essay date 1943)

Miss Millay belongs to the ages. Posterity, which is an

anachronism, may prove this strong impression an illusion. But we shall now know about that. Meanwhile Miss Millay has written a good many poems . . . which make her a great poet to most readers of poetry. These readers consider Edgar Allan Poe, Henry Wadsworth Longfellow, Blake, and Shakespeare great poets also; and if they read Poe, Longfellow, and Miss Millay, rather than Blake and Shakespeare, what else can be expected? How else can these readers sustain their view of what great poetry is? . . .

Miss Millay belongs to an age as well as to the ages. She is dated in a good sense. Like Scott Fitzgerald, H. L. Mencken, Sinclair Lewis, prohibition, and midget golf, she belongs to a particular period. No one interested in that period will fail to be interested in Miss Millay's poems. . . . Her lyrics were used by the period, and she was made famous by their usefulness; but now they are inseparable from the period, and they will always illuminate the liberated Vassar girl, the jazz age, bohemianism, and the halcyon days of Greenwich Village. Who can forget the famous quatrain in which a lady's candle burns at both ends, and will not last the night, but gives a lovely light? How could this point of view have been stated with greater economy of means or more memorably? Yet not all that is memorable is admirable. (p. 735)

Miss Millay has perhaps been defeated by her very success. "Fatal Interview" . . . is probably her best book, but there is nothing in it which represents an advance in perception or insight over her first book, which was published in 1917. To compare the two books is to see how all that is good in her work, all that is of permanent interest, is circumscribed by the period in which she became a famous poetess.

Consider, as an example, the view of love which recurs without exception in these lyrics and in many of Miss Millay's sonnets; in one of her best-known sonnets, "What lips my lips have touched and how and why / I have forgotten," Miss Millay compares the female protagonist of the poem to a tree and "the unremembered lads" who were her lovers to birds. Is this not the eternal feminine of the day when woman's suffrage was an issue and not yet an amendment? If one has a weakness for visualizing images, then the dominant image of the poem certainly presents the female and the lads in unfair proportions. Elsewhere some lovers are assured that a love affair is not any the less true love because it has been rapidly succeeded by several more love affairs, an assurance which might come gracefully from Catherine the Great, let us say, but which is not really the kind of attitude that makes great poetry. Is it not, indeed, just as shallow as its opposite, the squeezable mindless doll whom Hemingway celebrates? Yet just such attitudes explain Miss Millay's popular fame at the same time as they exhibit her essential failure. The late John Wheelwright remarked that Miss Millay had sold free love to the women's clubs. Yes, this has been at once her success and her failure; and one should add that another attribute of this kind of famous authoress is that of inspiring epigrams.

When we look closely at Miss Millay's poetic equipment—her images, diction, habits of style, and versification—we find the same twins of success and failure. Her diction especially is poetic in the wrong sense: the candles, arrows, towers, scullions, thou's, lads, girls, prithees, shepherds, and the often-capitalized Beauty and Death are words which come, not from a fresh perception of experience, but from the reading of many lyric poems. . . . If there is an al-

ternative, it is perhaps to be seen flickering in the poems in which Miss Millay draws upon what she has actually looked at on the New England coast or in the Maine woods. . . . (pp. 735-36)

But if Miss Millay had cultivated and searched out the actuality of this experience instead of using it as a stage set, she would not be the first text of all the girls who are going to write poetry; she would not have depended upon attitudes which are as characteristic of literate youth as the sophomore year; after her second volume she would have abandoned the obvious and banal poses she has struck in the face of love and death. She would not be the most famous poetess of our time, and she might have composed a body of poetry characterized by the nonesuch originality—however often warped, thin, fragmentary, exotic, or ingrown—of Marianne Moore, Leonie Adams, Louise Bogan, and Janet Lewis. . . . (p. 736)

Delmore Schwartz, "The Poetry of Millay," in The Nation *(copyright 1943* The Nation *magazine,* The Nation Associates, Inc.*), Vol. 157, No. 25, December 18, 1943, pp. 735-36.*

WINFIELD TOWNLEY SCOTT (essay date 1944)

A new attitude toward Edna St. Vincent Millay has pretty thoroughly been adopted by the literati, and if her popular audience is still not only faithful but large, she has—so far as I can determine—failed to excite any recent collegiate intelligentsia. The greatest insult you can offer any young woman poet in this country is to warn her that she may be the Edna Millay of her generation; which, being interpreted, means that she is in danger of glibness and of popularity.

Now if under the praise and the dispraise there are reasons for both to be found in Miss Millay's poetry, the fact remains that the adulation and the abuse have little to do with the worth of that poetry, since both have been excessive. They do merit preliminary mention because they make so difficult an attempt to write of a body of poetry that is neither the most unworthy nor the greatest since Sappho's. (p. 335)

All her poems may be said to be variations on a theme announced by Housman: "Let us endure awhile and see injustice done." Occasionally this injustice is political and social in the sense uppermost in Housman's line; but generally with Miss Millay it is personal, and at her best it is always personal. Here are some of the things she has said so often in her verse:

This is a lovely world, almost unbearably beautiful as a work of nature; but the poet is usually, in this expression, writing from some particular point on earth which is markedly less desirable than another she is recalling, and therefore she writes in sorrow. Sorrow in general is a constant mood with her, and its most typical expression is through sorrow in love. Though her love poetry has ranged from the flip to the marmoreal, from the casual to the frenzied, it has elaborated at both extremes and all the way between that love is (1) fickle and (2) irresistible. (p. 336)

From her poem *Mariposa* the conviction that

> Whether I be false or true,
> Death comes in a day or two.

was lightened and extenuated through the famous *A Few Figs From Thistles,* and this theme runs with its own small variations through her work, the impudence changing to bitterness and sometimes . . . to wholly humorless arrogance.

As deliberately as anywhere in her work, I suppose, Miss Millay seeks to objectify her conclusions in the eighteen sonnets called *Epitaph on the Race of Man.* I like a couple of these as well as anything Edna Millay has ever written, but as a whole it is a sequence that suffers from repetitiousness and from the later grand manner of the poet. No one can sound so profound as Miss Millay at her falsest! However, as I understand them, these sonnets portray man's victories over his environment and conclude that his tragedy lies in his inevitable defeat by himself. It is a great theme, and sometimes Miss Millay handles it with great beauty and genuine (not bogus) dignity. Two of the sonnets are certainly among her best: the much admired *See where Capella with her golden kids* and the not enough admired *Observe how Myanoshita cracked in two.* (pp. 337-38)

Her poems say a hundred times that life is sad. At least as often, her poems say that death is the bitterest pill of all; and they fight against it, wail upon it, and defy death. This, when you come to think of it, adds up to a lot of troubled emotion. Maybe if Miss Millay had ever made up her mind, we should have had less poetry from her, and that would be unfortunate; nonetheless, by these conflicting emotions she has remained in an intellectual jam. There is obvious sentimentality in this contradiction; it afflicts a great deal of her verse and explains, I think, why the verse leaves us dissatisfied. Here too I suspect we come closest to the reason for Miss Millay's attractiveness for the undergraduate, or adolescent, mind. (p. 338)

In other words, the mood of self-pity is exceptionally attractive to the young, and Miss Millay's verse has employed that mood (or vice versa) many, many times. The popularity of her poetry, of course, stems very largely from what we may call its familiarity: simple forms in rhyme and stanza, resemblances (whether or not fortunate) to poetry already well known, occasionally skillful reworkings of particular styles all the way from the Elizabethan to that of Robinson Jeffers. At her best, Miss Millay brings vigor and freshness to traditional forms and stamps them with a new personality more positively than any of her contemporaries has ever done. (pp. 338-39)

Edna Millay has pursued her art according to lights that have varied in her career, but according to those lights with integrity. This is not a small matter.

Where her poetry has, so to speak, gone wrong is where she has mistaken attitudes for convictions, or mere moods for profound truths (as we all do). Thus, you get the absurd blather, "O world, I cannot hold thee close enough!", in *God's World,* and the astounding insistence on so desiring the seashore that she is crying aloud for death by drowning. This is the common error of requiring an emotion to bear . . . a little more than it can bear. And along with such sentimentality in Miss Millay's work there has been a rapid loss of humor in its largest or smallest sense and a consequent gain in a grand manner that not only permits medieval impedimenta as aforesaid but even allows such solemn absurdities as celebrating the cleaning of a canary's cage. . . . (p. 340)

These elements were always in Miss Millay's poetry. The

humorless dullness of her early *Ode to Silence* is a pertinent example. The disproportionate overloading of an emotion was done full-length in *The Blue Flag in the Bog.* But the simpler elements have persisted, too, and it is those we come back to. (p. 341)

There is in the poem *Renascence* a simplicity which is at times girlish; legitimately so, of course. It holds the seed of Edna Millay's best poetry. In her subsequent work this girlishness sometimes became unpleasantly coy and mawkish, as for instance in the poem called *The Little Hill.* On the other hand, in *Elaine* and *A Visit to the Asylum,* bathos, however perilously, is really escaped; something pathetic and moving takes place. . . . (pp. 341-42)

> *Winfield Townley Scott, "Millay Collected," in* Poetry (© *1944 by The Modern Poetry Association; reprinted by permission of the Editor of* Poetry*), Vol. LXIII, No. VI, March, 1944, pp. 334-42.*

JOHN CIARDI (essay date 1950)

"The Goose Girl" [from "The Harp-Weaver"] still strikes me as the most typical of Edna Millay's poems, of the kind of presence she sought to invent. Its measure is cut to absolute simplicity; one thinks immediately of Housman, whose hand has surely touched Edna Millay's first poems. And immediately one senses a difference in the simplicity. "The Goose Girl" bears many surface resemblances to Housman's "Cherry Trees." The meter, the kind of language, the easy flow of the symbols, the imagery, all have a great deal in common. Yet Housman's poem remains convincing, and somehow "The Goose Girl" does not.

The difference occurs not in the way of saying but in the attitude of the saying. . . . One is finally forced to distrust the way Edna Millay takes herself in this poem. . . . [The] knowledge of Miss Millay's archness in so many of her other poems makes us wonder if this is not simply another pose. We doubt, and immediately the poem confirms our doubt. . . . This is not an experience, we conclude; it is a pose.

And poem after poem confirms this experience: there is always that element of the overdramatic about them, a fabrication of the words rather than of the feeling, of a posture rather than of an experience. It is, one suspects, exactly this in the poems that once set twenty years of undergraduates to imitating them. Something in the overstatement of the poems fitted our own imbalance. . . . Certainly something powerfully suited to our needs grew at that edge of bathos. . . .

It seems impossible now that we could have been so moved by such lines. . . .

Then somehow it was all over. (p. 9)

The simple fact seems to be that, having outgrown her youth, Edna Millay had outgrown the one subject she could make exciting. "Conversation at Midnight" was her attempt at intellectual reportage of an age, but it provided no subject for her gift. It seemed as if she had stopped living in order to talk—to talk endlessly and dully—about life. . . .

Then came the war, and the social consciousness that had first driven her to write some of her worst poetry in "Justice Denied in Massachusetts" (the Sacco-Vanzetti trial), betrayed her into such books as "Make Bright the Arrows." These are tragic books from which the last vestige of gift has disappeared; nobly to be sure, for reasons that all men of good will must be tempted to condone. But finally poetry must be protected from even the highest motives. . . . Moral indignation is no substitute for art. In these poems, unfortunately, only that substitution speaks: line after line of exhortations from the vocabulary of humanism, page after page of moral platitudes, but not a phrase of poetry. . . .

But to enumerate a poet's failures is not to judge him. A writer must be judged by his best. Edna Millay's best came at a time when many needed her excitement. Whether her capture of that audience was a good or a bad thing for the course of poetry one cannot say with any conviction. Certainly her intimate treatment of the frankly sensuous was some part of an age's contribution toward broadening the range of subjects permissible to poetry. That much is surely good. . . . But neither merit nor lack of merit defined her position in the poetry of the Twenties. It was not as a craftsman nor as an influence, but as the creator of her own legend that she was most alive for us. Her success was as a figure of passionate living. . . .

Perhaps her poems must be forgotten. Or perhaps they will become like "The Rubaiyat" and the "Sonnets from the Portuguese," poems that generation after generation of the young will be swept away by, gorgeously, overwhelmingly swept away by, and then outgrow. (p. 77)

> *John Ciardi, "Edna St. Vincent Millay: A Figure of Compassionate Living," in* The Saturday Review of Literature *(copyright, 1950, by The Saturday Review Co., Inc.; reprinted with permission), Vol. 33, No. 45, November 11, 1950, pp. 8-9, 77.*

EDMUND WILSON   (essay date 1952)

Edna Millay seems to me one of the only poets writing in English in our time who have attained to anything like the stature of great literary figures in an age in which prose has predominated. It is hard to know how to compare her to Eliot or Auden or Yeats—it would be even harder to compare her to Pound. There is always a certain incommensurability between men and women writers. But she does have it in common with the first three of these that, in giving supreme expression to profoundly felt personal experience, she was able to identify herself with more general human experience and stand forth as a spokesman for the human spirit, announcing its predicaments, its vicissitudes, but, as a master of human expression, by the splendor of expression itself, putting herself beyond common embarrassments, common oppressions and panics. (p. 752)

If one compares the contents of *Figs from Thistles,* written in the same year as the poems in *Second April,* with the contents of the other book, one can see that she imposed on herself a pretty rigorous critical standard. She would not mix with her serious work any of the merely cute feminine pieces . . . , nor any of the easier lyrics that reflected the tone of the women's magazines. This serious work, never loosely written, was tragic, almost pessimistic (though the best of her lighter verse had the same sort of implications). It was natural that Hardy and Housman should have been among her admirers. From Housman she partly derived

. . . , and she was closer to this masculine stoicism than to the heartbreak of Sara Teasdale. (pp. 767-68)

> *Edmund Wilson, "Epilogue, 1952: Edna St. Vincent Millay" (originally published in a slightly different form as "Edna St. Vincent Millay: A Memoir," in* The Nation, *Vol. 174, No. 16, April 19, 1952), in his* The Shores of Light: A Literary Chronicle of the Twenties and Thirties *(reprinted by permission of Farrar, Straus & Giroux, Inc.; copyright © 1952 by Edmund Wilson), Farrar, Straus & Giroux, 1952, pp. 744-93.*

MARY J. McKEE   (essay date 1966)

The more objective, the more representational a work of art, a piece of dramatic writing, the more clearly we can judge it against its model: truth of characterization, authenticity of language, verisimilitude of situation—all of these help the critic to judge a realistic play. In *Aria da Capo* we are deprived of all these criteria of judgment except in relation to its *commedia dell'arte* form. So here the artistry of form, of structural balance, of shaping of internal conflicts is the basis of evaluation. The psychological truth of the play is an equally important touchstone, but it is through the balance, the formal pattern of its structure, that we can best approach an assessment of its psychological truth. (p. 165)

This play deals with one of the "universals," man's relation to his fellow men and to the world. The meaning of the play is simple enough. In the cliché-ridden world of our empty, everyday lives, we are in danger of losing the capacity for the basic human awareness of the mystery of the universe, the transitoriness of our feelings, the constant presence of death. If this capacity atrophies, our lives become empty, mechanical; we lose one of the basic attributes of the dignity of man which has aptly been called "the tragic sense of life." This play inspires the search for genuine, authentic feeling and emotion, the striving to come to grips with reality despite all the cottonwool optimisms and euphemisms of our busy, purposeless lives. The playwright undertook to communicate what is most difficult to communicate—the callousness and heartlessness of human beings who have lost the basic sense of profound anguish at the thought of death and evanescence.

Pierrot and Columbine are the prototypes of all men and women cut off from the joy and sorrow of their fellowmen and from inquiry into the metaphysical sense of life. In *commedia dell'arte* and farcical *aria da capo* this servant and serving maid are bold externalizations of inner reality, visualizations of the underlying emptiness of life lived only to satisfy one's . . . desires. . . . They lack good will, warmth, love of fellowman, and easy emotional flow; instead, they have a certain kind of charming and disarming Charlie Chaplin helplessness.

The theatre of *commedia dell'arte* is basically a theater of laughter, and war could easily have been just another of its intriguing devices and comic tricks in *Aria da Capo*. But Millay did not choose the detachment which would have made war comic; on the contrary, she endeavored to do violence to that attitude. Within a Harlequinade setting she placed Cothurnus, a stock figure of Greek and Roman tragic drama, as the prompter for Corydon and Thyrsis, the protagonists in the war conflict. The tragedy on stage represents the human incapacity for a real confrontation with death—death is treated with playful disdain, maximum distance, with "the audience-will-forget" attitude. The insertion of the war tragedy into the *commedia dell'arte* setting is the very core and center of the play. (pp. 166-67)

Millay presented allegory, which essentially is a succession of events designed to illustrate a general idea. She chose to be direct rather than subtle, in opposition to modern taste. (p. 168)

The medium of *commedia dell'arte* provides characters through which we behold the tragic fate common to all men, but with a detachment which transforms frustration into laughter. We see the protagonists not with sympathy but as caricatures with a purely stage life. Yet in *Aria da Capo* these caricatures epitomize an attitude that we ourselves adopt at times, and hence they possess a strange and terrible significance. (p. 169)

> *Mary J. McKee, "Millay's 'Aria da Capo': Form and Meaning," in* Modern Drama *(copyright © 1966, University of Toronto, Graduate Centre for Study of Drama; with the permission of* Modern Drama*), Vol. 9, No. 2, September, 1966, pp. 165-69.*

NORMAN A. BRITTIN (essay date 1967)

In an age of criticism and poetical dryness, the lyrical intensity of personal revelation in [Millay's] poetry is striking. Her work is romantic and for the most part subjective. Though Millay, like other poets, puts on more than one *persona*, the reader always perceives the woman who identifies herself by her compassion, her love of beauty, her idealism, her tough unwillingness to compromise, her vehement defense of what she considers right. . . .

The bookishness of her poetry has been exaggerated. She was a well-read woman and had a wide range of vocabulary. Often, and especially in dramatic monologues, she wrote in colloquial style. Often, and especially in sonnets, she wrote in a formal style. It is a mistake to imply, as some critics have done, that the hallmark of her poetry is a kind of would-be grand manner that is faded and artificial. There are times when she is pompous and others when she indulges herself in girlish coyness. She has a tendency to use easy personifications which suggest centuries earlier than the twentieth; but for the most part, and increasingly through her whole career, her diction and style are not conspicuously "literary," old-fashioned, or derivative. Although she was at her mature best in elegiac poems, reflective sonnets and poems of exact description, Millay covered a considerable range in her work. In addition to her ambitious sonnet sequences, "Renascence," *Aria da Capo*, and *The King's Henchman* stand out as peaks of her success. (p. 165)

In technique she bridges the time of Tennyson and the twentieth century. . . . The Tennysonian and early Pre-Raphaelite attention to detail and sonority she adopted naturally. For use of the exact word and for subtle matchings of sound and sense her best work bears comparison with that of the finest masters of English poetic technique. In the line of poets who stress predication, she often uses long sentences with numerous qualifiers. Such sentences help to give a formal air to much of her poetry.

In her sonnets she soon reached a high level of achievement which she maintained throughout her career. Her example did much to restore the sonnet to respectability during her time. She deserves credit for success in the Petrarchan sonnet, which she wrote more and more with advancing years. (p. 166)

Although she is largely tied to tradition through her sonnets, her writing after 1928 is not bound to the traditional iambus and trochee or to traditional stanzas; she chooses her forms freely, sensitively exploring the possibilities of varied rhythms and lines of varied length. . . . Neither a hard-shelled traditionalist nor a fanatical experimenter, Millay followed an eclectic course.

Millay's constant theme is devotion to freedom. The freedom of the individual, the freedom of woman completely to be an individual—these values engage her complete loyalty. The ideals of freedom and justice, paramount among the traditional values of America, lead her to denounce threats to these ideals. As a supporter of freedom and justice she is a loyal citizen and a loyal critic of her country, although indignation unfortunately betrays her into shrillness. She became at times a prophetess-poet, never hesitating to speak her mind on public matters—thoroughly American in the tradition of Emerson, Whitman, Whittier, Lowell, and Moody. (pp. 166-67)

Hers is a radical creed. Meaningful freedom includes the freedom of the human being to be himself, to retain his integrity and fearlessly to express his individuality. Without belief in conventional religion Millay becomes a radical humanist, a Humanist-Stoic. Divisive modern forces, atomistic in their effects, have impelled many twentieth-century people along the same course. They find in Millay a poet who provides a moving record of a full-bodied participant in the twentieth century and who enunciates a credo for private lives and for public issues. (p. 167)

> *Norman A. Brittin, in his* Edna St. Vincent Millay *(copyright © 1967 by Twayne Publishers, Inc.; reprinted with the permission of Twayne Publishers, a Division of G. K. Hall & Co., Boston), Twayne, 1967, 192 p.*

JAMES GRAY (essay date 1967)

Seen whole [Edna St. Vincent Millay] emerges out of myth not as a gay figure but as a tragic one; not as a precocious perennial schoolgirl but as an artist born mature and burdened with a scrupulous sense of responsibility toward her gift; not as a changeling child of mysticism but as a creature whose essential desire was to find identity with the balanced order of nature; not as a woman merely but as a creator who inevitably contained within her persona masculine as well as feminine attributes.

The theme of all her poetry is the search for the integrity of the individual spirit. The campaign to conquer and control this realm of experience is conducted always in terms of positive and rigorous conflict—the duel with death, the duel with love, the duel of mind pitted against heart, the duel with "The spiteful and the stingy and the rude" who would steal away possession of beauty.

It is not too fanciful to say that she was born old while she remained forever young. . . . (pp. 5-6)

[Quiet] reverence for vitality under discipline is the distinguishing quality of her poetry. At its best it is characterized by a kind of orderly surrender to ecstasy. (p. 8)

It is often said of the major figures of the arts that each seems to create a universe all his own and to measure its vast dimensions with untransferable techniques. (pp. 9-10)

No such gigantic stature can be claimed for a poet like Edna Millay. Her theme was too personal, too intimate to herself to fill out the dimensions of a supernatural realm of imagination. Indeed it might be said that her unique effort was to perform the miracle of creation in reverse. A universe already made pressed its weight on the sensibility, the aptitude for awareness, of one individual. . . . (p. 10)

The journey in search of wholeness for the individual, an adventure which has obsessed the minds of the philosophers of the past and the psychiatrists of the present, cannot be left safely to further exploration by the computers of the future. It continues, therefore, to be of no trivial interest as it is presented in the poems of Edna St. Vincent Millay.

It should not be taken as an indication of a failure to grow that Edna Millay produced when she was only nineteen years old one of the most characteristic, most memorable, and most moving of her poems. The intuitions of artists do not reach them on any schedule of merely logical development. . . . In ''Renascence'' Edna Millay announced the theme to which four more decades of her life were to be spent in the most intense kind of concentration. ''The soul can split the sky in two, / And let the face of God shine through.'' This confrontation with the divine can be dared and endured because man is one with the divine.

Edna Millay presented the inner life of the spirit always as a conflict of powerful forces. The will to live and the will to die are elementally at war in ''Renascence.'' . . . The impulse toward surrender *itself* has roused the counter impulse toward a participation more passionate than ever before in the values of human existence. . . . The meaning of this battle of the wills is clear. The anguish of existence must be endured as the tribute owed to its beauty. (pp. 10-12)

An account of the running battle between life and death claimed first place among the poet's preoccupations through her writing career. The effectiveness of the report is heightened by an awareness, sometimes bitter and sometimes merely rueful, that now one side commands ascendancy over will and now the other. (p. 12)

[Variations] of tone in her report on the duel of life against death lend the best and most original of her personal qualities to the development of an old, familiar theme. The parallel may be suggested that, just as a mother must have faith in her child lacking any evidence to justify it, so the believer in life must show a similar courageous unreasonableness. Edna Millay is perhaps at her best when she casts her vote of No Confidence in death. (p. 14)

So many of Edna Millay's pages are devoted to critical moments of the love duel that it has been possible, even for reasonably well informed readers, to be aware only of her confidences about ''what arms have lain / Under my head till morning.'' To their loss they have ignored her equal preoccupation with other themes. Still it is true that some of her most searching observations about the human condition are concerned with the approach to ecstasy through the identification of man with woman. It would, however, be to deceive oneself to approach these poems as if they were exercises in eroticism. Despite the many sidelong references to the physical relationship, the enclosing interest is that of human love as a total experience of the psyche involving, on the positive side, intellectual communication and sympathy of taste and, on the negative side, the endless warfare of two egos that cannot effect a complete surrender into oneness.

The limp endorsement of correct and appropriate sentiments which has made up so much of love poetry, particularly that written by women, is conspicuous for its total absence from these ardent but anxious confrontations of man and woman. It is significant of Edna Millay's approach to the psychological crisis of love versus hate—and to the even more destructive tragicomedy of love slackening away into indifference by the influences of time, change, and disillusion—that she does not speak of these matters simply as a woman. Often in her highly dramatic representations of the love duel she assumes the man's role and she plays it with no nervous air of indulging in a masquerade. She is concerned with the mind as the retort in which all the chemical reactions of love take place and, because her own intelligence partook of both masculine and feminine characteristics, the poems convey the impression that the exactitude of science, in control of the impulses of intuition, has been brought to bear to reveal much that those changes involve in a man's temperament as well as in a woman's.

Again, as in her account of the conflict of the will to live and the will to die, the love duel is presented with high drama as one that is destined to go on and on indecisively because the adversaries are only too well matched in aggressiveness and submissiveness, in strength and weakness, in sympathy and treachery. (pp. 16-17)

[A reverential gaiety] which finds room for humor in the midst of the contemplation of bliss, characterizes much of Edna Millay's love poetry. Its popularity may be accounted for by the intoxicating quality that brings the immediacy of a highly personal emotion to the poetic statement. The merit that gives the work permanence is the fastidiousness of the style in which the spontaneity is captured.

In her younger days Edna Millay sometimes allowed her exuberant vitality to escape into verses the levity of which made her famous, perhaps to the injury of her reputation as a serious poet. (p. 18)

These flourishes of audacity do not touch at all closely on the center of her understanding of the love duel. There she held a formidable awareness of the power of change which is not in the least like the vague consciousness of impermanence in which so many poetic spirits have fluttered with languid futility. . . . Edna Millay used the sharpest tools of her intelligence to hew out for herself a unique place among poets by undertaking to discover *why* no love endures. What she says is that the loophole in commitment offers the necessary escape route by which the self saves its integrity. There can be no such thing as total surrender except with degradation or with, what is worse, dishonesty. In love the giving must be generous and free, but there must be withholding, too, if the self is to remain whole. (pp. 18-19)

The immediacy of experience is communicated in images that are piercingly personal. Very often the suggestions of the figurative language are so unexpected that they seem to spring out of an immediate passion which catches deliberately and desperately at punishing words. . . .

It is because she was bold enough to examine the problem of the psychological distance between man and woman—one that cannot be breached and should not be violated—that Edna Millay may be said to have made an original contribution to the literature of the love duel. (p. 19)

[It] is the ability to capture in colloquial language and in one brief thunderclap of drama the essence of a tragic psychological struggle that lends to Edna Millay's long discussion of the love duel its effects of variety and flexibility.

The tone of melancholy misgiving in the face of the emotional crisis is pervasive in these studies. but the warming, the nourishing, the half-maternal aspects of the experience of love are not neglected. (pp. 20-1)

It is characteristic of Edna Millay's temper—not merely its prevailing but its almost uninterrupted mood—that she enters upon the search for beauty as if this, too, were a struggle. (p. 21)

This is to say that the mind has its right to evaluate beauty. It should not yield in limp acceptance as if faced by something of divine origin and therefore, like a god of Greek mythology, not to be denied its will. What Edna Millay persuades a reader that she does indeed know is that beauty must be endured as well as enjoyed. To surrender to beauty without resistance would be to lose an exhilarating aspect of the experience. It must be participated in, but the terms of one's compact with beauty must be understood to be one-sided. "Beauty makes no pledges." In return for the awe that the observer feels in its presence nothing is promised other than awareness itself. . . .

That she is not entirely consistent in developing her religion of beauty need not be found disturbing. She is no more given to shifts of interpretation than mystics must ever be. Beauty may be aloof and impersonal but it is also an element in the process of rebirth, the faith in which the poet takes her deepest comfort. It even becomes in certain poems the food on which she feeds. Her figures of speech suggest again and again that, as a woman, she felt an almost organic closeness to the working of gestation. (p. 22)

Part of the nourishment that she receives from awareness of beauty is provided by what is for her the immediate actuality of sensuous experience. (p. 23)

She was always an actor in the drama: a militant defender of herself against beauty, a militant defender of beauty against its defilers. And she was resolutely faithful to the integrity of her own perceptions. She never attempts to encompass more of a sense of the wonder of the natural world than her own eyes can see. What moves her is the recollection of a familiar scene, fixed in memory by some small detail of local color. . . . Armed with awareness, the one who is "waylaid" by beauty may find exultation in the simplest of experiences. Edna Millay did indeed seem to write all her poems to give permanence to a moment of ecstasy. (pp. 23-4)

From first to last, through every phase of her development, Edna Millay continued to be intensely herself and no other. Whether her theme was death, love, beauty, or the refreshing impulse of the will to live she spoke always with an accent that was unique to her. Of language she made a homespun garment to clothe her passions and her faith.

That she was able to create effects of striking originality is discovered to be only the more remarkable when a characteristic poem is examined closely and its thought is found to wear "something old" and "something borrowed" from the left-over wardrobe of tradition. Edna Millay was a product as much of the nineteenth century as of the twentieth. The influence of tradition moved her a little backward in time. A too great reverence for her early instruction—not only at her mother's knee but also at Keats's—probably accounts for all the "O's" and "Ah's," the "would I were's," the "hast's," the "art's," the "wert's," the "Tis's." It must account also for the inversions of normal word order which sometimes impede the plunge of her hardihood in thought.

Even in more important matters of vocabulary, imagery, and symbolism her impulse toward expression was governed by convention. Despite her interest in science she felt its discipline to be alien to her always personal style of utterance. She did not find in its language a new source of imaginative power such as Auden has exploited. Despite her obsession in the late years with the crisis of war, such a reference as one to "Man and his engines" reveals an uninvolved attitude toward the special concerns of the machine age. . . . The familiar image, drawn from the treasury of metaphor upon which Shakespeare also depended for imaginative resource, seems never to have dismayed her. She was not inhibited by fear of intelligibility; she was not tempted to prod the imagination with tortured similes. For her, death still swung his scythe and the poems in which he does so with the old familiar ruthlessness betray no nervous apprehension that the instrument may have become rusty or blunted with the use of ages.

Because she absorbed tradition deeply into herself she seems able to revitalize its language with the warmth of her own temper. Her words become fertile from the nourishment which, as woman, she communicated to them as if by an umbilical link.

Simplicity, spontaneity, the seeming absence of calculation combine to produce her best effects. (pp. 27-8)

More often than with either definitely declared voice she speaks as a detached observer of natural sights and sounds. These souvenirs of experience are shared with a reader in language that seems entirely casual; it has been borrowed for the moment from more studied performers in the realm of poetry simply to convey a passing impression. . . . More typical of the poet's method is the device of catching a symbolic significance, some warning of the threat against survival, in an image that seems to be, all at once, spontaneous, startling, and inescapably true. (p. 29)

Edna Millay's wit was never petty. She was generous toward all her adversaries except mediocrity, war, and death. And in fashioning an epigram she revealed her most fastidious respect both for truth and for elegance. In the later poems her wit is so unobtrusive, so modest, that it might be missed entirely by a reader hoping to find a showy attribute identified by a capital letter. But it is always subtly present, embedded in a theme, as is the wit of Henry James. The tight-packed phrase, the unexpected revelation of how opposites of impulse may be found to blend, the sudden illumination of an ambiguity—these are the veins of wisdom through which wit runs in the sonnets. (p. 32)

A close examination of the work of any artist is certain to reveal flaws. The very urgency of the desire to communicate must tempt any poet sometimes to override obstacles recklessly. With Edna Millay the individual line seldom limps though it may now and again betray an obvious determination to be vigorous. There is little sense of strain in the use of rhyme and, even in the early poems when her effects threaten to become self-conscious, she avoids the temptation to indulge in the verbal acrobatics of clever versifiers as even Byron does. What troubles her appraisers most of all is the willingness to snatch up old trophies of metaphor and set them up among her own inspirations as if she were unaware of the difference of freshness between them.

But in the end vigor and spontaneity prevail in technique as they do in passion. The singing quality of the lyrics, of the free forms of verse and of the formal sonnets, too, is consistently clear and true. (pp. 33-4)

She wrote prose, as she wrote poetry, with an at once witty and intensely sober regard for her own values. The personal letters glow—sometimes they seem feverishly to glitter—with the élan that sustained her, however precariously, through the crucial moments of her experience. Her preface to the volume of Baudelaire translations reveals a critical intelligence of distinction. Only the adroit satiric sketches written under the pseudonym Nancy Boyd depart from her preoccupation with poetry. These exercises, too, display a kind of coloratura virtuosity. They draw freely on her gift of wit and have importance as lucid indirect reflections of her attitudes: her unwavering honesty, her distaste for pretense, sentimentality, and concessiveness. (p. 34)

Conversation at Midnight remains pseudo-drama, lacking a concentrated drive toward effective vicarious experience. . . .

The faults of the work are inherent in the original concept. This requires a group of men, met for a session of late-night drinking and ratiocination, to use the occasion for a kind of war game in which they fire rounds of ammunition over each other's heads, hitting only distant, theoretical targets. Each guest represents a point of view, aesthetic, social, or moral; each in turn has his say, in a piece of stylized elocution, about capitalism, Communism, commercialism, Nazism, and, of course, love in a world that is out of sorts with spontaneity. All is spoken in earnest; much of the talk is witty and stimulating; some of it inevitably seems trivial in its cloudy references to situations in the lives of the characters which there has been neither time nor occasion really to evoke. Nothing resembling dramatic tension can rise out of these arguments which never intermingle, never affect each other, never in the end manage to clarify idea. (p. 36)

There were crises of social life which gave gross affront to the most fundamental of her convictions and she could not withhold her protests. These took poetic form but—as she later knew to her chagrin—she was able at such times only to rear up the framework of a poem, gaunt and horrifying. To the lines with which she clothed the structure she could communicate her impotent rage but not the essence of compassion which she wished to memorialize.

There was, for example, her involvement in the Sacco and Vanzetti case. (p. 38)

When Sacco and Vanzetti were finally ordered to be executed, Edna Millay wrote the poem "Justice Denied in Massachusetts," a desperate and bitter threnody. . . . The unwilling, half-stifled protest that a reader makes in his turn against these utterances springs from the impression that a just and honest sentiment is being overdramatized. Is the abject surrender to despair really congenial to the poet's spirit or does this lamentation have to be brought under the charge of being tainted by hysteria? The conviction is clearly genuine but the excess of passion with which it is expressed still seems dubious. The literary crisis is not ameliorated when the poet yields her mind to the most cliché of imaginings: "We shall die in darkness, and be buried in the rain."

It is right for a poet to be a participant in the affairs of everyday living. With her special talent for doing precisely this, Edna Millay could not withhold her word. Nor is it relevant that the guilt or innocence of the two men whose part she took is still a moot question. The respect must be paid her of considering anything she wrote as a work of art. Viewed in that light it becomes evident that poems written for occasions come forth misshapen at their birth by the influence of propaganda. In work that was truly her own even her bitterest protests against the will to destroy were informed by a still abiding faith; such poems reveal her militant spirit at its most staunch. The weakness of "Justice Denied in Massachusetts" must be attributed to the fact that it was not nourished by an inner will but fed on the inadequate substitute of propaganda. (pp. 39-40)

Edna St. Vincent Millay has been praised extravagantly as the greatest woman poet since Sappho. She has also been dismissed with lofty forbearance as a renegade from the contemporary movement in poetry and sometimes been treated almost as a traitor because she never broke defiantly with the past. But both eulogy and denigration seem to hang upon her figure like whimsical investitures. Neither costume suits the occasion when her enduring presence rises up before us to bespeak a mind that has not lost its vigor. (p. 43)

She belongs to an impressive company of artists who came to maturity and found their voices during the second quarter of this century. Many of these have undertaken to explore the darkest caves of the secret mind of man and they have developed new poetic forms in which to record their experiences. Among them the figure of Edna St. Vincent Millay is conspicuous because she stands alone and in a blaze of light. It is impossible not to understand what she has to say, impossible not to be moved by the simple, direct, eloquent statements of her convictions. The world, which she had held no closer at the beginning of her life than she did at the end, gave her as much of pain as it did pleasure. Love, beauty, and life itself had all to be endured as well as enjoyed. But the human experience had meaning for her. The round of the seasons still kept to its pledge of rebirth and renewal. From that faith she drew the strength to impart dignity and beauty . . . to even the most cruel phases of the adventure of our time. (pp. 45-6)

James Gray, in his Edna St. Vincent Millay *(American Writers Pamphlet No. 64;* © *1967, University of Minnesota), University of Minnesota Press, Minneapolis, 1967, 48 p.*

ELIZABETH P. PERLMUTTER (essay date 1977)

Millay, assuming the existence of fixed conventions in lyric tradition, became virtually a crusader in the reclamation of the short lyric poem from its temporary submersion in the twin sloughs of Victorian sentiment and modernist gloom. . . . (p. 157)

In retrospect, Millay's actual achievement, which was not inconsiderable, was to conserve, in her early volumes, the melodic simplicity of the combined pastoral and personal lyric by breathing into it a hybridized diction we must ruefully call "poetic." That is, starting with her earliest verses, Millay's style was a resplendent pastiche of Sapphic simplicity, Catullan urbanity, homeless Chaucerian idiom, uprooted Shakespearean grammar, Cavalier sparkle, Wordsworthian magnanimity, Keatsian sensuousness, and Housemanian melancholy, not of course compounded all at once in a single lethal draught, but lightly dispersed here and there throughout her songs and sonnets. . . . Here was no fragmented, estranged, crumbling world, which to Millay's ears and eyes seemed more depressing than it actually was in the work of Eliot, Pound, and Aiken, but a universe to which the Aeolian strings of the poet's heart could still vibrate, her fingers all the while plucking an ancient lyre. . . . (p. 159)

In the long-familiar guise of the poet aching with the world's beauty, Millay uses an equally commonplace "poetic diction" of apostrophe and grammatical inversion, with touches of archaism ("thou" and "prithee") to construct a speaker at once reverent, breathless, and naïve. This persona becomes more fully rendered in the volumes following *Renascence* as the Girl, who as the analogue of the young, girlish poet herself, becomes the vehicle of the most "poetical" features of Millay's lyric diction. (pp. 159-60)

For the Girl, love—whether chaste or erotic, passionate or quiescent—was the whole of existence, subsuming her impetuous high-spiritedness and her thirst for intense sensation and meaning. Yet equally essential to the Girl's character was her self-abandon, and self-neglect. She would too often recklessly bestow herself upon some heartless lad who would, inevitably, betray her. Only then would she find at the very moment of heartbreak, at the very crisis of anguish, a terrible strength that would allow her to grieve but not to die. This combination of weakness and strength, of erotic susceptibility and unsuspected will, provided Millay's Girl with a basic affective strategy in which disappointment could change suddenly to ennui, and high lyric lamentation to shrugging colloquial gloom. Indeed, Millay's Girl was essentially a theatrical persona, a medium for the expression of sudden shifts in tone and implied bodily gestures. (p. 160)

[She spoke] of her love affairs, not with Sappho's brevity, nor with Catullus's candor, but with an allusiveness indebted to both and a coyness both would have shunned. Using a rhetoric of swift changes of mood, the Girl could turn the lightsome measures of impulse and intimacy into the acrid dismissals and recriminations of scorn and ennui. . . . (pp. 161-62)

Capable of moving readers and hearers, the skillful, charming verse through which the Girl had life was even so too dependent on implied gesture to be taken seriously as meant speech. If Millay's Girl defamed the "beautiful," or hinted at the improper, if in her excesses of feeling she occasionally rhymed bathetically or slithered around and over her meters, all it pointed to was her very modern right to

say or do anything she pleased. Emancipation was a matter of mood, not conviction. (p. 162)

> Elizabeth P. Perlmutter, "A Doll's Heart: The Girl in the Poetry of Edna St. Vincent Millay and Louise Bogan," in *Twentieth Century Literature* (copyright 1977, Hofstra University Press), Vol. 23, No. 2, May, 1977, pp. 157-79.*

ADDITIONAL BIBLIOGRAPHY

Brenner, Rica. "Edna St. Vincent Millay." In her *Ten Modern Poets*, pp. 61-82. New York: Harcourt, Brace and Co., 1930.
  Biographical account of Millay's growth as a poet and her publication career.

Cheney, Anne. *Millay in Greenwich Village*. University: The University of Alabama Press, 1975, 160 p.
  Biography of Millay's years in Greenwich Village that is only incidentally concerned with her poetry.

Colum, Mary M. "Edna Millay and Her Time." *The New Republic* 124, No. 11 (12 March 1951): 17-18.
  Discusses Millay as a poet who reflected the moods of her age and examines her failure to match her intellectual achievement with her technical one.

Dash, Joan. "Edna St. Vincent Millay." In her *A Life of One's Own: Three Gifted Women and the Men They Married*, pp. 115-228. New York: Harper & Row, 1973.
  A biographical sketch of Millay written with a psychological slant. The critic portrays Millay as ambivalent about being female and shows this ambivalence as critical to Millay's life and writings.

Davison, Edward. "Edna St. Vincent Millay." *The English Journal* XVI, No. 9 (November 1927): 671-82.
  Classifies Millay as a minor poet. The critic uses selections to illustrate her metrical skill and epigrammatic style as well as her exaggeration of language and emotion.

DuBois, Arthur E. "Edna St. Vincent Millay." *The Sewanee Review* 43, No. 1 (January-March 1935): 80-104.
  Emotional appraisal of Millay's various personalities: precocious child, woman, poet, and mystic.

Gould, Jean. *The Poet and Her Book: A Biography of Edna St. Vincent Millay*. New York: Dodd, Mead & Co., 1969, 308 p.
  Good biography of Millay.

Gurko, Miriam. *Restless Spirit: The Life of Edna St. Vincent Millay*. New York: Thomas Y. Crowell Co., 1962, 271 p.
  Biography that treats Millay's poetry in its autobiographical context.

Minot, Walter S. "Millay's 'Ungrafted Tree': The Problem of the Artist as Woman." *The New England Quarterly* XLVIII, No. 2 (June 1975): 260-69.
  Biographical study that attempts to determine why Millay, a poetic prodigy, never achieved lasting poetic greatness.

Sprague, Rosemary. "Edna St. Vincent Millay." In her *Imaginary Gardens: A Study of Five American Poets*, pp. 135-82. Philadelphia: Chilton Book Co., 1969.
  Biographical survey of Millay's career.

Tate, Allen. "Edna St. Vincent Millay." In his *Reactionary Essays on Poetry and Ideas*, pp. 221-27. New York: Charles Scribner's Sons, 1936.
  Describes Millay as a poet of the second order who lacks the power to create a whole world vision. Tate describes her as a poet of personal emotion with obvious limitations.

Wood, Clement. ''Edna St. Vincent Millay: A Clever Sappho.'' In his *Poets of America,* pp. 199-213. New York: E. P. Dutton & Co., 1925.

Review of Millay's first three volumes of poetry that praises her work but denigrates her self-conscious use of antiquated poetic techniques.

Luigi Pirandello

1867-1936

Italian dramatist, novelist, short story writer, essayist, and poet.

Pirandello was one of the most important innovators in twentieth-century drama. His philosophical themes and experiments with dramatic structure added a new dimension to traditional methods of theatrical production. Pirandello was closely identified with the *teatro del grottesco*, a movement in Italian drama that satirized society's shortcomings by stressing the grotesqueness of modern life. To do this, Pirandello developed techniques such as the play-within-the-play, the play-outside-the-play, and improvisation to present his themes of the relativity of truth, the tenuous line between sanity and madness, and the difficulty of communication. If a personal philosophy can be attributed to Pirandello, it is one of pessimism for the human condition tinged with compassion.

Pirandello was born in Sicily, the son of a prosperous sulfur merchant. Although his father wanted him to go into business, he decided to attend Bonn University, where he earned a doctorate in philology. Supported by an allowance from his father, he moved to Rome and began his literary career by contributing poems and short stories to various journals. When a catastrophic flood in the sulfur mines swept away the family fortune, he was forced to accept a professorship at a teacher's college for women. The bankruptcy led to his wife's emotional breakdown and subsequent insanity, a crisis which, in many critics' view, inspired his psychological themes.

Although Pirandello's early short stories and novels are strongly influenced by *verismo*, an Italian movement advocating literary realism, they reveal his obsession with the workings of inner consciousness. Critical success came in Italy with his third novel, *Il fu Mattia Pascal* (*The Late Mattia Pascal*), in which he observes a man's desperate attempt to shed his past and forge a new identity. It was as a dramatist, however, that Pirandello proved himself to be a brilliant innovator. The structural experiments of the trilogy of "theater-in-the-theater" plays brought Pirandello international renown. In these dramas he achieves a masterful synthesis of form and content. His themes—the fluidity of reality and the difficulty of establishing truth—are not only the subject of but also integral to the forms of *Sei personaggi in cerca d'autore* (*Six Characters in Search of an Author*), with its play-within-the-play; *Questa sera si recita a soggetto* (*Tonight We Improvise*), with its reliance on improvisation; *Ciascuno a suo modo* (*Each in His Own Way*), with its play-outside-the-play; and the frequent role reversals among actors and characters throughout the trilogy. In *Six Characters in Search of an Author*, his most popular and controversial work, six characters rejected by their author storm the stage and demand that their story be told. The resulting play-within-the-play reveals the inevitable distortion that actors impose on drama in the very act of presenting it. Pirandello's insistence on the relativity of personality and truth was so disturbing to

audiences of that time that the premiere of this play was accompanied by rioting.

The tragedy *Enrico IV* (*Henry IV*), considered his masterpiece by many critics, is the story of a madman's conscious decision to reject the sane world and remain fixed in his madness. In this drama Pirandello asks, Who is sane?—one who suffers the cruelties and humiliations of daily existence in contemporary society, or one who constructs his own world as an eleventh-century emperor. Pirandello probes in *Henry IV*, and in all his work, the conflicts between reality and appearance, the individual and society, art and life. Mirror and mask imagery, which he uses to explore these dichotomies, are ubiquitous not only in his dramas, but also in his earlier novels and short stories.

Pirandello was vitally concerned with the production and acting of his plays. Thus, following the success of *Six Characters in Search of an Author* and *Henry IV* he established his own acting company, which toured all over the world. He was awarded the Nobel Prize in literature in 1934.

Pirandello's work is criticized for being discursive, repetitious, and overly cerebral. Yet he is universally recognized as the leading architect of modern drama, and the precursor of the Theater of the Absurd.

PRINCIPAL WORKS

Mal giocondo   (poetry)   1889
Amori senza amore   (short stories)   1894
Beffe della morte e della vita   (short stories)   1902
Bianche e nere   (short stories)   1904
Il fu Mattia Pascal   (novel)   1904
   [*The Late Mattia Pascal*, 1923]
Erma bifronte   (short stories)   1906
L'esclusa   (novel)   1908
   [*The Outcast*, 1925]
L'umorismo   (essay)   1908
   [*On Humor*, 1974]
I vecchi e i giovani   (novel)   1913
   [*The Old and the Young*, 1928]
Liolà   (drama)   1916
   [*Liolà*, 1952]
Si gira   (novel)   1916
   [*Shoot*, 1926]
Cosí è (se vi pare)   (drama)   1917
   [*Right You Are! (If You Think So)* published in *Three
   Plays*, 1922]
Il piacere dell'onestà   (drama)   1917
   [*The Pleasure of Honesty* published in *Each in His Own
   Way, and Two Other Plays*, 1923]
Il carnevale dei morti   (short stories)   1919
L'uomo, la bestia e la virtù   (drama)   1919
Sei personaggi in cerca d'autore   (drama)   1921
   [*Six Characters in Search of an Author* published in
   Three Plays, 1922]
Enrico IV   (drama)   1922
   [*Henry IV* published in *Three Plays*, 1922]
Vestire gli ignudi   (drama)   1922
   [*Naked* published in *Each in His Own Way, and Two
   Other Plays*, 1923]
Novelle per un anno   (short stories)   1922-36
Ciascuno a suo modo   (drama)   1924
   [*Each in His Own Way* published in *Each in His Own
   Way, and Two Other Plays*, 1923]
Uno, nessuno e centomila   (novel)   1926
   [*One, No One, and a Hundred Thousand*, 1933]
Come tu mi vuoi   (drama)   1930
   [*As You Desire Me*, 1931]
Questa sera si recita a soggetto   (drama)   1930
   [*Tonight We Improvise*, 1932]
* *Horse in the Moon*   (short stories)   1931
* *Better Think Twice about It*   (short stories)   1934
* *Naked Truth*   (short stories)   1934
I giganti della montagna   (drama)   1937
   [*The Mountain Giants and Other Plays*, 1958]
* *Medals and Other Stories*   (short stories)   1939
Maschere Nude. 4 vols.   (dramas)   1948-49
Short Stories   (short stories)   1959
Short Stories   (short stories)   1965

*These stories have been selected from the series
   Novelle per un anno.

EDWARD STORER   (essay date 1921)

[The Sicilian Luigi Pirandello is] a weaver of fine dialectical
pieces, a creator of cerebral situations infused with a life
that is poetic and mystical, even philosophical. The language of his plays and novels in its occasional raciness and
explosive nervousness is often meridional, but the pains,
the doubts and the plaint which inspire this author's work

do not belong to the delightful but provincial island of Sicily, but are of our own modern day. (pp. 271-72)

The novel *The Late Mattia Pascal* has been rightly judged
to be the fecundating influence of the long series of so-
called grotesques which have held the boards of the Italian
theatre.... In *Mattia Pascal*, whom his family suppose
dead and who changes his name and becomes another man
with another history, we have the first appearance of a
theme dear to Pirandello: that of the man standing outside
of himself, the renouncer of life, spiritually beautiful in his
almost ascetic resignation. The type is sensitive and suffering, and one does not know if it be more patient in supporting life or more curious as to its puzzling developments.
(p. 273)

The central motive of *Il Fu Mattia Pascal*, which in its essence is poetry, since it holds life for a moment in a crystalline solution of thought, is repeated with greater poignancy
and with richer effect in the truly extraordinary play, *Cosi
e, si vi pare* (*It's So, if It Seems So*). This play, like most of
the author's later ones, has a poetic core from which, if
many thorns of unseizable dialectic grow, there exhales
also a pure spirit of poetry. The atmosphere of the comedy,
or "parabola," as Pirandello calls it, is tenderly human, and
though the play closes on a baffling note of interrogation,
only wilfully pragmatic spirits will be discontent with the
mystery under which truth always veils itself. For in *Cosi e,
se vi pare* we are perhaps only incidentally concerned with
the hopeless question: What is the truth? Pirandello is too
fine an artist to pose directly and brutally so disturbing a
conundrum to his audience of fellow human beings. He allows a suggestion of the question to reveal itself. (p. 274)

And here the poetry which tenuously haunts most of the
plays of Pirandello breathes forth from among the waspish
and humorous comments of the townsfolk all pettily determined "to get at the truth." (p. 275)

[Pirandello] began his dramatic period with some Sicilian
peasant plays: *Lumie di Sicilia* and *Liola*.... *Liola*, which
is one of his best plays, is a country comedy full of the
color, the shrill voices and the perfumes of Sicily. (p. 276)

But ..., it may be well to emphasize some of the faults
and weaknesses of the Pirandello comedies. They have
often a tendency to be too sophistic; the atmosphere is
sometimes so rarefied that there seems no possibility of
humanity and human manifestations existing in it. Pirandello, we must recognize, is not an author in his maturer
work to please the big public.... The laughs and smiles
which he brings to the faces of his audiences have often
something bitter about them, or rather they are too little
vulgar to please everyone. Again, Pirandello is often exag-
geratedly casuistic, and he requires on the part of his audience a mind rendered supple by a certain course of mental
gymnastics. He is not always an easy author, and even
those who admire him cannot but recognize that he is often
an exasperating author. But such are the inevitable faults of
this new school of "grotesques," or marionette dramas,
where seemingly volitionless puppets are moved by pains
and passions, that, torturing them, yet seem to leave them
cold. Nor is this impression without its inevitable reaction
on the audience which derives a refined, an intellectual
stimulus from the various manifestations of the Pirandellian conscience. Yet irony, as Nietzsche saw many years ago, is
the especial art of our epoch, self-conscious and spiritually

diffident, and the irony of Pirandello is fine and at the same time tender—a poet's irony, in fact.

In *Pensaci Giacomino! (Think About It, Jimmy!)* we have a typically Pirandellian theme, artificial, grotesque, not quite credible in fact. (pp. 277-78)

In *Come Prima, meglio di prima (As Before, but Better)*, we have another of Pirandello's curious inversions, this time of the traditional trio of husband, wife and lover. The personages do not seem to act from instinctive motives, but rather from prejudices or cerebral conceptions. This comedy is not one of the best works of Pirandello, but it exemplifies very clearly the peculiarities and the excesses of his style. The characters do not philosophize or make speeches, as they do in some of Shaw's plays, but a similar process seems to be going on inside their minds. The audience only gets glimpses of their exaggerated introspectiveness in a series of allusions, of ellipses, of swift changes of front.

In *Sei Personaggi in cerca d'Autore* . . . we have what is perhaps one of his most characteristic works. (p. 279)

This curious play, full of the wavering, acute and subtle spirit of its author, closes on this note of interrogation. What is reality? What is fiction? The author does not answer us: that is his secret, a secret which he, too, is unable to answer. (p. 281)

> *Edward Storer, "The 'Grotesques' of Pirandello,"*
> in Forum *(copyright, 1921, by Events Publishing Company, Inc.), Vol. 66, No. 4, October, 1921, pp. 271-81.*

MARIO PRAZ (essay date 1922)

Much might be said against the dramatist Luigi Pirandello; but at least he has introduced or tried to introduce to the stage a new point of view. . . .

Luigi Pirandello thought his assertion of the dissidence an original discovery. Had he been a philosopher he would have known better, and not merely asserted it, but tried to transcend it: but being an artist he has remained in front of the dissidence, impressed and moved by it; being a dramatist he has used it as a lever to overthrow the traditional convention of the theatre. A dramatist commonly aims to construct persons; to select among the various and often discordant gifts of life certain salient lines, and therefrom to compose characters. But Pirandello takes to pieces the abstractions which are called characters; he places the fictions called persons in contact with life, so that their illusory reality dissolves. . . . The traditional dramatist does all possible to make his puppets resemble living creatures; Pirandello, to make them appear as puppets, and thus he turns theatrical esthetic upside down. (p. 535)

[Before] attempting the stage [Pirandello] tried in stories and novels to give expression to the dissidence which now forms the nucleus of his art. He formulated it nearly twenty years ago in his novel *Il fu Mattia Pascal*. You might imagine he would choose his protagonist among the scientists, philosophers, rulers, for an intellect adequate to work out the grave problem. But no: herein lies his originality and freedom from pedantry. He lays his problem on the shoulders of a man less than mediocre. Mattia Pascal, a thoughtless native of a small town, behaves in early life so reck-

lessly that it becomes necessary for him suddenly to escape his surroundings. . . . [His] tragical dissidence appears to him in intense forms, but these suggest the profound significance of the story half symbolically, as in Chamisso's celebrated *Peter Schlemihl* a more hidden meaning lay in the man losing his shadow . . . , the man who no longer calls himself Mattia Pascal finds himself groping in the void. He is a fish out of water, knowing at once what to be a fish means, and no longer able to live. To return to life he must cease consciously to represent a determinate person, and reacquire his former name and clear up the misunderstanding of his presumed death.

The same dissidence appears in diverse forms, and very odd circumstances, in Pirandello's plays, complicated by an analogous motif. For beside our fashioning ourselves in our sight and the world's according to a fictitious picture, other people classify us according to the equally false picture which they have of us; and woe betide him who tries amid these pictures to discern truth. So in *Cosi e, come pare*, Signor Poza and his mother-in-law, Signora Frola, both call each other mad; which is lying? The district is thrown into confusion by the queer dilemma. How to discover the truth? Truth will issue from Poza's wife's mouth; ask her. So, being asked, she answers "To others I am what they believe me to be. To myself, no one," and the curtain is "Thus gentlemen, the truth is discovered."

Several of Pirandello's works involve these motives. But in *Six persons in search of an author, a comedy of action*, . . . he has attempted their concentration in an impressive and tragic vision. The whole set out of this play is original and odd. The spectators as they enter the theatre find the curtain raised, and the stage void of wings and scenery, as if ready for a rehearsal. A stage manager enters followed by actors, and he is beginning to arrange for the rehearsal of a play by Pirandello himself, when six persons are announced having urgent business with him. These six have together had a terrific experience, and wish now to fix it for ever immortally in the world of art. They therefore seek an author who will listen to them and compose a play from their monologues. So these six are before the mirror, watching themselves live. They see themselves as persons; and the dissidence is manifest. Each has envisaged the character of the others according to his own interpretation of a moment of his own life; and furthermore the actors, when they attempt to imitate the scenes which the six have lived through, and now reconstruct before them, give them their own interpretation, which is entirely different. The various fictitious realities thus stripped naked, contrast irreconcilably. The experience of the six is irreproducible. Life became a stage to them the moment they became conscious of their parts, and considered themselves as persons, and when towards the end life bursts forth anew, onrushing incontrollable, its actuality drags them in, and their consciousness vanishes.

I have tried to provide a skeleton key to Pirandello's work, but this last one is the most valuable, because his creations are not cold distilled abstractions, but really speak and suggest. His art presents a complexity and lifelikeness that formalism would try to achieve in vain. Their lack of pedantry distinguishes them completely from the so-called grotesques—our ordinary term for plays wherein plot and all are fantastic and downright absurd, and life appears deformed through the lens of a more or less banal allegory; to liken his plays to the grotesques of Rosso di San Secondo, or Luigi Antonelli is unjust, though even our best theatrical critics are doing it. (pp. 536-37)

Mario Praz, "A Letter from Italy," in The London Mercury, *Vol. VI, No. 35, September, 1922, pp. 535-37.*

LUDWIG LEWISOHN   (essay date 1922)

[In each of Pirandello's plays] there has been at work the same feeble and febrile fancy as of a more forlorn and less intense Maeterlinck who borrowed the outer garb of realism to hide from himself the futility of his own imaginings.

"Six Characters in Search of an Author" . . . is the best of his plays. It is the most frankly cerebral; it is less a play than a commentary; it abandons the creative for the ratiocinative. Among the works of a powerful dramatist it would occupy the place that "La Critique de l'Ecole des Femmes" does among those of Molière or "The Rats" among those of Hauptmann. It is, on the contrary, Pirandello's best performance. That fact defines the nature of his talent.

It is true that characters powerfully imagined and projected in literature have a changelessness and permanence that outlasts life. But it is curious and amazing rather than just and profound to illustrate that truth by letting six characters out of an unfinished play step on a stage during rehearsal and shame the mere theatric theater and the mere histrionic actor by the terrible reality of their passions and the eloquence of their discourse. For during the presentation of the piece these characters assume the nature of life; the stage and the actors are deliberately reduced to a more shadowy plane of stiff convention. The criticism thus constructed is no criticism at all. There are no players in the world that would not be confounded by the intrusion of men in the grip of some instant anguish of the living nerves or flesh. Art does not seek to compete with life on such terms. That is no reproach.

Ludwig Lewisohn, "Drama: Fantasies," in The Nation *(copyright 1922 The Nation magazine, The Nation Associates, Inc.), Vol. 115, No. 2994, November 22, 1922, p. 556.**

STARK YOUNG   (essay date 1922)

In *Six Characters in Search of an Author* Pirandello first of all manages to contrive a fine theatrical piece. It exhibits everywhere one of his most noticeable gifts—something that may be seen already even in so early a work as his *Sicilian Limes* . . .—the ability to set forth quite well enough what needs to be known and at the same time to clear it out shortly and make ready for what he really wishes to stay on and emphasize. *Six Characters in Search of an Author* shows a brilliant originality and invention in the situation. The machinery is highly expert with which the double line of incident is established. The transitions, which are so frequent and so varied in event and idea, are facile and profound. Pirandello's play is thought become theatric. And his thought is subtle, and subtle not through the sense of any vagueness but through luminous combinations of precise ideas and suggestions. This drama of his is satirical about the theatre but also in the same way about life. The blind and unending and unconcluded shifting of life is portrayed as it struggles against the accidents and illusion of society. No philosophy is pure, no theory gets a chance to exist in its clear reality, exactly as nothing that one of these characters thinks or feels or intends ever means to another character what it means to him.

Six Characters in Search of an Author has a plot suspense and a thought suspense. You are keen to see what happening will come next; your mind is excited by the play of thought till your head seems to hold a kind of cerebral melodrama. But the greatest achievement in Pirandello's play is that the sum of it is moving. It gives the sense of spiritual solitude. Under this fantasy and comedy and brilliant mockery and pity, it releases a poignant vitality, a pressure of life. It moves you with the tragic sense of a passionate hunger for reality and pause amid the flux of things. (p. 336)

Stark Young, "Brains," in The New Republic (© 1922 The New Republic, Inc.), *Vol. 32, No. 416, November 22, 1922, pp. 335-36.*

ORLO WILLIAMS   (essay date 1923)

A critic, with the great literature of the world in his mind, cannot praise unreservedly the work of Pirandello. It is the more important, therefore, to appreciate his merits justly. His chief merit, perhaps, is his inexhaustible vivacity in describing persons and scenes, and in presenting queer twists in ordinary human relations which bring about unexpected clashes. . . . His men and women, with all their quaintnesses of expression and habit, the oddities of their dress, their typical gestures and their pathetic blindness to the pitfalls of existence, come to his consciousness with a remarkable spontaneity, their story—one might say—already hung round their necks. (pp. 269-70)

[Pirandello] sees his fictitious characters as plainly as he sees flesh and blood. From this extraordinary immediacy of impression come his freshness and power of delineation: from it, too, comes his failure to penetrate beyond this first superficial reality and his willingness, in ironic contemplation of his 'bad company,' to rest contented with an attitude to life of derisive scepticism which, at first diverting, shows up before long its essential poverty.

The best of Pirandello's company, from an artistic point of view, is undoubtedly that which comes to him from rustic life: and in this he is not unique among Italian authors. Nobody can study Italian fiction for long without realising that the life of the village is its truest and strongest inspiration. (p. 270)

One of the best among Pirandello's short stories [in *Novelle per un anno*], 'Il Fumo,' is an admirable study of country life in Sicily, the action of which turns upon the inevitable damage wrought by the working of sulphur mines—Sicily's chief wealth—upon the vegetation of the neighbourhood; and the spiritual clash is between the land-love and land-hunger of a country proprietor and his hot desire for revenge. . . . [In many other stories] Pirandello exploits the inexhaustible vein of country passions and humours with a remarkable freshness and vivacity. His characters are not great, but they are striking and well observed; and there is conveyed throughout a vivid impression of active, varied, and pulsing human life rooted, like the vines and mulberries, in a rich soil. Moreover, when country life is his subject, Pirandello's humour has a spontaneity which contrasts advantageously with the weary pessimism of his reflections on middle-class life. (pp. 271-73)

The other side, however, of Pirandello's work—the side which is in many ways most typical of his peculiar talent and which preponderates in his later stories and plays—is not so unexceptionable. The same skill and vivacity are there, more evident than ever: the faces and shapes of his characters are made remorselessly plain, and they act, or their minds act, with an almost disconcerting energy. This electrical power carries Pirandello a long way: it imposes itself upon the reader the first time, the second time, even the third. Such a story as 'Notizie del Mondo'—which purports to be written in a mocking vein to an old friend who is dead, reproving him for getting married and regaling him with comic accounts of the narrator's relations with his widow—captures one with its extraordinary mixture of tenderness and cynicism; and the swift and powerful study, in 'La Toccatina,' of damaged humanity clinging, childlike, to a few poor sweets of life that remain has in it an originality and a movement that are truly refreshing. But those who read on become conscious, sooner or later, of a disillusionment which, when it comes, throws a shadow over the first keen appreciation. The reader is forced to realise that, when he turns his eye upon the spectacle of middle-class civilisation, Pirandello no longer sees clear. It is not life as a whole that he sees, but a phantasmagoria, extremely vivid but devoid of any significance; and from that phantasmagoria he draws a quasi-philosophy which is often amusing, but always sour and shallow. (pp. 273-74)

['La Trappola'] is a rhetorical harangue on the theme that human life is a trap, because every determined form of life is a corruption of life itself. . . . (p. 274)

Pirandello thinks 'meanly of the soul,' and we cannot accept his view of life as a ridiculous scurrying to and fro of miserable, foolish little creatures, tripping over one another and distracted by their own mean desires. There is a sense in which this view has truth, but it is not even partially true when it is an expression of blank discouragement or empty resignation. Only from the standpoint of a high faith or a profound philosophy is such a view permissible, and then it is transformed. Pirandello has neither faith nor philosophy, with the result that we are driven to reject his sorry masquerade of humanity as ingenious but unreal. We in England have a great author on whose mind the frequent futility of human effort has indelibly burnt itself: but between Thomas Hardy, author of 'Life's Little Ironies' but also of 'The Dynasts,' and Luigi Pirandello there is a world of difference. To Hardy the universe is a great and marvellous fabric, into which the ironies fit, to be understood by the intelligences and mourned by the pities. He is a poet, and poets do not think meanly of the soul. He looks on life as from a hill. Pirandello stands at the street corner and looks at life hurrying along the pavement through a rather cranky pair of glasses, and the crankiness of his vision impairs the value of his creations. The life which he presents whirls passionately round, but without a principle, even of evil, to give it significance; and the emotions he would evoke lose their edge because they too, on his showing, are part of a senseless flux. . . . By excluding every element of permanence from his conception of human life, Pirandello, with all his attractive gifts, his ingenuity and his dramatic sense, has banished the quality of greatness from his art. He cannot rise, since he has cut off his wings, and even his

style has to remain at the street level: it is just a pungent stream of everyday conversation. (p. 275)

Pirandello's limitations, as might be supposed, are least felt when his purpose is definitely fantastic, for one can then enjoy the lively movement, the quaint features, and the often exaggerated rhetoric of his characters without being obliged to measure their depth and consistency by exacting standards; and one can surrender oneself without uneasiness to his charm, as a man might pass from the street into some fantastic *cabaret* where a philosophic revue, illuminated by many brilliant approximations to subtle truths, might entertain him agreeably. For this reason Pirandello's novel, 'Il Fu Mattia Pascal,' is artistically the most satisfying of his works in fiction. Fantastic without being extravagant, it presents an illusion of reality sufficient to engage the imagination without deceiving the intelligence. (pp. 275-76)

[It] is interesting to note that the element of fantasy, to which much of the story's charm is due, is also its chief weakness. The one figure which has no solidity is the central one, Mattia Pascal himself. He remains in one's mind as a vague and backboneless person, almost inert, with a vein of intellectual buffoonery that has little counterpart in any exterior reactions. There is something impersonal about his reflections, and his actions are too few to give him a convincing personality. For the greater part of the book he is little more than a pair of spectacles, with a Pirandellian cast in them, through which to observe the oddities of life. . . . [Pirandello] often breaks the thread of his plot by those tirades on purely intellectual themes which thrill the author but dry up the emotions of his audience. One becomes veritably weary as old Signor Paleari drivels on— and it is the author speaking—about the illusion of life and the reality of death. But one forgives these lapses when one is laughing at the richly comic scene of the spiritualistic *séance* in the hero's room. . . . After this climax the interest declines, though the author tries to whip up a little laughter over the scene where the resuscitated hero chaffs his wife and her second husband on their situation: but this scene is out of tune, since the sympathies are not with Mattia Pascal. He has no right to crow over anybody, and these outbursts of rather crude buffoonery are inartistic. However, it is an original and amusing tale, though its central figure, taken all in all, is only a personification of nullity.

The consideration of Pirandello's plays leads, though by a slightly different route, to similar conclusions. Pirandello has the reputation of being a humourist: indeed, it is his most usual designation. . . . His 'umorismo,' which is not the same thing as humour, is his most striking quality, but he is apt to wear it as some headstrong knight might have worn a patch of gay silk where armour should have been. It attracts immediate attention, but it is an easy target in the tilt. He observes the characters of his plays through the same glasses as those of his stories, and over their antics he figuratively slaps his thigh and crows with ironic laughter. . . . The irresistible liveliness of [his] comic characters and scenes is wholly admirable, but it is impossible not to realise the weak spot in Pirandello's 'umorismo'; it is an attitude of derision, not of sympathy. The same posture of amused contempt for human futility which diverts but, in the long run, irritates the reader of his stories also disconcerts the spectator of his plays. He devises tragic conflicts, but displays them with a certain cold *bravura* which dissipates the appropriate emotions. The spectator is diverted, even thrilled, but—saving the power with which great actors can exalt imperfect creations—they feel neither pity nor fear. What else could be expected from an author who obviously despises his audience as much as he despises the rest of humanity. (pp. 277-79)

We come back then, in the plays as well as in the stories, to the fact that Pirandello's genius shines most purely when the fantastic element is openly admitted: and, after all, there may be a greater suggestion of truth in a fantasy than in a laborious travesty of reality. The plot of *Enrico IV* is fantastic, but it has a real tragic power because the atmosphere of unreality is insisted upon from the beginning. The central figure is a lunatic nobleman who, as the result of a fall from his horse during a pageant, imagined on returning to consciousness that he was really the character he represented, the tragic Emperor who went to Canossa; and the scene is laid at the country villa where he lives with four attendants dressed up as gentlemen of the period and with all the appurtenances that costumiers can devise to humour his delusion. . . . It is a bizarre theme worked up to an effective tragic conclusion, and the strangeness of the setting carries off the artificiality of the whole conception.

However, the gem of Pirandello's humour is the comedy *Sei Personaggi in cerca d'Autore,* a fantasy indeed, but one of seizing originality, extraordinarily ingenious in its mechanism, which sets a tragic drama inside a sheer comedy. It displays all Pirandello's remarkable sense of the stage and enables him, for once, to clothe with full and telling dramatic propriety those intriguing speculations of his on the nature of identity and reality. (p. 281)

The speeches of the Father throughout are worth studying as a revelation of Pirandello's own mental workings: he represents Pirandello's point of view against the Director—a delightfully comic part—who represents the average man. The Father's exclamation of indignation at the injustice of being discovered in an act of secret immorality, since he is otherwise a man of somewhat sentimental rectitude, his argument that all human beings are a bundle of different personalities, and his explanation of the essentials of the drama in which he is involved reveal more of their author than any amount of commentary. Fragments of purely intellectual discussion fill too great a place in the two succeeding acts, but it would be difficult not to enjoy the supreme comedy of the appalling old dressmaker's materialisation by the mere act of setting the scene to represent her back shop. Madama Pace with her Spanish jargon is a *tour de force,* and it is followed by a passage of considerable entertainment where the Father is pained and the Daughter bursts into fits of laughter when the leading actor and actress begin to rehearse the scene that has just been played before their eyes as it 'actually' was. It is almost a *reductio ad absurdum* of the theory of art as imitation. Act III drags at the beginning, but ends with sensational rapidity. The characters, as it were against their will, are forced by their inexorable 'reality' to enact the culmination of their tragedy. (pp. 282-83)

One might compare [Pirandello] to a billiard-player who should set out to make a break on the assumption that the balls are elliptical, whereas they are perfectly round and normal. He may bring off some astonishing shots, but his break will never reach the hundred. (p. 283)

Orlo Williams, "Luigi Pirandello," in The Corn-

hill Magazine *(reprinted by permission of John Murray (Publishers) Ltd.), Vol. LV, September, 1923, pp. 268-83.*

MERRITT Y. HUGHES (essay date 1927)

Pirandello humor is not merely a department of literature. It is a way of looking at life which has always had a few adepts and which he thinks very timely in the twentieth century. To judge by the response to his plays in Italy and beyond it, he has as good a claim as Shaw to be a prophet. And his plays are only half of Pirandello. (p. 175)

While he was still experimenting with his short stories, Pirandello wrote a book which he called *L'umorismo* and in which he tried to define what humor means to him as a principle both in criticism and in creation. . . . *L'umorismo* surveys the chaos of definitions of humor from China to Peru and faintly betrays its author's particular subspecies of wit by his unconsciously expressed affinities with men like Richter and Sterne. At the crucial point in the final section of the essay, where he undertakes to state his own idea, he abandons the crystal dialectic which he employs everywhere else throughout the monograph and falls into something very much like Platonic myth-making. Pirandello is too much an artist to define his humor adequately anywhere except in his stories and plays. (pp. 175-76)

In the scattered bits of fiction now being reprinted in *Novelle per un anno* Pirandello's peculiar humor had its first free expression. (p. 176)

His *Novelle,* in their way, are as complete a picture of contemporary Italy as Balzac drew of the France in which he lived. The art of the two men is altogether different, though the creative activity of both is the result of a fascinated recoil from life, and though the mood and method of both are realistic. Pirandello is a short story writer and Balzac was a novelist. The difference is a corollary of the fact that Balzac was a humorist in only a very secondary way while Pirandello is a humorist and nothing else. According to *L'umorismo,* humor expresses itself by decomposing situations, characters and everything that constructive artists combine to make their imposing fabrics. A man whose genius is disruptive rather than synthetic is likelier to write a bushel of short stories than one novel. That is what Pirandello has done. . . . [His single full-length novel, *Il fu Matteo Pascal,*] is an expanded short story, or rather, a collection of short stories about one person. As a novel the book may be a failure, but it is a marvellous combination of farce with tragedy and in the dialogue between Matteo's mother-in-law and his aunt Scolastica it has at least one scene worthy of Molière. The combination of farce with tragedy so that both are too vividly and distinctly felt for the emotions to yield to the appeal of either is the specific quality of Pirandello's work. (pp. 177-78)

Visiting the Sick [in *Novelle per un anno*] is a good story on which to try your taste for Pirandello's humor. Though it is capable of broad comedy, it is not the humor of Mark Twain nor that of Aristophanes. It consists in the drawing of grotesques which are convincing caricatures but which are not laughable. Naldi on his deathbed is a perfect gargoyle, too terrible to be funny, yet too much a caricature of himself to be pitiable. About him move a throng of spiritual gargoyles, all acting from motives weirdly perverting those which are presumed by convention to bring visitors to the sick. For background to this scene the title asks you to imagine the words of Christ, "sick and ye visited me", with their implication that the sick are worth visiting and will profit by it and that their visitors may escape from the closed circle of their own egotism.

Much finer grotesques in Pirandello's stories are the dropsical peasant on the hilltop silhouetted against a great bonfire in *Requiem aeternam dona eis. Domine,* and the miner, alone beside the pithead at midnight, insane with joy over the discovery of the existence of the moon, in *Ciaula discovers the Moon.* (p. 180)

Pity and indignation are the first responses to a reading of *Requiem,* yet the story is full of high comedy. Don Sarso talks like Peter the Hermit to the "Christians" outside the courthouse in its opening scene. The soldiers who escort him and his little delegation home are puppets belonging to a tyranny whose soul has been dead since the fall of the Kingdom of Naples. The old patriarch on the hilltop has the mind of a village chief of the Stone Age. They all belong to history and here they are posturing in the twentieth century in Italy. They are a bundle of contradictions which poignantly stimulate that conflict of emotions (*sentimento del contrario*) which Pirandello insists is the essence of the sense of humor. Humorists—both authors and readers—he believes, are always poised in an unstable equilibrium between laughter and sympathy. (p. 181)

In the abstract, Pirandellian humor is something like an Aristotelian virtue, geometrically poised between the extremes of pity and irony. It has some points of contact with the art of Sir James Barrie's short stories, if not very much with that of his later plays, which move in a world quite foreign to the Italian's imagination. The *Old Lady Shows her Medals* is a counterpart of *Le medaglie,* except that Pirandello's tale, though no longer, is on a bigger canvas. The vanities of a club of old Garibaldeans are made, with marvellous kindness, to grow out of the soil of their stale lives in a provincial seaport town. (p. 182)

Perhaps after all, Pirandello's humor is an expression of the Italian sensitivity to the disappointment of life, the Virgilian sense of the *lachrymae rerum.* Nearly all his plays are founded on the recognition that life inevitably crystallizes into forms which the flux of existence instantly overwhelms. The forms themselves are travesties of our desires, and the short fixation of our mortality which they give is a mockery. (p. 183)

The key to Pirandello's humor is its freedom from the familiar ironies. All irony, he reiterates in *L'umorismo,* is inartistic and rhetorical, the negation of humor, yet humor contains irony because it is always troubled by contrasts between ideals and reality. Pirandello insists that his two great gods, Cervantes and Manzoni, were idealists and that they could not have created Don Abbondio and Don Quixote, if they had not had respectively a religious and a chivalric ideal to serve as a foil for its human incarnations. . . . A comic writer laughs at our unconscious hypocrisy. A satirist is indignant over it. A humorist through what is funny sees what is painful and falls a prey to a peculiar esthetic emotion compounded of amusement, doubt and sympathy. That is why Pirandello writes comedies which are like tragedies and that also is why he is the most popular playwright in Italy. He understands the insignificance of life and knows how to make it significant for art. (pp. 184-85)

Pirandello is not primarily a *raconteur,* unlike Boccaccio. Like Chaucer, whom he misunderstands and underrates in *L'umorismo,* he has written numberless short stories and is finally stringing them together in a great series because it suits his discursively humorous genius to do so. He wrote them simply as an outlet for his master passion, his sense of humor. To many readers some of the stories may seem interesting for other qualities than humor, but that only proves that Pirandello is a competent observer and craftsman as well as a pioneer in translating into art some of the most elusive human intuitions. (p. 186)

Merritt Y. Hughes, "Pirandello's Humor," in The Sewanee Review *(reprinted by permission of the editor;* © *1927 by The University of the South), Vol. XXXV, No. 2, April-June, 1927, pp. 175-86.*

FREDERICK V. BLANKNER   (essay date 1928)

The force which regulates the phantasmagoria of persons and events we call "life" is resolved by this most distinguished dramatist of post-war Italy [Luigi Pirandello] into the two contesting impulses of form and movement. Since, as is natural, Pirandello's dream-creatures are dominated by these same impulses, a knowledge of their meaning is essential to an understanding of his art.

This form-movement concept, in which relativity plays a part, might be a derivative in art of modern philosophy and science, particularly of the *élan vital* and of Einstein. Yet one feels that in Pirandello the idea is spontaneous and personal, not a conscious derivation but an independent parallel discovery.

Pirandello feels that he was born with this vision. It was present in his first short-story thirty-five years ago and it is present in his latest drama. For such a concept of life could not change. The vision has clarified, there have been new "phantasms," as Pirandello calls his characters—the possible number of creatures and situations is infinite in art as it is in life—but there have been no new tendencies. The change has been in technique, a development which has reached its highest point thus far in one of Pirandello's latest produced plays, *Diana and Tuda.*

Compare *Diana and Tuda* with *Six Characters in Search of an Author,* for example. Although the earlier play is one of Pirandello's greatest, the light of his vision struggled there through clouds of tangled veils, smoke-red, purple, and grey, whirling and torn in a night-storm. In *Diana and Tuda* it gleams through a medium as clear and chaste as alabaster. Chaos has become creation.

The result is classic—pure in the Greek sense. Pirandello feels *Diana and Tuda* to be his masterpiece because in it he has most perfectly expressed his life-concept of form and movement. From this point of view it will probably remain so. In its simplicity there is a decided suggestion of the ultimate. (pp. 891-92)

[For Pirandello life] is a tragedy of inevitable, continual frustration, of man's tenacious, desperate struggle to accomplish the impossible, to conciliate the two necessities which are eternally in antithesis: to vitalize movement, casting it into form, to vitalize form, stirring it into movement. . . .

Of the two opposite tragedies, that of stability within the

fixed form of the body or of circumstance and that of change, man feels perhaps more painfully the tragedy of change—change in himself, in others, in all the values of life. (p. 892)

It is change that torments so many of Pirandello's women. When the knowledge of this ineluctable change in what she would conserve bursts upon the understanding of the mother in *Two in One,* her thwarted outcry is, *"Non voglio,"* "No, I do not want it, no, no, *no!"* But the feeble human negative is powerless: and change continues even while the soul is commanding it to stay.

Most disconcerting of the changes is that of personality: the ego is relative to all, even to itself, which varies with the varying moment. Its sanity, its Virtue, are relative. The relativity of sanity particularly, the question as to exactly who is mad—seed of the tricks and topsy-turvy in the famous *Henry IV* and in *Cap and Bells*—has peculiarly hypnotized Pirandello. This relativity, which one might call a corollary to the proposition of form and movement, is as penetrative in his drama as is the form-movement idea itself—and more obvious. The notable example is, of course, *Right You Are If You Think You Are,* where the relation between truth, sanity, and personality is the main theme. (p. 893)

To call Pirandello a cerebral dramatist is to define only his most obvious quality. Reason he considers "the light of the heart," but with Spinoza he knows that "the reason without the heart is void." Pirandello feels the law of form and movement as well as thinks it.

Though his phantasms often mirror relativity, though they are identified with form and movement, they exist not merely to be symbols for those ideas. Symbolism Pirandello holds to be the negation of art. (p. 897)

A superficial impression of Pirandello's theatre may suggest the contrary. But study of his art confirms the idea that form, movement, and relativity are not the protagonists of his drama. Nor yet are they its thesis. Rather they make its atmosphere. Like powerful searchlights they play over the mortals who are the protagonists and over their relationships, illuminating the meaning. The glare of the lights is cold, but if one persists in his scrutiny after the first blinding shock, there is the palpitation of living flesh-and-blood creatures, involved in human tragedy. (pp. 897-98)

> *Frederick V. Blankner, "Pirandello, Paradox," in* Theatre Arts Monthly *(copyright, 1928, by Theatre Arts, Inc.), Vol. 12, No. 12, December, 1928, pp. 891-902.*

GEORGE JEAN NATHAN (essay date 1928)

The major portion of the drama of Pirandello consists in a kind of metaphysical masochism. The Italian lays hold of a philosophical paradox and derives an intense orgastic pleasure from belaboring himself with it. Where Shaw takes the same paradox and uses it sadistically upon his audience, his Latin contemporary bares his own flesh to it. In his ability to laugh at his self-imposed torture lies the latter's genius.

The technique of the outstanding Pirandello drama is that of a philosophical detective play, with Truth as the mysterious and evasive culprit and with all the characters of the play as sleuths. The play called *Right You Are If You Think You*

Are, for example, is typical of the leading elements in the Pirandello canon. As a tour de force in mystification, it must rank as a noteworthy achievement. Composed of materials that are essentially of dubious dramatic value, it is so ingeniously contrived that time and again when it seems that the whole structure must be on the point of collapsing, the uncommon wit of the author astonishes one with its jugglery of the theme back into renewed life. . . . The fault of the play theatrically, as with the bulk of the author's work, lies in its prolonged and unrelieved argumentation. It is mentally dramatic, but, after all, the theatre calls for the use of the eye as well as the ear, and the Pirandello drama has the air of being written for intelligent blind men. I do not make a point of mere physical action, plainly enough; what I mean is that Pirandello seeks to dramatize abstraction in terms of abstraction rather than in terms of theatrical concreteness. One sees his characters move about the stage, but the movement always impresses one as having been wrought by the stage producer rather than by the dramatist himself. For all that it matters, the actors might just as well be wooden dummies and their lines spoken by a ventriloquist. (pp. 186-87)

> *George Jean Nathan, "Pirandello" (1928), in his* The Magic Mirror, *edited by Thomas Quinn Curtiss (copyright © 1935 by George Jean Nathan; reprinted by permission of Associated University Presses, Inc.), Knopf, 1960, pp. 186-88.*

DOMENICO VITTORINI (essay date 1930)

Luigi Pirandello . . . reacts against Naturalism. He gazes on the world of instinct which that school has studied and [Gabriele] D'Annunzio had glorified and he shows its tragic misery by contrasting it with the boundless ocean of life which flows unrestrained beyond the moulds within which man imprisons this divine power.

Pirandello's art is inwardly philosophical, and over it have passed all the stormy winds of modern thought from Descartes to Schopenhauer and Vaihinger. The problem of the unity or multiplicity of our "self," the absolute and relative value of reality are ever present in his works and are derived from the author's philosophical attitude towards life. His essay on humor, *L'umorismo* ("Humor") . . . , is a document in which we can study his philosophy and aesthetic principles. If, with the help of his book, we go beyond the apparent cynicism and grim laughter of the author, we discover that there exists in him a strong substratum of mysticism. (pp. 137-38)

Most of Pirandello's works are developments of the various aspects of the problem of Being and Becoming.

We can see in what relation Pirandello's idealism stands to its artistic expression in *La casa del Granella* ("Granella's House"), a short story, the motivation of which is the belief in the immortality of the soul. This subject, instead of being embodied in a philosophical dialogue in the fashion of Plato, becomes a humorous treatment of spiritualism. A lawyer, Signor Summo, "a serious and cultured man imbued with positivistic science," at first laughs at the story of a haunted house told by the three odd members of the Piccirilli family who find it impossible to live there. When, in order to defend his clients, Summo begins to study spiritualism, he discovers that a new light shines on him and on humanity. . . . He studies all the literature on the subject that is available to him. . . . He goes to court and makes an eloquent defense of his clients but is defeated by the cold indifference of the law. (pp. 138-39)

The impression has been given that Pirandello expresses a sort of categorical pessimism. His own statements in *L'- umorismo* repudiate this, and an analysis of his characters reveals that the grotesque situations in which they are placed are determined by their tortuous intellectualization of life. . . . [Pirandello's] idealism rises to the dizzy heights of mysticism, as he believes that man lives on this earth as if in exile and is tormented by a constant longing for the universal realm of which he is a stranded particle. (pp. 139-40)

How is it, then, that man estranges himself from life and loses himself in a maze of contradictions? . . . According to Pirandello, man, unlike plants and beasts, is endowed with intellect and "with an infernal mechanism called logic. Our brain pumps through it our sentiments and transforms them into concepts." . . . These abstractions deform reality, in so far as life is in a constant process of flux and change. Since our abstractions are subsequent to the reality that we conceive, it is evident that our concepts enclose a reality which is no longer existent.

The first of Pirandello's novels, *L'Esclusa,* already shows this philosophical trait of the author, who thereby infuses a new life into the provincial atmosphere and characters that, like [Giovanni] Verga and [Luigi] Capuana, he portrays. The whole novel pivots on the belief of Rocco Pentagora that every man in his family is destined to be betrayed by his wife. Having found some letters of an admirer, he sends his innocent wife back to her home. . . . Her husband, who had tried in vain to live without her, appears and receives her again in his home. It is in this fashion that Pirandello the humorist shows us with grim laughter what pranks our reasoning process can play. (pp. 140-41)

It is of paramount importance to point out that the grotesque presentation of man so much in evidence in his works is the result of the process of intellectualization to which man subjects life. These deformations are pictured against the lofty vision of the author, and behind the crowd of odd characters there looms the thoughtful and wistful countenance of Pirandello, both amused and grieved at the strange vicissitudes of man on this earth.

Most of Pirandello's works are carried on the plane of the inward contradiction that besets the tormented spirit of his characters. Contrast, studied in endless situations, is the chief source of his art, as evidenced by the very titles of his early books, such as [*Amori senz' amore* ("Love without Love"); *Beffe della morte e della vita* ("Jests of Death and of Life"); *Bianche e nere* ("Black and White Stories"); *Erma bifronte* ("Two-faced Hermes")]. . . . From contrast there springs humor and the greater the contrast between life as an ideal entity and life as a tangible expression, the more grotesque become the characters and the stranger their vicissitudes. We then find the characters who are an original and typical creation of Pirandello, beings in whom an idea becomes an obsession that transforms them into pitiful automata. They are the projection of the universal term "man" into a multitude of beings, grotesque yet throbbing with the tortured humanity that Pirandello lends to them. In a sense his characters are his antagonists, but since he realizes that they are human and a part of his own humanity,

his irony softens into pity for the ludicrous situations in which they are placed.

On the whole, we see a negative humanity portrayed in Pirandello's books, but now and then a breath of purity passes over his stories when a child or a queer looking vagabond appears, carrying in its heart all the original beauty and sweetness of life. Then we get a glimpse of the luminous idealism which grotesque and often obscene happenings seem to obscure.

Pirandello's art has gone through a process of clarification rather than evolution. Even in his first short stories and novels, his attitude appeared clearly outlined, and it has not substantially changed. . . . As years have passed, he has more clearly defined his position by illustrating its different phases. Dates are consequently of no avail to an understanding of his art. The task of the critic is to present the various stages of Pirandello's drama in considering the problem of Being and Becoming.

The first act of this gigantic and Dantesque drama pivots around a tragic realization on the part of the philosophical novelist: life as an ideal substance lacks expression, yet once it enters a human mould, it becomes dwarfed, deformed, and it is eventually destroyed. This motif is found in *I vecchi e i giovani* ("The Old and the Young"). . . . The plot is afforded by the vicissitudes of two generations, the one that fought the battles of Italian independence in the heroic days of Garibaldi, and the other that saw Italy's entry into the modern world of practical activity. . . . The contrast is not so much between the old and the young, as each generation is equally tormented, but between both of them and life conceived as a fluid sentiment. Pirandello embodies the ideal of life in Mauro Mortara, an old soldier who has kept pure the glory of his youth through the warmth of sentiment. When he realizes his long-cherished dream of visiting Rome, he refuses a guide and also refuses to learn anything about the different monuments. (pp. 141-44)

This is the ideal that Pirandello cherishes: to refuse, like the old veteran, to let life be crystallized in a given mould. (p. 144)

Quite different is the life of the other characters. . . . They cannot bear seeing themselves in a mirror, as their reflection shows the static ugliness of their life. They fear that image and they seek darkness like pursued beasts. The situation of these characters looking at themselves in a mirror returns again and again in the novel. (p. 145)

Mattia Pascal, who considers himself dead, brings before us a further development of Pirandello's dialectic drama: Is it possible to re-enter the stream of life to which we belong? The answer, which wavers between mysticism and humor, is: Yes, through death, through personal annihilation, through complete innocence, and mostly through illusion.

Many of his short stories illustrate these strange solutions and they are masterpieces on which chiefly rests Pirandello's greatness. They make one think of an oppressive and leaden sky in which there suddenly opens the horizon of the infinite.

To an even greater degree has Pirandello resumed this theme in his latest novel, *Uno, nessuno e centomila* ("One, No One, One Hundred Thousand"). . . . We find in it the problem of the complexity of human personality. Pirandello shows how tragic it is to realize that, although we believe we possess a distinct personality, we actually have no objective identity, as we vary according to the people who look at us. (p. 151)

[Angelo Moscarda, the hero,] decides to shake off all these false constructions which have enveloped and stifled his real self. He wants to destroy the fixity of his existence and to live in each aspect of life and nature, that is to say, to be a "hundred thousand" or as many as the manifold aspects of the universe. He is happy in this passive state of existence, as he is open to all impressions from the outside world. But in so doing he loses everything; his wife, his friends, his wealth. He ends in a poor-house, which he has built in order to make amends for his father's extortions. Yet in his "madness" he is completely happy.

This, which the world would call madness, is, in its last analysis, the "holy madness" of the mystics, as St. Francis characterized it. Moscarda, too, reaches the solution of the mystics—he loses his identity as a man of the world and becomes one of the poor sheltered in the home. But he is unfettered from every mould, free to live life in its primal fluidity. . . .

His holy madness begins when, rebelling against fictitious constructions of men who look upon him as a usurer, he discovers "a living point" in himself which he identifies with God. (p. 152)

In this fashion, Pirandello concludes his problem of Being and Becoming: destruction of the process of intellectualization to which we subject life, return to what is spontaneous, pure, and holy, even if we have to relinquish society and family, riches and pleasures, like the mystics. . . .

Although he transcends Naturalism, Pirandello follows the precepts of that school in studying the average man, and in the presenting of human passions in their natural proportions. A student of philosophy and an original thinker, he gives to naturalistic themes a background of ideas which lends to them a universal character. (p. 153)

Without [his] deep faith in and longing for the world of mysteries and shadows, Pirandello's art appears to be a form of comic art. Pictured against a background of his Idealism, it becomes a sublime epic of the human conscience, and it assumes the pathos of the drama of a man who, living in the time in which Positivism believed it had destroyed all religions, voices in a new and strange, but passionate way his faith in the infinite. (p. 154)

> *Domenico Vittorini, "Luigi Pirandello," in his* The Modern Italian Novel *(copyright 1930 University of Pennsylvania Press), University of Pennsylvania Press, 1930, pp. 137-53.*

MARK VAN DOREN (essay date 1931)

Pirandello's new play, "As You Desire Me" . . . , might be and has indeed been hailed as another contribution by this Italian intellectual to what we call our theater of ideas. For one who like myself found the piece merely pretentious and tiresome, nothing could be a more forcible reminder of the difficulties we get into when we use the word "idea" in connection with the drama. I found no ideas in it at all—or rather, I found a very rudimentary idea strutting around in fine clothes. The clothes could easily be identified as

coming from the shop of a fashionable phrase-maker. Here was a drama of phrases all right. But hardly a drama of ideas. . . .

Pirandello's play is stuck with a big and obvious moral—one large, abnormal clove. Pull that out and the meat must lose its savor, since there are no further ideas inside to season it as it might be seasoned. The moral is put into words—oh, many times—and runs somewhat to this effect: that if you can only believe me to be what I think I am, then I am what I think. . . .

The failure of the play is the failure to make all this doctrine either credible or palatable. It is so obviously a truth that is being thrust at us that with our customary perversity we refuse to accept it. And the reason for our refusal, I think, is that the truth has been put into words. Had it come in the form of action, in the form of feeling, we should have accepted it without knowing that we did so, and waited for some commentator to tell us what we had accepted. Pirandello is his own commentator; so we resist him. (p. 198)

> *Mark Van Doren, "The Theater of Phrases," in* The Nation *(copyright 1931 The Nation magazine, The Nation Associates, Inc.), Vol. 132, No. 3424, February 18, 1931, pp. 198-99.*

DOMENICO VITTORINI (essay date 1935)

The line of development followed by Luigi Pirandello in his art goes from a somewhat external and even picturesque naturalism to an introspective and tormented individualism. The two stages, however, are not separated by a clear-cut line of division. On the contrary, if one looks below the surface, he discovers that the early naturalism shows traces of the later individualism, just as the introspective stage has never lost at least the memory of the time when Pirandello's art was devoted to a direct analysis of life studied at close range. Whether in the elementary humanity of the earlier plays or in the complex individuals of the later ones, we find the reflection of his tormented spirit and sad existence. This is the essential part of Pirandello's drama, and it should be constantly seen behind the division to which we have subjected his large and imposing dramatic production. (p. 43)

The most naturalistic of Pirandello's plays is *Man, Beast, and Virtue,* in which the treatment of the theme of instinct has assumed an extremely ironical form. Rarely has the author indulged in such broad laughter and poked such malicious fun at man as in this play. (pp. 81-2)

The play involves Signor Paolino, a teacher who lives by giving private lessons, Signor Perrella, captain of a ship, who comes home only at long intervals, and the virtuous Signora Perrella. (p. 82)

The comedy has the appearance of being highly immoral, yet [the] light, ludicrous, and obscene events assume a deeper note as they pass through Pirandello's personality, and what seemed a scoffing mockery ends in serious implications. As a result of this undertone of seriousness, the author is lenient with Paolino and especially with the neglected Signora Perrella, while he is very severe with the captain. Pirandello puts on Paolino's lips a lengthy discourse to show that the responsibility is the husband's.

Paolino is the character who is closest to Pirandello's heart in this play. Not that he is a hero, an exceptional individual, or a great personality, however. He is as close to the average person as any of Pirandello's characters, but he shares with other characters that repressed, livid resentment against man and even against life. He, too, has been exasperated by experience, and he is always ready to pour his hatred on everything and on all. (p. 84)

In spite of his somewhat philosophical utterances and his excited gestures, Paolino is not yet endowed with a tragic soul. He still is, to a certain degree, external, which shows that Pirandello was forcing himself into the elementary psychology of an individual like the irascible teacher who is still too enveloped in the net of sensuous life to possess the fixity that a tormenting idea, arising from a sad experience, gives to individuals that Pirandello portrays in his best plays.

From characters that we have here and there met in these rudimentary attempts at drama, we can see that the author was tending towards more complex personalities. Our attention has already been attracted by solitary individuals crouched in a dark nook and revealing through their suffering and sneering posture their tragic sense of life. Such is the hero of *The Man with a Flower in His Mouth,* and such is Luca Fazio, whom death is pitilessly stalking.

When such characters appear we are nearing the portals of the majestic and tragic structure that Pirandello has created with the agonizing dramas he has revealed in his art, and we can truly say: Here begins the true and significant drama of Luigi Pirandello. (p. 85)

After the objective attitude towards reality shown in varying degree in the plays that give evidence of inspiration from Sicilian naturalism, Pirandello appears in a mood that he qualifies as humorous or grotesque. (p. 89)

Pirandello has shown in his plays that there are cases when loathing for life and for ourselves is so great that it transforms us into madmen. The typical Pirandellian character of this stage of his drama is a man distressed, with mobile eyes, tense, and unable to relieve that tension, for fear that his whole being, moral and physical, may disintegrate. When all alone, he grits his teeth and clenches his fists, while within him disgust rises like a polluted tide. Who could then show himself as he is, not only to others but to himself? It is then that reason begins to function, and it covers with idealistic hues a situation which is inwardly putrid. Reason lends to Pirandello's characters beautiful masks which they press against their faces while they walk among their fellow-men, composed and stately. However, there is the face and there is the mask which never become one, and Pirandello's characters know it. They feel from time to time that the face wants to appear or that circumstances in life threaten to remove the mask. They desperately cling to it, and press it with agonizing strength over their faces, feeling the hurt, the bruise, the burn, yet ready to endure that suffering because it is more bearable than the one inflicted on them by what they know about themselves.

This process, which has given life to immortal characters in Pirandello's drama, presupposes a ghastly moral shame and an acute and tormented sensitiveness. It is also predicated on the assumption that all men are, to a varying degree, theatrical, especially if highly intellectual. An intellectual man acquires in reflection what he loses in spontaneity. It is a law of life, and the mask that man dons is a logical means

of self-defense. Since Pirandello's drama begins when the voice of instinct has been silenced and his characters are stranded on the bleak shore of disillusionment, all their life centers in their intellectual raving. (pp. 91-2)

More than from his brain the drama derives from the heart of Pirandello, and his work is a delicate and passionate analysis of a humanity that suffers and tries to appear at least calm; that inwardly bleeds through shame and outwardly puts on the veneer of decency. . . .

Pirandellian humor . . . runs through *Right You Are if You Think You Are.* Humor, however, colors only the external side of the play, because the pathetic element affirms itself, and becomes larger and deeper as the play develops, till finally it culminates in the last scene, one of the most dramatic that Pirandello has created.

The play is constructed on clear-cut lines dividing a group of the *élite* of a provincial town, who are curious to the point of being cruel, from three individuals who are the victims of their morbid curiosity. There is a typical Pirandellian character between the two groups: Lamberto Laudisi.

In his looks, in his intellectual traits, he bears the marks of one of those characters in whom the author has embodied his wisdom of life. Laudisi stands on the boundary line of instinctive life and reflective intellect. He has reached the conclusion that the only solution for the tragic snares in which humans are caught is a complete categorical subjectivism. (p. 120)

The central idea of the play is the belief that we are absolutely subjective and that the only way to live and to let other people live is to accept this point of view. Lamberto Laudisi does so, and he respects the odd situation existing in the Ponza household. The others, totalitarian logicians, apply to this specific case a generic idea, and by so doing they create their own discomfort and destroy the peace which, even if based on illusion, allows three persons to live peacefully. (pp. 126-27)

Pirandello has projected in *Each in His Own Way* one of his most tormented and pessimistic moods, although his pessimism is the direct reaction of the belief that only humility and stoic silence can help man in the tragedy of being human.

The setting is laid in a more aristocratic atmosphere than in his earlier plays. His characters here are also more intellectual and, therefore, more tormented and complicated, since life for Pirandello becomes more tormented and complicated as it departs from a presupposed idyllic beginning where goodness and happiness reign. (p. 129)

In this play the aesthete and the moralist have come to the help of the dramatist in order to project on the screen of art pitiful and tragic events. The aesthetic considerations and the moral concern, however, do not destroy the dramatic character and the pathos of the vicissitudes that we witness. Pirandello in building up the play has been very much concerned with the relation between art and life. He has introduced in two intermezzi the real persons from whose life he took the idea of the comedy: Delia Morello and Baron Nuti, who are in the audience, mingle with the spectators, and witness their lives reënacted on the stage. They represent life as it is in its actuality, while the Delia of the play and Michele Rocca represent the way in which man interprets idealistically his shameful acts. The former are tragic and crushed by their tragedy; the latter gesticulate and find solace in their bubbling, excited chatter, until they are compelled to return to the plane of reality, whence a social incident had removed them. When Delia and Nuti see themselves in the fixity of art, in which is reflected all the ugliness of their deeds, they become outraged and violent. Delia Morello leaps on the stage and slaps the actress who is impersonating her. None the less violent is Baron Nuti, with the result that a confusion arises in the theatre and an imaginary third act, so Pirandello informs us, is not played. The public, after either admiring or condemning the play, goes home.

Outwardly the play seems involved, gloomy, and pessimistic. When we single out the various strands that Pirandello has woven into it and look at the intimate texture of the work, it becomes clear and faintly illuminated by the light of his idealistic philosophy of humility. All those tortuous constructions are due to the fact that Delia Morello and Michele Rocca do not possess resignation—the gift of the humble of spirit. (pp. 137-38)

The keynote of the play is given by the very title, *Each in His Own Way,* which refers to the duty that each has in creating his own reality. Reality is not a convention; it is not an object that everybody calls by a given name. Reality is something that we must create with our own souls, out of our own lives, in humility and candor. . . . (p. 139)

Henry the Fourth is pure tragedy and one of the greatest plays that Pirandello has written. Under the grandeur of history he has disguised an intensely touching human drama. When the Emperor Henry IV disappears and the man looms in all the agony that tortures him, his humanity is as complex and deep as the figure of the emperor was stately. (p. 150)

The drama is a subtle study of the interplay of the conscious and the subconscious, the rational and the irrational, as they may be observed in human actions. To what extent are our acts conscious? If we, without being seen, should look at the valets as they stand around the throne of Henry IV, we should believe, judging by their actions and words, that they were true and real. What difference is there between seeing them and seeing ordinary persons moving in the realm of actual life? As with grave mien they discuss matters of state with the emperor, we have no proof that they are acting. Conversely, we cannot ascertain that they are not acting when they speak and act in their capacity of men of today. We can be led in a most convincing manner to these paradoxical extremes by a process of logical and complete subjectiveness. Pirandello goes more deeply into the question of the reality of human personality. For twenty years, these valets have lived as men of the eleventh century. It is highly improbable that they have not merged to some extent with that superimposed rôle, even so far as to have their identity obliterated for hours at a time at least.

This play makes us realize more than any other how unjust is the accusation of abstract and cerebral so often applied to Pirandello. One feels constantly the author's reaction against those who lack spontaneity in life. (p. 157)

The power of the living reality is one of the strongest *motifs* in the play. What compelled Henry IV to leave the artificial groove into which he had gathered whatever débris of his life was left to him, was the call of the living life that reached him through the youth and charm of Frida. There was a violent clash between the desolate coldness of his solitude and the warm breath of the world that he had forsaken. That clash made it impossible for him to cling to his illusion and, therefore, it revealed the tragedy of his lucid madness. But it also made him feel that he was unfit to reënter the swift current of life that goes on and on, leaving behind all those who cannot keep pace with it. (p. 158)

All the characters in the play are molded with that vividness and clear-cut contour that Pirandello lends to the creatures of his imagination. Henry IV, however, towers above them all. His madness is a case of lucid madness, a madness that is kinder than sanity; a madness to which one goes for shelter when life becomes crushing and unbearable. Were we to view Henry IV as an ordinary man, feigning madness, he would arouse indignation in us for his prolonged pretending. If we accept his conscious madness, we stand before him appalled by the greatness of the sorrowful and tragic existence of one who has willfully cut himself off from life because he knew that life held no promise for him. We see him as a tragic figure, enmeshed in the contradictions of life, immobilized in the merciless fate of his madness, but surrounded by the warm sympathy and pity of the author. He stands unforgettable before us as one for whom a conscious, planned madness is more tragic, harrowing, and devastating than one of which an ordinary individual is unaware. The madman as illuminated by the poet has eclipsed the one diagnosed by the physician. (p. 159)

The social theme was implied in Pirandello's attitude of observer and critic of human acts. In analyzing man's actions he was logically and necessarily led to the consideration of the social environment.

Pirandello's social drama has distinct antisocial leanings. . . . [He] always viewed modern civilization in the light of corruption and profligacy. His exasperated idealism created an abyss between actuality and dream that never gave him the hope of a better condition. (p. 183)

The element that stands out in Pirandello's social plays and in the social implications of his drama is the moral inferiority of man, and, by way of a logical contrast, the superiority of woman. Pirandello, like most modern playwrights, has been very chivalrous with women and he contrasts the superficiality and fickleness of man's affections to the deeper feelings of woman. This attitude is the result of Pirandello's approach to the theme of instinct. He has never succeeded in overcoming a sense of loathing and revolt for sensuality. . . . Pirandello has never been able to free himself from the thought of the lowness of sexual instinct. (pp. 184-85)

In [*The Pleasure of Honesty*] we find ourselves before a strange, quixotic treatment of the theme of honesty. Pirandello, following the spirit of his times, when morality is more practised than preached, does not give us a treatise nor an oration about it. Rather he approaches the problem with his usual quizzical smile. He seems to be at first uncertain whether honesty is an impelling force of life or just an empty word. As events develop, he and his readers are led to the conclusion that something powerful abides in honesty, something that man can momentarily cast aside, but to which he must eventually turn to give consistency and support to his life.

The moral problem which constitutes the very texture of the play arises from an immoral situation. Agata Renni, a young woman who is approaching the age when the possibility of marriage becomes rather doubtful, has had a love affair with Marquis Fabio Colli, a man in his forties who is separated from his profligate wife. Agata's mother, to prevent a scandal, decides to marry her to Baldovino, member of a noble family in dire financial straits. (p. 187)

It is necessary to have clearly in mind the tragically fantastic character of Baldovino's mode of thinking and living in order to understand the play. He has renounced all that side of life that we may call material and concrete and which centers about instinct and obeys the dictates of sentiment. Baldovino is only "intellect," not because he delights in floating on the fleecy clouds of the irrational, but because the circumstances of his life have forced him to take refuge in the lonely castle of his imagination. (p. 190)

There is an undertone of social satire in the very events that form the warp of the play. Pirandello views with grieving mockery the attempt to hide the illegitimacy of the child under the cloak of a marriage ceremony. The clear-eyed Baldovino saw very well that the mother and Colli wanted to use honesty as a means of perpetuating a wrong situation. They wanted to use him as a soulless tool and then cast him aside. The author, half ironically and half thoughtfully, makes Baldovino don the armor of honesty and fight gallantly for it against the machinations of his enemies. (p. 197)

Pirandello is here a brilliant and ironical asserter of the power of honesty. As a genial and quixotic knight of Lady Honesty, he breaks his lance against those who preach of her in hollow voices and with solemn faces, while he attacks those who are inclined to think that honesty is just a prejudice of narrow-minded people. Pirandello the humorist begins by placing honesty in a man who lives outside the normal boundaries of life and by claiming that to be absolutely honest we must live as abstract formulas. Eventually he shows that honesty is imbedded in the very texture of social life to the extent that even when assumed as only a form it becomes a powerful reality and leads to the fullness that it is meant to afford to men. (p. 198)

[*Six Characters in Search of an Author* and *Tonight We Improvise*] present a decided change in the inspiration and state of mind of the author. Pirandello has freed himself from the preoccupation of instinct, and his eyes have limpidly gazed on a higher life. (p. 290)

In *Six Characters in Search of an Author,* one of the most complex and baffling of Pirandello's plays, a stirring dramatic action is so closely woven with keen and almost erudite discussions of art that one is at first uncertain as to the central idea of the work. The fact is that the motivation of the play is essentially literary, since there run through it various æsthetic considerations such as: Is life stronger than art? What happens when we attempt to enclose life in the mold of art? Is its reality increased or diminished? Does not the artist owe the reality of his art to the torment and anguish which have gnawed into the soul and the very flesh of the man? (p. 291)

[The] Six Characters are the projection of that fixity in mental agony and pain which is a typical state of mind of the central figures that Pirandello has made live in his drama. The play is, intrinsically and ultimately, a keen study of human personality to which Pirandello has accorded a most brilliant treatment. (p. 292)

[The Six Characters] are immortal in the fixity of their pain. Pirandello stresses their fantastic reality as well as their physical traits which they share with all humanity. (p. 293)

The tragic end of the play reintroduces the original theme of the relation between art and life. Life enclosed in the artificial mold of art breaks its narrow walls, sweeps away fiction, and rules with tragedy and grief. In the wake of a tragic life there lurks death.

Outwardly we find ourselves before a play within a play, a situation that has often been resorted to by playwrights. Actually it is a cleverly constructed play in three acts in which the first act gives the background, the second reënacts the ghastly scene between the Father and the Stepdaughter, and the third presents the life of the Six Characters in the home of the Father where tragedy overtakes them.

What makes the play difficult to understand and most difficult to act is the fact that Pirandello has unveiled before us his secret concern as an author, together with his sympathy for the pitiful plight of the Six Characters. (p. 300)

The *motif* of the closeness of art and life is ever recurring in Pirandello. It takes a strange form in that the man in him longs for life lived as actual experience, while the artist is fully conscious of the great power of art considered as a reflected activity.

The framework of *Tonight We Improvise* is constituted by showing a play in its making. The author contrasts the passion of the characters with the artificiality of the stage director in presenting a slight dramatic event that the latter has to stage. In its procedure and structure it bears a marked resemblance to *Six Characters in Search of an Author,* with the fundamental difference that it does not possess the striking characters that create the strength of that celebrated play. (p. 303)

In spite of the negative reactions that the play has inspired in us, we see in looking at it in retrospect that the play has a prologue that is followed by a first tableau introducing the characters and giving the situation as it stands when the drama begins. Then new tableaux give the death of the father, the marriage of Mommina, and the rage of the jealous Verri that leads to Mommina's death.

Over the æsthetic consideration, over the tragic life of modest and romantic Mommina, there floats the infinite sadness of the author before the mystery of life: "Life must obey two necessities that, because they are opposed to each other, do not allow it either to assume a definite form or to be forever fluid. If life moved eternally it would never acquire consistency; if it acquired consistency, it would never move. And yet life must have both consistency and motion." Still he realizes that life has ebbed away from the art that encloses Mommina's tragedy. Nothing will ever equal nor make live again the anguish of the poor girl who sang so beautifully the aria of *Trovatore* and shed real tears as she sang. (p. 310)

As I look at the crowd of characters who gesticulate and move in a frenzy in the perspective afforded by Pirandello's dramatic works, I think of the forest where Dante enclosed those who committed suicide. Dante created in it one of the most ghastly and powerful scenes of the *Commedia*. The poor human soul has been caught in the texture of the tree, becoming one with it, and writhing in it. On the judgment day those souls will reclaim their bodies, and they will hang them on the branches from which they will dangle all through eternity. Dante has been more compassionate than Pirandello. He has punished his characters after they have committed suicide, thereby dividing life and his inferno; Pirandello has denied his characters the interlude of a peaceful existence, and has obliterated the boundaries between life and suffering. (pp. 340-41)

By his intellectual aloofness, by the creations to which his sense of grieving isolation has given life, by his art that is as serene as it is unadulterated, Pirandello deserves a prominent place among the great spirits who have honored Italian letters and, indeed, since art is universal, the literature of the world. (p. 341)

> *Domenico Vittorini, in his* The Drama of Luigi Pirandello *(copyright © 1935 by University of Pennsylvania Press), University of Pennsylvania Press, 1935, 351 p.*

ERIC BENTLEY (essay date 1946)

[*Right You Are (if you care to think so!)*] has often been regarded as the quintessential Pirandello. . . . The basis of the play is some sort of "bourgeois tragedy." . . . The domestic unhappiness of a husband, a wife, and a mother makes up the tragic triangle. A commentator named Laudisi is the *raisonneur* à la Dumas.

The peculiar thing about the tragic situation in this domestic tragedy is that we do not know what it is: a fact that is as much second nature to Pirandellians as it is disconcerting to others. The peculiar thing about the *raisonneur* is that instead of giving us the correct view of the tragedy he tells us that all views are equally correct. But then, according to Pirandello, this is the correct view. (p. 178)

Like Shaw, Pirandello has not been averse to the report that his drama is all intellect—no man minds being thought a mighty brain. . . . (p. 180)

The essence of Pirandello is not his intellectuality. It is his conversion of the intellect into passion. Perhaps Strindberg had done that too; it is the theory behind his naturalistic tragedies; yet in Strindberg passion summons intellect to work its will, while in Pirandello passion and intellect torture each other and join in a mutual failure. The quintessence of Pirandellism is this peculiar relation of intellect to feeling.

Ostensibly Pirandello's plays and novels are about the relativity of truth, multiple personality, and the different levels of reality. But it is neither these subjects nor—precisely—his treatment of them that constitutes Pirandello's individuality. The themes grow tiresome after a time, and those who find nothing else in Pirandello give him up as a bad job. The novelist Franz Kafka was long neglected because his work also gave the impression of philosophic obsession and willful eccentricity. Then another and deeper Kafka was discovered. Another and deeper Pirandello awaits discovery.

Before he can be discovered the perpetual "cerebration" concerning truth, reality, and relativity will have to be dis-

missed as the hocus-pocus it is. At face value the argument of *Right You Are* is that, since both mother and husband give a contradictory but equally plausible account of the same events, and since the daughter jumbles the two incomprehensibly, therefore there is no objectively true version of the story. This is a complete *non sequitur*. All events can be reported in different ways. This might only mean that some reports must be wrong, not that there is no right view. There is actually nothing in the plot of *Right You Are* to indicate that there can be no correct version of the story. The unusual thing is that we do not know what it is. This is very Pirandellian—not only, however, in that it is used to bolster a rather confusing, if not confused, discussion of truth, but also because it leads us to what we might venture to think is the real Pirandello. (pp. 180-81)

There *is* a true version of the story but it must not be known lest the lives of three people concerned be shattered. But, someone will protest, could not Pirandello use the prerogative of the omniscient author and tell *us* without telling the characters what the remedy is which their love has found? He could. But his refusal to do so is more to his purpose. The truth, Pirandello wants to tell us again and again, is concealed, *concealed*, CONCEALED! It is not his business to uncover the problem and solve it for us as in a French *pièce à thèse*. The solution of the problem, the cure for these sick human beings, is to leave their problem unsolved and unrevealed. . . . On the superficial level Pirandello is protesting against the spurious helpfulness of the scandalmonger, the prying reporter, and the amateur psychoanalyst; at a deeper level he is asking that the human soul be left a little territory of its own—which also, perhaps, was one of the themes of Kafka. (pp. 181-82)

Actually the play is not about thinking but about suffering, a suffering that is only increased by those who give understanding and enquiry precedence over sympathy and help. Pirandello took from the *teatro del grottesco* the antithesis of mask and face, the mask being the outward form, the face being the suffering creature. At its crudest this is the theme of the clown with a tender heart. Already in Chiarelli the mask and the face had, however, the broader meaning of the social form, identified with tyranny, and the individual soul which it sought to crush. In his best-known plays Pirandello elaborates on this antithesis. We see a central group of people who are "real." They suffer, and need help, not analysis. Around these are grouped unreal busybodies who can only look on, criticize, and hinder. In *Naked*, which is the first Pirandello play to read since it does not lead one off on the false trail of relativity and truth, the mystery *is* dissolved, as in *Right You Are* it is not, and the result is the destruction of the protagonist. Note that this mystery, constituted by the illusions without which the heroine could not live, is not the Mask. The Mask is the social and antihuman tyranny of, for example, a novelist for whom the heroine's unhappy lot is grist to the mill. The Mask is the interference of the mechanical, the external, the static, the philosophical, with our lives. Thus not only the smug novelist of *Naked* and not only the disingenuous truth seekers of *Right You Are* are the Mask. Pirandello himself—and every novelist and playwright—is the Mask. His material is the flux of suffering; his art stops the flow; its stasis is at once its glory—in immortalizing the moment —and its limitation, since life, being essentially fluid, is inevitably misrepresented by art. In drama, life wears a double mask: the mask imposed by the dramatist and that imposed by stage production. Three plays are devoted to this fact. In the best of them—*Six Characters in Search of an Author*—the three levels of reality are played off against one another throughout, and a fourth level is implied when we find one character judging another by what he happened to be doing on one shameful occasion, in other words by one isolated fact, which, wrongly taken as typical, becomes a Mask on the face of the real man. What if all our characterizations are like this? Just as we found, Pirandello argues, that there is no objective truth, so we find also that there are no individuals. In the one case we have only a number of versions or opinions. In the other we have only a succession of states. (pp. 182-83)

Exactly as in the matter of truth, so in the analysis of character the extreme conclusion is a *reductio ad absurdum* too barren to be the real motive force of such powerful works as Pirandello's. His characters in fact are effective not in direct relation to these conceptions, but because these conceptions enable him to suggest beneath the Mask of the physical presence the steady ache of suffering humanity. What a pessimist Pirandello is! says someone. Certainly. But again the point of Pirandello is not his philosophy—of relativity, personality, or pessimism—it is his power to conceal behind the intellectual artillery barrage the great armies of fighters and the yet greater armies of noncombatants and refugees. (pp. 183-84)

[Pirandello's] subject is what might be called Twentieth-Century Blues, by which I mean not any particular, localized disillusionment such as that of the lost generation of the twenties or that of excommunists today. I mean the disillusionment that is common to all these: disillusionment over the failure, not so much of socialism or liberalism, as of humanness itself in our time. In Pirandello's world there is only littleness and suffering. Perhaps it was the realization that littleness and passive suffering are untragic that impelled Pirandello to make comedies out of them. As comedies they are more moving! (p. 188)

> Eric Bentley, "Varieties of Comic Experience," in his The Playwright As Thinker: A Study of Drama in Modern Times (copyright © 1946, 1967 by Eric Bentley; reprinted by permission of Harcourt Brace Jovanovich, Inc.), Reynal & Hitchcock, 1946, pp. 159-90.*

LANDER MacCLINTOCK (essay date 1951)

[When man] contemplates his image, what does he find? Distorted illusion and a duality of personality, amounting at times to schizophrenia, which are the twin bases for the emotional difficulties from which the characters of Pirandello's dramas suffer so subtly and so eloquently. Pirandello is indeed the perfect pessimist, and his subject is the grim absurdity of life. . . .

[Pirandello's] stories and plays are based on the sufferings of humanity in the presence of uncertainty, an uncertainty which derives from a long-recognized dichotomy or polytomy stated briefly in the phrase "man is a social animal." On the one hand he has the biological urges of any animal or plant, on the other he is forced to control, or at least mitigate, his primitive impulses because he must live with other men. Hence the strain and stresses which have long been recognized. . . . (p. 176)

The man or woman who flees from unbearable problems

into a world of illusion does what Pirandello calls "*costruirsi*" ("to build oneself up"). He becomes not one but many personalities, which he displays at different times, under differing circumstances, and so is unable to discriminate between his real self and his various illusory selves. The plays of Pirandello are filled with these neurotics who, like Enrico IV in the play of that name, Ersilia Drei in *Vestire gli ignudi* (*Naked*), Cia in *Come tu mi vuoi* (*As You Desire Me*), or Donn'Anna Lucia in *La Vita che ti diedi* (*The Life I Gave Thee*), attempt to delude themselves, or who, like the Father in *Sei personaggi in cerca d'autore* (*Six Characters in Search of an Author*), complain that they have been forced by society and circumstances into a role which shows them in an ignominious or ludicrous light. (pp. 177-78)

[Why] should Pirandello's shopkeepers, actors, professors, minor businessmen, novelists, artists, and plain people suffer the tortures of the damned at what they discover in themselves? Are they so bad that they recoil in horror from themselves? The answer is, yes. The life force, the libido, when we attempt to channel it into society, becomes baleful and maleficent; buried deep because of the necessity for social living, it plays all kinds of tricks on men. It destroys the ethical basis of their actions, resulting in complete moral anarchy; it ruins their faith in themselves by making them feel that they possess no continuity of being or character but change from day to day, from moment to moment, that they are "not one but many"; it forces them into situations in which they must sacrifice their ideals, their dignity, their integrity. For—and this is an essential point—Pirandello's suffering human beings all long for virtue; they want to *be* respectable, not only to be considered so; they see a vision of life in which they will be on the side of the angels. (p. 183)

By making his characters "*personaggi*," not human beings, by using the completely impersonal setting of the theatre . . . , Pirandello is able to concentrate upon his central theme: how can the dramatist create true characters and how can he truthfully convey his conceptions to an audience through the intermediary of speech, directors, and actors? . . . In his *Sei personaggi* Pirandello has fixed forever one terrible moment in the lives of his puppets. (pp. 193-94)

Pirandello has made it clear that the story of the characters is not his primary interest, nor is the philosophical question of reality versus illusion. His play is thought become theatric. I hope I do not misrepresent his idea when I state what seems to me the subject of *Sei personaggi* in this way: The dramatic writer cannot present "the truth" as he sees it because of two things: first, his thought must be filtered successively through speech, through the actor, through the director; and second, the blind, unending, and unconcluded shifting of life and of human character is destroyed when people are fixed unchangeably in the amber prison of a work of art. (pp. 195-96)

[In *Ciascuno a suo modo* (*Each in His Own Way*), Pirandello] returns once again to a discussion of the relationship between the author, the actor, and the public—in other words to the technique of the theatre—and again he develops his favorite theme that men do not understand themselves or their ethical principles and that they act from motives which are obscure both to themselves and to others, motives capable of contradictory interpretations. (p. 196)

[*Enrico IV*] is Pirandello's masterpiece, the play in which his manner and his matter pull together to bring about the creation of a genuine modern tragedy. It is not perfect—it has certain faults of construction and is too wordy (it is conducted almost entirely through the monologues of the protagonist)—but it possesses the authentic divine fire. (p. 198)

In *Enrico IV* Pirandello develops two of the ideas that . . . [are] fundamental to his dramatic thinking: the impossibility of distinguishing truth from illusion, and the necessity men feel to adopt a mask in order to be able to live. Then, too, in the protagonist there is a double personality. . . .

A comparison between Shakespeare's Hamlet and Pirandello's Henry IV springs almost inevitably to mind. Both characters have the same introspective tendencies, the analytical bent which interferes with their power of action, the same melancholy, the same tendency to cruel sarcasm. But there the analogy must end. Henry IV is a man of the twentieth century whose problems are the problems of his time. . . .

The third of the central trilogy is *Vestire gli ignudi* . . . , one of the most humanly touching of Pirandello's tragedies, containing, as it does, the pathetic, even tragic, figure of the woman Ersilia Drei. (p. 200)

Vestire gli ignudi lends itself to a clear, schematic explanation of certain points of Pirandello's psychology, but a performance of the play or a careful reading makes it clear that the essence of it is the presentation of the human, pitiful, sinful character of Ersilia. She is the victim of the world, the victim of herself, of her own nature and her own illusions. Certainly not by any means a heroine, she is a person any of us might know, with that instinct, to which Pirandello so often refers, to possess some kind of self-respect, even if only illusory. (p. 202)

In discussing the psychological basis for the suffering of Pirandello's characters I [must note] the similarity of his basic concept of human motivation to that of modern psychologists, particularly of Freud, to the effect that subconscious impulses and needs control man's every action and thought. *Non si sa come* (*No One Knows how it Happens* . . .) is an almost perfect example of the modern subjective drama in which the characters are spokesmen of this subconscious drive and its struggle with the forces of social responsibility. (pp. 212-13)

From the point of view of dramatic construction many of the plays are not impeccable. Pirandello often jumps *in medias res* without bothering with an adequate exposition, so that the spectator, already confused as to what is what, now suffers from further confusion as to who is who. . . . [On the other hand] some of the plays are superb technical accomplishments. I have in mind *Vestire gli ignudi*, in which, one by one, with successive incidents, the veils of illusion are torn from poor Ersilia to leave her naked. The cumulative dramatic effect here is superb, probably unequaled in Pirandello.

All critics are agreed that the dialogue is written by a master. . . . It *is* magnificent dialogue, to be sure, but what a mass of it there is! Every one of the characters in these forty-four plays is intensely articulate. Each knows not only how to analyze his own feelings and those of his fellows, but how to express even their finest shadings. There is

something fantastically unreal about the virtuosity in self-expression of these peasants, farmers, small shopkeepers, government clerks, prostitutes, minor schoolteachers, governesses. (pp. 218-19)

There is not one noble or heroic figure in the roster of his characters, not one who, herolike, struggles against his fate, not one generous soul, not one who asserts his dignity as a man; there are only victims rebelling against destiny in black desperation, lamenting the fact that they do not understand the plan of the universe, nor their own place in it. Pessimistic, analytical, self-critical, Pirandello finds lyrical notes only in self-pity, in people whose one imperious necessity is to communicate their suffering, their exasperation, and perhaps by this means to accomplish a catharsis.

Pirandello's attitude towards women is eminently and characteristically Italian; he looks upon them as inferior creatures, lower than men in the human hierarchy, more closely controlled by instinct and less by intelligence and morals. (pp. 222-23)

In Pirandello the role that women play is not a noble one, nor are the women noble. . . . They are weak, capricious, frivolous, and sensual, a source of temptation for men and the instrument of his moral destruction, his victim and his incubus. What a parade of whores, adulteresses, vixens, Xantippes, hypocrites, and neurotics move across his stage! (p. 223)

[There is] a curiously romantic notion which runs through many of the plays—the idea that there is some special potency in the relation between mother and child, that in some mysterious way motherhood is sanctified. This notion may be religious in origin and connected with the cult of Mary as mother of Jesus. . . . It is something of a surprise to find Pirandello developing this sentimental thesis. After all, there is nothing astonishing and certainly nothing meritorious about a woman's having a child, and the assumption that her character and outlook are completely changed by being pregnant seems gratuitous, but it is characteristically Italian. The word "mamma" is constantly on their lips, yet the position of mother in an Italian family is pathetic. (p. 225)

It is, I think, not overbold to say that in his dramas Pirandello dealt with no problems of religion. Implicit in them all is the realistic point of view that men are controlled by impulses and instincts over which they have no control, that these lead them to have feelings and to commit actions of which they are ashamed and at which they are frightened. His philosophy is one of absolute determinism, a nihilistic doctrine. There is no truth, no certainty, no hope of salvation, no virtue, no personality, no hope. . . .

[Like] Dante when he meets Francesca, our poet cannot restrain his sympathy. When he contemplates the sins, the shortcomings, the cruelty, the self-delusion of his fellow human beings he is moved not to wrath but to pity. (p. 228)

Eminently Italian, putting aside all foreign models, he was at the same time one of the most representative of modern European writers, for he expressed the moral and intellectual turmoil and confusion, the spiritual travail, of a whole generation. (p. 229)

Lander MacClintock, in his The Age of Pirandello *(copyright, 1951, by Lander MacClintock; © renewed 1975), Indiana University Press, 1951, 341 p.*

ERIC BENTLEY (essay date 1951)

A generation ago there was, notoriously, a literature of ideas. Most of it, like most literature of all movements, was bad; and fashion, which elevates the bad to the level of the good, subsequently turns its back on bad and good alike. Only if there is a body of readers interested in merit as such can anything like justice be done.

Such readers will rescue the better literature of ideas from beneath the fashionable ideas about it. Even authors like Ibsen and Shaw, who are by no means unread, need rescuing from ideas about their ideas. How much the more so Pirandello, who is suffering fashionable rejection without ever having had—outside Italy—widespread fashionable acceptance! (p. 296)

An artist, and no one was more aware of it than Pirandello, makes his ideas matter by rendering them artistically active; that is, by giving them the life of his chosen form in his chosen medium. The question for us here, then, is whether Pirandello's ideas become active in the dramatic form.

In reconsidering Pirandello today, fifteen years after his death, the first play to read is *Liolà*. . . . It is a play that lives by an evident loveliness. . . . Without any scene-painting whatsoever, and without . . . any attempt to create "poetic" peasant dialogue, Pirandello has contrived to let in the light and distill the essence of the charm.

If it especially commends itself to those who love Sicily, the play has a quality all can appreciate, the more so for its rarity both in life and art today, and that is joy. (p. 297)

Liolà, to be sure, is Pirandello on holiday. . . . It is a dream, if you wish, but in no Celtic twilight or Maeterlinckian mist: it is all actual; it is all concrete. . . . The breath of a happy paganism is felt in his comedy, which is the last Sicilian pastoral.

The greatest single creation of the piece is Liolà himself, from whom joy flows as from a fountain. . . . And Liolà is a holiday creation, a truancy on Pirandello's part, an exception to the rules of the Maestro's craft. He is one of the few gay characters in Pirandello, and perhaps the only positive one. By positive I mean morally positive, being an agent, not merely a victim; hammer, not merely anvil. There is positive will in Henry IV and in Baldovino (of *The Pleasure of Honesty*), but Life sweeps in like a flood and decides the issue. Neither of these protagonists is, like Liolà, master of his fate. He is master of his fate without being a hero, and that by steadfastly refusing to do what other Pirandello characters do: let himself be exploited. This fact is firmly fixed in Pirandello's plot. (pp. 298-99)

The play is about appearance and reality, and shows, in what readers have always regarded as Pirandello's characteristically tricky fashion, that reality is not more real than appearance. Further, there are real appearances and—merely apparent appearances. And just as appearance may be more real than reality, so merely apparent appearance may be more real than real appearance. (p. 300)

To Pirandello, form increasingly meant artistic form, and artistic form increasingly meant dramatic form. Theater and life are the theme. His standard version of it is the spatial pattern of the Sicilian village: a drama of suffering and a crowd of onlookers: Tuzza and all Agrigento looking on; the Ponza-Frola trio and the whole provincial capital looking on; Henry IV, a spectacle for his friends and his

servants; the six characters, a drama to amaze actors and stage manager; Delia Morello, with her double out front and actors on stage discussing the author; Mommina, dying in a play within a play while singing in a play within a play within a play.

The heterodox form of *Six Characters* is thus no freak, and has nothing to do with the Bohemian experimentalism of the twenties with which people still associate it. It closely corresponds to Pirandello's sense of life, and is but an extension of a pattern he had, as we have seen, used before. In *Liolà* and *Right You Are,* he juggles with reality and appearance, interchanging them, subdividing them, mixing them, always urgently aware of different degrees or levels of illusion. Having established a level midway between the audience and the essential drama—namely, that of the spectator characters—he could go a step farther and frankly use the device of the play within a play, which is all that we mean when we talk of the play's formal heterodoxy. (pp. 306-07)

As with Ibsen, as with Shaw, it is not the many more or less ostentatious ideas that matter, but one or two more persistent ideas that lie concealed behind them. This is the place to remember to how large an extent form is meaning. The degrees to which an idea gets expressed in an art—and not merely mentioned—depends on the artistic skill of the writer. For many years even Italian criticism of Pirandello was preoccupied with ideas as mentioned rather than as expressed. It is surprising how little has been said as yet of Pirandello's art.

Even against it. For there are lacunae in his equipment as a playwright, lacunae and deficiencies. A first reading of his forty-four plays leaves us with an impression of monotony. A second reading calls our attention to grave faults in dramatic structure and grave limitations in character portrayal. . . . *Tutto per bene (All for the Best)* has a central scene of the rankest ham melodrama. . . . [*Henry IV* and *The Pleasure of Honesty*] have an expository first act of such cumbersome explanatoriness that one would think the author a plodding mediocrity or a careless hack. Over-all structure? Pirandello forces all his full-length plays into the three-act mold whether they really fit it or not. Sometimes he has obvious difficulty (for example, in *L'Uomo, la bestia, e la virtú—Man, Beast, and Virtue*) in making the material spill out. More often one simply remains uncertain about the relation of act to act. How many *real* acts are there in *Six Characters* and *Each in His Own Way?* . . . Characters? How few of the personages in Pirandello's plays have an effective existence! Take two or three away during the intermission and no one would miss them afterward. Many of them are uninteresting in themselves and remarkably like most of the others.

Despite its reputation for experimentalism, the dramaturgy of Pirandello stays all too close to the French drawing-room play—we could more flatteringly say to Ibsen were it not precisely the "French" externals of Ibsenism that we find. . . . The Ibsenite exposition is admirable, not because the characters give us information without seeming to, but because the exposition is itself drama, furthering, even constituting, the action. Now, as Giacomo Debenedetti has pointed out, Pirandello destroys Time. His events do not grow in Time's womb. They erupt on the instant, arbitrarily; just as his characters do not approach, enter, present themselves, let alone have motivated entrances, but are suddenly there, dropped from the sky. (pp. 309-10)

[Pirandello's] strongest weapon is his prose. Its torrential eloquence and pungent force are unique in the whole range of modern drama, and recall the Elizabethans (in contrast with our verse playwrights who imitate the Elizabethans and do not in the least recall them). He gets effects that one would not have thought possible to colloquial prose, thus compelling us to reopen the discussion of poetry and drama, in which it has always been assumed that prose was a limitation.

Although it is not clear that the same feats could be performed in any language but Italian, Pirandello exploited the special resources of that marvelous tongue. (pp. 310-11)

It is clear that Pirandello, theorizing, did not view his prose in isolation from his characters and their activities (the plot). *Liolà, Right You Are,* and his other more successful plays show us that his practice could conform to his theory. Even the more discursive plays are discursive in order that the prose may fully express the nature of men—who, among other things, have brains and think. In Pirandello's dialogue, passion does not commit incest with passion as in D'Annunzio's. It meshes with the rest of life, and especially with thought; and benefits thereby, *even as passion.* . . .

Sometimes everything about a Pirandello play is weak except the central role. . . . The quality of the defect is that, when you have a star before you, the whole play takes on life, and you see that after all it is not a mere essay or speech, but poetry, theater, and even a drama *sui generis.* (p. 312)

At any rate it is poignant theater, and it conveys a vision of life that cuts below the celebrated ideas. Conversely: the ideas are a superstructure of the vision and of the pain of the vision. And what are they, after all, the ideas that Pirandello calls the pangs of his spirit? . . . The common denominator of these intellectual propositions is loneliness, isolation, alienation. As we break the bonds between man and man one after another, and find no other bonds to replace them with—or none that are compatible with our humanity —the sense of separateness in the individual grows from mild melancholy to frantic hysteria. As the invisible walls of our culture crumble, and the visible walls collapse in ever increasing quantity, a disintegration sets in within the individual personality and lags, not far perhaps, behind the general disintegration. Pirandello cannot claim the dubious privilege of being the only writer to dramatize this situation; all our profounder spirits have been busy doing so. But he has dramatized it with his own accent and that of his people. His Sicilian intensity and equally Sicilian speculativeness drive him into a sort of metaphysical agony, an arraignment of human life itself. For, if the great human gift is that of words, by what diabolic plan does it happen that words multiply misunderstanding? The very humanity of man increases his isolation. Such is the idea "behind" one of Pirandello's most famous ideas. "Multiple personality" is a similar instance: Pirandellian man is isolated not only from his fellows, but also from himself at other times. Farther than this, isolation cannot go. This is a "nihilistic vision," and no mistake.

Perhaps it would nowadays be called an existentialist vision: life is absurd; it fills us with nausea and dread and anguish; it gives us the metaphysical shudder; yet, without knowing why, perhaps just because we are *there,* in life, we face it, we fight back, we cry out in pain, in rage, in defi-

ance (if we are Sicilian existentialists), and because all living, all life, is improvisation, we improvise some values. Their Form will last until Living destroys them and we have to improvise some more.

Pirandello's plays grew from his own torment (I overlook for the moment the few precious pages that grew from his joy), but through his genius they came to speak for all the tormented and, potentially, *to* all the tormented—that is, to all men. And they will speak with particular immediacy until the present crisis of mankind—a crisis that trembles, feverishly or ever so gently, through all his plays—is past. (pp. 313-14)

Eric Bentley, "Pirandello's Joy and Torment" (1951), in Naked Masks: Five Plays *by Luigi Pirandello, edited by Eric Bentley (copyright 1952; renewal by Eric Bentley; by E. P. Dutton & Co., Inc.; reprinted by permission of the publisher, E. P. Dutton), Dutton, 1952 (and reprinted in his* In Search of Theatre, *Atheneum, 1975, pp. 296-314).*

IRVING HOWE (essay date 1959)

Not all the stories in [*Short Stories by Pirandello*] are first-rate; some show the marks of haste or fatigue, others are finger-exercises in which Pirandello plays with his main themes yet does not fully release them. But even in the slightest of these twenty-two stories . . . there is that uniqueness and assurance of voice which is the first sign of a major writer. And in the best of them there is writing which can bear comparison with the masters of the short story, Chekhov and Joyce. . . .

Pirandello's stories are in the main tradition of 19th Century European realism. Except for those set in Sicily, which have a distinctive regional flavor, they often seem close in manner and spirit to the writings of the French realists and naturalists. Ordinary social life forms their main setting. The frustrations of the city, the sourings of domesticity, the weariness of petty-bourgeois routines, provide their characteristic subjects. Like Flaubert, though with less fanatic insistence, Pirandello cuts himself out of his picture. His prose is neither elevated nor familiar; it is a middle style, denotative, austere and transparent, the style of an observer who achieves sympathy through distance rather than demonstration.

Far more than we have come to expect in the modern short story, the impact of Pirandello's stories depends upon their action, which sometimes contains enough incident to warrant a good deal of expansion. There are rarely Joycean epiphanies of insight or Chekhovian revelations through a massing of atmosphere. The function of Pirandello's style is to serve as a glass with a minimum of refraction or distortion; and whatever we may conclude as to his purpose or bias must come not from a fussing with details of metaphor but from a weighing of the totality of the action. In this respect, Pirandello the story writer is not quite a "modern" writer. . . .

The stories deal with human problems, but do not threaten the reader with a vision of human lot as beyond comprehension or as open to so many meanings that there follows a paralysis of relativism. Pirandello has a sharp eye for absurdities, but this is still far from the view that life is inherently absurd. One can find anticipations of existentialism in these stories, as one can find them in many writers of Pirandello's day who were oppressed by the collapse of 19th Century certainties; but precisely those writers, like Pirandello, who seem to have anticipated the existentialist posture of an affirmed insecurity, are the ones, in the end, who resist its full display. (p. 21)

Fantasy, playfulness, sexual pleasure, religious emotion, any sort of imaginative abandon or transcendence—these seldom break through in Pirandello's stories, though some of them can at times be heard pulsing quietly beneath the surface. A full tragic release is rare. Much more characteristic are stories in which the final sadness arises from the realization of characters that they will have to live on, without joy or hope. In a five-page masterpiece, "The Soft Touch of Grass," a bereaved, aging man is mistakenly suspected by a girl of having lewd intentions; overcome by a sense of the hopeless entanglements of life, he returns to his lonely room and "turned his face to the wall."

In "Such Is Life," a masterpiece that would do honor to Chekhov, a hopeless marriage, long broken, is hopelessly resumed. This story, written with a repressed austerity and unrelieved by a rebellious gesture or tragic resolution, stays terribly close to life; in a sense, the power depends upon Pirandello's scrupulous decision not to allow either his emotions or imagination to interfere with what he sees. . . .

There are humorous stories too, such as "The Examination," in which a good-tempered glutton studying for a state examination is regularly deflected from his work by friends tempting him to share their pleasures. One smiles at the end, for Pirandello manages it with suavity and tact. But it is a humor of sadness, a twist upon the idea of incongruity as the very heart of life, and it brings little gaiety or relief. Of the pleasure that can come from simply being alive, Pirandello's stories have little to say, certainly nothing to compare with his one marvellously lighthearted play *Liolà*, in which youthful energies bubble without restraint or theory. (p. 22)

[The stories] set in Sicily are comparatively buoyant and combative, not because Pirandello, himself a Sicilian, glosses over the misery of his homeland or indulges in peasant romanticism, but simply because here the human drama plays itself out with quick violence. Men rise, men fall; but they do not know the dribbling monotonies of an overly-rationalized mode of existence, as do so many characters in Pirandello's urban stories. In "Fumes," the best of the Sicilian group, a decent hard-working farmer, to frustrate the local money-lender, agrees to sell his land to a sulphur-mining company, appalled though he is at the thought of the fumes that will now blight the whole region. The spectacle of a man being pressed beyond endurance is a familiar one in Pirandello's stories; but the farmer, while hardly a Promethean figure, does cry out at the end, "Neither he nor I!"

Behind Pirandello stands his master in fiction, the Sicilian Giovanni Verga, from whom he learned to disdain rhetoric and grandeur. Reading Verga's stories one feels they are not so much "made-up" fictions as communal fables, the record of a people born to catastrophe. Reading Pirandello's stories one feels they have been wrought by a man increasingly estranged from a world he knows intimately. Pirandello does not achieve the virile spareness of Verga; no one does. In Verga everything is subordinated to the deci-

siveness of the event; in Pirandello one must always be aware of his psychological motives, even if these seldom appear on the surface of the story, and then mainly as a film of melancholy. Verga's happenings are much more terrible than Pirandello's, yet are easier to take, since in Verga men scream and howl as they suffer. Only a few decades separate the two writers, but the distance between them reflects a deep change in the spiritual temper of European life, a certain loss of zest and will.

Writers, like the rest of us, do not choose their moment of birth, and it would be absurd to relate Pirandello too closely with the depressing qualities of his stories. So quick an intelligence must have been aware of the difference in the literary possibilities open to Verga and himself, and realized that most of the advantage did not lie with him. But no serious writer chooses his subject; he can only choose whether to face it. And that Pirandello did with exemplary courage and honesty. (pp. 22-3)

Irving Howe, "Some Words for a Master," in The New Republic *(reprinted by permission of* The New Republic; © *1959 The New Republic, Inc.), Vol. 141, No. 13, September 28, 1959, pp. 21-4.*

A. L. De CASTRIS (essay date 1962)

In a climate of dejection and philosophical bitterness, of *taedium vitae* and cognitive engagement, there arises *Il fu Mattia Pascal (The Late Mattia Pascal)*, one of Pirandello's most remarkable inventions, which the writer himself later seemed to credit as a windfall of the mind, when, on reprinting it in 1921, he added the postscript on the Scruples of the Imagination (*Avvertenza sugli scrupoli della fantasia*). By emphasizing life's unpredictability and its superior inventiveness (or absurdity) vis-à-vis the imagination, he wanted above all to call attention to the bitter *truth* of that apparently paradoxical fable, to its flavor of real life and its significance as an exemplary experience of man. For this, and it starts actually with *Il fu Mattia Pascal*, is the conscious semantic duplicity of Pirandello, the figuration of a universal meaning (the human condition) in terms of an occasional life story.

From the objectively depicted and realistically colored aspects of life's inexplicability (seen in the grotesque situations and in the crisis of human relationships), there takes progressively shape and focus a new drama of everyman, a humorous epiphany of a diminutive Ulysses: the protagonist. He is an Orestes changed into Hamlet, because of his need to advance to the limelight from a background of masks devoid of objective reality, because of his useless will to see himself live and to measure with his consciousness the infinite solitude surrounding him; he is the witness of a failing dialectic, of inexorable rending in the paper heaven which had protected him and made existence finite and knowable. The grotesque scenery, thus rent asunder by man's revolt, suffers in the moans of its inhabitants, mediocre creatures withered by sorrow and by the solitude the writer himself compassionately saw. And yet this is no longer a central suffering to the impersonal witness, who from the crucial rending isolates a riper object of knowledge, a more inward "argument" of inquiry and portrayal. Pirandello's man, who has acquired the responsibility of a new dimension, i.e., of a consciousness mirroring and dramatizing himself, forced as he is from now on to experience the crisis personally, replaces the choral testimonial of the first Pirandellian "crowd."

The different fictional perspective is rendered by style, by the humorous detachment which renews the narrative's tone and structure. A deep decoloration of the milieu, to purge it of the earlier violent and distorting traits which imbued its figures and outlines with grimness, takes place here, in the new novel, through direct narration. Now consciousness sees itself live and confesses itself, and at the outset claims it wants to reduce the proportions of drama, as befits a perspective shaped by awareness of the petty scope of the human adventure. (pp. 91-2)

Thus, in the petty-bourgeois milieu of a Roman boarding house, that sense of an elusive something, of a life worn out in an ambiguous silence, stylistically signals the occasional nature of situations and persons vis-à-vis the subtle, inward and atomistic process of consciousness. In these creatures, cryptic in their several ways and as if brushed by an ancient, imperceptible folly; in Papiano, Anselmo, Adriana, and the singer, all expressions of a corruption and a misery rather stifled in the soul than cried out: something like a bloodless humanity is celebrated, a tortuous shyness which ideally fits them to deal with a shadow like Adriano Meis. This is the "feeling of contrast," which, objectified here for the first time in an independent character, prevents the violent dissociation of polemical irony and heartfeld compassion, for it is a feeling of contrast committed to extracting from all situations a "universal sense." And it makes for a nimble discursive tone, for a more rounded and light, almost serene syntax: a language of "lived" thought, of "thought" life—the language of an experience which is becoming, after Leopardi's fashion, a lucid and desperate consciousness.

The consciousness of living is, then, the new dimension in which Mattia Pascal moves. Life is an absurd prison of vain, provisional forms whose result for humanity is oppressive and alienating; society rivets man to a false individuation that warps his wishes and will, thereby breaking up his unity of consciousness into a deceitful multiplicity. He therefore rebels, escapes, refuses conventions and the artifice of a hated mask. He starts on his redemptive journey, seeking truer individuations, such as freedom, authentic love, justice, honor; and he finally does enjoy a sense of boundless availability, of having returned to a pure consciousness unfettered by any conditions. . . . But it is a short-lived rapture: for true love is rapport, justice is confrontation after all, *consciousness* is the others in us. The most tragic disappointment thwarts that quest of new selfhood, a definitive impossibility of individuation disillusions that pure will to choose: every experience leads man back to the necessity of a continuous bargaining for compromise outside which liberty becomes hopelessly arbitrary in the absence of foundations. (pp. 93-4)

Far from resolving the character's adventure in an accepted "triumph of the demands of State bureaucracy," as [B. Croce said in *Letteratura della nuova Italia*], Mattia Pascal's resigned conclusion actually constitutes the immediate premise to the final drama of Pirandellian man. For the failure of Mattia Pascal's anarchic attempt includes not merely the provisional escape of man from the prison of conventional forms, from mystifying society, in search of a genuineness of selfhood that will make him free and master of himself. It includes also, and above all, the discovery of

the tragic necessity for that oppressive form and inhuman prison. Beyond Mattia's humorous return, beyond his sulking reinsertion in the dark, alienating machinery of social pacts, it is actually his brief experience as disengaged man, as life's "foreigner" that strikingly foreshadows the real drama of Pirandello's great creatures. (p. 94)

．　．　．　．　．

Fictionally, I think, *Serafino Gubbio, Cameraman* constitutes Pirandello's most interesting and technically original experiment, for here the use of the diary form as an instrument of objectivity enables the protagonist to identify with the writer and makes the scattered contents of experience portrayable in a unified story. Historical continuity and narrative unity do not lie in the vicissitudes and actions of the characters, but exclusively in the experiencing consciousness, the reasoning diary-like structure which projects symbols and meanings onto those fragmentary events. The perspective of Serafino Gubbio coincides with Pirandello's consciousness: a consciousness engaged in reconstructing into an idiomatic or theatrical unity and continuity what psychologically and narratively is no longer to be reconstructed.

That is why, while Pirandello's other novels are valid as examples of his ideology (apart from their poetical results), *Serafino Gubbio, Cameraman* has value especially as a document of his poetics, as a very eloquent testimonial, in an artistically rich context, of Pirandello's natural yet laboring transition to theatrical experience. . . . I would say the overall movement is from a human to a "divine" feeling, from "narrative" pity to the tragic poet's high and invisible pity.

Pirandello's modern insight shows in his ability to make a valid myth of the imperturbable detachment which Serafino Gubbio pursues throughout the novel, by symbolizing such spiritual state in the unhuman impassiveness of the movie camera. At first Gubbio is upset by the paradoxical cruelty of this symbol of modern civilization; later he wishes to become worthy of it and attain a watching human insensitiveness which will suit the grotesque proportions of contemporary life; finally he knows that its apparent "inanimate silence" harbors the deepest meaning of his compassion. Facing up to the open and irreversible condemnation of man, this novel is exactly the graph of Pirandellian poetics, whose evolution it exhibits from an attitude of participation in the drama of his creatures to an attitude of pure contemplation.

A crisis of compassion, then. This crisis is set forth, to begin with, in terms of a concrete psychological situation with obvious motivations and historical circumstances. The initial meaning of the myth of the "machine" is polemical and negative, rife with the ironic and satirical tensions which reveal Pirandello to be the most mature awareness, in Italy as a whole, of the crisis of the bourgeoisie and of modern society's corruption. The first sections of the great diary contain, in fact, in the guise of a Chaplinesque figuration, a vibrant indictment of the frightful moral void into which modern civilization risks falling, since by the monstrous proliferation of "leviathan," by the inhuman, voracious growth of industrial mass standards, it confines within ever smaller boundaries, to the verge of insignificance, the ethical values of its history. . . . (pp. 96-7)

Man is the unknowing victim of his own violent inhumanity; for the dizzy mechanism produced by his ambition has reduced him to the non-life of inconsequential gestures, of progress without consciousness. The automatism of his moral life threatens to involve him in a total conflagration, salutary and regenerating though it may be. . . . (p. 98)

Serafino Gubbio is the awareness of this progressive inanition of man, of his inevitably self-destructive destiny. And yet he sees his own destiny in the others: while he humanly resists the fatal assimilation that the machine imposes on him, he slowly sinks in the abyss of impassiveness, of insensitive objectivity, as life persuades him of the uselessness of both compassion and conscience. (p. 99)

But the protest against modern man's reduction to amorphous mass is only the initial moment, and the figurative occasion, of Serafino Gubbio's consciousness. On a much deeper level we get the meaning of his renunciation of feeling and of the mechanical impassibility he thinks he is experiencing. The fact is that this novel conclusively summarizes Pirandello's ideological history to document an attitude by now ripe for the theatrical experience. It is the moment when the writer consciously sums up, so as to project them into a symbolic story, the essential phases of his philosophy, and thereby clarifies the meanings and inner tensions of his previous experiences. From the polemical recording of a historical world's collapse, his meditation has extracted the perennial, existential sense of the human condition. Now, from the universal compassion engendered by the conquest of what Leopardi would call the "horrible truth," there rises this significant need to "disappear": the will to objectify the drama in independent creatures, in absolute symbols.

That is the value of Serafino Gubbio's "seeing," a definitive clairvoyance by means of which, turning the handle of his little camera, he fixes in extreme symbols the spectacle of life—a spectacle of chaos and perdition, where the mechanically irrational quality of events and human acts seems to result from an ancient institutional doom. (p. 100)

This "seeing" of the cameraman, and the very objects of his visual recording, are the source of the novel's structure and style. The novel, in fact, is built on two different dimensions: on the inorganic, fragmentary time of the external story, and on the unified tissue of Serafino Gubbio's sentimental story, who comments on the former for the last time, and from the nausea of that moment invokes an absolute "disappearance." The mechanical bent of his point of view makes for the jumpy portrayal, and the story takes shape in a disconnected sequence of photographs, descriptive flashes, synthetic figurations. It is a conscious procedure, which lines up in an inorganic succession scenic openings, captions, theatrical and motion picture elements, scenarios, close-ups, often evincing that taste for what goes on behind the scenes which will make itself felt in Pirandello's future work. It pursues the fragmentary reality of characters and situations, in a mixed rhythm of memories and anxieties, of evasions and vivid mechanical illusions. But it registers above all the meaning of Gubbio's perspective, his evolution from polemical statements to instinctive sympathies, and from the disgust of these in turn to the frightful "stony" deliverance of consciousness, which is superbly envisaged in the objective rhythm, so violently and purposely scenographic, of the last sequence. . . . (pp. 100-01)

Here the monstrous process is accomplished. The terrifying

reality of man, that incongrous phenomenalism of his shreds of life, becomes the object of an absolute portrayal, of a timeless testimonial. And consciousness, brought to that extreme threshold by the gradual revelation of a wholesale failure of civilization—of which contemporary history represents the last act, in the sharpening of an irreversible process—becomes a silent, frightening clairvoyance. . . .

Serafino Gubbio's impassibility represents the definitive conquest of Pirandellian compassion, the terminal goal of a biographical itinerary which is entirely defined and resolved in the sphere of pity. The cognitive impulse, instinctively at work in the young writer's first, amazed glance, has aroused a need for understanding and clarity; but he who has understood life cannot prescribe for it, he can only refine his instruments of solace until he experiences them to the highest degree, in an utterly disinterested participation. Pirandello removes himself forever from the scene of his creatures, from the explanation of their drama. But this silent detachment, which burns up all human involvements to resolve his whole feeling of life in pure contemplation, is the last and greatest condition of his art. . . . (p. 102)

> A. L. De Castris, in two chapters in his Storia di Pirandello (© 1962 by Casa Editrice Giuseppe Laterza & Figli), Laterza, 1962 (translated by Glauco Cambon and reprinted as "The Experimental Novelist," in Pirandello: A Collection of Critical Essays, edited by Glauco Cambon, Prentice-Hall, Inc., 1967, pp. 91-102).

MORRIS FREEDMAN (essay date 1964)

Pirandello is first responded to in terms of his experimentalism, the *pirandellismo* which has made his name in the modern theater the counterpart of Joyce's in modern fiction, or of Yeats's in modern poetry. . . . Pirandello's experimentalism gains its force only through his substance, the fabric of plot, theme, character; his manipulation of the conventional dramatic structure reinforces, is often identical with, his subject matter. *How* Pirandello says what he has to say is a good part of *what* he says. What Pirandello has to say is, finally, why he is worth considering at all in other than a purely historical and technical way.

Pirandello is not simply engaged in writing an endless essay on the tensions between art and reality. . . . [His] unrelenting insistence on the art-reality opposition is subordinate to moral matters and has final meaning in the context of highly particularized human situations.

It Is So! (If You Think So) illustrates the point. It is tempting to take this play as simply another little treatise in dramatic form on the nature of truth, on the difficulty of ever ascertaining it precisely. We have Laudisi's snickering refrain on truth, and of course the long discussions that precede and follow the several revelations of the plot, which are concerned with "truth," the question of who is really the mad one, Signora Frola, or her son-in-law, Signor Ponza.

And, indeed, the examination of the question of truth is charming, especially brilliant, and lively, because it is so carefully embedded in the specific human arrangements of the drama. . . . Even more, we get a hint of one of Pirandello's major themes here: the unfixed state of truth in relation to the dramatic manipulation of it. (pp. 368-69)

Yet to take the play as only a treatise on truth is to fall into the same shortsighted and shallow intellectuality of the mob on the stage which is so intent on discovering the "truth." As the characters get involved in the triviality of the "plot," neglecting the human beings entangled in it who are entangling themselves all the more out of desperation, so our involvement with the question of truth turns us away from what, in the first place, makes the whole question such a compelling one: the quite awful circumstances of Ponza and his wife and his mother-in-law. Becoming involved in the macabre comedy of the curiosity seekers, we neglect the tragedy of the Ponza ménage, the wiping out of so many members of the family by the earthquake, and the attempts at adjustment by the survivors.... The complexity of the arrangements the three have worked out, a complexity that becomes fantastic, indicates how desperately they are trying to anchor themselves to some sort of reality and sanity, where mere truth must allow itself to be shaped freely, in the service of a more compelling exigency. (p. 369)

The horror which underlies the grotesque comedy comes from the brutal, insatiable, but always well-mannered prying of the officials of the town and their ladies into the affairs of Ponza. (p. 370)

Nor are the two tones of the play, the technical-abstract and the living-human, to be separated, for the essay on truth illuminates and is illuminated by the human agony. Truth emerges as less important than the need to accommodate to reality, in fact as subservient to it, so subservient that truth discards facts, that is, less important facts (like documents proving identity) for more important ones (needs that are not to be denied or catalogued or compromised). The one truth finally accepted by everyone, explicitly by the Ponzas, implicitly by the onlookers, is that some kind of deal by the Ponzas with the demands of reality was justified in the light of their circumstances.

Truth, then, has meaning only in specific human terms, which always take precedence over the requirements of evidence, of philosophy, of cold intellectuality. But the tragedy here, as elsewhere, comes from the hubris of human beings who think they can long act out a truth detached from the facts, abstracted from them.... Truth without regard to its human embodiment is meaningless, as Laudisi keeps saying; yet the human situation which leaps away, for good reason or bad, from the roots of truth risks tragedy. The meaning of the play is to be found in the blending of theme and technique, plot, and philosophy. (pp. 370-71)

Pirandello's sense of the absurdity and bleakness of the contemporary human situation is relieved only by his sympathy with any attempts to escape it or to mitigate it. Efforts like those of the Ponzas ..., however foredoomed they may be because of the unyielding demands made by the natural and possible, are at least heroic, for the human imagination is involved at its highest manifestation, creativity. Pirandello very nearly applauds the attempts although, with a hard sense of the inevitable, he does not bemoan the failure. (p. 377)

> *Morris Freedman, "Moral Perspective in Pirandello," in* Modern Drama *(copyright © 1964, University of Toronto, Graduate Centre for Study of Drama; with the permission of* Modern Drama*), Vol. VI, No. 4, February, 1964, pp. 368-77.*

ROBERT BRUSTEIN (essay date 1964)

[The autobiographical play *When One Is Somebody*] is flawed by traces of vanity and self-pity, but its final image is a stunning consummation of Pirandello's views about the individual's relationship to his life, and the artist's relationship to his art—two subjects which are really the same subject, and which continue to obsess him throughout his career. Pirandello knows that he is alive and changing, but, against his will, he has hardened into the stiff postures of the stereotyped public man, while his words, though formed in the mind of a living being, are etched in marble as soon as they are uttered. To accept a definition—to become a *somebody*—is to be frozen in time, just as art, the defined world of the artist, rigidifies in its prison of form. The typical Pirandellian drama is a drama of frustration which has at its core an irreconcilable conflict between time and timelessness or life and form; and whether the author is reflecting on human identity or (his other major subject) the identity of art, the terms of the conflict remain essentially the same.

Typical in this sense, *When One Is Somebody* is unusual in another: Pirandello very rarely wrote autobiographical plays. Yet, he is one of the most subjective dramatists in the modern theatre, and certainly the most self-conscious. Pirandello is a peculiarity of the theatre of revolt—an imperious messianic artist who writes compassionate existential plays. In him, the Romantic ego is strong, though usually sublimated. (pp. 281-82)

[It] is rare when . . . personal egotism informs his work. As a dramatist, Pirandello is a stern, uncompromising ironist, but his plays are full of pity for the fate of suffering mankind. It is true that the only playwright mentioned in Pirandello's theatre is Pirandello himself (his name is occasionally on the tongues of his characters). But the references are always ironic, and he always resists the temptation to glorify himself, like D'Annunzio, through the agency of superhuman heroes. Pirandello's messianic impulse, on the other hand, is channeled into a personal philosophical vision. If not present as a character, the author is always present as a hovering reflective intelligence—commenting, expostulating, conceptualizing. In this, he reminds us of Shaw, and he certainly fits Shaw's definition of the "artist-philosopher." (p. 283)

Pirandello's philosophy, however, is quite different than Shaw's, since it is pessimistic in the extreme, and based on the conviction that the problems of life are insoluble. Because of this conviction, Pirandello sees no possibility of salvation through social or community life. In fact, he is vigorously opposed to all forms of social engineering, and extremely contemptuous of Utopian ideals and idealists (he satirizes them, rather clumsily, in *The New Colony*). Pirandello, furthermore, considers the social-use of art to be a betrayal of art.... This would seem to put Pirandello at opposite poles from Shaw; but in one sense, they are very much alike. Both create plays in which plot and character are largely subordinate to theme; and both lean towards tendentious argumentation in enunciating their ideas. Indeed, Pirandello's weakness for ideas lays him open to the charge that his plays are too cerebral. This charge he does not deny, but he denies that cerebral plays have to be undramatic.... Pirandello is certainly the first to convert *abstract thought* into passion—to formulate an expository philosophy in theatrical terms.

It must be conceded, however, that these terms are not always very satisfactory. Pirandello is exceedingly interested in the *idea* of form, but rather indifferent to form itself. One tends to think of him as an experimental dramatist, but only his theatre trilogy can be called a formal breakthrough. The rest of his forty-four plays are relatively conventional in their use of dramatic materials. (pp. 283-84)

As for his dramatic structure, it is extremely conventional, when not downright haphazard. Almost all of his plays are crammed into three acts, ''whether they fit or not.'' Whenever the action flags, Pirandello contrives a new entrance or a new revelation; and each curtain comes down on a not always credible crisis. In the act of converting intellect into passion, Pirandello often tears the passion to tatters. His plots are bursting with operatic feelings and melodramatic climaxes in an exaggerated Sicilian vein. Hyperbolic expressions of grief, rage, and jealousy alternate with murders, suicides, and mortal accidents; wronged wives, maddened husbands, and bestial lovers foment adultery, incest, illegitimacy, plots, and duels. At times, his monologues turn into arias, and would be more appropriate set to Verdi's music.

The characters, furthermore, seem to lose psychological depth as they gain philosophical eloquence—occasionally, their identity is wholly swallowed up in the author's ideas. Pirandello is even more loquacious than Shaw, and has, therefore, less resistance to the *raisonneur*. Shaw is able to preserve aesthetic distance from a character like John Tanner, but Laudisi in *It Is So!* (*If You Think So*) and Diego Cinci in *Each in His Own Way* are hardly detached from their author at all. Shaw's drama is a drama of ideas, in which the ideas change from play to play, and the author can support two positions at the same time. Pirandello's drama is a drama of ideas based on a single underlying concept, consistent throughout his career and enjoying the author's wholehearted endorsement. Still, the basic Pirandellian concept is itself dialectical, and subject to endless combinations and permutations. The terms of the dialectic may not change, but the author's point of attack alternates from play to play, from thesis to antithesis, depending on the situation being considered.

The basic Pirandellian concept is borrowed from [Henri] Bergson, and, briefly stated, it is this. Life (or reality or time) is fluid, mobile, evanescent, and indeterminate. It lies beyond the reach of reason, and is reflected only through spontaneous action, or instinct. Yet man, endowed with reason, cannot live instinctually like the beasts, nor can he accept an existence which constantly changes. In consequence, he uses reason to fix life through ordering definitions. Since life is indefinable, such concepts are illusions. Man is occasionally aware of the illusionary nature of his concepts; but to be human is to desire form; anything formless fills man with dread and uncertainty. (pp. 285-86)

The drama Pirandello distills from this concept is usually described through reference to the face and the mask—a conflict he borrowed from the *teatro del grotesco*. (p. 286)

[In Pirandello's] work, the mask of appearances is shaped both by the self and others. The others constitute the social world, a world which owes its existence to the false assumption that its members adhere to narrow definitions. Man, like life, may be unknowable, and the human soul, like time, may be in constant flight, but society demands

certainty, and tries to imprison man in its fictitious concepts. To Pirandello, all social institutions and systems of thought—religion, law, government, science, morality, philosophy, sociology, even language itself—are means by which society creates masks, trying to catch the elusive face of man and fix it with a classification. (p. 287)

On the other hand, the mind of man, being stuffed with concepts, has no defense against these social definitions. Because he is uncertain of his identity, he accepts the identity given him by others—sometimes willingly, like the heroine of *As You Desire Me,* sometimes reluctantly, like the hero of *When One Is Somebody.* Looking for the elusive self, he sees it reflected in the eyes of others, and takes the reflection for the original. This acceptance of a superimposed identity is one side of Pirandello's *teatro dello specchio* (theatre of the looking glass)—aptly named, since the image of the mirror occurs in almost every one of his plays. (pp. 287-88)

The author—always identifying with the suffering individual in opposition to the collective mind—is in revolt against the social world, and all its theoretical, conceptual, institutional extensions.... Pirandello's social revolt has existential roots.... [In] Pirandello's view, the adoption of the mask is the inevitable consequence of being human. (p. 288)

To stop time, to achieve stasis, to locate the still point, Pirandello's characters put on their masks, hoping to hide their shameful faces by playing a role.

This is what Pirandello means by *costruirsi*, building yourself up. Man begins as nothing definite, and becomes a *costruzione*, creating himself according to predetermined patterns or roles. Thus, he plays family roles (husband, wife, father, mother), religious roles (saint, blasphemer, priest, atheist), psychological roles (madman, neurotic, normal man), and social roles (mayor, citizen, socialist, revolutionary). No matter how well these roles are played, however, none of them reveals the face of the actor. They are disguises, designed to give purpose and form to a meaningless existence—masks in an infinite comedy of illusion. The true self is revealed only in a moment of blind instinct, which has the power to break down all codes and concepts. But even then, the self is on the point of changing. Thus, Pirandello refuses to idealize the personality in the manner of the messianic rebels; for him, personality remains a fictional construct. Instead, he concentrates on the disintegration of personality in a scene of bondage and frustration—existential revolt in the ironic mode. Pirandellian man has freedom, but his freedom is unbearable; it beckons him towards the waste and void. Though he sometimes plunges into reality through spontaneous, instinctual action, he more often takes refuge from reality in a beneficial illusion. (pp. 289-90)

In Pirandello's drama ... the conflict between Art and Nature is translated into a conflict between life and form, while appearances become illusions; but with him, the conflict becomes a real dialectic. Pirandello evokes sympathy for the man who tries to hide from reality and sympathy for the man who tries to plunge back into it. Life and form—reality and illusion—are opposed, but they are the twin poles of human existence.

Pirandello is similarly ambivalent about the faculty of reason. His philosophy, founded as it is on the belief that real knowledge is unattainable, is profoundly anti-intellectual; yet, it is through the intellect that he reaches his conclusions. Such paradoxes proliferate in Pirandello's drama. Reason is both man's consolation and his curse; it creates a false identity which it can also destroy; it applies the masks to the face, and then rips them off. (p. 291)

This probably sounds impossibly abstruse, an exercise in epistemology rather than drama, but the wonder is the number of effective situations Pirandello is able to create out of such reflections. For Pirandello's concept always takes the form of conflict, and conflict remains the heart of his drama. . . . As an existential rebel, Pirandello explores the roles men play in order to escape from life—revolt turns inward against the elusiveness of human existence. As a social rebel, he attacks the busybodies, gossips, and scandalmongers who think they can understand the unknowable mystery of man—revolt turns outwards against the intruding social world. The two levels of Pirandello's revolt generally run parallel in each of his plays. . . . (pp. 291-92)

[Let] us call those in the outer circle *alazones* (impostors or buffoons) and those in the center *eirones* (self-deprecators). . . . In Pirandello's drama, the *alazon* is an agent of organized society, and is usually identified with one of its institutions—science, bureaucracy, or the state. He is sometimes a doctor, sometimes a petty official, sometimes a magistrate, sometimes a policeman—always a pretender, whose pretense lies in thinking himself a wise man when he is really a fool. The *eiron*, on the other hand, is a suffering individual who has hidden some private secret under a mask of appearances. Sometimes, he is unaware he is wearing a mask, in which case he is merely a pathetic sufferer—a *pharmakos*, or scapegoat. More often, he is a man of superior wisdom, because, like Socrates (the original *eiron*), he *knows* he knows nothing. Hounded and tormented by his persecutors, the buffoonish *alazones*, he replies with the dry mock: ironic laughter is his only weapon. (pp. 292-93)

The clash between the two groups occurs when the *alazones* try to peel off the masks of the *eirones*—an action which has both tragic and comic consequences. On the one hand, this impertinent invasion of another's privacy may be dangerous, since the *eiron's* illusion is necessary to his life; on the other, the attempt to discover another's secret self is ludicrously impossible, since the face beneath the mask cannot be known. The comic action, then, proceeds along the social level of the play where the *alazones* are frustrated in their curiosity, their state changing from knowledge to ignorance, from smug complacency to stupefied bafflement. The tragic action proceeds along the existential level of the play where the *eirones* are dragged under a painfully blinding spotlight which causes them terrible discomfort and suffering. . . .

One of the most famous, if not the most artful, of the plays in this mode is *It Is So! (If You Think So)*. . . . (p. 293)

[The] existential complaint is only suggested in *It Is So!*, then buried under a barrage of social satire. Instead of developing the deeper implications of his philosophy, Pirandello exercises the animus of his social revolt; and the tragedy which threatens is averted at the end. Their right to privacy affirmed, their secret still hidden from the gossips and the busybodies, the *pharmakoi* depart into darkness, while the *alazones* stand lost in amazement, whipped by the savage laughter of the *eiron*.

It Is So! (If You Think So) is a fairly conventional exercise in the mode of the grotesque. As an expression of social revolt, it has its power and relevance, but the split between the *pharmakoi* and the *eiron*—between the sufferers and their spokesman—shows that Pirandello has not yet perfected his structure. Furthermore, the prominence of Laudisi, the *raisonneur*, suggests that, at this early point, Pirandello is less interested in dramatizing his themes than in stating them flatly. In *Henry IV* . . . , however, Pirandello dispenses with the *raisonneur* entirely, embodying his ideas in a brilliant theatrical metaphor, and concentrating not so much on the social world of the dumbfounded buffoons as on the existential world of the chief sufferer. And now this world is wonderfully rich and varied. The central character of the play is both *pharmakos* and *eiron*, both a living person and an articulate personification, both the mechanism of the action and the source of the ideas. In Henry's character, Pirandello's reflections on the conflict between life and form, on the elusiveness of identity, and on man's revolt against time, achieve their consummation in a powerfully eerie manner. Henry is the culmination of Pirandello's concept of the mask and the face, as well as embodying Pirandello's notions (developed more elaborately in his theatre plays) about the timeless world of art. In trying to fix his changing life in significant form, Henry emerges as Actor, Artist, and Madman, and, besides this, possesses an extraordinary intellect, reflecting on all three. (pp. 295-96)

Henry IV is also significant for the hints it throws out about Pirandello's view of art—views which form the basis for another important group of his plays. For while Henry suggests certain characteristics of the actor and the artist, a good many of Pirandello's characters actually *are* actors and artists, reflecting self-consciously on the implications of their roles. Pirandello's attention is fixed not on the act but rather on the *process* of the act, as analyzed by the one who commits it. In his more conventional plays, Pirandello imagines men watching themselves live. In his more experimental drama, Pirandello imagines performers watching themselves perform and artists watching themselves create—the mirror remains the central prop of his theatre. Actually, Pirandello's views of art are an extension of his concept of the face and the mask. When man becomes a *costruzione*, placing a mask over his changing features, he stands in the same relationship to his new identity as the artist does to his art—for art is the artist's *costruzione*, the form he imposes on chaotic life. The construction, in each case, is built up by the human demand for order.

In each case, too, Pirandello's attitudes towards the product are split. Like the mask, the work of art is both a limiting and a liberating creation. Art is superior to life, because it has purpose, meaning, and organization—the illusion is deeper than the reality. But art is inferior to life because it can never capture the transitory, formless quality of existence. The work of art is thus a beneficial illusion, an ordered fiction—more harmonious than life, yet still a lie. When Pirandello finds the temporal world unbearable, he takes refuge in the timeless world of art; but when he finds the fixity of art unbearable, he longs to break out into spontaneous life. (pp. 301-02)

[The] agony of the artist in Pirandello's drama is that, for all his ingenuity, he cannot really create life—to make an artistic form is to deaden and kill. In *Diana and Tuda*, for example, the older sculptor, Giuncano, has destroyed all his statues because, as he grew old and changed, they remained perpetually the same. . . .

When Pirandello's messianism is the ascendant, however, he argues the opposite point—that the artist's work is superior to God's, because art, unlike man, is immortal. . . . (p. 303)

The contradictions multiply, and so do the Pirandellian paradoxes; only the basic conflict remains constant. Life and form are irretrievably at odds, and man suffers from his failure to reconcile them. Pirandello's desire to reconcile them explains, I think, his attraction to the theatre, because of all the literary forms, only theatrical art combines the spontaneous and accidental with the ordered and predetermined. (p. 304)

In Pirandello's view . . . dramatic characters are not alive at all until they have been bodied forth by actors; the action waits to burst into life, and passion to receive its cue. . . . Because the actor is only impersonating the character (*i.e.,* wearing his mask), the theatre performance cannot help but travesty the author's written conception; and much of the comedy in *Six Characters* is based on the disparity between the reality of Pirandello's six and the artificiality of the performers. Still, if the actor distorts his role, he is nevertheless essential to it—only he can make it live. This passion for life in art explains Pirandello's fondness for the idea of improvisation. In contrast with the author's writing, the actor's improvisation is vital, immediate, and spontaneous. And theatre, theoretically, reaches its ideal consummation when it springs, unprepared, from the imagination of the performer.

Thus, in *Tonight We Improvise,* the director, Hinkfuss, is pleased to announce that he has eliminated the author entirely. . . . Hinkfuss, a three-foot tyrant with a huge head of hair, is a caricature of the overbearing Reinhardtian *regisseur;* but he also functions as a Pirandellian *raisonneur* in outlining the author's theories. (p. 305)

[The] living actors proceed to improvise a drama, pulling in and out of character, commenting on their roles, expressing dissatisfaction with the director ("No one directs life")—until finally they are caught up entirely in their parts and play them to an unexpected conclusion. In the theatre, anything can happen, and the pattern of art is disturbed by the accidents of life. Thus, in *Each in His Own Way,* the play is not even completed, because among the spectators are the real-life counterparts of the characters on the stage; and angered by being represented in this *commedia a chiave,* they attack the author and the actors, and bring the curtain down. For Pirandello, plot and character are now totally subordinated to the theatrical process itself, for that process is life itself. The theory is courageous—but Pirandello is not courageous enough to put it into practice. In Pirandello's theatre, the playwright still exists. The "improvisations" of the actors are all composed beforehand, and the spectators are planted, their lines written too. Only through the disappearance of the author can the conflict between life and art be resolved, but Pirandello is unable to relinquish control over his work. Still dominated by his messianic obsession to create an organic art—changing from moment to moment, yet still formed by the hand of man—Pirandello refuses to complete his godlike function by withdrawing from the scene.

In his frustration over forming a statue that moves, Giun-

cano destroyed his art; Pirandello, frustrated but undaunted, continues to create, and the result is his "trilogy of the theatre in the theatre." [*Six Characters in Search of an Author, Each in His Own Way,* and *Tonight We Improvise*] . . . were all written at different stages of the author's career, but all are unified by a common purpose. Probing the complex relationships between the stage, the work of art, and reality itself, Pirandello attempts, in these plays, to forge out of the old theatrical artifacts a living theatre, destroying the traditional conventions of the stage by crossing the boundaries which separate art from life. In these plays, the illusions of the realistic theatre—where actors pretend to be real people, canvas and lumber pass for actual locations, and forged events are designed to seem real—no longer apply. Now the stage is a stage, actors are actors, and even the audience, formerly silent and half invisible in its willing suspension of disbelief, has been drawn into the action and implicated in the theatrical proceedings. As for the fourth wall, this fiction has been destroyed entirely— nothing separates the spectator from the stage except space, and even this space occasionally evaporates when the actors enter the audience, and the spectators come on stage. Having disintegrated reality in his more conventional plays, Pirandello is now disintegrating stage reality. Having scourged the peeping and prying of the social community, he is now attacking the community's peek-hole pastime, the theatre. For Pirandello, the fourth wall, designed for the entertainment of Peeping Toms, is an avenue that must be blocked. (pp. 306-07)

Pirandello goes further than any of his predecessors in breaking down the barriers between the inner and the outer plays; but he uses the [play within the play] convention for the same purpose as the Elizabethans—for commentary, criticism, and extradramatic remarks. Thus, Pirandello has not destroyed illusions; he has merely multiplied illusions. Contemptuous of imitation, he is unable to do without it. In his experimental drama, theory and practice fail to merge; idea and action fail to cohere. Unlike his companions in the theatre of revolt, Pirandello is never able to decide just to what extent he should enter his own work. Torn between messianic and existential demands, his Romantic ego is split wide open by its own contradictions.

Still, Pirandello's attacks on the deceptions of conventional realism and the narcotized stupor of the passive spectator had a revolutionary influence on the experimental theatre which followed. And if he does not ever solve the problem of life and form, he does open up a totally new side of it in each of his three plays. *Six Characters* examines the conflict between fictional characters and the actors who play their roles; *Each in His Own Way,* the conflict between stage characters and actual characters on whom they are based; and *Tonight We Improvise,* the conflict between actors who want to live their parts and the director who is always interrupting them. In each case, Pirandello preserves the pattern of the play within the play, preserving, besides, his earlier pattern of suffering *eirones* or *pharmakoi* surrounded by meddling *alazones.* (pp. 308-09)

Pirandello's most original achievement in his experimental plays . . . is the dramatization of the very act of creation. If he has not made a statue that moves, he has made a statue which is the living signature of the artist, being both his product and his process. The concept of the face and the mask has become the basis for a totally new relationship between the artist and his work. Thus, Pirandello completes that process of Romantic internalizing begun by Ibsen and Strindberg. . . . [For Pirandello] objective reality has become virtually inaccessible, and all one can be sure of is the illusion-making faculty of the subjective mind. After Pirandello, no dramatist has been able to write with quite the same certainty as before. In Pirandello's plays, the messianic impulse spends itself, before it even fully develops, in doubts, uncertainties, and confusions.

The playwrights who follow Pirandello are frequently better artists, but none would have been the same without him: Pirandello's influence on the drama of the twentieth century is immeasurable. (pp. 315-16)

> *Robert Brustein, "Luigi Pirandello," in his* The Theatre of Revolt: An Approach to the Modern Drama *(copyright © 1962, 1963, 1964 by Robert Brustein; reprinted by permission of Little, Brown and Company in association with the Atlantic Monthly Press), Atlantic-Little, Brown, 1964, pp. 281-317.*

FREDERICK MAY (essay date 1965)

There is . . . no clear-cut distinction to be drawn between Pirandello the playwright and Pirandello the *novelliere,* any more than we may separate his poetry, his novels, or his essays. His writing is one interpenetrating whole. . . . The dramatic feature of the *novelle* which is most immediately impressive is their dialogue. Here is an author who has mastered the secret of speech that can carry with ease and cogency plot, narrative, atmosphere, and character; here is an author who knows what pace is.

Pirandello's sureness of control issues from his perception that life—in which he always includes death, since that also is a state of being—is argument, a ceaseless polemic. He has no time to waste, therefore, on writing to a formula, and it is no use looking for 'typically Sicilian' tales, or stories that are free from his so-called obsessions. The *novelle* deal with the problems debated in the plays: the nature of identity; reality and illusion; the impossibility of communication; the possibility of a religion of compassion that springs from our common anguish; the ineluctable struggle between form and flux—and our inability to forgo the luxury of ideal images; coming to terms with and living out our aloneness; defining the role of paradox; and the unreasonableness of hope. These are universal problems, implicit in the human situation wherever man finds himself on the social scale. Pirandello refuses to allocate them by class or context, so that it is pointless to speak of middle-class or peasant *novelle.* True, he makes his characters elaborate their dialectic according to context, but he never allows us to believe that the central argument is generated by that context.

I have stressed the importance of dialogue in Pirandello because I feel it to be his especial contribution to the art of the short story. All but a few of the tales are shifting areas of conversation, either between Pirandello and the reader, or between character and character (or character and community). As a consequence, Nature, class, region, profession, and social institution are valued only in so far as they make it possible for him to thrust the sense of the debate tellingly upon us. (pp. ix-x)

The *novelle* of Pirandello may be seen as fairy-tales for modern grown-ups. That they are rooted in the great tradition of Italian story-telling takes away none of their disconcerting up-to-dateness. They belong to our era of disintegration, capturing its inflexions most acutely. The man whose dialectic is revealed in them is man coping with his multiple (and non-existent) identity, acquiescent in the realistic theory that the true events of life are the shades of becoming picked out by the mind, and eliciting his ethic from a compassionate inquiry into that constant dissolution which is the coherence of living. It is noteworthy how frequently he adopts the Dantesque journey, and nowhere more forcefully than in 'A Day Goes By'. . . . [It] is an allegory of the inner quest of contemporary man. (p. xii)

[Pirandello's very early story 'The Little Hut'] is a remarkable essay, with many hints of a personal style. The tautness may be a little overdone, the assembly of the elements be slightly too careful: the Paolo Veronese look of Màlia is bookish, and *romantically* bookish; while some of the dialogue is equally bookish. But its virtues easily outweigh its deficiencies. The behaviour of the little girl at the beginning of the story is not only finely observed, it is lived through. Papà Camillo's warning to Jeli reaches forward to the maturity of Pirandello as a writer of dialogue. The way in which so much is made to emerge from the very few words exchanged by the lovers; the vigil and prayer of Màlia, neatly straddled by the two uncomprehending vigils of the young girl; the observation of slight detail—the significance of the pipe—the juxtaposition of shut-upness and immensity (an early proof, this, of Pirandello's alertness to compressionism); all give hints of a unique gift. Already Pirandello is challenging the emptiness of form. (pp. xiii-xiv)

'Twelve Letters' bites very deep. There are affinities with Schnitzler, and Bourget is a wickedly employed catalyst, but this satire belongs to the Italian tradition. The situation is a network of Pirandellian traps. 'Hell is other people' is the tang of this story. And then, as we are released by and through its sophistication, we realize the tragedy of aloneness which is engaging all these characters. Why are they wearing these masks? Perhaps they're worthless. Nonetheless, they're suffering because society has made them into puppets. A typically Pirandellian reminder—and one we meet again and again in the plays—is the pointed use of the mirror. Tito Rossani sees himself living and at that moment dies. The dialogue is some of Pirandello's most intricate, and a nice counterpoint is maintained between its apparent simplicity (even triviality) and the real worlds which it is laying bare. A fine set-piece—comparable with the final speech in 'The Man with the Flower in his Mouth' or the Irish priest's speech in *Enrico IV*—is Rossani's re-evocation of his walk with Vidoni. If there were nothing else to convince us that Pirandello was aware from very early of the *novella* as theatre, this speech would do so. (p. xvi)

'Fear' resembles 'Twelve Letters' in its use of re-evocation, but this time Pirandello dispenses with satirical farce. The relationships between Andrea and Lillina, and Lillina and Antonio, have been too seriously constructed for them to be conveyed in other than a heavily claustrophobic idiom just lightly flecked with lyricism. The naked appeal by Lillina for sexual fulfilment, when she is caught in the trap of an exploiting society (symbolized for us by her husband and her lover), can only be answered by death. You must never ask to be allowed to live out your reality as you understand it—an admonition Pirandello reiterates in the *Sei person-*

aggi in cerca d'autore and *Enrico IV*. Sexual reality is the lost world of Pirandellian dreaming. (pp. xvi-xvii)

'The Best of Friends' is brilliantly comic. An obvious (almost *treacherously* obvious) piece of orthodox Pirandellianism, it tears along with gale-force till suddenly there is a stab of pain which pulls you up short. Gigi Mear doesn't *know* his friend from Padua, and *he* is once more annihilated. Not to worry, though! In this life you simply reconstruct yourself. You came back into Gigi's life as his friend. You'll go out of it again as his melancholy tormentor. Life's hell, so let's all have a good long laugh together. We're already in the world of *Enrico IV*.

The friend from Padua—and how perfect is his outrageous 'mask' name, 'Anthropophagus Goatsbeardhornyfoot'!—is among Pirandello's most vividly realized characters: an ironic wit, compassing his own tragedy, fully aware of himself, sardonically watching himself live, and punished with a clarity of intellect, whose nearness to insanity is manifest in the manic quality of his talk. (p. xvii)

'In the Abyss' [is] an astonishingly early and far-ranging exploration of the subconscious. What impresses most about this story—after we have taken in the assuredness with which Pirandello has distinguished the workings of the subconscious—is the way in which he has correlated the inner and outer lives of his characters, plucking them out of the general whirl . . . , driving down into them, till an image is forced to the surface. . . . The whole atmosphere of the story is one of hallucination, a world of contending shadows indicative of the contradictory layers of identity within the characters. (p. xx)

'The Man with the Flower in his Mouth' is, I think, unmatched among Pirandello's short stories, and great by any standards. Seldom can language have been so natural and so precise. Only a writer deeply aware of the processes of thought and image association could achieve such apparent casualness, at the same time as he exposed the desolation of two such divergent characters as the Man and the Other, and the annihilation of a third (the wife), who has not a word to say. It is not easy to pick out where the naturalistic fades into the incantational. Partly as a result of the milieu, partly as a result of the obvious tension informing the very first speech by the man with the flower in his mouth, we are taken straightaway into the brooding territory of loss. We shall not know until the last speech what it is we are mourning, but all the time our grief is personal. (p. xxii)

The man with the flower in his mouth and Nicola Petix in 'Destruction of the Man' are nearly related, but whereas Petix destroys the grotesque hope for the future begotten by others, the Man chooses the alternative commitment, pursuing the logic of illusion past the breaking-point, to a comprehension that even the act of destroying (as, to be sure, *all* action) is futile. Throughout the work of Pirandello this existentialist dualism prevails; some of his characters opt for the illusory form of death in suicide . . . ; others . . . either illogically refrain from killing themselves or someone else, or will their own survival in the moment of attempted suicide.

This is the dispute with life at its most ferocious, the questioning of the vision. The man with the flower in his mouth, having resisted self-destruction, goes on to capture the idyll of the apricot season, and the vision of the other customer's wife and daughters, dressed in blue and white, seated in the shade of a tree in a green field. For a few suspended and enchanted moments he has regained the earthly paradise. Petix is impelled to murder by an overwhelming sense of loss: the filth and animality of life in the tenement, following upon the barrenness of his relationship with his father, are a perpetual reminder of their antithesis, the golden age from which he is excluded. He is one of Pirandello's beggars—like the man we know as Henry IV, the boy in the *Sei personaggi in cerca d'autore*, Lillina in 'Fear', and the eponymous heroine of *Candelora*—who, asking for admittance into the lives of others, into life itself, are demolished, often by being driven mad, frequently by being forced into suicide.

'Destruction of the Man' is an inverted utopian story. It is also representative of a group of tales in which horror or revulsion finds relief in a horrifying action or horrible event. (pp. xxii-xxiii)

'A Day Goes By' is pure allegory, an intensification of the whole compass of the real life of Pirandello. Its events are the *meanings* of the things that have happened to him: his movement through life has been from the chaos of error . . . , the exile of society, to love in the tomb. His children, it is noticeable, are distinct from the ideal relationship with the beloved. She is the *fidanzata*, the promised bride of *Pasqua di Gea*, and the bed on which they have been united is the grave he foresaw. He is now old, but his child's eyes still scrutinize ironically and with paradoxical hope the stages of his journey and the condition of man. The tale is a direct conversation with the reader, a running commentary on life seen for the wandering and inquiry that it is. Technically, the eeriness of its time-suspended world, and the trance-like precise imprecision of outline of the owner of the restaurant, the clerks in the bank, the light that scurried to the train and away again (with no apparent agent to direct it)—all are brought off with complete success. There is an unflawed sincerity in their control. They *belong*, in fact. We are given the nakedness of the subconscious, human and vulnerable.

The outer world of Pirandello's stories—the appearance of its reality—has a deceptive monotony and a deceptive variety. The monotony is the mask which society exacts from us; the variety is the pathetic series of fragmentary masks in which we strut about the world: the peasant, the clerk, the editor, the landowner, the prostitute, the pseudo-veteran of Garibaldi's campaigns, the member of Parliament, the submissive daughter, the criminal, the usurer. . . . From this point of view, Pirandello has evolved an imposing range of characters. They are immaculately distinguished, for all the complexities of their interrelationships. But real character resides for him in the unique journey of search and realization, and to this the outer form is largely irrelevant. (pp. xxvii-xxviii)

Pirandello is . . . one of the most distinctive and characteristic voices of our age; the only great writer, I would suggest, who fully coheres with the relativistic propositions of modern science and modern philosophy. He provides their aesthetic analogue. (pp. xxviii-xxix)

Frederick May, in his introduction to Luigi Pirandello: Short Stories, *translated by Frederick May (© Oxford University Press 1965; reprinted by permission of Oxford University Press), Oxford University Press, London, 1965, pp. ix-xxix.*

OSCAR BÜDEL (essay date 1966)

Relativism is indeed the basic, fundamental category which informs all other dimensions of Pirandello's work. Pirandello thus opens perspectives on one of the most vital issues of his time. He appealed not because he flouted tradition but because his art mirrored, and put to discussion, the problems of his age. It is here that we have to see his importance; all other aspects of his work are secondary. The issues involved were those of his time; Pirandello had not created them. (p. 35)

Pirandello sees the basic evil in *ratio,* in human reason, which creates, indeed fabricates all the fictions with which man lives. To unmask all these rational fictions—or illusions, as the case may be—with the result that their opposites acquire the aspect of truth formerly associated with the fictions themselves is the fundamental aspect and the fundamental task of his work. Whatever the terms for the resulting dualistic aspect of Pirandellian thought, in which critics have seen the quintessence of his work—Form vs. Life, Movement vs. Form, Art vs. Life—here is their origin, their common denominator. This is the basis for the eminently analytical aspect of Pirandello's work. This is the reason why he called the collection of his theatre *Maschere nude,* naked masks. . . . (p. 36)

For Pirandello, all the fabricated fictions of human reason are thus relative, and in an untiring case history—as it were—he sets out to unmask and destroy them. The basic denouement in his stories and plays is usually the realization by one of the characters of the absolute relativity of his beliefs. (pp. 36-7)

With this crucial quest for truth, Pirandello's characters reach to the very foundations of their existence. Their relentless search for the truth of their proper identity harasses them, the suspicion of making uncomfortable discoveries lurks behind every thought. Existential despair is indeed the ever-present threat in all of Pirandello's work. . . . (p. 37)

Pirandello, however, stops short of the nothingness of an existential desperation. He leads his characters to the threshold of this realization, to the point where they make their basic discovery. The despair and nothingness which follow are in themselves of no interest. Pirandello is not treating, belabouring the mute question of the *absurde,* he is leading up to it. He is interested, as Pascal would say, in the hunt, not in the prey. He has forged ahead to the limits of the viable, he has arrived at the limits of the humanly bearable. What lies beyond it, the *gouffre,* the abyss, does not concern him. (p. 38)

For him, human existence, too, is only relatively that which it appears to be. Thus, even with man's basic concept of his own existence, it is—ironically—reason that prevents him from realizing the actual nature of this existence. Accordingly, Pirandello's concept of the illusion of human existence may be seen as fulfilling a giant hyperbolic function, that of foreshadowing, prefiguring, the kaleidoscopic fragmented appearances into which man 'organizes', 'fabricates' his everyday existence. (p. 40)

Pirandello took up [the] idea of human existence as a trap in the short story he appropriately called *La trappola.* . . . (p. 45)

The superficial aspects of the 'trap' may change in time, but its basic characteristics are the same: it imprisons, it immobilizes; thus, man is indeed 'dead' as long as he lives by his illusions and fictions, until he returns again to the stream of true life. . . .

[Appearance] or the mask, as Pirandello often refers to it—is both something created by man as well as something forced on him by his surroundings, his 'milieu'. Instances of the latter are infinitely more common in Pirandello's work. It is this appearance, this mask that prevents the 'exteriorization' or emergence of a real life. And whenever one of the Pirandellian characters throws away his mask, he is no longer understood by his surroundings; he no longer 'plays the game', and his action is interpreted as insanity. Thus the legion of Pirandellian 'fools'. (p. 46)

In Pirandello's view it is always the mask that suffocates, stifles life, and is synonymous with 'death'. The breaking out, the revolt, usually is short lived, for it is not possible to live this life of the dead—as Pirandello would say—without a mask. . . . Yet even if an individual seems to have outwitted fortune, chance, and society, which have foisted on him a certain image, there always ensues the most cruel repression. As a symbol of defeat almost, society will hold forth the relinquished mask, and the spell is cast again. This extreme case, where the mask is symbolized by a nickname, appears in the story *La maschera dimenticata* . . . , the forgotten mask. (p. 50)

The fiction, the mask alone, either self-imposed or, as in most cases, forced on man by society, makes life possible. If this mask is ever torn off, willingly or by force, man is no longer able to live, to function in a society based upon the law of common fictions: either he returns to wearing his mask, to 'living' the life of the dead, or he becomes 'crazy', 'insane' as far as society is concerned. By refusing to wear the mask, Pirandellian characters in the eyes of this world choose death. Thus they may die the symbolical death of insanity. They may choose to take their own life in earnest and throw away with it mask and imposed form, as does Ersilia Drei of *Vestire gli ignudi* . . . , who has no desire to be 'clothed' with a mask. They even may, willingly, choose a mask as a token of their freedom, as does the protagonist of *Enrico IV.* . . . He chooses to wear the mask of insanity in full consciousness, a decision he has sealed with a murder; and, ironically, society—the world of the masks—cannot hold him responsible because he has taken refuge behind a mask and beaten it at its own game.

A further way out for Pirandellian characters is to die the death of the *unio mystica.* Of the two modes of experience of life which, as Georg Lukács once remarked, in the end lead to a complete loss of the Self, the tragic and the mystic, Pirandello has chosen the latter. . . . [The] mystic, in fusing—as it were—with the All and One, gives up, renounces his individual essence. Thus, Pirandello's work has no heroes in the real sense of the word. The tragic situation necessarily and unavoidably includes, postulates an affirmation and assertion of Being, of the Self; it signifies, therefore, an assertion of Being in the highest degree. Yet man, living in this relativist state of being whatever the world sees in him, has no identity to assert, to defend; he has one only to give it up.

Thus, Moscarda of *Uno, nessuno e centomila* . . . draws the only possible conclusion from his realization that he is a different individual for whoever looks at him: since he is no longer *uno,* but *centomila*—a hundred thousand—he will henceforth be *nessuno,* no one. So he withdraws from 'life', founds a poorhouse with his money, and becomes its first inmate.... Henceforth he lives in some kind of mystical union with the All, and indeed he can only go on living at all if he subsumes himself in this mystical way within the All and One. (pp. 51-3)

This is Pirandello's logical conclusion and answer for man who has thrown overboard the fictions and conventions of society, who no longer wishes to be part of this world of human fictions and of the mask. Through an act of will he already, in a state of *unio mystica,* partakes of the life of the universe. From this point, physical death is only a transition of no consequence....

[Freedom] must be paid for with death, and death, whether physical, symbolical, or a *unio mystica* with the All and One, means freedom for all Pirandello's characters.... (p. 54)

Pirandello destroyed—always within his humorous creed—the form and structure of the play itself. (p. 81)

The dissolution on the structural level of the form of the play was not in itself a Pirandellian invention.... Yet Pirandello availed himself of it with the specific intent to destroy and make absurd any logical concatenation *from within,*—not simply in order to demolish an outer form. What lay behind this was the categorical rejection of one of the hitherto sacred characteristics of drama, its intentional finality. Again we see Pirandello's humorist conviction that any such design would be a mere construction or fabrication. (pp. 81-2)

Foremost among the devices Pirandello used to dissolve the form of the play on the structural level was the theatre-within-the-theatre technique. Again, this technique is in itself ... an ancient and venerable device; yet Pirandello uses it deliberately to destroy the form of the piece and any logical concatenation of events, of cause and effect, it might imply. (p. 82)

Pirandello's tendency to dissolve the dramatic form is evident especially in his fusion and blending of reality and illusion, of internal and external plays, of action and reflection on it, and in a constant shifting between these different levels. In many of Pirandello's plays the story as such is of only circumstantial importance and serves merely as a theme to be elaborated on; in short, it is used to prove a point which is not at all connected with the fabric of the plot itself. His pre-eminently analytical approach dominates the plays of his theatre-within-the-theatre trilogy. In *Sei personaggi,* the action is continuously interrupted by comments paralleling it, the characters themselves are drawn as types, and the stage directions even recommend that they wear masks. Their story is only incidental to the more important aspect of the play, the clash and exchange between the two worlds of art and life.... Whatever secondary considerations there may have been, it is clear that the primary aim of his dramatic writing is, as always, to forego direct representation and explosive action, in favour of the indirect approach of a reflective presentation of the filtered issues, as it were. Here, too, Pirandello follows his humoristic theory which implies a reflective attitude and postulates an analytical frame of mind.

In *Ciascuno a suo modo,* this analytical preoccupation

comes out even more clearly in that the dialectical approach is carried to the point where action and ensuing reflection on it are already sharply defined in the outer form of the play: after each of the two acts, there follow *intermezzi corali* in which the preceding action is discussed, and as a 'result' of this doubling and mirroring the third act does not even take place. The last play of the trilogy, *Questa sera si recita a soggetto,* draws the consequences of this approach; it no longer makes any pretence at taking seriously the play within the play: the director, Dr. Hinkfuss, has his actors improvise on a scenario—a short story by Pirandello. Whereas in *Sei personaggi* it was the director who interrupted, and commented on, the action, and in *Ciascuno a suo modo* the critics got their chance in the *intermezzi,* here in *Questa sera si recita a soggetto* it is the actors themselves who comment upon their own play. (pp. 87-9)

Wherever action does occur on the stage, Pirandello betrays some difficulty in handling—'orchestrating'—his characters within the framework of larger scenes.... [Many of Pirandello's plays] received their final form on the stage or were conditioned by his practical stage experience. Yet the deeper reason must be seen in Pirandello's infatuation with a dialectic approach, the ensuing tight dialogue, and his preference for arguing and reasoning. (pp. 90-1)

With Pirandello, too, action and final outcome of the play are ... often not at all important since they are relevant only in so far as they are conducive to an analytical approach. (p. 91)

[*Questa sera si recita a sog getto,*] perhaps more than any other, embodies the quintessence of Pirandello's attempts at analytically dissecting, as it were, the art of theatre. We would not wish to create the impression that Pirandello's theatre contains nothing else besides. But his originality lies in the way he imposed the principles of plurality and relativity upon the very art form of theatre itself, thereby questioning its validity while still using it as a medium. (p. 98)

Pirandello has toppled—as he said he would—the white columns erected by the Greeks over the dark abyss. The view is no longer obstructed. The spectator has indeed been 'liberated' from any fixed viewpoint.... As a result of works such as Pirandello's, the new drama perhaps will one day realize the portentous significance of what one of its ardent advocates, Brecht, once said, namely that the dynamics of representation should not be mistaken for the dynamics of the very matter to be represented. (pp. 105-06)

Oscar Büdel, in his Pirandello *(copyright © 1966 by Oscar Büdel; reprinted with permission of Bowes & Bowes), Bowes & Bowes, 1966, 126 p.*

MARTIN ESSLIN (essay date 1967)

Pirandello more than any other playwright has been responsible for a revolution in man's attitude to the world that is comparable to the revolution caused by Einstein's discovery of the concept of relativity in physics: Pirandello has transformed our attitude to human personality and the whole concept of *reality* in human relations by showing that the personality—character in stage terms—is not a fixed and static entity but an infinitely fluid, blurred, and *relative* concept. People appear different to different fellow human beings, they act differently in different contexts, they react differently to differing situations. And where is the Archimedean point outside that fluid reality from which we might judge which of these different manifestations of a human personality is the true, the *real* one? There is no such point, just as there is no fixed point in the physical universe from which all velocities could be measured. (p. 49)

[The] core of Pirandello's concern [is] the nature of human consciousness of itself, of reality as reflected in our minds. If it is impossible to find an objective yardstick of reality we are thrown back into a universe of interlocking subjective viewpoints between which it is impossible to determine a greater or lesser degree of objective truth. (pp. 51-2)

[While] he used the stage as a laboratory for the demonstration of a philosophical view of the world, Pirandello was anything but a cerebral dramatist. He was, above all, a man haunted by images. The subject matter of *Six Characters in Search of an Author* is, after all, basically a dramatization of the playwright's mind haunted, invaded, by characters who simply will not let him alone. The scene at the core of the play, that of the father, who furtively frequents houses of assignation, being confronted by his own stepdaughter, who is forced to eke out her existence by selling herself, is one the author does not want to deal with, that he discards, and yet one to which the figments of his subconscious mind force him to return. In that sense the stage itself that the characters invade is simply the author's own consciousness. He wants to repress the Oedipal, incestuous situation that haunts him, but he cannot do it, the play insists on being written. . . . (p. 54)

Pirandello's plays can therefore be studied, not merely as the product of a brilliant philosophical mind, but also as the expression of a personality haunted by images welling up from the depths of a deeply troubled soul. (pp. 54-5)

> *Martin Esslin, "Pirandello: Master of the Naked Masks" (originally published in* The New York Times, *June 25, 1967), in his* Reflections: Essays on Modern Theatre *(copyright © 1967, 1969 by Martin Esslin; reprinted by permission of Doubleday & Company, Inc.), Doubleday, 1969, pp. 49-55.*

NICOLA CHIAROMONTE (essay date 1967)

[In] Pirandello's view, man is a theatrical animal by nature, not by chance. According to him, the theatre must represent these basic facts: the relation between the action in which the individual finds himself involved and his conscience, as well as the conflict between his conscience and the vicissitudes of social life. This is the constant theme in all of Pirandello's plays from *Liolà, Cap and Bells* and *Right You Are—If You Think You Are,* through to *Six Characters, Henry IV* and *As You Desire Me.* The illusion of reality and the verisimilitude of the story are therefore of no importance in Pirandello's plays; what matters is the force of the initial situation and the logic with which the playwright is able to carry it to its ultimate conclusion. (p. 228)

[In] Pirandello, it is not a question of abandoning oneself (as he himself too often does) to the fiction-reality dialectic, but rather of fully exposing the irreparably ironical situation in which the individual finds himself in respect to the nature of things every time he takes seriously the role he chances to play in life at the expense of the incommensurable and at the same time ephemeral creature he is. This situation ap-

plies to everyone, Pirandello tells us, and the artist is no exception; indeed, he suffers more than the others, being unable to redeem it except through awareness. But this "redemption" is obtained at the price of relinquishing any attempt at being "somebody" (thus the flight from life of Mattia Pascal or of the protagonist of Henri IV) in order to become a mere vehicle of meaningful images: a theatre. (p. 231)

As to the "theatre within the theatre", which is rightly considered Pirandello's most original invention as a dramatist, when it is not construed as a mere stage device, it is a natural expression of that particularly modern sensibility which gives rise not only to the "theatre within the theatre", but to "poetry within poetry", "painting within painting" and even the "novel within the novel". Without entering into a discussion of the value of works based on the implied aesthetic principle, we can assert that all these forms are manifestations of one fundamental fact, namely, the solitude of the artist in modern times, a solitude which is the symptom and symbol of an even more serious fact: the devaluation of individual existence in contemporary society. This is the very fact that Pirandello exposes in his earliest dramatic works, *Cap and Bells* and *Right You Are*. . . .

Yet, if one comes to think of it, Pirandello's "theatre within the theatre" is nothing more than the return of drama to its pristine simplicity. (p. 233)

In the final analysis, Pirandello's "theatre within the theatre" is . . . nothing but the rediscovery of the theatre's basic nature, of its chief reason for existence, namely the bond between "I" and the others. He recaptured the freedom of the theatre in the same sense that Picasso may be said to have recaptured the freedom of plastic art. (pp. 234, 236)

> *Nicola Chiaromonte, "Pirandello and the Contemporary Theatre," in* World Theatre *(reprinted by permission of* World Theatre*), Vol. XVI, No. 3, 1967, pp. 224-37.*

JØRN MOESTRUP (essay date 1972)

[Luigi Pirandello's] years of apprenticeship are characterized by an inner schism that does not enrich what he writes —the possibility cannot be excluded—but which, on the contrary, makes him vacillate between various tendencies. The works of this period swing between contrasting feelings and ideas and lack completeness. Formal weaknesses are matched by lack of clarity, firmness or, simply, direction as regards content. (p. 14)

Of all Pirandello's novels "The Outcast" approaches most closely the nineteenth century narrative tradition and is his only more or less conventional novel. . . . The story begins with the failure of [Marta Ajala's] marriage. In fact she has done nothing more than to be so incautious as to receive letters from an admirer and answer them—without, however, giving him any grounds for hope. But her husband is so much a Sicilian that he immediately sends her home to her parents as soon as he has discovered the correspondence. . . . At the last moment, however, Marta is saved [from her planned suicide]—she meets her husband Rocco Pitagora at his mother's deathbed in Palermo, and they are reconciled. He still loves her and forgives her even when he learns that she is now guilty of the crime of which she had previously been unjustly accused.

This paradoxical ending, which is usually interpreted as a naive happy ending, contains the key to the understanding of the novel. From an artistic point of view it is unfortunate and conflicts with what has gone before; the criticism this ending has provoked is fully justified. Nevertheless it cannot be regarded as an unimportant appendix, to be dismissed as an unfortunate lapse, after which the rest of the novel can be judged without reference to the ending. An analysis of the ending will cast light on fundamental characteristics of Pirandello's writing in this period. Marta is a real romantic heroine, who in her refusal to give up in the face of difficulties stands for positive values; it is not until the end when she has been crushed by a malevolent fate that she resigns herself; she is treated with meaningless injustice, for she is innocent. She cannot even be blamed for her fall from grace when she commits adultery, for the author says several times that she is pursued by a fate that no one can resist. . . . In the end the author revolts against this pessimism, which is his own. Against all logic Marta and Rocco are reconciled and love conquers all conflicts, annuls all prejudice and all guilt. The struggle in Pirandello's mind between his increasing pessimism—the misfortunes to which Marta is subjected—and a passionate desire for a more positive view of life—Marta's salvation—reaches a climax in the conclusion of the novel. . . . [The contrast] is partly responsible for the failure of the novel as a work of art. The conflict is most clearly to be seen in the paradoxical conclusion, but it is also reflected elsewhere in the book, for example in its melodramatic structure and overwrought style. When she is driven away by her husband, Marta is pregnant, and the scene in which she gives birth to a stillborn child while her father dies of a paralytic stroke and the mob below celebrate Alvignani's election to parliament is a characteristic example of the way in which Pirandello piles up effects. (pp. 28-30)

The stylistic contrasts can be explained by reference to Pirandello's own inner struggle, the unresolvable conflict of which he is a prisoner. The contending elements are expressed in extremes: pessimism becomes total hopelessness, and the figures that motivate it become absurd grotesques. On the other hand belief in the positive elements manifests itself in a solution that runs counter to common sense and is, therefore, no less absurd, while the characters who represent these aspects of life are equipped with haloes. A slight but not insignificant detail in the conclusion deserves attention. When Marta and Rocco are reconciled, she does not tell him that she is pregnant. This act of deception clashes sharply with her total sincerity and her desire to make a clean breast of everything. But the author had difficulties. If an even greater sacrifice had been demanded of Rocco the discrepancy between the novel as a whole and the conclusion would have been even more striking, and the figure of Rocco himself would have become totally unconvincing. Nothing in the novel indicates that he, the prototype of the Sicilian husband, would have been able to accept a reconciliation with his *pregnant* wife. (pp. 30-1)

The above has demonstrated the connection between the dubious artistic quality of Pirandello's early works and the lack of unity in his attitudes in general. It cannot, of course, be maintained that to deserve the name a work of art can only be created in absolute tranquility of mind, but a certain philosophy of life or coherence of vision is necessary to prevent the work from falling apart. (p. 31)

Pirandello wrote his first completely perfect short stories around the turn of the century. This only became possible with the achievement of artistic maturity and inner balance. At the same time his lyric poetry, though it appears in a new form, gradually loses its importance in his writing. These are the factors that determine that a new period has begun, and it is clear that they are related. Pirandello's maturity can be seen both in the form and the content of his writing, and the latter is characterized by a spiritual balance that had previously been lacking. Both aspects are necessary conditions for the achievement of the high artistic level of the short stories of this period, while the movement towards a state of relative inner balance lessens Pirandello's need to write lyric poetry, the genre of confession, a genre for which he lacked natural talent. (p. 37)

"Sicilian Limes" is the first outstanding short story published by Pirandello. (p. 39)

The story is perfectly balanced. The author's sympathy for Micuccio and the mother and the milieu they represent, symbolized by the fragrant limes, is clear, but it is not accompanied by criticism or satire directed towards Teresina, who has betrayed her background. She can still appreciate the wonderful fruit, and her appropriation of the limes takes place with Pirandello's tacit acquiescence. A fate that neither of them could foresee or control has separated the two young people. In their youthful enthusiasm and self-sacrifice they had cut off the branch on which they were sitting. This is the first time Pirandello is artistically successful in depicting how fate deals with people without their having any chance of defending themselves. This bitter knowledge is communicated in a tone of sombre seriousness which does not, however, exclude humour. Deep insight and a profound knowledge of life have enabled the author to achieve a hard-won calm, which, in its turn, enables him to preserve the necessary distance between himself and his subject. Life can be regarded with resignation—never with coolness—and even with humour. Most of the best short stories of the decade are based on variations of this mood and subject matter—fate's role in human existence. (pp. 40-1)

["Quietly" deals] with the immediate effect of chance.

The main character in "Quietly" is a schoolboy, Cesare Brei, who is suddenly faced by problems that are more than he can manage, and which bring him disaster. (p. 47)

There is in this story a strangely heavy and menacing atmosphere that is also to be found elsewhere in Pirandello's short stories. It is not necessarily produced by the tragic events described. Pirandello depicts similar situations without this peculiarly closed and doomladen atmosphere, which seems to be bound up with the description of instinctual behaviour. . . .

For Pirandello the destructive instinct represents one of the ways in which malevolent chance wreaks havoc on human beings—from outside . . . , and from inside via instinct. (p. 48)

None of the novels [written during the period 1900 to 1910] are good, but the first and the last are at times amusing. "The Late Mattia Pascal" is the most renowned of Pirandello's novels and is considered by many critics to be his best. This is due to, among other things, the fact that the basic idea of the novel is an excellent one: it is the story of Mattia Pascal, who is inspired by chance to attempt to live a new life and obliterate his past. Another important reason for the novel's success . . . is its basic tone of sympathetic, controlled humour, which is now and again replaced by pathos (for example in the scene in which Pascal's child dies) or by irony. (p. 70)

"The Late Mattia Pascal" is amusing enough from time to time, but it is far from being as good as the best of the plays or short stories, or for that matter the best of the novels. . . . Large parts of the novel are in fact padding, which could be eliminated or replaced with other material without it making any difference. (pp. 71-2)

[The] novel disintegrates into a long series of unconnected episodes, some of which are amusing, others not. In the beginning there is a long and tedious account of Mattia's family, and later the plot is complicated by all kinds of unimportant additions like the episode in which Mattia chooses his new name, Adriano Meis, or his meeting with Tito Lenzi in Milan. The spiritualist scene is not particularly relevant either, but it is amusing and furthers the plot by bringing the relationship between Adriana and Mattia to a decisive point.—One of the few things that hold the novel together is, as mentioned above, the sympathetic tone of resigned humour, which is strengthened by the fact that the story is told in the first person. Mattia himself relates what happens, and the tone of the novel corresponds to and expresses the state of mind he has attained after many trials.

The next novel, "The Old and the Young", is Pirandello's weakest. It takes place in 1892-3, the first part in Sicily in and around Agrigento, the second part in Rome. The central theme of the novel is expressed in the title. The old are the generation that had united Italy, while the young are those whose turn it now is to succeed them. Pirandello's historical novel gives a picture of Italy as a bankrupt estate. There is, however, not much force in the description, since . . . he is devoid of historical insight. (pp. 72-3)

The novel is inordinately long. . . . The extreme feebleness of the plot makes the novel seem even longer. . . . The plot of "The Old and the Young" is made up of a number of ill-assorted and unorganized events that lack an organic inter-relationship. Underlying the novel, as a sort of vague background, is the idea of the conflict between the generations. —The novel is not rich in action in the traditional meaning of the word. There is little drama or variety, and its essential content is a large number of character descriptions and the commentary attached to these characters. . . . Pirandello is at his best as a psychological writer when his characters are placed in situations that have an existentialist perspective, that is when their fate is a direct expression of his own conception of the fundamental questions of life. This fact is of importance in evaluating Pirandello's achievements in the genre of the novel. . . . (pp. 74-5)

"One, None, A Hundred Thousand" is the fullest and most complete statement of Pirandello's position between 1910 and the beginning of the First World War. From an artistic point of view it is considerably inferior to the best of the short stories, but it is perhaps Pirandello's most impressive novel. The main character, Vitangelo, discovers one day that things are not as he has hitherto believed. Their existence is not as firm and unshakable as he has always

thought, and his own personality is also among the things that have suddenly become equivocal and uncertain. (pp. 121-22)

Vitangelo's reaction to the web of fictions that constitute conventional existence is of great artistic effect. It is spontaneous action, dictated by a moral requirement that suddenly breaks through from his innermost self, the actual and real, indefinable self, which also enables him to communicate with the hidden lifestream, or, rather, makes him a part of it. When he has tried to convince the others that he is not as they believe him to be, and the result is merely that they laugh at him, his protest breaks out, violently and directly, from inside him without his having willed or caused it. There is a deeply felt pathos in this moral absolutism, and once again it is demonstrated with unassailable clarity that the ethical moment, fused with the urge for cognition, is a constant and essential factor in Pirandello's work. Before 1910 it is experienced as part of a painful resignation, later frequently as a feeling of affinity with a real and *better* reality.

The structure is simple—there is a main character and some secondary figures; the plot is relevant and, on the whole, swift-moving. The novel is, nevertheless, not a masterpiece, which can be explained by, among other things, the fact that it is not short enough. . . . (p. 122)

The relativity thesis is put forward time and time again in an almost unchanged form and finally becomes flat and tedious. It is a matter of a simple idea, not of a complex philosophy, and it cannot stand up to being detached from the total view of life of which it is a part, nor from its ethical and metaphysical concomitants. The speculative aspect becomes impoverished and enfeebled when it is presented alone and repeated. Once again Pirandello demonstrates that the narrative form of the novel does not suit him, and "One, None, A Hundred Thousand" is, in fact, a short story that has been unfortunately expanded. (pp. 122-23)

The failure of Pirandello's novels, especially after 1900, is related to his fundamental views on life. As regards form he does not try to make a decisive break with the classic, that is the nineteenth century, novel, but the traditional elements of the latter do not harmonize with the basic elements of Pirandello's work. Development and analysis of character are alien to him. The concept of development, even in the sense of a meaningful temporal context, cannot gain a footing in a universe which, like Pirandello's is dominated by the idea of chance and total meaninglessness. This factor totally undermines a novel like "The Old and the Young", which is constructed as a confrontation between two generations because of its lack of coherence and continuity. In itself this idea harmonize poorly with the idea of absolute chance, and as a historical synthesis it is a naïve simplification.

The question of character description involves the problem of Pirandello as a psychological writer in general. It is necessary here to make a clear distinction between two aspects, character and situation. Pirandello's psychological analysis is in the first place never a goal itself. . . . The analysis is directed towards given existential situations, not towards the examination of certain people or characters. In Pirandello's work characters are not introduced at the beginning of the plot and then developed and rounded. His method is to place the character in certain conditions, like

Mattia Pascal, or to provide his figure with certain decisive traits. . . . (p. 126)

He does not create characters, but analyzes existential situations. There is nothing individualized about the psychological reactions provoked by these situations. The lack of individualization, of characterization, makes it even clearer why long narrative did not suit Pirandello's talent. It easily becomes monotonous or contradictory, while the short story, in which a simple situation and a corresponding figure are defined by a few dominant features, proved to be a far more fruitful genre. (pp. 127-28)

> *Jørn Moestrup, in his* The Structural Patterns of Pirandello's Work, *Odense University Press, 1972, 294 p.*

ANNE PAOLUCCI (essay date 1973)

Pirandello was the first dramatist to formulate and develop new stage techniques to express the profound existential questioning of our time. He did this not as a relativist (as is so often professed), but as a Socratic assessor of "reality," redefining experience as the expression of WILL. In his plays, questionings and doubts emerge as a dialectic, and his most memorable characters often verge on madness in their emotional opposition to and revolt against the "facts" of life and the abstract values of naive experience. Against "formal" acceptance of reality as predetermined "fact," is the dialectic of contradictory impulses working toward a resolution. *Six Characters in Search of an Author, Right You Are!, Henry IV,* and even an early play like *Liolà* are excellent examples of Pirandello's concern for new dramatic forms—the struggle to preserve basic stage conventions while undermining the outworn "statements" of Ibsen-like realism. Pirandello is the father of the Absurd in his insistence on the fragmentation of dramatic action and its corollary, fragmentation or dissolution of character. His new breed of stage personalities, although individualized and finished dramatically, are unique in their obsession with inner life, their exploration of motives, emotions, and states of mind. In this sense, they come closer to fragmented personalities, mirrors of seemingly contradictory impulses, but in final analysis such apparent contradiction is merely the vehicle for the definition of internal realities as they struggle for expression. It is this "examined" life, fully articulated, which ultimately emerges as "reality." (p. 404)

[Pirandello's] main interest was always the living human being in his painful self-confrontation: Man and his consciousness, and the infinite reflections of the mirrored image. Pirandello reached an absolute and firm conclusion: "facts" must mirror the inner man to be meaningful, and values must be accepted with Socratic certainty to be true. In thus redefining "reality," Pirandello reminds us that it is not an external state of things but the constant dialectic of the will, shaping and reshaping human intentions into completed deeds. (p. 405)

What makes the Pirandellian experience a giant step forward, dramatically, is not simply the playwright's insistence on the fragmentation of personality as traditionally conceived, but his way of going about it. We see the integrated or seemingly-integrated character collapse in slow stages before our eyes through the ever more intense oscillation between what IS and what APPEARS to be; and the

seemingly-erratic character by the power of his will slowly takes on shape before us in the process. (pp. 405-06)

[The] dramatic impulse to find objective correlatives for the fluctuations of internal life produces *maschere nude*—stripped semblances of character as traditionally understood. In the later plays, this impulse is a conscious and irresistible one; but even in earlier plays like *Liolà*, it is felt in the effort to see action as a conviction of the WILL. Like all the novelties he introduced, this one—for Pirandello—arose from a deep-rooted necessity to find the proper medium for the problem of restructuring reality. His great achievement is not giving expression to that much-abused polarity of realism versus illusion but his emphatic assertion that reality is a creation of the human WILL, the consent of the conscious mind to so-called facts. The later plays—particularly the "theater" plays and *Henry IV*—are the clearest expression of this constant theme. Throughout, Pirandello affirms the reality of the WILL as it shapes the world. In that process, he has created a new theater. Experimentation becomes—in this context—dramatic necessity.

The three plays about "theater" suggest the dissolution of character in the most complex way. In *Six Characters in Search of an Author* we have the fact of dramatic creation set before us as a suggestive paradox. Dramatic personality —Pirandello seems to be saying—exists like the David existed for Michelangelo in the block of marble from which the sculptor released him. Dramatically, this provocative notion is defined as the confrontation of the fully determined will of the character and that of the author, and the independence of the first as it emerges on the stage. Placed within the theater, this theme enables Pirandello to describe the various levels of the confrontation vividly and directly. . . . The particular circumstances which define the "plot" (if we wish to use that word) may or may not appeal to us, but they furnish the vehicle by means of which everyone on the stage and in the audience is forced into a confrontation with himself. They set up reverberations which move toward recognition. They reveal the secret of total commitment of will, a commitment which works like a magnet and draws everything else toward it which is essential, leaving all the unimportant details behind. The "fact" of incest is meant to be terrible, but even more terrible is the Oedipus-like unfolding of that fact. What is most terrible, ultimately, is the repudiation of self—which like a vengeful ghost seeks out the betrayer and forces him to acknowledge the lie buried inside him.

The process, dramatically, is a spiral-like movement in which each of the six characters must somehow come together in the characteristic act which is the core of their being and will, forcing the rest of us to acknowledge its reality. Their strength of purpose, Pirandello suggests, has guided even the author's hand, forcing him and the actors who are ready to put on his play to question their own purpose. No matter how often the single-minded characters are interrupted by the external mechanics of the professional group of actors, they invariably pick up their life-line, their own thrust, forcing everyone and everything else to retreat. Their irresistible impulse toward self-definition mirrors the larger theme; for life is expression, and each of us must find ways to give expression its one true form. (pp. 406-08)

They come seeking total expression, but they are, in fact, total expression from the beginning—their WILL having been fully determined and directed. The secret of the play lies in this: that Pirandello has recognized the single thrust of their being and the irresistible power of their unswerving commitment. The author keeps reminding us that the creator's will is not operating in these characters, but the paradox is only an apparent one. They are, in fact, fully defined in the only way possible. Their will is also the will of the dramatist, perfectly mirrored in the total absorption of everyone else—on and off stage—in their painful self-revelation. When their little drama is done, there is nothing left to do on stage, and the lights go out. (p. 408)

Reality, as created by the will of the man who retires from the world to live in a self-made historical past, assumes in [*Henry IV*] the aspect of madness. But the lucidity which flashes out of that apparent madness must give us pause. The isolation of Henry in his own private pageantry, his decision to abandon his friends (are they really his friends, we wonder?), his assumption of a stagepart made real for all time suggest an incurable amnesia. But confronted with his unexpected personal past, with those who accepted his living death and who perhaps contributed to it, Henry is tempted for a brief moment to repudiate his self-made play and return to the world of the living, as defined by his old friends. But history provides certainty and distance. The historical present IS reality in every sense of the word. What is unreal is the motions of life, the emptiness and distrust his old friends represent, the deception they practice on one another and on him. In the end, they must withdraw —like apparitions—before the fact of purpose and will. They are no match for him. And for a brief moment, he allows them to see once and for all the profound truth of his decision, explaining lucidly and with full rational powers the reasons for it. Madness, in this context, becomes the conventional label for something that cannot be understood on the face value of the facts. But Henry is no more mad than Hamlet is. He is the embodiment of willful purpose seeking expression and being shattered in the process. For Pirandello's Henry, as for Shakespeare's Hamlet, conventional reality and the appearances of things are death; what is lasting and true is the internal assumption of necessity, the conviction of internal consistency and purpose.

This unswerving commitment to explore in new dramatic forms the internal life of man as a means to understanding his emotional and spiritual make-up is present in Pirandello, from the very earliest plays. In *Liolà* we see, in effect, the triumph of will over conventions in the acceptance by Simone of a reality which seems on the surface to defy all facts. . . . Illusion here has all the force of revelation and mystical faith: the facts of the case retreat into insignificance as the will of Simone emerges as the positive force of the action. Tuzza has used Liolà for her own ends; but Liolà is spurred to contradict her by giving Mita the heir her husband longs for. In terms of traditional morality, it is all highly improper; but the conclusion does not undermine moral values in any way. Mita's purpose is not a selfish one, and Simone has recognized her essential goodness in accepting the child she bears as his own. . . . [The] wrong lies in the dualism of intention and action; Tuzza is thus convicted, and Mita absolved of all wrongdoing—although they accomplish the same identical end.

It is worth noting, in conclusion, that this complete fragmentation of conventional attitudes and dramatic techniques is fully contained within Pirandello's dramatic art.

He manages to reveal the dilemma and contradiction of human action within seemingly traditional stage conventions, reminding us that theater has its own imperatives and must retain its own distinct form. These new techniques are substantial and organic; they remind us that the great dramatist does not toy with gimmicks and use them as external means for effect. They convince us that in the great tradition of the innovators who produced Greek tragedy and the Elizabethan innovators who produced Shakespeare, Pirandello is faithful to his art and has created with the unerring instinct of the true dramatist the perfect vehicle for our time. . . . (pp. 412-14)

Anne Paolucci, *"Pirandello: Experience As the Expression of Will,"* in Forum Italicum *(copyright © 1973 by* Forum Italicum*), Vol. VII, No. 3, September, 1973, pp. 404-14.*

ADDITIONAL BIBLIOGRAPHY

Biasin, Gian-Paolo. "Moscarda's Mirror." In his *Literary Diseases: Theme and Metaphor in the Italian Novel*, pp. 100-26. Austin: University of Texas Press, 1975.
    Examination of the semantic and metaphoric meanings of mirror and mask imagery in Pirandello's novel *Uno, nessuno e centomila*.

Clark, Hoover W. "Existentialism and Pirandello's *Sei Personaggi*." *Italica* XLIII, No. 3 (September 1966): 276-84.
    Comparison of existentialist elements in *Sei Personaggi* with the tenets of existentialist thought.

Corrigan, Beatrice. "Pirandello and the Theatre of the Absurd." *Cesare Barbieri Courier* VIII, No. 1 (Spring 1966): 3-6.
    Shows how Pirandello's themes and techniques influenced such modern exponents of the Theater of the Absurd as Albee, Genet, and Beckett.

Della Terza, Dante. "On Pirandello's Humorism." In *Veins of Humor*, edited by Harry Levin, pp. 17-33. Cambridge: Harvard University Press, 1972.
    Discussion of Pirandello's theories of humor as put forth in his scholarly essay "L'Umorismo" and their application in his work.

Dombroski, Robert S. "Laudisi's Laughter and the Social Dimension of *Right You Are (If You Think So)*." *Modern Drama* 16, Nos. 3 and 4 (December 1973): 337-46.
    Examination of the role of Laudisi in *Right You Are (If You Think So)*.

Garzilli, Enrico. "Between the Circle and the Labyrinth: Mask, Personality, and Identity—Luigi Pirandello." In his *Circles without Center: Paths to the Discovery and Creation of Self in Modern Literature*, pp. 75-88. Cambridge: Harvard University Press, 1972.*
    Discussion of Pirandello's use of the mask to illuminate problems of identity as well as the relationship between art and life. The works studied are *Cosi e (se vi pare)*, *Enrico IV*, and *Sei personaggi in cerca d'autore*.

Gilman, Richard. "Pirandello." *Yale/Theatre* 5, No. 2 (Spring 1974): 94-117.
    Examination of Pirandello's themes and techniques, which challenged traditional ideas of dramaturgy, and which, in Gilman's view, ushered in a new phase of modern theater.

Groff, Edward. "Point of View in Modern Drama." *Modern Drama* 2, No. 3 (December 1959): 268-82.*
    Analysis of the complex points of view employed in *Six Characters in Search of an Author* and in *Each in His Own Way*.

Herman, William. "Pirandello and Possibility." *Tulane Drama Review* 10, No. 3 (Spring 1966): 91-111.

    Interpretation of religious symbolism in Pirandello's drama.

Krutch, Joseph Wood. "Pirandello and the Dissolution of the Ego." In his *"Modernism" in Modern Drama: A Definition and an Estimate*, pp. 65-87. Ithaca: Cornell University Press, 1953.

    Argues that Pirandello's theory of personality as continually in flux denies the Christian/classical conception of the ego.

May, Frederick. "Three Major Symbols in Four Plays by Pirandello." *Modern Drama* VI, No. 4 (February 1964): 378-96.

    A study of the role of three symbols (the mirror, water, and the color green) in *Six Characters in Search of an Author, Henry IV, A Dream (But Perhaps It Isn't)*, and *Man, Beast, and Virtue*.

McDonald, David. "Derrida and Pirandello: A Post-Structuralist Analysis of *Six Characters in Search of an Author*." *Modern Drama* XX, No. 4 (December 1977): 421-36.

    Applies a technical vocabulary derived from structuralist critic Jacques Derrida to elucidate the relationship between life and art as presented by the characters of this play.

Needler, Howard I. "On the Art of Pirandello: Theory and Praxis." *Texas Studies in Literature and Language* XV, No. 4 (Winter 1974): 735-58.

    Discusses Pirandello's methods of characterization and his arguments with traditional forms of characterization.

Radcliff-Umstead, Douglas. *The Mirror of Our Anguish: A Study of Luigi Pirandello's Narrative Writings*. London: Associated University Presses, 1978, 329 p.

    A study of Pirandello's novels.

Ragusa, Olga. *Luigi Pirandello*. New York: Columbia University Press, 1968, 48 p.

    A good introductory survey of Pirandello's work.

Sinicropi, Giovanni. "The Metaphysical Dimension and Pirandello's Theatre." *Modern Drama* XX, No. 4, (December 1977): 353-80.

    Discusses the ways in which Pirandello was able to make his dramatic action encompass metaphysical speculation.

Weiss, Auréliu. "The Remorseless Rush of Time." *Tulane Drama Review* 10, No. 3 (Spring 1966): 30-45.

    Focuses on the surrealistic nature of Pirandello's work.

Williams, Raymond. "Luigi Pirandello." In his *Drama: From Ibsen to Eliot*, pp. 185-95. London: Chatto & Windus, 1952.

    Examines Pirandello's dramas in relation to general trends in Italian theater from Romanticism to naturalism.

Marjorie Kinnan Rawlings

1896-1953

American novelist, short story writer, journalist, and poet.

Although Rawlings has been eclipsed by the greater luminaries of her generation, such as Hemingway, Faulkner, and Fitzgerald, she made a unique contribution to the genre of frontier regional literature. Having escaped the prevailing pessimism of the Lost Generation, she compassionately portrayed Florida's backwoods "crackers" and their relationship to the wild frontier country of north central Florida. Her best known work, *The Yearling*, made her enormously popular with the American reading public and became a successful motion picture.

Rawlings began her career as a journalist and worked for a time for the Hearst newspapers, but a move to Cross Creek, Florida, inspired her to write fiction. The wild and beautiful country of inland Florida made an indelible impression on Rawlings, and a preoccupation with this setting informs her work. A series of local color sketches published in *Scribner's* magazine brought her to the attention of Scribner's legendary editor, Maxwell Perkins, who became the guiding force in Rawlings's literary career and whose judgment she implicitly trusted.

In her first novel, *South Moon Under*, Rawlings portrays the special relationship the hunters and farmers of the Florida scrub country have to the land and to nature—a salient theme throughout this and all her work. *The Yearling*, for which she won the Pulitzer Prize in 1939, is her undisputed masterpiece. Twelve-year-old Jody Baxter, from whose point of view the story is told, is considered one of the most endearing boy-characters since Twain's Huckleberry Finn. In the autobiographical *Cross Creek*, reminiscent of Thoreau's *Walden* in technique, Rawlings describes the flora and fauna of her beloved home, underscoring her basic belief that to be happy one must find an environment in concert with one's nature.

Although Rawlings's work has been criticized for being overly sentimental and for relying too little on plot development and convincing characterization, her almost journalistic observation of place and dialect remains as a record of a vanishing frontier and the folkways of its inhabitants.

PRINCIPAL WORKS

South Moon Under (novel) 1933
Golden Apples (novel) 1935
The Yearling (novel) 1938
When the Whippoorwill (short stories) 1940
Cross Creek (autobiographical essays) 1942
The Sojourner (novel) 1953

JONATHAN DANIELS (essay date 1933)

Not the South moon lost under the earth but still darkly potent, nor the drama of men and persistent fear make Mar-

jorie Kinnan Rawlings's [*South Moon Under*] the splendid book that it is. She has written a vigorous story of murder and hiding, but, better than that, she has drawn in terms as lush and slow as the scrub grows a country and a people fresh in literature and rich in reality.

Her country, the Florida scrub of high pines and impenetrable stunted oak and myrtle rising from infertile sands and the surrounding tropical swamp of twisting water and bright flowers and bell-bottomed cypresses, is new in print, but the same implications of life in isolation lie in its tangle that have been drawn upon in the numerous stories of the coves and hollows of the Southern mountains. Her people, the Lantrys and Jacklins of the scrub and their piney woods kin, are related to the tradition of Southern and mountain whites who have been drawn in terms as diverse as dripping sentimentality and stark degeneracy. Mrs. Rawlings escapes both. In drawing her country and her Lantrys she has looked at the inhospitable earth and found it full of strangeness and beauty, and at the men and women of an old breed and seen in them dignity and the instinct that life, hard as it may be, is good. Also, and more profoundly, she has given her people an absolute integrity with their earth. . . .

This story Mrs. Rawlings has written well, but it is not her chief preoccupation. Chiefly she is interested in drawing the scrub and the people who live in it. She presses neither the country nor the people to the service of her plot. Slowly and with fine detail she has drawn the three generations of Lantrys who are the chief figures of the book. . . .

For these and around them, Mrs. Rawlings has created a world. She lingers as lovingly over the intimate details of their lives and the hard struggle for existence as she does over deer prancing in the moonlight. . . . In a sense the three generations represent not only a return of fate but also stages of acclimatization to the scrub. For Lantry, entry into the scrub is a step deliberately made; Piety grows into womanhood there; but the boy, Lant, born there, is a part of it. He knows all the craft of the savage in the forest, the ways of plants and beasts and fish, how to wring subsistence from its apparent forbiddingness. . . .

In drawing her characters Mrs. Rawlings has enlivened them with a strong masculine humor, racy and native. Neither in tragedy nor in fun is there any false note of primness about her people. . . .

Readers will welcome the freshness of Mrs. Rawlings's scene, but it is not mere new scene that gives her book its great distinction. What makes it one of the really fine books of the year is that the scene and the characters are drawn with a richness and vigor which makes them wholly alive. It is a book full of life, and of insistence that life with "love and lust, hate and friendship, grief and frolicking, even birthing and dying" is a choice thing. Out of that insistence in these simple people grows dignity and integrity and a strength equal to the irresistible growth of the scrub itself. . . .

> Jonathan Daniels, "Scrub Folk," in The Saturday Review of Literature (copyright © 1933 by Saturday Review; all rights reserved; reprinted by permission), Vol. IX, No. 33, March 4, 1933, p. 465.

PERCY HUTCHISON   (essay date 1935)

In "Golden Apples" Marjorie Kinnan Rawlings is again dealing with the poor whites of the Florida swamplands whom she portrayed so movingly in "South Moon Under." The swamps furnish a strange and wild locale, sinister, yet harboring exotic beauties. Mrs. Rawlings therefore has brought to American readers something new in backgrounds, as fit a setting for swift passions as the tropical lands of Conrad's earlier novels. Her work is romance of a kind, yet realistic; altogether, a rich combination of known and unknown ingredients.

Mrs. Rawlings in "South Moon Under" confined herself to the natives of her selected region; the story was what the theatrical world would call a natural. Naturals are not easy to come upon, either by playwrights or novelists. They are few and far between. If, then, in "Golden Apples" the author is unable to offer something quite so strikingly original as her earlier book, it does not mean that the reader has been let down: it means merely that she has been obliged to import into her story elements not native to the swamps. And, indeed, many may prefer this novel for the very reason that it is based on contrast, as "South Moon Under" was not. . . .

The author of "Golden Apples" knows her Florida Cracker inside and out; she understands both his emotions and his ethics. . . .

It would not be just to the reader not to say that "Golden Apples" has one defect, and this a considerable one. The novel lacks unity. . . . Mrs. Rawlings seems unable to draw her many threads together and make a finished ending to her narrative. The novel ends suspended in mid-air.

Yet it is so fine a piece of work in most of its parts that one does not wish to cavil unduly over the ending. Mrs. Rawlings at least brings us back to Luke, who for all his lack of "larnin," has such clarity of vision that her portrait of him is an impressive piece of character-drawing. . . . Indeed, the novel is honest, tender, enlightening—a fine achievement in literature about America done by an American imbued with deep feeling for a particular region and for an isolated and neglected population group. "Golden Apples" is also a novel one can enjoy. Nor need a reader shun the book because it is written for the most part in dialect. The near-Chaucerian dialect of the Southern poor white is not an annoyance but a delight.

> Percy Hutchison, "A Novel of the People in Florida's Swamps," in The New York Times Book Review (© 1935 by The New York Times Company; reprinted by permission), October 6, 1935, p. 3.

WILLIAM SOSKIN   (essay date 1938)

With Tom Sawyer, Huckleberry Finn and the lesser members of the fraternity of young boys in American literature well in mind, it is quite possible to maintain that Jody Baxter, son of the farmer and huntsman, Penny Baxter, in Marjorie Kinnan Rawlings' . . . "The Yearling" is the most charming boy in the entire national gallery. He may lack some of the sense of mischief and the adolescent wryness which have endeared Mark Twain's kids to our hearts. But Jody, roaming in the scrub forests of Mrs. Rawlings' favorite Florida country, living close to his animals with a sensitive emotional understanding of them, learning the subtleties of life which a child in sophisticated communities can never know, and reflecting that wholesomeness in his own spirit, has a gayety and a bubbling humor which run far deeper than that of any of the famous adolescents of our literature.

Jody is a young, laughing St. Francis in his own small world, and his unspoken conversations with his fawn, his dogs, his bear cubs, with the growing things and the deep pools and strong-flowing streams of Florida, are a communion with some spiritual core of the world. . . .

I find it difficult to convey the special importance of the history of this perky young Jody, for his quick, gentle humor, his intuitive intelligence and his bright courage, without resorting to an unbecoming effervescence of adjectives. . . . "The Yearling" is an education in life that is far removed from our dreary urban formulas; but it is fundamental and close to our own secret hopes, for all its romance and its frontier environment. (p. 1)

[This] story of a boy and an animal becomes one of the most exquisite I have ever read.

Out of this landscape of life in the Florida scrub, . . . Mrs. Rawlings draws a story with a tragic climax—that of the end of youth. It is because we have known the innermost recesses of Jody's heart and the intimacy of his dreams that the ultimate need to kill [his pet] fawn becomes a drama of overpowering proportions. It is written with a thorough poignance, and yet with a fine sense of detachment and of the normal flow of life that leavens all such tragedies of youth. As a result of the death of the fawn young Jody comes eventually to know that his yearling days are over, as are his pet's. . . . (p. 2)

> *William Soskin, "A Tom Sawyer of the Florida Scrub Lands," in* New York Herald Tribune Book Review *(© I.H.T. Corporation; reprinted by permission), Vol. 14, No. 31, April 3, 1938, pp. 1-2.*

LLOYD MORRIS (essay date 1938)

Among the rising generation of American novelists, none has given more valuable pledges to the future than Marjorie Kinnan Rawlings. . . . That her work received immediate praise from the critics is not surprising. It is strong, subtle, and exquisitely fashioned. . . .

Because Mrs. Rawlings locates her stories in the hammock country of Florida . . . most critics have reported her as a "regional" novelist, relating her work to that intensive study of local environment and folkways which today preoccupies many American writers. There is, of course, an obvious justice in this interpretation. But it is also misleading, and tends to obscure the major import of this author's work. (p. 179)

Few other contemporary American novelists exhibit so marked a detachment from the problems, the currents of opinion, the pressures and tensions which characterize American life today. So complete is her detachment from the specifically contemporary and the transient as, occasionally, to perplex her readers. It would be easy, for instance, to accept *The Yearling* as a story of today; nothing in the first half of the book contradicts this assumption; only one passage of dialogue, revealing that two middle-aged characters are Civil war veterans, identifies the period of the story as the past. In the case of so intelligent and meticulous a craftsman as Mrs. Rawlings, it is absurd to suppose that this detachment, and the rigorous exclusions which it imposes, are purely accidental. They are obviously dictated by a personal perception of life, by a concern for ultimate rather than relative values, and by an intention to present experience in its most simple and enduring forms.

To make this point is merely to suggest that Mrs. Rawlings is essentially a classicist, writing at a moment when the dominant accent of our fiction is romantic. Her work more closely resembles Miss [Willa] Cather's *My Antonia,* or Mrs. [Edith] Wharton's *Ethan Frome,* than it does the novels of Ernest Hemingway or Erskine Caldwell. But, although a classicist in her perception of life, she is a romantic in her literary endowment. Sensibility is its most impressive element, and imparts to Mrs. Rawlings's writing certain qualities more familiar in poetry than prose fiction. The sheer expressiveness of her prose will be noted by every reader. In passage after passage of her novels, a casual gesture or fleeting look is charged with meanings which her characters—by turns so eloquent and so reticent —cannot utter. Or a motive, a mood, a subtle complex of feelings and impulses, may be communicated by a minute modulation of light or color that transforms the landscape. And only a sensibility more than normally acute could register, with the astonishing rightness of Mrs. Rawlings's dialogue, the cadences and inflections of an idiom which some-

times rises to primitive poetry, and sometimes sinks to an inarticulate growl. This sensibility and this expressiveness are, in short, a kind of medium or instrument. For with them Mrs. Rawlings makes comprehensible and convincing a world that might otherwise seem part illusion, and part nostalgic memory. (pp. 180-81)

[Although] *South Moon Under* and, in less measure, *Golden Apples* may have justified a belief that [Mrs. Rawlings] was primarily concerned with [inland Florida's] local peculiarities, her use of it in *The Yearling* proves that this is not the case. For, in this latest and certainly finest of her three novels, she has written a universal parable. And in it, the world of Florida's hammock country is merely an archetype of all worlds in which man's spirit can emerge victorious or vanquished from the incessant conflict which is his life.

In choosing a subject at once so significant and so simple, Mrs. Rawlings reveals herself the mature artist, disciplined to complete awareness of her limitations and her resources. The minor blemishes which appeared in her two earlier novels, and which occurred only when she forced her talents to uncongenial tasks, are entirely absent from *The Yearling*. Within the terms of its intention, this is as nearly a perfect work of art as American fiction can display.

The story portrays the life of the Baxters, a family inhabiting an "island" or clearing in the depths of a forest which isolates them from their nearest neighbors, as well as from the world at large. (pp. 181-82)

One year of their experience is crystallized in the story, and its meaning made explicit at the end. Into that year Mrs. Rawlings has compressed the irreducible events which collectively furnish a common denominator for all human existence. Childhood and adolescence, the stern business of getting a livelihood, courtship and mating, the rearing of the young, the incidence of age, the passing of the torch, and finally death: all these are encompassed within four seasons of the Baxters' life. During that year, Jody passes from adolescence into manhood, Penny from vigorous maturity into age and decay. During it, likewise, the fortunes of the Baxters prosper and wane, flood devastates the hammock country, old Slewfoot the wily bear is pursued and finally slain in a passage that vividly recalls Ahab's pursuit of Moby Dick. And during it, we have been admitted to what is probably the most tender and beautiful love story recorded by American fiction: the love of Jody for Flag, the pet fawn which he captured in the forest, brought home and tamed. . . . (pp. 182-83)

[The parable that lies at the heart of *The Yearling* is] conceived strictly within the terms of a Puritan ethics, and represents a characteristically American attempt to reconcile the beauty, the pathos, and the indiscriminate cruelty of man's existence and nature's. To some readers, other aspects of Mrs. Rawlings's novel will seem more important. Docility, which is perhaps the end of all philosophy, may be only the beginning of wisdom: Mrs. Rawlings's intelligence makes no effort to carry us further. Her sensibility does. It plunges us deeply into the hearts and the perceptions of a child, a wise man, and a brave woman. It recreates for us those fundamental attitudes of the human spirit which make life endurable, and those inalienable experiences of love and beauty which enable us to live it without shame. With *The Yearling,* Mrs. Rawlings rightfully takes her place among our most accomplished writers of fiction. (p. 184)

Lloyd Morris, "New Classicist," in The North American Review *(copyright © 1938 by the University of Northern Iowa), Vol. 246, No. 1, Autumn, 1938, pp. 179-84.*

MARGARET GILLIS FIGH (essay date 1947)

In her books dealing with the Florida Cracker Mrs. Rawlings has created a regional fiction whose strength rests upon its sympathetic portrayal of the humor and the tragedy of the backwoods. . . . [She] has been able to write fiction that has its roots in the folk morality, customs, and beliefs. She realizes the inseparableness of the Cracker and his native setting, and she has shown in her books how his thinking has been molded through many generations by his primitive environment. Her use of superstitions, sayings, and similes in the native vernacular has aided greatly in making it possible for Mrs. Rawlings to create a picture of his everyday life and to reveal its significances. By this means she has portrayed both his stoical fatalism and his earthy humor, which enlivens even the grimmest poverty. (p. 201)

[She] has made effective use of [lore] in establishing atmosphere and characterization and . . . her work has been of value in preserving a record of this folk culture in the language which is its most fitting vehicle. (pp. 201-02)

Mrs. Rawlings has introduced the folk element into her work through describing customs such as fence raisings, frog hunting, cane grindings, peanut boilings, and log rafting. She shows the Cracker "making his crop," "marrying his wife," and "burying his dead;" but it is in recording his backwoods vernacular that her real claim to distinction lies, and his activities are most vivid when he is talking about them. Her best characterizations are made when her people express their folk wisdom and illuminate it with North Florida imagery. (pp. 208-09)

She can write about this scrub country, because she has based her work on a sound artistic foundation. She has made use of regional material, not merely to exploit the quaint or the odd, but to show how life has been molded from generation to generation by an environment. Her characters are individuals, but they bear the stamp of North Florida upon their faces, in their speech, and in the workings of their minds to such an extent that they are symbols of their community and embody the essence of its folk spirit. The use of folklore has contributed greatly to this end. And in turn, Mrs. Rawlings has been of service to the folklorist in that she has unearthed much hitherto unrecorded material and has preserved it in its own rhythmic language pattern. (p. 209)

Margaret Gillis Figh, "Folklore and Folk Speech in the Works of Marjorie Kinnan Rawlings," in Southern Folklore Quarterly, *Vol. XI, No. 3, September, 1947, pp. 201-09.*

GORDON E. BIGELOW (essay date 1966)

[Marjorie's attitude toward the Florida cracker] was remarkable in its insistence that these people were "beautiful," a view shared by so few others that she felt a kind of missionary drive to make others see the beauty she saw. (p. 100)

Her concern to present this people and their way of life—including the moonshining and the poaching of deer out of season—as something beautiful was so strong that she felt she had failed as an artist when anyone read her books and was left with a sense of ugliness. . . .

Like so many other aspects of her writing, her conception of these people is keyed to her theory about adjustment to environment. She recognized that the true crackers lived in unusually close harmony with their wild background, and this she felt must have an important molding influence on their character. (p. 101)

The cracker as she saw him was no dull-witted peasant but intelligent and sensitive to beauty. (p. 104)

[Marjorie] worked backward through time in her stories about the scrub. *South Moon Under* is chiefly about contemporary times, while *The Yearling* reflects a time fifty or sixty years earlier, before the partial despoiling of the wilderness. She was always scrupulous about historical accuracy, as about other details of the cracker way of life, and never confused horse-drawn times with later motor-driven times. . . . Still her treatment of cracker life in the scrub seems all of a piece because of a timelessness inherent in the material itself, because she depicts mainly those aspects of life which were the most traditional or the least affected by time. . . . Most of the events she chooses to record are part of a way of life which was itself isolated from the stream of history in the great world, so that while most of the action in *South Moon Under* takes place in the Roaring Twenties, almost nothing of that roar penetrates the silence of the scrub. One is so thoroughly immersed in the scrub point of view that the local dispute involving the fencing of cattle is of larger importance than the Wall Street Crash. Historical time can be established definitely in *The Yearling* only by two unobtrusive references to Penny's having served in the Confederate army during the Civil War. The effect of this timelessness in her books about the scrub is to produce a detachment which heightens immediacy and makes more convincing the characters and events within the books.

Taken together her stories of the Florida cracker depict an entire way of life from childhood through courtship and marriage and the pains and joys of mature life to old age and death. (pp. 109-10)

In most of her stories Marjorie uses cracker speech only in actual dialogue, the major portion of the narrative being given in standard English. In the early writings, like "Cracker Chidlings," she is obviously self-conscious about the dialect, still straining for accuracy, and she makes extensive use of misspellings and sprinkles apostrophes liberally across the page to show omitted sounds. Her transcription is accurate enough phonetically, but the "fly-speck" technique creates an impediment for the reader. . . .

In the later stories, she learned to make the dialect less obtrusive and used a more suggestive technique, letting idiom and syntax and grammar rather than distortions of spelling convey the flavor of the speech. (p. 113)

In *The Yearling* the dialect is handled so skillfully that one is seldom conscious of it, except for the occasional use of some archaic turn of phrase which has now passed entirely from the standard speech. (p. 114)

Marjorie's great gift for the vernacular is best seen in her comic stories [in *When the Whippoorwill*], which are in the tradition of the frontier tall tale. They have the classic elements established by Mark Twain—a folk narrator speaking in the vernacular, a surface realism coupled with wild exaggeration. The characters are grotesques. . . . But with all their grotesquerie, the people in these stories are humanly believable. Much of the comic comes from an indulgence in straight farce. . . . But as in other stories in this genre, much of the delight comes from a sheer relish in the vernacular language itself. (pp. 114-15)

These comic stories are a major literary accomplishment, good enough to be placed beside the best of Ring Lardner or Faulkner or the other American writers of this century who have followed Mark Twain's lead in using folk narration. . . .

Readers will detect a classic American note to Marjorie's writings in other ways than her skilled use of vernacular speech. Her books express many parts of what might be called a frontier archetype. (p. 116)

The central male figure in her stories has the same nostalgic familiarity. Penny Baxter, Lantry Jacklin, Luke Brinley, Mart, are, in differing proportions, blends of Cooper's Natty Bumppo and Jefferson's ideal husbandman. The woodsman-frontiersman has been depicted in a number of ways in American literature, from the savage mountain man who is a kind of white Indian, to the squalid, malaria-ridden, poor white. Marjorie's fiction contains no developed figure of the white savage, except possibly for the Forresters in *The Yearling,* who bear only approximate resemblance. And in like fashion, there are no more than brief glimpses of the degenerate clay-eater, even though her stories abound in figures who are in the lowest reaches of poverty. In her books even the most desperate poverty carries with it no necessary moral decline. Her people often look [starvation] in the face . . . but the experience teaches them hardihood and self-reliance rather than turpitude. Her cracker country contains few Snopeses or Jeeter Lesters.

One other conception of the frontiersman which has been most pervasive in literature, so pervasive as to achieve the dimension of a myth, is Cooper's conception of Natty Bumppo in *The Leatherstocking Tales.* . . . Cooper leaves no doubt that the reason this man is a paragon of physical and moral virtues is because he has been able to live at an ideally simple level in the great forest, far from the corrupting influences of civilization.

Several figures in the Rawlings stories, chiefly Penny Baxter and Lantry Jacklin, remind one of Natty. They show the same prowess as hunters and woodsmen, the same readiness and ability to meet crisis. They have little book learning, but are wise in the ways of the forest; they have the same quiet humor, the sensitivity to beauty, and the gentleness of spirit, combined with physical daring and skill. Each of these characters is also given his own individuality—Penny is diminutive in size from having been worked too hard on meager rations as a boy, and he is a farmer as much as he is a hunter; Lant is lean and gangling and is a moonshiner as well as a gifted woodsman. Both remind one of R.W.B. Lewis' "hero in space," the man like Natty Bumppo or Huck Finn who lights out for the territory when the irritants of civilization become too great. (pp. 117-18)

She applauds Penny Baxter's flight from the town into the

wild scrub, and she gives him in his role as hunter and woodsman many of the attributes of Natty Bumppo, those virtues which are the result of living close to nature, but she also makes Penny a knowing and hard working farmer, who successfully fights off the incursions of wild creatures and holds the wilderness at bay as the agent of civilization. Thus he falls squarely into the image of the idealized agrarian freeholder, which has been pervasive in American culture since the eighteenth century. . . . As an independent, self-reliant yeoman farmer living in a great forest, he is representative of a frontier condition midway between the savagery of the mountain men and the corruptions of sophisticated society, that agrarian middle ground esteemed by Crèvecoeur and Jefferson as the ideal condition for human happiness. To this frontier, so intimately associated with the American dream, Marjorie obviously has strong attachments, both theoretical and emotional. (p. 120)

[Ellen] Glasgow's insistence that character and not place should come first in regionalist fiction as in any other kind of fiction, highlights Marjorie Kinnan Rawlings' basic problem as a literary artist, since in most of her major writings *place* undoubtedly came first. When she began to write about Florida, her principal motive was to record rather than to create, and for a long time fiction was for her chiefly a vehicle by which to express fact. (pp. 130-31)

During her entire career Marjorie was caught in the regionalist's typical dilemma of how to strike the proper balance between fact and fiction. . . . (p. 131)

The Yearling was the first of her major works where she found the ideal point of balance between fact and fiction. She had already put the scrub on record in *South Moon Under,* so she was untroubled by this compulsion and free to make more purely literary use of the same materials. . . . [She] started for the first time with a primary concern for character rather than place, with the boy Jody as a single dominant character, and she gave the story a stiff backbone of theme, one of the oldest and most universal in literature, the painful passage of a boy from childhood into manhood.

She gave other aspects of the book a classic discipline. She placed point of view with Jody, and though she had a struggle after the story began to develop to keep Penny Baxter from taking it over, she persisted, and the narrative stayed with Jody. Time was strictly controlled to a single year's passage from April to April. The main characters were limited in number to the three members of the Baxter family—actually to Jody and the two beings he loved most, his father and his pet fawn. Ma Baxter, less fully realized, is a kind of scolding negative presence, full of duty and frugality and a puritanical distaste for pleasure. All other characters were held to minor supporting function and never allowed to obtrude upon the central grouping. Place was confined to the scrub, and chiefly to Baxter's Island within the scrub, except for brief excursions to Fort Volusia which lay just outside the scrub's boundaries. The important symbol of the flutter mill with which the book opens and closes gives an envelope structure to the action. The continuous parallel symbolism of the fawn reinforces the yearling status of Jody and makes more poignant his passage into manhood.

Marjorie's narrative talent was chiefly that of a raconteur, a teller of tales, and she always shows best in the short haul in particular scenes and anecdotes. Because of its controlling theme, there is a sense of steady progression in *The Yearling*, of a large inclusive action—Jody passes from boyhood to manhood, and his father from vigorous maturity to the beginning of broken old age. But within this structural pattern, because point of view resides with Jody, she is able to make the book a sequence of revelations and reflections, an indefinite series of carefully realized individual scenes, as if a spotlight were swung from one facet of life in the scrub to another. (pp. 135-37)

One reason for *The Yearling*'s excellence as fiction is that in this book the characters were conceived of as people first and as crackers second. (p. 137)

[With *The Sojourner*, Marjorie turned away from her depiction of the Florida scrub country and had] to encounter again, almost as if she were starting her whole apprenticeship once more, the vexing enigma of how to place the fulcrum of her story at the proper point between fact and fiction. (p. 144)

[Marjorie attempts in *The Sojourner*] to give a major restatement of the American dream, in a fully developed version of the pastoral myth of the ideal husbandman tilling the fertile garden of the symbolic middle landscape. This includes an intense polemic against modern bourgeois materialism, which she pictures as subverting and devouring the American nation. She also meant the book to have suggestive overtones of the story of Job, the man who suffers in silence; and she meant the book, finally, to be a statement of her own deepest penetration into the meaning of human life and destiny. For a vehicle to carry such heavy freight of serious idea, she fell back on the form traditionally used for this purpose in Protestant culture, the allegory, so that in spite of a surface realism detailing many aspects of farm life in the Middle West in the late nineteenth century, most of the major actions in the book and virtually all of the characters also exist at the symbolic level. [Asahel Linden] contains something of Everyman, Job, Abraham Lincoln, and a Fisher Indian. . . . His mother Amelia is a hard, selfish, narrow woman symbolic of the dominant American Puritanism of the past. . . . Ase's wife Nellie is the brisk, pert, pretty, capable American housewife and mother, cheerful, well-adjusted, pragmatic, materialistic, uncomplicated, completely at home in this world. Most of his children are monstrous devotees of Mammon who inherit materialism from both mother and grandmother. (pp. 146-47)

Like other allegories, the book displays a high degree of artifice. The characters are almost all types, if not personified abstractions. Though generally somber, the book is ultimately affirmative. Because of the natural wisdom imparted to him by his Indian "father," Ase is enabled to resist both the harsh puritan narrowness of his mother (the past) and the degenerate materialism of his son (the future) and save the American land from pollution by conveying it to its true heir, the still uncorrupted descendant of immigrants. (pp. 147-48)

The book represents a noble attempt to write the great American novel, but it must be counted more of a failure than a success—even when read as allegory rather than as a realist fiction. The plot is forced, the characters wooden, the prose often sententious and turgid. From the very beginning Marjorie was working with too large an ambition in an alien mode. Like all other writers, she used symbols, but except in this last novel and in a few of the late short stories

she was not a conscious symbolist in the sense that Joyce or Faulkner was. She had no gift for the subtleties, ambiguities, and ironies required of sustained symbolism, and her natural warmth and colloquial informality were smothered in this last novel by her self-conscious attempt to adopt the symbolic mode.

One of her greatest assets in the Florida writings was her style—open, energetic, vividly humane. Two things happened to release Marjorie's literary potential—the first was her discovery of Florida and the second was her learning from Hemingway the use of the blunt declarative sentence. She never acknowledged a specific debt, but there seems little question that in the late twenties or early thirties she went to school to Hemingway like so many other writers of her generation. In any case her style underwent a radical change, from overwritten journalese to a relatively chaste, unadorned style. (p. 148)

[She] made extensive and masterful use of dialect, but most of her stories except for the comic stories are narrated in third person in a voice which uses standard, and at times formal, language. In the early stories this sometimes resulted in a clash of tones. . . . (p. 149)

By the time she began *The Yearling*, she had learned to avoid such discrepancies and the style flows out with seamless integrity. In the early short stories she had learned to use several variations of stream of consciousness, and this book comes chiefly as a sequence of revelations to the alert, yet open and wondering mind of twelve-year-old Jody Baxter. To reveal Jody's inner consciousness she uses, not the cloud of impressions of Joyce or Virginia Woolf, the layered accumulation of thought upon thought, sense upon sense, but a modified third-person record of this process. She can thus be highly selective, can give a direct impression of Jody's mind or an edited version which includes his reaction to some impression, or she can move entirely outside the inner world of Jody's consciousness to interpretation or commentary or detached exposition. (p. 150)

[The autobiographical] *Cross Creek* was a similar triumph of style in which, using very different means and materials, she brought off a second time the precarious idyllic tone she had sought in *The Yearling*. . . . Because of the familiar tone, she was able in [*Cross Creek*], to make freest use of her gifts as raconteur, and she pours out anecdote after anecdote in a deceptively easy flow, story mixed with lyric nature description, character sketch with serious meditation, and the whole permeated by her own humanity and a bright glint of humor. (p. 153)

[In the Florida stories] she had a vision of life which she *had* to transmit, a pastoral vision of singular beauty and appeal. In a time when it was fashionable to be negative and despairing, her books were affirmative. In a time of great social and economic distress, of moral confusion and uncertainty, her stories quietly reasserted a familiar American ethic. In the heyday of the anti-hero, her Penny Baxter was an unobtrusive but true hero of the traditional sort. His virtues in abstraction sound like a rehearsal of the Boy Scout code—he was loyal, brave, honest, kindly, generous, and all the rest—but he was also sternly self-reliant and stoically tough. Her Jody Baxter undergoes a shattering of innocence not unlike that of Hemingway's Nick Adams figures or the young men in Sherwood Anderson's stories, but he comes to a much more satisfactory settlement with life's painful demands than they do. Hemingway's young men do not often recover from their "unreasonable wound," but go into a stasis or a flight to the wilderness or into frantic hedonism to escape a confrontation too painful to be lived with. Jody returns to Baxter's Island where he takes up manly responsibility for the family's support. (p. 156)

Nothing is more central to her statement than a tragic awareness that a boy's world contains loneliness as well as beauty and pain as well as purity, that innocence cannot last, and that its shattering is accompanied by a hard anguish. The pastoral vision in her books is of a world of natural beauty free from the stench and ugliness of modern cities, but it also includes Penny's stoic conviction that life will inevitably knock a man down, and when it does a man takes this for his share and goes on. This kind of pastoralism is neither an invitation to dalliance under the yum-yum tree nor to a wallowing in the pit of existentialist despair. Such a balanced view of human existence is more traditional than modern, and one might even say, more "classic." (p. 157)

> *Gordon E. Bigelow, in his* Frontier Eden *(copyright © 1966 by the Board of Commissioners of State Institutions of Florida), University of Florida Press, 1966, 162 p.*

W. J. STUCKEY (essay date 1966)

[*The Yearling*] is "local history" of pioneer life on the Florida frontier just after the Civil War, and . . . it is packed with homely detail about the lives of the rude, backwoods people and their houses, husbandry, and speech. Interwoven with these picturesque details is the sentimental story of a boy named Jody who finds a new-born deer, domesticates it, dotes upon it, and finally allows his mother to destroy it for trampling down the family's crops. In a rather amateurish attempt to give her story implications larger than it can bear, Mrs. Rawlings, at the close of the book, tries to make the death of the yearling deer be symbolic of the end of Jody's boyhood. . . . (p. 116)

[*The Yearling* is] too slight and sentimental to merit serious attention. Mrs. Rawlings' writing is generally amateurish. Her style owes much to Hemingway, but lacks Hemingway's precision and coherence of effect. Such artistic defects, of course, are not likely to bother the unsophisticated readers at whom the book seems, consciously or unconsciously, aimed. One can well imagine that . . . *The Yearling* will over the years continue to attract young readers. (p. 117)

> *W. J. Stuckey, "New Brands of Individualism," in his* The Pulitzer Prize Novels: A Critical Backward Look *(copyright 1966 by the University of Oklahoma Press), University of Oklahoma Press, 1966, pp. 94-121.*

SAMUEL I. BELLMAN (essay date 1974)

Perhaps the most important reason that *The Yearling* maintains so strong a hold on the reader is Mrs. Rawlings' profound sympathy for twelve-year-old Jody Baxter. Jody is a "natural" boy, not a *feminized* ideal of a boy; he is neither stereotypically good nor stereotypically bad. But because the author is so attached to him emotionally he is virtually an *animus* figure in the Jungian sense: a projection of the

masculine configuration of a woman's interior personality. Jody is Mrs. Rawlings' finest and most heart-warming literary expression of the boy she had always wanted but never had. All her life she had been describing this "dream child" in a variety of interesting ways, and she continued to do so long after completing Jody's story, but there is a special quality in *The Yearling* that sets it quite apart from those other works. (p. 54)

When we briefly review Mrs. Rawlings' novels, we find that her first book, *South Moon Under* . . . , is about a Florida Cracker woman, Piety Jacklin, and her beloved only son, Lant. The second novel, *Golden Apples* . . . , which has a great deal to say about maternity and child-parent relations, contains a subplot about a widower who worships his scapegrace son and then must endure the son's senseless death. *The Yearling* . . . is an unusually moving story of the closeness that is possible between a father and his son; aside from the Baxters, there are two other family groups (the Huttos and the Forresters) in which a beloved son plays an important role. The last novel, *The Sojourner* . . . , is essentially the story of an *unwanted* son who must abide his mother's single-minded dedication to his long-absent brother, as well as the griefs his own children bring him. This last work is also a veritable maze of parent-offspring relationships, natural and artificial. (p. 57)

[What] was touched on sketchily or with moderation in her other novels, was treated with consummate artistic skill in her finest book, *The Yearling*, which more than makes up for her weak and uninspired writings. By no means only a well-executed story about a father and son, or a boy and his pet deer, *The Yearling* has a kind of mythical quality which repays each successive reading. This novel elevates the writer to the rank of those special authors who at least once in their lives are capable of giving us dreams to dream by and words to shape those dreams. (p. 65)

If it were only a string of closely connected anecdotes about a young boy, *The Yearling* would be interesting and appealing enough, with its likable rascal Jody. . . . [But it is not] a mere "boy's book." Throughout *The Yearling* we are reminded that man is a lost soul here on earth, at the mercy of inscrutable, whimsical forces. (pp. 72-3)

Mrs. Rawlings describes a nightmare world where things continue to go wrong, and where the noblest resolve, the loftiest intention, and the most arduous toil are quite unavailing. Again and again, for all the surface sentimentality that has misled serious readers, the story echoes a frightened and lost child crying in the night, out of fear, disappointment, and despair. . . . [Since] this somewhat existentialist situation is seen largely through the Baxters, it is best to examine her dark, brooding drama through an analysis of the three protagonists—Ma Baxter, her husband Penny, and their son Jody.

Ma Baxter is a bitter, complaining woman who has little patience with anyone. From a casual reading of the book, she seems merely to be a dramatic foil for her husband Penny, whose deep and abiding love for his only child gives the story much of its beauty. Jody grows up father- and male-oriented, and his mother is a kind of stereotyped female ogre like the widows and aunts in *Tom Sawyer* and *Huckleberry Finn: She just won't let a boy have no fun nohow.* Most of the time, she gives Jody (and Penny too) "the miseries," and so the reader is tempted to write her off as a sorry example of a mother and wife. What natural boy wouldn't want to light out for the Territory? (p. 73)

Penny, for all his saintliness, is too soft for Ora Baxter, who is described as being about twice his size. His relationship with his wife is typical in certain respects of what one finds in many of Mrs. Rawlings' stories: the husband in some very important way disappoints or crosses his wife, and she reacts angrily and with deep bitterness. (p. 74)

Ora Baxter, for all her fierce energy, has been depleted by the early deaths of numerous children. Having anticipated a large family, she was forced to watch each pregnancy end in sorrow.

The thoughtful reader may discern a mirror-image contrast between the Baxters and their distant neighbors the Forresters. Fodder-wing, a saintly child who loved all the little animals of the scrub, was the seventh Forrester son and the only one too frail to survive. Jody Baxter, the last of the seven or so Baxter offspring, was the only one hardy enough to survive. But time, man's deadliest enemy . . . , has passed Ora by. (pp. 74-5)

It is not hard to understand why [Ora] was so unpleasant and formidable a person, or why she infused gloom and unhappiness into Jody's thirteenth year, just when the world was opening up to him. . . . [She] had been deprived, for a long time, of the opportunity for maternal expression. Even after Ma Baxter's great need had somehow been satisfied to an extent, force of habit . . . made her continue to project the customary baleful influence on those around her. It was almost as though she were lost between two worlds: the realm of *should have been* and the realm of *came too late*. . . . But the haunting aftereffects of a lost family constitute only part of the nightmare story that comprises *The Yearling*. (p. 75)

Penny is a man who has been severely injured by life—aside from the deaths of all the Baxter children who preceded Jody, his difficulties with his wife, and the snake-bite and the rupture that lay him low in the course of the story. His childhood, in a large farm family living near a village some distance from the Big Scrub, was characterized by adverse conditions: unremitting toil, short rations, and hookworm. His own father had been an austere preacher, and Penny's social growth was as severely stunted as his physical development. From this derived his trauma, which Mrs. Rawlings comments on vaguely but provocatively.

Why did this large-souled little man, who always wanted only what was properly his and would never kill wild game unless it was absolutely necessary, move into the primitive scrub country that was "populous with bears and wolves and panthers"? Because, the author explains mysteriously, wherever "neighbors were not too far apart, men's minds and actions and property overlapped. There were intrusions on the individual spirit." Despite all the social benefits of the settlements, there were also "bickerings and watchfulness, one man suspicious of another." Stern as his father's world had been, the world of men that Penny had grown into was "less direct, less honest, in its harshness, and therefore more disturbing." (pp. 75-6)

What lies behind this morbid sensitivity to social encroachment on the part of Penny, of Mrs. Rawlings, of many of her fictional characters? Was it merely a kind of paranoia,

finding its expression in a solitary existence supported by a philosophy of geographical primitivism? Actually, we are dealing with a peculiar physiological response, one not yet well understood. . . . [Given] our present state of knowledge, it is enough for our purposes merely to think that a deeper explanation exists for Penny's attitude . . . than simple touchiness or cantankerousness.

The novel derives a part of its beauty, in fact, from Mrs. Rawlings' sensitive treatment of Penny's lifelong burden which has to do with the "bad vibrations" he has gotten and will continue to get from other humans. . . . And Penny's basis for dealing with this burden, his hard-shelled stoicism, is the most valuable gift he is able to give to Jody. (p. 77)

Lastly, there is twelve-year-old Jody, growing up in isolation and molded by his father's morbid hypersensitivity to overcrowding and his mother's pervasive and bitter pessimism. But Jody emerges at the beginning of the story not as a neurotic, anti-social, emotional cripple, but as a wholesome country boy who is enormously excited by the renewed promise and glory of a North Florida April. The sensitive reader of any age and background cannot help but share Jody's delight in his woolgathering rambles and hunting and fishing trips, his worry over the calamities that befall his father, his fear over the threats to his family's food supply, and, finally, his ordeal in having to kill Flag, which had become a part of him and in effect a member of the family. (pp. 77-8)

The alienation, confusion, anxiety, and time-sensitivity that underlie the novel are most sharply focused at the end with Jody's killing of Flag. Why should life have to be this way? Well, it just is. (p. 78)

[There] is in *The Yearling* a series of intimations culminating in a strong final statement—*not* of stoic resignation toward the blighted world men are forced to live in (Penny's scrub had proven no more satisfactory than the "world of men" he had fled)—but of belief in a shadowy and sealed off parallel existence. Mrs. Rawlings' other novels, which end tragically or pathetically with the death of a relative, also suggest something of the sort, a very qualified existential solution to the spirit-breaking problem of life's bereavement pain. . . . Is this not actually the worst part of Jody's trial-by-fire initiation into young manhood: determining which is the sleep, the dream—and which is the waking, the quickening to tragic life? (pp. 79-80)

Some of the most effective writing in [*Cross Creek*] (most of which, actually, is beautifully rendered) deals with [Mrs. Rawlings'] perception of seasonal changes as they affected the flora and fauna of the Creek.

The memorable soliloquy at the end—dealing with the question of who really owns Cross Creek—is a fitting climax to the book. The birds own this region, she concludes; human claims are not as valid as theirs. In fact, the Creek belongs to the elements, "to the cosmic secrecy of seed, and beyond all, to time." . . . Mrs. Rawlings, like Faulkner, fell back on the ancient Anglo-Saxon idea of land*holding,* land *use,* land *loving, tending, tenancy,* rather than land *ownership.* And her soliloquy is worth memorizing and ranking with Faulkner's statements on landholding, with George Meredith's great poem, "Life is but a little holding, Lent to do a mighty labor," and with Robert Frost's poem "The Gift Outright." (p. 105)

Because *Cross Creek* is so intensely personal, it is difficult to summarize it in any systematic fashion. Mrs. Rawlings wrote as an amateur naturalist, and her frequent detailing of flora and fauna places her firmly within a given, meaningful space, while her occasional vagueness about time gives an odd impression of existential drift. (p. 106)

Cross Creek, like its predecessor *Walden* [by Henry David Thoreau], may be taken as a pastoral autobiography that harks back in certain ways to the ancient Theocritan-Virgilian tradition. (p. 114)

The *ruri-urbi* dichotomy—is life better up at the villa or down in the city?—can easily be overstated. . . . And there is no need here to become embroiled in the issues of geographical primitivism, the Noble Savage, and the teeter-totter of pastoral and anti-pastoral elements in our literature. Still, *Cross Creek* may be seen as a repudiation of one kind of sophistication in favor of another kind of sophistication. "Having left cities behind her," Mrs. Rawlings transferred her cultivated, reflective sensibility to the North Florida woods where she could, for all her occasional loneliness and frustration, make the best of two worlds. Far above the other inhabitants of the Creek area in education and refinement, she was a kind of reportorial visitor from another planet. . . .

Mrs. Rawlings' last novel, *The Sojourner,* is markedly different from her other novels in that it does not concern the harsh, earthy existence of the Florida Crackers. The locale is upstate New York. . . . Although *The Sojourner* is about people whose lives are dedicated to living on the soil and wresting a living from it, Mrs. Rawlings clearly was no longer in her element when she depicted their lives. Her message comes through somehow, but the story is weak in many places, and the characterization is often flat—in fact, painfully unimaginative. Yet the reader finds himself, after finishing the book, coming back again and again to the message; for it touches the very basis of human existence. (p. 119)

There is a haunting loneliness throughout the novel. . . . The mood of the book suggests, in fact, not only loneliness but also the sadness resulting from both an unappeased hunger and a bereavement whose wounds refuse to heal. We might even say that the book is pervaded by an existentialist feeling. (p. 123)

[Asahel Linden's] essential alienation and rootlessness are closely related to his deep-rootedness to a particular location and to a particular social group. Asahel does not—until the very end of his life—have a valid claim to the [land he farms] and thus he is in a painfully ambiguous position in regard to it. And he is a kind of outsider in his own family, to which he has also devoted a lifetime of service. (pp. 124-25)

Measure a man by his sense of loss, one thinks, in reading the story of this man's life. Asahel's predicament—which can never be resolved while he lives—is that something like a deep feeling of personal loss, perhaps a painful lack of affection from his closest kin (he repulses at least two of them—his mother and his son Nat—by his homeliness) impoverishes his life. Nothing seems to belong to him—neither wife, children, land, nor house: "He was a stranger." (p. 125)

Asahel, then, is an existentialist hero who spends his life

struggling to realize himself in his work and (sometimes ignoring logic and the demands of family) to establish a meaningful social relation. His efforts are often hampered and they may sometimes be tentative and uncertain; frustration is his frequent reward. But, far from being a total failure, Asahel's life has a certain grandeur, an imposing agrarian stature. In the very fact that his reach for spiritual fulfillment exceeded his grasp, he vindicates himself as a man. (p. 127)

[Mrs. Rawlings] lacked the genealogical milieu for a really significant body of fiction. Her family-farm tradition . . . was not nearly enough to offset this limitation. True, it helped her produce *The Sojourner,* but that novel, for all its strengths, is an abstraction of farm life conceived almost in Platonic terms that carries the reader from a simple, dedicated farmer's struggles with crops and family to the farmer's soul-flight toward the distant stars. And, the dialogue in the book is painfully flat, revealing the author's lack of understanding of people separated from her by a psychic distance. (pp. 134-35)

A greater degree of verbal skill might have carried her much farther. (p. 135)

[Yet], if we consider her Cracker fiction—and not her best, but the flawed though quite promising stories—we find hints of first-rate artistic expression, embedded in a matrix of raw, inchoate story materials. The gaunt, ill-used farm woman of "Gal Young Un" should have been brought to life instead of left as a symbol and a suggestion. The destitute Cracker couple in "Jacob's Ladder" should have been endowed with a much greater degree of vitality. . . . And, irony of ironies, Lant Jacklin in *South Moon Under,* one of the author's most important young boy idealizations, is largely a paper-doll figure. To judge from these and other works, it was extremely difficult for her to project her dramatis personae from the recesses of her mind onto the printed page so that they could enter the consciousness of her readers. (p. 137)

What do Mrs. Rawlings' stories seem to be saying? Man, the frail, struggling sojourner on this inhospitable planet, will *not* realize his fondest hopes and wishes—he will get knocked down by life—as Penny Baxter puts it—yet will have no choice but to get up again and keep on going every time the blow falls. Like Penny, again, he will be hurt at least "once too often" by his fellow humans. In this elemental story pattern (seen very clearly in "Jacob's Ladder," for example), with its overtones of the great folktales, there appears . . . [a consistent concern]: the failure of the romantic dream. (pp. 139-40)

Samuel I. Bellman, in his Marjorie Kinnan Rawlings *(copyright © 1974 by Twayne Publishers, Inc.; reprinted with the permission of Twayne Publishers, a Division of G. K. Hall & Co., Boston),* Twayne, 1974, 164 p.

LAMAR YORK (essay date 1977)

"Sense of place" is the most descriptive phrase to emerge from the relatively small amount of criticism on the works of Marjorie Kinnan Rawlings. (p. 91)

Rawlings uses rivers in her writings as the chief aspect of place and as the chief thematic element of setting. In all her stories in which man seeks to identify with his natural environment, there is a consciousness of the river either as the outside limits of the setting or as the connecting link between her setting and the rest of the world. (p. 92)

Though not a symbolist, despite her emergence as a writer during the fluent years of deliberate symbolists, she is indeed a strongly conscious literary artist. Dismissed lightly at times as merely descriptive, Rawlings's novels are carefully knit together through the use of description itself as a structural element in her plot, rather than as simply an elaboration of the real story. But all the geographical entities focused on in her writing—clearings, landings, hammocks, pine islands, homesteads—the description of rivers is the most significant to the course of her story-telling art. . . . Rivers were for her the perfect conceptualization of order because they offered structure without excessive orderliness. (pp. 92-3)

South Moon Under is her fullest exploration of a river as an architectonic element. The novel is about many of the basic forces operating on human life, all of which are summarized in the elemental pull of the moon on the scrub hunters and the animals they hunt, just as the moon manipulates the tides that rise and fall in the St. Johns River. The river is represented for the most part as beneficent. . . . But the river is also the same force that the sea is in Stephen Crane's "The Open Boat"; while it can be benevolent or malevolent, it leans toward neither. At times in the novel the river's role is uncertain. . . . (p. 95)

At other times the river seems to play a malevolent part, as when the simple-minded Ramrod Simpson is "afflicted" at his baptism in the river; the preacher falls in a hole and hits Ramrod's head on a rock getting him out of the river, leaving him "afflicted." The river is [also] a carrier of disease: "Early in March the influenza struck along the river." . . . [Similarly] Willy Jacklin meets his death on the river because he is unequal to its danger-filled challenge. (p. 96)

Although a passive character, seldom made to seem deliberately benevolent or malevolent, the river nevertheless operates as a deciding factor in the lives of those who live on or near its banks. In *South Moon Under* it is a line of demarcation outlining the edges of the scrub sanctuary. Lantry's life commences properly only when he "crosses the river" . . . into the safety and anonymity of the scrub. . . . [The] river is clearly a line of demarcation between two versions of the life of men in that the young boy Lant must cross the river to go to school. One side of the river holds for him the possibility of formal education; the other side, the scrub, makes possible a real education for the real world. The end of his formal schooling is signified when he recrosses the river from school for the last time after two years. (pp. 96-7)

[In] *The Yearling,* the river occupies less of Rawlings's attention, but it is as instrumental here in helping the characters find a sense of place as it was in any of the previous stories. The St. Johns River is the instrument of the young hero Jody's *rite de passage* from yearling to manhood. (pp. 100-01)

Jody senses the river's greatness even before it becomes the instrument of his self-discovery. He recognizes its character when he first sees it, though he cannot yet know the dramatic role the river will play in his own life. The St. Johns that Penny and Jody see as they arrive at Volusia

"was dark, and aloof. It seemed to slide toward the ocean indifferent to its own banks and to the men who crossed it or used it. Jody stared at it. It was a pathway to the world." . . . (p. 101)

[His] perception of the river in that episode is the motivation for his return to the river for help when the time comes that he must find his own identity.

This episode, which is Mrs. Rawlings's most poignant and dramatic use of the river in *The Yearling,* and perhaps anywhere in her fiction, appears in the closing pages of Jody's story. . . . Alone on the river [after he is forced to kill his pet fawn] he comes to understand what everyone must: the self he discovers is not a new one but the old self that had been awaiting discovery. But dissociation from the scrub home he knew so well has forced on him the consciousness that he will not find himself by getting away from the scrub. Life is a mystery anywhere, he discovers . . . , but he is now ready to move toward reconciliation with himself and with the place that he once called home. He is at his nadir, between his old childlike acceptance of life as a sure thing and his coming reconciliation with his adult role in the scrub homestead. He is, during the time he spends on the river, in that place between childhood and manhood, "suspended in a timeless space." (pp. 102-03)

[Returning] home, he can look back at the lake and river he had thought to use as his escape. It has been the instrument of his new understanding, and his actually participated beneficently in his growing up. . . . He passes the pathway leading down to the tiny crystal clear stream where he was seen daydreaming on the book's opening page. He wants to return now to that happy place. . . . But it is not the same place he remembers, any more than he is the person he was on the beginning page. Jody sees that he already has made the trip on that tiny stream of his childhood as far as it can take him; he has begun the journey now on an infinitely larger stream. . . . The river has taught him maturity; again the river encloses that universe which all of Marjorie Rawlings's characters inhabit. (pp. 103-04)

Lamar York, "Marjorie Kinnan Rawlings's Rivers," in The Southern Literary Journal (*copyright 1977 by the Department of English, University of North Carolina at Chapel Hill*), Vol. IX, No. 2, Spring, 1977, pp. 91-107.

ADDITIONAL BIBLIOGRAPHY

Bellman, Samuel Irving. "Marjorie Kinnan Rawlings: A Solitary Sojourner in the Florida Backwoods." *Kansas Quarterly* 2, No. 2 (Spring 1970): 78-87.
    Examination of Rawlings's personality as reflected in her work and her attitude toward regional literature.

Bellman, Samuel Irving. "Marjorie Kinnan Rawlings' Existentialist Nightmare: *The Yearling.*" *Costerus* 9 (1973): 9-18.
    Study of the existential conflicts in *The Yearling.*

Bigelow, Gordon E. "Marjorie Kinnan Rawlings' Wilderness." *The Sewanee Review* LXXIII, No. 2 (Spring 1965): 299-310.
    Places Rawlings's treatment of the Florida frontier and its inhabitants in the mainstream of the American frontier tradition by comparison with Cooper, Thoreau, and Faulkner.

Van Gelder, Robert. "A Talk with Marjorie Kinnan Rawlings."
The New York Times Book Review (30 November 1941): 2.

Interview with Rawlings discussing her home and work
methods.

Henry Handel Richardson

1870-1946

(Pseudonym of Ethel Florence Lindesay Richardson Robertson) Anglo-Australian novelist, short story writer, and essayist.

Richardson has been called the greatest British naturalist and is considered by many critics to be one of Australia's foremost novelists. Her fame rests primarily on two of her works, *Maurice Guest* and *The Fortunes of Richard Mahony*. Both demonstrate her naturalistic manner of characterization without authorial intrusion. She considered Flaubert to be her chief mentor in the formation of her impersonal style.

Richardson was born in East Melbourne, the daughter of a doctor who served as a model for Richard Mahony. After an unhappy childhood she left Australia and attended the Leipzig Conservatorium for musical studies. At Leipzig she met her husband, J. G. Robertson, and with his encouragement began writing. Fearful of being patronized by her readers because of her sex, she published her work as Henry Handel Richardson, the name of one of her relatives.

Richardson aptly described her artistic vision as one of "romanticism imbued with the scientific spirit and essentially based on realism." This spirit permeated her fiction, beginning with her first novel, *Maurice Guest,* which was at once a study of the destructive power of love, of artistic weakness, and of the Nietzschean ideal of genius which transcends ordinary morality. *The Getting of Wisdom* is also concerned with the artist's need for isolation from the mundane in order to search for truth. All of Richardson's novels, in fact, are concerned with isolation, the harshness of life, and the omnipresence of failure. Nowhere is this more apparent than in her trilogy *The Fortunes of Richard Mahony*, a tragic portrayal of one man's battle with environment and self.

After early praise, Richardson's critical reputation suffered a sharp setback. The argument concerned her artistic ability. It was felt by many critics that she had no power of invention, but simply reiterated her experiences in florid prose. These critics point to the similarity of *Maurice Guest* to her Leipzig experience, of *The Getting of Wisdom* to her girlhood, and of *The Fortunes of Richard Mahony* to the life of her father. Others disagree, offering Richardson's powers of structure and organization as evidence of her artistic skill. A critical reassessment of her work, begun during the 1960s, stresses the latter argument in portraying her strength as a novelist.

In spite of the dispute over Richardson's literary prowess, her work is important as one of the major products of the naturalist school in England. Some critics consider her the best exemplar of continental techniques of realism and naturalism in the English novel. For that reason alone her novels will remain important to the study of the tradition of the English novel.

PRINCIPAL WORKS

Maurice Guest (novel) 1908
The Getting of Wisdom (novel) 1910

The Fortunes of Richard Mahony (novel) 1917
The Way Home; Being the Second Part of the Chronicle of the Fortunes of Richard Mahony (novel) 1925
Ultima Thule; Being the Third Part of the Chronicle of the Fortunes of Richard Mahony (novel) 1929
The End of Childhood (short stories) 1934
The Young Cosima (novel) 1939
Myself When Young (autobiography) 1948

THE NATION (essay date 1909)

[*Maurice Guest*] is not a book to be lightly undertaken or lightly dismissed. . . . Mr. Richardson has manifestly chosen Balzac for his master and has shrunk from no elaboration of detail that will go to build up and furnish his environment, from no thrust of the analytic probe that will penetrate the innermost selves of his characters. . . . So abundant are the details, so frequent and apparently inconsequent the conversations, so continual the shifting, scattering, and regrouping of the minor characters, that for a while we really do not see the forest for the trees, and not till the clouds gather heavily over the coming end and the lesser actors begin to slip away, leaving Maurice and Louise to play out their tragedy of temperament and passion in comparative isolation, do we realize how intimate with them we have all the time been growing and how skilfully and artistically planned has been the long, slow passage from the soaring youthful hopes of the bright April morning with which the story opens, to the chill daybreak which brings an end to suffering beyond all remedy.

There is unquestionably much in the book to give more pain than pleasure. The theme itself, the demoralization and destruction of a hopeful young life by a great passion—the fatal, unreasoning, irresistible passion of the mediaeval romances—for a woman who has neither principle nor goodness of heart, who is a mere embodiment of the mystery and power of sex, is all the more distressing because of the complete lovableness, the loyal, trusting, pure, and tender nature of poor Maurice. Some of the realism is not only disagreeably, but unnecessarily, coarse, and the general picture of student life in Leipzig is not one to encourage the parents and guardians of young persons of either sex who propose to study there. In this realistic picture, by the way, though it has all the air of being done from the life, there is one absurdly false touch. All the American students speak that marvellous "Yankee" lingo which is never heard this side of the footlights of English theatres. . . . [After encountering examples of this false slang], it takes all the power and convincing quality of the book as a whole to win back the reader's confidence. That confidence is reconquered, however, and the book makes a very serious impression.

> *"Current Fiction: 'Maurice Guest',"* in The Nation *(copyright 1909 The Nation magazine, The Nation Associates, Inc.), Vol. 88, No. 2285, April 15, 1909, p. 387.*

J. G. ROBERTSON (essay date 1929)

Maurice Guest is the history of a young English provincial who aspires to be a master of the art and craft of music, betakes himself to the Conservatorium of Leipzig, and fails through lack of talent and temperament. Such a theme, the tragedy of the artist who is no artist, is obviously an old one. . . . Indeed, so well-worn is this theme of insufficient ability for the chosen calling that the author of *Maurice Guest* may have instinctively felt that it was too trite to provide a foundation for still another variation; and on to it she has grafted a love-story of such elemental force that the first conception of the 'stickit musician' has been dwarfed almost into insignificance. Imperiously unexpected and almost unwanted, love intrudes upon this 'musical novel'; and before very long it has ceased to be a 'musical novel' at all, but the relentless history of a devastating passion. The musician who lacks talent for his calling ceases to matter.

Maurice Guest is not then a 'musical novel' in the accepted sense: if its theme is set in the exotic *milieu* of a foreign city and among musicians and would-be musicians, it is only because such a *milieu* provides conditions not to be found, without a straining of probabilities, in conventional society, where the protagonists of the book would have stood outside the pale of respectability. Henry Handel Richardson has sought the musical *bohème* of a German city as writers of an earlier generation chose the Parisian *quartier latin*. So far, in fact, from *Maurice Guest* being a study of the musical temperament, the musical temperament is conspicuously absent from it: the tragedy of the two principal figures lies in the fact that they are not musicians: whereas the personages of the book who possess in a high degree the musical gift, Schilsky and Krafft, are depicted as abnormal and degenerate. For those who like to draw 'morals' from books, the moral of *Maurice Guest* is that, for young people who, without abundant talent, endeavour to acquire the art, it spells destruction. *Maurice Guest* is a book about an overwhelming passion in all its psychological aspects and vagaries. And love is here no thing of abiding happiness, no beneficent gift of the gods, but a veritable Pandora's box: no conciliator and harmoniser, but the enemy of man's peace of soul. (pp. 154-55)

[*Maurice Guest* is] no 'love-story' in the English acceptance of the word: its ruthless unveiling of the miseries of an unhappy passion lay outside our literary tradition; and still more, the manner of that unveiling. Love with us is rarely detached from sentiment: that is to say, if sincerely felt, it is never denied sympathy-awakening treatment; whereas here not a drop of sentiment is offered the parched reader, to assuage his intolerable suffering. *Maurice Guest* offers no hint of what its author thinks about her unhappy lovers; or on what side her sympathies lie. It is all so heartlessly impersonal, objective; presented with the cold scientific method of the physician diagnosing the symptoms of a patient struck down by an abnormal affliction.

No doubt, it was this lack of warmth, rather than its harrowing tragedy, that stood in the way of *Maurice Guest*'s being generally accepted by the average English novel-reader of its day. . . . [The] *technique* of *Maurice Guest*, the disappearance of the creator behind his creations, was strangely foreign to us, and little to our taste. (pp. 158-59)

[*Maurice Guest*] is essentially a book of literary provenance, a book that owed some of its power to the application of a foreign *technique*. In fact, as we see it now, it appears to gather up into itself the threads of the realistic movement of the previous generation; it is, in this continental sense, the greatest English naturalistic novel, the end and summary of the movement of which it is a part. It is the last link in the chain which practically began with *Madame Bovary* in 1856. (pp. 162-63)

From *Madame Bovary* comes the sombre conception of the devastating effects of a great passion on a soul that is not strong enough to bear it; from Flaubert, too,—perhaps also from an older master, Stendhal—that striving after objectivity and 'distance.' Flaubertian is the untiring effort to find the *juste mot*, that patient moulding of period and polishing of style; that endeavour to avoid every betrayal of the author's feelings, to expunge every thought from its pages that is not thinkable by the actors in the drama. (p. 163)

But conspicuous as is [her] debt to Flaubert, Henry Handel Richardson's art in this first book owes more to Russia. . . . [Some] of its earliest critics saw in it indeed a dubiously Russian novel. . . . [The] master that stands behind the most impressive pages of her work is unquestionably Dostoevsky. Without books such as *Crime and Punishment* and *The Brothers Karamasov*, it is safe to say that *Maurice Guest* would never have been written, or at least never have taken the form it took. And it is just this Dostoevsky element which gives *Maurice Guest* its particular niche in literature; it assimilates and reproduces in an English form all which Russia meant for the European novel in the foregoing generation.... What this apprenticeship in the school of the great Russian writer has meant for Henry Handel Richardson's art is first fully apparent when she emerges from dependence upon him, and in her *Richard Mahony* creates a type of novel that is peculiarly her own. (pp. 164-65)

The Getting of Wisdom is not a treatise on education; it is concerned merely with the experiences of a child. And it is comedy—ironic comedy—of a kind for which there had been little room in the emotional seriousness of *Maurice Guest.* (p. 168)

As *Maurice Guest* had been regarded as a 'musical novel,' and musical critics had solemnly pronounced judgment on its musical qualities and shortcomings, so *The Getting of Wisdom* was declared, just as irrelevantly, to be an educational thesis. (pp. 168-69)

What the critics of *The Getting of Wisdom* did not see, or were unwilling to admit, was that the school experiences of Laura Ramsbotham formed just as little the essential of the book as the musical experiences of Maurice Guest in the former work. This was not a school story as *Tom Brown* had been, or even Rudyard Kipling's *Stalky.* The school with all its realism is here merely *staffage,* as the musical world of Leipzig had been in *Maurice Guest.* The book is concerned in the first instance with the growing mind of a young girl in her early 'teens, not with the pros and cons of educational theory; and a child's trivial experiences in its first contact with the outside world have surely never been more shrewdly depicted than here. Sincerity, too—the same kind of ruthless sincerity that had constituted the strength of *Maurice Guest*—freedom from any taint of sentimentality, and from the suspicion that the author has a moral to impose on or squeeze out of her story, are equally conspicuous here. The book is amoral, even with a faintly immoral undertone. Henry Handel Richardson strips her little girl as spiritually naked as she had stripped her Maurice Guest.

Laura Ramsbotham's experiences are called 'the getting of wisdom''; they might perhaps more aptly have been entitled a child's tussle with the truth. A 'story' it hardly is, merely a series of kaleidoscopic—almost too kaleidoscopic—adventures of a child's school life: sharply cut little cameos, each marking a distinct step upward in the experience and worldly wisdom that is to fit it for life. All the steps . . . are at bottom concerned with the discovery that things are not what they seem; the note on which they harp is disillusionment—the disillusionment of a sensitive, imaginative child in its naïve unpreparedness for life's buffetings. (pp. 169-70)

These two books, *Maurice Guest* and *The Getting of Wisdom,* represent Henry Handel Richardson's apprenticeship to her art.... [With] the trilogy *Richard Mahony's Fortunes* she stands wholly on her own feet and conquers new land for the realm of imaginative prose. (pp. 174-75)

There is at bottom an undeniable similarity between *Richard Mahony* and *Maurice Guest;* they are both books the ultimate theme of which is disillusionment; both deal with spiritual and physical downfall and disintegration. The earlier work set out, as has been seen, with the purpose of

depicting the 'fortunes' of a young musician who turns out to be no musician, who comes to grief on the lack of sustaining genius. But it had not proceeded very far before the musical element became mere background and *staffage:* its character as a 'professional' novel was overshadowed by an obsessing emotional experience; it developed into a book not about music, but about the writhings of a soul in the grip of a great passion. Similarly *The Fortunes of Richard Mahony* opens as a professional novel—in respect not of Richard's profession as a physician, but as a colonist in the *El Dorado* of the new colony of Victoria; and similarly the centre of gravity shifts as the work proceeds. But whereas *Maurice Guest* leaves . . . the impression of having undergone a change of plan—as if the author had begun it without clear ideas of whither it was to lead—in *Richard Mahony* there is no wavering. . . . (p. 176)

It is a book about 19th-century colonisation, seen not in the rosy light of successful adventure, but with the cold eyes of a writer whose aim has ever been to see things as they are. For Henry Handel Richardson is not merely concerned, as she had been in *Maurice Guest,* with the tragedy and disintegration of personality under adverse conditions; she also deals with the multitudinous factors responsible for it; and she comes to grips with many problems and aspects of colonisation in the nineteenth century, and the building up of a new Britain beyond the seas.

To this end the first volume is largely concerned with what the aesthetics of realism called *milieu.* . . . The first volume of *Richard Mahony* [*Australia Felix*] is a kaleidoscope of motley adventure; and yet not adventure in the sense of the older colonial novel; for the events of this book are the quite commonplace experiences of early colonial life. . . . One feels that the author studied the early history of Australia with infinite care and endeavoured faithfully to depict things as they were. Glimpses of social development and political life are deftly woven into it; in the background is always present the rapid growth of the new colony from the cruel early days, through all the unsubstantial phases of easily acquired riches, to settled conditions and prosperous townships. And all this is not seen through the objective eyes of the historian, but through those of the participants themselves. Besides Mahony and his wife this volume is filled with a very motley crowd of living people—even more living than those of *Maurice Guest,* because less subjectively conceived; and Henry Handel Richardson, master of her puppet-show, has all the wires firmly in her hand; none, not even the most insignificant, comes short of his share of life. All this was clearly a most promising theme; it was thus not surprising that many of the early readers of *Australia Felix* greeted it as being at last a 'true' epic of colonisation; not one of colonisation seen through the coloured glasses of the romancer. But that promise has hardly been fulfilled; the 'epic of colonisation' hardly extends beyond this first volume; the historical background, as the work proceeds, becomes, if not forgotten, more and more faintly adumbrated. The *milieu* falls away, and the individual human fates usurp its place, just as had been the case in *Maurice Guest:* thus *Richard Mahony* has not become the novel of colonisation which many would have liked to see it become, any more than the earlier novel became a 'musical' novel. *The Fortunes of Richard Mahony* is the history of Richard Mahony, not of the land in which it is placed. (pp. 178-80)

The Way Home is a finer work than *Australia Felix;* richer and more varied in its changing scene; peopled with a wider range of clear-cut personalities; subtler in its psychology; and more carefully polished in its English style. (p. 183)

The best pages of *The Way Home* are perhaps just in those scenes in England with which it opens. Nothing Henry Handel Richardson has done shows the qualities of her peculiar art in a more engaging form than these. *Maurice Guest,* with its leisurely realistic way, its endeavour to leave nothing unsaid that might be said, had been reproached for a breadth and diffuseness of treatment which sometimes became even tedious; here everything is concentrated, reduced to the fewest possible words. (pp. 185-86)

The Way Home tempts to quotation, for it is the most multicoloured and varied of all Henry Handel Richardson's books; in no other has she given so rich and meaty a slice of life as here, or has been so lavish with her imagination. There are so many people and fates here which seem to cry out for expansion into independent books. So living are the subsidiary figures, so engaging are they, that she has exposed herself to the not unjustified criticism that the central theme, the ruthless downward progress of her central figure is—at least for the reader still unfamiliar with the final volume of his fortunes—at times obscured, and the vivid presentation of the Melbourne of the 'seventies of last century tempts us to forget the individual fate. (p. 190)

A change necessarily comes over the character and method of the work with [the tragic *Ultima Thule*]. The motley colonial world that had given variety and gaiety to *The Way Home* passes into a shadowy background, or, indeed, disappears altogether. The scene may change, and does change, more restlessly than before; . . . but this lonely man in his growing mental degeneration shuns his kind, and his kind plays less and less a rôle in his chronicle. The human *staffage* is reduced; it becomes more episodic and shadowy. (p. 196)

It is a very terrible book, this history of a mind diseased, one of the tragic books of our time. Looking back over the three volumes, one realises how firm and spacious was the plan of *Richard Mahony:* how his life-history, with the inevitableness of an impersonal fate, has been forged. One becomes aware of the constructive strength of its creator, of the art which never falters, which never fails to rise through a thousand pages to a fuller tragic music. Harrowing and poignant as are Mahony's sufferings from the beginning . . . there are always deeper depths, and greater tragic heights to come. (pp. 196-97)

[Compared to *Maurice Guest*,] Richard Mahony's personal tragedy may be deeper and more intolerable to the sensitive sympathiser; but it plays against a more positive background: one feels that the author recognises in the conduct of human things a 'somehow good' which balances the sufferings of the individual. (p. 200)

This positive element is provided by Richard's wife Mary, the personification of the forces that built and build up new communities. As Richard sinks, Mary rises; his mental disruption is balanced by the growing strength of will and purpose in his life-companion; and the book ends less with Richard Mahony's tragic passing through the night of insanity to the grave than in her spiritual and moral triumph. (pp. 200-01)

The realism of *Richard Mahony* . . . goes much further than that of *Maurice Guest.* The people of the later book are Englishmen and Englishwomen of the now so remote period we describe as Victorian. . . . It was accounted as a serious relapse on the part of the author that, after the realistic modernity of *Maurice Guest,* she should have filled her new book with the commonplace happenings and limited outlook, the old-fashioned things that might have been transferred from any novel of the older time. (p. 204)

But complete realism applied to the historical past is, and must always remain, something of a chimera; and it has been justly pointed out that the realism of *Richard Mahony* is after all only relative. With the best will in the world the author cannot suppress her twentieth-century standpoint and her twentieth-century art—as little here as in *The Getting of Wisdom.* (p. 207)

[There] is no 'plot' here in the sense in which the Victorians understood it. Henry Handel Richardson has dispensed with it; she has eschewed all erotic interest, and confronted the enormously difficult task of erecting a stupendous span without such adventitious aids. The construction of *Maurice Guest* was still the construction of a novel with a plot; the construction of *Richard Mahony* is stripped of all semblance to the arbitrary happenings of a novel. Everything has vital significance in this web of human fates; not one incident, however trivial, or apparently episodic and inessential, but takes its place, inexorably as in life itself. That she has achieved this structural unity, built an edifice of imposing proportions, in which every scene and personage dovetails with perfect fitness into the whole, seems to us the greatest achievement of *The Fortunes of Richard Mahony.* Yet in the end what holds the interest in this long book of human fates is not so much its architectural sureness and strength, qualities that only become apparent on reflection; but the intense life of its personages. (p. 210)

> J. G. Robertson, "The Art of Henry Handel Richardson" (1929), in Myself When Young by Henry Handel Richardson (reprinted by permission of W. W. Norton & Company, Inc.; in Canada by William Heinemann Limited; copyright 1948 by W. W. Norton & Company, Inc.; all rights reserved), Norton, 1948, pp. 153-210.

M. BARNARD ELDERSHAW [Marjorie Faith Barnard and Flora Sydney Patricia Eldershaw]   (essay date 1938)

Henry Handel Richardson is interested above all in people. Her preoccupation is not with ideas, philosophical or literary, but with her characters. She sees life as a dualism and a duel, between the ego and the alter, the alter being all that is not ego, the external world and its inhabitants. To her, as to Shakespeare, character is fate, and the individual life resolves itself like an equation. When a man of a certain temperament finds himself in a certain society and in certain circumstances the inevitable result works itself out with almost mathematical precision. A man's character is the product of his inheritance and the environment of his youth. . . . We are the victims not only of our characters but also of our bodies. The most tragic part of Mahony's tragedy is the mental and moral disintegration that accompany his physical decline. He was a man of honour, gentle, kind and sensitive, a loving husband and father, but his illness changes all that. . . . He was throughout his own victim. First his nature tormented him and then his body betrayed him. This is tragedy piled on tragedy. To be the victim of God or of Fate has something of nobility about it, an heroical touch. But to be one's own victim, forced to all one loathes by one's physical decay, is as ugly and humiliating a fate as a man can have. (pp. 9-10)

There is behind *The Fortunes of Richard Mahony* a relentless philosophy of life. Realism in presentation is the natural vestment of such a philosophy. We are shown every step of Mahony's *via crucis* and the author displays the deepest sympathy and understanding in her portrayal of the three lives most deeply involved, but that sympathy and understanding do not deflect her one inch from her purpose. She is pitiless. No trace of sentimentality or tinge of romanticism softens the outline of the story. An understanding that sees so clearly and shows so little sign of blenching is almost a function of cruelty. There is something god-like about it. It has a driving strength that makes the book, for all it deals of commonplace happenings, terrible and frightening.

Although *The Fortunes of Richard Mahony* is a black tragedy, it is neither defeatist nor pessimistic. Defeatism softens tragedy; there is nothing to soften this, least of all acquiescence. . . . The tragedy would have been deprived of some of its bitterness had the victims consented [to their crushing lot]. Conflict is the essence of it. Neither is the author's outlook pessimistic. Mahony's troubles come from within, not from without. The world is not hostile to him; it is indifferent. He is as he is and pulls his fate down on top of himself. (pp. 10-11)

Because of her general outlook, the author's interest is centred upon her characters, and it is upon the characterization that the value of the book depends. Richardson reveals her people gradually, not in analysis or statement but by showing us their reactions to the events of their daily life. We get to know them through their hopes, disappointments and irritations. We are given their innermost thoughts, and these thoughts and feelings are not removed a step from us by being passed through the medium of the author; we are shown them in the mind and heart of the character. . . . The reader grows to know the Mahonys very intimately, so intimately that for the duration of the book we almost live inside their skins. Every thing in the book is focused to illuminate the principal characters, Richard Mahony, Mary, and, in *Ultima Thule*, Cuffy. They loom large against a background that is composed of events and minor characters as well as of the natural scene. *Ultima Thule*, for all its vast cumulation of detail and incident, is a very concentrated book, for behind its richness is a single directed idea—the exploitation of Mahony's tragedy. It is safe to say that there is no event, no detail, no remark even, in the whole length of the novel that is not directed by irony, by contrast or by simple statement to further or to lay bare that tragedy. There are no irrelevancies. If there is no passage that does not affect the tragedy there is also no passage unaffected by it and yet the many-sided attack upon the story, the numerous minor characters, give the impression that here is a page torn out of life and presented unedited. This greatly enhances the power of the book and lends to the story an almost crushing sense of reality. The reader is overcome by volume. But the transcription *is* edited, and ruthlessly edited. Both event and natural background are entirely subjugated to the main object of the novel and the minor characters are allowed just sufficient irrelevance to make them appear like real people with

sharply drawn characteristics and an individual idiom. But they, too, are little more than obstacles in Mahony's path, exasperating incidents in his painful journey. Nothing and nobody is shown independently in relation to it but only in relation to Mahony. (pp. 12-13)

The first two books are told more objectively, but most of *Ultima Thule* is told subjectively, through the minds of Richard, Mary or Cuffy. As the story progresses Cuffy takes an ever larger part in it, events are shown more and more through his reactions to them. Because he is still a child, and because nothing is ever explained candidly to him, he does not fully understand what is going on; but he feels it none the less acutely for that. The poignancy of the story is greatly increased by the child's helpless part in it. Cuffy is no stock character, no 'innocent little child' of fiction. He is an individual drawn with delicacy, certainty and endless detail. He is the true and final measure of the author's pitiless attitude to her people. (pp. 18-19)

In the close-drawn unity of this book the prose plays its part. Prose and theme are closely modelled to one another. The prose does not compete with the narrative. It is in a way inconspicuous, because it is so much part of the story. Richardson is not a stylist, and this is a definite advantage in a book so intensely introspective and emotional. As the story is told largely from within, most of the prose is in character and a great deal of it is in broken sentences, the shorthand of the mind. (p. 20)

> *M. Barnard Eldershaw (pseudonym of Marjorie Faith Barnard and Flora Sydney Patricia Eldershaw), "Two Women Novelists," in her* Essays in Australian Fiction, *Melbourne University Press, 1938 (and reprinted by Books for Libraries Press, 1970), pp. 1-40.*

ELIZABETH BOWEN   (essay date 1948)

[Richardson's autobiography *Myself When Young*] is not a work of art. The style in which it is written is bluff, pedestrian; it could be the style of some honest, natural person who had not written before. At a first glance the object of the author might seem to be nothing more than to forge forward, at a steady pace, page by page, through time. Almost no passage directly illuminates the imagination of the reader; the selection of words would seem to have been, if not careless, utilitarian. The effect is domestic. And, in the matter of content, as to what has been set down, there could have been little discrimination other than memory's.

This was probably so. Henry Handel Richardson must have accepted that one remembers nothing that is not, somehow, important; that memory is the editor of one's sense of life. In that case, she submitted herself, when writing *Myself When Young,* to an inner, arbitrary dictation. To do this was an abnegation on the part of the artist, for whom creativeness means, most of all, choice. She may have begun writing with no design, no intention other than that of letting the submerged design of her life, like something hitherto written in invisible ink, appear. This could account for her abandonment, now that it was a matter of autobiography, of the whole illusory element comprehended in our idea of style: style in that sense notably served her when she wrote the novels—without that they could not have had their force. What she must have understood was, that in writing *Myself When Young* she was not creating, but, rather, contemplating what had created her. Her object, now, was not to set up illusion but, rather, to penetrate to its early source: she must, therefore, have fought shy of the magic that for any writer cannot but emanate from words. With the undiscriminating patience of a stenographer, she "took down."

The result is, an objectivity rare in autobiography—rarest of all in the autobiography of a novelist, for whom it is exceedingly difficult not to select, place, evaluate, dramatize and, thereby, virtually, invent.

> Elizabeth Bowen, "The Evolution of a Novelist," in The Times Literary Supplement (© Times Newspapers Ltd. (London) 1948; reproduced from The Times Literary Supplement by permission), No. 2424, July 17, 1948, p. 395.

NETTIE PALMER   (essay date 1950)

The Getting of Wisdom was mature, in spite of some roughness and unevenness of the style. H.H.R. had framed her work, not on conventional lines, but according to her own vision of the truth. In this it was an utterly unusual, an original book. For stories of school-life, like those of youth in general, had scarcely ever been written, at least in English-speaking countries, with even an approach to honesty. In them the emotion was misdirected to docility. They seemed to have been designed by teacherly persons, their object the concealment of the truth about the relations between young people themselves, or between young people and the grownups who expected their obedience and took for granted their delighted co-operation in adult schemes! (p. 30)

The outstanding quality of *The Getting of Wisdom* being this determination to get truth into a form unused to holding so eruptive an element . . . the result is a book for which only one comparison suggests itself in English. Even from that one "oceans divide it and the width of seas". The book is *Huckleberry Finn*. What they have in common is just this, that they were written with no holding back, no recognition of the conventions of the day or the attitudes decreed for young people. (pp. 31-2)

It is merely on the surface that *The Getting of Wisdom* seems as a school-story to be lifted safely above the quaking social ground of Huck Finn on the banks of the Mississippi. The apparently uniform security of the young ladies in the Melbourne boarding-school is riddled through and through by Laura's consciousness of poverty with its breath of social ostracism, and the school's and its scholars' insistence on orthodoxy in the matter of ideas and behaviour is again cut across by Laura's questionings, outspoken or silent. These questionings, in matters personal, social, even religious, are firmly and plainly made, though not pressed home at length; so that, by the end of the book, when Laura "dances away over her own self", the reader, through Laura, has passed through a subtly shattering experience. This, in spite of the ironic humour that plays over all the girl's experiences.

The book, then, was original in that it presented the realities of a girl's world not only with devastating truth but with gaiety. It took lightly things that were customarily treated with solemnity, took seriously things it was usual to

ignore. All the problems that confront a growing girl were met, but they were *not* framed so as to be solved successively as in some "Fairchild Family" thesis. They arose out of a natural scene or episode and had an air of inevitability. (pp. 32-3)

The book is as little concerned as *Huckleberry Finn* with the explicit ideas of a child's psyche that have become common since Freud. Novelists do not work from abstractions, following where psychologists have led the way. Often it is the other way about. Freud himself confessed that he frequently took his subject-matter from novels, since it was easier to study character and action in a small, ordered world than in the chaotic one presented to his daily vision. *The Getting of Wisdom*, then, is not a jumble of twentieth-century ideas in a nineteenth-century setting; it is an account of one girl's development, shown in a drama of small actions, conflicts, unforeseen consequences, and treated for the main part in a spirit of comedy. Laura blunders through school, making her mistakes, and the results are shown. (p. 41)

[The dominant force in *Maurice Guest* is] the magnetic and stormy figure of Louise Dufrayer. (p. 51)

But Louise is not only a more robust character than Maurice; she is a considerably more complicated one. As one of her friends remarks, she has a talent for suffering. If there is one word for her temperament, for her egoistic demands on life, it is "Bovarism"—that phenomenon of the nineteenth century, that map of the *femme fatale* outlined with such finality by Flaubert. Like Emma Bovary, Louise not merely wishes to be happy on her own terms; she takes it as her right, and at anyone's expense. It is as a wholly exceptional person, to whom extraordinary emotions occur, that she asserts herself. (pp. 58-9)

[Louise] depends for her charm largely on the author's sympathetic treatment of her, particularly in the way she is introduced, first as a legend (scandalous, it is true, but arresting), then as a vision whose radiance almost strikes Maurice blind. When he actually encounters her and they speak to each other, her behaviour could, in a person less favoured, be described as clumsy and self-conscious, but it is through his enamoured eyes that we see her. That same evening she declares to Maurice her "Bovarism", her assurance of her own rarity. . . . All with her is based on her own contention that whatever she does is bound to be extraordinary; that she is entitled to be made happy because she is beautiful and unusual, capable of great feeling, great suffering. (pp. 59-60)

[Louise has] a feverish vitality—a vitality much greater than in other modified or embryo Bovarys in English fiction, such as Thackeray's superficial young schemer, Blanche Amory, with her simpering, "*Il me faut des émotions*," or Rosamond, the greedy, empty little wife of Lydgate in [George Eliot's] *Middlemarch*. . . . (pp. 60-1)

Louise's ennui and exactingness of egoism are on a grander scale, lifted up out of the world of petty moods and reactions by the way they are shown as sombre reflections of her passion for Schilsky, a passion that has so consumed her that nothing counts beside it—reputation, security, or even self-respect. She has had many affairs, and yet she is not a light woman. The power of her feeling for this scoundrel of genius redeems her. (p. 61)

[*The Fortunes of Richard Mahoney* also shows concern for the growth of a strong woman in the depiction of] the emergence of Mary as a woman of initiative and courage, a positive support for the failing Richard. Without the vital principle she supplies to it the book would be a catalogue of unrelieved miseries—not a tragedy, but a mere study in decay and despair. Mary, with her developing strength of will and purpose, is a personification of all the forces that struggle to give life meaning and continuity. It is not only a matter of her common sense and physical vigour; it is something spiritual, something that arises from the depths of her nature. (p. 107)

Probably Henry Handel Richardson was not consciously affirming any general principle about the vitality of women, their greater toughness and tenacity than men's, when she made Mary rise to her full height after the breakdown of Richard. Mary's development in will and a sense of responsibility has something inevitable about it. It is in line with powers that had been visible in her all along; now dormant, now flickering into life; her capacity for smoothing out the many difficulties into which Mahony's temperament had landed them, her stoicism in the face of adversity, her quick adaptation to the role of mother after many childless years. In many ways she has markedly individual features and is not merely a type. (p. 112)

[It] is through her maternal instinct that [Mary] embodies the regenerative forces of woman. Very early in her life with Richard she had adopted the attitude of a mother towards a wayward child, and it is the thought that he is injuring the prospects of the other children that makes her heart harden towards him when he is going through his torments at Barambogie. . . . It would take little, it seems, to make her break from him altogether and set off to make some sort of separate life for herself and the children.

Yet when the blow falls and he is helpless, all the protective instincts of her nature make her rush to his support. The conventional lady, who has narrow, precise ideas about her place in society, recedes into the background, and the essential woman emerges. Spiritedly she accepts the responsibility of earning the family living, sets herself to learning the work of a small post-office, and by soliciting the help of old friends manages to get Richard into a private hospital where he can have every comfort. When it is plain that his case is hopeless and he has to be committed to an asylum, she follows every step of his descent with the eyes of a quickening imagination. . . . The scene in which she battles for possession of Richard with her old admirer, Henry Ocock, who has become an influential Minister, shows her at her fighting best. Outspoken to him about his hypocrisies as never before, she imposes her personality on him so effectively that he ends by complying with her demands. . . . Finally Mahony is released on probation and brought round by boat—a broken, distraught lunatic in the care of rough attendants—to the little port where she awaits him; her mother-love rushes out to receive his battered figure and enfolds it to the end. (pp. 113-14)

This insistence on the protective mother, undaunted by the many catastrophes of life, even stimulated by the shock of them, brings a positive element to the ending of the Mahony trilogy. Are there blind or sinister forces in the universe, battering down the innocent head? Perhaps so, but they are not more powerful, finally, than the reserves of human courage and tenderness. Mary's growth in the

ability to cope with all the disasters that fall upon her and Richard suggests something beyond her personal capacities or those of her sex. She is a symbol of the recuperative forces of humanity. The individual, you hear a quiet voice asserting as you watch her, may be overwhelmed and perish, but life goes on. (p. 115)

Nettie Palmer, in her Henry Handel Richardson *(reprinted with the permission of Angus & Robertson (UK) Ltd Publishers), Angus & Robertson, 1950, 214 p.*

A. D. HOPE (essay date 1955)

[*Maurice Guest*] is a novel which displays Henry Handel Richardson's characteristic gifts as a novelist and her even more characteristic defects: her uncertain, sometimes sloppy and often wooden prose style, which in *The Young Cosima* often degenerates into passages of sheer journalese; her distrust of, or paucity of imagination and her consequent rather tedious reliance on agglomerations of detail and a too careful 'documentation' of her effects; above all, her frequent failure to handle dialogue at important or critical moments of a novel. It is this, particularly, which spoils the effect of *Maurice Guest*. (p. 186)

In spite of its failings, *Maurice Guest* is a very interesting book and in many ways a profound book. It may be a spoiled work of genius but it *is* a work of genius nevertheless. And of all the works of Henry Handel Richardson it has most often been misrepresented and misunderstood. None of her critics, so far as I know, has been able to agree as to just what sort a novel it is. It has been described as a 'musical' novel, that is, as a novel whose main purpose is to give a picture of the world of music and musicians. And in one sense of course it is. This, in fact, seems to have been Henry Handel Richardson's main purpose in the first draft of the book. It is also plainly a study of tragic failure like *The Fortunes of Richard Mahony*. . . .

There has been some suggestion that the book is one of those novels which can be described as concealed biographies. There is something to support this view: all Henry Handel Richardsons' books, except *The Young Cosima*, are in one sense or another about herself. (p. 188)

But any attempt to look at *Maurice Guest* as an autobiographical novel must fail. . . . The argument that *Maurice Guest* is an autobiographical novel must fail, not because there is too little evidence for it but because there is too much. The essential difference between this book and *The Getting of Wisdom* is that in *Maurice Guest* the author enters into it everywhere. It is not a self-portrait or even a projection of herself into another character, but a whole world created out of herself, a world in which you can find parts of her everywhere and all of her nowhere.

Other critics have seen the book as a study of the nature of love—but love seen as a disruptive and destructive force in human life. And of course it *is*. What they have missed I think is that it is very much more than that.

H. M. Green in his *Outline of Australian Literature* describes the book as a story of tragic love, and he seems to think of Maurice and Louise as people whose obsessive and overwhelming passions imprison them and cut them off from the life around them and finally destroy them. Its theme, in fact, is the destructive effects of love. (pp. 189-90)

In spite of the fact that devastating and destructive passion takes up a very large part of it, [*Maurice Guest*] *is* a book about the musical temperament—or rather, about musical genius—and it is only a book about love inasmuch as the highest manifestation of love and of art have this in common that they require something that we call genius. Louise has the genius for love. Maurice has not. Schilsky has the genius for music. Maurice has not. What the book is about is what Maurice does not possess and cannot attain. What he neither possesses nor attains is made clear by what Schilsky and Louise and to a less extent Krafft are endowed with by their very natures. It is because the critics have misunderstood the meaning of this endowment that they have gone completely astray in their estimate of Maurice Guest himself.

They are not, perhaps, to be blamed for this. For the book presents readers with a deliberate trap for unwary players. It wears a mask, the mask which Nietzsche held to be a necessity of profound art to protect it from false and superficial interpretations. (pp. 191-92)

[*Maurice Guest*] is thoroughly imbued with some of Nietzsche's leading ideas. There is first of all the notion of two sorts of people. One is what Nietzsche calls the higher men or the free spirits, the other the members of the herd, the servile spirits, those who are incapable of the energy, the intellectual, artistic, or merely social will to power. Two moralities go with these two types of men. The 'free spirit' lives in a world beyond good and evil. More than that, the artist, as free spirit, will be what Nietzsche calls a *morbid* type. The test that he is a strong or superior spirit is the amount of morbidity, suffering and what (in ordinary terms) we call degeneracy he can absorb and yet remain strong and healthy and creative. The higher he rises above the spiritual values of ordinary humanity the deeper his roots will go down into the abyss. Now this is characteristic of Louise, Schilsky and Krafft. They not only represent each in his or her own way an aspect of genius, they are not only amoral and despise or ignore ordinary standards of behaviour, they not only have the single-mindedness of great men in pursuing their own peculiar genius, but they are also, from the ordinary point of view, morbid and degenerate types, sexually perverted, enjoying suffering in themselves and others. Schilsky is the creative genius, the Dionysiac artist par excellence; Krafft is the philosopher, the transvaluer of values. His discussion of Madeleine's moral views, of Maurice's shortcomings as an artist, and his defence of Louise are pure Nietzscheanism. Maurice's failure as an artist is total and absolute and it is shown to depend on more than mediocrity of talent. It depends also on his solid virtues, the limitations of his moral attitude, the lack of morbidity and the lack of power to transcend the conventions. (pp. 193-94)

Looked at in this way Maurice's passion for Louise is not what ruins his career as an artist. It is the last chance that fate offers him to break into the world of free spirits, to win his salvation as an artist. But it fails because, as Krafft observes, he has nothing of the artist in him. He has not even a *touch* of genius. And this comes out very clearly in his relations with Louise. His attitude is always servile. Even his attempts to force her to submit to him, his bullying, his beating of her are the actions of a petulant child. His nature is not elevated or freed by passion and suffering, it is simply disintegrated by coming into contact with something too powerful for it to deal with. (pp. 194-95)

Louise has the strength, the capacity for suffering, the single-mindedness and comprehension of genius. Once again this is Maurice's misfortune. He can neither understand it, cope with it nor rise to it. He remains on the level of servile and conventional passion. This I think is where Nettie Palmer, the only critic to recognise that Louise represents a type of genius, goes wrong when she compares Louise with Flaubert's *Madame Bovary* as an example of the *femme fatale* [see excerpt above]. Flaubert's heroine is much more like Maurice Guest, provincial, mediocre, the victim of circumstances rather than the maker and dominator of circumstance. . . . It is doubtful whether we should call even Maurice's fate a tragedy. Tragedy is for great souls. Those who confront their destiny adequately and are still defeated—what Aristotle calls the higher sorts of men. Maurice belongs to the lower sorts of men. His fate is not tragic: it is a grim comedy: it is at best pathetic.

The question might arise: Is Henry Handel Richardson simply giving us a picture of the Nietzschean cult and its effect, or does she subscribe to the views that Krafft expresses? Are they in fact the theme of the novel? It is impossible to tell. 'Everything that is profound,' to quote Nietzsche again, 'loves the mask.' *Maurice Guest* is a profound book and the mask of art is here inscrutable. But I would point out that if Henry Handel Richardson had *not* subscribed to the views I have put forward, it is remarkable that she has limited her pictures of genius to those types of people who meet Nietzsche's views exactly. (pp. 195-96)

A. D. Hope, "Henry Handel Richardson's 'Maurice Guest'," in Meanjin, *Vol. XIV, No. 2, June, 1955, pp. 186-99.*

VINCENT BUCKLEY (essay date 1961)

[Both *Maurice Guest* and *The Young Cosima*] move in a world of music and musicians, and have for their underlying theme—indeed, their first premiss—a contention about the extraordinary rights and privileges of "genius". (p. 9)

[But *Maurice Guest*] is not a mere account of how musicians live, a mere slice of exotically erotic life.

What are we to take it as being, then? Nettie Palmer calls it a great love story; but A. D. Hope rightly points out that it is also an analysis of the nature of genius [see excerpt above]. It is, in part at least, a translation into dramatic terms of certain Nietzschean categories; love and art are seen not as contradictory but as complementary; artistic genius and a "genius for love" are much the same thing in the end.

To me, this dimension of the novel is the most interesting thing about it, and Hope's essay establishes and defines it with enviable authority. But we must not allow a perception of its presence, or a personal interest in the questions it poses, to blind us to the fact that most of Richardson's emotional force, most of her insistent analysis, does in fact go into the presentation of a love-relationship. A thesis about the nature and prerogatives of genius is the most important premiss and theme of the novel; but so far as its surface workings are concerned, most of the creative energy goes into the depiction of a relationship which touches explicitly on the theme of genius only at moments. (pp. 9-10)

Also, since the modes in which it is written are naturalistic ones which appeared novel and revolutionary when Richardson was using them, we must recognise that love-story and genius-theme are both set in the context of a pretty factual account of student life. It does give much of the surface of that life, and dwells on its detail with a naturalist's curiosity. It seems to me, in fact, that the stress carried by the closing chapters is very different from that carried by the opening ones. It opens as an unequivocally naturalistic work, confident of its facts and interested in little else than facts. The very first paragraph of Chapter I has a posed, deliberate air, a quality of no-nonsense, let's-get-the-facts-straight-for-I'm-going-to-tell-you-a-story.... But if it gives the impression of being confident about the "facts", it seems to have little assurance with anything else. The prose in this opening chapter is too expository, too much a servant of "fact"; it has a laboured quality, as though the emotional effort to get everything into a factual perspective had robbed it of suppleness and drained it of any individuality which might have come to it from the sensibility of its author. Dullness sweeps in on a soft wave of cliché.... (p. 10)

The tensions of the artistic life are much more interesting as they appear in Louise than as they appear in Maurice: the love-story, the explicit theme of genius, and Richardson's preoccupation with emotional experience, all meet more richly in her than in Maurice. More richly, but more ambiguously. Despite all the people ... who give differing accounts of Louise, our sense of her remains clamped within the cloyingly romantic terms in which Maurice first sees her. Perhaps she is too marginally and arbitrarily presented, so that she never seems a full fictional person but only a function of other people's emotional lives. (p. 13)

The issues dramatised in the figure of Louise are important ones, and we do get some sense of their urgency. Patently, Richardson herself has an acute and generous awareness of what causes the rhythmic life-movement of such a person as Louise; the fluctuation in moods which seems arbitrary to everyone else no doubt has its own logic, which Richardson is aware of. But she doesn't adequately translate this awareness into dramatic terms.... Without adequate dramatisation of the figure who provides its subject, what does all the repetitive and fulsome analysis actually analyse? (p. 14)

Krafft is to my mind the most interesting figure in the book. I am not sure what it would mean to call him a "character", for he is simply a figure whom one sees in different stances of drollness, of unaffected friendliness, of absorption in the piano, of the man crucified by his own temperament, or pouring out different judgments on the world. He is always acting a part but, despite the cursory way in which he is presented, one is always conscious of him as an entity, a focus for values, a centre of anguish. Where Schilsky is the walking paragon of the Nietzschean philosophy, Krafft is its exponent. Judged by Madeleine's criteria, he is "our spoilt child"; but we learn that he is in fact an advanced nihilist, amoral, self-destructive, obsessed by death yet fascinated by the prospect of absorption into nothingness, the excitable ascetic of "art". Compared with him, Maurice is dull, and even his hero Schilsky is in a way mindless: possibly because he is presented in a surprisingly cursory way, and his "genius", which is so ardently talked about, is never really demonstrated.

Only in the figure of Krafft does Richardson break at all

purposively out of the wave of her own naturalistic exposition, on which her emotions bob like so many over-inflated balloons. (p. 15)

Richardson's method ensures that she will be at her strongest when recording physical or social events and at her weakest when seeking to catch the deepest pulse of the human being. The longer and more concentrated her gaze at the first, the weaker is her sense of the second. That is why, in the more emotional scenes, we are conscious of a lack of tact and a tendency to inflation. Even if her prose were much more flexible than it is, her perspective on human lives would still be inadequate.

But manners, social tendencies, release her talent and make her prose relatively supple.... On this level of generality, her sense of the human drama is released into a phrasing at times brilliantly expressive.... (p. 16)

But in general, the prose suffers as much as human understanding does from the earnest, insistent, inflationary habits of the naturalistic novelist. *Maurice Guest* is not the great tragedy it is often said to be. It is a lopsided half-grown giant which began as a slice of life, developed into a love-story, and ended as a dramatisation of certain Nietzschean ideas. Its hero begins as a middling-interesting, representative figure, but is soon rendered null by the size of the issues the author creates around him. She communicates a sense of the importance, even the urgency, of those issues; but her own preoccupations make it almost impossible for her to balance them against the other elements in the novel.

Nearly forty years after *Maurice Guest* was started, Richardson produced her last novel, *The Young Cosima*. There is some evidence that she had grown dissatisfied with her earlier treatment of the genius-theme, and had now decided to have another go at it. The story in itself is very different from that of *Maurice Guest*: it is a story not of failure but of success, not of artistic apprentices but of artistic masters, not of emotional decline but of personal fulfilment. But the underlying theme is the same: the theme of the prerogatives of genius, and of the immense gulf between genius and mere talent. Now these issues are embodied in the historical persons of Wagner, Liszt, Hans von Bülow, and Cosima von Bülow (née Liszt). (pp. 16-17)

It is true that by comparison with *Maurice Guest* the tone [of *The Young Cosima*] is more even, the author's attitude calmer, the sense of plot more balanced, and the focus on one figure more economically kept throughout. And it is likely that virtues have resulted from a quite deliberate choice by the author, who had decided to rectify the imbalance of *Maurice Guest*. But they are all craftsman's virtues: by themselves they signify very little. The novel lacks the sweep and the urgency which *Maurice Guest* had, in however ill-balanced a combination; and if the emotions are less melodramatically deployed in the later novel, it is not because they are more firmly controlled and directed, but because they are more coyly sentimentalised, more (in a word) domesticated. *Maurice Guest* was flawed by its novelese; *The Young Cosima* is built upon novelese. (p. 18)

The historical situation which Richardson recreates seems to me much more interesting than her recreation of it. Her method is as naturalistic as in any of her books, but her spirit is intolerably sentimental. Her pretence of intimacy with the inner lives of her characters is, in a way, a fraud, because she offers no evidence in the actual writing of being able to overcome her own quite disabling remoteness from those lives. From the opening conversation between Liszt and von Bulow, with its absurdly stilted and stagey quality, the writing keeps us at a distance from the human significance of the drama. Cosima is not romanticised as Louise was, but neither is she adequately explored.

And the prose cringes and limps under its burden of melodramatic emphasis. . . . Insignificant actions are inflated to an absurd size; and cliché abounds. These eminent musicians rack their brains, tear their hair, shake in their shoes, dash the back of their hands over their eyes, and throw up the sponge, while their women's eyes bore like gimlets. A sneeze is an heroic gesture, and Wagner blowing his nose actually causes "a trumpet-peal". Dialogue becomes a debased version of a set of speeches in an heroic drama. . . . (pp. 19-20)

It is hard to take seriously questions about the prerogatives of genius when they are presented in such a mode. The characters glide to their predictable ends on a long current of novelese, broken only here and there by a piece of sharp observation. And the issues themselves are cheapened; we don't feel anything equivalent to the urgency with which the power, and the ambiguities, of the Nietzschean ethic are expressed in the persons of Louise and Krafft. On the contrary, we are presented with a circulating-library dream of genius: a dream of unpredictability domesticated. The novel seems to me a nonentity, worth dealing with in any detail only because the claim has been made that it corrects the imbalance and imprecision which married *Maurice Guest*. (p. 20)

[*The Getting of Wisdom*] has generally been taken as marginal to [Richardson's] real achievement; but I am inclined to think that, in a definable though perhaps paradoxical sense, it is a much more serious work than either of the two "musical novels". In it, Richardson delves not into the ethos of the continental world of art but into her own Australian childhood; it is a fictional account of a young girl's education in the Melbourne of the 1880's. It has in common with *Maurice Guest* only these two facts: that it records and analyses a process of education, and that it is the education of an artist, or at the very least an artistically-inclined person. *The Getting of Wisdom* is her *Portrait of the Artist as a Young Girl*. (pp. 20-1)

The chief, the guiding demand [of the novel] is for honesty, that things should not be falsified. Only if you refuse to be content with appearances, with pressures towards hypocrisy and invitations to conform, can you "get wisdom, get understanding". But the temptation to be content with appearances is strong; it is particularly strong in a budding artist, for whom art may seem to be a glittering decoration on reality or a fantasy-substitute for reality. And since no one can become an artist unless he has met and faced and overcome this tendency in himself, the growth of the artist will be, in a particularly intense way, a growth in the sense of and concern for reality. The getting of wisdom is a learning to understand one's real self as well as the selves of others.

There is no need to trace the steps by which Laura Ramsbotham grows gradually and indirectly in understanding. . . . But it is necessary to stress that one basic datum in Laura's character is her foreign-ness. She is initially quite alien to the way of life followed and taught in the Ladies'

College; but that is a difference chiefly of manners. What is finally more important is the profoundly different sense of her own being and destiny with which she leaves the school; an incidental foreign-ness has become a vocationally necessary one.

It is thus not only a novel of social relationships but a novel of moral growth: of a growth which is painfully salutary precisely because Laura makes one desperate shift after another to conform to her companions' expectations but finds in the end that no shift will do; reality makes its own demands, and conformism, so tempting yet so inappropriate to the budding artist, is made impossible by those very demands.

The story opens *in medias res,* with nothing of that posed quality which makes the beginning of *Maurice Guest* and of *The Young Cosima* so much a stiff set-piece; and in this opening chapter the themes of the novel are held in embryo, much as they are held in the opening section of *A Portrait of the Artist as a Young Man.* Laura, aged 12, a stubborn and rebellious yet loving child, is the spinner of romantic fantasies for her younger brothers and sister. Yet she is much more acutely, much more feelingly aware of the domestic realities around her than of the stories she spins. Her translation to the city and its Ladies' College involves not only a physical shift to an alien environment but also a psychological change from the enjoyment of a privileged position among her inferiors to the endurance of an inferior status among girls who are superior to her in every respect that matters to them. At home, her independence of mind and her spontaneity of behaviour, though they led her into many social prickles, were an asset; at school, they appear as a combination of gaucherie, ill-breeding, and nonconformism. To conform, then, as she so desperately desires, involves a de-naturing of the unspoiled spoilt child. But the point is, that she proves incapable of conforming: her mind has too much integrity and her observation of people and manners too much acuteness. It is as though her vocation were built into her personality.

What she learns from her series of trials and self-trials is the lessons that are most valuable to an artist: that her mother's criterion of "niceness" is as irrelevant to the truth of things as the schoolgirl's criterion of "position"; that to yield too eagerly to the conventional expectations of you is to invite ridicule; that most people are unable to distinguish between fantasy and reality and on the whole prefer fantasy; and that while the world is concerned with "facts", the artist is concerned with truth. . . . But it is of little use to the artist who, after all, has no definable "place in the class"; what is important even to the twelve-year-old artist is neither fantasy nor "fact" but reality noted with a peculiar force and placed by her own individual personality. (pp. 21-3)

[So when] Laura leaves school, she does so in that ambiguous condition which is the most fruitful of all spiritual conditions for the growth of a young artist:

> She went out from school with the uncomfortable sense of being a square peg, which fitted into none of the round holes of her world; the wisdom she had got, the experience she was richer by, had, in the process of equipping her for life, merely seemed to disclose her unfitness. She could not then know that, even for the squarest peg, the

right hole may ultimately be found; seeming unfitness prove to be only another aspect of a peculiar and special fitness.   (p. 23)

[*The Getting of Wisdom*] is delightful in its very complexity. The first thing that strikes one about it is the very noticeable directness of attack and economy of means which, after a reading of the "musical novels", we should never have expected from Richardson. The prose never strains, and the story (it is hardly a "plot") never rambles. The observation is frequently acute, and is as often compassionate or intense as it is cosmic. We feel here, as we don't feel in *The Young Cosima*,that Richardson's gaze is fixed benignly yet penetratingly on the "reality" which she sets such store by. It is a minor masterpiece of compassionate comedy, but its concerns are refreshingly serious. (pp. 23-4)

> Vincent Buckley, in his Henry Handel Richardson *(reprinted by permission of the author), Lansdowne Press, 1961, 36 p.*

LEONIE KRAMER (essay date 1964)

The work of Henry Handel Richardson, . . . whether Australian or European in setting, displays a preoccupation with certain themes, and a consistent, though not uniformly successful approach to the writing of fiction. The world of Richardson is inhabited by two kinds of people—those who live and abide by the standards and demands of ordinary life, and those who legislate for themselves. Her failures—Maurice Guest and Richard Mahony—have aspirations beyond their talents. Her successes, Schilsky and Wagner, even Louise Dufrayer, succeed by a ruthless disregard for convention, and by surrendering themselves to what they believe to be a 'call'. It is ironical, though not perhaps surprising, that Richardson should have more success with her failures then with her geniuses. To the doomed aspirations of Maurice Guest and Mahony she gives eloquent expression; Wagner, even though speaking in words sometimes close to his own, seems more often frenzied than inspired.

Richardson was conscientious to a fault in her pursuit of objectivity and factual accuracy. Her imagination worked more freely at elaboration than invention. In *Maurice Guest* she drew not only on places, but on people she had known, with sufficient accuracy to give offence to some. . . . Hers is no impressionistic evocation of background and atmosphere, but a carefully constructed scenario, reliable as well as decorative.

This accuracy of detail, both in description of landscape and of character, is one of Richardson's great merits as a novelist. At the same time it imposes a restraint upon her writing, and makes for stylistic clumsiness. *Maurice Guest* and *The Getting of Wisdom* are freer from these faults than her other two novels. Though her writing, especially in scenes involving Louise Dufrayer, is sometimes extravagant and over-emphatic, the novel moves with ease and assurance, and it is easy to believe that, as she said, she found it no trouble to write. In *The Getting of Wisdom* too she displays the same easy stride, though her style is not free from awkwardness and the inversions which later became a mannerism. In *The Fortunes* the style is much more uneven, and at times is a serious obstacle to the appreciation of character and narrative comment. In *The Young Cosima* the constructional gaucheries, clichés and flatness

of language are even more noticeable, and lend to the novel a ponderous and stilted air. (pp. 374-75)

Not only is [Richardson] the objective recorder; she is also the impartial observer. She presents conflict without bias; on the important moral issues raised by her novels she passes no editorial comment. Only by a slight edge in her writing, and some external evidence, can it be assumed that her sympathies are with the dreamers of the world, not with the practical men and women of action, however worthy they might be. . . . She does not, it is true, reach the highest levels of achievement. Her imagination is constrained by her literal-mindedness, and her style does not permit her the penetration her theme often demands. But her searching analyses of human vulnerability, and her grasp of the nature of creative activity lend her novels a special distinction. . . . (p. 375)

> Leonie Kramer, "Henry Handel Richardson," in The Literature of Australia, *edited by Geoffrey Dutton (copyright © Penguin Books, 1964; reprinted by permission of Penguin Books Australia Limited), Penguin Books Australia, 1964, pp. 363-76.*

DOROTHY GREEN (essay date 1973)

[This writer sharply disagrees] with the critics who have complained of Richardson's literal-mindedness, her reliance on facts; . . . if her work received even a fraction of the close attention which is lavished on many lesser writers, it might be seen more clearly that she was, as she claimed to be, an imaginative novelist, not a mere chronicler. . . . [This writer holds] the conviction that her principal work can be read on many levels, as Dante said his *Paradise* should be read: the literal, the psychological, the moral, and the mythic; [and that], as all great writers have done, she threw a handful of facts into the crucible of imagination and produced two great works of art and some important lesser ones. (pp. 2-3)

All that can be done at present is to take more seriously two statements of Richardson's that have often been quoted and never properly examined: her remark to a fellow-novelist Brian Penton 'that an artist has all his material before he is ten years old' and her admission that in drawing Richard Mahony's portrait she was in fact drawing her own. If the first had been attended to, less critical emphasis might have been laid on peripheral material in her principal novel, such as the scenery. If the second had been accepted, it would not have been so easy to assume that Richard Mahony was identical with her father and Mary Mahony with her mother.

Another mischievous assumption which has distorted interpretation of her work is that because the principal characters in her first and her last novel are musicians and the heroine of the second novel shows some incipient literary ability, the main theme of her writing must be 'the problem of the artist' in relation to society. . . . [This writer, however, contends] that Richardson was interested in far more fundamental questions than this and that the characters were not designed to illustrate a theory; indeed that the characters were 'given', 'nearest to hand', rather than deliberately chosen, and that a concept of life arose from observing their behaviour, rather than that their behaviour illustrated a concept. (pp. 6-7)

What, then, was her principal preoccupation? In brief, to . . . attempt to understand how she came to be the kind of person she was, at the same time acquiring some insight into the general human condition. She portrays Richard Mahony as searching above all for the key to the mystery of life; self-knowledge is a painful by-product of his search. She herself reverses the order, following the Socratic injunction with, at times, quite scarifying honesty. Yet, in spite of the purpose behind the work, it remains, as she claimed, fiction. If some of the incidents that really matter in the novels, because they are those that most move us, are scrutinised as carefully as those for which she has been censured, it will be found that most of them contain material of a kind that could only have been invented or imagined, or which from a basis of fact are transmuted into poetry by a unifying act of imagination—and so the case about slavery to facts falls to the ground. It requires imagination of a peculiarly powerful kind to organise the seemingly disparate details accumulated in *Richard Mahony* into a massive structure in which each of these details has its own relevance to the whole, 'resonating' throughout the work, a work which makes a statement that has all the simplicity and clarity of a great myth without ever abandoning reality. It is well to keep in mind when reading the novels Richardson's great gift for music, especially for composition, and her thorough musical education. The time spent with her husband reading the scores of Wagner and Strauss was well spent; she could have learnt much from them about the deployment of vast resources. She belongs indeed in that company of nineteenth-century European writers who 'thought to music'.

The complaint about Richardson's lack of imagination and her dependence on facts is part and parcel of complaints about her style. Passages are torn out of context to prove that her language is stiff, awkward, and sometimes sentimental, even novelese, a procedure which is like condemning a tree because it has a few dead twigs. . . . Yet this kind of criticism, which has been applied mercilessly to Richardson, is based on the unexamined assumption that the principles of analysis which function for lyric poetry will do equally well for the novel. It is forgotten that a long novel is simply not the same thing as a lyric poem, which is wrecked if every word does not pull its weight. . . . Novels like Richardson's demand critical approaches that are specifically proper to prose fiction, techniques which do not confuse the suggestive speech appropriate to poetry with the more directly communicative language proper to prose; which do not demand excellence of style as the supreme novelistic virtue. Richardson's narrative method on the whole resembles the craft of a builder in random stone. She is less interested in the appearance and the feel of the individual stones than in the total structure she can make with them. She accumulates minute details and selects those which cohere into a general statement, focusing attention on that and not on the details, though if you do attend to them, you will find them appropriate. She proceeds on the assumption that if you have enough facts and stare at them long enough, their inner meaning will reveal itself; her perfection is the perfection of large masses compounded of tiny strokes; her aim is to shape insignificant ideas into mythic clarity rather than to achieve verbal felicity. (pp. 8-10)

But questions of style apart, what a novelist stands or falls by is his ability to create a self-consistent world, a world in which the inhabitants move as necessarily and inevitably as the inhabitants of the world in which we live. If the novelist can perform the miracle of making us accept this world, the occasional lapses, roughnesses, wrong notes, so to speak, will no more spoil it for us than specks of dust on a window-pane, however irritating, will spoil the view outside. Perfection of style will not perform this miracle unless there is intellectual pressure behind it, but if this pressure is powerful enough, it will accomplish its ends and in so doing create its own style. . . . We return [to *Richard Mahony* and *Maurice Guest*] because we accept their world and the people in them, as we accept the world of reality and the people we know; and we do so largely because of the pressure of ideas felt beneath the surface of the novels, and because, in presenting them, the author is conveying a deeply-considered conception of life, a philosophic attitude which gives shape and body to her fictional world in such a way that entry into it enlarges our own experience.

There are few Australian novels which create an autonomous world and which at the same time convey a vision of metaphysical life, but Richardson's are among them, and . . . still supreme among them. And though their central figures are far from heroic in the Aristotelian sense, their lives raise heroic issues and the feeling of having been in touch with these is powerfully present in the reader when he puts the books down. (pp. 11-12)

> *Dorothy Green, in her* Ulysses Bound: Henry Handel Richardson and Her Fiction *(© Dorothy Green 1973), Australian National University Press, 1973, 582 p.*

BRIAN McFARLANE   (essay date 1977)

Henry Handel Richardson presents the reader with a special difficulty. . . . Her prose has no edge to it; she often wields it like a blunt instrument and some fine effects in consequence elude her. *The Fortunes of Richard Mahony* is held together, not by its episodic narrative procedures, but by a careful, perhaps dogged, imagistic patterning—and by the steadiness with which Richardson holds to her grim vision. There is a sense in which, to put it crudely, one has to read *between* the lines to feel the book's full strength. Eugene O'Neill is perhaps another author whose power at its most impressive—in *Long Day's Journey into Night*—is to be felt only in the totality of a given work, and very difficult to pinpoint in local reference. Both he and Richardson, however, persuade us of the intensity of feeling in their best work despite nagging verbal incompetence.

If the reader can surmount this difficulty with Richardson, it seems to me that he is faced with a work very much in tune with the mid-twentieth century's preoccupation with the decline of social modes and the disintegration of individual lives. The patient charting of this disintegration—physical, mental, and social—in a man of more than usual sensitivity, and with a capacity for compassion at odds with his intolerant dismissal of the crude and the ordinary, is the essential interest of *The Fortunes of Richard Mahony*. (p. 211)

[Its first volume, *Australia Felix*,] is clogged with detail, much of it unrevealing about Mahony and miscalculated in the emphasis it throws on the colonial scene as a contributing factor in his breakdown. Even here, though, two or three of the briefly glimpsed lives—Glendinning, the gentleman-farmer become an alcoholic wreck, and Tangye, the disillusioned chemist for example—prepare us in some ways for the Mahony who is penultimately buried alive at Gymgurra. These are clearly men defeated by the colony whereas Mahony, a larger man, is defeated not by a place but by life itself; but they serve their purpose in the novel's organization. So, too, [does a finely handled episode] in the second volume, *The Way Home,* in which the novels' sense of enveloping gloom is intensified with every situation—Australian or European—that Mahony finds himself in. If the vision strikes one increasingly as narrow and unresponsive to large areas of human life, some of its manifestations are realized with a very moving accuracy.

The [episode] is a very brief one describing Mahony's journey to Dublin to see his mother and sisters. It is one of the book's small triumphs, both for its distillation of a death-in-life and for its place in the novel's imagistic pattern. (p. 212)

[This episode is written] with the author's clear-eyed approach to the details of disintegration and anticipates the power she will muster later. Equally, though, in recording the shifts to which their poverty has put these ladies, Richardson finds and applauds something durable and admirable in human life. Their standards of behaviour may be inappropriate to their means, impractical and absurd, but, in the rigidity of their stand, in confronting and defying rather than bowing before the circumstances of their lives, there is courage as well as bitterness and folly. The picture of dignified decay further exemplifies Richardson's view of life as a series of *culs-de-sac* (or premature burials, or traps) but, in its account of the assiduously preserved rituals of their days . . . , it provides a sharp if rare and momentary glimpse of man's capacity to rise above his environment. For Mahony, however, though "like spoke to like, blood to blood" in Dublin, his visit to his family offers no reassuring or viable code for himself. As in his much earlier conversation with Tangye, he unconsciously shrinks from bracketing himself with those most like himself or those who have shared his unhappiest experiences. (pp. 212-13)

Richardson's creative energies work most forcefully in the darkest places, and if her characteristic view of life is of a giant trap, her most impressive writing renders the closing of this trap on individual human lives. (I do not mean to use the metaphors implied in "trap", "buried alive" and "cul-de-sac" indiscriminately. I think they indicate quite specifically different aspects of the author's vision: respectively, its harshness, its terror and its sense of bleak futility. It is these I had in mind when I spoke of the novel's imagistic patterning.) If she is unable to give any real insight into what makes life so generally disturbing a process, she is able to make us feel how a particular life turns in on itself. Early adumbrations of this notion of life-as-trap have been seen in the opening image of the man buried alive in the mine-shaft (and quickly forgotten), in the carefully placed anecdotes of Glendinning and Tangye, and in the Dublin visit. Above all, it is the fates of Mahony, Mary, their son Cuffy, and Mary's politician brother John that dramatize this view at its most intensely felt and realized. Each is trapped in a different way, and on Richardson's exploration of the kinds of pain involved rests the main power of the novel.

In *The Fortunes of Richard Mahony,* though there is no persuasive evidence that the creative energies and passions may produce lasting good or hope for order in the universe, John Turnham has at least lived vigorously. His death, when he is very near the peak of his career, intensifies one's view of a malign fate at work in Richardson's world. If we could persuade ourselves that Mahony dies because of a physical condition over which he has no control, we could perhaps accept his as a harrowing case-study, but without any generalizing significance for man at large. The episode of John's death discredits this idea and prepares us in two ways for the greatness of *Ultima Thule*: first, in the sheer horror and pain which this author is able to face without flinching, which she can observe with an honesty that compels respect; and, second, in what her often ungainly prose can achieve when her imagination confronts some of life's most wracking passes. By the latter I mean the evidence that decay and disintegration are the irresistible processes of human life. (pp. 213-14)

The course of Mahony's relationship with his wife, closely linked with his decline into madness and death, becomes one of the book's major triumphs as it emerges from the novel's unwieldy structural procedures. It is tempting to see a kind of "compensation" in Mary's metamorphosis, and in a limited sense she does present a growth that provides a foil to Mahony's collapse; but Richardson is very well aware of the limitations inherent in Mary's growth. (p. 216)

Wherever one turns in this novel, there is the disturbing sense of the irrevocably flawed nature of all human life, of the susceptibility of all human potential to corruption and decay. However saddening this honestly faced view of life may be—and I find it painfully so—its final effect is that of a deep pessimism that is often very telling but lacks the grandeur of tragedy.

This limits the book's other major achievement—the careful recording of Mahony's collapse. However, if one accepts this limitation, I think one is still moved to admiration for the scrupulousness of the artistic integrity Richardson brings to bear on her subject. By the time she reaches the third volume, *Ultima Thule,* she has hit her stride and does not falter, at least not so that it matters. The ultimate images of trap and burial are of course those relating to Mahony, and these are worked out with a remarkable control that derives from the authenticity of the medical facts but goes well beyond this in its feeling. Though *The Way Home* focuses much more sharply on Mahony's personal position than does *Australia Felix,* it is not until the third volume that the process of concentration is complete. (pp. 220-21)

[*Ultima Thule's* greatness] lies in its author's dogged acceptance of what life seems to her to be. Mary's ready kindness, or Mahony's flashes of intuitive understanding, or Cuffy's sensitivity to the thrilling power of music are convincingly there, but they make little headway against the forces that debilitate, devitalise, and ultimately crush. It is these forces which command Richardson's most passionate belief and which account for the often terrifying power of the last volume. . . . It is a tribute to the strength and fixity of purpose in the last volume that one all but forgets the flabbiness that spoils so much of the first half but recalls what is significant to the novel's pattern. (p. 222)

The concentrated power of *Ultima Thule* derives from its author's fastening her attention on to these three sensibilities: Mahony's, Mary's and Cuffy's. She does not insist on their representativeness, but between them they constitute for her some of the chief forces that govern human life: aspiration which exceeds capacity and resists definition, and is therefore doomed to failure; devoted service so crippled by imaginative deficiencies that it helps to kill the thing it serves; and the exposed rawness of a sensitivity acute enough to apprehend the inadequacy of both these responses and to be abraded by them. In holding these forces in equilibrium, Richardson's courage excites our respect. She will not let us see Mahony's aspirations as other than vague and unrealizable; she denies us the commonplace comfort of Mary's strength grown out of adversity; and she makes clear that Cuffy's sensibilities are too often and too appallingly ravaged for us to trust in his ultimate resilience. This is far from the brutal negativism of *Madame Bovary*. Richardson faces these three instances of human decline with an unfaltering courage that really means something, because it grows out of an unyielding respect for their individuality, even though she cannot see this as productive in any of them, and out of a profound compassion for them as victims of "life the destroyer". She knows some of the most desperate blows life can deal, sees what they do to their victims, acknowledges that she can find no certain palliatives, and leaves us at the end with all that she honestly can find: that life is care and suffering, as Mary has said but also that life simply *is* and must be borne with whatever resources one has to hand. If she is obsessed with decay and disintegration, it is not an obsession that grows out of or leads to a contempt for human beings, but rather, leads to a pity which moves us because it is all that her integrity will allow her to offer. (p. 224)

Richardson pays only lip-service to the ideal of men making something of their lives, and the overwhelming impression in *The Fortunes of Richard Mahony* is of the pointlessness of their efforts. However, in *Ultima Thule*, where she makes us privy to the darkest recesses of her mind, she does so with such power, and shows them illumined with shafts of such unsentimental pity, that I want to call it a great achievement.

This is not the sort of greatness that draws one back to it again and again to see what more it may yield; there are indeed parts of it (almost all the Barambogie chapters and especially the death of the child, Lallie) that I hope never to read again. Equally I expect never to forget them, and if this is not the highest tribute one may pay to a writer, I think it is a substantial one. It recognizes the limitation of a life-view too preoccupied with disintegration to value human possibility adequately, and at the same time acknowledges the pity and integrity of the appraisal. (p. 228)

> *Brian McFarlane, "Power in Dark Places: 'The Fortunes of Richard Mahony',"* in Southerly, *Vol. 37, No. 2, 1977, pp. 211-28.*

ADDITIONAL BIBLIOGRAPHY

Elliot, William D. *Henry Handel Richardson.* Boston: Twayne Publishers, 1975, 174 p.

A biography, with descriptive and evaluative criticism of Richardson's canon.

Elliott, William. "French Influences in *The Fortunes of Richard Mahony*." *Discourse* XI, No. 1 (Winter 1968): 108-15.

Discusses the influence of Zola and Flaubert in *Richard Mahony*.

Green, H. M. "The Short Story" and "The Novel." In his *Australian Literature: 1900-1950*, pp. 22-6, pp. 26-34. Carlton, Australia: Melbourne University Press, 1951.*

Appraisal of Richardson's short stories as a "mere 'shaving from a great artist's workshop'." The second essay contains a brief critical overview of her canon, and finds *The Fortunes of Richard Mahony* to be the greatest Australian novel.

Jeffares, A. Norman. "The State of Letters: *The Fortunes of Richard Mahony* Reconsidered." *The Sewanee Review, Special Issue: Commonwealth Literature* LXXXVII, No. 1 (Winter 1979): 158-64.

An essay on *Richard Mahony* that concentrates on its theme of the wandering exile. *Maurice Guest* and *The Getting of Wisdom* are also briefly examined.

Kiernan, Brian. "Romantic Conventions and *Maurice Guest*." *Southerly* 28, No. 4 (1968): 286-94.

Study of Richardson's depiction of love as a destructive force in *Maurice Guest*.

Kramer, Leonie. *Henry Handel Richardson.* Melbourne: Oxford University Press, 1967, 30 p.

A biography of Richardson, including some criticism of her works. Kramer finds the theme of failure a common concern in Richardson's novels, and believes that theme reflects the novelist's own life.

Lewis, Sinclair. Foreword to *The Fortunes of Richard Mahony*, by Henry Handel Richardson, pp. v-vii. New York: The Press of the Readers Club, 1941.

A brief synopsis of the *Richard Mahony* trilogy, comparing it to the works of Wells, Dreiser, Galsworthy, and others. Lewis also discusses his feelings of kinship with Mahony.

Loder, Elizabeth. "*The Fortunes of Richard Mahony*: Dream and Nightmare." *Southerly* 25, No. 4 (1965): 251-63.

An examination of the themes of freedom, confinement, and suffering in Richardson's trilogy.

Palmer, Anthony J. "A Link with Late Nineteenth Century Decadence in *Maurice Guest*." *Australian Literary Studies* 5, No. 4 (October 1972): 366-73.

An essay that discusses the character Heinrich Krafft as the literary embodiment of a decadent artist.

Purdie, Edna, and Roncoroni, Olga M., eds. *Henry Handel Richardson: Some Personal Impressions.* Sydney: Angus & Robertson, 1957, 175 p.

Reminiscences of Richardson by nine of her friends and associates.

Richardson, Henry Handel. "Some Notes on My Books." *The Virginia Quarterly Review* 16, No. 3 (Summer 1940): 334-47.

Richardson's reminiscences of her life, the creation of her novels, and their critical reception.

Roderick, Colin. "Winning Independence." In his *An Introduction to Australian Fiction*, pp. 63-123. Sydney: Angus and Robertson, 1950.*

A critical overview of Richardson's works, discussing her morbid death obsession, the effects of an adolescent romantic interest on her writings, and her selective fitting of style to subject matter.

Arthur Schnitzler

1862-1931

Austrian dramatist, novelist, short story writer, and poet.

Schnitzler is known primarily for his psychological analysis of the decadent *fin de siècle* culture of pre-World War I Vienna. In his shrewd analyses of the subconscious motivations and longings of his characters, he gave literary expression to Freud's discoveries in depth psychology. Recurring themes in his work are the neurotic sex-obsession of the Viennese aristocracy, the inseparableness of illusion and reality, and the hypocrisy of the military honor-code—subjects which often shocked and outraged his contemporaries. A stylistic experimenter in both drama and prose, Schnitzler introduced the Viennese dialect to the Austrian stage and was one of the first practitioners of the stream-of-consciousness technique.

Schnitzler was born in Vienna into a cultivated, upper-middle-class, Jewish family. His father, a prominent physician, disapproved of his son's literary aspirations and persuaded him to study medicine instead. Schnitzler remained, however, deeply interested in drama and literature, and rose to the forefront of a literary movement known as "Young Vienna," which opposed the naturalism sweeping Berlin and the classicism of Franz Grillparzer. The principles of the emerging field of psychiatry, to which he was exposed through his medical practice, profoundly affected Schnitzler's philosophy and techniques as a writer. Although he never completely abandoned his medical practice, Schnitzler became increasingly absorbed in his literary career.

The refreshing wit of *Anatol*, a sequence of one-act comedies, brought Schnitzler to the attention of Viennese audiences. In these light-hearted vignettes he creates the stock characters which recur again and again in his work: the melancholy, effete, yet charming, young aristocrat always on the prowl for a new sexual conquest; the sardonic *raisonneur*, who analyzes and advises him; and the *suesse Maedel*, a pliant, lower-class suburban girl, who seeks glamour and excitement in the city and in upper-class life. The characters in his most notorious play, *Reigen* (*Hands Around*), form, in a series of ten interlocking dialogues, a chain of sexual union. Schnitzler grew increasingly judgmental of his dramatic characters, who seem to be neurotically driven by the fear of death and innate pessimism in their ceaseless pursuit of momentary sensation.

Stylistically, Schnitzler employed innovative dramatic and narrative techniques, which anticipated the work of more famous writers, such as Luigi Pirandello and James Joyce. For example, in *Der grüne Kakadu* (*The Duke and the Actress*), he incorporates a play-within-the-play to examine the uncertain boundaries between reality and illusion, and the psychology of sexual jealousy, thus presaging themes and methods more fully explored by Pirandello. He carried his psychological analysis still further in the novella *Leutnant Gustl* (*None but the Brave*) and produced the first masterpiece in the stream-of-consciousness mode in European literature. His mordant depiction of the fatuous lieutenant and the ridiculous intricacies of the military code governing duels raised

such a furor that he was forced to resign from the army medical reserve.

The advent of World War I marked the decline of the gay, pleasure-loving atmosphere Schnitzler portrayed in his work. While a mood of nostalgic sadness is often noted in his work antedating the war, depression seems to permeate his later fiction: the novella *Flucht in die Finsternis* (*Flight into Darkness*) is a clinical examination of a man's descent into madness.

Schnitzler's work was extremely popular in the years before the war, but he was always a controversial figure. Critics praised him for his subtle evocation of mood, deft characterization, and witty dialogue, but criticized him for the narrow circumscription of his subject—Vienna and the Viennese—and for his preoccupation with erotic themes. The anti-Semitic attacks which plagued him throughout his career culminated in the banning of his work by the Nazis. Although Schnitzler's fame has diminished, he is remembered for his wistful, yet penetrating, portrayal of a dying age.

PRINCIPAL WORKS

Das Abenteuer seines Lebens (drama) 1891

Anatol (drama) 1893
  [*Anatol*, 1911]
Das Märchen (drama) 1893
Liebelei (drama) 1895
  [*The Reckoning*, 1907; also published as *Light-o'-Love*, 1912; and *Playing with Love*, 1914]
Der grüne Kakadu (drama) 1899
  [*The Duke and the Actress*, 1910; published in England as *The Green Cockatoo*, 1913]
Der Schleier der Beatrice (drama) 1900
Leutnant Gustl (novella) 1901
  [*None but the Brave*, 1926]
Der einsame Weg (drama) 1904
  [*The Lonely Way*, 1915]
Zwischenspiel (drama) 1905
  [*Intermezzo*, 1915]
Der Weg ins Freie (novel) 1908
  [*The Road to the Open*, 1923]
Der junge Medardus (drama) 1910
Das weite Land (drama) 1911
  [*The Vast Domain*, 1923]
Professor Bernhardi (drama) 1912
  [*Professor Bernhardi*, 1927]
Reigen (drama) 1920
  [*Hands Around*, 1920; published in England as *Merry-Go-Round*, 1953]
Fräulein Else (novella) 1924
  [*Fraülein Else*, 1925]
Flucht in die Finsternis (novella) 1926
  [*Flight into Darkness*, 1931]
Therese (novel) 1928
  [*Theresa*, 1928]

MARTIN BIRNBAUM (essay date 1910)

It is significant that Arthur Schnitzler is a physician. A brilliant psychologist, his favourite themes are the foibles and weaknesses of humanity. He has achieved success with many prose forms, and all his best work has the nervous poetical grace and the heart-breaking quality of a Viennese Waltz by Strauss. He may be described as a lyric dramatist who uses prose as a medium. One of his most delightful, and perhaps his most characteristic book is a series of dialogues entitled *Anatol*, being the amorous campaigns of two young men about town.... In common with most of Schnitzler's men and women, no matter what their social status may be, they discuss wistfully and philosophise subtly about love, death, our ephemeral existence, or fear of the unknown,—and always in faultlessly elegant phraseology. *Liebelei*, the Vie de Boheme of Vienna, first made Schnitzler popular, but his greatest dramatic success artistically is *Zwischenspiel*.... Schnitzler strikes his characteristic feminine note in both plays. (p. 502)

Among Schnitzler's finest works are his short novels and one-act plays.... *Sterben*, which reminds one strongly of D'Annunzio, is an account of the last agonising days of a moody egoist, morbidly passionate and sensitive, who knows that he will soon be the victim of consumption. It exhibits Schnitzler's power of treating unpleasant subjects verging on tragedy with the utmost delicacy. *Lieutenant Gustl*, in gayer key, is a long monologue in which the dream expedient is cleverly used. It is an excellent example of that

lightness of touch which his distinguished friend Hugo von Hofmannsthal, also a Viennese, praises above all Schnitzler's qualities. (p. 503)

Martin Birnbaum "Some Contemporary German Tendencies: Arthur Schnitzler," in The Bookman (copyright, 1910, by George H. Doran Company), Vol. XXX, No. 5, January, 1910, pp. 502-03.

THE NEW YORK TIMES (essay date 1911)

If Ibsen could be imagined as collaborating with Anthony Hope on "The Dolly Dialogues," possibly the result might have, in some way, resembled Arthur Schnitzler's "Anatol." ... [These] dialogues are very sprightly reading—though they are in no sense intended for the ubiquitous young person.

Anatol is a Viennese bachelor of evident wealth and social position. He is a philanderer who takes himself rather seriously, whose excursions into the regions of sentiment are numerous and brief-lived. Schnitzler knows the type, and deals with it in a vein of good-natured satire. Yet the dialogues are not exaggerated into caricature; the author is far too clever and far too deeply in sympathy with every manifestation of human nature to deal so crudely with these vagaries of the wandering heart. At times his satire is a bit mordant, and there is a sting in his humor, but, on the whole, one is able to laugh with a frank enjoyment which leaves no bitter aftertaste....

Schnitzler is never coarse; nor is he insinuating—which is far worse. He seems to find men and women vastly amusing—as no doubt we are, and to a very human perception and sympathy he adds a note of Olympic laughter at our follies and frailties.

Technically, his construction of these dialogues is well-nigh faultless.... He is the foremost Viennese dramatist, and his work, while ultra-modern, is free from much that would condemn other present Continental production in the eyes of the more reserved Anglo-Saxon.

"Dialogues for Adults: There Is Much of Wit and Charm—and Spice—in 'Anatol'," in The New York Times (© 1911 by The New York Times Company; reprinted by permission), August 13, 1911, p. 496.

PERCIVAL POLLARD (essay date 1911)

The Austrian drama of to-day is typified in the work of Arthur Schnitzler. In his work were all those qualities which marked the contrast between the Viennese temper and the German. Where Berlin insisted on truth, at the expense of beauty, Vienna preferred beauty to everything else. As in its court and its lesser circles Vienna stands for all the aristocratic refinements, so the gestures and tones of the most sophisticated intelligence, of the most patrician outlook, are the paramount concerns in Viennese art.... Neither tremendous passion nor tremendous problems have stirred, to all appearances, those polite artists of Vienna. Passion might be there, but what was to be artistically expressed was, rather, the witty or ironically mournful surfaces of passion. Under the almost diabolically clever flippancies in dialogue there may be tragedy; but neither in life nor art is it good form, in Vienna, to let so middle-class an article as tragedy appear naked.

All these essentially Austrian qualities were markedly in Schnitzler. The ironies and mockeries in a sort of twilight land of love engaged him time and again. (pp. 271-72)

Always, in the Schnitzler plays, we move among delicate, amusing and intriguing love-affairs. No grim questions of right and wrong are allowed to assail us. How, most smoothly, most politely, most delicately, is this lover to say good-by to that sweetheart; or how is this lovely lady to inform her cavalier that she is tired of him—to all appearances we are never witnessing problems any deeper than those. We move in a realm of beauty; ugliness is never allowed to obtrude. Neither He nor She ever vows constancy; as long as the romance lasts, until the bloom of novelty and wit is off, in short; there is no more in these little love-affairs than that. The etiquette of the *liaison,* in short, is nowhere more charmingly expressed than in Schnitzler.

What in "Liebelei" was green, in this dramatist's later plays ripened to a far surer intellectual effect. In his cycle of one-act plays collected under the title "Anatol" we find him . . . at his most essential. Here is crystallized that viewpoint of the man-of-the-world and the witty sentimentalist which distinguishes Vienna aristocracy. . . . In spite of several longer plays, novels, etc., existing from Schnitzler's pen, his talent has found its fittest expression in the one-act drama. For just an episode, for the perfectly graceful exploitation of just one mood, his talent has sufficed. There are hardly any moods, whims or caprices in that twilight-land between passion and philandering, which he has not analyzed delicately for our diversion. He is supremely the analyst of light love. To read him is to understand the wit and the inconstancy, the politeness and the unscrupulousness, of the Viennese soul. (pp. 273-74)

Though Schnitzler seldom goes beyond the eternal duel between Her and Him—at the most he lets his witty lightnings flash about the eternal triangle which perpetually emphasizes the imperfectly monogamous nature of our kind—the dialogues he supplies for that duel are not easily surpassed for sheer cleverness; not even the Parisians are more skilful than he in the verbal scintillations of light love. (p. 275)

No writer of the first rank in any language has surpassed the ingenuity with which in "Reigen" the suggestion of the unprintable is welded into most brilliant conversations. "Reigen" expresses the last word in Schnitzler's erotic cynicism; it contains his mocking philosophy of life, which, as aforesaid, is all the more infectious through its faultless manner. In "Reigen" are ten dialogues; and I need do no more than tell you that the cycle of what most would call illegitimate eroticism is made into a perfect circle. . . . A vicious circle, literally; each episode . . . ends in just one and the same way. . . . Schnitzler was never more diabolically clever than in "Reigen," never more the mouthpiece of the utterly unmoral viveur's philosophy. Not Flaubert's *Emma Bovary* herself communicated more insidiously all the subtle poisons in human passion. Sheerly physical eroticism could hardly be more illusively cloaked in diverting words.

The people who have been wont to think German a clumsy medium for finesse should learn otherwise from Schnitzler. French has done nothing subtler than he with his Viennese temper and his quick ear for the very note of Vienna, whether of the palace or of the street (pp. 278-79)

Percival Pollard, "Vienna's Essence: Schnitzler," in his Masks and Minstrels of New Germany *(copyright, 1911 by L. E. Bassett), John W. Luce and Company, 1911, pp. 265-83.*

BAYARD QUINCY MORGAN   (essay date 1912)

Nothing is more characteristic of Schnitzler than the one-act piece. . . . None of his larger plays, with one exception, has proved really successful, several seem to be veritable fiascos. The reason is that his art is not monumental enough for the large sweep of a great tragedy. His chosen field is the sparkling, witty dialog. He uses this for all purposes: not merely to create atmosphere, and characterize subtly fine shades of personality, but also to outline stroke by stroke a dramatic setting and accompany a dramatic episode. But beyond the episode he rarely goes successfully. Take him into a more ambitious field and he flounders and splashes like an inexpert swimmer in deep water, and makes a great commotion, but little progress. (p. 5)

A priori one would not expect Schnitzler to achieve success in the historical drama. Yet he has twice tried his hand at it. In *Der junge Medardus* he takes us back to the Napoleonic wars. Medardus sets out to assassinate the emperor, but instead turns his dagger upon the woman who urges him on to the deed, because she has been accused of being Napoleon's mistress. The author's dialog is his undoing in this work. He is so concerned to produce atmosphere and setting that the dramatic action vanishes from view.

His most ambitious drama so far, though not his most successful, is the other historical play, *Der Schleier der Beatrice*("Beatrice's Veil"). In it he attempts a canvas of more than Shakespearean proportions. No less than fifty-three speaking parts are listed, besides all the mute figures which fill the background at various times. The scene is laid in Bologna of the sixteenth century, and the central figure, next to the Beatrice of the title, is the reigning duke, Leonardo Bentivoglio; and this again reminds of Shakespeare. If we add the great length of the drama, five acts, covering two hundred and fifteen pages, and the alternation of blank verse and prose, with an occasional happy turn of speech, we have all the elements that justify a comparison with Shakespearean art. Certainly any deeper similarity is lacking. The great canvas merely confuses; the verse, while smooth and even elegant at times, shows no sign of greatness; and the length deadens the effect and breaks up the unity of the conception. Worse than all, the magnificent reality and life of Shakespeare's characters is wholly lacking; the personages of this play are not convincing; they are not alive. (p. 8)

I now come to that type of subject which is evidently Schnitzler's favorite, and in which he has scored his greatest successes—and his greatest failures. Whether he merely follows one marked trend of the naturalistic school, or a strong individual bent, it is certain that his work is characterized by a steady, almost morbid, insistence upon man's sexual life. It crops out again and again, and amounts at times to a veritable obsession. No one will deny that the sexual impulse is one of the most powerful natural forces in the world. But to make sexual intercourse the equivalent of life itself, as Schnitzler does in *Der Ruf des Lebens* ("The Call of Life"), can only be called an outrageous distortion of normal humanity. . . .

Something of this unnatural emphasis on the sexual life is to be found in "Anatol," his first publication. This strange book consists of a series of seven one-act pieces, each of which centers about an affair between the young man of this name and a different woman. (p. 10)

Essentially sexual problems are also involved in his *Zwischenspiel* ("Intermezzo"). The plot consists of the separation, reunion, and second separation of a married couple, the wife being the prime mover in each case, and the motive force a thirst for "adventures," i.e., love affairs. . . .

Schnitzler's highest dramatic achievement thus far is his *Liebelei* ("Light-o'-Love"), of which *Das Vermächtnis* ("The Legacy") is a rather feeble echo. The "Legacy" is the posthumous illegitimate child of a young aristocratic rake; when the child dies, the mother is cast out of his family. In "Light-o'-Love" the action is more firmly knit, and the result is a superb achievement of its kind. (p. 11)

The [play has] firm, clear-cut lines . . . , steady and well-planned development, [and a] fine climax. But it has the further merit, which cannot be allowed all of Schnitzler's dramas, that the characters are really alive and convincing. . . . And the character drawing is executed with the lightest possible touch, built up line by line out of seemingly flimsy dialog, but with masterly precision.

One of Schnitzler's earliest works, *Liebelei* remains his high-water mark in the drama, and in view of the distinct limitations of his art, it may be doubted whether he will ever rise above it, or even reach it again. Certainly nothing he has done since has justified the hope it raised, that in Arthur Schnitzler might be found a new and powerful prophet of the naturalistic school. (p. 13)

Bayard Quincy Morgan, "Arthur Schnitzler," in The Drama *(copyright, 1912, by Drama League of America), Vol. II, No. 7, August, 1912, pp. 3-13.*

THE AMERICAN REVIEW OF REVIEWS (essay date 1915)

[Arthur Schnitzler] has taken middle-class life in the gayest capital of Europe and spread it before us, not as a theorist, but as one who observes minutely and is not deceived. His plays are parts of the great drama of life deflected by a lens of keen intellectuality upon the stage of our emotions and played by each man according to his perceptions. Schnitzler belongs to the latter-day prophets of truth,—those who would strip away all self-deception from the complexities of life wherein we moderns are enmeshed. His plays are the bulletins of the social conscience as it plays through the emotions. "The Lonely Way" values life for those who have never learned that love is service, and service love. For those who will not serve, there lies ahead the "lonely way" of desolate, disillusioned old age,—or suicide.

"Intermezzo" is one of the subtlest of the Schnitzler dramas. It weaves the question of a single moral standard for men and women into a domestic situation that falls into chaos through a lack of simple honesty and unquestioning faithfulness. (pp. 243-44)

In "The Countess Mizzie," the Countess, a ballet dancer, the Count, a coachman and a noble Prince for a brief hour, meet at the same level,—the recognition of identical emotional experience. Here Schnitzler's irony is leveled at the social conventions that outrage human emotions. All the

personages in this drama were social cowards; they dared not take what they wanted except clandestinely. One noble act would have saved all of them. Schnitzler's phrases are like scourges in the temples of desecrated gods. To him there is no hell like the hell of the coward who denies his own soul. (p. 244)

"A Great Austrian Dramatist," in The American Review of Reviews *(copyright 1915 by Review of Reviews, Co.), Vol. 52, No. 2, August, 1915, pp. 243-44.*

WINIFRED SMITH (essay date 1915)

The deep-seated American—or is it an Anglo-Saxon?—habit of judging all art, and especially literary art, by its conformity to conventional morality is almost certain to prevent for a long time the complete recognition here of one of the subtlest of modern European dramatists and poets, Arthur Schnitzler. Over all his work . . . there hangs what our popular critics are sure to interpret as the poisonous miasma from a very morbid kind of life,—it is so difficult for most of us to see in an artist's preoccupation with erotic psychology, and with other forms of nevrosity, anything but an unhealthy dwelling upon unpleasant subjects. In fact, this general impatience with attempts to express fine shades of temperament, this blindness in respect to artistic experiment and exploration in hazy borderlands of experience, may easily cause Schnitzler's books to be anathematized, unless they are cast aside as merely dull and unnatural, by those who fail to penetrate their allusive delicacy and their witty indirectness. . . .

[In "Anatol"] Anatol, the young aesthete of wealth and family, drifting from one exquisite moment to another, delighting in the analysis of fleeting sensations, demanding no purpose, no responsibility, no continuity, and no finality in love and life, is a figure that reappears again and again in Schnitzler's work. Under the name of Fritz, in "Playing at Love," he loses his superficial resemblance to an Oscar Wilde hero, and becomes at once more recognizable and more hateful, for this tragedy shows with the utmost poignancy the horror that may result from light loving when on one side there is serious passion and on the other merely a wish for diversion. Prince Egon, another version of the same type, who saunters not very gracefully through the play entitled "Countess Mizzie," has better luck than his fellows; but this is entirely because he is thrown into relations with a woman of strong nature, and not because he is self-controlled. . . .

In the five brief acts of "Professor Bernardi," Schnitzler comes as close as so detached an observer could ever come to working out a distinct thesis. . . . (p. 267)

[The] conclusion, which to the practical person might seem the ultimate destruction of all values, is actually the most positive kind of assertion of the modern individualist's creed. The self-sufficiency which results from wide comprehension, the independence born of a realization both of the individual's creative power and of the limits to that power, —these are the central themes focussing Schnitzler's as well as many another modern's work.

It is lack of strength, and so of self-sufficiency, that brings about Christine's tragedy in "Playing with Love" ("Liebelei"), and Robert's tragedy in "The Mate"; both go on living lies more or less consciously for want of independence and the force to make their lives sincere. . . . The positive and triumphant aspect of the creed is illustrated in "Dr. Bernardi," its tragedy in "The Lonely Way," most powerful of the later plays.

Ibsen never painted a tenser succession of scenes than the sequence of quiet conversations which in "The Lonely Way" reveal through skilful characterization the story of a long-dead passion and its fruits, and which lead finally to a double suicide and to the still more terrible destruction of cherished hopes and illusions. (p. 268)

Some minor studies of differing temperaments are exquisitely set in lower keys in the "Viennese Idylls,"—a very inappropriately titled collection of six unusually moving and various short stories. The influence of Freud and his school of psycho-analists is apparent in more than one passage of subtly presented mood, with its complex of emotion and of comparatively unmarked external action. In each of these stories, as in the plays, the drama is primarily internal; the tension is of the terrifying kind that holds during a nightmare; the characters are, many of them, endowed with the almost magical intuition which gives certain quiet and unimpressive persons the power to draw from commonplace events a very real aesthetic satisfaction, through their power to lose themselves in the effort of analysis and appreciation. For this satisfaction there can be no rule and no precise preparation, though incidentally there must be no prejudices,—there can only be power of the sort Schnitzler himself seems to possess to an unusual degree. Extraordinary receptiveness and sensitiveness, sympathies of the widest range, unusual intellect and cultivation, and a will determined to follow the intricate windings of the human spirit into shadowy corners of hitherto stubborn reticences, with a patience . . . in expressing his themes through a transparently suitable style, a style vigorously direct and natural, picturesque, suggestive or allusive as the case demands,—these are the marked characteristics of Schnitzler's work. Its whole effect is of a richness, a disinterested sincerity, and a subtlety which many of our thinner and cruder and more clamorous young writers could do no better than to study. (pp. 268-69)

Winifred Smith, "A Viennese Playwright in English," in The Dial *(copyright, 1915, by The Dial Publishing Company, Inc.), Vol. LIX, No. 702, September 30, 1915, pp. 267-69.*

EDWIN BJÖRKMAN (essay date 1917)

"Anatol" is nothing but seven sketches in dramatic form, each sketch picturing a new love affair of the kind supposed to be especially characteristic of Viennese life. . . . The story is told for the sake of the story, and its chief redeeming quality lies in the grace and charm and verve with which it is told. . . . There has been a strong tendency observable, both within and outside the author's native country, to regard him particularly as the creator of *Anatol,* and to question, if not to resent, his inevitable and unmistakable growth beyond that pleasing, but not very significant starting point.

And yet his next dramatic production, which was also his first serious effort as a playwright, ought to have proved sufficient warning that he was moved by something more than a desire to amuse. "A Piece of Fiction" (*Das*

Märchen) must be counted a failure and, in some ways, a step backward. But its very failure is a promise of greater things to come. It lacks the grace and facilty of "Anatol." Worse still, it lacks the good-humor and subtle irony of those first sketches. Instead it has purpose and a serious outlook on life. . . . Unfortunately the dialogue is heavy and stilted. The play is a tract rather than a piece of art. . . . Yet the play marks a step forward in outlook and spirit. (pp. xii-xiii)

"Amours" (*Liebelei*) may be regarded as a cross, or a compromise, between "Anatol" and "A Piece of Fiction." The crudeness of speech marking the latter play has given room to a very incisive dialogue that carries the action forward with unfailing precision. Some of the temporarily dropped charm has been recovered, and the gain in sincerity has been preserved. (pp. xiii-xiv)

"Outside the Game Laws" (*Freiwild*) is another step ahead —the first play, I think, where the real Arthur Schnitzler, the author of "The Lonely Way" and "Countess Mizzie," reveals himself. It has a thesis, but this is implied rather than obtruded. In style and character-drawing it is realistic in the best sense. It shows already the typical Schnitzlerian tendency of dealing with serious questions—with questions of life and death—in a casual fashion, as if they were but problems of which road to follow or which shop to enter. It has one fault that must appear as such everywhere, namely, a division of purpose. When the play starts, one imagines that those "outside the game laws" are the women of the stage, who are presented as the legitimate prey of any man caring to hunt them. As the play goes on, that starting point is almost lost sight of, and it becomes more and more plain that those "outside the game laws" are sensible, decent men who refuse to submit to the silly dictates of the dueling code. But what I have thus named a fault is mostly theoretical, and does not mar the effective appeal of the play. What must appear as a more serious shortcoming from an American viewpoint is the local nature of the evil attacked, which lessens the universal validity of the work. (pp. xiv-xv)

["Change Partners!" (*Reigen*)] attempts a degree of naturalism rarely equaled in France even. Yet those dialogues are anything but immoral in spirit. . . . The story is always the same (except in the final dialogue): desire, satisfaction, indifference. The idea underlying this "ring dance," as the title means literally, is the same one that recurs under a much more attractive aspect in "Countess Mizzie." It is the linking together of the entire social organism by man's natural cravings. And as a document bearing on the psychology of sex "Change Partners!" has not many equals.

In "The Legacy" (*Das Vermächtnis*) we meet with a forcible presentation and searching discussion of the world's attitude toward those ties that have been established without social sanction. . . . It is noticeable in this play, as in others written by Schnitzler, that the attitude of the women is more sensible and tolerant than that of the men.

The physician is one of the few members of that profession whom the author has painted in an unfavorable light. There is hardly one full-length play of his in which at least one representative of the medical profession does not appear. And almost invariably they seem destined to act as the particular mouthpieces of the author. (pp. xv-xvi)

The fundamental theme [of "The Veil of Beatrice" (*Der*

Schleier der Beatrice), a verse play in five acts,] is one dear to Schnitzler—the flaming up of passion under the shadow of impending death. The whole city, with the duke leading, surrenders to this outburst, the spirit of which finds its symbol in a ravishingly beautiful girl, *Beatrice Nardi*, who seems fated to spread desire and death wherever she appears. . . . The play holds much that is beautiful and much that is disappointing. To me its chief importance lies in the fact that it marks a breaking-point between the period when Schnitzler was trying to write "with a purpose," and that later and greater period when he has learned how to treat life sincerely and seriously without other purpose than to present it as it is. (pp. xvii-xviii)

["The Lonely Way" (*Der einsame Weg*)] is beyond all doubt Schnitzler's greatest and most powerful creation so far, representing a tremendous leap forward both in form and spirit. It has less passion than "The Call of Life," less subtlety than "Intermezzo," less tolerance than "Countess Mizzie." Instead it combines in perfect balance all the best qualities of those three plays—each dominant feature reduced a little to give the others scope as well. It is a wonderful specimen of what might be called the new realism—of that realism which is paying more attention to spiritual than to material actualities. Yet it is by no means lacking in the more superficial verisimilitude either. Its character-drawing and its whole atmosphere are startlingly faithful to life, even though the life portrayed may represent a clearly, defined and limited phase of universal human existence.

The keynote of the play lies in *Sala's* words to *Julian* in the closing scene of the fourth act: "The process of aging must needs be a lonely one to our kind." That's the main theme —not a thesis to be proved. This loneliness to which *Sala* refers, is common to all people, but it is more particularly the share of those who, like himself and *Julian,* have treasured their "freedom" above everything else and who, for that reason, have eschewed the human ties which to a man like *Wegrath* represent life's greatest good and deepest meaning. (pp. xxi-xxii)

The play has no thesis, as I have already said. It is not poised on the point of a single idea. Numerous subordinate themes are woven into the main one, giving the texture of the whole a richness resembling that of life itself. Woman's craving for experience and self-determination is one such theme, which we shall find again in "Intermezzo," where it practically becomes the dominant one. (p. xxiii)

With "The Lonely Way" begins a series of plays representing not only Schnitzler's highest achievements so far, but a new note in the modern drama. To a greater extent than any other modern plays—not even excepting those of Ibsen—they must be defined as psychological. The dramas of Strindberg come nearest in this respect, but they, too, lag behind in soul-revealing quality. Plots are almost lacking in the Schnitzler productions during his later period. Things happen, to be sure, and these happenings are violent, enough at times, but they do not constitute a sharply selected sequence of events leading up to a desired and foreshadowed end. In the further development of this period, even clearly defined themes are lost sight of, and the course of the play takes on an almost accidental aspect. This is puzzling, of course, and it must be especially provoking to those who expect each piece of art to have its narrow little lesson neatly tacked on in a spot where it cannot be missed. (p. xxiv)

"Intermezzo" (*Zwischenspiel*) might be interpreted as an attack on those new marital conventions which abolish the old-fashioned demand for mutual faithfulness and substitute mutual frankness. It would be more correct, however, to characterize it as a discussion of what constitutes true honesty in the ever delicate relationship between husband and wife. It shows, too, the growth of a woman's soul, once she has been forced to stand on her own feet. Viewed from this point, the play might very well be classified as feministic. It would be easy, for one thing, to read into it a plea for a single moral standard. But its ultimate bearing goes far beyond such a narrow construction. Here as elsewhere, Schnitzler shows himself more sympathetic toward the female than toward the male outlook on life. . . . (p. xxv)

Significant as this play is from any point viewed, I am inclined to treasure it most on account of the subtlety and delicacy of its dialogue. I don't think any dramatist of modern times has surpassed Schnitzler in his ability to find expression for the most refined nuances of thought and feeling. To me, at least, it is a constant joy to watch the iridescence of his sentences, which gives to each of them not merely one, but innumerable meanings. And through so much of this particular play runs a spirit that can only be called playful. . . . All the wit and sparkle with which we commonly credit the Gallic mind seems to me abundantly present in the scenes between *Albert* and *Amadeus.*

The poise and quiet characterizing "The Lonely Way" and "Intermezzo" appear lost to some extent in "The Call of Life" (*Der Ruf des Lebens*), which, on the other hand, is one of the intensest plays written by Schnitzler. The white heat of its passion sears the mind at times, so that the reader feels like raising a shield between himself and the words. (p. xxvi)

The weak point of "The Call to Life" is *Marie's* father, the old *Moser*—one of the most repulsive figures ever seen on the stage. It may have been made what it is in order that the girl's crime might not hopelessly prejudice the spectator at the start and thus render all the rest of the play futile. We must remember, too, that the monstrous egoism of *Moser* is not represented as a typical quality of that old age which feels itself robbed by the advance of triumphant youth. What Schnitzler shows is that egoism grows more repulsive as increasing age makes it less warranted. (pp. xxvii-xxviii)

If "The Lonely Way" be Schnitzler's greatest play all around, and "Intermezzo" his subtlest, "Countess Mizzie" is the sweetest, the best tempered, the one that leaves the most agreeable taste in the mouth. It gives us a concrete embodiment of the tolerance toward all life that is merely suggested by the closing sentences of *Dr. Schindler* in the last act of "The Call of Life." It brings back the gay spirit of "Anatol," but with a rare maturity supporting it. The simple socio-biological philosophy of "Change Partners!" is restated without the needless naturalism of those early dialogues. The idea of "Countess Mizzie" is that, if we look deep enough, all social distinctions are lost in a universal human kinship. (p. xxviii)

"Young Medardus" [*Der junge Medardus*] is Schnitzler's most ambitious attempt at historical playwriting. It seems to indicate that he belongs too wholly in the present age to succeed in that direction. . . . The central character, *Medardus Klähr,* is said to be historical. The re-created atmosphere of old Vienna is at once convincing and amusing.

But the play is too sprawling, to scattered, to get firm hold on the reader. . . . There is, too, a more deep-lying reason for the failure of the play as a whole, I think. The ironical outlook so dear to Schnitzler—or rather, so inseparable from his temperament—has betrayed him. Irony seems hopelessly out of place in a historical drama, where it tends to make us feel that the author does not believe in the actual existence of his own characters. (p. xxix)

Nowhere has Schnitzler been more casual in his use of what is commonly called plot [than in "The Vast Country" (*Das Weite Land*)]. Nowhere has he scorned more completely to build his work around any particular "red thread." Event follows event with seeming haphazardness. The only thing that keeps the play from falling apart is the logical development of each character. It is, in fact, principally, if not exclusively, a series of soul-studies. What happens serves merely as an excuse to reveal the reaction of a certain character to certain external pressures or internal promptings. But viewed in this light, the play has tremendous power and significance. (p. xxxi)

["Professor Bernhardi" is a remarkable play] in many respects. It deals largely with the internal affairs of a hospital. An overwhelming majority of the characters are physicians connected with the big hospital of which *Professor Bernhardi* is the head. They talk of nothing but what men of that profession in such a position would be likely to talk of. In other words, they are all the time "talking shop." This goes on through five acts. Throughout the entire play there is not the slightest suggestion of what the Broadway manager and the periodical editor call a "love interest." And yet the play holds you from beginning to end, and the dramatic tension could not be greater if its main theme were the unrequited love of the professor's son instead of his own right to place his duties as a physician above all other considerations. To one who has grown soul-weary of the "triangle" and all other combinations for the exploiting of illicit or legitimized love, "Professor Bernhardi" should come as a great relief and a bright promise. (p. xxxiii)

[Schnitzler's work indicates] a constant, steady growth, coupled with increased realization of his own possibilities and powers as well as of his limitations. In all but a very few of his plays, he has confined himself to the life immediately surrounding him—to the life of the Viennese middle class, and more particularly of the professional element to which he himself belongs. But on the basis of a wonderfully faithful portrayal of local characters and conditions, he has managed to rear a superstructure of emotional appeal and intellectual clarification that must render his work welcome to thinking men and women wherever it is introduced. (pp. xxxiii-xxxiv)

> *Edwin Björkman, in his introduction to "The Lonely Way," "Intermezzo," "Countess Mizzie": Three Plays by Arthur Schnitzler, translated by Edwin Björkman (copyright © 1915 by Little, Brown, and Company), Little, Brown, 1917, pp. vii-xxxiv.*

ASHLEY DUKES (essay date 1917)

Schnitzler, like most of the modern Viennese playwrights, is content to take as his theme only a few scenes from life, and even in those few scenes he recurs continually to a single passage. No wind instruments for him; he is a master

of the strings. To the Northern playwrights he leaves the wild barbaric march, to the Maeterlinckian symbolists the tone-poem. His dramatic method is the intellectualization, the refinement of the Viennese waltz. . . . His subject is always the same—the lover and a mistress or two. It is treated gracefully enough, with little passion and much gentle melancholy, little humor and much wit. His power lies chiefly in the creation of an atmosphere—a dim twilight atmosphere as of autumn evenings crowded with reminiscence. (pp. vii-viii)

That aristocrat-hero is Schnitzler's most charming characteristic figure. "New mistresses for old" is his eternal problem, and an imp is ever at his elbow, whispering that the old were better. Still he must obey the law of his own nature, and he accepts the necessity of change, as he accepts all else in his life, good-naturedly. (p. viii)

[Schnitzler's] drama depends upon a crisis in the lives of two people; the inevitable passing from old relationships to new. No flash of thought escapes him. He records every motive. In the crisis itself there can be no compromise. The break must come when one of the lovers desires it, however faintly. As long as Romance spreads her wings, the intimacy lasts; the instant they are folded it must come to an end at whatever cost of suffering. . . .

[Schnitzler] analyzes the transition moment in scenes such as those of *Anatol*. Outwardly, between the lovers, all is just as it was upon the first evening; inwardly everything is changed. The man must be free. Conversation grows lame. At last the explanation comes, and the woman departs; sometimes with frankly outstretched hand and a glance of understanding, sometimes helplessly in tears or riotously in a storm of indignation. . . . [These] are the Schnitzler hero and the Schnitzler heroine. They have most of the vices of their city and the quintessence of its charm; frivolity tinged with regret, and intrigue with grace. (p. ix)

Anatol represents the comedy of the lover-mistress motive, *Liebelei* the tragedy. In the former the man is the central figure; in the latter the woman. In *Liebelei* Christine meets her philanderer, and makes a hero of him. She becomes his mistress, and lives on in a dream-world of her own. Her hero is killed in a duel fought on behalf of another woman—and that is all. Of Christine it can only be said that she is as great a woman as is possible in the Schnitzler world: a world devised for men as surely as that of Strindberg, and in effect, although unconsciously, as contemptuous of women. The misogynist, indeed, is a lesser enemy of feminism than the philanderer. He is only the mouthpiece of ideas, not the arbiter of fates.

Liebelei was followed by the longer plays *Freiwild* and *Das Vermächtnis*. They represent the nearest approach that Austrian drama has made to the social problem play and the modernity movement of other countries. In social problems, however, Schnitzler is really out of his element. He has satirized the duel a thousand times more subtly than Sudermann in *Die Ehre*; he has ridiculed militarism, semitism, and anti-semitism, the government and the revolutionary parties. But his interests are not primarily political or social, any more than they are domestic. In *Reigen* he returns to the drama of personal moods. (p. x)

One can have too much of the twilight mood, the Viennese lover and his mistress, the melancholy and the grace. Everything that Schnitzler has written or imagined is summed up in the six hundred pages of his novel *Der Weg ins Freie*. There is the search for the "path of freedom" that he has never found. He has never made his way out of the half-world into the real world. But among the dramatists of the half-world he is supreme. (p. xi)

> *Ashley Dukes, in his introduction to "Reigen," "The Affairs of Antol" and Other Plays by Arthur Schnitzler, translated by Marya Mannes and Grace Isabel Colbron (copyright, 1917, by Boni & Liveright, Inc.; copyright, 1933, by The Modern Library, Inc.; reprinted by permission of Random House, Inc.), The Modern Library, 1933, pp. vii-xi.*

JOSEPH W. BAILEY (essay date 1920)

The shortcomings of Schnitzler as a literary artist are more in the nature of limitations than of actual faults. That is to say, the greatest weakness of his work is the narrowness of his scope. What he does he does with a grace and deftness which approaches perfection, but as we shall see, the range of his activity is not very wide. He has been called "the perfect Viennese", and those who are qualified to speak with authority have said that he has interpreted faithfully the Viennese life and atmosphere. . . . This, then, will constitute an important limitation to the scope of Schnitzler's work—it is restricted to city life and to the city life of Vienna in particular. Whether his scenes are laid in a suburb of Vienna or in some foreign city, his characters are distinctively urban and Viennese. In point of character types, he contents himself with dealing with those classes which he knew best—the cultured and idle representatives of the upper classes—and he deals with these only in their extra-official hours of recreation and love-making. Schnitzler does not concern himself with the *bürgerlich;* he is confined altogether to the aristocratic and artistic circles. His drama is always intensely personal; we find no suggestion of the social or economic problem in its broader aspects. The relation of sex to sex is his domain, and he reigns supreme within this province; but he seldom ventures beyond the limits which he has set for himself. . . . Schnitzler's work has also its scientific side. His dramas are, in the last analysis, little more than free studies in the psychology of sex, but let us remember that this field may ultimately be broadened to take in the whole of man's endeavor. (pp. 295-97)

I have said that the scope of Schnitzler's art is limited, and, from the standpoint of the materialist, this is true; but in so far as the passions of desire and pity may touch the heart of mankind, there is no limit to Schnitzler's appeal. The mystery of love and death is everywhere his theme. The tragedy of love—for love, as life, by reason of its very transiency, must have something of the tragic in it—and the tragedy of death . . . find expression, as it were, in ever-recurrent minor chords, and it is only in the lighter moments between that he allows himself, with a half playful air of cynical aloofness, to strike a major note. I do not wish to convey the impression that the dominant tone of his style is oppressively melancholy—quite to the contrary, it is replete with the tripping melody of wit and sarcasm—but, behind all his levity, we can sense the tell-tale note of pessimistic fatalism. . . . (pp. 299-300)

Schnitzler's manner of treatment in [*Anatol*] is intensely naturalistic. All the shades and subtleties of feeling are recorded, and no external detail is slighted. The action is

given a life-like accuracy. . . . The significant thing about *Anatol* is the proof it gives of the singular powers of Schnitzler as an artist: his delicate touch in the creation of an atmosphere, his supreme ability in the interpretation of emotion, and in the manufacture of dialogue.

In *Reigen,* Schnitzler has dealt even more candidly with the same theme: the amenability of all classes of mankind to the common passions. . . . Like *Anatol, Reigen* is expressive of the physician in Schnitzler, and is scientific in spirit as a study of the psychology of sex. In the broader significance it stresses the common nature of mankind and the fact that class distinctions are powerless before the onslaught of the basic passions of all men. (p. 302)

In *Liebelei,* one of Schnitzler's most powerful and far-reaching creations, although the theme is still the eternal passion of the love which is frowned upon by society, we see the other side of the shield—the tragic, sombre side. . . . The undercurrent of brooding sadness is felt everywhere in the play. Schnitzler's ever-present consciousness of the transiency of life and love is emphasized through every line. (p. 303)

Der Einsame Weg is, perhaps, Schnitzler's most powerful work. In this play, he rises to the height of his power in the depicting of human emotion. The inter-play of psychological reaction is so delicately subtle, the situations so realistic and lifelike in spite of the compression which is essential to the dramatic form, the appeal to the emotions of pity and regret so universal, that the play may be said to have ensured Schnitzler's reputation as a dramatist of the first order. The theme is still the same—the eternal tragedies of love and death, with the addition, as the title indicates, of the tragedy of loneliness, that twin shade and prelude to the final conqueror, Death—the unutterable pathos of continuing to breathe and to see when the passage of years has despoiled one's heart of all that life held dear. (p. 304)

[The] great fact behind all the minor sadnesses of life is the eternal tragedy of the passing of time—crushing and rending in its inexorable march all that it has made beautiful and strong—creating, nurturing, and then destroying, only to begin again its cycle of interminable labor. (p. 306)

> *Joseph W. Bailey, "Arthur Schnitzler's Dramatic Work," in* The Texas Review *(reprinted by permission of Southern Methodist University Press), Vol. V, No. 4, July, 1920, pp. 294-307.*

SIGMUND FREUD (essay date 1922)

I will make a confession which for my sake I must ask you to keep to yourself and share with neither friends nor strangers. I have tormented myself with the question why in all these years I have never attempted to make your acquaintance and to have a talk with you (ignoring the possibility, of course, that you might not have welcomed my overture).

The answer contains the confession which strikes me as too intimate. I think I have avoided you from a kind of reluctance to meet my double. Not that I am easily inclined to identify myself with another, or that I mean to overlook the difference in talent that separates me from you, but whenever I get deeply absorbed in your beautiful creations I invariably seem to find beneath their poetic surface the very presuppositions, interests, and conclusions which I know to be my own. Your determinism as well as your skepticism—what people call pessimism—your preoccupation with the truths of the unconscious and of the instinctual drives in man, your dissection of the cultural conventions of our society, the dwelling of your thoughts on the polarity of love and death; all this moves me with an uncanny feeling of familiarity. . . . So I have formed the impression that you know through intuition—or rather from detailed self-observation—everything that I have discovered by laborious work on other people. Indeed, I believe that fundamentally your nature is that of an explorer of psychological depths, as honestly impartial and undaunted as anyone has ever been, and that if you had not been so constituted your artistic abilities, your gift for language, and your creative power would have had free rein and made you into a writer of greater appeal to the taste of the masses. I am inclined to give preference to the explorer. But forgive me for drifting into psychoanalysis; I just can't help it. And I know that psychoanalysis is not the means of gaining popularity. (pp. 339-40)

> *Sigmund Freud, in his letter to Arthur Schnitzler on May 14, 1922, in* Letters of Sigmund Freud, *edited by Ernst L. Freud and translated by Tania & James Stern (© 1960 by Sigmund Freud Copyrights Ltd.),* Basic Books, Inc., Publishers, *1960, pp. 339-40.*

HUGO von HOFMANNSTHAL   (essay date 1922)

I cannot possibly speak of the Viennese theatre without coming immediately upon Arthur Schnitzler, . . . who has long been looked upon as Vienna's representative dramatic author in Germany as well as on the rest of the Continent, including Russia. (p. 307)

Schnitzler has assembled the mechanism of his larger and smaller pieces in the most skilful combinations and permutations of motives. Precisely in the construction and operation of these small but very subtle machines he showed his superiority as an artist.

The decisive element, the quality of international value, does not lie in these matters of structure, but in the vivid dialogue. Here great skill is employed to make the flow free and natural, while the characters analyse one another and frequently expose very deep undercurrents of thought and feeling; the conversation rolls on as though it were there simply for its own sake, to interest the people on the stage as well as those in the audience. For this reason it often happens that Schnitzler and Bernard Shaw are linked together, but they are fundamentally different in spirit and temperament. Their superficial point of contact is a preference for irony, but in this respect they could be classed with many men of genius. . . . [Those] pieces of [Schnitzler's] seem to me the best wherein this irony is situated not merely in the dialogue—as in all his more serious works where the *genre* comes quite close to the *comédie larmoyante*—but where irony also dominates the very nature of the action, as in the historical farce of *The Green Cockatoo,* or in several other of his one-act plays.

Physician and son of a physician, and thus a sceptic by calling, he is a product of the upper bourgeoisie at the close of the nineteenth century, a sceptical, observant, and historically-minded period not lacking in internal affinities with French life and culture of the eighteenth century; it is

to be expected, therefore, that this important and applauded dramatist should be a writer of distinguished short stories. Indeed, no two art forms have ever been closer to one another than the psychological play and the psychological story of the last generation. He is an unusual narrator; but it is not preëminently in the short form of which Maupassant and Kipling were masters, nor in the novel, but in the tale of medium length that he seems to me almost without a rival among his contemporaries. There is a peculiarly compelling force in the sheer narrative of these works. They hold the reader to the highest degree of suspense, and do this by an art which is rightly called sober, an epithet rarely applicable to a German author. But also in the case of his stories the strongest seem to me those in which his irony—with its constant touch of melancholy—is given a major importance. . . . (pp. 308-09)

> *Hugo von Hofmannsthal, "Vienna Letter," in* The Dial (*copyright, 1922, by The Dial Publishing Company, Inc.), Vol. LXXIII, No. 2, August, 1922 (and reprinted by Kraus Reprint Corporation, 1966), pp. 206-14.*

MALCOLM COWLEY   (essay date 1928)

For most writers of my generation, Schnitzler's early plays and novels are a romantic memory, associated with our first eager foray into modern literature. We read them in our college days, at a time when the modern drama was a prevailing fashion, when German seemed a language of the sophisticated, and when Vienna was the city of ultimate enchantment. Schnitzler to us was the modern drama, and he symbolized Vienna. Being very young, we failed to understand the half meanings in his plays; we disregarded most of their realistic elements; we prized them only for their glamour, for a sort of thick persistent charm, for their portrayal of a civilization that was tolerant, sentimental, rather witty and delightfully corrupt. We planned a visit to Vienna, we dreamt of young women—*süsse Mädl*—with yellow hair, brown eyes and a tolerant smile. . . .

That was, of course, before the war. The next ten years—lean years for every Austrian writer—have left hardly any direct reflection in Schnitzler's work. His later novels deal with the same characters, the same sort of incidents and substantially the same background as his early plays, but the glamour has disappeared. He has changed his method of approach. It is as if, instead of arriving through the porte-cochère, he opened the servants' door, climbed the back stairs and went poking through the closets for skeletons. He writes as a valet for whom no man is a hero. Héclassée his earlier heroes pursued their laughing careers. . . .

["Theresa"] is the story of a *déclassée* of a woman who descended from suitors to lovers and climbed from the parlor to a room under the eaves near the servants. . . .

One could write two reviews of this unpretentious novel. The first would be all praise—praise for its simplicity and straightforwardness, praise for the reality of all its characters, praise for the pitiless march of small events. One could congratulate Schnitzler for deserting the facile romanticism of his younger days, for stripping his work of all rhetoric and becoming an almost purely classical writer. The second review would present the same facts with a different interpretation: it would condemn the novel for being gray and monotonous; it would deplore the lack of dramatic or lyrical elements; it would suggest that the author is profoundly dispirited, tired of observing the human heart, tired of writing. . . . Personally I waver between the two attitudes; I respect Schnitzler's probity, but respect it coldly; I could wish him to be more vehement and less impeccable. At heart, I probably regret the glamour of his youthful books, which spoke so directly to the youth of our own generation.

Malcolm Cowley, "Backstairs" (copyright 1928 by I.H.T. Corporation; © renewed 1956 by Malcolm Cowley; used by permission), in New York Herald Tribune Books, *Vol. 88, No. 29911, October 7, 1928, p. 4.*

HARRY SLOCHOWER　(essay date 1931)

Arthur Schnitzler's permanent contribution to German literature lies in what might be called his French manner. To the turbid and difficult stylistic tradition in German writing, Schnitzler brought a light and clear idiom, carried along with taste, charm and wit. Even on those occasions when he turned toward close and minute psychological analyses, when Schnitzler the physician applied the microscope to the human soul (as in "Fraülein Else," "Lieutenant Gustl," "Daybreak"), his language preserves its freshness and lucidity. . . .

The mellow air of Vienna kept out [of Schnitzler's work] problems of dire poverty, of scientific determination, of economic maladjustments. . . . The sole mark that naturalism left on Austrian literature was the problem of *das süsse Mädel*—of the naïve suburban girl who enters the circle of the Viennese bohemia expecting love and becoming a light-o'-love instead. This theme almost exhausts the extent to which the Austrian writers were awakened to social consciousness.

Arthur Schnitzler represents perhaps the maturest expression of such light leanings. Courting and sex are the most dominant of his perplexities. This fact, by itself, hardly justifies an easy dismissal of the author: not the subject matter but its direction is decisive. For Strindberg and D. H. Lawrence, for Goethe and Richard Dehmel, sex also presents the most baffling material—but only because it is, to them, the tempest ground of the blindly irrational and unappeasable. They are concerned with sex because ultimately they are concerned with the cosmos. Schnitzler's arraignment of the transitoriness and uncertainty of life ("The Green Cockatoo," "Paracelsus") arises fundamentally out of his difficulty in solving the sex issue; he questions the cosmos primarily because he is in doubt about sex. His situations continually revolve about artist life in Vienna—bachelor apartments, cafés, soft lights and hushed voices. To be sure, Schnitzler's Anatol is not merely "light-minded"; he is also "melancholic." A note of *Weltschmerz* (or is it *Ichschmerz*?) runs through the greater part of Austrian literature. It is a nervous sensitiveness induced partly by the uncertain political fate of a country composed of differing nationalities, a country that was thus in constant, imminent danger of dissolution. There is in Schnitzler, too, a sad undercurrent ("Dying," "Beatrice," "Therese"). With mature reflection, he came to realize the limitations of his city's *Lebensstil*, the emptiness and hypocrisy of its social patterns. Yet he rests satisfied with a mere statement of his doubts regarding the value of the moment, and is content

with simply registering his perplexities as to the distinction between the real and the illusory ("Paracelsus"). His sadness is caused by a surface consideration of life's impermanence. His weariness and sense of futility are not preceded by a courageous search for enduring goods. His heroes, too, are passive creatures; they leave the arena before the gong is sounded.

Schnitzler's difficulties have sometimes been termed prewar problems. Yet even that seems an overstatement. Are his themes characteristic of the pre-war world as sketched in "The World's Illusion" or "The Magic Mountain"? Is there anywhere in Schnitzler's work a consideration of social inequalities, as in [Jakob] Wassermann's novel? Are Schnitzler's characters aware of such problems as trouble the Settembrinis and the Naphtas? The profound upheavals since 1914 seem to have brought about no inner disturbances, no shift of interests. The World War was not, to Schnitzler, what it was to most writers, a Rubicon to be crossed. Even the revolutionary social changes that visited Vienna failed to ruffle the surface of Schnitzler's literary individualism. From "Fräulein Else" to "Therese," from "Light-o'-Love" to "The Wide Land," we have but nuances—subtle, delicate, entertaining—of one inconsequential theme. While Thomas Mann was outgrowing his flirtations with the Tonio Krögers and the Hanno Buddenbrooks, turning his powers toward "The Demands of the Day"; while Alfred Doeblin and even Hugo von Hofmannsthal were growing critical of their esthetic individualism, Schnitzler was concerned with "Therese": the problem of a governess who is too weak to say "no" because the men of her particular milieu do not expect it of her. (p. 22)

Attempts have been made to show that there are unknown depths in Schnitzler; the trite and obvious "Sprüche und Bedenken" ought to serve as a warning. Attention is also called to his tinge of pessimism. A temper of despair deserves our admiration if it is reached through an earnest meeting with primary issues; Schnitzler's discontent arises out of the fact that lovers are generally not true to each other and that old age reduces man to impotence. . . . His work is the final charming embodiment of a culture, sweet, feminine and tired; it is the tactful expression of an age that is not unmourned. There is value in a closing chapter, well told.

"Flight into Darkness" . . . has the same characteristics as his earlier works, the faultless construction, the skillful analysis. Once more we are in Vienna; once more there is *Liebelei;* there are even sad melodies "hauntingly reminiscent of Chopin." The story concerns an incorrigible hypochondriac suffering from persecution mania. In dealing with this individual, the author's purpose is not to shed light on the abnormality in question; it is rather to suggest the darkness, baffling all analysis, in which "the disquieting complexity of individual cases" is hidden. This last of Schnitzler's novels is far from being the best; it is, indeed, a weak Danubian echo of Strindberg's "Inferno." (pp. 22-3)

Harry Slochower, "Arthur Schnitzler," in The New Republic *(© 1931 The New Republic, Inc.), Vol. 69, No. 885, November 18, 1931, pp. 22-3.*

SOL LIPTZIN　(essay date 1932)

[Arthur] Schnitzler's answers to various problems affecting

the relations between human beings, are presented by him merely as possibilities, and not as final solutions. No sooner is one possibility expressed than he becomes cognizant of another that is equally as plausible. He, then, often succumbs to the temptation of satirizing good-naturedly the very opinion that his hero or heroine has just as fervently defended. (p. 81)

The best manifestation of Schnitzler's sardonic tone is to be discerned in his *Reigen*. . . . (p. 97)

Reigen is a series of ten dialogues depicting the roundelay of sexuality. Like the dance of death, which the medieval artists were fond of portraying, the dance of sex may also lay claim to universality. In dispassionate, melancholy conversations, Schnitzler seeks to sketch the pettiness, the brutality, and the absurdity of the sex experience whenever it is purely a physical expression devoid of spiritual meaning. With painful accuracy, he dissects what some people dare to call love but what to him is a ghastly desecration of this sacred term. He points out how much of human life is wasted in pursuit of a moment's pleasure, how little this fleeting experience really should mean to reasoning creatures and how horrible and inevitable are the disappointments that such moments bring in their wake. With astounding courage, he tears off the mask of hypocrisy that covers sexuality. With amazing frankness, he reveals the technique of the game of sex as played by the many who seek the gratification of physical desires without the participation of their psychic personalities. He shows how the man pursues the woman until he succeeds in arousing in her a dangerous emotional wave, and how he then ruthlessly hurls her away. He portrays the woman for whom, whether she be huntress or hunted, the sensual experience always ends in utter disillusionment. He presents the young person who thinks he is entering on a grand adventure, but who, in the end, feels ridiculous and ashamed. He selects his characters from all social strata and all walks of life, and depicts everyone of them as equally pitiable. . . . Schnitzler's humor in these dialogues is bathed in sadness. His mirth is tinged with melancholy. The kind-hearted physician and dramatist sighs over our sick and sorrowful society in which healthy instincts are reduced to selfish lusts, and tragic passions degenerate into petty vices. . . . *Reigen* contains much of the wisdom of the unconventional Viennese thinker. (pp. 98-9)

Freedom is, to Schnitzler, that ideal state in which a person understands himself and the world about him. No person can enter on the road to freedom so long as he lies to himself, nor so long as he feels conscience-stricken when others condemn those actions of his which he deems justified. (p. 211)

[In *Der Weg ins Freie*] Baron Georg von Wergenthin, twenty-seven years old, drifts into an affair with Anna Rosner, a kind, respectable, middle-class girl. On the day on which she gives birth to their child, he leaves her. In doing so, he is aware that, though others might be blamed for acting thus in similar situations, no guilt is attaching itself to him. He is certain that he is behaving correctly. (p. 212)

Georg departs without remorse. He accepts the interpretation of the experience that Heinrich Bermann gives him: "Anna was, perhaps, fashioned to be your beloved, but not your wife. Who knows but what the person she will marry some day, will not have every reason to be grateful to you,

if only husbands were not so terribly stupid!" With this moral absolution from his best friend, Georg leaves the city of his youth; and, in a mild intoxication of pain and freedom, he sets out on the road toward his new center of activity.

Heinrich Bermann is left behind. The profoundest thinker among Schnitzler's young men, he is, also, the unhappiest, perhaps because he probes too deeply. Wanting to understand everything, he is at the same time aware that understanding exercises no appreciable influence upon our emotions, and rarely affects our actions. . . . Depth of insight does not lead to clarity, but rather it leads to a realization of the abysmal confusion within us. It does not make for happiness, but rather for a knowledge of our helplessness. It does not simplify our lives, but rather renders us aware of the infinite, uncontrollable threads that determine our acts. (pp. 221-24)

Does Schnitzler, then, wish to pave the way for moral anarchy by negating existing moral assumptions? Does he, by his merciless arraignment of conventional ethics, aim to undermine the pillars of family life and social institutions? Does he, by opening our eyes to infinite possibilities and by tearing down all taboos, also lend his approval to everything we may undertake, to every piece of villainy and every form of excess? Not at all! Schnitzler is not immoral, as his foes assert. On the contrary, he profoundly believes that every one of us has in his breast a moral seismograph that registers every minute deviation from the right path. In some mysterious way we know at every moment what we may or may not do. We even know when we may commit murder without sinning. But we also know that many of our acts for which we receive praise, are not necessarily good. Our chief moral fault lies in our not listening to the infallible measuring instrument in our souls, in our not trying to understand ourselves, in our seeking to ferret out justifiable motives for everything we do whether rightly or wrongly.

The only criminals for whom there is no atonement are, according to Schnitzler, those who act against their own nature. The only duties, the fulfillment of which may, perhaps, at times benefit others, are the duties one owes to oneself. All moral confusion results from the fact that but few people know their own true nature, and that only a very small minority of these have the courage to act in accordance with it. Yet, these alone are on the road to freedom. (pp. 224-25)

Sol Liptzin, in his Arthur Schnitzler *(copyright © 1932 by Prentice-Hall, Inc.), Prentice-Hall, Inc., 1932, 275 p.*

H. S. REISS (essay date 1945)

A study of the work of Arthur Schnitzler shows the important part which investigations into the various aspects of human life play in it. Among them the problems of personal relationships occupied his attention. In his consideration of those problems he is primarily an observer and as such he is never dogmatic; he considers the complexity of human nature, the various and infinite possibilities which exist in life. He merely states the problem, he shows its dependence on the character of the persons concerned, but he will never commit himself to any solution; for there never can be any solution to his problems for him. They are only discussed and illustrated, but not solved. They are problems of human life as complex and as flexible as they must be on account of the variety of circumstance and character. Thus each problem will require a different solution according to the different circumstances, and no standard solution can be drawn up; there never is a hard and fast guide to human conduct, for what may be right in one specific instance may be wrong in another, and what may be wrong in one may be right in another.

Schnitzler did not confine his study of problems to those of personal relationships. Other problems also occupied his mind, and among them the problems of fate and of religion must be considered as an essential basis of an understanding of his philosophy of life, which to so large an extent determined the value of his work. Schnitzler, as can be seen from his work, has studied the power of fate in human affairs throughout his life.

The principal conception which he has of fate is that we can never understand its working; it will always be incomprehensible to our minds. We are ignorant of its strange ways. Something may happen at any moment anywhere which may affect our future life, yet we cannot have the slightest notion of it. (p. 300)

Fate is inscrutable; thus we are to conclude from several of Schnitzler's short stories, such as *Die Weissagung,* a tale somewhat reminiscent of the romantic fate tragedy, where everything happens in the life of the hero, so that a picture a fortune-teller conjured up for him one day to forecast what was going to happen to the hero ten years later becomes reality, in spite of all the attempts of the hero to prevent its occurrence. (p. 303)

It would be wrong to identify Schnitzler's own opinions with those of any of his characters; one can only observe the general tendency in the outlook of his characters, the universal current of thought underlying all their ideas. Georg von Wergenthin thus has a feeling after the death of his child that its death was predetermined before its birth, that it had to die in order that some incomprehensible law of nature could be obeyed. Yet it would be a mistake to classify Schnitzler as a determinist because such statements appear in his work.

In order to gain a clearer picture of what Schnitzler's conception of fate was, one has to turn to *Das Buch der Sprüche und Bedenken.* Schnitzler is essentially a sceptic in outlook, and it is not surprising for a sceptic to be unable to hold a belief in a predestined way of life. Fate may appear to him as something mysterious, something incomprehensible, but he will not be able to view it as a preordained pattern. It is not surprising, therefore, that Schnitzler will not consider this world to be an ordered whole with a purpose, but will be a strong believer in the existence of free will. In the chapter *Schicksal und Wille* he expresses this strong conviction. Free will seems to him an essential part of life. He feels that there would have to be free will, even if one were to imagine that all actions had followed some law of causality; it strikes him as unimaginable that a choice was not made at the beginning and that some decision was not made by some will then. He feels that without a free will the world would not only lack any sense and purpose, but also be completely boring, because lack of responsibility destroys any ethical code. . . . (pp. 303-04)

Fate thus seems mysterious and inexplicable. This conclusion must be drawn from a study of Schnitzler's dramas and

his fiction, and it is also confirmed by a study of *Das Buch der Sprüche und Bedenken.* He states that the workings of fate are inexplicable; even that which appears to be a completely accidental event can be caused by one's own action and often the chance event will appear like fate; if considered from a higher point of view. Fate and chance will really appear identical, if viewed from this point of view. (p. 304)

From Schnitzler's drama and fiction one may receive the impression that he was in no way concerned with the problems of religion, with the conception of a reality which is greater than that of this world, and, in his eyes, religion seemed to play no part in life, as far as personal morals were concerned. For the world of his characters is a world without any morality of right and wrong, without any absolute standards. It is a world of reason and rationalization, an amoral world in which the inhabitants can only sin on account of their lack of wisdom and intelligence, but not on account of transgressing absolute standards of right and wrong. He never points out that an action is immoral or wrong in the higher sense. He only points out that certain actions, that a certain conduct, will lead to unhappiness or appear pointless in the eyes of reason, but he introduces nowhere the principles of a higher code of Christian ethics. No absolute standards of right and wrong are introduced anywhere into personal relationships or into any other part of his work. (p. 305)

Das Buch der Sprüche und Bedenken makes it clear that Schnitzler was occupied with the question of religion. Religion being so very much a matter of faith and belief, Schnitzler was in great difficulty. He finds it hard, if not impossible to believe. He can only doubt. As he himself admits the limitations of human reason, he feels that in his scepticism and his doubts he experiences devotion and worship, and that which others call faith can be found in them, too. It is not faith, he thinks, that is necessary, but our questions to the divine which make us spiritually rich. (p. 306)

A study of the problems which Schnitzler treated in his work makes it obvious that he is primarily an observer, that his vision is limited by the boundaries of this world, as he cannot reach by faith and spiritual guidance beyond them. His attitude towards fate and the divine in life is the attitude of the relativist, the man who will never commit himself to any definite point of view, who affirms the independence and individuality of the human being, as far as this world is concerned, but who can only reserve his judgment as to the world beyond. . . . (p. 307)

[This] observation of and commentary on the spectacle of the world, did not allow him to have a definite point of view which he could express in his work. . . . (pp. 307-08)

> *H. S. Reiss, "The Problem of Fate and of Religion in the Work of Arthur Schnitzler," in* The Modern Language Review *(© Modern Humanities Research Association 1945), Vol. XL, No. 4, October, 1945, pp. 300-08.*

RICHARD PLANT (essay date 1950)

One attitude [common in the criticism of Arthur Schnitzler's writings] seems to have survived with remarkable tenacity. Perhaps we may call it the Sunday-school approach. It reproves the author for his stories that deal with aspects of the erotic better left undiscussed; it takes him to task for discussing marital infidelity, the sexual awakening of young people, the promiscuity of his heroes and heroines and finally, for his lack of indignation while relating all these happenings. Emphatically, these crusaders disapprove of the philandering Anatols and Casanovas, scold the *süsse Mädel* for her lack of resistance and, carried away by their own zest, they do not bother to look at what Schnitzler really has achieved. (p. 13)

[It is] the vast domain of the soul which unceasingly occupied Arthur Schnitzler, a panorama that can never be charted completely. Never weary, he plumbed the depths of the human psyche, tracing its aberrations, soarings, downfalls, and duplicities. In his stories, he usually opens up the soul of one single person, registers every change and development of emotions, moods, fears, hopes, associating one with the other and using a palette of the finest shading. Thus even those *Novellen* which are recounted from several points of view can be called multiple "Ich-Novellen," since the workings of different characters are laid bare with equal omniscience. (pp. 16-17)

[There] is one element which plays and stories have in common, which, as effective on the stage as in a narrative, seems to me a primary element of Schnitzler's writings. It is, in a way, an instrument of technique, used so often that one might call it a signature of the author's productions. It is not the characters—they are not the central point of interest for the author because they repeat themselves too constantly. . . . The central point is, rather, a constellation of two or a few characters, an initial relationship, almost abstract, which is then wheeled around, switched back, turned in an unexpected direction until it is almost reversed. (p. 17)

This chain of cautiously calculated turnabouts we also find in one of Schnitzler's most moving, perhaps one of his best stories, *Der blinde Geronimo*. . . . Perhaps the reader senses even in [its] comparatively simple turnabout structure the intelligence of an engineer, of a mathematician rather than of an orthodox impressionist or lyricist. This is what gives Schnitzler's best plays their hardness, what prevents them from being *Stimmungsbilder,* evocations of mood, or case histories.

Schnitzler is a juggler of psychological situations which he wheels around and around, and in which usually someone's attempt to achieve a certain aim brings, ironically, the opposite result. Quite often, perhaps too often, the author uses erotic constellations as basic structures. However, he records mainly the dynamics of love, the eternally changing aspects of an affair, the self-deception and the deception of others, the shock of recognition of one's own possibilities and dangers. He has fashioned many of his plots as erotic puzzles to which he supplies surprising (or if one has come to know him, not so surprising) answers. He is lucid even when presenting chaos and turmoil, and his dramatic use of the *Umbruch* distinguishes, him from the archimpressionists, from Herman Bang, Jens Peter Jacobsen, or Maurice Maeterlinck. (pp. 17-18)

In Schnitzler's two monologue stories, *Leutnant Gustl* and *Fräulein Else,* these *Umbrüche* happen so frequently that it becomes impossible to count them. *Leutnant Gustl,* one of Schnitzler's most acid and most successful humorous stories, centers around the insult of a fat baker to what the

young lieutenant considers his honor. . . . Conveniently, Schnitzler mercilessly exposes the shallow and cold character of his slightly oversexed hero. As a matter of fact, the virtuoso technique of interlinked chains with which Schnitzler manages to convey Gustl's whole world might easily obscure the fact that the basic idea is again a reversal. . . .

That the basic blueprint of this *Liebesdenkspieler,* this mathematician of love, does not change from 1894 to the works of his later years can be most clearly illustrated by *Spiel im Morgengrauen,* published in 1926. Not only does Kasda constantly win and lose during the card games, whereby the perspectives of his future life are opened and closed in rapid succession, but after he has killed himself, the very uncle who had refused to advance the necessary money, rushes to the scene with the needed sum. The money was lent to his uncle by the woman who seemingly refused to pay Kasda and who has made him feel ashamed of himself. The speed of these reversals lends the story something mechanical, as though the characters were puppets. Schnitzler, if he was conscious of the puppet quality inherent in many of his works, must have been unable to change this pattern. Thus, in *Der grosse Wurstl* he drives this calculus of love and death to a point where it becomes a parody of itself. (p. 19)

Amadeus' infidelity [in *Zwischenspiel*]—a psychological, not an actual one—is as subtle as are the reactions of most Schnitzler characters to the known or feared, the provoked, witnessed, the purposely brought about, deception. Cäcilie pretends a betrayal in order to regain Amadeus whom, at the end, she no longer wants, whereby the initial situation is reversed. This *Liebesdenkspiel* is, it seems to me, much more typical of Schnitzler's work than his themes, his figures, his philosophy, or even his style. (pp. 20-1)

A glance at the seven published Anatol sketches reveals that each, using one or more turnabouts, centers around a past, present, or future duplicity. A catalogue of the plays and prose works in which some sort of deception furnishes the core, or at least a turning point of the plot would amount to a full list of Schnitlzer's writings. . . .

This sort of plot, centering around a betrayal, furnishes excellent possibilities for a complicated story exploring the psyche of one person. (p. 21)

[The] round of infidelities, mistaken identities and deceptions, driven forward by one turnabout after another [in *Casanova in Spa*] might be called a *Betrugsdenkspiel,* a game with all the imaginable facets of deceit. It represents the epitome of Schnitzler's dialectics of the erotic. Yet despite the wit of its brilliant verses, it defies its purpose, because the author has become so engrossed in his engineering that he has left little room for the portrayal of his personae, who seem smothered by pure mechanics.

A similar abundance of mechanics can be found in many of his longer stories. Fortunately, what the playwright presented as action or in self-analytical dialogues or monologues, the prose writer can develop cautiously in the "Ich-Novelle" with its interlocking links of associations. A peculiar brand of betrayal, a rather singular series of psychological equations, is revealed in *Frau Beate und ihr Sohn,* a much maligned story. Granted the *Betrugsdenkspiel* appears as tangled as that of *Casanova in Spa;* but the narrative method allows the author to X-ray his people in such a virtuoso manner that we forget the mathematics. This time, the betrayal is of a special nature. Beate, widow of the famous actor Ferdinand, mother of an adolescent boy, Hugo, has succumbed to the advances of her son's friend, Fritz. . . . As [Beate's] guilt feelings mount, she begins to feel responsible for her boy's strained love affair with the much older Baroness Fortunata. Very discreetly, Schnitzler makes us aware of the interchangeability of his figures. As to Beate herself, we guess that in young Fritz she has loved only her son Hugo: Schnitzler does not make it too explicit but the story's end, I think, hardly leaves any doubt. Hugo, in turn, stands for her actor husband Ferdinand, whose erratic nature had always confused and fascinated her. In addition, she is now certain that Ferdinand deceived her with many women, that he found in her only consolation, peace, protection against himself.

But Schnitzler does not stop here. Ferdinand was not simply one person with fixed qualities. A true actor, he was Hamlet, Don Carlos, Richard III, presenting a different face, a different character every night. . . . To the outside world, she was a devoted wife, but in reality she fulfilled her dangerous longings for adventure. (p. 23)

Characteristically, two main facts that Ferdinand was really Hamlet, Richard III, etc., and that he had many flirtations are furnished by Beate's memory. . . . The remembered deception thus brings about another mental turn, because the entire relationship between Beate and Ferdinand is revealed in a new light. But in a masterful manner, Schnitzler conveys to us that, of course, Beate is not quite sure of her suspicions: memory is most unreliable, as irresponsible as hope and wish. . . . *Frau Beate* seems as typical of Schnitzler's pattern as *Casanova in Spa,* but the monologue story helps the artist Schnitzler to triumph over the constructor. With everything enclosed within the sensibility of a single personality, *Beate* depicts the dialectics of the soul, with one *Umbruch* after another to propel the plot forward. The psychological equations are worked out intricately, but not to such a degree as to turn the figures to mere puppets. *Betrug*—actual, remembered, direct or oblique—causes the turnabouts which lead the psyche into a realization of its own abyss. (p. 24)

[The] *Liebesdenkspieler,* the engineer of psychological equations, whose constructions, though solidly built and firmly soldered, are easily overlooked, because Arthur Schnitzler has hidden them, obscured them by his stream-of-consciousness method. And it is this method with which he has brought the impressionist German short story to perfection while at the same time transcending it. (p. 25)

> Richard Plant, "Notes on Arthur Schnitzler's Literary Technique," in The Germanic Review (copyright 1950 by Helen Dwight Reed Foundation; reprinted by permission of Heldref Publications), Vol. XXV, No. 1, February, 1950, pp. 13-25.

CLAUDE HILL   (essay date 1961)

From the point of German literary history, Schnitzler's first book has remained his most important work. . . . In each of the short dialogues [in *Anatol*] we find the charming, blasé, frivolous and at the same time melancholy, philandering amateur-poet Anatol in the center, aided by his skeptic, realistic, raisoneur-friend Max. In each of the little scenes a different woman appears, each one a variation of the

"sweet girl" (Süsses Mädel) which has been associated with Vienna ever since and which Schnitzler has created again and again in many plays. Elegant escapism, nostalgia, resignation, slight neurosis, ever fleeting time, relativity of human feelings and experiences—these are the ingredients of Anatol's world. . . . [It] is the elegance and sophistication of the dialogue as well as the over-all enchantment of the mood that make this, Schnitzler's first work, an important literary document. In its emphasis on illusion rather than reality, and its fixation on the moment in the flux of time, *Anatol* is the best example of Impressionism in the history of German literature.

After a few rather pale attempts at the stage with topical plays (about duelling, about "fallen" girls, about society's attitude to illegitimate offspring), Schnitzler scored a great popular success with *Light-o'-Love* which he never surpassed with any other dramatic work. . . . The plot of this extremely touching drama is simple and developed with artistic economy; the characters . . . are well drawn; the bitter-sweet mood of love in the shadow of death places the play in the vicinity of genuine tragedy. Christine is the most touching "Süsses Mädel" that Schnitzler ever created.

Anatol and *Light-o'-Love* circumscribe the thematic range of most of Schnitzler's dramatic work. Love and flirtation, faithfulness and infidelity, upper-class man and lower-class woman, fleeting time and the finality of death, dreamy illusion and life's seeming reality—these are the conflicts and problems of the Austrian playwright's heroes and heroines, victims and bystanders. The impressionist's concentration on the moment as the only safe reality in the constant shift of appearances naturally led Schnitzler to the short form of drama, the one-act play, in which he brilliantly excelled. (pp. 82-3)

When Schnitzler dealt with topical problems in his plays, he was usually not too successful. He often piled one conflict on top of another, or even shifted his main interest suddenly in the middle of a drama to a new issue. . . . Schnitzler was at his best when he remained within the range of his personal and professional experiences. By far his best topical play is, therefore, *Professor Bernhardi* . . . , which deals with people and issues he knew well: doctors, clinical atmosphere, a problem of medical ethics, and the issue of anti-Semitism. . . . Of all of Schnitzler's mature full-length plays, *Professor Bernhardi* is by far his best work. The issues are sharply drawn, the plot logically developed, the characters superbly vivid. With the exception of one insignificant nurse part, there are no women in this drama, and no love conflict arises. Although written somewhat pro domo by an author who knew what it meant to be a Jew in the academic world of Imperial Austria, the anti-Semitic issue is never unduly stressed and only underlines the main problem of medical ethics. Although Schnitzler continued to produce dramas until the year of his death, he never equalled, in quality of plot development and individual characterization, his physician-drama of 1912.

Schnitzler's fiction comprises as many or more titles as his dramatic production, but its impact on the course of modern literature has been less notable. . . . Between 1890 and 1910 it is mainly the short story which attracted him, while in later years he was more interested in the longer forms of the novella and novel. The reason for this is simple: one-act play and short story were the proper vehicles of expression for the leader of "Young Vienna," who

. . . clung to the moment as the only safe reality. An exception is *Sterben* . . . , which, however, might be more properly called a psychological study than a novella. A man, given one more year to live by his doctor slowly adjusts himself to his fate and while he disintegrates, his bride, who was once ready to die with him, is gradually alienated and finally comes to hate and fear him. The piece is a superb clinical-psychological study, written at a time when the author was still close to the active practice of medicine. Most of the short stories are in the same sardonic, frivolous, flirtatious vein as are Schnitzler's short playlets. What makes them stand out among similar short fiction in German letters is un-Teutonic charm, gracefulness, and lucidity of style.

Of great importance for modern world literature is a satirical story, *Leutnant Gustl* . . . , which has often been dismissed as "just an amusing skit," although it represents an experiment in the modern stream-of-consciousness technique long before James Joyce. . . . The whole story is conceived from the lieutenant's point of view and is one gigantic "interior monologue," as some critics have called it. The author has recorded the complete chain of associations as they enter his hero's mind, with all the seemingly illogical jumps and shifts. Since Schnitzler handles the new technique with superb mastery, the whole background of a typically young, carefree, slightly foolish, and yet lovable officer of his time and class (Viennese society at the turn of the century) becomes transparent. . . . Schnitzler later repeated his tour-de-force in the well-known novella *Fräulein Else* . . . with great popular success. . . . The satirical and sardonic mood of *Leutnant Gustl* has become sad and tragic [in *Fräulein Else*], the technique is the same "interior monologue," and the psychological skill of the author, particularly in the passages prior to the girl's death, is extraordinary.

Fräulein Else reveals one of Schnitzler's strongest assets as a writer: his unusual and penetrating understanding of the female psyche. His women are generally more interesting and more alive than his men. (pp. 85-7)

Just as Schnitzler succeeded in writing one successful topical play, *Professor Bernhardi*, which turned out to become his best drama, so he reached his peak as a novelist with *The Road to the Open* (*Der Weg Ins Freie* . . .), his longest and most autobiographical work. . . . What makes the novel mainly interesting is the broad tapestry of Viennese pre-war society against which the thin plot is developed: men and women of the lower aristocracy and the upper middle class with a large sprinkling of Jews, social life in the salons and café-houses, and the issues of Austrian politics, anti-Semitism, the Zionist movement, (Schnitzler knew Herzl well), Chauvinism, tolerance, and art in its broad bearing on social culture. Schnitzler felt himself to be an Austrian writer within the broader stream of German civilization, and he presented his different Jewish types with great objectivity and often with a somewhat ironic condescension. In view of what was to happen in Austria three decades later, his novel is an important document of courage, insight, and artistic objectivity. (pp. 87-8)

Schnitzler as the poet of Vienna is not only to be viewed as the most charming portraitist of that city in German literature, but must be considered one of the first great urban writers from the focal point of comparative literature and sociology.

Some of Schnitzler's most engaging qualities might possibly be traced to his city background: his wit, sophistication, elegance of style, and artistic taste. He is one of the very few German authors who can make the *grosse Welt* believable. . . . His is a style of utmost lucidity, free of pompousness or sentimentality; his short stories call Somerset Maugham to mind. As Thomas Mann once remarked, Schnitzler's superb taste has prevented him from making a single mistake. Considering the delicate and daring nature of many of his themes, his sure artistic tact seems astonishing. He knew what to say, how much to say, and where to stop. His graceful, simple style ranks with the best masters of German prose.

What assures Schnitzler his place in the world literature of the current century is precisely that preoccupation with sex and depth-psychology which formerly shocked his critics. He was aware of the erratic nature of human behavior and saw the human soul as a "vast domain" (as he called it in one of his less successful dramas), at a time which still believed in the conventional psychology of the unified personality. He realized the importance of the dream as the gate to the subconscious. With the equipment of the psychiatrist, he expressed through the medium of literature what Freud arrived at through scientific research. . . . [He] was one of the first authors to probe into the hitherto hidden motivations of his characters. His concentration on sex, which was often misunderstood as a sign of frivolity by naïve critics, is only the proof of his affinity to Freudian psychoanalysis. While many of Schnitzler's plays are obsolete and beyond rescue because of issues dead today (duelling, illegitimate children, women's rights in marriage), his narrative work—or at least a great deal of it—must be considered part of living world literature, since it is still meaningful and modern in every aspect. Since Joyce's lonely attempts at isolating the particles of the human soul in the muddy stream of the subconscious seem to lead to the obliteration of literature, a study of Schnitzler's more moderate "interior monologue" may show a literary technique worth studying and developing. It could be that in this respect, too, he knew how far the artist should go. (pp. 89-91)

Claude Hill, "The Stature of Arthur Schnitzler," in Modern Drama *(copyright © 1961, University of Toronto, Graduate Centre for Study of Drama; with the permission of* Modern Drama*), Vol. 4, No. 1, May, 1961, pp. 80-91.*

HUNTER G. HANNUM (essay date 1962)

Reigen . . . is a masterful dramatic statement of Schnitzler's attitudes toward time. . . . The scenes, their Janus-faced composition pointing to both past and future, inexorably locate the characters in that context of time which they more or less consciously are always trying to escape. The aesthete's "day" has, as already anticipated in *Anatol*, been reduced to the most evanescent of moments, the moment of sexual satisfaction as experienced by two persons who are seeking only that from one another. (p. 198)

Like Felix in *Sterben* but without his reason for urgency, the people in *Reigen* realize that their living is a "Sein zum Tode" and act similarly to the earlier hero by seizing upon the moment of pleasurable sensation as their only guarantee of existence. The temporal aspect of this behavior has been described by Bernhard Blume as "aus der 'Zeit' in die

'Fülle' flüchten,'' and it is now necessary to examine this ''Fülle.''

''Fülle'' can of course be only a matter of minutes for Schnitzler's characters—a fleeting, momentary thing. The action of *Reigen* emphasizes this without the aid of any overt philosophizing on the part of the characters by building its brief scenes around a sexual act with no ''before'' or ''after'' (the ''before'' was with another partner as the ''after'' will be). The act refuses thus to ''acquire history,'' to become a part of time; it is discontinuous, its very nature precluding duration. (p. 199)

[Kierkegaard's] ''poetic infinitude, which can just as well be limited to an hour as to a month,'' is what Schnitzler's characters are seeking under the name of ''Fülle'': *Reigen* chronicles this search with its increasing and inevitable frustrations. It is usually felt that this particular play, with its title and analogous structure, precludes any form of dramatic development. Insofar as ''dramatic development'' suggests a progressive action with a beginning, middle, and end, and a cast of characters who to greater or lesser extents come to realizations of their human condition through this action, this usual skepticism about *Reigen* is well founded. . . . But to deny any kind of development in *Reigen* is to overlook the author's careful evolution and increasingly sharper statement of theme in the frenetic rondo of his ten scenes.

Among the more conventional deterrents to the full enjoyment of the present moment in *Reigen* is the characters' consciousness of the pasts of their partners. Anatol too had been tormented by the infidelity of others, but in the later play this sentiment is both more widespread (both male and female characters share it) and even more ironic; for Anatol is a model of constancy compared to these figures whose brief unions are so clearly framed for us by those of the preceding and following scenes. Anatol had found a sort of solution to the shock caused by his partners' infidelities: hasten to anticipate them in this sphere. (pp. 200-01)

The present was the most precarious among the chaos of tenses which defined Anatol's character. We recall that during the course of an erotic experience he already imagined it to himself as past, as a tender memory among many others. Another and even more effective way to undermine the present moment is to forget rather than remember it as it occurs. Anatol at least has his memories to shore up against his ruins; by browsing among the mementos of past love affairs which he deposited with Max, he can be sure that he has existed, although saddened by the consciousness of the tense. But if such a character has a bad memory, how can he be certain of his existence at all? ''Forgetting,'' then, becomes a motif which is stated with ever-increasing strength in *Reigen* until it represents the final and fatal triumph of time over the characters; for by robbing the aesthete of his consciousness of sensation, he is thereby robbed of his very existence. . . . By losing their grasp on the present moment . . . , the characters in *Reigen* also lose the clear contours of personality, also lose their identities. If the aesthete exists only for and in the present moment, he necessarily loses all reality when that moment loses reality. The first step in this process is the growing indistinctness of the partner in an erotic experience . . . ; the next and inevitable step for Schnitzler is the blurring of the experience itself for the subject.

[Although] *Reigen* has no *raisonneur* like Max, [in *Anatol*], who stands somewhat outside the action and comments upon it in neatly-turned epigrams, Schnitzler has given his later play a ''philosopher'' of sorts, and, by making him an integral part of the action, the author is able to give his play both increased dramatic objectivity and irony. The Count in the last two scenes is a near relation of those other aesthetes, Felix and Anatol, with the possible difference that his station in life permits him an even more exclusive and spectacular dedication to the pursuit of pleasure. As we would expect, then, his ''tungsind'' is even deeper than theirs. Through his practice of the ''rotation method,'' he has come to feel that all fields are equally unexciting and essentially interchangeable. When stationed in Hungary he looked forward to the diversions of Vienna; once arrived in Vienna he found that the only difference was that the crowds in that city were larger. He envies the Actress whom he is visiting because he assumes that she must know why she is living: she has the lofty goal of her art to pursue. When she denies any knowledge of purpose in her life, he points out that after all she is famous, celebrated. Then a highly significant conversation takes place about the central problem of ''happiness'' and its relation to time. . . . (pp. 201-02)

Here is the time philosophy of the characters in *Reigen* made explicit, but, as we shall see, this is not Schnitzler's own final statement on the theme in the play. The isolated moment with no before or after is the only element in which these characters can exist; and insofar as the moment is discontinuous, the character too must be discontinuous. For this reason . . . there can be no conventional development of character in a play such as *Reigen*. In the scenes toward the end involving the Actress and the Count, this discontinuity of character becomes so pronounced that we are confronted with a constant stream of non sequiturs. The figure of the actor or actress is supremely suited for the dramatic presentation of this inconstancy. The actor, as Nietzsche pointed out (and Schnitzler must have agreed with him), with his capacity for lightning-swift ''changes,'' typifies ''falseness with a good conscience,'' shows ''the joy in dissimulation breaking out'' to such an extent that it ''pushes the so-called 'character' to the side, drowns it, at times even extinguishes it.'' In her scene with the Poet, the Actress voices changing opinions in practically every speech, referring for example to her present lover as a ''whim,'' then as a man for whom she is ''dying'' with love. (p. 203)

Indeed, we cannot expect any consistency on the part of the aesthete, for whom the ''actors'' here are heightened representatives. The aesthete, in his turn, stands for man himself—for, as [Hugo von] Hofmannsthal defined him, he is a dovecote: impulses fly out like doves and others return, making it a metaphor to speak of the ''self'' at all. . . . Schnitzler illustrates this dissolution of the psychologically consistent traditional character most strikingly in the figures of the Actress and the Count; and with the latter he goes one step farther and shows the existential consequences of the discontinous ''I'' with a psychological sharpness equalling that demonstrated by Nietzsche in his fable of the herd. The aesthete-Count is sure of only one thing: the pleasure of the moment. . . . In the dim dawn scene which follows the interview with the Actress and is the final episode of *Reigen*, the intoxicated Count has accompanied the prostitute of the first episode home to her sordid room. He awakens and tries to orient himself in his at first unfamiliar surroundings. Schnitzler here shows us a character close to psychological annihilation and at the same time illuminates with mordant irony the paradoxical aestheticism of his characters. The Count, in the previous scene, had stated that the time before and the time after that of the most pleasurable sensations was essentially sad but that the time of that pleasure was something certain: "I know I enjoy . . . that is something certain," and he might have added: that is all that is certain. Now, throughout the scene with the Prostitute, he tries to establish with only halting success whether he has actually enjoyed her favors, whether the pleasure he is so sure of actually took place. The motif of forgetfulness takes on nihilistic proportions, for here, in the most real sense, is a man fighting for his existence and meeting only blank nothingness. As he regards the sleeping girl, the Count, "philosopher" still, speculates upon the similarity of sleep and death; he fails to realize, however, the similarity of his own state with death, for he too in this shadowy scene has lost contact with the real space and time surrounding him. He has reached the state of that "happy" member of Nietzsche's herd who always "forgets" his happiness of the moment before, and this state, as Nietzsche recognized, is psychological death for the human being. By seeking to isolate the "moment," which alone has meaning for him, he has succeeded in "killing" time in the real sense of that often thoughtlessly used phrase. Human existence at any given instant is contiguous with and dependent upon the coordinate points of past and future. Increasingly for the modern mind, there is no such thing as "absolute" time: a moment cannot be isolated from its surroundings, to which it is supremely relative, and then be spoken of as "real." Schnitzler here shows us characters seeking "fullness" of time outside the domain of measuring clocks and finding inevitably (and most dramatically in the case of the Count)—nothing. (pp. 203-04)

Schnitzler, like Kierkegaard, emphasizes the essential paradox of the aesthetic life by showing how such a life, so basically committed to time, inevitably comes to grief upon it. Like Kierkegaard and Nietzsche, Schnitzler realizes the inanity of the idolization of the moment, whatever form it may take. . . . (p. 205)

The characters in *Reigen* "forget" themselves so completely near the end of the play that we can refer to them only metaphorically as having conventional "selves." The circular structure suggests that the play might begin again at the ending with the same cast of characters (the Prostitute meeting the Soldier the evening after her episode with the Count, and so forth), for they have not developed or won any insights into themselves in the course of the action. These features must strike a modern theater-goer as amazingly like those of an "anti-play" such as *The Bald Soprano*. The seeds of absurdity present in Schnitzler have come to blossom in Ionesco's "Theater of the Absurd." . . . Schnitzler, like the scenes in his *Reigen,* is Janus-faced. He may indeed look back wistfully, as all the textbooks tell us, to the charms of a declining society, but he also assuredly looks forward to the peculiar confusions and torments of our own times. By devoting himself with such perspicacity to his own "moment," he succeeded at that feat which his characters were so signally unable to perform: he transcended his time. (pp. 205-06)

Hunter G. Hannum, ""Killing Time': Aspects of

Schnitzler's 'Reigen'," in The Germanic Review *(copyright 1962 by Helen Dwight Reed Foundation; reprinted by permission of Heldref Publications), Vol. XXXVII, No. 3, May, 1962, pp. 190-206.*

HEINZ POLITZER (essay date 1963)

[Schnitzler] was never more scientifically impartial and poetically undaunted than when he wrote . . . the first radical interior monologue in the German language, *Leutnant Gustl.* (p. 361)

For the sake of scientific objectivity Schnitzler dismisses here almost completely the narrator, that is: himself. The author no longer accompanies his figure, nor does he describe him in his own words. Instead, Gustl's thoughts and emotions, his reactions and conclusions are allowed to present themselves in their raw, natural, state. The designation "stream of consciousness" story does not apply here either, for Schnitzler succeeds in penetrating the lieutenant's consciousness and in opening up the sphere of his *pre-*conscious. Snippets of thought and shreds of sentiments are shown floating and bubbling, ostensibly without any sense or reason. The author observes this amorphous mass of associations from the outside, registering its fluctuations and vacillations as if he were looking into a witches' cauldron. It is no witches' cauldron, however, it is a very modern soul.

To perform this experiment Schnitzler has chosen the most neutral, most average object available to him at that time. Traditionally a young Austrian lieutenant around the turn of the century was a nondescript man. . . . He was distinguished neither by material riches nor intellectual gifts. The routine of peacetime service had left his inner life as blank as an empty mirror. At the same time he played a representative rôle in the society of his day. On him and his like rested the security of the empire. He was both smiled at and pampered like a pet. By taking this pet seriously for the short hours of one night, Schnitzler exposed the inner weakness of this guarantor of Austria's security. His experiment with Leutnant Gustl's soul touched a traumatic spot in the political unconscious of his fatherland. (pp. 361-62)

Gustl . . . experiences the night before his death. He is a young man, and the night is a spring night, enlivened by bells telling the hours which still separate him from his death. The problem is formulated now: How does man react in the imminence of his death? (In this respect *Leutnant Gustl* is a companion piece to *Reigen* where Schnitzler studied man under the impact of the love act.) Does Gustl, in the extremity of his situation, gain new insights? Is he led to extraordinary decisions by the inescapability of his death? Does the specific weight of his human nature change? What appears before the eyes of a drowning man during the last seconds of his existence unfolds before the observer's glance in the carefully registered convulsions of Gustl's psyche.

Although the lieutenant occasionally comes close to a better understanding of himself, he fails to learn from his experience, let alone to change. . . . Gustl's soul remains unaffected. Displaying the vitality of a cork tumbler, the lieutenant re-emerges as little scarred as he is bettered. His aggressiveness, his wantonness, his sluggishness of heart have successfully resisted the anguish, the proximity of death, and even the judgment of God, to which the experiment had exposed him. A hollow man has demonstrated his hollowness. Leutnant Gustl remains Leutnant Gustl. (pp. 362-63)

In Leutnant Gustl's mind Schnitzler read the pathological condition in which Austria, and perhaps Europe, found herself around the *fin de siècle*. And just as a correct diagnosis contains, to a certain degree, the prognosis, and anticipates the course the malady will take if it remains unchecked, so we are able to gather from Gustl's aimless and confused musings a warning of the catastrophe which was to befall the continent in 1914, fourteen years after the story was published. We discover in the young lieutenant's psyche an aggressiveness which drove him and his generation to the battlefields of the first world war. (p. 363)

Tragicomedy was the artistic means which Schnitzler selected to work out an acceptable approach to human affairs. For the sake of humanity he advocated as perfect as possible an understanding between man and man. But, for the sake of his art, he would not carry his rationality so far as Freud did. A moralist in a minor key, Schnitzler was occasionally heard to cry out against "this hodgepodge of restraint and insolence, of cowardly jealousy and fake equanimity—of raging passion and empty voluptuousness," which he saw around himself and projected onto the stage. It is no accident that this diagnosis is made by a physician and that it occurs toward the end of a play, *Das weite Land,* which Schnitzler specifically called a tragicomedy. But not only is Doctor Mauer the only decent human being in this drama, he is also the least interesting. In Schnitzler's work, the scientist, the doctor, the psychologist takes at best the place occupied by the chorus in the drama of the Greeks: he serves as the knowing witness of an inexorably absurd fate. This is even and especially true when the doctor turns dramatic hero and comments on the scene from the center of the stage, as is the case in the grim comedy *Professor Bernhardi* of 1912.

The poet Arthur Schnitzler was a wise doctor. Relentlessly he diagnosed the human absurdity in the tragicomedies that fill his books. He analyzed the psyche of a moribund society because he foresaw and dreaded the epidemic character of the neuroses that were bred and spread by it. But unlike his successors in the field of modern tragicomedy—from Jean Cocteau to Tennessee Williams and Samuel Beckett and beyond—he did not look down on the figures he had created. He lingered among them and suffered with them. He knew about their ultimate secret, and, knowingly, kept it. (p. 372)

> *Heinz Politzer, "Arthur Schnitzler: The Poetry of Psychology," in* MLN *(© copyright 1963 by The Johns Hopkins University Press), Vol. 78, No. 4, October, 1963, pp. 353-72.*

LORE B. FOLTIN (essay date 1963)

[Many critical] views seem to overlook . . . [an] aspect of death, as treated by Schnitzler, namely that rather than always being the inescapable pinnacle of loneliness or the punishment thereof, death is often inseparably linked with the theme of man's purification.

Death appears to us thus from two sides, that of the surviving and that of the dying. Those about to die sometimes rise in the last moments of their lives to a certain greatness; one might even say they rise to the challenge of death. In one of Schnitzler's one-act plays—a literary form in which he excelled—*Die letzten Masken,* the dying journalist Karl Rademacher has plotted revenge on a friend of his youth, the successful writer Weihgast. . . . When Weihgast appears [at his deathbed], however, [Rademacher] spends his time with him in small talk; he dismisses the desire for revenge. The approach of death has rendered such revenge small, foolish, insignificant. (p. 39)

Death as the great mitigator of human grief, the healer of human melancholy, and thus, the extreme opposite of the "pinnacle of loneliness' since it brings relief from it, assumes a dominant role in Schnitzler's work. (p. 40)

Further indication of Schnitzler's positive attitude toward imminent death may be seen in the novella *Casanovas Heimfahrt.* Schnitzler depicts a duel between the aging Casanova and his youthful, virile rival, lieutenant Lorenzi. While the duel has been motivated by quite ordinary reasons, . . . the manner in which the men duel is quite extraordinary. The opponents fence in the nude. In this, it would appear, Schnitzler indicates that life's external exigencies and petty concerns have been stripped away. Thus both men meet soul to soul. . . .

When we view death from the other perspective, that is of the survivors, it assumes a different appearance. It now serves to intensify the awareness of the beauty and sweetness of life.

In the beginning of the poignant novella *Sterben,* Marie, the mistress of a young man who has but one year to live, believes she wants to die with her lover. . . . When the time comes for him to die, however, and he, unable to bear the fact that Marie will live on, wants to take her with him, she . . . runs away. In spite of her lover's death, life is worth living for Marie. (p. 41)

Death may even establish a bond between the living and the dead, when such a bond did not exist while both were alive. The novella *Casanovas Heimfahrt* illustrates this beautifully in the scene when Casanova, before leaving his dead opponent bends down to the man whom he has just killed and kisses him on the forehead. (p. 42)

In Schnitzler's work . . . death may play the dual role of purifying and setting men free on the one hand, and of unifying and strengthening a bond on the other hand. With his preoccupation with death Schnitzler is linked with a tradition in German literature which goes back as far as Gottfried von Strassburg's *Tristan,* where we first encounter the dichotomy between "Lebensinstinkt," and "Todesinstinkt," if these Freudian terms may be used. This dichotomy is echoed through Schnitzler's work. . . . (pp. 42-3)

> *Lore B. Foltin, "The Meaning of Death in Schnitzler's Work," in* Studies in Arthur Schnitzler: Centennial Commemorative Volume, *edited by Herbert W. Reichert and Herman Salinger (copyright 1963, The University of North Carolina Press), University of North Carolina Press, 1963 (and reprinted by AMS Press Inc., 1966, pp. 35-44).*

MARTIN ESSLIN (essay date 1971)

My Youth in Vienna is a fragment of Schnitzler's unfinished—and also, clearly, unpolished—autobiography. . . . Clearly, neither in Schnitzler's own lifetime, nor in the decades since he died can there have been any compelling reason why this fragment should be published. Indeed, there must have been many for *not* publishing it: drawn from the author's diaries, it is an artless and rather dry account of the external circumstances of his life between his early childhood and the age of 27, when it breaks off; this was long before Schnitzler had reached his first major successes as a writer, or, indeed, met some of the people who played important parts in his life, like Hofmannsthal . . . , or his future wife.

Nevertheless *My Youth in Vienna* is a fascinating book, precisely because it is totally artless and unfinished; for, held against the subtlety and psychological depth of Schnitzler's works of fiction, it gives a most revealing insight into the raw material of his own experience.

And the astonishing thing is the utter triviality of these circumstances: this is a small world of largely Jewish bourgeois families—lawyers, merchants, doctors and their pretty dreary social round: balls, holiday outings, Sunday excursions, billiards in cafés—and love affairs, endless love affairs. (pp. 500-01)

In the period covered by *My Youth in Vienna*—the years up to 1889—Schnitzler himself seems to have been unaware of the iniquities and absurdities of this erotic class structure. And because the book is merely a first draft which has not progressed beyond a fairly literal transcription of his diaries, there is also no inkling in it that by the time he wrote it —during the First World War—he had in fact seen through the hypocrisy and falseness of this system of values and had bitterly satirised it in a number of plays and stories. *Reigen* was, after all, privately printed in 1900, only 11 years after the manuscript of *My Youth in Vienna* breaks off; and the point of that play is indeed that in the sex act the physical part is relatively unimportant compared to the social act of possession it represents. . . .

As a picture of a great writer, who was a late developer—he only came into his own well after the age of 30—in his early, as yet unreflecting, naïve phase, which provided him with the raw material for later insights, *My Youth in Vienna* is of considerable interest. (p. 501)

Martin Esslin, "Old Vienna," in New Statesman *(© 1971 The Statesman & Nation Publishing Co. Ltd.), Vol. 81, No. 2090, April 9, 1971, pp. 500-01.*

MARTIN SWALES (essay date 1971)

That the theatre recurs throughout Schnitzler's work—both narrative and dramatic—as an image for the existential situation of man has become by now almost a truism within Schnitzler criticism. Such a notion of the theatre is at once deeply traditional and strikingly modern. The image of the world as a stage has its roots in the Baroque, while the notion of man's practical existence as a form of role-playing appears as an image within a great number of contemporary novels which centre upon the problematic nature of modern man's identity. This is not, of course, to imply that there is complete thematic consonance between the literature of the Baroque and contemporary literature. There are, however, certain affinities between the two: both are concerned with the tension between a sheer delight in the colourful variety

and confusion of the world on the one hand, and on the other a sense of the corruption of this multifarious world, whereby value is divorced from event and is ultimately denied any substantial existence within the social world. (p. 253)

[In many of Schnitzler's works] the theatre functions as the central thematic concern. (p. 254)

[The one-act plays *Zum grossen Wurstel* and *Der grüne Kakadu*] are to be counted among Schnitzler's masterpieces. . . . *Zum grossen Wurstel* is set in the 'Prater'. As a curtain rises we see the public strolling around, talking to one another, eating. At the back of the stage is an enormous marionette-theatre which is about to present a new play. We are hence confronted by a play within a play. (p. 266)

[The] first scene—and the public's reaction to it—makes clear the satirical intention behind *Zum grossen Wurstel*. In the marionette-play Schnitzler creates a grotesque parody of his own works. The sombre, introspective hero, involved in countless love affairs and yet troubled by the shadow of death which falls over man's earthly joys, the 'süsses Mädel', the simple, passionate girl from the 'Vorstadt', such figures of course recur frequently in Schnitzler's own literary production. Here Schnitzler confronts the limitations of his own world, confronts the fact that the kind of characters that he creates so easily degenerate into mannered puppets. The jingling verse trivializes the 'philosophical' moments by revealing them as obvious, trite reflections that embody nothing but a facile 'profundity'. Yet Schnitzler here is giving us not only *his* caricature of his own work, but, more important, the kind of caricature of his own work that was established by his contemporary audience. Schnitzler was all too often identified with his Anatol figures, with the 'süsses Mädel', with Viennese 'Lokalpatriotismus'— and the extent of his critical relationship to the world he evoked became obscured. Hence, the marionette-play becomes a kind of 'all-purpose Schnitzler play' in which the typical figures from his world are simply taken at face value, without any differentiation of artistic illumination, and thereby emerge as jerky, stereotyped marionettes. (pp. 267-68)

One should mention here that *Zum grossen Wurstel* is important not simply as literary satire, as a kind of in-joke between author and public. Schnitzler's satire of the public response to his plays is more than a desperate attempt at artistic self-vindication. (p. 268)

Indeed, the process of making the play conform is seen in the reactions of the audience—and in the fact that the author frantically tries to cut out the passages that are not likely to be well received. At one point he appears at the window where the 'Räsoneur' is standing and orders him to cut some of his speeches. Unfortunately, the latter remains unimpressed and continues to intone couplets of immense banality. . . . [One] feels how insights, themes, statements that are part of a great literary tradition can be cheapened by glib usage. The debasement of literature, however, also indicates the existential debasement of those who practise it. (pp. 268-69)

Throughout *Zum grossen Wurstel* Schnitzler generates a sense of pressure behind the dialogue, as though at any minute the preposterous, creaky sequence of the marionette-play—and of the audience's speeches—can erupt into complete confusion. Both marionettes and spectators have an absurd energy; they are a menagerie that can easily get out of hand. Ultimately, the human reality of this menagerie is tested and found wanting. But the participants in this pandemonium are eminently convinced of their own strength and independence. (pp. 269-70)

In the climax of *Zum grossen Wurstel* 'der Unbekannte' passes his sword over the whole stage, and all the other characters . . . fall to the ground just as the marionettes have done. The mingling of the experiential reality of the puppet-play with the experiential reality of the audience, the falsity of the audience's response to the manifest falsity of the marionettes, the appearance of the 'Graf von Charolais' as one of the audience, all these features now receive explicit statement and commentary. The 'real' people are existentially as unreal as are the marionettes. . . . We are not, however, put to the test. We are saved by a theatrical convention, by the tradition that we are onlookers in the theatre, not participants. But implicitly, we are drawn into the kind of questioning with which 'Der Unbekannte' leaves the stage. Are we, in fact, any more real than the members of the 'audience' on stage? The theatre functions as a kind of existential judgement: if we can be persuaded that the theatre is an image for our actual experience, then how real is that experience? That it *seems* real is beyond doubt; but how, ultimately, can we test it? How can we step back from the stage of life and assess the kind of performance we have given? For the dramatists of the Baroque, for whom the theatre was an image of man's experience, there was, potentially, a moment of truth when one could judge one's performance. Death allowed man to review his life, and, however unreal he might find his own being, the ultimate critic, God, was real. He would judge with truth and compassion. For Schnitzler there is no such certainty. 'Der Unbekannte' himself does not know what power, what scale of values he represents. He only knows that by what he represents man's life is found wanting. He does not, in fact, wield the sword over the heads of the actual audience. But from his questioning of the audience's reality it is only a short step to the direct aggression of Brecht, to the 'Publikumsbeschimpfung' that is typical of so much *avant-garde* theatre.

At the end of *Zum grossen Wurstel* a question is asked, but no answer is received. As soon as the Unknown Man leaves, all the figures on the stage—both human beings and marionettes—spring to life again. As in Ionesco's *The Bald Prima-Donna* and Frisch's *Die chinesische Mauer,* the farce begins again. The cycle will be acted out once more to the point of ultimate questioning, will break down—and will then begin again.

The interrelationship between theatre and world, the agonized question as to the reality of either, such themes are also central to *Der grüne Kakadu*. (pp. 272-73)

As in *Zum grossen Wurstel,* the intense theatricality of *Der grüne Kakadu* is an integral part of the play's meaning. And this theatricality acquires an existential significance in that it is made to question the quality of 'reality' itself.

Both *Zum grossen Wurstel* and *Der grüne Kakadu* are works in which Schnitzler obviously draws on the baroque literary tradition from which he springs. At the same time, however, his reinterpretation of the tradition produces some of his most 'modern' achievements. In one sense, the

interrelation of illusion and reality, of theatre and life is a profoundly baroque notion. And yet it is a theme which is capable of an unequivocally modern resonance. (p. 277)

The typifying of characters until they become a series of theatrical clichés is clearly inherent in both *Zum grossen Wurstel* and *Der grüne Kakadu*. More important, however, is the notion of the fusion of tragedy and comedy. Both plays are in essence comedies, but comedies which radiate a bitter existential despair. The possibility of tragedy is far removed from such plays: there is, rather, a passionate sense of the squalid confusion of human experience. And confusion of this kind is conducive to comedy, not tragedy. These two plays are comedies in the sense that the contemporary Theatre of the Absurd produces comedies rather than tragedies. (p. 278)

Schnitzler's *Zum grossen Wurstel* and *Der grüne Kakadu* belong to contemporary dramaturgy. They are comedies, comedies that are plays about—and plays with—the insubstantial foundation of man's existential being. (p. 279)

Martin Swales, in his Arthur Schnitzler: A Critical Study *(© Oxford University Press 1971; reprinted by permission of Oxford University Press), Oxford University Press, London, 1971, 289 p.*

PAUL SCHLUETER   (essay date 1979)

The five stories [in *The Little Comedy and Other Stories*] are all radically different. . . . The title story is about a game of deception in which a fashionable Viennese couple individually pretend to be humble, poor folk, only to acknowledge their "true" selves at the same moment and, presumably, live "happily ever after." "Riches" is an allegorical account of a painter who wins great wealth by gambling, who hides the money and for twenty years cannot recall where, and who, on his deathbed, remembers the location in time to tell his son; the son, also an aspiring artist, has been forced, like his father before him, to do more mundane kinds of painting to survive. The neat conclusion in which the son prodigally loses his fortune in the presence of the same jaded millionaire who was responsible for the father's getting it in the first place is both predictable and yet affecting, not just in the sense that history repeats itself on a humble scale, but even more in the way in which two lives are utterly ruined by the love of money, one by not having it, the other by having it for only a moment.

The other three stories are more substantial than these first two. "The Son" is a brief account of a mother's compensation for a wastrel son's abuse, and is saturated with a sense of needless guilt. "The Judge's Wife," also somewhat allegorical or at least on the fairy-tale level, tells of a dedicated judge who has to sentence a life-long friend to prison; the judge makes the sentence more severe than necessary because of his duke's presence in the courtroom, but he discovers not only that the duke reverses the sentence, but also that he gains the judge's wife as a mistress. Whether or not the story . . . "strikes a blow for feminine liberation," is problematic; more likely, it merely suggests that not one of the principals in the story knows how to relate openly and candidly with another, except for the duke, and as a consequence all have their lives affected adversely.

The final story, "Dying," is by far the best—and longest. It is also the one with the greatest psychological depth and perplexity. A young man, knowing he is gradually dying, attempts by travel and other means to dramatize his plight; his fiancée who has sworn that she will die with him, accompanies him in a fruitless effort to find a peace otherwise denied him.... ''Dying'' captures remarkably well the self-induced despair and pity present in a man who cannot accept either his impending death or his unfullfilled life. The love the couple had shared thus becomes a form of mutual contempt. In all respects, the story is well told. . . .

Schnitzler, a very wise man, not only captured the moment of jaded, morbid self-defeat in his work, he also was able to embue this feeling with a sardonic, melancholic sense of pointless introspection. These five stories are a fine tribute to his talent. (pp. 245-46)

> Paul Schlueter ''Arthur Schnitzler: 'The Little Comedy and Other Stories','' in Studies in Short Fiction (copyright 1979 by Newberry College), Vol. 16, No. 3 Summer, 1979, pp. 244-46.

ADDITIONAL BIBLIOGRAPHY

Allen, Richard H. *An Annotated Arthur Schnitzler Bibliography: Editions and Criticism in German, French, and English 1879-1965.* Chapel Hill: The University of North Carolina Press, 1966, 150 p.
    Exhaustive bibliography which includes a brief survey of Schnitzler's life and works.

Beharriell, Frederick J. ''Schnitzler's Anticipation of Freud's Dream Theory.'' *Monatshefte* XLV, No. 2 (February 1953): 81-9.
    Argues that Schnitzler discovered certain principles of depth psychology before Freud.

Bentley, Eric. ''*Reigen* Comes Full Circle.'' In his *The Dramatic Event: An American Chronicle*, pp. 209-12. New York: Horizon Press, 1954.
    Comparison of *Reigen* with the film version *La Ronde*. Bentley concludes that the film offers a broad and superficial treatment of the play's serious themes.

Berlin, Jeffrey B. ''Arthur Schnitzler: A Bibliography of Criticism.'' *Modern Austrian Literature* 4, No. 4 (Winter 1971): 7-20.
    Bibliography of criticism in English, German, and French published from 1965 to 1971.

Berlin, Jeffrey B. ''Some Images of the Betrayer in Arthur Schnitzler's Work.'' *German Life & Letters* XXVI, No. 1 (October 1972): 20-4.
    Examines the motif of betrayal and deception in Schnitzler's work.

Garland, H.B. ''Arthur Schnitzler.'' In *German Men of Letters: Twelve Literary Essays, Vol. II*, edited by Alex Natan, pp. 55-75. London: Oswald Wolff (Publishers), 1963.
    In-depth thematic and structural analysis of Schnitzler's work.

Lederer, Herbert. ''Arthur Schnitzler: A Chronicle of Loneliness.'' *The German Quarterly* XXX, No. 2 (March 1957): 82-94.
    Argues that the frenetic sexual activity of Schnitzler's characters is due to their loneliness and alienation.

Lederer, Herbert. ''Arthur Schnitzler's Typology: An Excursion into Philosophy.'' *PMLA* LXXVIII, No. 4 (September 1963): 394-406.
    Analysis of Schnitzler's *Weltanschauung* as revealed in such nonfictional works as his philosophical treatise, *Der Geist im Wort und der Geist in der Tat*, and *Buch der Sprüche und Bedenken*, a collection of aphorisms.

Oswald, Victor A., Jr., and Mindess, Veronica Pinter. ''Schnitzler's *Fraulein Else* and the Psychoanalytic Theory of Neuroses.'' *The Germanic Review* 26, No. 4 (December 1951): 279-88.
    Freudian interpretation of *Fraulein Else*.

Schorske, Carl E. ''Politics and the Psyche in *fin de siècle* Vienna: Schnitzler and Hofmannsthal.'' *The American Historical Review* LXVI, No. 4 (July 1961): 930-46.*
    Study of the background and political crises of nineteenth-century Viennese culture. Schorske includes in his discussion an analysis of Schnitzler's treatment of politics in *The Green Cockatoo* and *Der Weg ins Freie*.

Stern, J. P. Introduction to *Libebelei, Leutnant Gustl, and Die Letzten Masken*, by Arthur Schnitzler, pp. 1-44. Cambridge: Cambridge University Press, 1966.
    Analyses of the main characters and themes in the dramas *Liebelei* and *Die Letzten Masken*, and the novella, *Leutnant Gustl*.

Swales, M. W. ''Arthur Schnitzler as a Moralist.'' *The Modern Language Review* 62, No. 3 (July 1967): 462-75.
    Examines Schnitzler's moral judgments in his work, concluding that he is not morally ambivalent as some critics have charged.

James Stephens
1882(?)-1950

Irish novelist, poet, short story writer, essayist, playwright, journalist, and editor.

A popular figure of the Irish Literary Revival, Stephens is best known for his fanciful tales based on Irish folklore and mythology. Through such disparate characters as tinkers, philosophers, gods, and charwomen, Stephens voiced his pantheistic philosophy and urged the Irish people to study Irish tradition and to revere the old Irish gods and mythic heroes.

Though information concerning Stephens's early life is uncertain, it is known that he was born in Dublin, that his childhood was impoverished, and that he worked for many years as a clerk-typist. He began his literary career by contributing poems, essays, and short stories to the newspaper *Sinn Féin*, published by nationalist Arthur Griffith. One of his poems impressed A.E., who exerted a profound and lasting influence over Stephens's career. Under A.E.'s tutelage Stephens studied Theosophical literature and became part of the Dublin literati, while Arthur Griffith directed his political education. During this time Stephens began a lifelong study of the Irish language and mythology.

The first period in Stephens's literary career was his most important and creative. A volume of poetry, *Insurrections*, followed in quick succession by the novels *The Charwoman's Daughter*, *The Crock of Gold*, and *The Demi-Gods* delighted his contemporaries with imaginative fancy, irreverent humor, and lyric power. Stephens shared with William Blake, whose themes and style he emulated, a distrust for authority, a belief in the happy innocence of childhood, and a concern for animals and the helpless. Although many of Stephens's themes are steeped in the legends of Ireland's past, his work also reflects his anger over the social evils of the present: the poems in *Insurrections* include powerful, realistic pictures of miserable conditions in the Dublin slums. In *The Charwoman's Daughter*, *The Crock of Gold*, and *The Demi-Gods* Stephens exhorts the Irish to remain faithful to their heritage and customs, while humorously depicting hostility and contention between the sexes. *The Crock of Gold*, considered his masterpiece by many critics, is a broad allegory, in which a young woman, representing Ireland, must choose between Angus Óg, the Irish god and the foreign god, Pan. The critical and commercial success of Stephens's early work allowed him to move to Paris, but depressed by the war, he accepted a post as Registrar of the National Gallery of Ireland and returned to Dublin.

Stephens's interest in Gaelic, Old Irish literature, and Theosophy deepened, and his literary efforts thereafter consist mostly of translations and adaptations from Irish saga cycles. *Irish Fairy Tales* is based on the Fenian cycle of Irish mythology; *Deirdre* and *In the Land of Youth* draw from the Ulster cycle and were to be part of a five-volume work. Discouraged—critical reaction to his adapations had been generally poor—Stephens abandoned his aim of producing an Irish epic and moved to London.

Stephens embarked on a second career as a lecturer and broadcaster. His tours and radio talks were a great success, but his literary output during this period, mostly poetry, was small. Saddened by the deaths of his closest friends and of his only son, Stephens dwelled on the themes of old age and loneliness in his last volume of poetry, *Kings and the Moon*.

Although Stephens's poetry is considered by many critics to be overly derivative of Blake and Browning, his early novels are still appreciated for their imaginative and lyric power.

PRINCIPAL WORKS

Insurrections (poetry) 1909
The Charwoman's Daughter (novel) 1912; published in the United States as *Mary, Mary,* 1912
The Crock of Gold (novel) 1912
The Hill of Vision (poetry) 1912
Here Are Ladies (short stories) 1913
The Demi-Gods (novel) 1914
Reincarnations (poetry) 1918
Irish Fairy Tales (fairy tales) 1920
Deirdre (novella) 1923
In the Land of Youth (novella) 1924

Collected Poems (poetry) 1926
Etched in Moonlight (short stories) 1928
Kings and the Moon (poetry) 1938

THE ATHENAEUM (essay date 1912)

It is not easy to decide precisely why ['The Charwoman's
Daughter'] is charming, but charming it certainly is, in spite
of a mixture of styles that might reasonably be expected to
spoil it. A very young girl, delicately and realistically drawn
from her own point of view, occupies the centre; slightly
behind stands the less fully indicated figure of her mother,
stronger, more passionate, perhaps more really interesting. . . . Through every scene runs a twisted thread of humorous observation and of kindliness somewhat akin to the
spirit of 'Wee Macgreegor'; but the humour of 'The Char-
womans Daughter' is subtler, and its literary style is far
finer. Some bits of description are exquisite. Page 135, for
instance, calls up all Dublin, and almost all Ireland, in a
single paragraph that contains the very essence of a grey
Irish as distinguished from a grey English day; and the
paragraph is not allowed to spread into and overwhelm the
history of a worthy woman's shopping. The women
throughout are the people of interest, the subjective figures.
The men matter only in so far as they affect the women.

Suddenly, all this sober story of real life collapses into a
fairy tale. The charwoman's illusive dream of unearned
wealth comes true, the curtain runs swiftly down, and the
reader perceives ruefully why the name of the heroine was
Mary Makebelieve.

> *"Poetic Criticism: 'The Charwoman's Daugh-
> ter',"* in The Athenaeum, *No. 4402, March 9,
> 1912, p. 278.*

THE ATHENAEUM (essay date 1912)

['Insurrections'] had poetry in it charged with vitality. It
cast away the swathings with which modern minor verse
screens itself from reality, and swept out upon us—a new
thing in full panoply of its own. The authors most potent
gift was poetic dramatization, the faculty of presentation in
condensed tabloids of thought. He rejoiced in elliptical expression, subtleties of transition, and daring strokes of
caustic irony that caught up the reader rudely into the mood
which engendered them. Occasionally, he achieved a harmony of rhythm almost as rounded and sonorous as the
Miltonic. He was an insurgent, and flung his gage, as the
insurgent minority should fling it, hard and straight in the
face of the adversary. His style, except where it gathered
speed and volume, was lean and lithe, stripped naked and
unabashed, admirably fitted for its rough and vigorous
work.

This prefatory explanation is necessary, not only on account of the rich promise and comparative neglect of Mr.
Stephens's first volume, but also because 'The Hill of Vision' marks a curious development of, and even departure
from, the territory he had mapped out for himself. His expression is now obviously more ripe, and has gained in deftness of handling and spontaneity what it has lost in ruthlessness, austerity, and grim stalking of the truth. In some
ways it would seem as if in this volume the poet was re-

creating himself, before, like Alastor, he girded himself
anew for the high places and solitudes of poetic endeavour.
But his emotional quality, always poignant and straining
eagerly at freedom, has been not so much diluted as deflected into other modes of poetic realization. Still warming
"both hands before the fire of life," he has, except for rare
impulses, ceased—we hope, momentarily—to bank it up
himself. We feel that other hands, greater and less than his,
have experienced a kindred glow before him. In 'A Prelude
and A Song,' for instance, there is a note of fresh joyous
aspiration, a sweet self-identification with natural phenomena, which reminds us vividly of Keats, when he tells us
how his spirit entered into that of the sparrow picking from
the gravel outside his window. Here and there is a touch of
that pellucid melody the cunning stops and keys of which
are well known to Mr. W. H. Davies; here and there a drop
into the soft melancholy of regret, which sounds in "Fair
Daffodils, we weep to see. . . ." But Mr. Stephens never
relapses into the mincing gait, exotic tonality, and spiritual
anaemia characteristic of the modern craft of verse. . . .

'Nora Criona' . . . and 'Danny Murphy' are in their fashion
perfect pieces of characterization, conveyed in broad, casual, yet secretly intimate strokes, the curt, fiercely direct,
concrete style, purged of all excrescence, fusing with and,
as it were, exhuming the general effects. But these lightning
flashes, rending open far, spacious, sombre horizons of
thought, are less numerous than in 'Insurrections.' More
frequently now is the spirit of the lyrist speeding after Joy
like Apollo after Daphne. . . .

> *"Literature: 'The Hill of Vision',"* in The Athen-
> aeum, *No. 4403, March 16, 1912, p. 303.*

THE LITERARY DIGEST (essay date 1912)

["The Hill of Vision" is] a book that has about it an air of
inspiration and a naive directness and intimacy that place it,
in spirit, very near to the work of William Blake.

As Blake was a voice crying in the solitary places against
everything that Lord Chesterfield and his age stood for, so
James Stephens is impatient of established education and
the prosy world of echoes and routine.

James Stephens, like [Emanuel] Swendenborg, seems
touched with vatic madness. His verse has humor of an
impish sort, but with always a bit of terror at the heart of it.
No modernism is in his poetry, no such attempt to poetize
the railroad, telephone, or automobile, as you might find,
for instance, in the work of John Neihardt, none of the passionate sympathy or the burning sense of sharing the priva-
tions of the unfortunate that you expect in James
Oppenheim—this is the solitary vision of a sojourner in the
wilderness. . . .

The power of Mr. Stephen's verse lies in the second
meaning that is always playing behind the first. An impish
immortal thought is ever grinning from somewhere between
the sentences, or is peering at us around a stanza. Mr. Stephens combines three words—and we have, not a sentence
but a star. (p. 546)

> *"Current Poetry: 'The Hill of Vision',"* in The
> Literary Digest *(copyright, 1912, by The Literary
> Digest, Inc.), Vol. 44, No. 11, March 16, 1912, pp.
> 546, 548-49.*

THE ATHENAEUM (essay date 1912)

[In] 'The Crock of Gold,' [James Stephens] gives the measure of a larger and more individual talent than could have been absolutely foretold. His work is neither a fairy tale, nor an essay, nor an allegory, nor a novel, although it has features of all these forms; there has been nothing hitherto quite like it, but it is safe to prophesy that by and by there will be plenty of imitators to take it for their pattern.

In some respects the book is characteristically Irish. Modern English writers can introduce fairies, but they cannot succeed in treating them quite as a matter of course. Even Mr. [J. M.] Barrie seems to be always hinting to us how pretty and quaint his fairies are. But to Mr. Stephens, as to Mr. Yeats—and formerly to Blake—fairies are as natural as sparrows; neither Irishman would feel a quiver of surprise at encountering a "leprecaun" in any woodland walk, nor deem that there was any incongruity in the association upon the same page of leprecauns and policemen.

Indeed, one of the triumphs of 'The Crock of Gold' is the mingling of the wildest fantasies with sudden gleams of melancholy realism.... The style which conveys these excellent things reminds us now of one good writer, now of another, but never of a bad one, and, in spite of these links of kindred, remains always personal in its flavour. In short, Mr. Stephens has produced a remarkably fine and attractive work of art.

> *"Literature: 'The Crock of Gold',"* in The Athenaeum, *No. 4435, October 26, 1912, p. 473.*

A. E. (essay date 1912)

For a generation the Irish bards have endeavoured to live in a palace of art, in chambers hung with the embroidered cloths and made dim with pale lights and Druid twilights, and the melodies they most sought for were half soundless. (p. 34)

It was a great relief to me, personally, who had lived in the palace of Irish art for a time, and had even contributed a little to its dimness, to hear outside the walls a few years ago a sturdy voice blaspheming against all the formulae, and violating the tenuous atmosphere with its "Insurrections." (p. 35)

There were evidences of such an art in *Insurrections....* In the poem called "Fossils," the girl who flies and the boy who hunts her are followed in flight and pursuit with a swift energy by the poet, and the lines pant and gasp, and the figures flare up and down the pages. The energy created a new form in verse, not an orthodox beauty, which the classic artists would have admitted, but such picturesque beauty as Marcus Aurelius found in the foam on the jaws of the wild boar. (p. 36)

I knew after reading "The Shell" that in James Stephens we were going to have no singer of the abstract. (p. 37)

From the tradition of the world too he breaks away, from the great murmuring shell which gives back to us our cries and questionings and protests soothed into soft, easeful things and smooth orthodox complacencies, for it was shaped by humanity to whisper back to it what it wished to hear. From all soft, easeful beliefs and silken complacencies the last Irish poet breaks away in a book of insurrections. He is doubtful even of love, the greatest orthodoxy of any, which so few have questioned, which has preceded all religions and will survive them all. When he writes of love in "The Red-haired Man's Wife" and "The Rebel" he is not sure that that old intoxication of self-surrender is not a wrong to the soul and a disloyalty to the highest in us. His "Dancer" revolts from the applauding crowd. The wind cries out against the inference that the beauty of nature points inevitably to an equal beauty of spirit within. His enemies revolt against their hate; his old man against his own grumblings, and the poet himself rebels against his own revolt.... (pp. 37-8)

He does not revolt against the abstract like so many because he is incapable of thinking. Indeed, he is one of the few Irish poets we have who is always thinking as he goes along. He does not rebel against love because he is not himself sweet at heart, for the best thing in the book is its unfeigned humanity. So we have a personal puzzle to solve with this perplexing writer which makes us all the more eager to hear him again. (p. 38)

["The City of Dreadful Night"] has all the vaporous horror of a Doré grotesque.... But our poet does not as a rule write with such unrelieved gloom. He keeps a stoical cheerfulness, and even when he faces terrible things we feel encouraged to take his hand and go with him, for he is master of his own soul, and you cannot get a whimper out of him. He likes the storm of things, and is out for it. He has a perfect craft in recording wild natural emotions. The verse in this first book has occasional faults, but as a rule the lines move, driven by that inner energy of emotion which will sometimes work more metrical wonders than the most conscious art. (p. 39)

[In his second volume of poetry, *The Hill of Vision,* he] has climbed a hill, indeed, but has found cross-roads there leading in many directions, and seems to be a little perplexed whether the storm of things was his destiny after all.... We enjoy his perplexity, for he has seated himself by his cross-roads, and has tried many tunes on his lute, obviously in doubt which sounds sweetest to his own ear. I am not at all in doubt as to what is best, and I hope he will go on like Whitman, carrying "the old delicious burdens, men and women," wherever he goes. For his references to Deity, Plato undoubtedly would have expelled him from his Republic; and justly so, for James Stephens treats his god very much as the African savage treats his fetish.... Sometimes our poet essays the pastoral, and in sheer gaiety flits like any bird under the boughs, and up into the sunlight. There are in his company imps and grotesques, and fauns and satyrs, who come summoned by his piping. Sometimes, as in "Eve," the poem of the mystery of womanhood, he is purely beautiful, but I find myself going back to his men and women; and I hope he will not be angry with me when I say I prefer his tinker drunken to his Deity sober. None of our Irish poets has found God, at least a god any but themselves would not be ashamed to acknowledge. But our poet does know his men and his women. They are not the shadowy, Whistler-like decorative suggestions of humanity made by our poetic dramatists. They have entered like living creatures into his mind, and they break out there in an instant's unforgettable passion or agony, and the wild words fly up to the poet's brain to match their emotion. I do not know whether the verses entitled "The Brute" are poetry, but they have an amazing energy of expression.

But our poet can be beautiful when he wills, and sometimes, too, he has largeness and grandeur of vision and expression. (pp. 41-2)

The Hill of Vision is a very unequal book. There are many verses full of power, which move with the free easy motion of the literary athlete. Others betray awkwardness, and stumble as if the writer had stepped too suddenly into the sunlight of his power, and was dazed and bewildered. There is some diffusion of his faculties in what I feel are byways of his mind, but the main current of his energies will, I am convinced, urge him on to his inevitable portrayal of humanity. With writers like Synge and Stephens the Celtic imagination is leaving its Tirnanoges, its Ildathachs, its Many Coloured Lands and impersonal moods, and is coming down to earth intent on vigorous life and individual humanity. (p. 43)

> *A. E., "The Poetry of James Stephens" (1912), in his* Imaginations and Reveries *(reprinted by permission of Russell & Volkening, Inc., as agents for the author; copyright © 1915 by George Russell), Maunsel & Company, Ltd., 1915, pp. 34-44.*

ROBERT SHAFER   (essay date 1913)

The verse in *Insurrections* varies in quality, as the earliest work of most young men does, and it contains echoes, more or less unmistakable, of Mr. Stephens' reading. His second volume of verse, *The Hill of Vision* . . . shows every sign of progress toward more complete mastery, and toward characteristic and individualized expression, though unevenness, as is perhaps to be expected, has by no means been entirely obviated. The most evident quality of this poetry is its artlessness—I use the word in its primary significance;—it is literally uncouth at times, and it is as far removed as possible from that polish and finish, that mastery of technique, which was so characteristic of the poetry of the nineties. (pp. 561-62)

Along with the artlessness of Mr. Stephens' poetry, however, there goes a great love of crudeness, of broad colors thickly laid on, of unlovely words and startling comparisons, a love of elemental things and of more primitive people. At first sight it appears to be a return to earlier, more elemental conditions; but the better we comprehend it the more clearly we see that this it is not, that it is rather one of the manifestations of a new spirit which is animating all European life and thought. (p. 562)

In *Said the Young-Young Man to the Old-Old Man* I seem to perceive not so much the voice of Mr. Stephens as that of youth itself incarnate. Certainly the quality of insight there displayed is something more than merely unusual. . . . In *The Sootherer*, again, Mr. Stephens shows us in a wholly delightful way his comprehension of childhood. . . . Mr. Stephens is usually, though not invariably, at his worst when dealing with age. What he says of old age seems at times to be so untrue as to be really comforting, at other times he appears to evade the question, and once or twice he becomes merely funny, as in *Nothing at All*. In his understanding of woman, however, he is again more than exceptional, even though when he is writing of Eve he does make her out to have been a surprisingly ontological person. And after all, the most consistent note of these poems is that of a fundamental, almost inarticulate joy, inherent in the nature of man. (pp. 563-64)

Mr. Stephens is not only a poet, however, he is a novelist as well. . . . His verse is significant, surely, but it is significant largely by way of promise, it is more in the nature of prophecy than fulfilment. It is as a guiding hand raised up in a desert, pointing the way toward a strange and new development. But in his novels there is more of visible fulfilment. (pp. 564-65)

Any attempt to describe the delights of [*Mary, Mary*] is doomed to absolute failure. . . . I really know of nothing just like it in the English language, save *The Crock of Gold*, and for the most part that is even better. . . . The book is simply overflowing from beginning to end with a naïve humor of the most delightful and individual kind, and with this there goes at times a real pathos that can never be mistaken for sentimentalism. Beyond that there is the pleasant fact that in it we have to do with real and indubitable human beings. I do not mean real in the sense that Mr. George Moore would—for these people are anything but stupid and mean and ugly. But at the same time they are infused with a spirit which is instinct with vital life, and their lives were conceived in a mind which has in it the rich fruitage of a loving and close observation of human character. (pp. 565-66)

[*The Crock of Gold*] is a novel by scarcely any known standard. It is a delightful fantasy rather, an Irish fairy tale. What I say may seem to be contradictory, for Irish fairy tales sometimes have a way of being stupid that is all their own. This book, however, is anything rather than stupid, it is literally packed with the most charming kind of humor, humor of a quality that has scarcely ever been equalled, I am sure. (p. 566)

Very often the words of Mr. Stephens, both in prose and verse, seem to have a meaning for me that is not to be connected directly with anything on the printed page; a spirit of which he is conscious and yet which cannot be defined in specific words seems to be speaking through him. (p. 567)

> *Robert Shafer, "James Stephens and the Poetry of the Day," in* Forum *(copyright, 1913, by Events Publishing Company, Inc.), Vol. 50, No. 4, October, 1913, pp. 560-69.*

THE ATHENAEUM   (essay date 1914)

The queerly composed fantasy before us [*The Demi-Gods*] is circumstantially more improbable than a fairy tale, and has that super-abundance of rhetoric which is, unfortunately, characteristic of Irish earnestness; but [James Stephens's] imaginative power compels his characters to stand out—human, idiosyncratic, and alive—unharmed by their creator's errors. . . .

Perhaps the peculiar attraction of this book can be best defined as a harmony between the sublime and the ridiculous, the esoteric and the simple. "What would the priest say," asks Patsy the tramp, "if he heard we were stravaiging the country with three big buck angels, and they full of tricks, may be?" It is safe to say that Patsy's phrasing would arouse in a gentleman, prepared to hear his story, an expectation of horrors of vulgarity. How extraordinary would be that gentleman's disappointment! Here we have a tenderness worthy of Francis of Assisi, a drollery and topsy-turviness as of Irish fairies, flashes of Indian mysticism and primitive brutality, poetic prose as artificial as a song, and a barbarian's dialect. It is a book of obstinate liveliness and charm.

"Fiction: 'The Demi-Gods'," in The Athenaeum, No. 4540, October 31, 1914, p. 453.

THE SATURDAY REVIEW (essay date 1914)

Mr. James Stephens has followed M. Anatole France in writing a story about the angels who descend to earth. . . . Of differences we found many, of resemblances not one. In the company of M. France's celestial visitors [in "La Révolte des Anges"] we experienced, as did the mortals of his tale, acute discomfort, but with Finaun, Caeltia, and Art [in "The Demi-Gods"] we were immediately at home. The reason is not far to seek. The angels who descended on Paris were cynical, disillusioned cosmopolitans who held us poor humans in contempt, whilst those who came down in Donegal were as good Irish as we could wish to meet. . . .

From Mr. Stephens's book we gather an idea that there is a heaven on earth, and particularly in Ireland, for those who have the wit to seize it. (p. 465)

"The Demi-Gods" is a book of miracles and at the same time a simple book. The angels are not at all pretentious people, not above conversation with a talkative spider and the company of tinkers, and the ass who went "to see if there was anything worth looking for" is an equally meritorious representative of his species. We have, in fact, but one complaint to make. The author allows Caeltia to tell a tale which he himself has told us before. This is unwise, for Mr. Stephens's books are not thrown away when read. One may keep them in a handy place for reference. (pp. 465-66)

"From The Sacred Hazel," in The Saturday Review, *London, Vol. 118, No. 3079, October 31, 1914, pp. 465-66.*

MARY C. STURGEON (essay date 1916)

[The] true poet will transcend his nation, as he does his manhood, at times of purest inspiration; and Mr Stephens has those happy seasons—happy, surely, for those to whom he sings, though, doubtless, each with its own agony to him. In many of the slighter poems, however, all of them good and most of them quite beautiful, the signs of nationality are obvious. They are comically clear, in fact, proceeding as they do directly from the quick, keen perception of the Comic Spirit itself. (p. 283)

[Mr Stephens'] lyric moods may be as tender and fanciful, though always more spontaneous, than those of Mr Yeats. And one may find the arrowy truth, the rich earthiness and the profound sense of tragedy of a Synge. But the filmy threads which seem to stretch between Mr Stephens and his compatriots have no strength to bind him. They are, indeed, only visible when he is ranging at some altitude that is lower than his highest reach. When he soars to the zenith, as in "The Lonely God" and "A Prelude and a Song," their tenuity snaps. He has gone beyond what is merely national and simply human; and has become just a Voice for the Spirit of Poetry.

Nevertheless the affinities of this poet with what is best in modern Irish literature would make a fascinating study. Foremost, of course, there is imagination. You will find in

him the true Hibernian blend of grotesquerie and grandeur, pure fantasy and shining vision. But each of these things is [in *Insurrections*] raised to a power which makes it notable in itself, while all of them may sometimes be found in astonishing combination in a single poem. . . . Already [in "What Tomas an Buile Said in a Pub"] we may see this complex quality at work. Tomas is protesting that he saw God; and that God was angry with the world. . . . You will see—a significant fact—that there is no nonsense about a dream or a transcendent waking apparition. In the opening lines Tomas says, with anxious emphasis, that he saw the 'Almighty Man'—and that is symbolical. It has its relation to the mellow tenderness with which the poem closes; but apart from that it is a sign of the way in which the creative energy always works in this poetry. It seizes upon concrete stuff; and that is fused, hammered and moulded into shapes so sharp and clear that we feel we could actually touch them as they spring up in our mental vision. This is not peculiar to Mr Stephens, of course. It would seem to be common to every poet—though to be sure they are not many—in whom sheer imagination, the first and last poetic gift, is pre-eminent. Mr. Stephens has many other qualities, which give his work depth, variety and significance; but fine as they are, they take a secondary place beside this ardent, plastic power. (pp. 284-86)

Yet there is something truly grotesque in this work. That is to say, there is a juxtaposition of ideas so violently contrasted that they would provoke instant mirth if it were not for the grave intensity of vision. Sometimes, indeed, they are frankly absurd. We are meant to laugh at them, as we do at Mac Dhoul, squirming with merriment on God's throne with the angels frozen in astonishment round him. But generally these extraordinary images are presented seriously, and often they are winged straight from the heart of the poet's philosophy. Then, the driving power of emotion and a passion of sincerity carry us safely over what seems to be their amazing irreverence. There is, for instance, in the piece called "The Fulness of Time," a complete philosophic conception of good and evil, boldly caught into sacred symbolism. The poet tells here how he found Satan, old and haggard, sitting on a rusty throne in a distant star. All his work was done; and God came to call him to Paradise. (pp. 287-88)

It is not irreverence, of course, but the audacity of poetic innocence. Only an imagination pure of convention and ceremonial would dare so greatly. And the remarkable thing is that this naïveté is intimately blended with a grandeur which sometimes rises to the sublime. The noblest and most complete expression of that is in "The Lonely God." That is probably the reason why this poem is the finest thing that Mr Stephens has done—that, and the magnitude of its central idea. There is, indeed, the closest relation here between the thought and the imagery in which it is made visible. (p. 288)

[This poet shares] in some measure, with Aeschylus and our own Milton and the unknown author of the Book of Job, a sublimity of vision. His conceptions have a grandeur of simplicity; and he makes us realize immensities—Eternity and Space and Force—by images which are almost primitive. Like those other poets too, whose philosophical conceptions were as different from his as their ages are remote, he also has made God in the image of man. But the comparison does not touch what we may call the human side of this newer genius; and it only serves to throw into bolder relief its perception of life's comedy, its waywardness, and its mischievous humour. This aspect, strongly contrasted as it is with the poet's imaginative power, is at least equally interesting. It is apparent, in the earlier work, in the realism of such pieces as "The Dancer" or "The Street." There is a touch of harshness in these poems which would amount to crudity if their realism were an outward thing only. But it is not a mere trick of style: it proceeds from indignation, from an outraged aesthetic sense, and from a mental courage which attains its height, rash but splendid, in "Optimist." . . . (pp. 290-91)

Returning . . . to the larger implications of this poetry, one may find a passion for liberty in it, and a courageous faith in the future of the race. Here we have, in fact, a pure idealist, one of the invincible few who have brought their ideals into touch with reality. (pp. 292-93)

It is . . . in "A Prelude and a Song" [in *The Hill of Vision*] that this ardour of freedom finds purest expression. Not that the poem was designed to that end. I believe that it was made for nothing on this earth but the sheer joy of singing. . . . In some degree at any rate it is a paean of freedom: delighted liberty lives in it. But we cannot apply our little distinctions here, saying that it is this or that or the other kind of freedom which is extolled: because we are now in a region where thought and feeling are one; in a golden age where good and evil are lost in innocency; in a blessed state where body and soul have forgotten their old feud in glad reunion. (pp. 296-97)

[Though] every stanza has a lightsome grace which makes it lovely in itself—though the whole chain, if broken up, would yield as many gems as there are stanzas, irregular in size and shape indeed, but each shining and complete—the great beauty of the poem is its beauty as a whole. (p. 297)

Subjective this poet may be—is it not a virtue in the lyricist?—but he does not confide his religion to us in so many words. He has an artistic conscience. But the avowal, though it is by way of allegory and grows up out of the imagery of the poem as naturally as a blossom from its stem, is clear enough. And is supported elsewhere, implicitly, or by a mental attitude, or outlined now and then in figurative brilliance. There can be no reason to doubt its strength and its sincerity—and there is every reason to rejoice in it—for it reveals Mr. Stephens as a poet of the future. (p. 298)

> *Mary C. Sturgeon, "James Stephens," in her* Studies of Contemporary Poets, *Dodd, Mead and Company, 1916, pp. 282-300.*

CORNELIUS WEYGANDT (essay date 1928)

James Stephens has been reborn into our troubled world from a previous existence in an age of innocence. His attitude toward life is irresponsible, primitive, incredibly optimistic, instinct with sunlight and the spirit of spring. His writing is rich in proverbs, in hidden sayings, in cryptic riddling. It would seem that there had been handed on to him, from his earlier incarnation, the secrets of some wizard of the little people of old time who appear in fairy-lore as leprechauns or gnomes or pucks. (p. 121)

A guess at the meaning of the leading motive of *The Crock of Gold* is that Caitilin is, like that other Cathleen of *Cathleenni-Houlihan*, a symbol of Ireland, and that her union with Pan before she finds happiness with Angus Og means that Ireland's way to happiness lies through a frank recognition of earthly joys. If this is the meaning of the story then Mr. Stephens is in close agreement with George Meredith in believing that the way to spiritual beings is through "good gross earth." Emerson, too, has had influence over Stephens, and "A. E.," the Irish Emerson, and Solomon. It is the happy philosophers that Mr. Stephens follows. You must not hold him to every one of the declarations of faith that he has made. You must devolve his creed from the whole of his sayings. It is these sayings that, with his lyric descriptions, are the best of Mr. Stephens. (pp. 124-25)

Mr. Stephens is a man of many points of view. Now he looks at things from one angle, now from another, now from still another. He can shift with the character he is making speak, he has dramatic sense, he can be now one person, and now another, and now a third.

Every once in a while Mr. Stephens translates one of his sayings from the symbolism in which he loves to speak into the English of the market-place understood of all men. (p. 125)

[He] pays his readers the compliment of considering them of this privileged company. Nor does he labor at all to support his maxims or his interpretations or his flashes of insight by illustrations or detailed statement of any kind. "What can be sensed requires no proof" he tells us in *The Crock of Gold,* in which, indeed, he has stored the half of the good things he has said. One is not concerned, in most cases, to question whether these good things are half-truths or whole-truths. One is content to take them for the stimulation to imagination and thought there is in them. One has, indeed, one reaction to them at one reading, another reaction at another. Each time you read him you find something new in Mr. Stephens, and no matter how many times you read him you cannot exhaust him. (p. 126)

Mr. Stephens has humor. Humor, indeed, he holds almost as necessary to man's well-being as freedom of thought. In *The Demi-Gods* he tells us that "Humour is the health of the mind." In *The Crock of Gold* he had referred to "the free will of mankind" as "the most jealously guarded and holy principle in life," and yet this philosopher and moralist is quick to turn from such declarations as these to such simple delights as hunting hen's eggs and romping with a dog. (p. 130)

Mr. Stephens, it seems to me, is unsurpassed today as a writer of fantastic stories. Mr. Stephens as a poet in verse is but a minor poet, not so good as Mr. Sturge Moore or Mr. Davies or Mr. Ralph Hodgson, and of only a slender talent as compared to such majors as Mr. Hardy and Mr. Masefield and Mr. Frost. Nor does it seem to me . . . that Mr. Stephens is at his best in his retellings of old Irish legends. (p. 131)

It is . . . in his three books of his first youthful mastery that he is at his best, in *The Crock of Gold* and *Here Are Ladies* and *The Demi-Gods.* . . . There is in these, a fresher revelation of the wonder of the world than in any story-teller of his generation. . . . The world of Mr. Stephens is lighted by the sun we know and the old familiar moon, but it is transfigured at intervals into a thing of strangeness and wild delight. Here, too, in Mr. Stephens is a humor we have not had before; a smiling delight in little things; a full-lunged heartiness that drives away doubt in a great gale of laughter. Here is a sympathy with all that is human; a welcome to all weathers, to the weathers of the spirit we call moods, and to the weathers of out-of-doors that bring rain in the face or sun to warm us. There are few figures against the sky in Mr. Stephens, only Patsy MacCann, maybe, and Mary, and the donkey, but there is a pageant of people of all sorts high and low, Mary Makebelieve and Mrs. Makebelieve in their high tenement in the Dublin slum, and the big policeman and the thin youth; philosophers and their wives out of fairy, Pan himself and the great god Angus Og, men of the royal Irish constabulary and leprechauns; publicans and sinners and twopenny clerks; thieving tinkers and brawling toughs; and a whole host of delightful animals from spiders to dogs and dogs to donkeys. Mr. Stephens may not be a great creator of character or a great story-teller, but he is a story-teller and creator of character who challenges comparison with the great. (p. 132)

> Cornelius Weygandt, "The Riddling of James Stephens," in his Tuesdays at Ten: A Garnering from The Talks of Thirty Years on Poets, Dramatists, and Essayists (copyright 1928 University of Pennsylvania Press), University of Pennsylvania Press, 1928, pp. 121-34.

FRANK SWINNERTON (essay date 1934)

[James Stephens's] work now very slightly resembles the poems which were published in *Insurrections* (these, I admit, have in the passage of years lost something of their first pungency, but not all of it); and in narrative has all the whispered assurance of the folk tale. Indeed, it is of the character of the folk tale, reinforced by an intricacy of saying and allusion such as only a witty mind could invent and keep of a piece with the whole. First it is a tale, and then it is philosophy, and then it is nonsense; but all these qualities are so merged and, for the reader, confounded, that the effect is one of profound laughter. At no time is there a hiatus between what is thought and what is said; all is of the same relish.

This is a very rare quality. It is not found even in [Gilbert Keith] Chesterton's fantastic narratives, for in such a book, for example, as *The Flying Inn,* Chesterton several times uses the word "absurd" or "ridiculous" in a conventional sense, as if imagination had failed him and he admitted his make-believe to be a fake. Stephens makes no such mistake. His imagining is unaffected by interruption from an outside and alien judgment. He never sniggers. For this reason he commands us entirely, as Lewis Carroll does, who for as long as a book lasts never interposes Kensington into Wonderland, Thus, where Chesterton's fairies are but figures of rhetoric, and [J. M.] Barrie's are little bells and flitting lights, Stephens's are as cunning as the elves in old tales, before cleverness came to quiz invention. (p. 128)

Stephens is one of the writers as to whose rank in the hierarchy there is no immediate question, and why Irishmen, who in general have no sense of humour whatever, must frequently laugh as they con lists of great English authors, to find in those lists the names of so many of their compatriots. (p. 129)

> Frank Swinnerton, "Fancy Fair: Barrie, Milne, James Stephens," in his The Georgian Scene: A Literary Panorama (copyright 1934 © 1962 by Frank Swinnerton; reprinted by permission of Holt, Rinehart and Winston, Publishers), Farrar & Rinehart, 1934, pp. 105-30.*

VIVIAN MERCIER (essay date 1951)

[Much] twentieth-century Irish writing, especially that of James Stephens, is in the pastoral convention; sometimes it takes the form of genuine pastoral, when the author dresses up as a small farmer or a fisherman; at other times it is mock-pastoral . . . , where the intention is mainly satirical or at least anti-social—in other words, playing at tinkers. . . .

[Authors] who use the pastoral convention are seeking to evade or criticize certain restraints imposed by society in their time: what the particular restraints are will vary from age to age, but ultimately all pastoral poetry implies a hankering for what one might call the ultimate in pastoral—namely, the return of the Golden Age, where there is freedom from all restraint. . . .

[*The Charwoman's Daughter, The Crock of Gold*, and *The Demi-Gods*] all fit into the pastoral category. . . .

[*The Charwoman's Daughter* is] an idyll, not a social indictment, nor even a documentary. . . . [It is] an excursion into, not the sordid, but the picturesque. . . . [The] occasional sordid details are seen to be nothing more sinister or tendentious than local colour. A great deal of the descriptive matter in the book deals, actually, with the fine dresses the Makebelieves would like to buy and the bourgeois appointments of the houses where the mother works as a charwoman. (p. 49)

[Stephens] was, to my mind, playing at being a charwoman, "dressing up," and the book's faults and virtues both spring from that source.

For the book has virtues, easy to see, but hard to define. . . . [We] have a calculated naiveté that nobody but Stephens can manage; whether it accurately represents the mental process of a simple girl of the people seems to me beside the point: almost certainly it doesn't; but it expresses the unique sensibility of one James Stephens to a T. (p. 50)

Passing over *The Crock of Gold* for the moment, let us take a quick look at *The Demi-Gods,* where we find not only Stephens, but a trio of angels, playing at tinkers. The descent of gods and demi-gods to earth is of course a well-worn pastoral theme; very often the cult of old gods survives only in the country, or else the country people are thought of as being the only ones sincere enough in their devotions and emotions to deserve the visits of the gods. Think of Philemon and Baucis, the country couple who were hosts to the gods Jupiter and Mercury, or of the Galilean fisherman who was the first to recognise the divinity of Christ. (p. 51)

In *The Demi-Gods* Stephens reveals a mastery of a certain type of dialogue that he had only occasionally achieved in *The Crock of Gold.* . . . It flows as freely between the human characters in *The Demi-Gods* as it does between them and the non-human. . . .

We may now turn back to *The Crock of Gold*, which begins as an Irish *Peter Pan*, but ends as something a little more profound—an allegory of the rescue of the Human Intellect, in bondage to Civilisation (the absurd and brutal Police-man), by the forces of the Divine Imagination. (p. 52)

When we come to the consideration of Stephens's poetry, we shall find ourselves wishing that he had more thoroughly learned the lessons of his own allegory. All too frequently the Human Intellect—and not too powerful a one at that—is offered to us in place of the Divine Imagination. Stephens unquestionably had ambitions of being a philosopher, but he is usually no better than a philosophizer. In the prose works, too, he constantly intrudes in his own person with bromides. . . . (p. 53)

Nowhere, perhaps, do Stephens's pastoral tendencies come out more clearly than in the selection and arrangement of the . . . *Collected Poems;* after a preface containing a spir-ited defence of lyric poetry, especially at the beginning of a new era such as he believes the present to be, he sets out all the poetry he wished to be preserved under six subject-headings. The first, ''In Green Ways'', covers his nature poetry, all those poems where he identifies himself with small or shy creatures like the rabbit of ''The Snare'' or the satyr who gives his name to one poem. . . . ''In Two Lights'' contains a series of twilight pictures from city and country; no reference to the Gaelic Twilight is intended; it seems rather that this time of day held a very personal symbolism for Stephens, a kind of moral significance. One such poem, ''The Holy Time'', which appears on the sur-face purely descriptive, ends with the assertion, *''there is no sin.''* Conventional morality seems here a creature of the broad daylight, whereas in the half-light innocence is pos-sible. In more traditional symbolism, sunlight and sinless-ness are usually equated. . . .

''Heels and Head'' contains the poems of vision, the core of Stephens. Very often the vision is conveyed through a character, some mad beggarman, Tomas An Buile or Mad Patsy, who is outside normal humanity and allows none of its preconceptions to come between him and his vision. At other times the poet himself is the visionary, reminding us of Blake. . . . (p. 55)

> Vivian Mercier, ''James Stephens: His Version of Pastoral,'' in *Irish Writing*, No. 14, March, 1951, pp. 48-57.

GEORGE EGON HATVARY (essay date 1952)

[James Stephens's] distrust of philosophical rationalism, of pure thought divorced from life, amounts to a major theme in *The Crock of Gold.* In a sense one may interpret this novel as the intellectual man's search for and successful winning of the spirit of life. (p. 58)

James Stephens's impatience with existing institutions has in this novel given rise to direct criticism in the form of so-cial protest and indirect criticism in the form of quiet depar-ture from orthodox theology. Undoubtedly the most pow-erful example of social revolt is constituted by the two autobiographical stories that the Philosopher hears in the darkness of his cell. While they have little to do with the plot formally, they possess power and beauty of their own, and one might consider them the microcosm of the entire latter part of the book. Both stories illustrate how deplor-able social and economic conditions will reduce honest men to thievery, but they are by no means mere sermons. . . . Stephens is more guilty of sermonizing elsewhere. Chapter

XIII begins, for example, with a little essay which sums up the author's philosophical position then turns into a critique of modern justice. This admittedly mars the narrative, al-though it may be pointed out in its favour that it does form a logical starting point of the second major theme, human versus natural justice, into which the first theme, abstract versus practical wisdom, resolves. These two themes, in fact, now blended into harmony, now contrapuntally, carry the novel to its conclusion. (pp. 59-60)

[It] is clear that the author's moral scheme is essentially Christian. In addition to the emphasis on love, charity, and humility, the Philosopher's arrest at a time when he has fully achieved these virtues may be looked on as an expres-sion of the tradition of martyrdom. Nevertheless, a purely Christian interpretation of the moral scheme will not do. . . . [In chapter II, the philosopher's query], ''Is it not possible that the ultimate end is gaiety and music and a dance of joy?'' smacks of paganism, and one cannot help recalling *cinque-cento* angels frolicking with unconscious sensuality.

The blending of the Christian and pagan elements, how-ever, receives a more poignant expression through the pres-ence in the novel of Pan. It is needless to emphasise that according to Christian theology lust is an improper way of love, and that it has no place in the soul's progress from a state of indifference and intellectual pride to a state of spiri-tual bliss. Here, however, as I pointed out before, the Phi-losopher becomes a human being through an awakening of his senses as well as through his conversation with the god of lust, Pan. In fact, one may say without exaggeration that lust in this novel becomes the first step toward salvation. (pp. 60-1)

The presence in this novel of Pan is furthermore an answer to the renaissance poet's inevitable interest in classical an-tiquity. This importation, however, of the Greek god of flocks and shepherds and his transformation into the god of lust imply a coming to terms with the demands of national tradition. Stephens's mythology is predominantly Irish, even if the pagan Pan and the Christian God and Holy Ghost become part of it. Although any specific attempt at creating order among this characteristically Celtic hodge-podge of deities is bound to result in theological absurdity, for purposes of analysis it seems possible to make a divi-sion between the world of the Leprecauns and the world of the gods. (p. 61)

The relationship between the world of Leprecauns and the world of gods is never made explicit; but, since the main action of the novel originates in a misunderstanding be-tween the Leprecauns and the human world and since hu-mans in their plight turn to the gods for succour, one is re-minded of the relationship between the Fates and the gods in Greek mythology. At any rate, the gods incline toward benevolence, with Angus Og designated as the chief deity, the god of love. (pp. 61-2)

[This] book was not written on the basis of a carefully con-ceived outline. Order in this work seems to lack so strik-ingly that some readers prefer to consider it a vaguely con-nected set of experiences rather than a novel. To be sure, in stories stretching over two hundred pages we have come to take form so much for granted that it is not design but the lack of it that tends to distinguish *The Crock of Gold* from other novels. . . .

Design and spontaneity tend to become reconciled as soon as we consider the work as characteristic of the renaissance tradition; but, since the artist is by definition concerned with form, we may legitimately inquire into the artist's reasons for deviation. What force makes a writer succumb to his momentary flights of fancy to an extent where he cannot resist their inclusion in an otherwise organized work? . . . Without attempting to go too far into the mysteries of the creative process, I think we may suggest a partial answer by considering Stephens's interest in philosophy, humour, and poetry. (p. 63)

[The] author enjoys philosophizing, but he is intelligent enough to know that this enjoyment is an excellent subject for satire; moreover he is enough of an artist to be able to satirize this tendency in himself. If we examine these philosophical bits of dialogue that are expounded by the Philosophers, I do not think we shall ever find them nonsensical. In themselves they are sensible and useful; the hilarity comes from their total irrelevance to the practical issue at hand. Similarly, alas!, when the author pours the remaining philosophy in his system into the reader's ear in order to illumine some aspect of the narrative, the result is often irrelevance. . . .

We pardon him primarily, I think, on account of his genius for humour. Whether it manifests itself in the form of exaggeration or oversimplification or juxtaposition, or in a special brand of delicate charm through which his children and Leprecauns and rabbits and squirrels become unforgettable, we willingly follow him into realms that become wholly disconnected from the main intention of the story. The conversation, for example, between the cow and the fly has no conceivable relationship even to the incident of which it is part. . . . If we allow our imagination to linger in a scene such as this we shall realize how successfully the very force that compelled the artist to succumb to a momentary flight of fancy is now communicated to the reader, with a similar result of irresistibility. (p. 64)

> George Egon Hatvary, "Re-reading 'The Crock of Gold'," in *Irish Writing, No. 22, March, 1952, pp. 57-65.*

CLARICE SHORT   (essay date 1956)

The return to primitivism in reaction against the complexities of modern life is represented in several aspects of James Stephens' work but in none more clearly than in his portrayal of women, their character and role in human life. In primitive belief the earth is feminine and as the source of life is strong. There is no escape from her tyranny which is sometimes beneficent, often harsh. To the female of the human species Stephens attributes the qualities of the maternal earth. There is something of Deirdre in all his women characters.

The role played by woman in the attainment of the good life, as Stephens sees it, explains his attractive portraits. Her power, which inspires both awe and fear, is his emphasis in the unflattering representations. (p. 285)

Because Stephens sees women as "the great impelling forces of life," his women characters often appear as personifications of natural law. They are phenomena like the change of seasons and the rise and fall of the tide. He may give some description of a woman's appearance, quote

some of her speeches, reveal her feelings upon particular occasions; but these details are only an introduction to generalizations about femininity. . . . The legendary Deirdre seems to have struck Stephens as the symbol of feminine essence.

She was irresistibly lovely. The women characters of Stephens do not all have her disturbing beauty; but when they do, their beauty carries all before it. (pp. 285-86)

Another of the sources of the legendary Deirdre's power was her intuitive wisdom, and Stephens bestows upon many of his women characters this same dark knowing. They are in touch with the fathomless currents which flow beneath man's conscious life. . . .

Another source of woman's power, in Stephens' opinion, is a singleness of purpose greater than that of most men. With terrifying intensity she can direct all of her energy toward one object. (p. 286)

Because of woman's beauty, elemental wisdom, singleness of purpose, she is strong. It is in her relationship to man that this strength becomes tyrannical and often fatal. Stephens often uses the spider as a symbol of the relationship of males and females, human and otherwise. The compulsion of sex drives the spider to his mate though she is very likely to devour him. (pp. 286-87)

It is in their association with men that women manifest their most dangerous quality: their desire for power. . . .

Marriage is a concession made by men to propitiate the fierce feminine spirit, but because this concession is often made unwillingly, the woman thenceforth gets her revenge. In the short stories, which are the most realistic part of Stephens' fiction, marriage is usually shown to be calamitous for men. The woman's desire to dominate the man is enhanced by her rights as legal wife. Often the men are shown as not knowing why they married. After marriage they grow fat and bored, or are driven to madness and violence, or rebel and run away. . . .

Fortunately for man, nature has put controls upon woman's desire to dominate. "There is a steadying influence; an irreconcilable desire and ambition; the desire of every woman to be the wife of a fool, her ambition to be the mother of a genius." Even beyond this desire and ambition is the maternal instinct, a powerful force for bringing women into subjection. (p. 287)

Two instances of the triumph of the woman motivated by pity for man's weaknesses occur in *The Crock of Gold*. The Thin Woman hates the philosopher so much that she marries him. But when he is imprisoned she exerts her influence upon the fairy world to bring about his release. Caitilin, a mortal, gives herself to Angus Og, a folk god, not with any view toward personal gain or because she is overcome by her awe of him, but "because his need of her was very great, and therefore she loved him." Moved by an innate compulsion to mother and protect, a few of Stephens' women characters are noteworthy for gentleness and self-sacrifice. Deirdre was not malicious; she would have saved her husband and his brothers had not masculine ego made them ignore her prophecy. But because of her they came to early and violent death.

Stephens' treatment of the woman character is a dramatization of the age-old paradox, man-propounded, that men can neither live with women nor without them. His concept of the woman spirit has its roots in the Celtic tradition of Maeve, ''Intoxication,'' and Deirdre, ''The Troubler.'' In his vision women keep the waters of life fresh by stirring them into motion, but men are often drowned in the turbulence of that flood. (p. 288)

Clarice Short, ''James Stephens' Women,'' in Western Humanities Review *(copyright, 1956, University of Utah), Vol. 10, No. 3, Summer, 1956, pp. 285-88.*

PADRAIC COLUM (essay date 1962)

[James Stephens] brought into Irish literature (it was then at the stage of being a movement) a naturalism that was fresh as it was engaging. . . . Into a poetry that was of the countryside or of a kingly past, James Stephens brought the streets of the town and the people of the streets. (pp. ix-x)

His first prose work, *The Charwoman's Daughter,* is, I take it, an idyll. . . . Leave the poetry out, let there be a demand on our credulity rather than an appeal to our imagination . . . and we have instead of the idyll, the sentimental story or poem. But make no mistake about it: the combination that makes the idyll is a rare thing in literature.

Well, James Stephens in his twenties made the combination and wrote *The Charwoman's Daughter.* The interior and exterior that Mary Makebelieve knows are equally memorable. (pp. x-xi)

[The] thing that *The Charwoman's Daughter* really gives us is a share in the happiness of the poor. (p. xiii)

[*The Crock of Gold* is about] seeing strange things, finding something to talk about, visiting the Shee of the Hills, and getting out of our daily lives to such an extent that we can become intimate with donkeys, goats and cows. . . . Why is this book more popular than any other of James Stephens' books? We all know that there is a world that is the other side of our day-by-day world: with all he has of intuition and reflection James Stephens in *The Crock of Gold* committed himself to this other side, and seeing him so wholeheartedly do this, we go wholeheartedly with him. This, I think, is the secret of *The Crock of Gold*'s appeal. (p. xiv)

The human entrants are refugees from Time. The leprecauns of course are, and have always been in that world. But the philosophers in *The Crock of Gold,* or at least the survivor of the pair, has a lien on it, too—else why should the leprecaun take it for granted he could come into it—for they are enemies of Time, and they talk day and night because they are talking against Time. The only villains in James Stephens' books of this genre are persons who have such an obsession about time that they interrupt and intercept the philosophers: they are the philosophers' wives. . . .

To retell the stories from the old epics, the sagas, the court romances was a challenge to Irish writers in James Stephens' early days. That challenge he took up in *Irish Fairy Tales, Deidre,* and *In the Land of Youth.* With his humour, poetry, fantasy, extravagance—the old storytellers combine these qualities, too—he made narratives out of them that have all his distinctiveness. Characteristically he makes shrewd use of the double time that is in the old stories—the time of the world of Faerie and the time of human computation. None except James Stephens could tell without hesita-

tion or embarrassment how the wife of the King of Ireland leaves her husband one Sunday morning, enters on a series of adventures that take a couple of chapters to recount, and is back before he notices that she has left the conjugal domicile. (p. xv)

The problem of transferring imaginative creations from one literature to another is first of all the problem of penetrating what has to be transferred with one's own imagination and then of finding an idiom and a pattern that will represent what is characteristic in the original. James Stephens did all this in *Irish Fairy Tales, Deirdre,* and *In the Land of Youth.* He made himself at ease with the strange stories of Maeve's or of Cormac's Ireland; his own idiom with its combination of humour, poetry, fantasy and extravagance was in line with that of the old storytellers; he found a pattern which brings over to us the peculiarities of the originals. And he went beyond all this by creating a society and a land in which such things can happen. Certainly his personages live according to strange customs, but who are we to compare theirs with ours? Their manners are kind and majestic; they have endowments of beauty, pride and nobility. The Tara of these stories is a grander place than any archeological measurements show us for it is what the storytellers dreamed it to be, ''the Lofty City, the Secret Place of the Road of Life,'' and whether it is possessed by Eochaid or Cormac or Dermod, has in it people who are natural even though their careers mingle with the careers of beings of another world.

Personally I think that *Irish Fairy Tales* is James Stephens' most fascinating book. (p. xvi)

The two that are my favorites in *Irish Fairy Tales* are ''Mongan's Frenzy'' and ''The Wooing of Becfola,'' and I think either would be hard to beat as a representative of the storyteller's art. It could be said that their originality is due to the peculiar pattern of the originals. Yes, but if one took the trouble to read the literal translations of these stories . . . one's admiration for James Stephens' art would be heightened. I have said that the pattern of these stories is peculiar. But the pattern of ''Mongan's Frenzy'' is so peculiar that one wonders how any storyteller could have related it without crazing his hearers. (pp. xvi-xvii)

How could one make [the plot] plausible enough for a story, find a centre for it and deliver it in a fashion that would be beguiling enough to hold us? If it hadn't been done I should be ready to assure the world that it couldn't be done. But there it is in *Irish Fairy Tales,* a brilliant and entertaining story. (p. xvii)

Padraic Colum, ''James Stephens As a Prose Artist,'' in A James Stephens Reader, *edited by Lloyd Frankenberg (reprinted by permission of the Estate of Padraic Colum), Macmillan Publishing Co., Inc., 1962, pp. ix-xix.*

LLOYD FRANKENBERG (essay date 1962)

We may come to recognize . . . James Stephens as one of the masters of looking-glass reality. Unlike the mirror, which casts back images, a looking-glass invites submergence. Its diverse classics include Lewis Carroll's *Alice* and Samuel Butler's *Erewhon,* Dean Swift's *Gulliver's Travels* and Jean Cocteau's *Blood of a Poet,* the wit of Oscar Wilde, of James Thurber and of Aristophanes. Each has his special slant of reversal, turning life upside down or inside out, paying the world left-handed compliments.

The particular genius of Stephens is to believe with equal vehemence inside and out. He doesn't avoid the outside world; he just won't go chasing after it. Contrariwise, a native direction for him, he makes it follow him about.

Life is alive for him in the proportion and to the degree that it commands the power of imagination. It can do this any time, anywhere. The surprising, the melancholy fact is that it does not always do so. Struck by this incomprehensible inactivity, Stephens must every now and again stop short in his tracks to regard it, much as one might regard an obstinate donkey.

Stephens has more patience with the donkey. Some fantasy, however dim, is working in that close-set mind. But not in the mind of the man without imagination. Worse, or more puzzling than roguery or malefaction is the abiding lack of this power.

Consider his police force: that limb of the law that pays court to Mary in *The Charwoman's Daughter;* his bumpkin counterparts in *The Crock of Gold.* None of them is villainous in the sense of deliberately vindictive, malicious or cruel. They are simply obtuse. . . . (pp. xxix-xxx)

The title story [of *Etched in Moonlight*], patently a dream, is written with such insight that for me its horror is more mounting than that of *The Turn of the Screw.* Perhaps this is because, while I find it hard to believe in ghosts, a dream is irresistible.

There could be no realer a dream than this shuddery, pellucid examination of motives so deep they are seldom translated into action. The dream is realer than waking reality; all its potentialities are realized. Reading it again I am inclined to feel, as so often on re-reading James Stephens, "Here, above all, is his masterpiece." (p. xxxi)

> Lloyd Frankenberg, "The Other End of the Rainbow," in his A James Stephens Reader, *edited by Lloyd Frankenberg (reprinted with permission of Macmillan Publishing Co., Inc.;* © *Macmillan Publishing Co., Inc. 1962), Macmillan, 1962, pp. xxi-xxxiv.*

RICHARD J. LOFTUS (essay date 1964)

[George] Russell introduced Stephens to the literati of Dublin and introduced him also to the spiritual "truths" which he and Yeats had found in theosophy and in eastern philosophy and had infused into their own poetics. It was no doubt inevitable that A. E.'s gospel of heterodox occultism should exert an influence upon Stephens' work, yet it is noteworthy that this influence is least apparent in Stephens' early period and that it grew more and more significant, in the end becoming the dominant factor in his aesthetic, as Stephens himself drew further and further apart from the popular nationalist movement.

One finds a sprinkling of occult material in *The Demigods,* but it is almost invariably treated humorously. For example, Stephens satirizes Madame Blavatsky's doctrine of reincarnation in the episode of Brien O'Brien, who, determined to have a "cosmic" joke, tries to disrupt the divine process of creation. (pp. 217-18)

The acceptance of eastern religious thought worked a marked change upon Stephen's poetry. His earlier work draws its substance and its inspiration from life itself; like [Padraic] Colum and Joseph Campbell, he concerns himself with the "stuff of existence," with the Irish people and with the environment in which they live, even though Stephens' point of view is certainly different from theirs. In some ways, the early volumes, *Insurrections, The Adventures of Seumas Beg, The Rocky Road to Dublin,* and *Reincarnations,* together comprise a chronicle of Irish life comparable to Colum's *The Poet's Circuits.* Eventually, however, Stephens came to equate the poet's function with that of the magician. . . . (p. 219)

Stephens incorporates into his mature poetry many of the same esoteric beliefs which one finds in the verse of Yeats and A. E. The "Theme" of "Theme and Variations," for example, celebrates the concept of *anima mundi.* . . . (p. 220)

Much of Stephens' mature verse, like that of Yeats, is concerned with the problem of unity of being, that is, with discovering the means by which mankind might achieve harmony with the natural universe. The underlying theme of the poem "Barbarians," for instance, is that of man's fall from grace and unity into degradation and division. A stream, a tree, and a wind speak to the poet, but he, as a human, is "deaf and dumb and blind" and cannot understand their message. Every wind and every tree and every stream knows directly and immediately its reason for being; only man is constrained to ask why, for man, having lost unity of being, has fallen into ignorance. . . . (p. 221)

Both Stephens and Yeats considered poetry to be a medium for the expression of mythico-religious truth. Yet there are important differences in the artistry employed by each to embody mystical "truth" in his poetry; and in these differences one perhaps may recognize why in the last analysis Yeats must be regarded as the greater of the two poets. (pp. 222-23)

Stephens is less successful than Yeats in applying the principle of *pars pro toto* to his poetry. Too frequently he fails to create a metaphor capable of absorbing his occult ideas and of communicating them to his reader. Too frequently he takes refuge in the circular rhetoric of abstraction. (p. 223)

There is implicit in Stephens' emphasis upon abstract values a rejection of Irish nationalism. In the later poetry one finds an occasional turn of phrase that is Irish in derivation, an isolated allusion now and again, a note of bitterness such as that sounded in "Tanist"; but there is no systematic treatment of Irish material. The poet has turned his gaze to the East, and Ireland and its people are excluded from his vision. (p. 224)

[Stephens] never managed to achieve the complete ascetic detachment that is the ideal of the mystic. There is always evident in his verse a deep and troubled sense of pity that has more relevance to man than to God. Stephens, like Yeats before him, took from eastern theosophical literature only those elements which gave substance and support to a philosophy of life which had long before ingrained itself upon his personality; and Stephens' personal philosophy of life begins and ends in the concept of humane love. (p. 225)

[As] far as Stephens was concerned, love offered the only possible hope for the future of mankind and the one possible solution to the enigma of human existence. . . . For Yeats, passion is at the center of all, and love is but one of its manifestations; passion is for Yeats the "universal principle" by which unity of being may be achieved. For Stephens, on the other hand, the universal principle is love; love envelops passion and conflict, and brings unity and harmony. . . . [A] message of deep-rooted, pervasive love is the element that gives essential unity to Stephens' collected poems. Indeed, it is the underlying theme of all his published works; but while in his late poetry the message is presented as a philosophic discourse, in his early work, prose and verse, it is given the form of a parable. The rarified vision of *Kings and the Moon* finds its origin in the earlier volumes of poetry and the novels, in which the ideal of love is given shape and substance. In these early works Stephens' philosophy of life is expressed in terms of physical reality and with specific reference to Ireland and the Irish people; and within the context of these early works, Stephens' vision of the ideal nation emerges—a nation of love and kindness and joy. (p. 227)

Stephens' vision of the ideal nation differs from that of Yeats, who desired the re-establishment of an aristocratic autocracy. . . . Stephens' nation, on the other hand—a nation without property rights or commerce, without education or religion, without law—is a nation without any authority whatsoever. In effect, Stephens rejects the concept of social order and advocates anarchy. His ideal nation is at best a practical absurdity, a never-never land. Yet who can read *The Crock of Gold* without half wishing that Stephens' dream were a reality? (p. 233)

> *Richard J. Loftus, "James Stephens: The Nation of Love," in his* Nationalism in Modern Anglo-Irish Poetry *(copyright © 1964 by the Regents of the University of Wisconsin), University of Wisconsin Press, 1964, pp. 199-233.*

FRANK O'CONNOR   (essay date 1967)

In describing Stephens as a genius I use the word deliberately, more deliberately than of any other Irish writer except perhaps Patrick Kavanagh. . . . If genius means anything it means the power of a natural force, and this was what Stephens had. In fact it was all that Stephens had, for though Joyce, when he forgot to be a talent might be a genius, Stephens, when his genius deserted him, was no talent. The genius was obvious in the conversation—that of a man who felt that if he stopped he might starve. Stephens sang for his supper; he sang for his breakfast and lunch as well. He sings like a bird through those two early books—through *The Charwoman's Daughter* more than through *The Crock of Gold* though the latter has acquired the reputation.

Like Stephens' conversation, *The Charwoman's Daughter* is life-giving. Without using clichés, I do not know how to describe this quality, but it is the book I prescribe for friends who are ill. I do this not because it is hearty and cheerful, but because it reminds me of Mozart's best music, written over an abyss of horror in which I should perish. By some special grace, both men suffered and survived. You have only to wait for the second paragraph to catch the powerful beat of some archangel's wings. (pp. 213-14)

The Charwoman's Daughter is as much a masterpiece as *Ulysses,* though there is no further resemblance. Joyce

does almost everything except sing; Stephens either sings or dithers. In the later books the singing note fails, and yet, just as a man who can swim never really loses his skill, a man who can sing never loses his. . . . (p. 214)

What makes *The Charwoman's Daughter* a masterpiece is that it is all an enormously delicate, witty variation on the themes of hunger and fear. Mrs. Makebelieve, the poor old charwoman, lives in an imaginary world of absolute security, but the horror is always there, implicit in every fantasy and reminiscence. For instance, her only memory of the brother who she hopes will come back some day from America and make her and her daughter rich is that even as a baby 'he would always say "no" if only half a potato remained in the dish or a solitary slice of bread was on the platter'. In other books and stories, even in the middle of gaiety the horror will suddenly swoop down, as in the dreadful incident of the unemployed man that jolts us in *The Crock of Gold.*

Of all the Irish writers Stephens had the most agile mind. He is a sort of literary acrobat, doing hair-raising swoops up in the roof of the tent. (p. 216)

> *Frank O'Connor, "Transition," in his* The Backward Look: A Survey of Irish Literature *(© 1967 by Frank O'Connor; reprinted by permission of Joan Daves, Literary Agents), Macmillan Publishing Co., Inc., 1967, pp. 212-21.*

GEORGE BRANDON SAUL   (essay date 1970)

Stephens' verse will, I think, be eventually approved as unforgettable in fewer instances than one might hope; the bulk of his indubitable poetry seems clearly to be found in his prose fiction—despite his personal critical terminology, which posits the usual illogical contrast of "poetry and prose", of spiritual element with verbal pattern. But certain pieces of verse have a timbre that, by any significant test, suggests permanence of echo. I, for one, should count "The Goat Paths", "Deirdre", "Nora Criona", "What Tomas Said in a Pub", and "A Glass of Beer" (formerly "Righteous Anger"!) . . . assured of future esteem. (p. 15)

Unfortunately, the casual taster of *Collected Poems* . . . may be discouraged by the sheer mass of ordinary material from searching for the really fine pieces. . . . [*Collected Poems*] is divided into six "books". The first of these, "In Green Ways", is an uneven section suggestive of motion under a wind full of leaves; it is exuberant—with the exuberance of animals gambolling, being apparently illustrative of the guiding principle suggested in the Blakean (Stephens owes much to Blake's example) "Dance", with its exhortation to singing and dancing by way of banishing "good and ill / With the laughter of the heart!" . . . It is verse that is sometimes technically interesting for its way of linking stanza to stanza by a device of repetition, sometimes appealing by virtue of its expression of humane and intimate regard for "Little Things." . . . But much of it is nevertheless trivial as poetry: a bounce is not necessarily a revelation. Only the vaguely brooding "The Goat Paths", its erratic metrical outline in itself a graph of such "paths", isolates itself in silver.

The second "book", "A Honeycombe", offers playful verses on love as well as a few love poems. An Elizabethan touch (in "To the Tree", a specifically Spenserian) is time and again discernible. So is an impish spirit (which nevertheless betrays an intelligent comprehension of the ways of woman—"life and law and dear delight!"). (pp. 15-16)

"In the Two Lights", the third division of the volume under consideration, stresses the note of nature, which can delight Stephens to the point of ecstatic proclamation that "There is no sin!" But its successor, "Heels and Head", is more characteristic of the individual Stephens, who writes as readily on "The Devil" as on man, "The Monkey's Cousin"; and who shows a cavalier humor on both divine and human subjects, as "The Merry Policeman" and "The Fur Coat" testify. Metaphysical and dramatic lyrics neighbor protest against the unimaginative side of Christianity and child-lyricism such as Stevenson might have achieved had he had more humor. . . . And here, outcrackling everything else in imaginative audacity, is "What Tomas Said in a Pub" about staying God's hand from threatened destruction of the earth.

The fifth book, "Less Than Daintily", deserves bracketing with "Heels and Head" for its humorous complaints at the current neglect of poets and at other conditions subject to bardic disapproval. Personal restatement, rather than strict translation, of matter originally in Irish verse may be recognized here, but the individual flavor is Stephens. (pp. 16-17)

Collected Poems concludes with "The Golden Bird", which presents a somewhat mystical series of conceptions relative to man and God in which one detects signs of Emerson and Æ, Emerson's debtor. But, whatever the complete philosophical content, or intent, there is, as in Synge, an obvious insistence on the element of joy—for "Joy" is "The Golden Bird". (p. 17)

Kings and the Moon is the one collection of his verse that counts substantially in the later Stephens, and this might be an unsurpassed volume if its individual lyrics measured up to their titles in quality. Actually, the book is a curious mixture of metaphysical speculation, aridity, and humility. The mind seems sometimes in confusion or paradox from trying to view an idea from all sides, whether at once or in turn. The verse-form is almost a lyrical shrug; sometimes it is merely a verbal skeleton, though it lacks the half-anticipated undertow of a chant. And the thought, though a bit wearily embittered, was early forecast. Memorable lyrics are few. . . . What impresses most is perhaps one's conviction that much of both best and worst, including the extensive speculations on love, still owes to Æ and—remotely— Emerson, despite an intimation of spiritual querulousness.

Much of Stephens' verse is little more than description, though even here there may be sudden revelation of character or moral implication; often, as its author's critical speculations would lead one to expect, it is concerned with a paradoxical insistence on the essential oneness of opposites—the compulsion and significance of contraries. With this reconciliation of opposites goes a stressing of onomatopoeia (sometimes, as in "The Main Deep", to the exclusion of practically everything else), resulting in a chant-like quality suggestive of woven texture, with the weft practically determining the symbolism in a process of throw and return. (p. 18)

What Stephens offers is—to put it crudely—the ejaculation of a rarely decent human spirit glowing through a delightfully unpredictable mind: the record of one who believed "All that is, is given to thee!"—that "Nothing is denied the

gay!"—but that the only true BEING (if I do not misread) lies in the freedom of abstracted isolation—in an existence thoughtless, effortless, and careless. Even more concerned with the moon than most of his tribe, he suggests variously the nature poet (in his imaginative identifications), the humorist, the poet of love, and the mystic with a joyous doctrine of man's finding a certain identity in God. Sometimes he seems a teaching commentator only—again in violation of his critical precepts; more frequently, a rider on the mercury of unpredictable currents, and a rider with voice modulated to the bells of a Celtic Faëry (pp. 19-20)

[*The Crock of Gold*] is a queer, delightful book. . . .

[The] book has, despite the wild disparity of its elements, a connected story to tell and a unified fabric of its own. (p. 21)

It is aphoristic ("A woman should be seen seldom but never heard"); it is whimsical (since thought is counted "a disease"); it is perversely wise—and wisely perverse—on a variety of subjects (from dancing to divintiy, from love to policemen); it is tender and inexhaustibly refreshing; it has marvelous dialogues between an ass and a spider, a cow and a fly; and it presents—in its opening pages—the most novel method of committing suicide ever devised! Which is to suggest that it is quite incomparable. It is. (p. 22)

[*The Demi-Gods*] is a wild and glorious—and deeply wise— book, with great fighting . . . , hilarious thievery, and the fierce and angry passion of the tinker and his doxy shouting through its pages. And the ranting fury of that passion covers as pitifully tender a relationship as only a most sensitive poet with an ear to the pulse—and an eye to the turmoil—of life could perceive.

Nor are the tender and the tragic missing from *Etched in Moonlight* (the etching is spectral), the volume of short stories . . . [This] is one of the great short-story collections of all time—a book that isolates itself in one's reading experience as few books of its category do. . . . The ghostly title story itself and "Hunger" . . . would be enough to argue the permanent significance of any author; but these neighbor tales only less effective. For there is also "Desire"—in which a man has dreadfully his wish to remain as he is at the age of forty-eight; there is "Schoolfellows", the chart of a terrifying experience of the utter shamelessness of the unmanned; and there are several others in which human psychology's unpredictable course is mapped by a mind as mercurial as that psychology itself. For no fictionist—unless Conrad—can be argued the equal of Stephens in ability at subtle identification of self with invented character.

It is here that Stephens achieves his greatest concentration and compactness as the prose art of the poet comes into perfect control. Scarcely a story but condenses the substance of a novel; none that is not essential drama. Indeed, even the short narrative and descriptive paragraphs have the impact of dramatic dialogue. Not a character is named: identification requires no labels as an aid to memory; and this elimination of names is in line with a practice frequently apparent in the early *Here Are Ladies*. *Etched in Moonlight* is a sobering—indeed, a frightening—book: what laughter it echoes is the laughter of hysteria; what dreams it reflects have the touch of cold madness. It is George Meredith's "tragic life" with a poet's sober and studied vengeance.

The re-creations of ancient Irish story . . . are another matter. . . . [Perhaps] only those who are aware of the almost incredible complications of content and structure of the original Irish stories can properly estimate the achievement [of *Irish Fairy Tales*]. For the mere organization and interweaving of themes would have been impossible if unabetted by genius.

In these retellings Stephens writes as a master of masters. He has all the audacity and imaginative exuberance of the aristocratic ancient *filid*—the princely order of poet-scholars—together with an artistic control and an instinct for selectiveness and integration which, so far as apparent evidence reveals, they never paralleled. Fortunately, too, he eschews their gnomic impulses. Indeed, since he writes as one who has sat brooding with the druids of his dreaming racial memory, he seems as one to whom all has become luminously simple. He is the wise innocent who has walked in Faëry; so he makes no problem of fusing poetry with philosophy. (pp. 23-5)

Of *Deirdre* . . . it is necessary to say little. This tale of the "troubler" whose elopement to Alba (Scotland) with the nephew (and his brothers) of a designing king wove the fabric of one of the great tragedies of world literature, and also explained the defection of many of that king's followers in his later war with Connacht, has been often retold —most movingly by Synge, Stephens, and (in part) Yeats. But the swift, clean-limbed, unsentimental telling of Stephens is perhaps the most wildly poetic and memorable of them all. Few poets have ever met the challenge of a great subject as Stephens met the challenge of this. It is like an exhilarating peal of triumphant bells.

And the tales of *In the Land of Youth* are, if anything, more lovely and exciting. Mad and wonderful achievements both, in them Stephens is unleashed as seldom before. Wit, humor, drollery, interplay of thought and emotion, light, ecstasy, poetry, and a breathless haste that nevertheless does not slight the story: the book has all these in golden abundance. Incidentally, it has more—and more originally glowing, fresh—descriptions of lovely women than any other book of its compass that I can call to mind. (p. 26)

What the secret of Stephens' power may be . . . will remain a matter of endless speculation. One may consider, in making his own guess, the knack of reducing narrative to its minimal essentials, the gift for exposing interrelationships of character, the economy which utilized and improved early essay in mature achievement, the dramatic character of concept and dialogue, the faculty for aphorism, the inner ecstasy and poetry of conception and impact, the recognition of the "romantic" as the "truth-telling", the amazing architectural sense, the loneliness brooding at the heart of laughter, the basically religious comprehension of joy, the seeming caprice rooted in great pity, the identification of writing as "a way of being". But it is not enough: the sandals were cobbled in Tír-na-nOg, "Land of the Young". The real secret of such pace, such naturalness and magic,— so far as I know, unmatched in any other prose,—remains elusive. But perhaps its key (except for *Etched in Moonlight,* and possible even there) is one to which Cornelius Weygandt long since pointed: is the remark of Billy the Music in *The Demi-Gods*—"There was no old age in that man's mind, and that's the secret of story-telling." (p. 28)

George Brandon Saul, "*Withdrawn in Gold: An Essay on James Stephens,*" in his **Withdrawn in Gold: Three Commentaries on Genius** (© copyright 1970 Mouton & Co. N. V., Publishers; reprinted by permission of the author), Mouton Publishers, The Hague, 1970, pp. 11-28.

PATRICIA McFATE (essay date 1979)

The Charwoman's Daughter is a remarkably harmonious blend of disparate styles and genres. It ranges in tone from whimsy to objectivity, from sentimentality to "philosophizing," and in approach from passages reminiscent of the nineteenth-century novelist to those peculiar to Stephens alone. At various times and in varying degrees it is a fairy tale about two characters called the Makebelieves, a realistic look at life in the Dublin slums, and a psychological analysis of the relationship between a widowed mother and her daughter. (p. 24)

The Charwoman's Daughter begins in the style of the *Märchen,* then becomes realistic and later aphoristic. In *The Crock of Gold* Stephens works these styles more closely together so that the account of Caitilin Ni Murrachu's union with Angus Óg is at once a fairy tale, a love story, and an object lesson.

This book is deliberately Irish in characterization, setting, and theme. . . . Angus Óg is not one of the Gaelic warriors such as Finn or Cúchulinn; rather he is the god of poetry, of love, of divine imagination. His setting is the forest, his followers are those who seek inspiration not revenge. His combat with Pan is philosophical in nature, his victory spiritual despite the physicality represented in Caitilin's naked body. Angus Óg's victory would not be what Arthur Griffith and his political compatriots envisioned; it comes closer to the belief of AE, Yeats, and others in old gods who inspire and teach the Irish people. Stephens will deal with the bloody battles of the Irish saga in later novels; here he celebrates the triumph of charity and creativity. (pp. 33-4)

The gaiety, the music, and the dance of joy envisioned by the Philosopher at the beginning of the book form the background for the ending. Moreover, the dancer's circular pattern, from countryside to city to a return to the home of the gods, is both descriptive of the plot and, Stephens hopes, prophetic of Ireland's future. *The Crock of Gold* is concerned with a descent into corrupt civilization and a return to beneficial nature. Ireland in the form of Caitilin, must make her way from Pan to Angus, from foreign to Gaelic gods, from base materialism to divine spirituality.

The Crock of Gold is, among other things, a prophecy and as such it is not surprising that Stephens, in writing the book, paid reverence to William Blake. (p. 39)

Stephens' admiration of Blake took the form of adaption of Blake's style, characters, and beliefs. In *The Crock of Gold* there are three themes which Stephens found in Blake's writings and made his own: the enmity between men and women, the happy innocence of childhood, and the need to embrace life's joys and its responsibilities. (p. 42)

In many ways, [*The Demi-Gods*] is not significantly different in structure from its predecessors. Symbolism and naturalism are compounded again in this story of angels who appear on earth to the bewilderment, delight, and occasional distress of a group who walk the Irish countryside. (p. 48)

The first three novels by Stephens deal with a basic conflict, the struggle between a maturing daughter and a strong parent. (p. 49)

[In his first] three novels, Stephens explores some favorite topics: the personality traits and behavior of animals, the tyrannies of a materialistic society, the conflict between the sexes, and certain Theosophical beliefs. (p. 50)

But *The Demi-Gods* is not a Theosophical document. It is a picaresque novel with a host of adventures and more than one rogue. (p. 53)

The Demi-Gods is not, moreover, only an extension of Stephens' first two novels. Its characters are new creations who afford Stephens an opportunity to demonstrate his increasing ability to capture speech and gesture humorously and effectively. Stephens is bolder in his characterizations here, and he achieves his descriptions in a less didactic fashion than before. He has learned to sketch a character succinctly. . . . (p. 54)

While the first novel centers around visual images and the second appeals to both the visual and auditory senses, the third encompasses all the senses. So, too, the setting expands as Stephens progresses from one work to another. *The Charwoman's Daughter* is bordered by the city limits of Dublin. While *The Crock of Gold* encompasses both city and nearby countryside, *The Demi-Gods* covers an even larger section of Ireland. But, however original and bold Stephens has been in *The Demi-Gods,* when he created the ending of his third novel, he looked back on his earlier works of fiction. *The Demi-Gods* closes with the attainment of goals which we find in *The Crock of Gold* and *The Charwoman's Daughter:* the unions of man and woman, of gods and men, and of fantasy and reality. (p. 55)

Although *Irish Fairy Tales* is a departure in setting and characterization from the earlier fiction of Stephens, there are certain thematic similarities to be found. Once again fantasy (magical dwellings, shape-changing, disguised gods) is combined with reality (conflicting emotions of lovers, boasting conversations between rivals, devotion to children). It is appropriate that the stories of Fionn dominate the collection because he embraced both worlds. Fionn was a hero, a giant, a descendant of the gods; but he was also, like Stephens, a father, a husband, and a man who loved "the music of what happens." (p. 72)

Stephens saw in Deirdre many of the traits of the modern heroine. In [*Deirdre,*] his version of the ancient tale, Deirdre joins the line of lonely young women who rebel against their parents. She is the most rebellious of the four, running away from her guardian and refusing to marry a king. Like Caitilin Ni Murrachu, she is a beautiful woman raised in the sunshine and peace of the Irish countryside. Like Mary Makebelieve who talks to ducklings, Deirdre converses with birds in their nests. When she puts her arms around "the shaggy mare and her dear, shy foaleen," one remembers Mary Mac Cann hugging her donkey. Deirdre's maternal instinct is aroused when she meets Naoise, for she knows that she can be both mother and wife to him.

Deirdre's guardian, Lavarcham, has a face of "ivory and jet," an abbreviated description recalling Mrs. Makebelieve and the Thin Woman. All three women hold strong opinions on domestic matters and are able counselors on the subject of the warfare between men and women. The male charac-

ters in the first four novels are also related. The lodger, the demi-god Art, and Naoise are boyish, handsome, and heroic. The villainous Policeman and Conachúr are spiders, waiting to catch Mary and Deirdre in their webs.

His insertions of "modernity" in *Deirdre* and *Irish Fairy Tales*—the humanizing of the saga figures by explanations of their emtoions, the addition of color and humor to the darker tales of treachery and murder, and the creation of dialogue which is comprehensible to the modern reader—do not prevent Stephens from maintaining the integrity of the legends by adhering to their essential plot and outlines. (pp. 80-1)

Stephens filled the earliest volume of his poetry, *Insurrections,* with bold, angry pictures of the Dublin slums and their inhabitants. In these poems garbage is "thick as blood," houses are black with soot, slum dwellers are "grim, noiseless things." This view of city life stands in marked contrast to the sweet innocence, the cheerful aspects, the sustaining camaraderie of *The Charwoman's Daughter.* Here one finds the old and the young cursing their enemies and their circumstances, a beaten down cabdriver, an exhausted clerk, a weary prostitute, a violent tramp. Life is harsh; violence and death are ever present. (pp. 88-9)

[A close source for Stephen's poetry] was Robert Browning, from whom he learned the technique of the dramatic monologue and its use as a means to reveal the eccentric, the striking, or the abnormal character reacting to a stressful situation. By his testimony, Stephens began writing poems after reading the Victorian poet for the first time. . . .

In one of the most original of the poems, "The Red-Haired Man's Wife," marriage and independence are examined from the standpoint of a woman. Although undoubtedly the poem owes something to Browning in its technique and to Cynthia Stephens [Stephen's wife] in its viewpoint, Stephens has produced a work which remains modern and fresh in its feminist concerns. . . . (p. 89)

Although some of its poems were written in the same period as those in *Insurrections, The Adventures of Seumas Beg / The Rocky Road to Dublin* represents a major shift in subject matter and tone from those vigorous portraits of life's cruelties. Engaging young spirits are apparent in "The Canal Bank" and "By Ana Liffey." A profoundly patriotic sentiment finds its way into "York Street," "Dublin Men," "The College of Science," and other poems which are reminiscent of the fervent statements contained in essays written for *Sinn Féin.* Among the last to be composed, the poems describing familiar settings, for example, Grafton and York Streets, Westland Row, and O'Connell Bridge, have the bright colors and humming sounds of the city scenes in *The Charwoman's Daughter.* (p. 92)

While the *Seumas Beg* poems described the terrors and joys of an imaginative young boy, works in *The Rocky Road* are aphoristic in tone, owing much to the writings of Blake. . . . (p. 93)

Completed in a period of intense productivity for the writer, *The Hill of Vision* holds works which demonstrate new poetic influences but also familiar, frequently-repeated subjects and themes. "A Prelude and a Song" is a good example; it finds its original sources in Spenser (the

''Epithalamion'' to be exact), but it recalls *The Charwoman's Daughter* and *The Crock of Gold* in its recording of the delights of nature. The poet expresses his joy in terms of the senses; he delights, as the Philosopher does after his meeting with Caitilin and Pan, in the songs of birds, the warmth of the sun, the wind at play. He sees the milkmaids and satyrs at play, a scene repeated in the second novel with the shepherdess and the Greek god. (pp. 93-4)

For the moment Stephens has stopped searching for meaning. In his delight in earthly pleasures and his love for the creatures who dance in the sunshine he has allied himself with Pan in thought and mood. (p. 94)

The best poems in this collection convey rustic joys through simple rhyme schemes, regular metres, plain language, and repetition—not unusual poetic devices, but Stephens adds to them a distinctive whimsical touch. (p. 95)

Despite several memorable poems, *The Hill of Vision* finds Stephens still in his apprenticeship. Even in the most carefully-wrought poems, he occasionally stumbles and uses an inelegant phrase or word. In ''A Prelude and a Song'' the ear is troubled by ''sad vagaries that make us weep,'' a hair ribbon being ''soused'' in a brook, ''exceeding jollity,'' ''happy minions,'' ''ye sing and hold carouse.'' Serious subject matter can also cause problems for the poet. Some of the solemn works in *The Hill of Vision* are ponderous and eminently forgettable, ''Said the Young-Young Man . . . ,'' ''Treason,'' ''The Lonely God,'' and ''Chopin's Funeral March,'' for example. And while there are poems happy in their description of life's pleasures, there are also ''philosophical'' ones which are dreary. Stephens rejected several when preparing for the third edition of this volume, including ''Poles,'' ''Mount Derision,'' ''The Spalpeen,'' and ''New Pinions,'' but the Blakean excesses in this volume are only exceeded by those in *Songs from the Clay*. (p. 96)

[*Reincarnations*,] based on works written by Irish poets of the seventeenth and eighteenth centuries, is the beginning point of an exploration of Gaelic materials which culminates in *Irish Fairy Tales, Deirdre,* and *In the Land of Youth*. The title of the collection reflects the fact that the poems are not Stephens' translations but rather new forms of old works. (pp. 100-01)

Stephens' adaptations are based on structural aspects of Irish poetry which he has modified to fit a modern audience. (p. 103)

Stephens' poems not only in *Reincarnations* but elsewhere clearly follow in the Gaelic tradition. In addition to metrical experimentation, there are certain qualities of Irish poetry which are found in abundance in Stephens' work: the presence of epigrammatic speech, epithets, wit, and hyperbole; concrete language and color in descriptive passages; a use of sharp words and curses; many lists of three items, emotions, or actions; impressionistic descriptions of nature or animals; a sense of refuge in the countryside; a lyricism which suggests music conveyed in words; a sentimental feeling toward an Ireland personified as a woman in need of protection; and moods of exuberance and melancholy.

Stephens' selections of works to adapt are interesting because their themes reflect his interests and preoccupations throughout his writing career with the relativity of time and man's mortality, love's manifold forms, beauty both human and in nature, Ireland's place in history, its legends, and the poet and his craft. He chose to work mainly with [Raftery, Egan O'Rahilly, and David O'Bruadair's] poems because they represented aspects of his own work: in Raftery he found a kindred spirit who loved the beauties of nature; in O'Bruadair and O'Rahilly he saw a point of view not unlike his own in their laments over the loss of heroic ideals. In O'Bruadair, particularly, he discovered a man who fought against materialism, foreign domination, and pro-British sentiment. Because of this sympathy in spirit, his adaptations of O'Bruadair's poems often come closer to the originals than his reworking of the other poets. (pp. 104-05)

Poems in *Kings and the Moon* are permeated with their author's mood of depression: they speak of lost love, of the coming of winter, of growing old. The poet ranges from weary dejection to cold indifference as he contrasts the arid modern times with the richness of the past. In one of the finest poems in the collection, ''I am Writer,'' however, Stephens escapes from his unhappiness into his work and describes the task of a poet in beautifully simple language. . . . If it is viewed in its entirety, Stephens' poetry may be seen as a progression from an early concentration on the real—natural rhythms, speech, figures, and situations—to a later search for the ideal—a dispensing of details, a desire to become bodiless, a need to expound, at most a qualified (''Strict'') Joy. (pp. 115-17)

The earliest poetry combines whimsy and coarseness, audacity and simplicity, the grotesque and the profound. An urban childhood is revealed in the harsh reality of poverty always just beneath the surface of his early poems, but the tone is often buoyant, frequently optimistic, always humane even as the subject matter ranges over earth and cosmos. Middle-period poems mirror childhood innocence, mourn the advance of a mechanical age, attack restrictive societal conventions such as law, religion, and government, and record a belief in the union of the Contraries. Those works written at the end of his life are less personal, more opaque in subject matter. (p. 117)

What connects Stephens' poetry early and late is the doctrine of correspondences. From his readings in Irish mythology and legend, Blake's prophetic books, Theosophical teachings, and the wisdom recorded in Eastern literature, he draws his belief in a heritage shared by all creatures. This belief in the connections among gods, tramps, animals, and trees, and between the living and the non-living, lightens the darkest moods and extends the impact of his poetry. Thus, we feel the sunshine on the winding goat paths, the coldness of the rain-soaked Dublin streets, the pain of a trapped rabbit. Thus, Deirdre's plight becomes our plight; we experience O'Bruadair's rage; and we share Stephens' wish for angels, his fears of growing old, and his need to be a poet. (p. 119)

In addition to being a collection of delightful short tales, *Here Are Ladies* is an interesting document because it contains works which are among the first examples of the modern Irish short story. Stephens' characters are clerks and employers, spinster landladies and frustrated housewives, nervous bachelors and smug husbands; the urban counterparts of the priests and peasants found in George Moore's *The Untiled Field*. Their stories are told in a lean, hard style: unnecessary details such as names, specific dates, and places are eliminated; little time is spent on distinguishing characteristics or on dialogue; the narrator gives the reader merely a brief look at a situation. Obvious literary ancestors are Moore, Chekhov, and Galsworthy, but in none of these writers do we find the variety of humor which pervades most of the stories. . . . (p. 123)

Of the short stories published in *Here Are Ladies*, "A Glass of Beer," "The Horses," and "The Blind Man" link most closely with the works of Stephens included in *Etched in Moonlight*. The emotions which were barely kept in control in the first book are now on a rampage; avarice, envy, despair, shame, jealousy, malice, guilt, anger consume the characters. Husband and wife clash or endure a grinding poverty with no release short of death. (pp. 132-33)

[There] are no happy endings in these stories. The mood ranges from irritability to desperation. Stephens' whimsy is gone; his humor is sardonic; there is no light touch to relieve the tension. The characters find no comfort in their settings. A husband seeks a different life and finds only death; a woman and her children cannot escape the horror of starvation; a man cannot avoid meeting a reminder of his past; another is forced by his obsessive thoughts to relive the past; in several works the indifference, the inhumanity of man toward his fellowman brings down the helpless victim. In the streets, in offices, in homes, in the countryside, there is no escape. (p. 133)

The stories in *Etched in Moonlight* provide evidence of Stephens' efforts to polish his short fiction: these are precisely cut, well-mounted gems. . . . The characters in Stephens' short stories are often anonymous; it is their deeds, their internal conflicts, or the events crushing them which the reader remembers. When this method works, in "Hunger" for example, where the anonymity is a counterpoint to a tale of immense human suffering, it produces a memorable short story. Too often, however, the story cannot survive such impersonal treatment and is quickly forgotten. (pp. 136-37)

Stephens' works reveal a personality like that of Ireland: brooding, highly comic, and bold. His novels and poems show us the gaiety and the loneliness of the Irish people: their estrangement from the land which was once theirs and their desire to return to an earlier, pastoral period; their animosities and suspicions; their flights of fantasy; and their love of words. His works are filled with the sunshine and thunder, lush vegetation and dirty slums, green trees and bloody combats of Ireland.

Although he had an ability to marry the opposites, including those of time and space, in one area he set up no contrasts. His best writing concentrates solely on Ireland. *Insurrections* and *The Charwoman's Daughter* provide affectionate or grimly accurate pictures of Dublin; *The Crock of Gold* and *The Demi-Gods* expand the setting to include the Irish countryside; *Deirdre*, *Irish Fairy Tales*, *Reincarnations*, and *In the Land of Youth* expand the time frame to include vivid, bold recreations of Ireland's past. Whatever the subject, it is an Irishman who is telling the story. (p. 148)

Stephens' love is for every creature and he displays this affection time and time again. All of his heroines are motivated by love in its manifold forms—maternal, charitable, sexual, marital. The secret of his successful works is that in them he embodies love; the later, more arid works only talk about it. In his last poems he no longer seeks Love the Magician; he is himself magician, dealing in mystical symbols, esoteric rites, mysterious rituals. Poetry is no longer a

manifestation of love; it comes from the poet's Will. The vitality one senses in the clash of emotions in *Insurrections*, *The Demi-Gods*, and *Deirdre* has vanished; whatever energy is left comes from idiosyncratic punctuation and capitalization. (p. 152)

In his best works he balances groups of two, three, or four characters in order to illustrate certain themes: the Contraries, sexual jealousy, and the divided self. These matters are also encompassed by the theme of love because fulfillment can only come through union. (pp. 152-53)

His works are all variations on this theme. Love is the motivation for patriotic essays and adaptations of Gaelic legends; it is the subject of stories concerning husbands and wives, parents and children, man and nature's creations. What shines through the prescriptions for a better world, the psychological analyses, the tales of the fantastic, the romantic, the grotesque, and the realistic is his first, his final, his over-arching theme—love. Stephens' works are his variations on this theme, his valentines to the world. (p. 154)

> *Patricia McFate, in her* The Writings of James Stephens: Variations on a Theme of Love *(© Patricia McFate 1979, reprinted by permission of St. Martin's Press, Inc., in Canada by Macmillan, London and Basingstoke), St. Martin's Press, 1979, Macmillan Press, 1979, 183 p.*

ADDITIONAL BIBLIOGRAPHY

Boyd, Ernest. "James Stephens." In his *Portraits: Real and Imaginary*, pp. 246-54. New York: George H. Doran Co., 1924.
    Anecdotal reminiscence of Stephens.

Bramsbäck, Birgit. *James Stephens: A Literary and Bibliographical Study*. Upsala, Sweden: Lundequist; Cambridge: Harvard University Press, 1959, 209 p.
    Contains valuable remarks on the Dublin cultural milieu and the political and literary influences from which Stephens's work arises. This seminal bibliographical study includes manuscript material, unpublished letters by Stephens, biography and criticism on Stephens, and a list of his B.B.C. recordings.

Colum, Padraic. "The Irish Literary Movement." *The Forum* LIII, No. 1 (January 1915): 133-43.*
    Discusses the genesis of the Irish Literary Movement and the stature of its various contributors, including Yeats, George Russell, Douglas Hyde, and Standish O'Grady, with brief mention of Stephens.

Dunsany, Lord. "Four Poets: AE, Kipling, Yeats, and Stephens." *The Atlantic Monthly* 201, No. 4 (April 1958): 77-8, 80.*
    Brief reminiscence of Stephens.

Finneran, Richard J. "Literature and Nationality in the Work of James Stephens." *South Atlantic Bulletin* XL, No. 4 (November 1975): 18-25.
    Traces the changes in Stephens's attitude toward the relationship between Irish literature and nationality.

Frankenberg, Lloyd. "For Seumas." In *James, Seumas & Jacques: Unpublished Writings of James Stephens*, edited by Lloyd Frankenberg, pp. ix-xxx. New York: The Macmillan Co., 1962.
    Discussion of the manuscripts of Stephens's B.B.C. broadcasts.

Gwynn, Stephen. "The Making of a Poet." *The Nineteenth-Century*, LXVII, No. 395 (January 1910): 65-78.*

Early review of *Insurrections* that suggests Stephens is consciously imitating the poetry of Robert Browning, Francis Thompson, and Rudyard Kipling.

McFate, Patricia Ann. "*Deirdre* and 'The Wooing of Becfola'." *Papers on Language and Literature* VIII, supp. (Fall 1972): 165-71.
Argues that *Irish Fairy Tales* and *Deirdre* are not faithful literary versions of the ancient Irish sagas, but creative adaptations.

Pyle, Hilary. *James Stephens: His Work and an Account of His Life*. London: Routledge & Kegan Paul, 1965, 196 p.
Biography containing lengthy discussion of the influence of Blake and Theosophy on Stephens's work.

Saul, George Brandon. "On Mercury and Reason: The Criticism of James Stephens." In his *In Praise of the Half-Forgotten and Other Ruminations*, pp. 119-25. Lewisburg, Pa.: Bucknell University Press; London: Associated University Presses, 1976.
Examines Stephens's theories of literary criticism as put forth in his *On Prose and Verse*, in his various introductions to anthologies, and in the preface to his *Collected Poems*.

Wall, J. "A. E. and James Stephens." *The Poetry Review* IV, No. 7 (January 1914): 29-36.*
Comparison of several poems by A. E. and Stephens.

Sara Teasdale

1884-1933

American poet.

Teasdale's poetry is noted for its lyric simplicity and delicate craftsmanship. Viewed in its entirety, her work chronicles a woman's emotional development from youthful idealism, through gradual disillusionment, to the final acceptance of death. Though considered a minor poet, Teasdale was quite popular in her day. She received the Pulitzer Prize in 1918 for her collection of poems titled *Love Songs*.

As a young woman, Teasdale joined a group of creative women in St. Louis called the Potters, publishing her first poetry in their monthly magazine, *The Potter's Wheel*. She gained her first significant exposure after being discovered by William Marion Reedy, who published some of her work in his widely read *Mirror*. As her literary reputation grew, she became part of the circle surrounding Harriet Monroe and the publication *Poetry*.

Teasdale's earliest influence was Christina Rossetti, whose lyric style and feminine point of view Teasdale greatly admired. Her first collection, *Sonnets to Duse and Other Poems*, illustrates the influence of Rossetti, Teasdale's early attraction to beauty, her sympathy with Sappho, and her admiration for the actress Eleanora Duse. The steady maturation of her lyric art becomes evident in her third collection, *Rivers to the Sea*, where she no longer speaks through ancient figures, and the emotions expressed are clearly her own.

Teasdale was unaffected by stylistic innovations in the works of her literary peers. Rejecting the experimental verse forms they used to examine the shallowness of twentieth-century life, she chose simple quatrains to explore her themes of love and beauty. Critics whose affinities lay with other styles dismissed this pure lyricism as sentimental naiveté. Although she is criticized for her limited range and conventional imagery, her best work is praised for its verbal precision and timeless exploration of human emotion.

As her life progressed, Teasdale's veneration of beauty and love gave way to frustration and a preoccupation with death. Torn between her desire for love and her need for solitude, she slowly withdrew from an active life and became increasingly unhappy. The effects of this conflict, which had persisted since childhood, are clearly evident in *Dark of the Moon*. Although her anguish is still obvious in *Strange Victory*, published posthumously, the poet demonstrates in this collection her confidence in the peaceful release found in death. At the time of her suicide, Teasdale was at work on a biography of Christina Rossetti.

PRINCIPAL WORKS

Sonnets to Duse and Other Poems (poetry) 1907
Helen of Troy and Other Poems (poetry) 1911
Rivers to the Sea (poetry) 1915
The Answering Voice: One Hundred Love Lyrics by Women [editor] (poetry) 1917

Love Songs (poetry) 1917
Flame and Shadow (poetry) 1920
Dark of the Moon (poetry) 1926
Strange Victory (poetry) 1933
The Collected Poems of Sara Teasdale (poetry) 1937

[ARTHUR SYMONS] (essay date 1907)

In this little American book ["Sonnets to Duse, and Other Poems"] there is poetry, a voice singing to itself and to a great woman, a woman's homage to Eleonora Duse. The sonnets to Madame Duse are hardly the best part of the book, for they speak and the lyrics sing; but they speak with a reverence which is filled with both tenderness and just admiration. . . . There are little songs for children, or about them, as lovely as [the sonnets and the lyrics], and with a quaint humour of their own. The book is a small, delightful thing, which one is not tempted to say much about, but to welcome.

> [Arthur Symons], "New Books and Reprints: Sonnets to Duse, and Other Poems," in The Saturday Review, London, Vol. 104, No. 2710, October 5, 1907, p. 426.

THE NEW YORK TIMES BOOK REVIEW   (essay date 1911)

One wonders: Is it the voice of the New woman, of the Old woman, or of woman Immemorial? In any case, it has the authentic accent of genius. The voice referred to sings in "Helen of Troy and Other Poems," by Sara Teasdale. . . . It is not too high praise to say that there is sufficient poetry in this small book to furnish forth a hundred volumes of the ordinary minor-poet variety: perhaps it is not high enough praise. . . .

[Not] since the day of Elizabeth Barrett Browning has any woman distilled a stronger essence of femininity into her verse. It is not at all unusual for women to write passionate love poetry; in fact, they have been accused of less reserve in such matters than male poets display. But, although Miss Teasdale's work shows a frank absorption in woman's great preoccupation, it is not passionate, in the common sense of the term, nor, though it deals almost exclusively with sentiment, is it sentimental.

The titles of the principal poems in the book, "Helen of Troy," "Beatrice," "Sappho," "The Portuguese Nun," "Guenevere," and "Erinna," hint at the author's point of view. Each pictures a revealing moment in the life of a woman who has sought after love as men seek after wealth or fame or honor. One fails to find it, another finds its fulfillment more bitter than failure—all breathe the sad and unconscious cynicism of noble natures foiled and beaten in their pursuit of the ideal, of weak natures the last stroke of whose fate is a knowledge of their own weakness. . . .

It will be seen that Miss Teasdale has courage. We do not recall any other similar indictment of the Great Lover in literature, and by a peculiarly feminine twist of the argument she does not even leave him a court of appeal!

The little songs following the larger efforts range from great tenuity of thought to great compression. All of them are intensely modern—and yet they are only Beatrice and Helen and Erinna over again. . . .

Among the "Sonnets and Lyrics" there is some verse beautiful in spirit and in form. . . . In the last poem, "On the Tower," Miss Teasdale returns to her feminism. It is a parable of man's love, which, having attained its desire, sleeps, to wake, no longer love, but ambition—and of woman's love, which, rather than decline from its high estate, destroys itself. Besides being a highly efficient parable, it is excellent satire, and would be praiseworthy as poetry were it not that, though it contains beautiful lines, the moral outstrips the tale. . . .

She has touched upon a phase of that strange and complex phenomenon we call the question of Woman's Rights, that is seldom mentioned—woman's right to love unsought and to suffer alone: a right too heavy for her to endure, but one that goes inevitably with the other rights for which some are clamoring and that seem likely to be thrust upon all, whether they will or no.

"Woman Articulate: The Strong Essence of Femininity in Sara Teasdale's Poetry," in The New York Times Book Review (© 1911 by The New York Times Company; reprinted by permission), December 3, 1911, p. 760.

JOYCE KILMER   (essay date 1915)

Sara Teasdale's first book established her as the maker of that sort of exquisite passionate epigram of which the greatest modern master is A. E. Housman. There was delicate and true art on every page of *Helen of Troy and Other Poems;* it had none of the looseness of thought and structure which sometimes is evident in a young poet's first offering. Miss Teasdale's new book, *Rivers to the Sea,* is full of poetry more finely wrought than any she has written before, and, furthermore, it has the virtues of variety in form and thought, and of a wholesome and joyous inspiration. Some of Miss Teasdale's earlier work was almost ostentatiously tragic; the poet seemed to be a devotee of melancholy for melancholy's sake. Now she has discovered the important fact that joy is not without its literary value, and the result is that ner new book will charm many more readers than its excellent, but depressing, predecessor. Some of Miss Teasdale's quatrains might be deft translations from the Greek Anthology; her accurate simplicity sometimes suggests Emily Dickinson; she is capable, at times, of expressing a passionate spirituality, but usually she is keenly and delightedly conscious of her own humanity. Now and then—all too rarely—she displays an elfin cynicism. . . . (pp. 457-58)

Joyce Kilmer, "This Autumn's Poetry," in The Bookman *(copyright, 1915, by George H. Doran Company), Vol. XLII, No. 4, December, 1915, pp. 457-62.**

WILLIAM STANLEY BRAITHWAITE   (essay date 1915)

There is in Miss Teasdale's art the purest song quality in American poetry. Her poems are brief, alluring and simple in expression. No mystery, no symbol, no inexplicable allusions, are woven into them. They are swift like swallows, with emotions; glittering and sparkling with the sunlight of love, on which an occasional shadow falls. The pain of love is no less exquisite than its joys. Love is her great theme. Though there is not a line in all these songs [*Rivers to the Sea*] that has a touch of the maudlin or sentimental. The mood is always a common mood, but spontaneous, sincere, fresh with a new experience, passionate but not sensuous, rapturous but not riotous, graceful without being elaborate, infectious, captivating, with the fresh and familiar emotions of humanity. In the Elizabethan song-books the love poetry was the natural speech of artistic emotions; those anonymous poets for the most part made love a delicate and exquisite decoration of moods; Miss Teasdale is natural in her moods and emotions, her speech is common language brightened and polished with simplicity, through which poignancy and exaltation runs like a golden weave. She is able to transmute any environment, any atmosphere, any circumstance, where the presence of love is found, into a fairyland of hope and surprise, into a sanctuary of human joy; and where the glory of love has faded, she has the power to make the sunshine a shadow because of it. Though she sings of love orchestrally in these many songs taken as a whole, it is not her only theme in this book. Her imagination is too vivacious, her visioning too curious not to see life many-motived, and so, but with the same melodious and evocative perceptions she sings of many experiences. There are the vignettes of travel, and in concluding her volume the splendid and passionate monologue on Sappho which is very ample evidence of her sustained imaginative powers. (pp. 250-51)

William Stanley Braithwaite, "The Best Poetry of 1915," in his Anthology of Magazine Verse for 1915 and Year Book of American Poetry (copyright © 1915 by Gomme and Marshall), Gomme & Marshall, 1915, pp. 223-55.*

O. W. FIRKINS (essay date 1916)

Sara Teasdale stands high among the living poets of America. In an age of outpour, her constitution and her method combine to reaffirm the beneficence of limitation. Nature, rich in her gifts to Miss Teasdale, has been wisely severe in her refusals, and the poet's forbearing and chary art has enforced the continence of nature. She writes brief poems on few subjects; her diction is culled rather than copious; her imagery is unmarked by range or change. Even the verse-forms are few and obvious, though certain unrhymed poems offer to the caprice of the hour the distant courtesy of a passing salutation. I find in her no proof of that more than Gallic unreserve which a press notice sent me by her publishers is sharp enough to discover in her work; if it be there, I applaud the cunning with which Miss Teasdale has hidden her openness. . . .

Her descriptions and monologues are forgettable; it is in her brief, passionate, unfalteringly modelled lyrics, at once flamelike and sculpturesque like fire in a Greek urn, that her true distinction becomes manifest.

The passion which these lyrics [*Rivers to the Sea*] embody is a strong, but also an unhurried, unimpetuous, clear-sighted, and self-guiding passion. . . . Hence the rare combination of fervor with a high, serene discretion, a poised and steadfast art, which makes the expression of feeling in these compact poems "half-ardent, half-austere." . . .

I should sum up Miss Teasdale as the inheritor rather than the copyist of the great English tradition, the tradition of refined vigor, vigor enclosed and ensheathed in comeliness, of feelings intensely personal yet delicately human, of a life whose springs are central and intimate, however great the variety of its individual outflowings. (p. 12)

O. W. Firkins, "Singers New and Old," in The Nation (copyright 1916 The Nation magazine, The Nation Associates, Inc.), Vol. 102, No. 2636, January 6, 1916, pp. 12-14.*

JESSIE B. RITTENHOUSE (essay date 1917)

[There is in *Love Songs*] the impulsive, wholly unconscious charm that belongs to everything Miss Teasdale writes. Indeed, the word "writes" is a misnomer, for these poems seem always to have been created by the lips and not the pen. And the reader soon finds them upon his own lips, for they are poems that become so quickly a part of the memory that one no longer needs to look for them upon the printed page. This is the lyric test; only poems which have at once music and magic become so instantly the possession of the reader.

Miss Teasdale is like a sensitive instrument responding to every emotion of life. These brief songs seem to be improvisations, catching the mood before it can depart. If a sonnet is a "moment's monument," much more are these lyrics which give you feeling while it is yet keen and alive. . . . In all of these poems there is a flame, a flame that

is unquenchable as a torch blowing in the wind. The accumulative effect of them is one of joy. Even the "Songs Out of Sorrow" serve but to enforce the truth that happiness is inherent and regenerative, the inner health of life. . . .

This period has few lyric poets like Sara Teasdale. She is the Elizabethan of to-day: one of the purest and clearest voices in our poetic literature. (p. 443)

Jessie B. Rittenhouse, "Contemporary Poetry: A Group of the Autumn Books," in The Bookman (copyright, 1917, by George H. Doran Company), Vol. XLVI, No. 4, December, 1917, pp. 438-44.*

LOUIS UNTERMEYER (essay date 1921)

[Sara Teasdale's "Flame and Shadow"] is by no means a series of facile melodies that live only to be set to music or to fill a page. . . . It is not even the same precise singing that one found in Miss Teasdale's previous work. Now that so many of the younger lyrists have learned her trick of tightening up an eight-line poem with a sudden twist, she has turned to something less patterned and more poignant. While other melodists are still copying the effects of Sara Teasdale, Miss Teasdale has stopped imitating herself. The clean, straightforward idiom of "Rivers to the Sea" has a warmer naturalism in "Flame and Shadow", a more spontaneous intensity. The subject-matter is still the same. Miss Teasdale seems limited to a preoccupation with death, landscapes, stars, the sea, life, longing, and Beauty—generalities that prevent her from exploring the rich details they contain. She is satisfied to use the old themes—but what surprising variations she weaves around them! Take, as examples, such poems as "What Do I Care", "Places", "The Sowing", "Water Lillies", and the magical threnody "Let it be forgotten". Here are new rhythms, far more subtle than those she has ever employed; here are words chosen with a keener sense of their actual as well as their musical value; here the line moves with a metrical inevitability. . . .

Radiance plays around these verses. Beneath the symbolism of such poems, one is conscious of a firmer artistry through a more flexible speech. This loosening up is the very proof of Miss Teasdale's advance. The flexibility of lines like "Water Lilies" and "The Long Hill" makes them all the lovelier; the slight (and logical) irregularities keep the pattern from hardening and . . . supply a fresh magic. (p. 362)

Louis Untermeyer, "Lyric Fire," in The Bookman (copyright, 1921, by George H. Doran Company), Vol. LII, No. 5, January, 1921, pp. 361-64.*

MARK VAN DOREN (essay date 1921)

A new volume by Sara Teasdale must be opened with anxiety—anxiety lest its author's old intensity of metaphor and meter be felt to have lessened, lest the glowing shapes of her love be seen to have paled and grown vague. The Sappho of this century and continent must be free, if anyone can be free, of poetical cant. Thus considered, at least a fourth or a third of "Flame and Shadow" meets the eagerest expectations. There is much in the book that is not fine, but there is enough that is. Sara Teasdale seems constantly assailed with two temptations, and it is only at intervals that she entirely surmounts them. One is the temptation to make effective endings, to save up points and appeals for a last line. This may come from having been set so often to music; she keeps her eye and ear too much, perhaps, on a possible singer whose audience will reward a neat conclusion with ripples of pleasure and applause. At any rate, it faintly tends to cheapen her product as poetry. The other temptation is to deal exclusively in stock love-lyric materials—in herself as "singer," in abstract Beauty, in the "call" of her love to this or that creature or thing, and in personified Pain. . . . Sara Taasdale only reaches her perfection when, defeating her temptations, she interpenetrates pain with metaphor and metaphor with pain, when she finds the proper balance between fire and form, between the complexity of a condition and the simplicity of a cry. . . .

Sara Teasdale draws her breath in ecstasy and pain among the time-old facts of poetry—the dark sea, the burning stars, the variable wind, the shining sun, and rain on flowers. Accepting a sphere of expression from a long past, she is content with living passionately and plaintively within it.

Mark Van Doren, "Sapphics," in The Nation *(copyright 1921* The Nation *magazine, The Nation Associates, Inc.), Vol. 112, No. 2896, January 5, 1921, p. 20.**

BABETTE DEUTSCH   (essay date 1926)

One has met [the poems of *Dark of the Moon*], if not themselves, then their blood-kin, on the pages of Miss Teasdale's previous books. Reading the volume through is like looking at a portrait in sepia of a woman remembered as flushed with wistful youth. It is the same person and yet not the same. Time has shadowed her eagerness, curtained her eyes, filled her quick hands with quietness, given her a dark serenity in exchange for her bright young agonies. (p. 48)

The measure of the difference between the younger and the older woman may be gauged by the difference between the poem Arcturus which appeared in her last book and the poem Arcturus in Autumn which appears in the present volume. . . . The second, more recent poem, has a slower beat, a mild-voiced bitterness lacking in the other. . . . This note of defeat—this shrinking yet dignified attendance upon intimations of mortality—was present even in the earlier book. But there it alternated with lighter moods; here it is the burden of nearly all the songs. On every page one reads the sorrowful wisdom which the years give in return for all they take. In the old days the poet, walking in fear of death, armored herself in song like the pure of heart in the leonine woods. Now she seems willing to put off even that hard and glimmering coat. . . . She is no longer frightened by the dark. Silence whines vainly at the door of her spirit, who is "self-complete as a flower or a stone."

Yet it is no gusty autumn that blows through the book. One is aware, rather, of Indian summer, the mellowness of whose sun is itself a foreboding of winter. The poet has drawn in upon herself, where the sounds of the world grow small and shrill, and the ache of the personal is endured without show.

Technically, the book offers little that is new. For the most part Miss Teasdale employs the tersely melodious quatrain which she has made peculiarly her own. There are a few

sonnets, and one or two interesting experiments with delayed rhymes, as in "Day's Ending" and "The Flight". The tempo is slower throughout than that to which she has accustomed us, to fit the more sombre thought. But the clear melody, the reverberant simplicity of statement are the same. Always Miss Teasdale has written songs. In other years they were songs which called for a Schumann. Now they demand the musicianship of Brahms. (pp. 48-9)

Babette Deutsch, "Indian Summer," in The New Republic *(© 1926 The New Republic, Inc.), Vol. 49, No. 626, December 1, 1926, pp. 48-9.*

LOUIS UNTERMEYER   (essay date 1933)

[Sara Teasdale's] "Helen of Troy and Other Poems" . . . revealed a self-sustaining lyricism and a blank verse that was as musical as her rhymes, but, though the volume was praised, no one predicted the fervor which would accompany her subsequent books. . . . Her unaffected quatrains, sparing of metaphor and almost bare of imagery, attracted a great following. . . .

In the late nineteen twenties popular taste underwent another of its unpredictable and inevitable metamorphoses. The fashion turned to keener edges, subtler byplay, a more shadowy metaphysic. Sara Teasdale was considered oversweet, over-emphatic if not over-emotional, suspiciously démodé. This was unfortunate and even ironic, for her later work is not only her most thoughtful but her best. "Dark of the Moon" . . . is slower-paced than anything she ever wrote, more avowedly autumnal. Yet even the outspoken clarity and the flexible cadences of "Flame and Shadow," which was the climax of her earlier work, are scarcely as compelling as the proud acceptance of change and the sombre reflections which add new dignity to the old lyricism.

This later poetry suggests, though it never quite reveals, that other aspect of Sara Teasdale which few, even among her intimates, ever came to know. . . . Those who charged her with being sentimental failed to realize that Sara Teasdale's quality was the translation of sentiment into sensibility, not into sentimentality, which is only the exploiting and cheapening of sentiment. . . .

Of this emotion Sara Teasdale had a surplus, but it was emotion stiffened with austerity, even, at times, with scorn. . . .

[Her verse] has what one must recognize as authenticity. And authenticity, rather than originality, was the gift which will, I believe, preserve a score of her simple poems long after much more pretentious work has perished. The best of her lyrics are fresh without being freakish; they are not dependent on the technical innovations or the manner of the moment. She was no Sibyl; her muse was frankly communicative. Hers was not the spell of strangeness and surprise, but the more immediate and more abiding charm of recognition.

Louis Untermeyer, "Sara Teasdale, 1884-1933," in The Saturday Review of Literature *(copyright © 1933 by* Saturday Review; *all rights reserved; reprinted by permission), Vol. IX, No. 30, February 11, 1933, p. 426.*

HARRIET MONROE (essay date 1933)

Sara Teasdale was feminine in the highest sense of that much-abused word. Her poems present the woman's point of view as authentically, as sincerely, as those of Shelley, Byron, Tennyson, any masculine lyrist of them all, present that of the man. She was "the answering voice" to many masculine singers of love, a voice which never lost its clear vibrance in expressing the feelings of a nobly disciplined woman through all love's joys and sorrows; as she was also the assertive voice in spiritual experiences not less feminine through which she moved with the serenity and dignity of complete conviction. As one reviews her life work now that death has set its seal upon it, one discerns its unity. Thought and experience developed the poet's character and deepened the essential motive of her songs, as practice and study of her craft developed the sure and adroit simplicity of her artistic method. But always we find the beautiful harmony of growth, never the violence of change.

To a degree rare even among women poets, Sara Teasdale's lyrics are a record of personal experience and emotion. She loved nature, continually drew inspiration from flowers, birds, the wind, the sea, the stars. Characters and episodes of the past interest her, as in *Fontainebleau* and *Effigy of a Nun*. But always the central motive of the poem is the poet herself under some stress of feeling, some dream or thought or emotion that reveals to her the glory of life. (pp. 30-1)

All experience became episodic and symbolic as she recognized the inevitable loneliness of the spirit; and through that loneliness she rose to rapturous flashes of joy, and to an acceptance of sorrow as serene as that "dark of the moon" which gave the title to her latest book. (p. 32)

[The] tune that her life played will not go out, for in it is the aspiration of a heroic spirit and the beauty of perfect utterance. (p. 33)

> Harriet Monroe, "Comment: Sara Teasdale," in
> Poetry (© 1933 by The Modern Poetry Association), Vol. XLII, No. 1, April, 1933, pp. 30-3.

LOUISE BOGAN (essay date 1933)

"Strange Victory," Sara Teasdale's last book, published posthumously, is the final expression of a purely lyrical talent and of a poetic career remarkable for its integrity throughout. . . . She correctly valued the quality of her talent from the start. Her matter—the record of a sensitive and gifted woman's emotions—was always rendered with clarity and justice definitely within the limits of her manner. Her range was far less wide than Emily Dickinson's: she never permitted herself any break with form or any flights into speculation; on the other hand, she added to a poetic equipment inherited in part from Emily Brontë and Christina Rossetti qualities peculiar to herself; a frankness of attack utterly lacking in her forerunners.

Miss Teasdale's sensibilities were completely sincere and therefore could function with freedom under the canons of her art. The pure lyric gift is notoriously narrow but notoriously strict as well. Its effects are based upon a true, subtle and naïve ear, and upon intensity rather than complexity of emotion. It is a medium that requires sincerity both in feeling and expression; inflation, cleverness and falsity show up only too plainly under its simple but inflexible demands. Sara Teasdale's poetry reflected, without dis-

tortion, every emotional change in her life from youth to late maturity. The two halves of her talent were delicately adjusted to one another to the end; her manner became clearer as her emotions became more calm. And because she had absolute faith in her own gift, she could eliminate from her work every effect of rhetoric. The twenty-two lyrics in her last book are poems reduced to the simplest terms. If a contemporary audience for lyric poetry may be postulated, the moving simplicity of these final poems must delight any responsive ear therein.

> Louise Bogan, "Sara Teasdale's Last Poems," in
> The New Republic (© 1933 The New Republic, Inc.), Vol. 77, No. 989, November 15, 1933, p. 25.

BABETTE DEUTSCH (essay date 1937)

[Sara Teasdale's early poems, which begin *The Collected Poems of Sara Teasdale*,] touched on recognized themes in the recognized way, they had nothing rough or foreign about them, and they possessed, beyond their pleasant familiarity, a fluent melodiousness. (p. 148)

Beauty and sorrow; love, happy or crossed; death, shrunk from as the end of love and beauty, or desired as the peace they cannot give—these are the recurrent motifs. A girlish wistfulness is the distinguishing feature of the early lyrics. . . . They are personal, without having the vice of privacy or the virtue of subtlety, honest but not profound. . . . Even where the poems bear titles that evoke common scenes—Union Square, Coney Island, Gramercy Park, the Metropolitan Museum—these are merely the background for a moment of sentimental drama or traditional romance. But always there is the subdued melody that redeems the easy imagery and the trite situation. . . . Repeatedly there is the slight ironic touch at the close, which, though the irony is gentle and all too feminine, is an index to a discriminating sensibility.

The chief faults of Miss Teasdale's work are the monotony of her matter and the explicitness of her statements. Often vague where she should have been precise, as in the delineation of background, she was apt to be overly exact where she should have been reticent, as in defining the nature of the grief that troubled or the joy that exalted her. It is almost incredible that the poet who was to write the lyrics in *Flame and Shadow*, and more particularly those in *Dark of the Moon*, the woman who was to become "self-complete as a flower or a stone," should have been capable of the banality of lines like "I love, I am loved, he is mine" or "And when I am with you, I am at rest."

The fascination of this volume lies in the fact that it exhibits so clearly the poet's development. As the years went by, the themes did not alter much, but the cadences became more varied, the mood more reflective, the expression more sensitive. Gradually, the irony that pointed the best of the early lyrics deepened and strengthened the poetry of Miss Teasdale's maturity. She was moved by the same things, rejoiced by the same natural beauties, overcome by the same loneliness, haunted by the same recurrent terror. But the personal relation is realized with a keener sense of the nuances of human intercourse, the terror is measured by a fuller awareness of man's fate, even the landscapes are viewed with a more perceptive eye. With these sharpened responses to the world about and the world within, came also a better control of her instrument. The later poems do not require, as so many of the early ones seem to do, the accompaniment of voice and strings in order to give them a suggestiveness that they fail to achieve. The riper pieces are, as their author came to be, self-sufficient. (pp. 148-50)

Aware, as every sensitive person must be, of the cruelties that beset mankind, Miss Teasdale scarcely ever touched upon the problems that are the subject of current poetry.... Even the poems written during the war show a signal ignorance of, if not quite aloofness from, the misery that eats the lives of the mass of humanity. Herself "not wholly joyous, proud or free," the circumstances of Sara Teasdale's life were yet sufficiently happy to enable her to savor the pleasures of travel and music, books and people, without too painful a realization of the disease infecting the society of which she was a part. It belongs, however, to a cultivated intelligence to appreciate the evils of existence as well as the gifts of fortune. But the later work, though it continues to be personal, harps upon a complaint so common to mankind as to raise the poetry to the level of the impersonal. There are still love poems that dwell upon the solace that perfect comradeship alone can give. The bulk of the later work, however, expresses an autumnal wisdom, or a craving for release from the burden of loneliness, the grief of lessening powers, the inevitable pain of living. (pp. 150-52)

[Miss Teasdale] plainly is no revolutionary, in any sense of the word. The technique is traditional. The prevailing temper is one of acceptance—joyous, mournful, or resigned. But though Sara Teasdale's scope was limited, it enlarged with the years, so that her mature work delights one with its deeper music and frosty beauty. Even the longed-for achievement of the good society will not appreciably lessen private griefs. While these remain, one can find some assuagement in the melody of such lyrics as these, and take courage from their quiet irony. (p. 153)

Babette Deutsch, "The Solitary Ironist," in Poetry *(© 1937 by The Modern Poetry Association; reprinted by permission of the Editor of* Poetry*), Vol. LI, No. 1, October, 1937, pp. 148-53.*

OSCAR CARGILL (essay date 1941)

Sara Teasdale's first two volumes of verse, [*Sonnets to Duse* and *Helen of Troy and Other Poems*] ..., are chiefly remarkable as the work of a young woman who was trying desperately to find other women interesting, whence earnest verses on the great Italian tragedienne, on the immortal Helen, and on Beatrice, Marianna Alcoforando, Erinna, and Guinevere. There are, to be sure, verses for Colin and Pierrot, who are innocuous enough males ..., yet one finds nothing truly arresting till he has all but put the volumes aside. (p. 633)

It is in *Rivers to the Sea,* four years later, that Sara Teasdale at once achieved stature as a poet and voiced what must be regarded as the characteristic attitude of the intellectual woman of her generation towards love. She insists, first of all, on her equal right to a completely passionate experience. She is not sorry for her soul, that it must go unsatisfied; she adopts instead an attitude that heretofore had been regarded as traditionally male.... [She] asserts as equal a right to experiment in love as the other sex has ever known.... Yet, with all her "new freedom," she demands a fidelity and completeness in love that woman

had hardly expected of man before.... It was this note in *Rivers to the Sea* which made it a tremendously exciting volume ..., rather than the exquisite music, or the happy turn of phrase. It is significant that the reviewers ignored altogether the long and labored pieces, Miss Teasdale's most ambitious "From the Sea" and "Sappho." And to tell the truth, Sara Teasdale could not manage a long line: her blank verse fails to move and her sonnets are mere exercises. She was effective only in the most lyrical forms, and now that her theme has no novelty, there is something tragic about her pretty little verses, as there is to fallen cherry blooms on the carpet.

Love Songs ... won both the Poetry Society and the Pulitzer awards, but no one, thumbing its pages today, if he is at all candid, will admit to being greatly moved by the volume.... [The poem "Barter" makes] us aware of Miss Teasdale's greatest fault as a poet—her willingness to be content with conventional imagery to fill out her pattern. Though the coiner of many beautiful images, Miss Teasdale was never notably prolific in imagery, and her poverty forced her to rely more and more on the traditional, to the ultimate damage of her reputation. While she never knew caustic criticism in her lifetime ..., she could not conceal from herself her own deficiencies, and a growing awareness of these may be responsible for the increased melancholy of her later volumes of verse [*Flame and Shadow, Dark of the Moon,* and *Strange Victory*].... Of her later verse, the better pieces are "I Have Loved Hours at Sea," "Pain," "There Will Come Soft Rains," "At Midnight," "A December Day," and "To the Sea." Yet in all of these is the note of frustration and defeat. For those who would trace this to its source one would suggest that the poem "Pain" and the poem "At Midnight" contain as complete an answer as could be desired. For one in ill health, to whom love was not ... a convenient spur for rhyming, but a passion, the wreck of love was the end of poetry. (pp. 633-36)

Oscar Cargill, "The Freudians," in his Intellectual America: Ideas on the March *(reprinted with permission of Macmillan Publishing Co., Inc.; copyright 1941 by Macmillan Publishing Co., Inc.; renewed 1969 by Oscar Cargill), Macmillan, 1941, pp. 537-763.**

GEORGE BRANDON SAUL (essay date 1957)

Despite some isolated good things, Miss Teasdale's first two books—[*Sonnets to Duse* and *Helen of Troy*] ...—are merely competent, commonplace work; her third, *Rivers to the Sea* ..., is, though nothing startling, better, and forecasts the later poet in its songlike quality and suggestion of artlessness. Fortunately, the cream of these early volumes was later incorporated in *Love Songs,* which seems to be Miss Teasdale's first clearly outstanding collection.... (p. 10)

[*Flame and Shadow*] though it contains more "shadow" than "flame", marks another advance.... I say "advance" because I feel this book shows more clearly than any of its predecessors the mature woman who has bitten on life, and because I feel its rhythms have in their emotional connotations more "natural falterings" than previously apparent. Presumably an experience of sorrow, and not only sorrow over the recent world war of 1914-18, helped produce these poems; but there is no wailing, bitterness, or rebellion—merely subdued pain and resignation.

As usual, whether in happiness or in trouble, Miss Teasdale returns meditatively to the stars; as usual, she indulges in a good deal of exclamatory writing; as usual, she is very musical. And despite a good deal of "sameness" characterizing poem after poem . . . there are a fair number of individualized lyrics, some of which ("Meadowlarks", "May Day", "A Little While", for example) prove tenaciously memorable. (pp. 11-12)

[*Dark of the Moon*]—the title is doubtless symbolic of the period leading directly to the author's divorce—is suggestive of anticlimax; there is nothing greatly significant or enriching to the earlier record. The verses are graceful, gracious, simple, and mild: the quiet meditations of a woman seemingly poured empty. . . . (p. 12)

There was little modulation necessary in moving from *Dark of the Moon* to *Strange Victory* [published posthumously]; the one led quietly and exquisitely to the other. As ever, the stars and the sea remained in the poet's thought, and her lines are as gracefully cadenced as before. . . . There is not a word of arraignment or blame in the book; merely an assured anticipation—a weary serenity that lacks even protest. . . . (p. 13)

[Sara Teasdale is] a poet eminently good to know, and—because of the naturalness of her expression, the simplicity of her technique—a good stylistic model for young poets learning their "trade", in Yeats's phrase. Little intellectual "depth" there admittedly is, and one concedes comparatively few notes; but there is certainly no pathos. And there is fragility of conception—exquisiteness of shading—genuine daintiness—a sense of dew and cobwebs—in her own phrase, "a delicate fabric of bird song". Further, while the greatest touch and the largest sweep are mostly absent, there is always present the infinitely fine feminine conception—and perception. . . . [There] are times when she has reached into the black waters whose chill brings wisdom, moments when the greater flame has blown at least briefly across her breast. One is assured that she was not born merely to feed oblivion. (pp. 13-14)

> *George Brandon Saul, "A Delicate Fabric of Bird Song: The Verse of Sara Teasdale," in* Arizona Quarterly *(copyright © 1957 by the* Arizona Quarterly*), Vol. 13, No. 1, Spring, 1957 (and reprinted in his* Quintet: Essays on Five American Women Poets, *Mouton Publishers, The Hague, 1967, pp. 9-14).*

MARGARET HALEY CARPENTER (essay date 1960)

[Sara Teasdale's] work is almost totally without figurative or ornamental imagery, without a large and pretentious vocabulary; it is not scholarly or cerebral. It is completely free of the influences that sifted through the poetic world during her lifetime: the awakening of a social conscience, the experimentation with new verse forms, new idioms of expression, poetry devoid of capitalization and clarity, and poetry depicting the emptiness and shallowness of the twentieth century. Essentially an individual in her life as in her art, she was affected by none of these.

For she did not see the world either through a social conscience or as an empty Waste Land; she wrote from the world within, a many-colored land whose shifting lights fell over the horizons of solitude, love, and beauty. The objective world was never as real or important to her as the castle of her own heart and mind.

It is true that her poetic latitude was limited. . . . But her range was wide enough to include the infinite spaces in the human heart—the eternal emotions of joy, sorrow, longing, and love that are of grave importance to every human being. (pp. 330-31)

Reading through her poems, one is struck with the number of times that the word "gray" (or "grey") appears. From the very first book where grey ashes of Japanese incense are mentioned, through all the others, this word is used over and over. . . . Perhaps this softly indefinite color was symbolic of the silver-gray solitude and peace that the poet's heart was seeking all her life.

Besides Sappho, Christina Rossetti was her first, last, and most enduring poetic influence, and many times the two poets have been compared. Both had the gift of pure and unaffected melodic grace and of distilling deep emotion into delicately written lines. But much of Christina Rossetti's ecstasy of spirit was channeled into a religious and moral dedication of life, while Sara Teasdale's consuming passion was for spiritual beauty—and this included love. (pp. 331-32)

Although Sara Teasdale was moved by the overwhelming passion of the [Elizabeth Barrett] Browning sonnets and intrigued by the romantic story of the English poet's life, her work itself was entirely untouched by the actual style of Mrs. Browning. . . . [Sara Teasdale] was born with a gift of flowing lyricism that Elizabeth Barrett Browning did not possess. There was never anything the least contrived, strained, or awkward in the poetry of Sara Teasdale; her work was like natural speech in a setting of song. (p. 333)

Sonnets to Duse was youthful testimony to the poet's overwhelming attraction to beauty, and in it are to be seen the three chief influences of her early period: the musical quality that she had absorbed from [Heinrich] Heine's poetry, her admiration for Eleonora Duse, and her identification with Sappho and deep love for ancient Greece. . . .

[*Helen of Troy*] represents a great step forward. . . .

The first six poems are monologues in blank verse, concerning some phase of love and spoken by various women. . . . Although there is no rhyme to enhance the lyric mood, and though the monologues are rather long, they are remarkable for their sustained moods and flowing quality; and they contain some memorably fine lines. (p. 335)

This book contains a number of poems that any talented young girl might have written; yet there are some that rise far above the average because of their simplicity, impulsive beauty, and emotional appeal. (p. 336)

[*Rivers to the Sea*] shows a still greater arc of achievement. The poet no longer speaks through characters of ancient times; the emotion is her own, and she writes of it in the pure music that was her native language. The very first poem ["Spring Nights"] in this candid volume marks the poet's awareness of the struggle that was to be apparent all through her life: the desire for beauty and the ability to enjoy it in solitude, and the conflicting desire for love and the presence of the lover. (p. 337)

These poems possess an eagerness and a spontaneity that reflect the fresh and passionate rapture of youth. . . . Love has now become an intensely personal experience, and its miracle sings through many of these lines. . . . Though these songs are a personal revelation of one young heart feeling the first stirring of romantic ecstasy and agony, they owe their great appeal to their universality; almost any reader can apply them to some point in his life. (pp. 337-38)

Again [in *Love Songs*], looking into her own spirit, Sara Teasdale brought forth from her personal universe poems of memory, delight, sorrow, and wisdom, set to her clear-voiced and graceful music. And again the poet proved her ability to handle . . . the prismatic moods of love—its burning joy and sadness, enchantment and disillusion, longing and fulfillment, ecstasy and suffering. Because of the lyrical spell of their musical appeal and their simple directness, these poems of love sing themselves into the heart. (pp. 339-40)

There are a spiritual enrichment, a new understanding and awareness of suffering, and a deepening sense of wisdom in the section of the book called "Songs Out of Sorrow." The lyric heart, momentarily turning from the rapture of love, observes now how something durable and triumphant may be salvaged from the anguish of the spirit. . . . In this group of poems is first foretold the new and more serious mood that was to absorb her so completely later. (p. 340)

[In *Flame and Shadow*], a book of still greater maturity of thought and spirit, both a radiance and a wisdom are evident. Now the eager and ecstatic tone of early youth has been tempered, though the music is still as liquid and melodious as it was before. This is a book of transition; the key is slowly and almost imperceptibly changing to a soft minor. Against the leaping flame of beauty, the poet now balances the gathering shadows of death. (pp. 340-41)

Over some of these poems fall the first shadows cast by thoughts of death, of loss, of grief, of inevitable endings, and the merciless passing of time—shadows that foretold the promise later fulfilled in the restrained and sombre music of *Dark of the Moon* and *Strange Victory*. And with the far-off promise of eventual winter, the faint stirring of an autumn wind prophesying a coming chill seems to blow gently across some of these lines. . . . Yet, in *Flame and Shadow*, she sings of love, though it is now in a slightly more subdued form. Occasionally, the tone of ecstatic emotion is still in evidence, for the autumn mood is only suggested, not wholly consummated yet. (p. 342)

In *Dark of the Moon* . . . , the book that brought her spiritual maturity to its fullest blossoming, the minor key that was suggested in *Flame and Shadow* has now become fully established; the music in these poems is as melodious and graceful as ever, but the pulse of the music has slowed to an autumnal measure. These poems are enriched with an austerity, a nobleness, a resignation with no self-pity and no bitterness; they are stripped down to the very essence of wisdom born out of suffering. Having drunk deeply from the cup of beauty and love in rapturous delight, the poet now turns her thoughts irrevocably to death; where autumn was once a whisper of coming loss, now the promise is fulfilled; now the winter landscape is a certain and inescapable thing. And the snow, the winter sadness, the sinking of Arcturus absorb her completely now. (pp. 343-44)

Her old passionate concern that the elements of nature—the sea, the stars, and the moon—will endure long after man has had his brief hour of joy on earth, is again mentioned, but now there is no struggle against this fact and no

distress in the acceptance of it. For in her maturity of spirit, her attitude toward death has undergone a change. No longer is she afraid of it; no longer does she rebel against it. The spirit is disciplined now to accept the inevitable. . . . (p. 344)

No longer is the poet absorbed with the dream, the promise, and the realization of love; for from her later wisdom she has evolved a philosophy that recognizes the poverty that makes the spirit rich. (pp. 344-45)

The old conflict within her own spirit, the old unresolved desire between solitude and love, are shown clearly within these pages. One section of poems called "The Crystal Gazer" reveals the essential and unchanging solitary quality of her spirit. (p. 345)

[*Strange Victory*], a small volume of only twenty-two poems, is an extension of the mood first felt so deeply in *Dark of the Moon*. Born, as its predecessor, of the winter of the spirit, this is a book that reflects deep emotional suffering and anguish, but it shows, too, a spirit that resolves its grief by the promise of the infinite peace and release that death is sure to bring. As in *Dark of the Moon*, the poet no longer wonders about death; she is preoccupied with it, and seems now, in these later days, to desire it and prepare for it. (p. 346)

Her touch that had always turned everything to song had not lost any of its artistry. Now the songs, however, are all set in an elegiac mood; a classic restraint and sombre grace enter into the very syllables. This poet had always sung from her heart, and when her heart was filled to overflowing with thoughts of imminent darkness, she sang as movingly of death as she had sung of love. (p. 347)

Dark of the Moon and *Strange Victory*, which were part of the same period of her growth, are the culminating volumes in which her genius was brought to the highest level of its artistry. She died at forty-eight at the height of her poetic achievement; though there was a turning toward the valley of the shadow from the high pinnacle of ecstatic romantic love, there was never any lessening of her lyric genius.

If one word could be used to describe the poetic artistry of Sara Teasdale, it would be the word *pure*. From a purity of spirit, she gave the world poems of pure music, pure emotion, and pure beauty. Even the suffering and resignation of later years could not mar this quality of purity; for as the darkness grew deeper, the true essence of the spirit shone even more luminously. . . .

The haunting melodies and the golden words [of her best work] will not be lost or forgotten; they will endure as long as man is conscious of his own heart and spirit. (p. 348)

Margaret Haley Carpenter, "The Work of Sara Teasdale," in her Sara Teasdale: A Biography *(copyright © 1960 by Margaret Haley Carpenter), The Schulte Publishing Company, 1960 (and reprinted by Pentelic Press, 1977), pp. 330-48.*

MARYA ZATURENSKA   (essay date 1966)

[There] is a mystery about Miss Teasdale's work—on the surface so slight, so simple, so conventional in form. It is only on rereading that one recognizes her *uniqueness*, that one encounters something that amounts to genius. (p. xviii)

When the poetry renaissance burst upon the scene shortly before the first World War, Miss Teasdale's language, her subject matter, her very traditional technique ought to have disqualified her from any honorable place among the innovators of the new poetry. Yet—and this was the mystery—her reputation spread among poetry lovers who were both critical and aware of the new poetry. She had in fact, like the poet who had most inspired her, Christina Rossetti, a gift that if it was not genius, certainly resembled it. It was a lyric gift as simple and natural as breathing. It caught one unaware and left the most critical mind astonished and helpless. It was a genuine cry of the heart, the anguish, the ecstacy, that cannot be counterfeited by art alone. (p. xxi)

Her first book . . . was called *Sonnets to Duse and Other Poems*. Her enthusiasm for Duse and her legend was pure Teasdale, a romantic vision out of which she drew an almost mystical meaning, a symbolic beauty. Though Duse kept her male critics in a trance, her chief adorers were women. (p. xxiii)

Sara Teasdale's enthusiasm for Duse did not lead to very distinguished poetry. But in these poems she was discovering her *tone* if not her real voice. That came later, slowly and so quietly that when her gifts had reached their ultimate distinction and even originality, very few of her admirers noticed it. One can say that they listened to the *sound* of her voice, but never troubled to discover the curious art and music of her song.

[Her *Love Songs*] began to show her increasing and individual promise. The *Love Songs* had their banalities, but she was the kind of poet whose critical processes as far as her own work was concerned flowed on unchecked and unheeded in her unconscious, far beneath the surface of instinctive artistry. She seemed to publish the same poem many times, deepening the tones and textures of her verse. But she remained clearly within her limitations, and her low-pitched variations upon a few themes were so persuasive and sensitive that the few banalities were forgotten, and in fact they almost completely disappear in her later work. (p. xxiv)

What then is the quality in Sara Teasdale's poems that defies critical silence and current fashion? . . . Clarity, emotional sincerity, technical simplicity that hid her art, and that indefinable something that is true poetry gave her work its strange appeal. (p. xxv)

There was more than a casual resemblance in Sara Teasdale's poems to Christina Rossetti's verse. Sara Teasdale had the same fine ear though not the same degree of subtlety for transmitting a faintly exotic music. Christina Rossetti had greater depths, she had passion where Teasdale had poignancy. Christina Rossetti's theme had been the transfiguration of love into religious devotion. . . . The experience and emotions of feminine love are enough for Sara Teasdale—that and the mysterious something that she derived from the 1890s, which she called Beauty. Her generation was still fond of invoking it, and it probably meant that she loved whatever was lovable and beautiful in life, the charm of landscape, of nature, of art. Unfortunately her weakest poems are often on this theme. When she invoked Beauty too self-consciously to a generation who had its own ideas about Beauty and did not always identify her with Helen of Troy, Sappho, or the acting of Duse but often rather in out-of-the-way places, she found herself misunder-

stood. It was in delicately expressing her changing feelings, her own depths and shifting moods that she began to speak with authority and with a Beauty that was more than a name. (pp. xxix-xxx)

In *Dark of the Moon* . . . one of her finest books, one begins to discover her rarity. It is really possible to think of it as one thinks of Jane Austen's last novel, *Persuasion*—its subtle sadness, its subtle difference to what has gone before, its preoccupation with autumn, with change, with darkening perceptions. (p. xxxi)

She had surpassed herself in *Dark of the Moon* and *Strange Victory*—her last book. . . . Her poetry had no wit, no dazzling technique innovations. The rising academic quarterlies would have had difficulty analyzing her. She seemed to have no social message. But she has outlived many more fashionable and showier reputations. She endures because she was, *is* unique. (p. xxxii)

> *Marya Zaturenska, "The Strange Victory of Sara Teasdale," in* Collected Poems of Sara Teasdale, *by Sara Teasdale (reprinted with permission of Macmillan Publishing Co., Inc.; copyright © 1966 by Macmillan Publishing Co., Inc.), Macmillan, 1966, pp. xvii-xxxii.*

ROSEMARY SPRAGUE (essay date 1969)

Sara Teasdale possessed both intuition and insight, in addition to imagination and an exquisite lyric gift. She indeed worked "in the changeless feelings of men," more particularly of women, and her theme was love, in all its facets of beauty, comfort, and tragedy. Her poetry is personal, drawn from her own deepest emotional experience, and it evokes an almost immediate empathetic response. (p. 99)

She was a "Romantic" in the Wordsworthian sense of prizing the immediacy of ordinary experience, and of finding in that experience—usually her own—the inspiration for her poetry. But she prized equally the quality of objectivity, and that objectivity permitted her to remain detached from personal involvement at the moment of writing. (p. 101)

Sara Teasdale obviously shared the view that the poet's task is to bring the imperfect to perfection, the chaotic into structure and order. Her reading of Emily Dickinson certainly influenced her; there are definite similarities to be found in their stanzaic patterns. . . . Not that her poetry is of uniform excellence; many poems, especially the early ones, can be justly criticized for over-sentimentality, and for describing, rather than evoking, emotion. But when she was at her best, as in *Dark of the Moon* and *Strange Victory*, the beautiful craftsmanship which was the distinctive quality of her poetry, was matched by an equally beautiful austerity and economy of language.

She said little about the craft of poetry, but what she did say was, as might be expected, highly subjective. Like Emily Dickinson, she would not lay down any hard and fast rules. (p. 120)

It is not surprising to discover that frequently her poems were not written down until they had been in her mind for a long time, and, once written, seldom needed altering. . . . She recognized the need for this period of contemplation between the immediate inspiration and the final work, in order to retain that objective view of the "emotional burden'' which would make the reader respond, without the presence of the poet intruding on that response. (pp. 120-21)

Though love in all its facets is the major theme of her poetry, wild, epic passion finds no place in it. She was no Emily Brontë or Christina Rossetti. Even when writing of such women as Guenevere or Maria Alcoforando, where wild bursts of emotion might be expected, we find characteristically restrained simplicity in the depths of despair. . . . (pp. 121-22)

The ability to transmit bitter experience without bitterness, and to laugh wisely, was one which Sara Teasdale possessed in the highest degree.

Nevertheless, when all is said and done, there is still a quality in her work which defies analysis. Her poetry does not lend itself to a frantic search for ambiguities or provide a forest for symbol hunters. It depends greatly for its impact upon the reader's empathy and imaginative response; it is not an intellectual exercise, but an experience. Like herself, her poetry is at times elusive, impossible to categorize, and therein lies its fascination and charm. . . . And,

though contemporary critics have tended to neglect her, thousands of others testify that, even in the cynical Sixties, her ''single songs'' are still lovely and still full of light, and still bring joy and often comfort to the heart. Which was all that she herself ever hoped or asked. (pp. 123-24)

Rosemary Sprague, ''Sara Teasdale,'' in her Imaginary Gardens: A Study of Five American Poets *(copyright © 1969 by Rosemary Sprague; reprinted with permission of the author), Chilton Book Company, 1969, pp. 97-125.*

ADDITIONAL BIBLIOGRAPHY

Untermeyer, Louis. ''Sappho, St. Louis, and the Dark Sea.'' In his *From Another World: The Autobiography of Louis Untermeyer,* pp. 159-83. New York: Harcourt, Brace, and Co., 1939.
    Account of Teasdale's life from the time she became involved with Harriet Monroe's literary circle up until her suicide. This chapter also provides an inside look at Vachel Lindsay's courtship of Teasdale, the latter's marriage, divorce, and consuming disillusionment.

Francis (Joseph) Thompson
1859-1907

English poet, critic, essayist, and biographer.

Thompson is one of the most important poets of the Catholic Revival in nineteenth-century literature. His best known poem, "The Hound of Heaven," displays the essence of his major work, with characteristic themes of spiritual struggle, redemption, and transcendent love. Often compared to the seventeenth-century metaphysical poets, especially Richard Crashaw, Thompson conforms to the pattern of *fin de siècle* letters for the extremes of aestheticism in his poetry and the chaotic style of his life.

Unlike numerous nineteenth-century authors who converted late in their lives, Thompson was raised a Roman Catholic. He attended a Catholic college with the intention of studying for the priesthood, a life for which he discovered himself temperamentally unsuited. During this period Thompson acquired the background of linguistic erudition which informs his poetry. After abandoning his hopes of entering the clergy, he enrolled in Owens College, where he studied medicine but failed his final examinations. His next years were spent in London working at menial jobs which barely supported him. An admirer of Thomas De Quincey's *Confessions of an English Opium Eater,* Thompson himself had a firmly established opium habit which he intermittently indulged throughout his life. Critics have debated the influence of opium upon Thompson's work, but he is usually thought to have written very few poems under the effects of the drug.

Thompson was rescued from his life of poverty by Wilfrid and Alice Meynell, who opened their home to him. It was in Wilfrid Meynell's literary magazine, *Merry England,* that the poet's work was first published. From the earliest appearance of Thompson's poetry, critics have repeatedly observed a few specific features: the poet's use of neologisms and uncommon word formations, esoteric diction, a striving for elaborate and unusual imagery, and a self-consciously exotic style, all of which contribute to the charge of obscurity often leveled at the poems. Critical persistence, along with an understanding of the poet's eccentric way of life, is generally conceded necessary for full appreciation of the poetry.

After publication of the collections *Poems, Sister Songs,* and *New Poems,* Thompson's poetry markedly diminished. His later work consisted primarily of critical essays and the biography *Saint Ignatius Loyola.* It is his relatively small output of poetry, however, that forms the foundation of his reputation as a minor author in the tradition of Christian mysticism.

PRINCIPAL WORKS

Poems (poetry) 1893
Sister Songs (poetry) 1895
New Poems (poetry) 1897
Health and Holiness (essay) 1905
Shelley (essay) 1909
A Renegade Poet, and Other Essays (essays) 1910

Saint Ignatius Loyola (biography) 1910
The Life and Labours of Saint John Baptist de la Salle
  (biography) 1911
Literary Criticisms (criticism) 1948
The Real Robert Louis Stevenson, and Other Essays
  (criticism and essays) 1959

COVENTRY PATMORE (essay date 1894)

The masculine intellect, which is the first constituent of all poetry having any pretentions to "greatness" . . . is as conspicuous and, alas, as predominant in Mr. Thompson's poetry as it is in that of Crashaw and Cowley. The feminine element, which is as essential to perfect poetry as a crust is to a pie, is in insufficient presence. Profound thought, and far-fetched splendour of imagery, and nimble-witted discernment of those analogies which are the "roots" of the poet's language, abound; but in the feminine faculties of "taste," of emotion that must have music for its rendering, of shy moderation which never says quite so much as it means, of quickness to "scent the ridiculous from afar," of the dainty conscience which sets "decorum" far above all other duties and knows that in poetry the manner is much more important than the matter, since manner is beautiful in itself, whereas, without it, it is no matter what the matter may be since it fails to express itself with feminine *feeling* and perfection;—in these qualities Mr. Thompson's poetry is as often deficient as is that of his two eminent predecessors. Even the barest sublimity cannot be adequately rendered in poetry without some measure of the chaste and timid reticence of womanhood. Mr. Thompson throws about him "handfuls of stars," and swings the earth as "a trinket from his wrist"; but these are very cheap sublimities. . . . (p. 20)

It is wonderful that, with such a truly splendid command of language as is possessed by this poet, he should have thought it expedient to search the dictionary for words many of which are not only archaic, but really extinct and incapable of resurrection. It is no excuse for the use for such a word as "cockshut-light" that it has been once or twice used by Marlowe, or somebody, for "twilight," and there is still less excuse for Mr. Thompson's abundant invention of entirely new words, which have not even the plea of being beautiful, but only that of being etymologically intelligible to those who know Latin. Only the very greatest poets have ever, so far as I recollect, succeeded in adding more than two or three new words to the language of English poetry; but Mr. Thompson's muse hatches them by the dozen, with the effect, in each case, of producing a shock of interruption, which spoils what might otherwise have been a delicate flow of thought and rhythm. One critic of note has condemned these inventions as "illiterate"; but this is quite unjust. Mr. Thompson is a good Latin and Greek scholar, and his linguistic freaks are only too "literate." (p. 21)

[Of all the] modern experimentalists, Mr. Thompson is, to my thinking, the only one who has, in some large measure, succeeded, notwithstanding his want of practice and his occasional defects and redundancies of language. The "Hound of Heaven" has so great and passionate and such a metre-creating motive, that we are carried over all obstructions of the rhythmical current, and are compelled to pronounce it, at the end, one of the very few "great" odes of which the language can boast. . . .

The main region of Mr. Thompson's poetry is the inexhaustible and hitherto almost unworked mine of Catholic philosophy. Not but that he knows better than to make his religion the direct subject of any of his poems, unless it presents itself to him as a human passion, and the most human of passions, as it does in the splendid ode just noticed, in which God's long pursuit and final conquest of the resisting soul is described in a torrent of as humanly impressive verse as was ever inspired by a natural affection. (p. 22)

Mr. Thompson's poetry is "spiritual" almost to a fault. He is always, even in love, upon mountain heights of perception, where it is difficult for even disciplined mortality to breathe for long together. . . . Mr. Thompson is a Titan among recent poets; but . . . a Titan may require and obtain renovation of his strength by occasional acquaintance with the earth. . . . (p. 23)

Since, however, Mr. Thompson's spirituality is a real ardour of life, and not the mere negation of life, which passes, with most people, for spirituality, it seems somewhat ungracious to complain of its predominance. It is the greatest and

noblest of defects, and shines rather as an eminent virtue. . . . (p. 24)

Coventry Patmore, "Mr. F. Thompson, a Poet," in The Fortnightly Review, Vol. LV, No. CCCXXV, January, 1894, pp. 19-24.

GREENOUGH WHITE　(essay date 1898)

[A] pleasurable sensation of expectancy, of excited curiosity, moved the present writer as he opened the volume of "New Poems," by Mr. Francis Thompson. . . . In the prevailing slang of the studios, they were decidedly "impressionistic." The first poem yielded an effect of vague perfume rather than of thought. As one worked further into the volume one became conscious of sensations melting into one another—of that blending of the reports of the various senses of which Shelley was fond. The author's psychology was indistinct—a blend of fancy and feeling—not imagination or passion; his prevailing mood was dreamy—he seemed to hover on a mystic borderland. His preference, among forms of verse, seemed to be for the irregular, ode-like strains known as dithyrambic. Ere long one was struck by strange words of Latin derivation, and by tortured syntax. The deepest point observed was a remarkable blend or transcendence of sex-distinctions—androgynous, shall we call it, or hermaphrodite? Such philosophy as was discoverable had a gnostic tang, and consisted in the ancient opposition of matter and spirit. This appeared most plainly in the "Anthem of Earth," the best piece in the collection. The deeply religious, Christian, even ecclesiastical tone, illustrated by many figures, struck one forcibly in an agnostic age. One felt disposed to ask: Are these verses a corollary of the ritual movement? A little further, it was made manifest that our author is a Roman Catholic, and the whole problem—diction, sentiment, and all—was resolved.

Right here one must record a conviction that this man has the essential thing, the true stuff and substance of poetry, however mixed with slag and dross. Serious indictments have been brought against him: that his lines are unmusical, that his phraseology is obscure, uncouth, even to the point of causing suspicion of affected obscurity; that in consequence it takes too much study to get at his meaning, that there is no pleasure in reading his verses. Damaging charges these—yet such as have been brought against every original poet; for it is inevitable that the fresher a man's message is the less will it be understood by the majority. Our author would do well, however, to heed these criticisms, and not soothe their sting with the flattering unction suggested; for they amount to this, that his verses lack *charm*—and the poetry, however great, that fails in grace, in natural magic, is doomed. . . . (pp. 39-40)

Greenough White, "A Poetical Problem," in The Sewanee Review (© 1898 by The University of the South), Vol. VI, No. 1, Winter, 1898, pp. 39-50.

WILLIAM ARCHER　(essay date 1902)

[In Mr. Francis Thompson we are] face to face with a poet of the first order—a man of imagination all compact, a seer and singer of rare genius. In the sheer essentials of poetry Mr. Thompson is rich to superfluity. . . . [Mr. Thompson] is something of a psychologist and a good deal of a metaphysician. There are noble passages of thought and cosmic vision in his work. But it is not primarily for thought, ethical, metaphysical, or mystical, that one turns to Mr. Thompson. It is for the inexhaustible opulence, the superb daring, of his imagery, and for the pomp and majesty (mannered though it may often be) of his diction. If ever there was a born poet, a poet in spite of himself, who lisped in metaphors for the metaphors came, this surely is he. His worst faults proceed from excess, not from defect, of poetic endowment. (pp. 431-32)

[The sequence of poems that *Sister Songs* comprises strikes] me as more superbly sustained, more evenly fraught with essential poetry, than the analogous sequence in [*Poems*], entitled *Love in Dian's Lap;* but while the resemblance is unmistakable, the difference may be fanciful. On the other hand, Mr. Thompson's third book, *New Poems,* shows a marked increase of power. There is more thought in it, less rhapsody; while the pressure of imagination to the square inch is, if possible, even higher than in the earlier volumes.

It is easy to attribute some of Mr. Thompson's peculiarities of style to the influence of Donne, Herbert, Crashaw, Vaughan, and other spiritual singers of the seventeenth century. Mr. Coventry Patmore, too, had indubitably some share in making him what he is. But it would be a grave critical error to dwell with any insistence on these influences. We must not mistake affinity for discipleship. Mr. Thompson is a voice, not an echo. His style was implicit in his organisation, or, in simpler terms, was born with him. It is the inevitable expression of a very individual mind—vividly perceptive, intensely sentient, and irrepressibly alert to recombine its perceptions in unexpected interplays of analogy. He may have been encouraged by seventeenth-century example to give the rein to certain tendencies, or to cultivate, instead of chastening, certain mannerisms. He may have picked up a measure here, a cadence there; but his style, in the main, is not a thing acquired from without. It is not the more or less artificial vesture, but the organic expression, of his mental processes. The undulant procession of images, of which almost all his work consists, is no mere decoration, but presents the very substance and texture of his thought. So, too, with the Latinisms of his diction. If they are a vice, they must be put down to original sin, not superinduced iniquity. The love of majestic sonorities is fundamental in the poet's idiosyncrasy, so that he tends instinctively to employ the more sonorous factor in our composite tongue. He Latinises, not because Milton Latinised, but because his mental ear is tuned to the Miltonic key. He does not follow that great precedent, but no doubt it helps to make him (as he might say) obsequious to the trend of his own impulse. (pp. 432-33)

It would be easy to multiply indefinitely . . . examples of Mr. Thompson's intense realisation of all the phenomena of Nature—both of her visual appearances, and of those vaster and minuter phenomena which are conceivable only to the imagination quickened by science. How comes it, then, that a poet who sees the material universe so intensely and, up to a certain point, so intrepidly, should, when that point is reached, plunge into the theological mysticism which speaks in *The Hound of Heaven* and *To the Dead Cardinal of Westminster,* in *Assumpta Maria* and *Any Saint,* and in a hundred incidental passages throughout his work? The explanation, I think, is not far to seek. Catholicism is Mr. Thompson's refuge from Pantheism, a creed, or

rather a philosophy, too cold to satisfy the poet within him. Pantheism makes no more picturesque or emotional appeal than a demonstration in Euclid. . . . Mr. Thompson, at all events, cannot stay his stomach upon it. Having realised the unity of the force underlying all phenomena, he proceeds to visualise, to dramatise it; or rather to accept the most gorgeously spectacular dramatisation of it ever evolved by the human intelligence. (p. 444)

It remains to note what seems to me the striking increase in virility and strength that distinguishes Mr. Thompson's *New Poems* from his two earlier publications. Writing of *Sister Songs* at the time of their appearance . . . I said: "His fantasies flash forth and fade away like streamers of the Aurora Borealis, with no apparent interdependence, and to no ascertainable end. Poetry more phantasmagoric does not exist in the language." This remark was perhaps too sweeping even then, but there was a considerable measure of truth in it. *Love in Dian's Lap* and *Sister Songs* are long-drawn hyperboles of homage, beautiful, but exceedingly insubstantial. We cannot see the Lady or the Children for the incense-fumes rolling up in ever-shifting arabesques from the poet-worshipper's censer. It is not intended that we should see his divinities: adoration, not portraiture or psychology, is his purpose: he achieves with mastery what he sets forth to do, but there is very little thought-substance, very little relation to life, in the long processions of imagery. What he aims at is rather the absolute beauty of music than the beauty-in-truth of the greatest poetry. (p. 446)

Concrete and very beautiful, too, are the five *Poems on Children—Daisy, The Making of Viola, To My God-child, The Poppy,* and *To Monica thought Dying.* But, on the whole, it may be said that in his first two books Mr. Thompson took no very firm hold upon life, suggesting rather Matthew Arnold's too-famous description of Shelley as "a beautiful ineffectual angel, beating in the void his luminous wings in vain."

To the poet of *New Poems,* on the other hand, this description would be grotesquely inapplicable. Here the great mass of the work is concrete and of universal relevance; no mere glorified coterie-speech, like *Love in Dian's Lap* and *Sister Songs.* Of the first poem—*The Mistress of Vision*—I shall say nothing. It contains impressive passages, but its purport, as a whole, entirely eludes me. Nor do I pretend that *Assumpta Maria* conveys much definite meaning to my mind: it probably is not intended to. One or two other poems, short and (I hope) unimportant, are too utterly spiritual for my grosser apprehension. But with the two exceptions above stated, all the longer poems convey definite and tangible, often profound and noble, thought, in language which, though loaded and overloaded with imagery, readily yields up its meaning to an attentive reader. *Contemplation, The Dread of Height,* the *Orient Ode, From the Night of Forebeing,* and the *Ode to the Setting Sun,* are philosophic poems of commanding power. The more one reads them, the more one is impressed by the vigour and fecundity of the mind which produced them. But the most important poem of this group is the before mentioned *Anthem of Earth*—a stately survey, in irregular, unrhymed verse, of man's destiny on earth. (p. 450)

I have said nothing of Mr. Thompson's rare gifts as a metrist, nothing of the singularly just instinct (to my thinking) with which in his rhymes he steers a middle course between pedantic accuracy and vulgar slovenliness.... [But my purpose] will have been fulfilled if I have brought home to the reader some realisation (however inadequate) of the wealth of essential poetry in Mr. Thompson's work, and proved him a poet not by personal choice but by divine election. (p. 456)

> *William Archer, "Francis Thompson," in his* Poets of the Younger Generation, *John Lane, 1902 (and reprinted by Scholarly Press, 1969), pp. 431-59.*

ALBERT A. COCK (essay date 1911)

Entering into possession of the field of poetry at the close of last century, what has Francis Thompson given us? Without its occasional prosiness and bathos, he has the intuitive and experiential grasp of the spiritual significance of Nature and the Child with which we associate the name of Wordsworth; the ecstasy of Shelley with the constructive synthesis which was Shelley's lack; Tennyson's melodies with richer harmonies, Tennyson's feeling for contemporary problems and aspirations with a power of interpretation rarely reached by the late Laureate; all the virility of Browning without his obstinate involutions of thought and lacunae of argument—the psychological penetration of Browning becomes in Thompson a spiritual realization more profound and satisfying, because more vital to the man himself. All that mystical longing for "infinite power of soul" which wrung from Richard Jefferies the anguished "Story of My Heart" is, in Francis Thompson accompanied and followed by a satisfaction (and knowledge of the means of satisfaction) which Jefferies never obtained, for he was not of that Church. Where [John Henry] Newman wins by logic vitalized by the passion of faith, Thompson masters and conquers by the poetry of faith. He is not to be studied as a formal treatise in direction and casuistry, but the director of souls will find in him many secrets and phenomena laid bare as few have done or can do. (pp. 248-49)

[In] the poems on children in [*Poem*], there are clear enough signs that of Childhood . . . Thompson was a master poet. . . .

Thompson's poems on children fall naturally into two groups. In *Sister Songs* he is largely autobiographical, and in his treatment breaks entirely new ground. He is there concerned not so much with the commoner aspects of child-life, as with his own discoveries of the primal Woman enfolded in the child-girl. On the other hand, the miscellaneous poems on children record and interpret such simple incidents as a child's gift or prayer. Did he succeed in stooping to the child?

The great charm of Blake's songs of Childhood lies in their artless, tender, naïve sincerity and in their perfectly simple yet wholly profound union of the children of men with the children of Nature and of God. (p. 251)

Children had come too near to the heart of Thompson's pain to permit him to sing of them with [Blake's] tremulous tenderness. Never could he forget that he was no longer a child, and so, though he sang of them, it was not as one of them. Moreover, he could not long forget that in his religion the Child of the world's desire is always and inseparably associated with the Maid of Bethlehem. Consequently, in only two of his poems ["The Making of Viola" and "Ex

Ore Infantium"] does he touch hands with Blake, in only two does he separate children from the heart of his pain. (p. 252)

Many of these poems on children are charged with a fatal self-conscious sadness and pessimism which makes their beauty like the later Rossetti's, death-hued. Thus, in "The Poppy," Thompson tells how among the southern downs he paced at eventide with a child hand in hand. A simple gift she gave, a poppy. How could she know its sombre symbolism? Would a Wordsworth have ignored the impulse of love and perceived only what the full man perceived, the symbolism of death? Yet so it was with Thompson. (p. 256)

[In Thompson there is] an attitude [which] may be described as that of objective subjectivity, an attitude in which the individual objectifies for admiration not the rightful other person from whom he draws his own breath, but his own finite self, which, whether sick or whole, he cherishes. This objective subjectivity is the fatal disease of much of Thompson's verse, though let us at once say that his greatest poetry is free from the blight. . . . (p. 260)

Nevertheless, Thompson does not stay in the mirage of self-objectification, for there is an opposite mood and a truer poetry, and into this he passes in the "Hound of Heaven." There, in language altogether imaginative, passionate and concrete, the transition from analysis to synthesis is clearly marked, the objective-subjective gives way to the subjective-objective, into a purged self at last enters from without the Person Who all along has been the only true sustainer. . . .

[Not] by the artistic contemplation of an alienated self did the poet find enduring life; only by the recognition that the exterior Infinite is *Person,* and that he was sustained by the everlasting arms thereof was he able to make peace. (p. 261)

This is the poetry which we accept with reverence. This is synthetic, constructive, the gateway to life. This is the fruit of will acting in, through and for, not itself, but another; this works not from within, outwards, for artistic delight, but from without, within, for peace and worship.

Ultimate synthesis, then, is that which alone can satisfy us in vital poetry, and this Thompson gives in the "Hound of Heaven." (p. 262)

The "Hound of Heaven" is the most synthetically representative of the movements of English and, perhaps, European thought in the nineteenth century that we have. We say synthetically representative and typical, because a careful examination of this poem will show that in his own individual experiences, there recorded, Thompson speculated, suffered and solved with his times. Consider the first eight lines alone. In them are suggested the reconstruction of history through the formative ideas of induction and development; the separation as a distinct study or science of psychology, whose work is generally agreed to be of the most vital importance to knowledge and religion together; and the alternative optimism and pessimism which, in turn and at times side by side, have dominated our literature, art, music and philosophy. The insistent refrain is not only of universal application, but of quite peculiar appositeness to the great longing of our day.

In the second section the whole octave of life's music is struck, the undeniable "sense of otherness," the eminently modern apotheosis of friendship, the specialization which separates subject from subject, so rigidly that only by faith can we maintain that knowledge is one; these further three characteristics, universal yet so eminently modern, find here their just and true expression.

The synthesis continues in the third section: the appeal of the children, never more widely felt than in our own day, the insufficiency of utter abandonment to the aesthetic appreciation of Nature, the imagery drawn at once from the altar and the mother, these further three are still more representative of modern interests, problems and solutions.

Similarly, the fourth great stanza. The failure of impersonal idealism, the dank stagnation of that peculiarly modern tendency to self-analysis, and the domination over all of the Figure whom all science and philosophy seek to explain—the only efficacy of the Victim, this Saving Victim, find here their fit and true expression.

The strength of this synthesis lies in its comprehension that love of Nature, home life and idealism are not separated from, but included in, the Christ-life. (pp. 263-64)

[Thompson's] works are penetrated, suffused, saturated and substantiated by a consciousness of the supernatural, of the symbolic mystery of life, of the secret affinities between stone and star which are not to be lightly defined but rather felt, lived and realized. Nevertheless, although mysticism has its field in every human heart, the instinct which orientates the heart to that love and search for the Absolute immanent in Nature and Man, and transcendent and personal in God, is intensified into a master principle in artists, musicians, poets and saints whom alike we call "mystics." To them, and especially is this observable in Thompson, the world and human life are crammed with Heaven and aflame with God. Their regard for Nature is, therefore, not for the unknowable, but rather for what is felt to be the indefinitely knowable, offering to Reason the marvellous hope that we may know her in her furthest depths. (p. 271)

> *Albert A. Cock, "Francis Thompson," in* The Dublin Review, *Vol. 149, No. 299, October, 1911, pp. 247-77.*

AUSTIN HARRISON   (essay date 1913)

To the mystic, to the religionist, Thompson may naturally be claimed as a great poet. Those of us who can detach art from creed, to whom art itself is the noblest of all religions, may reasonably hesitate. In the vision of the artist we want creation and not dogma; freedom, not theory; the love which is universal; we want personality. Thompson gives us only personification; he pontificates. He is never free to sing, like the lark. His very ecstasy is sacerdotal. His whole imagination is swaddled and gilded with ritualistic imagery and emotion. When he soars, it is into the nebulosity of Liturgy. His rhapsodical Rosicrucianisms (shall I say?) jar. It is not in Heaven that he sings, but of Heaven. Round his intellect always there is the aura of a theological imposition. (p. 106)

It is the persistency of this sacerdotal symbolism, metaphor, and jargon that is so exasperating in Thompson, for detach oneself as one may, it rises up and shakes its "Uranian censer" (as Thompson might have written) at the reader in almost every poem. (p. 107)

It is commonly said of Thompson's poetry that a man either loves or hates it. As criticism, however, that is not sufficient. No one can hate Shelley, though he may hate his Paganism. It is an evasion of criticism to apply the test to Thompson. I wish to say here that I grant Thompson at once vision, the afflatus and equipment of a poet, and above all intellect, for he is never rank or ordinary. But the peculiarities of his poetry are too marked and insistent to be passed over. All the time it "bumps." Like a funambulist of words, he is always trying to "show off." There is its constant and irritating sibilancy, its only too frequent cacophony, and again its turgidity, what I must call its strepitancy, and that despite the swell and grandeur of both metre and conception, as were the poet lacking in the music and beauty of language. It is like an over-gargoyled church. (p. 109)

As the poet of mysticism, Thompson will always appeal to the nebulous-minded, scarcely to those who seek music in poetry or clear and profound thinking. His catholicity was not of the mind, but of dogma; he is the carol-boy of Monasticism. (pp. 115-16)

His poetry lacks blood, which is the lubricant of the heart. Its soul is epicene. It has the restlessness of all epicenity. "The Hound of Heaven" is a Hydra, a work perhaps not lacking in genius, but as music ugly, in thought mediaeval—as a whole graceless. Those who believe in the Spirit of Man, which is the spirit of the modern scientific world, as it was of Shakespeare, can find little invigoration in the Thompsonian reaffirmation of cloistral cosmogony and but poor comfort in the verbal virtuosity of his inspiration. That he had power, insight, and, at times, an astonishing beauty and felicity of expression, all this we may grant; yet, in sum, as he was not himself of this world, so, neither in sympathy nor in melody, is he with us. He might have been for all that. The most human line in all Thompson, because so utterly unexpected and earthly, is the cry, "God send a mouth to every kiss," for which to all lovers—and who would not be a lover?—he will be for ever memorable. How the poet who associated human love with the Pit came to write that, one fails to understand. It is his solitary tribute to our frail humanity, uttered, as it were, in his own despite. (p. 116)

> *Austin Harrison, "The Poetry of Francis Thompson," in* The English Review, *Vol. 15, No. 1, August, 1913, pp. 103-16.*

CHARLTON M. LEWIS   (essay date 1914)

The poetry of Thompson's first period is a marvel of copious diction and imagery. When the fit is fully upon him, he achieves an Elizabethan pomp and grandeur. . . . One remembers, however, that Mr. Shaw defines Elizabethans as people with a tremendous way of saying things, but with nothing whatever to say. Thompson, indeed, has little to say; he has only a rapture to communicate. His most purple splendors, like the cloud-castles of a sunset, are very cunningly embroidered upon air. His first two volumes are for readers who can love imagery for its own sake, and whose mood will respond to mere opulence of diction.

In Thompson's poetry elaborate diction and elaborate imagery are found, as a rule, in close conjunction. Exceptions are to be explained as aberrations of his genius, induced by the attraction of some other star. When, for example, he wrote the "Song of the Hours" he was fresh from several weeks' work on his Shelley essay. The poem is not only one of Thompson's few pieces of out-and-out paganism, it is also composed throughout in a borrowed manner.... [It] is pure Shelley, even to plagiarism. If it is Thompson at all, it is at least far from Thompsonese. (pp. 101-02)

[It] was very fortunate that Thompson did not prolong his discipleship. He could never have succeeded in an effort to be somebody else. The "Song of the Hours" is a thoroughly uncomfortable poem; its etherial imaginings are disfigured by wretched lapses of taste. But when the poet pursues his own ends after his own fashion, he enjoys all the glory of freedom. It is true that lapses of taste occur even in the thick of Thompsonese.... And I have noticed as especially curious that when Thompson repeats himself (as he has a trick of doing) he repeats his mistakes as readily as his successes. Three times he uses the questionable epithet "snorting" to describe wild weather; and twice he calls infancy "newly-whelped existence,"—a term surely inappropriate to any infancy save that of a pachyderm. But these are exceptions. More often the far-fetched word vociferously justifies itself; and if his peculiar style has not the reticence of the highest art, neither is it unworthily artificial. Its very laboriousness is the perfectly sincere expression of the poet's nature. His intellect is eager but unfruitful, and wreaks its craving for adventure on the chase of the difficult word. When he finds it, he sometimes triumphs with shawms and cymbals, as intoxicated with his achievement as little Jack Horner; but even so we must be gray-gone in stolidity if we do not catch some of the contagion. (pp. 103-04)

[Thompson's "New Poems"] exhausted his poetic vein, and left him a hack-writer of miscellaneous prose for the weeklies.... [There was great change] in the content and purpose of his poetry. His earlier creed had been that the "true flower of poetry is beauty of language" and "the stringing together of ingenious images." "I had my great toy of imagination, whereby the world became to me my box of toys." During the rapture of his first great awakening this conception had satisfied him but it could satisfy him no longer. His later poetry still vibrates with natural ecstasy (only a little less poignant); his splendid imagery is still clothed in splendid diction (only a little less flamboyant); but the religious note, hitherto occasional, is now dominant. (p. 104)

Thompson's friendly critics make much of the superior genuineness of his mysticism; for while such poets as Maeterlinck have exploited their sense of mystery only for its artistic value, Thompson's aim was to discover truths that are dark. But I am not so sure that this distinction is sound as I am that any such defense of Thompson is superfluous. A poem like "The Mistress of Vision" needs no justification by analysis and argument. The gospel of renunciation, which Thompson borrows for it from Patmore, is, to be sure, more illuminating than some of his other gospels; but the glory of the poem is in its intricate melodiousness and the poppied warmth of its symbolism. Thompson's genius was lyrical, and it happily remained lyrical even after he had begun to think of it as philosophical.

The obscurity of these poems is of course Stygian. In Thompson's earlier work there were difficulties, but some of the "New Poems" seem like impossibilities. The reader who masters everything else in the volume may still have a hard struggle with "Grace of the Way," which I confess I do not at all understand. One might charge this obscurity to Thompson's imperfect grasp of his material.... (pp. 108-09)

The religious note in Thompson's poetry is distinct enough to need no special emphasis, and it has been rather overemphasized, I think, by some of his commentators. He need not be regarded as exclusively or even primarily a religious poet. He was a devout Catholic, but perhaps not altogether a good Catholic, and certainly not a complete one. Religion was to him chiefly a passion of adoration, and one feels that the divine objects of his adoration were secondary to the passion itself. That passion, moreover, was not so strong in him as the parent-passion of aloofness.... He needed to satisfy his intense craving for love without jarring the indolence of his soul's solitude; and he embraced so much of Catholicism as would supply this need, and embraced it with ardor like a saint's. He was attracted the more strongly by one aspect of the religious life because other aspects repelled him; and in his poetry, while we find frequent adoration of the Son and the Mother, we find little enthusiasm for the brotherhood of their children.

By calling his religion a passion of adoration and love, I mean also to distinguish Thompson from men whose religion is vivid and passionate belief. The assurances of Thompson's creed have but very loose hold on his imagination, which goes a-straying in purely pagan ways. We find the thought of death, for instance, more easily associated with cypress trees and the grave's quiet oblivion than with halleluiahs and palms. We find the Virgin invoked like a modernized Aphrodite Urania.... We find heaven charted in a Pre-Raphaelite manner not easily distinguishable from Rossetti's. And one of the most occult of the later poems,— "New Year's Chimes,"—rings new changes on the very pagan pantheism of Emerson's "Brahma".... Even in the best-known of all Thompson's poems, wherein he arrays his most grandiose imagery to celebrate the compulsive insistence of the divine love,—even in "The Hound of Heaven," it is not clear what parts of the strange fantasy were conceived as truth, and actually felt. I suspect that Thompson has here allowed his imagination to soar away from his thought, and that the magnificent opening is really irrelevant. The imagery is chiefly of the Heavenly Hound's pursuit of the soul, but the underlying thought is chiefly of the soul's quest of God. The chase that's chased is, indeed, confused with the Lord o' the chase. A theme of tenderness is thus masked under figures of Dantesque horror, and the human craving of the poet's own heart for sympathy and love becomes an enormous rout down Malebolgian steeps of fear.

But the uncertainty of aim which seems to obscure "The Hound of Heaven" is quite natural in Thompson. He is hardly the man to plot out his work in advance; he improvises. In a poem of any length it is never certain that his close will be in the original key, and the Protean metamorphoses of his purpose are often perplexing to an unwary truth-seeker. "Any Saint," for instance, is really two poems in one; and while we are making Herculean efforts to hold the antelope tight, it flutters to a sea-mew in our grasp. So, too, in the symbolism of the "Orient Ode," the Earth changes its sex oftener than did Tiresias. It figures first as a "joyous David" dancing before the Sun, next as a "poor maid" beautifying herself for his embraces, then yet again as the lover of the virgin Moon, and finally as a "gusty Maenad" whose domestic relations are not clearly defined. His tangential ramblings are hard to follow, and they are easy to ridicule; but except as they make for obscurity they need not provoke hostile criticism. Thompson felt no great concern for unity or precision; his imagination was not under intellectual control; but it is an anachronism to condemn a nineteenth-century poet for being unclassical.

Thompson's romantic genius could never adapt itself to the established verse-forms. His series of sonnets, for instance, is undistinguished. In only three of the fifteen does he attempt the classic model, and in none does he yield to the rigor of the law. His rhymed heroic verse is crabbed, with no sustained rhythm, no onward sweep. The form seems to tie up his inspiration. . . . And in blank verse he seems equally out of his element. There his inspiration sometimes forsakes him altogether, and he writes mere prose,—an offense with which he is hardly chargeable elsewhere. . . .

It is not easy to explain these comparative failures. It may be that Thompson lacked ear for the larger rhythms of the old forms; but my guess would rather be that he lacked rigor in self-discipline. It is hard to adjust phrases to a fixed form, and he therefore preferred to let his verse-form adjust itself to his phrases. He seems most at ease in metres of lawless irregularity. Even in the simplest kind of quatrains, like those of "The Cloud's Swan-Song," we find him perpetually in labor; his thoughts simply will not be said. (pp. 109-12)

In "The Cloud's Swan-Song" there was a special difficulty, for Thompson was consciously imitating Wordsworth's "Leech-Gatherer," and the effort to follow another's footprints threw him quite out of step. And yet, curiously enough, one of the most exquisite of all his poems, the well-known "Daisy," is commonly regarded as another imitation of Wordsworth, and is certainly composed in another fixed form. "Daisy," however, imitates Wordsworth only in being a poem about a child, and in manifesting for once a wholly charming simplicity. But the simplicity is not very Wordsworthian, and the essence of the poem is not Wordsworthian at all. Wordsworth studied children as the fathers of men, because he found their intuitions instructive. Thompson studied them not at all, he only contemplated them; and they figured in his reverie as beings of an order remote from ours. Most of his child poems are not really about childhood. They are about "the vanished hopes and the hopeless bliss" that the sight of childish innocence makes a grown man dream of; for in the presence of children Thompson's own sense of isolation from humankind became doubly poignant. (p. 113)

As Thompson is unlike Wordsworth, so he is unlike every other poet. "A greater Crashaw" and "a lesser Shelley" are convenient terms, but they express only half-truths about him; they are unjust to his uniqueness. If I wished to ticket him for classification, I would use the name of no other poet; I would try to define [his] ecstatic apprehension of nature . . . , for therein is seen Thompson's most marked individuality. Yet in any such labelling of his genius there would be danger of flagrant mis-description. His characteristic ecstasy is not really about nature, it is only expressed in terms of nature. He confounds enthusiasm for nature with enthusiasm for experience. It is not the wonder of the world that occasions his starriest showers of lyrical splendor, it is the wonder of life itself; and he has merely ex-

plored the world for adequate symbols of his delirium. It had been his lot to be born again to this life, and he saw it transfigured as a kingdom of glory. The "message" of his poetry is not the story of his mystical contemplations, but his translation of mere existence into spiritual rapture. (p. 114)

Charlton M. Lewis, "Francis Thompson," in The Yale Review *(© 1914 by Yale University; reprinted by permission of the editors), Vol. IV, No. 1, October, 1914, pp. 99-114.*

G. K. CHESTERTON (essay date 1949)

With Francis Thompson we lost the greatest poetic energy since Browning. His energy was of somewhat the same kind. Browning was intellectually intricate because he was morally simple. . . . But his real energy, and the real energy of Francis Thompson, was best expressed in the fact that both poets were at once fond of immensity and also fond of detail. . . . Great poets are obscure for two opposite reasons; now, because they are talking about something too large for any one to understand, and now again because they are talking about something too small for any one to see. Francis Thompson possessed both these infinities. He escaped by being too small, as the microbe escapes; or he escaped by being too large, as the universe escapes. Any one who knows Francis Thompson's poetry knows quite well the truth to which I refer. . . . [There was] one poem of which the image was so vast that it was literally difficult for a time to take it in; he was describing the evening earth with its mist and fume and fragrance, and represented the whole as rolling upwards like a smoke; then suddenly he called the whole ball of the earth a thurible, and said that some gigantic spirit swung it slowly before God. That is the case of the image too large for comprehension. Another instance sticks in my mind of the image which is too small. In one of his poems, he says that abyss between the known and the unknown is bridged by 'Pontifical death'. There are about ten historical and theological puns in that one word. That a priest means a pontiff, that a pontiff means a bridge-maker, that death is certainly a bridge, that death may turn out after all to be a reconcilling priest, that at least priests and bridges both attest to the fact that one thing can get separated from another thing—these ideas, and twenty more, are all actually concentrated in the word 'pontifical'. In Francis Thompson's poetry, as in the poetry of the universe, you can work infinitely out and out, but yet infinitely in and in. These two infinities are the mark of greatness; and he was a great poet. (pp. 277-78)

G. K. Chesterton, "A Dead Poet" (reprinted by permission of the Estate of G. K. Chesterton), in Selected Essays of G. K. Chesterton, *edited by Dorothy Collins, Methuen & Co., 1949, pp. 277-80.*

PETER BUTTER (essay date 1961)

[Francis Thompson's] poems can be roughly classified, as to content, into those which deal with (a) people, (b) nature, (c) poetry and (d) religion. Of course, nearly all of them are in a broad sense religious, but we can distinguish those which deal more directly with man's relationship to God from those which approach Him through people, nature and poetry. (p. 13)

The poems [in the first category] contain not only passionate feeling, but also quite clear and precise ideas as to the nature and function of love. Only intermittently does the expression rise to the height of the theme, but several of the poems contain touches at least of greatness, for instance *Before her Portrait in Youth, Manus Animam Pinxit, Love Declared, Grace of the Way, Arab Love Song* and *A Fallen Yew.* Collectively Thompson's love poetry is, for me, more valuable than the more perfect works of others who deal with the more superficial and obvious levels of experience; it widens horizons.

As a nature poet also Thompson has little to tell us of the surface appearance of things. He is capable of the occasional vivid descriptive line (e.g., 'Green spray showers lightly down the cascade of the larch') and of evoking the atmosphere of a scene (e.g., of London the night before the Diamond Jubilee: 'Night; and the street a corpse beneath the moon, Upon the threshold of the jubilant day'); but these are not the things at which he especially excels. He is not concerned to describe the surface of things, but to express an imaginative vision of all things as alive, as connected, and as the art of God. The landscape of his poems is a strange and violent one. Suns die weltering in their blood, stars are blown to a flare by great winds or are puffed out by the Morning Hours; large cosmic forces are handled with a sometimes too easy assurance which tends to trivialise them. But even the less good poems (even the, in parts absurd, *Corymbus for Autumn,* for example) have a Dionysian energy and joy behind them which most modern poems, with all their intelligence and control, lack.

They convey a vision of things rather similar to Van Gogh's, another neurotic who was also a true visionary and a true, if imperfect, artist. One of the best nature poems is *Contemplation,* which reveals a pattern of energy within calm existing in nature, in the spiritual life and in the life of the artist. (pp. 14-15)

Nature, for [Thompson], is the art of God and expresses, even in small things, something of His nature. But he is not, like many nineteenth century poets, sentimental about her. Many of his contemporaries, turning from their sorrows in the world of men, sought to lay their heads in the lap of mother Nature and to find there some response, some tenderness; even to find in her a guide, a teacher. Thompson replies that if one imagines that one hears any response from the great heart of nature to one's longing for sympathy, it is only the echo of one's own heart-beat that one hears. . . .

A considerable proportion of Thompson's poetry is concerned with his own experience as a poet. One sometimes gets impatient with his self-consciousness. . . ; but in a few passages (e.g., in parts of *Sister Songs,* in *Contemplation, From the Night of Forebeing* and *The Cloud's Swan Song*) he does succeed in conveying powerfully something of what it feels like to be a poet, and he has interesting things to say about the nature of poetic inspiration. . . . (p. 16)

The bulk of Thompson's poetry consists of longish poems, mostly odes written in no regular stanza form. The lack of a tight metrical pattern allows him to sprawl, but on the other hand enables him to achieve some of his most characteristic effects. The sections into which they are divided and the poems as wholes are seldom firmly enough constructed; but as one gets to know the poems better one usually comes to

see a more definite progression of thought and feeling and a greater density of meaning than one at first suspected.

The Hound of Heaven is the greatest of these Odes. Here we have a single great theme and a clear progression of feeling to give unity to the whole; and the sections, though some are too long, are given some shape by the refrain. The theme, of course, is God's pursuit of man—an unusual one in modern religious verse, which more commonly deals with man's fumbling search for God. The poem has a wonderful speed and urgency, expressing in its rhythms the restlessness of the soul's flight and the majestic instancy of God's pursuit. Criticism of details may seem niggling in face of the power with which it brings to the imagination a sense of the presence of the supernatural as alive and active. Very few, especially modern, religious poems do anything like this; most make us feel in contact only with the author, who tells us what he did, thought, felt, etc., not with any power outside him. Nevertheless, even here some of Thompson's weaknesses as well as his greatness are displayed. (pp. 22-3)

Thompson has been blamed for his 'passion for polysyllables', his too consistently high-coloured language and his too frequent use of archaic, poetical and coined words. There is some justification for these criticisms. His language is apt to be as grandiose when writing of a poppy or of some trivial event as of the largest subjects. Sometimes this is deliberate, when he is showing how great things are contained in small; but sometimes it is due to a sort of automatism. When not inspired by strong feeling or deep thought his writing seems turgid and verbose. Further, he is sometimes too concerned about the sound of words to the neglect of immediate intelligibility. Some of his best lines are those in which he uses simple and short words. (p. 29)

The trouble with using a more 'poetical' diction than is customary is that it tends at first to draw the reader's attention to itself. . . . But it is not fair to judge by first impressions only. The test is whether, as one gets to know a poet's work better, the words become more luminous, come to seem more and more the fitting expression of the author's personality and of what he intends to convey. A careful reader of Thompson will, I believe, find this happening—at any rate, with many of the poems—as he begins to feel his way into Thompson's world. One of the reasons for the dislike of Thompson's diction is failure to read him with enough care, failure to appreciate the density of meaning which his words often contain. (p. 30)

I believe Thompson was a major writer—a great flawed writer, much more interesting and valuable than lesser ones of more even quality. If one were to demand artistic perfection, one would have to discard nearly all his poems, and might be left with only one or two short ones. In so doing one would have to cast out much that is of great value. (p. 35)

> *Peter Butter, in his* Francis Thompson *(© Peter Butter 1961; Longman Group Ltd., for the British Council), British Council, 1961, 38 p.*

PAUL van KUYKENDALL THOMSON (essay date 1961)

That Thompson had a sense of religious mission cannot be anything but obvious, for he believed that it was a poet's duty to see and to restore the divine idea of things to a fallen world. Certain of his poems—most notably ''The Hound of Heaven''—have been almost constantly employed by preachers, both Protestant and Catholic. (p. 243)

There is, however, a certain danger in becoming absorbed in Thompson's religious message. It leads to the false impression that he believed poetry's chief importance lay in the service it could give to the spread of Catholic doctrine. A study of his critical work proves that if he was aware of what poetry can do for religion, he was even more conscious of those qualities which make poetry important in itself.

Thompson was driven to write poetry, not because it seemed to be a means for preaching the gospel, but because of an inner personal necessity. The artistic process, as T. S. Eliot has said, has an intensity, a pressure, of its own—by which the fusion of the component parts of its end product must be achieved. That pressure is not easily borne; yet without its demanding intensity there can be no signigicant re-creation of human experience in verse. (p. 244)

There can be no doubt about the fact that Thompson thought of poetry as a valuable ally of religion, but he never wanted it to be a domestic servant of the Church. (p. 253)

[Poetry] must be thought of as casting light upon areas of experience that no materialistic theory and no scientific analysis can fully explain or explore. Indirectly, it may strengthen the claims of religion, but its aim is not didactic. It is important for a right understanding of Thompson's developed critical theory to have this point clearly in mind, for there are passages in his writing which might suggest the contrary, especially to any reader who shares Thompson's belief in the truth of Catholic doctrines. (pp. 253-54)

Thompson says that poetry is ''essentially dogmatic or rather prophetic—a teaching instrument . . . when it assumes its highest function of dealing with truth.'' The question is: What is this ''truth'' with which poetry deals and how does it deal with it? Here the word *dogmatic* is especially dangerous, for Thompson was not using it in its technical, theological sense but in a more general and much less precise fashion. What he means is that poetry does not argue; it does not seek to persuade by the use of dialectics. It states what it states, as the ancient prophets did not argue, but proclaimed, ''Thus saith the Lord.''

The poet's ''vision of truth'' is his underlying theme; it is not equivalent to the ontological truth of philosophers. As Aristotle long ago made clear, the poet can deal in ''probable impossibility,'' which, for him is always preferable to the ''possible improbability.'' What he writes may not correspond to what actually is, for he may deal with what ought to be, or even with what can never be, except in the little world which the poet creates for us. What is required of the poet is an inner consistency, an interior probability of order, in the work he creates. He must be faithful to that in the development of his theme. In the last analysis, his poem will have an order which life itself never shows. (pp. 254-55)

Paul van Kuykendall Thomson, in his Francis

Thompson: A Critical Biography *(© 1961 by Paul van K. Thomson; reprinted by permission of the author), Thomas Nelson & Sons, 1961 (and reprinted by Gordian Press, 1973), 280 p.*

BRIGID BROPHY, MICHAEL LEVEY and CHARLES OSBORNE　(essay date 1967)

[People may be] puzzled as to how the over-written rhetoric of Thompson ever imposed itself. The date of the . . . publication [of *The Hound of Heaven*] is a clue. It appeared in 1893, at a period when purple sins were almost as much in vogue as purple passages. After the leaden materialism of the century's middle years came the filigree refinements and exotic escapades of the nineties. Religion itself was fashionable; penitence was as promising as sin. (p. 105)

To the weary, guilty hints and mystery—the passion of penitence—Thompson brought his own excited story: bursting on to the scene with a religious poem about being pursued by a *man*. . . . There is nothing even of magnificent baroque self-delusion in Thompson's over-written work. It is maudlin with self-pity, drenched in tears that have made a large but shallow pool where language constantly collapses into false poeticisms and archaic usage—'bruit' and 'wist,' with a steady repetition of 'Lo' as if to lull us into accepting as poetry [this] sort of beer-mat jingle. . . . [There] is a happy ending, of course. The flight (conducted *à la* Swinburne, 'down the arches of the years') seems the product only of some obscure lovers' quarrel and it closes with His hand 'outstretched caressingly'. A fade-out is inevitable. The first public, dispersing somewhat baffled by the performance, was probably divided: the critics being impressed by the mysticism, while the clergy gaily turned literary and approved as 'poetry' what was bolstered by a Christian message. Both today look equally bogus. The mysticism is sheer sentimentalism, and sentimentality has sugared the language to an intolerable sweetness and complete vagueness. Many of the lines do not make sense: they merely sound as if they do. Francis Thompson was running away from himself, shouting as he went that someone was after him. If anyone *was* chasing him, it was probably the personification of English Literature—stretching out its hand to give him not a caress but a well-deserved blow. (pp. 106-07)

> *Brigid Brophy, Michael Levey, and Charles Osborne, '''The Hound of Heaven','' in their* Fifty Works of English and American Literature We Could Do Without *(copyright © 1967 by Brigid Brophy, Michael Levey, Charles Osborne; reprinted with permission of Stein and Day Publishers), Stein and Day, 1967, pp. 105-07.*

ADDITIONAL BIBLIOGRAPHY

Alexander, Calvert, S.J. ''Middle Phase: Francis Thompson.'' In his *The Catholic Literary Revival: Three Phases in Its Development from 1845 to the Present*, pp. 150-74. Milwaukee: The Bruce Publishing Co., 1935.
　　Sketch of Thompson's life and work, emphasizing the religious qualities in each.

Armstrong, Robert. ''The Simplicity of Francis Thompson.'' *The Poetry Review* XII, No. 1 (January-February 1921): 13-16.

Critical essay suggesting a subsurface simplicity beneath Thompson's surface of obscurity in style and subject.

Connolly, Terence L., S.J. Foreword to *Literary Criticisms,* by Francis Thompson, pp. vii-x. New York: E. P. Dutton and Co., 1948.
Background to Thompson's literary criticism and a brief summary of its basic principles.

Dingle, Reginald J. "Francis Thompson's Centenary: The Fashionable Reaction." *The Dublin Review* 234, No. 483 (Spring 1960): 74-83.
Rebuttal of J. C. Reid's appraisal of Thompson in his *Francis Thompson: Man and Poet.*

Figgis, Darrell. "Francis Thompson." *The Contemporary Review* CIV, No. 72 (October 1913): 487-94.
Examines the mystic elements in Thompson's poetry.

Finberg, H.P.R. "Francis Thompson." *The English Review* XLI, No. 6 (December 1925): 822-31.
Overview of Thompson's poetry, its major themes, styles, and influences.

Kehoe, Monika. "Francis Thompson: Poet of Religious Romanticism." *Thought* XV, No. 56 (March 1940): 119-26.
Focuses on the Catholicism in Thompson's poetry.

LeBuffe, Francis P., S.J. *"The Hound of Heaven": An Interpretation.* New York: The Macmillan Co., 1922, 89 p.
Annotated version of the poem, supplying the reader with strictly theological and not literary commentary.

Madeleva, Sister M. "The Prose of Francis Thompson: Its Content and Style As Transitional from Patmore to Chesterton." In her *Chaucer's Nuns, and Other Essays,* pp. 45-88. New York, London: D. Appleton and Co., 1925.
Descriptive survey of Thompson's prose works and their various commentators, with extended comparisons to Coventry Patmore and G. K. Chesterton.

Meynell, Everard. *The Life of Francis Thompson.* London: Burns, Oates, & Washbourne, 1926, 280 p.
Provides useful sections surveying early critical reaction to Thompson's poetry.

Meynell, Wilfrid. "A Biographical Note on Francis Thompson." In *Selected Poems of Francis Thompson,* by Francis Thompson, pp. ix-xviii. London: Burns, Oates & Washbourne, 1908.
Sketch of Thompson's life, work, and early critical reputation.

Reid, J. C. *Francis Thompson: Man and Poet.* London: Routledge & Kegan Paul, 1959, 232 p.
Scholarly biography interwoven with commentary on Thompson's poetry. The critic extensively considers the role of opium in Thompson's life and work.

Tolles, Frederick B. "The Praetorian Cohorts: A Study of the Language of Francis Thompson's Poetry." *English Studies* XXII (1940): 49-64.
Sees Thompson's use of language as the culmination of Victorian poetics.

Walsh, John. *Strange Harp, Strange Symphony: The Life of Francis Thompson.* New York: Hawthorn Books, 1967, 298 p.
Biography pointing out the interdependence between Thompson's life and work, with an appended essay on cosmic imagery in the poetry.

Williamson, Claude. "Francis Thompson: A New Study." *Poetry Review* 27, No. 5 (1936): 375-85.
Discusses Thompson as a romantic poet, comparing his work to that of Blake, Coleridge, and Keats.

(Count) Leo (Lev Nikolaevich) Tolstoy

1828-1910

(Also transliterated as Lyof; also transliterated as Nikolay-evich; also transliterated as Tolstoi, Tolstoj, or Tolstoĭ) Russian novelist, dramatist, short story writer, essayist, and critic.

Tolstoy is regarded as one of the greatest novelists, and one of the few archetypal creative geniuses, in the history of world literature. His *Voina i mir* (*War and Peace*) and *Anna Karenina* are almost universally considered as all-encompassing documents of human existence and supreme examples of the realistic novel. Commentary on these novels frequently mentions Tolstoy's feat of successfully animating his fiction with the immediacy and variousness of life. Particularly esteemed are his insightful examinations of psychology and society, along with the religious and philosophical issues which occupied him later in his career.

Tolstoy was born and lived throughout his life on his family estate near Moscow. After attending the University of Kazan, he returned to the estate and continued his education through personal study. He later served in the army in the Caucasus, at this time working on his first novel, *Detstvo* (*Childhood*). This work gained notice in Russian literary circles, and elicited favorable reaction from Turgenev and Dostoevsky. The novel displays a feature that dominates Tolstoy's later work, that of autobiography. Short stories like "Nabey" ("A Raid") were the literary result of his experiences in the Caucasus, and his military service in the Crimean War is chronicled in the Sevastopol sketches. Subsequent short stories and short novels, including "Dva gusara" ("Two Hussars"), "Tri smerti" ("Three Deaths"), and *Kazaki* (*The Cossacks*), evidence a more characteristically Tolstoyan concern with issues of morality and the ideal of simple ways of life untainted by the complexity and temptations of society.

War and Peace has often been called the greatest novel ever written. Commentators point out that this work does not restrict itself to a single hero or point of view but ranges over all strata of human affairs, its subject being the whole of life. Tolstoy's characters are both realistically individualized figures and representatives of human types. From historical theory Tolstoy borrowed the idea of "the great man" in order to refute the notion that world events are primarily influenced by a few powerful individuals. For this theory he substituted his own conclusion that human life is determined by natural law and is not subject to the will of individuals, who in essence have no free choice. The passages of *War and Peace* in which Tolstoy elaborates his historical concepts are thought by some critics to be the weakest parts of the novel, further disjoining a work of many already detached parts.

While later critics have perceived a greater unity in *War and Peace* than previously supposed, most agree that Tolstoy's next work, *Anna Karenina*, displays a more purposeful structure. Henry James called these novels "loose, baggy monsters" of stylelessness, but Tolstoy stated of *Anna Karenina* "... I am very proud of its architecture—its vaults are joined so that one cannot even notice where the keystone is."

Evidence has shown that both of Tolstoy's most important works went through numerous reworkings and revisions, and critics are now more likely to emphasize Tolstoy's structural subtleties and stylistic nuances. Thematically, *Anna Karenina* parallels its heroine's conflict with social law with Levin's internal struggle to find meaning and guidance for his life. Levin's struggle is often said to be an embodiment of Tolstoy's moral dilemma.

But *Anna Karenina* reflects only the beginning of Tolstoy's crisis of meaning. In *Ispoved* (*A Confession*) he outlines a spiritual upheaval that caused him to question the basis of his existence. His attempt at a solution to this crisis took the form of a radical Christianity whose doctrines ultimately included nonresistance to evil and total abstinence from sex. The artistic repercussions of his conversion are spelled out in *Chto takoe iskusstvo* (*What Is Art?*). The major concern of this essay is to distinguish bogus art, which is mainly an elitist celebration of aesthetics, from universal art, which successfully "infects" its recipient with the highest sentiment an artist can transmit—that of religious feeling. This conception of art led Tolstoy to dismiss most of history's greatest creators, including Shakespeare and Wagner, and to repudiate all of his own previous work save for two short stories. During this phase of his career Tolstoy began writing his many moral and theological tracts, for which he was eventually excommunicated. His pamphleteering on social, political, and economic subjects resulted in the censorship of his work by the government.

Critics have traditionally regarded Tolstoy's post conversion works as artistically inferior to those of the earlier phase, disparaging his didactic intentions as injurious to his art. His last major novel, *Voskresenie (Resurrection)* is considered a lesser achievement than *War and Peace* and *Anna Karenina*. Still highly valued, however, are the later masterpieces like *Smert Ivana Ilyicha (The Death of Ivan Ilyitch)*, in which art and moral point are worked into greater accord. Tolstoy, who ultimately believed that art should serve a religious and ethical code, himself serves as a model of the consummate artist, and his two greatest works are exemplary of the nature and traditions of the modern realistic novel.

PRINCIPAL WORKS

Detstvo (novel) 1852
  [*Childhood* published in *Childhood and Youth*, 1862]
Otrochestvo (novel) 1854
  [*Boyhood* published in *Childhood, Boyhood, Youth*, 1886]
Yunost (novel) 1857
  [*Youth* published in *Childhood and Youth*, 1862]
Semeinoe schaste (novel) 1859
  [*Family Happiness*, 1888]
Kazaki (novel) 1863
  [*The Cossacks*, 1878]
Polikushka (novel) 1863
  [*Polikouchka*, 1888]
Voina i mir (novel) 1869
  [*War and Peace*, 1886]
Anna Karenina (novel) 1877
  [*Anna Karenina*, 1886]
Ispoved (essay) 1882
  [*A Confession*, 1885]
V chiom moya vera (essay) 1884
  [*What I Believe*, 1885]
Smert Ivana Ilyicha (novella) 1886
  [*Iván Ilyitch* published in *Iván Ilyitch, and Other Stories*, 1887]
Sebastopol (sketches) 1887
Vlast tmy (drama) 1888
  [*The Dominion of Darkness*, 1888; also published in the United States as *The Power of Darkness* in *Plays*, 1910]
Plody prosvesh cheniya (drama) 1889
  [*The Fruits of Enlightenment*, 1890]
Kreitserova sonata (novella) 1890
  [*The Kreutzer Sonata*, 1890]
Khozyain i rabotnik (novella) 1895
  [*Master and Man*, 1895]
Chto takoe iskusstvo (essay) 1898
  [*What Is Art?*, 1898]
Otetz sergii (novella) 1898
  [*Father Sergius* published in *Father Sergius, and Other Stories and Plays*, 1911]
Voskresenie (novel) 1899
  [*Resurrection*, 1899]
Khadzhi Murat (novella) 1911
  [*Hadji Murád, and Other Stories*, 1912]
Zhivoy trup (drama) 1911
  [*The Living Corpse*, 1912]

P. V. ANNENKOV (essay date 1855)

Count L.N.T.'s stories have a strict form of expression and in this lies the secret of the impression they make upon the reader. With unusual attention he follows [in 'Childhood' and 'Boyhood'] the impressions which are born in first a boy and then an adolescent and his every word is full of respect both for the task he has given himself and for that time of life which has so many more unanswered questions, moral lapses and turning-points than any other. All of this must have consequences. Fulness of expression in the characters and objects, profound psychological analysis, and finally a picture of the morals of a certain upper-class and strictly proper milieu, a picture painted with such a delicate touch, the like of which we have not seen for a long time in descriptions of high society, all are the fruits of a deep understanding by the author of his subject-matter. On top of this the depiction of the first waverings of the will and the recognition of thoughts in the boy are raised by the author, thanks to that same quality, to a history of all children of a particular place and time, and like a history written by a poet it includes, together with grounds for aesthetic pleasure, abundant food for every thinking man. . . . (p. 51)

With [Tolstoy] there are almost no external factors of little importance with the characters, no insignificant details with the events. On the contrary every characteristic of the one or the other is given such meaning, such intelligence, we dare to say, that it hits the eye even of those who by being used to the dark are little capable of making things out. Because of this we have a remarkable clarity of both characters and events. The author leads the reader with relentless verification of everything he meets to the conviction that man's soul can be seen in a single gesture, an unimportant mannerism or a careless word and that such things often disclose the personality of a character as truly and certainly as his most obvious and unambiguous actions. Both parts of the story are full of similar expressions of the role of secondary and tertiary signs in a person's life, but this is especially expressed through the presence of thought which fills with substance everything it touches in the chapters of the second story, 'Boyhood'. (p. 52)

The impressions and events of childhood are simple, more naive, more graceful than those of boyhood, which becomes more complicated, confused, rational and therefore more dramatic. That is why thoughts and their framework in the realm of art, i.e. the characters and events, are fused together in our author and present a unified whole, powerfully and beneficially affecting the reader. (p. 53)

> *P. V. Annenkov, "Annenkov on 'Childhood' and 'Boyhood'" (originally published under a different title in* Contemporary, *No. 1, 1855), in* Tolstoy: The Critical Heritage, *edited by A. V. Knowles (copyright © 1978 by A. V. Knowles), Routledge & Kegan Paul, 1978, pp. 50-3.*

N. G. CHERNYSHEVSKY (essay date 1856)

'Exceptional powers of observation, delicate analysis of the psychological processes, precision and poetry in describing nature, and elegant simplicity—these are the distinguishing features of Count Tolstoy's talent.' Such is the opinion you will hear from everyone who follows literature. The critics have repeated this evaluation suggested by the general consensus and have, in so doing, been completely true to the facts of the matter.

But can one limit oneself to this judgment, having noticed, it is true, the characteristics that distinguish Count Tolstoy's talent, and yet not show the special way in which these qualities appear in the works of the author of 'Childhood', 'Boyhood', 'The Memoirs of a Billiard-marker', 'The Snow Storm', 'Two Hussars' and 'The Military Tales'? Powers of observation, delicacy of psychological analysis, poetry in the description of nature, simplicity and elegance—you will find all of these in Pushkin, Lermontov and Mr Turgenev. To define the talent of each of these authors only by these epithets would be just, but completely inadequate to distinguish the one author from the other; and to repeat the very same things about Count Tolstoy is hardly to catch the distinguishing characteristics of his talent or show how his remarkable talent differs from many other equally remarkable talents. It has to be characterized more accurately. . . .

Count Tolstoy's attention is more than anything directed to how some feelings and thoughts develop out of others. He is interested in observing how a feeling immediately arising out of a given circumstance or impression and then, subjected to the influence of memory and the powers of association in the imagination, turns into different feelings and returns to its former starting point and again and again sets out and changes along the whole chain of memory; how a thought, born of an original sensation, leads to other thoughts, is carried further and further away, blends reverie with real sensations, dreams of the future with reflections on the present. Psychological analysis may take different directions; one poet is primarily occupied with outlining characters, another with the influence of social relationships and the conflicts of life on his characters, a third with the connection between feelings and actions, a fourth with the analysis of passions; Count Tolstoy is most of all concerned with the psychic process itself, its forms, its laws, with, to express it precisely, the dialectic of the soul. (p. 60)

Count Tolstoy's special talent lies in the fact that he does not limit himself to a description of the results of the psychic process; he is interested in the process itself, and the scarcely perceptible manifestations of this inner life, changing from one into another with great speed and an inexhaustible variety, are described by Count Tolstoy in masterly fashion. There are painters who are famous for their art in capturing the flickering reflection of the sun's rays on the fast-rolling waves, the shimmering light on rustling leaves and the play of colours on the changing shape of clouds, it is generally said of them that they can catch the life of nature. Count Tolstoy does something similar with the secret movements of the psychic life. It seems to us that it is in this that the completely original character of his talent consists. (p. 62)

> *N. G. Chernyshevsky, "Chernyshevsky on Tolstoy: Review of 'Childhood', 'Boyhood' and 'The Military Tales'" (originally published in* Contemporary, *No. 12, 1856), in* Tolstoy: The Critical Heritage, *edited by A. V. Knowles (copyright © 1978 by A. V. Knowles), Routledge & Kegan Paul, 1978, pp. 59-63.*

THE SATURDAY REVIEW   (essay date 1862)

[*Childhood and Youth*] is at the best a very thin narration of the early life of an affectionate and sensitive boy placed under such circumstances as must be very common in his class and country. . . . There is nothing to blame in the book. The incidents recorded are very trivial, and therefore, probably, true, and the whole production is insipid, unless we force an interest in it by reminding ourselves that it is improving to know how Russians write. But as a record of childhood it has its merits. It is not sickly or pretentious. Its merits are, however, mostly negative, and few compositions have less claim to philosophy. . . .

This is said to be a true history of Count Tolstoi's childhood, and the people introduced into it are real people. (p. 361)

It makes no difference whether a writer is a Russian, or a German, or an Englishman—whether he is or is not like a spring morning, or what may be his noble tendencies. He is not, we think, justified in telling his family history in this way, and in probing the failings of parents in order that he may have the satisfaction of sketching his own childhood. It is no excuse to say that, unless he puts in the dark shades, the picture cannot be truthful. There is no reason why he should draw the picture at all. The world can get on very well without criticisms written by a son on the behaviour of his father at his mother's funeral. It would destroy all family confidence if we were all of us liable to be sacrificed in this way to the exigencies of literary art; and if this is the style in which sons who are like spring mornings write, most fathers would devoutly wish their own offspring should be like autumn evenings. (p. 362)

> *"Reviews: 'Childhood and Youth'," in* The Saturday Review, *Vol. 13, No. 335, March 29, 1862, pp. 361-62.*

A. YA. PYATKOVSKY   (essay date 1865)

Count Tolstoy's literary talent, his powers of observation and his acute psychological analysis were all sufficiently expressed in his first work 'Childhood and Boyhood'. . . . On those occasions when Count Tolstoy does not propose some preconceived idea and does not strain to produce something new and startling to the whole universe he completely satisfies his readers with the accuracy of his observations and the masterly strokes he uses in the portrayal of his fictional characters. In a word the more humble the task and the further the author removes himself from any sly cleverness and deliberate manipulations of his artistic creations the better it is both for him and his public. To the number of works which present a truthful and unartificial combination of various facts from our lives belong 'Childhood and Boyhood', the memoirs of Sebastopol, the stories of the Caucasus ('The Raid' and 'The Woodfelling'), 'The Memoirs of a Billiardmarker' and the tale of 'Polikushka'. We would have included 'Family Happiness' had it not shown some ulterior motive in its idealization of a certain social class of an extremely bourgeois nature. . . . The story 'Lucerne' and the novel 'The Cossacks' suffered even more from tendentiousness and lyrical interpolations. The main character in 'Lucerne' is Prince Dmitriy Nekhlyudov who first appeared in 'Boyhood' and 'Youth'. It is true that this Nekhlyudov has developed somewhat since the time he was the guest of Ivan Yakovlevich Koreysha and was glad of the opportunity to make the acquaintance of that remarkable man. His development, though, is not of a very deep nature and the Schweizerhof hotel shelters the same spirit that in earlier days wandered the hills. (p. 86)

'The Cossacks' has the same virtues and faults as the stories in which Nekhlyudov appears. The pictures of nature and the descriptions of Cossack life are wonderful in their artistry; the impressions which the hero gains as he arrives in this half-savage country are accurately depicted; but the character of Olenin is indescribably weak and the central idea of the novel is even worse. As far as the latter is concerned the novel is no better than the 'Byronic' stories in our literature where our civilized Europeans set off to seek rest and oblivion in the countryside. . . .

But what was attractive and contemporary in the 1820s smells of anachronism in the 1860s. It is a little late for Count Tolstoy to restore ancient pictures. Furthermore he would seem to share Nekhlyudov's opinion that 'civilization is not a blessing nor is barbarism an evil', and that, given the opportunity, should one not exchange one for the other? (pp. 87-8)

> *A. Ya. Pyatkovsky, "Pyatkovsky Sums Up Tolstoy's Career" (originally published under a different title in* Contemporary, *No. 4, 1865), in* Tolstoy: The Critical Heritage, *edited by A. V. Knowles (copyright © 1978 by A. V. Knowles), Routledge & Kegan Paul, 1978, pp. 85-8.*

N. D. AKHSHARUMOV (essay date 1867)

We cannot place this work ['1805,' (the original title for the first parts of 'War and Peace')] categorically in any of the usual literary genres. It is neither a chronicle nor an historical novel. Although in form it is fairly close to the latter, in content it lacks any dramatic unity; the action has no central point; an opening, an intrigue, and a denouement are all missing; also it is clearly unfinished; but its general sense does not suffer in any way from these faults, and which we therefore cannot call faults. On the contrary it seems to us that a more strict framework would have been inhibiting and in order to be complete would have demanded things which the author neither had nor should have had in mind. His object was to write about Russian *society sixty years ago,* and we must admit to the correctness of the taste with which he rejected all superfluous decoration and every attempt at effect, sacrificing all to the demands of strict historical truth. The story has lost very little because of this, and has gained much. (pp. 91-2)

[The] author's method is almost irreproachable. The only thing that strikes us as always being the same and which is somewhat wearying in its monotonous impression is the eternal patch of shade, slowly following, always in its own way, always separately, every bright side of the description. This gives the impression that the author is afraid that the personages he has created will fly away into some abstract ideal and so he quickly weighs them down a little. It seems to us that there is no danger of this happening and the huge credit which the author enjoys with the mass of his readers could save him from the worry of paying with the small change of satire for every spark of poetry and every sign of beauty appearing in his portraits. (pp. 98-9)

[Even] the imagination of Shakespeare would not have been able to create such a clear and true story. (p. 99)

> *N. D. Akhsharumov, "Akhsharumov, Review of '1805'" (1867), in* Tolstoy: The Critical Heritage, *edited by A. V. Knowles (copyright © 1978 by A. V. Knowles), Routledge & Kegan Paul, 1978, pp. 91-9.*

V. G. AVSEENKO (essay date 1875)

The lack of new ideas, new types and new elements is reflected at the moment even in works written by authors who are above the average standard. This painting in dull colours has also affected 'Anna Karenina'; one can sense it through the freshness of the author's talent, through the poetry of his ideas and through the elegance of his pictures of his heroines. The basic idea behind the novel is an attempt to disown those manifestations of contemporary life which in their sum total [A. I.] Herzen called 'middle class'. Amid the general demand to mingle with the impersonal masses and to live for their everyday practical interests, the author has sought out a corner of contemporary society living as it were a separate life, filled with the traditions of that epoch before the middle class was knocking at everyone's door, a life which stands aloof and is foreign to the interests and concerns of the crowd and which seems to the majority of modern readers something quite empty and vulgar. In fact, of course, it is nothing of the kind. The author not only fills it with content but also gives it a certain charm. But whence this charm? How does the novelist create the magic with which he surrounds the delightful figure of Kitty Shcherbatsky, the passionate personality of Anna Karenina, the engaging nature of Konstantin Levin and the charmingly frivolous character of Stiva Oblonsky? Alas, all the magic, all the fascination, derives from the juxtaposition of these characters with elements of contemporary life, the life which is ruled by the middle classes. The secret of the fascination which surrounds the novel's heroes and heroines lies precisely in that it retains in itself and its life characteristics of outmoded people of a bygone age and that it is instinctively and organically opposed to the middle class. Thus all the delight of life is reduced to retaining its former charms and to sustaining the vitality of tradition. (pp. 261-62)

We note finally a strange fact: we have a great novel, written by the hand of a great artist and containing a multitude of contemporary characters—contemporary in the sense that such people actually exist today—but at the same time you will not only fail to see in this wonderful novel the main trends of contemporary life, you will not only fail to meet a single character who would be typical of modern society (with the sole exception of Nikolay Levin, who is a very minor character and who anyway destroys the general harmony of the story), but you will feel that all these people and their lives are organically opposed to the bases of our present-day reality and its main facet—the intelligent and moral middle class. . . .

Count Tolstoy, whatever convictions his turn of mind might have led him to in social questions, is above all a poet, i.e. a writer gifted with creative force. This creative force should have led him to create new ideals, if contemporary reality provided obvious material for him. But the fact is that this new material does not exist. (p. 263)

To accuse the author of a negative attitude to contemporary reality, to accuse him of neglecting to show us the new ideals, that the milieu he has painted is attractive only because it retains elements of a bygone society, is of course not possible. If life had shown some new positive aspects he would doubtless have shown them in the novel. (p. 264)

Count Tolstoy is one of those authors who pay very little attention to the exterior plot or plan of their works. We would not for a moment suggest that either is as important as a novel's inner content; but there is no doubt that a poverty of imagination which leads to an excess of prolixity and lack of balance in the plan of the work is a disadvantageous method even in such remarkable works as 'Anna Karenina'. This fault has become even more apparent in the chapters that have just appeared. The drama, so powerfully and vividly enacted through Anna and Vronsky, is brought to a halt by the fact that both these characters disappear from the scene for a time. It is true that Levin's life in the country, the scenes of work in the fields, the mowing and so on all breathe with fresh healthy poetry; but one feels that they lack the dramatic element and slow down the development of the story. Levin himself is partially the cause of this, or rather his passive nature, lacking in any drive. Such people are very engaging but in the main their lives are without much interest because there are so few facts to relate in them. In general one can state that the novel's male characters are far inferior to the female ones. Both Vronsky and Levin cannot help appearing comparatively insignificant when put alongside Kitty or Anna. Levin has too little initiative and Vronsky's personality is too shallow. His nature is brilliant only externally and if Anna is attracted to him it is only because our society is devoid of remarkable people. It is also impossible not to think that the lack of comprehension which our critics have shown with regard to Anna is caused by the character of Vronsky. In her choice of him they have seen evidence of her own emptiness . . . and immorality. We shall not comment on the latter because we strongly doubt the morality of the theories on the basis of which our critics have moralized about Anna. As for her emptiness and as our newspapers put it her 'vulgarity' one must note that 'vulgarity' is an extremely relative concept. She is, though, one of the most brilliant of all of Count Tolstoy's heroines. (pp. 265-66)

> *V. G. Avseenko, "Avseenko, Review" (1875), in* Tolstoy: The Critical Heritage, *edited by A. V. Knowles (copyright © 1978 by A. V. Knowles), Routledge & Kegan Paul, 1978, pp. 261-66.*

F. M. DOSTOIEVSKY (essay date 1877)

[A] month ago I came across so serious and characteristic a work in current literature that I have read even with surprise because I have long ceased to expect in fiction anything of this kind, and on such a scale. In a writer—artist *par excellence,* pre-eminently a belles-lettrist, I read three or four pages of genuine "topics of the day"—everything that is of the greatest moment in our Russian political and social problems being as it were brought into one focus. And what is most important—with the utterly characteristic nuance of the current moment, precisely as this question is being put at this very moment,—as it is being put and is being left unsolved. I am referring to several pages in *Anna Karenina* by Count Leo Tolstoy. . . .(p. 610)

Concerning the novel itself I shall say only a word, and this only in the way of a most necessary preface. I started reading it, as we all did, very long ago. At first, I liked it. Later, though the details continued to please me—so that I was unable to tear myself away from them—on the whole I began to like the novel less: I kept thinking that I had already read it somewhere —precisely in *Childhood and Youth,* by the same Count Tolstoy, and in his *War and Peace,* and that there it was even fresher. The same story of a Russian noble family, although the plot was different:

characters, such as Vronsky (one of the heroes of the romance), who can speak of nothing but horses, and who is even unable to find a subject for conversation other than about horses, are, of course, curious from the standpoint of ascertaining their type, but very monotonous and confined to a certain caste only. For instance, it seemed to me that the love of this "stallion in uniform," as a friend of mine called him, could have been depicted only in an ironical tone. However, when the author began to introduce me seriously into the inner world of his hero, I seemed to be bored. And then, suddenly, all my prejudices were shattered: the scene of the heroine's death (later she recovers) explained to me the essential part of the author's design. In the very center of that petty and insolent life there appeared a great and eternal living truth, at once illuminating everything. These petty, insignificant and deceitful beings suddenly became genuine and truthful people, worthy of being called men, solely because of a natural law, the law of human death. Their shell vanished, and truth alone appeared. The last ones developed into the first, while the first ones (Vronsky) all of a sudden became the last, losing their halo in humiliation; but having been humbled, they became infinitely better, worthier, more truthful than when they were the first and the eminent. Hatred and deceit began to speak in terms of forgiveness and love. Instead of worldly, beaumonde conceptions there appeared humaneness. They all forgave and acquitted one another. Caste and exclusiveness suddenly vanished and were rendered impossible, and these paper people began to resemble genuine human beings! There proved to be no guilty ones: they all accused themselves unconditionally, and thereby they at once acquitted themselves. The reader felt that there is a living truth, a most real and inescapable truth, which has to be believed, and that our whole life, all our troubles, both the petty and disgraceful ones and those which we often consider as our gravest ones,—they all are mostly but petty and fantastic vanity which falls and disappears even without defending itself before the moment of the living truth.

The most important thing was the indication that such a moment actually exists, although it rarely appears in its glaring fullness, and in some lives it does not appear at all. This moment was found and revealed to us by the novelist in all its terrible truth. He proved that this truth actually exists not merely as a matter of belief, not only as an ideal, but inevitably, inescapably, obviously. It seems that this is precisely what the novelist sought to prove to us when he was conceiving his novel. The Russian reader has to be often reminded about this eternal truth: in Russia many people begin to forget it. This reminder was a good act on the part of the author—to say nothing about the fact that he executed it as a sublime artist. (pp. 610-11)

> *F. M. Dostoievsky, "The Boy Celebrating His Saint's Day" (1877), in his* The Diary of a Writer, *translated by Boris Brasol (abridged by permission of Charles Scribner's Sons; copyright © 1949 Charles Scribner's Sons), Scribner's, 1949 (and reprinted by George Braziller, Inc., Publishers, 1954), pp. 588-92.**

W.R.S. RALSTON (essay date 1879)

[In "Voina i Mir" ("War and Peace") Count Tolstoy] has drawn a series of pictures of Russia, military and domestic, as it appeared during the first quarter of the present century, especially at the period when it bore up against the tremendous shock of Napoleon's invasion, and changed the course of European history. In ... "Anna Karenina" he has taken as his subject society as it exists at the present day in Russian aristocratic circles, combining with his graphic descriptions of the life now led by the upper classes, a series of subtle studies of an erring woman's heart. Neither of these works seems likely to be translated into English. Among other deterrent causes may be mentioned their length. . . . That they have many merits may be considered as proved by the unanimous and enthusiastic consent of Russian readers in their favor. (p. 409)

> *W.R.S. Ralston, "Count Leo Tolstoy's Novels," in* The Living Age *(copyright 1879, by the Living Age Co.), Vol. XXVI, No. 1822, May 17, 1879, pp. 409-20.*

IVAN TURGENEV   (essay date 1880)

War and Peace can easily be called one of the most remarkable books of our time. The spirit of an epic fills this vast work; in it the public and private life of Russia during the first years of our century is rendered by the hand of a true master. An entire epoch passes before the reader, rich in great events and important figures (the story begins shortly before the Battle of Austerlitz and goes to the engagement at Moscow), a whole world arises with a wealth of types taken from real life, from all levels of society. The manner in which Count Tolstoy works out his theme is as new as it is original. This is not the method of Walter Scott, and, it goes without saying, it is not that of Alexandre Dumas either. Count Tolstoy is a Russian writer to the very marrow of his bones; and those French readers who do not shun a few long tedious passages and the originality of some evaluations will justly say to themselves that *War and Peace* gave them a more immediate and faithful representation of the character and temperament of the Russian people, and of Russian life in general, than if they had read hundreds of works on ethnography and history. Here are whole chapters in which nothing will ever have to be changed; here are historical personages (such as Kutuzov, Rostopchin, and others) whose features are set for all times; this is unsurpassed. . . . [This] is a great work by a great writer—and this is real Russia. (pp. 1388-89)

> *Ivan Turgenev, in his letter to M. Abouton January 20, 1880, in* "War and Peace" *by Leo Tolstoy: The Maude Translation, Backgrounds and Sources, Essays in Criticism, edited by George Gibian (reprinted by permission of W. W. Norton & Company, Inc.; copyright © 1966 by W. W. Norton & Company, Inc.), Norton, 1966, pp. 1388-89.*

GUSTAVE FLAUBERT   (essay date 1880)

['War and Peace'] is first rate. What an artist and what a psychologist! The first two volumes are sublime, but the third goes downhill dreadfully. He repeats himself. And he philosophizes. In a word here one sees the gentlemen, the author, and the Russian, whereas hitherto one had seen only Nature and Humanity. It seems to me that there are some passages worthy of Shakespeare. I found myself crying out in admiration while reading, and that lasted a long time. Yes, it is powerful, very powerful!

> *Gustave Flaubert, "Gustave Flaubert on 'War and Peace'" (1880), in* Tolstoy: The Critical Heritage, *edited by A. V. Knowles (copyright © 1978 by A. V. Knowles), Routledge & Kegan Paul, 1978, p. 194.*

THE NATION   (essay date 1885)

This book of Tolstoi's ['War and Peace'] might be called with justice 'The Russian Comedy,' in the sense in which Balzac employed the word. It gave me exactly the same impression: I felt that I was thrown among new men and women, that I lived with them, that I knew them, that none of them could be indifferent to me, that I could never forget them. I entered into their souls, and it seemed almost as if they could enter into mine. Such a power in a writer is almost a miracle. How many novels have I not read, and, after having read them, and admired many qualities—the beauty of the style, the invention, the dialogues, the dramatic situations—have still felt that my knowledge of life had not increased, that I had gained no new experience. It was not so with 'War and Peace'. . . .

It would be difficult to give a proper definition of the talent of Tolstoi. First of all, he is an *homme du monde*. He makes great people, emperors, generals, diplomats, fine ladies, princes, talk and act as they do act and talk. He is a perfect gentleman, and as such he is thoroughly humane. He takes as much interest in the most humble of his actors as he does in the highest. He has lived in courts: the Saint-Andrés, the Saint-Vladimirs have no prestige for him—nor the gilded uniforms; he is not deceived by appearances. His aim is so high that whatever he sees is, in one sense, unsatisfactory. He looks for moral perfection, and there is nothing perfect. He is always disappointed in the end. The final impression of his work is a sort of despair. . . .

[A] fundamental idea of fatalism pervades the book. Fate governs empires as well as men: it plays with a Napoleon and an Alexander as it does with a private in the ranks; it hangs over all the world like a dark cloud, rent at times by lighting. We live in the night, like shadows; we are lost on the shore of an eternal Styx; we do not know whence we came or whither we go. Millions of men, led by a senseless man, go from west to east, killing, murdering, and burning, and it is called the invasion of Russia. Two thousand years before, millions of other men came from east to west, plundering, killing, and burning, and it was called the invasion of the barbarians. What becomes of the human will, of the proud *I*, in these dreadful events? We see the folly and the vanity of self-will in these great historical events; but it is just the same in all times, and the will gets lost in peace as well as in war, for there is no real peace, and the human wills are constantly devouring each other. . . . We are made to enjoy a little, to suffer much, and, when the end is approaching, we are all like one of Tolstoi's heroes, on the day of Borodino. . . .

[Tolstoi's book] is by far the most remarkable work of imagination that has been lately revealed to us. (p. 71)

> *"Tolstoi's 'Peace and War'," in* The Nation *(copyright 1885 The Nation magazine, The Nation Associates, Inc.), Vol. 40, No. 1021, January 22, 1885, pp. 70-1.*

THE NATION (essay date 1885)

'Anna Karénine' is purely a novel, and a Russian novel. But it is not a novel in the ordinary sense of the word; there is, so to speak, no story. It is not the development of a certain plot, with a beginning, a middle, and an end; it is rather a succession of pictures, of scenes, some of which seem hardly to have any connection with the principal scenes. Such is Tolstoi's manner, so far as he has a manner. He paints life such as it is, sometimes solemn and sometimes dull; tragical and commonplace—light and shadow constantly intermingled. His actors are numerous, their name is legion. The heroes and heroines are not always alone on the stage: they are constantly drawn among people who care nothing or who care little for their passions, their preoccupations. They move in a real atmosphere of dullness, of banality, of vulgarity, of levity, of indifference. It would seem as if the interest we took in them would be diminished by this juxtaposition or interposition; it is not so. On the contrary, the contrast between the tragical elements of life and the comical or dull elements increases our interest. Tolstoi shows us life as it really is, with its complexities, its necessary tedium, its frivolities. He does not deceive us: his finest characters have their weak points; he knows that perfection is not human. It would be an impossible task to give a suitable account of 'Anna Karénine,' considered as a novel. We must go a little beneath the surface, and try to find out if Tolstoi had an object in this extraordinary delineation of human life. He does not belong to the school of writers who let you know at once what their aim is, and where they are leading you; still, it seems as if he had been thinking of contrasting love, considered in its domestic aspects—legal love, if I may say so—observed in the family life, under common, ordinary, provincial circumstances; and love, as an uncontrollable passion—wild, lawless, destructive of the family affections and ties, of all social rules. (p. 112)

"Tolstoi's New Novel," in The Nation *(copyright 1885* The Nation *magazine, The Nation Associates, Inc.), Vol. 41, No. 1049, August 6, 1885, pp. 112-13.*

WILLIAM MORTON PAYNE (essay date 1886)

"Anna Karénina" (1875-1877) was first published in a Russian review. It is the most mature and probably the greatest of the products of its author's imagination. Unlike "War and Peace" it is purely domestic in its subject matter, but there is no lack of variety in its scenes and characters. It is, indeed, a world in itself, so comprehensive is its grasp, and so intimately does it bring us into relations with the manifold aspects of country and city life in Russia. Were this work the sole available document, it would be possible to construct from its pages a great deal of Russian contemporary civilization. It is, of course, realistic to the last degree. But its realism is not confined to minute descriptions of material objects, and is no less made use of in the treatment of emotion. There are few works of art in which the art is so well concealed; few works of fiction which give so strong a sense of reality as this. We seem to look upon life itself and forget the medium of the novelist's imagination through which we really view it. And right here we are brought to compare the methods of Tolstoï with those of his better known and unquestionably greater countryman, Tourguénieff. . . .

The work of Tourguénieff surpasses the work of Tolstoï, in revealing that final sublimation of thought and imagination which give to it an artistic value beyond that of almost any other imaginative prose. Tolstoï lacks this power of concentration and this unerring judgment in the choice of word or phrase. He cannot sum up a situation in a single pregnant sentence, but he can present it with great force in a chapter. Now that this story of "Anna Karénina" has been brought to the cognizance of the western world, it is not likely to be soon forgotten. It will be remembered for its minute and unstrained descriptions, for its deep tragedy, unfolded act after act as by the hand of fate, and for its undercurrent of gentle religious feeling, never falling to the offensive level of dogmatism, yet giving a marked character to the book, and revealing unmistakably the spiritual lineaments of the Russian apostle of quietism. (pp. 13-14)

William Morton Payne, "Recent Fiction: 'Anna Karenina',' in The Dial *(copyright, 1886, by The Dial Publishing Company, Inc.), Vol. VII, No. 73, May 1886, pp. 13-14.**

A. P. CHEKHOV (essay date 1890)

I won't say ['The Kreutzer Sonata'] is a work of genius, or one that will last for ever, I am no judge of these matters, but in my opinion, among everything being written here and abroad, you will hardly find anything as powerful in seriousness of conception and beauty of execution. Without mentioning its artistic merits, which in places are outstanding one must thank the story if only for the one thing that it is extremely thought-provoking. As I read it I could hardly stop myself crying out: 'That's true!' or 'That's wrong!' Of course it does have some very annoying defects. . . . [There is one] point which one will not readily forgive its author, namely the brashness with which Tolstoy pontificates on things he does not know and out of stubbornness does not want to understand. Thus his pronouncements on syphillis, foundling hospitals, women's repugnance for copulation and so on are not only debatable but also show him to be a complete ignoramus who has never taken the trouble during the course of his long life to read a couple of books written by specialists. Still these defects fly off like feathers in the wind; considering the merits of the story you simply do not notice them, or, if you do, it is only annoying that the story did not avoid the fate of all works of man, all of which are imperfect and possess faults. . . . (pp. 395-96)

A. P. Chekhov, in his letter to A. N. Pleshcheer on February 15, 1890, in Tolstoy: The Critical Heritage, *edited by A. V. Knowles (copyright © 1978 by A. V. Knowles), Routledge & Kegan Paul, 1978, pp. 395-96.*

NIKOLAI N. STRAKHOV (essay date 1895)

Anna Karenina is a work which is not free of artistic imperfections, but which represents a high artistic achievement. In the first place, its subject is so simple and general that for a long time many people were not able to find it interesting and did not imagine that contemporaneity and instructiveness could be found in a novel. The story falls into two parts, or two layers, only loosely connected in their outer form, but having a close inner connection. The first concerns the urban, metropolitan life, and tells how Anna fell in love with Vronsky, formed a relationship with him and left her husband for him, but after living with Vronsky became so weary of passion that she threw herself beneath a railroad car. The second plane, which is more general and has greater basic significance, is the story of the country dweller Levin: it tells how he made a declaration of love, proposed, fasted and prepared himself for his wedding, married, how a son was born to him and at last started to recognize his parents.

The great originality of the author is displayed in the striking significance and interest which these everyday events acquire because of the depth and clarity with which he presents them. The general idea of the novel, although not always conceived with equal force, appears very clearly: the reader cannot escape from its inexpressibly grave impression, in spite of the absence of any gloomy characters and events, and in spite of the abundance of absolutely idyllic scenes. Not only does Anna come to suicide without any striking outward reasons or sufferings, but Levin, who is blessed in everything and who leads such a normal life, also feels the inclination towards suicide at the end, and saves himself from it only with the religious thoughts suddenly awakened in him when a muzhik [a Russian peasant] tells him that it is necessary to remember God and to live for one's soul. (p. 794)

Levin finds salvation in religious thoughts, but Anna, who belongs to the artificial, upper strata of society, in spite of all her suffering, does not for one minute come to her senses and does not even know where to turn for salvation. This absence of all serious concepts in the so-called educated people, the absence of all that is called moral, is portrayed with great mastery in the picture of higher society. The whole novel is a representation of the general spiritual chaos reigning in all layers of society, except the very lowest. (p. 798)

> *Nikolai N. Strakhov, "Levin and Social Chaos" (1895), translated by Zoreslava Kushner, in "Anna Karenina" by Leo Tolstoy: The Maude Translation, Backgrounds and Sources, Essays in Criticism, edited by George Gibian (reprinted by permission of W. W. Norton & Company, Inc.; copyright © 1970 by W. W. Norton & Company, Inc.), Norton, 1970, pp. 794-97.*

W. D. HOWELLS   (essay date 1895)

Tolstoy awakens in his reader the will to be a man; not effectively, not spectacularly, but simply, really. He leads you back to the only true ideal, away from that false standard of the gentleman, to the Man who sought not to be distinguished from other men, but identified with them, to that Presence in which the finest gentleman shows his alloy of vanity, and the greatest genius shrinks to the measure of his miserable egotism. I learned from Tolstoy to try character and motive by no other test, and though I am perpetually false to that sublime ideal myself, still the ideal remains with me, to make me ashamed that I am not true to it. Tolstoy gave me heart to hope that the world may yet be made over in the image of Him who died for it, when all Caesar's things shall be finally rendered unto Caesar, and men shall come into their own, into the right to labor and the right to enjoy the fruits of their labor, each one master of himself and servant to every other. He taught me to see life not as a chase of a forever impossible personal happiness, but as a

field for endeavor toward the happiness of the whole human family; and I can never lose this vision, however I close my eyes, and strive to see my own interest as the highest good. He gave me new criterions, new principles, which after all, were those that are taught us in our earliest childhood, before we have come to the evil wisdom of the world. As I read his different ethical books, *What to Do, My Confession,* and *My Religion,* I recognized their truth with a rapture such as I have known in no other reading, and I rendered them my allegiance, heart and soul, with whatever sickness of the one and despair of the other. (pp. 250-52)

I have spoken first of the ethical works of Tolstoy, because they are of the first importance to me, but I think that his aesthetical works are as perfect. To my thinking they transcend in truth, which is the highest beauty, all other works of fiction that have been written, and I believe that they do this because they obey the law of the author's own life. His conscience is one ethically and one aesthetically; with his will to be true to himself he cannot be false to his knowledge of others. I thought the last word in literary art had been said to me by the novels of Tourguenief, but it seemed like the first, merely, when I began to acquaint myself with the simpler method of Tolstoy. (pp. 252-53)

His didactic stories, like all stories of the sort, dwindle into allegories; perhaps they do their work the better for this, with the simple intelligences they address; but I think that where Tolstoy becomes impatient of his office of artist, and prefers to be directly a teacher, he robs himself of more than half his strength with those he can move only through the realization of themselves in others. The simple pathos, and the apparent indirectness of such a tale as that of *Policoushka,* the peasant conscript, is of vastly more value to the world at large than all his parables; and *The Death of Ivan Ilyitch,* the Philistine worldling, will turn the hearts of many more from the love of the world than such pale fables of the early Christian life as *Work while ye have the Light.* A man's gifts are not given him for nothing, and the man who has the great gift of dramatic fiction has no right to cast it away or to let it rust out in disuse.

Terrible as the *Kreutzer Sonata* was, it had a moral effect dramatically which it lost altogether when the author descended to exegesis, and applied to marriage the lesson of one evil marriage. In fine, Tolstoy is certainly not to be held up as infallible. He is very distinctly fallible, but I think his life is not less instructive because in certain things it seems a failure. There was but one life ever lived upon the earth which was without failure, and that was Christ's, whose erring and stumbling follower Tolstoy is. There is no other example, no other ideal, and the chief use of Tolstoy is to enforce this fact in our age, after nineteen centuries of hopeless endeavor to substitute ceremony for character, and the creed for the life. I recognize the truth of this without pretending to have been changed in anything but my point of view of it. What I feel sure is that I can never look at life in the mean and sordid way that I did before I read Tolstoy. (pp. 256-57)

> *W. D. Howells, "Tolstoy," in his My Literary Passions (copyright © 1895 by William D. Howells), Harper, 1895, pp. 250-58.*

CONSTANCE GARNETT and EDWARD GARNETT (essay date 1901)

In looking at the countless ranks of writers to-day, writers of every degree, of genius, of talent, of excellence, of mediocrity, and at the ever-thronging crowd of imitators following close behind them, we see that here and there a writer stands out, whom men of different nations with one voice hail as a great figure of the age. (p. 504)

Leo Tolstoy is one of these giants among writers, to whom future ages will turn for their interpretation of nineteenth century Europe. The greatest novelist, perhaps, of his age, he will, one ventures to think, be studied not so much for the strength and beauty of his great art, as for the challenge flung at modernity by his creed and his spirit, making his life-work of greater significance to humanity than that of any of the great European artists since Byron's day. Tolstoy's development is well-known. The novelist, of whom the great artist Turgenieff said: "He is the greatest of contemporary novelists; Europe does not contain his equal;" the creator, whose analysis of the human soul, in every relation to life, shows a vaster range and deeper insight than is to be found in the work of any nineteenth century writer; the author, whose "War and Peace" and "Anna Karénina" sum up and typify the life of all classes of modern Russia; this man was brought to abandon this art, announcing that his old theory of life was meaningless, asserting that he had slowly gained a new perception of truth—the truth of Christ's Christianity—and he gave as his watchword, "The Kingdom of Heaven is within You." (pp. 504-05)

Polite society in Russia has tersely set Tolstoy down as mad. Statesmen, politicians, priests, military men, philosophers, and members of the learned professions generally have, with Turgenieff, looked on Tolstoy's philosophy as "mystical, childish and uncompromising," and as the ruin of his art. (p. 505)

Of late years, however, partly through Tolstoy's action in the Russian famine, and especially through the publication of his last work, "Resurrection," a certain number of men have come to ask themselves whether this educated European opinion in condemning Tolstoy and Tolstoyism was using science truly to determine what the appearance of Tolstoyism indicates, and what its value, what its significance, actually is in the development of the Russian soul. If Tolstoy's special value to humanity can be shown to turn on his life-creed's being a challenge to modernity, then the cultured and educated opinion that has condemned his action and his gospel may be said to have shown great blindness of understanding. (pp. 505-06)

Even if Tolstoy's teaching could be defined as a decadent force, and traced to fatalism and passivity springing from the old roots of Russian serfdom still in the soil, its appearance should, for the critic, be as significant, as to the healthy state of the community, as the breaking out of old ulcers is as to the health of a man's body. But, with few exceptions, the "world of culture" has preferred to see in Tolstoy's teaching simply the mystical aberrations of a great genius. So much for the perspicuity of latter-day "science!" (p. 507)

[The] whole tendency of Tolstoy's novels and tales is ethical; and, though the artist is always strong enough to state life impartially, the reader always feels that, behind these pictures of life, there is the author with his secret goal, faith in God, in goodness, in love of one's fellow-men. Thus, in "Anna Karénina" Levin's search for a moral basis for joy

and satisfaction in life is the secret standard against which most of the characters—Anna, Vronsky, Stepan, Kitty, Dolly—are measured, defined, adjudged; in "War and Peace" again, the whole marvellous analysis of modern war —war as a great, hypnotizing force, generated by fraud, vanity, vainglory, destructive of man's moral instincts, debauching the masses by the contagion of its cruel senselessness and far-reaching depravities—is really inspired by Tolstoy's central thought, Why is all this evil delirium and lust of cruelty, this senseless brutality, *glorified* by mankind?

"The Cossacks" enforces Tolstoy's favorite theme of the superiority of the simple, rude life of the peasant, or Cossack, over the cultured, artificial, complex outlook of the upper-class officer. "Childhood, Boyhood and Youth" is the most remorseless scrutiny of the affectation and self-consciousness of youth and youth's sentimentalism; and, already in this early book, the author is seeking the why and wherefore of life, seeking what can be found worthy under all these veils of illusions and worldly pretences. In "The Death of Ivan Ilyitch" we find again an extraordinarily acute analysis of the life of worldly success, and of the artificiality of the cultured, upper-class conception of life. "Family Happiness," with its presentation of the poetic glamor of romantic love, is as a half-way house of disillusionment on the road to Tolstoy's ascetic ideal of sexual relations, an ideal which we find, years afterward, developed into the absolute asceticism of the "Kreutzer Sonata." (pp. 507-08)

The chief difference between the Tolstoy of 1875 and the Tolstoy of 1895 is not that they are working toward a different goal, but that the latter alone thinks it his duty to tell all men the necessity of trying to reach it. The world, indeed, would like to see Tolstoy keep at the same stage as we see Levin is kept at in "Anna Karénina"—seeking the truth, but sceptical as to the use of teaching it to others. But the critics do not explain to us how it was possible that so great a hatred of war as Tolstoy's, so great a zeal for honesty and simplicity of life, so burning a desire for brotherliness and charity among all men, could find perpetual expression in the artist's mere joy in the representation of life as a spectacle. If we once grant that "Anna Karénina" and "War and Peace" owe their force and grandeur to the keenness of the moralist's vision, examining critically the great panorama of life moving inevitably onwards, then in Tolstoy's further development, either the moralist must have died down—in which case we cannot conceive what his art would have become—or else the moralist must have striven to apply his creed to actual life, finding pure contemplation of life, apart from this idea, less and less satisfactory. (pp. 508-09)

For ourselves, we see Tolstoy's ideas, life and work as forming a continuous, though irregular, advance down a series of commanding slopes, leaving behind the high vantage grounds of art, but finally reaching his destination in the vast plain stretching beneath, the common ground of the brotherhood of men. And it is our contention that "Resurrection" both demonstrates and vindicates the inner necessity of his life's final phase—as a great moral teacher. (p. 509)

Constance Garnett and Edward Garnett, "Tolstoy and 'Resurrection'," in The North American Review *(copyright © 1901 by the University of*

Northern Iowa), Vol. 172, No. 4, April, 1901, pp. 504-19.

G. K. CHESTERTON (essay date 1903)

["Tales from Tolstoy"] is calculated to draw particular attention to [the] ethical and ascetic side of Tolstoy's work. In one sense, and that the deepest sense, the work of Tolstoy is, of course, a genuine and noble appeal to simplicity. The narrow notion that an artist may not teach is pretty well exploded by now. But the truth of the matter is, that an artist teaches far more by his mere background and properties, his landscape, his costume, his idiom and technique—all the part of his work, in short, of which he is probably entirely unconscious, than by the elaborate and pompous moral dicta which he fondly imagines to be his opinions. The real distinction between the ethics of high art and the ethics of manufactured and didactic art lies in the simple fact that the bad fable has a moral, while the good fable is a moral. And the real moral of Tolstoy comes out constantly in these stories, the great moral which lies at the heart of all his work, of which he is probably unconscis, and of which it is quite likely that he would vehemently disapprove. The curious cold white light of morning that shines over all the tales, the folklore simplicity with which "a man or a woman" are spoken of without further identification, the love—one might almost say the lust for the qualities of brute materials, the hardness of wood, and the softness of mud, the ingrained belief in a certain ancient kindliness sitting beside the very cradle of the race of man —these influences are truly moral. When we put beside them the trumpeting and tearing nonsense of the didactic Tolstoy, screaming for an obscene purity, shouting for an inhuman peace, hacking up human life into small sins with a chopper, sneering at men, women, and children out of respect to humanity, combining in one chaos of contradictions an unmanly Puritan and an uncivilised prig, then, indeed, we scarcely know whither Tolstoy has vanished. We know not what to do with this small and noisy moralist who is inhabiting one corner of a great and good man.

It is difficult in every case to reconcile Tolstoy the great artist with Tolstoy the almost venomous reformer. It is difficult to believe that a man who draws in such noble outlines the dignity of the daily life of humanity regards as evil that divine act of procreation by which that dignity is renewed from age to age. It is difficult to beieve that a man who has painted with so frightful an honesty the heart-rending emptiness of the life of the poor can really grudge them every one of their pitiful pleasures, from courtship to tobacco. It is difficult to believe that a poet in prose who has so powerfully exhibited the earthborn air of man, the essential kinship of a human being, with the landscape in which he lives, can deny so elemental a virtue as that which attaches a man to his own ancestors and his own land. It is difficult to believe that the man who feels so poignantly the detestable insolence of oppression would not actually, if he had the chance, lay the oppressor flat with his fist. All, however, arises from the search after a false simplicity, the aim of being, if I may so express it, more natural than it is natural to be. (pp. 130-33)

> _G. K. Chesterton, "Tolstoy and The Cult of Simplicity" (1903), in his_ Varied Types _(reprinted by permission of the Estate of G. K. Chesterton), Dodd, Mead and Company, 1921, pp. 125-46._

V. I. LENIN (essay date 1908)

[The] contradictions in Tolstoy's works, views, teachings and school are glaring indeed. On the one hand we have the brilliant artist who has produced not only incomparable pictures of Russian life but also first-class works of world literature. On the other hand we have a country squire acting the fool in Christ. On the one hand we have a remarkably powerful, direct and sincere protest against social lies and falsehood, while on the other we have the "Tolstoyan," _i.e.,_ the washed-out, hysterical cry-baby known as the Russian intellectual, who publicly beats his breast and cries: "I am vile, I am wretched, but I am morally perfecting myself; I do not eat meat any more and now feed only on rice patties." On the one hand we have a ruthless criticism of capitalist exploitation, an exposure of the violence of the government, the farce of the courts and of the government administration, a revelation of the full profundity of the contradictions between increasing wealth and the achievements of civilisation and the increasing poverty, brutalisation and suffering of the working class masses; and on the other hand we have the fanatical preaching of "non-resistance to evil." On the one hand we have the most sober realism and the tearing away of all masks, while on the other hand we have the preaching of one of the most abominable things on earth—religion, the endeavour to replace priests officially appointed by priests who are priests by moral conviction, _i.e.,_ the cultivation of the most subtle, and therefore particularly disgusting, clericalism. (p. 682)

That in view of such contradictions Tolstoy was absolutely incapable of comprehending either the working class movement and its role in the struggle for Socialism or the Russian revolution, goes without saying. But the contradictions in Tolstoy's views and preachings are not fortuitous; they are an expression of the contradictions in the conditions of Russian life during the last third of the nineteenth century. The patriarchal village, which had only just been emancipated from serfdom, was literally delivered over to capital and the treasury to be despoiled and plundered. The old pillars of peasant economy and peasant life, pillars that had actually stood for centuries, were razed to the ground with unusual rapidity. And the contradictions in Tolstoy's views must be judged not from the standpoint of the modern working class movement and modern Socialism (such a judgment is of course necessary, but it is not enough), but rather from the standpoint of the protest that was bound to be raised by the patriarchal Russian village against the onmarch of capitalism, against the impoverishment of the masses and their loss of land. Tolstoy is ridiculous as a prophet who has discovered new recipes for the salvation of mankind—and therefore the foreign and Russian "Tolstoyans" who desire to transform what is actually the weakest aspect of his teaching into a dogma are absolutely contemptible. Tolstoy is great when he expressed the ideas and sentiments which were engendered in millions of Russian peasants at the time the bourgeois revolution began in Russia. Tolstoy is original because the ensemble of his views, which are harmful as a whole, expresses just the peculiarities that mark our revolution as a _peasant_ bourgeois revolution. From this standpoint the contradictions in Tolstoy's views are really a mirror of those contradictory conditions in which the historical activity of the peasantry was placed in our revolution. (pp. 682-83)

> _V. I. Lenin, "Leo Tolstoy As a Mirror of the Russian Revolution" (1908), in his_ Selected Works,

Vol. XI *(copyright, 1943, by International Publishers Co., Inc.), International Publishers, 1943, pp. 681-86.*

ASHLEY DUKES   (essay date 1911)

Of all the naturalists, Tolstoy conforms most nearly to the naturalistic ideal in his plays. There can be no doubt that this ideal was connected in the minds of its earlier followers with the decivilisation of art. The revolt against pseudo-romanticism drove them to represent the actual, and the revolt against upper-class drama led them to seek inspiration among the common people. . . . Tolstoy was able, as a Russian, to carry the naturalistic conception to its logical extreme. In his "Power of Darkness" . . . he portrayed what was to all intents and purposes a state of barbarism; a group of peasants, remote and primitive, unfamiliar to the rest of Europe, and yet monotonous; the whole picture relieved only by a certain crude individual power. "The Power of Darkness" has often been quoted as the masterpiece of naturalism. That it may be; but it is not a masterpiece of drama. It has a certain grand barbaric simplicity, and that is all. With Tolstoy's other play, "The Fruits of Culture," it was submerged by the coming of Ibsen, who gave to realism the note of distinction and differentiation which the drama of the Russian peasantry could never provide. It need hardly be said that the author of "Anna Karenina" proves himself to be a great creator of individual types in both of these plays, but what Europe awaited from drama at the time of the Théâtre Libre was not merely character-drawing, but direction. Ibsen showed the way, and Tolstoy was left far behind. With the passing of each year "The Power of Darkness" and "The Fruits of Culture" seem more remote; and this impression is the stronger when Tolstoy's own change of philosophy in his later years is taken into account. As far as Tolstoy the artist is concerned, the change no doubt represents a natural development rather than a conversion. He always believed in his peasantry, even though their simplicity of life should spell preference for squalor; their simplicity of thought, ingrained stupidity; their passions, primitive savagery and crimes of violence; their daily round, monotony relieved by superstition. He believed in their potentiality as a worldforce, and in the end he offered them a peasant gospel. His preoccupation with them was always at bottom ethical; in other words, he cared more for them as a mass of humanity than as a group of possibly unsocial, anarchical individuals. Unfortunately, as one writer has remarked, "it is easier to found an impossible religion than to write an 'Anna Karenina.'" And drama comes from the individual, not from the mass. (pp. 182-85)

Ashley Dukes, "Tolstoy and Gorky," in his Modern Dramatists *(reprinted by permission of the Estate of Ashley Dukes), Frank Palmer, 1911, pp. 181-90.**

JAMES HUNEKER   (essay date 1915)

Tolstoy the artist! When his vagaries are forgotten, when all his books are rags, when his very name shall be a vague memory, there will live the portrait of Anna Karenina. How dwarfted are his other achievements compared with the creation of this woman, and to create a living character is to be as the gods. Tolstoy has painted one of the three women in the fiction of the nineteenth century. If the roll-call of the century is ever sounded, these three women shall have endured "the drums and tramplings" of many conquests, and the contiguous dust of those fictional creatures not built for immortality. Balzac's Valérie Marneffe, the Emma Bovary of Flaubert, and the Russian's Anna Karenina are these daughters of earth—flesh and blood, tears and lust, and the pride of life that killeth. (p. 77)

How amateurish is the attitude of the Tolstoy disciple who cavils at his masterpieces. What is mere art compared to the message! And I say: what are all his vapourings and fatidical croonings on the tripod of pseudo-prophecy as compared to *Anna Karenina*? There is implicit drama, implicit morality in its noble pages, and a segment of the life of a nation in *War and Peace*. With preachers and saviours with quack nostrums the world is already well stocked. Great artists are rare. Every day a new religion is born somewhere—and it always finds followers. But art endures, it outlives dynasties, religions, divinities. It is with Tolstoy the artist we are enamoured. He may deliver his message of warning to a careless world—which only pricks up its ears when that message takes on questionable colour, as in the unpalatable *Kreutzer Sonata*. (Yes; that was eagerly devoured for its morbid eroticism.) We prefer the austerer Ibsen, who presents his men and women within the frame of the drama, absolutely without personal comment on *parti pris*—as before his decadence did Tolstoy in his novels. (pp. 78-9)

[With] Richard Wagner and Dostoïevsky, Tolstoy is one of the three most emotional temperaments of the nineteenth century. Unlike Ibsen or Nietzsche, he does not belong to the twentieth century; his religion, his social doctrines are atavistic, are of the past. Tolstoy is what the French call *un cérébral,* which, as Arthur Symons points out, is by no means a man of intellect. "*Un cérébral* is a man who feels through his brain, in whom emotion transforms itself into idea, rather than in whom idea is transformed by emotion." How well that phrase fits Tolstoy—the fever of the soul! He has had the fever of the soul, has subdued it, and his recital of his struggles makes breathless reading. They are depicted by an artist, an emotional artist, and, despite his protestations, by one who will die an artist and be remembered, not as the pontiff of a new dispensation, but as a great world artist. (p. 80)

James Huneker "Dostoïevsky and Tolstoy," in his Ivory Apes and Peacocks *(abridged by permission of Charles Scribner's Sons; copyright © 1915 Charles Scribner's Sons), Scribner's, 1915 (and reprinted by Charles Scribner's Sons, 1938, pp. 52-88).**

CLAYTON HAMILTON   (essay date 1920)

[Late in his life, Tolstoi] felt a strong impulse to express himself in the dramatic form; and, regardless of his lack of training in an unaccustomed craft, he wrote a few plays, of which the most ineresting is, perhaps, *The Living Corpse.* (p. 145)

The first important point to be observed is that the structure of *The Living Corpse* is utterly unconventional. It would appear that Count Tolstoi, at the outset of the twentieth century, was either ignorant or scornful of the trend which the dramaturgic art had taken throughout the three preceding generations. (p. 146)

Tolstoi was either ignorant of Ibsen or unimpressed by his laborious example. No effort has been made to pattern *The Living Corpse* in three acts or in four, with every moment revealing a logical relation to every other moment. Instead, the story is unfolded in a sequence of eleven episodes. Only two of these episodes happen in the same place, so that ten different stage-settings are required; and the author handles the category of time as freely as he handles the category of place. Undoubtedly this narrative method was employed because it seemed most natural to the mind of a novelist. He imagined his story in chapters, not in acts; and he set it forth in the form and order in which it had revealed itself to his imagination. (pp. 146-47)

The novelistic method of *The Living Corpse* is interesting from the outset because of its originality; and, as the play progresses, the spectator gradually realizes that the construction is not nearly so hap-hazard as it seems. The piece, in fact, is built like a huge pyramid. In the early episodes, the foundation is laid out upon a broad and ample base. Then, little by little, the superstructure is reared up, growing always narrower and sharper at the same time that it is growing higher, until at last the whole thing culminates in an acute point of dramatic agony.

The subject-matter of *The Living Corpse* is no less unconventional than the technical method. It was as long ago as 1893 that Ferdinand Brunetière made his famous empirical announcement that the essence of the drama was an assertion of the human will and that the most dramatic scenes were those in which opposing human wills were shown in conflict. Yet the hero of *The Living Corpse* may almost be described as a man without a will. He drifts through life along the line of least resistance, and never asserts himself at all. Any practical playwright of the eighteen-nineties would certainly have judged that the subject-matter of *The Living Corpse* was hopelessly undramatic; yet the undeniable fact remains that the play is intensely interesting in the theatre. (p. 148)

[As Count Tolstoi has treated the play], the characters are immeasurably more important than the plot. The accuracy of his observation, the intimacy of his analysis, the profundity of his sympathy, produce an impression of the immensity of life that is rarely to be met with in the modern theatre. Though *The Living Corpse,* according to the point of view, may or may not be regarded as a great play, there is no denying that it is a great work and that it was written by a great man. (p. 150)

Most modern Russian plays crowd an enormous canvas with a multitude of living figures, but are lacking in composition and design; but *The Power of Darkness* is patterned just as clearly as any play by Ibsen or by Dumas *fils.* . . . This piece reveals that unity of plot which is demanded by our western minds. It tells a single story with a cumulative intensity. No details are introduced which are extraneous to the essential pattern. A predestined climax is attained at the curtain-fall of the penultimate act; and the play closes with a logical catastrophe that might almost be described as a "happy ending." The piece is absorbing in its intellectual interest and overwhelming in its emotional appeal. (p. 151)

Nikita, the hero of this play, like Fedya, the hero of *The Living Corpse,* which was written nearly twenty years later than *The Power of Darkness,* is a man without a will. He drifts through life along the line of least resistance. He is

not deliberately vicious; yet he is impelled from crime to crime by influences that are stronger than himself. The germs of sin are fructified within his soul by the power of darkness. Before long, his tragic situation is akin to that of Macbeth, at that moment when he said, "I am in blood stepped in so far that, should I wade no more, returning were as tedious as go o'er." (p. 152)

This play is appallingly dramatic in the constantly increased intensity of its successive scenes. It is another *Macbeth,* composed in modern terms and reimagined in the mood of realism. The characters are terribly true; and the dialogue is impressively poignant. (p. 153)

> *Clayton Hamilton, "Two Plays by Count Leo Tolstoy," in his* Seen on the Stage *(copyright 1920 by Holt, Rinehart & Winston; reprinted by permission of Holt, Rinehart & Winston, Publishers), Holt, 1920, pp. 144-53.*

PERCY LUBBOCK (essay date 1921)

Of *War and Peace* it has never been suggested, I suppose, that Tolstoy here produced a model of perfect form. It is a panoramic vision of people and places, a huge expanse in which armies are marshalled; can one expect of such a book that it should be neatly composed? It is crowded with life, at whatever point we face it; intensely vivid, inexhaustibly stirring, the broad impression is made by the big prodigality of Tolstoy's invention. If a novel could really be as large as life, Tolstoy could easily fill it; his great masterful reach never seems near its limit; he is always ready to annex another and yet another tract of life, he is only restrained by the mere necessity of bringing a novel somewhere to an end. And then, too, this mighty command of spaces and masses is only half his power. He spreads further than any one else, but he also touches the detail of the scene, the single episode, the fine shade of character, with exquisite lightness and precision. Nobody surpasses, in some ways nobody approaches, the easy authority with which he handles the matter immediately before him at the moment, a roomful of people, the brilliance of youth, spring sunshine in a forest, a boy on a horse; whatever his shifting panorama brings into view, he makes of it an image of beauty and truth that is final, complete, unqualified. Before the profusion of *War and Peace* the question of its general form is scarcely raised. It is enough that such a world should have been pictured; it is idle to look for proportion and design in a book that contains a world.

But for this very reason, that there is so much in the book to distract attention from its form, it is particularly interesting to ask how it is made. (pp. 26-8)

If the total effect of his book is inconclusive, it is all lucidity and shapeliness in its parts. There is no faltering in his hold upon character; he never loses his way among the scores of men and women in the book; and in all the endless series of scenes and events there is not one which betrays a hesitating intention. The story rolls on and on, and it is long before the reader can begin to question its direction. . . . What is the subject of *War and Peace,* what is the novel *about?* There is no very ready answer; but if we are to discover what is wrong with the form, this is the question to press.

What is the story? There is first of all a succession of

phases in the lives of certain generations; youth that passes out into maturity, fortunes that meet and clash and re-form, hopes that flourish and wane and reappear in other lives, age that sinks and hands on the torch to youth again—such is the substance of the drama. The book, I take it, begins to grow out of the thought of the processional march of the generations, always changing, always renewed; its figures are sought and chosen for the clarity with which the drama is embodied in them. (pp. 28-9)

Youth and age, the flow and the ebb of the recurrent tide—this is the theme of Tolstoy's book. (p. 31)

Cutting across the big human motive I have indicated, there falls a second line of thought, and sometimes it is this, most clearly, that the author is following. Not the cycle of life everlasting, in which the rage of nations is an incident, a noise and an incursion from without—but the strife itself, the irrelevant uproar, becomes the motive of the fable. *War and Peace,* the drama of that ancient alternation, is now the subject out of which the form of the book is to grow. (pp. 31-2)

It is a mighty antinomy indeed, on a scale adapted to Tolstoy's giant imagination. With one hand he takes up the largest subject in the world, the story to which all other human stories are subordinate; and not content with this, in the other hand he produces the drama of a great historic collision, for which a scene is set with no less prodigious a gesture. And there is not a sign in the book to show that he knew what he was doing; apparently he was quite unconscious that he was writing two novels at once. (p. 32)

The long, slow, steady sweep of the story—the *first* story, as I call it—setting through the personal lives of a few young people, bringing them together, separating them, dimming their freshness, carrying them away from hopeful adventure to their appointed condition, where their part is only to transmit the gift of youth to others and to drop back while the adventure is repeated—this motive, in which the book opens and closes and to which it constantly returns, is broken into by the famous scenes of battle (by some of them, to be accurate, not by all), with the reverberation of imperial destinies, out of which Tolstoy makes a saga of his country's tempestuous past. (p. 34)

It is now the war, with the generals and the potentates in the forefront, that is the matter of the story. Alexander and Kutusov, Napoleon and Murat, become the chief actors, and between them the play is acted out. In this story the loves and ambitions of the young generation, which have hitherto been central, are relegated to the fringe; there are wide tracts in which they do not appear at all. Again and again Tolstoy forgets them entirely; he has discovered a fresh idea for the unification of this second book, a theory drummed into the reader with merciless iteration, desolating many a weary page. The meaning of the book—and it is extraordinary how Tolstoy's artistic sense deserts him in expounding it—lies in the relation between the man of destiny and the forces that he dreams he is directing; it is a high theme, but Tolstoy cannot leave it to make its own effect. (p. 35)

[The] cycle of the war and the peace, as distinguished from the cycle of youth and age, is broken and fragmentary. (p. 36)

In *War and Peace,* as it seems to me, the story suffers twice over for the imperfection of the form. It is damaged, in the first place, by the importation of another and an irrelevant story—damaged because it so loses the sharp and clear relief that it would have if it stood alone. Whether the story was to be the drama of youth and age, or the drama of war and peace, in either case it would have been imcomparably more impressive if *all* the great wealth of the material had been used for its purpose, all brought into one design. And furthermore, in either case again, the story is incomplete; neither of them is finished, neither of them is given its full development, for all the size of the book. (pp. 40-1)

[The] broad lines of Tolstoy's book have always seemed uncertain and confused. Neither his subject nor his method were fixed for him as he wrote; he ranged around his mountain of material, attacking it now here and now there, never deciding in his mind to what end he had amassed it. None of his various schemes is thus completed, none of them gets the full advantage of the profusion of life which he commands. At any moment great masses of that life are being wasted, turned to no account; and the result is not merely negative, for at any moment the wasted life, the stuff that is not being used, is dividing and weakening the effect of the picture created out of the rest. That so much remains, in spite of everything, gives the measure of Tolstoy's genius; *that* becomes the more extraordinary as the chaotic plan of his book is explored. He could work with such lordly neglect of his subject and yet he could produce such a book—it is surely as much as to say that Tolstoy's is the supreme genius among novelists. (p. 58)

> *Percy Lubbock, in his* The Craft of Fiction *(reprinted by permission of Jonathan Cape Ltd., on behalf of the Estate of Percy Lubbock), Jonathan Cape, 1921, 277 p.*

LAFCADIO HEARN (essay date 1922)

The wonderful art [of ''Resurrection''] is the analysis of the emotions of its characters, and the strange illustration which it affords of the possible result of a single selfish act, and of the tremendous difficulty in the way of repairing that act. There are several hundred figures in the story—real living figures—which must have been studies from life, and which are so very human that the reader forgets that he is reading about Russia. Characters are of the very same kind in every land. One cannot help thinking what a great dramatist Tolstoi might have been had he taken to that branch of literature. (pp. 305-06)

In calling your attention to this very terrible and wonderful book, however, it is my duty as a follower of Spencer, to tell you that some of its social theories will not bear scientific consideration. In this respect the work is certainly defective. It is not true, for example, that the practice of perfect brotherly love throughout all classes of society—the abolishing of prisons, the abolition of criminal law—it is not true that any of these things are possible in the present state of humanity. Everywhere throughout the book we meet doubtful and startling half-truths—for example, the statement that most of the unhappiness of life is caused by approaching men for motives of interest only, without sympathy and without love. If you can really love men and deal with them only in the loving spirit, the author tells us, you will not be unhappy; but if you mingle with men, and do not love them, if you do business with them without love, then the most frightful misfortunes will result. This sounds beautiful, and there is a good deal of truth in it, but by no means all the truth. The existing characters of men cannot be so changed, either by religious teaching or by education or law or by any other means, as to render such a policy of life even thinkable. And the book is full of utterances quite as remarkable and quite as illusive. But the defects which I have specified are after all, on the noble side; they do not really spoil the work in the least; and they make even men who cannot accept such teaching, who cannot help smiling at it, think in a generous way about matters which deserve the most careful consideration. (pp. 306-07)

> *Lafcadio Hearn, ''Note upon Tolstoi's 'Resurrection',''* in his Life and Literature, *edited by John Erskine, William Heinemann, 1922, pp. 300-07.*

BORIS EIKHENBAUM (essay date 1922)

The basic stance of the young Tolstoi is his rejection of romantic stereotypes in both style and genre. He does not think about plot and does not worry about the choice of a hero. The romantic story . . . with a central heroic figure, with peripetia of love creating a complex plot, with lyrical and conventional landscapes, fails to inspire him. He returns to the very simplest elements—''minuteness,'' elaboration of details, description and portrayal of people and things. In this respect, Tolstoi departs from the line of ''high'' art and at the very outset introduces a simplifying tendency into his creative work. Hence his intense self-observation and self-experimentation, his concern for the most direct transmission of sensations and his striving to free himself from every tradition. Characteristic in this regard is a passage from the diary: ''To people who look at things for the purpose of noting them down, things present themselves in a false light; I have experienced this with myself.'' Tolstoi examines himself and the world intently so as to convey the perception of the psychic life and of nature in new forms. It is natural, therefore, that the first formal problems he sets himself are problems of *description* and not of narration, problems of style and not of composition or genre.

In conjunction with this overall tendency of his poetics, the question of ''generalization'' arises. Tolstoi is not a narrator who links himself with his heroes in one way or another, but an outsider, a sharp-sighted observer and even an experimenter. His personal tone must be devoid of any emotional stress: he watches and reasons. Theoretical ''digressions'' become a necessary element of his poetics; its basic premises demand the deliberate, sharp rationality of tone. Generalization strengthens the position of the author as a detached observer—it provides the background for the details of the psychic life, which stand out paradoxically in their sharp minuteness. (p. 48)

The entire period before *War and Peace* is one not so much of attainment as of searching. In *Childhood* Tolstoi gives the impression of a practiced, finished writer, but only because he is still very careful and even timid here—he still needs to convince himself that he can write a ''good'' thing. It is typical, therefore, that precisely *after Childhood* there begins a period of études and experiments, a period of tormenting doubts and struggles. . . .

The idea for an autobiographical ''novel'' which would contain a description of four periods in life (*Childhood, Adoles-*cence, Youth *and* Young Manhood) is an organic outcome of Tolstoi's basic artistic tendencies. He does not contemplate any scheme of adventure, not even in the spirit of Dickens' *David Copperfield:* this should not be a ''life history,'' but something altogether different. Instead of linking novellas or events, Tolstoi will link separate scenes and impressions. He does not need a hero in the old sense of the word, because he does not have to string together a series of events. It is significant that the envisioned novel is to stop at the period of ''young manhood'' . . . ; Tolstoi does not worry at all about the end, as he needs only to have a certain perspective before him. The personality of the hero is drawn directly from self-observation, from the diaries; it is not a ''type,'' not even a personality, but the bearer of a generalization. Tolstoi uses the hero's perception to justify the minuteness of description. The personality of Nikolenka does not design the material of the novel, but rather the other way around—the material conditions the personality. It is characteristic, therefore, that Tolstoi begins to lose interest in his novel after *Childhood*, where Nikolenka is only a point which determines the lines of perception and where generalization and minuteness stand in equilibrium. In fact, Tolstoi does not really need the chronological progression of the novel, for he is not leading his hero anywhere and has nothing he wants to do with him. The necessity of directing more and more attention to the personality of the hero leads to a piling-up of generalizations. (p. 49)

After *Childhood* the ''autobiographical'' form itself virtually loses its meaning, because it commits the author to the centralization of his material, to its arrangement around the personality of the hero, which by no means corresponds to Tolstoi's artistic intentions. The concentration of psychological material around one personality is quite foreign to Tolstoi. *Childhood* proved not to be a part of a novel, but a finished thing, complete in itself. (p. 50)

> *Boris Eikhenbaum, ''The Style and Composition of 'Childhood''' (1922), in his* The Young Tolstoi, *translation edited by Gary Kern (copyright © 1972 by Ardis), Ardis, 1972, pp. 48-66.*

VIRGINIA WOOLF (essay date 1925)

[Tolstoi is the] greatest of all novelists—for what else can we call the author of *War and Peace*? Shall we find Tolstoi . . . alien, difficult, a foreigner? Is there some oddity in his angle of vision which, at any rate until we have become disciples and so lost our bearings, keeps us at arm's length in suspicion and bewilderment? From his first words we can be sure of one thing at any rate—here is a man who sees what we see, who proceeds, too, as we are accustomed to proceed, not from the inside outwards, but from the outside inwards. Here is a world in which the postman's knock is heard at eight o'clock, and people go to bed between ten and eleven. Here is a man, too, who is no savage, no child of nature; he is educated; he has had every sort of experience. He is one of those born aristocrats who have used their privileges to the full. He is metropolitan, not suburban. His senses, his intellect, are acute, powerful, and well nourished. There is something proud and superb in the attack of such a mind and such a body upon life. Nothing seems to escape him. Nothing glances off him unrecorded. Nobody, therefore, can so convey the excitement of sport, the beauty of horses, and all the fierce desirability of the world to the senses of a strong young man. Every twig, every feather sticks to his magnet. He notices the blue or red of a child's frock; the way a horse shifts its tail; the sound of a cough; the action of a man trying to put his hands into pockets that have been sewn up. And what his infallible eye reports of a cough or a trick of the hands his infallible brain refers to something hidden in the character so that we know his people, not only by the way they love and their views on politics and the immortality of the soul, but also by the way they sneeze and choke. Even in a translation we feel that we have been set on a mountain-top and had a telescope put into our hands. Everything is astonishingly clear and absolutely sharp. Then, suddenly, just as we are exulting, breathing deep, feeling at once braced and purified, some detail—perhaps the head of a man—comes at us out of the picture in an alarming way, as if extruded by the very intensity of its life. "Suddenly a strange thing happened to me: first I ceased to see what was around me; then his face seemed to vanish till only the eyes were left, shining over against mine; next the eyes seemed to be in my own head, and then all became confused—I could see nothing and was forced to shut my eyes, in order to break loose from the feeling of pleasure and fear which his gaze was producing in me...." Again and again we share Masha's feelings in *Family Happiness*. One shuts one's eyes to escape the feeling of pleasure and fear. Often it is pleasure that is uppermost. In this very story there are two descriptions, one of a girl walking in a garden at night with her lover, one of a newly married couple prancing down their drawing-room, which so convey the feeling of intense happiness that we shut the book to feel it better. But always there is an element of fear which makes us, like Masha, wish to escape from the gaze which Tolstoi fixes on us. Does it arise from the sense, which in real life might harass us, that such happiness as he describes is too intense to last, that we are on the edge of disaster? Or is it not that the very intensity of our pleasure is somehow questionable and forces us to ask, with Pozdnyshev in the *Kreutzer Sonata*, "But why live?" Life dominates Tolstoi as the soul dominates Dostoevsky. There is always at the centre of all the brilliant and flashing petals of the flower this scorpion, "Why live?" There is always at the centre of the book some Olenin, or Pierre, or Levin who gathers into himself all experience, turns the world round between his fingers, and never ceases to ask even as he enjoys it, what is the meaning of it, and what should be our aims. It is not the priest who shatters our desires most effectively; it is the man who has known them, and loved them himself. When he derides them, the world indeed turns to dust and ashes beneath our feet. Thus fear mingles with our pleasure, and of the three great Russian writers [Tchekov, Dostoevsky, and Tolstoi], it is Tolstoi who most enthralls us and most repels. (pp. 253-56)

> *Virginia Woolf, "The Russian Point of View," in her* The Common Reader *(copyright 1925 by Harcourt, Brace Jovanovich, Inc.; copyright 1953 by Leonard Woolf; reprinted by permission of the publisher), Harcourt, 1925, pp. 243-56.**

E. M. FORSTER (essay date 1927)

What about *War and Peace*? That is certainly great, that ... emphasizes the effects of time and the waxing and waning of a generation. Tolstoy ... has the courage to show us people getting old—the partial decay of Nicolay and Natasha is really more sinister than the complete decay of Constance and Sophia: more of our own youth seems to have perished in it. Then why is *War and Peace* not depressing? Probably because it has extended over space as well as over time, and the sense of space until it terrifies us is exhilarating, and leaves behind it an effect like music. After one has read *War and Peace* for a bit, great chords begin to sound, and we cannot say exactly what struck them. They do not arise from the story.... They do not come from the episodes nor yet from the characters. They come from the immense area of Russia, over which episodes and characters have been scattered, from the sum-total of bridges and frozen rivers, forests, roads, gardens, fields, which accumulate grandeur and sonority after we have passed them. Many novelists have the feeling for place.... Very few have the sense of space, and the possession of it ranks high in Tolstoy's divine equipment. Space is the lord of *War and Peace*, not time. (pp. 38-9)

> *E. M. Forster, "The Story," in his* Aspects of the Novel *(copyright 1927 by Harcourt Brace Jovanovich, Inc.; copyright 1955 by E. M. Forster; reprinted by permission of the publisher; in Canada by Edward Arnold Ltd. in connection with Kings College, Cambridge and The Society of Authors as the literary representatives of E. M. Forster's Estate), Harcourt, 1927, pp. 43-64.**

JOHN GALSWORTHY (essay date 1928)

In choosing a single novel to label with those words so dear to the confectioners of symposiums, "the greatest ever written," I would select "War and Peace." In it Tolstoi rides two themes, like a circus rider on his two piebald horses, and by a miracle reaches the stable door still mounted and still whole. The secret of his triumph lies in the sheer interest with which his creative energy has invested every passage. The book is six times as long as an ordinary novel, but it never flags, never wearies the reader; and the ground—of human interest and historical event, of social life and national life—covered in it is prodigious. A little, but not much, behind that masterwork comes "Anna Karenina." Also of stupendous length, this novel contains, in the old prince, in his daughter Kitty, in Stepan Arkadyevich, Vronsky, Levin, and Anna herself, six of Tolstoi's most striking characters. He never drew a better portrait than that of Stepan Arkadyevich—the perfect Russian man of the world.... The early parts of this great novel are the best, for I have never been convinced that Anna, in the circumstances shown, would have committed suicide. It is as if Tolstoi had drawn her for us with such color and solidity in the beginning that we cannot believe she is not in the end dismissed by him rather than by herself. Anna, in fact, is a warm pulsating person, with too much vitality to go out as she did. The finish strikes one as *voulu*, as if the creator had turned against his creature; and one forms the opinion that Tolstoi started on this book with the free hand of an unlimited sympathy and understanding, but during the years that passed before he finished it became subtly changed in his outlook over life, and ended in fact a preacher who had set out an artist.... With this reservation, "Anna Karenina" is a great study of Russian character and a great picture of Russian society—a picture that held good, with minor variations, up to the war....

The prime characteristic of Tolstoi as a novelist was certainly his unflinching sincerity, his resolute exposition of what seemed to him the truth at the moment. Remembering how he swung between the artist and the moralist we have in that trait at once his strength and his weakness. Frankly loyal, true to the vision and mood of the moment, he had a force that philosophic reflection lacks, together with its corollary—deficient balance. His native force is proved by the simple fact that, taking up again one of his stories after the lapse of many years, one will remember almost every paragraph. Dickens and Dumas are perhaps the only other writers who compare with him in this respect. (p. 218)

[The] Russia of Tolstoi's great novels, "War and Peace" and "Anna Karenina," is a Russia of the past, perhaps only the crust of that Russia of the past—now split and crumbled beyond repair. How fortunate we are, then, to have two such supreme pictures of the vanished fabric! (p. 219)

> *John Galsworthy, "Tolstoi As a Novelist," in* The Nation *(copyright 1928 The Nation magazine, The Nation Associates, Inc.), Vol. 127, No. 3296, September 5, 1928, pp. 218-19.*

STEFAN ZWEIG   (essay date 1928)

Were all artists like Tolstoy, we might readily come to believe that art is a simple matter; sincerity, a self-evident affair; imaginative writing, nothing more than a faithful account of reality, an effortless transcription. We might suppose that an author need merely possess (in Tolstoy's own words) "a negative quality, that of not being a liar." His writings have the self-sufficiency, the naïve naturalness of a landscape, they are as full of life and colour as nature itself. The mysterious powers of poetic frenzy, the fruitful ardours, the phosphorescent vision, the bold and often illogical fantasies, that are elemental in the creative artist, are to all appearance lacking in Tolstoy's epic work, and we fancy that he has no need of them. In his case, not a drunken demon, but a clear-sighted and perfectly sober man, has been at work, observing facts, recording them faithfully, and with perfect ease fashioning a replica of reality. (pp. 226-27)

War and Peace, which runs to two thousand pages, was written over and over again, seven times in all. Great chests were filled with the notes and references concerning this book.... We know that a writer of lyrics, such as Baudelaire, must polish every facet. Tolstoy, with the zeal of the artist who aims at perfection, was no less scrupulous in scouring and refining, in hammering and oiling and smoothing his prose.... But, as a crowning mercy, the toilsomeness of the process leaves no trace upon the finished product. Of our time, and yet transcending time, this prose which is the outcome of art that conceals art gives the impression of having always existed, of being self-created, ageless as nature. Nothing stamps it as belonging to any specific epoch. If one of his novels were to drop into your hands by chance, and you were to read it for the first time without knowing the name of the author, you would hesitate to guess in which decade or even in which century it had been penned. That is why I describe his writing as timeless. The folk-tales *Three Old Men* and *Does a Man want much Land?* might have been written, like the story of Ruth and the story of Job, a couple of thousand years before the invention of printing and when the alphabet was a

recent discovery. *The Death of Ivan Ilich* and *Polikoushka* and *Linen-Measurer* may belong to the nineteenth century or the twentieth or the thirtieth; for what finds expression here is not the contemporary mind as voiced by Stendhal and Rousseau and Dostoeffsky, but the primitive mind, which is changeless and perennial—the terrestrial pneuma, the primal sentiment, primal anxiety, primal sense of loneliness, felt by man brought face to face with the infinite. Perfect mastery frees itself from the trammels of time. Tolstoy never had to learn how to tell a tale, and he never lost the art. In this matter, his genius was of spontaneous growth. It could not wither, and could neither improve nor deteriorate. Take the descriptions of scenery in *The Cossacks*, written when the author was twenty-four, and compare them with the incomparably brilliant account of an Easter morning in *Resurrection*, penned when he was sixty, a storm-tossed generation later. Both of them are equally full of nature's direct and universal appeal, both are equally instinct with sensuous enjoyment.

For the very reason that his writing is thus perfected to a degree which lifts it above the realm of the individual and makes it timeless, we are scarcely aware of the personality of the artist in the work of art. We do not regard him as a writer of fiction; he is a master-recorder of realities. (pp. 229-30)

> *Stefan Zweig, "The Artist" (1928), in his* Adepts In Self-Portraiture, *translated by Eden and Cedar Paul (reprinted by permission of Williams Verlag AG, as agents for the Estate of Stefan Zweig), Cassell and Company Limited, 1952, pp. 226-43.*

AYLMER MAUDE   (essay date 1930)

Nothing can be simpler than most of the occurrences of 'War and Peace'. Everyday events of family life: conversations between brother and sister, or mother and daughter, separations and reunions, hunting, holiday festivities, dances, card-playing, and so forth, are all as lovingly shaped into artistic gems as is the battle of Borodino itself. Whatever the purpose of the book may be, its success depends not on that purpose but on what Tolstoy did under its influence, that is to say it depends on a highly artistic execution.

If Tolstoy succeeds in fixing our gaze on what occupied his soul it is because he had full command of his instrument—which was art. Not many readers probably are concerned about the thoughts that directed and animated the author, but all are impressed by his creation. Men of all camps—those who like as well as those who dislike his later works—unite in tribute to the extraordinary mastery shown in this remarkable production. It is a notable example of the irresistible and all-conquering power of art.

But such art does not arise of itself, nor can it exist apart from deep thought and deep feeling. What is it that strikes everyone in 'War and Peace'? It is its clearness of form and vividness of colour. It is as though one saw what is described and heard the sounds that are uttered. The author hardly speaks in his own person; he brings forward the characters and then allows them to speak, feel, and act; and they do it so that every movement is true and amazingly exact, in full accord with the character of those portrayed. It is as if we had to do with real people, and saw them more clearly than one can in real life. (pp. 225-26)

Similarly Tolstoy usually describes scenes or scenery only as reflected in the mind of one of his characters. He does not describe the oak that stood beside the road, or the moonlight night when neither Natasha nor Prince Andrew could sleep; but he describes the impressions the oak and the night made on Prince Andrew. The battles and historic events are usually described not by informing us of the author's conception of them, but by the impression they produce on the characters in the story.... Tolstoy nowhere appears behind the actors or draws events in the abstract; he shows them in the flesh and blood of those who supplied the material for the events.

In this respect the work is an artistic marvel. Tolstoy has seized not some separate traits but a whole living atmosphere, which varies around different individuals and different classes of society. (pp. 226-27)

The soul of man is depicted in 'War and Peace' with unparalleled reality. It is not life in the abstract that is shown, but creatures fully defined with all their limitations of place, time, and circumstance. For instance, we see how individuals *grow*. Natasha running into the drawing-room with her doll, in Book I, and Natasha entering the church, in Book IX, are really one and the same person at two different ages, and not merely two different ages attributed to a single person, such as one often encounters in fiction. The author has also shown us the intermediate stages of this development. In the same way Nicholas Rostov develops; Pierre from being a young man becomes a Moscow magnate; old Bolkonsky grows senile, and so forth. (p. 228)

In judging such a work one should tread with caution, but we think a Russian critic judged well when he said that the meaning of the book is best summed up in Tolstoy's own words: 'There is no greatness without simplicity, goodness and truth'. (pp. 231-32)

> *Aylmer Maude, in an excerpt from his* The Life of Tolstoy *(reprinted by permission of Oxford University Press), revised edition, Oxford University Press, London, 1930 (and reprinted in* Tolstoy: The Critical Heritage, *edited by A. V. Knowles, Routledge & Kegan Paul, 1978, pp. 225-32).*

A. E. (essay date 1938)

Tolstoi was an extraordinarily serious person. One gets the impression, perhaps wrongly, from his books that he could not play, that the child was dead in the man.... Tolstoi was not without humour or wit, but it was of the grimmest kind. Never does he play from sheer delight in being alive. When I read the volume [of] ... Tolstoi's writings on Art, I feel there is something fundamentally wrong because of that grim, unsmiling face which glowers at me all the time. Continually, as I read, I prostrate myself before a profound intelligence, and almost as continually do I find myself wondering at some incredible stupidity. It is doubtful whether any other man in the world could have secured publicity for the article on Shakespeare, whom he considers an insignificant writer, and the world worship which he receives Tolstoi regards as merely mass hallucination. Tolstoi had a power of concentration which was abnormal, but it was the concentration of one who seemed mentally short-sighted. He went too close to his subject, and, as I think, he saw it in wrong perspective. There is in what he writes the vividness and particularity of the man who looks closely at what

he sees, but his short-sightedness prevents him seeing objects bathed in light and air. Mountains are not appreciated with one's nose up to them, but at a distance where their grandeur can be seen. Tolstoi assures us of his sensitiveness to art and music and literature, and we believe him. In what way is he short-sighted? He sees everything from the moral angle.... To Tolstoi beauty was never its own excuse for being. It must toil and spin and, we might add, preach to justify its existence. Tolstoi was, first of all, a great novelist, perhaps the greatest of any; and, secondly, he was a preacher, and his criterion of art seems to be first, whether it tells its story well, and, secondly, whether it is a moral story, that is, his judgment of art and literature is conditioned psychologically by his own occupations. He makes great play with the definitions of beauty of the aesthetes and philosophers, and scoffs at those who regard beauty as a manifestation of spirit or Deity. (pp. 305-07)

We can agree with Tolstoi that the greatest art is religious, and when the spiritual element is lacking the art is inferior in substance. But I doubt the spirituality of Tolstoi even when he talks most about religion. Spirituality is the power of apprehending formless being or essence. When Wordsworth feels in Nature the sense of some being interfused with it, we think of his perception as spiritual. Tolstoi rarely gives us the impression of direct apprehension of anything spiritual. When he speaks scornfully about the philosophers to whom beauty is a manifestation of spirit, or when he shows a blindness to pure poetry in his criticism of Shakespeare, we feel that all he says comes from a lack of spirituality, and that feelings and moods which have moved humanity profoundly were incomprehensible to him.... Tolstoi's preaching leaves us cold, because somehow we feel this terrible old man is not in love with us. (p. 308)

I think Tolstoi wrong-headed, arrogant and blind in his criticism of art and literature; but a great genius, even in his aberrations, continually says things more profound than the man of mere talent who is always sane, and these profound things can be found in this which is perhaps the most wrong-headed of all Tolstoi's writing. I feel the distinction he makes is true when he says universal art arises when someone, having experienced a profound emotion, feels the necessity of transmitting it to others, while the art of the rich arises less from the artist's inner impulse than because wealthy people demand amusement and pay well for it, and there is much that is true in what he says about the counterfeits of art which are so created. Artists and literary men should brood on all that Tolstoi says about this. (pp. 308-09)

> *A. E., "Tolstoi," in his* The Living Torch, *edited by Monk Gibbon (reprinted with permission of Russell & Volkening, Inc., as agents for the author; in Canada by Colin Smythe Ltd, Gerrards Cross, Bucks, England; © 1938 by A.E.), Macmillan Publishing Co., Inc., 1938, pp. 305-09.*

THOMAS MANN (essay date 1939)

[Tolstoy] said of his early work *Childhood* and *Boyhood:* "Without false modesty, it is something like the Iliad." That is the merest statement of fact; only on exterior grounds does it fit still better the giant work of his maturity, *War and Peace*. It fits everything he wrote. The pure narrative power of his work is unequalled. Every contact with it, even when he wished no longer to be an artist, when he scorned and reviled art and only employed it as a means of communicating moral lessons; every contact with it, I say, rewards the talent that knows how to receive (for there is no other) with rich streams of power and refreshment, of creative primeval lustiness and health. Seldom did art work so much like nature; its immediate, natural power is only another manifestation of nature itself; and to read him again, to be played upon by the animal keenness of this eye, the sheer power of this creative attack, the entirely clear and true greatness, unclouded by any mysticism, of this epic, is to find one's way home, safe from every danger of affectation and morbid trifling; home to originality and health, to everything within us that is fundamental and sane. (p. 177)

But all that which later made [Tolstoy's] friends and admirers like Turgenyev weep, his denial of art and culture, his radical moralism, his highly questionable pose of prophet and confessor in his last period—all that begins much further back, it is quite wrong to imagine this process as something suddenly occurring in a crisis of conversion in later life, coincident with Tolstoy's old age. . . .

The course of Tolstoy's intellectual development had been present in the seed in *Childhood* and *Boyhood* and the psychology of Levin in *Anna Karenina* had marked out the path it would take.

So much is true, that Levin is Tolstoy, the real hero of the mighty novel, which is a glorious, indestructible signpost on the woeful Way of the Cross the poet was taking; a monument of an elemental and creative bear-strength, which was first heightened and then destroyed by the inner ferment of his subtilizing conscience and his fear of God. Yes, Levin is Tolstoy—almost altogether Tolstoy, this side Tolstoy the artist. To this character Tolstoy transferred not only the important facts and dates of his own life; his experiences as a farmer, his romance and betrothal (which are completely autobiographic), the sacred, beautiful, and awe-full experiences of the birth of his first child, and the death of his brother—which forms a pendant of equal and boundless significance—not only there but in his whole inner life, his crises of conscience, his groping after the whole duty of man and the meaning of life, his painful wrestling over the good life, which so decisively estranged him from the doings of urban society; his gnawing doubts about culture itself or that which his society called culture, doubts of all this brought him close to the anchorite and nihilist type. What Levin lacks of Tolstoy is only just that he is not a great artist besides. But to estimate *Anna Karenina* not only artistically but also humanly, the reader must saturate himself with the thesis that Constantin Levin himself wrote the novel. (p. 181)

What an extraordinary fellow he is, this surrogate of the author! . . . Strong and shy, defiant and dubious, with an intelligence of great anti-logical, natural, even helpless abundance, Levin is at bottom convinced that decency, uprightness, seriousness, and sincerity are possible only in singleness, in dumb isolation, each for himself; and that all social life turns him into a chatterer, a liar, and a fool. . . . Only life in the country is worthy of a man—though not the country life that the city man in sentimental relaxation finds "charming." (p. 185)

[Levin's] physical morality and conscientiousness is shaken to the depths by the experience of the physically transcendent and transparent mysteries of birth and death; and

all that the times teach him about organisms and their destruction, about the indestructibility of matter and the laws of conservation of energy, about evolution, and so forth, all that looks to him not only like utter ignorance of the whole problem of the meaning of life but also like a kind of thinking that makes it impossible for him to get the knowledge he needs. (p. 187)

So there is real humour in the fact that in *Anna Karenina* a simple little peasant shows the brooding man the way out of his despair. This little peasant teaches him, or recalls to his mind, something he has always known: true, he says, living for our physical well-being and in order to fill our bellies is natural and inborn and laid upon us all. But even so, it is not righteous or even important. What we have to do is to live for the "truth," "for our souls," "as God wills," for "the Good." . . . Knowledge of the good, asserts Levin, does not lie in the realm of reason; the good stands outside the scientific chain of cause and effect. The good is a miracle, because it is contrary to reason and yet everyone understands it. (pp. 187-88)

Levin is enchanted and soothed by this absurdly simple statement of the human being's supra-reasonable obligation to be good. In his joy he forgets that also that melancholy materialistic naturalistic science of the nineteenth century had, after all, as motive power, human striving for the good. He forgot that it was stern and bitter love of truth that made it deny meaning to life. . . . Art he does not need even to forget; he knows, it seems, nothing about it obviously thinking of it only as the society prattle of the "cultured". . . . Tolstoy knew art; he has suffered frightfully from and for it, achieved mightier things in it than the rest of us can hope to achieve. Perhaps it was just the violence of his artist personality that made him fail to see that knowledge of the good is just the opposite of a reason to deny art. (p. 188)

Thomas Mann, "Anna Karenina" (originally published as a preface to Anna Karenina *by Leo Tolstoy, Random House, 1939), in his* Essays of Three Decades, *translated by H. T. Lowe-Porter (copyright 1939 by Alfred A. Knopf, Inc.) Knopf, 1948, pp. 176-88.*

IVAN TURGENEV (essay date 1939)

I must admit that [*War and Peace*] strikes me as being positively bad, boring, and unsuccessful. Tolstoy left his bailiwick and all his defects thus came to light. All these little tricks, cleverly noticed and pretentiously presented, the petty psychological observations that, under the pretext of truth, he plucks out from under the armpits and other dark places of his heroes—how meager is all this on the broad canvas of a historical novel! And he places this unfortunate product higher than *The Cossacks*! So much the worse for him, if he says this sincerely. And how cold and dry all this is—how one feels the author's lack of imagination and naïvetée—how wearisomely a memory of the fleeting, the incidental, the unnecessary works on the reader. And what are these young ladies! Every one some sort of scrofulous, affected dame, No, this can not be; this is the way to fall, even with his talent.

Ivan Turgenev, "Comments on 'War and Peace'" (1939), translated by Virginia Van Wynen, in "War and Peace" *by Leo Tolstoy: The Maude*

Translation, Backgrounds and Sources, Essays in Criticism, *edited by George Gibian (reprinted by permission of W. W. Norton & Company, Inc.; copyright © 1966 by W. W. Norton & Company, Inc.), Norton, 1966, p. 1387.*

SEAN O'FAOLAIN (essay date 1940)

It may be an understatement to speak of Tolstoy's "War and Peace" as the greatest of all war books. It is certainly that; it may be the greatest novel, or one of a handful of the greatest novels, of all time. (p. 141)

Yet many readers of "War and Peace" say, "Yes, of course—a great book; but, my goodness, did it have to be so long? Was it necessary that it should be so long, seeing that it did not aim at this amazing, searching, clinical, symbolical subtlety of Proust?" In one word, that is the whole point and merit of Tolstoy; "War and Peace" is one of the best-planned books ever written. It is one of the very few long books of the world that could not easily have been shorter.

The whole conception of Tolstoy, if not one which, like Proust's, aimed at victory by slow and steady stealth, was one which aimed at victory by the width and spread of its attack. The conception was large and magnificent, as befitted a novel of action—or a novel, at any rate, which turned the searchlights on men in action. Tolstoy took life at the height of its magnificence. He took men at their healthiest in body and mind. He wrote in the open air, so to speak, where Proust, the asthmatic invalid wrote in a cork-lined chamber at night, with drawn blinds. But while Tolstoy's plan of attack could be outlined in a few broad and sweeping strokes, as in many an attack, it was the detail that counted: all the staff-work of the brains behind, the unbroken communications between the parts, the disposition of the units, and, above all, the author's general commissariat of ideas. But the simile betrays itself if it conveys any suggestion of mechanical planning and plotting. The individual characters are the chief detail.

And this is a thing which, incidentally, distinguishes Tolstoy from all the subjective novelists who succeeded him. For a novel is, inevitably, at once itself and its author: it is his personality, his innermost self, his nature recreated in terms of character, plot, idea, and so forth. The subjective novelists, like Proust and Joyce, are blatantly self-reproductive; Tolstoy, never. His individual characters all live and move in their own right.

The plan of the general attack is thus miraculously directed and controlled, while being at the same time something which each individual character seems to create by himself, for himself. It is this liberty and mobility of the individual inside a vast framework of idea which postulates a long book, as it is the consistency of the general conception which makes that long book a unity. (pp. 142-43)

Tolstoy wrote, as far as he could, in the definite tradition of the novel which permits its characters to speak for themselves. He added, like all the so-called "realists," an enormous amount to previous traditions. I do not say that he made any new discoveries about the nature of man—I do not believe in those books of criticism which hail modern literature as that sort of discovery: everything fundamental that may be said about man was said hundreds of years ago:

but Tolstoy did elaborate enormously, add new emphases, explore regions previously barely adumbrated. Like all the realist school of the last century, he dug out the gold which lies in the dark parts of the human mind, and which his predecessors had tended to refer to merely by the most vague and fastidious generalization, as something which was not gold but dross. Apart from the sex element he, and they, explored and refined all those dark regions: it remained only for our time to sublimate the unashamedly sensual, to find in horror not awe and mystical truth, as he did, but a new romanticism—to insist that there is poetry, even lyricism, in what was once thought obscene. (p. 148)

"War and Peace" takes us through the battle and brings us out to life at the other end. (p. 149)

Sean O'Faolain, "The Greatest of War Books," in The Yale Review *(© 1940 by Yale University; reprinted by permission of the editors), Vol. XXX, No. 1, September, 1940, pp. 141-49.*

JAMES T. FARRELL (essay date 1946)

Among the works of nineteenth-century Russian literature, *Anna Karenina* is focal. No other Russian novel of the entire century so concentrates the so-called Russian problem, images and represents it so vividly, so directly, so immediately in terms of direct, vigorously drawn, and humanly credible characterizations. The fact that it is set in the time of most intense change in Russia is significant in understanding the novel. The intensity of the change, the transitional character of the times, the fact that Levin, the most intelligent character in *Anna Karenina,* realizes that everything is upside down and just taking shape—all this helps us to understand the richness, the all-sidedness, the significance of this work.

The character Anna Karenina is not merely the wife of a high bureaucrat who falls in love with a rich army officer, leaves husband and child for her paramour, and, driven to despair, commits suicide. Nor is her story a mere tale of adultery. More than this, the novel is a presentation of the author's vision of humanity. When we consider the richness of detail, the fullness in the presentation of all the problems of Russia in the very narrative, in the very characterizations, it should be clear that there is a central importance in the fact that Anna's name serves for the title. Anna is the most representative figure in this novel. She is symbolic. She is Tolstoy's image of humanity. With the exception of some of the peasants in these crowded pages, we can observe a striking difference in Anna's motivations, and in those of every other important character. Her motivations come from inside herself, and are not seriously influenced by her role, her function in society. She acts in accordance with her inner nature, and she wants, above all else, to love and to be loved. We know from Tolstoy's entire literary output that he considered the need to love and to be loved fundamental in the character of the natural man and woman. Anna is, then, the most natural member of the upper classes to be found in this work. Her actions are inspired by her emotions. . . . Her tragedy is that of humanity seeking to express the full nature of its need to love and to be loved in material, sensory, sexual relationships; and this, it should be added, is sought amid a setting of luxury. (pp. 298-99)

Next to Anna, the other most important character in this

novel is Levin. It is striking to note in passing that these two do not meet until the latter portion of the narrative, but when they do, they immediately recognize each other's worth. Tolstoy's account of their meeting even suggests that, had they met under different circumstances, they could well have fallen in love.

Levin represents the landed nobility. In the city, he feels uncomfortable. He is often awkward, and is ill at ease even with intellectuals who are interested in the same problems as he is. . . . He needs to find a deeper meaning in life. Anna, in her way, seeks that deeper meaning in love. Levin, after a period of despair, discovers love. But unlike Anna's love, it is a spiritualized love, based on the example of Christ, and expressive of brotherhood for all men. In this respect Levin represents Tolstoy on the eve of the great religious change which occurred in the 1880's. He stands in contrapuntal relationship to Anna. Anna, as humanity, comes to a tragic end; Levin, the dissatisfied nobleman, grasps an image of humanity which permits him to go on living. In his period of despair he feared that he would destroy himself, and would not trust himself with a gun or a rope. Anna does destroy herself. When she can no longer love, she sees all of human life as motivated by hate.

These meanings can be brought out more clearly if *Anna Karenina* is related to *War and Peace.* Anna is a continuation of Natasha Rostov of the latter novel; she is like Natasha's older sister. In *War and Peace,* Natasha represents humanity, but as a girl becoming a woman. Natasha's motivations are similar to Anna's, and, like Anna's, different from those of most of the other aristocrats. Parallel to the similarity of Anna and Natasha, there is a correspondence between Pierre Bezuhov, the dissatisfied nobleman of *War and Peace,* and Levin. Neither of them can find occupation and meaning in life so long as they are motivated in terms of their class position and their social functions. They seek to discover humanity, and they find patriarchal peasants as models for this discovery. Unlike most of the other aristocrats in these novels, Pierre and Levin grow, develop in emotional depth. (pp. 301-02)

[The] conception of characters and events in *Anna Karenina* is based on the conception of history which Tolstoy formally stated at the end of *War and Peace.* The central problem treated is thus that of freedom, freedom and the self, or the personality. It is this same problem which concerns us at the present moment, in a further advanced period of our historical development; in fact, we can say we face this problem from the other side of progress. The satiety sometimes suggested when Anna and Vronsky are living in luxury has an almost contemporary ring. In like manner, many of the emotions of the characters of this novel seem almost contemporary. Russia at the dawn of its capitalist development and America at the peak of its development seem to reveal many parallels. This gives to *Anna Karenina* a strong contemporary appeal. (pp. 303-04)

Anna Karenina establishes [Tolstoy's] view in terms of the living images of human beings. Tolstoy's alternative, the so-called doctrine of Tolstoyism based on nonresistance and individual moral self-regeneration, has not, however, been historically successful. When we read him, then, we must do so not for some rigid solution but for insight. *Anna Karenina* brings us face to face with a great mind, a great artist, and a work of artistic greatness which is one of the true masterpieces of world literature. (p. 304)

James T. Farrell, "An Introduction to 'Anna Karenina'" (1946), in his Literature and Morality *(copyright © 1947, 1974, by James T. Farrell; reprinted by permission of the publisher, Vanguard Press, Inc.), Vanguard, 1947, pp. 296-304.*

GEORG LUKACS   (essay date 1950)

Tolstoy's oeuvre marks a step forward not only in Russian literature but in the literature of the world. This step forward was made, however, in rather peculiar circumstances. Although Tolstoy continued the great realistic traditions of the eighteenth and nineteenth centuries, the traditions of Fielding and Defoe, Balzac and Stendhal, he did so at a time when realism had already fallen into decay and the literary trends which were to sweep away realism had triumphed throughout Europe. Hence Tolstoy, in his literary work, had to swim against the current in world literature, and this current was the decline of realism.

But Tolstoy's position in world literature was unique for more reasons than this. It would be quite misleading to stress this divergence unduly and define Tolstoy's place in the literature of his age as though he had rejected all the literary trends and all the writers of his own time and had obstinately clung to the traditions of the great realists.

In the first place: what Tolstoy carried on was not the artistic and stylistic tradition bequeathed by the great realists. We do not wish to quote here Tolstoy's own judgments on the older and newer realists; these judgments are often contradictory and—like the judgments of most great writers—they vary a great deal according to the concrete requirements of each period of their work. What never varied, however, was Tolstoy's healthy—and angry—contempt of the petty naturalism of his own contemporaries. (p. 129)

The older great realists had no demonstrable immediate influence on Tolstoy's style. The principles he followed in his realism objectively represent a continuation of the great realist school, but subjectively they grew out of the problems of his own time and out of his attitude to the great problem of his time, the relationship between exploiter and exploited in rural Russia. Of course the study of the old realists had a considerable influence on the development of Tolstoy's style, but it would be wrong to attempt to derive the Tolstoian style of realism in art and literature in a straight line from the old great realists.

Although Tolstoy continued and developed the traditions of the older realism, he always did so in his own original way and in accordance with the needs of the age, never as an epigone. He was always in step with his time, not only in content, in the characters and social problems he presented, but also in the artistic sense. Hence there are many common traits in his literary method and that of his European contemporaries. But it is interesting and important to note in connection with this community of method that artistic traits which in Europe were the symptoms of the decline of realism and contributed to the dissolution of such literary forms as the drama, the novel and the short story, regained their vitality and originality in Tolstoy's hands and served as the elements of a nascent new form which, continuing the traditions of the old great realism in a novel manner and in relation to new problems, rose to heights unsurpassed by the realist literature of any nation. (pp. 129-30)

Tolstoy himself was well aware that his great novels were genuine epics. But it was not only he himself who compared *War and Peace* with Homer—many known and unknown readers of the book had the same feeling. Of course the comparison with Homer, while it shows the profound impression made by the truly epic quality of this novel, is more an indication of the general trend of its style than an actual characteristic of the style itself. For in spite of its epic sweep, *War and Peace* is still from first to last a true novel, although of course, not a novel with the dramatic concentration found in Balzac. Its loose, spacious composition, the cheerful, comfortable, leisurely relationships between the characters, the calm and yet animated abundance of the epic episodes indispensable to the true story-teller—all these are related more to the great provincial idylls of the eighteenth-century English novel than to Balzac. (p. 149)

Tolstoy's great novels differ from those of his English predecessors in the specific nature of the social reality which they mirror and are superior to their English parallels in artistic richness and depth precisely because of this specific character of the reality presented. The world depicted by Tolstoy is a world much less *bourgeois* than the world of the eighteenth-century English novelists, but—especially in *Anna Karenina*—it is a world in which the process of capitalist development is more strongly apparent than in the English novels which nearly always depict only one particular phase of it. (pp. 149-50)

Tolstoy's literary career began and ended in a period of approaching revolutionary storms. Tolstoy is a *pre-revolutionary* writer. And precisely because the central problem in his works was the Russian peasant problem, the decisive turning-point in the history of western literature, i.e. the defeat of the 1848 revolutions, left no traces on them. In this connection it matters little how far Tolstoy himself, in the various phases of his development, was aware or unaware of this cardinal issue. What is important is that this issue is at the core of all his works, that everything he wrote revolves around this issue; it is only for this reason that he still remained a pre-revolutionary writer even after the disaster of the European revolutions of 1848.

But the village idylls of Tolstoy's great novels are always threatened idylls. In *War and Peace* the financial disaster of the Rostov family is enacted before our eyes as the typical disaster of the old-fashioned provincial nobility; the spiritual crises of Bezukhov and Bolkonski are reflections of the great current which broadened politically into the Decembrist rising. In *Anna Karenina* even darker clouds menace the village idyll and the enemy has already openly shown its capitalist countenance. Now it is no longer a question of financial disaster alone—here one can already feel the undertow of capitalism, against which Tolstoy makes so passionate a protest.

Constantine Levin, who really takes up the problems where Nikolai Rostov left them in *War and Peace,* can no longer solve them as simply and light-heartedly. He fights not only to recover his material prosperity as a landowner (without falling a victim to the capitalisation of the land) but has to carry on an incessant inner struggle, a struggle moving from crisis to crisis in trying to convince himself that his existence as landowner is justified and that he has the right to exploit his peasants. The incomparable epic greatness of Tolstoy's novels is based on the illusions which caused him

to believe that this was not a tragic conflict out of which there was no way out for the honest representatives of the class, but a problem capable of solution.

In *Anna Karenina* these illusions were already shaken to a much greater extent than in *War and Peace*. This manifests itself among other things in the fact that the structure of *Anna Karenina* is much more 'European,' much more closely-knit and the unfolding of the story far less leisurely. The closer assimilation of the theme to those of the European novels of the nineteenth century is a further, even though external, indication of the approaching crisis; although the style of *Anna Karenina* still has the characteristics of Tolstoy's early period, certain traits of his later critical period are already showing themselves. *Anna Karenina* is far more novel-like than *War and Peace*.

In *The Kreutzer Sonata* Tolstoy takes another long step in the direction of the European novel. He creates for himself a great form of *novella* which resembles the perfected form produced by European realism and which is both broad and dramatically concentrated. He inclines more and more towards presenting the great catastrophes, the tragically-ending turning-points in human destinies by a detailed portrayal of all their manifold inner motives, i.e., in the most profound sense of the word, epically.

Thus Tolstoy approaches to some extent the form of composition used by Balzac. Not that Balzac had influenced his literary style; but the reality which they both experienced and the manner in which they experienced it drove both of them by an inner necessity to create such forms. *The Death of Ivan Ilyich* marks the culminating point of this later style of Tolstoy, but its effects can also be traced in his last great novel *Resurrection*. It is no accident that Tolstoy's dramatic works were also written in this period.

But the thematic assimilation to European literature does not mean artistic assimilation to the prevalent literary trends there, the very trends which broke up the artistic forms of the epic and the drama. On the contrary, to the end of his life Tolstoy remained, in all questions relating to art, a great realist of the old school, and a great creator of epic form. (pp. 150-51)

> *Georg Lukacs, "Tolstoy and the Development of Realism" (1950), in his* Studies in European Realism: A Sociological Survey of the Writings of Balzac, Stendhal, Zola, Tolstoy, Gorki and Others, *translated by Edith Bone (copyright © The Merlin Press; reprinted by permission), Merlin Press, 1972, pp. 126-205.*

ISAIAH BERLIN　(essay date 1953)

There is a line among the fragments of the Greek poet Archilochus which says: "The fox knows many things, but the hedgehog knows one big thing'. (p. 7)

The first kind of intellectual and artistic personality belongs to the hedgehogs, the second to the foxes; and without insisting on a rigid classification, we may, without too much fear of contradiction, say that, in this sense, Dante belongs to the first category, Shakespeare to the second; Plato, Lucretius, Pascal, Hegel, Dostoevsky, Nietzsche, Ibsen, Proust are, in varying degrees, hedgehogs; Herodotus, Aristotle, Montaigne, Erasmus, Molière, Goethe, Pushkin, Balzac, Joyce are foxes. (p. 8)

[When] we come to Count Lev Nikolaevich Tolstoy, and ask this of him—ask whether he belongs to the first category or the second, whether he is a monist or a pluralist, whether his vision is of one or of many, whether he is of a single substance or compounded of heterogeneous elements, there is no clear or immediate answer. The question does not, somehow, seem wholly appropriate; it seems to breed more darkness than it dispels. Yet it is not lack of information that makes us pause: Tolstoy has told us more about himself and his views and attitudes than any other Russian, more, almost, than any other European writer; nor can his art be called obscure in any normal sense: his universe has no dark corners, his stories are luminous with the light of day; he has explained them and himself, and argued about them and the methods by which they are constructed, more articulately and with greater force and sanity and lucidity than any other writer. Is he a fox or a hedgehog? What are we to say? Why is the answer so curiously difficult to find? Does he resemble Shakespeare or Pushkin more than Dante or Dostoevsky? Or is he wholly unlike either, and is the question therefore unanswerable because it is absurd? What is the mysterious obstacle with which our inquiry seems faced? (pp. 10-11)

The hypothesis I wish to offer is that Tolstoy was by nature a fox, but believed in being a hedgehog; that his gifts and achievement are one thing, and his beliefs, and consequently his interpretation of his own achievement, another; and that consequently his ideals have led him, and those whom his genius for persuasion has taken in, into a systematic misinterpretation of what he and others were doing or should be doing. No one can complain that he has left his readers in any doubt as to what he taught about this topic: his views on this subject permeate all his discursive writings—diaries, recorded *obiter dicta,* autobiographical essays and stories, social and religious tracts, literary criticism, letters to private and public correspondents. But the conflict between what he was and what he believed emerges nowhere so clearly as in his view of history to which some of his most brilliant and most paradoxical pages are devoted. (pp. 11-12)

Those who have treated Tolstoy primarily as a novelist have at times looked upon the historical and philosophical passages scattered through *War and Peace* as so much perverse interruption of the narrative, as a regrettable liability to irrelevant digression characteristic of this great, but excessively opinionated, writer, a lop-sided, homemade metaphysic of small or no intrinsic interest, deeply inartistic and thoroughly foreign to the purpose and structure of the work of art as a whole. (pp. 12-13)

Tolstoy's central thesis—in some respects not unlike the theory of the inevitable 'self-deception' of the *bourgeoisie* held by his contemporary Karl Marx, save that what Marx reserves for a class, Tolstoy sees in almost all mankind—is that there is a natural law whereby the lives of human beings no less than those of nature are determined; but that men, unable to face this inexorable process, seek to represent it as a succession of free choices, to fix responsibility for what occurs upon persons endowed by them with heroic virtues or heroic vices, and called by them 'great men'. What are great men? they are ordinary human beings, who are ignorant and vain enough to accept responsibility for the life of society, individuals who would rather take the blame for all the cruelties, injustices, disasters justified in

their name, than recognize their own insignificance and impotence in the cosmic flow which pursues its course irrespective of their wills and ideals. This is the central point of those passages (in which Tolstoy excelled) in which the actual course of events is described, side by side with the absurd, egocentric explanations which persons blown up with the sense of their own importance necessarily give to them; as well as of the wonderful descriptions of moments of illumination in which the truth about the human condition dawns upon those who have the humility to recognize their own unimportance and irrelevance. And this is the purpose, too, of those philosophical passages where, in language more ferocious than Spinoza's, but with intentions similar to his, the errors of the pseudo-sciences are exposed. (pp. 44-5)

In *War and Peace* Tolstoy treats facts cavalierly when it suits him, because he is above all obsessed by his thesis— the contrast between the universal and all-important but delusive experience of free will, the feeling of responsibility, the values of private life generally, on the one hand; and on the other, the reality of inexorable historical determinism, not, indeed, experienced directly, but known to be true on irrefutable theoretical grounds. This corresponds in its turn to a tormenting inner conflict, one of many, in Tolstoy himself, between the two systems of value, the public and the private. On the one hand, if those feelings and immediate experiences, upon which the ordinary values of private individuals and historians alike ultimately rest, are nothing but a vast illusion, this must, in the name of the truth, be ruthlessly demonstrated, and the values and the explanations which derive from the illusion exposed and discredited. And in a sense Tolstoy does try to do this, particularly when he is philosophizing, as in the great public scenes of the novel itself, the battle pieces, the descriptions of the movements of peoples, the metaphysical disquisitions. But, on the other hand, he also does the exact opposite of this when he contrasts with this panorama of public life the superior value of personal experience, the 'thoughts, knowledge, poetry, music, love, friendship, hates, passions' of which real life is compounded—when he contrasts the concrete and multi-coloured reality of individual lives with the pale abstractions of scientists or historians, particularly the latter, 'from Gibbon to Buckle', whom he denounces so harshly for mistaking their own empty categories for real facts. And yet the primacy of these private experiences and relationships and virtues presupposes that vision of life, with its sense of personal responsibility, and belief in freedom and possibility of spontaneous action, to which the best pages of *War and Peace* are devoted, and which is the very illusion to be exorcized, if the truth is to be faced.

This terrible dilemma is never finally resolved. Sometimes, as in the explanation of his intentions which he published before the final part of *War and Peace* had appeared, Tolstoy vacillates; the individual is 'in some sense' free when he alone is involved: thus, in raising his arm, he is free within physical limits. But once he is involved in relationships with others, he is no longer free, he is part of the inexorable stream. Freedom is real, but it is confined to trivial acts. At other times even this feeble ray of hope is extinguished: Tolstoy declares that he cannot admit even small exceptions to the universal law; causal determinism is either wholly pervasive or it is nothing, and chaos reigns. Men's acts may seem free of the social nexus, but they are not free, they cannot be free, they are part of it. Science cannot destroy the consciousness of freedom, without which there is no morality and no art, but it can refute it. 'Power' and 'accident' are but names of ignorance of the causal chains, but the chains exist whether we feel them or not; fortunately we do not; for if we felt their weight, we could scarcely act at all; the loss of illusion would paralyse the life which is lived on the basis of our happy ignorance. But all is well; for we never shall discover all the causal chains that operate: the number of such causes is infinitely great, the causes themselves infinitely small; historians select an absurdly small portion of them and attribute everything to this arbitrarily chosen tiny section. How would an ideal historical science operate? By using a kind of calculus whereby this 'differential', the infinitesimals—the infinitely small human and non-human actions and events—would be integrated, and in this way the continuum of history would no longer be distorted by being broken up into arbitrary segments. Tolstoy expresses this notion of calculation by infinitesimals with great lucidity, and with his habitual simple, vivid, precise use of words. (pp. 47-50)

It is not a mystical or an intuitionist view of life. Our ignorance of how things happen is not due to some inherent inaccessibility of the first causes, only to their multiplicity, the smallness of the ultimate units, and our own inability to see and hear and remember and record and co-ordinate enough of the available material. Omniscience is in principle possible even to empirical beings, but, of course, in practice unattainable. This alone, and nothing deeper or more interesting, is the source of human megalomania, of all our absurd delusions. Since we are not, in fact, free, but could not live without the conviction that we are, what are we to do? Tolstoy arrives at no clear conclusion, only at the view, in some respect like Burke's, that it is better to realize that we understand what goes on as we do in fact understand it—much as spontaneous, normal, simple people, uncorrupted by theories, not blinded by the dust raised by the scientific authorities, do, in fact, understand life—than to seek to subvert such common-sense beliefs, which at least have the merit of having been tested by long experience, in favour of pseudo-sciences, which, being founded on absurdly inadequate data, are only a snare and a delusion. That is his case against all forms of optimistic rationalism, the natural sciences, liberal theories of progress, German military *expertise,* French sociology, confident social engineering of all kinds. And this is his reason for inventing a Kutuzov who followed his simple, Russian, untutored instinct, and despised or ignored the German, French, and Italian experts; and for raising him to the status of a national hero which he has, partly as a result of Tolstoy's portrait, retained ever since. (pp. 50-1)

If we may recall once again our division of artists into foxes and hedgehogs: Tolstoy perceived reality in its multiplicity, as a collection of separate entities round and into which he saw with a clarity and penetration scarcely ever equalled, but he believed only in one vast, unitary whole. No author who has ever lived has shown such powers of insight into the variety of life—the differences, the contrasts, the collisions of persons and things and situations, each apprehended in its absolute uniqueness and conveyed with a degree of directness and a precision of concrete imagery to be found in no other writer. No one has ever excelled Tolstoy in expressing the specific flavour, the exact quality of a feeling—the degree of its 'oscillation', the ebb and flow, the

minute movements (which Turgenev mocked as a mere trick on his part)—the inner and outer texture and 'feel' of a look, a thought, a pang of sentiment, no less than that of the specific pattern of a situation, or an entire period, continuous segments of lives of individuals, families, communities, entire nations. The celebrated life-likeness of every object and every person in his world derives from this astonishing capacity of presenting every ingredient of it in its fullest individual essence, in all its many dimensions, as it were; never as a mere datum, however vivid, within some stream of consciousness, with blurred edges, an outline, a shadow, an impressionistic representation: nor yet calling for, and dependent on, some process of reasoning in the mind of the reader; but always as a solid object, seen simultaneously from near and far, in natural, unaltering daylight, from all possible angles of vision, set in an absolutely specific context in time and space—an event fully present to the senses or the imagination in all its facets, with every nuance sharply and firmly articulated.

Yet what he believed in was the opposite. He advocated a single embracing vision; he preached not variety but simplicity, not many levels of consciousness but reduction to some single level—in *War and Peace* to the standard of the good man, the single, spontaneous, open soul: as later to that of the peasants, or of a simple Christian ethic divorced from any complex theology or metaphysic, some simple, quasi-utilitarian criterion, whereby everything is interrelated directly, and all the items can be assessed in terms of one another by some simple measuring rod. Tolstoy's genius lies in a capacity for marvellously accurate reproduction of the irreproducible, the almost miraculous evocation of the full, untranslatable individuality of the individual, which induces in the reader an acute awareness of the presence of the object itself, and not of a mere description of it, employing for this purpose metaphors which fix the quality of a particular experience as such, and avoiding those general terms which relate it to similar instances by ignoring individual differences—'the oscillations of feeling'—in favour of what is common to them all. But then this same writer pleads for, indeed preaches with great fury, particularly in his last, religious phase, the exact opposite: the necessity of expelling everything that does not submit to some very general, very simple standard: say, what peasants like or dislike, or what the gospels declare to be good.

This violent contradiction between the data of experience from which he could not liberate himself, and which, of course, all his life he knew alone to be real, and his deeply metaphysical belief in the existence of a system to which they *must* belong, whether they appear to do so or not, this conflict between instinctive judgment and theoretical conviction—between his gifts and his opinions—mirrors the unresolved conflict between the reality of the moral life with its sense of responsibility, joys, sorrow, sense of guilt and sense of achievement—all of which is nevertheless illusion; and the laws which govern everything, although we cannot know more than a negligible portion of them—so that all scientists and historians who say that they do know them and are guided by them are lying and deceiving—but which nevertheless alone are real. Beside Tolstoy, Gogol and Dostoevsky, whose abnormality is so often contrasted with Tolstoy's 'sanity', are well-integrated personalities, with a coherent outlook and a single vision. Yet out of this violent conflict grew *War and Peace:* its marvellous solidity should not blind us to the deep cleavage which yawns open whenever Tolstoy remembers, or rather reminds himself—fails to forget—what he is doing, and why. (pp. 62-6)

Isaiah Berlin, in his The Hedgehog and The Fox: An Essay on Tolstoy's View of History *(copyright © 1953 by Isaiah Berlin; reprinted by permission of Simon & Schuster, a Division of Gulf & Western Corporation), Simon & Schuster, 1953, 86 p.*

MARCEL PROUST (essay date 1954)

Nowadays people set Balzac above Tolstoi. This is lunacy. Balzac's books are repulsive, posturing, full of absurdities; in them, humanity is judged by a literary man anxious to write a great book; in Tolstoi, by a serene god. Balzac succeeds in giving the impression of greatness; in Tolstoi everything is great by nature—the droppings of an elephant beside those of a goat. Those great harvest scenes in *Anna Karenina,* the hunting scenes, the skating scenes, etc., are like vast unbroken surfaces that space out the rest, and make everything seem on an ampler scale. It seems as though there were the whole meadow of standing hay, the whole summer, between two conversations of Levine's. One loves different things by turns in this great world, and scenes that are like nothing else—the emotion of the man riding a race (O my beauty, my beauty!), of the man who has laid a wager, sitting on the window-sill, the gaiety of life under canvas . . . , of the aristocratic spendthrift (Natasha's brother) in *War and Peace,* of old Prince Bolkonski. This is not the work of an observing eye but of a thinking mind. Every so-called stroke of observation is simply the clothing, the proof, the instance, of a law, a law of reason or of unreason, which the novelist has laid bare. And our impression of breadth and life is due precisely to the fact that none of this is the fruit of observation, but that every deed, every action, being no other than an expression of a law, one feels oneself moving amid a throng of laws—only, since the truth of these laws is established for Tolstoi by the inward authority they have exercised over his thinking, there are some which we are still baffled by. It is not easy to understand what he means when he speaks of Kitty's sly look when she talked about religion, nor when he speaks of Anna's delight at humbling Vronsky's pride.

We are pleased to see how the man of splendid intellect really draws on much the same kind of wit we often draw on ourselves (Ruskin's witticisms about his dog Vizir and his servant Anne, Tolstoi's witticisms setting the tone of the opening of *Anna Karenina*). And for all that, in this apparently inexhaustible fund of creation it seems as though Tolstoi were repeating himself, as though he had no more than a few themes at his disposal, disguised and reshaped, but the same in both novels. The stars, and the sky that Levine rivets his gaze on are pretty much the same as the comet that Peter saw, as Prince Andrew's wide blue sky. What is more, Levine, first discarded by Kitty in favour of Vronsky, then loved by her, reminds one of Natasha leaving Prince Andrew for Peter's brother-in-law, then going back to him. And might not the same memory have "sat" for Kitty passing by in the carriage and Natasha in the carriage following the army? (pp. 378-79)

Marcel Proust, "Tolstoi" (1954), in his Marcel Proust on Art and Literature 1896-1919, *translated by Sylvia Townsend Warner (© 1958 by Meridian Books, Inc.; reprinted by permission of Georges Borchardt, Inc., as agents for the author), Meridian Books, 1958, pp. 378-79.*

DMITRI PISAREV (essay date 1956)

The new, not-yet-completed novel of Count L. Tolstoy ["War and Peace"] can be called the best work on the pathology of Russian society. In this novel there is a whole series of sharp and varied pictures, drawn with the majestic and imperturbable calm of an epic, that ask and answer the question: "What happens to human minds and characters under conditions that make it possible for people to get along without knowledge, without ideas, without energy, and without work?"

It is very possible and even very probable that Count Tolstoy does not have in mind the posing and the solving of such a question. It is likely that he simply wishes to draw a series of pictures out of the life of the Russian gentry in the time of Alexander I. He himself sees and tries to show to others, precisely, down to the smallest details and nuances, all the special characteristics of that time and of the people of those days, members of that circle which interests him more than any other and which is accessible to his investigation. He wishes only to be truthful and exact. His efforts are not directed to the support or rejection of any theoretical idea whatever through the pictures he creates. In all probability, his relationship to the object of his prolonged and careful research is that involuntary, natural tenderness a talented historian ordinarily feels for the remote or near past which he resurrects. He perhaps even finds, in the peculiarities of that past, in the characters he investigates, in the concepts and customs of the society he represents, many traits worthy of love and respect. All that is possible; all that is even really probable. But it is precisely because the author has spent a great deal of time, work, and love in the study and representation of the epoch and its representatives that the characters he creates live their own lives, independent of the author's intention. They themselves enter into an immediate relationship with the readers. They speak for themselves and lead the reader irresistibly to thoughts and conclusions which the author did not have in mind and of which he perhaps would not even have approved.

This truth, springing in lively fashion out of the facts themselves, this truth breaking through the personal sympathies and convictions of the author, is especially precious because it is so irresistibly convincing. (pp. 1377-78)

Dmitri Pisarev, "The Old Gentry" (originally published in Sochineniya, *Vol. IV, 1956), translated by George Gibian, in "War and Peace" by Leo Tolstoy: The Maude Translation, Backgrounds and Sources, Essays in Criticism, edited by George Gibian (reprinted by permission of W. W. Norton & Company, Inc.; copyright © 1966 by W. W. Norton & Company, Inc.), Norton, 1966, pp. 1377-81.*

CLIFTON FADIMAN (essay date 1957)

In a way writing about *War and Peace* is a self-defeating activity. Criticism in our day has become largely the making of finer and finer discriminations. But *War and Peace* does not lend itself to such an exercise. If you say the book is about the effect of the Napoleonic Wars on a certain group of Russians, most of them aristocrats, you are not telling an untruth. But you are not telling the truth either. Its subject has been variously described—even Tolstoy tried his hand at the job—but none of the descriptions leaves one satisfied.

You can't even call the book a historical novel. It describes events that are part of history, but to say that it is about the past is to utter a half-turth. *Ivanhoe, Gone With the Wind*—these are historical novels. Kipling (a part of him, I mean) has suddenly become for us a historical novelist: Gandhi made him one. But the only sections of *War and Peace* that seem historical are the battle pieces. War is now apocalyptic; it was not so in Tolstoy's time. Austerlitz and Cannae are equally historical, equally antique, equally part of the springtime of war. Now our weapons think for us; that is the revolutionary change that has outmoded all previous narratives of conflict.

But, except for these battle pieces, *War and Peace* is no more a historical novel than is the *Iliad*. Homer is not history, not Greek history, not Trojan history, he is—Homer. So with Tolstoy.

No, you say little when you say that *War and Peace* has to do with the Napoleonic Wars, Borodino, the burning of Moscow, the retreat of 1812. As a matter of fact the vaguer your critical vocabulary, the less precisely you describe the subject of *War and Peace,* the nearer you get to the truth. It is really—yes, let us use un-twentieth-century words—about Life and People and Love: those abhorred capital-letter abstractions that irritate our modern novelists and against which they persistently warn us. (pp. 363-64)

Tolstoy is not an artist at all, as, let us say, Virginia Woolf, Hemingway, Faulkner, Proust, are artists. He does not appear, at least in translation, to have any "style." There is no such thing as a Tolstoyan sentence or a Tolstoyan vocabulary. The poor chap has no technique. He knows nothing of flash-backs, streams of consciousness, symbols, objective correlatives. He introduces his people flatly and blurts out at once their dominant characteristics. He has unending insight but no subtlety. Compared to such a great master as Henry James, or such a little master as Kafka, he seems deficient in sheer brain power, the power to analyze, the power to discriminate.

He never surprises you. All his characters are recognizable, most of them are normal. Even his villain, Anatole Kuragin, seems merely an impetuous fool compared to the monsters of labyrinthine viciousness that our Southern novelists can create with a touch of the pen.

He isn't even a good storyteller, if by a good storyteller one means a master of suspense. You do not read *War and Peace* in order to see "how it comes out," any more than you live your life in order to see how it will end. His people grow, love, suffer, die, commit wise or foolish actions, beget more people who are clearly going to pass through the same universal experiences; and that's about all there is to the "story." There are plenty of events, but they are not arranged or balanced or patterned. Tolstoy is not a neat writer, any more than your biography or mine is neat. He is as shapeless as the Russian land itself.

I found myself struck with the originality of *War and Peace,* but by a kind of reverse English. It is original because it is unoriginal. Kafka is original. Faulkner is original.

Eudora Welty is original. In fact most of our most admired modern writing is original, full of strange people, strange feelings, strange ideas, strange confrontations. But Tolstoy portrays pleasant, lively, ordinary girls like Natasha. His book is crowded with people who are above the average in intelligence or wealth or insight—but not extraordinarily so. He balks at portraying genius: he makes of Napoleon a fatuity, and of the slow-thinking, almost vacant-minded Kutuzov the military hero of the war. And when he writes about war, he does not describe its horrors or its glories. He seizes upon the simplest of the truths about war and sticks to that truth: that war is *foolish.*

Tolstoy has a genius for the ordinary, which does not mean the commonplace. It is this ordinariness that to us moderns, living on a literary diet of paprika, truffles, and cantharides, makes him seem so unusual. When we read him we seem to be escaping into that almost forgotten country, the real world.

Another odd thing—Tolstoy does not seem to have any "personality." Many fine writers are full of personality, Hemingway for instance; but the *very* finest write books that seem to conceal themselves, books like the *Iliad* or *Don Quixote* or *War and Peace.* I do not mean that Tolstoy writes like an impersonal god, but that he seems to intrude into his book only in the sense that he and the book are one and the same. I believe this effect of desingularization springs from his instinctive refusal to load any scene or indeed any sentence with more meaning than it will bear. He has no "effects." He is unable to call attention to his own mastery. He knows what he is doing, but he does not know how to make *you* know what he is doing. The consequence is that, despite the enormous cast of characters, everything (once you have waded through the rather difficult opening chapters) is simple, understandable, recognizable, like someone you have known a long time. In our own day the good novelists tend to be not very clear, and the clear novelists tend to be not very good. Tolstoy is clear and he is good. (pp. 364-66)

> *Clifton Fadiman, "'War and Peace', Fifteen Years After," in his* Any Number Can Play *(copyright © 1957 by Clifton Fadiman; reprinted by permission of Harper & Row, Publishers, Inc.), World Publishing Co., 1957, pp. 361-69.*

GEORGE STEINER (essay date 1959)

The history of Tolstoy's mind and of the growth of Tolstoyan Christianity has often been misread. Tolstoy's condemnation of literature in the winter of 1879-80 was so emphatic that it suggested a radical dissociation between two eras in his life. Actually, most of the ideas and beliefs expounded by the later Tolstoy appear in his earliest writings and the live substance of his morality was plainly discernible during the years of apprenticeship. As [Léon] Shestov points out, in his essay on *Tolstoy and Nietzsche,* the remarkable fact is not the seeming contrast between the early and the late Tolstoy, but rather the unity and consequentiality of Tolstoyan thought.

But it would also be erroneous to distinguish three chapters in Tolstoy's life—a period of literary creation circumscribed on either hand by decades of philosophic and religious activity. In Tolstoy we cannot separate the two shaping powers; the moralist and the poet co-exist in anguished and creative proximity. Throughout his career, the religious and the artistic impulse grappled for supremacy. The struggle was particularly acute at the time when Tolstoy was in the midst of writing *Anna Karenina*. At one moment his capacious spirit inclined towards the life of the imagination; in another it yielded to what Ibsen called the "claims of the ideal." One has the impression that Tolstoy found tranquillity and equilibrium only through physical action and in the wild play of physical energy; through exhaustion of body he was able to silence momentarily the debate raging in his mind. (p. 242)

The perception of the specific and integral is the characteristic mark of Tolstoy's artistry, of his unrivalled concreteness. In his novels each piece of the world's furniture is distinctive and stands with individual solidity. But simultaneously Tolstoy was possessed by the hunger for final understanding, for the all-inclusive and justifying disclosure of the ways of God. It was this hunger which impelled him to his polemic and exegetic labours. . . .

[The] quest for unity, for the revelation of total meaning, underlies Tolstoy's art even where his sensuous perception is most enthralled by the boundless diversity of life. (p. 243)

It was Tolstoy's peculiar tragedy that he should have come to regard his poetic genius as corrupt and as an agent of betrayal. By virtue of their comprehensiveness and vitality, *War and Peace* and *Anna Karenina* had splintered yet further an image of reality in which Tolstoy was determined to discover a single meaning and a perfect coherence. They had opposed the disorder of beauty to his desperate search for the philosopher's stone. (p. 246)

Anyone familiar with Tolstoy's personal life and with the history of his mind will be sensible—perhaps too sensible—to the problematic and doctrinal implications inherent in everything he wrote. Perceived in their total context, the novels and tales play the part of poetic tropes and exploratory myths in an essentially moral and religious dialectic. They are stages of vision in the long pilgrimage. But if we set *Resurrection* to one side, it is clear that religious themes and acts of a religious character occupy a minor place in Tolstoyan fiction. Both *War and Peace* and *Anna Karenina* are images of the empiric world and chronicles of men's temporal works and days.

Even a momentary glance at Dostoevsky provides the contrasting note. In the novels of Dostoevsky, images and situations, the names of the characters and their habits of speech, the general terms of reference, and the qualities of action are prevailingly and dramatically religious. Dostoevsky portrayed men in crises of belief or denial, and often it is through denial that his characters bear witness most forcefully to the incursions of God. . . . The same cannot be asserted of Tolstoy. One may read *War and Peace* and *Anna Karenina* as the foremost of historical and social novels with only a vague awareness of their philosophic and religious tenor. (pp. 246-47)

Must we suppose that the conventional image of Tolstoy is, after all, accurate? Was there a decisive break (possibly in the period from 1874 to 1878) between the "pagan" creator of *War and Peace* and the Christian asectic of *Resurrection* and the later years? I think not. Tolstoy's biography and the record he has left us of his spiritual life bear out the impression of an underlying unity. If we are right in supposing that *War and Peace* and *Anna Karenina* are nearer

to Homer than to Flaubert, then the notion of paganism is not unexpected; indeed, it becomes a vital part of the metaphysics to which the analogies between Homer and Tolstoy refer us. There are in Tolstoyan Christianity, and particularly in Tolstoy's image of God, pagan elements; if the *Iliad* and *War and Peace* are comparable on formal grounds (as we have seen them to be), then their governing mythologies are comparable also. By keeping our attention responsive and uncommitted, we shall, I think, come to realize that Tolstoyan paganism and Tolstoyan Christianity were not diametrical opposites, but successive and interrelated acts in the drama of a single intelligence. *War and Peace, Anna Karenina,* and the tales of the early and middle years, sensuous, wondrously serene in their effect, were nevertheless forerunners and preparers of Tolstoy's sacrificial theology. They establish the world image which that theology will seek to interpret. Conversely, the doctrines of the later Tolstoy carry to the folly of conclusion premises laid down in the writings of his golden period. (pp. 247-48)

Much of the perfection of *Anna Karenina* lies in the fact that the poetic form resisted the demands of the didactic purpose; thus there is between them a constant equilibrium and harmonious tension. In the double plot the duality of Tolstoy's intent is both expressed and organized. The Pauline epigraph initiates and colours the story of Anna but does not utterly control it. Anna's tragic fate yields values and enrichments of sensibility that challenge the moral code which Tolstoy generally held and was seeking to dramatize. It is as if two deities had been invoked: an ancient, patriarchal God of vengeance and a God who sets nothing above the tragic candour of a bruised spirit. Or to put it otherwise: Tolstoy grew enamoured of his heroine, and through the liberality of his passion she achieved a rare freedom. Nearly alone among Tolstoyan characters, Anna appears to develop in directions which point away from the novelist's control and prescience. Thomas Mann was right in asserting that the commanding impulse behind *Anna Karenina* is moralistic; Tolstoy framed an indictment against a society which seized for its own upon a vegeance reserved to God. But for once, Tolstoy's own moral position was ambivalent; his condemnation of adultery was rather close to current social judgment. Like the other spectators at the opera—however mundane or acrimonious they may appear—Tolstoy could not help being shocked by Anna's behavior, by her tentative advances towards a freer code. And in his own perplexity—in the lack of a perfectly lucid case such as is argued in *Resurrection*—lay opportunities for narrative freedom and for the predominance of the poet. In *Anna Karenina* Tolstoy succumbed to his imagination rather than to his reason. . . . (p. 282)

After *Anna Karenina,* the moralistic and pedagogic strains in Tolstoy's inspiration, with their attendant techniques of rhetoric, became increasingly dominant. . . . Both *The Death of Ivan Ilych* and *The Kreutzer Sonata* are masterpieces, but masterpieces of a singular order. Their terrible intensity arises not out of a prevalence of imaginative vision but out of its narrowing; they possess, like the dwarf-figures in the paintings of Bosch, the violent energies of compression. *The Death of Ivan Ilych* is a counterpart to [Dostoevsky's] *Letters from the Underworld;* instead of descending into the dark places of the soul, it descends, with agonizing leisure and precision, into the dark places of the body. It is a poem—one of the most harrowing ever conceived—of the insurgent flesh, of the manner in which carnality, with its pains and corruptions, penetrates and dissolves the tenuous discipline of reason. *The Kreutzer Sonata* is, technically, less perfect because the elements of articulate morality have become too massive to be entirely absorbed into the narrative structure. The meaning is enforced upon us, with extraordinary eloquence; but it has not been given complete imaginative form. (p. 283)

It is difficult to think of *Resurrection* as a novel in the ordinary sense. . . . Tolstoy could not reconcile himself to the idea of fiction, particularly on a large scale. It was only when he saw in the work a chance to convey his religious and social program in an accessible and persuasive form that he could compel himself to the task. . . . It reflects these changes of mood and a puritanical conception of art. But there are wondrous pages in it, and moments in which Tolstoy gave rein to his unchanging powers. The account of the eastward transportation of the prisoners is handled with a breadth of design and aliveness which transcend any programmatic purpose. When Tolstoy opened his eyes on actual scenes and events, instead of keeping them fixed inward on the workings of his anger, his hand moved with matchless artistry.

This is no accident. In a full-length novel, even the late Tolstoy could allow himself a measure of freedom. Through the repeated exemplifications that a long novel makes possible, abstractions assume a colour of life. Ample flesh surrounds the bones of argument. In a short story, on the contrary, time and space are lacking. The elements of rhetoric cannot be absorbed into the fictional medium. Thus, the didactic motifs, the mythology of conduct in Tolstoy's late stories remain visible and oppressive. Through their sheer length, *War and Peace, Anna Karenina,* and *Resurrection* enable Tolstoy to approach that idea of unity which he pursued with such obstinate passion. (pp. 284-85)

> George Steiner, in his Tolstoy or Dostoevsky: An Essay in the Old Criticism *(copyright © 1959 by George Steiner; reprinted by permission of Alfred A. Knopf, Inc.), Knopf, 1959, 354 p.**

RAYMOND ROSENTHAL (essay date 1962)

Leo Tolstoy wrote fables and fairy tales throughout his adult life. It is incorrect therefore to associate them solely with the later period of his writing career, when his religious conversion led him to regard what he called the "religious" and "universal" arts as the only arts worth the trouble of creation. (p. ix)

Now Tolstoy's life is usually divided into three distinct periods: his youth, when he wrote the stories of his literary apprenticeship, such as "Childhood," "Tales of Sevastopol," and "The Cossacks"; his maturity, when the fresh, keen-sighted realism that characterized his first work took on a deeper, intellectual dimension in his masterpieces *War and Peace* and *Anna Karenina;* and his old age, when his religious conversion seemed to transform a spontaneous artist into a single-minded and almost compulsive moral teacher. . . . [In] his last period, when he devoted himself almost entirely to writing fables and folktales, he was in fact trying to give universal form to a mythic experience which was exquisitely intimate and personal.

This accounts for the way in which his last tales, such as "Ivan the Fool," "Esarhaddon, King of Assyria," and

"Emelyan and the Empty Drum," are at once similar to the run of fables and fairy tales yet very much unlike them. The manner of their difference lies in Tolstoy's effort to allegorize and explain the mythic content of his original childhood experience. In most fairy tales, the hero's humility and kindness are the human traits which permit him to overcome the dangers and obstacles in his path and win his just reward; and he is rewarded with wealth or happiness or the princess's hand because he is humble and kind. In Tolstoy's tales, however, the hero's humility and kindness are simply the preconditions for the achievement of greater wisdom and self-awareness, and his reward is never wealth or personal success but rather his ability to conquer, both for himself and others, a new and deeper area of human value and responsibility. Thus, if one believes that a folktale or fable is merely an entertainment, providing the same sort of formal pleasure that one gets from Mallarmé's poetry or abstract painting, then Tolstoy's tales, which above all intend to "prove" the reality and urgency of a whole moral world, can only be criticized as a misuse of the form.

I must admit that I am not at all disturbed by Tolstoy's manhandling of the fabulistic proprieties. One could expect just that when a genius of his particular gifts encounters an ancient form and bends it to his special purposes. The wonder of it is that these stories, despite all the ideological and moral preachments they carry, are yet so successful as sheer stories. Much has been made in recent years of the lacerating conflicts that plagued Tolstoy in his old age. But none of these critics have turned their analytical attention to the fables and folktales. If they had considered them, they would quickly have seen that Tolstoy's realism, the acute and absolute perception which operates so directly and beautifully in his great novels and, at the same time, made it so difficult for him to find an all-embracing intellectual system that would satisfy his heart as well as his head, has here achieved an ideal, well-nigh perfect transfiguration. It is a starkly simple transfiguration, but with all the Tolstoy's essential personal qualities still intact—his straightforwardness, his shrewdness, his incisive intellectual power, his mordant humor. (pp. xi-xii)

I am not trying to unravel Tolstoy's enormous complexity by offering a quaint, fairy-tale view of him. The colossal creator who composed the great novelistic symphonies will not yield up his secret so easily. But the fact remains that side by side with this titan stands the humble, unassuming man who wrote the simple tales. And the simplicity that speaks in these tales is quite palpably not a contrived or affected simplicity, for, as every writer knows, of all literary genres the simple tale is the hardest to fake and the easiest in which to detect the insincere and false. What's more, Tolstoy's simplicity was not a facile achievement. It arose out of a vastly complicated intellectual ferment. Consider: Tolstoy was a rationalist and a desperate God-seeker, a hater of all orthodoxy and a stifled dogmatist, a steadfast believer in the essential goodness and creativity of man and one of the keenest intellects ever to expose man's vices and duplicities. And yet, though pulled in so many divergent directions, Tolstoy somehow managed "to become as a child" and to write the slight, pellucid, sardonic tales that one reads in [*Fables and Fairy Tales*]. (p. xiii)

[The] truth of the matter is that Tolstoy was able to write these tales with such purity and grace because he possessed that Biblical virtue—loving-kindness. It was his supreme virtue, both as a man and as an artist. (p. xiv)

Raymond Rosenthal, "Foreword" (copyright © 1962 by the New American Library, Inc.; reprinted by arrangement with the author), in Fables and Fairy Tales by Leo Tolstoy, translated by Ann Dunnigan, The New American Library, 1962, pp. ix-xvi.

R. F. CHRISTIAN (essay date 1962)

It is not easy to express in words the focal point of Tolstoy's [*War and Peace*]. Broadly speaking it is the contrast between two opposite states: on the one hand selfishness, self-indulgence, self-importance, and the attendant evils of careerism, nepotism, vanity, affectation and the pursuit of purely private pleasures; on the other hand a turning outwards from the self, a groping towards something bigger, an endeavour to surmount individualism, a recognition that the cult of the self is an unworthy alternative to the service of one's neighbours, one's family, the community and the country at large. Most people, Tolstoy appears to be saying, are preoccupied most of the time with their own selfish cares. Some are incorrigible careerists like Boris Drubetskoy or Napoleon, place-seekers and intriguers. Some such as Hélène or Anatole Kuragin think only of their own pleasure and are not restrained by any scruples of conscience from gratifying it. They are superb animals—handsome, graceful, lithe—with the senses and the appetite of an animal, and a total lack of consideration for human beings. What is more, they are not at all disturbed by their selfishness and would no doubt be offended if it were suggested that they were anything but normal, decent people—not saints certainly, but no worse than their neighbours. To this category of people belong the statesmen and military leaders who believe that their work is important and devoted to the public cause, but who are really only implementing their selfish desires for fame, power and decorations.

Others again such as Natasha and Nikolai Rostov are fond of themselves and of the normal round of upper class entertainment, the accepted and unquestioned way of life of the gentry. They are not troubled by profound thoughts; they are not moved to ask themselves difficult questions about the purpose of life in general or their own lives in particular. But although they may be a little vain, a little too complacent at times, they unquestionably create a favourable impression on the reader by virtue among other things of their simple, forthright characters, their ability to share in the universal pleasures and obligations of everyday life and their freedom from hypocrisy and intrigue. (pp. 1456-57)

If the focal point of *War and Peace* is the problem of the sublimation of the self, this problem is capable of being answered in the way in which Tolstoy was himself trying to answer it as he wrote his novel, and in which Pierre and Natasha, and Nikolai and Princess Marya answer it in the closing chapters of their story. The solution to the problem is the sober acceptance of family responsibility at the sacrifice to some extent of the uninhibited individual personality, work which brings its own reward, and the pursuit of simple pleasures accessible to all; the recognition that it is right and natural that the sparkling, vivacious Natasha should become a somewhat staid and lustreless mother of children, and that her husband and her brother and her brother's wife should arrive at a happy state of active and fruitful domesticity. Tolstoy has an unfortunate tendency from time to time to call the virtues he admires specifically Russian: he writes, for example, with reference to Pierre that he felt a 'vague, exclusively Russian feeling of contempt for everything conventional and artificial'; and he tells how the diplomat Bilibin described a certain campaign with 'a fearless self-censure and self-derision genuinely Russian'. But since he himself provides many examples of Russians who *are* conventional, artificial and egotistical, one must take these passing observations of his with a grain of salt. (pp. 1457-58)

War and Peace is too big a novel, and written over too long a period of time, for its author to be expected to be able to carry the whole work in his mind and merely concern himself with putting the different parts together. The book grew with Tolstoy, and its composition must be looked at in terms of growth, dynamically, not in terms of completion, statically. That is to say it is not a finished work. One thing leads on to the next, and there is no real ending. It seems to me that the principle of composition is to think of people and phenomena in terms of their opposites and then to contrive the juxtaposition and interaction of these opposites. The principle operates, in the long view, as a series of sharp contrasts between two dissimilar groups—family and social—which, as groups, each reveal a corporate uniformity. Within these contrasted groups, and in the short view, there is individuality and variety. But ultimately the individual, however many-sided his personality, remains basically true to his group and does not transfer his allegiance to the other side. The flow of the novel is maintained by this constant juxtaposition of contrasting groups, the individual members of which are in continual contact as they move to and fro and mix with each other. But group solidarity triumphs; the individual is only free within the limits of the group.

The basic contrast in *War and Peace* is the one inherent in the title. This is not simply a contrast between periods when the country is at war and periods when it is not (by this calculation most of the scenes in *War and Peace* take place when the country is at war). War means military actions; peace means non-military actions whether in peacetime or in war. There is a balance held in the composition of the book between military and non-military scenes, even towards the end, when a state of war is permanent. Even then the presence of Pierre, the civilian, the spiritual seeker, towers above that of the soldiers and prisoners among whom he finds himself. Although Pierre and Karataev are both prisoners-of-war one does not think of the episodes in which they appear as belonging to the 'war' side of *War and Peace*. (p. 1460)

Structurally speaking . . . there is a serious unbalance in Tolstoy's novel—not a high-handed disregard of 'architecture', but a lapse on the part of a novelist who nevertheless strove after the 'architectural' virtues of order, balance, harmony, contrast, and focus. A major weakness of the digressive passages is that they are concerned so much with the big groups—whether nations, armies, or historians, which as groups make far less impression on the reader than the individual heroes who, forming the stuff of the novel, are, nevertheless, as individuals, given only the scantiest treatment in the digressions and have the small area of freedom ascribed to them inadequately defined. In his article on *War and Peace* Tolstoy wrote: 'there are two kinds of actions: some that do and others that do not depend on my will.' This crucial statement ought to be both illustrated in the text of the novel and elaborated in the commentary in order to give that *balance* between reflection and action, between thesis and illustration of thesis, which, for all Tolstoy's preoccupation with compositional problems, seems to me to be inadequately maintained in *War and Peace*.

In drawing attention to the evidence that Tolstoy was far from indifferent to problems of form, a final reservation must be made. Despite all the 'links' and 'connexions', the inadequately explored structural subtleties of Tolstoy, *War and Peace* remains a sprawling work—vast, all-embracing, life-like, unrounded. To many West European writers of the twentieth century—to Proust, Thomas Mann and others—this was the fact which really counted. This was the great lesson which the Russian novel had to offer. It was the shapelessness, variety and richness of life, not the shapes and graces of architecture, which was Tolstoy's literary bequest to posterity. (pp. 1479-80)

> *R. F. Christian, "The Theme and the Art of 'War and Peace'," in his* Tolstoy's "War and Peace": A Study *(© Oxford University Press 1962; reprinted by permission of Oxford University Press), Oxford University Press, Oxford, 1962 (and reprinted in* "War and Peace" *by Leo Tolstoy: The Maude Translation, Backgrounds and Sources, Essays in Criticism, edited by George Gibian, W. W. Norton & Company, Inc., 1966, pp. 1456-80).*

R. P. BLACKMUR (essay date 1964)

If there is one notion which represents what Tolstoi is up to in his novels—emphatically in *Anna Karenina* and *War and Peace*—it is this. He exposes his created men and women to the "terrible ambiguity of an immediate experience" (Jung's phrase in his *Psychology and Religion*), and then, by the mimetic power of his imagination, expresses their reactions and responses to that experience. Some reactions are merely protective and make false responses; some reactions are so deep as to amount to a change in the phase of being and make honest responses. The reactions are mechanical or instinctive, the responses personal or spiritual. But both the reactions and the responses have to do with that force greater than ourselves, outside ourselves, and working on ourselves, which whether we call it God or Nature is the force of life, what is shaped or misshaped, construed or misconstrued, in the process of living. Both each individual life and also that life in fellowship which we call society are so to speak partial incarnations of that force; but neither is ever complete; thus the great human struggle, for the individual or for the society, is so to react and so to respond to "the terrible ambiguity of an immediate experience" as to approach the conditions of rebirth, the change of heart, or even the fresh start. Tragedy comes about from the failure to apprehend the character or the direction of that force, either by an exaggeration of the self alone or of the self in society. That is why in Tolstoi the peasants, the simple family people, and the good-natured wastrels furnish the background and the foils for the tragedy, for these move according to the momentum of things and although they are by no means complete incarnations of the force behind the momentum are yet in an equal, rough relation to it. The others, the tragic figures, move rather, by their own mighty effort, in relation, reaction, response to that force, some with its momentum, some against it; some falsifying it in themselves, some falsifying it in society, but each a special incarnation of it; some cutting their losses; some consolidating their gains; some balancing, some teetering, in a permanent labor of rebirth. There is thus at work in the novels of Tolstoi a kind of dialectic of incarnation: the bodying forth in aesthetic form by contrasted human spirits of "the terrible ambiguity of an immediate experience" through their reactions and responses to it. It is this dialectic which gives buoyancy and sanity to Tolstoi's novels. (pp. 3-4)

Tolstoi begins his novel [*Anna Karenina*], by showing his people through the motion of their manners, first those of Stiva and Dolly, then those of the others. By the end of the first Part of the novel, we know very well the manner of life of each person and could extend it to suit any further accident of life: we know the probable critical point in the temperament of each which rises or descends to some old or new form of action or inaction, and we know it by the kind of manners each exhibits and by how far into the being of each the manners seem to penetrate: into all that is on the surface of Stiva, into all there is anywhere for Dolly, into a layer of permanent irritation for Levin, into a layer of perpetual possibility for Anna, into the radiant sweep of things not yet her own for Kitty, and into the animal vitality of things for Vronsky (who is at the beginning, and always, less a man than a sensual force inhabiting a man). (p. 5)

But for Levin, the other half of Vronsky, there is enough to make up for all the rest. He is, in his unmannerliness, in his steady breach of the expected manner, an effort at declaring what the manners are about; but he is only one effort, one declaration, which can by no means minimize or defeat the others should they come to make their declarations. Levin's very breaches of manners are organized into manners themselves, as organized as the fools and the plain-spoken men in Shakespeare. He is a foil, a contrast, a light to Anna, Stiva, Karenin, Kitty, and Vronsky; and he is a successful foil by the accident of the condition of his temperament, by what he misses or ignores of what they all see. (p. 7)

[Manners] are the medium in which the struggle between the institutions of society and the needs of individuals is conducted. Viable dramatic manners exist so long as the struggle has not become too one-sided, so long as no total credit is given either to one side or the other. (p. 8)

It is through manners that the needs and possibilities of each person are seen in shifting conflict with the available or relevant institutions, including the twilight institutions—the illicit, amorphous institutions—which stand at the edges of the institutions of broad day. Stiva, Anna, and Vronsky depend on the twilight institutions of marriage and general social conduct which encroach on the edges of the broad day institutions upon which Dolly, Kitty, and Levin depend. . . . In actuality the struggle is conducted in the medium of manners between individuals trying from their different needs to shape institutions into some tolerable relation to their own partial apprehensions of reality. Here again it is Levin who has the first illumination; he knows there can be no victory and that there must be a balance. Himself a disbeliever in institutions, and therefore the more apprehensive of their force, he resents the maimed and maiming complaints of his brother Nicolay against the need of institutions: the forever need of make-shift. But best of all are the brother and sister Oblonsky, Stiva and Anna of the voided marriages: the one whose manners will last him forever, the other whose manners will be less and less good to her where they lead her, until at last she creates a fatal manner of her own. (pp. 8-9)

At first Anna *uses* the manners of the fashionable set to promote her relations with Vronsky, then she *breaches* manners to solidify them, and at last—with her husband, with society, with Vronsky—she throws manners away, and the force which has been there all along takes over although she does not as yet wholly know it. (p. 11)

Tolstoi has many skills in the dialectic of incarnation. Here is one where the incarnation is of raw force itself, but it must be thought of in its setting. Consider how he surrounds the affair of Anna and Vronksy—the seduction, pregnancy and declaration—on the one side with the true idyll of Levin in the spring and on the other side the false idyll of Kitty at the watering place. It is across Vronsky and Anna that Kitty and Levin reach. At the very center lies Frou Frou, the mare, with her broken back, struggling up on her forelegs, then falling: all because Vronsky could not keep pace with her. Vronsky kicked her with his heel in the stomach. (pp. 14-15)

Vronsky's unpardonable act was no accident; neither was it done by intention. It was rather that, at a moment of high arbitrary human skill, at a moment of death-risk and momentary glory, the center of all eyes and the heart of an almost universal act of mimetic participation—at that moment something like fate broke the rhythm. . . .

But what is even more terrifying about Tolstoi's honesty—or let us say what is more astonishing about his genius—is that he could have broken the back of a mare in the midst of the crisis in the passion of Anna and Vronsky without either adding or diminishing *human* significance but rather deepening the reality. It is as if in this image he had gotten into the conditions of life from which the conditions we know of emerge: into conditions purer and conditions more intolerable: into an order which includes all human disorders. (p. 15)

[Both Anna and Levin] need the identification of force with love, the one outside society and nature, the other through society and nature. Anna needs to become herself standing for everybody, Levin needs to become everybody in order to find himself represented. That is why both Anna and Levin are subject to fearful jealousies. Their rebirth into new life is never complete and the identification of force with love is never complete. (p. 16)

[The nature of Anna's tragedy is] that her own strength cannot be equal to her cause. The independence of the individual is never equal to the cause of independence. (p. 18)

Levin in new life, Levin on wings, has also singled his life, has made an act of devotion, to which he will necessarily turn out inadequate, not so much because of inadequate strength but because the cause itself (in the form of his original impulse) will desert him. (p. 19)

[We] see Anna, Vronsky, Karenin, and Levin tied in the hard knot of individual goodness, and each, in that goodness, in a different relation to the manners and momentum of society. I mean, by goodness, that each has been reborn into a man or woman for once, and at last, proper to his or her own nature. . . .

We see Levin in doubt and delight about everything, desiring not to desire, as we see Vronsky equally in doubt, but so full of *ennui* that he desires desire. We see that Anna's problem is to maintain that state of crisis in love, to be always a young girl in love, and that Vronsky's problem is to find substitutes, caprices of action, to prevent *ennui* from absorbing crisis. (p. 20)

We cannot live at crisis, at the turning point, but must make out of it either a birth or a death in the face of ordinary life. (p. 23)

It is in contest and concert with the ordinary world that crisis is reached and given worth; and it is into the ordinary world that things break through and are bodied forth, visibly in crisis, actually all along. The last two parts of *Anna Karenina* put into parallel and analogy such recognitions as these. (p. 24)

It is their manners, failing, that keep Anna and Vronsky from joining their emotions. They neither do their part nor keep pace. It is when her manners wholly fail that Anna brims over, sees herself clear, and comes on that unintermediated force which makes her suffer, and it is in desperate pursuit of some manners into which she can deliver that suffering that she finds her death. . . . (p. 25)

With no less of the force in him that drove Anna, Levin turned the other way. He too had been at the point of death and for months at a time, but through the death of his brother and the delivery of his wife found himself alive instead. It could have been the other way; Levin and Anna were aimed equally at life or at death. Human life cannot stand the intensity of Anna, but works toward it; human life requires the diminution of intensity into faith and of faith into momentum which is Levin. The one is very near the other. Only Anna's face was stone and more beautiful than ever. Yet it is in the likeness not the difference that the genuineness and the dialectic of Tolstoi's incarnation lies. (pp. 25-6)

R. P. Blackmur, "The Dialectic of Incarnation: Tolstoi's 'Anna Karenina'," in his Eleven Essays in the European Novel *(copyright 1950, by R. P. Blackmur; copyright 1978 by Betty Bredemier Davison; reprinted by permission of Harcourt Brace Jovanovich, Inc.), Harcourt, 1964, pp. 3-26.*

IRVING HOWE (essay date 1968)

The Death of Ivan Ilych is one of the most ambitious pieces of fiction ever written. Tolstoy set out not merely to describe a single segment of society or to present a single example of humanity but to *encompass within one story the fundamental patterns of human existence.* Tolstoy wished to write a story about which a fool might say, "True enough, but, after all, this does not concern me, for I am not like Ivan Ilych." More accurately, he wished to write a story to which all of us would first respond like the fool but about which we would finally be forced to harbor a second thought: "Ivan Ilych *is* me, not insofar as I am young or old, pretty or ugly, rich or poor, silly or wise, but insofar as I share with other men one overriding condition: I am mortal, I must die." And this realization of our common fate stabs our hearts. (p. 113)

Tolstoy wished to shake us out of our routine response and to assault our private self-deception (*you and you may die, but not me*). To do this he had to find a way of making his abstract intention come to pulsing life. For he was not concerned merely with showing the death of some particular character, a circumstance from which the reader could soon find a way of squirming loose emotionally. Instead, Tolstoy wanted to render a universal experience but not as a mere abstraction, since abstraction has a tendency to become a psychological anesthetic. (pp. 113-14)

The strategy Tolstoy hit upon was to create a figure who, in his absolutely commonplace life and character, would indeed seem universal—he would be a man stripped of all those traits that distinguish one person from another, and there would be almost nothing left to him but the fact that he is a man. Almost anyone can feel superior to Ivan Ilych, that good gray nonentity; yet all of us share at least some of those trivialities and vanities that make up the bulk of Ivan Ilych's existence. By thus embodying his abstract idea in the life of an utterly ordinary man, Tolstoy hoped to make each detail of his story take on a universal significance. The concrete would become a way of conveying the abstract, and the life of Ivan Ilych would become—or seem to become—the life of all of us. (p. 114)

In looking back on this remarkable story, we can hardly suppose that it is through a particular device or technique that Tolstoy establishes his mastery over our imaginations. At the end, I think we must fall back upon an idea which in the criticism of literature ought to be advanced with great caution and only in a few instances: the idea that we have submitted ourselves to the voice of a man who has reached the innermost depths of experience, who has purchased his wisdom at a heavy price in suffering, and who has thereby burned out of his writing all vanity and pretension. For if we must conclude that each of us is Ivan Ilych, we must not forget that Tolstoy was but another version of Ivan Ilych. And from the pain of that recognition, the story has been written. (p. 121)

> *Irving Howe, in his introduction to "The Death of Ivan Ilych" by Leo Tolstoy, in* Classics of Modern Fiction: Eight Short Novels, *edited by Irving Howe (© 1968 by Harcourt Brace Jovanovich, Inc.; reprinted by permission of the publisher), Harcourt, 1968, pp. 113-21.*

ERNEST J. SIMMONS (essay date 1968)

No novelist was more acutely aware of the reality around him than Tolstoy or more exhaustively absorbed, through the intellect and senses, in all its manifestations. Unlike Dostoevsky, who creates a world of his own in the image of the real world, Tolstoy accepts the real world, and his picture of it is fresh and interesting because he sees so much more of it than his readers, but its commonplaces, observed through the prism of his imagination, take on new meaning. That is, he is able to perceive genuine poetry in the average which so often embodies the reality of man's dreams and hopes. (p. 2)

Though *Childhood* is in the tradition of classical Russian realism begun by Pushkin, one can detect curious traces of foreign influences in the work. As in the case of "A History

of Yesterday" certain aspects of the *Sentimental Journey*, especially Sterne's love of humanity and pervasive sensibility, as well as tricks of style, are clearly reflected in *Childhood*. (p. 15)

But in most respects this first short novel is a highly original work. Tolstoy once remarked: "When I wrote *Childhood* it seemed that no one before me had so felt and depicted all the charms and poetry of childhood." And this is an admirable brief description of the work, which is simply the story of a child's life up to the age of about fourteen. What especially impresses the reader is Tolstoy's wonderful skill in evoking childhood memories and associations that all have forgotten or only dimly remember, but which, when recalled with feeling, seem infallibly true and altogether delightful. If he criticized Pushkin's historical novel, *The Captain's Daughter,* because the interest in events predominates over the interest in feeling, it was precisely in the feelings of his characters that Tolstoy was primarily interested, and in the psychological reasons why they feel as they do. (pp. 15-16)

Of course, there is a great deal of Tolstoy's own childhood in this work, especially in the thoughts and feelings expressed by the central character, Nicholas. More so perhaps than that of any major novelist, Tolstoy's fiction is unusually autobiographical. This is no reflection upon his imagination or powers of invention, which were very considerable. But the life he transposed into art was largely his own life of recorded experience and observation, rendered infinitely effective artistically by penetrating analysis and by his subtle choice of significant psychological detail. In short, the convincing, unexaggerated realism of his fiction is rooted in autobiography. (p. 16)

[There is] less of the autobiographical in the sequels—*Boyhood* . . . and *Youth*. . . . In them, however, the poetic and evocative atmosphere of *Childhood* is not so much in evidence, and elements of intellection and psychological analysis are more dominant. Yet in these three connected short novels one savors the happy ease and self-sufficiency of large gentry families. Their intimate understanding of one another is curiously transformed into an intimate understanding between Tolstoy and the reader, a pleasurable familiarity that is carried over in his handling of the many similar families portrayed in the great novels of the future. How memorable are some of the scenes in *Childhood, Boyhood,* and *Youth,* in which the commonplace experiences of the young are made to seem "strange" by the witchery of art. . . . (pp. 16-17)

Many of the characteristic qualities of Tolstoy's mature art are already apparent in these early works. The customary initial period of imitation and immature fumbling is avoided. All the ineffable charm of childhood, boyhood, and youth is recaptured with compelling authenticity, and we live over again in these pages our own youthful joys and sorrows, dreams and hopes. With little faltering and no false moves, Tolstoy mounted at the first try the immortal steed of great art. (pp. 17-18)

All four of Russia's most celebrated novelists, Gogol, Dostoevsky, Turgenev, and Tolstoy, began their literary careers with the short story. . . . Tolstoy continued to write short stories throughout his long life, but several of his earliest efforts are particularly important, not only for their intrinsic worth and charm, but also for an understanding of the inception and development of a narrative art which found its fullest expression in the great novels. (p. 18)

Each of the Caucasian stories ("The Raid," "The Wood-Felling," and "Meeting a Moscow Acquaintance in the Detachment") . . . is an outgrowth of personal experience in fighting with the Russian forces against the hill tribes, or of some adventure on his furloughs. (pp. 18-19)

Within the limitations of the short-story form, the principal characterizations of the military figures in the Caucasian tales are studies in some depth, and the significant action is nearly always narrated with a realism quite fresh for that time. In this military environment it was almost inevitable that the youthful Tolstoy, with his restless questing mind, should reveal an interest in such abstract questions as: What constitutes bravery? ("The Raid"), or: Into what categories should soldiers be classified? ("The Wood-Felling"). Yet these concerns are never allowed to obtrude on the essential unity of the stories. And the subject that was to dominate so much of his thinking in later years—the rightness or wrongness of war—is also touched upon. In fact, in "The Raid," and to a certain extent in "The Wood-Felling," there is more than a suggestion of his later ruthless analysis of conventional thinking about military glory. But he was not yet blind to the heroism of the simple plain soldier or officer, and his accounts of incidents in this connection in "The Raid" provide the main attraction of the tale. (p. 19)

Purists might well reject Tolstoy's three Sevastopol "sketches" ["Sevastopol in December 1854," "Sevastopol in May 1855," and "Sevastopol in August 1855"], as they are sometimes erroneously called, as fiction. On the other hand, one could hardly regard them as articles of a talented war correspondent. Whatever else they may be they are art of the highest quality, in the same sense that Dostoevsky's *House of the Dead* is art and not simply a reporter's write-up of his life in a Siberian prison. If these pieces are mostly accounts of what Tolstoy observed and experienced at Sevastopol, he renders them immeasurably effective by employing artistic devices of fiction—setting, careful selection of precise detail in description, dialogue, development of characters through analysis of human motivation and feelings, and in the third narrative, possibly also in the second, there is as much plot as one finds in most of his indubitable short stories. (p. 21)

Though Tolstoy excelled in the short-story form from the beginning of his writing career, its artistic restrictions were alien to the natural bent of his expansive genius. Hence his early efforts in the short novel, often brilliantly realized, represent a transition to the more artistically congenial, spacious, and complex world of *War and Peace* and *Anna Karenina*. Specifically, he began to reveal more care for settings, greater psychological density, and the ability to cope with a larger number of characters in intricate human relations.

In *Two Hussars* . . . , the earliest of this group of short novels and Tolstoy's first piece of fiction based on a theme outside his personal experience, one is immediately aware, in comparison with his previous writing, of maturing artistic powers. The juxtaposition of two generations reflecting alternating contrasts in the personalities and adventures of father and son became a favorite fictional device which Tolstoy later used in his long novels on a much more elaborate scale. (p. 31)

In *A Landlord's Morning* and *Polikushka*, Tolstoy for the first time is mainly concerned with peasants, a class that played a role, but not a dominant one, in his later fiction. And in *A Landlord's Morning* . . . he also returns to events of his personal life, which had furnished themes for so many of his early tales. (pp. 32-3)

Though *Polikushka* . . . was published after the emancipation of the serfs in 1861, it is concerned, like *A Landlord's Morning*, with peasant existence before they obtained their freedom. But here the emphasis is quite different. There is no autobiographical element, no personal thesis to develop. Tolstoy's concentration is entirely upon telling a gripping story of peasant life, and he does it with infinite art. The result is a masterpiece in the genre of the short novel. (p. 35)

Without being tendentious, *Polikushka* exposes the hard features of peasant life. The tone of refined humor that aimed to ridicule the false and insincere in art appeared for the first time in his fiction. On this same high level of performance, he continued to write about the peasant and his relation to the landowner in brilliant sections of *War and Peace* and *Anna Karenina*.

Family Happiness . . . is a most interesting example of the manner in which Tolstoy transposes the facts of real life into the substance of art. (p. 36)

It is a delicate psychological study in depth, a worthy forerunner of the moving love stories of his great novels. We observe how the mysterious chemistry of love gradually and insensibly alters the nature of the youthful, inexperienced Masha. . . . (pp. 37-8)

The Cossacks is the final work of Tolstoy's first literary period, and no doubt it is his finest. . . . Turgenev did not hesitate to pronounce it "the best story that has been written in our language." Though there are artistic flaws in the portrait of Olenin, the principal Cossack characters, Eroshka, Lukashka, and Maryanka, are among the most memorable of Tolstoy's creations. With them, one experiences that baffling impression, which is the quintessence of his realism, that somehow these characters are telling their own stories without the author's intervention beyond that of acting as an occasional commentator. And that inner truth of a work of fiction, which must come from life itself, seems more fully developed in *The Cossacks* than in any other tale of Tolstoy's first literary period. (p. 41)

The common complaint that *War and Peace* is devoid of form recalls eighteenth-century criticism of the shapelessness of the Alps. In the first place such a complaint overlooks the unique totality of life indigenous, so to speak, to the novel. Given this fact, one naturally asks: What other form, or what changes in the present one, would have resulted in greater aesthetic unity of design in so huge a work? Of course, the logical answer is that Tolstoy surrendered the possibility of satisfactory form by attempting to do too much in a single novel. However, if he had radically reduced its scope, the work would probably not be the *War and Peace* which so many modern writers of stature have acclaimed as the greatest novel in the world. (p. 67)

But what is the subject of Tolstoy's great novel? Many have remarked that it has no subject other than life itself and no single hero. The work has such an immediacy for us that we tend to forget what Tolstoy never forgot, that he was writing a historical novel. . . . In short, to write a history of the people, understanding history both as a theory of knowledge and as the principal integrating factor in a vast wealth of material, is the real subject of *War and Peace.* (pp. 67-8)

It is important to realize that Tolstoy's theory of history applies to the activities of [the] numerous fictional characters as well as to the purely historical ones. To paraphrase his lengthy and rather involved statement in the novel, he contends that in order to understand the process of history, one must begin not with a consideration of the deeds of supposed great men, but with the integration of an infinitely large number of infinitesimally small actions, what Tolstoy calls "the differential of history."

If Tolstoy tends to deflate the historical reputations of those who are credited with shaping great events by insisting that the events themselves are beyond their active control, the actions of his fictional characters are conditioned by the same lack of freedom. But these tremendously vital, well-rounded, and intensely real men and women enjoy the illusion of freedom, the full consciousness that they are directing their own destinies. Yet fate, chance, accident, lady luck, or decisions thrust upon them by others often determine crucial events in the lives of Natasha, Nicholas, Sonya, Pierre, Princess Mary, Prince Andrew, and others. Tolstoy wisely avoids arguing his thesis on the limitations of man's conscious will in connection with his fictional characters, which may be one reason why its pervasiveness in the total design is often overlooked.

However, the integration of the Napoleonic campaign into the design of the novel, whose subject is the history of the people, is accompanied by lengthy sections of theorizing about war, its leaders, and the historical implications of their actions. Though opinions differ sharply on the necessity of this extensive theorizing, and on its intellectual quality and connection with major and minor fictional characters, Tolstoy obviously regarded it as of the utmost consequence in the definite plan of *War and Peace.* In this sense these sections are not extraneous and may be considered as necessary and extremely informative. To convey knowledge was for Tolstoy an essential concomitant of the novel. (pp. 69-70)

Once the main theme of the novel is grasped, a history of the people and the manner in which all the elements involved in it are integrated by Tolstoy's theory of history, the basic structure becomes apparent and stands as a refutation of the notion that the work is formless. A history of the people is told in terms of the two broad areas of human experience identified in the title—war, symbolizing the vast world of public affairs, and peace, the private manifold activities of the family. A careful examination of the amazingly rich thematic multiplicity of the novel reveals a deliberate and meaningful series of juxtapositions and alternating contrasts, first between war and peace, and then, within this framework, series of alternating contrasts of scenes, situations, events, and characters under each of these two divisions. (pp. 72-3)

So attached is Tolstoy to this device of antithesis, which he regards as a touchstone of the reality of things, that he creates a series of contrasting characters, and in a few individual characters, such as Pierre and Natasha, he stresses their contrasting moods and thoughts as important traits in

their natures. This elaborate pattern of juxtapositions and alternating contrasts serves to create an illusion of ceaseless movement involving an endless variety of action, people, moods, and thought. (p. 73)

Unlike *War and Peace, Anna Karenina,* despite its considerable length, is limited in scope and subject matter, has a definite beginning and end, and preserves an inner unity. (p. 85)

Some critics assert that the one flaw in the characterization of Anna is Tolstoy's failure to motivate her seemingly sudden passion for Vronsky. . . . Her falling in love, however, is not sudden, and a careful reading reveals how what Anna regards as a harmless flirtation slowly develops into an irresistible passion, a process which in no sense contradicts anything we know of her character up to that point. (p. 87)

Although *Anna Karenina* is one of the great love stories of world literature, it is a tribute to Tolstoy's infallible instinct for reality that he so successfully keeps overt manifestations of love out of the novel. For profound love between two such mature and refined people as Anna and Vronsky is a secret thing, expansive only in hidden ways. The moral and physical effects of their guilty passion are constantly before the eyes of their world, but verbal expression of it is carefully restrained. Their affection for each other is suggested by some kind of mental telepathy in their chats on indifferent topics, or it is conveyed by hints or implications, but rarely by direct declarations.

Tolstoy's art of individualizing his numerous characters, so evident in *War and Peace,* loses none of its effectiveness in *Anna Karenina.* If anything, he adds to his psychologizing a deeper, more searching moral probing. And even more so than in *War and Peace,* he creates in *Anna Karenina* the baffling impression, which is the quintessence of his realism, that somehow the characters are telling their own stories without the author's interposition beyond that of acting as an occasional commentator. At times this effect seems to be something less than illusory. That is, characters appear to retain their freedom of action and behave in ways not anticipated by their creator, or they act a new part in a new situation without ceasing to be themselves. (p. 90)

Throughout *Anna Karenina* one perceives Tolstoy's ability to combine a sense of the accidental and inevitable which is the result not of happy chance, but of the novelist's art. He uses a variety of technical procedures, some of them designed to create a kind of symbolic atmosphere, such as the divorce lawyer who catches moths or the pattern of significant actions that take place at railway stations or in trains. Failure to savor this atmosphere is to miss an important unifying factor in the narrative schema. To some, the symbolic effects may seem too obvious, as in the case of the candle whose light, before Anna's suicide, helped her to read the book of her life and then wavered and went out forever. The force of the passage is not in the rather commonplace image, but in the rhythm and depth of the language, the words of which seem to be uttered for the first time. For rugged and solid grandeur there are few passages to compare with it in Russian literature. (p. 92)

There can be no question, however, that shortly after finishing *Anna Karenina* in 1877, Tolstoy experienced a shattering moral and spiritual crisis which brought him to the verge of suicide. *A Confession,* one of the noblest utterances of man, is the chronicle of his doubts and merciless self-examination. He admitted that he had everything to live for—a loving wife, family, wealth, fame, and good health. Yet life seemed stupid, a spiteful joke that someone had played on him. Why should he go on living, he asked himself? Did life have any meaning which the inevitability of death did not destroy?

In *A Confession* . . . Tolstoy records the unique and overwhelming personal experience of a man perplexed in the extreme by life's most agonizing problem—the relation of man to the infinite. The result is a masterpiece of the highest art, comparable to the Book of Job in its terrible human urgency of the need to know, as well as in its wonderful language, with biblical echoes, and its compelling use of parables to illustrate ideas. With courage not devoid of a certain humility he dared to tell cynical unbelievers that religion contained the only explanation of the meaning of life, and to believers in dogmatic and popular religions he declared that the very foundations of their faith were erroneous. With complete sincerity, he made it clear that he was uncompromisingly turning his back on all the joys and fame and magnificent artistic achievements of his fifty years of existence in the search for a new way of life that would enable him to seek moral perfection in service to God and humanity. (pp. 95-6)

[In Tolstoy's last short stories] he reverts to his early manner of fiction-writing before his spiritual conversion, with the difference that he still remains influenced by the special concerns of his new faith. At times he draws upon personal experiences as he did in so many of his previous creative works. This is especially true of "Memoirs of a Madman." . . . It is a rather thinly disguised fictionized treatment of the oppressive fear of death, which he experienced before his religious change, and its relation to his growing belief that the kind of life he led then was irrational, fit only for a madman, and must be abandoned. Scenes of the visitation of death are as intensely and brilliantly realized as Prince Andrew's striking encounter with death in *War and Peace*. (p. 143)

In addition to the short story, Tolstoy also devoted a substantial amount of creative effort, after *War and Peace* and *Anna Karenina,* to that longer type of fiction which he had attempted in his earlier period—the short novel. (p. 146)

[*The Death of Ivan Ilych* and *Master and Man* are] two of his greatest masterpieces in the genre of the short novel. (p. 148)

[*The Death of Ivan Ilych*], which is an account of the spiritual conversion of a judge, an ordinary, unthinking, vulgar man, in the face of the terrible fear of approaching death, is a problem story in which Tolstoy does not so much preach as communicate experience. In it he not only reverts to the wonderful realism of his early fiction, but adds an emphasis new and startling in the development of Russian literature. Although Gorky is often credited with freeing nineteenth-century Russian realism from its genteel tradition of inoffensiveness, a tradition not unlike that of English Victorian fiction, Tolstoy preceded him in this respect in *The Death of Ivan Ilych,* where he dwells with unsparing detail on the physical horrors of disease and death. But the story is also filled with those psychologically realistic and perceptive touches made familiar to us by earlier novels—Peter Ivanovich's efforts, at a solemn moment, to suppress the rebel-

lious metal springs of the pouf on which he sits at Ivan Ilych's funeral; the subtle indications of the mourners' insincerity, suggested by their concentration on unrelated trivia; the indirect hints of the dissimulation and hypocrisy of Ivan Ilych's grieving wife and colleagues, who barely disguise their secret concern over the advantages or disadvantages that will accrue to them because of his death. Yet we somehow know that Ivan Ilych would have behaved in similar fashion in the event of the decease of his wife or of one of his partners in the law. (p. 149)

[Shortly] before his death an inner light mystically illumines the clouded understanding of Ivan Ilych. He suddenly perceives that man's essential life belongs to the spirit, a realm of feeling where well-being is achieved in the loving community of people. In truth, death for Ivan Ilych ultimately becomes an awakening. He asks forgiveness of his family for his sins and welcomes death, transported by the inner light of faith, renunciation, and love.

In *Master and Man* the same theme is treated with equal effectiveness in a totally different setting of peasants and merchants, and the story is told in a style that falls between Tolstoy's earlier method of saturated realism and his post-conversion manner of simple unadorned narrative designed to appeal to the mass reader. Here and elsewhere we sense that his aim is to relate facts with as much warmth and persuasiveness as possible and hence the prose he creates is magnificent. (pp. 150-51)

Master and Man embodies Tolstoy's ideal of religious art that has a universal appeal more successfully than other tales which he expressly designed for this purpose. Here truth is achieved by spiritual conviction rather than by the intellectual conviction that brings about the conversion of Tolstoy's hero in his novel *Resurrection*—a patent artistic error. (pp. 152-53)

As in *The Death of Ivan Ilych,* the emancipated realism of *The Kreutzer Sonata* shocked readers and also held them spellbound. Never before in Russian literature had sex, marriage, and the physical foundations of it been discussed so frankly. (p. 155)

The new ideal that had appealed to Tolstoy, for the expression of which his distraught hero Pozdnyshev in *The Kreutzer Sonata* became the mouthpiece, was the necessity of absolute chastity not only for unmarried, but even for married people. . . .

Though Tolstoy's original story of "sexual love" acquired some of the characteristics of a treatise on celibacy and chastity, his extraordinary artistic sense prevented it from turning into a mere didactic tract. Despite the half-mad behavior of Pozdnyshev nothing could be more realistically and psychologically compelling than the narrative of his moral and spiritual struggle against former personal convictions and the conventional taboos of society. The detailed account of the moves and countermoves and of all the reasons for them which step by step drive him on to kill his wife, and the description of the murder itself, are positively gripping. The story is an amazing example of Tolstoy's ability to elucidate a moral ideal of his own through the medium of artistic narrative. (p. 156)

Walk in the Light While There Is Light . . . and *Father Sergius* . . . are short novels that bear a direct relation to the short moral and religious stories and legends that Tolstoy wrote not long after his spiritual conversion. That is, they are much longer and more complex efforts to employ fiction to teach and illustrate the dogmas of Tolstoy's new faith. (p. 158)

As in Tolstoy's previous full-length novels, there is a great deal of autobiographical matter in *Resurrection*. (pp. 191-92)

Resurrection naturally forces comparison with those supreme works, *War and Peace* and *Anna Karenina,* and it must be admitted that it falls below the lofty artistic achievements of these earlier novels. However, its best things, artistically speaking, belong to the narrative method of Tolstoy's earlier fiction rather than to the compressed, direct, and stylistically unadorned manner of the later period after *What Is Art?* was written. In *Resurrection* there is that same wealth of precise realistic detail which conveys the appearance of indubitable actuality to imagined situations, as well as roundness, completeness, and the vitality of life to his characters. (p. 193)

Tolstoy turned his back on [the] admirable credo of relative objectivity in art in writing *Resurrection*—an unashamedly purpose novel. To be sure, most great novels are in one sense or another purpose novels, but the purpose is sublimated in a depiction of life free of any special pleading that distorts the essential artistic unity of the whole. In *Resurrection* Tolstoy's purpose of condemning the violence of government, the injustice of man-made laws, the hypocrisy of the Church, and of pleading the biblical injunction to judge not that you be not judged, obtrudes in a rather scholastic manner throughout the novel. (p. 194)

According to Tolstoy's principal criterion of real art, namely, infectiousness, which he developed in his treatise *What Is Art?, Resurrection* holds up quite well. That is, the novel deals with feelings sincerely expressed by the author, and so artistically conveyed that they infect readers and cause them to share these feelings with him and with each other. And certainly more than any of his other novels, *Resurrection* fulfils Tolstoy's definition of the best art, for it evokes in us feelings of brotherly love and of the common purpose of the life of all humanity—a striving to achieve spiritual and moral perfection through service to others. (p. 198)

> *Ernest J. Simmons, in his* Introduction to Tolstoy's Writings *(reprinted by permission of the University of Chicago Press; © 1968 by The University of Chicago), University of Chicago Press, 1968, 215 p.*

HARRY J. MOONEY, JR. (essay date 1968)

Leo Tolstoy is probably most effectively approached in terms of his relationship not to the conventions of the novel but rather to those of the epic. (p. 1)

The quality of Leo Tolstoy's imagination as a novelist is so pervasively epic that it seems clear that his two greatest novels, *War and Peace* and *Anna Karenina,* are often most rewardingly approached in terms of their relationship to this great, though by no means rigid, literary pattern. Like their Homeric and Virgilian prototypes, Tolstoy's characters are often developed with a density which is at least partly owing to their profound commitment to land and nature, family and society. Constantine Levin in *Anna Karenina* is

of course the exemplification of Tolstoy's sense of man's necessary relationship to the natural world. Moreover, the basic ethic of *Anna Karenina* is sharpened by Tolstoy's structural insistence upon contrasting the artificial, attenuated culture of the city with the primary, organic spiritual challenge of the country. (p. 2)

Like the earliest epic writers, and in a way which has become representative of their kind of vision, Tolstoy in some of his greatest moments unites man and nature at a level of almost mystical communication. The hunting scenes in *Anna Karenina,* the extended episode of the wolf hunt in *War and Peace,* are metaphors for expressing this unity in a way which also dramatizes Tolstoy's unique sense of the lyrical, joyful quality of the release of man's physical energy. At still more important levels of meaning, the direct perception of the natural world arouses in man luminous and revelatory sensations which could come to him in no other way. (p. 3)

Equally central to Tolstoy's vision is the family, the unit in which, in both *War and Peace* and *Anna Karenina,* man's most vital relationships are lived, those relationships the fracture of which produces the most drastic consequences in his life. *Anna Karenina* opens with a line which, although it was added after the original draft of the novel, focusses all that is to follow: "All happy families resemble one another, but each unhappy family is unhappy in its own way." By opening the novel with the scenes in the Oblonsky's home immediately after the wife has discovered her husband's infidelity, and by creating in Dolly a profound sense of the role of wife and mother in contrast to her husband's unreckoning libertinage, Tolstoy not only introduces proleptically the two major themes of the novel as they will be represented by Levin and Anna (thought only in general terms: no one could call Anna a libertine), but also provides in the study of the Oblonskys themselves the structural means by which the two halves of the novel are made to join. (pp. 7-8)

War and Peace, although more diffuse by its very nature, is nevertheless pervaded by family relationships and their vitality. In the multiplicity of situations and characters represented by its plot, this novel also creates its thematic emphases by contrast and counter-statement. Some of its greatest, most densely epic scenes are those the power of which derives from Tolstoy's ability to suggest the variety, the joy, the tension and the anxiety of family relationships. . . . (pp. 12-13)

The family occurrences of *War and Peace,* however, carry an emphasis very different from those of *Anna Karenina,* for over all the relationships of the novel hang the heavy and transforming shadows of war, time and death. . . . The family therefore acquires a preternatural sharpness of definition because of Tolstoy's method of giving it a density and solidity which, though unique, are nevertheless threatened by the attenuations of time and distance. (pp. 13-14)

To allude to the primacy of the family in Tolstoy, then, is to define a part of the epic force and clarity with which he focusses on life, death, love, sexuality, birth, war and peace, for the family is nothing less than the unit by which Tolstoy conveys what it means to be human, and to be deeply involved with other human beings.

Such an option for the epic focus upon all these areas of human existence, since it constitutes above all a way of looking at life, must inevitably have large results for the question of style. In Tolstoy perhaps the first of these, and certainly one of his most distinguishing characteristics, is the moral energy—whether in approbation or disapprobation, though the effect is most obvious, but no more important, in the latter—with which style itself is often invested. (p. 15)

Joy and reverence, qualities evoked by Tolstoy with extraordinary clarity and power, transform completely all those objects the perception of which they influence. (p. 18)

This joy sounds the dominant note in the closing sections of *Anna Karenina* and if it is joy in God it is simultaneously joy in existence. It springs logically from that experience of wonder so central to [Tolstoy]. (p. 88)

> *Harry J. Mooney, Jr., in his* Tolstoy's Epic Vision: A Study of "War and Peace" and "Anna Karenina" *(copyright 1968 by the University of Tulsa), University of Tulsa, 1968, 88 p.*

LEV SHESTOV (essay date 1969)

In his book *What Is Art?* Tolstoy—not, indeed, for the first time, but with all the passion of a man freshly entering the struggle—attacks contemporary society. (p. 11)

This tendency is already strongly manifested in *Anna Karenina*. As a motto for this novel Tolstoy took the Biblical verse "Vengeance is mine, and I will recompense, saith the Lord." We are accustomed to understand these words in the sense that the final, decisive judgment over men cannot be pronounced by men and that the success or failure of our earthly life proves neither our innocence nor our guilt. But in *Anna Karenina* we feel a completely different understanding of the Biblical text. Already in this novel Tolstoy does not restrict himself to describing human life but also undertakes to judge it—and to judge not as a calm and impartial judge who knows neither pity nor anger, but as a man deeply and passionately interested in the outcome of the trial. Every line of this magnificent work is directed against an invisible but definite enemy and defends an equally invisible and definite ally. And the stronger the enemy is, the more cutting and refined is the weapon with which Tolstoy strikes him, the more clever, complex, and inconspicuous is the mine-work with which he attacks him. Oblonsky is easily disposed of by some ironic remarks and by the comic situations in which the author constantly involves his characters. Karenin, of course, is a more serious case, but even against him the battle is not too difficult. But it is different with Vronsky and Koznyshov. These are men of greater caliber. Even if they do not have enough initiative to succeed in creating anything new, they at least have enough energy to further the things they wish and to promote those persons with whom an inner relationship binds them. They support a certain social order; they are the pillars whose solidity guarantees the solidity of the entire structure. And it is upon these representatives of society that Tolstoy throws himself with all the power of his tremendous genius. Not only their activity but their entire being is reduced to nothing. They struggle, they strive, they get excited, but everything is as fruitless and purposeless as the running around of a squirrel in a cage. They serve a senseless idol whose name is Delusion. (pp. 12-13)

The most important person, however, among the accused,

for whose sake the Biblical verse was obviously set at the beginning of the work, is Anna. It is her whom vengeance awaits, her whom Tolstoy wishes to punish. She has sinned and must accept the punishment.

In all Russian literature, perhaps even in all world literature, there is not to be found another novelist who has shown such a complete lack of pity and such cold-bloodedness in leading his heroine toward the terrible death that awaits her. And it is not enough to call him pitiless and cold-blooded; it was joyously, triumphantly that Tolstoy sacrificed Anna. Her shameful and sorrowful end is for him a sign—and a sign that fills him with hope. After having led Anna to death, he brings Levin to faith in God, and then ends his novel. Had Anna been able to survive her shame, had she retained a consciousness of her human rights, had she died not broken and bowed down but maintaining her innocence and pride, the point of support which permitted Tolstoy to preserve his spiritual equilibrium would have been taken away from him. He found himself before the alternative: Anna or himself, her destruction or his own salvation. And he sacrificed Anna—Anna who had left her lawful husband and gone to Vronsky. Tolstoy knows perfectly well what kind of a husband Karenin is for Anna; he has described better than anyone the terrible situation of this woman—well-endowed, intelligent, delicate, full of life —whom the bonds of marriage had chained to an automaton. But Tolstoy had to regard these bonds as holy and obligatory, for in the very existence of the universally obligatory lay for him the proof of a higher harmony. To the defense of this obligatory he rises with all the power of his literary genius. Anna, having disregarded the "rule," must die a horrible death.

The characters of *Anna Karenina* are divided into two categories. Some follow the rule or rules and go with Levin toward the good and toward salvation. The others follow their own inclinations, break the rules, and suffer, according to the audacity and deliberateness of their actions, more or less severe punishment. (pp. 13-14)

In *Anna Karenina* the number of rules that Tolstoy regards as obligatory is still relatively quite small. At the time that he conceived this novel, the author gave the "good" only relative power over human life. Even more: he still refuses to think that the service of the good must be the exclusive and conscious goal of our life. In *Anna Karenina*, as in *War and Peace*, Tolstoy disavows the possibility of exchanging life for the good; indeed, he believes that such an exchange would be against nature, that it would be false and affected, and that, in the final analysis, it must lead even the best of men to a reaction. (pp. 14-15)

Levin was tormented that he did not know for what or how he should live. Nevertheless, he firmly followed his own definite way in life and finally convinced himself that, even though he was not seeking the good but his own happiness, his life—despite this, or much more precisely, because of this—not only was not void of meaning, as it had been formerly, *but had the indubitable sense of the good.*

Whence did this "sense of the good" suddenly come? Why did this good come to Levin to bless him and not to the other characters of the novel? Why did Anna perish—and rightly? Why did Vronsky come to ruin, why did Koznyshov lead an illusory existence, while Levin not only enjoyed all the goods of life but also acquired the right to deep spiritual peace—a privilege accorded only to very few and extraordinary men? Why did fate so unjustly deal mildly with Levin and so cruelly with Anna? For another writer—a naturalist, for example—all these questions would be inappropriate. For such a man the injustice of fate is the fundamental principle of human existence, a law deriving so clearly from natural evolution that there is no occasion to be surprised by it. But such a writer does not quote the gospel and does not speak of retribution. With Tolstoy, however, his entire novel is born out of these questions. In *Anna Karenina* he does not simply describe life, he interrogates it, demands answers of it. His literary creativity awoke at the need to find a solution for the problems that tormented him.

This is why all his works, the long as well as the short, *War and Peace* as well as "The Death of Ivan Ilyitch" and his journalistic articles, always have the character of complete settledness. Tolstoy always presents himself to the public with finished answers, and these answers are given in a form so precise that they satisfy the most demanding of men. Obviously this is not and cannot be a matter of chance. In it lies the fundamental point of all of Tolstoy's creativity. All the tremendous inner travail that was necessary to create *Anna Karenina* and *War and Peace* had been provoked by the need, carried to the furthest extreme, of understanding himself and the world surrounding him, of ridding himself of all the doubts that tormented him, and of finding—at least for a time—stable ground under his feet. These needs are too serious and too persistent for one to be able to hide behind a simple painting of images of immediately perceived reality or the setting down of one's reminiscences. Something else is necessary. One's right to live must be found. It is necessary to find a power greater than human which can sustain and defend this right. Personal tastes, sympathies, enthusiasms, passions—all these elements, into which realist writers are accustomed to divide human life—guarantee nothing and cannot satisfy a Tolstoy. He seeks a strong and omnipotent ally, in order to speak in its name of his right. All the power of Tolstoy's genius is applied to finding this ally and drawing it to himself. In this undertaking Tolstoy is merciless. There is nothing that he is not willing to destroy in order to arrive at his goal. There are no limits to the tension of his soul when this interest that is most sacred to him is involved. (pp. 18-19)

[After *Anna Karenina*] Count Tolstoy has so solemnly renounced his past that it is altogether impossible to accuse him of contradiction and inconsistency. He himself admits having been "bad" before. What more is needed? But I do not in the least wish to reproach Tolstoy. He was, is, and will always be "the great writer of the Russian land." If I seek to investigate his past, it is not to accuse him but only better to understand the meaning and scope of his doctrine. And I am less struck by the difference between the former and the present Count Tolstoy than by the unity and consistency that characterize the development of his philosophy. One finds in it, to be sure, some essential contradictions, and these ought not to be ignored. Tolstoy from the time he created *War and Peace* and *Anna Karenina* is for us in any case an important witness, to whom one not only can listen but to whom it is our duty to listen. Especially in view of the fact that this extraordinary man, as has already been shown above, always, throughout all his life, stubbornly

professed the conviction that outside the "good" there is no salvation.

All the transformations in his philosophy never pass beyond the limits of "life in the sign of the good"; they touch only the question of knowing in what the good consists and how one must act to have the good on his side. This explains Tolstoy's purely sectarian intolerance toward the opinion of others, toward those who led a life different from his own. Such is the nature of the good; he who is not for it is against it! And whoever has recognized the sovereignty of the good is compelled to divide his neighbors into good and wicked men, i.e., friends and enemies. It is true that Tolstoy always expresses his preparedness to pardon his neighbor, to let him pass from the category of wicked into that of good, but only on the strict condition that he repent. "Acknowledge that you have been wrong, that you have been bad, live as I do, then I will call you good." He knows no other way of reconciliation. Even more, if the condition of repentance is lacking, eternal enmity is declared. Not, obviously, enmity in the ordinary sense of the word. Count Tolstoy will neither strike his enemy nor try to do any harm to him. On the contrary, he will turn the other cheek when anyone strikes him; he will accept insult and suffering and will be all the more happy the more he can yield. He reserves one thing only: his right to the "good."

To every attack against this right Tolstoy shows a greediness like that of Shakespeare's Henry V, when it is a question of glory. Both Tolstoy and Henry V believe that in this case greed is not a vice, that no one can be reproached for it, that, on the contrary, it must be counted an excellence. We can gladly let the English king rest, but when a Tolstoy shows himself eager to defend his right, like a knight of the Middle Ages, one is led to serious reflections. That virtue, that good, which we have always believed to be beyond the hereditary activity of egoism, suddenly shows itself to be just as human, just as inalienable, as all the other purely pagan goods—glory, power, wealth. For the sake of the good, just as implacable a struggle is possible—by means, of course, of other weapons.

All of Tolstoy's life is an example of this; all of his preaching is proof of it. In his last work, *What Is Art?,* Tolstoy, an old man of seventy, undertakes a battle for his right against an entire generation. And how this struggle inspires him! The sole purpose of this work is to declare to men: "you are immoral but I am moral, i.e., I, not you, possess the highest good." And this work is written with such mastery that one can find nothing like it, not only in Russian literature but in contemporary world literature. Despite the external calm of the almost epic tone, the passionate excitement and indignation which agitated Tolstoy make themselves felt only too strongly, even by those whom the sources of the brilliant writer's creativity do not interest greatly. One does not find in it any trace of the insulting words that ordinarily betray human anger. Tolstoy even avoids open sarcasm. He has no weapons other than his delicate irony and a few epithets of—at first blush—inoffensive character, such as "wicked," "immoral," "depraved." The word "impudence" is used only once, in relation to Nietzsche. It might be thought that one could not do anything in this way, especially in our day when the word "immoral" seems to have long since lost its former sharpness and its opposite, "virtuous," that Tolstoy was not afraid to use to designate those spiritually close to him, has become almost synonymous with "comical." And yet, what can a genius not accomplish! *What Is Art?* is the model of a polemical work. To express with greater power what Tolstoy has expressed is impossible, even without the framework of mild Christian apologetic to which he voluntarily limited himself. I am profoundly convinced that most readers, especially Russian readers, however far they may be from Tolstoy's ideals, however little inclined they may be to renounce their privileges, must experience, in reading his book, true pleasure and even find that "basically" he is completely right. (pp. 41-3)

> *Lev Shestov, "The Good in the Teaching of Tolstoy and Nietzsche: Philosophy and Preaching," in his* Dostoevsky, Tolstoy and Nietzsche, *translated by Bernard Martin (© 1969 by Ohio University Press; reprinted by permission of Ohio University Press, Athens), Ohio University Press, 1969, pp. 11-140.**

EDMUND WILSON   (essay date 1971)

The difference between Tolstoy's great early novels and his so much less satisfactory late ones is due to his having been able, in the former, to split up his own complicated personality into the several personalities of his characters—as in Pierre Bezukhov, Prince André, and Nicholas Rostov— each true to its own laws and each more or less of a piece. When he falls back on dramatizing his own mixed nature in an attempt to reduce it to something more easily acceptable, he produces such relatively implausible creations as Ivan Ilyich, Father Sergius and Prince Nekhlyudov. (p. 176)

[In] general, it seems to me that most of [Tolstoy's] post-conversion stories suffer from their being deformed by the moralistic bias. *The Death of Ivan Ilyich* has often been much admired; but I cannot believe that a provincial judge, even ill and on the verge of death, would have felt to an extent so demoralizing the futility of his life. Tolstoy would have had—he did have when he wrote *A Confession*—such broodings as he attributes to Ivan Ilyich, but I cannot believe that Ivan would have had them or that Tolstoy, in his early phase, would have invented so implausible a character.

In his other famous late story, *Father Sergius,* the main character becomes preposterous. (p. 178)

Tolstoy was of course well qualified to understand the spiritual pride of Sergius, his ungovernable sensuality, and his equally ungovernable determination that no one should ever top him. But he is quite unable to imagine his hero's existence in the cave—which, to a non-Russian non-religious reader is equally unimaginable. What is the use of these endless sessions of prayer and worshipful meditation? Would they not certainly pall on a man who had enjoyed all the pleasures of society? (p. 179)

Resurrection is more impressive because it deals with actuality, a situation much less of fantasy. It seems to me an underrated book. It has become a critics' cliché to say that it is by no means equal to its more celebrated predecessors. . . . Tolstoy said of the novel that he did not have time to make it what it ought to be; but what he seems to have meant was not that he did not have time to polish and prune it but that he ought to have brought it closer to his conception of the kind of thing that could be easily understood by an unsophisticated audience. (p. 180)

In all Tolstoy's talk about love and God, it is a little hard to know what he means by either. He does not seem very much to love others; and what is his communion with god? . . . [The] cult of love and God seems often, as with Father Sergius, an arid self-directed exercise that simply raises the worshipper in his own esteem. (p. 183)

> *Edmund Wilson, "Notes on Tolstoy" (1971), in his* A Window on Russia, for the Use of Foreign Readers *(reprinted by permission of Farrar, Straus & Giroux, Inc.; copyright © 1943, 1944, 1952, 1957, 1965, 1967, 1969, 1970, 1972 by Edmund Wilson; copyright renewed © 1971, 1972 by Edmund Wilson), Farrar, Straus & Giroux, 1972, pp. 160-83.*

ELIZABETH HARDWICK   (essay date 1973)

The Kreutzer Sonata by Tolstoy is a work of great peculiarity. It is not of the first interest imaginatively, and there is a dense, frantic distortion in this pedagogic monologue on sex and the ills of marriage. It is a tract, inchoate, and yet noble, impractical, original. There are moments of dramatic genius: a wracking vision of marriage as jealousy nourished, hatred voluptuously fed, rage taken for breakfast. The whole of a man's sexual life comes under Tolstoy's agitated scrutiny—from the arrogant encounters of youth to the fevered tournaments of conventional unions. Tolstoy sees the line of "immorality" beginning in the young man's first relations with prostitutes and girls toward whom he feels no obligation; from there all of the later life of the sexes is either grossly or subtly poisoned. Life among men and women is a debauch the young are led to accept, even to expect, by custom, example, social convenience.

The actions the nineteenth century gathered together under the name of "debauchery" are never, in fiction, made entirely clear, but it seems very likely that many of them are understood in our time as healthy exertions of vital being. Debauchery, of course, still exists in our minds as a designation of brutal excess and deviation, even if it cannot stand as the name of the experiences of the man in *The Kreutzer Sonata.* . . .

Tolstoy was in his seventies when he wrote *Resurrection.* The indulgences of his youth thus presented themselves to his imagination as moral and social delinquencies, rather than as mere instances of man's inevitable practice. For this reason and despite the marvelous truthfulness of a great deal of the novel, it relies upon the silky transcendences of persons in the grip of a spiritual idea, characters who must go from flaw to virtue under the rule of justice and ethical revelation. . . .

The title of the novel is accurate—drastic breaks with the customs ruling men and women are to be understood as a "resurrection," a surpassing. It is, after all, only an ideal, the dream of an old man in love with humility and longing to achieve a personal reformation upon which a reformation of society might begin. The novel was based on an incident that appeared in the press and stirred Tolstoy's thoughts and imagination. In spite of this it is realistic only in the grand, elevated Russian novel sense, in that landscape where obsession and transfiguring guilt and expiation are real. No subsequent novel decided to gaze so directly into the abyss of sexual responsibility, to turn a limpid, child-like, old-man's eye upon the chaos of youth, to undertake a day of judgment accounting. (p. 6)

Elizabeth Hardwick, "Seduction and Betrayal II," in The New York Review of Books (*reprinted with permission from* The New York Review of Books; *copyright* © *1973 Nyrev, Inc.*), Vol. XX, No. 10, June 14, 1973, p. 6-10.*

RUTH CREGO BENSON (essay date 1973)

The conflict between his instincts and his conscience that characterized Tolstoy's entire life was reflected in his double view of woman as both angel and devil. In his life and in his fiction, Tolstoy believed that women at their best could be loving companions to their husbands, devoted mothers to their children, and the guardians of household and family. Woman's selfish interests, however, and particularly her sexuality, constantly threatened Tolstoy's own and his heroes' search for moral perfection and an ideal of purity. (p. vii)

Of Tolstoy's early works, *The Cossacks* and Part I of *Family Happiness* share an unflawed vision of an ideal love relationship. (p. 16)

Family Happiness was not a hastily executed literary venture but rather one which isolated and explored a theme from the projected third part of *The Cossacks*. The heroine of *Family Happiness* is, like Olenin [in *The Cossacks*], moved by the romantic impulse toward pure love and moral perfection. But once married, her romantic illusions are destroyed and eventually transformed into a subdued, chastened adaptation to domestic reality. The themes of moral retribution and homicidal jealousy, also present in the original plan for *The Cossacks,* were of course fully elaborated in *Anna Karenina* and *The Kreutzer Sonata.* . . . [The Cossacks represents] a unique attempt in Tolstoy to legitimize the sexual relationship of man and woman by associating it with nature and the "natural ideal." By itself, *The Cossacks* remains, in fact, so pure, stark, and finally unreal, that it strays from the conventions of the short story into the abstract world of myth. (p. 17)

Although the first part of *Family Happiness* is, like *The Cossacks,* a tale of romantic love, its second half proceeds to the disillusionment with romantic love which Tolstoy foresaw but never described for Olenin and Maryanka. In this story Tolstoy conforms to his own conviction that while most love stories usually end with marriage, that is where they should begin. From Masha's wedding he proceeds to her married and family life. It is the contrast between her expectations of love and the actual experience of her marriage that provides the substance and mood of the story. Beyond that, *Family Happiness* is a fictionalized treatise on the appropriate roles and behavior for women. (p. 23)

In his characterization of Natasha Rostov, Tolstoy states some of the most important themes of *War and Peace*. In her, life fights against death, humanity against materialism, spontaneity against manipulation, intuition against reason, endurance and continuity against disorder and chaos, private experience against civic, and truth against disguise. In short, Tolstoy has created a conventionally positive and sympathetic heroine. But because Tolstoy identifies Natasha's most attractive qualities and roles specifically with her womanhood, his attitudes toward her are colored by his ambivalent views of women in general. Not even Natasha fully escapes the "implacable hostility" toward women that Gorky saw in Tolstoy.

Crucial to Natasha's character is her nonintellectual temperament. In one of his sketches for *War and Peace,* Tolstoy describes Natasha as "stupid, but nice, uneducated, knows nothing. . . ." . . . Natasha's nonintellectuality, her lack of formal education, and her political naiveté serve a polemical purpose: these traits challenge the achievements and the aspirations of the feminists of the 1860s. . . . Tolstoy thought that women should not be involved with political and social problems; they had a more important function to fulfill at home in serving their husbands and educating their children. Masha of *Family Happiness,* for example, seriously endangered her marriage by living independently of her husband and children. (pp. 45-6)

Tolstoy presents in the Epilogue [of *War and Peace*] a bizarre theory of marital equilibrium: the role of the individual man or woman acting on the demands of will, conscience, or passions, is lost as one mate absorbs the other and as both are consumed by the family. In the absorption of the individual into the family, Tolstoy is in fact striving toward the selfless ideal of life most characteristic of his late period, but present even in the young Tolstoy. . . . [Although] Tolstoy viewed his marriage in the Epilogue with approval and enthusiasm, the happy resolution of *War and Peace* for Natasha and Pierre is not a thoroughly satisfying one. It is, in fact, only one of a double image, the second of which Tolstoy was compelled to expose in his greatest and most complex treatment of marriage: *Anna Karenina*. (pp. 73-4)

[Like] Masha of *Family Happiness,* Anna wants not to play at life but to experience it directly. She mistakenly believes that the "achievement of her desires" in romantic love will assure her happiness; but in Tolstoy's view, it can only guarantee her disillusion and isolation.

This inner demand for love and happiness is instinctive, part of Anna's nature; she, therefore, cannot control it or its consequences. Also beyond her control is that "mysterious force" which colludes with her own and Vronsky's limitations to confine and destroy them. It is that "harsh, mysterious force" which, Karenin believes, governs life and "demands the fulfillment of its decrees." Its symbol is the terrifying blizzard which engulfs Anna and Vronsky when, at the train station, Vronsky makes his confession of love to Anna. It is an immutable, nonrational logic of events which does not lead people to their destiny, but surrounds them, like amniotic fluid, as they themselves proceed to it.

But Anna herself conspires with this mysterious force by consciously choosing alternatives which can only lead to her death. These choices are influenced both by her own feeling of guilt and her "literary" conception of her fate. Whether or not the reader may judge Anna "guilty" she herself certainly does. When she reflects on her life she realizes that she "would always remain the guilty wife." . . . Her guilt is the source of her schizophrenic reaction to Karenin at the birth of her daughter: she clutches him to her with one hand and pushes him away with the other. She wants, in addition, to be punished for her guilt. . . . (pp. 103-04)

The question, then, of judgment and moral retribution in *Anna Karenina* is finally one that centers around Anna herself. She judges herself guilty, chooses to continue an impossible way of life, and executes her own death sentence.

When Anna throws herself under the wheels of the train, she both punishes herself and takes revenge on Vronsky and all the others whom she blames for her condition. But just as Levin felt that there was something ''not quite right'' in the pity he felt for Anna, so the reader is left with the uncomfortable feeling that the harsh verdict of the wheels is also ''not quite right.'' That feeling derives from the fact that Tolstoy ''allowed'' Anna, one can only feel, to seek a conclusion, not a resolution, to her life. And not simply because any resolution that one could devise would inevitably be untenable, but rather because Tolstoy himself could not fully resolve the tension between Anna's personal charisma and her own morality. (pp. 105-06)

In contrast to his earlier work, the two distinctive motifs of *The Kreutzer Sonata*, and equally of ''The Devil'' and ''Father Sergius,'' are Tolstoy's explicit and exacerbated preoccupation with sex as central to the relations between men and women, and the barely concealed hysteria which provides the tone of the stories. They are the fulfillment of and the self-indulgent absorption in the dark content of *Family Happiness*, *War and Peace*, and, of course, *Anna Karenina*. Of the three pieces, *The Kreutzer Sonata* is the most developed and the most powerful. If one were not aware that the other two were written subsequently, one might consider them preliminary sketches for the first, so similar are the concerns and details. They are, however, more appropriately described as abortive attempts to re-make the statements so compellingly rendered in *The Kreutzer Sonata*. (p. 112)

The later Tolstoy, as we know, regarded sexual intercourse, even between married partners, as disgusting and absurd, a shameful, ''animal'' act that separated the partners spiritually and emotionally. But that did not eliminate the basic problem of sexuality, the recognition of oneself and others as sexual creatures, fully available to each other. This might be called the ''no barriers'' theme in Tolstoy's thought, for he uses the phrase again and again to denote such recognition. This phrase indicates the mutual sudden awareness of attraction between many couples in Tolstoy's works: Pierre and Ellen, Natasha and Anatole, Anna and Vronsky, and so on. In short, throughout Tolstoy's literary work, he defines sexual attraction with a phrase connoting the consciousness of a naked confrontation between the two persons and of an uncontrolled force drawing them together. (p. 126)

Of course this naked confrontation is not always matched by a frank admission of the basically erotic content of sex. The men of these stories invent verbal subterfuges, like the ''safety valve'' metaphor that occurs so often in Tolstoy, or better yet, they repeat the maxim that sex is necessary for the sake of one's health. In the notion that sex is necessary to the health, the mechanical idea of sex as a ''safety valve'' is simply rendered more explicit and concrete. Expressing these attitudes, Tolstoy was not merely reflecting his society: he was stating previous or present personal convictions. (p. 127)

Basic to the shared content of the [*The Kreutzer Sonata*, ''The Devil,'' and ''Father Sergius''] is Tolstoy's assurance that women, and the sexuality that women represent, project, and provoke, are the source of man's downfall. Because of them, careers are destroyed, character is corrupted, sexual desire flares out of control. In *War and Peace* and *Anna Karenina* Tolstoy was still willing to repre-

sent marriage as an effective and acceptable way to organize sex for the purpose of bearing children. In two of these three stories, however, though the marriages could have taken such a form, Tolstoy's characters dismiss this possibility without serious consideration. In each of the three stories, when the main character faces a dilemma that is mainly sexual in nature, he feels a profound fear, distrust, or contempt of sexuality, or of intimacy of any kind. And in all three, as a direct consequence of, and indeed in direct response to, the sexual dilemma of the male tempted by the female, alienation and violence follow relentlessly.

Natasha and Pierre and Kitty and Levin had escaped this fate; Anna and Vronsky had succumbed to it. Yet there was adequate warning of this nihilism even as early as *Family Happiness*, where the possibility of happiness is concrete at the beginning, but where the deterioration of romantic illusion and the isolation of mates is inexorable. In *The Kreutzer Sonata* and its satellites, the possibility of alternatives or adjustment to this process appears as delusion or hallucination. But *The Kreutzer Sonata* penetrates beyond a tragic view of experience: like Tolstoy's own *Confession*, its orgiastic tone and its insistent self-contempt invite us to celebrate, with the penitents, their capacity for evil and their pride of guilt. In these three stories, the consistent single message is the inevitable failure of human relationships and the inescapable recognition of human alienation. In this world, like Pashenka and Father Sergius, who come together only for aid and comfort, men and women no longer live and act in concert, but in isolation. (pp. 137-38)

[Tolstoy's] power was tragically flawed by his consistently limited and distorted view of the nature of sex, of women, and, therefore, of the men who were his chief concern. So that, by the end of his life, the dream of the young Tolstoy —of a warm family life in the country, of a productive and benevolent estate, of friendships, of literary success, of the pursuit of culture—had vanished entirely. For this ideal, the spent but still aspiring old man finally substituted his heterodox-Christian vision of an emotionally and erotically anaesthetic world. (p. 138)

> *Ruth Crego Benson, in her* Women in Tolstoy: The Ideal and the Erotic (© *1973 by the Board of Trustees of the University of Illinois; reprinted by permission of the author and the University of Illinois Press*), *University of Illinois Press, 1973, 141 p.*

A.D.P. BRIGGS (essay date 1978)

Any casual assessment of Tolstoyan scholarship would conclude that the pioneering work was out of the way, at least as far as the major works are concerned. The historical tale *Hadji Murat* is an interesting exception; it is probably the only work of this eminent writer which deserves a position in the front rank of his achievement. . . . (p. 109)

The idea that the work is somehow inchoate because Tolstoy never finished revising the story is manifestly wrong. . . . The anomalous nature of the work is, on the other hand, difficult to pronounce upon. It is amusing to recall the famous old man working at his manuscript on the sly for days on end, troubled by his own conscience which told him it was wrong to waste his time on historical adventure stories when he ought really to be using his talent for the improvement of the moral condition of his fellow men. (p. 110)

Time after time he caught himself going into much detail, labouring a point or making his moral too obvious. His artistic self-control is truly surprising, and the rewards of it have proved very considerable. *Hadji Murat* emerged as a near perfect blend of narrative skill and moral argument, the latter amounting to a summation of many well-known Tolstoyan preoccupations presented with an altogether new sense of restraint, balance and apparent objectivity. In this work Tolstoy fascinates his reader by his excellent story-telling and propels him only with the gentlest of nudges, which pass unnoticed in the wealth of interest or excitement, in the required directions of moral judgement. One exceptional chapter . . . , devoted to the hated Nicholas I, overbrims with sarcastic venom and is spoiled because of it; this section—which was itself drastically pruned—has the useful function of emphasising how subtly entertainment and dialectic are intermingled elsewhere. Tolstoy seems to have used *Hadji Murat* as a repository for excellent, disciplined writing on the side during a period when his conscious mind was busy denying the value of anything that was not simply and overtly instructional. There is little value in wondering why this came about, whether the urge to write well simply reasserted itself or whether Tolstoy experienced the rare, subconscious awareness of an obvious truth, namely that nagging instruction is a less powerful method of persuasion than gentle guidance masked by entertainment. The extent and the manner of the achievement, however, remain open to analysis.

The signal accomplishment of *Hadji Murat* is not only that it triumphs in characterisation, content and form but that each of these aspects of the serious narrator's art, and every other temptation towards an extreme to which Tolstoy often succumbs on other occasions, is thwarted in its attempt to predominate. First, characterisation. . . . Tolstoy provides a strong sense of Hadji Murat's physicality. He is glimpsed in action and negotiation, not in reflection. At the end of it all we are left with a powerful impression of how this strong man has moved, ridden, fought, paced up and down in impatience, washed, dressed and undressed, prayed, buckled on his weapons and performed other bodily functions, including that of dying a cruel death. It was a wise decision by the author to eschew his normal method of characterisation, that of amassing much detail and assisting the reader with the interpretation of it. Instead he opted consciously for an impressionistic manner to which he referred as the 'peep-show' technique. . . . Many subsequent critics have made much of this statement of intent as well as of Tolstoy's avowed plan to depict his hero in the round rather than in the single dimension of military hero or religious fanatic. They have been right to do so because this is what gives the story its pace and its style; moreover it is wholly appropriate that a man of exceptional vitality should be portrayed in a dynamic manner.

The other important decision taken by Tolstoy was to widen the scope of his story beyond its main hero, yet to restrain and organise his amplification so that it added both depth of meaning and greater suspense without at the same time dragging the reader off into irrelevant action or tedious theorising. The effect of this upon the characterisation alone is remarkable. The tale extends to no more than 35,000 words and yet it swarms with vitally interesting characters. (pp. 111-12)

[The] characterisation of *Hadji Murat* imparts an amplitude

to the work which, taken together with other qualities yet to be discussed, sets it on a level not with *The Death of Ivan Il'ich*, *The Kreutzer Sonata* or *Master and Man*, significant as these stories are each in its own way, but with *Anna Karenina*, *War and Peace* and *Resurrection*.

Such a large claim needs further substantiation in terms of the ideas and themes explored by the author. (p. 113)

Where, then, are the hidden meanings, conflicting insights and larger moral view? It is true that they do not clamour for attention, nor do they present themselves in the simplified, pre-digested or exaggerated forms to which the accustomed reader of Tolstoy becomes resigned. They are certainly not to be found packaged in epigrams as silly as the opening sentence of *Anna Karenina*. Nevertheless it is scarcely possible to read *Hadji Murat* without searching one's mind over a number of profound matters, some of them amounting to age-old questions of philosophy and religion: the relationship between civilised man and nature, the wonderful phenomenon of the force of life which animates all of us, the ordering of attitudes to inevitable death, the effect of religion upon mentality and behaviour, the proper arrangement of moral standards, the universality of falsehood, the need for altruism, the all too easily suppressed instinct for brotherly love, the pleasant usefulness of family life, the propensity of those in government to misuse their power and become corrupt, the awful arbitrariness of the workings of nature and history, and, perhaps most obviously in this story, the ease with which men have recourse to violence, allowing it to become an enjoyable and honourable way of life and disregarding its many horrific consequences. On all of these issues, and on others, we are invited by tacit suggestion to form a judgement. For once, Tolstoy has not told us what conclusions must be drawn, he has not even asked straight questions, he has apparently set out his hidden arguments dispassionately, and yet *Hadji Murat* contains an inbuilt guarantee that a large majority of its readers, if they reflect at all, will not only arrive at certain important convictions but that those convictions will be similar to the ones which this same author insists upon elsewhere with greater stridency and commensurately less chance of persuading his audience. (pp. 114-15)

Such are the main characteristics of *Hadji Murat*, the last really important work of Tolstoy's life and one of the finest that he ever wrote in view of its triumphant reconciliation of the competing claims of history, literature and moral instruction. (p. 126)

> *A.D.P. Briggs, "'Hadji Murat': The Power of Understatement," in* New Essays on Tolstoy, *edited by Malcolm Jones (copyright © 1978 by Cambridge University Press), Cambridge University Press, 1978, pp. 109-30.*

ADDITIONAL BIBLIOGRAPHY

Arnold, Matthew. "Count Leo Tolstoi." In his *Essays in Criticism: Second Series*, pp. 253-99. London: Macmillan and Co., 1921.
    Primarily an examination of *Anna Karenina* and Tolstoy's religious ideology.

Bayley, John. *Tolstoy and the Novel*. New York: The Viking Press, 1966, 316 p.
    Examines Tolstoy's major fiction with respect to the traditions

and devices of the nineteenth-century European novel, focusing primarily on *War and Peace.*

Christian, R. F. *Tolstoy's "War and Peace": A Study.* Oxford: Clarendon Press, 1962, 184 p.
An account of the successive stages in the writing of *War and Peace,* with an analysis of its sources, structure, style, and methods of characterization.

Christian, R. F. *Tolstoy: A Critical Introduction.* Cambridge: Cambridge University Press, 1969, 291 p.
Chronicle of Tolstoy's literary career and descriptive survey of his works and their major themes, offering much relevant background information.

Crosby, Ernest Howard. *Tolstoy and His Message.* New York: Funk and Wagnall's, 1904, 93 p.
Identifies the origins of Tolstoy's spiritual crisis and summarizes his religious, philosophical, and moral views.

Davie, Donald, ed. *Russian Literature and Modern English Fiction.* Chicago: The University of Chicago Press, 1965, 244 p.*
Includes essays on Tolstoy by George Saintsbury, George Moore, D. S. Merezhkovsky, and D. H. Lawrence.

Fausset, Hugh I'Anson. *Tolstoy: The Inner Drama.* New York: Harcourt, Brace & Co., 1968, 320 p.
Examines the effect wrought on Tolstoy's writings and personal life by an inner struggle between instinct and consciousness.

Fedin, Konstantin. "The Genius of Leo Tolstoy," *The Atlantic Monthly* 205, No. 4 (June 1960): 85-6.
Discusses as characteristic Tolstoy's device of testing the moral value of his hero at the decisive point of life and death.

Gorky, Maxim. "Reminiscences of Leo Tolstoy." In his *Reminiscences,* pp. 4-68. New York: Dover, 1946.
Personal recollection.

Greenwood, E. B. *Tolstoy: The Comprehensive Vision.* New York: St. Martin's Press, 1975, 184 p.
Study designed "to outline the striving on the part of Tolstoy and of many of his characters for a comprehensive vision which holds the many-sided confusion of life in a single luminous intuition."

Gunn, Elizabeth. *A Daring Coiffeur: Reflections on "War and Peace" and "Anna Karenina."* Totowa, NJ: Rowman and Littlefield, 1971, 146 p.
Reveals the inconsistency of Tolstoy's dictum that one must not judge others by reviewing several novels in which Tolstoy himself moralizes at length.

Jones, Malcolm, ed. *New Essays on Tolstoy.* Cambridge: Cambridge University Press, 1978, 253 p.
Collection of essays by British scholars, including Henry Gifford, A. V. Knowles, W. Gareth Jones, E. B. Greenwood, and F. F. Seeley. The editor states that each essay "constitutes a reassessment of some aspect of Tolstoy's legacy to the modern reader. . . ."

Knowles, A. V., ed. *Tolstoy: The Critical Heritage.* London: Routledge & Kegan Paul, 1978, 457 p.
Compendium of early criticism on Tolstoy's major works, especially useful for its translation of Russian critics.

Lamm, Martin. "Leo Tolstoy." In his *Modern Drama,* pp. 182-93. Oxford: Basil Blackwell, 1952.
Descriptive survey of Tolstoy's major dramas.

Lavrin, Janko. *Tolstoy: An Approach.* New York: The Macmillan Co., 1946, 166 p.
Introduction to Tolstoy's fiction and philosophy.

Leavis, F. R. "*Anna Karenina:* Thought and Significance in a Great Creative Work." In his *Anna Karenina and Other Essays,* pp. 9-32. London: Chatto & Windus, 1967.
Analysis of the themes and artistic structure of *Anna Karenina,* examining in part the reaction of D. H. Lawrence to this novel.

Matlaw, Ralph E., ed. *Tolstoy: A Collection of Critical Essays.* Englewood Cliffs, NJ: Prentice-Hall, 1967, 178 p.
Includes seminal essays by B. M. Eikhenbaum, George Lukács, R. F. Christian, R. P. Blackmur, and Lev Shestov.

Maude, Aylmer. *Tolstoy and His Problems.* London: Grant Richards, 1902, 220 p.
Designed to elucidate Tolstoy's ideas on art, religion, politics, and economics among other subjects.

Maude, Aylmer. Introduction to *Recollections and Essays,* by Leo Tolstoy, translated by Aylmer Maude, pp. vii-xxviii. London: Oxford University Press, 1937.
Descriptive survey of the essays in this volume, with a rebuttal to critics of *What Is Art?*

Merejkowski, Dmitri. *Tolstoi As Man and Artist: With an Essay on Dostoïevski.* New York and London: G. P. Putnam's Sons, 1902, 310 p.*
Analyzes Tolstoy's life and work in relation to his religious ideology. This study also examines Tolstoy's use of narrative detail and discusses the importance of art and religion in the thought of Tolstoy and Dostoevsky.

Mirsky, D. S. "The Age of Realism: The Novelists (II): Tolstoy (Before 1880)." In his *A History of Russian Literature,* pp. 245-63. New York: Alfred A. Knopf, 1949.
Biographical sketch and survey of the major works.

Nordau, Max. "Tolstoism." In his *Degeneration,* pp. 144-71. New York: D. Appleton and Co., 1895.
Sees Tolstoy as an example of "degeneracy" for his views on sexuality and religion.

Orwell, George. "Lear, Tolstoy and the Fool." In his *Shooting an Elephant and Other Essays,* pp. 32-52. New York: Harcourt, Brace & World, 1950.
Examination of Tolstoy's critique of Shakespeare.

Phelps, William Lyon. "Tolstoi." In his *Essays on Russian Novelists,* pp. 170-214. New York: The Macmillan Co., 1922.
Critical overview of the major fiction.

Redpath, Theodore. *Tolstoy.* London: Bowes & Bowes, 1960, 126 p.
Survey of Tolstoy's thought and fiction.

Slonim, Marc. "Leo Tolstoy." In his *The Epic of Russian Literature: From Its Origins through Tolstoy,* pp. 309-46. New York: Oxford University Press, 1950.
Biographical sketch with an examination of major works and themes.

Symons, Arthur. "Tolstoi on Art." In his *Studies in Prose and Verse,* pp. 173-82. New York: Dutton, 1922.
Discussion of Tolstoy's theories of art which acknowledges the integrity of his argument while bemoaning the narrowness of his vision.

Troyat, Henri. *Tolstoy.* Garden City, NY; Doubleday & Co., 1967, 762 p.
Biography emphasizing the development of Tolstoy's philosophical and ethical beliefs.

Zweers, Alexander F. *Grown-up Narrator and Childlike Hero: An Analysis of the Literary Devices Employed in Tolstoj's Trilogy "Childhood," "Boyhood" and "Youth."* The Hague: Mouton, 1971, 165 p.

Includes a survey of the critical literature on the trilogy and compares it to other treatments of childhood found in Russian literature.

Paul (Ambroise Toussaint Jules) Valéry

1871-1945

French poet, critic, essayist, and dramatist.

Valéry is one of the leading examples in modern literature of nineteenth-century Symbolist aestheticism. His work particularly reflects this movement's concern with artistic form. The foundation of his work is a desire for total control over his creation. He directed his attention to the process of creativity itself and attempted to grasp its logic. This absorption with the creative process forms the method behind his poetry and appears as a subject in his prose. Valéry revered Edgar Allan Poe's ideal of the poet who creates solely by the power of his intellect, without dependence upon inspiration. From this ideal Valéry derived his own theory of composition.

As a young man Valéry studied law at the University of Montpellier. In this city he met Pierre Louys, who afterward introduced him to the Parisian literary scene. Later Valéry became one of a group of writers who gathered at the home of the Symbolist poet Stephane Mallarmé for his Tuesday evening sessions of literary discourse. Mallarmé was influential in directing Valéry's future emphasis on aesthetic sensibility, though the younger poet did not adopt the idolatry of art which is associated with his mentor. Valéry was concerned more with the process of poetic composition than with the poem itself, which he considered necessarily imperfect. A skepticism about the value of poetry eventually led to his abandonment of art for the study of mathematics and the natural sciences.

After his initial appearances in French literary journals during the 1890s Valéry wrote practically no poetry and published very little prose for a period of almost two decades. His writing during these years took the form of personal notebooks, the *Cahiers*. In them he hoped to definitively document the workings of the mind, thereby gaining insight into his lifelong field of study: human consciousness. What is commonly referred to as Valéry's "silent period" ended with the publication of a new poem, *La jeune parque*, which was immediately recognized for its highly technical beauty. The poem is evidence of an extremely subtle poetic genius, though it has also been criticized as rarefied and obscure. Publication of the collections *Album de vers anciens, 1890-1900* and *Charmes*, which includes Valéry's famous "Le cimetiere marin," secured Valéry's position as a major poet, and in 1925 he was elected to the French Academy.

Valéry's prose displays what is perhaps his most fundamental talent: the ability to apply a well-disciplined mind to a diversity of subjects, including art, politics, science, dance, architecture, and aesthetics. The prose may be divided principally into the essays found in the five volumes of *Variété* (*Variety*) and dialogues such as *L'idée fixe* (*Idee Fixe*) and *Eupalinos, ou l'architecte* (*Eupalinos; or, The Architect*). Whatever the ostensible themes of these works taken individually, there is always present a concern with form and the activity of the critical mind—an examination of the examination. Even in his sole dramatic work, *Mon Faust* (*My Faust*), the drama is not one of action but of self-examining intellection. The

achievement of Valéry as a profound investigator of mental phenomena, an undertaking to which he remained faithful throughout his life, has earned him critical regard as one of those few writers and thinkers who are indispensible to literature in the twentieth century.

PRINCIPAL WORKS

La jeune parque (poetry) 1917
La soirée avec M. Teste (short stories) 1919
 [*An Evening with Mr. Teste*, 1925]
Album de vers anciens, 1890-1900 (poetry) 1920
Charmes (poetry) 1922
Eupalinos, ou l'architecte; precede de l'âme et la danse (prose dialogues) 1923
 [*Eupalinos; or, The Architect*, 1932; *Dance and the Soul*, 1951]
Variété I-V (essays) 1924-44
 [*Variety*, 1927; *Variety: Second Series*, 1938]
Regards sur le monde actuel (essays) 1931
 [*Reflections on the World Today*, 1948]
L'idée fixe (prose dialogue) 1932
 [*Idee Fixe*, 1965]
Tel quel. 2 vols. (essays and notebooks) 1941-1943

Mon Faust (drama) 1946
  [*My Faust* published in *Plays,* 1960]
Cahiers. 29 vols. (notebooks) 1957-61
Plays (dramas) 1960
Poems (poetry) 1971

ALYSE GREGORY (essay date 1927)

[M Paul Valéry] has sought to recapture in his poetry the virginity of the French language, and like Mallarmé he makes no concessions, no effort to become popular; "To shine in others' eyes is only to see the glitter of false gems." Discarding the sly and accredited admonitions of the emotions, wily accomplices of our instinctive wishes, he has exercised his intellect in the interests of elucidation and restraint, and in translating into unusually melodious poetry the almost avid response of his senses to the images which he imagines or contemplates. Thus his thought carries within it a kind of sensuality of its own, in which images and ideas pursue each other in harmonious swiftness. . . . (p. 430)

Like many famous poets before him, like Goethe, Poe, Baudelaire, Shelley, and Leopardi, to mention but a few, Paul Valéry is impelled to seek a meaning in a universe disconcerting and unassimilable. First of all a poet, he becomes later a philosopher through necessity, and thus develops in its nervous, haughty indifference that same superb eclecticism so nurtured and elucidated by Pater. . . . [The similarity between these two authors] is clear: each has learned to nourish, maintain, and multiply those inner moments of realization and scrutiny which are the crowning rewards of the intellectual life, each seeks in music the perfect structure of poetry, each achieves that "quietude of mind," that absence of discourteous confusion which makes it possible for them to disentangle and transcribe their intimate revelations. But in the calm and delicate complexity of Pater's style, fugitive and explicit, like winter sunshine on perfect stained glass, there is more correspondence to one's aesthetic taste, while the lucid and literary prose style, virile, weighty, and trenchant of M Valéry stimulates to a greater degree one's intellectual participation. The quality is indeed rare that is able to join in so brilliant a manner science with poetry, and force them, these seemingly alien companions, to run with so invincible a front, neck to neck, for one's interest and enlightenment. (p. 431)

If one desires to find in M Valéry's philosophical utterances an affirmative system of thought more ample and defined than a mere statement of personal values one will be disappointed. M Valéry draws about himself that bright hazardous circle of security in which thoughts, arrested on the march, are held in a state of perfect equilibrium. (p. 432)

[M Valéry's] ambition is the discovery of the common origin of all operations of the mind, above all the important relationship between art and science. In consciousness alone he sees the supreme power and resistance to "the fascination of the senses, the dissipation of the ideas, the fading of memories, the slow variation of the organism." Each person possesses "the fundamental permanence of a consciousness which depends on nothing," and yet this consciousness is powerless to furnish proofs which we

need, for it is the will which affirms, and our power of knowledge is circumscribed. "Even our most profound thought is limited by the insuperable conditions which make all thought superficial."

And so in the end one feels that M Valéry's desire for precision and clarity is the admonition he imposes on a multiform disorder which, though crystallizing in many harmonious patterns, escapes at last even the sharpest descent of his trained and scornful attacks.

It is the property, however, of distinguished literature to leave within the mind, side by side with a store of rich and fertile perspectives, questions that live on without an answer, questions that have, indeed, their odd separate flowerings. (pp. 432-33)

>   *Alyse Gregory, "A New Academician," in* The
>   Dial *(copyright, 1927, by The Dial Publishing
>   Company, Inc.), Vol. LXXXIII, No. 5, November,
>   1927 (and reprinted by Krause Reprint Corporation, 1966), pp. 429-33.*

EDMUND WILSON (essay date 1931)

[In] spite of its title, its heroic grand manner and its reverberating alexandrines, "La Jeune Parque" is no conventional French poem on a subject from Greek mythology. Valéry speaks of the "rather monstrous copulation of my system, my methods and my musical exigencies with the classical conventions." And it is certain that his mysterious poem represents a genre which has never appeared in literature before. Mallarmé's Hérodiade and his Faun are the precursors of Valéry's young Fate: they have already a certain ambiguity and seem at moments less imaginary personages than names attached to metaphysical reveries. But Valéry has carried the subtleties of conception, the complexities of presentation, of this characteristically Symbolist form much further than Mallarmé. Is "La Jeune Parque" the monologue of a young Fate, who has just been bitten by a snake? Is it the reverie of the poet himself, awakening early one morning in bed and lying more or less awake till dawn? Is it the voyage of the human consciousness testing out all its limitations, exploring all its horizons: love, solitary thought, action, sleep, death?—the drama of the mind which would withdraw from the world and rise superior to it but which is inevitably pulled back into life and involved in the processes of nature? It is all of these—yet the various strata, "physical, psychological and esoteric," as Francis de Miomandre describes them, are not overlaid one upon the other as in a conventional allegory or fable. They are confused and are always melting into one another—and it is this which makes the obscurity of the poem. The things that happen in "La Jeune Parque" and in Paul Valéry's other mythological monologues . . . are never, on the one hand, quite imaginable as incidents which are actually taking place and never, on the other hand, quite reducible merely to thoughts in the poet's mind. The picture never quite emerges; the idea is never formulated quite. And for all the magnificences of sound, colour, and suggestion which we find in these poems stanza by stanza, it seems to me that they are unsatisfactory because they are somehow not assimilable as wholes.

Yet Paul Valéry, when we put him beside Mallarmé, whom he echoes in these poems so often, is seen to possess the more vigorous intellect and the more solid imagination.

Mallarmé is always a painter, usually a water-colourist—he wrote verses for ladies' fans as he might have painted little figures and flowers on them. He has his brightness and relief, but it is only such brightness and relief as is possible to someone working in the flat—whereas Valéry's genius is sculptural rather: these mythological poems have a density of cloud-shapes heavily massed—if they were not clouds, we should call them marmoreal. He gives us figures and groups half disengaged—and he runs to effects less of colour than of light: the silvery, the sombre, the sunny, the translucent, the crystalline. And his verses carry off with the emphasis of an heroic resounding diction reminiscent of Alfred de Vigny the fluid waverings, the coy ambiguities and the delicately caught nuances which he has learned from Mallarmé. If Mallarmé was to supply subjects for Debussy, Valéry, outliving Debussy's vogue, was to be inspired in "La Jeune Parque" by Gluck. Valéry is, indeed, a sort of masculine of an art of which Mallarmé is the feminine. The elements in Mallarmé which made it possible for him to edit a woman's magazine and to write with his characteristic daintiness about styles in women's clothes is complemented, in Valéry, by a genius more powerful and stout which has a natural affinity with that of the architect.

And there is more substance in Valéry than in Mallarmé. In spite of his insistence that it is only the form, only the method in his work which interests him, Valéry's poetry has a certain dramatic quality. He is preoccupied with a particular conflict—the conflict between that part of man's existence which is represented by the abstraction of M. Teste and that part which is submerged in the sensations, distracted by the accidents, of the everyday world. If one were to read only "M. Teste"—though M. Teste is presented with some humour—or if one were to read only Valéry's prose, one might take him for one of the dryest and one of the most relentlessly abstract of minds. And it is true that the point of view of M. Teste figures conspicuously in the poetry of Valéry, as it predominates in his prose—that none of his characters is ever allowed to have a life independent of the intellectual world where at any moment he may appear as an abstraction, and that we suspect Valéry of preferring to human subjects, or at least of finding more satisfactory, the marble columns and stately palms which he makes the heroes of certain of his poems. (pp. 62-4)

Valéry's poetry is . . . always shifting back and forth between [the] palpable and visible world and a realm of intellectual abstraction. And the contrast between them, the conflict implied between the absolute laws of the mind and the limiting contingencies of life, opposites impossible to dissociate from one another, is . . . the real subject of his poems. Rather an unpromising subject, one might suppose —one, at any rate, entirely remote from the emotions of Romantic poetry. Yet this queer antagonism has inspired Valéry to some of the most original poetry ever written, to some of the indubitably great poetry of our time. We may take as an example of this theme treated on Valéry's full scale his most popular and perhaps his most satisfactory poem, "Le Cimetière Marin". . . . Here the poet has stopped at noon beside a graveyard by the sea: the sun seems to stand still above him; the water looks as level as a roof on which the boats are doves walking. The external world at the moment seems to figure that absolute toward which Valéry is always turning, with which he has been for so many years obsessed. Yet, "O Noonday!" he cries, "for all your immobility, I am the secret change in you—I am

the flaw in your enormous diamond!"—But the dead, there below, they have gone to join the void—they have become a part of inanimate nature. And suppose he himself, the living man, has, alive, merely the illusion of movement— like the runner or the arrow of Zeno's paradoxes?—"But no!" he exhorts himself. "Break up that brooding, that immobility, which has all but absorbed you!" The salt wind is already rising to break up the tranquil roof of the sea, and to dash it against the rocks. The world enters into movement again and the poet must go back to life!

It is quite impossible, however, in other language, to provide a scenario for one of Valéry's poems: in doing so, one must leave out almost all that is most characteristic of Valéry. In trying to clear up his meaning, one clears it up too much. The truth is that there are no real ideas, no real general reflections, in such a poem as "Le Cimetière Marin": Valéry presents, even more completely than Yeats in such a poem as "Among School Children," the emotion merged with the idea and both embedded in the scene where they have occurred. . . . In such a poem as "Le Cimetière Marin," there is no simple second meaning: there is a marvellously close reproduction of the very complex and continually changing relation of human consciousness to the things of which it is conscious. The noonday is inorganic Nature, but it is also the absolute in the poet's mind, it is also his twenty years of inaction—and it is also merely the noonday itself, which in a moment will no longer exist, which will be no longer either tranquil or noon. And the sea, which, during those moments of calm, forms a part of that great diamond of nature in which the poet finds himself the single blemish, because the single change, is also the image of the poet's silence, which in a moment, as the wind comes up to lash the sea, will give way to a sudden gust of utterance, the utterance of the poem itself. World and poet are always overlapping, are always interpenetrating, as they might in a Romantic poem; but the Symbolist will not even try, as the Romantic would be likely to do, to keep their relations consistent. The conventions of the poem's imagery change as quickly and as naturally as the images passing through the poet's mind. (pp. 66-8)

Valéry's prose, in spite of the extravagant respect with which it is treated by his admirers, is by no means so remarkable as his verse. In the first place, it seems doubtful whether Valéry has ever really mastered a prose style. There are many admirable things in his essays, passages of a fine terseness, tightness and wit, but the prose is always liable to get snarled in a knot of words which balks the understanding at the same time that it exasperates the taste.

The opacities of Valéry's prose are usually attributed by Valéry's admirers, who in this only follow the intimations of the master himself, to the originality and profundity of his ideas. But the truth is that, when we go through Valéry's essays, we are unable to find many ideas. We find simply, as we do in his poetry, the presentation of intellectual situations, instead of the development of lines of thought. A French critic has already taxed Valéry with being a philosopher who won't philosophise; and it is true that the "rigour" of which he is always talking is rather an artistic effect of his prose, produced by certain devices of style like the artistic effects of his poems, than a quality of his logic. In spite of his passion for method, Valéry seems to have taken singularly little trouble to sort out or set in order his ideas: like M. Teste, he is occupied rather with savouring his intellectual sensations and in coining more or less mixed metaphors to convey them. And though it is possible to a certain extent to share his enjoyment of this pastime, in the long run we find it dreary and even repellent. What, we ask, has Valéry-Teste succeeded in dredging up by that abysmal self-scrutiny of his? Why, not much more than the realisation, which he is hardly the first to have arrived at, that all forms of intellectual activity—even those which seem on the surface very different: poetry and mathematics, for example—are fundamentally the same sort of thing, merely arrangements or organisations of selected elements of experience. In so far as Valéry really deals in ideas, he is, in fact, a sort of super-dilettante, who, though he has many passages of pungent writing and stimulating insight, is just as likely, with groans of heavy labour, to unload a ponderous platitude. Most of Valéry's reputation for profundity comes, I believe, from the fact that he was one of the first literary men to acquire a smattering of the new mathematical and physical theory. Valéry has, it is true, made interesting use of this, but one wishes sometimes that he would either go further with it or leave philosophy alone. He never seems to have got over his first excitement at reading Poincaré, and he is still rather snobbish about it: he is always telling us how difficult it is going to be to make us understand this or that, and then the portentous thought, when it comes, turns out to be one of the commonplaces of modern scientific philosophy. . . . (pp. 68-9)

As a literary critic, however, Valéry has both interest and importance. He is perhaps the principal exponent in France of a peculiar point of view about poetry which has gained currency with the progress of modern Symbolism. The Romantics thought of a poem as primarily a piece of self-expression—a gushing forth of emotion, a bursting into song. The conception fashionable to-day is quite different: the doctrines of Symbolism were in some ways closely analogous to the doctrines of Romanticism, but in this respect the later Symbolists are at the opposite pole from the Romantics. Paul Valéry's attitude toward poetry is both more esoteric and more scientific than that of Romantic criticism.

Valéry had already . . . , in his "Introduction to the Method of Leonardo da Vinci," defined a work of art as "a machine intended to excite and combine the individual formations" of a particular "category of minds." And from the time of "La Jeune Parque," he has never ceased to insist that a poem is an intricate intellectual problem, a struggle with self-imposed conditions—that it is, above all, something *constructed*. Or, according to a favourite simile of Valéry's, a poem is like a heavy weight which the poet has carried to the roof bit by bit—the reader is the passer-by upon whom the weight is dropped all at once and who consequently receives from it in a moment an overwhelming impression, a complete aesthetic effect, such as the poet has never known in composing it. (pp. 69-70)

This apparently cool and analytic attitude, however, is accompanied, curiously enough, by an excessively esoteric conception of poetry. . . . Here we find, as usual, the scientific approach—which it occurs to us, as we read, is largely a matter of scientific similes: "There are certain rather mysterious bodies which physics studies and which chemistry uses: I always think of them when I reflect upon works of art." These are the catalytic agents, which precipitate chemical changes without being affected themselves. So the work of art, says Valéry, acts upon the mind into which it is introduced. Even when chemically considered, then, the work of art remains something "mysterious." And by "works of art," it further appears that, in the department of literature, Valéry means poetry exclusively. Prose, he says, has "sense" for its sole object—but the object of poetry is something not only more mysterious, but also apparently more occult: "There is absolutely no question in poetry of one person's transmitting to another something intelligible that is going on in his mind. It is a question of creating in the latter a state whose expression is precisely and uniquely that which communicates it to him. Whatever image or emotion is formed in the amateur of poems, it is valid and sufficient if it produces in him this reciprocal relation between the word-cause and the word-effect. The result is that the reader enjoys a very great freedom in regard to ideas, a freedom analogous to that which one recognises in the case of the hearer of music, though not so intensive."

It seems to me that a pretence to exactitude is here used to cover a number of ridiculously false assumptions, and to promote a kind of aesthetic mysticism rather than to effect a scientific analysis. In the first place, is it not absurd to assert that prose deals exclusively in "sense" as distinguished from suggestion, and that one has no right to expect from poetry, as Valéry says in another passage, "any definite notion at all"? Is verse really an intellectual product absolutely different in kind from prose? Has it really an absolutely different function? Are not both prose and verse, after all, merely techniques of human intercommunication, and techniques which have played various rôles, have been used for various purposes, in different periods and civilisations? The early Greeks used verse for their histories, their romances and their laws—the Greeks and the Elizabethans used it for their dramas. If Valéry's definitions are correct, what becomes of Homer, Virgil, Dante, Shakespeare and Goethe? They all of them deal in sense as well as suggestion and aim to convey "definite notions." These definitions have, however, obviously been framed to apply to the poetry of Valéry himself and of Mallarmé and the other Symbolists. Yet it does not really apply even to them. As we have seen, Valéry's poetry does make sense, it does deal with definite subjects, it does transmit to us "something intelligible that is going on inside his mind." Even though in calling his book of poems "Charmes," he has tried to emphasise its esoteric, magical, non-utilitarian character, we cannot admit that it is anything but an effort like another of articulate human speech. . . . But Valéry has already let us see—it is even one of his favourite ideas— that he understands the basic similarity between the various forms of intellectual activity; he has taken pride in pointing out the kinship between poetry and mathematics. And if the function and methods of poetry are similar to those of mathematics, they must surely be similar to those of prose. . . . Valéry betrays himself here, it seems to me, as a thinker anything but "rigorous"; and he betrays also, I believe, a desire, defensive no doubt at the same time as snobbish, to make it appear that verse, a technique now no longer much used for history, story-telling or drama and consequently not much in popular demand, has some inherent superiority to prose. He has not hesitated even to assure us elsewhere that "poetry is the most difficult of the arts"!

With all respect for Valéry's intelligence, for his candour and independence, it must be admitted that he is taken too seriously—and perhaps takes himself too seriously—as a universal sage. (pp. 70-3)

Edmund Wilson, "Paul Valéry," in his Axel's Castle: A Study in the Imaginative Literature of 1870-1930 *(abridged by permission of Charles Scribner's Sons; copyright © 1931 by Charles Scribner's Sons; renewal copyright © 1959 by Edmund Wilson), Scribner's, 1931 (and reprinted by Collins, 1961, pp. 58-79).*

G. TURQUET-MILNES   (essay date 1934)

[M. Valéry] is really, in essentials, an eighteenth century man. It is reading Condillac, and Detutt de Tracy, and Buffon, and Diderot, which will help you to understand the philosophical attitude of Valéry. In *La Soirée avec M. Teste* he says, '*Je rature le vif*', by which he means he does not want to trouble himself about the *living*. You will not find him writing novels, or historical studies. Keep the phrase in mind when reading his book called *Variété*, or the *Introduction à la Méthode de Léonard de Vinci*, and you will see at once that M. Valéry is a direct descendant of Condillac and that what he is after is the mechanism of the mind in its pure state. Like Condillac, he is always trying to find out what our self is, to see it stripped of all the foreign elements in which life wraps it. He wants to discover our real personality underneath all the physical human contingencies which enslave our thought. The affiliation between the sensualist school of philosophy and M. Valéry is very clear. But the odd thing is that this writer who has so great a horror of any kind of servitude for our self, who detests all formulae which might imprison our individuality, seems to be an extreme sensualist. Therein he is like Diderot. On the one hand he is Condillac's pupil, but on the other still more Diderot's. In his thought, and in his art, he clearly inclines to a kind of Lucretian materialism. More clearly still, he acknowledges and denies in turn existence of an external world which directs the inner world. That is one of the great sources of his strength and originality.... And surely no man ever loved words so dearly for their own sake. In his work words seem to feel an invincible attraction for one another. *La Fausse Morte* is a masterpiece in this manner. Everything here is the outcome of the senses, is the product of feeling, and as he is in the habit of subjecting himself to the strictest self-study, he arrives at what some critics call the metaphysics of nothingness. There is always a great conflict raging in Valéry between intellect and what we call vulgarly 'heart'. (pp. 11-13)

Valéry brings to the art of poetry the love of nothingness. He who loves life so dearly, worships it in so many forms, would despise existence, and to such an extent that he would cross it out, erase it. In reality this so-called nihilism is of no more use for composing a portrait of M. Valéry than it would be for painting Diderot. Because the poet in him is persistently alive—especially when he is writing in prose—a poet full of reminiscences so far-reaching that it is as if his literary antennae reached to the very confines of the universe: a poet combining in one being a very great number of human beings.... In order to understand him it is absolutely necessary to know M. Teste. (pp. 13-14)

M. Teste is a consciousness which has discovered itself, self-possessing and self-sufficient—hence its singularity, its indifference towards the outside world, its weariness and its pride. M. Teste would seem to be the ultimate Romantic,

the spirit which believes in nothing except in himself, so that he is able to dispense with the Romantic background so necessary to Chateaubriand or Victor Hugo. So away with storms, mountains, and deserted heaths! M. Teste lives in a dreadfully commonplace flat, his room is as dull as an algebraic formula. His one pleasure is in thought. He does not want to dwell like Baudelaire in a forest of symbols, but amid algebraic thoughts, scientific formulae, and there compose a kind of grammar of Self. A sort of hermit, a profoundly philosophical St. Anthony.... There we are in the pure mechanism of the mind.... (pp. 14-15)

When we are confronted with a personality so difficult to grasp as M. Valéry, a mind which seems in a sense detached from all human substance, we cannot refuse the help of criticism inspired by Bergsonian philosophy. For there are two ways of studying an author: from without, as he appears to the public, analysing his thoughts and his artistic method in order to deduce therefrom a system: and from within as a living being developing in Duration, ever changing since he must submit to the urge of earthly things. It is in the second way that M. Valéry should be studied, wishes to be studied. Thought is an eminently mobile changing thing which we take up or set aside according to our humour. It 'romances' truth. And the more we study Valéry, the more convinced are we that he is much less interested in finding a solution by means of abstract concepts, than in discovering a new vital impulsion on any given problem—new ideas. Perhaps that is why he dislikes the philosophers so much.

It has been said that M. Valéry's talent evokes only images of desolation: cemetries, annihilation, death. This would indeed appear to be the case: as we read certain lines in *La Jeune Parque* in praise of purity, calling down curses upon existence, M. Valéry here appears as a new Hippolytus Coronatus. But the great difference between him and the hero of Euripides is, that the Frenchman, living as he does in the most troublous of our times, perhaps the most troublous of all times, seeks to wrest classical culture from the clutches of that dissolution which has renounced it.

Even his enemies acknowledge in him that love of humanism, love of sincerity, love of perfection, which combine to make the true Classic. (pp. 41-2)

G. Turquet-Milnes, in his Paul Valéry, *Jonathan Cape, 1934, 163 p.*

C. M. BOWRA   (essay date 1943)

La Jeune Parque has been acclaimed as the most obscure poem in French. It has been variously interpreted as the monologue of a Young Fate who has to choose between celestial seclusion and earthly responsibilities, as the revery of the poet lying in bed, as a voyage of the human consciousness through vast issues of life and death. It is all these things, and none of them. Valéry's subject cannot be stated with precision; for by its very nature it is formless and indefinable. The poem does not state a thesis but makes an effect. It might be said to record a series of states of mind, but these melt into one another, and the contour of each is dim. It is natural to compare it with Mallarmé's *Hérodiade*. Just as Mallarmé found a subject in the human instinct which desires remoteness and coldness and found a centre for his symbols in the ice-cold virgin Hérodiade, so Valéry, it might be thought, makes his symbolical Young

Fate the mouthpiece of a conflict between desires for an active life and for independent, passionless contemplation. There is truth in this, but it is not the whole truth. Mallarmé's dramatic method, with its contrast between Hérodiade and the Nurse, serves to emphasise two sides of a struggle which may ultimately be his own. Valéry has no drama, and with reason. In the movements of his poem the issues are not clearly cut. The uniting thread is of a half-dreaming consciousness, in which what counts is not contrast but continuity. It begins and ends without any marked event. It is a section of a complex poetical experience. To appreciate it we need not so much a vigilant intelligence as a receptive sensibility which marks symbols for their associative and imaginative worth and responds to the subtle changes of atmosphere which pass across the dreaming landscape. In reading *La Jeune Parque* we may forget the character who holds it together; we may even feel that the poet forgets her. In both cases we are right. For in the last analysis the poet deals with matters for which even his central symbol is inadequate, with feelings so little definable that they resist attempts to arrange them in a system or to relate them to ordered thought. (pp. 21-2)

The art of *La Jeune Parque* lies in an evocation of atmosphere in which some things are seen with unusual clearness, others fade into mist and lose their contours. In so far as it does this, it does its special task. It can do more than this, and it does. But this is its first and essential characteristic.

In this half-dreaming state the mind sees matters of great importance in a special way. Images that rise before it seem to have a remarkable significance, to be symbolical of things far greater than themselves. In such a mood we may well see ourselves in a new light, as figures of cosmic import. And this happens in *La Jeune Parque*. The poet transposes the movements of his consciousness into a strange *milieu*. He sees himself as a divine figure who has left a serene supraterrestrial dwelling for the chances and passions of mortal life. So may a man dramatise himself who is torn between his thoughts and his actions. In this state the ordinary limits set to out powers seem not to exist. We feel that we are the centre, if not of the universe, at least of some enormous scheme, and that anything we do or that happens to us is pregnant with huge issues. (p. 24)

In the half-dreaming state which pervades *La Jeune Parque* what counts most is the sustained tone. In this lies its chief poetry. But this tone varies as the thoughts of a man vary in trance-like meditation. Half the pleasure lies in the delicate adjustment of tone, in the transition from one shade to another. Though the whole pattern is made of subdued colours, it has many strands and patterns. To isolate one or the other is necessarily an artificial process which may damage our appreciation of the whole. (pp. 24-5)

The half-consciousness which permeates *La Jeune Parque* is certainly fit matter for poetry, especially for a poet whose analytical intelligence has closed the way to many themes. But this dream-world is only part of his self. There remains much outside it no less important, no less adaptable to poetry. Valéry is still a divided personality in so far as his poetic activity lies outside the sphere of this ranging intelligence. This is no criticism of it as poetry. It is still a triumph in a peculiarly difficult kind of art. But until Valéry puts more of himself into his verse we feel that his success is not complete, that he has not mastered all the material at his disposal.

In *Charmes* he has done this. At first sight it is clear that his whole manner has changed from that of *La Jeune Parque*. A series of poems composed in a wide range of metres show that he has found a new way to express himself, an adaptation of the Symbolist method which is his own. The dreaming atmosphere of *La Jeune Parque* has given place to something much clearer, much more readily grasped by the intelligence. Instead of a tone he presents a series of themes, sometimes stated in such a title as *Poésie*, usually clear enough on reading. The ambiguity has disappeared. Each poem has its own temper and atmosphere, but in the sum of them there is much variety and divergence. The deliberately mixed metaphors which contribute so much to the effect of *La Jeune Parque* have almost gone. Their place has been taken by a new art in which a single figure or symbol is elaborated throughout a whole poem, gives consistency to it and holds it together. In *Palme* all that matters is the tree that promises a rich harvest of fruit, in *Les Pas* the feet of the beloved that hesitate. Such a tree and such feet have a special significance; they are symbols of no common importance. But because they are sustained through whole poems, they make it easier to appreciate an abstract and impalpable experience, and add to the force of the poetry by this very consistency. A defect in the Symbolist method was that in its concentration on a single point and the mixture of symbols which it used to secure this it sometimes lacked exactness in presenting, not thoughts, which do not matter, but states of imaginative experience, which do. This defect is not altogether absent from *La Jeune Parque*. In the delicate and subtle presentation of special states it does not always yield a full and satisfying effect. No doubt this matters less in a poem which is concerned with a half-conscious condition. But when the poet advances into the daylight of consciousness this vagueness of outline may impede him. With his poet's instinct Valéry saw this, and in *Charmes* his symbols are either strictly self-consistent or else chosen in such a way that we know what each one means and does.

This advance in method is accompanied by what look like concessions to the common reader. Valéry is now more ready to explain what he means, to give hints in his titles and elsewhere about a poem's subject, to make statements of fact which are not in the spirit of Mallarmé. A title like *Poésie* is in the best classical tradition; *Ode Secrète* at least warns us that we may fail to understand the contents; *Cantique des Colonnes* is what it claims to be; a quotation from Pindar at the beginning of *Le Cimetière Marin* is a useful clue. So too in the poems themselves those lines of explanation which Mallarmé abhorred are not wanting. Not all are so clear as the end of *La Pythie* with its emphatic statement of fact, but with rare exceptions these poems have definable subjects to which the poet leads by different means. Nor is this method merely or truly a concession to our desire to understand. It is dictated by a more reputable and more artistic motive. In *Charmes* Valéry writes about matters on which clear thought is in some degree possible. This is not to say that he writes didactic or explanatory verse. He writes indubitably as a poet. But since his subjects are those about which thought is possible, then thought has its part in poetry about them. To present these themes in the manner of *La Jeune Parque* would be to mutilate or falsify them. In so far as they arise from the poet's conscious meditation and have their place in it, it is right to maintain this element of thought, even of explanation. For

Mallarmé such a situation hardly existed. The aesthetic state of which he wrote is divorced from ordinary analytical thought. Prose cannot describe it except in the language of poetry. But Valéry is concerned with other matters, more mundane perhaps but not less poetical. He is therefore entitled to make himself clear to the intellect as well as to create an effect through the imagination. (pp. 26-8)

[In most of the poems of *Charmes*] Valéry has moved far from Mallarmé. He may use some of the same symbols . . . , but the intention and the effect are different. The mystical view of poetry has been replaced by the acceptance of it as a fact like other facts. The special place of the poet in society is not mentioned. Indeed the poet moves nearer to other men as his art finds its capacities. The desire for "pure poetry" is tempered by a realisation that in poetry the intellect must have its place and that poetry may gain by admitting elements of reason and almost of argument. The difficulties of Mallarmé's grammar, the abrupt breaks in syntax, the deliberate obscurities, are not to be found in Valéry. His poetry is difficult. His symbols are not always easy to grasp. But the grammar and the sense are there. On the other hand, Valéry's debt to Mallarmé remains incalculable. His poetry is intensely personal. It is also extremely poetical, in the sense that subjects proper to prose are excluded from it and that it aims not at instruction but at creating an effect. The poet has found his relation to life, but on the whole he lives in a rare and special atmosphere. He writes for the few. Such poetry is only possible when there exists a cultivated society able to face its difficulties and to understand its subtleties. Above all it is the poetry of an extremely intelligent man, who knows what things are and is not afraid to see them in their true nature. It demands the sacrifice of many false or romantic notions. It needs a considerable adjustment of mind before its full strength is revealed. As such it is representative of the age in which it was written, scientific and sceptical of transcendental hypotheses but willing to admit that in the varied pattern of life there is much that calls for wonder. (pp. 54-5)

> *C. M. Bowra, "Paul Valéry," in his* The Heritage of Symbolism *(copyright; reprinted by permission of St. Martin's Press, Inc.; in Canada by Macmillan, London and Basingstoke), Macmillan, 1943, pp. 17-55.*

WALLACE FOWLIE (essay date 1946)

Valéry has three poems on the theme of Narcissus. The second of these, and the most profound, *Fragments du Narcisse*, does not deal with the myth as a simple story of metamorphosis, but as a complex drama, central to the thought of Valéry and to the psychological enquiry of the contemporary artist.

Inaccessible to himself, this Narcissus created by Valéry, is a kind of philosopher in his search for self-knowledge. He is also the hero of sterility, bearing spiritual affinities with Hamlet, with Gide's André Walter and with the contemporary hero of inaction and self-analysis. Valéry's twenty years silence is reduced in *Narcisse* to an afternoon, but the briefer silence is also pregnant with thought and meditation. The cool body of Narcissus is his sole defense against the dead who await him. He can therefore love only himself, and pray the gods to arrest the daylight as it diminishes. The poem ends in the disorder of evening shadows. The

inaccessible love of Narcissus disappears as his lips touch the darkening waters and scatter the image he loved.

If *Narcisse* is the poem of . . . gardens and shadows, of self-love and youth,—*Le Cimetière Marin* is the poem of . . . Valéry's return to his native city on the sea, to his ancestors in their marine graveyard. Immobility in this poem is not that of a single individual, as it was in *Fragments du Narcisse*; it is the immobility of nature: of the sea and of the sun poised on the zenith. Always throughout the work of Valéry, persists the mirage of power, the possible omnipotence of the human mind. The problem explored is that of the soul, of whether it is one of the myths of mankind, or the great reality of man. The contemplation of the sea, ever stable and enduring, gives to the poet the experience of an ecstasy in which the "pure" self and the "pure" cosmos meet, or derive their existence one from the other.

These two poems . . . illustrate the two states of being in which Valéry studies his favorite subject; the principle of his own functioning, the autonomy and the potency of his own mind. First, as Narcissus, he studies the multiple selves of a single man, the constant changes in the nature which surrounds him, and the duration of time with its endless vicissitudes and intermittences. Secondly, as the poet walking over the tombs of his ancestors and contemplating the constancy of the sea, he studies the image of stability and the non-temporal. On the one hand, he analyzes the principle itself of living, of all that is personal and transitory in an individual. And on the other hand, he abstracts himself from life, in his search for the universal and the permanent. (pp. 255-56)

Mallarmé taught the modern world how to read poetry. Valéry will teach the future world how to consider behind the poem the spiritual depths from which it rises. It is the new dialogue between rigor and profundity. Between rigor taught by Mallarmé, rigor of form, of architecture, of symbol, and profundity taught by Valéry, profundity of source, of mystery, of knowledge. (p. 257)

> *Wallace Fowlie, "Homage to Valéry," in* The Sewanee Review *(reprinted by permission of the editor; © 1946 by The University of the South), Vol. LIV, No. 2, April-June, 1946, pp. 250-57.*

JACKSON MATHEWS (essay date 1947)

Monsieur Teste is, in a sense, Valéry's novel. Teste himself, on the one hand, is an ordinary fictional character, someone anyone might know, the lonely figure of modern city life, a problem in everyday human relations. On the other, he is a mind behaving as a man, or, to put it the other way, "a man regulated by his own powers of thought." *Monsieur Teste* is the story of consciousness and its effort to push *being* off the stage, to use it up. "The character of man," said Valéry, "is consciousness; and the character of consciousness is to consume, perpetually, . . . *the man of mind* must finally reduce himself knowingly to an endless refusal *to be* anything whatever." But is it possible for man to be all mind? Is M. Teste possible? If not, *why is he impossible?* That question, Valéry says, is the *soul* of M. Teste. He is impossible because . . . (shall I presume to answer, in straight prose?) because consciousness cannot entirely consume being and still continue to exist. It depends on being. Sensibility is its home, knowledge is its profession; that is why Valéry had to invent Mme Teste (all soul and sensibility) and Teste's friend (his knowledge of the world).

The pieces that make up [*Monsieur Teste*] then, are the occasional results of a lifetime of meditation on the question: *How would a complete mind behave as an everday man?* It is amazing how much we see of Teste in so few pages; in each part, a different view of him: his author's, his wife's, his young friend's, his own. We see him at the café, the theater, at home, even in bed; we watch him think, make love, sleep, stroll in the park; we witness a vivid re-creation of his milieu, the Paris that contained him; and in his logbook, "the sacrifice of his thought."

Some readers find the logbook an anticlimax. Led to expect so much of this extraordinary man, it is natural that they should find his actual thought not so extraordinary after all. If this little book were to be held strictly to laws of fiction this would have to be counted one of its flaws; but actually, anticlimax is here calculated and necessary, for it reinforces just that impression of the ordinary, the everyday, which is a large part of Valéry's theme: the mind's involvement in daily modes of existence. In the end, the effect makes one of his main points, that it is always "a sacrifice of thought" to write it down; the very act of writing stops thought by making it dependent on words for its expression. M. Teste's logbook is no exception.

The legend identifying M. Teste with Valéry himself has naturally grown up, and has already made perhaps too much of the autobiographical aspects of the work. This is a very personal book indeed, but Valéry was probably no more M. Teste than he was Leonardo, Mallarmé, or Descartes; he was all of these in his own way. Teste is simply the most persistent image of that unknown man, his author's consciousness. He remains, said Valéry toward the end of his life, "the most satisfactory being I have met . . . the only person who endures in my mind." (pp. xi-xiii)

Jackson Mathews, "A Note on Valéry," in Monsieur Teste, *by Paul Valéry, translated by Jackson Mathews (copyright © 1947 by Alfred A. Knopf, Inc.; renewed 1975 by Alfred A. Knopf, Inc.; reprinted by permission of Alfred A. Knopf, Inc.), Knopf, 1947, pp. v-xiv.*

WARREN RAMSEY (essay date 1948)

[In *Reflections on the World Today* we have] a whole book about subjects which Valéry did not like, did not, in any very meaningful way, understand.

He begins by indicting history for failing to provide verifiable truths. None of the myths out of the histories should be imitated, says the Foreword, though many are, with disastrous results. In a world characterized by *"increase in clarity and precision, and an increase in power,"* political judgments and actions based upon historical myths are notably inept and haphazard. But since the effects of events can no longer be confined, since technical developments bring about novel repercussions everywhere in the world, "there is no prudence, wisdom, or genius but is soon baffled by this complexity of affairs, for there is no recognizable pattern of duration, continuity or causality in this world of multiplied relationships and contacts." So *any* mind, not only the historico-political, is insufficient.

For its manner rather than its matter this is an interesting

presentation of a familiar point of view, and we might let it go at that. Valéry does not. "Notes on the Greatness and Decadence of Europe" and "Of History" simply rephrase the Foreword, adding that Europe will be punished for improvising wildly on mythical themes. "Remarks on Progress" comes to a conclusion which served as one step in the argument of the Foreword: progress is defined as increase in precision and power. . . .

[That and the other ideas contained in this volume] are not numerous or remarkable. Above all they do not stand the variations to which Valéry subjects them in article after repetitious article marred by exclamations about the absence of "scientific" truth in fields where nobody claims that it exists, patent contradictions, clumsy admissions. . . .

On the face of them, Valéry's political ideas are insignificant. But in summing up this last and least book of a great poet it is fair to recall that it is never the face of an idea which is important with Valéry, but, so to speak, its body. Even in this volume the course of Valéry's reflections is interesting. . . . What Valéry provides us with is a series of disorganized, permutating opinions in process of formation. They can no more be paraphrased than a poem can be. (p. 478)

Warren Ramsey, "Books: 'Reflections on the World Today'," in Commonweal *(copyright © 1948 Commonweal Publishing Co., Inc.; reprinted by permission of Commonweal Publishing Co., Inc.), Vol. XLVIII, No. 20, August 27, 1948, pp. 478-79.*

JEAN COCTEAU (essay date 1950)

Paul Valéry turned figures into gold in the noble fire of his soul. He was an alchemist and a goldsmith, a cabinetmaker and a spiritualist, the man who puts the table together and the man who forces it to speak.

No one knew so many secrets; no one more effectively brought order into disorder and turned order into disorder; no one laid a more prudent and more imprudent hand on the cunning explosives of poetry.

This wise man respected madmen. He had preserved his childhood. For he knew that without children and madmen literature would lose the unwonted in all its spontaneity. He proclaimed this. He said "Suppress the race of scandal and literature will become a dread thing." Fancy a paradoxical blend of wise man and madman, of child and philosopher, of teacher and pupil. Add to this mixture the enigmatic fluid in which poetry bathes and shake the elixir dangerously. There results a pure and flawless metal . . . with that object-purity which is so remote from the subject-purity that critics confuse with it.

Occasionally it happens that a writer possesses this privilege and makes use of it spontaneously. I wonder at times whether Paul Valéry originally possessed this privilege or whether he created it out of whole cloth; in short, whether he (and he alone) did not discover the secret of gold and the means of using it.

Unless I am wrong, he is the prototype of the artist-artisan, the prince of that famous breathing-out which is called breathing-in (inspiration), of that phenomenon that starts not from the outside but from the inside, giving a legible form to the vague shadows that dwell within us.

Jean Cocteau, "Alchemist of Words," in The New York Times Book Review *(© 1950 by The New York Times Company; reprinted by permission), May 7, 1950, p. 6.*

ELIZABETH SEWELL   (essay date 1952)

Valéry is of the same poetic generation as Yeats and Rilke, and is often to be found classed in works of literary history and criticism as a symbolist, the faithful disciple of Mallarmé, whose poetic methods he is supposed to have extended both in time and in scope. The label of 'symbolism' is no more useful than such labels usually are, and there is little to be gained by calling Valéry a symbolist if by that is meant an adherent of an ill-defined poetic group existing in France at the end of the last century. The word 'symbol' is in any case misleading. It suggests that a poet is putting down something for something else, using a certain image which is a direct substitute for whatever it is that he is talking about, a rose to stand for Love, for example. This in turn is likely to suggest that the symbols and the poem need interpreting; and indeed Valéry has been much interpreted. His obscurity is not of this kind, however, and it is important to sweep the symbols off the floor before we begin, lest there should be any misunderstanding about the nature of Valéry's work, or of the work that confronts us in trying to appreciate it, with the mirror as starting point. (pp. 7-8)

What was the shape of Valéry's mind? He was continually trying to discover that himself, not because it was his own mind but because he was fascinated by the ways of thought in general, of which, as he says, we know so little. He was a poet and a precise and rigorous thinker, but at the same time he was always watching himself making poetry, watching his mind thinking and making a form and structure out of its thoughts. Valéry's mind watches itself in the mirror. (p. 8)

Judging by the range of subjects which Valéry deals with in his writing, one might think that his mind was a peculiarly far-reaching one, capable of being interested in almost anything. In one sense this is true. Valéry was a great believer in universality, but indirectly. He was interested in everything because he was interested only in one. 'As soon as the mind is involved, everything is involved' . . . ; but Valéry was interested in so much only because he was passionately interested in the mind. In one sense his range was very narrow, if his mind was not. . . . He seems almost to suffer, in his own words, from an *idée fixe;* but in the book with that title he defines the *idée fixe* in terms of movement. 'An idea cannot be fixed. The only thing that can be fixed (if anything can be) is something that is not an idea. An idea is an alteration—or rather, a mode of alteration— indeed the most discontinuous mode of alteration.' Valéry's *idée fixe* is the movement and play of thought. (pp. 10-11)

If his aim was not content but form, not the product of a mind so much as its exercise, this may account both for his obscurity and for the astonishing effect his work has on the reader's thought. If Valéry's work was a mirror, for himself and others, that does not mean that the one looking into the mirror is passive. In *Au Sujet d'*EURÉKA, from *Variété,* Valéry says, 'A woman modifies herself in front of her mirror.' So does Valéry; and we are compelled to do likewise, caught up as we are within the framework of his own reflection. (p. 15)

[It is] one of the strange things about the mind—and Valéry, I suspect, knew it—that extreme precision generates its own mystery. He speaks in *L'Idée Fixe* of physicists who have carried analysis so far that they reach an order which resembles nothing. A little later in the same work he throws doubt on the adequacy of the phrase 'One and one make two.' Our difficulty is that we are faced, in Valéry, with that very problem, the apparent equivalence in the mind of two and one, a straightforward contradiction. (p. 17)

The progress in the mind from two to one is set out most clearly in the *Note et Digression* to the Leonardo essay in *Variété.* The passage is too long to quote in full, but it is an attempt to answer the question: What is the nature of the inalterability of the mind, through all its own activity, the action of the universe upon it, the slow decay of the organism to which it is attached? . . . Valéry makes a distinction between consciousness and the personality which, he says, 'is only a thing, mutable and accidental beside this most naked *self* . . . only a secondary psychological divinity, which inhabits our mirror and answers to our name.' He goes on to say that it is the hidden but essential work of the greatest minds to define themselves, not in terms of the personality but in those of 'this self to which no words can be applied, which has no name and no history, which is no more perceptible and no less real than the centre of mass of a ring or of a planetary system.' This is for Valéry the goal to be attained, where the mind 'feels itself to be pure consciousness: there cannot be two.' It is in a sense the goal of all knowledge and study. (p. 18)

Elizabeth Sewell, in her Paul Valéry: The Mind in the Mirror *(copyright 1952 by Yale University Press; reprinted by permission of Anthony Sheil Associates Ltd.; as agents for the author), Yale University Press, 1952, 61 p.*

WALLACE STEVENS   (essay date 1956)

[What] are the ideas that Valéry has chosen to be discussed by the shades of Socrates and his friend Phaedrus, [*In Eupalinos, or the Architect*], as they meet, in our time, in their "dim habitation" on the bank of Ilissus? They are alone and remain alone. Eupalinos does not appear and takes no part in the discussion, unless, as he is spoken of, an image of him passes, like the shade of a shade. The talk is prolonged, and during its course, one or the other speaker propounds ideas. If we attempt to group a number of the ideas propounded, we have something like the following:

> There are no details in execution.

> Nothing beautiful is separable from life, and life is that which dies.

> We must now know what is truly beautiful, what is ugly; what befits man; what can fill him with wonder without confounding him, possess him without stupefying him. . . . It is that which puts him, without effort, above his own nature   (p. xii)

This is the substance of the dialogue between Socrates and Phaedrus, or, at least, these sayings, taken from their talk, indicate what they have been talking about. And what in fact have they been talking about? And why is Valéry justified when, in his closing words, Socrates says: ". . . all that we have been saying is as much a natural sport of the silence of these nether regions as the fantasy of some rhetorician of the other world who has used us as puppets!'' Have we been listening to the talk or men or of puppets? These questions are parts of the fundamental question, What should the shades of men talk about, or in any case what may they be expected, categorically, to talk about, in the Elysian fields? Socrates answers this question in the following manner:

> Think you not that we ought now to employ this boundless leisure which death leaves us, in judging and rejudging ourselves unwearyingly, revising, correcting, attempting other answers to the events that took place, seeking, in fine, to defend ourselves by illusions against nonexistence, as the living do against their existence?

This Socratic question (and answer) seems empty. The Elysian fields would be the merest penal habitude, if existence in them was not as absolute as it is supposed to be eternal and if our disillusioned shades were dependent, there, on some fresh illusion to be engendered by them for themselves in that transparent realm. It cannot be said freely that Valéry himself fails to exhibit Socrates and Phaedrus engaged in any such discussion, for as the talk begins to reach its end, there emerges from it an Anti-Socrates, to whom an Anti-Phaedrus is listening, as if their conversation had been, after all, a process of judging and rejudging what they had done in the past, with the object of arriving at a state of mind equivalent to an illusion. The dialogue does not create this impression. It does not seem to us, as we read it, that we are concerned with the fortunes of the selves of Socrates and Phaedrus, notwithstanding that that would be a great concern.

We might well expect an existence after death to consist of the revelation of the truth about life, whether the revelation was instantaneous, complete, and dazzling, or whether it was a continuity of discoveries made at will. Hence when a conversation between Socrates and Phaedrus after death occurs, we somehow expect it to consist of resolutions of our severest philosophical or religious difficulties, or of some of them. The present dialogue, however, is a discussion of aesthetics. It may even be said to be the apotheosis of aesthetics, which is not at all what we have had in mind as that which phantoms talk about. It makes the scene seem more like a place in provincial France than either an archaeological or poetic afterworld.... The trouble is that our sense of what ought to be discussed in the afterworld is derived from specimens that have fallen into disuse. Analysis of the point would be irrelevant. It seems enough to suppose that to the extent that the dead exist in the mind of the living, they discuss whatever the living discuss.... (pp. xv-xvi)

This elevation of aesthetics is typical of Valéry's thought. It is itself an act of construction. It is not an imbalance attributable to his nature as a poet. It is a consequence of reasonable conviction on his part. His partiality for architecture was instinctive and declared itself in his youthful *Introduction to the Method of Leonardo da Vinci*. It was not an artificiality contrived to please the company of architects who had commanded *Eupalinos*. It seems most natural that a thinker who had traced so much of man's art to man's body should extend man's art itself to the place of God and in that way should relate man's body to God, in the manner in which this is done in *Eupalinos*. (p. xvi)

Wallace Stevens, "Two Prefaces," in The Collected Works in English: Dialogues, Vol. 4 *by Paul Valéry, Bollingen Series XLV, translated by William McCausland Stewart (copyright © 1956 by Princeton University Press; reprinted by permission of Princeton University Press), Pantheon Books, 1956, pp. ix-xxvi.*

T. S. ELIOT (essay date 1958)

If the best of [Valéry's] poems are among the masterpieces, the best of his critical essays are among the most remarkable curiosities of French literature. (p. viii)

[In his literary essays Valéry] is perpetually engaged in solving an insoluble puzzle—the puzzle of how poetry gets written; and the material upon which he works is his own poetry. In the end, the question is simply: how did I write *La Jeune Parque* (or *Le Cimetière marin*)? The questions with which he is concerned are questions which no poet of an earlier generation would have raised; they are questions that belong to the present self-conscious century. This gives to Valéry's thought a singular documentary value. (p. xi)

So far, however, I have not approached the essential problem, which is that of the characteristics distinguishing Valéry's *art poétique* from that of anyone else. His purpose is not to teach the writing of poetry or to improve the understanding of it; his purpose is not primarily to facilitate the understanding of his own poetry—though it will very soon strike the attention of the perceptive reader, that much of what he predicates of ''poetry'' is applicable only to his own poetry. The best approach, I believe, is through a little essay, of very early date . . . entitled ''On Literary Technique.'' The date is 1889, but this early credo gives a clue to his later development. What it announces is no less than a new style for poets, as well as a new style for poetry. The satanist, the dandy, the *poète maudit* have had their day: eleven years before the end of the nineteenth century Valéry invents the role which is to make him representative of the twentieth:

> . . . a totally new and modern conception of the poet. He is no longer the disheveled madman who writes a whole poem in the course of one feverish night; he is a cool scientist, almost an algebraist, in the service of a subtle dreamer. . . .

We must remember that Valéry was a very young man when he wrote these enthusiastic words; but in making this allowance, we are all the more struck by the fact that this is essentially the point of view to which he was to adhere throughout his life. The association of the ''dreamer'' and the ''algebraist,'' for example, was to remain unbroken. . . . But what is most impressive about the passage I have just quoted, is that it discloses, behind Valéry's Idea of Poetry, another and perhaps the controlling Idea—Valéry's Idea of the Poet. It is from the conception of the poet that he proceeds to the conception of poetry, and not the other way about. Now this Idea of the Poet was a prophetic one, prophetic not only of the mature Valéry, but of the ideals and the idols of the coming age. Looked at in this way, the ''cool scientist'' is an alternative, rather than the antithesis to the ''disheveled madman'': a different mask for the same actor. (pp. xvii-xix)

Valéry in fact invented, and was to impose upon his age, not so much a new conception of poetry as a new conception of the poet. The tower of ivory has been fitted up as a laboratory—a solitary laboratory, for Valéry never went so far as to advocate "teamwork" in the writing of poetry. The poet is comparable to the mathematical physicist, or else to the biologist or chemist. He is to carry out the role of scientist as studiously as Sherlock Holmes did: this is the aspect of himself to which he calls the public's attention. Our picture of the poet is to be very like that of the austere, bespectacled man in a white coat, whose portrait appears in advertisements, weighing out or testing the drugs of which is compounded some medicine with an impressive name.

What I have said above is what I may call the primary aspect of Valéry's poetics. The secondary aspect is its relation to his own poetry. Everything that he says about the writing of poetry must be read, of course, with constant reference to the poetry that he wrote. No one, I think, will find [his literary] essays fully intelligible until he has read Valéry's most important poems. To some extent, I see his essays on poetry as a kind of defense and vindication of his own poems—a justification of their being the kind of poems they are, of their being as brief as they are, and of their being as few as they are. And to some extent the essays seem to me a kind of substitute for the poems he did not write. (pp. xix-xx)

We do not turn to Valéry's *art poétique* in the hope of learning how to write poetry or how to read it. We do not even turn to it primarily for the light it throws on Valéry's poetry: certainly we can say as truly that if the prose throws light on the poems, the poems also illuminate the prose. I think that we read these essays, and I think people will continue to read them, because we find Valéry to be a singularly interesting, enigmatic, and disturbing author, a poet who has realized in his life and work one conception of the role of the poet so amply as to have acquired also a kind of mythological status. We read the essays because, as Valéry himself says, "there is no theory that is not a fragment, carefully prepared, of some autobiography." We could almost say that Valéry's essays form a part of his poetical works. We read them for their own sake, for the delight in following the subtleties of thought which moves like a trained dancer, and which has every resource of language at its command; for the pleasure of sudden illuminations even when they turn out to be *feux follets;* for the excitement of an activity which always seems on the point of catching the inapprehensible, as the mind continues indefatigably to weave its fine logodaedal web. (p. xxii)

The one complaint which I am tempted to lodge against Valéry's poetics, is that it provides us with no criterion of *seriousness*. He is deeply concerned with the problem of process, of how the poem is made, but not with the question of how it is related to the rest of life in such a way as to give the reader the shock of feeling that the poem has been to him, not merely an experience, but a serious experience. . . . But in mentioning something of which I notice the absence in Valéry's poetics, I am not questioning the seriousness of his own finest poems. If some of Valéry's poems were not very serious poems indeed—if two of them, at least, were not likely to last as long as the French language—there could have been no interest for him in studying the process of their composition, and no delight for us in studying the result of his study. (pp. xxiii-xxiv)

T. S. Eliot, in his introduction to The Collected Works in English: The Art of Poetry, *Vol. 7 by Paul Valéry, Bollingen Series XLV, translated by Denise Folliot (copyright © 1958 by Princeton University Press; reprinted by permission of Princeton University Press), Pantheon Books, Inc., 1958, pp. vii-xxiv.*

FRANCIS FERGUSSON (essay date 1960)

What does the master of pure poetry propose to do with the impure medium of the theater? How does Valéry, whose deepest aim is the ultimate abstraction, come to terms with the stubborn concreteness of stage, audience, and performers?

He does so in various ways, for he was led to write for the theater at different times and for several different reasons. In the fragments entitled "*My Faust*" it is the theme of Faust which inspires him, and the dramatic form in which they appear is accidental. The librettos on the other hand are occasional pieces written for particular composers or performers, and in writing them Valéry was trying primarily to make entertainments which would actually work in the theater.

The legend of Amphion, who first received the lyre from Apollo, and through the formative power of music became the father of the arts, inspired Valéry in his youth with its operatic possibilities, as he explains in his illuminating lecture on the libretto he finally wrote. The legend seemed to be the perfect illustration of the young Valéry's own theories of the creative process. (pp. viii-ix)

Valéry tells us that this *Amphion* embodies a "bizarre conception born of a theory-making mind"—and that conception represents another and more intellectual kind of despotic ideal; it bespeaks the authentic Valerian passion for pushing art to its theoretical limit. Pushed to the limit, as he says, *Amphion* in this version would approach liturgy. Liturgy has its abstractness too: it presents the generalized scenario of some mode or moment of human experience, and it is enacted by agents of little significance in themselves. The unindividualized figures in the pretty Greek tale are not themselves the substance of *Amphion*. Through them, as through a conventional sign language, we must read a "liturgical" enactment of the birth of the arts—if not a religious meaning, at least a scheme of final authority, a theoretic "limit" of human experience. (p. x)

[*Semiramis* and *The Narcissus Cantata*] were composed for the theater. Valéry's Preface to *Semiramis* explains his intentions in that work: he was dreaming, as usual, of a theater-poem in which all the elements would be strictly unified, as in a lyric; but he ruefully foresaw that the conceptions of collaborating performers, designers, and musicians would have to be taken into account. We also have the lyric poems, the *Air de Sémiramis* and the *Fragments du Narcisse*, on the themes of the librettos. The lyrics are certainly close to Valéry's own inspiration, and by comparing them with the librettos we may see what he did to meet the somewhat alien requirements of the stage.

The *Air de Sémiramis*, the song of the legendary savage queen as she dreams of absolute power, is an early work of Valéry's, but it has some of the musical beauty and allusive richness which we associate with his most famous poems. Absolute power is one phase, or face, of his notion of the mind's creative power. In the poem this theme is conveyed by the appropriate magic of the word, which creates the queen's terrible aspiration in the reader's imagination as the Word of God is supposed to have created the world. But in making the libretto Valéry was obliged to rely on the composer, the designer, and the performers to produce effects like those of the words and imagery of the poem. "The music should create an atmosphere of power and sovereign pride," he says; and he calls upon the designer to present to the physical eye the gigantic palace, the parapet in the morning light, and the smoking and swarming kingdom spread below. The poem has no narrative movement, but for the performers he provides a story: the queen's triumph over the neighboring kings; her lustful enjoyment of one of them; her rejection of lust in favor of murder, and her final ecstatic self-immolation in the rays of the morning sun. (pp. xi-xii)

The conception of *Semiramis* is clear, especially when compared with the poem; but to what extent is it realizable in the theater?

That depends of course on both audience and performers, and perhaps Valéry could ask the utmost of both. In his dialogue *Dance and the Soul* he describes a ballet with that combination of abstractness and richest allusiveness which we find in his verse. He believes that the inspired dancer might come as close as the musician himself to the invisible root of life. Perhaps he counted on such a dancer for *Semiramis*. But the role he wrote for her is not, like the ballet he describes, "pure" dance, corresponding to his own pure poetry, but a narrative sequence in which a human individual is all to scandalously visible. Could an audience, however accustomed to literary and theatrical conventions, watch the queen and her captive king wrestling among the cushions without a little unwanted laughter? It is when the concretely human shows through the conventional stage figure that Valéry's plan falters. The other side of his kind of intellectual rigor, the price of his theoretic strictness, is a kind of solemn and sensational crudity, which we feel whenever we are reminded of actual human relationships. In all his librettos there is a tension between the theoretic ideal and the perversity of the human image, which the public and all too human medium of the theater continually threatens to reveal. Choreographer and dancers would have to beware of this tension, treading with the utmost tact a tightrope course; and the written libretto does not give them much help with this problem: that of the *style* of the performance.

In *The Narcissus Cantata* this problem of style or convention is much less acute. It is the last of the librettos, the farthest from Valéry's deepest sources, and the easiest theatrically. (pp. xii-xiii)

The librettos are not equally successful, but they are all, in intention at least, "poetry of the theater" as Cocteau defined it. One may get this poetry by thinking over the sequence, not of words, but of the theatrically perceptible scenes and images as the librettos call for them. It is poetry akin to that of ballet, with a comparable economy and concentration, dependent like it upon a conventional vocabulary. But unlike ballet it appeals also to the mind, reflecting as it does the author's brilliant and despairing spirit.

In the prefatory note to "*My Faust*," which Valéry addresses "to the wary but not unwilling reader," he gives us the clue to the proper reading. Goethe, he says, having taken Faust and Mephistopheles at the puppet stage, and by his genius raised them to the highest point of poetic existence, has made them available as instruments of the universal spirit: "He put them to the immortal purpose of expressing certain extremes of humanity and the inhuman; and in so doing he liberated them from any particular plot." Valéry proposes to place the two in our time . . . which is so different from Goethe's. It is, in short, the Faust theme at its highest level of abstraction which interests him. As for the plays themselves, he sketched them in quickly, he says, "with little care for plot, action, or ultimate scope." The use of the play form seems to have been chance, perhaps only an echo of Goethe's long conversation with himself.

The Faust theme offers a natural challenge to Valéry, especially as Goethe had handled it. What he says of Leonardo da Vinci applies to this Faust: "I regarded him as the principal character of that Intellectual Comedy which has still to find its poet and would, in my judgment, be far more precious than the *Comédie humaine;* more precious, even, than the *Divine Comedy*." The comedy, the challenge, and the difficulty of the post-Goethian Faust is that when Faust is abstracted from the Christian framework of belief in which early versions had their being, it becomes impossible to define his form or meaning. Faust himself is regarded as a "limit," and so comes to mean or include everything—or nothing. Marlowe's Faust (whatever Marlowe's own belief) had a real devil to sell his soul to, a real soul, a real world to enjoy, and a real God to end his story in damnation. But in Goethe's *Faust* all these elements tend to lose their solidity. They fuse, change places, and begin to "mean" each other, as they are digested into Faust's mind. And if we then try to define or limit Faust himself, we are led back to Goethe as he thinks over his experiences and the books he has been reading. Though much has changed since Goethe, as Valéry reminds us, the "comic" plight of Faust remains essentially the same; and the question is how a contemporary author can reawaken the tired theme. . . . (pp. xv-xvi)

Thomas Mann felt the renewed pull of Faust at about the same time as Valéry. He too is bitten by the appetite for the limits of human experience, and he inhabits the same dehumanized *espace* of contemporary intellectual Europe. But the stratagems he employs in writing *Doctor Faustus* are the exact opposite of those Valéry uses in "*My Faust*." Mann makes a massive frontal assault upon the Faust theme, to *prove* that it is really the hidden machinery, the sinister fatality, of the whole of contemporary culture. He is too serious and voluble to bother with what used to be called "taste"; and though he flirts with the reader, his purpose is not to charm, but to exhaust and overpower him. Valéry, on the contrary, implies that he has himself politely done the work in advance, and now presents us with the result which we may take as lightly as we please: a harmless-looking tube, in which (we are assured) absolute vacuum has been approached as nearly as the most refined modern methods for exhausting the air can do it; a sample of the atmosphere at his and Faust's ultimate summit.

By settling for mere samples of Faustianism, Valéry eludes Mann's unmanageable encyclopedism, and also his worst problems of form. But the basic difficulty, that of objectifying Faust dramatically, remains: if he has "read all the books," tasted and rejected all experience, and seen through all the arts and sciences, what (of any significance) can possibly happen to him? In *Luste, or The Crystal Girl,* Valéry leaves Faust in his motionless and invisible plight, but brings three more tangible characters into his orbit: Luste, his charming secretary, an agile version of the eternal feminine; a young disciple who seems bent on repeating the patterns of Faust's own distant youth; and Mephistopheles, now helpless and superannuated. It is these three who give the comedy its movement, and the audience its *frisson nouveau.*

We cannot tell how Valéry might have contrived an end to *Luste,* if he had been interested enough to finish it for the stage. It is perhaps *essentially* fragmentary in form, a sample of conversation: Valéry talking to himself "in two voices," as he puts it. But the genre of this sample is intellectual comedy akin to that of Shaw or Giraudoux, and Valéry masters its tone and movement with extraordinary ease. He weaves a texture which is both witty and delicately lyrical; perhaps the most promising and congenial theatrical vein he discovered. (pp. xvii-xviii)

Perhaps most of us who read Valéry's theater works on this side of the Atlantic, and in another generation, must feel that his "extremes of humanity and the inhuman" are somewhat alien to us when he spells them out for the stage. The great lyrics may be enjoyed as "pure" poetry, on the analogy of music: with little regard to their provenance or their concrete relevance. But in the theater pieces we are reminded, from time to time, that we have not read all the books, and that the "Mind" we know something about is suffering from malnutrition rather than the frustration of omniscience. And then a difficult effort of sympathy is required if we are to see the effects Valéry intended, his ironic and suggestive play with the limits of his thought, at the limit of the theater medium. (p. xix)

> *Francis Fergusson, in his introduction to* The Collected Works in English: Plays, Vol. 3 *by Paul Valéry, Bollingen Series XLV, translated by David Paul and Robert Fitzgerald (copyright © 1960 by Princeton University Press; reprinted by permission of Princeton University Press), Pantheon Books, 1960, pp. vii-xix.*

PRISCILLA WASHBURN SHAW (essay date 1964)

In view of the fact that the single volume *Poésies* includes poetry written over approximately four decades, its relative homogeneity of language and manner is striking. Moreover, the numerous volumes of prose reveal a comparable uniformity of point of view and suggest in many ways exercises of a high order, virtuoso applications of a personal intellectual algebra, in which the similarity of operations and terms seems far more significant than the ostensible variety of subject. To be sure, it is possible to trace a line of development in the poetry, especially between the *Album des vers anciens* and *La Jeune Parque,* but the curve that it follows is in many respects a familiar one, common to most poets as they slough off the external part of early influences and gradually come into their own style. There is no genuine bifurcation of interests or manner in the mature verse, no suggestion that a poetic vein has been exhausted or a style outgrown, no evidence, from within the poems or without, of a dissatisfaction which might have forced the exploration of different areas of discourse or experience.

A partial explanation of the apparent uniformity of tone and effect may lie in the relatively small number of poems Valéry has written. It seems at least probable that mere quantity heightens our awareness of nuances in treatment or subject, in so far as repetition clarifies what is specific to a particular poem and what appeals to a more permanent strain in the poet's imagination. Thus, the experience of variety depends to some degree on number, and additional examples of Valéry's work might well have suggested groupings within the whole which are not readily apparent as it stands. Yet, there is much in Valéry's explicit statements on poetic theory, as in the poetry itself, that convinces us that this homogeneity was not accidental, but something consciously sought after and desired. It is my belief that it grew out of his way of seeing the world and the self. . . . (pp. 107-08)

Valéry's particular use of language affects considerably the relations of the external to the internal in his poetry and contributes, fully as much as his special presentation of the world, to the merging of these two terms. . . . [In "Le Sylphe" and "Le vin perdu,"] Valéry avoided specifying the exact level on which these poems should be read, preferring to keep them open so that their suggestiveness would not be confined to any one domain. Such, in fact, is the message and warning of "Le Sylphe." Later a related use of language will be seen in *La Jeune Parque,* where words with definite emotional coloring are chosen which can apply to several objects at once, because the syntax does not anchor them conclusively to any one object. The "Cantique des colonnes" makes clear that Valéry also selects adjectives and detail to shape tone and attitude rather than to achieve sharp descriptive effects. . . . Similarly, although Valéry exploits the dimension of the erotic quite frequently, he rarely uses explicitly sensuous images, but rather tends toward more diffuse effects like provocativeness, tenderness, lassitude, gallantry. These parallel tendencies are best explained by the fact that, as Valéry himself has said, he wanted to avoid in his poetry any kind of mental translation, whether into the realm of ideas or of the senses. . . . But one of the consequences of this attitude is his weakening of the denotative meaning of words while strengthening their connotative meaning. This is particularly apparent in a passage like the opening of *La Jeune Parque,* where the ambiguity of the references permits the precise communication of something imprecise—a groping towards awareness, still unlocalized, still largely premonition and intimation.

But it is also more generally true of Valéry's poems that words stand in a looser relation to their referents than is necessarily the case even in poetry. (pp. 146-47)

Words can, it seems, point in two directions: They not only designate an object; they also reveal a speaker. When an expression is not dissoluble on one level, we automatically read it on the other. Valéry quite consistently exploits both these dimensions together, because he wishes to give, not the sensory world in itself, but the affective tone of the person experiencing that world. He thus undermines somewhat the independent reality, the out-thereness of the world, in order to communicate the consciousness assimilating that world, reacting to it and transforming it.

The point can be retraced from a number of different angles. For instance, most critics refer at some time or other to Racine in their discussions of Valéry, because of the remarkable similarity of tone, vocabulary, and metrical phrasing apparent in many lines and pervasive in the Narcissus poems. Or Guiraud, in classifying Valéry's vocabulary, groups a large number of terms under the heading of "poetic words," i.e., words of noble or high style which are considered intrinsically poetic within the tradition of the language. (p. 152)

Certainly one of the reasons Valéry favors high-style words is that they are admirably suited to this purpose. Colloquially speaking, they do not call a spade a spade; they substitute for the common word an expression that has greater emotive overtones, without necessarily transforming our perception of the object itself. (p. 154)

Valéry often selects words among these high-style expressions, not to further descriptive ends, not to provide a sharp illumination of the world, but to create a certain tone, to release affective resonance, to communicate the general emotive overtones which can and do color our perception of the world. The other side of this quality is that there may arise a slight uncertainty as to the referent; when a term is left partially independent of its context, when its specific meaning is not enhanced by the surrounding words, when it cannot be explained by common usage, we simply may not be quite sure what Valéry is referring to. (p. 156)

Valéry is frequently considered obscure. Since, however, there are perhaps as many types of obscurity as there are poets, this general judgment requires elaboration. Moreover, it is often true that the nature of the difficulty is significantly related to other aspects of the poetry, in so far as a poet's focus can be defined by what he leaves unspecified, as well as by what he presents in sharp outline. There are certainly many ways in which Valéry is not obscure at all. There is never any question of tone, for instance, no problem in determining point of view, of deciding whether a poem is ironical or not. . . . It would be inaccurate to say that there is a pervasive difficulty of content—we usually know what the poems say in a general way, and we understand the problems with which they deal. The type of experiences presented is fairly clear, whether in "Fragments du Narcisse," "La pythie," or *La Jeune Parque.* . . . None the less, several of Valéry's poems resist a detailed line-by-line reading, and to this extent they may appear obscure. This obscurity comes from two sources—from the difficulty of establishing references and from the shifting, fluctuating movement of the poems, which frustrates a desire for clear logical, chronological, or even psychological progression. (pp. 156-57)

In other words, it is the obscuring of the exact referent which often permits Valéry to let into his poetry a cluster of feelings and possible relations which considerably enhance the affective tone, even while they may somewhat obstruct a clear orientation in the sensory world. (p. 160)

> *Priscilla Washburn Shaw, "Paul Valery: The World in the Mind," in her* Rilke, Valéry and Yeats: The Domain of the Self *(copyright © 1964 by Rutgers, The State University; reprinted by permission of Rutgers University Press), Rutgers, 1964, pp. 105-74.*

W. H. AUDEN (essay date 1969)

[Valéry's *Notebooks*] form one of the most interesting and original documents of "the inner life" in existence.

Most of such documents are concerned with the so-called personal, that is, with the confession of sins and vices, memories of childhood, the feelings of the subject about God, the weather, his mistress, gossip, self-reproach, and the ordinary motive for producing them is a desire to demonstrate that their author is more interesting, more unique, more *human* than other folks.

For the personal in this sense, Valéry had nothing but contempt. It is in what they show, he believed, that men differ, what they hide is always the same. Confession, therefore, is like undressing in public; everyone knows what he is going to see. Further, a man's secrets are often much more apparent to others than to himself. (p. 360)

The task which Valéry set himself was to observe the human mind in the action of thinking; the only mind that he can observe is, of course, his own, but this is irrelevant. He is not a philosopher, except in the etymological meaning of that word, nor a psychologist insofar as psychology is concerned with hidden depths—for Valéry, humanity is confined to the skin and consciousness; below that is physiological machinery—but an amazingly keen and *rusé* observer of conscious processes of thinking. For this neither a special talent, like a talent for mathematics, nor esoteric learning is required, but only what might be called intellectual virtue, which it is possible for every man to develop, if he chooses.

For the cultivation of such an *Ethique sportive,* as Valéry once called it, one must develop a vigilance that immediately distinguishes between fictions and real psychic events, between the seen, the thought, the reasoned and the felt, and a precision of description that resists all temptation to fine literary effects. Hence Valéry's repeated attacks on the popular notion of "profundity." A thought, he says, can properly be called profound only if it profoundly changes a question or a given situation, and such a thought is never found at the bottom of the mind which contains only a few stock proverbs. (p. 361)

Valéry's attitude to life is more consistent than he admits, and begins with a conviction of the essential inconsistency of the mind and the need to react against it. The following three notes might be taken as mottoes for all his work.

> Cognition reigns but does not rule.

> Sometimes I think; and sometimes I *am.*

> I invoke no inspiration except that element of chance, which is common to every mind; then comes an unremitting toil, which wars against this element of chance.

Valéry's observations cover a wide range of subjects. As one might expect, the least interesting, the ones in which he sounds least like Valéry and most like just one more French writer of mordant aphorisms, are those concerned with love, self-love, good, and evil.

He has extremely interesting things to say about our consciousness of our bodies, about those curious psycho-physical expressions, laughing, crying, and blushing, about the physical behavior of people when they are concentrating on a mental problem. He is excellent on dreams—he observes, for instance, that in dreams there is "practically no present tense." But for poets, naturally, and for many others too, I believe, his most valuable contributions are his remarks on the art of poetry. (p. 362)

For Valéry, a poem ought to be a festival of the intellect, that is, a game, but a solemn, ordered, and significant game, and a poet is someone to whom arbitrary difficulties suggest ideas. It is the glory of poetry that the lack of a single word can ruin everything, that the poet cannot continue until he discovers a word, say, in two syllables, containing P or F, synonymous with *breaking-up,* yet not too uncommon. The formal restrictions of poetry teach us that the thoughts which arise from our needs, feelings, and experiences are only a small part of the thoughts of which we are capable. In any poem some lines were "given" the poet, which he then tried to perfect, and others which he had to calculate and at the same time make them sound as "natural" as possible. It is more becoming in a poet to talk of versification than of mysterious voices, and his genius should be so well hidden in his talent that the reader attributes to his art what comes from his nature.

Needless to say, Valéry found very little in the French poetry of his age which seemed to him anything more than a worship of chance and novelty, and concluded that poetry was a freak survival, that no one today would be capable of arriving at the notion of verse if it were not already there.

In his general principles I am convinced that Valéry is right past all possibility of discussion, but I cannot help wondering if I should also agree in daily practice as much as I do, if I were a Frenchman trying to write French poetry. For polemical reasons, probably, Valéry overstresses, I think, the arbitrariness of poetic formal restrictions, and overdramatizes the opposition between them and the "Natural." If they really were purely arbitrary, then the prosodies of different languages would be interchangeable, and the experience which every poet has had, of being unable to get on with a poem because he was trying to use the "wrong" form for this particular poem until, having found the right form, the *natural* form, composition proceeded freely, would be unknown. (pp. 363-64)

> *W. H. Auden, "Un homme d'esprit" (originally published in* Hudson Review, *Vol. XXII, No. 3, Autumn, 1969), in* Forewords and Afterwords, *edited by Edward Mendelson (copyright © 1973 by W. H. Auden; reprinted by permission of Random House, Inc.), Random House, 1973, pp. 358-66.*

E. M. CIORAN (essay date 1969)

To be understood is a veritable misfortune for a writer; it was Valéry's, both during his lifetime and afterward. Is it possible that he could have been as simple, as *penetrable* as all that? Surely not, but he was improvidently generous with information about his life and work, he divulged himself, he freely distributed keys, he dissipated a good many of those misunderstandings on which the secret prestige of a writer is founded; instead of leaving to others the labor of ferreting him out, he performed it himself, indulging to a fault his mania for self-explanation. His commentators thus found their burden singularly reduced: by initiating them straightaway into the nub of his preoccupations and gestures, he invited them to ponder not so much his work as his remarks about it. Subsequently, the goal of every enquiry concerning him was to learn whether, on a given point, he had been the victim of a delusion or, on the contrary, of *excessive* clairvoyance, but in either case of a judgment dissociated from the real. Not only was he his own commentator, his very works amount to an autobiography more or less camouflaged, a learned introspection, a *diary* of his mind, an elevation of his experience, however ordinary, to the rank of intellectual events, an inquisition against whatever traces of the *unreflected* he sensed within himself, a revolt against his depths.

Knowing how to dismantle the mechanism of a thing—everything being a mechanism, a sum of artifices, of gimmicks or, to use a more dignified term, of operations—getting at the springs, behaving like a clockmaker, peering *inside,* refusing to be a dupe, that is what counted in his view. Man, as he conceives him, is noteworthy only in proportion to his capacity for non-acquiescence, to the degree of lucidity he has achieved. This demand for lucidity brings to mind the *alertness* which underlies every spiritual experience, the measure of it being one's response to the paramount question: "How far have you progressed in your perception of unreality?" (pp. 411-12)

[In Valéry's evolution as a poet, Poe's] "The Philosophy of Composition" is a major event, an encounter of capital importance. In it are to be found all the ideas he later promulgated about the poetic act. He must have been ecstatic on reading that the composition of "The Raven" can in no way be attributed to chance or intuition, that the poem was conceived with "the precision and rigid consequence of a mathematical problem."

But "The Philosophy of Composition" was one of Poe's mystifications: all of Valéry sprang from a naive understanding of it, from his enthusiasm for a text in which a poet was poking fun at his credulous readers. That he supported with such juvenile ardor a demonstration fundamentally anti-poetic proves that at the outset, deep down, Valéry was not a poet, for otherwise his whole being would have rebelled against this cold, pitiless dismantling of delirium, against this indictment of the most basic poetic reflex, of poetry's *raison d'être;* undoubtedly he needed this cunning incrimination, this trial of all spontaneous creation to justify, to excuse his own lack of spontaneity.... Here was a catechism not for poets but for versifiers which was bound to flatter the virtuoso in Valéry, his penchant for intellectual one-upmanship, for art at one remove, for art *in art*—this religion of the niggling, as well as his determination to stand, at every moment, outside all lapses of reason, poetic or otherwise. Only a maniac of lucidity could relish this cynical trek backward to the sources of the poem, which contradicts every law of literary production, this infinitely fussy pre-meditation, these unheard-of acrobatics from which Valéry derived the first article of his poetic credo. He elevated into a theory his inaptitude for being a poet naturally, and proposed it as a model, he fastened to a technique in order to hide his congenital defects, he placed —an unforgivable crime—poetics above poetry. There is reason to believe that all his theses would have been quite different had he been capable of producing a less intricate body of work. He endorsed the difficult out of *impotence:* all his requirements are those of an artist, not of a poet. What was merely a game in Poe becomes a dogma in Valéry, a literary dogma, which is to say an *accepted* fiction. As a good technician, he tried to rehabilitate procedure and skill at the expense of *gift*. From every theory (in art that is), he sought to extract the most unpoetic conclusion, and to it he would hold fast, seduced as he was, to the point of obnubilation, by *craft*, by invention devoid of fatality, of the ineluctable, of destiny. (pp. 415-16)

Valéry's cult of rigor does not go beyond the appropriateness of terms and the conscious striving for an *abstract* brilliance in sentences. Rigor of form, not of matter. The *Jeune Parque* is said to have required more than a hundred drafts: the author is proud of it, offering this statistic as proof of a rigorous method. Leaving nothing to improvisation or inspiration (odious synonyms in his view), supervising words, weighing them, never forgetting that language is the one and only reality—all this characterized his will to expression, carried to such extremes that it turns into hair-splitting, into an exhausting quest for infinitesimal precision. Valéry is a galley-slave of the Nuance.

He advanced to the most remote limits of language where, dangerously tenuous, it is but *essence* of lace, the last degree *before* unreality. It would be impossible to imagine a language more chastened than his, more miraculously bloodless. Why deny that in more than one instance it is over-elaborate or clearly precious? . . . It would all in all be excessive to consider Valéry a precious writer, but correct to say that he has *fits* of preciosity, which was quite natural in someone who saw nothing behind language, no substratum or residue of reality. Only words save us from nothingness, such would seem to be the *rock-bottom* of his thought, though rock-bottom is something whose existence he rejected both metaphysically and rhetorically. The fact remains that he wagered his all on words and thereby proved that he still believed in something. Had he ended up by estranging himself from them, only then could one treat him as a "nihilist." (pp. 421-22)

The effort to define oneself, to dwell on one's own mental operations represented for Valéry true knowledge. But *knowing oneself* is not *knowing,* or rather, it is but one variety of knowing. Valéry always confused *knowledge* and *clear-sightedness.* And in him, the will to be clear-sighted, to be inhumanly disabused, goes hand in hand with a thinly disguised pride: he knows himself and he admires himself for knowing himself. Let us be fair: it is not that he admires his mind—he admires himself insofar as he *is* Mind. His narcissism, inseparable from what he designated as "emotions" and "pathos" of the intellect, is not a narcissism of private diaries, it is not the attachment to oneself as a *unique* aberration, nor is it the self of those who like to brood on their ailments; no, it is, to be more precise, an abstract self: the self of an abstract individual, far from the indulgences of introspection or the impurities of psychoanalysis. . . . History, the idol he sought to demolish, is largely responsible for his enduring, for what currency he enjoys—his remarks bearing on it are those most often quoted: an irony which he might have appreciated. His poems are questioned, his poetics rejected, but as moralist and analyst attentive to events he is is granted more and more authority. This self-lover had the makings of an extrovert. One senses that appearances did not displease him, that with him nothing assumed a morbid, profound, consummately private aspect, and that even the Void, which he inherited from Mallarmé, was merely a fascination exempt from vertigo, and by no means an opening onto horror or ecstasy. It is written, in I forget which Upanishad, that "the essence of man is the word, the essence of the word is the hymn." Valéry would have subscribed to the first assertion and denied the second. It is in this assent and this refusal that one must look for the key to his accomplishments and his limits. (p. 424)

E. M. Cioran, "Valéry before His Idols," in The

Hudson Review *(copyright © 1969 by The Hudson Review, Inc.; reprinted by permission), Vol. XXII, No. 3, Autumn, 1969, pp. 411-24.*

ROGER SHATTUCK   (essay date 1970)

What characterizes [Valéry's] prose most is the variety, in kind and quality, of the styles [he] can muster. All the formal speeches are larded with asides, brief skirmishes with the audience that play for a laugh. In these passages, Valéry's "I" hovers between the mocking Academician, the serious "man in the mind," and the straightforward human being. . . . [For example,] the short text on suicide and the somewhat more developed article on "The Future of Literature" waste no time on preliminaries or lengthy transitions. Valéry divides suicides into three classes and examines them one after another as if before a class. Then, instead of imagining himself in the situation of delivering a speech and padding it out with dramatic asides, he imagines himself convincingly in the very act of committing suicide. As a result his two columns are more arresting than the surrounding texts by surrealist activists in the pages of *La Révolution surréaliste.* When he bends his attention to the social evolution of literature there is a kind of comic grace in the ease with which he reaches his conclusion: "I sometimes catch myself thinking that in the future the role of literature will be close to that of a *sport.*"

Before long one notices that Valéry rarely fails to plant such a key sentence at intervals in every sustained prose piece. . . . In the dizzy spaces of thought a distant light shines forth toward which one can sight and slowly make one's way. A single thought, a profound platitude, or a verbal formula is enough. Then the rest of the essay comes together around that spark. One could, of course, take the contrary position and argue that these startling simplicities are not what he started with as isolated markers in the wilderness, but are rather the final results of the pressure of thinking patiently applied to anything whatsoever.

But in either case we are led to a related question that particularly concerns the "occasional" writer. Did Valéry have something like a method, a sequence of mental steps to which he could submit any raw material and produce a presentable written result? Frequently he leaves precisely that impression. . . . By 1924—give or take a year or two— he had organized his ideas, found a method of work, and discovered that he could turn his mind to any subject without wasting his time. . . . His most seminal essays— "Introduction to the Method of Leonardo da Vinci," "Conquest by Method"—were twenty years behind him; their titles are not without significance. His debut as a public figure required that he be prepared to speak on all topics. It turned out to be possible, even rewarding. He already had a profound intellectual faith in the act of attention, and from the very earliest of his writings on Leonardo he had expressed a belief in the relationship between all things and all events. Given that attitude, he did have a kind of method or process.

Valéry's "method" had the effect of reducing the infinite variety of his subject matter to three themes: the mind, language, and everything else. His earliest metaphors for mind (a theater; a smoke ring) depict its turbulent equilibrium as circular and self-beholding. As time goes on he rejects with increasing vehemence any theory of separable mental faculties and portrays consciousness as a rhythm. . . . [In] a beautifully turned page he asks . . . doctors: how, since you know so much about the organic functioning of the reproductive organs, can you bring yourselves to make love? He suggests that the solution lies in the existence of an alternating rhythm of being: "Now I think, now I am." We cannot be everything at once. This functional rhythm had already been described in a pithy little essay called "The Aesthetic Infinite": "To justify the word *infinite* and give it a precise meaning, we need only recall that in the aesthetic order *satisfaction* revives *need, response* renews *demand, presence* generates *absence,* and *possession* gives rise to *desire.*"

In these most critical pronouncements about mind, Valéry falls back on the sexual metaphor, or rather on the erotic ritual with which man, more than any other animal, has sanctified the act of mere coupling. . . . In his theoretical statements, Valéry contrasts the aesthetic realm of infinitely renewable pleasure with the practical realm, where satisfaction obeys the entropy principle and returns everything to zero.

But most important of all to Valéry and to us are two intermediate realms where pleasure and delight arise under circumstances of restraint and reticence, two realms where we come to the threshold both of ourselves and of another person. Those realms are love and language. They lead us to the most precious and fragile acts of mind and body that we can know. (pp. xx-xxiv)

> *Roger Shattuck, in his introduction to* The Collected Works in English: Occasions, Vol 11 *by Paul Valéry, Bollingen Series XLV, translated by Roger Shattuck and Frederick Brown (copyright © 1970 by Princeton University Press; reprinted by permission of Princeton University Press), Princeton University Press, 1970, pp. ix-xxx.*

WILLIAM H. GASS (essay date 1972)

[Despite Valéry's] "intellectualized" view of poetry, the poetry he wrote was predominately erotic.

In addition to the predictable appearance of Venus, Orpheus, Helen and their friends, the use of films and gauze, the dreary azures, lilies, fountains, fruit, hair, swans and roses of conventional symbolist poetry, the moon and the murmurous wood, the ritual expostulations (hollow ohs and fatuous ahs), the early poems are stuffed, as though for Christmas, with images of images: tree, leaf and sun shadows, dream and fire flicker, countless kinds of reflection. Here the footprint has more substance than the foot; the face finds its resemblance in another medium, floats in fountain water like a flower, trembles independently of its owner as if it had its own sorrows, looks back from the language of its own description like a lover or an accusation. The Narcissus theme has already been introduced: "I can love nothing now but the bewitching water." (p. 160)

Valéry chose a world where he could be, as he repeatedly said, master in his own house: his head. It was a world of wait and watch.

Order, clarity, precision, shape: these properties seem so often an enemy of powerful feelings that, although they may usefully employ them the way steam is put to work by the piston, to invoke them is the same as calling the police.

Anything—the starry heavens which so terrified Pascal (the one author for whom Valéry exhibits contempt)—can be scientifically observed, but the man of science, Valéry believed, "*switches off* the whole emotive system of his personality. He tries to turn himself into a kind of machine which, after recording observations, sets about formulating definitions and laws, finally replacing phenomena by their expression in terms of conscious, deliberate, and definite potentials."

Valéry's error here, and one he makes repeatedly, is the conflation of method with mind. He supposes that if the scientist or mathematician employs an objective method and pursues disinterested ends, that the mind so engaged must become objective and disinterested too. This is clearly not the case. One must play by the rules, but passionately by them; someone whose emotive system is switched off will hardly be able to think creatively.

Nevertheless, the strategy of withdrawal was shrewd. Let the poet continue to compose; let the man, Valéry, love if he needed to; let him entertain confused ideas—marry, work, worry; he, the other Paul, would observe carefully, allowing the value of each enterprise to detach itself from its original aim and fasten instead to the successive acts which the undertaking may have required and then finally to reach for something principled and abstract which, if it were mastered, would render writing unnecessary: namely, the method of composition itself. To have the power, yet withhold its use; to be divine, and not create, is to possess a double strength. It is to say: I could if I would, and I *can,* so I won't. It is also the ultimate in fastidious disdain. (pp. 161-62)

Odd, mannered, doctrinaire, yet exquisitely wrought, "Monsieur Teste," from its famous opening line ("Stupidity is not my strong suit"), has seemed to its critics to show Valéry at his most arrogant and exasperating. Scarcely a fiction, it is scarcely anything else. Certainly it contains one of the more curious, though forthrightly named, characters in . . . in . . . what shall we say? fictosophy? "Mr. Head?" is that the right address? No, the wrong resonances. "Mr. Headstrong?" No, that's out of balance. Taken from an old French form of *tête* (shell, pot, head), *teste* also means "will / witness / testament," and thus combines, with only a little distortion, three qualities Valéry valued most at the time. In addition, *teste* refers to the *testes cerebri,* the optic lobes, which are called the testicles of the brain.

Although Valéry treats him with characteristically amused and skeptical reservations, Monsieur Teste nevertheless represents the ideal man of mind. He is a monster, and is meant to be—an awesome, wholly individualized machine —yet in a sense he is also the sort of inhuman being Valéry aimed to become himself: a Narcissus of the best kind, a scientific observer of consciousness, a man untroubled by inroads of worldly trivia (remember Villier de Lisle-Adam's symbolist slogan, "as for living, our servants will do that for us"?), who vacations in his head the way a Platonist finds his Florida in the realm of Forms. Like the good analytic philosopher he also resembles, Monsieur Teste complains constantly about the treacheries of words and the salad-forked tongue wagged so loosely by language (while his own name, perversely, is an excellent example of ambiguity well used). Teste has become almost pure potentiality, and a man in whom knowledge has finally made unnecessary the necessity to act. (pp. 164-65)

Edmund Wilson once wrote [see excerpt above] that Valéry's prose, "in spite of the extravagant respect with which it is treated by his admirers, is by no means so remarkable as his verse," but I find myself unable to agree.... [The "Eupalinos," one of Valéry's dialogues, is one] of the most original and moving pieces of prose in any language.

The empirical distinction between poetry and prose is a wholly illusory one, a fact of which Valéry was at times perfectly aware, for the French have pioneered the prose poem; Valéry admired Rimbaud's, and wrote not a few himself; he also dabbled in the story, wrote "Monsieur Teste," of course, made jots of plots, especially fancying the kind of flat, weird, metaphysically menacing situations Lettau could find stimulating, as Borges certainly did.

Valéry could never quite give himself up to prose (prose as he had got in the bad habit of defining it), and this accounts, at least in part, for the flicker in his thought which one often finds in the essays. Perhaps his mind was too playful, perhaps it danced when it should have walked or harshly stomped, yet what is striking in even his most occasional pieces—let alone the famous ones like "The Crises of the Mind" or "The Outlook for Intelligence"—is his remarkable prescience, so that even brief asides ("Perhaps waste itself has become a public and permanent necessity"), made in 1940, or 1932, or 1929, fall further over and into the present than any wholesome shadow should. It's not just his style alone that sometimes causes the scalp to prickle.

I suspect that Valéry's success as a wise man was not due to his Leonardo-like ambitions, because his studies were not as universal or as thorough as he liked to let on, and the central concern of his life was a stubbornly restricted one; nor was it because he reasoned like a Teste, for his mind was essentially metaphoric in its operation (what he knew and liked most about architecture, for example, was almost wholly embodied in the very idea of "building"); and although his sovereign detachment certainly helped him and he was instinctively right about what to despise, he was particularly a master of the sidelong look, and the practice of composition over many years had taught him to attend to "little" things and small steps, for there, in scrupulosities only a spider might otherwise pain itself with, were the opportunities for genius. It is Valéry, himself, who writes:

> Great events are perhaps so only for small minds. For more attentive minds, it is the unnoticed, continual events that count.

It was these small movements of which Valéry was such a master, if we think of them as the movements of a mind which has practiced passage to the point of total purity, compressing those steps, those postures and attitudes which were learned at the mirror so painfully, into one unwinding line of motion; and as we follow the body of his thought as we might that of an inspired dancer, leaving the source of his energy like flame, we have presented almost to our eye other qualities in addition to those normally thought vital and sufficient for the mind, though rare and prized like clarity and rigor, honesty, openness, interest, penetration and brevity, truth; that is to say, lightness, tact in particular, and above all, elegance and grace. (pp. 174-76)

William H. Gass, "Paul Valéry" (1972), in his The World within the Word *(copyright © 1978 by William H. Gass; reprinted by permission of Alfred A. Knopf, Inc.), Knopf, 1978, pp. 158-76.*

ADDITIONAL BIBLIOGRAPHY

Bosanquet, Theodora. *Paul Valéry.* New York: Haskell House Publishers, 1974, 136 p.
    Biographical background to Valéry's literary career, with a descriptive and interpretive survey of his poetry and prose. This is a reprint of a study first published in 1933.

Chisholm, A. R. *An Approach to M. Valery's "Jeune Parque."* Melbourne: Melbourne University Press, 1938, 66 p.
    Detailed analysis interpreting the poem as "mainly the symbol of human consciousness."

Crow, Christine M. *Paul Valéry: Consciousness and Nature.* Cambridge: Cambridge University Press, 1972, 271 p.
    Study examining the relationship between human consciousness and nature in Valéry's work, questioning critical assumptions that the author was less responsive to the world of nature and emotion than to the world of pure intellect.

Eliot, T. S. *From Poe to Valery.* New York: Harcourt, Brace and Co., 1948, 32 p.
    Examines Valéry's interest in Poe's poetic theories.

Fisher, H.A.L. *Paul Valéry.* Oxford: The Clarendon Press, 1927, 22 p.
    Traces Valéry's development as a poet, his influences, and major themes.

Franklin, Ursula. *The Rhetoric of Valéry's Prose "Aubades."* Toronto: University of Toronto Press, 1979, 154 p.
    Close reading of Valéry's prose poems and fragments dealing with the theme of dawn.

Garzilli, Enrico. "Man Alone: Monsieur Teste—Paul Valéry." In his *Circles Without Center: Paths to the Discovery and Creation of Self in Modern Literature,* pp. 11-18. Cambridge: Harvard University Press, 1972.
    Considers Valéry's ideas on human consciousness as represented by Monsieur Teste.

Grubbs, Henry A. *Paul Valéry.* New York: Twayne Publishers, 1968, 153 p.
    Critical study designed as an introductory survey of Valéry's work.

Ince, W. N. *The Poetic Theory of Paul Valéry: Inspiration and Technique.* Leicester, England: Leicester University Press, 1961, 187 p.
    Study analyzing Valéry's theoretical views regarding the artist's use of technique and craftsmanship as opposed to his submission to various kinds of inspirational forces.

Jones, Rhys S. "Paul Valéry." *Contemporary Review* 193, No. 1105 (January 1958): 29-33.
    Examines Valéry as a prophet warning humanity against the perils of reason and science.

Lawler, James R. Introduction to *Paul Valéry: An Anthology,* by Paul Valéry, translated by Stuart Gilbert, pp. vii-xiii. Princeton: Princeton University Press, 1956.
    Survey of Valéry's work and the phases of his literary career.

Lawler, James R. *Form and Meaning in Valéry's "Le Cimetière marin."* Melbourne: Melbourne University Press, 1959, 41 p.
    Examines compositional background and evolution of the poem, analyzing its successive revisions and its final form.

Lawler, James R. *The Poet as Analyst: Essays on Paul Valéry.* Los Angeles: University of California Press, 1974, 353 p.
    Essays representing, according to critic, "an attempt to describe the methods, and to explain the sensibility, of a poet and thinker whom I hold to be one of the most important in French literature." These studies focus on Valéry's lesser known works and include examinations of the critical opinions of T. S. Eliot and E. M. Cioran.

McLaren, James C. "Criticism and Creativity: Poetic Themes in Mallarmé and Valéry." *L'Esprit Créateur* IV, No. 4 (Winter 1964): 222-27.*
   Discusses themes of the poetic ideal in the works of these two writers.

Read, Herbert. Introduction to *Aesthetics,* by Paul Valéry, translated by Ralph Manheim, pp. vii-xiv. New York: Pantheon Books, 1964.
   Summarizes Valéry's thoughts on artistic creativity.

Suckling, Norman. *Paul Valéry and the Civilized Mind.* London: Oxford University Press, 1954, 285 p.
   Examines the influence on Valéry of various authors and thinkers, including Mallarmé, Poe, Descartes, Goethe, and Bergson.

Turnell, Martin. "Paul Valéry and the Universal Self." *The American Scholar* 45, No. 2 (Spring 1976): 262-70.
   Biographical sketch and descriptive survey of the major poetry and prose.

Valéry, François. Preface to *History and Politics,* by Paul Valéry, translated by Denise Folliot and Jackson Mathews, pp. ix-xx. New York: Pantheon Books, 1962.
   Character sketch and examination of Valéry's political thought by his son.

Whiting, Charles G. *Paul Valery.* London: The Athlone Press, 1978, 147 p.
   Descriptive survey of Valéry's work and its major themes.

Thomas (Clayton) Wolfe

1900-1938

American novelist, short story writer, essayist, dramatist, and poet.

Wolfe, one of the foremost southern writers of this century, took the facts of his life and, with an intensity and lyricism not witnessed in American literature since Whitman, wove them into an epic celebration of the American dream. His books are often critically perceived as a single *künstlerroman*, evoking the essential isolation of the hero as he grows toward artistic and personal maturity.

Wolfe's work is informed by an epic quality—every thought, feeling, and action is of monumental importance—and an all-encompassing empathy for humanity, brought about by his own attempts to read all, sense all, and experience all. Awash in adjectives and description, his stories are told in a variety of styles ranging from Elizabethan lyricism to satiric rhetoric to stream-of-consciousness. His varying styles indicate the influence of many authors, notably James Joyce, Samuel Taylor Coleridge, and Sherwood Anderson.

Born in Asheville, North Carolina, which served as a model for Altamont and Libya Hill, Wolfe grew up among the people who later appeared in various guises within his fiction. He began his career as a playwright at the University of North Carolina, continuing at Harvard. There he studied English under John Livingstone Lowes. The latter's theories on the importance of the subconscious fusion of previous experiences and influences with imagination in the creative process shaped the young man's writing.

Aline Bernstein was central to Wolfe's personal life and career. Close to twenty years his senior, she provided him with the emotional and financial support that enabled him to give up his teaching position at New York University and write the first, and many believe best, of his novels, *Look Homeward, Angel*. Their involvement lasted five years and provided the material for the George Webber-Esther Jack relationship in *The Web and the Rock* and *You Can't Go Home Again*. Appearing in the persona of Eugene Gant, Wolfe traced his own story in *Look Homeward, Angel*, introducing his theory of life as a lonely search for "a stone, a leaf, an unfound door": a sign which will reveal a universe of fulfilling purpose left behind at birth. The book's acceptance by editor Maxwell E. Perkins of Charles Scribner's Sons and publication in 1929 brought Wolfe instant critical acclaim (except in his offended home town) and began one of the most intense and controversial editor-author relationships of the century. After several years of artistic floundering Wolfe conceived of a multi-volume series titled "The October Fair," in which Eugene's story and that of his family would be continued. His theme of the loneliness of the individual was expanded to include what he considered a universal quest: the search for a spiritual father, or "someone who can help you, save you, ease the burden for you." This theme surfaced in the turbulent, myth-ridden *Of Time and the River*.

After the publication of his second novel in 1935, Wolfe fell

P. Buller

out of favor with many critics, who objected to his strident, epic stance, the autobiographical aspect of his novels, and the increasing intrusion of the authorial voice in the narrative. One essay in particular, Bernard DeVoto's "Genius Is Not Enough," rankled Wolfe, as the critic accused him of utter dependence on Maxwell Perkins and "the assembly line at Scribner's" to give form to his lengthy novels. Stung by such criticism and intent on proving himself an author dependent on no one, Wolfe left Scribner's in 1937 for a new publisher, announced the abandonment of his autobiographical mode, and set to work on an objective novel. The resulting mass of manuscript was honed down by Edward C. Aswell of Harper and Brothers to the two novels published after Wolfe's death. While *The Web and the Rock* and *You Can't Go Home Again* exhibited little evidence of progression to objectivity, they did contain a powerful, more mature retelling of Wolfe's story, with Eugene Gant now in the guise of George Webber, and Aline Bernstein appearing as Esther Jack. Wolfe's vision had expanded to include social concerns as well as the individual's quest for fulfillment. Wolfe, through Webber, explained his outlook on life to editor Foxhall Edwards (Maxwell Perkins) in *You Can't Go Home Again*: "Man was born to live, to suffer and to die, and what befalls him is a tragic lot. There is no denying this in the final end. *But we must, dear Fox, deny it all along the way.*"

Critics remain sharply divided regarding Wolfe's stature. While some see in his work the high-flown artiness of an eternal adolescent, others contend, as Wolfe himself had written of his father, that "though a man's work may be as full of flaws as a Swiss cheese it will somehow continue to endure if only it has fire. . . ."

PRINCIPAL WORKS

Look Homeward, Angel (novel) 1929
From Death to Morning (short stories) 1935
Of Time and the River (novel) 1935
The Story of a Novel (essay) 1936
The Web and the Rock (novel) 1939
You Can't Go Home Again (novel) 1940
The Hills Beyond (short stories, sketches, and unfinished novel) 1941
A Stone, a Leaf, a Door (poetry) 1945
Mannerhouse (drama) 1948
Short Novels (novellas) 1961

WALTER S. ADAMS (essay date 1929)

An amazing new novel is just off the press which is of great and unique interest to Asheville. This community in fact, is going to be astounded by it. Some few well known residents may be shocked into chills. Others will probably be severely annoyed. Many others will snicker and laugh.

The reason is that ["Look Homeward, Angel"] is written about Asheville and Asheville people in the plainest of plain language. It is the autobiography of an Asheville boy. The story of the first twenty years of his life is bared with a frankness and detail rarely ever seen in print. The author paints himself and his home circle, as well as neighbors, friends and acquaintances with bold, daring lines, sparing nothing and shielding nothing. . . .

It is quite apparent from the book that the author was not happy. His life here, as he boldly sketches it, was crowded with pain, bitterness and ugliness.

While the characters in the book are undoubtedly painted true to life, according to the author's idea of it, the names are changed and juggled around. However, any resident of Asheville who knew this city and its people during the period 1900 to 1920, will not have the slightest trouble in filling in the names of the real persons whom Wolfe made characters in his book. Asheville in this novel goes by the name of Altamount. (p. 1)

To the outlander, "Look Homeward, Angel" is an outstanding novel possessed of unquestioned literary merit. The portraiture is vivid, the style is incisive, the narrative flows with a freedom that sweeps along the most resisting reader. . . .

Most of the Asheville people who appear in the novel wear their most unpleasant guises. If there attaches to them any scandal which has enjoyed only a subterranean circulation, it is dragged forth into the light. If they have any weaknesses which more tolerant friends are considerate enough to overlook, these defects are faithfully described. In describing them, the author must often convey the impression to the unknowing that these weaknesses were the distinguishing characteristics of the persons.

The novel will be acclaimed to literary critics as a work of real distinction. But the suspicion is strong that Asheville people will read it not because of its literary worth but rather in spite of any artistic merit which it may possess. They will read it because it is the story, told with bitterness and without compassion, of many Asheville people. (p. 2)

> *Walter S. Adams, "Amazing New Novel Is Realistic Story of Asheville People," in* Asheville Times *(reprinted by permission of* Asheville Citizen-Times), *October 20, 1929 (and reprinted as "'Look Homeward, Angel'," in* Thomas Wolfe: The Critical Reception, *edited by Paschal Reeves, David Lewis, Inc., 1974, pp. 1-32).*

JOHN CHAMBERLAIN (essay date 1929)

Among young American writers who have made impressive debuts in recent years, Thomas Wolfe is a distinct anomaly: he has not a nostalgic temperament. *Look Homeward, Angel* is not the book of a frayed spirit who is trying his level best to escape through elegiac writing; it is a rich, positive grappling with life, a remembrance of things past untinged by the shadow of regret, of one who has found his youthful experiences full of savor. No more sensuous (not to be construed as sensual) novel has been written in the United States. There is an easy, unforced strength to it that should be the despair of those beginners of the *New American Caravan* who have tossed overboard one genteel tradition only to fall into another. Inasmuch as it is not a novelist's novel, there will be quite intelligent devotees of fiction who will find its rough, fluid pattern too easy for their tastes. The answer to them would be that it is unfair to condemn a good chronicle novel simply because the chronicle, through over-emphasis, is now falling out of fashion.

For a good chronicle novel is precisely what *Look Homeward, Angel* is. The story is a familiar one: the life of a family set down as it progresses in time, with particular attention to one member who serves as a focal point. . . . Eugene Gant is born at the opening of the century, and his experiences have probably been matched by any number of our contemporaries. But Mr. Wolfe writes of Eugene's days with a difference. The sensitivity of the book is enormous, and it is not a sick sensitivity. There is either gusto or intensity to all of Eugene's activities. . . .

Mr. Wolfe's grasp of character is unhurried—a firm grasp in the old Thackeray sense. His people are "flat"; they are tagged by their idiosyncrasies of speech and action. They do not change greatly . . . , but because they are the sort of people who are set in their ways (excepting Eugene) the imputation of flatness is no derogation. As for Mr. Wolfe's sheer dramatic power, we ask you to read the death of Ben and then compare it, as we did, with the death of Madame Bovary. Mr. Wolfe's scene is more intimate, it brings a sharper emotion of recognition to one who has been through such a ghastly ordeal. We do not say that it is greater artistically; we merely submit that it is substantially richer.

Look Homeward, Angel has its faults, but they are not those springing from a poverty of material. We might point out that a more logical effect would have been gained if Ben's adventure in the Greasy Spoon (which sets fineness against vulgarity in the manner of the Walpurgisnacht of *Ulysses*) had been left open somehow to the observation of

Eugene, or if Gant's trip to California had been assimilated in some way to the narrative of Eugene's life. There are sentences that debouch here and there into meaningless rhetoric. But why seek flaws in the midst of abundance? Mr. Wolfe gives the impression of being inexhaustible, even though the book is largely autobiographical. His second novel will be his real test; for in it he will be forced to think more in terms of pattern and idea than he has in his first. But his observance is so inclusive, his antennae so sensitive to the world about him, that one can hardly regard *Look Homeward, Angel* as a flash in the pan. (pp. 344-46)

> *John Chamberlain, "Fiction: 'Look Homeward, Angel'," in* The Bookman *(copyright, 1929, by George H. Doran Company), Vol. 70, No. 4, December, 1929 (and reprinted as "Thomas Wolfe," in* The Idea of an American Novel, *edited by Louis D. Rubin, Jr. and John Rees Moore, Thomas Y. Crowell Company, 1961, pp. 344-46).*

ROBERT PENN WARREN (essay date 1935)

The root of Mr. Wolfe's talent is his ability at portraiture. The figures of Eliza Gant and old Gant, of Ben and Helen, in *Look Homeward, Angel*, are permanent properties of the reader's imagination. Mr. Wolfe has managed to convey the great central vitality of the old man, for whom fires would roar up the chimney and plants would grow, . . . whose quality is perpetually heroic, mythical, and symbolic. It is the same with Eliza. . . . These two figures dominate both [*Look Homeward, Angel* and *Of Time and the River*]; even after old Gant is dead the force of his personality, or rather the force of the symbol into which that personality has been elevated, is an active agent, and a point of reference for interpretation.

These two characters, and Ben and Helen in a lesser degree, are triumphs of poetic conception. (pp. 171-72)

[The] figures of the Gant family are powerful and overwhelming as symbols, as an emotional focus for the novel, and as a point of reference. But the method collapses completely when applied to Starwick, a character of equal importance in Mr. Wolfe's scheme.

We amass a great fund of information concerning Francis Starwick. (pp. 172-73)

But this body of information is not all that the writer intends. F. Scott Fitzgerald and Ernest Hemingway have been able to use effectively such characters as Starwick and to extract their meaning, because as novelists they were willing to work strictly in terms of character. But in *Of Time and the River* the writer is forever straining to convince the reader of some value in Starwick that is not perceptible, that the writer himself cannot define; he tries, since he is writing an autobiography, to make Starwick a symbol, a kind of alter ego, for a certain period of his own experience. The strain is tremendous; and without conviction. (p. 173)

The potency of the figures from the family and the failure with Starwick may derive from the autobiographical nature of Mr. Wolfe's work. Eliza and old Gant come from a more primary level of experience, figures of motherhood and fatherhood that gradually, as the book progresses, assume a wider significance and become at the same time a reference for the hero's personal experience. And the author,

knowing them first on that level, has a way of knowing them more intimately and profoundly as people than he ever knows Starwick. Starwick is more artificial, because he is at the same time a social symbol and a symbol for a purely private confusion of which the roots are never clear. (p. 174)

[Some] of Mr. Wolfe's material is not subordinated to the intention of [*Of Time and the River*]. What is his intention? On what is the mass of material focused? What is to give it form? His novels are obviously autobiographical. This means that the binding factor should be, at least in part, the personality of the narrator, or, since Mr. Wolfe adopts a disguise, of the hero, Eugene Gant. The two books are, in short, an account of the development of a sensibility; obviously something more is intended than the looseness and irresponsibility of pure memoirs or observations. The work demands comparison with such works as Joyce's *Portrait of the Artist as a Young Man* or Lawrence's *Sons and Lovers;* it may even demand comparison with proper autobiographies, such as Rousseau's *Confessions* or *The Education of Henry Adams.* But the comparison with these books is not to the advantage of Mr. Wolfe's performance. It has not the artistry of the first two, the constant and dramatic relation of incident to a developing consciousness of the world, nor has it the historical importance of the third, or the philosophical and intellectual interest of the last.

The hero of *Look Homeward, Angel*, though a child and adolescent, is essentially more interesting than the Eugene of *Of Time and the River*. He is more comprehensible, because there is a real (and necessarily conventional) pattern to his developing awareness of the world around him. Further, the life of the Gant household, and even of the community, is patterned with a certain amount of strictness in relation to Eugene. . . . There is a progress toward maturity, a fairly precise psychological interest. The novel contains much pure baggage and much material that is out of tone, usually in the form of an ironic commentary that violates the point of view; but the book is more of a unit, and is, for that reason perhaps, more exciting and forceful. (pp. 176-77)

The reader amasses a large body of facts about [Eugene], as about Starwick, but with something of the same result. He knows that Eugene is big; that he is a creature of enormous appetites of which he is rather proud; . . . that he is obsessed by the idea of devouring all of life. Then, the reader knows the facts of Eugene's comings and goings, and knows the people he meets and what they say. But the Eugene susceptible of such definition is not the hero of the book, or at least does not function adequately as such. The hero is really that nameless fury that drives Eugene. The book is an effort to name that fury, and perhaps by naming it, to tame it. But the fury goes unnamed and untamed. Since the book is formless otherwise, only a proper emotional reference to such a center could give it form. Instead, at the center there is this chaos that steams and bubbles in rhetoric and apocalyptic apostrophe, sometimes grand and sometimes febrile and empty; the center is a maelstrom, perhaps artificially generated at times; and the other, tangible items are the flotsam and jetsam and dead wood spewed up, iridescent or soggy, as the case may be. (p. 178)

There are two other factors in the character of Eugene that may deserve mention. The hero feels a sense of destiny and direction, the sense of being "chosen" in the midst of a world of defeated, aimless, snobbish, vulgar, depleted, or suicidal people. (This is, apparently, the source of much of the interpolated irony in both books, an irony almost regularly derivative and mechanical.) In real life this conviction of a high calling may be enough to make a "hero" feel that life does have form and meaning; but the mere fact that a hero in a novel professes the high calling and is contrasted in his social contacts with an inferior breed does not, in itself, give the novel form and meaning. The transference of the matter from the actuality of life to the actuality of art cannot be accomplished so easily. Second, at the very end of the novel, Eugene, about to embark for America, sees a woman who, according to the somewhat extended lyrical epilogue, makes him "lose" self and so be "found":

> After all the blind, tormented wanderings of youth, that woman would become his heart's centre and the target of his life, the image of immortal one-ness that again collected him to one, and hurled the whole collection passion, power, and might of his one life into the blazing certitude, the immortal governance and unity, of love.

Certainly this is what we call fine writing; it may or may not be good writing. And probably, falling in love may make a man "find himself"; but this epilogue scarcely makes the novel find itself.

It is possible sometimes that a novel possessing no structure in the ordinary sense of the word, or not properly dominated by its hero's personality or fortunes, may be given a focus by the concrete incorporation of an idea, or related ideas. Now, *Of Time and the River* has such a leading idea, but an idea insufficient in its operation. The leading symbol of the father, old Gant, gradually assumes another aspect, not purely personal; he becomes, in other words, a kind of symbol of the fatherland, the source, the land of violence, drunkenness, fecundity, beauty, and vigor, on which the hero occasionally reflects during his wanderings and to which in the end he returns. But this symbol is not the total expression of the idea, which is worked out more explicitly and at length. There are long series of cinematic flashes of "phases of American life". . . . Or there are more lyrical passages, less effective in pictorial detail. . . . (pp. 179-80)

This kind of material alternates with the more sedate or realistic progress of the chronicle, a kind of running commentary of patriotic mysticism on the more tangible events and perceptions. For Mr. Wolfe has the mysticism of the American idea that we find in Whitman, Sandburg, Masters, Crane, and Benét. He pants for the Word, the union that will clarify all the disparate and confused elements which he enumerates and many of which fill him with revulsion and disgust. (p. 180)

The other promulgators of the American vision have been poets. Mr. Wolfe, in addition to being a poet in instinct, is, as well, the owner on a large scale of many of the gifts of the novelist. He attempts to bolster, or as it were, to prove, the mystical and poetic vision by fusing it with a body of everyday experience of which the novelist ordinarily treats. But there is scarcely a fusion or a correlation; rather, an oscillation. (pp. 180-81)

Mr. Wolfe is astonishingly diffuse, astonishingly loose in his rhetoric—qualities that, for the moment, may provoke more praise than blame. That rhetoric is sometimes grand, but probably more often tedious and tinged with hysteria. Because he is officially writing prose and not poetry, he has no caution of the clichés of phrase or rhythm, and no compunction about pilfering from other poets.

His vocabulary itself is worth comment. . . . [The reader] will observe a constant quality of strain, a fancy for the violent word or phrase (but often conventionally poetic as well as violent): "wild, sweet, casual, savage . . . ," "haunted them like legends," "no rest or peace or certitude of fury," "target of his life," "blazing certitude, the immortal governance and unity, of love." Mr. Wolfe often shows very powerfully the poetic instinct, and the praise given by a number of critics to his "sensuousness" and "gusto" is not without justification in the fact; but even more often his prose simply shows the poetic instinct unbuckled on a kind of week-end debauch. He sometimes wants it both ways: the structural irresponsibility of prose and the emotional intensity of poetry. He may overlook the fact that the intensity is rarely to be achieved without a certain rigor in selection and structure.

Further, Mr. Wolfe, we understand from blurbs and reviewers, is attempting a kind of prose epic. American literature has produced one, *Moby Dick*. There is much in common between *Moby Dick* and *Of Time and the River*, but there is one major difference. Melville had a powerful fable, a myth of human destiny, which saved his work from the centrifugal impulses of his genius, and which gave it structure and climax. Its dignity is inherent in the fable itself. No such dignity is inherent in Mr. Wolfe's scheme, if it can properly be termed a scheme. The nearest approach to it is in the character of old Gant, but that is scarcely adequate. And Mr. Wolfe has not been able to compensate for the lack of a fable by all his well-directed and misdirected attempts to endow his subject with a proper dignity, by all his rhetorical insistence, all the clarity and justice of his incidental poetic perceptions, all the hysteria or magnificent hypnosis.

Probably all of these defects, or most of them, are inherent in fiction which derives so innocently from the autobiographical impulse. In the first place, all the impurities and baggage in the novel must strike the author as of peculiar and necessary value because they were observed or actually occurred. But he is not writing a strict autobiography in which all observations or experiences, however vague, might conceivably find a justification. He is trying, and this in the second place, to erect the autobiographical material into an epical and symbolic importance, to make of it a fable, a "Legend of Man's Hunger in His Youth." This much is declared by the subtitle.

Mr. Wolfe promises to write some historical novels, and they may well be crucial in the definition of his genius, because he may be required to reorder the use of his powers. What, thus far, he has produced is fine fragments, several brilliant pieces of portraiture, and many sharp observations on men and nature: in other words, these books are really voluminous notes from which a fine novel, or several fine novels, might be written. If he never writes these novels, it may yet be that his books will retain a value as documents of some historical importance and as confused records of an unusual personality. Meanwhile, despite his admirable energies and his powerful literary endowments, his work illustrates once more the limitations, perhaps the necessary limitations, of an attempt to exploit directly and naïvely the personal experience and the self-defined personality in art.

And meanwhile it may be well to recollect that Shakespeare merely wrote *Hamlet;* he was *not* Hamlet. (pp. 181-83)

Robert Penn Warren, "A Note on the Hamlet of Thomas Wolfe" (originally published in The American Review, Vol. 5, No. 1, April, 1935), in his Selected Essays (copyright © 1958 by Robert Penn Warren; reprinted by permission of Random House, Inc.), Random House, 1958, pp. 170-83.

BERNARD DeVOTO (essay date 1936)

["The Story of a Novel"] is one of the most appealing books of our time. No one who reads it can doubt Mr. Wolfe's complete dedication to his job or regard with anything but respect his attempt to describe the dark and nameless fury of the million-footed life swarming in his dark unknown soul. So honest or so exhaustive an effort at self-analysis in the interest of esthetics has seldom been made in the history of American literature, and "The Story of a Novel" is likely to have a long life as a source-book for students of literature and for psychologists as well. But also it brings into the public domain material that has been hitherto outside the privilege of criticism. Our first essay must be to examine it in relation to Mr. Wolfe's novels, to see what continuities and determinants it may reveal, and to inquire into their bearing on the art of fiction.

Let us begin with one of many aspects of Mr. Wolfe's novels that impress the reader, the frequent recurrence of material to which one must apply the adjective placental. (The birth metaphors are imposed by Mr. Wolfe himself. In "The Story of a Novel" he finds himself big with first a thunder cloud and then a river. The symbolism of waters is obviously important to him, and the title of his latest novel is to be that of the series as a whole.) A great part of "Look Homeward, Angel" was just the routine first-novel of the period, ... the story of a sensitive and rebellious adolescent who was headed toward the writing of novels. The rest of it was not so easily catalogued. Parts of it showed intuition, understanding, and ecstasy, and an ability to realize all three in character and scene, whose equal it would have been hard to point out anywhere in the fiction of the time. These looked like great talent, and in such passages as the lunchroom scene in the dawn that Mr. Wolfe called nacreous some fifty times, they seemed to exist on both a higher and a deeper level of realization than any of Mr. Wolfe's contemporaries had attained. But also there were parts that looked very dubious indeed—long, whirling discharges of words, unabsorbed in the novel, unrelated to the proper business of fiction, badly if not altogether unacceptably written, raw gobs of emotion, aimless and quite meaningless jabber, claptrap, belches, grunts, and Tarzanlike screams. Their rawness, their unshaped quality, must be insisted upon; it was as if the birth of the novel had been accompanied by a lot of the material that had nourished its gestation. The material which nature and most novelists discard when its use has been served. It looked like one of two things, there was no telling which. It looked like the self-consciously literary posturing of a novelist too young and too naive to have learned his trade. Or, from another point of view, it looked like a document in psychic disintegration. And one of the most important questions in contemporary literature was: would the proportion of fiction to placenta increase or decrease in Mr. Wolfe's next book?

It decreased. If fiction of the quality of that lunchroom scene made up about one-fifth of "Look Homeward, Angel," it constituted, in "Of Time and the River," hardly more than a tenth. The placental material had enormously grown and, what was even more ominous, it now had a rationalization. It was as unshaped as before, but it had now been retroactively associated with the dark and nameless heaving of the voiceless and unknown womb of Time, and with the unknown and voiceless fury of the dark and lonely and lost America. (pp. 72-3)

Certain other aspects of the new book seemed revealing. For one thing, there was a shocking contempt of the medium. Some passages were not completely translated from the "I" in which they had apparently been written to the "he" of Eugene Gant. Other passages alluded to incidents which had probably appeared in an earlier draft but could not be found in the final one. Others contradictorily reported scenes which had already appeared, and at least once a passage that had seen service already was re-enlisted for a second hitch in a quite different context, apparently with no recollection that it had been used before.

Again, a state of mind that had been appropriate to the puberty of Eugene seemed inappropriate as the boy grew older, and might therefore be significant. I mean the giantism of the characters. Eugene himself, in "Of Time and the River," was clearly a borderline manic-depressive: he exhibited the classic cycle in his alternation between "fury" and "despair," and the classic accompaniment of obsessional neurosis in the compulsions he was under to read all the books in the world, see all the people in Boston, observe all the lives of the man-swarm, and list all the names and places in America. That was simple enough, but practically every other character in the book also suffered from fury and compulsions; and, what was more suggestive, they were all twenty feet tall, ... laughed like Falstaff, and bellowed like the bulls of Bashan. The significant thing was that we were seeing them all through Eugene's eyes. To a child all adults are giants: their voices are thunderous, their actions are portentous and grotesquely magnified, and all their exhibited emotions are seismic. It looked as if part of Eugene's condition was an infantile regression.

This appearance was reinforced by what seemed to be another stigma of infantilism: that all the experiences in "Of Time and the River" were on the same level and had the same value. When Mr. Gant died (of enough cancer to have exterminated an army corps), the reader accepted the accompanying frenzy as proper to the death of a man's father—which is one of the most important events in anyone's life. But when the same frenzy accompanied nearly everything else in the book—a ride on a railroad train, a literary tea fight, a midnight lunch in the kitchen, ... the discovery of Eugene's true love—one could only decide that something was dreadfully wrong. If the death of one's father comes out emotionally even with a ham-on-rye, then the art of fiction is cockeyed.

Well, "The Story of a Novel" puts an end to speculation and supplies some unexpected but very welcome light. To think of these matters as contempt of the medium, regression, and infantilism is to be too complex and subtle. The truth shows up in two much simpler facts: that Mr. Wolfe is still astonishingly immature, and that he has mastered neither the psychic material out of which a novel is made nor the technique of writing fiction. He does not seem aware of the first fact, but he acknowledges the second with a frankness and an understanding that are the finest promise to date for his future books. (pp. 74-5)

The most flagrant evidence of his incompleteness is the fact that, so far, one indispensable part of the artist has existed not in Mr. Wolfe but in Maxwell Perkins [his editor]. Such organizing faculty and such critical intelligence as have been applied to the book have come not from inside the artist, not from the artist's feeling for form and esthetic integrity, but from the office of Charles Scribner's Sons. . . . [The] artist goes on writing till Mr. Perkins tells him that the novel is finished. But the end of a novel is, properly, dictated by the internal pressure, osmosis, metabolism—what you will—of the novel itself, of which only the novelist can have a first-hand knowledge. There comes a point where the necessities of the book are satisfied, where its organic processes have reached completion. It is hard to see how awareness of that point can manifest itself at an editor's desk—and harder still to trust the integrity of a work of art in which not the artist but the publisher has determined where the true ends and the false begins. (pp. 75-6)

The placental passages are now explained. They consist of psychic material which the novelist has proved unable to shape into fiction. The failure may be due either to immature understanding or to insufficient technical skill: probably both causes operate here and cannot be separated. The principle is very simple. When Mr. Wolfe gives us his doctors, undertakers, and newspapermen talking in a lunchroom at dawn, he does his job—magnificently. There they are, and the reader revels in the dynamic presentation of human beings, and in something else as well that should have the greatest possible significance for Mr. Wolfe. For while the doctors and undertakers are chaffing one another, the reader gets that feeling of the glamour and mystery of American life which Mr. Wolfe elsewhere unsuccessfully labors to evoke in thousands of rhapsodic words. The novelist makes his point in the lives of his characters, not in tidal surges of rhetoric.

Is America lost, lonely, nameless, and unknown? Maybe, and maybe not. But if it is, the condition of the novelist's medium requires him to make it lost and lonely in the lives of his characters, not in blank verse, bombast, and apocalyptic delirium. You cannot represent America by hurling adjectives at it. Do "the rats of death and age and dark oblivion feed forever at the roots of sleep?" It sounds like a high school valedictory, but if in fact they do then the novelist is constrained to show them feeding so by means of what his characters do and say and feel in relation to one another, and not by chasing the ghosts of Whitman and Ezekiel through fifty pages of disembodied emotion. Such emotion is certainly the material that fiction works with, but until it is embodied in character and scene it is not fiction—it is only logorrhea. . . . A novelist represents life. When he does anything else, no matter how beautiful or furious or ecstatic the way in which he does it, he is not writing fiction. Mr. Wolfe can write fiction—has written some of the finest fiction of our day. But a great part of what he writes is not fiction at all: it is only material with which the novelist has struggled but which has defeated him. The most important question in American fiction today, probably, is whether he can win that encounter in his next book. . . . If he does win it, he must do so inside himself; Mr. Perkins and the assembly line at Scribner's can do nothing to help him. (pp. 76-7)

[However] useful genius may be in the writing of novels, it is not enough in itself—it never has been enough, in any art, and it never will be. At the very least it must be supported by an ability to impart shape to material, simple competence in the use of tools. Until Mr. Wolfe develops more craftsmanship, he will not be the important novelist he is now widely accepted as being. In order to be a great novelist he must also mature his emotions till he can see more profoundly into character than he now does, and he must learn to put a corset on his prose. (p. 79)

> *Bernard DeVoto, "Genius Is Not Enough" (reprinted by permission of Mrs. Bernard DeVoto), in* Saturday Review of Literature, *Vol. XIII, No. 26, April 25, 1936 (and reprinted in* Thomas Wolfe: A Collection of Critical Essays, *edited by Louis D. Rubin, Jr., Prentice-Hall, Inc., 1973, pp. 72-9).*

THOMAS WOLFE   (essay date 1938)

Many people see in the last great war a kind of great dividing line in their own lives—a kind of great tale of two worlds, a world before the War, and a world after the War; but in my own experience, if I had to write my own tale of two worlds, I think I should be more inclined to use 1929 as the dividing line. (p. 47)

Before that . . . my experience as a man and as a writer had passed through certain well-defined stages, all of which were very familiar to the times and to the lives of many other young men of the times. . . . I passed into the period when I had to go to work, and where I learned for the first time what work—hard, creative work—was like, and where at last I began to spend more time in an effort to create "art" and "beauty" than in talking about it. And now finally, I had reached the stage of first accomplishment—where at last I had accomplished something, got it completed, accepted, printed, and put between the covers of a book, where for the first time the general public, if it so desired, could look at it.

This is certainly a definite and closely linked chain of clear development, and for me it marked the end of one great cycle. . . . I was a lot closer to life, to people, to the world around me, to America in 1929, than I had ever been before; although I was still too detached from it, not nearly close enough. . . . For one thing, [Look Homeward, Angel] still showed unmistakably the evidence of the stages I had gone through, the periods of development, the special aesthetic faiths and creeds of the time. It is what is called an autobiographical novel—a definition with which I have never agreed, simply because it seems to me every novel, every piece of creative writing that anyone can do, is autobiographical. Nevertheless, it is true that this book was autobiographical in the personal and special sense: it was possible, for example, to identify the life of the hero with the life of the author—to suspect that a great many of the characters and incidents in the book were drawn pretty closely and directly from the writer's own experience. And, although I have not read the book for years, I believe that in this sense of the word—in this special autobiographical sense—was the book's greatest weakness: I believe the character of the hero was the weakest and least convincing one in the whole book, because he had been derived not only from experience but colored a good deal by the romantic aestheticism of the period. He was, in short, "the artist'' in pretty much the Harvard Forty-seven Workshop sense of the word—the wounded sensitive, the extraordinary creature in conflict with his environment, with the Babbitt, the Philistine, the small town, the family. I know that I was not satisfied with this character even at the time: he seemed to me to be uneasy and self-conscious, probably because I was myself uneasy and self-conscious about him. In this sense, therefore, the book followed a familiar pattern—a pattern made familiar by Joyce in *A Portrait of the Artist as a Young Man,* and later in *Ulysses*—a book which at that time strongly influenced my own work. But I think the book also had been conceived and created with some of the blazing intensity of youth: although I did not know it at the time, in that sense of the word the book was a kind of passionate expletive—a fiery ejaculation hurled down upon a page of print because it had to come out, it had to be said. Here, too, my real education was beginning, for as yet I did not know these things. Again, the book had a rather extraordinary career: although it was on the whole well-reviewed and well-received throughout the rest of the country, and had, for a first book, a moderately good sale, in my own home town it was received with an outburst of fury and indignation that in my own experience has not been surpassed, and that I believe is even extraordinary in anyone's experience. (pp. 48-51)

I did not realize, . . . even in 1929, that those images and figures of my experience and training—the image of "the artist" and of "art," of "beauty" and of "love," of the wounded sensitive, driven out and fleeing away from the Philistines of the tribe—all of which had seemed so fixed and everlasting in the scheme of things, were really just the transient images of the times, a portion of the aesthetic belief and doctrine of the period. I did not realize that the year 1929, which was so important to me in such immediate personal ways concerning my own life and my immediate career, was to be a fatal and important year in so many other ways I did not even know about at that time, in so many ways affecting the life of the nation and of all the people in it, affecting human beliefs, that it seems now to mark a dividing line between two worlds. About the organized structure of society in 1929—its systems of finance economy, politics and government—and how they shaped and affected the lives of people, I knew almost nothing, and had never considered it a part of my interest to question or examine them. Certainly, if anyone should have suggested to me, in 1929, that it was not only a part of the purpose and function of an artist to examine them, but that if he continued to produce, his participation and examination would be inescapable, I should have denied the proposition utterly. I should have said that the purpose and the function of the artist was to create, to create what was true and beautiful, without reference to its social implications as regards the world around him; I think that I should probably have further said that the interest of the artist in such things as economics, politics, government, the organized structure of society, was not only outside the province of his life and work—to create the beautiful and true—but would probably be alien and injurious to it, if he allowed it to intrude in what he did.

The fact that I no longer feel this way, and how and why, and by what degrees and stages I have come to feel differently, marks the last stage of my development at which I have now arrived. . . . (pp. 53-4)

Thomas Wolfe, ''Writing and Living'' (originally a

speech delivered at Purdue University on May 19, 1938), in Thomas Wolfe's Purdue Speech: ''Writing and Living,'' *edited by William Braswell and Leslie A. Field (copyright © 1964 by Purdue Research Foundation; reprinted by permission of Paul Gitlin, administrator C.T.A. of the Estate of Thomas Wolfe), Purdue University Studies, 1964, pp. 25-78.*

JOHN PEALE BISHOP (essay date 1939)

[Wolfe's] aim was to set down America as far as it can belong to the experience of one man. Wolfe came early on what was for him the one available truth about this continent—that it was contained in himself. There was no America which could not be made out—mountains, rivers, trains, cities, people—in the memory of an American. If the contours were misty, then they must be made clear. It was in flight from a certain experience of America, as unhappy as it had been apparently sterile, it was in Paris, in an alien land, that Wolfe first understood with hate and with love the horror and the wonder of his native country. (pp. 3-4)

This is not an uncommon experience, but what made it rewarding in Wolfe's case was that his memory was anything but common. (p. 4)

From the time of *Look Homeward, Angel,* [Wolfe was critically] regarded, and rightly, as a young man of incomparable promise. *Of Time and the River* seemed to many to have borne out that promise and, since its faults were taken as due merely to an excess of fecundity, it was met with praise as though it were the consummation of all Wolfe's talents. Yet the faults are fundamental. The force of Wolfe's talents is indubitable; yet he did not find for that novel, nor do I believe he could ever have found, a structure of form which would have been capable of giving shape and meaning to his emotional experience. He was not without intelligence; but he could not trust his intelligence, since for him to do so would have been to succumb to conscience. And it was conscience, with its convictions of guilt, that he was continually trying to elude.

His position as an artist is very like that of Hart Crane. . . . Both had what we must call genius; both conceived that genius had been given them that they might celebrate, the one in poetry, the other in prose, the greatness of their country. But Wolfe no more than Crane was able to give any other coherence to his work than that which comes from the personal quality of his writing. And he found, as Crane did before him, that the America he longed to celebrate did not exist. He could record, and none better, its sights, its sounds and its odors, as they can be caught in a moment of time; he could try, as the poet of *The Bridge* did, to absorb that moment and endow it with the permanence of a myth. But he could not create a continuous America. He could not, for all that he was prepared to cover one hundred and fifty of its years, conceive its history. He can record what comes to his sensibility, but he cannot give us the continuity of experience. Everything for Wolfe is in the moment; he can so try to impress us with the immensity of the moment that it will take on some sort of transcendental meaning. But what that meaning is, escapes him, as it does us. And once it has passed from his mind, he can do nothing but recall another moment, which as it descends into his memory seems always about to deliver itself, by a miracle, of some tremendous import.

Both Crane and Wolfe belonged to a world that is indeed living from moment to moment. And it is because they voice its breakdown in the consciousness of continuity that they have significance for it.

Of the two, Wolfe, I should say, was the more aware of his plight. He was, he tells us, while writing *Of Time and the River,* tormented by a dream in which the sense of guilt was associated with the forgetting of time. (pp. 5-6)

It can be said of Wolfe, as Allen Tate has said of Hart Crane, that he was playing a game in which any move was possible, because none was compulsory. There is no idea which would serve as discipline to the event. For what Wolfe tells us was the idea that furiously pursued him during the composition of *Of Time and the River,* the search for a father, can scarcely be said to appear in the novel, or else it is so incidentally that it seems to no purpose. It does not certainly, as the same search on the part of Stephen Dedalus does in *Ulysses,* prepare a point toward which the whole narrative moves. There was nothing indeed in Wolfe's upbringing to make discipline acceptable to him. He acts always as though his own capacity for feeling, for anguished hope and continual frustration, was what made him superior, as no doubt, along with his romantic propensity for expression, it was. But he was wrong in assuming that those who accept any form of discipline are therefore lacking in vigor. He apparently did not understand that there are those who might say with Yeats, "I could recover if I shrieked my heart's agony," and yet like him are dumb "from human dignity." And his failure to understand was due to no fault of the intelligence, but to a lack of love. The Gant family always strikes us, with its howls of rage, its loud Hah-hahs of hate and derision, as something less than human. And Eugene is a Gant. While in his case we are ready to admit that genius is a law unto itself, we have every right to demand that it discover its own law.

Again like Crane, Wolfe failed to see that at the present time so extreme a manifestation of individualism could not but be morbid. Both came too late into a world too mechanic; they lacked a wilderness and constantly tried to create one as wild as their hearts. It was all very well for them, since both were in the way of being poets, to start out to proclaim the grandeur of America. Such a task seemed superb. But both were led at last, on proud romantic feet, to Brooklyn. And what they found there they abhorred.

They represent, each in his way, a culmination of the romantic spirit in America. There was in both a tremendous desire to impose the will on experience. Wolfe had no uncommon will. . . . For Wolfe the rewards of experience were always such that he was turned back upon himself. Isolated in his sensations, there was no way out. He continually sought for a door, and there was really none, or only one, the door of death. (pp. 7-8)

[At] the center of all Wolfe's writing is a single character, and it was certainly the aim of that writing to present this character in all his manifold contacts with the world of our time. Eugene has, we are told, the craving of a Faust to know all experience, to be able to record all the races and all the social classes which may be said to exist in America. Actually Eugene's experience is not confined to America.

But when we actually come to consider Eugene closely, we see that, once he is beyond the overwhelming presence of his family, his contacts with other people are all casual. The perfect experience for Eugene is to see someone in the throes of an emotion which he can imagine, but in which he has no responsible part. (p. 8)

He sees from a train a boy trying to decide to go after a girl; . . . through one of his students at the university, he comes in contact with an old Jewess wailing a son dead for a year. Each of these moments is completely done; most of them, indeed, overwrought. From the country seen from a train he derives "a wild and solemn joy—the sense of nameless hope, impossible desire, and man's tragic brevity." He reacts to most circumstances, it must seem to us, excessively. But to men and women he does not really answer. The old Jewess's grief fills him "with horror, anger, a sense of cruelty, disgust, and pity." The passion aroused returns to himself. And it is precisely because his passions cannot attain their object, and in one person know peace, that he turns in rage and desire toward the millions. There is in Eugene every emotion you wish but one; there is no love.

The most striking passages in Wolfe's novels always represent these moments of comprehension. For a moment, but a moment only, there is a sudden release of compassion, when some aspect of suffering and bewildered humanity is seized, when the other's emotion is in a timeless completion known. Then the moment passes, and compassion fails. For Eugene Gant, the only satisfactory relationship with another human creature is one which can have no continuity. (pp. 9-10)

The only human relationship which endures is that of the child to his family. And that is inescapable; once having been, it cannot cease to be. His father is still his father, though dying; and his brother Ben, though dead, remains his brother. He loves and he hates and knows why no more than the poet he quotes. What he does know is that love has been forbidden him.

The only contemporary literary influence on Wolfe which was at all strong is that of Joyce. I shall consider it here only to note that while we know that Joyce could only have created Stephen Dedalus out of the conflicts of his own youth, we never think of Stephen simply as the young Joyce, any more than we think of Hamlet as Shakespeare. He is a creation. But in Wolfe's novels it is impossible to feel that the central figure has any existence apart from the author. He is called Eugene Gant, but that does not deceive any one for a moment; he is, beyond all doubt, Thomas Wolfe. There is, however, one important distinction to be made between them, and one which we should not allow ourselves to forget: Eugene Gant is always younger, by at least ten years, than Thomas Wolfe.

Wolfe described *Of Time and the River* as being devoted to "the period of wandering and hunger in a man's youth." And in it we are meant to take Eugene as every young man. The following volume would, Wolfe said, declare "a period of greater certitude, which would be dominated by a single passion." That, however, still remains to be seen. So far, Eugene has shown no capacity as a lover, except in casual contact with whores. . . . The one contact which lasts for any time [is with Starwick]. . . . (pp. 10-11)

It ends when he discovers that Starwick is a homosexual. . . . What we have been told about Starwick from his first appearance in the book is that, despite a certain affection and oddity of manner, he is, as Eugene is not, a person capable of loving and being loved. What is suddenly revealed in Paris is that for him, too, love is a thing the world has forbidden. In Starwick's face Eugene sees his own fate. Just as in his brother Ben's complaint at his neglect, he had looked back through another's sight at his own neglected childhood and in his brother's death foremourned his own, so now, when he beats Starwick's head against the wall, he is but raging against his own frustration and despair.

In his father's yard, among the tombstones, stood for years a marble angel. . . . It stands a magnificent reminder of the time when as a boy, with winged ambition, he had wanted to be not merely a stone cutter but a sculptor. . . . The one symbol of the divine in the workshop is [eventually] sold to adorn the grave of a prostitute; what the boy might have been the man lets go for such a purpose. It cannot be said that Thomas Wolfe ever sold his angel. But the faults of the artist are all of them traceable to the failures of the man. He achieved probably the utmost intensity of which incoherent writing is capable; he proved that an art founded solely on the individual, however strong his will, however vivid his sensations, cannot be sound, or whole, or even passionate, in a world such as ours, in which "the integrity of the individual consciousness has been broken down." How far it has broken down, I do not believe he ever knew, yet all that he did is made of its fragments. (pp. 11-12)

John Peale Bishop, "The Sorrows of Thomas Wolfe" (originally published in The Kenyon Review, *Vol. 1, No. 1, Winter, 1939), in* The Kenyon Critics: Studies in Modern Literature from "The Kenyon Review," *edited by John Crowe Ransom (copyright 1951 by* The Kenyon Review), World Publishing Co., 1951, pp. 3-12.

CLIFTON FADIMAN   (essay date 1939)

[*The Web and the Rock,*] except for some hundred-odd scattered and magnificent pages, marks no particular advance, either in power or objectivity, over *Of Time and the River.* The central character, though he is called George Webber, is still the Eugene Gant of the previous books. One may at last freely and sadly say both George Webber and Eugene Gant are Thomas Wolfe. George Webber is, again, the young writer who wishes to experience everything and is driven to frenzy because he cannot. All the motifs we are used to from the other books repeat themselves here: the attraction-repulsion exerted on the provincial by New York. the voyage-and-return pattern that marked *Of Time and the River,* the sonorous but vague celebration of America, the insistence on man's "aloneness" and on the "strangeness" of "time." You even feel that certain characters are only seemingly new and have their roots in the other books. The style, too, remains unchanged —distended, straining for impossible effects, often capable of high (but never the highest) beauty, often reminiscent of old-time movie-caption prose. . . . [*The Web and the Rock*] is simply more of the same Wolfe, which is to say more of the most gifted young American writer produced during the last fifteen years. It is not a self-contained novel any more than the others were. It is a cut-off length of the endless experiences of Thomas Wolfe. (pp. 149-50)

[It] is not George Webber who makes the first sections of the book wonderful—for they are wonderful. It is the townsfolk he describes—seen, it is true, through a very

special vision, but seen unforgettably. I should say, for example, that Nebraska Crane, the Cherokee boy, is almost as great a characterization as Huckleberry Finn. The terrible outsize Lampley family comprise the most memorable grotesques in the whole Wolfe gallery. Magnificent, too, is the whole account of Dick Prosser, the gentlemanly Negro who ran amok—a story that, to my mind, brings out more of the underlying violence of the Southern temperament than do all the novels of William Faulkner combined.

Much of this small-town material is magnificent, but not all. The further the event from George's own experience, the more moving it is; the nearer it approaches his own life and mind, the more tedious it becomes—and the harder Wolfe works to prevent it from becoming tedious. Thus, when Wolfe describes a dogfight, you see it before your own eyes, but when young George reflects on the dogfight, unreality sets in. I seem to be in a pathetic minority here, but it seems to me that the one crucial defect of the Wolfe books is that the central character, despite the hundreds of pages devoted to him, despite his endless monologues, despite all the introspection, never quite becomes believable. The most boring pages in Wolfe are the most personal ones; the most fascinating are devoted to people and scenes he remembers vividly, but which he does not incorporate within his gigantic sense of self.

If *The Web and the Rock* had stopped at page 170, it would have been a far finer book. Not that the succeeding 525 pages are without interest, but one must pick and choose among them, wade through overwritten passages, repetitions, and almost incredible naïvetés of thought and feeling. The college sections—though there is some extremely funny if exaggerated satire here—are formless and inferior to those in *Look Homeward, Angel.* Also, the chapters dealing with George's early days in New York are dragged out beyond their natural length. Wolfe remembered with almost painful particularity everything that had happened to him. He committed the fallacy of assuming that the intensity of his memory would naturally awaken an equally intense reaction in the reader. He never seems to have asked himself the simple question: Is this detail worthy of being remembered? He could write fervently about anything, but he never knew what things one ought to be fervent about.

The second half of the book deals almost entirely with a love affair and with George Webber's introduction to the "smart" life of New York. . . . I guess I may as well confess that most of this seemed to me a crashing bore. I'm not sure why. I think it's simply that there's just too much of everything—too much recrimination, too much ecstasy, too many scenes, too many reconciliations. Enough is enough.

The book ends, rather oddly, with a European-travel section, sufficiently interesting in itself but somehow tacked on, superfluous. (pp. 150-52)

It is impossible to say what would have happened to [Wolfe] had he lived, but it is certainly possible to say that this book shows no growth, save an increase in confusion. (p. 153)

Clifton Fadiman, "'The Web and the Rock'" (reprinted by permission of the author), in The New Yorker, *Vol. XV, No. 19, June 24, 1939 (and reprinted in* The Enigma of Thomas Wolfe: Biographical and Critical Selections, *edited by Richard Walser, Harvard University Press, 1953, pp. 149-53).*

E. K. BROWN (essay date 1941)

The fall of 1940 has brought the second and last of [Wolfe's] posthumous novels, *You Can't Go Home Again*. Significant in many ways, it shows that Wolfe had clearly seen, at the end, that his formula for fiction was not viable. In all his earlier novels he tried to present life as a continuous process, the slave of time and memory; at the end he was willing to be representative, although he could never be brief. He would show the reef of love by a single party—it occupies almost half as many words as make up an average novel; two or three instances, varied in stress, set before the reader with immense detail, would show the reef of fame. As design the book may dissatisfy: it is rough and above all it is lumpy. Still it has a workable formula, and its roughness and lumpiness are accidental, and might well have disappeared in a second attempt.

Whatever may have been wrong with the formula on which his earlier novels were constructed—and it is on them, not on *You Can't Go Home Again*, that his reputation will chiefly rest—they had a fusion of qualities never even juxtaposed by any other American novelist of his time. Wolfe had the realist's regard for the particularity of a shape or a colour, a glance or a voice. . . . He joined with this perceptive and devouring eye of the master-realist the imaginative symbolist's regard for relationships, occult and profound. In each generation he sought to uncover the qualities of those before and those to come; all civilization he regarded as a natural unity to whose base he was always trying to dig. . . . Realism and imaginative symbolism he brought together within the roomy formula of autobiographical fiction. His conception of the novel led him to make his autobiographical presentation highly imaginative, to shape the progress of his book not by particular facts but by essential meanings. In such imaginative autobiography there was a place for all the instances of his sensitivity to appearances, and nevertheless the limits of realism could be transcended.

Most of Wolfe's achievements will come under view if one pauses over the three notions: realism, symbolism, roomy autobiography. (pp. 154-55)

[The] novels are essentially autobiographical. We know that his father was a stone-cutter; that Wolfe's life developed in the same fashion as that of the hero of the first two novels, Eugene Gant, and that of the hero of the two later, George Webber. But the main reason for accounting the novels autobiographical is something that we know of the temper of Wolfe's mind.

He had a very strong and very acute equipment for sense-experience. (p. 156)

The magnificent result of [his] preoccupation with sense-experience is shown in [the lengthy and detailed] passage which tells of the food at the Gant table. . . . [The] author of this passage has a need to recall the whole of his sensuous experience—he can be content with no typical representation. Nor can he be content with a dry catalogue: he must recall not only the objects of his experience, but also its quality in all its rich complexity. The power of so recalling experience is one of Wolfe's chief powers. . . .

The character who bestrides *Look Homeward, Angel* and a large part of its sequel is undoubtedly Wolfe's own father, put before us with all the resources of a realist. But Mr Gant is not only a remembered character, he is also the creation of a powerful symbolic imagination. The central idea of the sequel, *Of Time and the River*, Wolfe has himself described: "The deepest search in life, it seemed to me, the thing that in one way or another was central to all living, was man's search to find a father, not merely the father of his flesh, the lost father of his youth, but the image of a strength and wisdom external to his need and superior to his hunger, to which the belief and power of his own life could be united." (p. 157)

In Mr Gant, the perfect expression of the demonic in man, the realist and the symbolist have worked together within the formula of imaginative autobiography to reveal the whole force of Wolfe's characterizing power. The realist has a delighted awareness of the comic quality in his tirades of invective. (p. 158)

[Mr Gant's] tirades are not, however, wholly comic: they are his means of expressing his frustration and his resentments, his awareness of his tragic failure as a person. The tragic aspect of his tirades Wolfe's imagination seizes as a symbol of fury. (pp. 158-59)

Frustration in the central quest of his life is the key to Mr Gant's fury which at once sets him apart from his fellow-townsmen and gives them an imperfect awareness of a hidden affinity—of something in Mr Gant which is going beyond them on a path that they too ideally would follow.

By his intense emotionalism, his wild energies, his inarticulate awareness of a meaning in life which he cannot fathom, Mr Gant is raised into a symbol of the American adventure. Wolfe believed that there was a peculiar American tragedy, that on this continent life made specially heavy demands which man was specially inadequate to meet. (pp. 159-60)

All personal relationships Wolfe brought to one major test: what had the other person experienced and how much of his experience could he communicate? In *The Web and the Rock* he puts love itself to that test. In the earlier novels his treatment of love had been episodic, fumbling, and extremely shabby. The reader of *The Web and the Rock* knows why. Wolfe could love—in fact or in imagination—only when a woman could add to his store of vicarious experience. . . . None of the women in the earlier novels could do so. It is significant that his first striking portrait of a loved woman—Esther Jack, whom he sets beside his hero in *The Web*—is a person much older than the man, much more travelled, more cultivated and involved in a criss-cross of intimate relationships with half the most interesting people in New York, where he is a stranger. (pp. 161-62)

The relation between Esther and Webber had developed over more than a year before its undoing began. Her range of experience had been so rich, her hold on it was so firm, that Webber, absorbing that body of experience, was confronted with something stronger than he was. He became uncentred. . . . To preserve "his own proper vision" he breaks with Esther; the recognition that another's range of experience could be so rich and could be communicated so fully that it became a peril, not simply an opportunity, this was the most smashing blow that a man of Wolfe's temper could meet. . . . He had now to live with the knowledge that he must accept the limitations imposed upon him by the flaws and strains in his individual nature. He could console himself—but it was inadequate—in the assurance that "he had done all with his hunger and his flesh that one man could. And he knew also, although his bleared and battered face might seem to be the visage of a madman, the spirit that dwelt behind this ruined mask now looked calmly and sanely forth upon the earth for the first time in ten years.'' Such a recognition is the psychological end of *The Web and the Rock.*

The year 1940 has brought its sequel, telling what a man does when he has bought such bitter knowledge. Wolfe redefines the will's role in the individual's life. One cannot assimilate all: the will must be trained (and trusted) to determine what one shall try to assimilate. One must not be a blotter: the good life is one of conflict, in the service of loyalties chosen by the will. It had been Wolfe's belief that art could not properly be representative: the full record of one experience, he had thought, could not stand for a dozen distinct experiences, no matter how similar they might have been. Wolfe, at the end, recognized that his temperamental repudiation of the representative had been at the root of his difficulties as artist, and as person. He could admit it, but the tendency—the strongest if not the finest in his nature—was too strong to be dominated.

Still he did come to see quite early that if he could not describe America without reaching out for experience on all sides of his life and into all the lives he could touch, nevertheless the heaping up of experience brought one but a short way toward that ''door'' into the chamber of perfect awareness, of which, like Mr Gant, he was in quest.

It could bring one but a short way because the exploration of the universe through specific experiences, even in great number, leads only to fragmentary knowledge, and not to the *articulation* which is the second phase in the artist's quest. The person with fragmentary knowledge will suffer from loneliness, the philosophical loneliness which a man may feel in the presence, or under the weight, of an unexplained universe. Such loneliness is in Wolfe's view specially the destiny of the American; and the frame of mind I am attempting to describe he has set forth in a meditation at the end of a passage in *Of Time and the River* where he has sought to record his knowledge of America: ''And always America is the place of the deathless and enraptured moments, the eye that looked, the mouth that smiled and vanished, and the word; the stone, the leaf, the door we never found and never have forgotten. And these are the things that we remember of America, for we have known all her thousand lights and weathers, and we walk the streets, we walk the streets forever, we walk the streets of life alone.'' In this passage in which Wolfe records the loneliness so movingly, he points to the escape from it, the way to articulation. Throughout the first three novels, at least, as a refrain come the references, usually grouped as here, to ''the stone, the leaf, the door.''

These are three central symbols for the nature of life. And at this moment one turns wholly away from the realistic method, the method of faithfully recording experiences, to the method of the imaginative symbolist.

The *stone* is the angel which dominates not only the title but the text of the first novel. . . . The carving in stone of an angel's head came to represent for [Mr Gant] the full realization of the possibilities of life. He never learned to carve an angel's head: [his] big statue was sold to become a prostitute's memorial; and [his] energies waned until of all that huge and muscular body only the hands preserved their strength. . . . So completely is Mr Gant's quest of meanings symbolized in his carving that for his son those huge hands

''seemed to rest there upon . . . the corpse with a kind of terrible reality as if there really is, in death, some energy of life that will not die, some element of man's life that must persist, and that resumes into a single feature of his life the core and essence of his character.'' For Mr Gant the medium of stone which he had chosen for his grapple with the meaning of the universe was too resistant: the faculty within him on which he had staked all was too clumsy.

''All of our lives is written in the twisting of a leaf upon a bough, a door that opened, a stone.'' . . . The leaf is allied with the constant reference to October which, as *Of Time and the River* proceeds, becomes a mighty chorus: October when life dries up even in Mr Gant whose vitality for so long seemed inexhaustible.

The *door,* the chief of the three symbols, is the thin barrier between personalities. It is to be remembered that for Wolfe personalities mattered not because of what they might in themselves be (it is doubtful if for him the conception of a personality as something in itself bore any clear sense) but because of the range of experiences which they had undergone, and might communicate. An individual is confined to a fragment of space and a moment of time: his continual need is to make at least a momentary escape through one of the doors that surround him. If he cannot go through all these doors—and ideally he would—he can perhaps go through the few which are most important for him, as the door leading to Esther Jack was for Webber, or the door leading to Bascom Pentland for Eugene. (pp. 162-65)

The use of such symbols, not spasmodically but throughout his fiction, enabled Wolfe to rise above the inadequate apprehensions of the universe open to him as a faithful realist. Through them he was often able to illuminate places which to the realist in him remained impenetrable. These symbols are securely rooted in his sensuous experience: they are not imposed from the intelligence, but impressed upon the perceptions. The reader of his novels, knows that they abound in sharp experiences of sculpture, trees, and entrances. What Wolfe was unable to clarify, either for himself or for his readers, was the exact mode in which he passed from the level of faithful realism to the higher, dimmer level of imaginative symbolism. His struggle towards clarification, both in the analysis of his own nature and in the presentation of relationships, is central to *You Can't Go Home Again;* but the success—and it is not complete—is bought at the cost of great emotional and sensuous impoverishment. He could not even then make the round of his own being. His loss is irreparable if one believes, as I do, that with time he could have achieved perfect clarification without important impoverishment. He would then have been the model—he is already the pioneer—of a profounder kind of fiction than America has yet had. (p. 166)

E. K. Brown, ''Thomas Wolfe: Realist and Symbolist,'' in University of Toronto Quarterly *(reprinted by permission of University of Toronto Press), Vol. X, No. 2, January, 1941, pp. 153-66.*

EDWARD C. ASWELL (essay date 1941)

[*The Hills Beyond*] deserves to stand beside the other books of Thomas Wolfe. Some of his finest short stories are here. Some of the pieces also have considerable biographical interest. All of them fit somewhere into the single unified pattern of his work. (pp. 376-77)

Tom used to say that he wrote a book in order to forget what it was about. *Look Homeward, Angel* contains a brief account of Grover's death. Tom felt later that he had not dealt adequately with that tragedy, which had occurred when he was still a mere infant. So he kept thinking about it, and the result was ["The Last Boy," a] fine and moving story. One of its interesting points is that it illustrates Tom's desire to extract the whole substance of an experience by getting at it on four levels at once. (p. 377)

["Gentlemen of the Press"] belongs to Wolfe's experimental period, the Brooklyn period as he described it in *You Can't Go Home Again*. That was the time when, after having published his first book, he was testing out new methods of writing and trying everything. . . . He believed that Americans are a nighttime people, that there is something in the chemistry of our blood that makes us come more alive at night than in the daytime. He wanted to find out what it was, so he started writing the series and did twelve or thirteen episodes. "Gentlemen of the Press" is one of them, the best of the lot. . . . (p. 378)

One of the best stories Tom ever wrote, ["Chickamauga"] belongs somewhere in the Pentland background of Eugene Gant, although it was not written until 1937, when the Gants and Pentlands were no more. (p. 379)

The two parts of ["The Return of the Prodigal"] were written at different times—"The Thing Imagined" around 1934, "The Real Thing" in 1937. One interesting point about the two pieces is the contrast they afford between pure imagination and an almost straight factual record. Another is that they contain the germ of *You Can't Go Home Again* on its most literal level. . . .

In mood and feeling ["The Lion at Morning"] fits into the pre-depression parts of *You Can't Go Home Again*. It is a superb analysis of character, and illustrates Tom's belief that you can tell best what a person is like by watching him get up in the morning and prepare to go about his day's work. In *You Can't Go Home Again* he applied this same technique in his descriptions of Mr. Jack, of Esther Jack, and of Foxhall Edwards. (p. 380)

Written in the first person, ["On Loneliness at Twenty-three"] is straight autobiography.

It is a very beautiful and tragic essay, and proves, I think, if further proof is needed beyond his books themselves, that Tom was a deeply religious man in the unconventional and truest sense of the word. (p. 381)

In some respects the title piece of this volume is one of the most interesting things he ever wrote. ["The Hills Beyond"] is without a doubt his most objective work. In some parts of it the style is lean and bare beyond anything one would have expected to find in Wolfe. There is both a gain and a loss in this—a gain of compactness along with objectivity; a loss of the lyrical and poetic intensity of his earlier writing. . . . Moreover, "The Hills Beyond" is a work of almost pure imagination, with only a few traces here and there of factual identity with the history of his own family. Most of it represents the very last work he did. (p. 383)

As it stands, "The Hills Beyond" brings the story of [George Webber's] ancestors down to about 1880. *The Web and the Rock* begins with George Webber's birth in 1900. Tom was going to fill this gap of twenty years and make "The Hills Beyond" a complete book in itself. It would

then have ended where *The Web and the Rock* begins, thus rounding out the Webber-Joyner cycle. (p. 386)

Edward C. Aswell, "A Note on Thomas Wolfe" (1941), in The Hills Beyond *by Thomas Wolfe (copyright 1935, 1936, 1937, 1939, 1941, by Maxwell Perkins as Executor; reprinted by permission of Harper & Row, Publishers, Inc.), Harper & Brothers, 1944, pp. 349-86.*

ALFRED KAZIN   (essay date 1942)

From the very first the long epic of self to which [Wolfe] devoted his life became the history of his tribulations, a history of his self's struggle against all the manifold threats, humiliations, paralyzing cautions and frustrations, which composed his outer experience—the enemy which he had to destroy in order to conquer—that is, to live truly, at all. The theme, then, was the conflict between the "I" and the world, that first person in which he began to write *Look Homeward, Angel,* and which slipped, like a Freudian gamin, through the rough disguise of Eugene Gant in *Of Time and the River.* In his first novel the enemy was the world narrowed to the first horizon of a child's sensations, and found its abundant representation in his mother Eliza, her greed and lovelessness and talk, the burning acquisitiveness which found its symbol in the boardinghouse that supplanted their home, the family's slow disintegration, his newspaper route in the early winter mornings—a mother in whom he recognized a fateful source of his torment, as he saw its theatrical reflection in his father. And struggling against his mother and the experience she at once represented and imposed upon him, Wolfe was struggling with even more painful ardor and bewilderment against those in his own family—Ben and Helen particularly—who had submitted and been defeated. Or, in making his newspaper rounds in the Negro quarters, he was rebelling simultaneously against the hysterical "success" of his brother Luke, the frenzied Oliver Optic mind stammering its way to the forlorn middle-class victory of money and status.

"Lost, lost, forever lost," he wrote of his kind in the anguished little prose lyric that became the leit-motif of his work. *"Naked and alone we came into exile. In her dark womb we did not know our mother's face; from the prison of her flesh have we come into the unspeakable and incommunicable prison of this earth."* Doomed as they all were, they represented even more the threat of his own doom, the enemy made symbol, the symbol made flesh. (pp. 472-73)

In this struggle between two absolutes, the "I" and the Enemy world, Wolfe found the theme of his rhetoric, and the source of the imagery—swollen and turgid, yet curiously dramatic—that illuminated the struggle in his own mind and sustained it by symbols. The prime symbol, always, was the image of the Father, the gate that would open the doors of the prison house for him. . . . The image of the Gate that recurred in his works . . . became the theme of his pilgrimage, the gateway to reality and happiness. But with it was united in Wolfe's mind the sense that this was somehow related to the American loneliness, the perpetual American migration, the loneliness of the artist-spirit in America that could so easily become the loneliness of all its young men and ardent spirits. . . . The Romantic "I" he remained to the end, consciously writing the story of his life and of all existence within the framework of that personal epic struggle; but the "I" became more than

Thomas Eugene Gant Wolfe, or Thomas George Webber Wolfe. It became (with the same facile incandescence with which Whitman had associated himself with the hero of *Leaves of Grass,* and *Leaves of Grass* with all America) the moral history of the Young American, even of modern American life. For the second of his primal symbols was the Rock, the city world and the city darkness, the flowing river of time that absorbed and dissipated life; and as the Father image represented the yearning for freedom, and the Rock the waste and chagrin of experience, so only the artist's "I" could mediate between them and conquer the Enemy.

In this light Wolfe's perpetual recourse to America as an idea, the seeming paradox between his frenzied self-interest and his assumption of a moral authority in which he spoke for all the lost young men in America, even for all America itself, was not a paradox or a sentimentally expansive gesture at all, but the necessary consequence of his situation and his understanding. For though he used his life and art interchangeably in this quest (so that the relations between them were perhaps as dark and radiantly confused as they are to us), they were, taken together, a reflection of Wolfe's conviction that he himself was a prime symbol of American experience and of a perpetual American ambition.... Hence the further significance of his need to set all of America down on paper, as Whitman had done. Hence his recurrent effort (always using his life and art interchangeably, always using his life not as the material of art but as the very voice of his art) to capture America as an idea and to master it as one, since in his own mind he was a spiritual agent, speaking and acting for others, and always in the name of nationality and destiny. (pp. 474-75)

He was not "celebrating" America, as Whitman had done; he was trying to record it, to assimilate it, to echo it in himself. This, the very quality and turn of his abundant energy, was the source of his frenzied passion for American details, of his need to reproduce them exactly for the substance of his art. Sitting in a Paris café, he would remember the railing on the Atlantic City boardwalk, an iron bridge across an American river, the clink of a milkman's horse going slowly up the morning street. (p. 476)

[His] passion for accumulation was not, however, a sentimental habit or even the mere reflex of his energy. He was offering America, or the possible idea of America, as a standard and as a reaction against all the sloth, degeneration, weakness, and cynicism which he saw in that Enemy which had become the symbol of everything he hated and feared. It is precisely because he was not merely "celebrating" America, in Whitman's sense, that he thought of his own struggle and of the necessary moral struggle in contemporary life in the same terms. Believing rapturously in the Romantic "I," he extended that faith, as he extended almost everything else, into a counterpoise to chaos. As Whitman had come at the beginning, when America was shapeless and nascent, so Wolfe thought of himself as coming at the climacteric, when the choice between the promise and its disillusionment, between life and death even, summoned all a man's resources—his own resources above all.... Where Whitman had identified himself with his America out of a supreme act of fellowship, the radiant confidence possible only to him and his time, Wolfe made his self equal to the communal tragedy he saw and wished to describe; he kept to the "I" as Whitman never did. This,

perhaps, is the larger significance of his inveterate self-interest, and the reason why he became the least interesting character in his work, and certainly the character in all his books one knows least. He could prove himself a striking realist of contemporary society, but at bottom his sense of tragedy was always a personal complaint, an imperial maladjustment. For if he knew the significance behind "the malady of the ideal," knew it with an excruciating pain and intensity and livid precision unmatched by his contemporaries, it was always, at bottom, because his experience was what sustained and afflicted *him;* it was because he wanted, consciously and dynamically, more of America than it was prepared to give him. He thought of himself as writing the last great epic of American nationality, certainly the last great American romance, as perhaps he did; but the epic was a personal quarrel, and the romance a vast inchoate yearning to the end.

That Wolfe proved himself the most self-centered and most inclusive novelist of the day is thus no paradox. His imagination was a perpetual tension between his devotion to himself and his devotion to his self's interests and symbolism, and he made his art out of the equation he drew. It is this that explains why Wolfe, in no real sense an objective novelist, was yet one who incorporated the best methods of American realism and passed beyond them; and it is this that explains why, though he often seemed determined to prove himself the sickliest of romantic egotists, he was, ironically enough, the most alert and brilliant novelist of depression America, and an extraordinarily imaginative analyst of American types and the social disorganization of the thirties. Though the feverish surface of his work hardly suggests it, he did write on several levels. Just as his imagination had presented his own situation and the American situation as coeval, so he was not always the stricken child wailing through thousands of pages of epic unhappiness—lost, lost, forever lost—but a prophetic voice who brought the same shattering intensity to his studies of contemporary demoralization, the climate of Fascism in Europe and America, the confusion and rout of the masses, that he did to his self-torment and yearning for personal freedom and redemption; brought it, indeed, with a conviction of absolute harrowing need and sense of achievement that made him seem the richest in spirit of contemporary American novelists. Though what he saw in society was always refracted through his own self, was always tangential to his own situation and his private agony, the force behind that agony broke through, enveloped and absorbed the life of contemporary society, as no social realist of the time, not even Dos Passos, ever did. He had come to believe that the Enemy was as much the nemesis of his America as it was of himself; and in that identification lay half his strength, and as has too often been forgotten, something as representative of his spirit as his lack of artistic discipline.

In one sense, then, there were two forces in Wolfe, mutually accommodating, springing from the same source, yet different in tone and effect. One was the mountaineer's son who wrote with a hard, driving force of the people he had hated as a child.... It was [this] Wolfe who proved himself a richly comic novelist, with an ear for dialogue, a sense of timing ... that were remarkable in their nervous power.... He saw them always—Hitler Germany and the baseball players out of his boyhood, the Jewish students at "The School for Utility Cultures" and Esther Jack, the mountain folk and Foxhall Edwards—as segments of that outer world that had significance only in its relation to Eugene Gant-George Webber, saw them often with a disproportionate intensity and strident wit that were literally fantastic in their excess; but he saw them always with great acuteness and wit, and they became, for all their stridency or angularity, as vivid and true as he had seen them in his mind.

The "other" Wolfe, always the centripetal Wolfe who related everything to the dead center of his own fate, was the Asheville, North Carolina Hamlet who dramatized himself perpetually in pride and suffering, rose in his books above the world he was trying to discover and redeem, and could never save himself. For at the bottom of all his frenzy, his herculean misery, the millions of words that spurted out of his pen without drawing him closer to the salvation, the answer he needed so desperately, lay an extraordinary fear of himself and the world he lived in. (pp. 476-79)

You Can't Go Home Again, his last novel, was pieced together out of fragments he left at his death; but for all its gaps and editorial interpolations it did represent this last and most fateful period in Wolfe's life faithfully. He had reached the end, as in his mind America and the world had reached the end, and for all his talk of "going on," of writing "greater and greater," he almost unconsciously told what he wished most to tell when he wrote into the fragments of the book a long study in dissolution. For *You Can't Go Home Again,* a climax to the one long book he wrote all his life, was rooted in a conviction of decline and fall, of emptiness and dissolution.... And since he was writing with something more than his old fury, with what seemed almost a new sense of prophecy and scorn, he was able to invest the poverty of New York, the crash back home, the bitterness his family and old neighbors felt against him, the very boom psychology of business itself as he saw it rotting away before him, with a terrible and incandescent loathing.

Something of the old romantic naïveté, always implicit in the absolute conflict he posed between the world and himself, remained to the end, as when he wrote of the sudden humiliation of the middle-class "successes" at home that "he had found out something about life that he had not known before." Yet that naïveté, as always, was the source of half his power.... A raging naïf to the end, Wolfe had the naïve curiosity as well as the naïve credulity and bombast; and that curiosity enabled him to see the depression and its atmosphere as a type of universal experience, a cataclysm not merely rooted in the facts of social change but inexpressibly more significant than them. He was discovering the mass agony as he had hitherto explored only his own, and though that larger world was still only a reflection of his own, he proved, almost by the depth of his self-absorption, that his romantic conception of a world that seemed to exist only to oppress Thomas Wolfe *had* actually led him somewhere, had justified his stricken devotion to Thomas Wolfe and his fate.

The two worlds had converged at last, if only in that last projection of himself which he offered to the world and the Enemy. And having achieved that much of the essential victory, he proved—it seems at once so little and so much —that in making his "I" equal to all America, he could speak for that essential truth in it which only a certain spirit could know, and suffer. (pp. 482-84)

Alfred Kazin, "The Rhetoric and the Agony," in

his On Native Grounds: An Interpretation of Modern American Prose Literature (copyright 1942, 1970, by Alfred Kazin; reprinted by permission of Harcourt Brace Jovanovich, Inc.), Reynal & Hitchcock, 1942, pp. 453-84.

ALFRED KREYMBORG (essay date 1945)

It is possible to read and enjoy "A Stone, A Leaf, A Door" as a book of poems and to disregard the novels from which they were drawn. Here, from beginning to end, one is confronted by an impassioned youth imprisoned in flesh and spirit seeking escape from personal exile and ranging from the womb to the grave in a rhapsodic state of despair and exultation. The book is a theme with variations, and the theme is the author himself seizing on natural images to symbolize his embattled existence and destiny. At times he sounds like one of the Hebrew mystics. . . .

While the book is primarily concerned with time and eternity and there is hardly any reference to specific events, [certain] lines are prophetic of the dilemmas of mankind in a second post-war world. The loneliness of Wolfe in a state of perpetual autointoxication belongs to an age when individualism and isolation were paramount. In a sense, the poet inherited the mood of the first post-war world which gave rise to Gertrude Stein's "lost generation." And yet, in reaching out from an inner to an outer self, or to a personal universe, he was never guilty of the petty disdain and cynicism of most of his fellows. His vision of an age in decline was larger and more heroic than theirs and, [at times,] reminds one of Ecclesiastes. . . .

The poems are generally composed in broad running lines which remind us of Whitman as well, and of Hart Crane and his belief in rivers, bridges, and the sea. And Wolfe, in the midst of his tumult and rhapsodic vein, was capable of carving an image in the manner of the supposedly out-dated Imagists. . . .

In one of his many unrhymed odes, Thomas Wolfe, after arraigning mankind for its bestiality and destructiveness, concludes that "it is impossible to scorn this creature."

Alfred Kreymborg, "Thomas Wolfe, Poet," in The Saturday Review of Literature (copyright © 1945 by Saturday Review; all rights reserved; reprinted by permission), Vol. XXVIII, No. 44, November 3, 1945, p. 32.

MAXWELL E. PERKINS (essay date 1947)

[Thomas Wolfe dedicated *Of Time and the River*] to me in most extravagant terms. I never saw the dedication until the book was published and though I was most grateful for it, I had forebodings when I heard of his intention. I think it was that dedication that threw him off his stride and broke his magnificent scheme. It gave shallow people the impression that Wolfe could not function as a writer without collaboration, and one critic even used some such phrases as, "Wolfe and Perkins—Perkins and Wolfe, what way is that to write a novel." Nobody with the slightest comprehension of the nature of a writer could accept such an assumption. No writer could possibly tolerate the assumption, which perhaps Tom almost himself did, that he was dependent as a writer upon anyone else. He had to prove to himself and to the world that this was not so.

And that was the fundamental reason that he turned to another publisher. If he had not—but by the time he did it was plain that he had to tell, in the medium of fiction and through the transmutation of his amazing imagination, the story of his own life—he never would have broken his own great plan by distorting Eugene Gant into George Webber. That was a horrible mistake. (pp. 143-44)

[If] Tom had held to his scheme and completed the whole story of his life as transmuted into fiction through his imagination, I think the [common] accusation that he had no sense of form could not have stood. He wrote one long story, "The Web of Earth," which had perfect form, for all its intricacy.... One might say that as his own physical dimensions were huge so was his conception of a book. He had one book to write about a vast, sprawling, turbulent land—America—as perceived by Eugene Gant.... If he had not been diverted and had lived to complete it, I think it would have had the form that was suited to the subject.

His detractors say he could only write about himself, but all that he wrote of was transformed by his imagination. For instance, in *You Can't Go Home Again* he shows the character Foxhall Edwards at breakfast. Edwards's young daughter enters "as swiftly and silently as a ray of light." She is very shy and in a hurry to get to school. She tells of a theme she has written on Walt Whitman and what the teacher said of Whitman. When Edwards urges her not to hurry and makes various observations, she says, "Oh, Daddy, you're so funny!" What Tom did was to make one unforgettable little character out of three daughters of Foxhall Edwards.

He got the ray of light many years ago when he was with me in my house in New Canaan, Connecticut, and one daughter, at the age of about eight or ten, came in and met this gigantic stranger. After she was introduced she fluttered all about the room in her embarrassment, but radiant, like a sunbeam. Then Tom was present when another daughter, in Radcliffe, consulted me about a paper she was writing on Whitman, but he put this back into her school days. The third, of which he composed a single character, was the youngest, who often did say, partly perhaps because she was not at ease when Tom was there, "Oh, Daddy, you're so silly." That is how Tom worked. He created something new and something meaningful through a transmutation of what he saw, heard, and realized.

I think no one could understand Thomas Wolfe who had not seen or properly imagined the place in which he was born and grew up. Asheville, N.C., is encircled by mountains. The trains wind in and out through labyrinths of passes. (pp. 145-46)

[I] think that those mountainous walls which his imagination vaulted gave him the vision of an America with which his books are fundamentally concerned. He often spoke of the artist in America—how the whole color and character of the country was completely new—never interpreted; how in England, for instance, the writer inherited a long accretion of accepted expression from which he could start. But Tom would say—and he had seen the world—"who has ever made you know the color of an American box car?" (pp. 146-47)

It was with America he was most deeply concerned and I believe he opened it up as no other writer ever did for the people of his time and for the writers and artists and poets of tomorrow. Surely he had a thing to tell us. (p. 147)

Maxwell E. Perkins, "Thomas Wolfe," in Harvard Library Bulletin *(copyright 1947 by the President and Fellows of Harvard College; reprinted by permission of the* Harvard Library Bulletin*), Vol. 1, No. 3, Autumn, 1947 (and reprinted in* Thomas Wolfe: Three Decades of Criticism, *edited by Leslie A. Field, New York University Press, 1968, pp. 139-47).*

HERBERT J. MULLER (essay date 1947)

Up to a point, *Of Time and the River* may be considered as of a piece with *Look Homeward, Angel*—another huge length sliced off the story that Wolfe apparently will go on writing forever.... I should pause to remark that he is indeed taking an unconscionably long time in growing up. *Of Time and the River* still reads like a first novel. Although published six years after *Look Homeward, Angel,* it is full of the same extravagances and is not a more finished technical performance; Wolfe appears to have learned little or nothing about his craft. Offhand, in fact, *Look Homeward, Angel* comes off better in a comparison. It remains the most unified of his novels, lyrically and dramatically, because it naturally falls into a simple pattern. It covers a natural stage in a man's life; it tells with whole-hearted intensity the story of growing pains, which to the youth are very complicated but to the grown man an old story. By contrast, *Of Time and the River* is an arbitrary slice of a man's life, with practically no plot unity, no climax, no dramatic beginning, middle and end. It has more breadth and variety because Eugene Gant has got out into the great world; it also seems more formless and muddled because he is lost there, at the end appearing to be just about where he was at the beginning. (p. 55)

[*From Death to Morning*] is a collection of short pieces which, with a few exceptions, add little to his stature or to our understanding of him. Mostly they are not complete, self-contained short stories but sketches, little pieces of novel. They are in fact pieces that he was unable to fit into his novels, or forced to edit out, and are worth salvaging chiefly because they have the same substance and quality as the novels. In addition there are a few exercises from a writer's notebook: "Only the Dead Know Brooklyn," a tiresome exercise in Brooklynese; "One of the Girls in Our Party," an experiment in the Ring Lardner manner, but less amusing and more obvious than Lardner; "The Far and the Near," a bare outline for a potentially good short story. On the whole, the collection emphasizes that Wolfe needed plenty of room, and was seldom capable of the artistry required by the confinement of the short story. A little Wolfe is not apt to go a long way.

The best thing in this volume, accordingly, is a novelette, "The Web of Earth." It is a monologue by Eliza, who talks to her son and is allowed to tell her own story, without benefit of comment or chant by the author. It is perhaps Wolfe's most expert technical performance, for he achieves form through the method of apparent formlessness. Eliza talks out of her inexhaustible memory; one thing leads to another, by psychological rather than logical association; but by the end she has woven the complete pattern of a personality and a life, against the background of the good earth. (pp. 77-8)

Far more significant, however, is *The Story of a Novel*.... [In this book] he reviews his accomplishment and outlines the task ahead. It is an unassuming, utterly truthful little book. No writer, not even Trollope, has written about his own work with more quiet, unaffected honesty; an honesty the more difficult because Wolfe's work had been conceived and wrought with such passion. He is not only humble but free from false modesty, and not only earnest but clear-sighted; he gives a very just statement of his methods and aims, his failures and successes. In particular, he clearly defines and explains the mature attitudes that in *Of Time and the River* might be overlooked, or discounted as passing moods, because they do not clearly govern the conception of the work as a whole. His story of his novel makes it much plainer that he has grown considerably. (pp. 79-80)

"Through free creation," [Wolfe] announces in the Author's Note to [*The Web and the Rock*], he has sought a release of his "inventive power"; this is the "most objective novel" he has written, and marks a "turning away" from his previous work, "a genuine spiritual and artistic change."

At first glance, this is a ludicrously naïve pretense, the more pathetic because as usual Wolfe was quite sincere, and had high hopes of his new enterprise. He is still writing his autobiography. He has not turned away from his early work but has done it over again, gone back over the same ground. (pp. 94-5)

The most genuine artistic change in *The Web and the Rock* itself gives away Wolfe's "new" enterprise. It is a change not in his materials but in his attitude toward them; he relates the early history of George Webber far more coolly and objectively than he had the history of Eugene Gant. Midway in the novel, however, there is an abrupt break. George has seemed like an ordinary young man, enjoying himself in college and in New York; then, suddenly, he boils over with hunger and fury, turns into Eugene Gant. The last half of the novel is centered on his love affair with Mrs. Esther Jack. . . . Wolfe had not only introduced Esther at the end of *Of Time and the River* but had completed the story of their love in his old vein, for his original purposes, before conceiving his new project. . . . Because he felt spiritually changed, he decided to make a fresh start; but because his central theme was the same, and much of the later chronicle already written, his new introduction could not be substantially new. George Webber would have to be like Eugene Gant because he had to become Eugene Gant. His early life could differ only superficially because it had to lead to the same maturity, or immaturity. In short, the first half of *The Web and the Rock* was merely grafted on to Wolfe's original legend; and the grafting is a rather crude job. The result is the least impressive of his novels. (pp. 96-7)

As the [two posthumous] novels stand, the sequel, *You Can't Go Home Again,* is by far the better. It is more nearly finished, and almost all of it is in Wolfe's mature manner. *The Web and the Rock* is a transitional work, uncertain in intention and uneven in accomplishment. Not only does it break into two different parts, but the last half in turn is an incomplete fusion of two versions of the love affair. The original version was a complete defense of Eugene Gant; Wolfe altered portions of it, to expose George Webber in a much less agreeable light, but did not revise it thoroughly. Nevertheless he was in fact undergoing a spiritual change and attempting an artistic change, striving ear-

nestly for impersonality and restraint. His efforts were not wholly successful, nor wholly unsuccessful; they entailed both gains and losses. As a transitional work, *The Web and the Rock* makes an interesting text for the study of Wolfe's growth. (p. 98)

The manuscript that Wolfe turned over to his editor before his death contained not only his last "novels" but all his unpublished writing—material left over from his first novels, early drafts of sections later rewritten, experimental pieces, miscellaneous fragments. . . . After Aswell extracted *The Web and the Rock* and *You Can't Go Home Again* there was still enough material to fill several more books, and from this he salvaged a final volume, *The Hills Beyond.* . . . Most important of these selected pieces is the title piece, a 150-page fragment of a novel on George Webber's maternal ancestors. (p. 155)

This is unquestionably Wolfe's most "objective" fiction, impersonal even by high critical standards. With one or two exceptions, his characters are inventions; he is not himself the hero, nor does he identify himself with any one character; and though he comments freely on the narrative, he comments as the omniscient, dispassionate author. Likewise his style is modest and quiet. His setting is Zebulon, the wild mountain country of Old Catawba, but no demented winds go howling over the hills, nothing demoniacal haunts the savage wilderness. His characters are lusty, uninhibited backwoodsmen, but neither do they howl, snarl, or yell. In short, Wolfe is no longer possessed, but in full possession of his materials and his powers.

Hence I regret the necessity of [stating] that these materials and powers are considerably less impressive than those he once struggled to control. *The Hills Beyond* is a respectable professional performance that will interest many readers but excite few, if any; I doubt that the most ardent lovers of Wolfe can find in it signs of genius, for to them in particular it is apt to seem simply dispirited. . . . [Actually his] characterization is generally sharp and vivid, especially because his dialogue is often rich. Nor is he actually dispirited. If his style is too often restrained to the point of prosiness, he nevertheless has an evident relish for his folk materials, even too obvious a relish for their picturesqueness—some of the local color is laid on with a trowel. In any event, the merits of the novel are on the surface. There is only occasional suggestion of latent depths of thought and feeling, powers in reserve. Wolfe's restraint here is seldom impressive because he does not seem to be restraining much. (pp. 156-57)

[There] are no hints of new directions in this final volume. *The Hills Beyond* itself not only covers ground that Wolfe had previously explored but naturally introduces much the same themes as in the novels it was designed to preface. (p. 158)

Likewise the shorter pieces in the volume contain familiar materials. Perhaps the best of them, a monologue called "Chickamauga" in which a Confederate veteran pours out his memories of the Civil War, belongs in the Pentland-Joyner cycle; Wolfe got the story from one of his maternal great-uncles, and told it in the old man's words. Several other sketches are relics of Wolfe's immaturity, and it might have been more pious to have left them unpublished. "On Leprechauns," for example, is a bitter, labored satire on the deference shown foreign writers, while "the usual reception of our young native artist . . . is a good, swift kick in the teeth''; it is untrue as well as unamusing. Still another sketch, ''The Lost Boy,'' is at first glance an interesting experiment in technique. It presents young Grover Gant . . . as he seemed to himself, to his mother Eliza, to his sister Helen, and to Wolfe when revisiting the scene of his death years later; Edward Aswell notes that Wolfe here tries ''to extract the whole substance of an experience by getting at it on four levels at once'' [see excerpt above]. But though it is a touching story, its texture is not actually so subtle or so complex. Grover looks essentially the same in all four views; we get not four levels but four characters on one level. Wolfe never handled point of view with anything like the subtlety of Henry James or Conrad, nor is there any clear indication that he ever would have developed into a fine craftsman.

More significant is a wholly characteristic essay, ''God's Lonely Man,'' which Wolfe rewrote at several stages of his career, and passages from which are scattered throughout *You Can't Go Home Again*. It is a final, comprehensive statement of a major theme of his life and work. He has lived, he says, ''about as solitary a life as a modern man can have.'' . . . [All] his experience has taught him that loneliness is ''the everlasting weather of man's life,'' love only ''the rare, the precious flower.'' This is indeed the consistent meaning of Wolfe's entire book. Among modern writers, only Conrad leaves so deep, persistent, haunting a sense of man's loneliness. (pp. 158-60)

> *Herbert J. Muller, in his* Thomas Wolfe *(copyright 1947 by New Directions; all rights reserved; reprinted by permission of New Directions Publishing Corporation), New Directions, 1947, 196 p.*

MARK SCHORER (essay date 1948)

The books of Thomas Wolfe were, of course, journals, and the primary role of his publisher in transforming these journals into the semblance of novels is notorious. For the crucial act of the artist, the unique act which is composition, a sympathetic editorial blue pencil and scissors were substituted. The result has excited many people, especially the young, and the ostensibly critical have observed the prodigal talent with the wish that it might have been controlled. Talent there was, if one means by talent inexhaustible verbal energy, excessive response to personal experience, and a great capacity for auditory imitativeness, yet all of this has nothing to do with the novelistic quality of the written result; for until the talent is controlled, the material organized, the content achieved, there is simply the man and his life. It remains to be demonstrated that Wolfe's conversations were any less interesting as novels than his books, which is to say that his books are without interest as novels. As with Lawrence, our response to the books is determined, not by their qualities as novels, but by our response to him and his qualities as a temperament.

This is another way of saying that Thomas Wolfe never really knew what he was writing *about*. *Of Time and the River* is merely a euphemism for ''Of a Man and his Ego.'' It is possible that had his conception of himself and of art included an adequate respect for technique and the capacity to pursue it, Wolfe would have written a great novel on his true subject—the dilemma of romantic genius; it was his true subject, but it remains his undiscovered subject, it is

the subject which *we* must dig out for him, because he himself had neither the lamp nor the pick to find it in and mine it out of the labyrinths of his experience. Like Emily Brontë, Wolfe needed a point of view beyond his own which would separate his material and its effect. (p. 23)

> *Mark Schorer, ''Technique As Discovery'' (copyright © 1948; reprinted by permission of the Estate of Mark Schorer), in* The Hudson Review, *Vol. 1, No. 1, Spring, 1948 (and reprinted in* Forms of Modern Fiction, *edited by William Van O'Connor, The University of Minnesota Press, 1948, pp. 9-29).**

JOHN WOODBURN (essay date 1949)

[Wolfe's] publishers state on the jacket of ''Mannerhouse'' that it is not autobiographical and hence is of special significance to an understanding of his development as an artist. It seems to me that it could be said rather that this understanding can be gained from the fact that ''Mannerhouse'' is, although not in the conventional sense of time and place, essentially autobiographical, and that it is possible to move easily and with recognition from the Eugene Ramsay of the play to the Eugene Gant of *Look Homeward, Angel*. Both are concerned with the defense and perpetuation of myth, as was Wolfe, who was always in both of these and in all of his novels, Wolfe-Eugene. These three share the same conflict, because they are the same: and indeed throughout all the great lumbering novels, in which Wolfe strove so mightily to encompass life and express it truly, there is the triumphant entrance and reëntrance, the bright, airy sound and the aura of myth. (pp. 24-5)

Peering at this play across the massive novels which followed, it is difficult to evaluate it in terms of itself, to bring it out from under the long shadows of Eugene Gant and of Thomas Wolfe. . . . As a play, considered technically and judged by really good ones, it is not, I suppose, very good. It is somber, sometimes tense, often moving and nearly always eloquent, frequently topheavy with a symbolism which misses absurdity only because the scale is grand and it is passionate and filled with the vitality that quickened everything Wolfe wrote. It is interesting to see Wolfe working under the discipline of the play form, which demands a succinctness, a condensation which he did not have, or did not choose, to consider in his novels. It is only in the stage directions, some of which read like prose passages, that he can indulge his tendency to be prolix.

Wolfe's stamp is on this play, there is no doubt about it— the excitement, the energy, the eloquence and the kind of shine that is in his writing is here, on every page, and the play lies beneath them, secondary and shadowed. (p. 25)

> *John Woodburn, ''Wolfe's Hamlet,'' in* The New Republic *(© 1949 The New Republic, Inc.), Vol. 120, No. 3, January 17, 1949, pp. 24-5.*

WILLIAM FAULKNER (essay date 1953)

[Contrary to the claims of the press, I] never said Wolfe was 'the greatest American writer of modern times.' I said, and this was several years ago, that among his and my contemporaries, I rated Wolfe first because we had all failed but Wolfe had made the best failure because he had tried hardest to say the most—a generalisation made rather in conversation than as a public statement, or so I thought at the time. I still support the statement, of course. Man has but one short life to write in, and there is so much to be said, and of course he wants to say it all before he dies. My admiration for Wolfe is that he tried his best to get it all said; he was willing to throw away style, coherence, all the rules of preciseness, to try to put all the experience of the human heart on the head of a pin, as it were. He may have had the best talent of us, he may have been 'the greatest American writer' if he had lived longer, though I have never held much with the 'mute inglorious Milton' theory; I believe it all gets said: that is, unless you are run down by a hit-and-run car, you say what you are capable of before you can persuade yourself to let go and die.

> *William Faulkner, in his undated letter to Richard Walser (excerpted by permission of the Estate of William Faulkner), in* The Enigma of Thomas Wolfe: Biographical and Critical Selections, *edited by Richard Walser, Cambridge, Mass.: Harvard University Press, 1953, p. vii.*

B. R. McELDERRY, JR. (essay date 1955)

[Wolfe's] untimely death in 1938 cast a Keatsian halo around his memory, and in 1939 [he] was a minor literary cult.

The Keatsian halo has proved unfortunate, for it has prevented recognition of Wolfe as one of the finest humorous writers in America since Mark Twain, perhaps even better than Twain in range and variety. . . . There has been an over-zealous concern with the "serious" side of his work. . . . It is time to re-read *Look Homeward, Angel,* his best novel, not so much as the agonizing search for maturity by an adolescent genius, as for the wonderful gallery of comic characters remembered and created from Wolfe's journey through the early years of this century. Eugene Gant's struggle to escape from family and environment is a thoroughly American pattern, and it gives intelligible direction to the story, but it is not the main attraction, any more than the freeing of the negro slave Jim is the main attraction of *Huckleberry Finn.* In both books it is the rich panorama and the lively episodes that enthrall. (pp. 91-2)

It is the tolerance, the lack of malice, that gives distinction to Wolfe's humor in this novel. In this he is often superior to Twain, for much of Twain's humor is overshadowed by his obvious desire to score off somebody else as more stupid than himself, or sometimes to get even with himself for being stupid. Either way the temptation to bludgeon his way in is strong. Wolfe is more natural, and more varied. How easily he gets his effect as he describes the meeting of Eliza Pentland and W. O. Gant. (pp. 92-3)

[The scene contains] humor drawn from nature, requiring nothing but selection and the restraint of accurate reporting. Another passage illustrates humorous interpretation. Gant has just called his four sons for breakfast.

> "When I was your age, I had milked four cows, done all the chores, and walked eight miles through the snow by this time."

> Indeed, when he described his early schooling he furnished a landscape that was constantly three feet deep in snow, and frozen hard. He seemed never to have attended school save under polar conditions.
>
> (p. 93)

Old man Gant is Wolfe's greatest character, and it is time to recognize him as one of the most varied comic characters in American literature. Beside him, Twain's Beriah Sellers is a shallow and tiresome stereotype. Gant's feud with Eliza is counterpointed by his even greater rage at her brother, Major Will Pentland. Gant's tirades, his passion for food and drink, his fear of the automobile he absentmindedly purchased, his unblinking support of the temperance movement, his pride in his children—these are but a few of the comic materials. But Gant is not the only source of humor. Eliza herself, literal-minded and obsessed with greed, is a wonderful foil to her turbulent husband. (p. 94)

Besides Gant and Eliza, there is young Luke Gant, energetically stuttering the townspeople into buying the *Saturday Evening Post.* There are Doc Maguire and Horse Hines (the undertaker), frequently found at Uneeda Lunch No. 3. There are Eugene's teachers: Mr. Leonard clumsily justifying the study of the classics he so unimaginatively taught; Professor Torrington, the pompous Rhodes Scholar who thought Barrie more important than Shaw; and Buck Benson, who said, "Mister Gant, you make me so damned mad I could throw you out the window," but left Eugene with a permanent love of Greek. . . . And—years before Walter Mitty—there are the skillful parodies of youthful daydreaming in which Eugene Gant sees himself . . . as Bruce Glendenning, the beachcomber who saves Veronica from a band of yelling natives; and as "The Dixie Ghost," beating Faro Jim to the draw.

Despite these shining riches, there remains what Kipling called "The Conundrum of the Workshops." The work may be clever, striking, human—but "Is it Art?" It is a hard question with respect to humor. . . . And as for *Huckleberry Finn,* Twain himself authorized the shooting of persons attempting to find a motive, moral, or plot in it. It is generally thought that without these you cannot have Art. Whether they are in fact present in *Huckleberry Finn* I shall not go into, but motive, moral, and plot are reasonably in evidence in *Look Homeward, Angel.* Eugene Gant is a sensitive boy, and his journey to adulthood has point and interest. For readers today it has more point than Huck's journey on the raft. At any rate it is a more difficult journey, for Twain took care that Huck never underwent the pangs of adolescence, in which, as Keats said, "the soul is in ferment." (pp. 95-6)

> *B. R. McElderry, Jr., "The Durable Humor of 'Look Homeward, Angel'" (copyright © 1955 by the* Arizona Quarterly; *reprinted by permission of the* Arizona Quarterly), *in* Arizona Quarterly, *Vol. 11, No. 2, Summer, 1955 (and reprinted in* The Merrill Studies in "Look Homeward, Angel," *edited by Paschal Reeves, Charles E. Merrill Publishing Company, 1970, pp. 91-6).*

W. M. FROHOCK (essay date 1957)

The greatest praise we give to a poet who in mature years writes lyrics of freshness and originality is that he "seems so young." This strikes me as one of the most helpful keys to Wolfe; his vision of life and the world in which he makes his characters live are the vision and the world of a very young man.

He felt himself so wretchedly, so miserably, and so magnificently alone. Despite all his use of the second person plural, Eugene Gant and George Webber never escape the feeling that their enterprises are personal and special, their cases unique. (p. 54)

The record of the autobiographical character's inability to establish satisfactory communication with other human beings suggests a fundamental difficulty, a failure to understand and to be understood, which may in turn be related to the state of compulsive frenzy in which Wolfe appears to have done much of his writing. With Wolfe, as with Céline, the other novelist of our time who approaches Wolfe in this matter of being repelled by people, one cannot help feeling that the drive to write, and to keep on writing at whatever cost in prolixity and reiteration, is tied up with some sort of despair of ever being fully understood. (p. 55)

We have come, of late, to feel that the presence of [a] theme of isolation makes the mood of a novel tragic. In Wolfe's case, however, it seems clear that the exaggerated feeling of man's loneliness which permeates his work, and which conditions his whole somewhat neurotic vision of life, prevents that vision from being a truly tragic one. At this point, a comparison with the work of André Malraux becomes almost inevitable.

Wolfe and Malraux, better than any other contemporaries who come to mind, have caught up and made their own the feeling of man's solitude. (p. 56)

Malraux's mature awareness of the two faces to [solitude, man's loneliness and man's essential solidarity,] is what Wolfe seems to me never to have attained. He never convinced himself that no man is an island. Wolfe's feeling of solitude—together with his awareness of the erosions of time and the imminent presence of death—appears, in comparison with Malraux's later work, as a badge of immaturity. Not that this condemns him; many writers as great as and greater than Wolfe have been immature in this sense. But their achievement has nothing to do with tragedy. The feeling of loneliness, and of the individual's being so bafflingly penned within himself, prevents it. The first person singular, as has often been remarked, is not the appropriate pronoun for tragedy.

It would be pointless, of course, to worry such a question unless in the process we got a fresh view of what Wolfe was and of what he did. It is very likely that his chronic immaturity—moral and aesthetic—warped his vision of life. (p. 57)

In his books he sounds like one of the people—Stendhal was another—who spend their lives trying to see themselves as they are without ever quite penetrating the thick wall of self-delusion.

His ability to make incredible things seem credible is itself almost incredible. It is only when one goes back to *Look Homeward, Angel* that the Aeschylean family of the early book shows itself for what it is and the whole Pentland-Gant clan becomes implausible if not preposterous. W. O. Gant as Agamemnon home from the wars to die, . . . Eugene as the wretched Orestes . . . one feels that Wolfe cannot really have intended these things, and yet, vaguely, there they are! The people, if hardly the setting, of an *Oresteia*. The family taint on which Eliza and Helen dwell is the Curse upon the House. And on first reading, or if one has read *Look Homeward, Angel* and no more, one accepts these things unthinkingly; the Gant-Pentland tribe seems plausible indeed when taken by itself.

But when one gets out of Altamont into the wider world of *Of Time and the River,* he begins to see that too many people are like the Gants and the Pentlands; there are simply too many queer ducks. . . . [It] is impossible not to feel that we have strayed into some gallery of eccentrics. At times it seems as if everyone Wolfe writes about is abnormal, or else downright insane. And after we have seen [the people of *Of Time and the River*] we look back at Altamont and are much less impressed by the extraordinary population of *Look Homeward, Angel;* the Aeschylean family now appear as only the first in a long succession of crackpot figures. There is small doubt that something in Wolfe's vision has warped them. (pp. 58-9)

Reading *Of Time and the River* directly after *Look Homeward, Angel* throws a revealing light on the people of the latter book. The Gants and Pentlands become not tragic but queer; not people working out their destiny, but frustrate victims of time. Their violence, instead of being the inevitable result of forces which drive them in a given direction, is merely the inevitable result of frazzled nerves. A typical case of this, perhaps the most eloquent that Wolfe ever invented, is the struggle between Eugene and his brother Luke, which takes place in their mother's living room. There is no point to the fight, nothing is at stake; doing physical damage to each other will accomplish no more than the temporary relief of their exasperation. This is violence without significance. Compare it with the fighting in *The Grapes of Wrath* or with the last chapter of *For Whom the Bell Tolls* and the distinction is clear. These are eccentrics clawing at each other; they are frustrated even in the attempt to do lasting harm; and this is the best proof possible that the people Wolfe sees, as he sees them, are not tragic figures.

Straightway we also doubt the reality of the places where Wolfe makes them move. Originally we accepted Altamont without question, but just as we suspect that the people are distorted as soon as we leave Altamont for Cambridge, so we also suspect Altamont itself as soon as we can put it in the new perspective. Wolfe's New England makes Altamont a never-never land. (pp. 60-1)

Wolfe's New York is probably better. New York is at least so various that nothing said of it can be convicted of falsehood. But here again, as Wolfe watches the gray-faced, hostile millions stream through the subways, he is an outsider. (p. 62)

It is in the nature of his talent that he should see things from the outside only, and be forced always to guess what is inside them; his vision is the vision of the outsider. Thus the question naturally arises, after we have finished looking at his middle books, whether his view of Altamont is not the vision of an outsider also. Did this youth of sixteen ever read all the books Wolfe talks about, or are these the reading experiences of a mature man, garnered at the University of North Carolina and at Harvard and thrown back in memory to be associated with the wrong age? (pp. 62-3)

Thus, to the earlier remark that the first person singular is not the appropriate pronoun for tragedy, we must add that the perfect is not the appropriate tense. Recollection of tragic events does not make tragedy. To get the full force of the tragic situation we need to feel contemporaneous with it; the author has to show the action as it takes place, not as it is rebuilt in retrospect. And so for this reason also

Wolfe's novels are not tragic; his attitude toward his material, with special respect to time, is not a tragic attitude. It is dominantly emotion recollected.

But not emotion recollected in tranquillity. Wolfe's poetry is not calmly and quietly intense; his main theme is the theme of being lost in America, and it is treated by a poet who is still lost. . . . He has some of the naturalistic pantheism, the feeling that man and the soil are intimately bound together in essence, which marks so much Western literature since Zola and which makes him sound occasionally like Jean Giono, just as he shows at times some of the enthusiasm for being American, if not for the faith democratic, of Walt Whitman. Now and again he reveals a feeling for, though not much knowledge of, the history of our people—the feeling that this land is something apart because the dust of his ancestors is mixed with its dust. But mostly his complaint is that these things do not mean more to him than they do, that he really has no place and "no door where he can enter," and that meanwhile he is being swept along by the stream of time. . . . The one thing that he can be sure of, the one door that must open for him, is death.

Wolfe is the writer of our century who has written most eloquently about death—the death of Grover, the death of Ben, of old Gant; and of the overwhelming imminence of death everywhere. As each individual submerges beneath the river of time, something of Wolfe himself is lost; each was a parcel of his consciousness. More surely than anything else the thought of death looses that remarkable flow of his language . . . and also the extraordinary resources of his rhetoric.

The rhetoric is essential. One reads much more about Wolfe's breadth of vocabulary and his obviously sensuous pleasure in words, and of what someone has called his multitudinous garrulity, than about the way he used his gift. He has the distinction of being the one writer of his generation who truly dared pull out all the stops. (pp. 63-4)

There is no point in denying that often Wolfe let go to print much that should never have gone. Those of us who like him believe that there was a god in him, but a very unruly god who gave him no peace and at times went away without warning, as people sometimes go away and leave a radio with the switch turned on playing in an empty tenement. He was an enthusiast who had, as old Gant had, "a tragic consciousness of time," and of death. Like the people in *Look Homeward, Angel* he was a fanatic, and time and death were his obsessions. Consequently, in those moments when the god is absent he sounds like a hysterical woman who insists on feeling unloved, . . . whose life is a great conspiracy to frustrate her. (p. 67)

Much that he wrote proves that the critics who were hellbent to show what really needed no demonstration, i.e., that he did not know how to compose, were right, and is evidence of the compulsive frenzy in which he worked. . . . Our criticism of him will become more cogent as we give over arguing about this incontrovertible weakness and go on to define, as precisely as we can, Wolfe's great strength. (p. 68)

W. M. Frohock, "Thomas Wolfe: Time and the National Neurosis," in his The Novel of Violence in America *(copyright © 1953, 1957 by Southern Methodist University Press; copyright © 1950,*

1957 by W. M. Frohock), revised edition, Southern Methodist University Press, 1957 (and reprinted by Beacon Press, 1964, pp. 52-68).

FLOYD C. WATKINS (essay date 1958)

The varying judgments by different critics, the frequent changes in the attitude of the reader toward Wolfe, and the tendency to like a passage from Wolfe at one time and to dislike it at another—all these are understandable if we view him as a poet—particularly a primitive or natural poet. Perhaps the most basic characteristic of Wolfe's prose is that it reveals a love for primitivistic sound and phrase. . . . Much of his writing reveals an attraction to the mere words and rhythms of a sentence not entirely unlike the appeal to the primitive in Vachel Lindsay's "The Congo." His elaborate repetitions and pointing words and phrases are occasionally as inept as the dull reiterations of a freshman theme, often as primitive as the incremental repetition of a folk ballad, and sometimes as infinitely various as the work of a careful poet.

The long description of Altamont waking at dawn in *Look Homeward, Angel* contains an example of how Wolfe repeated phrases and figures and achieved an unusual effect by varying the combinations of colors and images. "Spring," he wrote, "lay strewn lightly like a fragrant gauzy scarf upon the earth; the night was a cool bowl of lilac darkness, filled with fresh orchard scents." In the following twelve pages he repeats in many combinations such terms as *lilac darkness, pearl light, nacreous dawn,* and *blue-pearl* until the repetitions lead gradually to the full light of day, which appears suddenly in the new term *virginal sunlight.* Without such extended development, some of the descriptive passages would seem overwritten, but the activities of the waking citizens as well as the repetitions prepare for a rhapsody like the following: "Nacreous pearl light swam faintly about the hem of the lilac darkness; the edges of light and darkness were stitched upon the hills. Morning moved like a pearl-gray tide across the fields and up the hillflanks, flowing rapidly down into the soluble dark." This is one of the best examples of Wolfe's characteristic rhetorical patterning of phrases throughout a unified passage. (pp. 79-80)

Look Homeward, Angel is Wolfe's most subtle novel in imagery. He describes wonder as "the union of the ordinary and the miraculous," and in many instances he succeeds in blending the two poetically and almost metaphysically in the poetic sense. Destiny, he says for example in the first paragraph, leads "into the hills that shut in Altamont over the proud coral cry of the cock, and the soft stone smile of an angel. . . ." *Coral cry* metaphysically yokes heterogeneous elements by violence together; it may involve a description of the color of the cock, or the description of the sound as a color, or the description of the color of the dawn. And "the soft stone smile of the angel" merges paradoxical terms. Oxymorons and conceits of this kind are almost omnipresent in the first novel but rather infrequent in later works.

Wolfe's turbulent emotions and extravagant figures of speech often counterbalance his successes. That cow in *Look Homeward, Angel* which is "singing in her strong deep voice her Sunday exuberance" is an unhappy example of Wolfe's own occasional bovine mooings; and she even suggests the ineptness of the squeal and the goat-cry in the love story in *The Web and the Rock* or of characters "holding [their] . . . entrails thoughtfully in [their] . . . hands" in *Of Time and the River*. (pp. 80-1)

What most of us too often fail to see, however, is Wolfe's frequent comic intent in his rhetorical passages. Often he succeeds in making his adult readers nostalgically long for childhood, and he amuses them in the same passages by creating comic melodrama about childhood, using deliberately high-flown rhetoric. When young Eugene Gant visualizes himself as the Dixie Ghost in a motion picture, Wolfe is not only portraying a child's imagination but also sympathetically laughing at the child and the movie. When the Ghost "found himself face to face with the little dancing girl," there was as much comedy as childhood romance: "Two smoking globes of brine welled from the pellucid depths of her pure eyes and fell with a hot splash on his bronzed hand." Later, the Ghost "pondered on love's mystery. Pure but passionate. Appearances against her, 'tis true. The foul breath of slander. She worked in a bawdy-house but her heart was clean. Outside of that, what can one say against her?" (p. 81)

Look Homeward, Angel exhibits the major tendencies in Wolfe's rhetoric. It is his best book, because his rhetorical flourishes are most happily employed to describe the emotions and the imagination of a sensitive child or youth. In the next two books, the rhetoric frequently becomes bombastic descriptions of adolescent emotions of an older if not more mature hero. *You Can't Go Home Again* marks in many respects a new stage. The rhetoric appears in panoramic descriptions of the landscape of America and in passages where a lyrical style is appropriate.

The decline evident in *Of Time and the River* and *The Web and the Rock* is significantly offset by Wolfe's increasing use of his Southern origins and of Southern speech and oratory. "The Web of Earth" is one of his best works because Wolfe presents so ably the mountaineer rhetoric of Eliza Gant in what might be called a stream of conversation. Uncle John's account of the battle of Chickamauga in *The Hills Beyond* is one of the most effective representations of mountaineer speech in American literature. And the political oratory and backwoods humor of Zachariah Joyner in *The Hills Beyond* are other examples of Wolfe's growing consciousness of his Southern heritage, including Southern rhetoric.

Wolfe must be viewed as a Southern rhetorician. He was a poet in his love of sound and his use of sensuous imagery. At his worst, he is "full of sound and fury, signifying nothing"; at his best, as one of his characters says of W. O. Gant, he could "tie a knot in the tail of the English language." (p. 82)

> Floyd C. Watkins, "Rhetoric in Southern Writing," in The Georgia Review (copyright, 1958, by the University of Georgia), Vol. XII, No. 1, Spring, 1958, pp. 74-86.*

LOUIS J. BUDD (essay date 1960)

[Sherwood Anderson was] a major figure during the years that Wolfe switched from drama to fiction; just about every critic who has commented on Wolfe recognizes this fact and then develops a contrast between the two. However,

Wolfe's praises for the older man justify a search for a deep-running relationship that, it turns out, shaped *Look Homeward, Angel* in basic ways.

His earliest letter to Anderson declared: "It seemed to me ever since I first began to read your books when I was a kid of twenty that you got down below the surface of our lives and got at some of the terror and mystery and ugliness and beauty in America better than anyone else." This meant that he had started to read Anderson not too long after the appearance in 1919 of *Winesburg*, which in its dedication spoke of the "hunger to see beneath the surface of lives." Wolfe was to subtitle his first book "A Story of the Buried Life." It repeats Anderson's search into the psychic center, into the most breathing reality—which lies in the emotions that control the now symbolic actions, not in humdrum and workaday routine. When Wolfe grandly gave credit to Anderson for "anything I know of writing," he must have referred partly to this intentness on hiddden feeling. (p. 128)

[Wolfe] deeply sensed Anderson's unique, complex tone. To the confusion of hometown friends, *Look Homeward* like *Winesburg* highlights the sometimes agonized, sometimes exalted upthrusts through drab normality. In the note attached to his manuscript as it was being peddled in 1928, Wolfe insisted that his characters were the "richest and strangest" yet the "greatest people" he had known and that his "painful and ugly" treatment of "terror and darkness" vibrated with a "strong joy." Although some personal bitterness lurked behind the book's making, he was genuinely disappointed that Ashevillians should resent it as a betrayal. He intended the same warmth that ran through *Winesburg*; the theme of life's frightening meaninglessness was linked with a tender belief in life's magic that in Anderson and Wolfe mounted to a crude religiosity.

The "terror" that Wolfe savored in Anderson's fiction rose primarily from the vision they shared of man's loneliness. People in Winesburg and Altamont have lost their ancestral moorings and their sense of belonging. But the inner man at his best resists annihilation and pursues his right to emotional fulfillment. Painfully, he seeks the unifying word and embrace; too often the violent promptings of his need drive him into self-defeating excesses. However, the chance that he can succeed sets Anderson and Wolfe apart from the psychological realists of the twenties who can promise nothing. The terrible doggedness of the quest in itself affirms human creativity.

Nevertheless, most people meet denials that deform them emotionally. Their plight aroused in Anderson a tenderness that Wolfe magnified into agonized sympathy. Both pitied expecially the warping that results when men are baffled in their desire to get truly close to other men. Winesburg has its Elizabeth Willard, Dr. Reefy, Louise Hardy, and Wing Biddlebaum. Altamont has their counterparts in profusion, climaxed by W. O. Gant. His strength never feels honest release, his appetites miss an adequate outlet; he never carves his ideal stone angel or finds peaceful love. . . . In its searching, bewildered, and deeply agitated characters, *Look Homeward* is a second "Book of the Grotesque."

Anderson's most influential maneuver had been to make the adolescent his touchstone. . . . By making the adolescent's struggle toward discovery uncover a common tension between cruelty and understanding, Wolfe stood much closer to Anderson than to Joyce. George Willard and Eugene Gant hope to resolve the dilemmas of feeling by becoming writers; but in their hunger for emotional richness and their ambivalent, often frustrated intercourse with their townsmen, they typify the travail of any innocent spirit. Much more than Stephen Dedalus, they also seem likely to find some day the words of insight that redeem their experiences; leaving the hometown does not mean that they renounce the past. (pp. 128-29)

Like Winesburg, Altamont is seen through a shocked nostalgia that indicts Main Street's hidden tragedies and deformities much more than its clichés.

This indictment never leaped into a rejection of American society, however destructive the gap between private needs and public codes. . . . In its jabs at our Anglophiles, in its attempts to give a national backdrop to the Gants' doings, in its panoramic chapters, Look Homeward shows the old desire to epitomize our best qualities. Anderson and Wolfe kept a faith in the democratic dream that set them apart from the expatriate of the twenties; in the proletarian thirties their social analysis would appeal to native liberalism. If this proves mere agreement rather than the influence of the older man, it still makes other borrowings more likely.

Along with the finer similarities in attitude, it makes more reasonable the view that Wolfe followed Anderson in some devices of method. As belated romantics, they valued emotion and idea over rigid architecture. Written well within the era of the well-made novel, Winesburg avoids ordered symmetry and Look Homeward leans toward shapelessness. Both books approach the effect of sketches held in the loose autobiographical cycle that Anderson, as much as anyone, established during the twenties as a prose form. The tenuous plot line of both is even closer: a boy gropes toward understanding the quivering inward life of his town; softened by new insight but increasingly restless after the death of a loved member of the family, he takes the train to the shining city and to adulthood. (pp. 129-30)

The tie between Anderson and Wolfe rests mainly on the fact that while he was still unfledged in writing fiction the younger man read Winesburg with delighted receptivity. He admired its descent into the hidden emotional world, its counterpoint of terror and beauty, its poignant sense of man's isolation and the psychic deformities caused by his drive to communicate, its symbolic use of the adolescent's struggle toward identity, and its somber yet loving concern with American life. Although Wolfe later complained about having "every name in the library hurled at my head" and although he slowly grew away from Anderson, Winesburg contributed to the viewpoint, structure, and even the rhetoric of Look Homeward. (p. 132)

> Louis J. Budd, "The Grotesques of Anderson and Wolfe," in Modern Fiction Studies (© copyright 1960 by Purdue Research Foundation, West Lafayette, Indiana), Vol. V, No. 4, Winter, 1959-60 (and reprinted in The Merrill Studies in 'Look Homeward, Angel,' edited by Paschal Reeves, Charles E. Merrill Publishing Company, 1970, pp. 126-33).

C. HUGH HOLMAN (essay date 1961)

[Look Homeward, Angel] assumed a simple but effective narrative form. The record of childhood and youth, cast at least semi-consciously in the bildungsroman pattern of James Joyce's A Portrait of the Artist as a Young Man, had found its theme and taken its shape from the sequential flow of lyric feeling which it expressed. After its publication, Wolfe began a desperate search for another form into which to pour his materials. (p. 166)

By the fall of 1931 Wolfe found himself immersed in a struggle for form whose magnitude and difficulty, as well as spiritual and emotional anguish, he recorded touchingly in The Story of a Novel. In November, badly in need of money and in black despair over "the book," he turned to a body of materials in which he had earlier worked and began shaping them into a short novel. These materials dealt with his experiences in Cambridge and with his uncle, Henry Westall. In its finished form the short novel, A Portrait of Bascom Hawke, pictured an old man resigned to the death of dreams as he is seen through the eyes of a youth still half blinded by the visions of glory which the old man has given up. The two points of view, the youth's and the old man's, together gave a sense of the flow and corrosion of time. The result was a portrait in depth, done with irony, poignance, and tolerant laughter, of an eccentric who might have stepped from the pages of Dickens. (pp. 166-67)

[The Web of Earth], the longest of Wolfe's short novels, comes to the reader entirely through the voice of its narrator, Delia Hawke (later changed to Eliza Gant when the novel was reprinted in From Death to Morning). . . . The seemingly disparate elements of the story—disjointed in temporal and logical sequence—are effectively knit together by the powerful personality of the narrator and by her obsessive search in the events of her life for the meaning of the spectral voices that spoke "Two . . . Two" and "Twenty . . . Twenty" in "the year that the locusts came."

In writing The Web of Earth Wolfe followed James Joyce again, as he had done in Look Homeward, Angel. He compared his "old woman" with Molly Bloom and seemingly felt that his short novel had a structure like that of the interior monologue at the conclusion of Ulysses. In her resilience, her undefeatable energy, and her vitality Eliza (or Delia) approaches "the earth goddess" and is, as Louis D. Rubin, Jr. has pointed out, reminiscent of the end of the "Anna Livia Plurabelle" sequence of Finnegans Wake. . . . In this short novel one understands what Wolfe meant when he referred to Eliza Gant's people as "time-devouring." Thus, The Web of Earth becomes a fascinating counterpiece to A Portrait of Bascom Hawke; for each is a character sketch of an elderly person, but where Bascom Hawke is defeated and despairingly resigned, Eliza Gant is triumphant and dominant; where Bascom is the male victim of time, Eliza is the female devourer of time; where Bascom's is the vain grasp of intellect and reason in a mad and fury-driven world, Eliza's is the groping of mystery, passion, and fear in a world where reason always falls victim to the decay of time. Never did Wolfe articulate more effectively than in these two short novels the fundamental polarities of his childhood and youth. (pp. 168-69)

[Death the Proud Brother] was a skillfull attempt to unify a group of seemingly disparate incidents in the city through their common themes of loneliness and death, "the proud brother of loneliness." . . . Although it is a successful effort to impose thematic unity upon disconnected instances of death in the city, it is less effective than Wolfe's other novellas. . . .

In arranging the materials of [*No Door*], Wolfe selected a group of intensely autobiographical incidents all centering on his sense of incommunicable loneliness and insularity, dislocated them in time, and bound them together by a group of recurring symbols arranged in *leitmotif* patterns, extending and enriching a method he had used in *Death the Proud Brother*. Through the recurring images and the repeated phrases of a prose poem used as a prologue, he knit together one portion of his life. In its concluding episode are united the themes of youth's exuberance and age's sad wisdom, which had been central to *A Portrait of Bascom Hawke,* and the enduring earth, which had been central to *The Web of Earth*. . . .

Since the structure of *No Door* is essentially that of *Of Time and the River,* since the prologue to *No Door* reappears with only minor changes as the prologue to the long novel, and since the writing of *No Door* coincides with the finding of a "way to begin the book," it is probable that the short novel was the door through which Wolfe entered *Of Time and the River*. (p. 170)

No Door represents as sure a mastery as Wolfe ever demonstrated of the subjective, autobiographical materials for which he is best known. . . .

One other short novel resulted from Wolfe's arranging of materials from the "big book" during this period. It was *Boom Town,* a story of approximately 20,000 words, portraying the real estate craze in Asheville in the satiric manner of Sinclair Lewis. (p. 171)

[Two years later] he used the short novel form to dramatize this perception of the truth about Hitler's Germany, and he elected to give his account, which he entitled "*I Have a Thing to Tell You,*" the sharp intensity and the almost stark directness of the action story. At this time Wolfe had great admiration for the directness and simplicity of Ernest Hemingway's style, and in this short novel of Germany he came closest to adopting some of its characteristics. Nothing Wolfe ever wrote has greater narrative drive or more straightforward action than this novella. The simplicity and objectivity of "*I Have a Thing to Tell You*" were seldom sustained for any length of time in Wolfe's work before 1936.

This short novel also displays clearly the growing concern with the issues of the outer world which had begun to shape Wolfe's thinking. (pp. 172-73)

[He] was led by his growing sense of social injustice to attempt another experiment with a short novel as a vehicle of social criticism. . . .

Wolfe felt that he was attempting in *The Party at Jack's* "one of the most curious and difficult problems that I have been faced with in a long time," the presentation of a cross-section of society through a representation of many people, ranging from policemen, servants, and entertainers to the leaders in the literary world and the rich in the events of a single evening during which they were brought together through a party and a fire in the apartment house in which the party occurred. He used several devices, including the recurring quivering of the apartment house as the trains run in tunnels through its seemingly solid rock foundations and the conversations of the doormen and elevator operators, to underscore the contrast among the characters and to comment on society. (p. 173)

The Party at Jack's is, as Wolfe asserted, free of autobiography, except in the most incidental ways. It is also in Wolfe's late, more economical style. Its taut prose and its rapid movement, together with its effective but implicit statement of social doctrine, make it one of Wolfe's most impressive accomplishments. (pp. 173-74)

Wolfe was forever reshuffling the parts of his work and assembling them in different patterns, in a way not unlike the shifting elements of the Snopes material in Faulkner's continuing legend of Yoknapatawpha County. Thus Wolfe took the materials he had presented first as short novels and interwove them into the larger frames and subject matters of his "big books," fragmenting, expanding, and modifying them, and often destroying their separate integrity. Only two of his short novels escaped this process; and these two —*Death the Proud Brother* and *The Web of Earth*—were published in a collection of his shorter works, *From Death to Morning,* which has never received the critical attention that it deserves. (p. 175)

Wolfe's treatment of his short novels when he incorporated them later into his long books . . . is a key to one of Wolfe's central problems, the finding of a large form sufficient to unify his massive imaginative picture of experience. This large form that he sought would give, apparently, not the representation of a series of sharply realized dramatic moments in the life of his protagonist (and through him of America) but an actual and significant interweaving of these moments into a complex fabric of event, time, and feeling. That he struggled unceasingly for the mastery of this vast structure is obvious from his letters, from *The Story of a Novel,* and from the long books themselves. Whether he was moving toward its realization is a matter of critical debate today, as it was at the time of his death. However much one may feel that he was (and I share that belief), the fact remains that none of the published novels after *Look Homeward, Angel* succeeded in finding a clearly demonstrable unity, in being "a single thing."

The intrinsic qualities of the short novel were remarkably well adapted to Wolfe's special talents and creative methods. Although he was skilled at the revelatory vignette, in which he imprisoned a character in an instance in time, those characters and actions which were central to his effort and experience he saw in relation to the expanding pattern of life. Experience and life itself were for him, as Herbert Muller has noted, remarkably "in process." One of the distinctive aspects of Wolfe's imagination is its tendency to see life as a thing of "becoming." He saw time—"dark time," he called it—as being at the center of the mystery of experience, and its representation on three complex levels [actual present time, past time, and time immutable] was a major concern of his work. The individual scene or person had little value to him; it had to be put back in time to assume meaning. (pp. 175-76)

Ultimately in the portrayal of an incident or an individual against this complex pattern of time, that incident or individual must be seen through a perceiving and remembering self, such as David Hawke, the youth who can read the corrosion of time in the contrast between his exuberance and his uncle's resignation, in *A Portrait of Bascom Hawke.* Eliza Gant's fabric of memories in *The Web of Earth* is a record of the impact of time on her. The individual incidents of *No Door* assume their importance as portions of a personal history as they are reflected in the narrator's memory. To be fully understood, such events and people must be set against the innumerable other events and people which the perceiving self has known; it is this larger context in time which Wolfe attempts to give these short novels when he incorporates them in his longer works. We can think of an event as being an objective experience which is perceived and recalled later by the self that first knew it directly; then it, as fact and as memory, becomes a part of the totality of experience that makes the web of meaning for that self. Wolfe's short novels represent that portion of the process in which the incident is remembered, isolated, organized, and understood as incident by the self. Their later fragmentation and inclusion in the long novels represent his attempt to absorb them into his total experience and to use them in all the complexity of life as elements in his search for ultimate meaning. Hence he breaks up the sequence of actions, introduces new incidents, and frequently expands the wordage of the short novels when they are incorporated into the larger structures. These incidents thereby lose some of their artistic and inherent right to achieve unity by exclusion, and they tend to become diffuse.

Since Wolfe's success in achieving the larger unity for which he strove in the last three long novels is considerably less than total, the materials which he had organized into short novels have an integrity and a consummate craftsmanship which they seem to lack in the long books. . . . In the short novel form Wolfe was a master of his craft, and these successful products of his efforts should not be forgotten. (pp. 176-77)

> C. Hugh Holman, "Introduction," in his The Short
> Novels of Thomas Wolfe, edited by C. Hugh Holman
> (abridged by permission of Charles Scribner's Sons;
> copyright 1947 by Charles Scribner's Sons), Charles
> Scribner's Sons, 1961 (and reprinted in Thomas
> Wolfe: A Collection of Critical Essays, edited by
> Louis D. Rubin, Jr., Prentice-Hall, Inc., 1973, pp.
> 165-77).

C. HUGH HOLMAN (essay date 1961)

What he said of his character George Webber is true of Wolfe himself: "He was a Southerner, and he knew that there was something wounded in the South. He knew that there was something twisted, dark, and full of pain which Southerners have known all their lives—something rooted in their souls beyond all contradiction." But all his knowledge of her darkness and damnation could not stifle his love for the lost and ruined and burning Helen in his blood. . . .

Ambiguous and contradictory though his views of his native region were, the South was a theme and a subject matter for much of Wolfe's work, and it existed for him in a sensuous, irrational emotional state of mutual attraction and repulsion. (p. 179)

In his efforts . . . to realize the self as generic American and make his personal pilgrimage the national odyssey, Wolfe functioned with uneven effectiveness. He magnificently realized individual scenes and sections of his mammoth work, especially in the form of short novels, but he only imperfectly formed the faint outlines of the larger task. That the elements which made up his all-encompassing effort were woven from the filaments of his self and that that self was both woven and torn by his Southern heritage should be

beyond dispute; but in the interest of illuminating a little of both Wolfe and the literature of his region it may be worth while to point to some of the Southern qualities in his work.

The urge to represent America, to embody it in a work of art, although by no means unique to the region, has been persistent in Southern literature. . . . In 1856, for example, William Gilmore Simms, of South Carolina, had written: ". . . to be *national* in literature, one must needs be *sectional*. No one mind can fully or fairly illustrate the characteristics of any great country; and he who shall depict *one section* faithfully, has made his proper and sufficient contribution to the great work of *national* literature." . . . This view is not far from Wolfe's own, when he insists upon the representation of his unique self as the proper subject for a national art. (pp. 182-83)

It is also typical of the Southern writer that this epic portrayal of America should constitute a project of great magnitude and tremendous complexity. . . . *The Story of a Novel* [carries] the evidence of the vastness of scope and the complexity of design of the "work in progress" on which he expended his days and hours and which he left incomplete. It is startling to one who has accepted the standard view of Wolfe's works as the spontaneous and unpremeditated overflow of the author's powerful feeling, recollected in abnormal intensity, to find him writing to Maxwell E. Perkins, "I think you may be a little inclined to underestimate the importance of arrangement and presentation, and may feel that the stories can go in any way, and that the order doesn't matter much." In the light of his efforts to get on paper the theme, the argument, the structure of the large work as he labored on its parts, such a statement—although it does not redeem his novels from formlessness—makes poignant and telling Wolfe's protests against the publication of *Of Time and the River* in the form in which Perkins sent it to the press. (pp. 183-84)

The scope of [Wolfe's] ambitious plan—which was to be no less than the record of his nation and his people told through one representative man—merits in its magnitude comparison with the master projects of literary history, with Balzac and Zola and with Tolstoy. To embark upon such vast projects has also been typically, although by no means exclusively, Southern, perhaps because the Southerner tends to distrust abstraction. . . . (p. 184)

The artist's problem, [Wolfe] believed, is the resolution of a three-fold consciousness of time into a single moment so that scenes can represent "characters as acting and as being acted upon by all the accumulated impact of man's experience so that each moment of their lives was conditioned not only by what they experienced in that moment, but by all that they had experienced up to that moment," and with these actions set somehow against a consciousness of "a kind of eternal and unchanging universe of time against which must be projected the transience of man's life, the bitter briefness of his day." Whether or not Wolfe is indebted to Proust and Bergson for these ideas, he certainly envisions his characters as set in a complex fabric of time, and their actions as having remote roots and immeasurable forward extensions. . . .

Wolfe shares with many Southern writers his concerns with the reality of the past in the present and with the nature of time. One can find examples of the Southern writer's concern with time and his belief that it is, not only fact or sequence, but, more important, a key to the nature of human experience. . . . (p. 185)

The mixture of styles in which Wolfe wrote is also not uncommon in Southern writing. On one level Wolfe illustrates with great effectiveness the concrete, the immediate, the sensuous. (p. 186)

Closely associated with this concern for the concrete is Wolfe's delight in folk speech, dialect, and speech mannerisms. His works are full of accurate transcriptions of vivid speech. His characters seem sometimes to talk endlessly, but they always talk with vigor and with great distinctiveness of diction, syntax, and idiom.

Yet the same writer who displays these startlingly effective qualities of lyric concreteness and speech accuracy is also guilty of excesses in both quantity and quality of rhetoric perhaps unequaled by any other American novelist. With the power to evoke a particular object, scene, or character with remarkable clarity, he is unwilling to let these creations speak for themselves, but must try by the sheer force of rhetoric to give expression to the peculiar meanings that they suggest, to define ineffable feelings, to formulate the inchoate longings and the uncertain stirrings of spirit which he feels that all men share. (p. 187)

The drift toward rhetoric is the aspect of Wolfe's work most frequently called Southern. (p. 188)

Wolfe likewise shares the Southerner's willingness to accept and find delight in paradox. (p. 189)

Wolfe saw his world and himself through an only semilogical application to life of the Hegelian dialectic. He seemed to need to define a thing's opposite before he could comprehend the thing, and to have a naïve faith that somehow the meaning was manifest if the opposites were stated. Hence, there is in his work on practically every level—sentence, paragraph, scene, theme, large project—a structure of paradox.

But all these attributes of Wolfe's work individually are essentially superficial qualities of his "Southernness." So strong a combination of these attributes as he displays does not often occur in America outside the South; yet these qualities suggest rather than define a distinctively Southern quality. In certain other respects, however, Wolfe seems definitively Southern. One of these is his attitude toward capitalistic industrialism; another is his sense of the tragic implications of experience; and a third is his deep-seated sense of human guilt. (pp. 189-90)

Wolfe looked upon himself as a radical, even, as he once called himself, a "Revolutionary," and he angrily expressed his hatred of the gross injustice and inhumanity that the depression produced. But to him the solution was never material; indeed, the substitution of the material for the spiritual was the cause for his belief "that we are lost here in America," and only his confidence that ultimately America would put aside the material for the spiritual made it possible for him to add, "but I believe we shall be found."

Wolfe is peculiarly Southern, too, in the degree to which he sees the darkness, pain, and evil in life, and yet does not succumb to the naturalistic answer of despair. (p. 193)

[When] the nation as a whole began to experience the cataclysms of the twentieth century and to react to scientific

and philosophic views of man that were less optimistic, the American artist outside the South tended to turn to programs of Utopian reform, or satiric correction, or naturalistic despair. The Southern writer on the other hand, older in the experience of calamity and defeat, saw the tragic grandeur of man, the magnificence of his will in the face of disaster, and the glory with which he maintained the integrity of his spirit in a world of material defeat. (pp. 194-95)

Thomas Wolfe's view of man and life had this tragic sense. . . . At the conclusion of Chapter 27 of *You Can't Go Home Again,* in what is a too-obvious extension of a speech by Hamlet, Wolfe attempts to answer the question, "What is man?" and in his answer states as clearly as he ever did the extent to which his vision of experience had tragic magnitude. Man to him is "a foul, wretched, abominable creature . . . and it is impossible to say the worst of him . . . this moth of time, this dupe of brevity and numbered hours, this travesty of waste and sterile breath." Yet Wolfe stands in awe of man's accomplishments. "For there is one belief, one faith, that is man's glory, his triumph, his immortality—and that is his belief in life. . . . So this is man —the worst and best of him—this frail and petty thing who lives his days and dies like all the other animals and is forgotten. And yet, he is immortal, too, for both the good and evil that he does live after him."

The Southern writer is often obsessed with a sense of guilt and the need for expiation. . . . This sense of guilt may be the product of the pervasive Calvinism of the region; it may be the product of the poverty and suffering that the region has known; it is certainly in part the result of the guilt associated with slavery in the nineteenth century and the Negro's second-class citizenship in the twentieth—a guilt most thoughtful Southerners have felt. In any case, it appears to be a hallmark of the serious twentieth-century Southern writer. And it is a hallmark that Thomas Wolfe's work certainly bears. (pp. 195-96)

In *You Can't Go Home Again* he explicitly links this sense of guilt with the South, and in turn sees the South as a symbol and in a sense a scapegoat for the national hurt. (p. 196)

Thomas Wolfe did not live to complete his representation of his America through the portrait of himself as generic man, and out of the novels, short stories, and letters we piece out the pattern he was trying to follow and we guess at meanings and intentions. One thing seems clear: Wolfe was a Southerner, torn by the tensions and issues that thoughtful Southerners feel, oppressed as they tend to be with the tragic nature of life, and feeling as they often do a sense of guilt that demands some kind of expiating action. The work he completed had demonstrable Southern qualities; the total work, had he lived to complete it, would probably have had these qualities too. The South did, indeed, burn in his blood and on his pages like a "ruined Helen"—beautiful, passionate, and dark with violence and guilt. (p. 197)

C. Hugh Holman, "'The Dark, Ruined Helen of His Blood': Thomas Wolfe and the South," in South: Modern Southern Literature in Its Cultural Setting, *edited by Louis D. Rubin, Jr. and Robert D. Jacobs (copyright © 1961 by Louis D. Rubin, Jr. and Robert D. Jacobs; reprinted by permission of C. Hugh Holman and Louis D. Rubin), Doubleday & Company, Inc., 1961 (and reprinted by Greenwood Press, 1974, pp. 177-97).*

RICHARD WALSER (essay date 1961)

Wolfe's novels . . . constitute a reaction against the *romans bien faits* with their neat, proper, thin-blooded outlines. True, Wolfe did not often think of himself as a novelist, and he did not write in terms of stories supplied with the expected pseudoplots and conventional paraphernalia. He wished, rather, to follow life with its seemingly patternless movements, and he did not push for answers with which experience had not provided him. Nothing must be implied; everything must be told. Yet his pattern, as it turned out, was a constant progression from romanticism toward realism, from rebellion toward maturity, from youth toward responsibility.

To give unity to this progression throughout the four major novels and all the shorter pieces, Wolfe evolved a theme inherent in the material itself. In America—strange, vast, poetic—the individual was a wanderer, lonely and set apart. The autobiographical heroes Eugene Gant and George Webber were artists spurned by a collective society whose prosperous, callous mechanization had forced them into exile. The heroes struggled with town and family and school, with New York esthetes and Brooklyn philistines, with all those elements forgetful of their American heritage.

The image of the lonely, ostracized wanderer moving here and there, touching life passionately yet always readying himself for departure, is a constant one beginning with *Look Homeward, Angel.* (p. 4)

It is movement, perhaps, which most characterizes Wolfe's novels. Automobiles, boats, and trains hurl Eugene-George on to new experience. The seductive woman smoothing her legs in an upper Pullman berth is image and part of the fantasy and wish fulfillment of America. "Through you," Wolfe wrote Aline Bernstein after his first voyage to Europe, "I slid back into America again."

On the move, somewhere, would be found the glorious dream, symbolized by that beautiful, enticing woman. She (the idea of America, the woman) would be security against all degradations and failures. In her were longing and love, and Wolfe poured into his books a return of that love, even when she had to bear up under his chastisement; for only through love and desire was fulfillment possible. (p. 6)

For the straight narrative scenes he had the tried-and-true techniques of realistic fiction, valid and versatile enough to carry the burden of his intention. Infused with Wolfe's peculiar ironic commentary, it served well. Yet, for those pages where a more rhapsodic expression was indicated to unfold emotional themes, he turned to poetry. (p. 7)

In his paeans to Time and America, his hymns to Death, Loneliness and Sleep, his salutes to trains and rivers, and his tributes to night, Wolfe swept past the lyric optimism of Whitman into an epic abundance. The picture was completely there, as it always has been in the best poetry.

Perhaps he was able to write in rhapsodic vein because he was willing to be neglectful of current trends and fashionable dicta. But the reason is more that he was young with a young man's vision. It has been said that Wolfe retained his adolescence until the end, that he never worked away from a boyhood with its ideals and hopes, that he kept the pain and poetry of youth even when, in the later novels, he tried to send them on their way. There is some truth in the observation. Poetry—the best lyric poetry—is concomitant with

morning, and Wolfe wrote out of the morning of his life. Disillusionments which eventually disturbed him were soon replaced by faith.

The prose poems introducing each of the four major novels return and ring and give emphasis to the stories to be told. In them and in the colors they create, one may observe Wolfe's essential quality. (pp. 9-10)

Look Homeward, Angel carries as its subtitle "A Story of the Buried Life." What did Wolfe mean by this? Evidently the phrase was borrowed from Matthew Arnold's short poem beginning "Light flows our war of mocking words," in which Arnold comments on that part of man's life hidden behind the disguises he wears and on his inability, except in moments of love, to reveal himself. This buried life, even so, is the real one, the essential one which lends meaning to existence. Wolfe extended this notion into what he called his "plan" for the book. Before the novel was accepted for publication, he wrote that in it "There are two essential movements—one outward and one downward. The outward movement describes the effort of a child, a boy, and a youth for release, freedom, and loneliness in new lands. . . . The downward movement is represented by a constant excavation into the buried life of a group of people, and describes the cyclic curve of a family's life—genesis, union, decay, and dissolution." The buried life was a secret life, and though even Gant and Eliza had such a side, it is mainly Eugene, and to a lesser degree, Ben, who are shown to be strangers to the world.

With Eugene the secret life had much to do with imagination, by means of which he daydreamed of huge ships and faraway cities and lands which opened out. In his imagination there was belief in the great virtues: tenderness and gentleness, beauty and love and goodness, valiance and glory. (p. 61)

The essence of the buried life was a continuation of prenatal existence. If Wolfe borrowed Arnold's phrase for his subtitle, he was even more influenced by the Neoplatonic romanticism of Wordsworth and Coleridge. In the prose-poem facing the first chapter are these well remembered words: "Naked and alone we came into exile. In her dark womb we did not know our mother's face; from the prison of her flesh have we come into the unspeakable and incommunicable prison of this earth." Eugene was born trailing Wordsworthian clouds of glory, but all too soon he was suspended in time, caught in life's prison house, and the sound of the great bell ringing underseas was dimmer and dimmer. As time went on, the prison house became more stifling, and though he sought to escape the prison gates, he came to realize that his incarceration was complete and he found comfort in the fantasy of the buried life. Thus walled in, he projected "an acceptable counterfeit of himself which would protect him from intrusion." At birth he knew the word—the lost key opening the prison gates, the lane-end into heaven"—but eventually, like all who are born, he forgot it.

Re-echoes of pre-existence and the buried life persist throughout the novel and give it unity. To go a step further, [it has been contended] that Wolfe utilized, besides the pre-existence-and-return myth, other Platonic contrasts: dark and light, many and one, isolation and union, imprisonment and freedom, shadow and reality. His study and love of the romantic poets left their mark.

While the subtitle and opening sentences of *Look Home-ward, Angel* established a mood for the story to follow, they do not state a theme. Almost from the first days when Wolfe started writing the novel, there was no doubt in his mind what his intent would be. Though the materials would come from his own life, he planned to tell . . . "the story of a powerful creative element trying to work its way toward an essential isolation; a creative solitude; a secret life—its fierce struggles to wall this part of its life away from birth, first against the public and savage glare of an unbalanced, nervous brawling family group; later against school, society, all the barbarous invasions of the world." (pp. 62-3)

Throughout the novel, the mood and theme are enriched by a number of symbols which must be understood if the poetic nature of the fiction is to be fully realized. . . . [The] symbolic words *are* something at the same time they carry another intention. Moreover, like the whale in Melville, the intention is constantly shifting, rarely static.

A good example is the Angel of the title. Here are the lines from Milton's "Lycidas":

> Or whether thou [the poet's college friend who has
>   drowned], to our moist vows denied,
> Sleep'st by the fable of Bellerus old,
> Where the great Vision of the guarded mount
> Looks toward Namancos and Bayona's hold.
> Look homeward, Angel, now, and melt with ruth:
> And, O ye dolphins, waft the hapless youth.

Here Milton invokes the protector angel St. Michael to turn from foreign threats in order to weep for a disaster at home. The same meaning may be applied to Wolfe's novel. Heaven is urged to look toward home and "melt with ruth" rather than gaze afar for tragic possibilities. Altamont and the Gant family have their own pathetic lives. This poetic interpretation of the word *angel* is balanced by a palpable image: the stone angel on the porch of Gant's shop. . . . In this instance, the angel is the symbol of the creativity which, though throbbing, is suppressed in most men.

A third and more compelling interpretation, and in no way unconnected with the other two, is the angel of Ben and Eugene. Wolfe generally substituted the word ghost, the ghost being the spirit from some pre-existence. "O lost, and by the wind grieved, ghost, come back again," Wolfe reiterated. The ghost is a lonely spirit. It is sometimes synonymous with the loss of innocence as when, after Eugene's first visit to a prostitute, he "was haunted by his own lost ghost: he knew it to be irrecoverable." But the angel-ghost image, like any wraith, shifts and changes. Often it stands for corporeal life, which is not real at all, but a zombie taking the place of the real. At such times the ghost wails for a return into life from exile. The ghost therefore is lost. Eugene, himself a ghost, seeks the way of returning. "The way is here, Eugene. Have you forgotten? The leaf, the rock, the wall of light. Lift up the rock, Eugene, the leaf, the stone, the unfound door. Return, return." Then, after Ben's death, Ben *becomes* Eugene's ghost, and Ben's answer to the question "Where is the world?" is the simple one "*You* are your world." In that last chapter, the dead Ben finally has life, and he is therefore no longer a ghost. The stone angels begin to move, and with them Eugene believes himself freed. The ghost-angel reappears as creative power. (pp. 64-6)

The central and simplest theme of *Look Homeward, Angel*

is the revolt of the individual from the small town, a theme uppermost in the minds of other writers of the 1920's—Zona Gale, Sherwood Anderson, and Sinclair Lewis, to name a few. But unlike the works of these authors, *Look Homeward, Angel* was written at a time when the clouds of glory had not entirely passed away, at a time before the prison house had completely closed in. The stars were right; the union of Boy and Man was as nearly perfect as could ever be expected, and from this union came a lyrical quality rare in fiction. (pp. 70-1)

Though *Of Time and the River* does not have the unity of *Look Homeward, Angel*, it is the most typically Wolfean of the four major novels, for it has all the qualities popularly associated with its author. Poetry is still abundantly present, a youth still looks with wonder and pain and elation as he seeks fulfillment in the world, the novel is pleasantly diffuse, and it is long. . . . (pp. 72-3)

While there is no suspense or plot-involvement in the ordinary literary sense, the book is constructed on a deliberate plan. Wolfe wished, as the subtitle indicates, to write "A Legend of Man's Hunger in His Youth." Beneath the subtitle he cited Ecclesiastes 3:21, "Who knoweth the spirit of man that goeth upward, and the spirit of the beast that goeth downward to the earth?"—calling attention to the godlike nature of the sublime quest. (p. 73)

Eugene's adventures are those of a youth trying to find a mooring for his trusts and beliefs. The image has genuine force. In practically all fiction, a human being is looking for that which he does not have. Eugene lacked a knowledge of life's meaning. If he could find the Father, the understanding might be his; and so Eugene (and Wolfe, through an act of creation) sifted his experiences to see whether he might not come upon a solution of the puzzle.

From the first outline of the book, initially titled "The October Fair," Wolfe decided to give shape to Eugene's search by the use of certain Greek legends which would almost never be mentioned except in the eight section headings. From time to time, the hero would be Orestes, Telemachus, Proteus, Jason, Antaeus, and Kronos; twice, departing from the Greek myths, he would be Faust. Each would suggest the nature of the journey in that particular segment.

Before embarking on the Orestean course, Wolfe affixed a prose-poem in which with Biblical cadences he repeated some of the symbols of *Look Homeward, Angel* and then spoke of the search for the Father. The main emphasis, however, was on the endurance of the earth in contrast to the passing and death of the flesh. Only immortal love endured as the earth endured. From these poetic paragraphs the phrase most echoed throughout the novel is ". . . of wandering forever and the earth again. . . ." By "earth again" Wolfe explained that he meant simply "a place for the heart to come to," but according to Virginia Stevens there is more to the phrase than that. The "wandering" is equivalent to the North, to the Father, and to the eternal seeking; the "earth" is the South, the mother, the need for roots. These opposites were combined in Eugene, and from their unresolved contradistinction the events of the narrative develop. (pp. 74-5)

Throughout *The Web and the Rock* there is a duality which operates on a number of levels. In the first place, there are the two unconnected parts which seem even more disjointed because of the lapse of time between their writing. The Monk of Libya Hill and the Monk of New York are almost two different persons. Second, two cultures are always opposed: among others, town and city, Gentile simplicity and Jewish opulence. Then, too, in Monk and Esther, Wolfe contrasts youth and age, innocence and sophistication.

This duality, even so, fails to build a new character out of Monk. Unlike Eugene Gant, he is shadowy and objectionably egocentric. It is difficult for a reader to sympathize with his self-torture, his invented prejudices, his madness, and most of all his shabby treatment of Esther. If his sensitivity and physical strangeness set him apart from other people, if acquaintances and those who loved him failed always to bow immediately before his unproved genius, Monk was no different from thousands of other American youths. Monk's agonies are more culpable, by far, than the bouncing hungers of Eugene Gant.

Unsatisfactory as all these things are, *The Web and the Rock* is, of course, a necessary link in the Wolfe saga. In that last chapter, one feels, Monk (or Wolfe-Gant) looks at himself honestly and sensibly for the first time. Within a half hour he is no longer a boy, but has become a man. Romanticism (subjectivity) has been altered, regrettably perhaps, into realism (objectivity). The transition was made quietly but it was finally made. And the one who is basically responsible for it is Esther Jack, one of Wolfe's great living creations. Her tragic misfortune was to love a man almost twenty years younger than she, and to love him beyond his belief in himself.

Aside from the incompletely realized hero of the book, other weaknesses are obvious. Excursive essays, like those in the first sections, continue intruding upon the narrative. Often there is no preparation for some significant phase of the story: as when suddenly Monk, without apprenticeship, is said to be putting his main strength into writing a novel; or when in the Old Pinakothek in Munich, never having been warned that he had any interest in art, we are abruptly given paragraphs on Monk's sensuous appreciation of painting.... And not once in Munich—after Monk's convulsive pangs in England and France—is there a mention of Esther, though we were told so defiantly that in Europe "he did nothing but remember her." But, then, much of "Oktoberfest" belongs to *Of Time and the River.* This fault of Wolfe's in looking backward is awkwardly balanced by a looking forward: for instance, Monk's sympathy, following the break with Esther, for the downtrodden—a distinguishing characteristic of *You Can't Go Home Again* but not of its predecessors. (pp. 102-03)

Because his desire for objectivity was so determined, there are fewer strains of prose-poetry in the book. Yet Wolfe (through George Webber) was still exploring for "the substance of his own America ... still seeking home." In the last pages the poetic fantasy of Body and spirit foreshadows an end of the search. The great discovery, finally, would be made in *You Can't Go Home Again.* (p. 104)

Although the action of Wolfe's fourth novel follows hard upon the action of the third, there is a change of emphasis. As Wolfe carried his autobiographical story forward, a theme which persisted and recurred and hammered away in his brain without his knowing exactly what it meant was the notion that there is no going home again, no turning back,

no reliving time. In *You Can't Go Home Again,* this theme seems, finally, to crystallize the notion. (p. 105)

On its publication ... *You Can't Go Home Again* was joyfully received in some quarters as long-awaited evidence that Thomas Wolfe had at last matured. It was this book, not *The Web and the Rock,* which discharged his promise of objectivity. While it is difficult to define literary maturity, and it is speculative, certainly, to attest whether maturity is always desirable, no one can deny Wolfe's shift in emphasis. Like a scholar, George Webber began to see relationships and associations and resemblances in all aspects of life.... Instead of nursing a passionate solicitude for himself, Webber had thoughts and eyes always turning outwards. In a Christian sense, he found himself when he looked with pity and sympathy upon others.

This lessening of self-concentration was accompanied by a diminishing of lyric exuberance in style. Only occasionally in *You Can't Go Home Again* does youthful enthusiasm bubble through into poetry. In its place was a personal research into problems about him, into situations in which he was merely a single minor character or a lone observer: American business practices, economic fluctuations, race, international politics. One does not write poetry when reporting the findings of investigation.

Examination of one type of episode after another ... shows that Wolfe had his hero Webber reach a conclusion following each of them. The novel, on this plan, is a series of rejections and a final acceptance. Discarded as insufficient are (in this order): blind hometown allegiance, privilege and love, praise and success, social uninvolvement, Fame, man's inhumanity to his fellows, and fatalistic determinism. At the end, by a process of elimination, Webber can cry out his Whitmanian belief in a "mystical evolution" toward betterment.

In the poetic statement which prefaces the first chapter, Wolfe recorded that it "seemed to him that all man's life was like a tiny spurt of flame that blazed out briefly in an illimitable and terrifying darkness, and that all man's grandeur, tragic dignity, his heroic glory, came from the brevity and smallness of this flame." *You Can't Go Home Again* is the affirmation of this tragic glory. (pp. 106-07)

In the final analysis ... Wolfe's success or failure rests on his adventure with the American Dream, as this Dream was developed from the time of Jefferson on through Emerson and Whitman up to the first quarter of the twentieth century. The Dream encompassed the hopes of young men everywhere for democracy and liberty and equality and individuality. It was an ideal and a promise. Wolfe was an American writer, not only because his problems were those of an American within America, but because his youth demanded fulfillment in a land where individual fulfillment was possible. In this Dream, it was Whitman who was his nearest spirit. Each of them spoke poetically out of his loneliness for all the young artists—and every young man is an artist to himself—across the sweep and breadth of the great land.

Before he completed his investigation into the nature of permanent acceptance in America, Wolfe had won within himself the struggle which is the essence of all human drama. With courage and honor, he had discovered through experience that his lot was common to that of all men. Out of his life and out of this discovery came the books. (p. 143)

Richard Walser, in his Thomas Wolfe: An Introduction and Interpretation *(copyright © Barnes & Noble, Inc. 1961; by permission of Barnes & Noble Books, a Division of Littlefield, Adams & Co., Inc.), Barnes & Noble, 1961, 152 p.*

CLYDE C. CLEMENTS, JR.   (essay date 1965)

[The] real concern of *You Can't Go Home Again* is] the development of the protagonist, George Webber, who is a conscientious artist struggling with his life material to find a philosophic purpose, that is, where he can go spiritually with his allegiances. The process of rejecting personal and social illusions as he matures is essential to the ultimate veracity of his vision. Thus Wolfe's book lies in a literary tradition with the short stories of Hawthorne and James, which trace the development of the artistic credo.

These syndromes in the artist-philosopher's search are structured by symbolic patterns, in each case Webber feels attraction, undergoes enlightenment and then forces severance of an illusion which he had held to be all-sufficient. The symbolic patterns fall into three groupings, Reminiscence, Progression, and Projection, reflecting stages in his search. I have identified the following symbolic patterns in *You Can't Go Home Again:*

> *Symbolic Patterns of Reminiscence*
>   The Pattern of the Family
>   The Pattern of the Hometown
> *Symbolic Patterns of Progression*
>   The Pattern of the Business Ethic
>   The Pattern of Love and Art
> *Symbolic Patterns of Projection*
>   The Pattern of Fame in Exile
>   The Pattern of the Father   (p. 231)

[*Pattern of the Family:*] Although the novel starts out with George Webber in the city, the first significant action occurs when he is summoned home for the funeral of Aunt Maw. Webber feels the pull of a powerful sense of family ties. . . .

In the cemetery Webber encounters Delia Flood, an old friend of the family, who reminds him: "'Your Aunt Maw always hoped you'd come home again. And you *will!*'."' . . .

But the young writer rejects the entreaty to return to the family, for George Webber is *not* Eugene Gant, nor is Aunt Maw an eternal mother symbol like Eliza Gant whom the son will always feel drawn back to. When Wolfe changed the history of his protagonist, he replaced the fecund Eliza with Aunt Maw, a virgin who regards any interest in the flesh with suspicion, and substituted John Webber, a shadowy figure who ran away from his responsibilities as a father, for the monumental W. O. Gant. With his foster mother dead and his father gone, Webber painfully realizes that there can be no lasting relationship between an educated writer who moved in fashionable New York society and his half-mad mountain kin. Thus the illusion of the family which seemed to represent security, understanding, and everlasting ties is not sufficient, and Webber has experienced attraction, enlightenment, and severance in this symbolic pattern. (p. 232)

[*Pattern of the Hometown:*] If Webber feels a lost security in his family, he anticipates in the familiar rural landmarks of his hometown, a symbol of permanence in a life of muta-

bility. . . . Yet no sooner does he board the train for Libya Hill than Webber hears talking of burgeoning real-estate developments, of remaking his hometown into something bigger and better. Wolfe has drawn portraits in the social satire mold of Sinclair Lewis of the corrupt townsmen who relate the "progress" in Libya Hill. . . . However, the changes in his hometown are scored upon Webber's consciousness by his encounter with three symbolic characters: Nebraska Cane, J. Timothy Wagner, and Judge Rumford Bland.

Nebraska Crane, a character of pure invention, the Cherokee Indian who was a boyhood friend of Webber, has become a famous baseball star, wealthy and able to retire wherever he wants. On the train, when Wolfe asks him if he will be bored by life back on a farm in Zebulon, he reveals an attitude directly opposite to the corrupt town leaders. Crane is the only one of Webber's hometown acquaintances who conceives of land as a place to live and work on.

Still another meaning is evident in J. Timothy Wagner, "the high priest and prophet of this insanity of waste," . . . a symbol of the complete derangement of values of the town. . . . (pp. 232-33)

If the townspeople flung paper fortunes away on the whim of a false prophet, they failed to heed another local prophet, Judge Rumford Bland. In a short number of pages, Wolfe has created a symbolic figure of the proportions of the Gant family. Bland is a mixture of good and evil, "a fallen angel" who has tasted the fruits of forbidden knowledge. Blind now, an unmistakable parallel to Tiresias, he had started with all the advantages of a distinguished family. . . . (pp. 233-34)

The tragedy of Judge Bland, a potentially great man who had ruined himself, was symbolic of the basically honest and rural Libya Hill, a town that had ruined itself. Webber has learned that the hometown of his spirit has changed radically in form and values, and he cannot go back to any certainty there. (p. 234)

[*Pattern of the Business Ethic:*] Disappointed in his philosophic search in reminiscence, Webber, an activist, turns to the present for answers—to the values of the new "American way" of the 1920's, the business ethic. The symbolic pattern of the business ethic goes beyond "the city" as a stronghold of dishonest privilege, being a folly of all America from Libya Hill to New York City, eventually bringing economic and moral collapse. (pp. 234-35)

In New York City Webber feels [an] attraction to the world of society, supported by the business ethic, before he senses enlightenment about its values and forces severance. The wealthy Mr. Jack and his friends delight in the animal-like struggle of laissez faire, convinced that their professional hardness and amorality selects them for privilege. . . .

Wolfe uses the party at Jack's, which ends in a climactic fire, as a symbolic device to represent both the privilege and the disintegration of society based on the business ethic. He juxtaposes the events at the party just one week before the stock market crash, which ushered in the depression. The figures from the world of finance, the theatrical, literary and international set are superficial, jaded with power, or perverse. Their phony liberalism is exposed by such business practices as child labor and strike-breaking.

The eventual failure of the business ethic is foreshadowed by the accidental fire in the apartment building, which reveals the impotence of their wealth, and the leveling of social classes in the depression, as all types and classes seek refuge and mingle in the sidewalk below. Ironically, and to the point, the only persons killed in the fire are two working men, Enborg and Anderson. Corrosion of moral values becomes more apparent in the attitude of the management, concerned only with protecting their wealthy tenants from unpleasant news.

After the party Webber rejects the world of the business ethic. . . . (p. 235)

[Pattern of Love and Art:] Love and art function closely as a single symbolic pattern in You Can't Go Home Again. Webber has a selfish and self-justifying attitude toward love, and toward art for the sake of art; these are tied up with his sexual relationship to Mrs. Jack. . . .

As the novel opens, Webber returns to New York, finding Esther Jack and feeling again their tremendous pull of love. (p. 236)

As symbolic device, the party at Jack's functions to show him that personal bonds of love are wrong because they bind him to a world with twisted values about life and art. The characters at the party treat love as an experiment or as a purchasable commodity. The beautiful Lily Mandell's aversion toward the wealthy Mr. Hirsch is calculated to raise the price of her eventual seduction. Even the extravagant critical acclaim given to Piggy Logan's circus cannot blunt the inanity of this tedious spectacle. The pièce de résistance of Logan's circus, an act in which he persists in pressing a pin down the doll's throat until the stuffed entrails spill out, suggests the hollowness of the society approving this spectacle. Piggy Logan's circus, which has been held up as the ultimate measure of sensibility and culture, is a symbol of the inner emptiness of Esther's society. Since the illusion of love means condoning the twisted values of Esther Jack's society, Wolfe writes, "The fire was over," . . . ambiguously suggesting the extinguishment of Webber's love as well as the apartment conflagration.

After his break with Esther Jack, Webber is free to reevaluate his artistic credo—his pained reaction to hometown disapproval has been to assume the role of the artist, sensitive and misunderstood. . . . Under Randy Shepperton's questioning he begins to realize that his arrogant posture may have marred his art. . . . (pp. 236-37)

From now on, Webber resolves to be as objective about himself as he would be about any material for fiction. In rejecting the illusions of the young provincial, he finds he "can't go home again" to art for the sake of art, or to love for the sake of love. The rejection of these values within this symbolic pattern helps to prepare Webber for a broader vision. (p. 237)

[Pattern of Fame in Exile:] Failing to find a purpose in reminiscence or progression, Webber seeks in a projection, the idea of fame in exile, an answer to his quest. Since the main outline of this symbolic pattern is given in the introduction, a few corroborative details will be presented. Bound for Europe, Webber seeks renewal in a search for fame: "And by his side was that stern friend, the only one to whom he spoke what in his secret heart he most desired. To Loneliness he whispered, 'Fame!'" . . . His projection assumes

grandiose proportions, Milton and Goethe are cited as authority, and even the American Dream becomes the chance for anyone to achieve fame.

But his trip through the English countryside with the embodiment of fame, McHarg, is a fiasco, compared to the Walpurgis Night of Faust, and Webber perceives fame has given his idol no security or peace. Nevertheless, he cannot resist fame in Germany where he receives adulation and praise for his work, although he becomes uneasy at the Olympic games of 1936, which seem to be chosen as "a symbol of the new collective might." . . . The fear, suspicion, and tyranny of the Nazis are concretized in the abduction of the Jewish banker on Webber's train. . . . Wolfe seems to use traditional Christian symbolism to emphasize the inner torment Webber experiences as he conceals the money the banker had given him to hide: "Turning half away, he thrust his hands into his pockets—and drew them out as though his fingers had been burned. The man's money—he still had it! . . . felt the five two-mark pieces. The coins seemed greasy, as if they were covered with sweat." . . . There can be no return to the illusory place that promised identity and purpose for the writer. (pp. 237-38)

[Pattern of the Father:] When Webber leaves Germany, one illusion still binds him to a pattern of return: that of the symbolic father. . . . In You Can't Go Home Again Webber's editor, Foxhall Edwards, assumes this role. . . . Wolfe also provides a suitable fictional background by giving Webber a most indistinct father and making Edwards a father without a son.

But after this attraction, the emotional Webber begins to tire of Edwards' rationalistic fatalism. Edwards' intelligence is described in animal imagery usually reserved for unsympathetic characters like Piggy Logan. . . . (pp. 238-39)

In his letter of resignation to Edwards' publishing house, Webber rejects the editor's fatalistic attitude, which he equates with Ecclesiasticus, for a philosophy of activism. . . . Webber realizes that the search for the symbolic father is over; there exists no magical "someone who can help you, save you, ease the burden for you." Again Webber's reaction to the father figure has been in the customary form: attraction, enlightenment, and severance.

The meaning of the final symbolic statement of "you can't go home again" is found in the summation of the individual symbol patterns of reminiscence, progression, and projection. By the process of attraction, enlightenment, and severance Webber has suggested six major illusions that may prevent a meaningful vision for the artist. Divested of his false personal and social symbols, he is liberated to concern himself with the problems of his fellow man. And just as for him there is no going back, there can be no return of America to old ways and solutions. Only if society is ever ready "to look into the face of fear itself, to probe behind it, to see what caused it, and then to speak the truth about it," . . . will the recurring "single selfishness and compulsive greed" . . . be overcome, in short, be willing to discard its own illusions.

Where can Webber find the purpose he so earnestly desires? The answer lies where the quest began, in America—in the promise and true discovery of the American Dream. Finally, Webber stands as the artist firmly within his society, not alienated from it. (pp. 239-40)

Clyde C. Clements, Jr., "Symbolic Patterns in 'You Can't Go Home Again'," in Modern Fiction Studies (© *copyright 1965 by the Purdue Research Foundation, West Lafayette, Indiana), Vol. XI, No. 3, Autumn, 1965 (and reprinted in* Thomas Wolfe: Three Decades of Criticism, *edited by Leslie A. Field, New York University Press, 1968, pp. 229-40).*

WILLIAM STYRON　(essay date 1968)

Rereading Wolfe is like visiting again a cherished landscape or town of bygone years where one is simultaneously moved that much could remain so appealingly the same and wonderstruck that one could ever have thought that such-and-such a corner or this or that view had any charm at all. It is not really that Wolfe is dated (I mean the fact of being dated as having to do with basically insincere postures and attitudes: already a lot of Hemingway is dated in a way Wolfe could never be); it is rather that when we now begin to realize how unpulled-together Wolfe's work really is—that same shapelessness that mattered so little to us when we were younger—and how this shapelessness causes or at least allows for a lack of inner dramatic tension without which no writer, not even Proust, can engage our mature attention for long, we see that he is simply telling us, often rather badly, things we no longer care about knowing or need to know. So much that once seemed grand and authoritative now comes off as merely obtrusive, strenuously willed, and superfluous. Which of course makes it all the more disturbing that in the midst of this chaotically verbose and sprawling world there stand out here and there truly remarkable edifices of imaginative cohesion.

Wolfe's first novel, *Look Homeward, Angel,* withstands the rigors of time most successfully and remains his best book, taken as a whole. Here the powers of mind and heart most smoothly find their confluence, while a sense of place (mainly Altamont, or Asheville) and time (a boy's life between infancy and the beginning of adulthood) lend to the book a genuine unity that Wolfe never recaptured in his later works. Flaws now appear, however. A recent rereading of the book caused me to wince from time to time in a way that I cannot recall having done during my first reading at eighteen. Wolfe at that point was deeply under the power of Joyce . . . and if the influence of *Ulysses* can be discerned in the book's many strengths it can also be seen in its gaucheries. (p. 100)

But *Look Homeward, Angel* can be forgiven such lapses precisely because it is a youthful book, as impressive in its sheer lyricism and hymnal celebration of youth and life as is the Mendelssohn *Violin Concerto,* from which we do not expect profundities either. In addition, the novel is quite extraordinarily *alive*—alive in the vitality of its words (Wolfe wrote many bad sentences but *never* a dead one) in its splendid evocation of small-town sights and sounds and smells and, above all and most importantly, in the characters that spring out fully fleshed and breathing from the pages. The figures of W. O. and Eliza Gant are as infuriatingly garrulous and convincing now as when I first made their acquaintance, and the death of the tragic older brother Ben is fully as moving for the simple reason that Wolfe has made me believe in his existence. With all of its topheaviness and the juvenile extravagances that occasionally mar the surface of the narrative, *Look Homeward, Angel* seems likely to stand as long as any novel will as a record of early twentieth-century provincial American life.

It is when we run into *Of Time and the River* and its elephantine successors, *The Web and the Rock* and *You Can't Go Home Again,* that the real trouble begins. One of the crucial struggles that any writer of significance has had to endure is his involvement in the search for a meaningful theme, and Wolfe was no exception. The evidence is that Wolfe, though superbly gifted at imaginative projection, was practically incapable of extended dramatic invention, his creative process being akin to the setting into motion of some marvelous mnemonic tape recorder deep within his cerebrum, from which he unspooled reel after reel of the murmurous, living past. Such a technique served him beautifully in *Look Homeward, Angel,* unified as it was in time and space and from both of which it derived its dramatic tension; but in the later works as Tom-Eugene-George moved into other environments—the ambience of Harvard and New York and, later, of Europe—the theme which at first had been so fresh and compelling lost its wings and the narrator became a solipsistic groundling. Certainly the last three books are still well worth reading; there is still the powerful, inexorable rush of language, a Niagara of words astonishing simply by virtue of its primal energy; many of the great set pieces hold up with their original force: old Gant's death, the *Oktoberfest* sequence in Munich, the apartment-house fire in New York. . . . These scenes and characterizations would alone guarantee Wolfe a kind of permanence, even if one must sift through a lot of detritus to find them. But there is so much now that palls and irritates. That furrow-browed, earnest sense of discovery in which the reader participates willingly in *Look Homeward, Angel* loses a great deal of its vivacity when the same protagonist has begun to pass into adulthood. (pp. 100-01)

[An] exaggerated sensibility, [a] club-footed gawky boy's style, becomes increasingly apparent throughout all of Wolfe's later work, in which the author-protagonist, now out in the world of Northern sophisticates, falls unconsciously into the role of the suspicious young hick from Buncombe County, North Carolina. (p. 101)

[Another] trait which crops up increasingly in the later books . . . is a tendency to generalize promiscuously about places and things which demand, if anything, narrow and delicate particularization—especially about a place as various and as chaotically complex as America. . . . Wolfe's writing is filled with . . . silly hyperbole. . . . [A] statement such as "we are so lost, so naked, and so lonely in America"—a refrain that reappears over and over again in Wolfe's work—seems to me the worst sort of empty rant, all the more so because Wolfe himself surely knew better, knew that lostness, nakedness, loneliness are not American but part of the whole human condition.

It is sad that so much disappoints on a rereading of Wolfe, sad that the "magic and the singing and the gold" which he celebrated so passionately seem now, within his multitudinous pages, to possess a lackluster quality to which the middle-aging heart can no longer respond. It is especially sad because we can now see (possibly because of the very contrast with all that is so prolix and adolescent and unfelt and labored) that at his best Wolfe was capable of those epiphanies that only writers of a very high order have ever achieved. (p. 102)

Wolfe would have to be cherished if only for the power he exerted upon a whole generation. But even if this were not enough, the clear glimpses he had at certain moments of man as a strange, suffering animal alone beneath the blazing and indifferent stars would suffice to earn him honor, and a flawed but undeniable greatness. (p. 104)

> *William Styron, "The Shade of Thomas Wolfe" (reprinted by permission of The Harold Matson Co.), in Harper's, Vol. 236, No. 1415, April, 1968, pp. 96, 98-102, 104.*

LOUIS D. RUBIN, JR.   (essay date 1973)

Encountering Wolfe, particularly if one is young and a would-be writer, has often turned out to be not merely an event; it is an emotional experience. There have been few American authors, I think, who have been capable of affording just this particular kind of intense experience. . . . What Wolfe did was not merely to dramatize the stories of his protagonists' lives; he also dramatized his desire to tell about those lives. . . . In a sense, all of Wolfe's novels are about the feelings of a young man who wants to write, and it is to this that so many of his readers have responded. (pp. 2-3)

[At the age of nineteen I first] read *Look Homeward, Angel,* and straightaway was transported into a realm of literary experience that I had not known could exist. No writer, as Thoreau once remarked of Whitman, can communicate a new experience to us; but what he can do is to make us recognize the importance of our own experience, so that we become aware, for the first time, of what it is that we feel and think and what it can mean for us. That is what Thomas Wolfe did for me. He described a young man whose sensuous apprehension of life was matched by his appetite for feeling. Not only did he render the concrete details of experience in brilliant specificity, but he responded to the details lavishly and lyrically. Everything he thought, observed, and did was suffused with feeling. For a young reader such as myself there could be an instantaneous and quite exhilarating identification, not only with the youthful protagonist Eugene Gant, but with the autobiographical author who was describing Eugene's experience with so much approval and pride. And it was on emotional response—not in its subtlety or discrimination, but in its intensity—that the highest premium was placed. (p. 3)

What Wolfe was saying was that feeling counted for everything and that if you could feel intensely enough about the things of your world, it was all the proof needed to know that you were virtuous.

It was the description, the concrete emotional evocation of the space and color and time of a young man's developing experience of himself and his world, that gave body to the Wolfe novels, anchored the rhetoric, and . . . ultimately helped to protect the art against the weakness of the rhetoric when, as sometimes in the early work and more frequently later, it tended to dissolve into empty assertion. (pp. 4-5)

Thomas Wolfe was brilliantly able, for readers such as . . . myself, to render the sense of being young. He did this in part with the rhetoric, to be sure—but most of all it was the world of experience that he opened up to vision. For a young man the world is apt to seem imminently there for the taking—and Thomas Wolfe portrayed it in glowing color and brilliant detail, shot full of emotional response. . . . Wolfe took the mundane, the ordinary, the humdrum and recreated them so sharply in language that you saw them for almost the first time. Or rather, he drew together and articulated the diffused and latent emotional impressions you had about something so that for the first time you recognized what you really saw and felt.

Wolfe's great subject, especially after *Look Homeward, Angel,* was America. He rendered in poetically, gave it a glamor and mystery, and made the places you were living in, and just beginning to explore, seem full of promise and excitement. (pp. 6-7)

In *Look Homeward, Angel,* he sent Eugene Gant on a walk through downtown Altamont, and described dentist's offices, laundrywomen, undertaker's parlors, Y.M.C.A. secretaries, milliner's shops, and the like in a series of little vignettes of vivid color, and, concluded each with a quotation from a poem, as much as to say that in such mundane, everyday activities the same aesthetic response was appropriate as in the more literarily respectable objects depicted by the English poets. (p. 7)

No one could depict a train trip with more excitement than Wolfe. The poetry of motion was his forte; it was not merely a matter of making a trip in order to arrive at this destination or that, but the experience of going for its own sake that enthralled him, and he portrayed it in a way that caught the imagination. (p. 8)

Many of the most moving lyrical passages in Wolfe's work after *Look Homeward, Angel* involve . . . moments in which Eugene Gant, and less occasionally George Webber, look on people from a train window and recognize their kinship and their own loneliness. Such moments, however, are transitory; the human contact is limited to the momentary glimpse, whereupon the train moves on. (p. 9)

On the one hand there is, especially in *Look Homeward, Angel* but often elsewhere as well, a portrayal of aspects of the American scene that are concrete, evocative, enormously affective. And there is also, in the work after the first novel, a deliberate and cumulative attempt to depict the idea of America itself—an attempt which, though involving much itemization and often long catalogs, is usually singularly impersonal in nature, in that the numerous specific items are chosen as typical examples rather than for themselves. The human contacts, in other words, are as viewed through a train window, and neither lasting nor individualized. Wolfe seeks to give them meaning through emotional rhetoric, the emotion belonging to his protagonist as he views them and to the novelist as he remembers viewing them. In page after page of *Of Time and the River* Eugene Gant is shown "experiencing" America, both while travelling across it and afterward through memory while in France. His longing for it while abroad is agonizing, his view of it as seen from train windows is full of love, compassion, desire. But when viewed in this way, as *America.* it consists entirely of lists, catalogs, assemblages of examples. It is, in other words, almost entirely quantitative, a collection of items, scenes, themes, names. There is little or no sorting out, no choosing of some of the items as more or less uniquely or typically American, more or less beautiful or meaningful, than others. And at the end what has been given is an abstraction, "America," along with a display of items that are proposed as typical examples of its makeup. (p. 10)

What the "America" episodes do is to dramatize both the Wolfean protagonist's and, importantly, the authorial personality's yearning for experience. The very fact that the emotional hunger is there in such abundance and that it cannot quite make contact with—or, to continue the metaphor, find adequate spiritual nourishment in—the substance at which it is being so urgently directed is itself a device for imaging the sense of loneliness and spiritual yearning that lies at the heart of the experience of reading the novels. And we go wrong, I think, if we refuse to accept that dimension and dismiss such a viewpoint as an example of the so-called "imitative fallacy." For the experience of fiction is a subtle and complex affair, and if we try to leave out the "rhetoric" of the art, the formal function of the presence of the storyteller in our reading of the story he is telling, we may impoverish our relationship with a work of fiction.

What I am getting at is that in his fiction, . . . Wolfe *dramatizes himself as author,* warts and all. Or more precisely, he dramatizes himself in the act of looking at himself. What is involved here is not just a biographical matter, a formal, literary relationship. Not only was Wolfe's protagonist a dramatized version of himself when a bit younger, but the rhetoric of the interpretative description serves to set up a myself-when-younger relationship between the storyteller and the protagonist. (pp. 10-11)

This dual identity as character and chronicler, enforced through rhetoric and attitude, is both the strength and the weakness of the Wolfe books. It enables Wolfe to bring to bear on his youthful protagonist's experience the impressive powers of his rhetoric. He can recognize, explore, and delineate the particularities of that experience. He can use the affective possibilities of rhetoric to intensify the meaning of the experience, and guide our response to it. He can, in other words, both show and persuade. Because the persuasion is coming from a formally established point of view, a recreating authorial personality, . . . it takes on an authority that would otherwise be lacking if it were merely arbitrary authorial embellishment. . . . (p. 12)

But just as surely, it can work that way only if we are willing to believe in the validity of both the youthful protagonist's experience and the recreating interpreter's delineation of its importance. If ever we feel that what the speaker tells us about the meaning of what happened is exaggerated, or confused, or actually inaccurate, and the whole relationship breaks down. For the rhetorical stance of this remembering sensibility has got to be plausible, too. When the author says that Eugene did or thought such and such, we accept that; but when he insists that what Eugene did or thought signifies this or that about human experience, and we believe that it doesn't so signify, he is in trouble; and when he tries to enforce his interpretation by cascades of affective rhetoric, what results is something very different from what he intends. Let me cite [an] example, from the material posthumously published as a novel, *The Web and the Rock.* [The passage contains the scene in which] Wolfe is describing young George Webber's feeling and behavior at a time when he had been quarreling with his mistress. His novel has been rejected, he is in bad shape emotionally, and sometimes, when he telephones his mistress' home to find her not in, he imagines that Esther is betraying him. (pp. 12-13)

[In this passage] there are two levels of experience. One is that of George Webber in love, as he suspects his mistress and suffers. However, by use of the conditional tense—George "*would* leave the phone to drain the bottle," and "*would* be hurled through tunnels"—the author makes it clear that the experience is one that happened to George on characteristic occasions, rather than just the time being described. Clearly, therefore, it is the authorial personality who is speaking to us, recapitulating and summarizing his protagonist's experience over a period of time. Now presumably what the author is doing is showing us how it was with young George Webber at a bad time. It is not that Esther Jack is really betraying George; rather, George, in his pain and torment, imagines that she is, and on such occasions goes off like a madman into the night to wander about the city in his anguish. Under such conditions, his behavior could hardly be termed inexplicable. Nor would it be improbable that at such a time, drunk, distraught, despondent, George might well envision the city through which he is wandering in just such [a hellish] fashion as described. But exactly who is it that sees the walk as a "prowl" along "a hundred streets," during which George looks "into a million livid faces seeing death in all of them"? To whom does "the ragged edge of Brooklyn" appear as "some hideous outpost," as "a wasteland horror of bare lots and rust and rubbish," and of "dismal little houses flung rawly down upon the barren earth"? Is it the distraught young protagonist or the supposedly more objective authorial personality who interprets what happened? The answer, syntactically and emotionally, is that both of them see and evaluate it that way. . . . [There] is thus little or no difference between the two perspectives. At such moments, all too frequent after *Look Homeward, Angel,* the reader is likely to refuse to accept the interpretation of George Webber's experience which the author is insisting upon. He can go along with the notion that young George Webber may have felt this way about the city at the time, and that George may indeed have imagined he was prowling a hundred streets and looking into a million livid faces, but when the story-teller, the remembering author who as interpreter and judge ought not still to feel betrayed and overcome with a sense of failure, also interprets and evaluates the experience in that fashion, without irony or humor or reservation of any sort, it is something else again. The sympathy and understanding the reader might have for the youthful George Webber at such times of torment is seriously undercut when he realizes that the author is in complete agreement with his protagonist, that he sees nothing excessive, nothing pathological, nothing childish or histrionic in George's attitude, but is recounting it with complete approval and endorsement.

The experience of Thomas Wolfe's fiction, therefore, involves two factors. One is the way in which the doings of the protagonists of the novels are described and communicated to us. The other is the way in which the authorial voice interprets and evaluates those doings. But these two factors cannot be separated from each other and considered in isolation. The impact of the first, as we have seen, is made possible in part by the second. (pp. 13-15)

[While] many readers will agree with the burden of De Voto's strictures [see excerpt above], which is that *Of Time and the River* is an overwritten and unstructured book that would have profited greatly by a great deal more cutting and revising than the author was willing to give it, it should be recognized that De Voto's memorable assault fails to comprehend how the Wolfe novels actually work as fiction. De Voto's theory of fiction dismissed absolutely what we have seen is a necessary dimension to the art of fiction as practiced by Wolfe—that conscious presence of the authorial voice interpreting the doings of the protagonist. . . . De Voto said, "A novelist represents life. When he does anything else, no matter how beautiful or furious or ecstatic the way in which he does it, he is not writing fiction." . . . [But] part of the representing—in Aristotelian terms, the imitation—happens to be the act of giving order and meaning, and when Wolfe uses his authorial rhetoric to reinforce, interpret, comment upon his protagonist's actions and thoughts, we object not when the rhetoric as such shows up, but only as it fails to enhance our interpretation and evaluation of what the protagonist's life means. When it does fit the occasion, when what the authorial personality says about the protagonist seems believable and appropriate, then, far from being disconcerted by the presence of the rhetoric, we accept it and let it help us take part in the experience of the fiction. What I think De Voto really objected to was not the asserting, ranting, or detonating rhetoric of the novelist; it was the inappropriateness of such rhetoric as an accurate and believable interpretation of the experience being chronicled. . . . [The] more the author goes on . . . the less convincing he seems.

The intense experience that reading Wolfe can be for the young . . . is possible precisely because of the ability and the willingness of a certain kind of younger reader to accept, at face value and as a version of the truth, just the signification that the narrator is attaching to it. This reader identifies with the author. For him a rhetorical exercise such as that involving the spirit of America [represented by Eugene's train trip northward] isn't "placental" at all rather, it is an important part of the experience of reading *Of Time and the River,* because it pronounces the meaning and significance of the train trip and reinforces the feelings of the younger Eugene Gant who made the trip with the more "mature" rhetorical approval of the author telling about it. The book works by an alternation of viewpoint between the younger Eugene and his older writing self, in which the younger man acts and feels and thinks and then the older man not only expresses his approval but confirms the verdict in emotive rhetoric. The charm, for the younger reader, lies in the fact that although the older, commenting narrator is, by dint of his rhetorical skill and the obvious fact that he wrote the book, no mere youth first undergoing the experience, he nevertheless not only accepts and ratifies the younger viewpoint but extols it as being even more significant than the younger protagonist himself had realized. The verve, the self-importance, the romantic insistence upon uniqueness of sensibility, the essentially uncritical, quantitative hunger for sensation of the adolescent and post-adolescent, free of qualification or ironic presentation by the older narrator, are enthusiastically received by many younger readers. (pp. 17-19)

The difficulty for the adult reader of the Wolfe novels, in particular after *Look Homeward, Angel,* is that not only does the autobiographical protagonist insist upon holding on to his immaturity, but the interpreting author equally insists upon the entire appropriateness of his doing so and upon the spiritual insensitivity of all who refuse to go along with him when he does it. Furthermore, the authorial commentator, for all his approval, appears to become increasingly apprehensive that others may not share his approba-

tion, and his response is to double and treble his own rhetorical assertion of the rightness of Eugene's behavior, attempting to sweep away all possible objections, including perhaps his own, in a torrent of words. This is the material that De Voto calls placental. It is not that, so much as simply superfluous. (p. 21)

What we have in the Wolfe fiction, then, is the dramatized record of a talented and romantic young writer's encounter with the experience of being an artist in America, as it forced itself upon him. He described it happening, and he told us what he thought it meant. Especially after his first book, what he said it meant is often not what we think it really did mean, but there can be no mistaking the earnestness with which he presented his case or any questioning of the artistic honesty of the attempt. We may disagree with the interpretation, may feel sometimes that he is trying to justify what cannot and should not be justified, and sometimes even that he is using his rhetoric to persuade himself as well as the reader. But let this be said: he never spares himself, never hides behind cheap deceits or clever, modish poses. His aim, as Faulkner says, was to tell it all, and though by no means always sure of what it was he was telling, he did his best. This is why it seems to me that even *Of Time and the River,* for all its excess and its attitudinizing, comes out as a pretty good book. We may not like all of what we see in it, but there can be no doubt we have experienced something very formidable and very honest. What we have experienced is Thomas Wolfe trying to tell about himself as Eugene Gant; and I submit that this is worth having, and we should let no theory of the effaced narrator prevent us from recognizing that this is the formal experience of the encounter with *Of Time and the River.* What one may think about the experience may change a great deal over the decades, but there can be no doubt that the transaction is there to be read. . . . (pp. 24-5)

> *Louis D. Rubin, Jr., "Introduction: The Sense of Being Young" (a revision of a speech originally delivered to the North Carolina Historical and Literary Society, Raleigh, December 1, 1972; reprinted by permission of Louis D. Rubin, Jr.), in* Thomas Wolfe: A Collection of Critical Essays, *edited by Louis D. Rubin, Jr., Prentice-Hall, Inc., 1973, pp. 1-30.*

JAMES ATLAS (essay date 1979)

Shelley, Wolfe wrote in "Of Time and the River," was the poet "of that time of life when men feel most strongly a sense of proud and lonely inviolability," "when we were twenty and could never die." And Wolfe himself is the novelist of that time. His work constitutes a vast sensory catalogue of childhood reminiscence, that exultation in landscapes, weather, awakening on a train late at night in some forgotten town. . . .

What animates Wolfe's novels is the conviction that art can recover and illuminate experience. Milton's stately line at the close of "Paradise Lost," "The world was all before them, where to choose," found a deliberate echo in "Of Time and the River," where Eugene Gant—Wolfe's persona in the first two novels—delights in "a sense of being triumphant and of having before him the whole unvisited plantation of the world to explore, possess and do with as he would." That same eager longing was what made Wolfe's novels live, and one gradually comes to appreciate his rhapsodic prose as if it were a faculty long dormant, suppressed by the now-dominant modernist sensibility. Fitzgerald and Hemingway were no less sentimental than Wolfe—is there a more grandly romantic passage in American fiction than the last words of "The Great Gatsby"?—but they were more tightlipped about it. Wolfe's florid effusions are doomed to seem archaic in an age that finds its reflection in the laconic plays of Samuel Beckett.

Nor is it fashionable to write fervently about America, that brooding landscape that figured so prominently in Wolfe's imagination. . . . No other novelist of his generation wrote so poignantly about the land, the cities, the people of America before it became a chaos of shopping centers and urban blight. . . .

Nostalgia was Wolfe's major theme, and that it could become a wearisome refrain is undeniable. "Naïve, self-absorbed, full of homespun mysticism and adolescent grandeur"—"the Tarzan of rhetoric," in Kazin's shrewd assessment—he crammed his novels with lavish apostrophes to Life and Death and Loneliness and Sorrow, covering page after page with grandiose rhetorical flourishes ("O death in life that turns men to stone! O change that levels down our gods!"), pseudo-Homeric epithets ("the great man-swarm," "the million-footed crowd"), wooden dialogue and pious homilies about "the brevity of our days." At its worst, his prose was mere portentous babble. . . .

[An] autobiographical impulse dominated all other considerations. Wolfe's "awful secret," F. Scott Fitzgerald wrote to his daughter, was that "he did not have anything particular to say"—surely a damning fault in a novelist. But he was a brilliant observer despite his self-absorption; the people of Asheville became in "Look Homeward, Angel" a populous tapestry of American lives. . . . (p. 3)

Whenever he strayed from the Whitmanesque, incessantly self-reflective chronicle he could sustain with such hypnotic force, Wolfe found himself mired in melodrama. Time and again, he squandered hundreds of pages on scenes that were simply not credible. The visit to his wealthy classmate's estate on the Hudson in "Of Time and the River," the literary parasites at a Park Avenue dinner party in "The Web and the Rock": Wolfe was utterly hopeless as a chronicler of *moeurs,* and when he tried his hand at it only succeeded in producing implausible types who could never have existed anywhere. Rage, the force that animated so many novelists from Dickens to Wyndham Lewis, was in Wolfe a strangulated cry that made those he caricatured seem freakish, gloating, maniacal.

When it came to the depiction of ordinary people, he was more confident. Wolfe hated the crowd, whose ignorant guttural speech he cruelly mimed, but he was also fiercely democratic, quick to repudiate the Romantic idea that artists were privileged and contemptuous of estheticism, preciosity, literary pose. The artist had to be "subject to the same desires, the same feelings, the same passions" that ruled other men, he declared. Some of the finest scenes in his later novels are about oppression: the young black, humiliated by whites to the point of madness, who goes on a shooting spree and is tracked down by a vicious posse; the Nazis' persecution of a Jew in prewar Germany attempting to escape across the border. . . .

The last two novels, assembled from the thousands of pages

of manuscript Wolfe left behind when he died, evoked the solitary life he had led in Brooklyn during the 1930's. . . . Four months [after their completion], desperately ill, Wolfe wrote Perkins: "No matter what happens, I shall always think of you and feel about you the way it was that Fourth of July day three years ago when you met me at the boat, and we went out on the cafe on the river and had a drink and later went on top of the tall building, and all the strangeness and the glory and the power of life and of the city was below." For all their grave imperfections—their bluster, their histrionic pose, their ostentatious displays of sensibility—Wolfe's novels still show forth that power. (p. 53)

> *James Atlas, "The Case for Thomas Wolfe," in* The New York Times Book Review *(© 1979 by The New York Times Company; reprinted by permission), December 2, 1979, pp. 3, 52-3.*

ADDITIONAL BIBLIOGRAPHY

Beach, Joseph Warren. "Discovery of Brotherhood." In his *American Fiction 1920-1940*, pp. 197-215. New York: The Macmillan Co., 1941.
    A critical examination of *You Can't Go Home Again.* Beach places the book alongside its three predecessors in importance, noting Wolfe's progression from "a Byronic sentimentalist" to "a social-minded realist."

Bowden, Edwin T. "The Mighty Individual." In his *The Dungeon of the Heart: Human Isolation and the American Novel,* pp. 66-102. New York: The Macmillan Co., 1961.*
    An examination of *Look Homeward, Angel* as "a direct exploitation of the American sense of isolation," in the tradition of the frontier novel. The book is found to be poor in its handling of Eugene Gant's role as the besieged individualist.

Cowley, Malcolm. "Wolfe: Homo Scribens." In his *A Second Flowering: Works and Days of the Lost Generation,* pp. 156-90. New York: The Viking Press, 1973.
    A study of Wolfe's writing methods, answering critical charges against him by showing the close link between his outlook and method of composition, and the faults and virtues of his work.

Fagin, N. Bryllion. "In Search of an American *Cherry Orchard.*" *The Texas Quarterly* 1, No. 3 (Summer-Autumn 1958): 132-41.*
    An exposition of Wolfe's *Mannerhouse* as a drama containing borrowings from Chekhov's *The Cherry Orchard.*

Field, Leslie, ed. *Thomas Wolfe: Three Decades of Criticism.* New York: New York University Press; London: University of London Press, 1968, 304 p.
    A well-chosen collection of critical essays on Wolfe's major themes and style, and on specific novels and short stories. Included are essays by Paschal Reeves, Oscar Cargill, Louis D. Rubin, Jr., and many others.

Forrey, Robert. "Whitman to Wolfe." *Mainstream* 13, No. 10 (October 1960): 19-27.
    Finds Wolfe's writings to be at the end of the American liberal tradition, which dates back to the work of Thoreau, Melville, and Whitman. The critic finds Wolfe a failure in his attempts to exalt the common person in his novels.

Geismar, Maxwell. Introduction to *The Portable Thomas Wolfe,* by Thomas Wolfe, edited by Maxwell Geismar, pp. 1-27. New York: The Viking Press, 1946.
    An excellent introduction to Wolfe's tormented life and career, finding him "one of the most acute and entertaining social commentators of [the 1920s]—and a prime chronicler of the

national mind during the decade of the bust and the hang-over."

Gilman, Richard. "The Worship of Thomas Wolfe." *The New Republic* 158, No. 8 (24 February 1968): 31-2, 34.
A critical attack on Andrew Turnbull's biography of Wolfe. The critic believes Wolfe's critical reputation to be grossly inflated and sees the novelist as neither an artist nor an important writer.

Holman, C. Hugh. *Thomas Wolfe.* University of Minnesota Pamphlets on American Writers, edited by William Van O'Connor, Allen Tate, Leonard Unger, and Robert Penn Warren, no. 6. Minneapolis: University of Minnesota Press, 1960, 47 p.
A brief biographical and critical introduction to Wolfe's life and work.

Kennedy, Richard S. *The Window of Memory: The Literary Career of Thomas Wolfe.* Chapel Hill: The University of North Carolina Press, 1962, 461 p.
An important, well-documented, biographical and critical study of Wolfe.

Kussy, Bella. "The Vitalist Trend and Thomas Wolfe." *The Sewanee Review* L, No. 3 (July-September 1942): 306-24.
An essay finding Wolfe's novels steeped in his vitalist beliefs: the doctrine of life as an all-pervading force or presence not bound by physical limitations. The works of Whitman, Nietzsche, and Hitler are also discussed, and the vitalist ideas contained within them are compared and contrasted with those of Wolfe.

McElderry, B. R., Jr. *Thomas Wolfe.* New York: Twayne Publishers, 1964, 207 p.
A brief biography and critical appraisal of Wolfe, examining his use of autobiographical material and finding the claim exaggerated which accuses him of uncreative use of that material. Wolfe is also favorably compared to Mark Twain.

Powell, W. Allen. "Thomas Wolfe's Phoenix Nest: The Plays of Thomas Wolfe as Related to His Fiction." *The Markham Review* 2, No. 6 (May 1971): 104-10.
An essay identifying elements of Wolfe's novels that originally appeared in his dramas.

Reeves, Paschal, ed. *Thomas Wolfe and the Glass of Time.* Athens: University of Georgia Press, 1971, 166 p.
Papers on Wolfe and his art, originally read at the first South Atlantic Graduate English (SAGE) symposium. Contributors include Richard S. Kennedy, Richard Walser, C. Hugh Holman, Ladell Payne, Paschal Reeves, and Wolfe's brother, Fred.

Rothman, Nathan L. "Thomas Wolfe and James Joyce: A Study in Literary Influence." In *A Southern Vanguard: The John Peale Bishop Memorial Volume,* edited by Allen Tate, pp. 52-77. New York: Prentice-Hall, Inc., 1947.
An important essay on Wolfe's great debt to Joyce. The critic cites many instances of Joycean influence in Wolfe's work and sees Eugene Gant as the twin of Stephen Dedalus.

Rubin, Larry. "Thomas Wolfe and the Lost Paradise." *Modern Fiction Studies* XI, No. 3 (Autumn 1965): 250-58.
Traces the theme of man as an exile from paradise through Wolfe's four novels. The critic contends that most of the major themes of those novels spring from this main theme.

Rubin, Louis D., Jr. *Thomas Wolfe: The Weather of His Youth.* Baton Rouge: Louisiana State University Press, 1955, 183 p.
A critical appraisal by one of the nation's foremost Wolfe scholars, examining Wolfe's use of time and autobiography in his novels, and highlighting Wolfe's dedication to his craft.

Schoenberger, Franz. "Wolfe's Genius Seen Afresh: A European Recounts His Discovery of an Eloquent Voice of the New World." *The New York Times Book Review* (4 August 1946): 1, 25.
Laudatory appraisal of Wolfe by a German emigrant. The critic finds Wolfe's ominous impressions of Germany's nazism in *You Can't Go Home Again* superior to the reports of American news correspondents writing from that country during the prewar era.

Schramm, Wilbur L. "Careers at Crossroads." *The Virginia Quarterly Review* 15, No. 4 (Autumn 1939): 627-32.*
A review finding *The Web and the Rock* a disappointment. The critic sees Wolfe's writing career marked by "the uneven power of a thunderstorm, rather than the sustained sweep of a hurricane."

Steele, Richard. *Thomas Wolfe: A Study in Psychoanalytic Criticism.* Philadelphia: Dorrance & Co., 1976, 214 p.
A psychoanalytic study of Wolfe's works, examining the narcissism, racism, sense of alienation, and other aspects found in them.

Turnbull, Andrew. *Thomas Wolfe.* New York: Charles Scribner's Sons, 1967, 374 p.
The most complete biography of Wolfe to date.

Walser, Richard, ed. *The Enigma of Thomas Wolfe: Biographical and Critical Selections.* Cambridge: Harvard University Press, 1953, 313 p.
A collection of essays on Wolfe's life and work, containing important writings by his editors, Margaret Church, W. P. Albrecht, and others.

Appendix

THE EXCERPTS IN TCLC, VOLUME 4, WERE REPRINTED FROM THE FOLLOWING PERIODICALS:

The Academy
The Acolyte
American Literature
American Quarterly
The American Review
The American Review of Reviews
The American-Scandinavian Review
Approach
Ariel
Arizona Quarterly
Asheville Times
The Athenaeum
The Atlantic Monthly
Blackwood's Magazine
Book Week—New York Herald Tribune
The Bookman (London)
The Bookman (New York)
Books Abroad
Calendar of Modern Letters
The Canadian Forum
College English
Commonweal
Comparative Literature
Contemporary
Contemporary Review
Cornhill Magazine
The Crisis
The Dalhousie Review
The Dial
Domiskussty
The Drama
The Dublin Review
Encounter
The English Review
Essays in Criticism
Extrapolation

The Fortnightly Review
Forum
Forum Italicum
The Freeman
The Georgia Review
The Germanic Review
Harper's
Harper's Weekly
Harvard Library Bulletin
Haunted
Hispania
Horizon
The Hudson Review
Irish Writing
The Kenyon Review
Latin American Literary Review
The Listener
The Literary Digest
The Living Age
The London Mercury
Meanjin
The Measure
The Mississippi Quarterly
MLN
Modern Drama
Modern Fiction Studies
The Modern Language Journal
Modern Language Notes
The Modern Language Review
Monatshefte
The Nation
The Nation and The Athenaeum
The New Republic
New Statesman
New York Herald Tribune Book Review
New York Herald Tribune Books

The New Yorker
The New York Review of Books
The New York Times
The New York Times Book Review
The Nineteenth-Century
The North American Review
Opportunity
Papers on Language and Literature
PHYLON
PMLA
Poet Lore
Poetry
Poetry Review
Polish Perspectives
The Polish Review
Proceedings and Transactions of The
  Royal Society of Canada
Renascence
Revista Hispánica Moderna
The Russian Review
Saturday Review
The Saturday Review (London)
The Saturday Review (New York)
The Saturday Review of Literature
The Scandinavian Review
Scandinavian Studies
Scottish Literary Journal
The Sewanee Review
Slavic and East European Journal
Slavic and East European Studies
The Slavic Review
The Slavonic and East European
  Review
The Slavonic Review
Smart Set
South Atlantic Quarterly

Southerly
Southern Folklore Quarterly
The Southern Literary Journal
The Southern Review
The Speaker
The Spectator
Studies in Modern German Literature
Studies in the Novel
Studies in Scottish Literature

Studies in Short Fiction
Survey
The Texas Review
Theatre Arts Monthly
The Times Literary Supplement
Twentieth Century Literature
The University of New Mexico
    Bulletin
University of Toronto Quarterly

Vanity Fair
The Virginia Quarterly Review
Western Folklore
Western Humanities Review
The Westminster Review
Whispers
World Literature Today
World Theatre
The Yale Review

THE EXCERPTS IN TCLC, VOLUME 4, WERE REPRINTED FROM THE FOLLOWING BOOKS:

Abercrombie, Lascelles. Thomas Hardy: A Critical Study. *Secker, 1912, Russell & Russell, 1964.*

Adams, Henry. The Selected Letters of Henry Adams. *Edited by Newton Arvin. Farrar, Straus & Giroux, 1951.*

A. E. Imaginations and Reveries. *Maunsel, 1915.*

A. E. The Living Torch. *Edited by Monk Gibbon. Macmillan, 1938.*

Aiken, Conrad. Scepticisms: Notes on Contemporary Poetry. *Knopf, 1919, Books for Libraries, 1967.*

Aiken, Conrad. Collected Criticism. *Oxford University Press, 1968.*

Alexandrova, Vera. A History of Soviet Literature. *Translated by Mirra Ginsburg. Doubleday, 1963.*

Archer, William. Poets of the Younger Generation. *Lane, 1902, Scholarly Press, 1969.*

Atkins, Elizabeth. Edna St. Vincent Millay and Her Times. *University of Chicago Press, 1936.*

Atkins, John. Walter de la Mare: An Explanation. *Temple, 1947.*

Auden, W. H. Forewords and Afterwords. *Edited by Edward Mendelson. Random House, 1973.*

Baker, Denys Val, ed. Modern British Writing. *Vanguard, 1947.*

Baker, Houston A., Jr. A Many-Colored Coat of Dreams. *Broadside, 1974.*

Barclay, Glen St John. Anatomy of Horror: The Masters of Occult Fiction. *Weidenfeld & Nicholson, 1978, St. Martin's, 1979.*

Baskervill, William Malone. Southern Writers: Biographical and Critical Studies, Vol. I. *Publishing House of M. E. Church, 1897, Gordian, 1970.*

Bates, H. E. The Modern Short Story: A Critical Survey. *Nelson, 1941, Joseph, 1972.*

Bayley, John. An Essay on Hardy. *Cambridge University Press, 1978.*

Beach, Joseph Warren. The Technique of Thomas Hardy. *University of Chicago Press, 1922, Russell & Russell, 1962.*

Bell, Aubrey F. G. Contemporary Spanish Literature. *Knopf, 1925.*

Bellman, Samuel I. Marjorie Kinnan Rawlings. *Twayne, 1974.*

Benson, Ruth Crego. Women in Tolstoy: The Ideal and the Erotic. *University of Illinois Press, 1973.*

Bentley, Eric. In Search of Theatre. *Atheneum, 1975.*

Bentley, Eric. The Playwright As Thinker: A Study of Drama in Modern Times. *Reynal & Hitchcock, 1946.*

Berendsohn, Walter A. Selma Lagerlöf: Her Life and Work. *Translated by George F. Timpson. Nicholson & Watson, 1931, Kennikat, 1968.*

Berlin, Isaiah. The Hedgehog and The Fox: An Essay on Tolstoy's View of History. *Simon & Schuster, 1953.*

Bigelow, Gordon E. Frontier Eden. *University of Florida Press, 1966.*

Björkman, Edwin. Voices of To-morrow: Critical Studies of the New Spirit in Literature. *Mitchell Kennerley, 1913.*

Blackmur, R. P. The Expense of Greatness. *Arrow, 1940, Smith, 1958.*

Blackmur, R. P. Eleven Essays in the European Novel. *Harcourt, 1964.*

Blackmur, R. P. A Primer of Ignorance. *Edited by Joseph Frank. Harcourt, 1967.*

Bone, Robert. The Negro Novel in America. *Rev. ed. Yale University Press, 1965.*

Borges, Jorge Luis. Other Inquisitions: 1937-1952. *Translated by Ruth L. C. Simms. University of Texas Press, 1964.*

Bowra, C. M. The Heritage of Symbolism. *Macmillan, 1943.*

Bowra, C. M. The Creative Experiment. *Macmillan, 1949.*

Boyesen, Hjalmar Hjorth. Essays on Scandinavian Literature. *Scribner's, 1911.*

Boynton, Percy H. More Contemporary Americans. *University of Chicago Press, 1927.*

Braithwaite, William Stanley. Anthology of Magazine Verse for 1915 and Year Book of American Poetry. *Gomme & Marshall, 1915.*

Brawley, Benjamin. The Negro Genius: A New Appraisal of the Achievement of the American Negro in Literature and the Fine Arts. *Dodd, Mead, 1937.*

Braybrooke, Patrick. Philosophies in Modern Fiction. *Daniel, 1929, Books for Libraries, 1965.*

Brégy, Katherine. Poets and Pilgrims. *Benziger Brothers, 1925.*

Brenan, Gerald. The Literature of the Spanish People from Roman Times to the Present Day. *Cambridge University Press, 1951.*

Brennan, Joseph Payne. H. P. Lovecraft: An Evaluation. *Macabre House, 1955.*

Brittin, Norman A. Edna St. Vincent Millay. *Twayne, 1967.*

Brophy, Brigid; Levey, Michael; and Osborne, Charles. Fifty Works of English and American Literature We Could Do Without. *Stein and Day, 1967.*

Brotherston, Gordon. Latin American Poetry: Origins and Presence. *Cambridge University Press, 1975.*

Brown, Edward J. Mayakovsky: A Poet in the Revolution. *Princeton University Press, 1973.*

Brown, Edward J., ed. Major Soviet Writers: Essays in Criticism. *Oxford University Press, 1973.*

Brustein, Robert. The Theatre of Revolt: An Approach to the Modern Drama. *Atlantic-Little, Brown, 1964.*

Buckley, Vincent. Henry Handel Richardson. *Lansdowne, 1961.*

Büdel, Oscar. Pirandello. *Bowes and Bowes, 1966.*

Butcher, Philip. George W. Cable: The Northampton Years. *Columbia University Press, 1959.*

Butler, Lance St. John, ed. Thomas Hardy after Fifty Years. *Rowman and Littlefield, 1977.*

Butter, Peter. Francis Thompson. *British Council, 1961.*

Cambon, Glauco, ed. Pirandello: A Collection of Critical Essays. *Prentice-Hall, 1967.*

Cargill, Oscar. Intellectual America: Ideas on the March. *Macmillan, 1941.*

Carpenter, Margaret Haley. Sara Teasdale: A Biography. *Schulte, 1960, Pentelic, 1977.*

Cecil, David. The Fine Art of Reading and Other Literary Studies. *Bobbs-Merrill, 1957.*

Chakravarty, Amiya. ''The Dynasts'' and the Post-War Age in Poetry: A Study in Modern Ideas. *Oxford University Press, 1938.*

Chandler, Frank W. Modern Continental Playwrights. *Harper, 1931.*

Chesterton, G. K. Varied Types. *Dodd, Mead, 1921.*

Chesterton, G. K. Selected Essays of G. K. Chesterton. *Edited by Dorothy Collins. Methuen, 1949.*

Chesterton, G. K. Heretics. *Lane, 1950, Books for Libraries, 1970.*

Chew, Samuel C. Thomas Hardy: Poet and Novelist. *Knopf, 1928.*

Christian, R. F. Tolstoy's "War and Peace": A Study. *Oxford University Press, 1962.*

Cole, Leo R. The Religious Instinct in the Poetry of Juan Ramón Jiménez. *Dolphin, 1967.*

Collins, Joseph. Taking the Literary Pulse: Psychological Studies of Life and Letters. *Doran, 1924.*

Cowley, Malcolm, ed. After the Genteel Tradition: American Writers since 1910. *Smith, 1959.*

Cowley, Malcolm, and Smith, Bernard, eds. Books That Changed Our Minds. *Doubleday, 1939.*

Cox, R. G., ed. Thomas Hardy: The Critical Heritage. *Barnes & Noble, 1970.*

Craig, G. Dundas. The Modernist Trend in Spanish-American Poetry: A Collection of Representative Poems of the Modernist Movement and the Reaction. *University of California Press, 1934.*

Davison, Edward. Some Modern Poets and Other Critical Essays. *Harper, 1928.*

Derleth, August. H.P.L.: A Memoir. *Abramson, 1945.*

Deutsch, Babette. This Modern Poetry. *Norton, 1935.*

Dostoievsky, F. M. The Diary of a Writer. *Translated by Boris Brasol. Scribner's, 1949, Braziller, 1954.*

Duffin, Henry Charles. Walter de la Mare: A Study of His Poetry. *Sidgewick and Jackson, 1949.*

Dukes, Ashley. Modern Dramatists. ***Palmer, 1911, Sergel, 1912.***

Dutton, Geoffrey, ed. The Literature of Australia. *Penguin, 1964.*

Eikhenbaum, Boris. The Young Tolstoi. *Edited by Gary Kern. Ardis, 1972.*

Ekström, Kjell. George Washington Cable: A Study of His Early Life and Work. *Harvard University Press, 1950.*

Eldershaw, M. Barnard. Essays in Australian Fiction. *Melbourne University Press, 1938, Books for Libraries, 1970.*

Eliot, T. S. Points of View. *Faber and Faber, 1941.*

Elledge, Scott, ed. "Tess of the d'Urbervilles" by Thomas Hardy: An Authoritative Text, Hardy and the Novel, Criticism. *Norton, 1965.*

Erlich, Victor, ed. Twentieth-Century Russian Literary Criticism. *Yale University Press, 1975.*

Esslin, Martin. Reflections: Essays on Modern Theatre. *Doubleday, 1969.*

Fadiman, Clifton. Any Number Can Play. *World, 1957.*

Farrell, James T. Literature and Morality. *Vanguard, 1947.*

Fiedler, Leslie A. Unfinished Business. *Stein and Day, 1972.*

Field, Leslie A., ed. Thomas Wolfe: Three Decades of Criticism. *New York University Press, 1968.*

Forster, E. M. Aspects of the Novel. *Harcourt, 1927.*

Freud, Ernst L., ed. Letters of Sigmund Freud. *Translated by Tania Stern and James Stern. Basic, 1960.*

Frohock, W. M. The Novel of Violence in America. *Rev. ed. Southern Methodist University Press, 1957, Beacon, 1964.*

Frynta, Emanuel. Hasek: The Creator of Schweik. *Translated by Jean Layton and George Theiner. Artia, 1965.*

Garten, H. F. Gerhart Hauptmann. *Yale University Press, 1954.*

Gass, William H. The World within the Word. *Knopf, 1978.*

Geismar, Maxwell. The Last of the Provincials: The American Novels, 1915-1925. *Houghton, 1947, Hill and Wang, 1959.*

Goldberg, Isaac. Studies in Spanish-American Literature. *Brentano's, 1920, Kennikat, 1968.*

Goldstone, Adrian, and Sweetser, Wesley. A Bibliography of Arthur Machen. *University of Texas Press, 1965.*

Gorky, Maxim. On Literature. *University of Washington Press, 1973.*

Grant, Donald M., and Handley, Thomas P. Rhode Island on Lovecraft. *Grant-Handley, 1945.*

Gray, James. Edna St. Vincent Millay. *University of Minnesota Press, 1967.*

Grebstein, Sheldon Norman. Sinclair Lewis. *Twayne, 1962.*

Green, Dorothy. Ulysses Bound: Henry Handel Richardson and Her Fiction. *Australian National University, 1973.*

Gregor, Ian. The Moral and the Story. *Faber and Faber, 1962.*

Grøndahl, Illit, and Raknes, Ola. Chapters in Norwegian Literature. *Gyldendal, 1923, Books for Libraries, 1969.*

Guerard, Albert J. Thomas Hardy. *Rev. ed. New Directions, 1964.*

Gustafson, Alrik. Six Scandinavian Novelists. *American Scandinavian Foundation, 1940.*

Hamilton, Clayton. Seen on the Stage. *Holt, 1920.*

Hardy, Thomas. ''Jude the Obscure'' by Thomas Hardy: An Authoritive Text, Backgrounds and Sources, Criticism. *Edited by Norman Page, Norton, 1978.*

Hearn, Lafcadio. Life and Literature. *Edited by John Erskine. Heinemann, 1922.*

Hewett-Thayer, Harvey W. The Modern German Novel: A Series of Studies and Appreciations. *Jones, 1924.*

Hicks, Granville. The Great Tradition: An Interpretation of American Literature since the Civil War. *Rev. ed. Macmillan, 1935, Quadrangle, 1969.*

Hochfield, George. Henry Adams: An Introduction and Interpretation. *Barnes & Noble, 1962.*

Holl, Karl. Gerhart Hauptmann: His Life and His Work, 1862-1912. *Gay and Hancock, 1913, Books for Libraries, 1972.*

Hopkins, Kenneth. Walter de la Mare. *Rev. ed. British Council, 1957.*

Howe, Irving, ed. Classics of Modern Fiction: Eight Short Novels. *Harcourt, 1968.*

Howells, W. D. My Literary Passions. *Harper, 1895.*

Howells, W. D. Heroines of Fiction, Vol. II. *Harper, 1901.*

Howells, W. D. Criticism and Fiction and Other Essays. *Edited by Clara Marbury Kirk and Rudolph Kirk. New York University Press, 1959.*

Huneker, James. Ivory Apes and Peacocks. *Scribner's, 1938.*

Hynes, Samuel. The Pattern of Hardy's Poetry. *The University of North Carolina Press, 1961.*

Jackson, Blyden, and Rubin, Louis D., Jr. Black Poetry in America: Two Essays in Historical Interpretation. *Louisiana State University Press, 1974.*

James, Henry. The Letters of Henry James. *Edited by Percy Lubbock. Scribner's, 1920.*

James, Henry. Literary Reviews and Essays. *Edited by Albert Mordell. Twayne, 1957.*

Jameson, Storm. Modern Drama in Europe. *Collins, 1920.*

Jarrell, Randall. Poetry and the Age. *Knopf, 1953.*

Jean-Aubry, G. Joseph Conrad: Life and Letters, Vol. I. *Doubleday, 1927.*

Johnson, James Weldon, ed. The Book of American Negro Poetry. *Rev. ed. Harcourt, 1931.*

Johnson, Robert Underwood; Blashfield, Edwin Howland; and Van Dyke, John Charles. Commemorative Tributes to Cable, Sargent, Pennell. *American Academy of Arts and Letters, 1927.*

Jones, Malcolm, ed. New Essays on Tolstoy. *Cambridge University Press, 1978.*

Jordy, William H. Henry Adams: Scientific Historian. *Yale University Press, 1952.*

Joshi, S. T., ed. H. P. Lovecraft: Four Decades of Criticism. *Ohio University Press, 1980.*

Kaun, Alexander. Soviet Poets and Poetry. *University of California Press, 1943.*

Kazin, Alfred. On Native Grounds: An Interpretation of American Prose Literature. *Reynal & Hitchcock, 1942.*

Knight, K. G., and Norman, F. Hauptmann. *University of London Institute of Germanic Studies, 1964.*

Knowles, A. V., ed. Tolstoy: The Critical Heritage. *Routledge & Kegan Paul, 1978.*

Larsen, Hanna Astrup. Selma Lagerlöf. *Doubleday, Doran, 1936.*

Lavrin, Janko. From Pushkin to Mayakovsky: A Study in the Evolution of a Literature. *Sylvan, 1948.*

Lawrence, D. H. Phoenix: The Posthumous Papers of D. H. Lawrence. *Edited by Edward D. McDonald. Viking Penguin, 1936.*

Lehmann, John. New Writing in Europe. *Penguin, 1940.*

Lenin, V. I. Selected Works, Vol. XI. *International Publishers, 1943.*

Lewisohn, Ludwig. The Modern Drama. *Huebsch, 1915.*

Liptzin, Sol. Arthur Schnitzler. *Prentice-Hall, 1932.*

Loftus, Richard J. Nationalism in Modern Anglo-Irish Poetry. *University of Wisconsin Press, 1964.*

Lovecraft, Howard Phillips. Supernatural Horror in Literature. *Dover, 1973.*

Lubbock, Percy. The Craft of Fiction. *Cape, 1921.*

Lukacs, Georg. Studies in European Realism: A Sociological Survey of the Writings of Balzac, Stendhal, Zola, Tolstoy, Gorki and Others. *Translated by Edith Bone. Merlin, 1972.*

Lundquist, James. Sinclair Lewis. *Ungar, 1973.*

Lyon, Melvin. Symbol and Idea in Henry Adams. *University of Nebraska Press, 1970.*

APPENDIX

MacClintock, Lander. The Age of Pirandello. *Indiana University Press, 1951.*

Madeleva, Sister M. Chaucer's Nuns and Other Essays. *Appleton, 1925, Kennikat, 1965.*

Mann, Thomas. Essays of Three Decades. *Translated by H. T. Lowe-Porter. Knopf, 1948.*

Maude, Aylmer. The Life of Tolstoy. *Rev. ed. Oxford University Press, 1930.*

McFarlane, James Walter. Ibsen and the Temper of Norwegian Literature. *Oxford University Press, 1960.*

McFate, Patricia. The Writings of James Stephens: Variations on a Theme of Love. *St. Martin's, 1979.*

Mencken, H. L. Prejudices, first series. *Knopf, 1919.*

Michael, D.P.M. Arthur Machen. *University of Wales Press, 1971.*

Mickelson, Anne Z. Thomas Hardy's Women and Men: The Defeat of Nature. *Scarecrow, 1976.*

Miller, J. Hillis. Thomas Hardy: Distance and Desire. *Harvard University Press, 1970.*

Mirsky, D. S. A History of Russian Literature. *Edited by Francis J. Whitefield. Rev. ed. Knopf, 1955.*

Moestrup, Jørn. The Structural Patterns of Pirandello's Work. *Odense University Press, 1972.*

Monroe, N. Elizabeth. The Novel and Society: A Critical Study of the Modern Novel. *University of North Carolina Press, 1941.*

Mooney, Harry J., Jr. Tolstoy's Epic Vision: A Study of "War and Peace" and "Anna Karenina." *University of Tulsa, 1968.*

Muchnic, Helen. From Gorky to Pasternak: Six Writers in Soviet Russia. *Random House, 1961.*

Muir, Edwin. Essays on Literature and Society. *Rev. ed. Harvard University Press, 1965.*

Muller, Herbert J. Thomas Wolfe. *New Directions, 1947.*

Nash, Berta. Minor British Novelists. *Edited by Charles Alva Hoyt. Southern Illinois University Press, 1967.*

Nathan, George Jean. The Magic Mirror. *Edited by Thomas Quinn Curtiss. Knopf, 1960.*

Nause, John, ed. The Grove Symposium. *University of Ottawa Press, 1974.*

O'Connor, Frank. The Mirror in the Roadway: A Study of the Modern Novel. *Knopf, 1956.*

O'Connor, Frank. The Lonely Voice: A Study of the Short Story. *World, 1963.*

O'Connor, Frank. The Backward Look: A Survey of Irish Literature. *Macmillan, 1967.*

O'Connor, William Van, ed. Forms of Modern Fiction. *University of Minnesota Press, 1948.*

Olson, Paul R. Circle of Paradox: Time and Essence in the Poetry of Juan Ramón Jiménez. *Johns Hopkins University Press, 1967.*

Orage, A. R. Readers and Writers. *Knopf, 1922.*

Orwell, George. The Collected Essays, Journalism and Letters of George Orwell: My Country Right or Left, 1940-1943, Vol. II. *Edited by Sonia Orwell and Ian Angus. Secker & Warburg, 1968.*

Palmer, Nettie. Henry Handel Richardson. *Angus & Robertson, 1950.*

Pasternak, Boris. I Remember: Sketch for an Autobiography. *Translated by David Magarshack. Pantheon, 1959.*

Peers, E. Allison. A Critical Anthology of Spanish Verse. *University of California Press, 1949, Greenwood, 1968.*

Peers, E. Allison. A History of the Romantic Movement in Spain, Vol. II. *Cambridge University Press, 1940.*

Penzoldt, Peter. The Supernatural in Fiction. *Nevill, 1952, Humanities, 1965.*

Poggioli, Renato. The Poets of Russia: 1890-1930. *Harvard University Press, 1960.*

Pollard, Percival. Masks and Minstrels of New Germany. *Luce, 1911.*

Ponomareff, Constantin V. Sergey Esenin. *Twayne, 1978.*

Pound, Ezra. Guide to Kulchur. *New Directions, 1970.*

Priestley, J. B. Literature and Western Man. *Harper & Row, 1960.*

Pritchett, V. S. In My Good Books. *Chatto & Windus, 1942.*

Pritchett, V. S. The Living Novel. *Chatto and Windus, 1946.*

Proust, Marcel. Marcel Proust on Art and Literature 1896-1919. *Translated by Sylvia Townsend Warner. Meridian, 1958.*

Ransom, John Crowe, ed. The Kenyon Critics: Studies in Modern Literature from "The Kenyon Review." *World, 1951.*

Redding, J. Saunders. To Make a Poet Black. *University of North Carolina Press, 1939, McGrath, 1968.*

Reeves, Paschal, ed. Thomas Wolfe: The Critical Reception. *Lewis, 1974.*

Reeves, Paschal, ed. The Merrill Studies in "Look Homeward, Angel." *Merrill, 1970.*

Reichert, Herbert W., and Salinger, Herman, eds. Studies in Arthur Schnitzler: Centennial Commemorative Volume. *University of North Carolina Press, 1963, AMS Press, 1966.*

Rubin, Louis D., Jr. George W. Cable: The Life and Times of a Southern Heretic. *Bobbs-Merrill—Pegasus, 1969.*

Rubin, Louis D., Jr., ed. Thomas Wolfe: A Collection of Critical Essays. *Prentice-Hall, 1973.*

Rubin, Louis D., Jr., and Jacobs, Robert D. South: Modern Southern Literature in Its Cultural Setting. *Doubleday, 1961, Greenwood Press, 1974.*

Rubin, Louis D., Jr., and Moore, John Rees. The Idea of an American Novel. *Crowell, 1961.*

Russell, Bertrand. Portraits from Memory: And Other Essays. *Simon & Schuster, 1956.*

Saul, George Brandon. Quintet: Essays on Five American Women Poets. *Mouton, 1967.*

Saul, George Brandon. Withdrawn in Gold: Three Commentaries on Genius. *Mouton, 1970.*

Saul, George Brandon. In Praise of the Half-Forgotten and Other Ruminations. *Bucknell University Press, 1976.*

Scarborough, Dorothy. The Supernatural in Modern English Fiction. *Putnam's, 1917, Octagon, 1967.*

Schmidt, Michael. A Reader's Guide to Fifty Modern British Poets. *Barnes & Noble, 1979.*

Schorer, Mark. Sinclair Lewis. *University of Minnesota Press, 1963.*

Schorer, Mark, ed. Sinclair Lewis: A Collection of Critical Essays. *Prentice-Hall, 1962.*

Schweitzer, Darrell. The Dream Quest of H. P. Lovecraft. *Borgo Press, 1978.*

Scott, Winfield Townley. Exiles and Fabrication. *Doubleday, 1961.*

Segel, Harold B. Twentieth-Century Russian Drama: From Gorky to the Present. *Columbia University Press, 1979.*

Sewell, Elizabeth. Paul Valéry: The Mind in the Mirror. *Yale University Press, 1952.*

Shaw, Bernard. Dramatic Opinions and Essays, Vol. I. *Bretano's, 1906.*

Shaw, Donald L. The Nineteenth Century. *Barnes & Noble, 1972.*

Shaw, Priscilla Washburn. Rilke, Valéry and Yeats: The Domain of the Self. *Rutgers, 1964.*

Shestov, Lev. Dostoevsky, Tolstoy and Nietzsche. *Translated by Bernard Martin. Ohio University Press, 1969.*

Shreffler, Philip A. The H. P. Lovecraft Companion. *Greenwood, 1977.*

Simmons, Ernest J. Introduction to Tolstoy's Writings. *University of Chicago Press, 1968.*

Southworth, James Granville. The Poetry of Thomas Hardy. *Columbia University Press, 1947.*

Spettigue, Douglas O. Frederick Philip Grove. *Copp Clark, 1969.*

Spettigue, Douglas O. F.P.G.: The European Years. **Oberon Press, 1973.**

Sprague, Rosemary. Imaginary Gardens: A Study of Five American Poets. *Chilton, 1969.*

Squire, J. C. Books Reviewed: Critical Essays on Books and Authors. *Doran, 1922, Kennikat, 1968.*

Starrett, Vincent. Buried Caesars: Essays in Literary Appreciation. *Covici-McGee, 1923.*

Steiner, George. Tolstoy or Dostoevsky: An Essay in the Old Criticism. *Knopf, 1959.*

Strachey, Lytton. Literary Essays. *Chatto and Windus, 1948.*

Stuckey, W. J. The Pulitzer Prize Novels: A Critical Backward Look. *University of Oklahoma Press, 1966.*

Sturgeon, Mary C. Studies of Contemporary Poets. *Dodd, Mead, 1916.*

Sutherland, Ronald. Frederick Philip Grove. *McClelland, 1969.*

Swales, Martin. Arthur Schnitzler: A Critical Study. *Oxford University Press, 1971.*

Swann, Thomas Burnett. Ernest Dowson. *Twayne, 1964.*

Swinnerton, Frank. The Georgian Literary Scene, 1910-1935: A Panorama. *Hutchinson, 1950.*

Swinnerton, Frank. The Georgian Scene: A Literary Panorama. *Farrar & Rinehart, 1934.*

Thompson, Francis. Literary Criticism. *Edited by Terence L. Connolly, S. J. Dutton, 1948.*

Thomson, Paul van Kuykendall. Francis Thompson: A Critical Biography. **Nelson, 1961, Gordian, 1973.**

Tillotson, Geoffrey. Essays in Criticism and Research. *Archon Books, 1967.*

Tolstoy, Leo. "Anna Karenina" by Leo Tolstoy: The Maude Translation, Backgrounds and Sources, Essays in Criticism. *Edited by George Gibian. Norton, 1970.*

Tolstoy, Leo. "War and Peace" by Leo Tolstoy: The Maude Translation, Backgrounds and Sources, Essays in Criticism. *Edited by George Gibian. Norton, 1966.*

Trotsky, Leon. Literature and Revolution. *Translated by Rose Strunsky. Russell & Russell, 1957.*

Turner, Arlin. George W. Cable: A Biography. *Duke University Press, 1956.*

Turner, Darwin T. In a Minor Chord: Three Afro-American Writers and Their Search for Identity. *Southern Illinois University Press, 1971.*

Turquet-Milnes, G. Paul Valéry. *Cape, 1934.*

Untermeyer, Louis. American Poetry Since 1900. *Holt, 1923.*

Van Doren, Carl. Many Minds. *Knopf, 1924.*

Van Doren, Mark. Four Poets on Poetry. *Johns Hopkins Press, 1955.*

Van Doren, Mark. The Happy Critic and Other Essays. *Farrar, Straus & Giroux, 1961.*

Vedder, Henry C. American Writers of To-day. *Silver, Burdett, 1894.*

Verschoyle, Derek, ed. The English Novelists: A Survey of the Novel by Twenty Contemporary Novelists. *Chatto & Windus, 1936.*

Vigar, Penelope. The Novels of Thomas Hardy: Illusion and Reality. *Athlone, 1974.*

Vittorini, Domenico. The Modern Italian Novel. *University of Pennsylvania Press, 1930.*

Vittorini, Domenico. The Drama of Luigi Pirandello. *University of Pennsylvania Press, 1935.*

Wagenknecht, Edward. Cavalcade of the English Novel: From Elizabeth to George VI. *Holt, Rinehart and Winston, 1948.*

Wagner, Jean. Black Poets of the United States: From Paul Laurence Dunbar to Langston Hughes. *Translated by Kenneth Douglas. University of Illinois Press, 1973.*

Walser, Richard. Thomas Wolfe: An Introduction and Interpretation. *Barnes & Noble, 1961.*

Walser, Richard, ed. The Enigma of Thomas Wolfe: Biographical and Critical Selections. *Harvard University Press, 1953.*

Ward, Thomas Humphry, ed. The English Poets: Browning to Rupert Brooke, Vol. V. *Macmillan, 1923.*

Warren, Austin. The New England Conscience. *University of Michigan Press, 1966.*

Warren, Robert Penn. Selected Essays. *Random House, 1958.*

Webster, Harvey Curtis. On a Darkling Plain: The Art and Thought of Thomas Hardy. *University of Chicago Press, 1947.*

West, Anthony. Principles and Persuasions: The Literary Essays of Anthony West. *Harcourt, 1957.*

Weygandt, Cornelius. Tuesdays at Ten: A Garnering from the Talks of Thirty Years on Poets, Dramatists, and Essayists. *University of Pennsylvania Press, 1928.*

Whipple, T. K. Spokesmen: Modern Writers and American Life. *Appleton, 1928.*

Wilson, Colin. The Strength to Dream: Literature and the Imagination. *Houghton, 1962.*

Wilson, Edmund. Axel's Castle: A Study in the Imaginative Literature of 1870-1930. *Scribner's, 1931, Collins, 1961.*

Wilson, Edmund. Classics and Commercials: A Literary Chronicle of the Forties. *Farrar, Straus & Giroux, 1950.*

Wilson, Edmund. The Shores of Light: A Literary Chronicle of the Twenties and Thirties. *Farrar, Straus & Giroux, 1952.*

Wilson, Edmund. Patriotic Gore: Studies in the Literature of the American Civil War. *Oxford University Press, 1962.*

Wilson, Edmund. A Window on Russia, for the Use of Foreign Readers. *Farrar, Straus & Giroux, 1972.*

Wilson, Edmund, ed. The Shock of Recognition: The Development of Literature in the United States by the Men Who Made It. *Farrar, Straus and Cudahy, 1955.*

Winters, Ivor. The Anatomy of Nonsense. *New Directions, 1943.*

Winters, Ivor. In Defense of Reason. *Swallow, 1947.*

Wittig, Kurt. The Scottish Tradition in Literature. *Oliver and Boyd, 1958.*

Wolfe, Thomas. Thomas Wolfe's Purdue Speech: "Writing and Living." *Edited by William Braswell and Leslie A. Field. Purdue University Studies, 1964.*

Woolf, Virginia. The Second Common Reader. *Harcourt, 1932.*

Woolf, Virginia. The Moment and Other Essays. *Harcourt, 1948.*

Woolf, Virginia. Contemporary Writers. *Hogarth, 1965.*

Young, Douglas F. Beyond the Sunset: A Study of James Leslie Mitchell. *Impulse, 1973.*

Young, Howard T. The Victorious Expression: A Study of Four Contemporary Spanish Poets. *University of Wisconsin Press, 1964.*

Zweig, Stefan. Adepts In Self-Portraiture. *Translated by Eden Paul and Cedar Paul. Cassell, 1952.*

Cumulative Index to Authors

Cumulative Index to Critics

Aaron, Daniel
Nathanael West 1:485

Abcarian, Richard
Sherwood Anderson 1:59

Abel, Lionel
Bertolt Brecht 1:109
Henrik Ibsen 2:232

Abercrombie, Lascelles
Thomas Hardy 4:153

Abrams, Ivan B.
Sholom Aleichem 1:24

Abril, Xavier
Cesar Vallejo 3:526

Adams, J. Donald
F. Scott Fitzgerald 1:239

Adams, Marion
Gottfried Benn 3:111

Adams, Robert Martin
James Joyce 3:273

Adams, Walter S.
Thomas Wolfe 4:506

Adcock, A. St. John
O. Henry 1:347
George Bernard Shaw 3:386

Aguirre, Ángel Manuel
Juan Ramón Jiménez 4:223

Aguinaga, Carlos Blanco
Miguel de Unamuno 2:561

Aiken, Conrad
Sherwood Anderson 1:37
Robert Bridges 1:127
Walter de la Mare 4:71
F. Scott Fitzgerald 1:237
John Galsworthy 1:296
Federico García Lorca 1:308
Thomas Hardy 4:155
D. H. Lawrence 2:344
Edgar Lee Masters 2:460
Eugene O'Neill 1:383
Dorothy Richardson 3:349
Rainer Maria Rilke 1:414
Dylan Thomas 1:466
Virginia Woolf 1:529

Akhsharumov, N. D.
Leo Tolstoy 4:446

Aldington, Richard
Oscar Wilde 1:499

Aldridge, John
F. Scott Fitzgerald 1:246

Alexandrova, Vera
Sergei Esenin 4:113

Allen, Walter
Wyndham Lewis 2:394
Dorothy Richardson 3:358

Alpert, Hollis
O. Henry 1:350

Alsen, Eberhard
Hamlin Garland 3:200

Alvarez, A.
Hart Crane 2:118
D. H. Lawrence 2:364
Wallace Stevens 3:454
William Butler Yeats 1:564

Amann, Clarence A.
James Weldon Johnson 3:247

Amis, Kingsley
G. K. Chesterton 1:185

Anders, Gunther
Franz Kafka 2:302

Anderson, David D.
Sherwood Anderson 1:52

Anderson, Maxwell
Edna St. Vincent Millay 4:306

Anderson, Quentin
Willa Cather 1:163

Annenkov, P. V.
Leo Tolstoy 4:444

Antoninus, Brother
Hart Crane 2:119

Aratari, Anthony
Federico García Lorca 1:316

Arce de Vazquez, Margot
Gabriela Mistral 2:477

Archer, William
W. S. Gilbert 3:207
Henrik Ibsen 2:224
Selma Lagerlöf 4:229
Francis Thompson 4:434

Arendt, Hannah
Bertolt Brecht 1:114
Franz Kafka 2:301

Armstrong, Martin
Katherine Mansfield 2:446

Arrowsmith, William
Cesare Pavese 3:334
Dylan Thomas 1:468

Arvin, Newton
Henry Adams 4:12

Ashbery, John
Gertrude Stein 1:442

Aswell, Edward C.
Thomas Wolfe 4:515

Atherton, Gertrude
May Sinclair 3:434

Atkins, Elizabeth
Edna St. Vincent Millay 4:311

Atkins, John
Walter de la Mare 4:75

Atlas, James
Gertrude Stein 1:442
Thomas Wolfe 4:538

Auchincloss, Louis
Willa Cather 1:164
Ellen Glasgow 2:188
Henry James 2:275
Sarah Orne Jewett 1:367
Edith Wharton 3:570

Auden, W. H.
Max Beerbohm 1:72
C. P. Cavafy 2:90
G. K. Chesterton 1:184, 186
Walter de la Mare 4:81
A. E. Housman 1:358
George Orwell 2:512
George Bernard Shaw 3:389
Paul Valéry 4:499
Nathanael West 1:480
Oscar Wilde 1:504, 507
Charles Williams 1:516
Virginia Woolf 1:546
William Butler Yeats 1:562

CRITIC INDEX

CRITIC INDEX

CRITIC INDEX

CRITIC INDEX

CRITIC INDEX

CRITIC INDEX

CRITIC INDEX

CRITIC INDEX